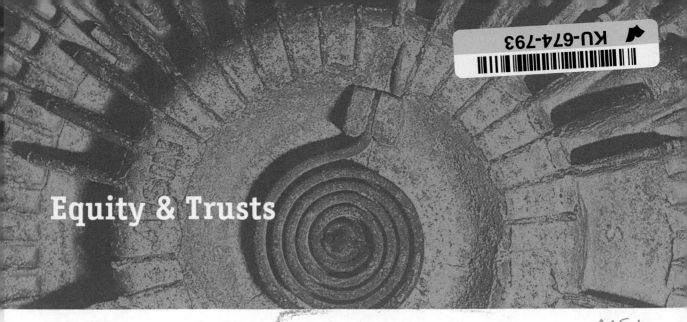

Equity & Trusts

Other Titles in the Textbook Series

Cretney's Family Law
Employment Law
Environment Law
Criminal Law
Land Law
Public Law
Tort
Contract

Equity & Trusts

Sweet & Maxwell's Textbook Series

SIXTH EDITION

by
Professor Michael Haley
School of Law, Keele University

and

Dr Lara McMurtry
School of Law, Keele University

SWEET & MAXWELL
LONDON • 2020

First edition 2006 by Michael Haley and Lara McMurtry
Second edition 2009 by Michael Haley and Lara McMurtry
Third edition 2011 by Michael Haley and Lara McMurtry
Fourth edition 2014 by Michael Haley and Lara McMurtry
Fifth edition 2017 by Michael Haley and Lara McMurtry
Sixth edition 2020 by Michael Haley and Lara McMurtry

Published in 2020 by
Thomson Reuters, trading as Sweet & Maxwell. Registered in England & Wales,
Company No. 1679046. Registered Office and address for service:
5 Canada Square
Canary Wharf
London E14 5AQ

For further information on our products and services, visit *www.sweetandmaxwell.co.uk*

Typeset by Servis Filmsetting Ltd, Stockport, Cheshire
Printed in Great Britain by CPI Group (UK) Ltd, Croydon, CR0 4YY

A C.I.P. catalogue record for this book is available from the British Library

ISBN (print): 978-0-414-07829-1
ISBN (e-book): 978-0-414-07831-4
ISBN (proview): 978-0-414-07832-1
ISBN (print & proview): 978-0-414-07830-7

Acknowledgements

Grateful acknowledgement is made to the following authors and publishers for permission to quote from their works:

THE INCORPORATED COUNCIL OF LAW REPORTING FOR ENGLAND AND WALES: Law Reports and Weekly Law Reports.

LEXISNEXIS: All England Law Reports and Family Law Reports extracts reproduced by permission of RELX (UK) Limited trading as LexisNexis.

Bloomsbury Professional: Family Court Reports.

Cambridge University Press: Cambridge Law Journal.

Oxford University Press: Cranston (ed.), *Making Commercial Law*, 1997; Gardner, *An Introduction to the Law of Trusts*, 2003; Gray and Gray, *Elements of Land Law*, 2008; Reports of Patent, Design and Trade Mark Cases.

While every care has been taken to establish and acknowledge copyright, and contact the copyright owners, the publishers tender their apologies for any accidental infringement. They would be pleased to come to a suitable arrangement with the rightful owners in each case.

Dedication

With much love to Adrienne, Fiona and Jordan as ever

Preface

The law of equity and trusts represents notoriously difficult territory for students to navigate. This is not surprising considering the highly technical rules, arcane and uncertain principles, ancient wisdoms and contradictory judicial utterances which characterise the subject area. Unlike subjects such as crime and tort, it is also difficult for students to identify readily with the real-life issues that underpin the law of equity and trusts. Nevertheless, it is necessary to overcome these obstacles in order to achieve a sound understanding of the law and perhaps for some, more pressingly, to perform successfully in examinations and other forms of assessment. This is where (we hope) this sixth edition of our textbook assumes relevance.

When writing this book, we remain very aware of the strength and depth of other texts on equity and trusts that are available for purchase. As a result, we have strived to fashion a book that is distinctive and which provides a valuable and interesting alternative to its competitors. We have been selective as to the topics included and, when making this choice, were guided by our own maxim that "the product bought should reflect the product taught". For example, the book offers only a succinct introduction to history, but does provide comprehensive and detailed analytical coverage of the key substantive topics. This analysis is designed to blend a rigorous scrutiny of up-to-date case law authorities (both reported and unreported) with an appreciation of the published views of commentators. The text also considers a variety of out-of-court lectures given by individual members of the Supreme Court, which help to explain the policy underlying both the past and the contemporary development of Equity. Our ambition is to offer a book that will benefit students of equity and trusts whatever their ability and level. Although the initial assumption is that the reader has no pre-existing knowledge of the subject area (hence a basic glossary and guide to further reading is incorporated), we aim to offer a text that stimulates and educates at all stages of academic development.

In the three years since the last edition, there have been many changes to the law which fall to be incorporated within this edition. We have seized the opportunity to overhaul Chapter 9 (Resulting Trusts), which is now refreshed and restructured to include a more comprehensive and focused coverage of *Quistclose* trusts. Chapter 17 (Breach of Trust) has also been refashioned to deal more effectively with the personal liability of trustees and equitable compensation.

There is also a range of modern caselaw developments that have been incorporated. The Supreme Court decision in *Ivey* confirming that an objective standard of dishonesty applies in cases of dishonest assistance is considered. The subsequent Court of Appeal decision in *Group Seven Ltd* features in a revamped and streamlined analysis of accessory liability. Chapter 7 (Charities), benefits from the inclusion of various First-tier Tribunal (Charity) cases. In addition, noteworthy case law developments have occurred in relation to constructive and resulting trusts, for example, *Macmillan Cancer Support v Hayes, Re Ninian (Deceased)* and *Re Estate* of *Amos (Deceased)* on the application of the forfeiture rule and its modification; *Generator Developments Ltd v Lidl UK Gmbh* concerning the scope of the *Pallant v Morgan* equity; and *Wood v Watkin* and *Farrell v Burden* regarding the scope of the presumption of advancement. In the context of injunctions, the availability of search orders and freezing injunctions continues to trouble the courts. On the availability of "Wrotham Park" negotiating damages (granted in lieu of injunction), moreover, the Supreme Court decision in *Morris-Garner v One Step (Support) Ltd* proves highly instructive. There are too many other illustrations to mention.

We would especially like to thank the editorial team at Sweet & Maxwell, particularly Nikki and Sarah, as they worked from home to assist us in the later stages of this process, at a time when COVID-19 and the national lockdown created unprecedented challenges for us all.

Lara McMurtry and Michael Haley
August 2020

Table of Contents

1   An Introduction to Equity and Trusts

2 The Three Certainties

3   Constitution of Trusts

4   Formalities and the Perpetuity Rules

5 Post-Mortem Trusts: Mutual Wills and Secret Trusts

6   Non-Charitable Purpose Trusts

7 Charitable Trusts

8   Cy-près

9   Resulting Trusts

10   Constructive Trusts

11   Trusts of the Family Home

12   The Appointment, Retirement and Removal of Trustees

13   The Duties of a Trustee

14   Trustees' Powers: Investment, Maintenance and Advancement

15   Variation of Trusts

16   Setting Trusts Aside

17   Breach of Trust and Associated Remedies

19 Specific Performance

A Selective Glossary of Terms

AB INITIO: from the beginning.

ACCUMULATION: an increase of principal or capital sum through re-investment of income.

ACQUIESCENCE: an assent to an infringement of rights which can be express or implied from conduct.

ACTUAL NOTICE: actual subjective awareness of another's rights.

AD VALOREM: tax payable on instruments transferring property proportionate to the value of the property.

ADMINISTRATIVE UNWORKABILITY: the size of the beneficiaries must not be so large as to make the administration of the trust unworkable.

ADMINISTRATOR: where a person dies without leaving a will an application must be made to the court for "letters of administration" appointing an administrator. His duties are similar to those of an executor under a will.

ADMINISTRATRIX: a female administrator.

ADMISSIBILITY: the question as to whether evidence is allowable before a court.

ADVANCEMENT, PRESUMPTION OF: a rebuttable presumption whereby a transfer of property is deemed to be by way of advancement, that is under an equitable obligation to provide for another. Applies only to certain special relationships, e.g. from parent to child, from husband to wife.

ADVANCEMENT, POWER OF: a power by which a trustee may apply capital moneys for the advancement or benefit of a beneficiary.

AFTER-ACQUIRED PROPERTY: property acquired after a settlement is created. It was a common feature of marriage settlements to promise to convey to trustees after-acquired property.

AGENCY, AGENT: an arrangement (usually contractual) whereby one person acts on behalf of another (his principal). An act of an agent binds his principal.

ALIENATION: disposition of an interest (e.g. by gift, sale or other transfer).

ANNUITY: provision of an annual payment.

ANTE-NUPTUAL SETTLEMENT: settlement made in contemplation of marriage.

ANTON PILLER ORDER: see search order.

APPOINTMENT, POWER OF: a power, given by deed or will, to appoint a person or persons to take an estate or interest in property, whether real or personal.

ASSIGNMENT: the transfer of property. The transfer of a subsisting equitable interest must be in writing: s53(1)(c) of the Law of Property Act 1925.

ATTESTATION: witness of a signature (e.g. on the execution of a will).

ATTORNEY: a person appointed by another to act in his place or represent him. An attorney can represent his principal for the purpose of executing deeds.

BAILMENT: an arrangement (often contractual) whereby an owner (bailor) entrusts possession of his property to another (bailee).

BARE TRUST: a trust where the trustee's duty is simply to convey the property, when required, to the beneficiary.

BENEFICIARY: the party for whose benefit property is held by trustees or executors (sometimes called the cestui que trust).

BENEFICIAL INTEREST: the interest of the beneficiary under the trust.

BEQUEST: a testamentary gift of personal property (i.e. a legacy). A testamentary gift of realty is known as a devise.

BONA FIDE: in good faith.

BONA VACANTIA: property without an owner accrues to the Crown.

BREACH OF TRUST: a trustee is liable for breach of trust if he fails to carry out his duties or commits an unauthorised act.

CAPITAL: the fund or property as opposed to income or profits generated from the fund or property.

CAPITAL GAINS TAX: a tax upon gains accruing on the disposal of an asset, other than on death.

CAPITAL MONEY: the proceeds of sale of an asset by a trustee.

CERTAINTIES: the basic requirements of a trust are the certainties of intention, subject matter and objects.

CESTUI QUE USE / CESTUI QUE TRUST: old descriptions for a beneficiary.

CHARGE: a form of security for the payment of a debt or the performance of an obligation where there is a right to receive payment out of a specific fund or out of the proceeds of the realisation of specific property.

CHARITABLE TRUST: a trust of public character such as a trust for the prevention or relief of poverty, the advancement of education, the advancement of religion and a range of other purposes specified in the Charities Act 2011.

CHATTEL: an item of personal property such as a car or a watch. This is sometimes termed a chose in possession.

CHOSE IN ACTION: a right of proceeding in a court of law to procure payment of a sum of money or to recover damages for wrongdoing (e.g. debts, bank accounts, shares, copyright, patents or contract rights).

CIVIL PARTNERSHIP: a registered same sex relationship.

CLAIMANT: person bringing a legal action formerly known as the plaintiff.

CLEAN HANDS: reference to an equitable maxim that requires that the claimant in equity must be free from fraud or sharp practice.

COHABITANT: a person who lives with a person in a relationship other than husband and wife or same sex registered partnership.

COMMITTAL: the sending of a person to prison (e.g. for contempt of court).

CONDITIONAL INTEREST: an interest dependent upon the fulfilment of some condition precedent.

CONDITION PRECEDENT: this arises where a gift is to take place on the occurrence of some event (e.g. to X if she marries).

CONDITION SUBSEQUENT: this arises where the gift takes place but is to be forfeited on the occurrence of some event (e.g. to X on condition that she does not marry).

CONSIDERATION: payment under a contract.

CONSTITUTION OF TRUST: this concerns whether the trustee has legal title to the trust property (i.e. where the trust is created by transferring legal title to the trustee, all the necessary formalities to transfer the property must be complied with).

CONSTRUCTIVE NOTICE: knowledge of the rights of a third party that would have been acquired if reasonable care had been taken.

CONSTRUCTIVE TRUST: a trust arising by operation of law imposed as a result of fraudulent or unconscionable conduct or to give effect to the common intentions of the parties.

CONTEMPT OF COURT: conduct which impedes the administration of justice.

CONVERSION, DOCTRINE OF: "equity looks on that as done, that which ought to be done". On entry into a specifically enforceable contract to buy land, the interest of the vendor is treated as an interest in the proceeds of sale and the interest of the buyer is treated as an equitable interest in land.

CONVEYANCE: an instrument (other than a will) transferring property.

CONTINGENT: something which depends on the happening of an event (e.g. reaching the age of 21 years).

COVENANT: traditionally a promise under seal, but in its modern form means a promise contained in a covenant in a formally drafted deed. Covenants are not recognised in equity and are enforceable only in common law.

CUSTODIAN TRUSTEE: a trustee who has care and control of trust property and documents, while leaving the day to day management to a managing trustee. New managing trustees can thus be appointed without vesting trust property in them.

CY-PRÈS: the cy-près doctrine allows gifts for charitable purposes which cannot be carried out to be applied for other purposes as near as possible to those intended by the donor.

DEBT: usually a contractual obligation of one party (the debtor) to pay money to another (the creditor).

DECLARATION OF TRUST: one of the two ways of constituting a trust (the other being the transfer of legal title to the trustee). Although declarations of trust usually require no formality, a trust of land must be proved by some writing signed by the person who is able to declare such a trust (s.53(1)(b) of the Law of Property Act 1925).

DEED: traditionally a document signed, sealed and delivered. The Law of Property (Miscellaneous Provisions) Act 1989 removes the requirement of a seal, but the document must make clear on its face that it is intended to be a deed, is signed in the presence of a witness who attests the signature and is delivered by its creator or someone authorised by him.

DEHORS THE WILL: outside the will.

DELEGATUS NON POTEST DELEGARE: a delegate cannot delegate. The traditional rule is that a trustee may not, in general, delegate his powers or duties.

DETERMINABLE INTEREST: an interest which comes to an end upon the happening of some contingency which may never occur.

DEVISE: a testamentary gift of realty.

DISCLAIMER: the refusal by a nominated trustee to act in that capacity.

DISCRETIONARY TRUST: a trust where trustees have a duty to apply the trust property for the benefit of the members of a class of beneficiaries in such proportions as the trustees in their discretion think fit.

DISHONEST ASSISTANCE: where a third party dishonestly participates in a breach of trust without the trust property vesting in him, he is accountable in equity to make good the loss to the trust.

DISPOSITION: a transfer of title by way of sale, assignment, gift etc.

DIVIDEND: payment out of profits to the shareholders of a company.

DONEE: a person receiving a gift.

DONOR: a person making a gift.

DONATIO MORTIS CAUSA: a conditional gift made in contemplation of death.

ELECTION: equitable doctrine which prevents a person who accepts a benefit from taking free from an associated burden.

ENDOWMENT: property given in permanent provision (e.g. for educational purposes).

ENTAIL: a settlement whereby property descends exclusively to lineal descendants of the original donee.

EQUITABLE ASSIGNMENT: transfer of property taking effect in equity.

EQUITABLE INTEREST: a right enforceable only in equity.

EQUITABLE MAXIMS: founding and general principles of equity.

EQUITABLE REMEDIES: discretionary remedies created by the Court of Chancery.

EQUITY: the system of principles and rules formulated in the Court of Chancery prior to the Judicature Acts or fairness or natural justice, or a right to an equitable remedy (e.g. where an estoppel arises).

ESTATE: a proprietary stake in the land that varies in quality according to whether it is leasehold or freehold. It is also used to describe a deceased person's assets.

ESTATE CONTRACT: a contract for the sale, lease or other disposition of land.

EX PARTE: a "without notice" application to the court—by one party in the absence of the other.

EXECUTOR: a person (personal representative) who carries the provisions of a will into effect. An executor owes fiduciary obligations to the beneficiaries under a will.

EXEMPTION CLAUSE: a clause in an agreement excluding or limiting the liability of one or more of the parties.

EXPRESS TRUST: a trust voluntarily and intentionally granted.

FAIR DEALING RULE: sometimes called the rule against insider dealing. It operates where a trustee / fiduciary intends to purchase the interest of a beneficiary.

FALSIFICATION OF ACCOUNTS: the right of a beneficiary to show that an entry in the account is false or erroneous and should be disallowed.

FEE SIMPLE: a freehold estate in land.

FEOFFEE TO USES: forerunner of the trustee who held property subject to a use.

FIDUCIARY: a person who holds a position of trust in relation to another and who must act for their benefit. Typical fiduciary relationships are trustee and beneficiary, principal and agent, director and company, but the categories are not closed.

FIDUCIARY POWER: a power of appointment given to a person in a fiduciary position.

FIXED TRUST: a trust where the beneficiaries and their interests are prescribed.

FORMALITIES: the legal requirements to be satisfied before a transaction becomes effective. Formalities usually focus upon the requirement of signed writing.

FREEHOLD: a legal estate of land, unlimited in duration, sometimes called the fee simple.

FREEZING INJUNCTION: formerly known as the "Mareva" injunction, and issued to prevent specified assets from being removed form the jurisdiction of the court.

FULLY SECRET TRUST: a testamentary trust which is not disclosed on the face of the will.

FUTURE PROPERTY: a right or title which has not yet been acquired, but which might be acquired in future (e.g. a covenant to settle after-acquired property on the trusts of a marriage settlement).

GENERAL POWER: a power exercisable in favour of anyone, including the donee of the power (e.g. a gift to X for life with remainder to whomsoever he shall appoint).

GIFT: transfer of absolute title to property to another without consideration.

GIFT OVER IN DEFAULT: a provision in a will or settlement providing for a specified gift in the case where a donee of a power fails to exercise that power (e.g. on trust for my wife for life, then to such of our children as she may appoint, but if she fails to do so, to my eldest son absolutely).

GOOD FAITH: acting in a genuine and honest manner. Sometimes referred to as acting bona fide.

GRATUITOUS: a transfer without consideration—a gift.

HALF-SECRET TRUST: a trust the existence of which is disclosed in a will where the beneficiary is undisclosed.

HYBRID POWER: sometimes called an intermediate power, this is a power to appoint anyone except a defined group (e.g. to X for life, with remainder to whomsoever X appoints, but X may not appoint himself or his wife).

ILLEGALITY: undertaking an act forbidden by law.

INALIENABILITY: rights or property that cannot be transferred.

INJUNCTION: an order by the court that the defendant shall do or refrain from doing a particular act.

IN LOCO PARENTIS: a non-parent viewed in the eyes of the law as being in the position of parent.

IN PERSONAM: rights enforceable only as against the person.

IN REM: rights enforceable against the world.

IMPLIED TRUST: a trust, which is not express, that is, a resulting or constructive trust.

INTANGIBLE ASSET: something which does not have a physical form such as goodwill or shares in a company or intellectual property rights.

INTER PARTES: between the parties.

INTERIM INJUNCTION: a temporary injunction restraining the defendant until trial. Also referred to as an interlocutory injunction.

INTERMEDIATE POWER: a power to appoint anyone except those within a certain group. Also known as a hybrid power.

INTER VIVOS: in one's lifetime.

INTESTACY: where a deceased person dies leaving no effective will, he is wholly intestate; if he dies leaving a will which applies only to some of his property he is partly intestate.

JOINT TENANCY: a form of co-ownership of property which is characterised by the right of survivorship.

JUDICIAL TRUSTEE: the High Court may appoint a person as judicial trustee under the Judicial Trustees Act 1896.

JUSTIFICATION: a plea in defence of an action which admits the allegations of the claimant, but pleads that they are lawful or justifiable.

KNOWING RECEIPT: personal liability imposed on a third party recipient of trust property in circumstances where the third party either knew or ought to have known of the breach of trust.

LACHES: a defence to equitable claims whereby the claimant is deemed to have delayed unreasonably in bringing his case.

LANDLORD: a person who allows another exclusive possession of land for a term at a rent (sometimes called a lessor).

LAPSE: the failure of a gift, e.g. where a person to whom property is bequeathed dies before the testator and the property falls into residue.

LEGATEE: a beneficiary under a will.

LETTERS OF ADMINISTRATION: court authorisation to a person to administer the estate of a deceased person who has died intestate.

LIEN: the right to hold property of another as security for performance of an obligation.

LIFE INTEREST: interest in property for the benefit of a person for the duration of his life.

LIVES IN BEING: the common law perpetuity period may be measured by reference to a life or lives in being i.e. of an ascertainable individual or group of individuals living at the time of the disposition plus an additional period of 21 years after the date of the last surviving member.

MAINTENANCE: the provision of payments to cover the costs of life's necessities for a person.

***MAREVA* INJUNCTION:** see freezing injunction.

MARRIAGE SETTLEMENT: a conveyance of property for the benefit of the parties to, and any prospective issue of, a marriage.

MISREPRESENTATION: a representation which is untrue—where a person is induced to enter into a contract on the basis of a false statement of fact. A misrepresentation may be innocent, negligent or fraudulent.

MONEY HAD AND RECEIVED: a common law action available where money is paid to one person which rightfully belongs to another.

MORTGAGE: a charge by way of legal mortgage providing security for a loan.

NOTICE, DOCTRINE OF: the principle that equitable rights do not bind a bona fide purchaser of a legal estate for value without notice. This covers actual notice (knowledge), constructive notice (knowledge that would have been acquired if reasonable enquiries has been made) and imputed notice (the actual or constructive notice of an agent).

OBJECTS: beneficiaries under a trust.

OFF-SHORE TRUST: trust situated outside the jurisdiction of the court.

OPTION: a right conferred by agreement to buy property at will according to the terms of the agreement.

OVERREACHING: occurs where the proceeds of sale of land are paid to at least two trustees or a trust corporation. The beneficiaries' interests shift to interests in the proceeds of sale and no longer constitute equitable proprietary interests in the land capable of binding a purchaser.

PARI PASSU: equally without preference (i.e. an equal percentage of what is owed).

PAROL: oral (e.g. parol/oral evidence).

PERPETUITIES, RULE AGAINST: the rule against remoteness of vesting requires that the gift must vest within prescribed time limits under the common law (lives in being plus 21 years); under the Perpetuities and Accumulations Act 1964 (maximum of 80 years) or under the Perpetuities and Accumulations Act 2009 (125 years). The rule against inalienability restricts the duration of private trusts to lives in being plus 21 years and is not affected by the 1964 and 2009 Acts.

PERSONAL PROPERTY: property other than real property (e.g. goods, chattels or choses in action).

PERSONAL REPRESENTATIVES: the executors under a will.

PLAINTIFF: old descriptive label for the claimant.

POSSESSION, INTEREST IN: a person with an immediate right to income produced by settled property has an interest in possession.

POWER OF ADVANCEMENT: the payment or application of capital sums to the beneficiary before he is entitled to demand the fund.

POWER OF APPOINTMENT: a permissive authority to allocate property amongst a class of beneficiaries.

POWER OF ATTORNEY: an instrument empowering one person to represent another.

PRECATORY WORDS: words of hope or confidence which impose merely a moral obligation.

PRIORITY: the right to enforce a claim in preference to others.

PRIVITY: the common law rule by which only those party to a contract can enforce it and have it enforced against them.

PROBATE: a certificate granted by the High Court stating that the will of a person has been proved and registered.

PROPRIETARY ESTOPPEL: equitable doctrine enforcing an informal expectation generated by a representor and relied upon to the detriment of the representee in circumstances where it would be unconscionable to allow the representor to rely on his strict legal rights.

PROTECTIVE TRUST: a trust determinable on the bankruptcy of the beneficiary or other specified event, whereupon a discretionary trust usually in favour of the beneficiary's family arises.

PUBLIC TRUSTEE: a corporation sole under the Public Trustee Act 1906 which acts as custodian or judicial trustee.

PURPOSE TRUST: a trust designed to promote a purpose or object which is prima facie void for want of a beneficiary.

QUIA TIMET INJUCTION: an injunction to prevent a future or threatened act which would cause the claimant serious damage.

QUISTCLOSE TRUST: arises in a situation in which a lender lends money to a borrower subject to a condition that the money will be used only for the specified purpose. Classified as a resulting trust.

REAL PROPERTY: land.

RECEIVER: a person appointed to receive rents and profits (e.g. for the court or the mortgagee).

RECTIFICATION: an equitable remedy whereby a written contract or other document can, following a mistake, be rewritten by the court to reflect the true agreement of the parties.

REDEMPTION: the discharge of a mortgage debt.

REMAINDER: an interest or estate expectant upon another's estate (e.g. to A for life, remainder to B).

RESCISSION: an equitable remedy used to set aside contracts and to restore the parties to the positions that they had previously occupied.

RESIDUARY ESTATE: the property left by the deceased after discharge of debts and expenses etc and the payment of specific legacies in a will.

RESTITUTION: in its narrow form, a common law process of restoring specific property to its rightful owner or, in its liberal form, the rules concerned with reversing a defendant's unjust enrichment.

RESULTING TRUST: an implied trust where the beneficial interest in property reverts back to the person who transferred the property.

RETENTION OF TITLE: where a supplier of goods stipulates that the property in the goods shall not pass until payment or until the buyer's obligations have been fulfilled.

REVERSION: where land is granted by the owner for an estate less than he himself holds, the undisposed of interest is termed the reversion.

SEARCH ORDER: an interim order which requires a person to admit another to premises for the purposes of preserving evidence formerly known as an *Anton Piller* order.

SECRET TRUST: a testamentary trust which is fully secret (i.e. not disclosed on the face of a will), or half secret (i.e. where the existence of a trust but not its beneficiary is disclosed on the face of the will).

SELF-DEALING RULE: a rule which prevents the trustee dealing with trust property and taking a profit from the transaction.

SEISIN: feudal possession.

SET OFF: a claim by a defendant to a sum of money which is relied on as a defence in whole or in part to an action by the claimant.

SETTLOR, SETTLEMENT: the settlor is the person who creates the trust by conveying property upon trust by way of succession (e.g. to my wife for life, then to my children equally).

SHARE CERTIFICATE: a document certifying that the person named is entitled to a certain number of shares in a company.

SPECIAL POWER: where the field of potential appointees is limited to a class (e.g. to such of the settlor's children as his wife shall appoint).

SPECIFIC PERFORMANCE: equitable remedy enforcing the performance of positive contractual obligations.

SUBROGATION: X taking over the legal rights of Y, so that Y stands in the shoes of X able to assert X's remedies against a third party.

SUB-TRUST: a trust of an existing beneficial interest.

SUI JURIS: of full legal capacity.

SURVIVORSHIP: principle operative in the context of joint tenancies whereby on the death of a joint tenant, the property accrues to the surviving joint tenants.

TENANCY IN COMMON: a form of co-ownership in equity whereby each co-owner has a distinct share in the property.

TESTAMENTARY DISPOSITION: a transfer of property on death.

TESTATOR: a male who executes a will.

TESTATRIX: a female who executes a will.

TITLE: a right to ownership of property.

TITLE DEEDS: documents conferring or evidencing the title to land.

TRACING: the process of locating the value of misappropriated assets into a substitute asset (e.g. a car purchased with money from trust funds) or in a new mixture of property (e.g. a bank account into which the value has passed).

TRUSTEE: person who has a duty to administer property for the benefit of others.

TRUSTEE DE SON TORT: one who intermeddles in a trust without authority and, thereby, assumes the duties of a trustee.

TRUST OF LAND: a trust the subject matter of which is land.

ULTRA VIRES: beyond powers or in excess of authority.

UNINCORPORATED ASSOCIATION: Two or more persons bound together for one or more common purposes by mutual undertakings, each having mutual duties and obligations, in an organisation which has rules identifying in whom control of the organisation and its funds is vested, and which can be joined or left at will.

USE: the forerunner of the trust.

VARIATION OF TRUSTS: the ability of the court to approve an arrangement varying or revoking a trust or the powers of a trustee in the interest of the beneficiaries.

VEST: an estate is said to have vested when it gives present rights.

VOID: of no legal effect.

VOIDABLE: a transaction which is capable of being set aside on the basis of misrepresentation, undue influence or mistake etc.

VOLUNTEER: a person who provides no consideration.

WILL: documentary disposition of property on death.

Table of Cases

Table of Statutes

Table of Statutory Instruments

Table of National Legislation

1

An Introduction to Equity and Trusts

The term "equity" is, in a general sense, associated with notions of fairness, morality and justice. It is an ethical jurisdiction, originally of canon law descent.[1] On a more legalistic level, however, "equity" is the branch of law that was administered in the Court of Chancery prior to the Judicature Acts 1873 and 1875.[2] This was a jurisdiction evolved to achieve justice and to overcome the rigours and deficiencies of the common law.[3] Lord Sales points out that "The common lawyers and the Chancery lawyers were different personnel and formed different cadres with distinct esoteric knowledge. They litigated in their own distinct courts".[4]

As Lord Cowper LC rather grandly explained in *Lord Dudley v Lady Dudley*:

> **"Now equity is no part of the law, but a moral virtue, which qualifies, moderates, and reforms the rigour, hardness, and edge of the law, and is a universal truth; it does also assist the law where it is**

---

1   See generally, H. Coing, "English Equity and the Denunciatio Evangelica of the Canon Law" (1955) 71 L.Q.R. 223.

2   Equity was, as Lord Neuberger MR noted in his Keating lecture (delivered at Lincoln's Inn on 19 May 2010) entitled "Equity, ADR, Arbitration and the Law: Different Dimensions of Justice", para.30, "the common law's twin administered by the Court of Chancery, its jurisdiction arising from the prerogative of grace". This is available at *http://webarchive.nationalarchives.gov.uk/20131202164909/http://judiciary.gov.uk/media/speeches/2010/speech-lord-neuberger-19052010* [Accessed 31 July 2020].

3   As Lord Neuberger MR observed in his lecture "Equity, ADR, Arbitration and the Law: Different Dimensions of Justice", 19 May 2010, para.31, "Equity arose as a second doorway to justice as a consequence of defects, weaknesses and limits in the common law". It was fashioned so that "the justice system could properly ensure that substantive justice could be done" (para.30).

4   "The Interface between Contract and Equity" the Lehane Memorial Lecture, 28 August 2019, p.5. This is available at *https://www.supremecourt.uk/docs/speech-190828.pdf* [Accessed 31 July 2020].

> defective and weak . . . and defends the law from crafty evasions, delusions, and new subtleties intended as contrived to evade and delude the common law, whereby such as have undoubted right are made remediless; and this is the office of equity, to support and protect the common law from shifts and crafty contrivances against the justice of law. Equity therefore does not destroy the law, nor create it, but assists it."[5]

Although an ethos of conscience pervades this aspect of the law,[6] equity never bestowed a totally unfettered jurisdiction on the Court of Chancery to do what was fair in the settlement of a dispute.[7] Embodying aspects of ecclesiastical law and Roman law, equity developed and gradually emerged as a distinct body of law. In time, the system became as hidebound by rules and principles as its common law counterpart.[8]

It was not until 1875 that equity was practised in the common law courts. The existence of a dual system entailed that, for example, when a defendant had an equitable defence to a common law action, he would have to go to the Court of Chancery to obtain an injunction to suspend the proceedings in the common law court. He would then begin a fresh action for relief in the Court of Chancery. No court had the ability to offer a complete resolution. This duality persisted until the Judicature Acts 1873, 1875 which created the Supreme Court of Judicature and allowed all courts to exercise both a common law and equitable jurisdiction. Although the jurisdictions have been amalgamated for administrative purposes, it remains a matter of some contention as to whether the two streams of law have been substantively fused.[9] As will become clear, the traditional view is that fusion in this full sense did not occur because both jurisdictions retain their distinctive features and maintain very different rules, remedies and principles. As Lord Neuberger MR noted, "Equity had not disappeared, as the 1873 Judicature Act intended, it was simply administered by one and the same court which administered law; and administered in a way which was intended to render it easier, cheaper and quicker to enter the temple of justice than before".[10]

---

5   (1705) Prec. Ch. 241 at 244.

6   Lord Browne-Wilkinson explained that, "Equity operates on the conscience of the owner of the legal interest" (*Westdeutsche Landesbank Girozentrale v Islington LBC* (1996) A.C. 669 at 705).

7   Sir George Jessel MR explained in *Re National Funds Assurance Co* (1878) 10 Ch. D. 118 at 128 that "This court is not, as I have often said, a Court of Conscience, but a Court of Law".

8   Lord Neuberger MR admitted in his lecture "Equity, ADR, Arbitration and the Law: Different Dimensions of Justice", 19 May 2010, para.33 that, "by the 19th Century equity procedure had become so like common law procedure in its technicality, complexity and expense that it struck terror in the hearts of litigants".

9   See generally, K. Mason, "Fusion: Fallacy, Future or Finished?" a paper presented at the Fusion Conference, 16 December 2004, *http://www.supremecourt.justice.nsw.gov.au/Documents/Publications/Speeches/Pre-2015%20 Speeches/Assorted%20-%20L%20to%20Z/mason_speeches.pdf* [Accessed 31 July 2020].

10 Lord Neuberger MR, "Equity, ADR, Arbitration and the Law: Different Dimensions of Justice", 19 May 2010, para.35.

The History of Equity—A Shortened Version[11]

1-002

In medieval times, the Chancellor (originally a clergyman) was the second most important figure in the country. He was the King's premier minister and presided over the Chancery Court. This court was responsible for the issue of royal writs (i.e. claim forms) which were necessary to commence actions in the common law courts. A defect with the writ system was that a claimant could bring an action only if the complaint corresponded in type to an existing writ. If there was no writ, there was no remedy. At the time of the thirteenth century, the range of writs available was limited and, following the Provisions of Oxford 1258, new writs were rarely innovated. The system was to become fixed and rigid and could no longer adapt to changing needs and changing times. As a consequence, hardship and injustice increased. This set the scene for the development of equity for, as Lord Sales explained speaking extra-judicially, "Equity grew up because of the reification and rigidity of the common law, which split apart from social understandings of justice and acceptable conduct. The common law was born out of a formulary system based on the established and time-honoured forms of action. It also tended to favour strict, brightline rules of property and obligation".[12]

In cases of injustice, the King had long enjoyed the discretion to interfere for the benefit of his subjects. In order to obtain this discretionary relief, the claimant would need to petition the King or the King's Council. The King dispensed a brand of extraordinary justice in cases where the common law failed the claimant. The Kings of this period were often fighting abroad or too young to deal with petitions. From early times, therefore, the Chancellor was instructed to deal with these petitions. He became the keeper of the King's conscience. The Chancery was the Chancellor's administrative department and operated to process the petitions. By the beginning of the fifteenth century, the petitions were addressed directly to the Chancellor. They became so numerous that it was necessary to establish the Court of Chancery.

The Chancellor heard claims in circumstances where the law was defective because of the inadequacy of damages as a remedy or the slavish insistence upon the satisfaction of formalities. Claims might follow an allegation of bias in favour of a wealthy and powerful individual who might be able to influence proceedings or juries in the common law courts. As Lord Ellesmere acknowledged, "men's actions are so diverse and infinite, That it is impossible to make any general Law which may aptly meet with every particular Act and not fail in some Circumstances. The office of the Chancellor is to correct men's consciences for Frauds, Breach of Trusts, wrongs and oppression of what Nature soever they be, and to soften and mollify the extremity of the law".[13] Understandably, the interference of the Chancellor was not always well received by the common law judges.

1-003

During the thirteenth and fourteenth centuries, there was no body of law known as "equity". The Chancellor operated to grant relief on an individual case-by-case basis and, in

---

11   For a full account see W.S. Holdsworth, *A History of English Law*, Vol.1 (London: Sweet & Maxwell, 1938).
12   "The Interface between Contract and Equity" the Lehane Memorial Lecture, 28 August 2019, p.3.
13   *Earl of Oxford's Case* (1615) 1 Rep. Ch. 1 at 6.

this way, offered a speedier and less costly jurisdiction. The Chancellor would grant or withhold assistance to a petitioner according to his own sense of what was just. Originally, there were no rules or fixed procedures and justice was geared according to notions of fairness and conscience. This element of subjectivism and idiosyncrasy explains the criticism levied against Chancery justice that it varied with the size of the Chancellor's foot. Hence, equity operated as a gloss on the common law, offering novel solutions to well-worn problems. It was, therefore, a supplementary jurisdiction which complemented the common law.[14] Indeed, Chancellors tended to consult with the common law judges as to the sorts of case where relief should be granted to a petitioner. This avoided much potential conflict between the competing camps. The Chancery did not deny the common law and the Chancellor's jurisdiction was framed as being against the person (i.e. in personam). For example, as subsequently became clear as regards the trust, the Chancery has never denied that legal ownership rested with the trustee, but it imposes obligations upon the legal owner to use the trust property for the benefit of a third party. This meant that the Chancellor was making orders to respond to the consciences of the individual parties.

Due to the personal nature of the Chancery's work, it was necessary that the Chancellor could secure the attendance before him of the defendant. The Chancery developed the subpoena as a means of securing such attendance. The subpoena was an order to attend with the sanction that the defendant who failed to comply would forfeit a stipulated amount of money. Similarly, the Chancery required the disclosure of documents by the parties as regards disputes before it. To this day, this remains a central aspect of civil litigation. It also became necessary to devise methods by which the Chancellor's decisions could be enforced. The Chancellor claimed for himself the ability to imprison those who failed to comply on the basis of their contempt of court. In addition, the Chancellor fashioned a novel remedy in the form of injunctive relief. This was an order which either restrained parties to a common law action or prevented a successful claimant in the common law courts from enforcing the judgment. Not surprisingly, the ability of the Chancellor to grant such "common injunctions" was perceived as a direct attack on the common law. The injunction had the potential to render the common law sterile.

Matters came to a head in the sixteenth century when a major conflict developed between Coke LCJ and Lord Ellesmere, the Chancellor. The battle took place as to whether the Chancellor would continue to be able to grant these injunctions. The Lord Chief Justice asserted that they were unlawful and should be prohibited. Lord Ellesmere claimed that he was not intermeddling and that equity acted only in personam. In this contest for supremacy, the King (James I) favoured the Chancellor. Thereafter, the jurisdiction of the Chancellor was rarely challenged.

The key feature in the transformation of equity into a system of set rules, precedents and principles was the appointment of lawyers as Chancellors. Thereafter, there was a discernible movement from a conscience-based jurisdiction to a precedent-driven style of decision making. Lord Nottingham is thought to be the father of the present system of equity. In his nine

14   As Lord Evershed MR put it, "The function of equity was . . . to fulfil the common law: not so much as to correct it as to perfect it" ("Reflections on the Fusion of Law and Equity after 75 Years" (1954) 70 L.Q.R. 326 at 328).

years (1673–82) as Chancellor, he began the process of moulding a settled system of law.[15] The process of systemisation continued under successive Chancellors, particularly Lord Hardwicke (1736–56) and Lord Eldon (1801–27). The reach of equity was, moreover, wide and extended into the law of mortgages, probate and business law and, of course, the fast-developing law of trusts. The impact of equity was also significant in the range of novel remedies that it developed. At common law, the remedy was compensation and this was available as of right. Equity, however, had no power until Lord Cairns' Act 1858 to award damages. Instead, equity had by then long fashioned a number of discretionary remedies which included, most notably, specific performance and injunctions.

The Judicature Acts and the Fusion Debate

1-004

It is ironic that, during the seventeenth and eighteenth centuries, the Court of Chancery itself became bogged down in procedure, disorganisation, corruption and administrative incompetence. This is what Lord Sales regards as "a hardening of the arteries and what is sometimes referred to as the decline of Equity, as it became more an assembly of technical rules".[16] Until 1813 there were only two judges overseeing matters and, when the court was abandoned in 1873, this number had risen only to seven. Understaffed and overburdened, it became a source of expense and injustice. There had also developed an alliance of sorts between the chancery and common law camps for, as Lord Edmund-Davies admitted: "The fact is that for some years before the Judicature Acts of 1873 and 1875 the common law and Chancery courts had been mutually making increasingly friendly overtures, and these had modified the attitudes of each".[17] Although it was subject to piecemeal reform, the Judicature Acts 1873–1875 eventually abolished the Court of Chancery. Most of its jurisdiction was transferred to the Chancery Division of the newly formed High Court, but all courts subsequently had the ability to exercise both equitable and common law jurisdictions.[18] The Judicature Acts were, therefore, designed to end the conflicts of jurisdiction between the common law and chancery courts. By virtue of s.25(11) of the 1873 Act, Parliament achieved an administrative balance which ensured that, in the rare circumstances that a conflict arose between equity and the common law,

---

15 "[Lord Nottingham] took equity by the scruff of the neck and gave it coherence—or so we were all taught. Whether it is as coherent as we all had thought must be a matter of debate" (Lord Neuberger, the Lehane Lecture, "Equity—The Soul and Spirit of the Law or a Rough Thing?", Supreme Court of New South Wales, Sydney, 4 August 2014, para.31, *https://www.supremecourt.uk/docs/speech-140804.pdf* [Accessed 31 July 2020].

16 "The Interface between Contract and Equity" the Lehane Memorial Lecture, 28 August 2019, p.3.

17 *Raineri v Miles* [1981] A.C. 1050 at 1082.

18 As occurred famously in *Walsh v Lonsdale* (1882) 21 Ch. D. 9, where a specifically enforceable contract to grant a seven-year lease was held to be as good as the lease itself.

the equitable rules were to prevail.[19] Speaking extra-judicially, however, Lord Neuberger MR observed that:

> **"It is difficult to conceive how the rules of equity could prevail over those of Law, if there were no longer any rules of Equity or Law; if the Judicature Acts had assimilated the two in order to create the successor to Equity and Law what conflict could there be?"[20]**

Despite Lord Neuberger's clearly stated view, there remains a lively debate as to whether the Judicature Acts achieved substantive fusion of the common law and equity or merely effected procedural fusion.[21] Substantive fusion involves a complete merging of the common law and equity and its administration by a single omni-competent court and a single procedural code. Although still administered by a single omni-competent court and a single procedural code, procedural fusion entails that substantive common law and substantive equity remain separate jurisdictions.

In the substantive fusion corner stand some heavyweight judicial figures. As Keith Mason, President of the New South Wales Court of Appeal commented, "Fusionists come in all shapes and sizes, generally united by concerns for coherence, rationality, efficiency and respect for general principles that serve as guides in legal education and appellate decision-making. Anti-fusionists may also share these goals, but they are generally united in their greater respect for a static legal framework and their love of history".[22] For example, Sir George Jessel became a believer that law and equity were fused.[23] Denning J was also of the opinion that it was unhelpful to draw a distinction between law and equity and that "problems have to be approached in a combined sense".[24] Lord Diplock spoke authoritatively that it was wrong to perpetuate any dichotomy between rules of equity and rules of common law.[25] Lord Simon was similarly

---

19 Now enshrined within s.49(1) of the Senior Courts Act 1981 (previously known as the Supreme Court Act 1981).

20 "Has equity had its day?" Hong Kong University Common Law Lecture, 12 October 2010, p.14, *http://webarchive. nationalarchives.gov.uk/20131202164909/http://judiciary.gov.uk/media/speeches/2010/mr-speech-hong-kong-lecture-12102010* [Accessed 31 July 2020].

21 See generally, A. Burrows, "We Do This At Common Law But That In Equity" (2002) 22 O.J.L.S. 1.

22 See K. Mason, "Fusion: Fallacy, Future or Finished?" *http://www.supremecourt.justice.nsw.gov.au/Documents/ Publications/Speeches/Pre-2015%20Speeches/Assorted%20-%20L%20to%20Z/mason_speeches.pdf* [Accessed 31 July 2020]. He added that, "The fusing of law and equity has been going on for centuries. It has generally been encouraged by all branches of government since the time that Chancery began behaving like a court of law. It reflects the law's striving for coherence and consistency".

23 *Walsh v Lonsdale* (1882) 21 Ch. D. 9 at 14.

24 *Central London Property Trust Ltd v High Trees House Ltd* [1956] 1 All E.R. 256 at 259. He had previously expressed a similar view in *Errington v Errington* [1952] 1 K.B. 290 and was to reiterate it again in *Boyer v Warbey* [1953] 1 Q.B. 234.

25 *United Scientific Holdings Ltd v Burnley BC* [1978] A.C. 904. His view was unflatteringly described in *Meagher, Gummow & Lehane's Equity, Doctrines & Remedies*, 4th edn (London: Butterworths LexisNexis, 2002), p.xv as being "the low water-mark of modern English jurisprudence".

prepared to endorse this sentiment.[26] The pro-fusionist school accepts that the respective rules can be harmonised and that the law should develop on the basis that the common law can inform equity and vice versa. As Burrows puts it:

> **"to support fusion seems self-evident, resting, as it does, on not being slaves to history and on recognising the importance of coherence in the law . . .".[27]**

In the opposite corner, Lord Brandon denied that the Judicature Acts had in any way altered the substantive common law or equity.[28] This view was championed originally by Sir George Jessel MR (before he himself was converted to the fusionist cause)[29] and, more recently, Mummery LJ expressed the firm belief that there had been no substantive fusion, but merely administrative and procedural improvements.[30] By means of a lecture delivered at Hong Kong University, Lord Neuberger MR also made his anti-fusionist views known.[31] He reasoned that substantive fusion is a fallacy and emphasised that "The Judicature Acts . . . did not, nor were they intended to, effect substantive fusion".[32] Common law and equity, therefore, continue to operate alongside one another. Lord Neuberger MR added that:

> **"The substantive Common Law would continue to exist insofar as it did not conflict with Equity. The twin streams of English substantive law were thus intended to continue to flow separately, even though the common law stream would narrow at those points where it overlapped, but did not mingle, with flowing waters of Equity".[33]**

The conventional understanding is that the Judicature Acts did not sweep aside the intellectual distinctions between equity and the common law. It remains the case that, for example, legal ownership is very different from equitable ownership, legal interests are stronger than their equitable counterparts, equitable remedies are discretionary, equity has no regard for a covenant and the common law does not recognise a trust. An equitable claim may offer an equitable remedy (e.g. rectification, rescission, specific performance and injunction) and different rules apply to the tracing of assets according to whether this process is

---

26   *United Scientific Holdings Ltd v Burnley BC* [1978] A.C. 904 at 944.
27   A. Burrows, "We Do This At Common Law" (2002) 22 O.J.L.S. 1, 4. He advocates "a principled product which may combine elements of law and equity" (p.7).
28   *Bank of Boston Connecticut v European Grain & Shipping Ltd* [1989] A.C. 1056 at 1109.
29   *Salt v Cooper* (1880) 16 Ch. D. 544.
30   *MCC Proceeds Inc v Lehman Bros International (Europe)* [1998] 4 All E.R. 675 at 691.
31   Lord Neuberger MR, "Has equity had its day?", Hong Kong University Common Law Lecture, 12 October 2010.
32   Lord Neuberger MR, "Has equity had its day?", Hong Kong University Common Law Lecture, 12 October 2010, p.13.
33   Lord Neuberger MR, "Has equity had its day?", Hong Kong University Common Law Lecture, 12 October 2010, p.14.

undertaken at common law or equity. The existing differences, therefore, are numerous and pronounced.[34]

A related area for debate concerns whether the Judicature Acts stripped away the ability of equity to devise new rights and remedies. The traditional view is that, as stated by Megaw LJ in *Western Fish Products Ltd v Penwith DC*, "the creation of new rights and remedies is a matter for Parliament, not the judges".[35] Bagnall J developed this theme further in *Cowcher v Cowcher*: "This does not mean that equity is past childbearing; simply that its progeny must be legitimate—by precedent out of principle".[36] If correct, this entails that equity has shifted from invention to the refinement of existing principles on a case-by-case basis. Not all judges, however, agree. Lord Denning MR repeatedly attempted to extend the reach of equity in the area of constructive trusts,[37] the deserted wife's equity,[38] and the availability of injunctive relief.[39] In his 2010 lecture, Lord Neuberger MR accepted that there are various ways in which judges can be thought to legislate. He referred to the Human Rights Act 1998 and the highly contentious right to respect for privacy, where "The judiciary has been left to fill in the gaps; to bring those high principles down to earth and give them concrete application".[40] He acknowledged that Parliament might set general principles and leave it for the judges to develop both law and policy. Lord Neuberger explained that a degree of judicial activism and imaginative interpretation was necessary and beneficial due to the legislature suffering from two disabilities: "The first problem is that of too much ill thought-out legislation; the second is avoidance of failing to legislate in controversial and sensitive areas".[41] At the conclusion of his lecture, Lord Neuberger emphasised that equity had not had its day and was, most certainly, not ossified. He suggested that the difference between refinement and development was more an issue of degree than principle. In his view, the Judicature Acts did not operate as a bar on invention. As evidenced by the maxim "Equity will not suffer a wrong to be without a remedy", equity is not intended to be a static jurisdiction. The downside of this was highlighted in a further lecture by Lord Neuberger:

> **"Indeed, equity may sometimes look like a minefield of unpredictability rather than, as its fans like to suggest, a haven of principle. Far**

34   See Lord Sales: "The Interface between Contract and Equity" the Lehane Memorial Lecture 28 August 2019, pp.6,7. He observed (p.23) that, "The resulting pattern of law is not one of outright fusion of law and Equity, but of a degree of confluence and of significant, though nuanced and subtle, interaction between them".

35   [1981] 2 All E.R. 204 at 218.

36   [1972] 1 All E.R. 943 at 948.

37   *Eves v Eves* [1975] 1 W.L.R. 1338.

38   *Bendall v McWhirter* [1952] 2 Q.B. 638.

39   Particularly, the freezing order (*Mareva Compania Naveiera v International Bulkcarriers SA* [1980] 1 All E.R. 213) and the search order (*Anton Piller KG v Manufacturing Processes Ltd* [1976] 2 W.L.R. 162).

40   Lord Neuberger MR, "Has equity had its day?", Hong Kong University Common Law Lecture, 12 October 2010, p.17.

41   Lord Neuberger MR, "Has equity had its day?", Hong Kong University Common Law Lecture, 12 October 2010, p.20. He cited the criminal law as an example of the former and co-ownership as an illustration of the latter.

> from being a seamless collection of clear principles, equity some-
> times appears to be a hot-bed of uncertainty where the judicial foot
> not merely comes in all shapes and sizes, but seems to set off in
> opposite directions".[42]

Particular concern has been expressed as to the role of equity in the commercial field.[43] As Lord Briggs acknowledged, "Most judges who pronounce on the question agree at least that equitable principles and remedies need to be kept from getting out of control in the market place".[44] Gloster LJ agreed that "it is impracticable and unreal to introduce into commercial transactions the moral standards of the vicarage . . .".[45]

The Maxims of Equity

1-005

The maxims of equity are a series of core principles devised by the Court of Chancery and designed to offer general and overarching guidance for judges as to when and how to exercise their equitable jurisdiction. The maxims reflect equity's general approach to the solution of legal problems. As Lord Neuberger MR put it, "Without Equity and its famous maxims . . . the common law would be an incomplete means to achieve justice".[46] Not everyone, however, shares this enthusiasm. In *Yarmouth v France*, Lord Esher MR admitted that ". . . I detest the attempt to fetter the law by maxims. They are almost invariably misleading: they are for the most part so large and general in their language that they always include something which really is not intended to be included in them".[47] It will become clear that these principles sometimes overlap and conflict and are often too vague to be of practical value. Nevertheless, the major maxims are:

- equity will not suffer a wrong to be without a remedy;

- equity follows the law;

---

42 Lord Neuberger, "Equity—The soul and spirit of all law or a roguish thing?", the Lehane Lecture 2014, para.10.
43 *UBS AG v Kommunale Wasserwerke Leipzig GmbH* [2017] EWCA Civ 1567 at [347].
44 "Equity in Business" The Denning Society Annual Lecture, 8 November 2018, para.2. Available at *https://www.supremecourt.uk/docs/speech-181108.pdf* [Accessed 31 July 2020].
45 *UBS AG v Kommunale Wasserwerke Leipzig GmbH* [2017] EWCA Civ 1567 at [347].
46 Lord Neuberger MR, "Has equity had its day?", Hong Kong University Common Law Lecture, 12 October 2010, p.1; see generally M. Harding, "Equity and the Rule of Law"' (2016) 132 L.Q.R. 278.
47 (1887) L.R. 19 Q.B.D. 647 at 653. In *Lissenden v CA v Bosch Ltd* [1940] A.C. 412 at 435, Lord Wright voiced his dissatisfaction: "Indeed these general formulae are found in experience often to distract the court's mind from the actual exigencies of the case, and to induce the court to quote them as offering a readymade solution".

- he who seeks equity must do equity;

- he who comes to equity must do so with clean hands;

- equity is equality;

- where the equities are equal the first in time prevails;

- equity imputes an intention to fulfil an obligation;

- equity regards as done that which ought to be done;

- equity looks to substance rather than form;

- delay defeats equity;

- equity acts in personam;

- equity will not allow a statute to be used as an instrument of fraud;

- equity will not assist a volunteer; and

- equity will not perfect an imperfect gift.

Equity will not suffer a wrong to be without a remedy

1-006

This maxim is not to be taken too literally as equitable remedies are geared only to strike against unconscionable behaviour and to operate only if that behaviour constitutes a legal (as opposed to merely moral) wrongdoing. As Mann J commented in *Dubey v HM Revenue & Customs* in relation to the disappointed Farepak customers who received neither their Christmas goods nor a refund of their money, "at the end of the day their claims have to be based in law, not sympathy . . . No amount of sympathy can entitle them to be paid moneys to which they are not, or may not be, legally entitled".[48] The underlying rationale of this rule is that equity will strive to interfere in order to remedy a legal wrong when the common law is inadequate to do so. In other words, equity will attempt to ensure that deserving claimants obtain redress. A broad-based illustration is the law of trusts under which the beneficiary has no remedy at common law. In the eyes of the common law, it is the trustee who has legal ownership of the trust property and not the beneficiary. The latter could, therefore, only enforce his beneficial interest in equity. A more specific example concerns quia timet injunctions which can

---

48   [2006] EWHC 3272 (Ch) at [28].

be employed to prevent an anticipated wrong whereas there is no remedy at common law until the wrongful act has been performed. Modern developments include the evolution of estoppel and the deployment of the constructive trust.

Equity follows the law

The general rule is that equity will adhere to the common law unless there is some exceptional justification for not doing so (i.e. where it would be unconscionable as, say, in relation to secret trusts and deathbed gifts). If possible, equity will harmonise its own rules with those of the common law. For example, in *Stack v Dowden* the majority of the House of Lords promoted the presumption that equity follows the law.[49] There the House had to consider the effect of a conveyance of the family home into the joint names of a cohabiting couple, but without an explicit declaration of their respective beneficial interests. In such joint names cases, Baroness Hale concluded that:

1-007

> **"The starting point where there is joint legal ownership is joint beneficial ownership. The onus is upon the person seeking to show that the beneficial ownership is different from the legal ownership".[50]**

Accordingly, the common law presumption of a joint tenancy in relation to the co-ownership of land in joint names, as discussed in Ch.11, will prevail unless the facts are unusual or the property was purchased as part of a commercial venture.[51] In the latter circumstances, equity deems the right of survivorship, which arises automatically on the death of a joint tenant, to be unsuited to the transaction and presumes a tenancy in common.

A further illustration of this maxim concerns the refusal of equity to contradict the common law rule that a third party cannot be made to perform a contract. Hence, the general rule is that specific performance is available only as against a party to the contract.

He who seeks equity must do equity

A claimant who seeks the relief of equity must himself be willing to act fairly towards the other party. A person seeking equity must be prepared to do equity (i.e. act conscionably).[52] For

1-008

---

49   [2007] 2 A.C. 432. Lord Neuberger gave a strong dissenting speech. In *Jones v Kernott* [2012] 1 A.C. 776, Lord Walker and Lady Hale reiterated that the starting point is that equity follows the law and that, in joint names cases, the parties are joint tenants both in law and in equity.

50   [2007] 2 A.C. 432 at [56]. She added at [69], "cases in which the joint legal owners are to be taken to have intended that their beneficial interests should be different from their legal interests will be very unusual".

51   *Stack v Dowden* [2007] 2 A.C. 432; *Jones v Kernott* [2012] 1 A.C. 776.

52   The court is not bound by any contractual terms which purport to allow the claimant to take free from any

example, a person seeking the grant of an injunction or specific performance must be willing and able to perform his own future obligations.[53] Similarly, if the claimant seeks to rescind (i.e. withdraw from) a contract, the court will ensure that the claimant acts equitably by, say, returning any deposit paid under the contract. If the claimant cannot or will not perform his obligations, the court will not grant equitable relief. The doctrine of election, which prevents a person who accepts a benefit from taking free from an associated burden, is based upon this maxim.[54] As Lord Cairns explained:

> "where a deed or will professes to make a general disposition of property for the benefit of the person named in it, such person cannot accept a benefit under the instrument without at the same time conforming to all its provisions, and renouncing every right inconsistent with them".[55]

For example, Adrienne by will purports to leave a valuable painting to her grandson, Jordan, and by a separate legacy leaves her daughter, Fiona, £50,000. Adrienne, however, is mistaken in that the painting already belongs to Fiona. Under the doctrine of election, Fiona must elect either to transfer her painting to Jordan or to forgo the legacy. She cannot have both.[56]

He who comes to equity must come with clean hands

1-009

While the previous maxim focuses upon future conduct, this maxim concentrates upon the claimant's past actions. As equitable remedies are discretionary in nature, the claimant has to be deserving of equitable intervention (i.e. have acted in good faith).[57] Hence, there will be no specific performance of a contract if the claimant himself is in breach or if the claimant brought about the contract by misrepresentation or fraud.[58] If it were otherwise, equity would be imposing a dual standard.[59] For these purposes, it is the claimant's conduct that is to be examined[60] and not the other party's behaviour. Accordingly, there is no balancing out of fault and bad

---

equity or cross-claim and its discretion is unaffected by such a term: *Quadrant Visual Communications Ltd v Hutchinson Telephone (UK) Ltd*, *The Times*, 4 December 1991.

53   See *Chappell v Times Newspapers* [1975] 2 All E.R. 233.

54   *Birmingham v Kirwan* (1805) 2 Sch. & Led. 444. One cannot, therefore, both approbate and reprobate (*qui approbat non reprobat*).

55   *Codrington v Codrington* (1875) L.R. 7 H.L. 854 at 861, 862.

56   See *Douglas v Douglas* (1871) L.R. 12 Eq. 617.

57   See P.H. Pettit [1990] Conv. 416; M. Halliwell [2004] Conv. 439.

58   *Cross v Cross* (1983) 4 F.L.R. 235. Similarly, the unclean hands defence can be employed to resist an injunction: *Royal Bank of Scotland v Highland Financial Partners LP* [2013] EWCA Civ 328.

59   See *Guinness v Saunders* [1990] 2 A.C. 663, where a director had his claim for remuneration (£5.2 million) for work done turned down because of his breach of fiduciary duty.

60   In *Boulding Group Plc v Newett* unreported 16 May 1991, CA, a wife who sought specific performance was not affected by her husband's misconduct. There is no doctrine of dirty hands by affection.

behaviour between the parties. For example, if a landlord seeks to forfeit the tenant's lease for the latter's breach of covenant, the court has a jurisdiction to grant the tenant relief from forfeiture. Regardless of the landlord's conduct, the tenant will be denied the intervention of equity if the past breach was flagrant. It is to be appreciated, moreover, that the "lack of cleanliness" must relate to the dispute and not to unconnected matters. This means that a general depravity and corruptness does not bar a claim in equity.[61] As Eyre CB put it in *Dering v Earl of Winchelsea*, "it must be depravity in a legal as well as moral sense".[62] It must concern the equity sought.[63] Accordingly, in J *Willis & Son v Willis*[64] the claimant knowingly put forward a false document in support of an estoppel claim and was thus barred from equitable intervention.

For example, in *Fiona Trust & Holding Corp v Privalov* the defendants pleaded that the claimants should not be granted equitable relief of any kind because of their misconduct in relation to non-disclosure of documents and the improper carrying out of background investigations.[65] In rejecting the defendants' assertions, Andrew Smith J made several points. First, the maxim is directed usually to conduct that is in some way immoral and deliberate. Secondly, not all misconduct deprives a claimant of equitable relief. The conduct may be too trivial for it to have this effect. Thirdly, the court will assess the gravity and effect of the misconduct cumulatively, "so that, while the elements of misconduct taken individually might be too trivial for the maxim to be applied, they might be sufficient taken together".[66] On the facts before him there was an insufficiently immediate relationship between the misconduct and the relief claimed. It is, moreover, possible for a party who has acted with unclean hands to "wash them" before seeking the relevant equitable relief.[67]

Equity is equality

1-010

As regards claims to property under a fixed trust, if the shares are not allocated between the claimants, equity generally presumes that each was intended to have an equal share.[68] For example, in *Jones v Maynard* a husband and wife opened a joint bank account together, but made no reference as to how the money was to be shared.[69] The court applied this maxim and determined that each was entitled to an equal share. It has been held that the maxim goes

---

61 See *Ball v De Marzo* [2019] EWHC 1587 (Ch) where a forged will was relied upon in order to obtain grant of probate. Nevertheless, the clean hands principle did not apply to a claim to a trust interest in property belonging to the estate.
62 (1878) 1 Cox 318 at 320.
63 See *Grobbelaar v News Group Newspapers* [2002] 4 All E.R. 732.
64 [1986] 1 E.G.L.R. 62.
65 [2008] EWHC 1748 (Comm).
66 [2008] EWHC 1748 (Comm) at [19].
67 *Royal Bank of Scotland v Highland Financial Partners LP* [2013] EWCA Civ 328.
68 *Burrough v Philcox* (1840) 5 My. & Cr. 72. The presumption gives way in the face of evidence to the contrary: *McPhail v Doulton* [1971] A.C. 424.
69 [1951] 1 All E.R. 802.

beyond mere mathematical equality and extends also to proportionate equality.[70] Put simply, this approach would entail that if there were legacies to three individuals in different amounts (say £1,000, £10,000 and £100,000), and the residuary estate was to be divided between them, their entitlement would be in proportionate equality to their respective legacies. It is, however, doubtful whether this alternative version of equality is correct.[71]

If no other way forward is outlined by the donor/settlor, this somewhat rough and ready presumption is employed to achieve fairness. It is, however, a default mechanism of last resort.[72] In many cases, equality is most certainly not what was intended.[73]

Where the equities are equal the first in time prevails

1-011

Time assumes importance to equity. In circumstances where two parties have equally strong cases, the party who acquired his equitable rights first will have priority. For example, if two equitable mortgagees are competing for priority in order to determine who will have first claim to the proceeds of sale then, in the eyes of equity, priority will lie with the mortgagee whose interest was created first. This maxim is the founding stone of the doctrine of notice which, prior to any system of registration, regulated the priority between equitable interests in land.

Equity imputes an intention to fulfil an obligation

1-012

This maxim means that where a person is obliged to do something, but instead does something else that could be regarded as a performance of the obligation, equity will regard this as fulfilling the obligation. For example, where a debtor leaves a legacy by will to his creditor, the legacy will be viewed as the satisfaction of the debt. Unless the presumption is rebutted, the creditor will not be able both to sue on the debt and keep the legacy. The debt must, however, be incurred before the will was made, the legacy must be as large as or larger than the debt and the will must not contain a direction to pay debts.[74]

Equity regards as done that which ought to be done

1-013

In the situation where there is a specifically enforceable obligation (e.g. a contract to create a legal lease), equity regards the parties as already being in the position which they would be in

---

70   *Re Bower's ST* [1942] Ch. 197.

71   *Re Steel* [1979] Ch. 218.

72   The maxim has frequently been applied to the distribution of surplus funds on the dissolution of an association: see *Re Bucks Constabulary Widows' Fund (No.2)* [1979] 1 W.L.R. 936.

73   See Lord Reid in *Gissing v Gissing* [1971] A.C. 886 at 897 (a case decided in the context of the beneficial ownership of the family home).

74   *Sowden v Sowden* (1875) 1 Bro. C.C. 582.

following the performance of the obligation (e.g. as if the legal lease had been granted). This maxim is well demonstrated in *Walsh v Lonsdale*[75] where a seven-year lease was granted to the tenant, but no deed was executed. The fixed-term lease was, therefore, equitable. In the light that specific performance of the contract to create a legal lease was available, the court admitted that an equitable lease is as good as a legal lease. This was because equity looked on the lease as "legal" as soon as it was informally created. Law and Equity must also have the power to correct what had been an obvious administrative error.[76] Another example of this maxim is the "doctrine of conversion" that arises on a binding contract, say, for the sale of land. As soon as the contract is entered, the vendor becomes the trustee of the legal estate for the benefit of the purchaser. This ensures that the vendor's interest has been "converted" into the agreed proceeds of sale. Accordingly, if the property is damaged after the contract, the risk potentially falls on the shoulders of the purchaser and the vendor is entitled to the full purchase price.

Equity looks to substance rather than form

1-014

The principle here is that equity will look to substance and not be deceived by the outward appearance of a transaction.[77] This is evident in relation to the intention to create a trust where it is not necessary that the word "trust" be used and it is not conclusive even if the term is employed. Accordingly, in *Singha v Heer* the language used was inconsistent with the declaration of trust even though the words "on trust" were utilised.[78] The court must always look for the true relationship that was created. It will, moreover, unravel any sham or pretence trusts[79] and order rectification of a document that does not represent the true intentions of the parties (see para.**1-024**). Similarly, as regards mortgage law and the special protection that is afforded to the mortgagor, the court will look to see the real nature of the bargain entered and whether it is truly a mortgage transaction.[80] By way of a further illustration, a freehold covenant may be construed as being negative even though it is framed in positive language (and, indeed, vice versa).[81]

Delay defeats equity

1-015

This is a further illustration of how time is important to equity. It is often said that equity aids the vigilant and not the indolent and the overarching expectation is that the claimant is to

---

75   (1882) 21 Ch. D. 9.
76   In *HR Trustees Ltd v Wembley Plc* [2011] EWHC 2974 (Ch), a declaration signed by four trustees (but not the fifth trustee) was treated as having been signed properly by all five trustees.
77   *Parkin v Thorold* (1852) 16 Beav. 59.
78   [2016] EWCA Civ 424.
79   *Midland Bank v Wyatt* [1995] 1 F.L.R. 696.
80   *Grangeside Properties Ltd v Collingwoods Securities Ltd* [1964] 1 W.L.R. 139.
81   *Tulk v Moxhay* (1848) 2 Ph. 774.

act expeditiously. [82] The rule is that, if the court concludes that the claimant has allowed too much time to elapse between the wrongdoing and the commencement of legal proceedings, equity will not protect the claimant's rights. Hence, the doctrine of "laches" developed in order to prevent stale claims.[83] The court's decision should be based upon notions of good conscience in light of the delay. Hence, the respondent will have to show that the effect of the claimant's delay made it equitable to deny him relief. In practice, the role of this maxim has been largely subsumed by the Limitation Acts (which set out time limits within which actions must be commenced), but is still relevant when dealing with fraudulent breach of trust cases,[84] undue influence[85] and deciding whether equitable remedies should be granted.[86] For example, in *Hughes v La Baia Ltd*,[87] the Privy Council had to consider whether equitable relief should be declined under the doctrine of laches. Lord Walker acknowledged that a degree of delay, when coupled with prejudice to the defendant, may operate as a defence in equity. Nevertheless, the Privy Council emphasised that the onus is on the defendant to prove that it would be inequitable to grant the claimant the relief to which he was otherwise entitled.[88]

Equity acts in personam

1-016

At the heart of equity is the notion that it acts in personam which means that it is designed to prevent a specified individual from acting unconscionably. It strikes at the conduct and conscience of the defendant. This means that equitable remedies are personal in that they are exercised against specific persons. They compel or permit a person to do something or not to do something, for example, search orders and freezing injunctions.[89] In relation to a breach of trust, the beneficiary's redress strikes against the trustees personally. A failure to comply with an order of specific performance or an injunction is viewed as a contempt of court and punishable by a purging visit to the prison cells.[90] It also explains why equity can make an order

---

82 *Lester v Woodgate* [2010] EWCA Civ 199.

83 *Smith v Clay* (1767) 3 Bro. C.C. 639.

84 Section 21(1)(a) of the Limitation Act 1980; see generally J. Stevens, "Too Late to Face the Music? Limitation and Laches as Defences to an Action for Breach of Fiduciary Duty" [1997] Conv. 225.

85 Although no limitation period runs in relation to claims based upon undue influence or unconscionable transactions, in *Evans v Lloyd* [2013] EWHC 1725 (Ch) the High Court felt that a delay of 15 years before the gifts were challenged on the basis of wrongdoing would invoke the laches defence.

86 See *Leaf v International Galleries* [1950] 1 All E.R. 693 (a claim for rescission).

87 [2011] UKPC 9.

88 In *Whatley v Lougher* unreported 6 April 2020 (HC), the claimant issued proceedings for fraud years after the six-year limitation period had expired. The claimant had known of the fraud in 2007, but issued proceedings only in 2019. The claimant was statute barred and the equitable doctrine of laches also applied.

89 See generally, Ch.18.

90 Section 14 of the Contempt of Court Act 1981. A fine is an alternative punishment.

relating to property situated outside the jurisdiction, provided that the defendant is within the jurisdiction.[91]

Equity will not allow a statute to be used as an instrument of fraud

1-017

This maxim is designed to prevent one party relying on an absence of statutory formalities (e.g. relating to land contracts, wills, the creation of legal leases and express trusts and the registration of land charges), if to do so would be unconscionable and unfair.[92] For example, in *Bannister v Bannister*[93] an elderly woman conveyed a house on the understanding that she would be able to continue to reside there rent free. Whether viewed as a land contract or an express trust, there was no documentation concerning the transaction. Hence, the underlying bargain was not enforceable by her. The purchaser then fraudulently set up the absolute nature of the conveyance with the intention of defeating her beneficial interest. Nevertheless, equity stepped in and imposed a constructive trust which gave her a life interest in the property. The consequences of the statutory requirement of writing would otherwise have inflicted injustice upon the woman.[94] Accordingly, as Critchley concludes, "the usage of the maxim gradually shifted from interpretation to circumvention of statutory provisions. The change was subtle but significant".[95]

Equity will not assist a volunteer

1-018

The general rule is that the court is prevented from coming to the aid of a volunteer regardless of how undesirable the outcome might appear.[96] Equity will not, therefore, grant specific performance of a gratuitous promise (i.e. an agreement that is unsupported by consideration). Equity will not enforce a covenant ("equity has no regard for a seal"[97]), whereas the common law embodies no such inhibition.[98] In relation to trusts, equity will assist a beneficiary only when there is a perfectly constituted trust (i.e. once legal title to the trust property has vested in the trustee).[99] As Lord Browne-Wilkinson noted, "Once a trust relationship Is established . . . the fact that the beneficiary has given no value is irrelevant".[100]

---

91 See *Penn v Lord Baltimore* (1750) 1 Ves. Sen. 444, where specific performance of a contract relating to land in North America was granted.
92 See *Shah v Shah* [2001] 3 W.L.R. 31 where an improperly attested deed was upheld under this maxim.
93 [1948] 2 All E.R. 133.
94 See also secret trusts (Ch.5) which may be upheld despite non-compliance with the Wills Act 1837.
95 P. Critchley, "Instruments of fraud, testamentary dispositions, and the doctrine of secret trusts" (1999) 115 L.Q.R. 631.
96 *Jones v Lock* (1865) L.R. 1 Ch. App. 25.
97 *Jeffreys v Jeffreys* (1841) Cr. & Ph. 135.
98 *Cannon v Hartley* [1949] Ch. 213.
99 *Milroy v Lord* (1862) 4 De. G.F. & J. 264; see Ch.3.
100 *T. Choithram International SA v Pagarani* [2001] 1 W.L.R. 1 at 12.

Equity will not perfect an imperfect gift

1-019

The underlying notion here is that to make a perfect gift the donor must comply with the requirements necessary to transfer legal title to the property. There are numerous examples where equity has not interfered when, although a transfer was intended, the transferor did not follow the appropriate transfer process. In *Jones v Lock*,[101] a father intended to make a gift of a cheque to his child, but failed to endorse the cheque with the result that legal title did not pass. Equity refused to cure the defect and the gift failed. Similarly, in *Milroy v Lord*[102] an attempt to establish a trust of 50 shares in a bank failed because legal title to the shares never became vested in the trustee. The settlor did not take any steps to transfer the shares before his death. Equity could not perfect the transfer.

As considered in Ch.3, however, this general rule has its exceptions and these include deathbed gifts, fortuitous vesting, proprietary estoppel, unconscionability and the so-called every effort rule.

Key Equitable Remedies

1-020

At common law, the usual remedy is the award of damages and this is available as of right. One of the most significant contributions of equity is the wide range of remedies that it has fostered. These remedies are discretionary and, as indicated above, their availability in any given case may hinge upon the application of the maxims of equity. They are granted in circumstances where common law damages are inadequate and are in personam, that is, they are targeted at the defendant personally. The major types of equitable remedy will now be considered. These are:

- specific performance;

- injunctions;

- rectification;

- rescission; and

- subrogation.

---

101 (1865) L.R. 1 Ch. App. 25.
102 (1862) 4 De. G.F. & J. 264.

Specific performance

The remedy of specific performance is analysed in detail in Ch.19. For present purposes, it is to be appreciated that specific performance is an order of the court which directs the defendant to perform his side of a contract. Specific performance operates in relation to the entire contract and not merely a part of the agreement. The claimant has to come with "clean hands"[103] and to apply for relief without unreasonable delay. When granted, this will be either as an alternative to or in addition to damages for breach of contract. The remedy will not be granted if damages would adequately compensate the claimant. An example of where specific performance will be readily granted concerns contracts for the sale of land. This is because each piece of land is considered to be unique and damages will not normally be sufficient to compensate a potential purchaser. Although damages may be suitable for the vendor, a need for mutuality allows the vendor to claim specific performance of a land contract. An action for specific performance, moreover, may be commenced even before there has been an actual breach of contract. This would arise where there is an anticipatory breach, for example when one party has stated his intention not to perform his side of the contract.

Specific performance is not, however, available for all types of contract. As regards contracts for the sale of goods, such as a car or a television, specific performance will not usually be an appropriate remedy. This rule will give way only when the goods are rare, unique or difficult to acquire (e.g. a work of art or shares in a private company) or where special circumstances make the payment of damages inadequate (e.g. petrol in a time of world shortage). Obviously, illegal or immoral contracts will not be enforced in this way and contracts involving personal services (e.g. an agreement under which a singer is to appear on a television show) or services which require constant supervision (e.g. an agreement to provide cleaning services in an office block) usually fall beyond the reach of specific performance.[104]

1-021

Injunctions

An injunction is an order of the court which requires a person either to do something (i.e. a positive or mandatory injunction) or to refrain from doing something (i.e. a negative or prohibitory injunction). Injunctions are considered in detail in Ch.18. Although the remedy is discretionary, any person who suffers from an infringement of an equitable or legal right may apply for injunctive relief. Damages may be awarded in lieu of or in addition to an injunction.

There are various types of injunction, each of which has been designed to achieve a different function. It is perhaps useful at this stage to outline the major categories of injunction:

1-022

---

103 See *Coatsworth v Johnson* (1886) 54 L.T. 520 where a breach of covenant disqualified the plaintiff from equitable relief.
104 See *Co-operative Insurance Society Ltd v Argyll Stores ((Holdings) Ltd* [1998] A.C. 1 where the House of Lords refused specific performance of a "keep open" covenant in relation to the continued operation of a supermarket.

- the prohibitory injunction is an injunction which forbids the party to do or to continue to do an unlawful act (e.g. not to build upon land in breach of a restrictive covenant);

- the mandatory injunction is an order that an act be undone (e.g. to demolish a building which has been built in breach of a restrictive covenant). Hence, a mandatory injunction when granted is likely to undo a wrongful act rather than to order the defendant to carry out a positive obligation. This type of injunction is uncommon;

- the perpetual or "final" injunction is an order made in final settlement of the dispute between the parties and issued at the completion of the court proceedings;

- the interim injunction (sometimes known as an interlocutory junction) is an injunction made during the course of legal proceedings and which is effective only until the trial of the action takes place. It is primarily used to restrain the defendant immediately while waiting for a full court hearing;

- the without notice (or ex parte) injunction. This is an injunction granted in an emergency without the other side having been informed or given the opportunity to attend the hearing of the application;

- the quia timet injunction is an injunction designed to prevent an anticipatory infringement of the claimant's rights where such an infringement is a realistic threat;

- a search order (formerly known as an *Anton Piller* order) authorises the entry to the defendant's premises to inspect and seize documents relevant to the case. The aim is to protect evidence in relation to impending litigation; and

- a freezing injunction (formerly known as a *Mareva* injunction). This is an injunction that prevents the defendant from removing his assets out of the jurisdiction of the court before the completion of litigation.

1-023 As indicated, in certain circumstances the courts may, under s.50 of the Senior Courts Act 1981, award damages instead of injunctive relief. Although the rule of thumb is that if a right is infringed an injunction may be granted, damages may be substituted where the claimant's loss is small, the loss can be valued in money terms, money would provide the claimant with adequate compensation and an injunction would be oppressive, unduly harsh or disproportionate.[105]

---

105 *Shelfer v City of London Electric Lighting Co* [1895] 1 Ch. 287.

Rectification

The remedy of rectification (which Lord Briggs described as "another not-so-good part of the curate's egg")[106] concerns the rewriting of documents to accord with what the parties agreed in bilateral transactions (such as contracts) or, in the case of a voluntary deed (such as a trust or will), with what the settlor truly intended.[107] As Lord Toulson put it, "Rectification is an equitable means of correcting the text of a written form of contract or other legal instrument by changing or inserting words which the court is satisfied have been included or omitted by mistake".[108] It operates so as to prevent injustice.

The remedy is, therefore, designed to rectify mistakes made. Understandably, there must be convincing proof to counteract the evidence of a different intention as represented by the document. Accordingly, there must be a flaw in the written document, such that it does not give effect to the true intention of the parties or the settlor, as appropriate. It is crucial that it was intended that the term appear in the written agreement. If it was deliberately omitted or the mistake is merely as to the legal consequences of the document, rectification is not available.[109] The purpose of rectification is, therefore, to correct mistakes in the way the transaction has been recorded. It does not allow the parties to change the substance of the agreement reached. It is simply equity's way of setting the record straight.[110] Although it is a discretionary remedy that must be treated with caution,[111] rectification will usually be awarded unless damages are a suitable alternative.[112]

As regards bilateral transactions (such as contracts), the remedy operates usually when the mistake is common to both parties; for example, when both parties intend that a term appear in a written contract, but the term is mistakenly omitted from the final draft. As the contract fails to record what was agreed, the contract may be rectified by the court. It is no longer

---

106 Lord Briggs, "Equity in Business" (2019) 135 L.Q.R. 567 at 580.

107 See *Re Butlin's Settlement* [1976] Ch. 251 where the rewriting sought was to introduce a power for a majority of trustees to make decisions binding upon the minority.

108 "Does Rectification require Rectifying?", TECBAR Annual Lecture, 31 October 2013, p.1, available at *https://www.supremecourt.uk/docs/speech-131031.pdf* [Accessed 31 July 2020].

109 *Oun v Ahmad* [2008] EWHC 545 (Ch); *Transview Property Ltd v City Site Properties Ltd* [2008] EWHC 1221 (Ch). Rectification will not be available, therefore, merely because the document fails to achieve a desired fiscal objective (e.g. a tax saving).

110 For an overview of the principles involved, see Arden LJ's judgment in *Ahmad v Secret Garden (Cheshire) Ltd* [2013] EWCA Civ 1005 and the judgment of Barling J in *Giles v Royal National Institute for the Blind* [2014] EWHC 1373.

111 *RBC Trustees (CI) Ltd v Stubbs* [2017] EWHC 180 (Ch). There Rose J emphasised that the claimant's case must be established on a balance of probability by clear evidence of the true intention and that, in addition, there must be an issue capable of being contested between the parties. The latter is required notwithstanding that all the relevant parties consented to the rectification of the document.

112 Rectification can be denied on the basis that there has been undue delay in seeking the remedy. In *Bullard v Bullard* [2017] EWHC 3 (Ch), however, the application was made some 14 years after the creation of the trust, but there was no evidence that the claimant had sat on her hands once she had discovered the problem. Rectification of the trust deed was granted.

necessary that the signed contract mark a mistaken departure from actual common intention. Instead, a mistaken departure from the deemed common intention as objectively assessed will also suffice.[113] As Lord Briggs acknowledged, "The result is that a party can now obtain rectification where previously he could not, in particular in a case where, in fact, and as in *Chartbrook*, the parties were never truly *ad idem* about the matter in issue".[114] Writing extra-judicially, Lord Briggs added that this shift was, "what many judges and academics regard as earth-shattering change in a previously quiet and untroubled area of the law".[115]

It is less common for a contract to be rectified because of the mistake of one party only. Indeed, rectification for a unilateral mistake will be allowed only when there has been some fraud, sharp practice or other unconscionable conduct on the part of the other contracting party.[116] As Arnold J explained in *Classic Property Developments (South East Ltd) v Islam*, "Rectification is available as a remedy for unilateral mistake if one party to a transaction knows that the instrument contains a mistake in his favour, but does nothing to correct it and seeks to take advantage of the other's mistake . . .".[117]

Rectification of a voluntary settlement can, however, occur when there is convincing evidence that, say, a will did not express the clear intention of the testator because of a drafting error by the testator's solicitor.[118] Accordingly, in *Girls' Day School Trust v GDST Pension Trustees* an unamended draft deed was executed by mistake and rectification followed.[119] In *Marley v Rawlings*,[120] a husband and wife mistakenly signed each other's wills. Lord Neuberger felt able to order rectification of Mr Rawling's will so that it contained the typed parts of the will signed by the late Mrs Rawlings in place of the typed parts of the will signed by him. The Supreme Court simply substituted references to the husband for references to the wife and vice versa.[121] Understandably, the burden of proof lies on the shoulders of those seeking rectification.[122] As regards lifetime settlements, rectification can be ordered at the behest of the settlor or, indeed, a beneficiary.[123] The mistake here will usually be of a unilateral nature.

---

113   *Chartbrook Ltd v Persimmon Homes Ltd* [2009] UKHL 38.

114   "Equity in Business" The Denning Society Annual Lecture, 8 November 2018, [46]. He lamented that, as a result, "equity may have taken a course which detracts from commercial certainty . . ." ([50]).

115   Lord Briggs, "Equity in Business" (2019) 135 L.Q.R. 567 at 580.

116   *Commission for New Towns v Cooper (GB) Ltd* [1995] Ch. 259; *Transview Properties Ltd v City Site Properties Ltd* [2008] 2 P. & CR. D 13.

117   [2015] EWHC 2958 (Ch) at [48].

118   *Lawie v Lawie* [2012] EWHC 2940 (Ch). In *ABC v JKL* [2019] EWHC 2416 (Ch), it was emphasised that it is not necessary for the parties to have had a precise form of wording in mind. Rectification can follow if the intended objective of the document is not achieved.

119   [2016] EWHC 1254 (Ch).

120   [2014] UKSC 2.

121   See further Lord Hodge's extra-curial speech, "The Rectification of Wills: *Marley v Rawlings*", The Edinburgh Tax Network and Trust Bar, 12 February 2015, available at *https://www.supremecourt.uk/docs/speech-150212.pdf* [Accessed 31 July 2020].

122   *Joscelyne v Nissen* [1970] 2 Q.B. 86.

123   *Thompson v Whitmore* (1860) 1 John & H. 268.

Rescission

Rescission is a remedy employed to set aside a contract or deed and to restore the parties to their pre-existing positions. The contract/deed is, therefore, voidable and remains, until rescinded, perfectly valid. Accordingly, rescission reflects the desire of one party no longer to be bound by the transaction. As this is a discretionary remedy, the right to rescind may be lost and this will occur when there has been delay,[124] the contract/deed has been affirmed in full knowledge of the facts or it is no longer possible to restore the status quo ante.

Equity claims the ability to set aside a contract where the transaction is tainted by what is known as a vitiating factor. The grounds for rescission include:

- Misrepresentation. A contract/deed may be rescinded if it was induced by misrepresentation. The misrepresentation can be fraudulent, negligent or innocent. Other than with innocent misrepresentation, the victim may also obtain damages.

- Mistake as to fact or law. In *Cooper v Phibbs*,[125] a contract to lease property was entered under the common mistake that the purchaser did not already have an equitable interest in the property. The purchaser later discovered that he had an equitable interest and was entitled to rescind the contract. As regards unilateral mistake, there must be some element of unconscionability arising from the other party's conduct. In both situations, the mistake must have induced the contract.[126]

- Undue influence. Where one party exerts undue influence over the other this takes away the free and voluntary will of the victim. Not surprisingly, therefore, the transaction can be rescinded on this basis.[127]

- Breach of fiduciary duty. A fiduciary duty exists, for example, between trustee and beneficiary. In contracts between these parties, the trustee owes a duty of undivided loyalty and utmost good faith and is obliged to make full disclosure (see Ch.13). If the fiduciary does not satisfy these duties, a contract may be rescinded.[128]

Rescission is not, however, limited to contracts and can be employed to set aside the exercise of a power by a trustee. Although it was once thought that the exercise of a discretionary power

---

124 For example, a delay of 10 years in *Hawkes v County Leasing Asset Management Ltd* unreported 24 February 2015 (HC).

125 (1867) L.R. 2 H.L. 149.

126 *Oscar Chess v Williams* [1957] 1 W.L.R. 370. In *Payne v Tyler* [2019] EWHC 2347 (Ch), a deed of appointment that resulted in a greater liability to inheritance tax was rescinded due to the mistake on the part of the specialist tax adviser to the trust.

127 *Allcard v Skinner* (1837) 36 Ch. D. 145.

128 See the Australian case of *Maguire v Makaronis* (1997) 188 C.L.R. 449, where clients of a solicitor successfully sought rescission of a contract due the solicitor's breach of fiduciary duty.

by a trustee could be rendered void on the basis that the trustees had not taken on board all relevant matters,[129] this is no longer good law. The Supreme Court in the conjoined appeals of *Pitt v Holt; Futter v Futter*[130] made clear that acts which are within the power of trustees can be rescinded if the beneficiary can demonstrate a serious breach of fiduciary duty by the trustees. Acts outside their powers are ultra vires and are necessarily void. Rescission for a trustee's mistake is, moreover, possible. The Supreme Court accepted that a voluntary disposition can be set aside if it would be unconscionable and unjust to allow the mistake to be uncorrected.

Subrogation

1-026

The equitable remedy of subrogation allows one person to be subrogated to the existing rights of another.[131] This means that there is a substitution of one claimant by another. It enables the acquisition of the other's rights against a third party. In its simple form, subrogation allows, say, an insurance company who has paid out under a policy to take over the legal rights of the insured and sue any wrongdoer for the loss it has incurred. Subrogation is also a useful remedy where the claimant's money is employed by the defendant to discharge a secured creditor.[132] The idea, which is reliant upon tracing, is that the claimant can stand in the shoes of the secured creditor. As Walton J observed, "It is simply that where A's money is used to pay off the claim of B, who is a secured creditor, A is entitled to be regarded in equity as having an assignment to him of B's rights as a secured creditor".[133] The claimant will then be able to enforce the security and take priority over the general creditors of the defendant. In *Banque Financiere de la Cite v Parc (Battersea) Ltd*, Lord Hoffmann emphasised that subrogation is a remedy that is primarily restitutionary in nature and designed to reverse the defendant's unjust enrichment.[134] In *Boscawen v Bajwa*,[135] Mr Bajwa intended to sell his house. The purchasers took a £140,000 mortgage from the Abbey National Building Society. From the proceeds of sale, Mr Bajwa intended to redeem a legal charge held by the Halifax Building Society on his property. The purchase money was transferred to Mr Bajwa's solicitors pending completion. Mr Bajwa's solicitors went bankrupt with the purchase money in their client account and the purchase fell through. In breach of trust, the Halifax charge had already been discharged by the solicitors using Abbey National money. Mr Bajwa, therefore, ended up with an unmortgaged property. The Abbey National claimed to be subrogated to the rights of the Halifax in relation

---

129   Re Hastings-Bass [1975] Ch. 25.
130   [2013] 2 A.C. 108; see further, para.**14.43**.
131   Equitable defences can be raised against a claim for subrogation: *Cheltenham & Gloucester Plc v Appleyard* [2004] EWCA Civ 291.
132   See *Day v Tiuta International Ltd* [2014] EWCA Civ 1246. Although the party does not actually acquire the creditor's interest, as Gloster LJ explained (at [43]), "[he] obtains a new and independent equitable security interest which prima facie replicates the creditor's old interest".
133   *Burston Finance Ltd v Speirway Ltd* [1974] 1 W.L.R. 1644 at 1652.
134   [1999] 1 A.C. 221 at 231; see also *Anfield (UK) Ltd v Bank of Scotland Plc* [2011] 1 W.L.R. 2414.
135   [1995] 4 All E.R. 769; see also *Filby v Mortgage Express (No.2) Ltd* [2004] 2 P. & C.R. D16 (mortgage fraud).

to the charge on the property. The Abbey National could trace its money and employed sub-rogation to deprive Mr Bajwa of the unjust enrichment that he would otherwise have obtained at its expense.[136] The Abbey National was treated as if it had been the mortgagee under the extinguished mortgage. By paying off the legal charge, the Abbey National had in effect "purchased" Halifax's right against the property.

A further example of subrogation is where a trustee brings an unsuccessful legal action against a third party. Costs awarded against the trustee can be charged against the trust property and the third party can stand in the shoes of the trustee and, by way of subrogation, claim the trustee's right to indemnity against the trust property.[137]

Remedies in the Context of a Breach of Trust

1-027

In addition to the key equitable remedies, it is necessary to consider the range of personal and proprietary remedies available when there has been a breach of trust.[138] Breaches of trust are many and various, including fraudulent acts, misapplication of trust assets and the failure to act with requisite care and skill. In the case of a breach of trust the beneficiary may require the trustee to account for his stewardship of the trust property. The trustee will be obliged to disclose what trust assets have been in his possession and provide an account of what he has done with such assets. If the beneficiary is not satisfied with the trustee's actions, he has the right to "falsify" or to "surcharge" the account. The account will be "falsified" when the trustee has misapplied trust property, i.e. the trustee has done something that he was not authorised to do. This will entail that the trustee has to account to the trust for the full amount, i.e. the trustee is liable to restore the trust property or its value. As Lord Browne-Wilkinson pointed out in *Target Holdings Ltd v Redferns*, "the basic rule is that a trustee in breach of trust must restore or pay to the trust estate either the assets which have been lost to the estate by reason of the breach or compensation for such loss".[139] Accordingly, if the trustee invests in unauthorised investments and makes a loss, the beneficiaries can insist that the account be falsified and that the money be restored.

The account will be "surcharged" when the trustee has failed to obtain all that should have been obtained for the benefit of the trust. As Peter Millett (writing extra-judicially) explains,

---

136 See also *Bank of Cyprus v Menelaou* [2015] UKSC 66 where the respondent bank was entitled by subrogation to an unpaid vendor's lien over the appellant's property because she had been unjustly enriched at its expense. Similarly, in *Bank of Scotland Plc v Joseph* [2014] EWCA Civ 28, the Bank's money had been used to pay the property developer and it followed that the Bank had a subrogated claim to an unpaid vendor's lien.
137 *Barnett v Semenyuk* [2008] B.P.I.R. 1427.
138 These are considered in detail in Ch.17.
139 [1996] A.C. 421 at 434.

"The trustee is made to account not only for what he has in fact received, but also for what he might in due diligence have received".[140] Hence, the trustee is accountable for what the value of the trust should have been. The beneficiary will, however, have to prove that the loss would not have happened but for the trustee's failure.

In the case of misapplication of the trust property, the beneficiary may make a proprietary claim to the specific assets or their traceable proceeds.

The Trust and its Origins

1-028

Albeit with some structural differences, the forerunner of the trust was known as the "use" and this had existed, at least in a very basic form, since the eleventh century.[141] By the thirteenth century, however, the "use" had become more sophisticated. At the heart of the "use" was the conveyance of property to a third party (the "feoffee to uses") subject to the proviso that the property was to be held for the benefit of a beneficiary (*"cestuis que use"*). In this way, the use fragmented legal and equitable ownership.[142] The feoffee was usually a passive recipient of legal title and held under the duty to account for profits to the beneficiary. In some cases, the feoffee would be under the positive duty to convey the property to another. The popularity of the use in medieval times has been ascribed to the Crusades, which encouraged landowners to give control of their property to a feoffee while they fought abroad. The Franciscan monks have also been held responsible for the growth of the use in that it allowed them to retain the benefit of property without contravening their vow of poverty. The use was also employed to facilitate simple frauds whereby property could be put beyond the claims of creditors and feudal lords. Indeed, the avoidance of feudal incidents, such as wardship, marriage and escheat, was a main influence in the growth of the use. As a precautionary measure, it was usual for there to be more than one feoffee appointed and they were directed to hold as joint tenants. As the existing feoffees died, new ones could be appointed by the settlor.

The use did not suit the common law which did not recognise the divide between legal and beneficial ownership. The beneficiary had no *"seisin"*, i.e. he had no estate in possession, and fell beyond the reach of the common law. Hence, the success of the use rested entirely upon the degree to which the feoffees could be trusted or otherwise enforced to carry out their duties. With the growing popularity of the use in fifteenth-century society, the Chancellor was to play a key role. The settlor was reposing trust and confidence in the feoffee which, although

---

140   P. Millett (1998) "Equity's Place in the Law of Commerce" 114 L.Q.R. 214 at 226.

141   See generally, N. Jones, "Uses and 'Automatic' Resulting Trusts of Freehold" [2013] 72 C.L.J. 91.

142   For a fuller narrative see the Hayton Report, "Trusts and their Commercial Counterparts in Continental Europe" (2002) (commissioned by the Association of Corporate Trustees), paras 3.1–3.8, available at *www.tact.uk.net/ wp-content/uploads/2015/02/The-Hayton-Report.doc* [Accessed 31 July 2020].

not illegal for the feoffee to break, was clearly unconscionable for him to do so. As Simpson puts it:

> "Thus it was the very impotence of the common law which provided the basis upon which the Chancellor could intervene in the name of good conscience and equity and require the feoffee to hold the land for the benefit of the *cestuis que use* and allow him to take the profits."[143]

The Chancellors fashioned rules and principles which were designed to protect the interests of the beneficiary under both an express use and also an implied "resulting use" that arose by operation of law on conveyance for no value or no good reason (e.g. a good reason would be a charitable gift or transfer on marriage). One principle became known as the "doctrine of notice" which was originated to prevent the feoffee transferring use of property to a third party and the latter claiming not to be bound by the use. A further rule was that uses could be disposed of by will, whereas common law estates could not. This ability to make testamentary dispositions became an attractive feature of the use.

1-029

A number of statutes were passed so as to deal with the evasions of creditors and feudal incidents. These provisions were easily sidestepped by the use. The Statute of Uses 1535, however, made a dramatic change in that the legal estate was to be taken away from the feoffees and, instead, vested in the beneficiary. This vesting was termed as "executing the use". It was, in effect, a statutory conveyance of the legal estate and threatened to put an end to the fragmentation of legal and equitable ownership. The application of feudal incidents was again restored. The power to leave the estate by will was also eroded. In the face of political pressure, however, this ability was quickly reinstated and, indeed, extended by the Statute of Wills Act 1540.

Medieval lawyers were keen to identify ways in which the effect of the Statute of Uses could be avoided. First, the statute did not apply to leasehold uses. A settlement to Fred for 1,000 years to the use of Jordan entailed that the legal estate would still be vested in Fred. Jordan's beneficial interest would still need to be enforced in equity. Secondly, it quickly became clear that the Statute of Uses did not apply to so-called "active" uses, that is, where the feoffee had to perform some positive duty under the terms of the use. For example, to Fred subject to the obligation that he pay rents and profits from the land to Jordan. Thirdly, a new type of relationship was gradually innovated and this became known as "the use upon a use". A simple example of this new type of relationship would arise where there was a grant to Fred to the use of Jordan to the use of Fiona. In time, the second use was recognised by equity and this entailed that Jordan became the legal owner (by virtue of the first use) for the benefit of Fiona (under the second use). The use upon a use was, therefore, employed to keep alive the distinction between legal ownership and beneficial ownership.[144] With the recognition that the use upon a use was

---

143 A.W.B. Simpson, *An Introduction to the History of Land Law* (Oxford: Oxford University Press, 1961), p.166.
144 Accordingly, and as Lord Hardwicke observed in *Hopkins v Hopkins* (1738) 1 Atk. 581 at 591, "A statute made

a mere device to outflank the Statute of Uses, a new terminology assumed popularity. By 1700, the relationship had become known as the "trust" and the legal title was held by the "trustee". The terms "use", "feoffee" and *"cestuis que use"* faded into the background. It was then possible to create a "trust" which not being a use, albeit in name only, was not within the Statute of Uses.

1-030

During the eighteenth century, the trust became a vehicle by which wealthy landowners could tie up their property for the benefit of future generations of their families. The technique adopted was to settle land successively on the eldest son of each generation for life with the trustees having the flexibility to raise capital for other members of the family. The Settled Land Act 1882 was designed to give the tenant for life powers to dispose of and manage the land and overcome the problem of the land being sterile for substantial periods of time. The Industrial Revolution and the shifting nature of wealth and investment entailed that the trust was to adopt a more dynamic approach in modern times.[145]

Key Characteristics of a Trust

1-031

Although the trust may be the most important invention of equity, it has proved resistant to precise and exhaustive definition.[146] As Parkinson points out: "There can be no area of law in which there is more confusion about basic definitions than the law of trusts".[147] Although trusts are usually to do with the promotion and safeguarding of wealth, the trust concept arises in a variety of contexts and its ingredient features vary accordingly.[148] It is, therefore, safer to describe what a trust is rather than to go in pursuit of a definitional chimera.[149] As Nolan comments, "A unifying, defining characteristic is sought where none exists, nor ever can exist, given the flexibility of trusts in allocating and apportioning benefit from trust assets".[150] Reduced to its basics, a trust is either a self-imposed obligation or an obligation imposed on a third party (in whom legal title in the property becomes vested) to act for the benefit of another,

---

upon great consideration, introduced in a solemn and pompous manner . . . has no other effect than to add at most three words to a conveyance".

145 See generally, C. Stebbings, "Trustees, Tribunals and Taxes: Creativity in Victorian law", (2007) 70(2) *Amicus Curiae 2*.

146 See W.G. Hart, "What is a Trust?" [1899] 15 L.Q.R. 294 who acknowledges (at 294) that, "ideas which seem to be most simple are really the most difficult to grasp with certainty and express with accuracy".

147 P. Parkinson, "Reconceptualising the express trust" (2002) C.L.J. 657, 657.

148 As Roxburgh J commented in *Re a Solicitor* [1952] Ch. 328 at 332: "As the principles of equity permeate the complications of modern life, the nature and variety of trusts ever grow". D. Hayton, "Developing the Obligation Characteristic of the Trust" (2001) 117 L.Q.R. 96, 97 agrees that, "In the twenty-first century it seems likely that the English Trust concept will be seen to be a more flexible obligation than is currently considered to be the case so that out-dated descriptions or definitions of the trust will need to be re-cast".

149 See generally *Investec Trust (Guernsey) Ltd v Glenalla Properties Ltd* [2018] UKPC 7.

150 R.C. Nolan, "Equitable Property" (2006) 122 L.Q.R. 232, 253.

which is enforceable in equity.[151] The trust may be created inter vivos (i.e. during the lifetime of the settlor) or may be post-mortem (i.e. on the death of the settlor). It might be express or implied in nature. The striking characteristic is that identifiable property is held for the benefit of others.[152] The trustee (or his nominee) holds legal title and the beneficiary will usually enjoy a proprietary equitable interest in the trust property.[153] The beneficial interest is, thereby, both different and distinct from the paper legal title. It is possible, therefore, to appraise the trust either in terms of the property rights conferred on the beneficiaries or the obligations imposed on the legal owner to act for the benefit of others. The core idea, as Parkinson explains, "lies in the notion of equitable obligations in relation to property, which in most cases will also give to beneficiaries commensurate property rights in equity".[154]

The trustee labours under a wide range of duties designed to protect the trust assets and to distribute trust income and capital in accordance with the terms of the trust. Indeed, the trustee owes a special equitable obligation to the beneficiaries, which is known as a fiduciary duty of good faith and loyalty. This ensures that the trustee must always prioritise the interests of the trust over personal interests.[155] If the trustee is in breach of duty, he will be personally liable for the breach of trust. The obligations, moreover, attach to the trust property and can bind anyone in whom that property becomes vested at a later date.[156] In order that the beneficiaries can police the trust, the trustee is under specific duties to maintain financial accounts and to provide other information at their request.[157] As Parkinson observes, "a definition of the trust in terms of obligation and enforcement does offer a way of understanding the irreducible core of the trust concept".[158]

Ratifying art.2 of the Hague Convention on the Law Applicable to Trusts and their Recognition 1984, the Recognition of Trusts Act 1987 promotes a uniform understanding of a trust as a legal relationship created by a settlor for the benefit of a person or purpose and which possesses the following characteristics:

1-032

- the assets are a separate fund and not part of the trustee's own estate;

- legal title to the assets is vested in the name of the trustee or another acting on behalf of the trustee;

---

151 *Raynor v Preston* (1881) 18 Ch. D. 1.
152 Lord Browne-Wilkinson explained in *Westdeutsche Landesbank v Islington* [1996] A.C. 669 at 705 that, "Equity operates on the conscience of the owner of the legal interest. In the case of a trust, the conscience of the legal owner requires him to carry out the purposes for which the property was vested in him (express or implied trust) or which the law imposes on him by reason of his unconscionable conduct (constructive trust)".
153 Different rules apply to certain private purpose trusts (see Ch.6), charitable trusts (see Ch.7) and discretionary trusts (*Gartside v IRC* [1968] A.C. 553).
154 P. Parkinson, "Reconceptualising the express trust" (2002) C.L.J. 657, 663.
155 See Ch.13.
156 Except a bona fide purchaser of value of the legal estate without notice (see Ch.17).
157 Put simply, trustees must be ready to account to the beneficiaries for what they have done with the trust assets: *The Royal National Lifeboat Institution v Headley* [2016] EWHC 1948 (Ch).
158 P. Parkinson, "Reconceptualising the express trust" (2002) C.L.J. 657, 683.

■ the trustee has the power and the duty to manage, employ or dispose of the assets in accordance with the terms of the trust.[159]

Types of Trust

1-033

As indicated, the major reason why the concept of the trust cannot comfortably slot within any promoted definition is that there are various types of trust and various objectives that trusts are designed to achieve. As Hayton observes:

> **"Births, marriages, divorces, or intimations of mortality often lead to the creation of trusts. Tax considerations will play a major role in encouraging a settlor to divest himself of his property and in determining the type of trust to be created to preserve the family wealth from the clutches of the taxman and of improvident spendthrift beneficiaries".[160]**

Although the major classification is between an express trust and an implied trust, a variety of sub-divisions exist within each class. It is useful to consider these categories at this early stage.

The express trust

1-034

Express trusts are created deliberately by the settlor and, as a general rule, may be created by deed, will, writing or orally. The overwhelming majority of trusts are expressly created. The settlor will either declare himself to be a trustee (uncommon) or nominate a third party to act as his trustee. If the latter option is adopted, the settlor must always ensure that the trustee obtains legal title to the trust property by, as appropriate, an inter vivos transfer or by will. The basic ingredients for an express trust are that there is the certainty of intention to create a trust, certainty of subject matter forming the trust and certainty of beneficiary under the trust. By way of an exception to the general rule, some trusts (e.g. those relating to land) must also satisfy additional formalities which usually relate to the need for signed writing. As will now be demonstrated, there are several brands of express trust.

---

159 See generally *Schechter v The Commissioners for Her Majesty's Revenue & Customs* [2017] UKFTT 189 (TC).
160 D. Hayton, *The Law of Trusts* 4th edn (London: Sweet & Maxwell, 2003), p.49.

Bare trusts

A bare or simple trust arises when the trustee holds property for a sole beneficiary who is entitled to the entire beneficial interest without any contingency or encumbrance. The beneficiary can call for a conveyance of the trust property at any time.[161] The trustee has no duties to perform other than holding the property as a nominee for the beneficiary. A bare trust arises where, for example, a solicitor holds client account money in its bank account on trust for its client.[162] Trusts which require the trustee to perform duties are sometimes described as "special trusts".

Fixed trusts

A fixed trust arises where the trustee holds property on trust for a number of specified beneficiaries and their respective shares under the trust are identified in the trust instrument. For example, "£33,000 on trust for Fiona, Jordan and Adrienne equally". There is no discretion in the trustees as to the beneficiaries and their beneficial shares as everything has been predetermined by the settlor.

Executed and executory trusts

This is a further division of express trusts. An executed trust is one where the settlor has made clear exactly what interests are to be taken by each beneficiary, for example "£5,000 on trust for each of my two children". The entitlement of the beneficiaries is, therefore, set out in a final form.

An executory trust arises where the settlor has merely expressed a general intention as to how the property is to be applied. Some other document is intended to be executed so as to define more exactly the beneficial interests to be taken. In *Davis v Richards & Wallington Industries Ltd*,[163] a pension scheme was established by an interim (i.e. temporary) trust instrument. This provided for the later execution of a final trust deed. The validity of the later instrument when executed was challenged. Although the court upheld the later deed, it accepted that, had the deed been defective, the interim instrument would have been a valid executory trust. If necessary, the court could have ordered the execution of a new and final instrument corresponding to the terms of the defective one.

---

161   *Clarence House Ltd v National Westminster Bank Plc* [2010] 1 W.L.R. 1216.
162   *Target Holdings Ltd v Redferns* [1996] A.C. 421.
163   [1990] 1 W.L.R. 1511.

Discretionary trusts

1-038

A discretionary trust arises where the trustee is given some power of selecting who is to get what under the trust. For example, "£100,000 to be divided between my children as my trustee sees fit". There the trustee has to divide the money between my children, but is allowed the discretion as to which child will receive what amount. The trustee cannot fetter his discretion by giving any undertaking as to how discretions and powers will be exercised at a future date.[164] The discretionary trust offers flexibility and can reflect changes in the circumstances and needs of the beneficiaries. Obviously, this makes the job of trustee more difficult and this is particularly so when there is a large class of potential claimants (e.g. a discretionary trust for past and present employees of a particular company). No beneficiary has any property rights until the trustee exercises his discretion. All the beneficiary has is an expectation. As Lewison LJ put it in *SC Mezhdunarodniy Promyshlenniy Bank v Pugachev*, "A beneficiary under a discretionary trust has a right to be considered as a potential recipient of benefit by the trustees. That is an interest which equity will protect".[165]

There is a further sub-classification of "exhaustive" and "non-exhaustive" discretionary trusts. The former arises where the trustee is under the obligation to distribute all the trust property, and the discretion concerns only who should be selected as a recipient of the property. The "non-exhaustive" strain of discretionary trust differs in that the trustee is not under an obligation to distribute all the trust property and is given the power to accumulate income.

Sometimes the distinction between a fixed trust and a discretionary trust is not strikingly apparent. For example, "£200,000 to my trustee so that he will divide it fairly between my children". Although this might appear to be a discretionary trust, it is in fact a fixed trust. As the maxim, "equity is equality" can be brought into play, it will be valid. If, however, the trust is instead "£200,000 to be divided in a fair manner between such of my children as my trustee shall select", this will create a discretionary trust because the trustee is given the choice of who gets what.

Public trusts

1-039

A private (or non-charitable) trust is one which is to benefit people named or described by the settlor (e.g. "my relatives") whereas a public (or charitable) trust is designed to promote a purpose which is beneficial in some way to society (e.g. the relief of poverty).[166] Charitable trusts are, not surprisingly, treated differently from private trusts. They enjoy fiscal advantages, are capable of enforcement by the Attorney General or the Charity Commission (and, hence, do not need to satisfy the rules which require certainty of beneficiary) and need not comply

---

164 *Fielden v Christie-Miller* [2015] EWHC 87 (Ch).
165 [2016] 1 W.L.R. 160 at [13].
166 Charitable purposes are as listed in s.3(1) of the Charities Act 2011.

with the rule against inalienability.[167] In order to be a charitable trust, the purpose must be one that the law recognises as charitable; it must have a public benefit and be exclusively charitable.[168]

Secret trusts

A secret trust is one which is created on the death of the settlor with the element of secrecy being that the existence of the trust is either not evident at all on the face of the settlor's will (a fully secret trust) or where the trust is disclosed in the will, but the identity of the beneficiary is not (a half-secret trust).[169] The secret trust offers a vehicle by which, say, a married man can provide for his clandestine lover or illegitimate child after his death and is discussed in Ch.5.

1-040

Statutory trusts

Statutory trusts are imposed in certain circumstances. The major example is where there are joint legal owners of land. By virtue of the Trusts of Land and Appointment of Trustees Act 1996, the joint owners must necessarily hold the legal title on statutory trust for themselves and/or others (see Ch.11). Statutory trusts arise, for example, on the conveyance of land to minor, on bankruptcy, on intestacy and under the Financial Services and Markets Act 2000. A statutory trust arises also under the Solicitors Act 1974 on the intervention of the Law Society with a solicitor's practice.[170]

1-041

Employee trusts

Employee trusts have become common in recent years and are often known as "Employee Share Ownership Trusts". Such trusts when coupled with approved profit-sharing schemes provide an attractive option for companies and their employees. The company establishes the trust fund with tax deductible money and the trustees acquire shares in the company which are then distributed to the employees. The dividends subsequently paid on those shares are taxed in the hands of the employees.

1-042

---

167   See Ch.4.
168   This is discussed further in Ch.7.
169   See *Rawstron v Freud* [2014] EWHC 2577 (Ch).
170   See *Law Society v Pathania* [2017] EWHC 2469 (Ch).

Pension trusts

1-043

It is common for an individual who is, say, self-employed to maintain a private pension scheme with an insurance company. The individual will pay premiums to the company who will act as trustee, invest the money and, it is to be hoped, provide an adequate pension on the retirement of the individual. As regards the employed sector, there exist contributory pension schemes. These involve its members, in their capacity as employees, contributing a percentage of their earnings to the scheme. The employer will top up their contributions. Such occupational pension trusts (otherwise known as superannuation schemes) are central to modern life and an individual's provision for the future. Indeed, since the Pensions Act 2011 employers are required to enrol their employees, with low or moderate earnings, into an occupational or workplace pension scheme as selected by the employer.[171] Unusually, therefore, occupational pension trusts are rooted in the contractual relationship of employer and employee and, due to the employee's financial contributions, the beneficiary is not simply a volunteer.[172] The trust concept is utilised as a means of managing and investing those substantial payments into the scheme. The beneficiaries, therefore, have rights both in contract and under the trust instrument.[173]

In order to maximise fiscal advantages, the scheme must be approved by the Pensions Regulator and the Inland Revenue. Under such superannuation schemes, the employee makes financial contributions through the "pay as you earn" scheme administered by the employer on behalf of the Inland Revenue. The employee receives income tax relief as regards these pay as you go payments. The employer will also make contributions to the pension scheme. The trustees will invest the entire pension fund and, on the retirement of an employee, the idea is that there should be sufficient funds to provide a taxable pension for the retirement years.[174] The payment may be calculated as a percentage of the employee's final salary (final salary schemes) or may reflect the money earned as a result of the individual's total contributions to the fund (money purchase schemes). The use of a trust, therefore, operates to segregate the pension funds from the employer's funds and to maximise tax advantages.

As mentioned, the choice of scheme to be adopted is up to the employer and, hence, it is the employer who will make the initial appointment of the trustees and determine their powers and duties. The danger, of course, is that the employer may be able to exert too much influence

---

171   For example, a pension scheme entitled the "National Employment Savings Trust" (NEST) was set up by this Act in order to ensure that every employer has free access to a workplace pension scheme that meets the requirements of the new workplace pension rules in operation since the Pensions Act 2008.

172   See generally, Law Commission, *Fiduciary Duties of Investment Intermediaries* (2013) Consultation Paper No.215.

173   See *Air Jamaica Ltd v Charlton* [1991] 1 W.L.R. 1399.

174   The Occupational Pension Scheme (Investment) Regulations 2005 (as amended in 2010) require investments to be made in a manner calculated to ensure the security, quality, liquidity and profitability of the investment portfolio as a whole. The Regulations also call for the diversification of investments and impose a 5% limit on the amount of resources an occupational pension scheme can invest in the sponsoring employer.

and prejudice the interests of the employees. The employer, however, owes a fiduciary duty and is obliged to act in good faith towards its employees.[175] Following the Robert Maxwell scandal in 1991, where some £453 million disappeared from the Mirror Group pension trust, additional safeguards were imposed to prevent the misuse and misappropriation of pension trust funds.[176] The primary aim of the subsequent Pensions Acts is to protect beneficiaries from the effects of poor administration, fraud and insolvency.[177] Basic safeguards such as the keeping of proper books and the maintenance of a separate bank account for trust money, and the imposition of criminal liability on an employer who fails to pay over the employee contributions within a set period, were put in place under the legislation. Parliament introduced the Pensions Regulator who can police pension schemes and can appoint and remove trustees and even bar a person from acting as a trustee. The Pensions Regulator can also impose financial penalties on trustees and, for example, may seek an injunction to restrain a misuse of trust assets and/or apply to court for restitution of assets which have been misused. The Pensions Regulator can even wind up an occupational pension scheme in order to protect the scheme's members. In addition, the Pensions Ombudsman may investigate complaints and disputes concerning maladministration. The legislation also introduced the Pension Protection Fund which is designed to provide limited compensation for loss suffered by members of a pension scheme when the employer has become insolvent leaving a final salary scheme in deficit. It is expected that Parliament will eventually remove the current cap on compensation.

Although governed by the same core principles as other trusts,[178] funded pension trusts are undoubtedly distinctive and specialist in nature.[179] As Hayton explains, "the species of pension trust should be regarded as having evolved from the trust genus as a drastically different species from the species of the traditional family trust".[180] They are rooted in a contractual relationship existing between the employee and the employer/pension provider, involve large sums of money and large numbers of beneficiaries and are regulated by discrete statutory controls.[181] Hence, pension trusts have a distinct character and reflect situations not encountered by other trustees.[182] As Lord Walker put it, "pensions trusts, burdened by increasingly complex regulatory statutes, are another enclave reserved for pensions specialists".[183] As such, their detailed regulation falls beyond the scope of this general text.

---

175 *Imperial Group Pension Trust Ltd v Imperial Tobacco Ltd* [1991] 2 All E.R. 597.

176 See generally, *Pension Law Reform: Pension Law Review Committee Report* (1993) Cmnd.2342.

177 See R. Nobles, "Pensions Act 1995" (1996) 59 M.L.R. 241.

178 See *Cowan v Scargill* [1984] 2 All E.R. 750; *Re Drexel Burnham Lambert UK Pension Plan* [1995] 1 W.L.R. 32.

179 See the views of Browne-Wilkinson VC in *Imperial Group Pension Trust Ltd v Imperial Tobacco Ltd* [1991] 2 All E.R. 597.

180 D. Hayton, "Pension Trusts and Traditional Trusts: Dramatically Different Species of Trust" [2005] Conv. 229, 245.

181 See *In the Matter of Merchant Navy Ratings Pension Fund* [2015] Pens. L.R. 239.

182 See D.M. Fox, "Discretion and Moral Hazard in Pension Funds" (2010) 69 C.L.J. 240.

183 *Pitt v Holt; Futter v Futter* [2013] 2 A.C. 108 at [15].

Protective trusts

1-044

A protective trust is aimed at ensuring that a feckless beneficiary will not lose the trust property to his creditors or sell his trust interest to someone else.[184] The way in which this protection is achieved is by giving the beneficiary a life interest in the property which is made determinable on a given event (e.g. bankruptcy or assignment) and followed by a discretionary trust in favour of specified beneficiaries.[185] Hence, there are two trusts. The first is designed to benefit the main beneficiary (e.g. a son) until the happening of the determining event. The second trust bites once the event has occurred and, thereby, preserves the trust property and allows the discretionary beneficiaries (which may include the son) to benefit without bothering about the claims of creditors or the trustee in bankruptcy. One limitation is that the settlor cannot create a protective trust with himself having a determinable life interest.[186] In addition, while the forfeiture might operate so as to shield the money against the claims of creditors, it is not always free from negative consequences for the main beneficiary. In *Re Baring's ST*, for example, on forfeiture occurring a wife lost her income from the trust property, which then went to others under the second trust.[187]

Implied Resulting and Constructive Trusts

1-045

There are two types of implied trust: the resulting trust (see Ch.9) and the constructive trust (see Ch.10). It is helpful for the distinction between the two styles of implied trust to be understood at this early stage.

The resulting trust takes its name from the fact that it operates to ensure that beneficial title "results back" to a transferor. This is more easily understood by considering the circumstances in which the resulting trust will arise. First, where one party transfers legal title of property to another in return for no consideration a presumption of a resulting trust is raised, but may be displaced by the outmoded and gender-biased counter-presumption of advancement (i.e. gift) (see Ch.9).[188] This type of resulting trust is sometimes called a "voluntary conveyance resulting trust". The equitable interest will result back to the transferor.

---

184 See L.A. Sheridan, "Protective Trusts" [1957] Conv. 110.
185 This is facilitated by s.33 of the Trustee Act 1925 which allows such a trust to be created by merely directing the trustees to hold on "protective trust". Section 33 of the Act sets out a traditional template for the protective trust.
186 See *Re Detmold* (1889) 40 Ch. D. 585.
187 [1940] Ch. 737.
188 Advancement is to be abolished if and when s.199 of the Equality Act 2010 is implemented: see J. Glister, "Section 199 of the Equality Act 2010: How Not to Abolish the Presumption of Advancement" (2010) 73 M.L.R. 80.

Secondly, it arises where property is purchased by Fiona with some financial assistance from Jordan. Jordan may acquire an interest in the property by virtue of a purchase money resulting trust. Such a trust will be relevant only when there is no common intention to share the property beneficially and when the payments were made to the acquisition cost of the property. The examples so far concern what is traditionally called the "presumed intention resulting trust".

Thirdly, when a settlor who intends to create an express trust fails in some way to dispose of the entire equitable interest that which remains results back to the settlor. This third class is often called an "automatic resulting trust" because it is traditionally perceived to be an automatic response to the failure to deal with the property fully and effectively. For example:

- Fred transfers legal title to shares to Jordan to hold on trust for Adrienne. If Adrienne dies before the transfer, the trust fails and the beneficial interest in those shares results back to Fred[189];

- as occurred in *Vandervell v IRC*,[190] when Mr Vandervell retained an option to purchase back shares transferred to the Royal College of Surgeons, the entire beneficial interest was not dealt with and, because of this failure to declare in whom the beneficial interest of the option was vested, a resulting trust arose in favour of a very unhappy and heavily taxed Mr Vandervell;

- in *Barclays Bank v Quistclose Investments Ltd*,[191] what appeared to be a loan was subject to the condition that the money could only be used to pay dividends to shareholders of a particular company. As the money was never used for these purposes, it was held on resulting trust for the "lender"; and

- if there is a trust under which specified allocated annuities are to be paid, say, to elderly beneficiaries who die before the fund is exhausted, the surplus will result back to the settlor.[192]

The constructive trust is very different from the resulting trust. It is a trust imposed by the court as a result of conduct and, being designed to ensure good conscience, originally had nothing to do with the intention of the parties. For example, in *Keech v Sandford*[193] a trustee of leasehold property abused his position by negotiating the grant of a new lease of a market in his own favour. Although the landlord had refused to grant a renewal to the trust, his personal interests conflicted with the interests of the trust. Hence, a constructive trust was imposed under which the original trustee held the lease for the benefit of the beneficiaries under the

---

189   The objects of the trust failed: see *Bankes v Salisbury Diocesan Council* [1960] Ch. 631.
190   [1967] 2 A.C. 291.
191   [1968] 3 All E.R. 651. This case is discussed in detail in Ch.9.
192   See *Re Llanover Settled Estates* [1926] Ch. 626.
193   (1726) Sel. Cas. Ch. 61.

express trust. If the property has been disposed of, the constructive trust will attach to the proceeds of sale.[194] These trusts arise by operation of law and are framed to prevent unconscionable dealings.[195] As Sir Terence Etherton explained at the Court of Appeal stage in *FHR European Ventures LLP v Mankarious*, "The constructive trust is a feature of equity which arises in many different areas of the law. They include, among others, contracts for the sale of land, the perfection of imperfect gifts, gifts in contemplation of death (donatio mortis causa), testamentary secret trusts, mutual wills, common intention constructive trusts, fraud and undue influence, estoppel, specific performance, joint ventures, breach of trust, and breach of fiduciary duty".[196]

1-046

Time has, however, marched on and the constructive trust has a modern sphere in which to operate, and this is in relation to the joint purchase of the family home. As is demonstrated in Ch.11, the constructive trust has largely subsumed the relevance of the resulting trust in this area of the law. There are two scenarios where this so-called "common intention constructive trust" will arise.[197] The first is when there has been some discussion, arrangement or understanding between the parties as to beneficial ownership of the property. If a non-owning party acts to his detriment on the strength of that express bargain, a constructive trust will arise and the court will give effect to the bargain reached. The second instance of a family home constructive trust is when the parties have no discussion at all about the fate of the beneficial ownership of the property, but the non-owner makes a direct financial contribution to the purchase of the property. In such circumstances there will be an implied bargain constructive trust arising from the presumed common intentions of the parties as evidenced by the course of dealings between them.

Distinguishing a Trust from Other Legal Concepts

1-047

Due to the very different legal consequences that attach to a trust relationship than operate in relation to other types of relationship, it is necessary to make some key distinctions at the outset. The alternative concepts that will be considered are debt, bailment, agency, gift and

---

194 *Royal Brunei Airlines v Tan* [1995] 2 A.C. 378.

195 See *Westdeutsche Landesbank Girozentrale v Islington BC* [1996] A.C. 669.

196 [2013] 3 W.L.R. 466 at [75]. He added at [75]: "Although it may be said at the most general level that the constructive trust is a feature of equity to prevent or remedy unconscionable conduct, there is no generally accepted set of principles governing the existence of a constructive trust across all the different areas of the law where it is to be found".

197 See *Lloyds Bank v Rosset* [1991] 1 A.C. 107.

the thornier distinction between a trust and a power. It is to be appreciated, however, that, as the use of the trust concept develops, the boundaries between the trust and other categories of legal relationships are inevitably shifting. This is particularly evident with the distinction between trusteeship and agency.

Debt

A debt is usually rooted in a bilateral contractual relationship between the debtor and the creditor. The law of contract is underpinned by the concept of privity of contract which, subject to certain statutory exceptions (e.g. the Contracts (Rights of Third Parties) Act 1999), entails that only a party to a contract can bring an action for breach of contract. Even though no consideration has been provided and no privity of contract exists, a beneficiary can still enforce a trust in equity. The rights afforded under a contract are, moreover, personal whereas a trust interest is a property right. This entails that a trust can be enforced against third parties whereas, due to privity of contract, a contract is not usually enforceable against a non-contracting party. This is important when the recipient of money becomes bankrupt. If the recipient is a debtor and the money is paid under a contract, then the creditor has no special claim and must compete for repayment with other creditors. If the property was trust property, however, the beneficiaries have a prior claim over other creditors. The distinction between a contractual debt and a trust is not, however, always easy to draw. For example, in *First City Monument Bank Plc v Zumax Nigeria Ltd*,[198] it was argued that ten transfers (totalling $3,752,000) by the Bank were subject to a liability to account as a constructive trustee. The Court of Appeal could discern no trust. Newey & Lewison LJJ emphasised that the basic banker–customer relationship was one of debtor and creditor and not that of trustee and beneficiary. The money placed in the custody of a banker was, to all intents and purposes, the money of the banker to do with as it pleased. The Bank received the monies as the agent of its customer to whom it owed duties arising purely from their contractual relationship.

By way of contrast, in *Barclays Bank v Quistclose Investments Ltd*[199] money was loaned by Quistclose to a company known as Rolls Razor Ltd specifically in order that the latter could pay its shareholders dividends. The money was placed in a separate account at Barclays Bank by Rolls Razor. Before any dividend was paid, Rolls Razor went into liquidation and Barclays Bank laid siege to the money loaned in order to discharge a debt owed to it by the defunct company. If this had merely been a contractual loan, Quistclose's position would have been hopeless. The House of Lords, however, discerned the existence of an implied trust (later identified as

198 [2019] EWCA Civ 294.
199 [1968] 3 All E.R. 651.

a resulting trust).[200] The beneficiary of that resulting trust, Quistclose, could thus reclaim its money in priority to the bank's claims. As examined in Ch.9, numerous cases have been decided in the wake of *Quistclose* and all turn upon there being the finding of some condition that has yet to be satisfied.

1-049

Albeit in a different setting, the tension between contract and trust is evident in the cases where there has been no segregation of trust property (examined in Ch.2). In *Re Goldcorp Exchange Ltd*,[201] customers had paid money for precious metals which were stored for convenience and safekeeping at the dealer's premises. The metals, however, were not separated or segregated in any way. The dealer ceased trading and competing claims arose as to the precious metals. Those that had bought the stored metals claimed the existence of a trust so as to facilitate their claims in advance of the creditors. The court concluded that there could be no trust of tangible objects unless they were clearly identifiable and, as that was not the case here, the owners could not claim priority. It was purely a matter of contract.

Bailment

1-050

If goods are entrusted to another for safe keeping or repair, the relationship at common law is one of bailment. Bailment can be contractual (e.g. as with valet parking of a car) or gratuitous (e.g. when a friend borrows the car). It can even be involuntary as when a mortgagor leaves chattels in property to be repossessed by the mortgage lender.[202] There is, admittedly, some similarity with the trust in that the property is handed over to another and the recipient is under a duty in relation to that property. Nevertheless, they are very different creatures.[203] In the above examples, legal title to the car does not pass to the third party and it always remains with the original owner. There is no intention to fragment legal and equitable ownership. The bailee cannot pass title to the property. The duty owed by the bailee is also comparatively slight (i.e. a duty to take reasonable care) when compared to the diverse and onerous equitable duties of a trustee.[204]

---

200 Lord Millett in *Twinsectra Ltd v Yardley* [2002] 2 A.C. 164.
201 [1994] 2 All E.R. 806.
202 See *Campbell v Redstone Mortgages Ltd* [2014] EWHC 3081 (Ch).
203 See *Day v Royal College of Music* [2013] 3 W.L.R. 1560 where the distinction was held to turn on the intention objectively ascertained from the property owner's words and conduct.
204 See *Da Rocha-Afodu v Mortgage Express Ltd* [2014] EWCA Civ 454.

Agency

The key distinction between an agent and a trustee is that an agency is a relationship based upon a contract between principal and agent and, therefore, only offers personal rights in favour of the principal. An agency usually passes no title to the property and legal and beneficial ownership is unaffected.[205] An agent is empowered to commit his principal within the limits of his authority as if the principal had agreed personally. The extent of the liabilities of an agent will depend primarily upon the terms of the contract as will the duration of the agency.[206] As should now be clear, a trust bestows property rights on the beneficiary which, if necessary, can be enforced against third parties. Like a trustee, an agent owes a fiduciary duty to her principal. This is the most striking similarity as both are prevented from making unauthorised profits and becoming unduly enriched from their position. It is a confidential relationship importing a duty normally of undivided loyalty on the part of the agent. If an agent makes such a profit, she will hold the money made on constructive trust for her principal. As with a beneficiary, a principal can employ the equitable rules of tracing so as to claim back misappropriated assets, secret commissions and bribes in the hands of a third party.[207]

Gifts

A gift is the complete transfer of property to another. Both legal and equitable titles pass and the donee becomes the absolute owner of the property. A gift is not dependent upon consideration and is voluntary in nature. To perfect a gift, it is necessary that the relevant form of transfer relating to the type of property involved is employed. If not, there is an imperfect gift which equity will not perfect and, as there is no consideration given, equity cannot assist a volunteer. By way of a simple example, Fred approaches Jordan and passes across a £20 note saying something akin to: "I want you to have this as a birthday present". Absolute ownership has passed to Jordan by the parting with possession and the intention to make a gift. If Fred then seeks to claim the money back it is simply too late. Compare this with Fred giving Jordan a £20 note until Jordan gets paid at the end of the week. This is not a gift, but is instead a loan. A contract exists between Fred and Jordan which can be enforced as a debt. In contrast, Fred gives Jordan a £20 note and says, "Will you give this to Fiona when you see her tonight". This is

---

205 If the agent acquires property on behalf of the principal, this may give rise to a trust in favour of the latter: *Re Lehman Brothers International (Europe)* [2012] 3 All E.R. 1.

206 See *Bailey v Angove's Pty Ltd* [2016] UKSC 47. There Lord Sumption emphasised that to allow the agent to exercise authority, after it has been revoked, would amount to the specific enforcement of a relationship, which is by its nature not specifically enforceable.

207 *FHR European Ventures LLP v Cedar Capital Partners LLC* [2015] A.C. 250.

not a gift to Jordan nor is it a loan. There is no contract, but there is a trust. Jordan has the legal title to the money, but holds that £20 on trust for Fiona.

Powers of Appointment

1-053

A trust will always place mandatory obligations, admittedly of varying degree, on the shoulders of the trustee. As regards a fixed trust, the duty of the trustee is to distribute according to the precise allocation made by the settlor. In relation to a discretionary trust, the duty of the trustee is to exercise his discretion in accordance with the guidance provided by the settlor and to distribute accordingly. The beneficiary under a fixed trust has an entitlement to the distribution of his share as laid out in the trust instrument. The beneficiary under a discretionary trust has no more than a mere expectation that she will be allocated a beneficial share. She can, however, demand that trustees exercise discretion in accordance with the trust. A survey of the key duties of trustees is provided in Ch.13.

A trust will frequently give the trustee powers that are dispositive in nature. Trusts and powers are different creatures. These dispositive powers are those that authorise the trustee to apply trust property (e.g. the powers of advancement and maintenance) in a different manner than is obligatory under the terms of the trust.[208] The major dispositive power is the power of appointment. Usually operating behind a trust, it allows the donee the discretion to divert trust money from the beneficiaries or otherwise dispose of trust property in favour of another person or purpose, but only to the extent permitted by the settlor. Unlike non-charitable trusts it is, therefore, possible to have a power to promote a purpose.[209] The idea is to promote flexibility without imposing onerous obligations on the donee of the power.

Distinguishing a power from a discretionary trust

1-054

It is essential to distinguish a power from a discretionary trust. Although this task is usually a straightforward matter of construction of the words used, a power of appointment and a discretionary trust may share similar characteristics.[210] In both there may be provision for the distribution of assets between members of a class, the selection of who is to benefit and the fixing of the amounts each is to receive. The difference is that under a discretionary trust the trustees are obliged to apply the trust property in the prescribed manner (even with a non-

---

208 See Ch.14.
209 *Re Douglas* (1887) 35 Ch. D. 472; *Re Shaw* [1957] 1 W.L.R. 729.
210 For a catalogue of differences and similarities see *Breadner v Granville-Gossman* [2001] Ch. 523; see further J. Hopkins, "Certain Uncertainties of Trusts and Powers" (1971) 29 C.L.J. 68.

exhaustive discretionary trust where the trustees have the power to accumulate income). If the intention is that the discretion must be exercised, then the relationship is a trust. As demonstrated in Ch.16, the beneficiaries together (provided they are of the age of majority and in sound mind) can collectively put an end to the trust, even a discretionary trust, and divide the property between them.[211]

As regards a power of appointment, appointors are not under an obligation to apply the fund. As Emery explains, "A power of appointment differs from a trust primarily in that a donee of a power (unlike a trustee) has no duty whatever to make any appointments of the settlement property".[212] Powers are always exercisable at the election of the donee. They are simply permissive in nature. The discretion is whether to exercise it or not. Where a power is not exercised, the property goes to those entitled in default of appointment (e.g. the beneficiaries under the trust). A potential object under a power has no entitlement, whether individual or collective, and must be content to live in hope that the power will be exercised in his favour.[213] As to whether a trust or a power has been created, all turns upon the intention, actual or presumed, of the settlor as divined from the language of the instrument. Hence, if there is a gift over in default of appointment then this will demonstrate the lack of intention to create a trust.[214] In *Re Weekes*,[215] a testatrix left her husband a life interest in property and gave him the power to dispose of all such property by will amongst their children. He died intestate. The court could not discern a trust and concluded that the intention had been to create a power.

Powers may be fiduciary or personal. Fiduciary powers are powers vested in an office holder such as the trustee. In *Mettoy Pension Trustees Ltd v Evans*,[216] for example, a large company had stood in a fiduciary relationship with the beneficiaries under an occupational pension scheme. Under the pension scheme rules, any surplus of the pension fund could be applied to further benefits at the discretion of the employer. On the liquidation of Mettoy there were 2,500 entitled to benefits and a £9 million surplus. Two issues arose. First, whether the power was fiduciary in nature. The High Court held that the power was fiduciary and, hence, the beneficiaries had a right to be considered for discretionary benefits. Secondly, whether the power could be exercised by liquidators. The High Court concluded that, as the power was not an asset of the Company, it could not be exercised by the liquidator. Nevertheless, the court was able to enforce the power on behalf of the Company in a manner best suited to carry out the purposes of the pension scheme.

Where discretion is exercised under a fiduciary power, the donee must do so responsibly. The duty is to consider periodically, whether or not to exercise discretion to benefit beneficiaries

1-055

---

211 *Saunders v Vautier* (1841) 49 E.R. 282.
212 C.T. Emery, "The Most Hallowed Principle: Certainty of Trusts and Powers of Appointment" (1982) 98 L.Q.R. 551, 579, 580.
213 *Re Sayer* [1957] Ch. 423.
214 *Re Mills* [1930] 1 Ch. 654. There is no intention to benefit the objects of the power if it is not exercised. The intention is to benefit someone else on default of appointment.
215 [1897] 1 Ch. 289.
216 [1991] 2 All E.R. 513.

or objects of the power.[217] The fiduciary power must be exercised in good faith and not in a manner that negates the sensible expectation of the settlor.[218] Such appointors, as Lord Reid observed, "cannot simply push aside the power and refuse to consider whether it ought in their judgment to be exercised".[219] By contrast, a personal (or mere/bare) power is vested in an individual in a personal capacity. Here the donee is not required to consider periodically whether to exercise the power. In the absence of a fraud on the power (i.e. where the power has been exercised for an improper purpose) the exercise of discretion cannot be challenged in court. The court is not in a position to take away a personal power from a donee.

A power of appointment may be "general" in that the donee is allowed to exercise it in favour of anyone he chooses (including himself), "special" in that it can be exercised only in favour of specified persons or purposes or "intermediate" or "hybrid" in that it is exercisable in favour of anyone except for specified persons or purposes.[220] For example, a fixed trust of £100,000 in favour of Jordan and Fiona might allow the trustee the special power to pay, at his discretion, income or capital to Adrienne or Fred. Hence, the donee is permitted to siphon away trust money for the benefit of these persons. Similarly, the power might allow the donee the capacity to make charitable donations from trust money. This means that the donee is under no obligation to pay money to Adrienne or Fred or to make a charitable donation, but because the donee is a fiduciary she is obliged to consider from time to time whether or not to do so.[221] As has been discussed, the donee simply cannot ignore the existence of the power and, if it is exercised, it must be exercised reasonably and responsibly. Accordingly, if the power allowed an appointment of property to Adrienne or Fred, the trustee would act outside the power if she appointed to Noel. This would be a "patent" incorrect use of the power. If the donee of the power acted in a clandestine manner to subvert the intended use of the power, this would be a "latent" incorrect use of the power.[222] Of course, if the power is not exercised the money remains on trust for Jordan and Fiona.

Sometimes, the label "trust power" is employed. This description is, however, apt to confuse and, as it lacks real significance in modern times, should be used sparingly.[223] If the obligation imposed is mandatory, the existence of a discretionary trust must be recognised. If it is, instead, a mere permission, then it is a power. It is to be recalled that all turns on the intentions of the settlor, the construction by the court of the language employed and whether mandatory

---

217 *Re Hay's ST* [1981] 3 All E.R. 788.
218 *Re Pauling's ST* [1964] Ch. 303.
219 *Re Gulbenkian* [1970] A.C. 508 at 518. He added at 518: "And they cannot give money to a person who is not within the classes of persons designated by the settlor . . .".
220 *Re Manisty's Settlement* [1973] 3 W.L.R. 34; see J. Hopkins, "A New Shape or Form of Power of Appointment" (1974) 33 C.L.J. 66.
221 *Re Charteris* [1917] 2 Ch. 379.
222 See generally the lecture of Lord Sales presented to the Chancery Bar Association entitled "Fraud on a Power: the interface between contract and equity" (2 April 2019), p.7. This is available at *https://www.supremecourt.uk/docs/speech-190402.pdf* [Accessed 31 July 2020].
223 As J. Hopkins, "Certain Uncertainties of Trusts and Powers" (1971) 29 C.L.J. 68 put it, at 70, "the so-called power in the nature of a trust is regarded really as a trust, which masquerades under the guise of a power . . .".

words are used.[224] For example, in *Burrough v Philcox*[225] the testator gave life interests to his two children with remainder to their issue. The will stipulated that, if the children did not have issue, the survivor had power to distribute the property by will amongst the original testator's nephews and nieces as the survivor should select. It was held that the original testator had, thereby, created a trust in favour of his nephews and nieces. The trust was subject to the survivor's power of selection, which lapsed when the survivor himself died. The general intention to benefit a class overrode the failure of the survivor to exercise his particular power to select.[226] In *Re Weekes ST*, however, no such general intention was discernible and so, when the donee of the power died without making an appointment, the property remained in the donee's estate.[227]

Guide to Further Reading

A. Burrows, "We Do This At Common Law But That In Equity" (2002) 22 O.J.L.S. 1.

A.J. Duggan, "Is Equity Efficient?" (1997) 113 L.Q.R. 601.

S. Gardner, "Two Maxims of Equity" (1995) C.L.J. 60.

W.G. Hart, "What is a Trust?" (1899) 15 L.Q.R. 294.

A. Mason, "The Place of Equity and Equitable Remedies in the Contemporary Common Law World" (1994) 110 L.Q.R. 238.

P. Parkinson, "Reconceptualising the Express Trust" (2002) C.L.J. 657.

---

224 See *McPhail v Doulton* [1971] A.C. 424 where Lord Wilberforce had to determine whether a clause, which stated that the trustees "Shall apply the net income . . . in such amounts at such times and subject to such conditions (if any) as they think fit", created a power or a trust. The House of Lords upheld a discretionary trust.

225 (1840) 5 My. & Cr. 72.

226 See also *Borwon v Higgs* (1803) 8 Ves. 561.

227 [1897] 1 Ch. 289. Romer J held that there must be a clear indication that the donor intended the power to be regarded in the nature of a trust so that the class should take.

2

The Three Certainties

As shown in Ch.1, the key characteristic of a trust lies in its fragmentation of legal and equitable ownership. Legal (i.e. nominal) title rests with the trustee (or his nominee), whereas equitable (i.e. substantive or real) title vests in the beneficiary. In all cases, the trustee is under a fiduciary duty to use the property according to the terms of the trust and is personally liable to a beneficiary for any breach of trust conditions. Accordingly, it is necessary that the settlor demonstrates that a trust was intended, demarcates the property that is to be the subject of that trust, and identifies who is to benefit under its terms. To cater for this, the law has evolved a test known as the "three certainties" which requires certainty of intention, certainty of subject matter and certainty of objects.[1] The general rule is that the three certainties need to be present so that a trust can be practicable, enforceable and capable of supervision by the court. As these certainties are conceptually separate, different requirements apply to each head of certainty. Accordingly, each will be examined in turn.

Initial Observations

It is to be appreciated that all three certainties must be present as regards express private trusts. In relation to public (i.e. charitable) trusts, however, there is no need to establish certainty of objects (i.e. beneficiaries) because the Attorney General (on behalf of the Crown) and the independent body known as the Charity Commission have the legal authority to enforce charitable trusts.

The test as to "certainty of objects" varies between fixed trusts (i.e. where the beneficiaries

1   See Lord Langdale MR in *Knight v Knight* (1840) 3 Beav. 148 at 173.

and their shares are identified) and discretionary trusts (where the trustee selects who exactly is to benefit from a wider class specified by the settlor). Except for charitable trusts, which are the subject of special treatment, the objects must be living individuals. Private purpose trusts (e.g. to care for pets) are thought to have no place in the modern law. This is because of the "beneficiary principle" which requires that there be someone with locus standi (i.e. the legal capacity) to apply to the court to enforce the trust.[2]

And gifts?

2-003

Issues of certainty might arise also in relation to gifts. This is particularly so with conditions that are attached to a gift, for example a condition precedent[3] or a condition subsequent.[4] Although these eventualities must be conceptually certain,[5] a less strict test applies to these types of gift than applies to trusts.[6] In *Re Allen*,[7] the Court of Appeal was invited to decide whether a devise "to the eldest of the sons of [A] who shall be a member of the Church of England and an adherent to the doctrine of that church" was void for lack of certainty. By a majority, it was held that the personal representative could establish as fact whether the eldest son (the appellant) satisfied the conditions. In *Blathhwayt v Baron* Cawley,[8] a condition for forfeiture if the recipient of a gift should be or become a Roman Catholic was upheld. A further illustration of this liberality emerges from *Re Barlow's Will Trust*.[9] There, a testatrix bequeathed a number of valuable paintings to specified individuals. As to the remainder of her collection, she directed her executor to sell the paintings with the proviso that "any friends of mine who may wish to do so" could buy any of the paintings at less than market value. This direction was upheld because a complete list of friends was not needed. Browne-Wilkinson J understood the term "friend" to be someone with whom the deceased had a social relationship and had met frequently when circumstances allowed. The friends so defined had options to purchase the artwork. This is a tolerant approach that does not extend to trusts. As will become clear, the term "friend" is insufficiently certain for the creation of a trust.

---

2 See *Re Astor's ST* [1952] Ch. 534.

3 For example, an interest vesting only on the donee becoming a solicitor.

4 For example, an interest ceasing on the donee's bankruptcy. This type of condition is often referred to as a forfeiture clause.

5 For example, a condition that a person, as appropriate, merely resides or ceases to reside in a particular area will be void for uncertainty: *Re Gape* [1952] Ch. 743. Cf. a condition subsequent that the donees "take up permanent residence in England" where the reference to "permanent" and a country render it sufficiently certain.

6 See *Re Allen* [1953] Ch. 810, where, as regards certainty of objects, the test is that the gift is valid if it is possible to show that at least one person qualifies even though there may be uncertainty as to others; see generally C.T. Emery, "The Most Hallowed Principle: Certainty of Trusts and Powers of Appointment" (1982) 98 L.Q.R. 551.

7 [1953] Ch. 810.

8 [1976] A.C. 397.

9 [1979] 1 W.L.R. 278.

Consequences of a lack of certainty

The consequences of an absence of certainty may vary according to which certainty is lacking.[10] First, as regards an absence of the *certainty of intention* to create a trust and depending upon the circumstances, there are alternative options as to what will become of the property. If the property was given or bequeathed to a third party, it will be viewed as an absolute gift to that person.[11] Legal and beneficial title will be transferred to the recipient without the recipient's being subject to any legal obligation to do anything with the property. If, however, the settlor has retained legal title to the property,[12] the property will simply remain in the settlor's estate. This is illustrated in *Re TXU Europe Group Plc*.[13] There the key issue was whether an investment portfolio (valued at more than £8 million) was held by the company on trust to provide top-up benefits to certain senior employees. The High Court held that there was an absence of any positive indication of the intention to hold it on trust. Indeed, such indicators as there were pointed towards the opposite conclusion.[14] Accordingly, the money stayed with the company and was available to its general creditors.

2-004

Secondly, if there is a lack of *certainty of subject matter* there are again alternative possibilities. Where there is no certainty of trust property whatsoever, there can be no trust. Applying common sense, and as there is nothing sufficiently identifiable that can leave the legal owner, the property will remain with the settlor (or the settlor's estate). As such, the property will remain susceptible to the claims of the settlor's creditors or next of kin. In the scenario where there is a lack of certainty of beneficial share, the trust will also fail. If the settlor had intended to act as trustee, the property will obviously remain with her (or her estate). If, however, legal title to the trust property has already left the settlor and become vested in a third-party trustee, the trustee will hold the trust property on what is called a "resulting trust". This entails that the property automatically reverts to the settlor (or her estate).

Thirdly, as regards an absence of *certainty of objects*, if the settlor is the trustee, then nothing at all happens. No property has left the estate of the settlor. If, however, a third party has been appointed as trustee, then, on failure of the trust, the property is again to be held upon automatic resulting trust for the settlor (or her estate).

2-005

---

10   See G. Williams, "*The Three Certainties*" (1940) 4 M.L.R. 20.
11   *Lassence v Tierney* (1849) 1 Mac. & G. 551; *Hancock v Watson* [1902] A.C. 14.
12   For example, where the settlor had attempted unsuccessfully to declare himself as a trustee of the property for the benefit of another (see Ch.3).
13   [2003] EWHC 3105 (Ch).
14   For example, the company's accounts referred to the investment as an asset. It was also clear that the company's directors (the potential beneficiaries) did not, at the time of the investment, wish for a trust to be created because each would have incurred an immediate liability to tax.

Certainty of Intention

2-006   It is necessary for the settlor[15] to intend to create a trust as opposed to some other type of legal relationship (e.g. a gift, a power, bailment or agency). There is, however, no magic formula required to demonstrate the intention to create a trust. It is a well-established principle that equity looks to substance not form. Hence, it is the finding of intention rather than the precise form of expression employed that assumes importance. Trusts can be expressly declared or even inferred from the conduct of the parties and the surrounding circumstances. The test is whether, on a construction of the words used and/or from the behaviour of the parties, there is discernible a clear intention that the property is to be held on trust for the benefit of a third party.[16] The court is advised against taking an unduly technical approach to the interpretation of a homemade document.[17] A mere expression of desire to make a gift or to confer a benefit is insufficient. The unequivocal intention must be to separate legal and equitable ownership and to impose the obligations of trusteeship on the holder of the legal title.[18] This raises issues of fact and degree.[19] Although desirable, the use of the word "trust" is not essential.[20] Indeed, as in *Singha v Heer*, even if the term is employed it offers no guarantee that a trust will have been created.[21] It is a word that is capable of various meanings.[22] As Marcus Smith J explained in *The High Commissioner for Pakistan v Prince Mukarram Jah*, " the use of the term 'trust' is by no means conclusive as to the existence of an express trust: it is one of the factors that must be taken into account when considering whether or not a trust has been created".[23]

---

15   The intention of a third-party trustee is irrelevant: *The High Commissioner for Pakistan v Prince Mukarram Jah* [2020] 2 W.L.R. 699.

16   See *North v Wilkinson* [2018] EWCA Civ 161 where the language of the document was inapposite to create a trust of a business in favour of investors.

17   *Wallbank v Price* [2007] EWHC 3001 (Ch); see also *Kynnersley v Wolverhampton City Council* [2008] W.T.L.R. 65.

18   See *Wright v Atkyns* (1823) Turn. & R. 143.

19   In *Hilton v Cosnier* [2018] EWHC 2728 (Ch), for example, the expression "I have bought it for you to live in for the rest of your life but I am not giving it to you it is to go to my grandchildren" did not demonstrate the intention to create a trust in favour of the grandchildren. The words merely indicated that on the grandfather's death his grandchildren were likely to inherit.

20   As Megarry J put it in *Re Kayford* [1975] 1 All E.R. 604 at 607, "it is well settled that a trust can be created without using the words 'trust' or 'confidence' or the like: the question is whether in substance a sufficient intention to create a trust has been manifested".

21   [2016] EWCA Civ 424. There the language used in correspondence was inconsistent with the declaration of a trust.

22   See e.g. *Tito v Waddell (No.2)* [1977] Ch. 106 where government documents referred to a "trust" in the context of mining rights, but no trust was found to have been created. Megarry J observed (at 211) that, "terms such as 'Brains Trust', 'Anti-trust and 'Trust Territories', though commonly used, are not understood as relating to a trust as enforced in a court of equity"; see also *Harrison v Gibson* [2006] 1 W.L.R. 1212.

23   [2020] 2 W.L.R. 699 at [267].

It is to be noted, moreover, that there is no general requirement that a trust be created[24] or even evidenced[25] in writing.

Gift, trust or both?

The authorities emphasise that an imperfect gift is not to be rebranded as a valid declaration of trust or vice versa. This is so regardless of the injustice that may follow. The two styles of intention are usually distinct. With an immediate gift, the donor means to dispose of all entitlement to the property, whereas with a trust the trustee intends to retain rights subject to the obligations of the trust. If a gift is intended but fails, then there is nothing the court can do because of the traditional maxims, "equity will not assist a volunteer" and "equity cannot perfect an imperfect gift". This inability is well illustrated in two cases. First, in *Jones v Lock*[26] a father held out a cheque for £900, which was payable to him, and placed it in the hand of his child. The father said: "I give this to baby and I am going to put it away for him". The father died a few days later and the issue was whether the child was entitled to the cheque. The court held that this was a failed gift (the title to the cheque did not pass because it was not endorsed in favour of the child) and could not be construed as a declaration of trust because no trust had been intended. As Lord Carnworth LC added:

> **"I think it would be a very dangerous example if loose conversations of this sort, in important transactions of this kind, should have the effect of declarations of trust".[27]**

Secondly, a similar sentiment was expressed in *Richards v Delbridge*.[28] There a tenant sought to transfer his business premises (he was a bone manure merchant) and stock-in-trade to his grandson. Unfortunately, before his death he did not execute a conveyance necessary to complete the transfer of legal title to land. The gift, therefore, failed. The grandson argued that the court should instead discern an intention to create a trust. Sir George Jessel MR rejected this reasoning and made clear that, if it is intended to be a gift, the court cannot regard the failed transfer as amounting to a declaration of trust.

A potential blurring of these boundaries occurred in *Shah v Shah*.[29] In the context of a single transaction involving the transfer of shares, the Court of Appeal held that both inten-

2-007

---

24   An exception to this rule concerns sub-trusts which involve the disposition of a subsisting equitable interest (e.g. the transfer of an existing trust interest or the declaration of new beneficiaries) which must be in writing and signed by the settlor: s.53(1)(c) of the Law of Property Act 1925; see Ch.4.

25   An exception to this rule relates to express trusts of land which need to be evidenced in writing and signed on behalf of the settlor: s.53(1)(b) of the Law of Property Act 1925, see Ch.4.

26   (1865) L.R. 1 Ch. App. 25.

27   (1865) L.R. 1 Ch. App. 25 at 29.

28   (1874) L.R. 18 Eq. 11.

29   [2010] EWCA Civ 1408.

tions might coexist. On the facts of *Shah*, Dinesh delivered a signed letter to his brother, which attempted to make a disposition of 4,000 shares in a company in the latter's favour.[30] The letter enclosed a signed stock transfer form, but no share certificate. Dinesh later sought to withdraw from the arrangement, claiming that he had intended to make a gift which, because it had never been completely constituted, was ineffective. In his letter, Dinesh admitted that "I am from today holding 4,000 shares in the above company for you". Although the letter described itself as "a declaration", its author submitted that any reasonable person would interpret this as being no more than a simple statement of gift. Dinesh also contended that it was legally impossible for him to intend both a gift and a trust at the same time. Arden LJ was unimpressed and held that "this line of argument starts from the wrong point".[31] The court should not look to the subjective intentions of the maker of a document, "but to the intentions of the maker as manifested by the words he has used in the context of all the relevant facts".[32] By his use of the expression "I am from today holding" in the letter, Dinesh had manifested the clearest intention that the transfer should take effect immediately. He had not employed a phrase such as "I am assigning" or "I am giving". The attachment of the stock transfer form indicated the intention that registration would occur in due course. It followed that, to give effect to the wording of the letter, there had to be a disposition of the beneficial interest until legal title passed. This could occur only by the imposition of a trust that would survive until registration was complete. On the admittedly unusual facts before her, Arden LJ felt able to conclude that, "One of the ways of making an immediate gift is for the donor to declare a trust".[33]

Precatory words

2-008

Precatory words are words merely of hope and desire (e.g. "in the hope that", "I would like that", "in the expectation that", "I desire that" and "I feel confident that"). Usually, such words appear in non-professionally drafted wills that deal with what is to happen to property on the death of the testator. Since the late-nineteenth century, such expressions alone are insufficient to show the necessary intention to create a trust. Older cases are, therefore, no sure guide to modern understanding.[34] The modern approach is to look for imperative words that impose

---

30 Legal title to a share in a limited company is traditionally transferred by the execution of a share transfer form, the passing over of the share certificate and the subsequent registration of the transfer in the company's shareholding register: see para.**3-004**.

31 [2010] EWCA Civ 1408 at [13].

32 [2010] EWCA Civ 1408 at [13].

33 [2010] EWCA Civ 1408 at [22]. This was a sentiment shared by Lord Browne-Wilkinson in *T. Choithram International SA v Pagarani* [2001] 1 W.L.R. 1 when (at 11) he spoke of "words of gift on trust".

34 As Cotton LJ admitted in *Re Adams and Kensington Vestry* (1884) 27 Ch. D. 394 at 410, "some of the older authorities went a great deal too far in holding that some particular words appearing in a will were sufficient to create a trust . . . what we have to look at is the whole of the will which we have to construe . . . we must not extend the old cases in any way, or rely upon the mere use of particular words . . .".

a mandatory legal obligation on the trustee. A moral obligation or mere request is simply not enough.[35] Although sometimes allusion is made to a "precatory trust", care should be taken with this expression. All that this unhelpful descriptive label means is that the intention to create a trust can be discerned from conduct and surrounding circumstances even when the language employed is itself insufficiently imperative. It is, however, to be remembered that there can now be no trust based on precatory words alone.[36] It is, moreover, sometimes argued that there is an interrelationship between the three types of certainty. This is traditionally described as the "reflex action" and emanates from *Mussoorie Bank Ltd v Raynor* where Sir Arthur Hobhouse said:

> **"Uncertainty in the subject of the gift has a reflex action upon the previous words . . . and seems to show that he could not possibly have intended his words of confidence, hope or whatever they may be . . . to be imperative words".[37]**

There the House of Lords was cementing the proposition that the use of "precatory" words cannot alone show the intention to create a trust. As this is now well-established law, the "reflex action" appears to lack contemporary significance.[38] It is to be appreciated, however, that a trust can fail for a lack of more than one certainty.

There are two classic examples of the rule that precatory words do not work to create a trust. First, in *Lambe v Eames*[39] the testator left his estate to his widow "to be at her disposal in any way she may think best, for the benefit of herself and her family". It was held that this was a precatory expression and did not connote the necessary intention to create a trust. In relation to the more liberal approach advocated in some earlier cases, James LJ commented:

> **"I could not help feeling that the officious kindness of the Court of Chancery in interposing trusts where in many cases the father of the family never meant to create trusts must have been a very cruel kindness indeed".[40]**

---

35 *Sweeney v Coghill* (1999) 77 P. & C.R. D14, but as Lewison J accepted in *Wallbank v Price* [2007] EWHC 3001 (Ch), "if there is one interpretation which will produce a valid instrument and another rival interpretation which will make it ineffective, the court should, in my judgment, prefer the former interpretation" (at [44]).

36 *Kynnersley v Wolverhampton City Council* [2008] WTLR. 65. There the will spoke of the imposition of an obligation and not merely the expression of a hope or desire. The funds were not at the free disposal of the Council and were held on trust for the staff of a named care home.

37 (1882) 7 App. Cas. 321 at 331.

38 See the views of Rigby LJ in *Re Williams* [1897] 2 Ch. 12 at 35; but see Nourse LJ in *Margulies v Margulies* unreported 16 March 2000 at [98], where he accepted that a lack of specificity as to subject matter inevitably reflects on the instructions or wishes themselves and whether they are imperative in form.

39 (1871) 6 Ch. App. 597.

40 (1871) 6 Ch. App. 597 at 599.

Secondly, in *Re Adams and the Kensington Vestry*[41] the testator's estate was devised by will to the absolute use of his widow, "in full confidence that she will do what is right as to the disposal thereof between my children, either in her lifetime or by will after her decease". These again were merely words of aspiration and did not impose a legal obligation on the widow.

There are many other case law examples that show the inefficacy of precatory words. These include:

- *Re Hamilton*,[42] where the testator left legacies to his two nieces and added the words: "I wish them to bequeath them equally between the families of [X] and [Y] in such mode as they shall consider right". No trust was created in favour of X and Y because the words employed did not impose the obligations of a trustee upon the nieces.[43]

- *Re Diggles*,[44] where the testatrix left her property to her daughter with the rider that "it is my desire that she allows to A.G. an annuity of £25 during her life". The added words did not create a trust and the daughter took the property free from this qualification.

- *Margulies v Margulies*,[45] where a legacy of the residuary estate was left to one son and expressed to be in confidence that, "if in the interests of achieving family harmony", he would make provision for his brother and sister. The language of the testator did not disclose a sufficient certainty of intention to create a trust. As the words used were precatory in nature, the son could keep the money for himself. He had laboured merely under a moral obligation.

- *Mussoorie Bank v Raynor*,[46] where a husband left land to his widow, "feeling confident that she will act justly to our children in dividing the same when no longer required by her". The widow mortgaged the land and, eventually, the Bank sought to sell it to recoup the loan. She argued that, as she was a trustee of the land, the mortgage was invalid. The House of Lords held that no trust existed because the husband had used precatory words. She was the legal and beneficial owner of the property and, hence, the mortgagee could sell the property.

There are three cases that might, at first glance, be viewed as contradicting the accepted wisdom as to the effect of precatory language. The temptation to interpret these cases in this way should, however, be resisted. The first case to be considered is *Comiskey v Bowring-*

---

41 (1884) 27 Ch. D. 394.
42 [1895] 2 Ch. 370; see also *Green v Marsden* (1853) 1 Drew. 646 ("I beg and request").
43 See also *Re Johnson* [1939] 2 All E.R. 458 ("I request that . . .").
44 (1888) 39 Ch. D. 253. See also *Re Conolly* [1910] 1 Ch. 219 ("I specially desire that. . .").
45 Unreported 16 March 2000.
46 (1882) 7 App. Cas. 321.

Hanbury.[47] There a legacy was left to a widow "in full confidence" that she would leave the property on her death to one or more of the testator's nieces. As these were precatory words, they were in themselves ineffective to create a trust.[48] The will, however, went on to declare that, "in default of any disposition by her thereof by her will . . . I hereby direct that all my estate and property acquired by her under this my will shall at her death be equally divided among the surviving said nieces". These added words proved crucial because the House of Lords held that, in looking for certainty of intention, it was necessary to consider the trust document as a whole. The imperative wording of the gift over imposed the mandatory obligation upon the widow. She held the property on trust for herself for life and then in remainder for the nieces equally. It is to be emphasised that this case is not authority for saying that precatory words can constitute a trust. All that it shows is that the provision made clear the widow could not keep the property for herself.

The second case is that of *Re Steele's Will Trusts.*[49] This involved a solicitor drafting a trust deed for a client, but unfortunately utilising an outmoded precedent that featured precatory words ("I request my said son to do all in his power"). Although this precedent had worked in the past,[50] in the more contemporary setting there should have been no trust because of a lack of certainty of intention. Nevertheless, Wynn-Parry J concluded that the deliberate use of the precedent (albeit itself defective) demonstrated the necessary intention to declare a trust of a diamond necklace. This is, undoubtedly, a rogue decision and is thoroughly unsafe.[51] It disregards the actual wording of the deed, seemingly imputes an artificial intention to the settlor and departs from the general rule that extrinsic evidence is inadmissible in the construction of a trust deed.[52]

Finally, in *Vucicevic v Aleksic*[53] the issue arose as to whether there was an absolute gift of three houses for the benefit of the Serbian Orthodox church or, instead, a trust of those houses for needy children in Kosovo. In his homemade will, the testator had expressed his "full confidence" in the senior bishop of the church that the latter would ensure that the benefit went to the right place. The church claimed the houses on the basis that precatory words had been used. The High Court held that the wording had to be viewed in context. As Judge Paul Matthews explained, "the question is one, not of principle, but simply of gathering the intention of the testator the words used in that context".[54] The legacy was from a testator with no

---

47 [1905] A.C. 84; see also *Gibbs v Harding* [2008] Ch. 235 where the words "it is my wish" were followed by the expression "to hold in trust". A trust was upheld.

48 Indeed, s.22 of the Administration of Justice Act 1982 provides that, unless there is a contrary intention demonstrated, a bequest to a spouse will be regarded as an absolute gift even though it purports to give their children an interest in the same property.

49 [1948] Ch. 603.

50 *Shelley v Shelley* (1868) L.R. 6 Eq. 540.

51 See P. Langan, "A Note on *Re Steele's Will Trusts*" (1968) 32 Conv. 361.

52 See *Rabin v Gerson Berger Association Ltd* [1986] 1 W.L.R. 526. Extrinsic evidence is allowed to ascertain the testator's intention where there is ambiguity or doubt as to meaning of a provision in a will: s.21 of the Administration of Justice Act 1982. Where there is no will, therefore, s.21 cannot apply.

53 [2017] EWHC 2335 (Ch).

54 [2017] EWHC 2335 (Ch) at [35].

wife, partner or children to an institution for charitable purposes. The testator, moreover, spoke poor English and intended the funding to be long-lasting. The confidence he expressed was not placed in the legatee, but rather in someone who was in a position of authority and whom he trusted to make the right kind of decision in the trust's administration. The testator had not intended the houses as an absolute gift.

Fictitious intentions

2-011

The working rule is that an express declaration of trust will be conclusive. This rule gives way, however, where the intention to create a trust is palpably false or when an intended beneficiary is different from the named beneficiary (i.e. a "sham" or "pretence" trust has been created).[55] If regarded by the court as a fiction, the trust fails and the title to the property remains with the settlor.[56] Such an outcome will arise where the subjective intention of the parties to the "trust" is that the acts or documents are not to create the rights and obligations that they appear to create.[57] The onus of showing that the purported trust is not genuine, however, rests squarely upon the party who alleges the sham.[58] In *ND v SD*,[59] a wife failed to prove as a matter of law that an offshore trust set up by the husband was a sham. The parties had intended their arrangements to be given effect in the form in which they were recorded, and the courts would not enquire into their motives. In order to demonstrate a sham, it would have to be shown on a balance of probabilities that both the husband and wife had intended that the trust assets would be held on terms other than those set out in the trust deed. This would require each of them to give a false impression of the position to outsiders.[60] Nevertheless, the court is not restricted to examining the four corners of the document and may examine external evidence, such as evidence of the subsequent conduct of the parties.[61] While the court should be slow in finding a sham trust,[62]

---

55 *Hitch v Stone* [2001] EWCA Civ 63; see M. Conaglen, "Sham Trusts" (2008) 67(1) C.L.J. 176.

56 *Schechter v The Commissioners for Her Majesty's Revenue & Customs* [2017] UKFTT 189 (TC).

57 See *Snook v London & West Riding Investments Ltd* [1967] 2 Q.B. 786. In *Swift Advances Plc v Ahmed* [2015] EWHC 3265 (Ch), Norris J referred to these instances as the deed in a drawer cases.

58 *Erlam v Rahman* [2016] EWHC 111 (Ch). This case also demonstrates that the fact that the act or document is unfavourable or appears artificial does necessarily entail that it is a sham provided that the parties intend the agreement to take effect according to its tenor.

59 [2017] EWHC 1507 (Fam).

60 See also *JSC Mezhdunarodniy Promyshlenniy Bank v Pugachev* [2017] EWHC 2426 (Ch). This case was analysed by Lady Arden in her speech entitled "Family Trusts Today" at the Trusts and Wealth Management Conference, Singapore Asian Wealth and the Global Context, 1 August 2019. This is available at *https://www.supremecourt. uk/docs/speech-190801.pdf* [Accessed 31 July 2020].

61 *Erlam v Rahman* [2016] EWHC 111 (Ch). The High Court emphasised that the mere fact that parties subsequently departed from an agreement did not necessarily mean that they never intended that agreement to be effective and binding.

62 *National Westminster Bank v Jones* unreported 22 June 2000 (HC) where (at [59]) Neuberger J explained that "there is a very strong presumption indeed that parties intend to be bound by the provisions of agreements into

it must be wary of self-serving evidence of subjective intention which is adduced without corroboration.[63]

Often a fictitious transaction will be created to prevent creditors[64] or an estranged spouse from making a claim against property.[65] In *Thandi v Sands*,[66] Mr Thandi claimed to be the beneficial owner of 16 properties which were registered in his son's name. He produced a previously unknown deed of trust (as the judge put it, "rather like a rabbit out of a hat") purporting to show that the son's apparent wealth was illusory. The court concluded that it was merely an insurance document designed to defeat potential creditors by showing an intention that was not the actual intention of the parties. In *Liscott v CPS*, a property transfer to a third party was set aside as a sham designed to avoid the reach of a court confiscation order.[67] In *JSC BTA Bank v Albyazov* the pretence trust was designed to avoid a judgment debt and to sidestep a worldwide freezing order.[68] Similarly, in *Rahman v Chase Bank Trust Co Ltd* it was held that the settlor (who secreted money in an offshore trust based in Jersey) had retained total control over the trust funds and, therefore, could never have genuinely intended to set up a trust.[69]

A classic example is *Midland Bank v Wyatt*,[70] where a husband and wife declared a trust in respect of the matrimonial home. The beneficial interest was to be shared equally between the wife and their daughters. The property was mortgaged to the Midland Bank and the husband continued to borrow on the security of the family home. He did not inform the Bank of the trust. The Bank eventually sought to sell the property to recover the husband's outstanding debt. In the High Court, the Deputy Judge held that the husband had never had the intention truly to divest himself of his interest in the property. He had declared the trust merely as a means of shielding the family home from the claims of the Bank. Put simply, there was no real intention to create a trust. The declaration was a mere pretence and, therefore, the trust was void. This outcome is not dependent upon there being a finding of fraud and can arise even if the settlor has acted honestly following deficient financial or legal advice. It remains necessary, however, that the evidence shows that the trustee as well as the settlor is aware of the pretence.[71]

---

which they enter, and, even more, intend the agreements they enter into to take effect", and added that "there is a strong and natural presumption against holding a provision or a document a sham".

63 *Thandi v Sands* [2014] EWHC 2378 (Ch).
64 See *Vickers v Jackson* [2011] EWCA Civ 725 where the fictitious transaction (i.e. a fake charge on land) was designed to encourage creditors to look elsewhere for the payment of their debts.
65 In *Minwalla v Minwalla* [2004] EWHC 2823 (Fam), a husband purported to create an offshore trust with a Jersey company (which he controlled) acting as trustee. As neither party had intended to act upon the trust deed, it was a sham. The husband remained the sole and true owner of the property which was to be included as a marital asset for the purposes of divorce proceedings.
66 [2014] EWHC 2378 (Ch).
67 [2013] EWHC 501 (Admin); see also *Earp v Seamer* [2014] EWHC 3776 (Admin).
68 Unreported 14 July 2014 (HC).
69 [1991] J.L.R. 103 (a Channel Islands' case).
70 [1995] 1 F.L.R. 696.
71 *Alliance Bank JSC v Zhunus* unreported 30 January 2015 (HC); see generally A. See, "Revisiting sham trusts: common intention, estoppel and illegality" (2018) Conv. 31.

Inferred intention

2-012

Even though there may be no express verbal recognition that a trust is intended, the requisite intention may still be inferred. Obviously, much here turns upon the perception of the court and less upon the subjective intentions of the parties.[72] Writing in an extra-judicial capacity, Lord Millett explained that this type of trust "arises only partly from the language used. In most cases it arises largely, and in some cases wholly, by implication of law . . . inferred from the language and conduct of the parties and the circumstances of the case".[73] There is no requirement that the settlor be actually aware that what he is creating is a trust. Instead, the court will investigate whether he intended to make the property subject to an obligation that the law acknowledges as a trust obligation.[74] It is always assumed that the settlor intends the legal consequences of his actions.

2-013

The primary example of an inferred intention trust is to be found in *Paul v Constance*.[75] Mr Constance repeatedly said to Mrs Paul of a bank account in his sole name: "The money is as much yours as mine". Special arrangements were made so that she could draw on the account and she paid her bingo winnings into it. Mr Constance subsequently died. There was found to be a declaration of an express trust that gave Mrs Paul an equal share in the bank account with the widow of Mr Constance. Scarman LJ admitted that there was no need for "stilted lawyers' language" and that the court must remember that it is "dealing with simple people, unaware of the subtleties of equity, but understanding very well indeed their own domestic situation".[76] The words and conduct of Mr Constance had to be viewed against their own background and in their own circumstances. It did not matter that Mr Constance was ignorant of the consequences of his actions.[77] There are, however, two potential difficulties with this case.

First, it was not made clear exactly when the express trust was created. As Scarman LJ admitted:

> **"It might, however, be thought that this is a borderline case, since it is not easy to pin-point a specific moment of declaration, and one must exclude from one's mind any case built upon the existence of an implied or constructive trust, for this case was put forward at the trial and is now argued by the plaintiff as one of express declaration of trust".**[78]

---

72 Indeed, the subjective intentions of a settlor have been held to be irrelevant: *RP Medplant Ltd v Pensions Regulator* [2017] UKUT 385 (TCC).

73 (1985) 101 L.Q.R. 269 at 284.

74 See *Duggan v Governor of Full Sutton Prison* [2004] 1 W.L.R. 1010, where the court held that a governor who held prisoner's money was not a trustee, but was instead merely a debtor.

75 [1977] 1 W.L.R. 527.

76 [1977] 1 W.L.R. 527 at 530.

77 See also, *Rowe v Prance* [1999] 2 F.L.R. 787 where frequent reference to a boat (purchased by Mr Prance) as "ours" gave his partner (Ms Rowe) a beneficial interest in the vessel.

78 [1977] 1 W.L.R. 527 at 532.

Presumably, the trust was created on the first utterance of joint ownership. If so, the relevance of future utterances might be that they serve to embrace the additional payments made into the account by Mr Constance.

Secondly, it was not clear what occurred in relation to the bingo winnings paid into the account by Mrs Paul. Imagine a scenario where Mrs Paul won £1 million on the lottery and paid it into the account. There is no way that this additional money would become trust property shared with Mr Constance. The account holder would hold it on resulting trust for the payer. As Mr Constance could not declare a trust in favour of himself over someone else's property, it must be that the £1 million would fall outside the scope of the trust. Any future payments made by him might, however, fall within the subject matter of the trust if that is deemed to have been his intention. As mentioned, his further utterances of trust may indicate this. This divergence of treatment seems to explain why the widow Constance could claim a share of the account (as her deceased husband's next of kin) and why the contents of the bank account were not regarded solely as the property of Mrs Paul. Mr Constance and Mrs Paul could not be regarded as beneficial joint tenants.[79] The unilateral declaration of trust, coupled with the fluctuating nature of the account and the payments in made by her, undermined any intention that they be beneficial joint tenants of the contents of the account.[80] It is also arguable that the words used by Mr Constance amounted to words of severance, which again would prevent the existence of a beneficial joint tenancy. A different outcome would, seemingly, be reached if the couple had opened the bank account together and, although they made unequal contributions, had intended to pool their resources.[81]

The inference of the intention to create a trust was drawn more recently in *Gold v Hill*.[82] In 1993, Mr Gilbert took out a life assurance policy. Mr Gilbert named the beneficiary of the policy as Max Gold and identified Mr Gold as executor under his will. Although a valid will was in existence (it had been executed in 1983), it did not name Mr Gold as executor. It was alleged that Mr Gilbert had said to Mr Gold that he wanted the insurance money to be used to look after his mistress, Carol, and her children. Mr Gilbert was not as charitable towards his wife, Antoinette, stating "Don't let that bitch get anything". Antoinette was, however, the major beneficiary under his will. Mr Gilbert died in 1995. Mr Gold claimed the money in an individual capacity. The issue was whether he would then be under a duty to pay the money to Carol. Carnwath J held that the earlier conversation had the effect of nominating Mr Gold as a trustee and that Mr Gilbert had informally explained what he was doing and why.[83]

---

79   See generally D. Capper, "Survivorship rights in joint deposit accounts: a matter of construction?" [2018] Conv. 395.

80   See *Standing v Bowring* (1885) 31 Ch. D. 282 where stocks were transferred into the joint names of a widow and her godson. The manifest intention was that they were not to be joint tenants and that the godson was to have sole beneficial entitlement.

81   See *Re Bishop* [1965] Ch. 450.

82   [1999] 1 F.L.R. 54.

83   In *Charity Commission For England & Wales v Framjee* [2014] EWHC 2507 (Ch), charitable donations made to a website created a trust even though there was no express statement of intention. The necessary intention was inferred from the contextual evidence.

2-015   In *Ong v Ping*,[84] a claim that a house and the proceeds of its sale were held on a discretionary trust was upheld. This was so even though a defective trust deed had been executed. The Court of Appeal found clear evidence of an intention to create a trust from what was said and done. The background circumstances (including correspondence leading up to the signing of the deed) would lead a reasonable person to believe that the settlor had made a valid declaration of trust in respect of the house. Accordingly, the inference was that, while something had gone wrong with the drafting of the settlement, it was intended that the house was to be held on trust. The correspondence operated to satisfy s.53(1)(b) of the Law of Property Act 1925 by providing the necessary signed writing to evidence the trust of land.

Inferred intention and the commercial context

2-016   As in the domestic setting, the courts can infer an express trust from words and conduct arising in commercial transactions. Such is illustrated in *Don King Productions Inc v Warren (No.1)*[85] where a partnership was entered under which the benefit of any existing and future sports management agreements acquired by the parties was to become partnership property. It was argued that certain agreements were non-assignable and could not, therefore, be regarded as partnership property. Lightman J held that the poor drafting of the partnership agreement obscured the parties' true intentions. Nevertheless, and despite the wording of individual management agreements, the inferred mutual intention was that the benefit of such agreements be held on trust for the partnership.

2-017   A further scenario in which an intention to create a trust can be inferred is where the recipient unilaterally acts in a way that evinces the necessary intention to hold the property on trust. The most prominent authority for this proposition is *Re Kayford*.[86] This decision concerned a mail order company that received advance payments from its customers.[87] The company feared insolvency and unilaterally paid these payments into a special Customers' Trust Deposit Account. The company became insolvent and the general creditors laid claim to the money. In the normal course of events, the creditors would be so entitled. On the present facts, however, Megarry J held that the steps taken by the company overtly demonstrated its intention to create a trust. He viewed this as an express trust for persons with the necessary intention being inferred from the unilateral conduct of the settlor. The trust was not viewed as a resulting trust. Due to segregation being a useful, albeit inconclusive, indication of the intention to create a trust, there must be an investigation into why there was segregation.[88] As Megarry J

---

84   [2017] EWCA Civ 2069.

85   [1998] 2 All E.R. 608.

86   [1975] 1 All E.R. 604.

87   The Law Commission, "Consumer Prepayments on Retailer Insolvency" (2016) Law Com. No.368 made a series of recommendations designed to lessen the impact of retail insolvencies on prepaying consumers.

88   See *Mills v Sportsdirect.com Retail Ltd* [2010] EWHC 1072 (Ch) where Lewison J at [58] noted that usually, "the segregation in question still results in an account in the name of the alleged trustee with no express indication that the account is held for the benefit of someone".

commented, "The whole purpose of what was done was to ensure that the moneys remained in the beneficial ownership of those who sent them, and a trust is the obvious means of achieving this".[89] Until the goods were delivered, therefore, the equitable interest in the money remained with the customers.[90] The company had made it clear that it had given up the right to use the money itself. The court viewed this as a proper and honourable act for a company to take. Although there was an absence of any bilateral understanding between the parties, there was a trust that was clearly intended by the settlor company.[91]

A similar approach was adopted in *Re Chelsea Cloisters Ltd*[92] where the dispute concerned deposits paid by tenants as regards potential liabilities for damages and breakage. The landlord experienced financial problems and new deposits were paid into an account ("Tenants' Deposit Account") which was opened for the purposes of keeping the money separate. The Court of Appeal held that the nature of the transaction created a trust in favour of the tenants and that the funds were not to be claimed by the landlord's creditors.[93] In *Brazzill v Willoughby*,[94] a trust was created over monies paid into a Bank of England account by a bank, prior to being placed in administration. The beneficiaries of this trust were all account holders of the bank in administration who had made deposits between the issuing of the supervisory notice by the Financial Services Authority and the bank being placed in administration.

In *Re Challoner Club Ltd*,[95] however, the company was incorporated to take over the business of an unincorporated club and to carry on the business of, essentially, a social club for members who were of the Roman Catholic religion. A separate account was set up and monies were transferred into it. It was argued that the funds were not to be available to the general creditors of the club. Lloyd J could not, however, discern the terms of the alleged trust. In contrast with *Re Kayford* where it was clear when the monies segregated were to be used to satisfy the customer orders, here it was uncertain when the money was to be repaid to the members.[96] Hence, the trust failed because there was no adequately precise definition of the circumstances in which the alleged trust was to operate.

---

89 *Re Kayford* [1975] 1 All E.R. 604 at 607.

90 While it is generally accepted that a requirement to keep money separately from other funds is indicative of a trust (*R. v Clowes (No.2)* [1994] 2 All E.R. 316) this will not be so where the evidence shows that the customers are to accept the risk of insolvency (*Customs and Excise Commissioners v Richmond Theatre Management Ltd* [1995] S.T.C. 257).

91 Cf. *Re Crown Holdings (London) Ltd (In Liquidation)* [2015] EWHC 1876 (Ch) where no *Kayford* style trust existed because the liquidated company's banker, who held its customers' money, was merely a third party acting to protect its own position, was not the agent of the company and did not take on the role of trustee or seek to establish a trust.

92 (1980) 41 P. & C.R. 98.

93 See also *Hill v Phillips* [1999] 1 All E.R. (Comm) 289, which dealt with money put into a designated "Money Requirement Account". The money was held on trust for investor clients and was not available to general creditors.

94 [2010] EWCA Civ 561.

95 *The Times*, 4 November 1997 (Ch).

96 See also *Re Multi Guarantee Ltd* [1987] B.C.L.C. 257 where, although the money (i.e. warranty premiums) was paid into a separate joint account, there was no trust because there was no relinquishing of control of the funds

Certainty of Subject Matter

2-018   Any existing property may be the subject matter of a trust. It is, for example, permissible to have a trust of land, personal goods, shares, cheques, money, debts and covenants. Existing property must be distinguished from future or after acquired property which (without consideration being provided) cannot be the subject matter of a trust.[97] The concept of existing property, however, includes property that has not yet become vested in the settlor and is awaiting the determination of some other prior interest. This would be the case where, for example, the settlor is entitled absolutely to the property following the death of a life tenant or where the settlor is entitled to the property which is to vest on her reaching a certain age. In both scenarios, the settlor's interest is regarded as being in existing property. After acquired property refers to property that may vest in the future, but about which there is no certainty. It is a mere expectation that some property may accrue. Future royalties of a book or an anticipated legacy under a living-relative's will cannot, therefore, be the subject matter of a trust.[98]

In all cases, the requirement is that the trust property must be identifiable. The settlor must also provide the means by which the interest of the beneficiaries can be ascertained. If either feature is absent, the trust must fail because it cannot be enforced. For example:

- "£100,000 to be divided equally between my children, Jordan & Fiona". This is a fixed trust that identifies the trust fund (£100,000) and the beneficial entitlement of the children (equal shares).

- "£100,000 to be divided between such of my children as my trustee sees fit". This is a discretionary trust that identifies the trust fund (£100,000) and provides the mechanism by which beneficial entitlement is to be allocated (who gets what is left to the discretion of the trustee).

Trust property

2-019   The entire property that is to be the subject of the trust must be described in such a way that it becomes certain and ascertainable. The straightforward reasoning is that a trustee can perform his duties only if he knows exactly what is trust property and the trust can be enforced only if both the beneficiary and the court are similarly aware. This simply stated rule has, however, caused difficulty both in the family and the commercial context. Three possibilities emerge:

---

deposited therein. Multi Guarantee Ltd, "never did manifest a sufficient intention to create a trust and the requisite certainty of words was simply not there" (per Nourse LJ at 268).

97   *Williams v IRC* [1947] A.C. 447, the logic being that it is impossible to own something that does not yet exist.

98   See respectively *Performing Right Society v London Theatre of Varieties* (1924) A.C. 1 and *Re Lind* [1915] 2 Ch. 345.

- the fund from which the beneficiary's interest is to be carved out may not itself be identifiable. For example, money paid into an overdrawn account will disappear and cannot be the subject matter of a trust;

- the language used by the settlor may be so vague as to offer no definite meaning whatsoever. This could arise from the use of an uncertain descriptive label (e.g. "most of my money"). This is to be contrasted with a trust of the residue of an estate, which will usually be valid. For example, if a testator leaves a will containing a number of legacies and creates a trust of "whatever is left", then there is certainty of subject matter. The executors can eventually calculate the exact value of the residual estate; and

- uncertainty might arise from a failure to segregate the trust property from other property owned by the settlor (e.g. "50 stamps from my collection". This problem has arisen following the purchase of goods from a supplier who does not identify specifically the goods bought from general stock.[99] The general rule is that there can be no trust as it is impossible to determine the goods that are to be its subject. A different approach, however, is currently adopted by the courts according to whether the trust property is tangible (e.g. a car, painting or jewels) or intangible (e.g. shares or money in a bank account).

Two cases illustrate the workings of this requirement that there be an identifiable trust fund. First, in *Hemmens v Wilson Browne*[100] a document which the draftsman described as "akin to a trust" failed to give Ms Hemmens (the settlor's former mistress) any enforceable legal right to a set sum of money promised to her by her ex-lover (Mr Panter) to enable her to purchase a house. Mr Panter subsequently had a change of heart and refused to pay. Consequently, the plaintiff unsuccessfully claimed damages for negligence against the defendant solicitors. Although the document purported to give Mrs Hemmens the right to a monetary payment of £110,000 at any time from Mr Panter, it was not a promissory note nor a contract (because there was no consideration) and it was not under seal. It did not create a trust because there was no fund identified which could form the subject matter of the trust nor was there the intention to create a trust.

Secondly, in *MacJordan Construction Ltd v Brookmount Erostin Ltd*[101] a building contract provided that the employer would retain 3 per cent of the price as trustee for the builder. No separate retention fund was set up. On the insolvency of the employer, the builder claimed

2-020

---

99 The Sale of Goods (Amendment) Act 1995 now offers help to such a purchaser because, in conjunction with the other purchasers, they will be regarded as having proprietary rights against the property as tenants in common. This arises as soon as the contract is entered and allows the purchasers to make a joint claim against the property.

100 [1995] Ch. 223.

101 (1991) 56 B.L.R. 1.

to have a trust interest and to have priority over a floating charge in favour of a bank. As the source of the money was not identified, there was nothing upon which a trust could be based. The employer had never agreed to set up the retention fund out of its general bank account and, therefore, the builder could make no beneficial claim against the money therein. It follows that, if Fred sets up a trust of a particular bank account, but that account does not exist, the trust must fail.

In search of meaning

2-021

The words employed by the settlor must be such that they identify with clarity the property to be held on trust or, at least, provide the machinery through which such property can be ascertained (e.g. such furniture as my trustee shall select). The subject matter must be conceptually certain. The following authorities provide useful illustrations of this requirement. In *Palmer v Simmonds*[102] a testatrix by her will left the residue of her estate to her friend, Mr Harrison, subject to the proviso that, if he died childless, "he will . . . leave the bulk of my said residuary estate unto" four named persons. The reference to "bulk" was held to be ineffective to create a trust. It has no clear meaning and is thoroughly uncertain. It could mean anything between 51 per cent and 99 per cent. There was nothing designated to which a trust could attach. As Kindersley VC explained, she had failed to identify "a definite, clear, certain part of her estate".[103] In *Re Kolb's Will Trusts*[104] the testator (a stockbroker) died and instructed his trustees of his residuary estate to sell trust property and from the proceeds to buy "first class" and "blue chip" investments. The reference to "first class" and "blue chip" investments was too subjective in meaning and, therefore, rendered the testamentary direction void for uncertainty. As it did not establish an objective standard, the trustees could not know what the testator intended. The trustees, moreover, were not given a power of selection. As Cross J admitted:

> "[T]here is no strict definition of the term and the opinions of different stockbrokers and others differ as to what stocks and shares can properly be called 'blue chips' at any given time . . . The testator might have made his trustees the judge; but, as he has not done so, that part of the clause is, in my judgment, void for uncertainty".[105]

Similarly, in *Peck v Halsey*[106] a gift of "some of my best linen" failed and, in *Jubber v Jubber*,[107] the expression "a handsome gratuity" was held to be conceptually uncertain.

---

102 (1854) 2 Drew. 221.
103 (1854) 2 Drew. 221 at 227.
104 [1962] Ch. 531.
105 [1961] 3 All E.R. 811 at 814.
106 (1720) 2 P.W. 387.
107 (1839) 9 Sim. 503.

A trust of whatever is left

2-022

There should, normally, be no problem in establishing a trust of "whatever remains" in a deceased's estate after, say, funeral expenses, taxes and legacies have been paid. As Briggs J noted in *Re Lehman Brothers International (Europe)*, "the terms of the trust are sufficient to identify its subject matter in the future".[108] Indeed, setting up a trust of the residue of an estate is a common practice. Provided the net residue is ascertainable, the trust will be upheld. Despite this straightforward proposition, the area is not entirely liberated from difficulty. Two cases serve to illustrate this tension and demonstrate that much may turn upon the court's construction of the terms of the disposition.

In *Sprange v Barnard*,[109] a testatrix left her husband shares valued at £300, "for his sole use; and at his death, the remaining part of what is left, that he does not want for his own wants and use, to be divided between . . ." her brother and sisters. The widower sought to cash in the shares and the dispute arose as to whether he was a trustee of those shares for his deceased wife's siblings. The Court of Appeal held that he was absolutely entitled to the shares. As it would be uncertain as to what would be left on the husband's death, it was a trust that would be impossible to execute. The capital might be wasted away during the lifetime of Mr Sprange.[110] This is an example of where the residue could not be ascertained. Hence, there was no certainty of subject matter.

2-023

This case is, however, to be contrasted with *In the Estate of Last*.[111] There property was left by a testatrix to her brother on terms that "at his death anything that is left, that came from me" was to pass on to specified persons. The court adopted a very different attitude from that in the *Sprange* case because it held that the brother was given merely a life interest in the property.[112] It was significant that he could not leave any remaining property under his own will. As the trust (albeit with successive interests) was created on the death of the testatrix, the trust property was sufficiently certain at that date. Consequently, any property not disposed of during his lifetime was to be held on trust. The beneficial interest of the specified beneficiaries was, therefore, suspended during the lifetime of the brother, attaching to the property only on his death.[113] If the brother's interest had not been so limited, the trust would clearly have failed. This decision, therefore, can be understood only in the light that the court was able to find that a life interest, as opposed to an absolute gift, had been created. It will not normally be the case that successive interests can be discerned in this way.[114]

---

108   [2010] EWHC 2914 (Ch) at [225].
109   (1789) 2 Bro. CC 585.
110   See also *Re Jones* [1898] 1 Ch. 438, where a trust of "such parts of my . . . estate as she shall not have sold" also failed for uncertainty of subject matter. It was viewed as being an absolute gift to the legatee.
111   [1958] 1 All E.R. 316.
112   See also *Re Richards* [1902] 1 Ch. 76 where a widow was held to have a life interest. Named legatees under her husband's will were able to claim their entitlement on her death.
113   See Brightman J in *Ottaway v Norman* [1972] Ch. 698.
114   See *Flint v Hughes* (1843) 6 Beav. 342 where a gift expressed to be for life with the proviso that her daughters then take "whatever she can transfer" failed to create a trust.

A trust of part of property: tangibles

2-024

As will become clear, a trust of part only of the settlor's property can give rise to difficulties, when it comes to identifying what exactly is the subject matter of the trust. A different approach applies also according to whether the property is tangible (e.g. two of my cars) or intangible (half of my shareholding in a particular company). Before grappling with the problematic nature of that distinction, two initial observations might be helpful. First, there is no problem where Fred declares himself to be a trustee of, say, his entire share portfolio for the benefit of Fiona and Jordan whether equally or in other specified proportions. The subject matter of the trust is certain, as are the beneficiaries' equitable interests. They can jointly end the trusts, sell the shares and divide the proceeds in the specified proportions between themselves.[115] With an eye on *Hunter v Moss* (see para.**2-026**), Hayton admits that the settlor could have declared himself to be a trustee of all the 950 shares with himself and the plaintiff as tenants in common in specified proportions.[116] The shares defined as a proportional interest in the entire bulk is, therefore, unobjectionable. As will become clear, however, what Hayton denies is that the settlor could declare himself to be a trustee of 50 shares only without segregating the particular shares intended for the claimant as a separate parcel. In his view, it is not possible for the shares to be defined as a numerical quantity.[117]

Secondly, where the item is what can be described as a physical mass (e.g. a vat of molten gold or a tanker-load of petrol[118]), it would appear that a trust of, say, half of that mass of gold or petrol can be upheld. As Briggs J put it at the High Court stage in *Re Lehman Brothers International (Europe)*, "A trust of part of a fungible mass without the appropriation of any specific part of it for the beneficiary does not fail for uncertainty of subject matter, provided that the mass itself is sufficiently identified and provided also that the beneficiary's proportionate share of it is not itself uncertain".[119] This would not apply to a trust, for example, of half of my art collection because that is not a homogeneous mass.

2-025

Fortunately, the case law relating to a trust of part of physical property is generally more straightforward. Segregation of the trust property from the remaining bulk is usually necessary.[120] The judicial approach is encapsulated in *Re London Wine Co.*[121] There a company carried substantial stocks of wine in a number of warehouses. It was common practice that the wine would be sold, but remain stored by the company. The customer received a certificate of title, but the customer's wine was not separated from the rest of the stock. Although the company went into receivership, there were sufficient stocks to satisfy all orders. The issue was

---

115   *Saunders v Vautier* (1841) 49 E.R. 282.

116   D. Hayton, "Uncertainty of Subject-Matter of Trusts" (1994) 110 L.Q.R. 335. This approach is shared also by A. Jones [1994] Conv. 466 and M. Ockleton [1994] C.L.J. 448.

117   See further S. Worthington, "Sorting out ownership interests in a bulk: gifts, shares and trusts" [1999] J.B.L. 1, 15: "A trust of 20 per cent of a parcel of 1,000 shares is seen as unproblematic, whereas a trust of 200 shares out of the same parcel is seen as impossible".

118   See *Indian Oil Corp Ltd v Greenstone Shipping S.A.* [1988] Q.B. 345.

119   [2010] EWHC 2914 (Ch) at [225].

120   *Re Wait* [1927] 1 Ch. 606.

121   [1986] P.C.C. 121 (HC).

whether the wine sold was held on trust for the customers or whether the wine was available to the company's creditors. Oliver J held that, because the property sold was not singled out in any way from the remainder of the company's stock, a customer could not say of any given bottle of wine that he had bought that bottle. Hence, no trust could be created in favour of the customers. He explained that:

> "It seems to me that in order to create a trust it must be possible to ascertain with certainty not only what the interest of the beneficiary is to be but also to what property it is to attach".[122]

In *Re Goldcorp Exchange Ltd*,[123] an appeal to the Privy Council concerned a dealership in precious metals that went into receivership. The dealer acted to purchase gold bullion and other metals on behalf of clients and offered a storage service. The usual style of contract entered with clients required the dealer to hold the whole of an order in its vaults. It transpired that there were woefully insufficient stocks of bullion to meet its obligations. The Bank of New Zealand sought to claim these stocks under a floating charge over the dealer's assets. The customers claimed that the contracts created a series of trusts and that they, as beneficiaries, had first claim to the gold. On the facts, three categories of client emerged.

- Those clients who had claims to identified stocks that had been acquired specifically for them by the dealer. These claimants were successful in establishing a trust because the bullion had been physically and unconditionally segregated from the rest of the stock. This demarcation entailed that the subject matter of these trusts was certain.[124]

- Those customers who had purchased gold for future delivery, but had not been allocated any specific parcel of bullion before the bank's floating charge crystallised. All these claimants could show was a contractual entitlement to an amount of bullion representing a certain value. As they were unable to point to any specific bullion as being purchased under their respective contracts, there could be no trust. There was a total absence of certainty of subject matter.

- An individual customer had agreed to purchase 1,000 gold maple coins. The dealer did not carry such large stocks of coinage. The dealer bought in a larger stock than was required for this order. The coins bought for the client were not, however, segregated

122 [1986] P.C.C. 121 (HC) at 137. He added (at 137) that, "I cannot see how, for instance, a farmer who declares himself to be a trustee of two sheep (without identifying them) can be said to have created a perfect and complete trust whatever rights he may confer by such declaration as a matter of contract. And it would seem to me to be immaterial that at the time he has a flock of sheep out of which he could satisfy the interest".
123 [1995] 1 A.C. 74.
124 See also, *Re Stapylton Fletcher Ltd* [1995] 1 All E.R. 192, where the trust property (again wine) was separated from the rest of the stock in a distinct part of the warehouse and documentary records identified it as the property of the beneficiary.

from the additional coins that the dealer purchased. There was no certainty of subject matter here as the customer's property could not be specifically identified from the total stock. Of course, if no extra coins had been bought in there would not then be a problem with ascertainment of trust property.

In short, *Re Goldcorp Exchange Ltd* emphasises that a commercial contract for the purchase and storage of goods does not, without more, give rise to a relationship of trustee and beneficiary. As Lord Mustill observed, "the essence of a fiduciary relationship is that it creates obligations of a different character from the contract itself".[125] He concluded that no property in the goods could be transferred to the buyers unless the goods themselves were ascertained.

A trust of part of property: intangibles

2-026

The degree of certainty of subject matter required for trusts of so called "choses in action" or intangible assets (such as shares, money in bank accounts and debts[126]) is different from that which is required of trusts of tangible assets. Hayton describes this as an "old fashioned, but surely specious, distinction".[127] Nevertheless, it is now generally accepted that a trust of, say, shares falls to be treated differently from a trust of chattels.[128] The major case is *Hunter v Moss*,[129] where Mr Hunter was entitled, under his contract of employment with Mr Moss, to claim 50 shares out of 950 shares in a company held by his employer. Although this showed the intention to create a trust, Mr Moss did not identify which shares were the subject of this arrangement. Mr Moss later sold the 950 shares and kept the proceeds of sale for himself. Mr Hunter claimed a proportion of those proceeds. The central issue was whether, in these circumstances, Mr Hunter could assert beneficial rights over 50 shares under a trust. A series of points are to be appreciated.

First, if the orthodox approach (as considered above in relation to tangibles) fell to be applied, the outcome would be against Mr Hunter. It would be impossible to identify precisely which 50 shares were to be the subject matter of the trust. There had been no segregation whatsoever and, seemingly, no certainty of subject matter. This would, most certainly, be the

---

125 [1995] 1 A.C. 74 at 98; see also, *Commissioners of Customs & Excise v Richmond Theatre Management Ltd, The Times* 1 February 1995, where it was held by Dyson J that, on paying money over for a theatre ticket, a patron retained no proprietary interest in the payment.

126 It might also embrace a trust of a share of a sole trader's business: see *North v Wilkinson* [2018] EWCA Civ 161.

127 D. Hayton, "Uncertainty of Subject-Matter of Trusts" (1994) 110 L.Q.R. 335, 337. His view is that segregation should always be necessary whatever the nature of property involved. Cf. J. Martin [1996] Conv. 223, who suggests that the tracing rules relating to mixed assets can apply in cases of identifiable mixed funds to negate the need for segregation in every case.

128 See *Re Harvard Securities Ltd* [1997] 2 B.C.L.C. 369 (HC), where Neuberger J held that it was possible to create a trust of a particular number of shares even though they formed an unidentified part of a bulk of shares; see also the Hong Kong case *CA Pacific Finance Ltd* [2000] 1 B.C.L.C. 494.

129 (1994) 1 W.L.R. 452. In *Re Harvard Securities Ltd* [1997] 2 B.C.L.C. 369 (HC), Neuberger J followed the *Hunter* approach, but admitted to little enthusiasm in doing so.

outcome if, say, Fred (a writer) attempts to create a trust of "50 copies of my latest textbook from my personal stock". Although the books are identical, the trust will still fail because they are tangibles and there has been no identification of the exact 50 books to be taken. The only discernible difference between the books and, say, shares is that the books could be physically separated and are, thereby, distinguishable.[130]

Secondly, and nevertheless, the Court of Appeal held that there was a valid trust.[131] The reasoning employed was that, since the shares were essentially identical and indistinguishable, any 50 shares in the company can form the subject matter of the trust. The same would apply to an unsegregated share of a credit balance on a bank account.[132] Dillon LJ distanced himself from *Re London Wine Co* ("that case is a long way from the present")[133] and concluded that, "as a person can give by will a specified number of shares in a certain company, so equally, in my judgment, he can declare himself a trustee of 50 of his ordinary shares and that is effective to give a beneficial proprietary interest to the beneficiary under the trust".[134] It is to be appreciated that, if the arrangement had been to give Mr Hunter 50 shares from 950 shares held by Mr Moss in a range of companies, the lack of a homogeneous whole would have prevented the existence of an inter vivos trust.[135]

Thirdly, any analogy drawn with what occurs on death has proved controversial because, with a testamentary disposition, the shares are to be allocated by the executors of the will.[136] There is no immediate interest vested in the legatee. In contrast, a trust brings with it an immediate interest and, therefore, requires an immediate means of identifying exactly which shares are the subject matter of the trust.[137] In addition, the same post mortem justification can equally be invoked in relation to tangibles (e.g. leaving a legacy of "50 copies of my latest textbook").

2-027

Hunter v Moss was revisited and extended in *Lehman Brothers International (Europe)*.[138] This highly technical case concerned the collapse of Lehman Brothers International (Europe) (LBIE). The company's administrators sought directions as to the beneficial ownership of a broad and constantly changing range of securities which LBIE had, prior to the onset of its administration, acquired on behalf of a number of affiliates within the Lehman group. The affiliates argued that a trust existed under which they were the beneficiaries. The administrators asserted that any such trust would necessarily fail due to uncertainty of subject matter

2-028

---

130   See *Re Wait* [1927] 1 Ch. 606 (1000 tons of wheat).
131   Leave to appeal to the House of Lords was refused.
132   See *North v Wilkinson* [2018] EWCA Civ 161.
133   (1994) 1 W.L.R. 452 at 458.
134   (1994) 1 W.L.R. 452 at 458, 459.
135   *Wright v National Westminster Bank* [2014] EWHC 3158 (Ch).
136   In *Re Clifford* [1912] 1 Ch. 29, the court considered the concept of ademption (where specifically bequeathed property is no longer in the testator's estate) and whether or not the shares that were gifted in the will were still in existence in substance at the time of death. The testator gave a specific legacy of shares in a named company, which subsequently changed its name and subdivided its shares. It was held that the legacy was not adeemed since, although its name and form had changed, the subject matter remained the same. The executors had to acquire such an item and give it to the beneficiary.
137   See D. Hayton, "Uncertainty of Subject-Matter of Trusts" (1994) 110 L.Q.R. 335, 338.
138   [2010] EWCA Civ 917.

because the securities had been pooled in LBIE's unsegregated house deposit accounts and could be loaned or otherwise used by LBIE. At any moment in time the supposed trust fund might consist either of shares originally acquired, equivalent shares subsequently acquired or no shares at all.

In the High Court, Briggs J admitted to difficulty in applying *Hunter v Moss* outside its original and simple facts because he could not identify a clearly expressed rationale as to how such a trust works in practice. He felt that such a trust works by creating a beneficial co-ownership share in the identified fund,[139] rather than in the conceptually more difficult task of seeking to identify a particular part of the fund that the beneficiary owns outright. Briggs J accepted that there was no objection that the fund is shared beneficially with the trustee (as in *Hunter v Moss*) or that a segregated fund (i.e. one in which the trustee does not share) is a constantly changing fund beneficially co-owned by a constantly changing class of clients of the trustee.[140] He held that there was no fatal uncertainty in subject matter as each affiliate's beneficial co-ownership interest could, in principle, be readily ascertained from LBIE's records and be expressed as a proportion of the whole. Hence the trust is not defeated by the mingling of shares belonging to different parties. In the Court of Appeal, the decision was upheld with Lord Neuberger MR emphasising that "the basis, for sharing in the pool is the amount which ought to have been segregated for each client, rather than the amount which was in fact segregated for each client".[141]

2-029

Not surprisingly, the decision in *Hunter v Moss* has received widespread criticism. Most notably, Hayton sees no logical distinction to justify the divergent treatment of tangibles and intangibles and views *Hunter v Moss* as a controversial decision that, seemingly, flies in the face of traditional understanding.[142] Hayton writing elsewhere suggests also that the court was "perhaps blinded by the merits of the donee, who had done an awful lot for the subsequently ungrateful donor".[143] Nevertheless, there are defenders of the decision. Jill Martin views it as, "fair, sensible and workable . . . a welcome example of the court's policy of preventing a clearly intended trust from failing for uncertainty".[144] She adds:

> **"The chattels rule does not apply to money, shares and other choses in action because, in the nature of things, there is no difference between one pound and another pound, or one share and another share of the same class in the same company".[145]**

With some hesitation, Neuberger J in *Re Harvard Securities Ltd* also concluded that the distinction was justifiable and that it was the subject matter (i.e. shares rather than goods) which

---

139   See further, R. Goode, "Are Intangible Assets Fungible?" [2003] L.M.C.L.Q. 379.
140   See *Re CA Pacific Finance Ltd* [2000] 1 B.C.L.C. 494.
141   Re *Lehman Brothers International (Europe)* [2010] EWCA Civ 917 at [234].
142   D. Hayton, "Uncertainty of Subject-Matter of Trusts" (1994) 110 L.Q.R. 335.
143   D. Hayton, *The Law of Trusts*, 4th edn (London: Sweet and Maxwell, 2003), p.85.
144   J. Martin, "Certainty of subject matter: a defence of *Hunter v Moss*" [1996] Conv. 223, 227; see also S. Worthington [1999] J.B.L. 1.
145   J. Martin, "Certainty of subject matter: a defence of *Hunter v Moss*" [1996] Conv. 223, 224.

allowed for this divergence of treatment.[146] Put simply, intangible property should be treated differently because it does not lend itself to physical division and segregation.[147]

Certainty of beneficial share

Not only must the trust property be certain and ascertainable, but (except as regards discretionary trusts[148]) each beneficiary's share under the trust must also be allocated in some way when the trust is established.[149] This is the task of the settlor and the court cannot rewrite the trust instrument in order that the trust can be upheld.[150] As is illustrated by the following cases, this simple proposition as to beneficial share is apt to cause major problems:

- In *Boyce v Boyce*,[151] a fixed trust was set up by will on the death of the testator. The trust property consisted of two houses and there were two named beneficiaries, Maria and Charlotte. Maria was to choose which house she wanted. The other house was to be held on trust for Charlotte. Unfortunately, Maria predeceased the testator and died without making any selection. As it was now impossible to say which house Charlotte should have, the entire trust had to fail for uncertainty of beneficial share. As neither the court nor the trustees could decide which house each was to have, both properties stayed in the settlor's estate. The difficulty here was that the testator had prescribed a method of -allocation that had subsequently become impossible. Albeit a harsh decision, the court felt unable to disregard the settlor's instructions by implying an alternative method of selection.

- In *Re Knapton*,[152] the testatrix provided that a number of houses were to be distributed among "my nieces and nephews" and various named relatives and friends. Unlike in the *Boyce* case, she did not provide any machinery through which the properties were to be divided between them. In these circumstances, the High Court held that the beneficiaries had a right to choose which house they wanted and the order of choice was according to the order that their names appeared in the will. As to those who were described merely as "my nieces and nephews", the order of selection was worked out by the drawing of lots. The court, therefore, felt able to imply a right of selection to save the bequests and, importantly, without contradicting the express provision of the settlor.

---

146 [1997] 2 B.C.L.C. 369.
147 See *Holland v Newbury* [1997] 2 B.C.L.C. 369.
148 In relation to discretionary trusts, the very nature of such trusts entails that the beneficial interests are never certain. The essence of a discretionary trust is that the trustees exercise discretion as to who is to get what under its terms.
149 *Curtis v Rippon* (1820) 5 Madd. 434; *Asten v Asten* [1894] 3 Ch. 260.
150 *Richardson v Watson* (1833) 4 B. & Ad. 787.
151 (1849) 16 Sim. 476.
152 [1941] 2 All E.R. 573.

- In *Waddington v Waddington*,[153] the testator died leaving to his wife by will, "such articles of furniture not otherwise hereby bequeathed as she shall require". She chose some items and then later sought to choose more. Her step-children argued that her initial selection was irrevocable and limiting. In the High Court, Deputy Judge Mackie QC held that she had irrevocably made her choice and was not free to make any further choice. Her share had crystallised on the initial selection.

Equity is equality

2-031

The principle "equity is equality" can be applied where there is a fixed trust that does not declare expressly the beneficial interest to be taken by each beneficiary.[154] The classic example is *Burrough v Philcox*[155] where a trust was set up to benefit the settlor's son and daughter. Their beneficial shares, however, remained unspecified. As such, it might be thought that the trust was irredeemably flawed. The court was, however, able to uphold this trust by invoking the equitable maxim "equity is equality". Hence, each child was deemed to have an equal share. The maxim can be invoked only where there is no contrary intention demonstrated. In the unlikely event that the trust had been worded "to benefit my children unequally", the maxim could not then apply and the trust would necessarily fail.[156]

Although there is authority that that the maxim is not limited to mathematical equality, and might instead refer to proportionate equality,[157] the validity of this proposition has been doubted.[158] Mathematical division is, undoubtedly, the normal outcome.

An objective calculus

2-032

A difficult case is *Re Golay's Will Trusts*[159] where the testator set up a trust under which Tossy was "to enjoy one of my flats during her lifetime and to receive a reasonable income from my other properties". As to the flat, there was no problem as the executors were, on the testator's death, able to choose in which property she could live. The difficulty concerned the calcula-

---

153 [1999] All E.R. 557.
154 Although usually associated with fixed trusts, the principle that "equity is equality" could arise in relation to a discretionary trust, but only in the highly unlikely event that the trustees fail to exercise their discretion.
155 (1840) 5 My. & C.R. 72.
156 See *Margulies v Margulies* unreported 16 March 2000, where the terms of a will contradicted the presumption that the children were to take equally.
157 *Re Bower's ST* [1942] Ch. 197; *Steel v Dixon* (1881) 17 Ch. D. 825. For example, if there are two legacies of £100 and £200 and the legatees are to take the residuary estate in unspecified shares then, using proportionate equality, the latter will get twice as much as the former.
158 See *Re Steel* [1979] Ch. 218 where (at 226) Sir Robert Megarry VC explained, "the simplicity of mathematical equality is to be preferred to any process of proportionate division".
159 [1965] 1 W.L.R. 969.

tion of a "reasonable income" and whether that expression rendered that aspect of the trust thoroughly uncertain. Ungoed-Thomas J held that the word "reasonable" gave the court an objective yardstick by which to assess what was an income tailored for any particular person. Ungoed-Thomas J explained:

> "In this case, however, the yardstick indicated by the testator is not what he or some other specified person subjectively considers to be reasonable but what he identifies objectively as 'reasonable income'. The court is constantly involved in making such objective assessments of what is reasonable and it is not to be deterred from doing so because subjective influences can never be wholly excluded. In my view the testator intended by 'reasonable income' the yardstick which the court could and would apply in quantifying the amount so that the direction in the will is not in my view defeated by uncertainty".[160]

There are two observations that flow from this decision. First, if the word "reasonable" had not been employed, the trust of the income would have failed. It was the use of this term which gave the court the ability to undertake the calculation.[161] As Ungoed-Thomas J acknowledged, this offered "an effective determinant".[162] The court could, thereby, look at Tossy's age, her present income and current outgoings and conjure up a figure that was reasonable for her.

Secondly, if the testator had, for example, wanted to give Tossy a "reasonable share", "reasonable sum" or "reasonable legacy", then such arrangements would have clearly failed for uncertainty of beneficial share.[163] The difference is that a "reasonable income" (or, it is submitted, "reasonable maintenance" or "reasonable financial provision"[164]) is measured solely by taking on board the personal circumstances of the individual concerned. Accordingly, whether the testator's estate was worth £50,000 or £2 million, the income calculated would remain constant (i.e. certain). As regards the alternative and ineffective expressions, the calculation would necessarily reflect the size of the deceased's estate. Put in a slightly different context, say Jordan agrees with Fred that, if Fred gives Jordan a winning tip on a horse race, Jordan will give Fred a "reasonable share" of the proceeds. At the time the understanding is reached, it is impossible to quantify what would amount to a "reasonable share". All would depend upon how much money Jordan placed on the winning horse and the betting odds prevailing at the

2-033

---

160 [1965] 1 W.L.R. 969 at 972.
161 As also occurred in *Jackson v Hamilton* (1846) 3 J. & Lat. 702.
162 [1965] 1 W.L.R. 969 at 971. It is to be appreciated that, as this was not a discretionary trust, her entitlement was not at the subjective determination of the trustees. Accordingly, if the court could not ascribe meaning to the subject matter then the trust would fail.
163 These expressions simply have no clear meaning.
164 In *McNulty v McNulty* [2002] EWHC 123 (Ch), which concerned an application for "reasonable financial provision" under the Inheritance (Provision for Family and Dependants) Act 1975, the court appeared to equate this with a "reasonable income".

time. Unlike "income", therefore, the court has there to look beyond the beneficiary's needs and wants. If, however, Jordan had stated that Fred would have 50 per cent of any winnings, then that would at least offer sufficient certainty of intended entitlement.

Certainty of Objects

2-034
In order for a trust or, indeed, a power to exist there have to be beneficiaries (i.e. the objects of the trust) who are certain or capable of being rendered certain.[165] As Lord Evershed MR put it, "No principle perhaps has greater sanction or authority behind it than the general proposition that a trust by English law, not being a charitable trust, in order to be effective must have ascertained or ascertainable beneficiaries".[166] There must be someone who can enforce the trust or someone in whose favour the court can enforce the trust.[167] If there are no ascertainable beneficiaries there is no trust.[168] As to future interests, the beneficiaries must also be ascertainable within the perpetuity period.[169] The general requirements are that, first, except for charitable trusts, there must be human beneficiaries. A private purpose trust (e.g. the promotion of good relations between nations and the preservation of the independence and integrity of newspapers[170]) cannot be upheld. This is because there would be no one entitled to enforce such a trust. Secondly, the beneficiaries must be identified individually (e.g. "to hold on trust for Adrienne and Fiona") or identifiable as a member of a clearly defined class (e.g. "to hold on trust for my children"). Such was demonstrated in *Re TXU Europe Group Plc (In Administration)*[171] where it was unclear who were the intended objects of the alleged trust. Some evidence suggested that it was to benefit only existing executives and did not extend to future employees. Other evidence indicated that it was to benefit any employee whether past, present or future. As Blackburne J explained, "There is no reason, of course, why there should not be a trust for a class of persons which may increase in number. The evidence, however, must make this clear".[172]

---

165   The hallowed principle is that, as Lord Upjohn explained in Re *Gulbenkian* [1970] A.C. 508 at 524, "the Court of Chancery, which acts in default of trustees, must know with sufficient certainty the objects of the beneficence of the donor so as to execute the trust".

166   *Re Endacott* [1959] 3 All E.R. 562 at 568. It is to be remembered that what follows does not apply to charitable trusts, as the Attorney General and Charity Commission can enforce such public trusts.

167   See *Morice v Bishop of Durham* (1805) 10 Ves. 522.

168   *Tackaberry v Hollis* [2007] EWHC 2633 (Ch).

169   See Ch.4.

170   *Re Astor's ST* [1952] Ch. 534; see Ch.6.

171   [2003] EWHC 3105 (Ch).

172   [2003] EWHC 3105 (Ch) at [29].

By way of contrast, in *RoadChef (Employee Benefits Trustees) Ltd v Hill*[173] the expression "employees from time to time" of a company was given the meaning that it referred to employees existing at the time of the distribution and did not include former employees.

Conceptual uncertainty?

The description of the beneficiaries must, as regards both fixed and discretionary trusts, be conceptually certain at the time that the trust is created. This refers to semantic or linguistic expression (i.e. precision of language) about the individual or class that is to benefit. The description of beneficiaries must, therefore, be capable of having some ascertainable meaning. There must be provided sufficient definitional criteria so that the trustee can carry out the settlor's instructions. To achieve this end, the court will strain to make sense of the formula that has been used to define the objects. Lord Wilberforce illustrated this in *Blathwayt v Baron Cawley* when he counselled that judges should undertake the task of construction, "without excessive astuteness to discover ambiguities".[174] In *Re Gulbenkian's Settlements*, Lord Upjohn added that the court must exercise, "its judicial knowledge and experience in the relevant matter, innate common sense and desire to make sense of the settlor's or party's expressed intentions, however obscure and ambiguous the language that may have been used, to give a reasonable meaning to that language if it can do so without doing violence to it".[175]

It was argued in *Public Trustee v Butler*[176] that the conceptually uncertain reference to "deserving" relatives should be regarded as merely a guide to the trustee and not as part of the definition of the class. Sir Andrew Morritt rejected this distinction, concluding that, "If the word is added as a guide to the trustee it is part of the qualification to be enjoyed by the beneficiary. If such qualification as a concept is inherently uncertain then it invalidates the trust or the power".[177] This is to be contrasted with the scenario where the problematic terms are regarded merely as words of explanation. In *Re Steel*, for example, the trust of the residuary estate was bequeathed to benefit "those beneficiaries who have only received small amounts".[178] Sir Robert Megarry VC felt able to construe the words employed as embracing all beneficiaries and the reference to small amounts was not defining the class, but was an explanation of motive.[179] The distinction is not always easy to draw and, as in *Steel*, will hinge

---

173 [2014] EWHC 3109 (Ch).
174 [1976] A.C. 397 at 425.
175 [1970] A.C. 508 at 552.
176 [2012] EWHC 858 (Ch).
177 [2012] EWHC 858 (Ch) at [19].
178 [1979] Ch 218. The beneficiaries were the pecuniary legatees under the testator's will.
179 As Megarry VC explained [1979] Ch 218 at 223, "On this interpretation the testator is giving his residue for division between all the legatees, and he is adding the explanation that he is doing this because they will all be receiving small amounts; if his estate is large enough, he is therefore increasing what they get, up to the limit of his estate".

upon punctuation, the language employed in the specific legacies and the arrangement of the words in the testator's will.

If sense cannot be made of the language used, the trustee will be unable to perform his duties and the trust will be entirely void. For example, a fixed trust to distribute money between "my favourite people", "my relatives who are handsome" or "good citizens of Keele" would be conceptually uncertain because it would be impossible to ascertain who the settlor truly intended to benefit. The boundaries of meaning are simply too imprecise.[180]

Examples of conceptual uncertainty

2-036

The most effective way of understanding what will amount to conceptual uncertainty is to consider the authorities. The following cases provide a useful demonstration:

- In *Re Barlow's Will Trusts*,[181] Browne-Wilkinson J discussed, albeit by way of obiter, the validity of a trust to benefit "old friends" and concluded that, while such expressions would not invalidate a gift subject to a condition precedent, they would render a trust conceptually uncertain. The terms "old" and "friend" have so many shades of meaning that, whether applying the complete list or the given postulant tests (see below), it was impossible to say who was intended to benefit. If the court was unable to discern any precise meaning, then the trustee would similarly be unable to do so. As Browne-Wilkinson J put it, "many people, if asked to draw up a complete list of their friends, would probably have some difficulty in deciding whether certain of the people they knew were really 'friends' as opposed to 'acquaintances'".[182]

- In *Re Wright's Will Trust*,[183] a trust was designed to benefit "such people and institutions as have helped me or my late husband". Not surprisingly, this was held to be conceptually uncertain. Templeman J concluded that "help" was a term that "could mean anything from helping the testatrix across the road to saving her from death, dishonour or bankruptcy".

---

180 Context is important as in *Public Trustee v Butler* [2012] EWHC 858 (Ch) where "my promising relatives" was held to be certain. The word "promising" was not to be construed in a vacuum and referred to scholarships for education. As Sir Andrew Morritt explained at [15], "A person liable to benefit from the education for which the scholarship was offered would be 'promising'". He went on to consider the further expression "to help . . . the deserving materially hardship cases amongst my relatives" and concluded hesitatingly that "material hardship" was conceptually certain, but emphasised that "deserving" was not.
181 [1979] 1 W.L.R. 278.
182 [1979] 1 W.L.R. 278 at 280; see also, Lord Wilberforce in *McPhail v Doulton* [1971] A.C. 424 at 457 where he said: "If there is a trust for 'my old friends', all concerned are faced with uncertainty as to the concept or idea enshrined in these words. It may not be difficult to resolve that 'old' means not 'aged' but 'of long standing'; but then there is the question how long is 'long'. Friendship, too, is a concept with almost infinite shades of meaning".
183 Unreported 29 July 1982 (CA).

■ In *Re Astor's ST*,[184] a trust failed on two fronts. First, it was a non-charitable purpose trust that had no living beneficiaries. Secondly, the trust also failed because of conceptual uncertainty. The testator's wishes were to maintain "good understanding, sympathy and co-operation between nations" as well as "the independence and integrity of newspapers". The concepts employed here were incapable of any precise meaning.

■ *Re Endacott*[185] offers a further example of a failed purpose trust. The testator left money to the local council, "for the purpose of providing some suitable monument to myself". The trust failed also for a lack of conceptual certainty as it was unclear what the term "suitable" encompassed.

■ In *Public Trustee v Butler*,[186] trust was intended to benefit "the deserving materially hardship cases amongst my relatives". The reference to those who suffered "material hardship" was sufficiently certain, but the concept which divided those within that subset, that is, those who were "deserving", rendered the entire clause conceptually uncertain.

Relatives, dependants and children

2-037

It is helpful to consider a couple of cases where the trust was determined to be conceptually certain in circumstances that might be thought of as borderline.

In *Re Baden's Deed Trusts* (*No.2*),[187] the issue arose as to whether the definition of the beneficiaries as "relatives" and "dependants" made the trust void for conceptual uncertainty. The Court of Appeal found these expressions to be conceptually certain. The term "dependants" caused the least trouble and, having been employed over many years in trust deeds, lent itself well to conceptualisation. As Sachs LJ admitted, "I confess that the suggestion that it is uncertain seems no longer arguable".[188] It was, as Megaw LJ put it, an "ordinary, well understood word".[189] The expression "relatives" was, however, to prove more problematic. Stamp LJ thought that the term "relatives" was synonymous with next of kin and nearest blood relations. The other members of the Court of Appeal adopted the broader definition of descendants from a common ancestor. Either way, the Court of Appeal could uphold the trust. Although such terms might cause evidential difficulties,[190] they are conceptually certain.[191]

---

184 [1952] Ch. 534.
185 [1959] 3 All E.R. 562.
186 [2012] EWHC 858 (Ch).
187 [1973] Ch. 9.
188 [1973] Ch. 9 at 21.
189 [1973] Ch. 9 at 22. Stamp LJ did not doubt that the word "connotes financial dependence" and agreed that it did not introduce linguistic uncertainty (at 30).
190 As Lord Evershed MR commented of "relations" in *Re Scarisbrick* [1951] Ch. 622, 632, "That class is, in theory, capable of almost indefinite expansion, but proof of relationship soon becomes extremely difficult in fact".
191 *Public Trustee v Butler* [2012] EWHC 858 (Ch).

In *Gold v Hill*,[192] the beneficiaries were described as "Carol and the kids". It was contended that "kids" was uncertain because Mr Gilbert had various children from various relationships. In the context of this trust, Carnwath J concluded that there was no serious doubt as to whom the "kids" referred, i.e. Carol's children.

Fixed trusts: the complete list rule

2-038

It will become clear that a different approach is adopted according to whether the trust is a fixed trust or a discretionary trust. A fixed trust is one where both the identity and the interests of the beneficiaries are set out in the trust instrument. The beneficiaries might be named individually or defined by reference to a class (e.g. "my employees" or "my children"). The essence of such a trust is to confer fixed benefits upon fixed beneficiaries. Each beneficiary, therefore, is to benefit under a fixed trust. The trustee enjoys no discretion as to the distribution of the trust property.

As the trustee labours under a duty to distribute according to the settlor's expressed wishes, the courts understandably take a strict approach. There can be no division unless all beneficiaries are known. Hence, the rule is that a fixed trust is void unless each and every beneficiary is ascertainable. This is sometimes called the "complete list" test, which demands that the trustee must be able to draw up an exhaustive list of the beneficiaries. If the trustee cannot compile such a comprehensive catalogue, the trust must fail. It was emphasised in *Re Eden*[193] that, although it might be time consuming and expensive, an exhaustive catalogue of beneficiaries must still be compiled. As Wynn-Parry J accepted, "it may well be that a large part, even the whole of the funds available, would be consumed in the inquiry . . . that would be very unfortunate, but that cannot of itself constitute any reason why such an inquiry, whether by the trustees or the court, should not be undertaken".[194]

2-039

A useful illustration of the operation of the complete list test is *OT Computers Ltd v First National Tricity Finance Ltd*.[195] There the claimant (OT Computers) was a retailer of computer products. In 2002, the claimant instructed its bank to open two separate trust accounts for the payment of customer deposits and moneys owed to "urgent suppliers". The claimant compiled two schedules: one containing the names of the customers and the other listing a number of its suppliers. On the claimant going into receivership, the bank sought to discharge a loan due to it from the money in the two accounts. A trust in favour of the customers was upheld because the beneficiaries could be identified in the context of the payments made by them to the company.[196] Pumfrey J concluded, however, that the trust

---

192 [1999] 1 F.L.R. 54.
193 [1957] 2 All E.R. 430.
194 [1957] 2 All E.R. 430 at 435.
195 [2003] EWHC 1010 (Ch).
196 This was a *Re Kayford*-style of trust whereby the company by unilateral conduct made itself a trustee of the funds.

in favour of the suppliers failed because of a lack of certainty of objects. It was not possible to draw up a complete list of urgent suppliers. The term "urgent" was simply too conceptually vague to identify any class of beneficiary and, therefore, the trustees could draw up no complete list. As Pumfrey J admitted, "It is not sufficient to be able to say whether or not any identified person is or is not a member of the class entitled to be considered: the purpose of the trust in the present case is to vest an immediate interest in the suppliers in question . . .".[197] The money in the suppliers' account remained in the beneficial ownership of the company.

Untraceable beneficiaries

2-040

It is possible that a fixed trust might be created or a statutory trust exist[198] in circumstances where it is unclear either where a particular beneficiary is or, indeed, whether a particular beneficiary is still alive. In such situations, the trustees potentially face a difficult and legally risky choice, i.e. to delay distribution indefinitely until the facts become established or to make an immediate distribution in ignorance of the true facts. The trustee has been helped considerably by a pragmatic solution offered in *Re Benjamin*.[199] There it was demonstrated that, provided the beneficiaries are defined with adequate precision, every reasonable step has been taken to trace entitled individuals, and it is improbable that any other individual would ever establish a title, the court can exercise its supervisory jurisdiction to enable the trust property to be distributed. This means that the trust will not fail simply because a beneficiary cannot be found or because there are doubts as to a beneficiary's continued existence. In such cases, the court can authorise the trustees to distribute the trust property amongst the known beneficiaries on the assumption that the beneficiary is dead (i.e. make a *"Benjamin* order"). This order does not, however, disturb the entitlement of the missing beneficiary.[200] It merely facilitates a speedier distribution. If the beneficiary later reappears, his share can then be recovered from the other beneficiaries. It is common for the court to take an express legal undertaking from the identified beneficiaries to repay the money to any new claimant. If a Benjamin order is not obtained, the trustees run the risk of personal liability to the newly discovered beneficiary. The trustees can, however, take out missing beneficiary insurance to shield themselves against any potential liability. Indeed, such a policy is often more effective than the limited protection provided by a costlier application for a *Benjamin* order.[201]

---

197 [2003] EWHC 1010 (Ch) at [21].

198 *Re Pritchard Stockbrokers Ltd* [2019] EWHC 137 (Ch) where a statutory trust arose following the Financial Services Authority intervention with an insolvent company. The trustees sought to make a final distribution amongst known clients with potential claims.

199 [1902] 1 Ch. 723. This is, as Norris J acknowledged *Re Pritchard Stockbrokers Ltd* at [14], "well established in the sphere of private trusts, and is of equal utility in the context of 'commercial trusts'".

200 See *Re Green's Trusts* [1985] 3 All E.R. 455. The Lazarus-style beneficiary may then trace the trust property into the hands of the others: *In the matter of Marconi Corp Plc* [2013] EWHC 324 (Ch).

201 This is a perfectly proper expense for the trustee to incur: *Evans v Westcombe* [1999] 2 All E.R. 777. As Deputy

Fixed trusts: evidential certainty

2-041

Whereas conceptual uncertainty deals with meaning, evidential uncertainty concerns the practical difficulty of proving as a fact whether a person is or is not within the class of beneficiaries.[202] It is, therefore, a totally separate issue from conceptual uncertainty. This requirement of evidential certainty applies only to fixed trusts, which require the trustees to draw up a complete list of the beneficiaries. As demonstrated by the majority in *Re Badens Deed Trusts (No.2)*, because of the employment of the class test (or any given postulant test), a discretionary trust should never fail on this ground.[203] An example of evidential uncertainty would be where the settlor establishes a fixed trust to benefit such students of Larne University who graduated in 1969 with a first-class degree in law. If the records of Larne University have been destroyed by fire, it will be impossible to draw up a complete list of beneficiaries and, therefore, the trust will fail for evidential uncertainty. In approaching its task, the court is not to insist upon absolute certainty and, instead, must adopt a pragmatic stance and look to probability rather than theoretic possibility.[204] In *Re Eden*, Wynn-Parry J explained, "it is only when one reaches, on the evidence, a conclusion that is so vague, or that the difficulty is so great that it must be treated as virtually incapable of resolution, that one is entitled, to my mind, to say that a gift of that nature is void for uncertainty".[205]

Rendering the evidentially uncertain certain?

2-042

The trust deed may, however, expressly allow the trustee or a third party to settle any evidential dispute as to whether a given individual is a beneficiary. Seemingly, this liberality does not appear to extend to conceptual uncertainty,[206] which remains a matter solely for the court.[207] Three cases offer an insight into the workings of this proposition:

- In *Re Tuck's Settlement Trusts*,[208] money was put on trust for "the Baronet for the time being if and when and so long as he shall be of the Jewish faith and be married to an approved wife". Such a wife was defined as: "a wife of Jewish blood by one or both of her

---

Judge McCombe explained at [24], "The missing beneficiary policy does provide, at relatively small cost, a practical answer to such problems. Such a policy provides a fund to meet the claim of such a beneficiary in exoneration of the representative and of the overpaid beneficiary".

202 As C.T. Emery, "The Most Hallowed Principle: Certainty of Trusts and Powers of Appointment" (1982) 98 L.Q.R. 551, 556 put it, "Evidential certainty exists when it is possible to gather facts which will demonstrate of a particular person that he does, or does not fulfil those criteria".

203 [1973] Ch. 9. As will become clear below, this is achieved whether through the reversal of the burden of proof (as advocated by Sachs LJ) or the substantial numbers approach (as canvassed by Megaw LJ).

204 See Cross J in *Re Saxone Shoe Co* [1962] 2 All E.R. 904 at 912.

205 [1957] 2 All E.R. 430 at 433.

206 *Re Coxen* [1948] 2 All E.R. 492. Cf. Lord Denning MR in *Re Tuck's ST* [1978] Ch. 49.

207 *Re Wynn* [1952] Ch. 271.

208 [1978] Ch. 49.

parents and who has been brought up in and has never departed from and at the date of her marriage continues to worship according to the Jewish faith". Lord Denning MR could see no reason why a settlor should not provide that any dispute or doubt should be resolved by his executors or trustees, or even by a third person. He concluded that the Chief Rabbi was able more than anyone else to determine whether a wife was of Jewish blood and had been brought up according to the Jewish faith. Unless it could be shown that the arbiter was guilty of misconduct or arrived at a decision that was wholly unreasonable, his decision should stand.[209] Lord Denning expressed the unconventional opinion that the same approach should apply equally to conceptual uncertainty and to evidential uncertainty as well as to conditions whether subsequent or precedent.

■ In *Re Coxen*,[210] the testator by a codicil devised a dwelling-house to his trustees with a direction to permit his wife to "reside therein during her life, or for so long as she shall desire to reside therein" and declared that "from and after her death or if in the opinion of the trustees she shall have ceased permanently to reside therein" the house was to fall into his residuary trusts. Jenkins J held that this double provision for the determination of the wife's interest was sufficiently defined to enable the trustees to come to a proper decision and that it constituted a valid limitation of the gift. Any potential evidential uncertainty (as to whether the event occurred) was removed by making the trustees' opinion decisive.[211] In contrast, Jenkins J added that, if the condition had been conceptually uncertain, making the trustees' opinion the criterion would not have saved it.

■ In *Re Leek*,[212] the objects of the trust were expressed to be "such other persons as the company may consider to have a moral claim". The trust was upheld because, as Harman J put it, "The trustees are made the arbiters and the objects are such persons as they may consider to have a moral claim; and I do not see why they should not be able on this footing to make up their minds and arrive at a decision".[213]

Discretionary trusts: the class test

Under a discretionary trust, the trustee is given the discretion to select, from amongst a specified class of beneficiaries, who will benefit under the trust and often when and to what extent.

2-043

---

209 See also *Re Tepper's Will Trusts* [1987] Ch. 358, where beneficiaries were directed that "they shall not marry outside the Jewish faith". The court was able to hear extrinsic evidence of the surrounding circumstances to show the meaning attributed by the testator.
210 [1948] 2 All E.R. 492.
211 See also, *Re Jones* [1953] Ch. 125, where a daughter was to lose her inheritance if, in the opinion of the trustees, she struck up a relationship with a particular man.
212 [1968] 2 W.L.R. 1385.
213 [1968] 2 W.L.R. 1385 at 1390.

In modern times, the discretionary trust is used to benefit substantial groups of people, such as employees and their dependants. It is prized as providing a more tax-effective means of settling property, maintaining flexibility and offering administrative benefits. The settlor will not usually intend that each person within the designated class will benefit directly under the trust. The settlor will, most certainly, not intend that they each receive an equal share. As Lord Wilberforce explained in *McPhail v Doulton*, "Equal division is surely the last thing the settlor ever intended: equal division among all may, probably would, produce a result beneficial to no one. Why suppose that the court would lend itself to a whimsical execution?"[214] Accordingly, it should follow that it is not necessary for every potential beneficiary to be identified by the trustee.[215] Indeed, a complete list might often be a practical impossibility. Nevertheless, until the majority decision of the House of Lords in *McPhail v Doulton* the rule for certainty of objects for discretionary trusts was the same as for fixed trusts (i.e. the complete list approach).[216]

In the *McPhail* case, Lord Wilberforce rejected the traditional rule, explaining that the duties of a trustee of a discretionary trust are very different from those under a fixed trust. With a fixed trust, each beneficiary has a specific claim to a specific share of the trust fund and, therefore, the trustee must discover each and every beneficiary. As regards a discretionary trust, however, the trustee is required merely to act as a reasonable trustee and survey the field of potential beneficiaries. As Lord Wilberforce put it:

"a trustee with a duty to distribute, particularly among a potentially very large class, would surely never require the preparation of a complete list of names, which anyhow would tell him little that he needs to know. He would examine the field, by class and category; might indeed make diligent and careful inquiries, depending upon how much money he had to give away and the means at his disposal, as to the composition and needs of particular categories and of individuals within them; decide upon certain priorities or proportions, and then select individuals according to their needs or qualifications. If he acts in this manner, can it really be said that he is not carrying out the trust?"[217]

2-044

The facts before Lord Wilberforce concerned a discretionary trust established to provide benefits for the staff of Matthew Hall & Co Ltd, their relatives and dependants. The objects of the trust, therefore, were so numerous and wide-ranging that it was impossible for the trustee to draw up an exhaustive list of potential beneficiaries. The House of Lords, however, applied a different test that is sometimes referred to as the "class test", the "any given postulant test",

214 [1971] A.C. 424 at 451.
215 See J.W. Harris, "Discretionary Trusts—An End and a Beginning?" (1970) 33 M.L.R. 686.
216 See *IRC v Broadway Cottages Trust* [1955] Ch. 20.
217 [1971] A.C. 424 at 449; see also, Megarry VC in *Re Hay's Settlement Trusts* [1982] 1 W.L.R. 202 at 209, 210 who spoke of the necessity of the discretionary trustee to address "the size of the problem".

or the "is or is not test".[218] Put simply, the issue is whether it could be said with certainty of any given individual that he is or is not a member of the class.[219] Unfortunately, the House of Lords in *McPhail* felt unable to apply this test on the evidence before it and, instead, referred the case back to the High Court to determine whether the test was satisfied. Eventually, it proceeded to the Court of Appeal under the alternative name of *Re Baden's Deed Trusts (No.2)*.[220]

> ## The class test in operation

2-045

The operation of the class test has proved more difficult than, perhaps, might be expected. Although in *Re Baden's Deed Trusts (No.2)* the Court of Appeal tackled the issue directly, each judge gave quite a different interpretation.[221] The major stumbling block concerns the inherent difficulty in proving a negative: how can a trustee prove that a particular person is not, for example, a relative of an employee? Ironically, none of the three approaches is entirely convincing and each is open to criticism. Surprisingly, it remains unclear which approach will be favoured by the courts:

- Stamp LJ thought that the class test was to be applied literally, that is, it can be satisfied only when it can be said of any given postulant that he is or is not a member of the class. There is no room for any doubt with this approach. As Stamp LJ explained, "Validity or invalidity is to depend on whether you can say of any individual—and the accent must be on that word 'any' for it is not simply the individual whose claim you are considering who is spoken of—'is or is not a member of the class', for only thus can you make a survey of the range of objects or possible beneficiaries".[222] The obvious problem with this formulation is that it marks what is, essentially, a retreat to the complete list test previously jettisoned by the House of Lords in *McPhail v Doulton*. It would be remarkable if a discretionary trust, under which only some beneficiaries were intended to benefit, failed because of an inability to say categorically of one person whether he is or is not in a class. Nevertheless, Stamp LJ believed that the entire class of objects had to be surveyed: "Any survey of the range of objects or possible beneficiaries would certainly be incomplete, and I am able to discern no principle on which such a survey could be conducted or where it should start or finish".[223] Hence, the existence of even a single "don't know" would mean that the trust is doomed.

---

218 This test had previously operated only in relation to powers of appointment: see *Re Gulbenkian's ST* [1968] 3 All E.R. 785. Lord Wilberforce saw no difference between the way in which a discretionary trust and a power operate while the selection process is ongoing.

219 See Lord Wilberforce in *McPhail v Doulton* [1971] A.C. 424 at 454, 456.

220 [1973] Ch. 9.

221 See J. Hopkins, "Continuing Uncertainty as to Certainty of Objects of Trust Powers" (1973) 32 C.L.J. 36.

222 [1973] Ch. 9 at 28.

223 [1973] Ch. 9 at 28.

- Sachs LJ adopted a more liberal view and stated that it was up to a claimant to prove positively that he is within a class. If he fails to do so, then he is regarded as falling outside the class.[224] Sachs LJ was promoting the argument that the court should, as regards a discretionary trust, never be defeated by evidential uncertainty. To avoid such an outcome, the burden of proving the negative should be reversed. The weakness of this approach is that, when pushed to extremes, it produces some distinctly odd outcomes. It allows for the fact that there might be numerous individuals who cannot prove their entitlement. It also caters for the possibility of a discretionary trust being upheld in circumstances where only one beneficiary can prove positively that he is in the class. This is clearly not what the settlor would ever have intended.

- Megaw LJ was also prepared to reject a strict approach. He felt that it sufficed that the trustee could say about a substantial number of beneficiaries that they fell within the scope of the trust. This would be so even where there were others about whom it could not be said with certainty whether they were inside or outside the class.[225] Accordingly, it does not matter that there is a category of "don't knows". This approach overcomes the possibility of there being only one beneficiary under a discretionary trust. Nevertheless, it may mean that the trustee is selecting from a narrower class than that intended by the settlor.[226]

Administratively unworkable trusts

2-046

This issue is concerned with the width of the class specified (i.e. it is to do with the numerative range of potential beneficiaries). In *McPhail v Doulton*, Lord Wilberforce acknowledged, albeit by way of obiter, that a class of beneficiaries might be, "so hopelessly wide as not to form 'anything like a class' so that the trust is administratively unworkable or . . . one that cannot be executed".[227] By way of illustration, he suggested that a trust for "all the residents of Greater London" would necessarily be void.[228] In *Gibbs v Harding*,[229] the objects were defined as "The Black Community of Hackney, Haringey, Islington and Tower Hamlets". [230]Although the trust was upheld as a charitable trust, Lewison J admitted that the class would be too

---

224 [1973] Ch. 9 at 19.

225 As Megaw LJ concluded, "If it does not mean that, I do not know where the line is supposed to be drawn . . ." ([1973] Ch. 9 at 24).

226 See the dissenting speech of Lord Hodson in *McPhail v Doulton* [1971] A.C. 424 at 443, which (with Lord Guest) approved the traditional reasoning that a trust would be void for uncertainty since no complete ascertainment of all the objects of the trust was practicable.

227 [1971] A.C. 424 at 457.

228 [1971] A.C. 424 at 457. He added that a trust for "relatives" (even of a living person) did not fall within this category.

229 [2008] Ch. 235; see C. Harpum "Administrative Unworkability and Purpose Trusts" (1986) 45(3) C.L.J. 391.

230 The reference to colour was deleted by virtue of s.34 of the Race Relations Act 1976.

wide to sustain a private trust.[231] The class would be too extensive for the trustees to perform their duties and for the court to enforce the beneficiaries' claims if the trustees failed in those duties. Logically, therefore, the case for invalidity appears stronger with a fixed trust than it is with a discretionary trust.[232] For example, a fixed trust to benefit employees of a huge multinational company and their children might be a ready candidate for classification as an administratively unworkable trust. A discretionary trust, however, in favour of the same beneficiaries would, it is submitted, be less likely to be struck down on this ground.[233] The notion of administrative unworkability appears, therefore, not to be driven solely by numbers, but is concerned with the overarching ability of the trustee to carry out his duty of inquiry and ascertainment.[234]

The only decision directly on this issue is *R. v District Auditor Ex p. West Yorkshire Metropolitan CC*.[235] An attempt was there made by the soon to be defunct council to benefit in specified ways "any or all or some of the inhabitants of the County of West Yorkshire". Lloyd LJ held that the discretionary trust failed because the class (approximately 2.5 million people) was far too large to be workable. He also found it to be a private purpose trust which, as a general rule, will offend the beneficiary principle and fail also on that basis. In *Re Hay's Settlement Trust*,[236] Megarry VC accepted (not surprisingly) that a trust to benefit anyone in the world would be ineffective. He did, however, acknowledge that a power of appointment on similar terms might be valid.[237] This distinction was based upon the premise that a trustee's duties are imperative and more stringent than those who are called upon to exercise a power.

Capriciousness

There is no general rule of law that requires a disposition to be sensible and rational. As Wigram VC famously remarked, "No man is bound to make a will in such a manner as to deserve approbation from the prudent, the wise and the good".[238] Although this approach

2-047

---

231   Administrative unworkability is thought not to affect powers: *Re Manisty's Settlement* [1973] 2 All E.R. 1203; *Re Hay's Settlement Trust* [1982] 1 W.L.R. 202.

232   See generally, I.M. Hardcastle, "Administrative unworkability: a reassessment of an abiding problem" [1990] Conv. 24, who considers it best to treat the notion of unworkability as a logical extension of evidential certainty.

233   It would not, to employ the words of C.T. Emery in "The Most Hallowed Principle: Certainty of Trusts and Powers of Appointment" (1982) 98 L.Q.R. 551, 558, "render meaningless the notion of a duty of discretionary distribution owed to its members".

234   L. McKay ([1974] 38 Conv. 269, 283), however, argues that there is no substance to the requirement that a trust must be administratively workable. This author concludes that there are no insurmountable difficulties associated with having a large class of beneficiaries.

235   [1986] R.V.R. 24 (QB).

236   [1981] 3 All E.R. 786.

237   See also, *Re Manisty's Settlement* [1973] 2 All E.R. 1203.

238   (1850) Hare 301. It matters not that the disposition is unexpected, inexplicable, unfair and improper (*Gill v Woodall* [2011] Ch 380) or motivated by surprising, vindictive or perverse reasoning (*Hawes v Burgess* [2013] EWCA Civ 94).

extends to testamentary dispositions and gifts, it does not apply to trusts. Due to the nature of the obligations placed upon a trustee, a trust is void if it is capricious, i.e. it reflects a nonsensical intention on the part of the settlor and precludes any proper consideration by the trustees.[239] For example, a trust to benefit red-haired men would be struck down in this way.[240] It is submitted that a trust could also be viewed as capricious if the trust fund was woefully inadequate to justify the expense and enquiries of distributing it amongst the specified class of beneficiaries.[241] Although there has, as yet, been no case decided specifically on the basis of capriciousness, it has been the subject of some judicial consideration.

In *Re Manisty's Settlement*, Templeman J provided the example of an attempt to benefit the residents of Greater London as being capricious because the terms, "negative any sensible intention on the part of the settlor".[242] While this view may have some merit where the settlor is a private individual, it would surely not apply where the settlor is a local authority. This was the stance adopted by Lloyd LJ in the *West Yorkshire Metropolitan CC* case where he concluded that a trust to benefit 2.5 million inhabitants was not capricious. Following the lead of Templeman J, Lloyd LJ felt that capriciousness would arise where the class was merely, "an accidental conglomeration of persons who had no discernible link with the settlor".[243] On the facts before him, he concluded that, "The council had every reason for wishing to benefit the inhabitants of West Yorkshire".[244]

2-048 Two other cases might be invoked as illustrations of when a trust might be classified as capricious. First, in *M'Caig v University of Glasgow* a private purpose trust to establish various monuments in memory of the settlor was viewed as "perpetuating at great cost, and in an absurd manner, the idiosyncrasies of an eccentric testator".[245] Although the trust failed because of want of beneficiary, it could have failed also because of capriciousness. Secondly, in *Brown v Burdett* the trustees were directed to block up the doors and windows of a house for 20 years.[246] Although the trust was held to fail because it was to advance a private purpose, the direction was undeniably capricious in nature.

---

239 As I.M. Hardcastle, "Administrative unworkability: a reassessment of an abiding problem" [1990] Conv. 24, 32, 33 explains, "a settlor is permitted to earmark whomsoever he pleases to be the objects of his benefaction, but, as a matter of policy, the court will not aid the settlor in all his eccentricities. If the disposition is devoid of any sensible purpose, then it will be avoided as capricious".
240 A power will also be rendered void if it is capricious.
241 See Lord Reid in *Re Gulbenkian's Settlement Trusts* [1970] A.C. 508.
242 [1973] 2 All E.R. 1203 at 1211.
243 [1986] R.V.R. 24 (QB).
244 [1986] R.V.R. 24 (QB).
245 [1907] S.C. 231 at 242 per Lord Kyllachy.
246 (1882) 21 Ch. D. 667.

Guide to Further Reading

C.T. Emery, "Certainty of Beneficiaries of Trusts and Powers of Appointment" (1982) 98 L.Q.R. 551.

Y. Grbich, "*Baden*: Awakening the Conceptually Moribund Trust" (1974) 37 M.L.R. 643.

C. Harpum, "Administrative Unworkability and Purpose Trusts" (1986) 45(3) C.L.J. 391.

D. Hayton, "Uncertainty of Subject-Matter of Trusts" (1994) 110 L.Q.R. 335.

L. McKay, "*Re Baden* and the Third Class of Uncertainty" (1974) 38 Conv. 269.

3

Constitution of Trusts

This chapter focuses upon the circumstances in which a trust may be properly constituted or, put more simply, it considers the circumstances in which a trustee will have sufficient title to the property for the trust to be effective. Constitution can occur by means of an effective self-declaration of trust or an effective transfer of property to the trustees. The classic exposition of this rule of constitution is that of Turner LJ in *Milroy v Lord*:

> "In order to render a voluntary settlement valid and effectual, the settlor must have done everything which according to the nature of the property comprised in the settlement was necessary to be done in order to render the settlement binding upon him. He may, of course, do this by actually transferring the property to the persons for whom he intends to provide and the provision will then be effectual and it will be equally effectual if he transfers the property to a trustee for the purposes of the settlement, or declares that he himself holds it on trust for those purposes . . . but, in order to render the settlement binding one of these modes must, as I understand the law of this court, be resorted to for there is no equity in this court to perfect an imperfect gift".[1]

The requirement of constitution is straightforward and suggests that only if the trust is completely constituted will the trust bind the settlor and be enforceable by the beneficiary. If the trust is not completely constituted then, as a general rule, it will be ineffective.[2] In the latter scenario, the intended beneficiaries have no interest that they can enforce. This is because, unlike a contracting party, the beneficiary usually provides no consideration -what-

---

1   (1862) 4 De. G.F. & J. 264 at 274.
2   See *Deslauriers v Guardian Asset Management Ltd* [2017] UKPC 34.

soever.[3] Equity, moreover, cannot offer assistance because of two interrelated and venerated maxims "equity will not assist a volunteer" and "equity will not perfect an imperfect gift". Hence, the general rule is that the court is prevented from coming to the aid of a volunteer beneficiary regardless of how undesirable the outcome might appear. In *Jones v Lock*, for example, Lord Carnworth LC was unable to identify a trust of a cheque in favour of a baby and lamented that, "by an act of God, this unfortunate child has been deprived of a provision which his father meant to make for him".[4] Obviously, the courts will, if possible, uphold a trust for, as Lord Browne-Wilkinson put it, "Although equity will not aid a volunteer, it will not strive officiously to defeat a gift".[5] In addition, this lack of assistance to a volunteer is not a hard and fast rule and there are, as will become clear, well-established exceptions to it. As Arden LJ explained in *Pennington v Waine*, "The principle against imperfectly constituted gifts led to harsh and seemingly paradoxical results. Before long, equity had tempered the wind to the shorn lamb (i.e. the donee). It did so on more than one occasion and in more than one way".[6]

3-002

The exceptions to the general rule that equity will not perfect an imperfect gift are listed below. In *Curtis v Pulbrook*, however, Briggs J expressed some dissatisfaction with the present rules and doubted that "the circumstances when equity will and will not perfect an apparently imperfect gift . . . serve any clearly identifiable or rational policy objective".[7]

- the conveyance of land to a minor. Under the Trusts of Land and Appointment of Trustees Act 1996, the conveyance will operate as a declaration that the land is held on trust for that minor. This is the only statutory exception to the rule that equity will not assist a volunteer;

- the so-called every effort rule or the rule in *Re Rose* (see para.**3-009**);

- as promoted by Arden LJ in the *Pennington* case, when it would be unconscionable for the donor to change his mind (see para.**3-013**);

- *donationes mortis causa* or deathbed gifts (see para.**3-015**);

- the rules as to fortuitous vesting contained in *Strong v Bird* and *Re Ralli's WT* (see paras **3-021**; **3-025**, respectively); and

---

3 Cf. the bare trust of mortgage monies that arises when a solicitor is retained to act on behalf of the mortgage lender in a conveyancing transaction: *Santander UK Plc v RA Legal Solicitors* [2014] EWCA Civ 183.
4 (1865) L.R. 1 Ch. App. 25 CA at 29.
5 *T. Choithram International SA v Pagarani* [2001] W.L.R. 1 at 11, where the Privy Council construed the words used by the settlor as amounting to a declaration of trust even though they were couched in the language of a gift. See further J. Hopkins, "Constitution of Trusts—A Novel Point" (2001) 60 C.L.J. 441.
6 [2002] 4 All E.R. 215 at 226, 227.
7 [2011] EWHC 167 (Ch) at [47].

- proprietary estoppel (see para.**3-027**). Although most of the reported cases of proprietary estoppel involve claims to land, there is no authority preventing its applying to other kinds of property (except the payment of money alone).[8]

Methods of Constitution

As Sir George Jessel MR explained in *Richards v Delbridge*, there are two methods through which a trust will be perfectly constituted by a settlor:

3-003

> "he may either do such acts as amount in law to a conveyance or assignment of the property, and thus completely divest himself of the legal ownership . . . or the legal owner of the property may, by one or other of the modes recognised as amounting to a valid declaration of trust, constitute himself a trustee, and, without an actual transfer of the legal title, may so deal with the property as to deprive himself of its beneficial ownership, and declare that he will hold it from that time forward on trust for the other person".[9]

The first method, therefore, is by transfer of legal title of the property to a third party. This can occur by a valid will[10] or by lifetime (inter vivos) transfer. It applies equally to gifts as it does to the setting up of a trust with a third-party trustee.

The second method is for the settlor to declare himself as a trustee of his own property. This latter method is obviously more straightforward as the settlor already has legal title and, hence, no transfer is necessary. The declaration will, therefore, operate to strip the settlor of his beneficial interest in the property. He will, of course, retain nominal, legal title to the property. It is to be appreciated that, as a general rule, the two methods will be mutually exclusive in that a trust to be constituted by a transfer to third parties cannot be construed as a self-declaration of trust.[11]

Transfer of legal title

It is necessary for the settlor to comply with the appropriate formalities in order to transfer legal title to a third-party trustee. This, not surprisingly, hinges upon the settlor's having legal

3-004

8   See *Sami v Hammit* [2018] EWHC 1400 (Ch).
9   (1874) L.R. 18 Eq. 11 at 14.
10 That is, one which satisfies the requirements of the Wills Act 1837.
11 *Deslauriers v Guardian Asset Management Ltd* [2017] UKPC 34.

title in the first place.[12] As will now become clear, the precise mechanism of transfer to be adopted varies according to the nature of the property concerned. As mentioned, the same rules apply also to the making of gifts:

- *Land*. Subject to exceptions relating to short leases,[13] to transfer legal title to land a deed of conveyance is needed.[14] In the case of registered land, the transfer becomes complete only on its registration at the Land Registry.[15]

- *Shares*. Legal title to shares is transferred traditionally by executing what is called a share transfer form and handing over the relevant share certificate, followed by registration[16] of the new owner in the company's shareholding register.[17] It is upon registration that the transfer is complete. The transferee will require both documents to apply to be registered in place of the transferor.[18] Registration is usually outside the donor's control. As regards a public company, registration will automatically follow on from the documentary transfer. A private company, however, often has the discretion bestowed in its articles of association to refuse to register a share transfer dealing and, instead, to exercise a right of pre-emption. If registration is declined, legal title cannot pass and the express trust will be incompletely constituted. In such circumstances, and if the trust is testamentary, the executors will hold on bare trust for the intended beneficiaries until sale occurs.[19] If the trust is inter vivos, it may amount to an assignment of the beneficial interest rather than a transfer of legal title.[20] There exists, however, a class of shares that are called "bearer" shares and these are treated differently. Legal title of bearer shares passes to whoever has physical possession of the share certificates.

- *Chattels*. Title to chattels is transferred either by deed of gift (uncommon) or by physical delivery of the item to the recipient coupled with the intention to effect a transfer.

---

12 *Re Brook's ST* [1939] 1 Ch. 993.
13 Section 54(2) of the Law of Property Act 1925 exempts the creation of periodic tenancies and leases not exceeding three years. This exception does not, however, apply to the assignment of such leases.
14 Section 52 of the Law of Property Act 1925.
15 Sections 7 and 27 of the Land Registration Act 2002.
16 No registration can take effect until a proper instrument of title has been sent to the company concerned: s.770 Companies Act 2006. Registration offers prima facie evidence of title: s.127 of the 2006 Act.
17 Section 1 of the Stock Transfer Act 1963. Although registration remains key, it is now possible to dispense with a document of transfer. If adopted, the CREST system of share transfer dispenses with paper and allows the transfer to occur electronically. There is no share certificate and title is recorded in a computer-based system called a central securities depository.
18 *Zeital v Kaye* [2010] EWCA Civ 159.
19 In *Pennington v Crampton* [2003] EWHC 2691 (Ch), however, the company's articles permitted the shares to be registered in the names of the executors. The company then enjoyed the right to purchase the shares from the executors.
20 See *Shah v Shah* [2010] EWCA Civ 1408; *Zeital v Kaye* [2010] EWCA Civ 159.

Delivery includes parting with dominion over an article (e.g. passing over the key to a jewellery box). In *Re Cole*,[21] a husband arranged for furniture to be delivered to the address that he then shared with his wife. She argued that the furniture was a gift to her, but the Court of Appeal held that this delivery did not coincide with an intention to transfer title. There was no gift. The appellate court also explained that a transfer does not occur by merely showing the intended donee the goods and uttering words such as "these are now yours".

- *Cheques.* Legal title to a cheque passes on endorsement by the transferor and delivery of the cheque to the third party. This, seemingly, is not possible when the cheque is crossed "account payee only".

- *Copyright.* Signed writing is necessary for the transfer of copyright.[22]

Ineffective transfers

3-005

If the correct procedure is not followed, the gift or the transfer to the trustees will be ineffective.[23] Accordingly, the imperfect gift can be simply revoked by the donor. In *Collins v Simonsen*,[24] Ms Simonsen transferred £42,000 to a letting agent in order to pay for her former partner's rent. He claimed it as a gift, but she sought the return of the funds. Although she had originally intended to make a gift, the funds were received by the letting agent from an unknown payer and with no instructions. Accordingly, the recipient had no authority to allocate those funds to either the landlord or Mr Collins. This was fatal to his claim. She had not done everything that it was in her power to do to complete the gift .The £42,000 was held on resulting trust by the agent for the benefit of Ms Simonsen. The maxim "equity cannot perfect an imperfect gift" applied. This approach reflects a paternalistic stance that ensures that a donor who acts unwisely and informally can have a change of mind. It is also important to appreciate that, as *Jones v Lock*[25] demonstrates, a failed gift will not, without more, be regarded as a declaration of trust. Examples of ineffective transfers are readily available from decided case law.

In *Richards v Delbridge*,[26] Mr Delbridge purported to assign legal title of a lease to his grandson. He wrote on the back of the original lease, "This deed and all thereto belonging I give to Edward Burnetto Richards from this time forth with all the stock in trade". The gift failed because there was no deed specifically created to convey the property (see para.**3-004**). It

21 [1964] Ch. 175.
22 Section 90(3) of the Copyright Designs and Patents Act 1988.
23 *Williams v Ball* [1917] 1 Ch.1.
24 [2019] EWHC 2214 (QB).
25 (1865) L.R. 1 Ch. App. 25 CA.
26 (1874) L.R. 18 Eq. 11.

could not, moreover, be argued that Mr Delbridge declared himself to be a trustee as there was no intention to create a trust. He intended throughout for there to be an outright gift.

3-006
In *Antrobus v Smith*,[27] an attempted transfer of shares by the mere endorsement on the back of a share certificate was clearly ineffective to pass legal title to the intended transferee. In *Milroy v Lord*,[28] an attempt to establish a trust of 50 shares in a bank failed because legal title to the shares never became vested in the trustee. The settlor did not take any steps to transfer the shares before his death and, although the intended trustee had previously held an unexercised power of attorney to transfer the shares, this power was revoked by the settlor's death. The shares, therefore, remained in the deceased's estate.[29] In *Zeital v Kaye*, Rimer LJ held that there had been an ineffective transfer in circumstances where the donor had handed to the donee a blank stock transfer form signed by a non-agent third party which did not add the donee's name and was undated.[30] Similarly, *Curtis v Pulbrook*[31] involved two gifts of shares which failed due to an absence of proper transfer of title. In relation to both transactions, the donor had passed over the share certificate, but not the stock transfer form. It followed that legal title to the shares did not pass to the intended donees.[32] More recently, in *Yusuf v Yusuf* there was no formal share transfer agreement and only a signed letter existed, which was no more than an instruction to prepare the transfer documentation.[33]

A slightly more difficult case is *Re Fry*.[34] There the intended donor executed a share transfer document before his death. As he was resident abroad, the Defence (Finance) Regulations (Amendment No.2) (SI 1939/1620) required the consent of the Treasury before the transfer could take place. The donor had completed the necessary forms and returned them. He had also applied for the necessary consent, but this was not given before his untimely demise. With regret, Romer J held that the transfer was ineffective because the donor had not done everything that he needed to do to pass title. It remained possible that the Treasury would require further information or supplemental answers from the donor or, indeed, refuse its consent altogether. As Romer J pointed out, if the donor had been asked for further details, he would have been under no compulsion to proceed with the transfer and "he might have refused to concern himself with the matter further".[35] *Re Fry* is often regarded a harsh decision, particularly when contrasted with the two *Re Rose* cases (see para.**3-009**).[36] Nevertheless, the

---

27 (1806) 12 Ves. 39.
28 (1862) 4 De. G.F. & J. 264.
29 See also *Letts v IRC* [1957] 1 W.L.R. 201, whereby a father merely directed that a company transfer shares to his children. He had not done enough to transfer legal title.
30 [2010] EWCA Civ 159; see G. Griffiths, "Zeital v Kaye: doing everything necessary—a recent manifestation of an ongoing issue" [2010] Conv. 321.
31 [2011] EWHC 167 (Ch).
32 As Briggs J [2011] EWHC 167 (Ch) at [44] put it, "he did his incompetent best to transfer both legal and beneficial title to the shares".
33 [2019] EWHC 90 (Ch).
34 [1946] Ch. 312.
35 [1946] Ch. 312 at 318.
36 See generally L. McKay, "Share Transfers and the Complete and Perfect Rule" [1976] Conv. 139.

Defence Finance Regulations ensured that Mr Fry had no power to affect a transfer without Treasury consent. Hence, he attempted to achieve that which was legally impossible and there was no way for the court comfortably to condone such a contravention of the Regulations.

Self-declaration as trustee

A settlor with a legal interest in property can declare himself a trustee of that property for a beneficiary.[37] This is the less popular method of creating a trust because, somewhat obviously, it can only be created during the lifetime of the settlor (i.e. it relates only to inter vivos trusts). It will also entail that the onerous, and usually unwelcome, duties of a trustee will rest with the person who has just divested himself of beneficial ownership of the property. Several initial points need to be appreciated. First, the general rule is that such a declaration can be oral without the need for any additional formality. An exception applies in the case of land where the trust must be evidenced in writing and signed by the settlor or his agent.[38]

Secondly, the settlor can use any form of words to demonstrate the intention to create a trust,[39] or this intention might even be inferred from conduct. In *Richards v Delbridge*, Jessel MR admitted, "the settlor need not use the words 'I declare myself a trustee' but he must do something which is equivalent to it and use expressions which have meaning; for however anxious the court may be to carry out a man's intention, it is not at liberty to construe words other than according to their proper meaning".[40]

Finally, it is crucial to bear in mind that an ineffective gift cannot without more be construed as a declaration of trust. This is because the settlor has shown the intention to give the property away absolutely and has evinced no intention to retain the legal estate on trust for the intended donee. Accordingly, in *Jones v Lock* the purported gift to a child of a cheque failed because the cheque was not endorsed and the court was unable to distil from the facts any declaration of trust.[41] Lord Cranworth LC explained:

> **"It all turns upon the facts, which do not lead me to the conclusion that the testator meant to deprive himself of all property in the note, or to declare himself a trustee of the money for the child".[42]**

3-007

3-008

---

37 See generally S. Agnew & S. Douglas, "Self-declarations of trust" (2019) 135 L.Q.R. 67.
38 Section 53(1)(b) of the Law of Property Act 1925; see Ch.4.
39 See *Paul v Constance* [1977] 1 W.L.R. 527, where it was held that Mr Constance had declared a trust, albeit informally, of a bank account for himself and his mistress. He had used words that, coupled with his conduct, indicated an intention to create a trust.
40 (1874) L.R. 18 Eq. 11 at 14.
41 (1865) L.R. 1 Ch. App. 25 CA. See also *Pappadakis v Pappadakis* [2000] W.T.L.R. 719, where the intention to assign a life assurance policy could not be construed as a declaration of a trust.
42 (1865) L.R. 1 Ch. App. 25 CA at 29.

If in doubt, the court will if possible adopt a benevolent construction in order to give effect to the wishes of the donor/settlor.[43] In limited circumstances, it is also possible that the two intentions can co-exist within the framework of the same transaction. As discussed earlier (see para.**2-007**), this coalescence was identifiable on the facts of *Shah v Shah*.[44]

The Every Effort Rule

3-009

This rule entails that, if the donor has done everything necessary for him to do to transfer title, the gift or trust will not fail simply because the donor dies before the process of transfer is finalised.[45] This is also known as the rule in *Re Rose*.[46] Put simply, if the only outstanding task is to be carried out by a third party, then the settlor has taken all the steps that he personally needs to take. In this way, it is properly to be viewed as an exception to the general rule that a transfer that fails at law will not take effect in equity. As Rimer LJ explained in *Zeital v Kaye*:

> **"once the donor has done all in his own power to transfer the shares, he will be regarded as holding the legal title to them upon trust for the donee, who will thereupon become their beneficial owner".**[47]

In *Re Rose*, the donor executed a share transfer form in favour of his wife and handed it, together with the share certificate, over to her. He died before the transfer was registered. Although the transfer of the legal title was not concluded at the time of his death, the gift was upheld.[48] In the eyes of equity, the transfer was concluded when the signed document was given to the wife for delivery to the company. As there was nothing more for the donor to do to perfect the gift, his death was not fatal to the transfer process. This explains why it is called the "every effort"

---

43   *T. Choithram International SA v Pagarani* [2001] 1 W.L.R. 1.

44   [2010] EWCA Civ 1408.

45   See generally A. Ollikainen-Read "Assignments of equitable interests and the origins of Re Rose" [2018] Conv. 63.

46   [1952] Ch. 499; see also the decision of Jenkins J in the earlier and unrelated case coincidentally bearing the similar name: *Midland Bank Executor & Trustee Co Ltd v Rose* [1949] 1 Ch. 78.

47   [2010] EWCA Civ 159 at [40]. Here the donor had not done all in his power to transfer the share in question because the whereabouts of the share certificate was unknown. If it was lost, a replacement would have to be procured by the legal owner. The donee was not, therefore, equipped with the title documentation that she needed to be registered as a member of the company.

48   Unlike in *Collins v Simonsen* [2019] EWHC 2214 (QB) where no directions were given to the recipient as to the use of the funds transferred, here the wife clearly knew of her husband's plans for the shares.

rule. The same approach has been adopted also in relation to the transfer of registered land. For example, in *Mascall v Mascall*[49] a father delivered an executed land transfer form and land certificate to his son. Following an argument, and before the transfer was registered, the father sought to resile from the transaction. It was held that the every effort rule applied and that it was too late to withdraw from the process.[50] A different outcome, however, arose in *Smith v Charles Building Services Ltd*[51] where the shareholder signed, but did not date, a share transfer form and then almost immediately tore it up. The transferee pieced the form together and had the transfer registered. Subsequently, the validity of the transfer was successfully challenged. It was held that the execution was never complete because the filling in of the form had been conditional and had been torn up by the transferor. Accordingly, the transfer should not have been registered.

Re Rose stands in striking contrast to *Re Fry* and *Milroy v Lord* where, in both cases, it was held that the donor still had something left to do to effect the transfer. Consequently, it could not be said that the transferor had made every effort. The rule, therefore, entails that the settlor need do more than merely sign a document of transfer. The last step in the process will usually be making arrangements for its delivery to, for example, the company or the Land Registry. Accordingly, executing the document and merely placing it in a desk drawer should not, without more, suffice. At this stage, the settlor would surely be free to have a change of heart and tear up the transfer document.[52] There is obviously no question of the transfer being complete in law and it should also follow that there has been no assignment of the equitable interest to the beneficiary/donee.

3-010

Although simple to state, the rule has proved at times difficult to apply. The Court of Appeal decision in *Pennington v Waine* has further muddied the waters.[53] This case concerned a purported gift of 400 shares in a private company by Ada Crampton to her nephew, Harold Crampton. The donor signed the appropriate share transfer form and gave the documentation to her adviser to deal with. Prior to the donor's death, the adviser had written to the donee stating that he had been instructed to transfer the shares to him and inviting him to become a director of the company. The donee then signed a form agreeing to become a director and was assured that there was nothing else for him to do. Unfortunately, no further action was taken by the adviser. On the donor's death, the issue arose as to whether the 400 shares formed part of the donor's residual estate or were, instead, held on trust for the donee, pending registration of the transaction.

Arden LJ admitted that there is no clear answer to the question when the last step necessary is taken by a donor and the equitable assignment of shares takes place. She explained:

3-011

---

49 (1984) 50 P. & C.R. 119.
50 See also, *Brown & Root Technology v Sun Alliance & London Assurance Co* [1996] Ch. 51, where Judge Paul Baker QC applied the every effort rule in relation to an assignment of a lease.
51 [2005] EWHC 654 (Ch).
52 *Smith v Charles Building Services Ltd* [2005] EWHC 654 (Ch).
53 [2002] 4 All E.R. 215. Murray J spoke kindlier of the decision stating that, "the case tested the border line between completion and incompletion in relation to a gift . . ."(*Collins v Simonsen* [2019] EWHC 2214 (QB) at 58).

> "The equitable assignment clearly occurs at some stage before the shares are registered. But does it occur when the share transfer is executed, or when the share transfer is delivered to the transferee, or when the transfer is lodged for registration, or when the pre-emption procedure . . . is satisfied or the directors resolve that the transfer should be registered?"[54]

As to whether it was necessary at law for the donor to deliver the documentation of transfer, Clarke LJ felt that this was not a prerequisite of a valid equitable assignment. Arden LJ agreed that delivery could, in some circumstances, be dispensed with. In the interests of legal certainty, she accepted that there must be an ascertainable point at which it can be said that a gift is completed and that point of no return must be identified on a principled basis. Arden LJ concluded that this stage is reached when it becomes unconscionable for the donor to renege on the gift. She added:

> "There can be no comprehensive list of factors which makes it unconscionable for the donor to change his or her mind: it must depend on the court's evaluation of all the relevant considerations".[55]

3-012

In the context of the every effort rule, this is an unhelpful and questionable decision that flies in the face of well-established authority and, because it turned on special facts as to delivery, is readily distinguishable.[56] It also introduces notions of fairness of outcome into a rule that previously focused exclusively upon the physical process of transfer. Surely, and unless some arrangement has been made for delivery, the donor truly cannot be said to have taken every step that he must take.[57] Arden LJ did, however, accept that, if wrong on the issue of unconscionability, the same end could be reached by finding that the adviser became the agent for the donor for the purpose of submitting the share transfer to the company. It is, perhaps, unfortunate that the decision was not founded solely upon this more traditional basis.

The every effort rule most certainly conflicts with the traditional stance that equity does not regard an ineffective transfer as a declaration of trust. This tension is not, however, major where the role of the third party is merely a formality, i.e. as with a public company where registration is inevitable. In that situation, there is implied a constructive trust which assigns the equitable interest to the donee and is timed to span the interim period until the transfer is completed. It is not a trust that is created expressly or permanently. As with a private company, however, it remains possible that the transfer will never be registered because the directors will, in all likelihood, enjoy a veto. Although in both *Re Rose* cases the shares were of a private

---

54   [2002] 4 All E.R. 215 at 227.
55   [2002] 4 All E.R. 215 at 230.
56   See Rimer LJ *Zeital v Kaye* [2010] EWCA Civ 159 at [40]. He also noted (at [40]) that the court in *Pennington* did not speak with one voice as to why the appeal should be dismissed.
57   See *Brown & Root Technology v Sun Alliance & London Assurance Co* [1996] Ch. 51 at 67.

company, registration did eventually occur.[58] The problem to be addressed is what happens if registration is subsequently denied. If the implied trust is to be maintained beyond the refusal of registration, is it not blatantly upholding an ineffective transfer as a declaration of trust? Nevertheless, this is the outcome generated by the every effort rule. Such is confirmed on the facts of *Pennington* where the donee was never registered as the owner of the shares because the directors exercised a right of pre-emption. Although the transfer of legal title was never completed, the donee was entitled to the proceeds of sale of those shares.

The Role of Unconscionability

In *Pennington v Waine*, the Court of Appeal concluded that, on the facts, it would have been unconscionable for the donor to recall the gift once the donee had agreed to become a director. The argument ran that, by withdrawing, the donor would have been taking unconscientious advantage of the donee. It followed, therefore, that it would be equally unconscionable for her personal representative to refuse to hand over the share transfer form to the donee.[59] As Arden LJ pointed out, "In those circumstances . . . delivery of the share transfer before her death was unnecessary so far as perfection of the gift was concerned".[60] Legal title was to remain vested in the donor's estate pending registration of the transaction. Arden LJ admitted that, during the intervening period, the donor's personal representative became the constructive trustee of the legal title to the shares for the donee. Both Arden and Schiemann LJJ advocated the notion of unconscionability as being a standalone exception to the general rule that equity will not intervene. It was utilised solely as a means of engineering a just outcome. Indeed, such was accepted by the High Court in *Jordan v Roberts*.[61] There, Deputy Judge George Bompas QC acknowledged that an otherwise imperfect gift of shares could be treated as having been completely constituted if it would be inequitable for the donor to resile from the transaction.

The prevailing view, however, is that Arden LJ adopted a mistaken interpretation of previous authority.[62] Halliwell, for example, believes that the stance adopted by the Court of Appeal may "give courts of equity an unfettered discretion as to whether a voluntary gift or trust should take effect".[63] She observes that this is "completely irreconcilable with previous authorities"[64]

3-013

---

58 Albeit in the earlier *Re Rose* it took 18 months for registration of the share transfer to occur.
59 For an overview of the principle of unconscionability as a touchstone in equitable intervention, see H. Delany and D. Ryan, "Unconscionability: A Unifying Theme in Equity" [2008] 72 Conv. 401.
60 [2002] 4 All E.R. 215 at 231.
61 [2009] EWHC 2313 (Ch).
62 See A.J. Oakley, *Parker and Mellows: The Modern Law of Trusts*, 9th edn (London: Sweet & Maxwell, 2008), who at p.156 describes Arden LJ's judgment as "a complete misunderstanding"; cf. J. Garton [2003] Conv. 364.
63 M. Halliwell [2003] Conv. 192, 193.
64 [2003] Conv. 192, 195.

and spotlights the key authority relied on by Arden LJ, which was the Privy Council decision in *T. Choithram International v Pagarani*.[65] There, on facts considered below, Lord Browne-Wilkinson admitted that it would be unconscionable for the settlor, who had validly declared a trust, to have a change of heart.[66] The comparison with *Pennington* is, therefore, unconvincing. Parker and Mellows agree and argue that, "in contrast, in *Pennington v Waine*, the donor had neither declared a trust nor made a gift nor done everything in her power to make a gift".[67] Delany and Ryan describe the "now notorious" *Pennington v Waine* as an example of the courts utilising unconscionability "as a means of explaining or arriving at a particular result, even where the principle appears to have no (or at least no obvious) connection with the substantive equitable principles at stake".[68] Accordingly, the prevailing wisdom is that *Pennington* is a flawed decision, dogged by imprecision, uncertainty and the absence of any legitimate, doctrinal underpinning. As Delany and Ryan conclude, "it is just such an approach to the principle of unconscionability espoused in *Pennington* that ought to be avoided if the principle is not to be irreparably damaged on the grounds of growing concerns about legitimacy and doctrinal transparency".[69] It also overlaps unhelpfully with the role of estoppel in this area, as regards which the principle of unconscionability provides, as Delany and Ryan note, "the axis on which proprietary estoppel revolved".[70] Indeed, Briggs J in *Curtis v Pulbrook* viewed this unconscionability test as being merely an illustration of proprietary estoppel.[71]

The settlor as one of several trustees

3-014

In *T. Choithram International SA v Pagarani*, the settlor (Mr Pagarani) executed a deed of trust in favour of a charitable organisation which he established. He nominated himself and nine others as trustees. Shortly before his death, the settlor purported orally to settle money and shares on the organisation. He did not, however, transfer the title of the assets to the other trustees. On his death, it was argued that the trust was incompletely constituted and that the assets would pass on intestacy to his next of kin. In the Privy Council, however, Lord Browne-Wilkinson upheld the trust. Admitting that the facts were "novel and raise a new point,"[72] it

---

65   [2001] 1 W.L.R. 1 PC; see J. Hopkins, "Constitution of Trusts—A Novel Point" (2001) 60 C.L.J. 441.

66   While in the process of dying, the settlor spoke in terms of having made a gift to the charity. Nothing turned on this as the trust was already constituted.

67   A. Oakley, *Parker and Mellows: The Modern Law of Trusts*, 9th edn (London: Sweet & Maxwell, 2008), p.156; see also *Deslauriers v Guardian Asset Management Ltd* [2017] UKPC 34.

68   H. Delany and D. Ryan, "Unconscionability: A Unifying Theme in Equity" [2008] 72 Conv. 401, 430, 431; see also P. Luxton, "In Search of Perfection: the *Re Rose* Rule Rationale" [2012] 76 Conv. 70.

69   H. Delany and D. Ryan, "Unconscionability: A Unifying Theme in Equity" [2008] 72 Conv. 401, 433.

70   H. Delany and D. Ryan, "Unconscionability: A Unifying Theme in Equity" [2008] 72 Conv. 401, 404.

71   [2011] EWHC 167 (Ch); see P. Luxton [2012] Conv. 70. A. Doggett, "Explaining *Re Rose*: The Search goes on" [2003] 62 (2) C.L.J. 263 makes the point, however, that the donee suffered no real detriment on the facts of *Pennington*.

72   [2001] 1 W.L.R. 1 PC at 11; see J. Hopkins, "Constitution of Trusts—A Novel Point" (2001) 60 C.L.J. 441.

was held that the settlor had done enough to declare himself a trustee. It did not matter that he intended to be one of several trustees (and not a sole trustee). Lord Browne-Wilkinson explained:

> "There can in principle be no distinction between the case where the donor declares himself to be the sole trustee for a donee or a purpose and the case where he declares himself to be one of the trustees for that donee or purpose. In both cases his conscience is affected and it would be unconscionable and contrary to the principle of equity to allow such a donor to resile from his gift".[73]

On these unusual facts, he accepted that it would be unconscionable for the settlor to renege on the declaration of trust. There was nothing to show that the settlor wanted the trust to come into effect only when all trustees had legal title. This is a very different scenario from that which faced the Court of Appeal in *Pennington v Waine*.

Donationes Mortis Causa

3-015

As shown, the general rule is that equity will not assist a volunteer. One judge-made exception to this rule is *donationes mortis causa* (DMC) or deathbed gifts.[74] This rule, which has its origins in Roman law, may have the consequence of constituting what would otherwise be viewed as an incomplete gift to a donee or an incomplete transfer to a trustee. If a DMC is upheld, the donor's personal representatives will be obliged formally to complete the gift or transfer. It will, therefore, take priority over the terms of the will itself. The DMC rule concerns a conditional, lifetime gift that is made by the donor in contemplation of death. It is, therefore, a present gift that remains conditional and inchoate until the death of the donor. As Buckley J put it in *Re Beaumont*:

> "A *donatio mortis causa* is a singular form of gift. It may be said to be of an amphibious nature being a gift which is neither entirely *inter vivos* nor testamentary. It is an act *inter vivos* by which the donee is to have the absolute title to the subject of the gift not at once but if the donor dies. If the donor dies the title becomes absolute as against

73   [2001] 1 W.L.R. 1 at 12. See C. Rickett, "Completely Constituting an Inter Vivos Trust: Property Rules?" (2001) 65 Conv. 515.
74   This doctrine assumed importance following the Statute of Frauds 1677, which abolished the legal ability to make an oral will.

> **his executor. In order to make the gift valid it must be made so as to take complete effect on the donor's death".[75]**

Since the defrosting exercise undertaken by Nourse LJ in *Sen v Headley*,[76] any type of property can, seemingly, be the subject of a DMC: cheques, promissory notes, chattels, shares (even if in a private company[77]), bonds, insurance policies, land, etc. As Nourse LJ commented: "Anomalies do not justify anomalous exceptions".[78]

The central notion is that a gift by reason of death may, in certain circumstances, be perfected even though the necessary formalities of transfer have not been followed. It reflects a sentimentality of the court shown towards the dying and the desperate. As such it is an anomaly and, not surprisingly, has been the subject of criticism. For example, as early as 1752 Lord Hardwicke bemoaned the fact that the rule was not abolished in the Statute of Frauds 1677.[79] Lord Eldon later echoed this sentiment and expressed the view that DMC should be "struck out of our law altogether".[80] Rolfe B also alluded to the "evils" of this method of side-stepping the formalities of transfer.[81] More recently, in *King v Dubrey*[82] Jackson LJ accepted that the doctrine of DMC was a legal anomaly because it enabled a donor to transfer property upon death without complying with any of the formalities usually attendant on such a transfer. Hence, a need for the strictest scrutiny of the factual evidence and a refusal to allow DMC to be used as a device to validate ineffective wills and to side-step other formalities.[83] As Jackson LJ added, "Indeed I must confess to some mystification as to why the common law has adopted the doctrine of DMC at all. The doctrine obviously served a useful purpose in the social conditions prevailing under the later Roman Empire. But it serves little useful purpose today save possibly as a means of validating death bed gifts. Even then considerable caution is required".[84]

Nevertheless, the rule remains and, ironically, with regard to the criticism levied against it, attempts (albeit unsuccessful) have been made to enlarge it in modern times.[85]

---

75   [1902] 1 Ch. 892 at 893.

76   [1991] 2 All E.R. 636; see M. Halliwell [1991] Conv. 307.

77   Following *Pennington v Waine* [2002] 4 All E.R. 215, if the donee under a DMC is never registered by the company as the shareholder, the donee will still enjoy an equitable interest in the shares and will be entitled to the proceeds of their eventual sale.

78   [1991] 2 All E.R. 636 at 647; see further P.V. Baker, "Land as a donatio mortis causa" (1993) 109 L.Q.R. 19.

79   *Ward v Turner* [1752] 28 E.R. 275.

80   *Duffield v Elwes* [1827] 4 E.R. 959 at 972.

81   *Hills v Hills* (1841) 151 E.R. 1095 at 1096. It has already been abolished in Scotland: s.25 of the Succession (Scotland) Act 2016.

82   [2016] 2 W.L.R. 1; noted by H. Cumber [2016] Conv. 56. This case is sometimes referred to as *King v Chiltern Dog Rescue, Redwings Horse Sanctuary*.

83   [2016] 2 W.L.R. 1. He warned (at [51]) that, "Thus the doctrine paves the way for all of the abuses which those statutes are intended to prevent".

84   [2016] 2 W.L.R. 1 at [53]. The prospect of the abolition of DMCs was mooted (but not decided upon) by the Law Commission in its Consultation Paper "Making Wills Work" (2017) Law Com. 231.

85   A notable example of this being the (now overruled) decision in *Vallee v Birchwood* [2014] 2 W.L.R. 543. As Jackson LJ observed in *King v* Dubrey [2016] 2 W.L.R. 1 at [54], "In my view therefore it is important to keep DMC

3-016

There are, however, certain conditions that are necessary for an effectual DMC to occur. As Russell CJ demonstrated in *Cain v Moon*[86]:

- the gift or donation must have been made in contemplation, though not necessarily in expectation, of death;

- the gift must be made under such circumstances as show that the property is to revert to the donor in the case that death does not occur; and

- there must have been delivery to the donee of the subject matter of the gift.

The burden of proof rests on the donee and, if the claim is unsupported by evidence of any person other than the donee, the court must have before it all material which may be relevant.[87] As acknowledged by Lord Chelmsford in the Privy Council in *Cosnahan v Grice*:

> **"Cases of this kind demand the strictest scrutiny. So many opportunities, and such strong temptations, present themselves to unscrupulous persons to pretend these death-bed donations, that there is always the danger of having an entirely fabricated case set up. And without any imputation of a fraudulent contrivance, it is so easy to mistake the meaning of a person languishing in a mortal illness, and, by a slight change of words, to convert their expressions of intended benefit into an actual gift of property, that no case of this description ought to prevail, unless it is supported by evidence of the clearest and most unequivocal character".[88]**

In contemplation of death

3-017

The requirement is that the gift be because of or on account of death. In *Duffield v Elwes*, Lord Eldon spoke in terms of "the conceived approach of death".[89] There must be an impending risk of death occurring and this requires more than mere philosophical musing or some general contemplation of death. In *Re Craven's Estate*, it was said by Farwell J that the contemplation

---

within its proper bounds. The court should resist the temptation to extend the doctrine to an ever-wider range of situations".

86   [1896] 2 Q.B. 283 at 286; see also the similar formulation of Farwell J in *Re Craven's Estate* [1937] 1 Ch. 423 at 426.

87   *Calvert v Scholes* [2002] EWHC 2333 (Ch); *Keeling v Keeling* [2017] EWHC 1189 (Ch) (brother taking title deeds to sister's house for safekeeping).

88   (1862) 15 Moo. P.C. 215 at 216.

89   [1827] 4 E.R. 959 at 971.

must be of "death within the near future".[90] As Jackson LJ explained in *King v Dubrey*, "That means D should be contemplating death in the near future for a specific reason . . . D must have good reason to anticipate death in the near future from an identified cause".[91] Once made, the gift does not run for ever more. As Jackson LJ emphasised, "It comes to an end if D fails to succumb to the death which was anticipated when he made the DMC".[92] Similarly, in *Keeling v Keeling* the donor did not, at the time the alleged discussion took place, have good reason to anticipate death from an identified source. In any event, she had recovered from any possible contemplated cause (here a heart attack).[93]

The donor does not have to be *in extremis* or at death's door when the gift is made. For example, a patient admitted to hospital for a routine operation may make a DMC in contemplation of death even though death might not be the expected outcome.[94] Death must, however, be contemplated from an identified source. Such a source could be, for example, illness,[95] the result of an accident,[96] the fear of an air crash[97] or, possibly, suicide.[98] The gift will still be perfected in the unlikely event of the deceased dying from a different cause than was anticipated.[99] In *Wilkes v Allington*, the donor was dying of cancer and made a valid DMC in contemplation of death, even though he eventually died of pneumonia.[100] It is not enough, however, for the donor to be approaching the end of his life without having an anticipation of death in the near future from a known cause.[101]

It is the subjective state of mind of the donor that appears to be relevant. The donor's actual motivation must surely be the crucial issue and this should not readily be supplanted by the fictitious motivations of a reasonable man in the donor's position. Often there will be an express reference to death (the "if I die, I want you to have this" style of case), but this is not necessary. Such contemplation can be inferred from the circumstances in which the gift is made.[102] In

90   [1937] 1 Ch. 423 at 426.
91   [2016] 2 W.L.R. 1 at [55].
92   [2016] 2 W.L.R. 1 at [57]. The Court of Appeal thereby overruled *Vallee v Birchwood* [2014] 2 W.L.R. 543 where the gift of a house was made in contemplation of death even though the time gap between the gift and the death was four months. Normally, it is only a few days.
93   [2017] EWHC 1189 (Ch).
94   For example, in *Re Craven's Estate* [1937] 1 Ch. 423 had the operation been successful the donor would have recovered.
95   *Re Beaumont* [1902] 1 Ch. 892 where the donor was in hospital and seriously ill. Similarly, in *Sen v Headley* [1991] 2 All E.R. 636 the donor was in hospital suffering from inoperable pancreatic cancer.
96   In *Birch v Treasury Solicitor* [1950] 2 All E.R. 1198, the donor was an elderly woman in hospital after suffering a serious accident.
97   See *Re Miller* (1961) 105 Sol. Jo. 207.
98   See *Mills v Shields* [1948] I.R. 367. See also C. Towl, "Donatio mortis causa and suicide—an anomaly within an anomaly?" (2018) Conv. 367.
99   This rule might give way when the donor specifies the risk (e.g. "if my plane crashes I want you to have this"), but then dies of a different cause (e.g. of a heart attack on the way to the airport): see *Re Richards* [1921] 1 Ch. 513.
100 [1931] 2 Ch. 104.
101 *King v Dubrey* [2016] 2 W.L.R. 1.
102 *Walter v Hodge* [1818] 36 E.R. 549.

Gardner v Parker, the connection between the gift and the contemplation of death was inferred from the fact that the donor was terminally ill when he made the gift and died shortly after the making of it.[103] The circumstances surrounding the gift demonstrated clearly that this had been the motivation underlying the gift. A different conclusion, however, was manufactured in *Re Kirkley*.[104] There a gift made by an aged and bedridden donor was not inferred to be in contemplation of death because the donor, although worn out, was not ill. The reference to death in this case would have had to be express for an effectual DMC to be created.

Conditional on death

The gift must be made in circumstances that show that the property is to revert to the donor if he recovers. As in *Staniland v Willot*,[105] the gift lapses if the donor recovers from his illness. Over a century later, Nourse LJ accepted in *Sen v Headley* that the gift becomes absolute only on the donor's death, "being revocable until that event occurs and ineffective if it does not".[106] Accordingly, there can be no DMC if the donor intends to make an absolute and immediate gift.[107] In *Tate v Hilbert*, for example, an elderly donor purported to give money to his two nieces, claiming that he had too much money just for himself.[108] He did not adopt the appropriate method of transfer and died before he could do so. The court held that he had attempted to make an immediate and unconditional gift and, hence, the nieces were denied as there could be no effectual DMC.

The conditional nature of the gift can be expressed (e.g. "if I die this is yours") or inferred from the circumstances. Indeed, the general rule is that if the gift is made in expectation of death then, absent contrary evidence, it will be regarded as being conditional on the death of the donor.[109] In *King v Dubrey*, the words "this will be yours when I go" were more consistent with a statement of testamentary intent, than a gift which was conditional upon the donor's death within a limited period of time.[110] The court will not entertain any argument that, if imminent death is thought to be a certainty, this provides evidence of the intention to create an immediate gift.[111] As Lord Tomlin put it, "when a man is smitten with a mortal disease, he may

---

103 [1818] 56 E.R. 478.
104 [1909] 25 T.L.R. 522.
105 [1850] 42 E.R. 416.
106 [1991] 2 All E.R. 636 at 639.
107 *Edwards v Jones* [1836] 40 E.R. 361.
108 (1793) 30 E.R. 548.
109 *Gardner v Parker* [1818] 56 E.R. 478; *Re Lillingston* [1951] 2 All E.R. 184.
110 [2016] 2 W.L.R. 1. The parties had acted as if their conversation constituted a statement of testamentary intent. The ineffective attempt subsequently to make a new will indicated that the aunt was trying to dispose of her assets by means of a will. As Jackson LJ pointed out at [71], "Those actions were inconsistent with the proposition that June had already disposed of her assets by means of a DMC".
111 See *Re Mustapha* (1891) 8 T.L.R. 160.

know, in fact, that there cannot be any recovery; yet I apprehend that a man in that situation . . . is capable of creating a good *donatio mortis causa*".[112]

3-019
At any time prior to death, the gift can be revoked. This can occur expressly by words[113] (e.g. "I no longer want you to have my watch") or may be implied from the circumstances[114] (e.g. taking back possession of the watch). In *Hawkins v Blewett*,[115] however, the donor took back physical possession of a box containing money (the subject matter of the gift) to keep it safely hidden under his bed. This did not evince any intention to revoke the DMC. It is the traditional wisdom that revocation cannot occur by the donor's will,[116] but this is not an unchallengeable proposition. While the legal effects of the will arise only post mortem, nevertheless logic suggests that when drafted it could serve to evidence the donor's change of heart.[117]

Delivery and Dominion

3-020
The requirement is that, for a valid DMC to exist, dominion (i.e. control and possession) of the subject matter must pass from the donor to the donee before the donor's death.[118] Hence, if delivery occurs after the donor's death, there will be no DMC.[119] There must be something done that demonstrates the intention to transfer the property.[120] Words alone, however, do not suffice for these purposes.[121] Instead, there must be actual and physical delivery of an item[122] or constructive delivery by passing over the means of obtaining the property or some indicia of title to the item.[123] Examples of the latter method include handing over the keys to a safety deposit box kept at a bank[124]; passing over of a savings book[125]; handing over the title deeds to

---

112 *Wilkes v Allington* [1931] 2 Ch. 104 at 111.
113 *Jones v Selby* (1710) Prec. Ch. 300.
114 *Bunn v Markham* [1816] 129 E.R. 90.
115 [1798] 170 E.R. 489; see also *Re Hawkins* [1924] 2 Ch. 47 (taking back of bank notes for safe keeping).
116 *Jones v Selby* (1710) Prec. Ch. 300.
117 See H Cumber, "Donationes mortis causa; a doctrine on its deathbed?" [2016] Conv. 56.
118 *Ward v Turner* [1752] 28 E.R. 275. Delivery can be made by the donor's agent and accepted by the donee's agent: *Moore v Darton* [1851] 64 E.R. 938.
119 *Hardy v Baker* [1738] 25 E.R. 1063. Delivery can, however, precede the gift: *Cain v Moon* [1896] 2 Q.B. 283.
120 *Miller v Miller* (1735) 3 P. Wms. 356. There a DMC of a coach and horses failed in the absence of any evidence of delivery.
121 *Bunn v Markham* [1816] 129 E.R. 90.
122 *Birch v Treasury Solicitor* [1950] 2 All E.R. 1198.
123 *Cain v Moon* [1896] 2 Q.B. 283.
124 *Re Wasserberg* [1915] 1 Ch. 195; see generally A.C.H. Barlow, "Gifts inter vivos of a chose in possession by delivery of a key'" (1956) 19 M.L.R. 394.
125 *Re Weston* [1902] 1 Ch. 680; *Birch v Treasury Solicitor* [1950] 2 All E.R. 1198.

a house[126]; delivery of mortgage deeds[127]; delivery of share certificates[128] and giving over the keys to a car.[129] If there is no change of possession, whether real or constructive, there can be no DMC. Accordingly, the mere execution of a deed of transfer without passing the document to the donee will be insufficient.[130] Similarly, if the donee refuses to accept delivery there can be no DMC.[131] In *Reddel v Dobree*,[132] the donor delivered to the donee a locked cash box, but the donor wanted the box back every three months. The donor reserved dominion by retaining the right to deal with the box until his death. It has been argued by Roberts that problems may arise in connection with accessing a dematerialised asset electronically and he notes that "The traditional indicia of investments—the passbook and the certificate—are clearly now of less importance. The question then arises of whether there is anything which fulfils the same function when accessing a 'dematerialised' asset electronically, and so would enable one to make a DMC of it".[133] It remains to be seen whether the disclosure of a password to, say, an online bank account can amount to the passing of dominion over that account.

In the now discredited decision in *Vallee v Birchwood*,[134] the High Court was faced with a novel problem concerning the passing of dominion. In 2003, Ms Vallee went to visit her elderly father, Mr Bogusz. Mr Bogusz told her that he wanted her to have the house when he died and passed her the deeds to the property and a key. Mr Bogusz later died and Ms Vallee claimed the property on the basis that it had been given to her by a DMC. The administrator of the estate argued that dominion had not passed because Mr Bogusz had remained living in the property after passing over the deeds and key.[135] The Deputy Judge emphasised that it is not necessary that the donee be given exclusive physical possession or control over land. Hence, there was no reason why the donor could not continue to enjoy his own property until death. By handing over the title deeds by way of gift, the donor has put it outside his power (without revoking the gift) to transfer legal title or alter the interest that is the subject matter of the gift.

Although the administrator argued that the donor could still have carried out physical alterations to the house, the Deputy Judge cautioned that, "for this purpose the Court should look at the practical, and not the theoretical, possibilities".[136] He did, however, accept that

---

126   *Sen v Headley* [1991] 2 All E.R. 636.

127   *Duffield v Elwes* [1827] 4 E.R. 959.

128   See A. Samuels, "Donatio mortis causa of a share certificate" [1966] 30 Conv. 189.

129   *Woodard v Woodard* [1995] 3 All E.R. 980. A cheque handed to the donee and cashed after the death of the donor can be a valid DMC: *Rolls v Pearce* (1877) L.R. 5 Ch. D. 730.

130   See *Re Hughes* (1888) 59 L.T. 586.

131   *Cant v Gregory* (1894) 10 T.L.R. 584.

132   [1839] 10 Sim. 244.

133   N. Roberts, "Donationes Mortis Causa in a Dematerialised World" [2013] Conv. 113, 123. He casts doubt upon whether there can be a DMC of registered land (now that land certificates have been abolished), a legal charge (in the absence of a charge certificate) or shares subject to the CREST system (where no share certificate is produced).

134   [2014] 2 W.L.R. 543.

135   Cf. *Sen v Headley* [1991] 2 All E.R. 636 where the donor was in hospital and unable to return to his home. He died three days after making the gift.

136   [2014] 2 W.L.R. 543 at [41].

the concept of dominion in this context was "a slippery one".[137] The fundamental rationale is that something must be done that demonstrates that what is intended is a conditional gift and not something that falls short of that. The Deputy Judge added, "There does not have to be delivery or transfer which would suffice at law to effect a gift *inter vivos* . . .".[138] The delivery by Mr Bogusz of the title deeds and key to the house to his daughter in contemplation of his impending death, coupled with what he said, was a sufficient passing of dominion. It is arguable that this aspect of the decision remains, in principle at least, correct subject to the caveat that death must occur within a reasonable time of the donation. Otherwise the donor will have ample time to take advice and make a will.

The Rule in Strong v Bird

3-021

A further exception to the rule that equity will not perfect an imperfect gift is the rule regarding fortuitous vesting of which the leading example is the case of *Strong v Bird*.[139] Simply put, in its original and narrow form the rule is that, where there is the forgiveness of a debt and the donee subsequently obtains legal title to the property in the capacity of an executor, the gift (i.e. the release from liability) will then be perfected. This is what is known as "fortuitous vesting" because equity is unconcerned with how the relevant title became vested in, say, a trustee. Accordingly, and if it can be shown that the intention to make the gift was sustained until the donor's death, the necessary transfer of legal title occurs automatically by operation of law when the donee becomes the executor.[140] It does not matter whether the donee is the sole executor or merely one of a number of executors. As Neville J acknowledged:

> **"The whole of the property in the personal estate in the eye of the law vesting in each executor, it seems to me immaterial whether the donee is the only executor or one of several . . .".[141]**

The facts of *Strong v Bird* concerned a stepson who borrowed £1,100 from his stepmother. She lived in his house and paid £212 every three months for her board. It was agreed that the loan was to be paid off by making a £100 deduction from each of the next 11 payments. The deduc-

---

137 [2014] 2 W.L.R. 543 at [42].
138 [2014] 2 W.L.R. 543 at [42].
139 (1874) 18 Eq. 315. As J. Jaconelli notes in "Problems in the rule in *Strong v Bird*" [2006] Conv. 432, 434, "Yet, of all the exceptions to the application of that maxim, the rule in *Strong v Bird* is surely the strangest".
140 In *Day v Royal College of Music* [2013] 3 W.L.R. 1560 a gift of music manuscripts was initially incomplete because there was no delivery. It was, however, perfected when the recipient became the executor under the donor's will.
141 *Re Stewart* [1908] 2 Ch. 251 at 254, 255.

tions were made on two occasions following which the stepmother orally released the stepson from the remainder of the debt. She paid the £212 each quarter thereafter until her death. The stepson was appointed her executor under her will. Her residuary legatees, however, sought to recover the outstanding debt from the executor. Although there was no formal release made, the intention to forgo the debt was evident and maintained until the stepmother's death. It is to be appreciated that the intention alone would have proved insufficient to effect release of the debt. Without more, her estate would be entitled to claim the remainder of the debt. As Cozens Hardy MR said of it in *Re Pink*, "There is no consideration for it. It is not a perfect release; it is not a release at law; and therefore if there is nothing more it would have no operation or effect".[142]

3-022

The stepson being appointed as executor was, however, crucial. It is long established that, at common law, the coincidental appointment of the debtor as an executor (alone or with others) will operate to extinguish the debt.[143] The reasoning is that, as the executors become the owner of the deceased's estate (including the right to bring actions on a debt), it is impossible for the executors to sue themselves. This approach did not, however, originally apply in equity where the deceased's estate would always be allowed to claim against an executor.[144] *Strong v Bird* modified the traditional stance of equity and allowed the common law rule to operate when it was the intention of the deceased to release the debt and that intention continued until death.[145] Accordingly, the oral release of the debt was perfected when the debtor became the executor, i.e. on the death of the testatrix. Sir George Jessel MR explained that, "There being the continuing intention to give and there being a legal act which transferred the ownership . . . the transaction is perfected, and he does not want the aid of a Court of Equity to carry it out, or to make it complete, because it is complete already, and there is no equity against him to take the property away from him".[146] Hence, *Strong v Bird* offers an example of a donor inadvertently completing an otherwise imperfect gift. Such was accepted by Astbury J in *Carter v Hungerford*, in that, "if a donor makes an incomplete gift of real estate and afterwards, though unintentionally, includes it in a conveyance of real estate to the donee, the conveyance perfects the intended gift, and prevents the donor from reclaiming it on the ground of resulting trust or otherwise".[147]

The rule in *Strong v Bird* was widened considerably in *Re Stewart*[148] where it was held that the rule was not limited merely to the release of a debt and, indeed, applied to any imperfect, inter vivos gift. There it was a failed lifetime gift of bonds. As Neville J explained:

> "the vesting of the property in the executor at the testator's death completes the imperfect gift made in the lifetime, and . . . the

---

142 [1912] 2 Ch. 528 at 535.
143 *Wankford v Wankford* (1704) 1 Salk 299.
144 See *Re Bourne* [1906] 1 Ch. 697.
145 See *Jenkins v Jenkins* [1928] 2 K.B. 501.
146 (1874) 18 Eq. 315 at 318.
147 [1917] 1 Ch. 260 at 273.
148 [1908] 2 Ch. 251.

> intention of the testator to give the beneficial interest to the executor is sufficient to countervail the equity of the beneficiaries under the will, the testator having vested the legal estate in the executor".[149]

3-023

Re Stewart, therefore, extends the equitable rules relating to fortuitous vesting much further than catered for by the common law.

In *Re James*,[150] it was held that the rule in *Strong v Bird* applied also in the situation where the donor dies intestate (i.e. without leaving a will) and the donee takes out letters of administration (i.e. becomes the administrator of the deceased's estate). There the deceased handed over the deeds of a house to a housekeeper. It will be recalled from *Richards v Delbridge* that this is woefully insufficient to pass legal title to land. On the death of the donor, the housekeeper was granted letters of administration and legal title to the house then became automatically vested in her by virtue of her capacity as administratrix. As she now had legal title, albeit by this circuitous route, the gift was perfected. This extension to intestacy cases is, however, contentious and was doubted by Walton J in *Re Gonin*.[151] The debate focuses upon the fact that, unlike executors under a will, the deceased does not nominate an administrator. Instead, probate rules (i.e. a matter of law) govern who, usually from amongst the deceased's next of kin, can apply to be an administrator. Accordingly, it is unpredictable who eventually will become the administrator(s) of the estate. In addition, at common law (and unlike with an executor) the debt is not extinguished upon the debtor becoming an administrator.[152] It is, instead, merely suspended. This is, therefore, fortuitous vesting at its most fortuitous. It is, as Walton J put it, "to treat what ought to be a simple rule of equity . . . as something of a lottery".[153]

The intention of the donor must be to make an immediate gift. In *Re Freeland*,[154] the promise to give a car at a future date fell outside the rule in *Strong v Bird*. There was no intention to make a present and absolute gift of the property. Accordingly, when the donee became the executrix under the donor's will, the gift was not perfected and failed. As Parker J admitted in *Re Innes*, "it would be extremely dangerous to try to give effect by the appointment of an executor to what is at most an announcement of what a man intends to do in the future, and is not intended by him as a gift in the present . . .".[155] The property subject to the gift must, moreover, be in existence at the time of the gift (the rule does not apply to after acquired property) and the property must be specifically identified (e.g. a debt, a bond, shares, land, a specific sum of money or chattels). It is thought that the rule cannot apply to a gift of an unspecified sum of money or unidentified goods (e.g. a gift to Jordan of one of my paintings).

---

149 [1908] 2 Ch. 251 at 254.
150 [1935] Ch. 449.
151 [1977] 2 All E.R. 720.
152 Hence, *Strong v Bird* would have been decided differently if the donee had been an administrator and not an executor.
153 [1977] 2 All E.R. 720 at 734. The extension is defended, however, by G. Kodilinye [1982] Conv. 14.
154 [1952] Ch. 110.
155 [1910] 1 Ch. 188 at 193.

3-024

The intention to make the gift, moreover, must persist until the death of the donor. If not, the rule in *Strong v Bird* cannot apply.[156] As Kennedy LJ commented in *Re Pink*, this requires "a continuing intention that the gift should have been given at the time it was given".[157] In *Re Wale*,[158] the testatrix had intended to constitute a trust, but forgot to transfer all the trust property to the trustees. It was held that the subsequent failure to transfer the trust property showed that she did not have the necessary continuing intention for the rule in *Strong v Bird* to apply. In a like vein, in *Re Gonin* a mother sold the land that was to be gifted to her daughter and drafted a cheque in her favour instead. This denied any continuing intention that the daughter (also the administratrix) should have the land.[159] A similar approach might be adopted where, after the gift, the donor leaves the same property by will to another party. It is uncertain whether a temporary change of mind will prevent the rule from operating. Nevertheless, the better view is that there would need to be a fresh attempt to make the gift again for it to be brought back within the scope of the rule. Accordingly, a fluctuating intention should prove fatal to a claim under *Strong v Bird*. The issue of whether the intention has continued is an issue of fact and the burden of proof rests with the donee.

Although the rule has been explained in relation to gifts, it will apply equally to the transfer of property to trustees. Accordingly, if the trustee obtains legal title in the capacity of executor or administrator, then the trust will be constituted and rendered effective. This possibility was accepted in *Re Wale*.

Re Ralli's Will Trusts

3-025

In *Re Ralli's WT*,[160] a testator (Ambrose Ralli) left his estate on trust for his wife for life and then for his daughters, Helen and Irene, absolutely. Subsequently, Helen entered a covenant to transfer existing and subsequently acquired property to the trustees of her marriage settlement. The subsequent property referred to represented the interest that was to come to her, following her mother's death, under her father's will. No transfer was ever made to her trustees. The daughter, however, predeceased the mother. On the mother's death, the trust property reverted to the father's estate and title vested in the sole executor under the father's will. The executor (Irene's husband) was, by coincidence, also the remaining trustee under Helen's marriage settlement. The case was decided on the non-contentious ground that the marriage settlement was a declaration of trust of Helen's existing property and that the reversionary

156 *Vavasseur v Vavasseur* (1909) 25 T.L.R. 250.
157 [1912] 2 Ch. 528 at 538.
158 [1956] 1 W.L.R. 1346.
159 [1977] 2 All E.R. 720.
160 [1964] Ch. 288.

interest under her father's will was existing property at the time of the declaration. Hence, her executor held the property on the same trust when he obtained legal title. As Buckley J explained, "the rule that equity will not assist a volunteer to enforce an executory contract to make a settlement has no application to this case, for the relevant trust has been completely declared by the defendants' predecessor in title and such declaration is binding on them and is enforceable by and for the benefit of the beneficiaries under the settlement, whether they are volunteers or not".[161]

By way of obiter, Buckley J advanced a broader and more controversial proposition. He believed that, absent an effective declaration of trust of her reversionary interest by the daughter, the trust would still have been perfected. His reasoning was that, as legal title was now (albeit fortuitously) vested in the trustee, the trust of the reversionary interest had become perfectly constituted.[162] The fact that the trustee obtained that title from a different source (i.e. as executor under the father's will) would operate to perfect what might otherwise be an imperfect trust. It should not matter how the trustee acquired title, the key issue was that title had now been acquired. As Buckley J observed, "He is at law the owner of the fund, and the means by which he became so have no effect upon the quality of his legal ownership".[163]

3-026

At first blush, *Re Ralli's WT* might be seen as merely marking an extension to the rule in *Strong v Bird*. It is thought, however, that because of the differences between them, the two rules should be regarded as distinct. First, *Re Ralli's WT* does not require the trustee to be the executor under the settlor's will. There it sufficed that he was the executor under her father's will. *Strong v Bird* would not apply in that instance. Secondly, *Re Ralli's WT* does not require a continuing intention on the part of the settlor and can apply to unspecified and future (i.e. after acquired) property. *Strong v Bird* would be inapplicable in such circumstances. Thirdly, it is to be appreciated, moreover, that *Re Ralli's WT* has never been followed and doubts are raised as to whether it is good law.

Re Ralli's WT appears to contradict the earlier authority of *Re Brook's ST*[164] where, even though the trustees acquired title through a different route, the trust was not perfected. In that case, Lloyds Bank were the trustees of a marriage settlement under which the wife enjoyed a power of appointment. One of her children made a voluntary settlement of property that he might acquire under his mother's power of appointment. His mother later made the anticipated appointment in his favour. At the time of the appointment Lloyds Bank held legal title

---

161 [1964] Ch. 288 at 298.

162 As Buckley J acknowledged at 302, "it may seem strange that the rights of the parties should depend upon the appointment of the plaintiff as a trustee of the will in 1946, which for present purposes may have been a quite fortuitous event. The result, however, in my judgment, flows—and flows, I think, quite rationally—from the consideration that the rules of equity derive from the tenderness of a court of equity for the consciences of the parties".

163 [1964] Ch. 288 at 301. As Buckley J explained at 302, "it is not unconscientious in the plaintiff to withhold from Helen's estate the fund which Helen covenanted that he should receive: on the contrary, it would have been unconscientious in Helen to seek to deprive the plaintiff of that fund, and her personal representatives can be in no better position".

164 [1939] 1 Ch. 993.

to the property on behalf of the mother. The issue was whether the Bank now held the property under the terms of the son's voluntary settlement (the second trust) or whether the son could claim the property absolutely. The court determined that, even though the title to the property was fortuitously vested in the Bank, the second trust was incompletely constituted. The decision of Farwell J turned on the fact that the case concerned the assignment (by way of voluntary settlement) of a future expected interest. Hence, the son had no more than a mere expectancy under the marriage settlement until the appointment was made. Hence, he purported to assign something to which he may or may not become entitled in the future. This is not a contingent interest and amounted to a mere expectancy. As there was no consideration given for the assignment, it could not be enforced in equity.[165] The beneficial interest was, thereby, retained by the son. This decision underscores the maxim that equity will not assist a volunteer. Perhaps significantly, *Re Brook's ST* was not cited before the court in *Re Ralli's WT*.

Proprietary Estoppel

The doctrine of estoppel can be employed as a mechanism to sidestep formalities and, hence, perfect an otherwise imperfect gift or imperfectly constituted trust.[166] In *Yeoman's Row Management Ltd v Cobbe*, Lord Scott acknowledged that:

3-027

> "An 'estoppel' bars the object of it from asserting some facts or facts, or, sometimes, something that is a mixture of fact and law, that stands in the way of some right claimed by the person entitled to the benefit of the estoppel. The estoppel becomes a 'proprietary' estoppel—a sub-species of a 'promissory' estoppel—if the right claimed is a proprietary right, usually a right to or over land but, in principle, equally available in relation to chattels or choses in action".[167]

This reflects an expansive jurisdiction of the court to prevent the assertion of a party's strict legal rights in circumstances where it would be unconscionable for that party to rely on such

---

165   If there had been consideration found, Lloyds Bank could have enforced the contract to assign future property if and when it was received: *Re Ellenborough* [1903] 1 Ch. 697.

166   For example, the doctrine of proprietary estoppel extends to an oral assurance to leave property in a will (*Gillett v Holt* [2001] Ch. 210) and, indeed, can override the terms of an otherwise effective will (*Todd v Parsons* [2019] EWHC 3366 (Ch).

167   [2008] 1 W.L.R. 1752 at 1761. While accepting that estoppel is a flexible doctrine that is designed to prevent injustice, Lord Walker added at 1774, "it is not a sort of joker or wild card to be used whenever the Court disapproves of the conduct of a litigant who seems to have the law on his side. Flexible though it is, the doctrine must be formulated and applied in a disciplined and principled way".

rights.[168] The key characteristics of proprietary estoppel are assurance, reliance and detriment. These are not, however, watertight compartments and are often interconnected.[169]

The assurance made by one party to the other might be express (e.g. "the house is yours") or might in more limited circumstances be implied from conduct (e.g. by making payments to the purchase price of the house).[170] In *Greasley v Cooke*,[171] for example, the assurance given to a maid was that she could live in the house for as long as she wished, provided that she continued to care for the family without payment. She could establish an estoppel which, when satisfied, entitled her to occupy the house rent-free for as long as she wanted. It is also to be appreciated that, although estoppel cases usually feature some express assurance or representation, it is possible that an estoppel by acquiescence can arise. The general idea there is that if A, knowing that B is under a mistaken belief as to the acquisition of a right, allows B to act to his detriment on the basis of his erroneous belief that an estoppel might arise as a result of A's acquiescence.[172] The understanding between the parties must, however, be both certain and complete. As Lord Scott pointed out:

> "Proprietary estoppel requires, in my opinion, clarity as to what it is that the object of the estoppel is to be estopped from denying, or asserting, and clarity as to the interest in the property in question that that denial, or assertion, would otherwise defeat".[173]

Although there must be the belief that the representation is binding and irrevocable, this does not mean that there must be an exact specification of what the estoppel claimant is to receive.[174] A general assurance may, therefore, suffice whereas a mere hope will not.[175] Hence, in *McDonald v Rose* the estoppel claim failed because nothing had been said to give the claimant the understanding that he would inherit a business on the death of his parents.[176]

3-028

The reliant conduct of B must, moreover, be referable to A's express or implied assur-

---

168 See *Taylor Fashions Ltd v Liverpool Victoria Trustees Co Ltd* [1982] Q.B. 133.
169 As Mummery LJ explained in *Uglow v Uglow* [2004] W.T.L.R. 1183 at [9], "The overriding concern of the equity to prevent unconscionable conduct permeates all the different elements of the doctrine of proprietary estoppel: assurances, reliance, detriment and satisfaction are all intertwined". See also the views of Floyd LJ in *Davies v Davies* [2016] EWCA Civ 568.
170 *Thorner v Major* [2009] 1 W.L.R. 776.
171 [1980] 3 All E.R. 710; see also *Lothian v Dixon* unreported 28 November 2014 CA where the representation was that the claimants would inherit the representor's entire estate.
172 See *Lester v Woodgate* [2010] EWCA Civ 919.
173 *Yeoman's Row Management Ltd v Cobbe* [2008] 1 W.L.R. 1752 at 1768; see also *Herbert v Doyle* [2010] EWCA Civ 1095.
174 *Thorner v Major* [2009] 1 W.L.R. 776. Exact specification is, however, common: see *Grundy v Ottey* [2003] W.T.L.R. 1253 (a particular flat in Jamaica).
175 See *Re Knowles* [2008] UKPC 30, where it was emphasised that the courts should not penalise those who, through kindness, simply allow other family members to live in property rent free. Nothing had been done to encourage any belief that the brother and sister in law could treat the property as their own.
176 [2018] EWHC 445 (Ch).

ance. There must be a causal link between the two.[177] The reliance must necessarily involve a change of position or disadvantage incurred by the claimant on account of the representation that was made.[178] Accordingly, in *Coombes v Smith*[179] the estoppel claimant failed to show reliance because she had done nothing more than was to be expected of a woman who was leaving her husband to live with her lover. A more liberal approach was, however, adopted in *Wayling v Jones*.[180] There Mr Jones contributed his unpaid labour in reliance on a promise that he would inherit his cohabitee's business. Although he readily admitted that, had the promise never been made, he would have remained in the relationship, an estoppel interest still arose. In these circumstances, an inference of reliance was drawn from Mr Jones' contribution of 16 years' labour. Once the inference is raised, the burden of proof shifts to the representor to show that the claimant's actions were not in reliance on the promise. The cohabitee's estate failed to rebut the presumption of reliance because it became clear that Mr Jones would have quit the relationship had the promise, once made, been subsequently withdrawn.

The reliance must be detrimental to B and this must be judged at the time that the other party seeks to do back on the assurance. It is, therefore, retrospective in nature.[181] Typical acts of reliance will involve expenditure of money or labour, but can also include acts of personal sacrifice.[182] The change of position in *Greasley v Cooke*, for example, was evident from her lengthy service in the family home and sacrificing her career opportunities. In *Lothian v Dixon*,[183] the detriment included running a hotel and looking after an elderly relative on a full-time basis and acting as a general dogsbody. In *Gee v Gee*,[184] as a result of the representations made by his father, a son agreed to be paid the minimum wage throughout his 20 years of working on a farm.[185] Although a change of position can be evidenced from a wide range of circumstances, the claimant's actions must be substantial.[186] In *Brown & Root Technology v Sun Alliance & London Assurance Co*, the High Court held that a landlord changing his records and collecting rent from the putative assignee was insufficient for, as Judge Paul Baker QC explained, "The differences were too trivial to satisfy the test of reliance".[187] As emphasised in cases such as *Stallion v Albert Stallion Holdings (GB) Ltd*,[188] the role played by unconscion-

---

177   *Thorner v Major* [2009] 1 W.L.R. 776; *Cook v Thomas* [2010] EWCA Civ 227.

178   *Gillett v Holt* [2001] Ch. 210.

179   [1986] 1 W.L.R. 808.

180   (1993) 69 P. & C.R. 170.

181   *Davies v Davies* [2016] EWCA Civ 463.

182   In *Jones v Jones* [1977] 1 W.L.R. 438, the detriment comprised of the giving up of a job and home in order to live with the representor. In *Henry v Henry* [2010] UKPC 3, working the land, caring for its owner and depriving himself of the chance of a better life sufficed.

183   Unreported 28 November 2014 CA.

184   [2018] EWHC 1393 (Ch).

185   See also *Thompson v Thompson* [2018] EWHC 1338 (Ch) where the successful claimant had dedicated his life to working his father's farm, which entailed low wages, long hours and the sacrifice of financial independence.

186   See *Shaw v Shaw* [2018] EWHC 3196 (Ch).

187   [1996] Ch. 51 at 68; see also *Davies v Davies* [2016] EWCA Civ 568 where the daughter working on her parents' farm for years on a low wage was evaluated in terms of a substantial detriment.

188   [2009] EWHC 1950 (Ch).

ability must not be overlooked and, in order for equity to intervene, the conscience of the court must be shocked. The determination of whether the detriment is sufficiently substantial is to be judged by whether it would be unjust or inequitable for the assurance to be disregarded. As Judge Robert Kaye noted in *Lothian v Dixon*, "ultimately the matter is to be viewed at the moment of crystallisation, namely whether, looked at in the round, in the circumstances that have happened, it would be unconscionable for the promise or assurance not to be kept . . .".[189]

3-029

Once an estoppel is invoked, it is for the court, in the exercise of a largely unfettered discretion, to decide in hindsight how best it is to be satisfied.[190] As will become clear, expectation is not determinative of the relief to be granted.[191] Judge Robert Kaye observed that, following a broad inquiry, "the task of the court is to do justice, to do what is necessary to avoid an unconscionable result".[192] The claimant cannot, however, recover more than that which was assured. The court will examine matters in the round (i.e. assess the value of the representation, evaluate the extent of the detriment incurred, factor in any benefits already obtained and consider the conduct of the parties and the interests of others) and then determine what remedy (if any) will be awarded.[193] In some cases, the court may order the donor to complete the gift or transfer (i.e. to perform the representation).[194] The consensual element of what has happened might suggest that the parties regarded the expected benefit and the accepted detriment as being rough and ready equivalents.[195] This is as occurred in *Pascoe v Turner*[196] where a couple cohabited in a house owned by one partner. He encouraged the other to spend her savings and improve the house in the belief that she would then become the owner. The relationship broke down and he wanted her out of the property. Even though there was no binding contract or express trust declared, the court compelled him to transfer the house to his partner. Similarly, in *Dillwyn v Llewelyn*[197] a father assured his son that certain land now belonged to the son. The father did not, however, transfer the land to his son. The son built a house on the land, but later

---

189   Unreported 28 November 2014 CA at [19]; see also *Raza v Chaudhary* [2019] EWHC 1720 (Ch) where it was emphasised that unconscionability was a value judgment for the court to make and as assessed at the time the representor refused to go through with the assurance.

190   *Guest v Guest* [2019] EWHC 869 (Ch).

191   *Habberfield v Habberfield* [2019] EWCA Civ 890.

192   *Lothian v Dixon* unreported 28 November 2014 CA at [32]; see further S. Gardner, "The Remedial Discretion in Proprietary Estoppel" (1999) 115 L.Q.R. 438; S. Gardner, "The Remedial Discretion in Proprietary Estoppel—Again" (2006) 122 L.Q.R. 492.

193   In *Lothian v Dixon* unreported 28 November 2014 CA, the claimants sought the residuary estate of the deceased, whereas the other surviving relatives argued that their award be capped at £40,000 plus travel expenses. The High Court favoured the claimants' claim.

194   Such occurred in *Gee v Gee* [2018] EWHC 1393 (Ch) where the representation was that the claimant would obtain shares in a company.

195   As expressed by Robert Walker LJ in *Jennings v Rice* [2003] 1 P. & C.R. 8 at [45], "Sometimes the assurances, and the claimant's reliance on them, have a consensual character falling not far short of an enforceable contract".

196   [1979] 1 W.L.R. 431.

197   (1862) 4 De. G.F. & J. 517.

the validity of the gift was challenged. The son was able to invoke an estoppel and compel the gift to be perfected. The son acquired a right to call on his father's estate to perform the bargain and complete the otherwise imperfect gift.[198] Again, in *Crabb v Arun DC*[199] the Council led Mr Crabb to believe that he could have a right of way over the Council's land. In reliance, Mr Crabb allowed his land to become land-locked. The Council was estopped from denying the right of way. In the same way as an imperfect donation can be perfected by estoppel, so might an otherwise incomplete transfer of legal title to a trustee.

In other cases where the expectation is disproportionate to the detriment, the court should satisfy the equity in a more limited way, for example, by making a financial award.[200] This represents the modern view which incorporates a notion of proportionality.[201] As Norris J observed in *Sutcliffe v Lloyd*:

> **"The task is to identify the minimum equity to do justice (the qualification 'minimum' not requiring the court to be constitutionally parsimonious, but simply being an express recognition of the need to do justice not only to the claimant but also to the defendant)".[202]**

Hence, the court must consider a whole range of events embracing expectations, reliance and unconscionability. In *Jennings v Rice*,[203] for example, the representation was that the claimant would be left a property worth £420,000 in the representor's will. The property was, however, left to someone else. The claimant invoked an estoppel on the basis that, on the strength of this assurance, he had resided with the deceased and had cared for her during her lifetime. The court held that the extent of his detriment warranted a cash payment of £200,000. It was pointed out by Robert Walker LJ that a disproportionate remedy did not avoid an unconscionable result. He explained that:

> **"if the claimant's expectations are uncertain, or extravagant, or out of all proportion to the detriment . . . the court can and should recognise that the claimant's equity should be satisfied in another (and generally more limited) way".[204]**

---

198 See also *Jiggins v Brisley* [2003] EWHC 841 (Ch), where the court awarded the full extent of the claimant's expectation (i.e. the transfer of a flat) as the understanding between them was focused upon specific property and clearly expressed.

199 [1976] Ch. 179. In *Manton Securities Ltd v Nazam* [2008] EWCA Civ 805, Mr Nazam claimed that his landlord had led him to expect that he would be granted a new 21-year lease if he carried out works of repair and improvement on the premises. The landlord was estopped from denying the new lease.

200 See *Davies v Davies* [2016] EWCA Civ 568.

201 *Moore v Moore* [2018] EWCA Civ 2669.

202 [2008] EWHC 1329 (Ch) at [4]; see also *Suggitt v Suggitt* [2012] EWCA Civ 1140.

203 [2003] 1 P. & C.R. 8.

204 [2003] 1 P. & C.R. 8 at 22.

3-030

In *Sledmore v Dalby*,[205] Mr and Mrs Sledmore encouraged their son-in-law to carry out repair works on a cottage that they owned. In return, he was assured that the property would be left by will to him and his wife (Mr and Mrs Sledmore's daughter). The daughter, however, predeceased her parents. Eventually Mrs Sledmore sought possession of the cottage and the son-in-law advanced an estoppel claim. Although it was clear that there had been an expectation, coupled with detrimental reliance, the son-in-law was awarded nothing. The principal reason was that he had already lived in the property rent-free for over 15 years and that the benefit received satisfied the equity he asserted. In that case, therefore, the remedy fell well below that expected by the claimant. It should be noted that the enjoyment of rent-free accommodation does not always extinguish the equity, but it is factored in to how the equity is to be satisfied. Hence, in *Campbell v Griffin* such free accommodation militated against a finding of a life interest, but produced an outcome where the equity was satisfied by a fixed monetary sum.[206] The court should always compare the advantages obtained with the detriment incurred.[207] In *McGuane v Welch*[208] the representation was that Mr Welch would acquire Mr McGuane's flat. The flat was purchased at a discounted price under the Right to Buy scheme contained in the Housing Act 1985. Mr Welch contributed to the mortgage repayments and expended around £10,000 on the modernisation of the property. Although an estoppel was successfully raised by Mr Welch, minimum equity required that he obtain a charge on the property so that he could be reimbursed for his past expenditure.[209]

Guide to Further Reading

D. Delany and D. Ryan, "Unconscionability: A Unifying Theme in Equity" [2008] Conv. 401.

S. Gardner, "The Remedial Discretion in Proprietary Estoppel" (1999) 115 L.Q.R. 438.

S. Gardner, "The Remedial Discretion in Proprietary Estoppel—Again" (2006) 122 L.Q.R. 492.

M. Halliwell, "Perfecting Imperfect Gifts and Trusts: Have We Reached the End of the Chancellor's Foot?" [2003] Conv. 192.

J. Jaconelli, "Problems in the rule of Strong v Bird" [2006] Conv. 432.

G. Kodilinye, "A Fresh Look at the Rule in Strong v Bird" [1982] Conv. 14.

N. Roberts, "Donationes Mortis Causa in a Dematerialised World" [2013] Conv. 113.

---

205 (1996) 72 P. & C.R. 196.

206 [2001] EWCA Civ 990.

207 *Henry v Henry* [2010] UKPC 3; *Bradbury v Taylor* [2012] EWCA Civ 1208.

208 [2008] EWCA Civ 785.

209 This is clearly not an easy task for the court to perform. In *Davies v Davies* [2016] EWCA Civ 463, for example, the lower court awarded the claimant £1.3 million to satisfy the estoppel, but this was reduced on appeal to £500,000.

4

Formalities and the Perpetuity Rules

The general rule is that, once the three certainties are present and legal title to the trust property is vested in the trustee, there is nothing more demanded of the settlor. By way of exceptions to this rule, however, Parliament has decreed that certain types of disposition require additional formalities before they can become effective. The most usual insistence is that the transaction either be in writing or, at the least, be evidenced (i.e. recorded) in writing and that such writing be signed. All testamentary dispositions (i.e. dispositions by will) are regulated by s.9 of the Wills Act 1837 (as amended)[1] whereas inter vivos trusts (i.e. lifetime trusts) are governed by s.53 of the Law of Property Act 1925. These statutory formalities as they apply to lifetime trusts will be considered in detail. The latter part of the chapter, however, will serve as an introduction to the arid and complex perpetuity rules relating to vesting, inalienability and accumulation of income.

The Function of Formalities

There are three broad and interconnected functions which are said to underlie the requirement for added formalities[2]:

- ■ The evidentiary function. The clearest justification for legal formality is to provide documentary evidence of the existence and terms of the transaction. As such, it offers some

---

1 Testamentary trusts are considered in Ch.5.
2 See generally, L.L. Fuller, "Consideration and Form" (1941) 41 Colom. L. Rev. 799.

protection against fraud, undue influence and other types of wrongdoing. Formalities also provide a provable record of transactions and, in particular, lead a paper trail to the individual who currently holds the equitable interest under the trust. This is valuable because equitable interests are intangible (i.e. without physical form) and, thereby, difficult to keep track of. Documentation also helps to establish the obligations of the trustee/executor so that the risk of an inadvertent breach of trust is minimised.

■ The cautionary function. This operates to focus the mind of the settlor/testator and to offer a "cooling off" period until the formalities have been attended to. As property rights are often valuable rights, they are not expected to be created or disposed of casually, secretly or informally.

■ The channelling function. The presence of authenticated writing relieves the court of the need to enquire whether a legal transaction was intended and, if so, to explore its nature. Fuller explains that, "form offers a legal framework into which the party may fit his actions . . . it offers channels for the legally effective expression of intention".[3] This provides administrative assistance in that the court has some document to look at to divine the settlor/testator's true intentions. In this way, the court does not have to rely solely upon the (often unreliable) testimony and (often incomplete) recollections of witnesses and, thereby, this may avoid costly controversy.

The disadvantage of formalities

4-003

The major problem with formalities is that, if they are not complied with, the genuine intentions of a settlor can be frustrated. For example, the settlor may in the clearest terms declare a trust of land, but fail to adhere to the necessary formalities in providing signed written evidence of the terms of the trust. In this situation, the general rule is that the trust will then be unenforceable and the informal disposition rendered of no effect. For example, this may mean that land intended for Jordan will remain in the settlor's estate and, on the settlor's death, pass by will or on intestacy to Adrienne as residual legatee or next of kin. Hence, it may generate an unintended outcome that runs contrary both to the wishes of the settlor and, in our example, the expectations of Jordan. Gulliver and Tilson describe this as "enthroning formality over frustrated intent".[4] Nevertheless, it is for the legislature to draw a balance between these conflicting interests and for the judiciary to ensure that the balance is maintained. As Gardner puts it:

> **"Deciding whether to require formality involves assessing the advantages and disadvantages either way, and comparing them, to see where the greater benefit lies. So, for example, in having the rule**

3   L.L. Fuller, "Consideration and Form" (1941) 41 Colom. L. Rev. 799, 801.
4   A.G. Gulliver and C.J. Tilson, "Classification of Gratuitous Transfers" (1941) 51 Yale L.J. 1, 3.

> that any attempt to dispose of property on death other than by using the ordained formalities is ineffective, the law takes it that the balance lies in favour of such insistence; that the potential ineffectiveness of attempted informal dispositions is an acceptable price to pay for the advantages of minimising uncertainty".[5]

Lifetime Trusts of Land

Inter vivos trusts of land are subject to the additional formalities prescribed in s.53(1)(b) of the Law of Property Act 1925. This provides that "a declaration of trust respecting any land or any interest therein must be manifested and proved by some writing signed by some person who is able to declare such a trust or by his will".[6] These extra requirements are imposed because of both the value of land and the highly technical rules that attend its transfer. The settlor is saved, as Hayton puts it, "from the perils of oral evidence being (mis)used to deprive him of his land".[7] Hence, land is traditionally treated differently from other types of property. In contrast, no additional formalities are necessary to create an inter vivos trust of personalty.[8] Gardner argues that the singling out of trusts of land in this way is justifiable:

4-004

> "Trusts of land are particularly likely to be made formally in practice. People making dispositions of land are especially likely to perceive that they are doing something significant, and will almost certainly use professional advisers, who will always want to put important matters down on paper. So, as with wills, the danger of a requirement of formality frustrating settlors' intentions is slight, allowing the balance of advantage to come down in favour of its imposition".[9]

---

5   S. Gardner, *An Introduction to the Law of Trusts,* 3rd edn (Oxford: Oxford University Press, 2011), p.88. Reproduced with permission of the Licensor through PLSclear.

6   In *Princess Tessy of Luxembourg v Prince Louis of Luxembourg* [2018] EWFC 77, the purported declaration of a trust in writing was ineffective for the purposes of s.53(1)(b) because the purported settlor had no legal or beneficial ownership in the property.

7   D. Hayton, *The Law of Trusts*, 4th edn (London: Sweet and Maxwell, 2003), p.130.

8   See *Paul v Constance* [1977] 1 All E.R. 195. As A. Oakley, *Parker & Mellows The Modern Law Of Trusts*, 9th edn (London: Sweet & Maxwell, 2008) observes, p.109, "It is indeed rather surprising that a declaration of trust requires the appropriate writing even if it relates to as little as a square foot of land while a declaration of trust of millions of pounds worth of cash or investments does not; however, that is what the statutory provisions provide".

9   S. Gardner, *An Introduction to the Law of Trusts,* 3rd edn (Oxford: Oxford University Press, 2011), p.91. Reproduced with permission of the Licensor through PLSclear.

Section 53(1)(b) applies to a declaration of a trust of land regardless of whether the title is freehold or leasehold and whether the land is registered or unregistered. The section will catch a trust of land even if the land is situated outside the jurisdiction of the domestic courts. For these purposes, land is widely defined as embracing mines, minerals, buildings and incorporeal hereditaments (e.g. easements and profits).[10] It is to be appreciated, however, that s.53(1)(b) does not require that the trust of land be created in writing. Instead, it demands that such trusts merely be evidenced in writing. This requires a documentary memorandum of the existence of the trust, the trust property[11] and the beneficiaries of the trust.[12] There is no requirement for a deed or for the signature to be witnessed.[13] Hence, in *Taylor v Taylor* the trust document was unsigned, but a subsequent notice of severance of the joint tenancy provided the necessary signed writing.[14]

4-005

The consequence of a failure to adhere to s.53(1)(b) is that, although the trust of land remains valid, the trust is rendered unenforceable by the beneficiary.[15] This distinction can assume significance where the timing of the creation of the trust is important. For example, in *Gardner v Rowe*[16] the settlor orally declared certain trusts of land. Subsequently, he became bankrupt and only then did he decide to commit the terms of the trust to writing. Although the creditors laid claim to the trust property, the court held that the trusts had been validly created and, due to the presence of writing, were now enforceable by the beneficiaries. If, of course, the settlor had declined to provide signed documentary evidence of the trust, then the creditors could have claimed the land. As shown in Ch.3, however, this general rule might give way where the beneficiary can establish, for example, an estoppel interest[17] (see para.**3-027)** or, following the dubious reasoning in *Pennington v Waine*,[18] demonstrate that it would be unconscionable for the settlor to renege on the arrangement (see para. **3.013**).

There must be writing and this includes typing, printing, lithography, photography and other modes of representing or reproducing words in a visible form.[19] This definition is wide enough to embrace the modern manifestations of writing found in telex, fax and email. The writing may well come into existence contemporaneously with the declaration of the trust. This is not, however, a necessary requirement. The documentary evidence can be created

---

10   Section 205(1)(ix) of the Law of Property Act 1925.

11   In *Ong v Ping* [2017] EWCA Civ 2069, the trust property (a house) was not identified in the signed document, but was disclosed in a subsequent letter. It was held that when reading the documents together all the necessary terms were set out in writing.

12   *Smith v Matthews* (1891) 3 De. G.F. & J. 139.

13   *Close Invoice Finance Ltd v Abaowa* [2010] EWHC 1920 (QB).

14   [2017] EWHC 1080 (Ch).

15   *Spencer v Strickland* [2009] EWHC 3033 (Ch).

16   (1828) 5 Russ 258 which was decided in relation to s.7 of the Statute of Frauds 1677 (the precursor to s.53(1) (b)).

17   *Gledhill's Trustee v Gledhill* [2011] B.P.I.R. 918.

18   [2002] 4 All E.R. 215.

19   Interpretation Act 1978 Sch.1.

either before[20] or, as demonstrated in *Gardner v Rowe*, after the trust has been declared. Nevertheless, and regardless of when it is brought into being, the writing must recite all the terms of the trust. As Deputy Judge Simon Picken QC explained in *Close Invoice Finance Ltd v Abaowa*, "it seems obvious to me that it is wrong to seek to divorce the question of proof from the issue of what s.53(1)(b) requires; as I see it, the two are essentially the same and it is not accurate to characterise the latter as being merely a matter of form".[21] There a document created 13 years after the purported declaration of trust and in the course of the dispute concerning the very issue to which it related, did not satisfy s.53(1)(b).[22]

As there is no prescribed form for this writing to adopt, it can be pieced together from more than one document.[23] It may, for example, take the form of correspondence, documents used in court proceedings[24] or a will (valid or otherwise). Indeed, although unlikely, the terms of the trust could even be scrawled on the back of a cigarette packet or beer mat. Understandably, and as demonstrated in *Close Invoice Finance Ltd v Abaowa*,[25] the document must, however, be genuine. In *Random House UK Ltd v Allason*, it was claimed that the original document had been lost and a copy was adduced in evidence.[26] David Richards J considered the so-called secondary evidence rule and concluded that the trustees must satisfy the court that the original document existed or had existed, that it had been lost or destroyed and that a reasonable explanation of this had been given. Here, however, the evidence showed that there had never been a genuine declaration of trust.

The writing must, moreover, be "signed". It is not, however, relevant that the signatory did not analyse the precise wording of the document signed.[27] Traditionally, the courts have adopted a liberal approach as to what amounts to a signature,[28] but in recent years there has been a tightening up of this requirement as regards wet ink signatures. The old cases are, therefore, no sure guide to future decisions.[29] Nevertheless, there remain certain conditions that need to be satisfied:

4-006

- there must be some physical manifestation on the document that is intended to identify the declarant. This will entail the presence of the declarant's mark whether

---

20 *Kaki v Kaki* [2015] EWHC 3692 (Ch).
21 [2010] EWHC 1920 (QB) at [87].
22 In *Ong v Ping* [2017] EWCA Civ 2069, the letter could still provide the missing term although it stated that Madam Lim would like to cancel the trust. This letter recognised that the discretionary trust existed at the date of the letter and prior to the proposed cancellation.
23 See *Sandhar v Sandhar & Kang Ltd* [2008] EWCA Civ 238. This is provided that the document can be clearly connected with, and is referred to in, the document that is signed: *Forster v Hale* (1798) 3 Ves. Jr. 696.
24 See *Wright v Wright* [2010] EWHC 1808 (Ch) where a party's affidavit supplied the necessary signed evidence.
25 [2010] EWHC 1920 (QB).
26 [2008] EWHC 2854 (Ch).
27 *Rollerteam Ltd v Riley* [2015] EWHC 1545Ch (upheld on appeal [2016] EWCA Civ 1291).
28 See further, C.T. Emery, "Statute of Frauds: The Authenticated Signature Fiction—An Illogical Distinction" (1975) 39 Conv. 336.
29 See *Firstpost Homes Ltd v Johnson* [1995] 4 All E.R. 355, where Balcombe LJ admitted (at 363) that "there was every reason for consigning the old law to the limbo where it clearly belongs".

represented by a cross, full signature or initials. The mark can be handwritten, typed, made by a rubber stamp, or an electronic signature[30];

■ the declarant's cipher may be placed anywhere on the document provided that it is designed to authenticate and to adopt the document. In *Firstpost Homes Ltd v Johnson*, for example, the typed insertion of a party's name at the top of a letter as addressee was woefully insufficient to amount to a signature. In *Simpson v Simpson*,[31] the writing relied upon to evidence an oral trust was signed by a person with severe dyslexia. It was argued before the High Court that, because of this disability, he could not be taken to have agreed the contents of the documents. The court was unimpressed and concluded that the dyslexic party would have had the documents explained to him at the time of his signature. In order to escape the effect of signing the document, he would have to show that the content was untrue and that he was improperly persuaded to add his signature. Hence, even though the signatory cannot read or understand the documents without assistance, they remain sufficient evidence of the oral trust; and

■ the signature of the individual able to declare the trust is necessary. In relation to a company, however, the document must be signed "by" the company and not merely signed "on behalf of" the company. As recognised by Lloyd LJ in *Hilmi & Associates Ltd v 20 Pembridge Villas Freehold Ltd*:

"In relation to a corporate entity which cannot itself hold a pen and apply it to a piece of paper, this may seem a somewhat metaphysical inquiry. But it is one which the law requires to be considered, on occasion, although perhaps only very rarely".[32]

■ Section 44 of the Companies Act 2006 concerns the execution of documents by a company and allows for more informal methods than the affixing of the company's common seal. It provides that a document may be effectively signed by two authorised signatories (i.e. directors and company secretary) or by the attested signature of a director. This process is deemed to have the same effect as if the document was executed under the common seal of the company.[33]

---

30 There is a growing use of electronic signatures and their effectiveness was confirmed by the Law Commission Report, "Electronic execution of documents" (2019) Law Com No. 386. This has the Government's support.
31 [2005] EWHC 2098 (Ch).
32 [2010] 1 W.L.R. 2750 at 2755.
33 *Redcard Ltd v Williams* [2011] EWCA Civ 466.

The signature envisaged will usually be that of the settlor. It has, however, been argued that, if legal title to the property has already been transferred, it is the owner of the equitable interest who must sign and not the original settlor.[34] If the trustee were given the mandate to declare new trusts, in that scenario it would appear that the trustee's signature would be required. There is no express mention made in s.53(1)(b) of the ability of an agent to sign the document. This limitation exists, presumably, because the written evidence of a trust of land can emerge informally and unintentionally and, hence, requires the declarant's direct involvement.

Section 53(2): An exception

As Gray and Gray comment:

4-007

> **"However compelling the policy motivation behind the statutory requirement of written evidence of an express trust of land, there are nevertheless certain circumstances where even this potent rationale is displaced by concerns ranking higher in the scale of values which animate equitable jurisdiction".[35]**

Such an exception is expressly catered for in s.53(2), which states that the formalities prescribed elsewhere in s.53 as to writing apply only to express trusts and do not extend to resulting,[36] implied[37] or constructive trusts. The latter types of trust are usually informal and may never have been contemplated by the parties. Such implied trusts exist to achieve fairness and to prevent unconscionable outcomes. They concern, as Glidewell LJ explained in *Ivin v Blake*:

> **"a transaction between the trustee and the *cestui que trust* in connection with the acquisition by the trustee of a legal estate in land, whenever the trustee has so conducted himself that it would be inequitable to allow him to deny to the *cestui que trust* a beneficial interest in the land acquired, and he will be held so to have conducted himself if by his words or conduct he has induced the *cestui***

---

34 T. Youdan, "Formalities for Trusts of Land, and the Doctrine in *Rochefoucauld v Boustead*" (1984) 43 C.L.J. 306. See *Taylor v Taylor* [2017] EWHC 1080 (Ch).

35 Gray and Gray, *Elements of Land Law*, 5th edn (Oxford: Oxford University Press, 2008), p.830. Reproduced with permission of the Licensor through PLSclear. See also J.D. Feltham, "Informal Trusts and Third Parties" [1987] Conv. 246.

36 For example, in *Solomon v McCarthy* [2020] 1 P & CR DG.22 the beneficiary was defeated because the intended trust of land was not evidenced in writing, but the court was still able to conclude that the property was held on resulting trust for that beneficiary.

37 It is, however, unclear whether there is a class of "implied trust" that is totally distinct from the resulting or constructive trust.

> *que trust* to act to his own detriment in the reasonable belief that by so acting he was acquiring a beneficial interest in the land".[38]

Hence, to require formalities for the creation of such trusts would undermine the reason for their very existence. Consequently, it is possible for what is originally an unenforceable express trust of land to adopt the guise of an enforceable resulting or constructive trust on the same terms.[39] Of course, if there is no writing and no resulting or constructive trust, then the trust will remain unenforceable.[40]

A classic case is *Hodgson v Marks*,[41] where a widow was influenced by her lodger to transfer the title to her house into his name on the basis that this would prevent his eviction following her death. The lodger later sold the house to a third party. The Court of Appeal decided that the lodger had held the house on resulting trust for the widow and, as this implied trust fell outside s.53(1)(b), it was enforceable against the third party. Sometimes the court will imply a constructive trust from the facts to take an otherwise unenforceable transaction outside the ambit of the formalities. In *Bannister v Bannister*,[42] two cottages were conveyed to a trustee on the basis that the beneficiary would be allowed to live in one of them for the rest of her life. The court would not allow the trustee to rely upon an absence of writing in these circumstances and invoked a constructive trust.[43]

4-008

A similar outcome was achieved in *Rochefoucauld v Boustead*[44] which also concerned an oral trust of land that was, at face value, unenforceable. The claimant had, however, relied detrimentally on the strength of this otherwise unenforceable bargain. The court concluded that not to enforce the claimant's rights would amount to a fraud. As Lindley LJ explained, "it is a fraud on the part of the person to whom land is conveyed as trustee, and who knows that it was so conveyed, to deny the trust and claim the land himself".[45] Accordingly, as the maxim of equity is that a "statute cannot be used as an instrument of fraud" the need for formality was, thereby, sidestepped.[46] The Court of Appeal, however, spoke in terms of the express trust remaining valid because of the maxim and did not contemplate any new constructive

---

38 (1994) 67 P. & C.R. 263 at 269.
39 See *Simpson v Simpson* [2005] EWHC 2098 (Ch).
40 *Al-Khayat v Al-Khayat* [2005] EWHC 3465 (Ch).
41 [1971] Ch. 892.
42 [1948] 2 All E.R. 133.
43 See also *Taylor v Taylor* [2017] EWHC 1080 (Ch) where, regardless of whether signed writing existed, the High Court determined that there was ample evidence of an agreement that the parties were to hold equally to fuel a constructive trust.
44 [1897] 1 Ch. 197.
45 [1897] 1 Ch. 197 at 206. Note that these cases concern a constructive trust imposed on the transferee in favour of the transferor because of the terms on which the property was acquired.
46 See also, *Lyus v Prowsa Developments* [1982] 1 W.L.R. 1044, where land was sold on the express oral understanding that it would be subject to the rights of a third party. The third party acquired enforceable rights under a constructive trust because it would otherwise entail that statute (there the Land Registration Act 1925) was being employed as an engine of fraud.

trust arising. Nevertheless, the better view is that the court will, in such cases, be enforcing a constructive trust and not the original express trust.[47] At the least, this disregard of s.53 is expressly condoned in the 1925 Act itself. As whichever route is adopted the outcome remains the same, it appears that nothing much turns upon the correctness of this classification.[48]

A major area for the operation of resulting and constructive trusts concerns informal arrangements relating to the family home. This is discussed in detail in Ch.11. For example, where the title to, say, a house is registered in the name of one partner only, but the other has contributed 20 per cent towards the purchase price, traditionally a resulting trust would arise without any need for formality. The beneficial interest under this resulting trust will be throughout fixed at 20 per cent of the value of the property and that, of course, is itself likely to fluctuate over future years. If the legal owner later allows the other, say, to finance repairs or to give up work to look after their children, a constructive trust may then arise which will subsume the original resulting trust. The attraction of this alternative mechanism is that the assessment of entitlement is not driven solely by monetary contributions towards the acquisition of the property and can reflect what the court deems to be fair and reasonable over the whole course of dealings between the parties.[49]

Dealing with an Existing Trust Interest

Section 53(1)(c) of the Law of Property Act 1925 provides that "a disposition of an equitable interest or trust subsisting at the time of the disposition, must be in writing signed by the person disposing of the same or by his agent thereunto lawfully authorised in writing or by will".[50] This is a far from straightforward provision and, as Nolan laments, "Every year, those who teach the law of trusts face a dry and difficult task: explaining the formalities which govern the creation and disposition of equitable interests".[51]

4-009

Several initial observations about this provision may be made:

- a failure to comply with s.53(1)(c) makes the transfer entirely void[52];

47 See Millett LJ in *Banner Homes Group Plc v Luff Developments Ltd* [2000] 2 W.L.R. 772 at 780.
48 See *Neale v Willis* (1968) 19 P. & C.R. 836; *Simpson v Simpson* [2005] EWHC 2098 (Ch).
49 See *Oxley v Hiscock* (2004) 3 All E.R. 703; *Curley v Parkes* [2004] EWCA Civ 1515.
50 For example, in *Smith v Crawshay* [2019] EWHC 2507 (Ch) the court concluded that the defendant's signature on the relevant partnership accounts satisfied s.53(1)(c).
51 R.C. Nolan, "*Vandervell v IRC*: A Case of Overreaching" [2002] C.L.J. 169.
52 Parliament has exempted a limited number of transactions from s.53(1)(c): for example, the Financial Collateral Arrangements (No.2) Regulations 2003 (SI 2003/3226) which operate in relation to financial collateral arrangements (which include repurchase agreements) and the Collective Investment in Transferable. Securities (Contractual Scheme) Regulations 2013 (SI 2013/1388) (which deal with electronic dispositions of units in co-ownership schemes).

■ s.53(1)(c) applies to all property, that is, personal property as well as land;

■ the formalities do not apply to resulting or constructive trusts: s.53(2). In *Neville v Wilson*,[53] a dispute arose between the shareholders of a small company as to a series of informal agreements and whether two directors had effectively disposed of their equitable interest in shares of a parent company. Each agreement was oral and the issue, of course, became whether the agreements were rendered ineffectual by s.53(1)(c). It was successfully contended that the effect of each individual agreement was to constitute the two directors as constructive trustees for the other shareholders so that the writing requirement was dispensed with by virtue of s.53(2) (which exempts such implied trusts from the formal requirements). Nourse LJ could see no reason why s.53(2) should not extend to these constructive trusts.[54] Such a trust would, therefore, prevent a party who has legal title from benefiting wrongfully from the transaction.[55] The onus, of course, lies with the claimant to demonstrate the existence of an implied trust[56];

■ for the purposes of writing, two documents can be read together in order to satisfy s.53(1)(c). By way of illustration, in *Re Danish Bacon Co Ltd Staff Pension Fund Trust*[57] an employee nominated his wife to receive benefits under a pension scheme should he die before he was entitled. He signed the approved form. Later the employee changed the identity of the nominated beneficiary by amending the original form and sending an explanatory letter to the trustee of the pension fund. The issue arose as to whether this was a valid nomination. It was held that the alteration was effective. Although doubtful as to whether the nomination was an assignment of a subsisting equitable interest within s.53(1)(c), Megarry J held that, even if it was, the two documents (i.e. the form and the letter) were sufficiently interconnected that they could together constitute the necessary writing. The document(s) must, however, purport to be an immediate assignment of the equitable interest.[58] In *Young v Dawson*,[59] an argument that a signed witness statement sufficed to satisfy s.53(1)(c) was rejected as it spoke in the past tense ("I have relinquished my status as a secured creditor"). The act to which it referred had taken place before the making of the statement;

---

53   [1997] Ch. 144.
54   Hence, it need not be in writing: *Singh v Anand* [2007] EWHC 3346 (Ch); *Rashid v Ayub* (2001) 81 P. & C.R. D17.
55   *Hniazdzilau v Vajgel* [2016] EWHC 15 (Ch). There a company was acquired by Mr Vajgel with money provided by the claimant, Mr Hniazdzilau. It was held that, despite an absence of writing, the company was held on trust for the claimant.
56   *Arif v Anwar* [2013] EWHC 624 (Fam).
57   [1971] 1 All E.R. 486.
58   *Zeital v Kaye* [2010] EWCA Civ 159. There a signed stock transfer form enabling a future transfer of the legal title to a share, which did not purport to assign the equitable interest, did not constitute a written assignment for the purposes of s.53(1)(c).
59   [2012] EWHC 196 (Ch).

■ where an assignee of an equitable interest is to hold in a fiduciary capacity, there is no need for the writing to contain all the terms of the trust. In *Re Tyler*,[60] Miss Tyler appointed King and Green the executors under her will. Shortly afterwards, she gave £1,500 to King. As she did not intend King to have beneficial ownership of the money, and had given no directions as to its application, this gave rise to a resulting trust in her favour. Subsequently, she wrote to King instructing him to use the money for Green as she had previously directed. Although the letter did not contain every detail of the assignment, the letter amounted to a valid disposition of her equitable interest. As Pennycuick J observed, "There is nothing in s.53 which requires that, where the assignee is to hold in a fiduciary capacity, the writing shall comprise the particulars of the trust"[61]; and

■ in contrast with s.53(1)(b), the signature of an agent will suffice for the purposes of s.53(1)(c). This reflects the fact that express written assignments are unlikely to occur inadvertently. The agent must, however, be authorised in writing to sign the document.[62]

Disposition of a subsisting equitable interest?

It is crucial to understand that s.53(1)(c) applies only after a trust has been created. It has no relevance whatsoever to the original creation of the trust under which the equitable interest arises.[63] This entails that, if both legal and equitable titles are vested in the same person, the law does not regard the equitable title as having an existence distinct from the legal title.[64] Put in other terms, s.53(1)(c) can apply only where the legal and equitable interests in the property are already divorced.[65] Accordingly, the formalities are designed to bite on the transfer of an equitable interest by a beneficiary to someone else, or the direction of a beneficiary to the trustee to hold the trust property on behalf of another. The purpose is to maintain a written record of such transfers. As Deputy Judge Robertson explained, "One can see that trustees would be exposed if beneficiaries could dispose of their beneficial interest by notifying the trustee orally of that change and then later renege, leaving the trustee without ready means of proof that the trustee had paid out to the correct beneficiary".[66]

It is the disposition (i.e. the transfer itself) of the equitable interest that must be in documen-

4-010

---

60 [1967] 1 W.L.R. 1269.

61 [1967] 1 W.L.R. 1269 at 1275.

62 *See Zeital v Kaye* [2010] EWCA Civ 159 where there was no authorisation, no written assignment and, hence, no transfer of the equitable interest in shares.

63 *Drakeford v Cotton* [2012] 3 All E.R. 1138.

64 See *Commissioner of Stamp Duties (Queensland) v Livingstone* [1965] A.C. 694 PC.

65 See *Kinane v Mackie-Conteh* [2005] EWCA Civ 45, where Arden and Neuberger LJJ held that s.53(1)(c) did not apply when the legal and equitable estates had not been divided prior to the disposition.

66 *JSC VTB Bank v Skurikhin* [2019] EWHC 1407 (Comm) at [212]. There an existing beneficiary under an express trust attempted to transfer his interest to another beneficiary while the legal interest remained where it was. It fell squarely within s.53(1)(c).

tary form.[67] Hence, it is not enough that the transfer is merely evidenced in writing. Similarly, there can be no scope for any subsequent written ratification of the disposition. It is void from the outset.[68] Unfortunately, it is not always clear whether a transaction amounts to a declaration of trust (outside s.53(1)(c)) or is, instead, the disposition of an equitable interest (within s.53(1)(c)). The latter is a term of wide import. The cases, moreover, appear inconsistent and illogical. As Nolan put it, "sadly, common-sense and s.53(1)(c) share only a nodding acquaintance".[69] Indeed, Green criticises the judiciary for confining their attention to adjudicating the facts as appear before them and this entails that judges, "often fail to perceive the wider implications of their particular determinations".[70] Many of the decisions concern tax avoidance cases and involve the body formerly known as the Inland Revenue (now HM Revenue & Customs) as a major player in the litigation. As dispositions must be in writing and writing attracts stamp duty, the Inland Revenue tends to argue for a disposition rather than a declaration. This is because stamp duty is charged on an instrument rather than on the transaction itself. In *Bishop Square Ltd v IRC*,[71] for example, the Inland Revenue sought stamp duty of £372,230 whereas the taxpayer claimed that only nominal duty was payable (a mere 50 pence).[72] The outcome (which favoured the Inland Revenue) turned upon an oral transfer being invalid under s.53(1)(c). Similarly, in the *Vandervell* cases (see below), it was in the interest of the Inland Revenue to establish that an oral disposition had been ineffective due to an absence of writing.

4-011
Section 53(1)(c) does not apply to the outright disclaimer of an equitable interest by a beneficiary. This is demonstrated in *Re Paradise Motor Co Ltd*,[73] where a stepfather gave an equitable interest in certain shares to his stepson. When the stepson discovered this, he made it clear he did not want them. Subsequently, the stepson changed his mind and argued that his disclaimer was ineffective because it was not in writing to comply with s.53(1)(c). The court rejected this reasoning and held that the disclaimer had been effective and stripped him of any rights he might otherwise have had in relation to the shares.[74] It also appears from the views expressed by Megarry J in *Re Danish Bacon Company Staff Pension Fund* (see para.**4-009**) that the nomination of a person to receive payment under a pension scheme is not captured by s.53(1)(c). It is unlikely that the nomination could be regarded as a disposition because it is revocable and transfers nothing at the time it is made. Similarly, in *Gold v Hill*[75] the holder of

---

67 In *Chandler v Clark* [2002] EWCA Civ 1249, it was emphasised that the disposition needs to be unconditional and in final form.

68 *JSC VTB Bank v Skurikhin* [2019] EWHC 1407 (Comm).

69 R.C. Nolan, "*Vandervell v IRC*: A Case of Overreaching" [2002] C.L.J. 169, 176.

70 B. Green, "Grey, Oughtred and Vandervell—A Contextual Reappraisal" (1984) 47 M.L.R. 385, 395.

71 (1999) 78 P. & C.R. 169.

72 Although less eye-catching, in *Henty & Constable (Brewers) Ltd v Inland Revenue Commissioners* [1961] 1 W.L.R. 1018 duty was originally assessed on a conveyance on sale of land at £985, but the High Court held that it was instead a transfer of shares and carried duty at 10 shillings (i.e. 50 new pence).

73 [1968] 1 W.L.R. 1125.

74 Once the equitable interest is accepted, however, there can be no informal disclaimer: *Hameed v Qayyum* [2008] EWHC 2274 (Ch).

75 [1999] 1 F.L.R. 54.

the life policy orally directed the nominated beneficiary of the policy that, in the event of the policyholder's death, the nominated beneficiary should hold the policy for the benefit of the deceased's family. As nothing was transferred until the death of the policyholder, this was not regarded as an assignment of the existing equitable interest. In *Young v Dawson*,[76] Mr Young applied to participate in the prescribed part of realised assets available for the benefit of the unsecured creditors of JT Frith Limited. To do so it was necessary for him to prove that he had effectively surrendered his security in respect of the debts owed to him. The issue was whether he could effect such a surrender by omitting to disclose those interests in the submission of his proof of debt. The High Court felt that he could do this without complying with s.53(1)(c).[77]

In circumstances where an equitable owner declares a sub-trust of his own entire equitable interest, it appears that the application of s.53(1)(c) turns upon whether the equitable owner has active duties to perform (e.g. the exercise of discretion on the creation of a discretionary sub-trust). If there are active duties to perform, or only part of the equitable interest is the subject of the sub-trust, it should be treated as a valid declaration and outside the reach of the formalities.[78] It is to be regarded as a new trust and not merely the transfer of an existing equitable interest. If, however, there are no active duties to perform (i.e. it is a passive or bare sub-trust), the beneficiary will drop from the picture and be regarded as merely having assigned his equitable interest.[79] Hence, the disposition will be invalid unless it satisfies the requirements of s.53(1)(c). Not everyone, however, is happy with this line of reasoning. Green describes it as involving a "somewhat inelegant distinction" and argues that it is a distinction not truly justified on the authorities.[80] Nevertheless, it still reflects the conventional wisdom.

Section 53(1)(c): Four Seminal Cases

Case 1: *Grey v IRC*

In *Grey v IRC*,[81] the issue was whether a direction by a settlor to his existing trustees to hold shares on trust for a third party fell within s.53(1)(c). In this case, Mr Hunter created six settlements in favour of his grandchildren. Some years later, he transferred legal title in 18,000

4-012

---

76 [2012] EWHC 196 (Ch).
77 This was because of r.4.96 of the Insolvency Rules 1986, which provides that, if the creditor states that he has no security, he loses the right to rely on his security and is to be treated as an unsecured creditor, subject only to the court's power to grant relief.
78 *Grainge v Wilberforce* (1889) 5 T.L.R. 436.
79 See *Re Lashmar* [1891] 1 Ch. 258.
80 (1984) 47 M.L.R. 385, 397. In *Singh v Anand* [2007] EWHC 3346 (Ch) at [144], Judge Norris QC refused "to enter upon this controversy".
81 [1960] A.C. 1.

shares in Sun Engraving Co Ltd to his trustees (one of whom was Mr Grey) to hold on an express bare trust for himself. Shortly afterwards, Mr Hunter orally and irrevocably directed his trustees to hold those shares on trust in six parcels for new beneficiaries (his grandchildren). The same trustees were the trustees of the grandchildren's pre-existing settlements. Mr Hunter attempted to do everything orally so as to escape liability to ad valorem stamp duty. Some five weeks later, the trustees executed six documents confirming that they now held the shares on trust for the grandchildren. There was no doubting that the new trusts were valid. The real issue, however, was when the equitable interest in the shares passed: was it on the oral direction or subsequently on the trustees' written confirmation?

The House of Lords had to consider what amounted to a "disposition" for the purposes of s.53(1)(c). The initial stumbling block concerned the forerunner of this provision as contained in s.9 of the Statute of Frauds 1677. It was argued by the trustees that the Law of Property Act 1925 was merely a consolidating Act and, as such, did not amend the earlier legislation. As s.9 dealt only with "grants and assignments", it was contended that s.53(1)(c) must be similarly limited in scope. It followed that, as the creation of a trust was outside s.9,[82] the present transaction must fall outside s.53(1)(c) because it was neither a grant nor an assignment and was, instead, the declaration of an entirely new trust. This argument was destined to fail.

Although only by way of obiter, Lord Radcliffe was of the opinion that, even if the restricted meaning was adopted, Mr Hunter's direction would still amount to an assignment:

> **"Something had to happen to that equitable interest in order to displace it in favour of the new interests created by the direction: and it would be at any rate logical to treat the direction as being an assignment of the subsisting interest . . .".[83]**

4-013

Both Viscount Simonds and Lord Radcliffe noted that there were substantial differences in language and subject matter between the two statutory provisions and that there had been interceding legislation in the form of s.3 of the Law of Property (Amendment) Act 1924. Lord Radcliffe emphasised that the 1924 Act had made alterations to the Statute of Frauds and it was these amended provisions that were consolidated in the 1925 Act. These changes were too overt to be ignored and there was no direct link between the two provisions. Lord Radcliffe concluded that the meaning of "disposition" was not to be limited or controlled by the old Act and claimed that, "It is impossible to regard s.53 . . . as a consolidating enactment in this sense . . .".[84]

With that argument out of the way, Viscount Simonds felt that the term "disposition" had to be given its ordinary meaning and concluded that, "It cannot, I think, be denied that the direction given by Mr Hunter, whereby the beneficial interest in the shares theretofore vested in him became vested in another or others, is a disposition".[85] Similarly, Lord Radcliffe held no

---

82 *M'Fadden v Jenkyns* (1842) 1 Hare 458.
83 [1960] A.C. 1 at 16.
84 [1960] A.C. 1 at 17.
85 [1960] A.C. 1 at 12, 13.

doubts that this was a disposition for the purposes of s.53(1)(c), stating, "Whether we describe what happened in technical or in more general terms the full equitable interest in the 18,000 shares concerned, which at the time was his, was (subject to any statutory invalidity) diverted by his direction from his ownership into the beneficial ownership of the various equitable owners, present and future, entitled under his six existing settlements".[86] Accordingly, the nomination of the new beneficiaries was a disposition of Mr Hunter's equitable interest for the purposes of s.53(1)(c). Mr Hunter had held a subsisting equitable interest at the outset and claimed no longer to hold such an interest. Common sense dictated, therefore, that there had been a purported disposition of that interest. As the oral direction could not achieve this transfer, the documents executed by the trustees operated to effect the disposition. Stamp duty was, therefore, payable on those documents.

Case 2: *Oughtred v IRC*

In *Oughtred v IRC*,[87] the House of Lords had to consider whether a formal transfer of shares following an oral agreement amounted to an assignment for the purposes of s.53(1)(c). The trustees held 200,000 shares in William Jackson & Son Ltd (a private company) for the benefit of Mrs Oughtred for life with remainder absolute to her son, Peter. Between mother and son, they owned the whole equitable interest in those shares. In return for 72,700 of his mother's own shares in the same company, Peter made an oral contract to transfer his trust interest in remainder to her. Her life interest under the trust would, thereby, become an absolute interest. Following the oral agreement, the mother transferred her shares to Peter. On the same day, two documents were executed. First, a deed of release between the trustees, the mother and Peter was executed which recited that his shares were now to be held on trust absolutely for the mother. Secondly, and in order to ensure that she was the registered owner of them, the trust shares were transferred to the mother by deed made between her and the trustees. The consideration was expressed to be 10 shillings.

The Inland Revenue claimed ad valorem duty of £663 on the document of transfer, asserting that it was a conveyance on sale that transferred Peter's reversionary interest in the 200,000 shares. The mother contended that she fell outside the catchment of s.53(1)(c) because a contract of this sort was not a disposition of an equitable interest. It was, she argued, not a complete disposition of Peter's reversionary interest and was instead the creation of a new equitable interest. In addition, and by virtue of the doctrine of conversion that operates on a specifically enforceable contract, she argued that a constructive sub-trust had arisen under which the equitable interest had already passed to her.[88] This reflects the maxim that "equity looks on

4-014

---

86 [1960] A.C. 1 at 15.
87 [1960] A.C. 206; see also the similar case of *Bishop Square Ltd v Commissioners of Inland Revenue* (1999) 78 P. & C.R. 169.
88 See *Lysaght v Edwards* (1876) 2 Ch. D. 499 (the entry into a contract to sell land passing an equitable interest from vendor to purchaser). As Sir George Jessel MR explained (at 506), "the moment you have a valid

that as done that which ought to be done".[89] It is to be appreciated, however, that a contract for the sale of shares in a publicly quoted company will not usually be specifically enforceable. Damages will generally be an adequate remedy.[90] The position is, however, different where the shares are in a private unquoted company. In such a case, the contract is specifically enforceable.[91] Accordingly, the mother claimed that, following the oral contract, the son was no longer the beneficial owner of the shares. All that the later transfer conveyed was the legal title to the shares. Her case was, therefore, that the disposition of the equitable interest fell within the exception in s.53(2) because of the constructive sub-trust attendant to the contract.

4-015

The majority of the House of Lords rejected the mother's appeal and held that the documentary transfer was assessable under the Stamp Act 1891 to stamp duty.[92] The majority held that, even if the oral agreement passed some equitable interest to the mother, the later transfer was a conveyance on sale.[93] Lord Denning took the view that, "stripped of all trimmings" the case was simple.[94] He had no doubt that this was a transfer such as to attract stamp duty. Although it was the trustees and not Peter who transferred the shares to the mother,

> "It is clear to me that, by the transfer so made by his authority, she acquired his reversionary interest as effectively as if he had conveyed it directly to her. And that is quite enough to attract stamp duty . . . the instrument is the means by which the parties choose to implement the bargain they have made".[95]

The release dealt with the equitable interest and the transfer dealt with the legal title to the shares. It did not matter that the transaction was designed to wind up the existence of the trust.

As to the constructive trust argument, Lord Denning said little, but did comment that:

> "I do not think the oral agreement was effective to transfer Peter's reversionary interest to his mother . . . s.53(1)(c) of the Law of

contract for sale the vendor becomes in equity a trustee for the purchaser of the estate sold, and the beneficial ownership passes to the purchaser, the vendor having a right to the purchase-money . . .".

89 See *Walsh v Lonsdale* (1882) 21 Ch. D. 9.

90 An exception to this is where the shares cannot be acquired readily in the open market: *Duncuft v Albrecht* (1841) 12 Sim. 189.

91 See *Mills v Sportsdirect.com Retail Ltd* [2010] EWHC 1072 (Ch). Lewison J assumed (but did not decide) that the same principles applied in the case of shares traded electronically through CREST.

92 In a like manner, the High Court in *Keston v IRC* [2004] EWHC 59 (Ch) held that a conveyance from a vendor to a sub-purchaser was chargeable to stamp duty. This could not be avoided by the interposition of a shell company and a sub-sale by that company on instalment terms.

93 Cf. *Henty & Constable (Brewers) Ltd v Inland Revenue Commissioners* [1961] 1 W.L.R. 1018, where the transaction was not categorised as a conveyance on sale and *Oughtred* was distinguished accordingly. It was, as Buckley J concluded at 1029, "a conveyance made in consequence of the sale, but not as part of the sale".

94 [1960] A.C. 206 at 232. Of these s.53(1)(c) cases, M.P. Thompson, ("Mere Formalities" [1996] Conv. 366, 369) describes *Oughtred* as being, "traditionally the hardest to explain . . .".

95 [1960] A.C. 206 at 233.

> Property Act, 1925, clearly made writing necessary to effect a transfer: and s.53(2) does not do away with that necessity".[96]

Lord Radcliffe, however, thought that s.53(2) did apply and Lords Keith and Jenkins expressed no view either way. This lack of a majority view enabled Nourse LJ in *Neville v Wilson*[97] to depart from Lord Denning's view and, following Lord Radcliffe's lead, to apply the statutory exemption to an equitable interest arising under a specifically enforceable contract.[98] He felt that to deny the application of s.53(2) would be to restrict the effect of the general words employed therein without justification and to signal problems for the future.[99]

Lord Jenkins (with whom Lord Keith agreed) took the view that, even if the oral contract did give rise to a constructive trust, the disputed transfer still operated as a transfer of the shares to the mother. He explained:

4-016

> "This interest under the contract is no doubt a proprietary interest of a sort . . . But its existence has never (so far as I know) been held to prevent a subsequent transfer, in performance of the contract, of the property contracted to be sold from constituting for stamp duty purposes a transfer on sale of the property in question".[100]

Lord Jenkins emphasised that the contract did not pass the full equitable interest in the shares:

> "In truth, the title secured by the purchaser by means of an actual transfer is different in kind from, and may well be far superior to, the special form of proprietary interest which equity confers on a purchaser in anticipation of such transfer".[101]

---

96 [1960] A.C. 206 at 233.
97 [1997] Ch. 144. It is what M.P. Thompson, "Mere Formalities" [1996] Conv. 366, 371 calls "another example of the difficulties that the doctrine of conversion can create when one is considering the position of the parties under an uncompleted contract of sale".
98 This was an approach followed also by the High Court in *Singh v Anand* [2007] EWHC 3346 (Ch) where the principle expressed in the dissenting opinion of Lord Radcliffe in *Oughtred* was thought to be the correct interpretation. As Judge Norris QC concluded at [144], "as soon as the promise to transfer the equitable interest is made for consideration there arises a constructive trust which . . . renders compliance with s.53(1)(c) unnecessary".
99 See also, *Chinn v Collins* [1981] A.C. 533. P. Milne, "Oughtred revisited" (1997) 113 L.Q.R. 213, however, argues that the decision in *Neville* is unclear as to whether the original equitable interest is completely wiped out once the consideration has been paid or, instead, some equitable interest is retained by the original equitable owner.
100 [1960] A.C. 206 at 240. The vendor has been described as, "a trustee in a qualified sense only" (per Cotton LJ in *Rayner v Preston* (1881) 18 Ch. D. 1 at 6) and "a quasi trustee" (per Lord Greene MR in *Cumberland Consolidated Holdings Ltd v Ireland* [1946] K.B. 264 at 269).
101 [1960] A.C. 206 at 240; see also Lord Walker in *Jerome v Kelly* [2004] 1 W.L.R. 1409 who (at [32]) spoke of the provisional nature of this trust.

In this scenario, the equitable interest that exists in the purchaser until the contract is performed is of an interim and incomplete nature. This potential vulnerability is what Lord Jenkins was referring to and he was responding to an argument put forward by counsel as to what would happen if the contract were not performed. Lord Jenkins was accepting that, if the contract had been rescinded or specific performance for some reason ceased to be available (e.g. the son sold his reversionary interest to a bona fide purchaser), the constructive trust would be discharged. It could not be said that the mother ever had the entire equitable interest until the transfer of the legal title to her.

Battersby, however, argues that this approach is true when the property being purchased (as in *Oughtred*) includes the legal title, "but is not true where the property is a mere equitable interest".[102] This argument enjoys some appeal. It is obvious that a contract to purchase the legal estate in property will, pending completion of the transaction, only pass an equitable interest in that property. Full legal and beneficial title cannot, of course, pass by virtue of the doctrine of conversion. As Millett LJ explained in *Bishop Square Ltd v Commissioners of Inland Revenue*:

> **"A transfer to a purchaser of the legal estate in property contracted to be sold is nevertheless a 'conveyance on sale', notwithstanding that the beneficial interest in the property has already passed to the transferee under a preceding contract for sale and even though the whole of the purchase consideration has been paid to the transferor before the transfer . . .".[103]**

Hence, in *Oughtred* the majority of the House of Lords were correct in the conclusion that the full equitable title was transferred only in writing, which was then subject to stamp duty.

4-017

If, however, the contract involves the transfer of the equitable interest only (i.e. it is not to be followed by the transfer of the legal estate), different considerations should, arguably, apply. There appears no reason why such a contract should not pass the full equitable title to the purchaser. If so, the equitable interest will transfer under the contract without the need for any written transfer. The vehicle of the constructive trust will, following the approach adopted by the Court of Appeal in *Neville v Wilson*, ensure that s.53(1)(c) is entirely bypassed.[104]

The minority of the House of Lords, namely Lord Radcliffe and Lord Cohen dissented from the majority thinking. Lord Radcliffe accepted that the whole point of the appeal was whether it was open to the court to deduce from the documentation that Mrs Oughtred's title to Peter's reversionary interest rested upon anything more than an oral agreement. He concluded, "my opinion is that such a deduction is not open to a court of law. The materials that would support

---

102 G. Battersby, "Formalities for the Disposition of Equitable Interests under a Trust" [1979] Conv. 17, 27.
103 (1999) 78 P. & C.R. 169 at 173.
104 This view enjoys some currency: see *Singh v Anand* [2007] EWHC 3346 (Ch); *Rashid v Ayub* (2001) 81 P. & C.R. D17.

it are simply not there".[105] On the oral contract, Peter created an equitable interest in his reversion in favour of his mother. He then became a constructive trustee for her of that interest and, having regard to s.53(2), the absence of writing did not prevent that trusteeship arising. In the words of Lord Radcliffe, "She was the effective owner of all outstanding equitable interests".[106] As to the transfer of legal title in the shares to the mother, this followed on the heels of the release which wound up the trust. Lord Radcliffe reasoned that the release acquitted the trustees from their duties. They were called on to transfer legal title only to the mother. He explained:

> "this transfer cannot be treated as a conveyance of the son's equitable reversion at all. The trustees had not got it: he never transferred or released it to them: how could they convey it?"[107]

The other dissentient, Lord Cohen, adopted a similar approach. Although the mother ended up as the absolute owner of the shares, as Lord Radcliffe emphasised:

> "that is description, not analysis. The question that is relevant . . . is how she came to occupy that position; a position which, under English law, could be reached by more than one road".[108]

Case 3: *Vandervell v IRC*

In *Vandervell v IRC*,[109] the House of Lords had to decide whether a direction by a settlor to his existing trustees to transfer legal and beneficial title to trust property to a third party was within s.53(1)(c). The National Provincial Bank held 100,000 shares in Vandervell Products Ltd on bare trust for Mr Vandervell. In 1958, he directed the Bank to transfer the shares to the Royal College of Surgeons to finance (at the expense of £150,000) a chair in pharmacology. The money was to be derived from the dividends paid on these shares. It was decided that the shares should not be given outright to the College and that an option to repurchase them for £5,000 should be granted to Vandervell Trustees Ltd. It was not, therefore, an unconditional transfer. Lord Reid took the view that:

4-018

> "this case provides yet another illustration of the folly of entering into an important transaction of an unusual character without

---

105 [1960] A.C. 206 at 227.
106 [1960] A.C. 206 at 228.
107 [1960] A.C. 206 at 228.
108 [1960] A.C. 206 at 228.
109 [1967] 2 A.C. 291.

> **first obtaining expert advice regarding tax liabilities which it may create".[110]**

The Inland Revenue mounted two alternative arguments. First, it was argued that the transfer of the shares was caught by s.53(1)(c). This argument was destined to fail. Secondly, the option to repurchase entailed that Mr Vandervell retained some equitable interest in the shares. This argument proved to be more fruitful for the Inland Revenue.

Was the transfer caught by s.53(1)(c)?

4-019

The Inland Revenue argued that there was no written disposition necessary to satisfy s.53(1) (c) and, accordingly, Mr Vandervell had failed to dispose of his equitable interest in the shares and was liable to pay surtax on the dividends paid under those shares. The contention failed because, on the facts, the legal and equitable title to the shares had moved within the same transaction. This was beyond the mischief of the provision which was to prevent hidden oral transactions and fraud which would, in turn, make it difficult for the trustees to ascertain who the true beneficiary is. It is interesting to consider how each of the Law Lords reasoned this outcome. Unfortunately, as Nolan points out, the decision is "far from easy to understand" and "equally difficult to justify as a matter of legal principle".[111]

Lord Upjohn took the view that:

> **"when the beneficial owner owns the whole beneficial estate and is in the position to give directions to his bare trustee with regard to the legal as well as the equitable estate there can be no possible ground for invoking the section where the beneficial owner wants to deal with the legal estate as well as the equitable estate".[112]**

Lord Upjohn emphasised that "the section is, in my opinion, directed to cases where dealings with the equitable estate are divorced from the legal estate . . .".[113] Lord Reid agreed that the first argument of the Inland Revenue was unsound, but did not take the matter further.[114]

4-020

Lord Donovan put forward the view that:

> **"If, owning the entire estate, legal and beneficial, in a piece of property, and desiring to transfer that entire interest to another, I do so by means of a disposition which ex facie deals only with the**

---

110 [1967] 2 A.C. 291 at 305.
111 R.C. Nolan, "*Vandervell v IRC*: A Case of Overreaching" [2002] C.L.J. 169, 169.
112 [1967] 2 A.C. 291 at 311.
113 [1967] 2 A.C. 291 at 312; see *Soomro v Khuhawar* [2015] 30 January unreported (HC).
114 [1967] 2 A.C. 291 at 307.

> **legal estate, it would be ridiculous to argue that s.53(1)(c) has not been complied with, and that therefore the legal estate alone has passed".[115]**

It did not matter that here the legal and equitable interest in the shares was in separate ownership. Mr Vandervell had the legal competence to direct his trustees to transfer both legal and equitable title to the College and when the trustees did so they disposed of the entire estate in the shares.[116]

Lord Wilberforce acknowledged that s.53(1)(c) "is certainly not easy to apply to the varied transactions in equitable interests that now occur", but concluded, "However, in this case no problem arises".[117] Mr Vandervell was the absolute master of the shares and could easily have made himself the sole legal and equitable owner of the shares.[118] Instead, he made a gift of them to the College. As Lord Wilberforce explained:

> **"The case should then be regarded as one in which the appellant himself has, with the intention to make a gift, put the College in a position to become the legal owner of the shares, which the College in fact became".[119]**

No separate transfer of the equitable interest was, therefore, necessary.

Following this unanimous conclusion of the House of Lords in *Vandervell*, it is relevant to revisit both *Grey v IRC* and *Oughtred v IRC*. It is seductive to argue that in *Grey*, although the identities of the trustees were unchanged, legal title was subsequently held by them in a different capacity (i.e. as trustees for the grandchildren instead of as trustees for Mr Hunter). If this equation is correct, should this not be treated the same as the directions in *Vandervell*? It would then follow that, because of this perceived movement of equitable and legal title, if *Grey* came before the courts today it would be held that s.53(1)(c) does not apply. This argument is, however, specious.[120] It is clear from the speeches of the Law Lords in *Vandervell* that what was envisaged was the transfer to one entity of the entire estate in the property. In this light, the transfer of the legal estate subsumes and carries in its wake the equitable estate. There is no separate disposition of a subsisting equitable interest. There is not a shred of support therein for the contention that the legal and equitable titles could remain distinct once the transaction is completed. Similarly, it would have been insufficient for Mr Hunter to direct his trustees to

4-021

---

115   [1967] 2 A.C. 291 at 317.
116   See also *Whitlock v Moree* [2017] UKPC 4.
117   [1967] 2 A.C. 291 at 329.
118   Under the rule in *Saunders v Vautier* (1841) 49 E.R. 282 collectively the beneficiaries can call for legal title and put an end to the trust. There is nothing to stop a new trust being declared and this would clearly be outside the scope of s.53(1)(c).
119   [1967] 2 A.C. 291 at 330.
120   See *JSC VTB Bank v Skurikhin* [2019] EWHC 1407 (Comm).

transfer legal title to new trustees and transfer equitable title to his grandchildren. Although there is a clear movement of both within the same transaction, the two species of title are treated differently and distinctly. This must amount to a disposition of an equitable interest for the purposes of s.53(1)(c). If it were otherwise, it would drive the proverbial coach and four through the provision. Accordingly, the outcome would, it is submitted, have been very different had Mr Vandervell attempted to move legal title one way and equitable title another.

In *Oughtred v IRC*, it would now appear possible (in the post-*Vandervell* era) for the mother and son to have sidestepped s.53(1)(c) altogether by orally directing the trustees to transfer both legal and equitable title to Mrs Oughtred. As legal and equitable title would then move at the same time to the same person, this would surely be a scenario where there would be nothing to which the provision could apply. Of course, the transfer of legal title to the shares would need to be effected by the completion of a share transfer form.

Nolan argues that the decision in *Vandervell v IRC* is best considered from the perspective of "overreaching", that is, the gift of the shares overreached Vandervell's equitable interest in them and, as a result, the Royal College acquired the shares free of that interest.[121] This is so even though the trustee received nothing in return for the shares.[122] Nolan concludes that, "if *Vandervell* is correctly understood as a case of overreaching, then law relating to overreaching can be used to determine what happens in various circumstances when a nominee, acting on instructions from his beneficiary, deals with an asset he holds for that beneficiary".[123] Although the concept of overreaching was not considered by the House of Lords, Nolan's alternative take (be it right or be it wrong) is convincingly argued and offers an attractive spin on the decision in *Vandervell*.

What of the option to purchase?

4-022

By a majority decision, Mr Vandervell lost the appeal on the second ground advanced by the Inland Revenue. This alternative argument was that Mr Vandervell had failed to divest himself completely of his equitable interest in the shares because of the option retained to repurchase them.[124] For these purposes, Mr Vandervell and not the College must be regarded as the real grantor of the option. Although the legal title to the option was validly vested in Vandervell

---

121 R.C. Nolan, "*Vandervell v IRC*: A Case of Overreaching" [2002] C.L.J. 169. As the author observes, p.175, "It is clear that an overreaching conveyance by trustees does not amount to a disposition within s. 53(1)(c) of the Law of Property Act 1925: such a conveyance is a disposition of legal title, free of an equitable interest".

122 As R.C. Nolan explains [2002] C.L.J. 169, 175, "gratuitous overreaching is not as unusual as might be thought. It often happens when trustees exercise a power of theirs to pay or transfer trust assets to someone who is not absolutely entitled to that property. Such 'powers to advance capital' or 'powers of advancement' are commonplace in settlements . . .".

123 R.C. Nolan [2002] C.L.J. 169, 170.

124 This prompted Megarry J to observe in *Re Vandervell* (*No.2*) [1974] 1 All E.R. 47 at 55 that "the consequences of granting the option had proved lamentable to all save the Inland Revenue. It was the option which had, I am told, prevented the College from recovering the income tax on the dividends which had constituted the gift, and

Trustees Ltd, no mention whatsoever was made of where the equitable title in the option was to lie. The option deed was too short and too simple. This omission ensured that the title to the option was held on resulting trust for Mr Vandervell. He was, therefore, liable to pay surtax on the dividends. The majority of the Law Lords reasoned as follows.

Lord Upjohn (with whom Lord Pearce agreed) acknowledged that the law relating to resulting trusts was not in doubt, but admitted that "The difficulty, and it is very great, lies in the application of those well-settled principles to the facts of the case".[125] Lord Upjohn outlined the basic principles to be applied:

> **"Where A transfers, or directs a trustee for him to transfer, the legal estate in property to B otherwise than for valuable consideration it is a question of the intention of A in making the transfer whether B was to take beneficially or on trust and, if the latter, on what trusts. If, as a matter of construction of the document transferring the legal estate, it is possible to discern A's intentions, that is an end of the matter . . . But, if, as in this case . . . the document is silent, then there is said to arise a resulting trust in favour of A".[126]**

In Lord Upjohn's eyes, Mr Vandervell had subjectively intended to give away all his beneficial interest in the shares, but had failed to do so because he retained the equitable interest in the option to repurchase them. It followed that, "If the beneficial interest was in A and he fails to give it away effectively to another . . . it must remain in him".[127] The trustee company, therefore, held the option on trust for Mr Vandervell until either he or the trustee company (as it was empowered to do) declared new trusts.

Lord Wilberforce admitted that whether or not a resulting trust arose in favour of Mr Vandervell hinged upon the interpretation placed on the facts as found. He had no difficulty in concluding as fact that Mr Vandervell had "failed to bring about the total divestiture" of his interest in the shares.[128] As there had been a failure securely to place the beneficial interest in the option elsewhere, Lord Wilberforce concluded that "the equitable or beneficial interest cannot remain in the air: the consequence in law must be that it remains with the settlor".[129] The trustee company necessarily held legal title on resulting trust for Mr Vandervell.

Lords Reid and Donovan (the minority voices on this point) both felt that there had been an outright grant of the option to the trustee company and that the company owned the option absolutely. Although Lord Reid agreed that "the beneficial interest must belong to or be held

4-023

---

it was the option which resulted in Mr Vandervell having to pay surtax on dividends that had never been his in any real sense of the word".

125 [1967] 2 A.C. 291 at 312.
126 [1967] 2 A.C. 291 at 312.
127 [1967] 2 A.C. 291 at 313.
128 [1967] 2 A.C. 291 at 324.
129 [1967] 2 A.C. 291 at 329.

for somebody: so if it was not to belong to the donee or to be held by him in trust for somebody it must remain with the donor",[130] on an examination of the transaction he concluded that the trustee company took an absolute right to the option. He could see nothing on which the inference of a resulting trust could be based. Lord Donovan advanced the view that the onus of proof lay with the Inland Revenue to establish a resulting trust of the option and that it had failed to discharge this burden. In any event, there was no hint of any trust evident on the face of the option deed and the language employed was of an absolute grant. There were also compelling fiscal reasons why Mr Vandervell would want the trustee company to hold the option absolutely. In these circumstances, Lord Donovan observed, "it is clear that one must walk a little warily upon the path leading to a resulting trust".[131] Looking at the situation objectively, he concluded that there was no scope for a resulting trust. As he explained, "There was no reason why the option should be held on trust for the appellant either expressly or by implication. On the contrary there were weighty reasons why it should not".[132]

Case 4: *Re Vandervell Trusts (No.2)*

4-024

To continue the Vandervell saga, Mr Vandervell wanted finally to rid himself entirely of any interest that he had in the shares. In 1961, he instructed his trustees to exercise the option given to them and orally directed them to hold the shares so repurchased on trust for his children. The trustees used £5,000 from a trust fund already established to benefit Mr Vandervell's children. Subsequently, the dividends of those shares were transferred to the children's trust fund. In 1965, and to resolve any doubts, Mr Vandervell executed a deed of release by which he transferred to Vandervell Trustees Ltd his equitable interest in the shares, expressly declaring that the shares were to be held on trust for his children. Mr Vandervell died in 1967 and made no further provision for his children in the belief that they were well provided for under the trust. Later that year, the Inland Revenue claimed tax from his executors on the dividends that had been paid between 1962 and 1965 (£769,580 net). The Inland Revenue asserted that Mr Vandervell had not disposed of his equitable interest in the shares until the execution of the deed of release. The executors commenced proceedings against Vandervell Trustees Ltd (the trustees of the children's settlement), claiming that the estate was entitled to the dividends paid (prior to 1965) to the trustee company, less the £5,000 paid on the exercise of the option by the trustee company. The Inland Revenue was not, however, allowed to join in the litigation.[133] The executors succeeded at first instance before Megarry J, but an appeal from this decision was unanimously upheld in the Court of Appeal.

---

130   [1967] 2 A.C. 291 at 307, 308.
131   [1967] 2 A.C. 291 at 322.
132   [1967] 2 A.C. 291 at 323.
133   As Megarry J put it in the High Court [1974] 1 All E.R. 47 at 55, "the Inland Revenue is awaiting the outcome of this case in the wings rather than being on the stage".

The reasoning of Megarry J

Megarry J considered the option to purchase the shares and concluded that "it would be quite unreal to say that in substance it was the college that provided the option; it was Mr Vandervell".[134] The option was, moreover, clearly held on automatic resulting trust for Mr Vandervell. As Megarry J argued, "What a man fails effectively to dispose of remains automatically vested in him . . .".[135] It could not be said that the option was held on trust for the children's settlement. Megarry J acknowledged that Mr Vandervell had wanted to rid himself of the shares and did not wish to retain any interest under the option. He continued:

> "Yet I cannot see how an intention not to get the shares back can negative a resulting trust . . . I do not see how the donor's intention not to have the beneficial interest can prevail when the resulting trust is automatic".[136]

He next considered the effect of the children's £5,000 used to exercise the option and explained:

> "That issue is, in essence, whether trustees who hold an option on trust for X will hold the shares obtained by exercising that option on trust for Y merely because they used Y's money in exercising the option. Authority apart, my answer would be an unhesitating No. The option belongs to X beneficially, and the money merely exercises rights that belong to X. Let the shares be worth £50,000, so that an option to purchase those shares for £5,000 is worth £45,000, and it will at once be seen what a monstrous result would be produced by allowing trustees to divert from their beneficiary X the benefits of what they hold on trust for him merely because they used Y's money instead of X's".[137]

In his opinion, the children had, instead, what is known as a "lien" (a charge) over the shares for the repayment of £5,000 plus interest, adding, "This in effect will restore the status quo ante as regards this payment".[138]

Megarry J then turned his attention to the issue of estoppel. It was claimed by the trustee company that Mr Vandervell knew that the exercise of the option was to be financed out of the funds of the children's settlement, intending and agreeing that the shares should become part of that settlement. The trustee company did this in reliance on Mr Vandervell's agreement

---

134   [1974] 1 All E.R. 47 at 61.
135   [1974] 1 All E.R. 47 at 64.
136   [1974] 1 All E.R. 47 at 72.
137   [1974] 1 All E.R. 47 at 72.
138   [1974] 1 All E.R. 47 at 73.

and, therefore, he (and, thereby, his estate) was estopped from asserting any claim to the shares. Megarry J was unimpressed with this argument. At the time the option was exercised, Mr Vandervell had not known that he was the beneficial owner of it. There could be no estoppel claim made out as:

> **"There is nothing inequitable in a man who has no knowledge that an option is his standing by while the option is exercised for the benefit of a settlement which he has some grounds for believing to be entitled to the option".[139]**

4-026

The final aspect of Megarry J's judgment concerned the now outmoded presumption of advancement. The trustee company submitted that the payment of the dividends over to the children's settlement gave rise to the presumption of a gift and prevented Mr Vandervell and his estate from claiming them back. Megarry J was again unimpressed:

> **"The dividends came from the ... Company and not from Mr Vandervell; there could therefore be no advancement, for the ... Company was neither the father of Mr Vandervell's children nor stood in loco parentis to them".[140]**

The divination of a new trust

4-027

The reasoning of Megarry J was not to be followed by the Court of Appeal. Lord Denning MR recognised that, when the option was exercised, the trustee company became the legal owner of the shares and held those shares on trust. Seizing upon Lord Upjohn's acceptance that the trust interest remained with Mr Vandervell until new trusts were declared by himself or the trustee company, Lord Denning regarded the children as the beneficiaries under a new trust declared by the trustee. He explained:

> **"This was a different kind of property altogether ... On this occasion a valid trust was created at the time of the transfer. It was manifested in clear and unmistakable fashion. It was precisely defined. The shares were to be held on the trusts of the children's settlement".[141]**

As the option rights had disappeared when the option was exercised, it was open for Mr Vandervell to direct the trustees to hold the property on new trusts without having to comply with s.53(1)(c).

---

139 [1974] 1 All E.R. 47 at 75.
140 [1974] 1 All E.R. 47 at 75.
141 [1974] Ch. 269 at 319.

The evidence of the intention to create a new trust was, in Lord Denning's view, indisputable. The key indicators of this intention were several-fold. First, that the trustee company had used the children's money to acquire the shares. Lord Denning noted that this would be a breach of trust unless it was intended that the shares were added to the children's settlement. Secondly, the trustee company had written to the Inland Revenue declaring that the shares were held by it on trust for the children. Thirdly, all the dividends subsequently received by the trustee company were paid into the children's settlement and treated as part of those funds. This was all done with the full assent of Mr Vandervell. In these circumstances Lord Denning concluded that, "Such being the intention, clear and manifest, at the time when the shares were conveyed to the trustee company, it is sufficient to create a trust".[142] It is, however, unclear how the trustee company could have declared a trust when it already believed that it was a trustee of the shares. There was not, as Harris points out, "a conscious dispositive *animus* of any kind".[143] The payment from the children's settlement, moreover, need not be decisive as the general rule (demonstrated by Megarry J in the High Court) is that he who merely pays will not own. In addition, it could be argued that both the notification to the Inland Revenue and the payment of dividends merely represented what the trustees thought the position was and should not be regarded as declarative of a trust. These actions could have been made under a mistake and, as Megarry J again demonstrated in the High Court, to yearn is not to transfer.

Stephenson LJ admitted that he was treading, what was for him, a "dark and unfamiliar path",[144] but was content to uphold the appeal, "as it seems to me to be in accordance with the justice and reality of the case".[145] Lawton LJ took the view that the children were the beneficiaries of a new trust which arose from the fact that their money had been used to exercise the option. He concluded:

> **"It follows that once the transfer of the shares had been registered the beneficial interest in them was held by the trustee company on trusts of the children's settlement so that no declaration of trust was necessary".[146]**

So what about s.53(1)(c)?

4-028

Not surprisingly, it was submitted that, despite this intention, there could be no trust because Mr Vandervell did not (until the deed of release) comply with s.53(1)(c) and could not, therefore, dispose of his subsisting equitable interest under the resulting trust. Lord Denning could not accept this approach:

---

142   [1974] Ch. 269 at 320.
143   J.W. Harris, "The Case of the Slippery Equity" [1985] 38 M.L.R. 557, 559.
144   [1974] Ch. 269 at 322.
145   [1974] Ch. 269 at 323.
146   [1974] Ch. 269 at 325.

> "There is a complete fallacy in that argument. A resulting trust for the settlor is born and dies without any writing at all. It comes into existence whenever there is a gap in the beneficial ownership. It ceases to exist whenever that gap is filled by someone becoming beneficially entitled. As soon as the gap is filled by the creation or declaration of a valid trust, the resulting trust comes to an end. In this case, before the option was exercised, there was a gap in beneficial ownership. So there was a resulting trust for Mr Vandervell. But as soon as the option was exercised and the shares registered in the trustees' name, there was created a valid trust of the shares in favour of the children's settlement. Not being a trust of land, it could be created without writing".[147]

The central notion, therefore, was that Mr Vandervell had not disposed of his equitable interest in 1961 (i.e. on the exercise of the option). As Lord Denning made clear, "All that happened was that his resulting trust came to an end—because there was created a new valid trust of the shares for the children's settlement".[148] Lawton LJ adopted a similar stance and reasoned that:

> "The exercise of the option and the transfer of the shares to the trustee company necessarily put an end to the resulting trust of the option. There could not be a resulting trust of a chose in action which was no more".[149]

Accordingly, neither the extinction of the resulting trust of the option nor the declaration of the new trust fell within the scope of s.53(1)(c). The conclusion that the termination of a resulting trust falls entirely outside the formality provisions is convenient. Although s.53(2) expressly exempts only the "creation" and "operation" of resulting trusts, the gloss applied by the Court of Appeal means that it also encompasses termination. Harris makes the astute observation that the case is authority for the following and novel proposition:

> "No disposition of an equitable interest needs to be in writing if the interest subsisted only by virtue of a resulting, implied or constructive trust, provided that the disposition brings the trust to an end. This would mean that someone in the position of the settlor in *Grey's* case could avoid the necessity for writing by transferring assets to persons named as trustees, avoiding declaring any trusts

---

147 [1974] Ch. 269 at 320.
148 [1974] Ch. 269 at 320.
149 [1974] Ch. 269 at 320.

> and relying on an automatic resulting trust to leave the beneficial interest in him; thereafter, he could make oral declarations shifting the beneficial interest".[150]

The role of estoppel

Lord Denning consolidated his decision by adding that, even if Mr Vandervell had retained a post-option equitable interest in the shares, he would have been estopped from asserting a claim against his children. This was to militate against the possibility that the resulting trust had not been extinguished, but had survived the exercise of the option.[151] Lord Denning explained:

4-029

> "Just see what happened. He himself arranged for the option to be exercised. He himself agreed to the shares being transferred to the trustee company. He himself procured his products company to declare dividends on the shares and to pay them to the trustee company for the benefit of the children. Thenceforward the trustee company invested the money and treated it as part of the children's settlement. If he himself had lived, and not died, he could not have claimed it back. He could not be heard to say that he did not intend the children's trust to have it. Even a court of equity would not allow him to do anything so inequitable and unjust. Now that he has died, his executors are in no better position".[152]

Put simply, Lord Denning concluded that Mr Vandervell's conduct was such that it would be inequitable for him to be able to rely upon his strict legal rights under the resulting trust. The children had acted to their detriment by sourcing the purchase money for the shares. Lawton LJ agreed that Mr Vandervell (and now his executors) would be estopped from denying the existence of a beneficial interest for the children.

A further example is *Singh v Anand*[153] where an estoppel arose following a promise that the representee would acquire a 33 per cent interest in a company. To the knowledge of the existing beneficial owner, the representee acted to his detriment on the strength of that representation. Although he received some payment, it did not fully compensate him for the work

---

150 [1985] 38 M.L.R. 557, 561.
151 It could not be invoked to prevent a challenge to a disposition that had been found to fall squarely within s.53(1)(c): *JSC VTB Bank v Skurikhin* [2019] EWHC 1407 (Comm). Mr Skurikhin could not claim that he had disposed of the legal interest in a manner that carried with it the beneficial interest and he was not the beneficiary under a resulting trust.
152 [1974] Ch. 269 at 321.
153 [2007] EWHC 3346 (Ch).

done. The court concluded that, despite an absence of signed writing, the representee ought to have had what he was promised.

There are, however, two problems with this approach on the facts of *Vandervell*. First, when enforcing an estoppel claim the court must afford the "minimum equity" necessary to redress the unconscionable treatment of the claimant.[154] As regards the equity afforded to the children, it is clearly over-generous. The payment of £5,000 as detriment is clearly dispro-portionate to the eventual benefit of the substantial dividends produced from the shares. By any lights, this is not representative of the "minimum equity" yardstick usually employed in the valuation of the claimant's interest under an estoppel.

Secondly, it is difficult to see what detriment (other than the payment of £5,000 which could easily be refunded) the children had suffered as a result of the representation that they were the beneficial owners of the shares. Indeed, Green argues that the only person who acted to his substantial detriment was Mr Vandervell himself. He had made his will on the basis that his children were otherwise provided for. This mistaken belief, it is contended, could justify an estoppel being raised against Mr Vandervell's executors. As Green admits, however, this would make Mr Vandervell "the only person in English law ever to have stood in the shoes of both 'estopped' and 'estopper' at one and the same time".[155]

Is Re Vandervell (No.2) correctly decided?

4-030

The decision of the appellate court in *Re Vandervell* (*No.2*) has been heavily criticised. For example, Battersby states that the decision of the Court of Appeal is "unsatisfactory and should be approached with caution by trust lawyers and tax planners".[156] It is, indeed, difficult on the facts to find that there was a genuine declaration of trust by the company who already thought that it was a trustee. It is also difficult to understand why, as there was a resulting trust of the option, there was not also a resulting trust of the shares that resulted from the exercise of the option. The practical consequence was that the beneficial interest passed from Mr Vandervell to his children under their settlements. This, however, appears very much like a disposition. Perhaps a major clue is to be found from the consideration by Lord Denning of what can be called the "hard cases" point. He commented:

> "Every unjust decision is a reproach to the law or to the judge who administers it. If the law should be in danger of doing injustice, then equity should be called in to remedy it. Equity was introduced to mitigate the rigour of the law. But in the present case it has been prayed in aid to do injustice on a large scale—to defeat the intentions of a dead man—to deprive his children of the benefits he pro-

154 See *Crabb v Arun DC* [1976] Ch. 179.
155 B. Green (1984) 47 M.L.R. 385, 420.
156 G. Battersby [1979] Conv. 17, 36.

> vided for them—and to expose his estate to the payment of tax of over £600,000. I am glad that we can overcome this most unjust result".[157]

The Court of Appeal, therefore, felt that it would be unfair to both Mr Vandervell and his children not to uphold the trust. As a result, the Inland Revenue withdrew its tax assessment for the period up to 1965. Any other outcome, as Gardner concludes,

> "would clearly have been unmeritorious in its disjuncture with the true nature and import of the circumstances. The fact that such distorted reasoning was required to circumvent s.53(1)(c) in aid of a more appropriate result, confirms the sense that the law would do better without the section".[158]

The problem, of course, is that this form of intuitive justice introduces uncertainty to the law and provides a dubious precedent for future cases. As Clarke comments of the Vandervell saga, "Charles Dickens would perhaps make a second Bleak House from it, but who, apart from the lawyers or the Revenue, really benefits from all this".[159]

Section 53(1)(c): A Synopsis

The operation of s.53(1)(c) is undeniably complex and defies ready understanding. It is, therefore, convenient to rehearse the key points concerning its application.

4-031

- ■ It is the transfer/disposition of an existing equitable interest under a trust that must be in signed writing.

- ■ The transfer of the beneficial interest of one beneficiary to another requires writing (*Grey v IRC; Oughtred v IRC*). This is so whether the transfer takes the form of an assignment or a direction to trustees.

- ■ Section 53(1)(c) does not apply when the entire legal and equitable interest in the property passes to a single entity (*Vandervell v IRC*). It is a dubious proposition to sug-

---

157 [1974] Ch. 269 at 322. Care must be taken to ensure that s.53(1)(c) is not itself used as an instrument of fraud: *Singh v Anand* [2007] EWHC 3346 (Ch).

158 S. Gardner, *An Introduction to the Law of Trusts*, 3rd edn (Oxford: Oxford University Press, 2011), p.107.

159 P.J. Clarke, "Mr Vandervell Again" [1974] Conv. 405, 413.

gest that the section similarly does not apply where legal title moves one way and equitable title another in the same transaction.

■ The provision does not apply to a disclaimer of an equitable interest. Hence, an attempted gift is ineffective if the donee disclaims before he has accepted it: *Re Paradise Motor Co.*[160]

■ If a sub-trust is created under which the beneficiary retains some function and thereby does not dispose of the entire beneficial interest, the traditional understanding is that this sub-trust is beyond the reach of s.53(1)(c). If the sub-trust involves a complete disposal of the beneficial interest, however, it is thought that this requires a written transfer.[161]

■ It was recognised in *Re Vandervell (No.2)* that the interest under a resulting trust can be disposed of without the need for writing. Similarly, in *Levi v Levi* it was held that the relinquishment of an interest under a constructive trust did not have to be in writing.[162]

■ It was also recognised in *Re Vandervell (No.2)* that, even though it is not specifically identified as an exception in s.53(2), an estoppel can circumvent the need for writing.

■ As regards a contract to transfer both legal and equitable title in, say, land or shares in a private company, the constructive trust that arises does not pass the full beneficial interest to the purchaser (*Oughtred v IRC*; *Bishop Square Ltd v Commissioners of Inland Revenue*). If it is only the equitable interest that is to be transferred, however, the constructive trust will operate outside the parameters of s.53(1)(c) (*Neville v Wilson*).

■ The operation of s.53(1)(c) can be excluded by Parliament as it does, for example, in relation to financial collateral arrangements[163] and to dispositions of units in unit trust schemes, so as to make transfers of such units possible by electronic communication.[164]

---

160 [1968] 1 W.L.R. 1125.
161 *Grainge v Wilberforce* (1889) 5 T.L.R. 436.
162 [2008] 2 P. & C.R. D1.
163 The Financial Collateral Arrangements (No.2) Regulations 2003 (SI 2003/3226); see *Mills v Sportsdirect.com Retail Ltd* [2010] EWHC 1072 (Ch).
164 The Unit Trusts (Electronic Communications) Order 2009 (SI 2009/555).

The Rules Against Perpetuity

An express trust that satisfies the requirements as to certainty, constitution and, when necessary, formality will, as a general rule, be valid. By way of an exception there exist the rules against perpetuity. These rules impose temporal limitations on trusts and operate to restrict the duration that property can be tied up by the settlor.[165] The rules are based on notions of public policy that property, particularly land, should not be rendered inalienable for an indefinite period. To allow such sterilisation would prove economically and socially undesirable. As Emery asks, "why should the dead rather than the living prescribe indefinitely who should be entitled to the use and enjoyment of property (the dead hand argument)?"[166] Accordingly, the law has, through the rules against perpetuity, achieved a compromise between settlor's wishing to restrict the use of property usually with a dead hand (i.e. from the grave) and the ability of future beneficiaries to dispose of the property free from any restraints imposed.[167] This compromise recognises that one person's freedom may well amount to another person's restriction. As Gardner explains:

4-032

> **"a settlor cannot legally provide for assets to remain subject to a trust for longer than legal policy will tolerate: there comes a point at which they must return into absolute ownership, and hence full marketability".[168]**

The law has, therefore, confined such settlements within narrow limits and invalidates them when they attempt to extend too far into the future.

Perpetuity has, at common law, traditionally been a major cause of trust failure. As will become clear, however, as regards dispositions occurring after the coming into force of the Perpetuities and Accumulations Acts 1964 and 2009, markedly fewer now fall foul of the perpetuity rules. There are three distinct rules, each of which will be considered in turn:

- the *rule against remoteness of future vesting*, which deals with future gifts and focuses upon how long the property can lie dormant before having to vest in a donee. Put simply, this is to do with the commencement of future interests and relates solely to what may be described as "people trusts";

- the *rule against inalienability* (sometimes referred to as the rule against perpetual purpose trusts), which deals with how long property can be rendered unmarketable

---

165 The rules, as P. Mathews, "The comparative importance of the Rule in *Saunders v Vautier*" (2006) 122 L.Q.R. 266 puts it, 278, "compromise between allowing land to be tied up forever, and not allowing it to be tied up at all".

166 C. Emery, "Do we need a Rule Against Perpetuities?" (1994) 57 M.L.R. 602, 603. For a useful snapshot of the development of the rules against perpetuity and accumulation, see P. Matthews, "The comparative importance of the rule in *Saunders v Vautier*" (2006) 122 L.Q.R. 266, 276–285.

167 See generally R. Deech, "Lives in Being Revived" (1981) 97 L.Q.R. 593.

168 Gardner, *An Introduction to the Law of Trusts,* 3rd edn (2011), p.45.

by the donor. As this rule concerns "purpose trusts", the rule against inalienability and the rule against remoteness of vesting operate in mutually exclusive spheres; and

- the *rule against accumulations*, which concerns how long the donor can insist that income be added to the capital and, for that period, effectively put income beyond the reach of the donee.

Remoteness of Vesting

4-033
The rule against remoteness of vesting strikes at trust provisions that attempt to sterilise capital (whether real or personal) either indefinitely or for a long period of time. The rule operates, as Emery explains, by "limiting the period of time for which the identity of persons unconditionally entitled to property in trust funds is permitted by law to be unascertainable".[169] All future gifts of property must occur behind a trust whether that trust is testamentary or inter vivos, private or charitable or fixed or discretionary. The rule applies also to powers of appointment. The rule against remoteness of vesting does not, however, have application to unconditional gifts that vest immediately. The rule is to do with interests that are contingent and not with those that are vested.

The rule against remoteness of vesting demands that the intended recipient must acquire his interest in the property (i.e. it must vest in interest) within a finite time frame. It is, therefore, aimed at future gifts that are subject to a condition or contingency that may or may not eventually be satisfied. For example, the donor might make a conditional or contingent gift under which the identity of the beneficiary will be unknown for years to come (e.g. a gift to my first descendant who qualifies as a barrister). Until a descendant qualifies as a barrister, the property will be tied up (i.e. it cannot be sold or otherwise disposed of). As it is possible that not one of the descendants ever becomes a barrister, it would be absurd if the property was frozen for hundreds of years awaiting the mere possibility that one of them might one day qualify. The requirement that the gift must vest (i.e. take effect) within the perpetuity period is, therefore, designed to avoid property being tied up for longer than a prescribed time. It ensures that the identity of any potential claimant will be ascertained within the permitted perpetuity time frame.

4-034
As will become clear, the applicable perpetuity period may differ according to whether the gift is governed by the common law perpetuity rules or, being made after 15 July 1964 and before 6 April 2010, is governed by the Perpetuities and Accumulations Act 1964. If the gift is made on or after 6 April 2010, then it is subject to the refashioned rules set out in the Perpetuities and Accumulations Act 2009. Accordingly, there are three codes that may apply

---

169 (1994) 57 M.L.R. 602, 602.

according to the date that the gift was created. As the Law Commission put it, "The existence of three distinct sets of rules is far from ideal, but it is preferable to the alternatives of no reform at all or retrospective reform".[170] Under either code, if the gift does not vest within the chosen period it is void.

A vested interest?

It is necessary that the property must "vest" within the perpetuity period. Remoteness of vesting is not concerned with the time that property may be kept once it has vested in the recipient. The example provided by Parker and Mellows is of when "an outright gift is made to a limited company so that the gift vests in the company immediately, that company may hold the property for more than a thousand years without ever infringing the rule against remoteness".[171] It is, therefore, crucial to understand what is meant by an interest having "vested" for these purposes. The requirement is that the property "vest in interest" within the perpetuity period. The time that it "vests in possession" is irrelevant.

    Vesting in interest occurs when a prior interest is all that stands between the interest holder and full enjoyment of the property. For example, consider a trust of property "to Jordan for life with remainder to Adrienne". Jordan's prior life interest is one vested both in interest and in possession (i.e. he has the right to the present enjoyment and use of the property). While Jordan remains in the land of the living, Adrienne's interest is one vested in interest, but not vested in possession (i.e. she does not have a present right to the use and enjoyment of the property). Both Jordan and Adrienne and their respective interests are ascertained and there are no conditions to be satisfied.

    In contrast, if the trust had been "to Jordan for life with remainder to Adrienne provided that she qualifies as a barrister", different considerations then apply to Adrienne. Her interest is now merely a contingent interest and does not become vested in any sense until the condition is fulfilled (i.e. until she qualifies as a barrister). It is with this type of contingent interest the rule against remoteness of vesting is concerned.

The common law perpetuity period

At common law, every gift of property must vest in its intended recipient within the duration of a finite period of 21 years or specified life or lives in being (i.e. a life or lives existing at the date the gift is made) plus 21 years. Put in a different way, the perpetuity period can extend 21 years beyond the death of the relevant life(s) in being. A life in being may include an embryonic child (*en ventre sa mere*) if this is relevant. For example, if the lives in being are expressed to be "my children", this will include a child who at the time of the gift is merely an embryo. It is not,

---

170 *The Rules against Perpetuities and Excessive Accumulations* (1998) Law Com. No.251, para.1.20.

171 Oakley, *Parker & Mellows The Modern Law Of Trusts*, 9th edn (2008), p.257.

4-035

4-036

4-037

however, possible to nominate, say, a tortoise or a tree as the life in being. The basic idea was to allow a testator to make provision for his future grandchildren in a way that the property would vest when those grandchildren reached the age of 21. Hayton and Mitchell provide a useful example of a testator who leaves his estate on trust for his widow for life, remainder to his only son for life with remainder to such of his grandchildren who attain 21 years of age.[172] As the authors demonstrate, these trusts are valid:

- the widow has a life interest that is a present right of present enjoyment (i.e. it is vested in both interest and possession);

- the son also has a vested interest in that it is a present right, but of future enjoyment (i.e. it is not yet vested in possession); and

- the grandchildren under 21 years of age merely have a contingent interest and not a present right (i.e. they have a contingent right to future enjoyment and have no right vested in interest). As the contingent right must necessarily vest in the grandchildren within 21 years of the death of the specified lives in being (the widow and the son) the perpetuity rule is satisfied.[173]

In principle, the donor can expressly select any living person or persons as the chosen yardstick.[174] For example, the trust for grandchildren might nominate the lives in being as the settlor's children (i.e. the parents of the intended beneficiaries). As shown above, this would ensure that all grandchildren who achieve 21 years will do so within the perpetuity period. Nevertheless, it became common practice to adopt what is termed a "royal lives clause". This election entails that the perpetuity period is keyed into the lifetime of members of the Royal Family.[175] By way of illustration, the perpetuity period could at common law expire 21 years after the death of the last survivor of all the lineal descendants of Queen Elizabeth II alive at the date of the gift. The Royal Family would, thereby, constitute the lives in being.

If no life in being is expressly selected, a life in being might be chosen implicitly. For example, "to the first child of Jordan to attain the age of 21 years" would be valid because it is undeniably certain that Jordan's first child will attain the required age within 21 years of the death of Jordan. Jordan would be the measuring life in being.

---

172 B. McFarlane and C. Mitchell, *Hayton and Mitchell Commentary and Cases on the Law of Trusts and Equitable Remedies*, 14th edn (London: Sweet and Maxwell, 2015), p.301.

173 If the testator had, instead, sought to benefit his grandchildren who reached the age of 22 years, this would have been invalid as running contrary to the common law rule against remoteness of vesting.

174 In *Re Moore* [1901] 1 Ch. 936, however, the settlor selected a perpetuity period as "21 years from the death of the last survivor of all persons who shall be living at my death". This failed for uncertainty because it would be impossible to say when the last person had died.

175 See *Re Villar* [1928] Ch. 471.

The wait and see rule

4-038

At common law, the vaguest possibility (however ludicrous) that the gift might not vest within the permitted period was enough to invalidate it ab initio. For example, in *Re Dawson* the possibility of a 60-year-old woman giving birth was factored in to the equation and rendered the trust void.[176] This was clearly an unsatisfactory state of affairs and entailed that, as Parker and Mellows put it, "common sense has gone straight out of the window and Alice has walked in the front door".[177] As regards the earlier example concerning the first descendant to qualify as a barrister, the gift would be void at common law because it is a possibility that it might not vest within the perpetuity period.

The Perpetuities and Accumulation Act 1964, however, counters the problem of the gift being invalidated at common law by the merest possibility of its failing to vest within the perpetuity period. Section 3 introduces what is styled a "wait and see" approach and this ensures that, if the gift eventually vests within the perpetuity period, it will be upheld. If it transpires that, at the end of the period, the gift has not vested then (and only then) will it become void. The wait and see approach, therefore, focuses upon actual events and not abstract possibilities. For example, a trust to benefit my first grandchild will be rendered void only if and when no grandchild emerges within the relevant perpetuity period.

4-039

The wait and see rule, however, only applies to dispositions made after 15 July 1964. The provision, moreover, embodies a major complication. It operates fully only to save gifts that would otherwise be void at common law when the perpetuity period is geared to the "statutory lives in being" listed in s.3(5). If there is no statutory life in being (e.g. a legacy by will to the first person who journeys to the centre of the earth, or where a royal lives clause is employed in a will), the perpetuity period for the wait and see provisions is 21 years.[178]

Section 4 of the 1964 Act contains a series of other gift-saving provisions, including the so-called "class-closing rule". This allows a gift to be upheld by the exclusion of a beneficiary whose inclusion would otherwise invalidate the gift. This imposes a cut-off point at the end of the perpetuity period that maintains the validity of the gift and closes the class of beneficiaries at that point.

Statutory lives in being for the wait and see provisions

4-040

For the purposes of the wait and see rule (and only for this rule), the 1964 Act defines the lives in being. These statutory lives in being are not identical to their common law counterparts. This means that if the interest would be void at common law on the basis that it might vest outside the perpetuity period, the interest will not be void until it is established that it will vest

---

176 (1888) 39 Ch. D. 155. A similar absence of reality was present in *Re Gaite* [1949] 1 All E.R. 459, where the court based its calculation on the basis that a girl below the age of five years could give birth.

177 Oakley, *Parker & Mellows The Modern Law Of Trusts*, 9th edn (2008), p.256.

178 Perpetuities and Accumulation Act 1964 s.3(4)(b).

outside the perpetuity period as measured by the statutory lives in being. Section 3(5) provides that, for the purposes of the wait and see provision, only the following who are living and ascertainable can be the life or lives in being:

- as regards a lifetime gift, the grantor (s.3(5)(a));

- in the case of a gift to a class, a beneficiary or potential beneficiary (s.3(5)(b)(i));

- the person upon whom any power, option or other right is conferred (s.3(5)(b)(v)); and

- any person on the failure or determination of whose prior interest the disposition is to take effect. For example, "to my wife for life with the remainder to be divided between my nephews who marry". The life in being may be the person having that prior interest, i.e. the wife (s.3(5)(d)).[179]

The 1964 Act

4-041

The Perpetuities and Accumulations Act 1964 retains the common law method of stating a perpetuity period with reference to a life or lives in being. It is possible, therefore, that a "royal lives clause" could still be used. Nevertheless, the most attractive feature of the 1964 Act is that it offered an alternative and more practical method of specifying the perpetuity period that is to operate. Section 1 offered the donor the straightforward option of stipulating a fixed period not exceeding 80 years within which the gift must vest in interest. Although the maximum period might be selected, it could manufacture a perpetuity period shorter than that available under common law. The benefit of simplicity outweighs this potential disadvantage. At least, it will be known in advance precisely when the trust will end.

It is hard to escape the conclusion that Parliament should have seized this opportunity to jettison entirely the common law rules. There is no doubt that, in maintaining a dual system, Parliament promoted what might be regarded as unnecessary complexity in an already difficult area of the law.

The 2009 Act

4-042

The Perpetuities and Accumulations Act 2009 adds a third level to the perpetuity rules. It is to be recalled that the 2009 Act applies only to trusts and wills created on or after 6 April 2010 and is, therefore, not retrospective in effect. The legislation represents an attempt to

---

179 Further provisions apply to powers of appointment and discretionary trusts. In short, the Perpetuities and Accumulation Act 1964 ss.3(3) and 15(2) ensure that these remain valid to the extent that the trustees exercise their power or discretion within the statutory perpetuity period.

modernise this aspect of the law and to bring it more into line with offshore jurisdictions. It was introduced following the deliberations of the Law Commission[180] and was designed to tackle the following problems:

- the conceptual difficulties arising from the inconsistency between the definitions of the common law lives in being and their statutory counterparts;

- the fact that the default position of a 21-year perpetuity period was too short to reflect what the parties would have actually intended, particularly so in the commercial arena;

- the unfairness of the present rules in circumstances, say, where a provision in a will is void for offending the perpetuity rules as to vesting. The failure would entail that the property would pass instead to the residuary estate and to someone who is unlikely to be the person who was to have benefited under the invalid disposition. In other words, the rules are capable of producing a result that the testator simply did not intend;

- the potential that the rules constituted a trap for the unwary settlor and generated increased legal costs for those sufficiently knowledgeable to ensure compliance with them; and

- the fact that the rules were out of step with contemporary attitudes to property ownership.

4-043

The 2009 Act retains the rule against remoteness of future vesting, but makes it more straightforward and easier to understand and operate. Section 5 provides that (as regards wills and trusts created on or after 6 April 2010)[181] the perpetuity period is 125 years. This period applies whether or not the instrument specifies a different perpetuity period.[182] It jettisons entirely the notion of a "life in being". This simplification will reduce difficulties faced by trustees in administering trust property subject to different perpetuity periods. The rule is now limited to future estates and interests in property that are held on trust.[183]

The "wait and see" rule is maintained by s.7 with the result that interests are treated as being valid until it is clear that they cannot vest within the perpetuity period. As with its prede-

---

180 See *The Law of Trusts: The Rules against Perpetuities and Excessive Accumulations* (1993) Consultation Paper No.133 and the Final Report, *The Rules against Perpetuities and Excessive Accumulations* (1998) Law Com. No.251.

181 Testamentary dispositions take effect at the date of death: Perpetuities and Accumulations Act 2009 s.20(6).

182 As regards trusts created prior to 6 April 2010, an application to vary the perpetuity period to 125 years can be made under the Variation of Trusts Act 1958: *A v B* [2016] EWHC 340 (Ch); *Allfrey v Allfrey* [2015] EWHC 1717 (Ch).

183 The rule no longer applies to commercial interests such as future easements, options and rights of pre-emption: see *Cosmichome Ltd v Southampton City Council* [2013] 1 W.L.R. 2436. Charitable trusts and pension schemes are exempted by s.2.

cessor, the 2009 Act also provides in s.8 for the exclusion of certain beneficiaries from a class of beneficiaries whose inclusion would cause an interest or estate to become void for remoteness. This class-closing rule allows a gift to be saved by the exclusion of a beneficiary whose inclusion would invalidate a gift.

There is, however, a retrospective facility offered by s.12 and this enables the trustees of existing trusts to opt for a perpetuity period of 100 years. This fiduciary power arises only when the existing perpetuity period is based on a specified life or lives in being and in circumstances where it is difficult or not reasonably practicable to ascertain whether or not the lives have ended. In such cases, the trust will be treated as if this had been the perpetuity period since the trust was established.[184]

The Rule Against Inalienability

4-044

The second rule (sometimes described as a rule against excessive duration or perpetual trusts) is that trust property shall not be subject to limitations that effectively render it inalienable. The driving force underlying the rule against inalienability is economic based and reflects the policy that property, particularly land, should not be tied up indefinitely.[185] As Emery comments, "The dead hand argument is another public interest argument based ultimately on the proposition that the deployment of the nation's wealth should not be entirely governed by the wishes and designs of the dead".[186]

The Perpetuities and Accumulations Acts of 1964 and 2009 have no effect on the rule against inalienability.[187] Accordingly, the common law period of a specified life or lives in being plus 21 years operates as the relevant perpetuity period. If no life is chosen, the perpetuity period will then be 21 years. No election for an 80-year fixed period is, therefore, possible. Similarly, there is no wait and see rule to be applied. Hence, such purpose trusts will be void unless it is certain from the outset that persons will become absolutely entitled to the property by the end of the perpetuity period.

4-045

The rule is directed against non-charitable purpose trusts.[188] As discussed in Ch.6, the general rule is that a private purpose trust will be void for want of a beneficiary. There exist, however, anomalous exceptions, which relate to, for example, the maintenance of tombs and monuments and horses and hounds. Hence, the settlor may attempt to set up a fund to

---

184 This will not affect the accumulation period of the trust.
185 See generally, I. Dawson, "The Rule Against Inalienability—A Rule Without a Purpose" (2006) 26 L.S. 414.
186 C. Emery, "Do we need a Rule Against Perpetuities?" (1994) 57 M.L.R. 602, 604.
187 Section 15(4) of the Perpetuities and Accumulation Act 1964; s.18 of the Perpetuities and Accumulations Act 2009.
188 Note that charities and most pension funds are exempted from the operation of the rule against inalienability.

maintain his own gravestone by directing his trustee to invest £10,000 and to use the interest obtained solely for this maintenance work. In this example, the settlor is attempting to keep the capital sum (£10,000) locked up permanently and well beyond the perpetuity period. The trust would, therefore, clearly offend the rule against inalienability. The need for a specific rule to cater for these admittedly rare circumstances is promoted by Hayton and Mitchell:

"Such a rule was necessary because purposes unlike individuals can last forever and because a rule against remoteness of vesting is inappropriate when interests cannot vest in purposes as opposed to persons".[189]

The Rule Against Excessive Accumulations

4-046

The underlying idea of the rule against accumulations is that it is to sidestep any requirement that income be added to capital (i.e. accumulated) for a period exceeding the perpetuity period. The ambition is to prevent the property (this time income) from being tied up indefinitely and to tackle what may be described as posthumous avarice.[190] This rule is again based upon the broad policy edict that property must not be rendered inalienable. The rule applies both to charitable and private trusts.

At common law, and in the same way as with the rules against remoteness of vesting and against inalienability, this rule was keyed into the perpetuity period of a life or lives in being plus 21 years. The 80-year term offered by the 1964 Act does not extend to accumulations. As a result of creative drafting of settlements, it became apparent to Parliament that the common law rule alone was insufficient to prevent excessive accumulations.[191]

4-047

Since the Accumulations Act 1800, Parliament has imposed additional restrictions. Their present incarnation is to be found within s.164 of the Law of Property Act 1925 and s.13 of the Perpetuities and Accumulations Act 1964. These provisions add a gloss to the common law and permit accumulation only for the restricted periods allowed therein. The settlor must expressly or impliedly choose one of the following periods for the duration of the accumulation:

- the life of the grantor or settlor;

- 21 years from the death of the grantor, settlor or testator;

189 McFarlane and Mitchell, *Hayton and Mitchell Commentary and Cases on the Law of Trusts and Equitable Remedies*, 14th edn (2015), p.303.
190 See *Re Earl of Berkeley* [1968] Ch. 744.
191 This realisation emerged from the decision in *Thellusson v Woodford* (1798) 4 Ves. Jun. 227, where the income was accumulated for almost 80 years and yet remained valid.

- the minority of any person(s) alive (or *en ventre sa mere*) at the death of the grantor, settlor or testator;

- the minority of any person(s) who would, if of full age, be entitled to the income to be accumulated;

- 21 years from the making of an inter vivos disposition;

- the minority of any person(s) in being at the date of making the inter vivos settlement.

Effect of excessive accumulation

4-048

In circumstances where an excessive accumulation has been directed, the outcome varies according to whether the direction violates the common law perpetuity period or one of the six statutory periods. A direction that contravenes the common law perpetuity period will be totally void and no income can be accumulated.[192] A direction that satisfies the common law, but exceeds the statutory time frame, will be valid until the lapse of the statutory period. Beyond this cut-off point, the income must be distributed.[193] For example, a direction to accumulate for the life of a member of the Royal Family, while effective at common law, is not one of the listed statutory periods and, therefore, the direction will be valid for 21 years.[194]

Accumulations and the 2009 Act

4-049

There is no doubt that the rule against accumulations is overly complex, uncertain and inconsistent. Unsurprisingly, therefore, major change was promoted in the Perpetuities and Accumulations Act 2009. Although not prospective in application, s.13 abolishes the rule against excessive accumulations for all non-charitable trusts created on or after 6 April 2010. A clause limiting accumulations need not now be included in the trust instrument. As regards charitable trusts, two accumulation periods are now available under s.14. The choice is narrowed to 21 years or the life of the settlor. This reflects the view that there is no longer a solid policy basis for restricting a settlor's ability to direct or allow for the accumulation of income, except in the case of charitable trusts. In relation to the latter, there is a public interest in limiting the time for accumulations and facilitating the spending of income for the public benefit.

---

192   *Curtis v Lukin* (1842) 5 Beav. 147.
193   *Re Watt's WT* [1936] 2 All E.R. 1555.
194   *Longden v Simson* (1806) 12 Ves. 295.

Guide to Further Reading

G. Battersby, "Formalities for the Disposition of Equitable Interests under a Trust" [1979] Conv. 17.

P.J. Clarke, "Mr Vandervell Again" [1974] Conv. 405.

C. Emery, "Do we Need a Rule Against Perpetuities?" (1994) 57 M.L.R. 602.

B. Green, "Grey, Oughtred and Vandervell—A Contextual Reappraisal" (1984) 47 M.L.R. 385.

J.W. Harris, "The Case of the Slippery Equity" (1985) 38 M.L.R. 557.

R.C. Nolan, "*Vandervell v IRC*: A Case of Overreaching" [2002] C.L.J. 169.

S.M. Spencer, "Of Concurring Beneficiaries and Transferring Trustees" [1967] Conv. 175.

5

Post-Mortem Trusts: Mutual Wills and Secret Trusts

5-001

A testamentary disposition, whether by gift or by trust, must comply with s.9 of the Wills Act 1837 (as amended). If it does not, the will fails and the gift or trust cannot take effect.[1] It is to be appreciated, moreover, that the formalities prescribed in s.53 of the Law of Property Act 1925 (as discussed in Ch.4) will not invalidate a trust created by will.[2] Hence the validity of a testamentary trust hinges upon whether the will itself was validly executed. The policy justification underlying s.9 is to prevent fraudulent claims being made against the deceased's estate when, of course, the testator is no longer able to disprove such claims. As Gulliver and Tilson observe, "The Statute of Wills may therefore reasonably incorporate unusual probative safeguards requiring evidence of testamentary intent to be cast in reliable and permanent form".[3] In the light that most people are aware that there are some formalities attendant upon the making of a will, "the problem of frustrating settlors ignorant of a certainty requirement is negligible, leaving very little to be said against the obvious advantages of imposing such a requirement: as the law does".[4]

A will has no legal significance until the demise of the testator and hence it can be modified or, indeed, revoked at any time prior to death.[5] Provided that it is valid, a later version automatically revokes any predecessor. Marriage also has an invalidating effect.[6] The requirements imposed by s.9 are that no will shall be valid unless:

---

1   A will can, however, be rectified under s.20 of the Administration of Justice Act 1982 to correct a clerical error. This can even be utilised to save an otherwise invalid will: *Marley v Rawlings* [2015] A.C. 129; see generally D. Hodge, "The correction of mirror wills: interpretation versus rectification" [2017] Conv. 45.
2   Section 55 of the 1925 Act.
3   A.G. Gulliver and C.J. Tilson, "Classification of Gratuitous Transfers" (1941) 51 Yale L.J. 1, 6.
4   S. Gardner, *An Introduction to the Law of Trusts* 3rd edn (Oxford: Oxford University Press, 2011), p.90.
5   *Re Heys* [1914] P. 192.
6   Section 18(1) of the Wills Act 1837. Divorce, however, does not automatically invalidate a will, but absent a

■ it is in writing;

■ it is signed either by the testator or, alternatively, by some other person provided that it is made in the presence of and at the direction of the testator;

■ this signature is made or, alternatively, acknowledged by the testator in the presence of at least two witnesses present at the same time; and

■ each witness signs his name in the presence of the testator, but not necessarily in the presence of the other witness.[7] It suffices for witnesses merely to write their names with the intention that this should operate as an attestation.[8]

5-002

Two key principles underpinning probate law are, first, that the testator enjoys the freedom of testamentary disposition which, as indicated, entails that he is free to revoke a will at his pleasure. A major exception to this rule, however, takes the form of the doctrine of "mutual wills". This operates to curtail the ability of the testator to change his plans. Secondly, the terms of a legacy or a testamentary trust must be disclosed on the face of a validly executed will. If not, the legacy or trust will be invalid. An exception to this rule exists in the doctrine of secret trusts which, at least in appearance, drives the proverbial coach and horses through the provisions of the Wills Act. As Patten LJ explained in *De Bruyne v De Bruyne*:

> **"These cases do not depend on some form of detrimental reliance in order to re-balance the equities between competing claimants for the property. They concentrate instead on the circumstances in which the transferee came to acquire the property in order to provide the justification for the imposition of a trust. The most obvious examples are secret trusts and mutual wills in which property is transferred by will pursuant to an agreement that the transferee will hold the property on trust for a third party. In neither case does the intended beneficiary rely in any sense on the agreement (he may not even be aware of it) but, in both cases, equity will regard it as against conscience for the owner of the property to deny the terms upon which he received it".[9]**

---

contrary intention expressed in the will a former spouse cannot benefit (see generally the deliberations in the Law Commission Report, "Family Law: The Effect of Divorce on Wills" (1993) Law Com. No.217). A former spouse may claim instead under the discretionary jurisdiction afforded by the Inheritance (Provision for Family and Dependants) Act 1975.

7 It is likely that these formalities will be relaxed following the Law Commission's Consultation Paper, "Making a Will" (2017) Law Com. 231.

8 *Re Payne* [2018] EWCA Civ 985; see generally B. Sloan, "Testing times for attestation" [2019] Conv. 182.

9 [2010] EWCA Civ 519 at [51].

The Doctrine of Mutual Wills

Mutual wills arise where two or more parties (usually, but not necessarily, husband and wife) enter into a binding agreement that they will execute wills in a mutual form (or rarely a joint will) on the understanding that those wills are irrevocable and with the intention of benefiting a third party. It is much more than merely having mirror wills. For example, Adrienne and Fred may enter into an agreement that each executes a will under which the surviving spouse will inherit the property of the deceased spouse. The condition attached is that the surviving spouse must bequeath his or her property to their children. Of course, neither Fred nor Adrienne will know which of them will die first, but on the death of the first the other's estate will be increased. The increased estate will then, on the death of the surviving spouse, devolve to the children as per the arrangement. The parties having entered what might be called a "mutual wills contract".[10] In 1980, the Law Reform Committee considered whether mutual wills should be abolished and decided against such reform or, indeed, any form of statutory regulation.[11] It is to be appreciated, however, that mutual wills are anomalous, uncommon and only occasionally cause problems in the real world. As Pawlowski and Brown point out, "Although much space is devoted in the textbooks on equity and trusts to a discussion of mutual wills, the reality is that such wills are seldom used in practice . . . mutual wills are seen by most solicitors as having a number of inherent flaws and practical difficulties which make their use highly unattractive in the vast majority of cases".[12] An obvious defect is that mutual wills prevent the surviving testator from responding to changes of lifestyle that occur after the first testator's death. Similarly, such irrevocable wills might also energise family tensions and might be viewed as reflecting a Victorian sentiment that a surviving spouse (usually female) should be tethered by the wishes of the of the deceased.[13] It also entails that the survivor's estate cannot be challenged under the Inheritance (Provision for Family and Dependants) Act 1975.[14]

On the date of death of the first testator, equity regards the mutual wills as being irrevocable.[15] This inflexibility prevents the survivor from having a change of heart and leaving the property elsewhere (e.g. to a new spouse).[16] For example, in *Legg v Burton* a father and mother

---

10 As Rimer J observed in *Birch v Curtis* [2002] EWHC 1158 (Ch) at [62], "If there is no such contract, then the doctrine of mutual wills will simply not apply at all". See also *Davies v The Commissioners for Her Majesty's Revenue and Customs* [2009] UKFTT 138 (TC).

11 Law Reform Committee, *Twenty-second Report of the Law Reform Committee on the Making and Revocation of Wills* (1980) Cmnd.7902, paras 3.50–3.52. The Committee felt it was best for the courts to monitor the operation of mutual wills. Reforms are again on the agenda following the Law Commission's Consultation Paper, "Making a Will" (2017) Law Com. 231.

12 M. Pawlowski and J. Brown, "Problems with Mutual Wills—A Study of Probate Practice" [2012] Conv. 467 at 467, 468.

13 See the Law Commission's Consultation Paper, "Making a Will" (2017) Law Com. 231, para.122.

14 The Law Commission did not propose abolition, but felt that property subject to a mutual will should be within the definition of an estate for the purposes of the 1975 Act.

15 *Birmingham v Renfrew* (1937) 57 C.L.R. 666; *Fry v Densham-Smith* [2010] EWCA Civ 1410.

16 *Dufour v Pereira* (1769) 1 Dick 419; *Olins v Walters* [2009] Ch. 212.

each made a will (the one the mirror of the other) under which each left their estate to the surviving spouse absolutely on condition that the surviving spouse would leave his or her property to their two daughters.[17] The mutual wills doctrine operated and a subsequent will made by the widow was ineffective to defeat the entitlement of the daughters. In order to manufacture this result, equity imposes a constructive trust that binds the survivor and prevents disposal otherwise than under the terms of the mutual agreement.[18] As the agreement between the parties need not be contained in the wills themselves, the imposition of the constructive trust operates by way of an exception to s.9 of the Wills Act and curtails the freedom of testamentary disposition of the survivor.[19] This consequence is justified on the basis that equity will intervene in order to prevent the fraud that would arise if the survivor were able to take the benefit of the agreement without performing his obligations. For example, in *Re Dale*,[20] a husband and wife entered into mutual wills under which their estates were to be left to their son and daughter equally. The husband died first and his estate devolved according to the agreement. Subsequently, the wife executed a new will under which she left most of her estate to her son. The later will was disputed and the court held that, as the husband and wife had entered into a binding agreement to create mutual wills, the son became the constructive trustee of his mother's estate, holding the property on trust for himself and his sister equally. More recently in *Olins v Walters*, Mummery LJ emphasised that:

> "The obligation on the surviving testator is equitable. It is in the nature of a trust of the property affected so the constructive trust label is attached to it. The equitable obligation is imposed for the benefit of third parties, who were intended by the parties to benefit from it. It arises by operation of law on the death of the first testator to die so as to bind the conscience of the surviving testator in relation to the property affected".[21]

A binding agreement

5-004

For mutual wills to be recognised by the court, there must be a legally binding agreement between the parties that the wills are to be irrevocable.[22] The doctrine is not founded upon

---

17   [2017] EWHC 2088 (Ch).
18   See *Re Cleaver* [1981] 1 W.L.R. 939. This element of trust law was necessary because of the general rule that only a party to a contract can sue on the contract. Hence, without the trust the beneficiaries would, at common law, be unable to enforce the terms of a revoked mutual will: *Olins v Walters* [2009] Ch. 212.
19   As Judge Paul Matthews explained in *Legg v Burton* [2017] EWHC 2088 (Ch) at [71], "In equity at least, the clock of her testamentary freedom had stopped with the death of her husband, and thereafter she no longer retained the unilateral right to dispose of her assets that she had once enjoyed".
20   [1994] Ch. 31.
21   [2009] Ch. 212 at [37].
22   *Re Oldham* [1925] Ch. 75.

some broad-based equitable notion of benefit and burden.[23] As Judge Paul Matthews noted, "there is a crucial difference between an obligation which is legally binding, and which will be enforced by the court, and an obligation binding in honour only".[24] The agreement, of course, must be sufficiently certain so that it can be enforced.[25] As Viscount Haldane put it in *Gray v Perpetual Trustee Co Ltd*, "without such a definite agreement there can no more be a trust in equity than a right to damages at law".[26] The agreement must, moreover, be proved and, as Latham LJ stated, "Those who undertake to establish such an agreement assume a heavy burden of proof. It is easy to allege such an agreement after the parties to it have both died, and any court should be very careful in accepting the evidence of interested persons upon such a question".[27] Dixon J shared this sentiment that, "Such an agreement can be established only by clear and satisfactory evidence. It is obvious that there is a great need for caution in accepting proofs advanced in support of an agreement affecting and possibly defeating testamentary dispositions of valuable property".[28]

It is a matter of construction as to what was agreed that determines the terms of the trust. The terms will, of course, differ on a case by case basis. As Leggatt LJ explained in *Re Goodchild*, "A key feature of the concept of mutual wills is the irrevocability of the mutual intentions. Not only must they be binding when made, but the testators must have undertaken, and so must be bound, not to change their intentions after the death of the first testator".[29] The existence of an agreement must be established on a balance of probabilities. If there is no contract, the survivor retains the ability to dispose of the property under a new will at a future date.[30]

As in *Re Hagger*,[31] it is a much more straightforward matter if the agreement not to revoke is recited in the wills themselves. It is not, however, necessary that the wills make any reference to the agreement. Nevertheless, as Astbury J demonstrated in *Re Oldham*, a trust is not to be inferred merely because the wills share corresponding terms as this, "does not necessarily connote any agreement beyond that of so making them".[32] He further observed:

5-005

---

23   *Birch v Curtis* [2002] EWHC 1158 (Ch).
24   *Legg v Burton* [2017] EWHC 2088 (Ch) at [20].
25   As explained by Mummery LJ in *Olins v Walters* [2009] Ch. 212 at [36], "it is a legally necessary condition of mutual wills that there is clear and satisfactory evidence of a contract between two testators . . .".
26   [1928] A.C. 391 PC at 400.
27   *Birmingham v Renfrew* (1937) 57 C.L.R. 666 at 674. Unusually in *Olins v Walters* the agreement was challenged by the surviving testator. Most cases concern the period after the death of the survivor.
28   (1937) 57 C.L.R. 666 at 681.
29   [1997] 3 All E.R. 63 at 71. Leggatt LJ could find no mutual intention that both wills remain unaltered on the facts before him. Although the wife had thought that this would be so, the husband had not.
30   See *Re Oldham* [1925] Ch. 75.
31   [1930] 2 Ch. 190.
32   [1925] Ch. 75 at 88. As Astbury J explained at 88, "there are many reasons which may have operated on the minds of these mutual will makers. Each may have thought it quite safe to trust the other, and to believe that, having regard to their ages, nothing was likely to occur in the future substantially to diminish the property taken by the survivor, who could be trusted to give effect to the other's obvious wishes. But that is a very different thing from saying that they bound themselves by a trust that should be operative in all circumstances and all cases".

> "Of course it is a strong thing that these two parties came together, agreed to make their wills in identical terms and in fact so made them. But that does not go nearly far enough".[33]

The court can, however, scout elsewhere for evidence of the legally binding obligation. In *Re Dale*, Morritt J commented upon the nature of this agreement, reflecting that, "for the doctrine to apply there must be a contract at law . . . it is necessary to establish an agreement to make and not to revoke mutual wills, some understanding or arrangement being insufficient . . . it is necessary to find consideration sufficient to support a contract at law . . . The performance of that promise by the execution of the will by the first testator is in my judgment sufficient consideration by itself".[34] If the property includes land, the normal rule is that the contract must be in writing and signed by both parties: s.2 of the Law of Property (Miscellaneous) Provisions Act 1989. Nevertheless, this formality may also be overridden in order to prevent fraud[35] and, in any event, a constructive trust does not need to satisfy the formalities.[36]

It is not necessary that the disposition favours the survivor and it suffices that the mutual agreement is to benefit a third party (e.g. a child or a charitable body). In addition, it appears unnecessary for the wills to be in similar forms. There is no reason why there cannot be mutual wills where the agreement is that Adrienne leaves a will benefiting Fred on condition that Fred leaves a will benefiting Fiona.[37]

Acting on the agreement?

5-006

It is necessary that there must be a disposition in consequence of the agreement to create mutual wills. This gives rise to a number of issues. First, it means that equity will intervene only once one of the parties has died leaving a will as agreed with the other. Until that time, the wills can be revoked by mutual agreement. Unilateral revocation, however, would amount to a breach of contract. The problem with the latter course of action is that damages recovered are likely to be nominal because the claimant has suffered no real loss.[38]

Secondly, if the first party to die does not leave a will as agreed, it is possible that a survivor can claim (usually only nominal) damages for breach of contract against the deceased's

---

33 [1925] Ch. 75 at 87. A sentiment echoed by Deputy Judge Anthony Elleray QC in *Jiggins v Brisley* [2003] EWHC 841 (Ch) at [68], "The making of wills in similar terms, is merely part of the evidence which must be considered, if it is to be established that the testators had the intention to create a binding contract".
34 [1994] Ch. 31 at 38.
35 *Healey v Brown* [2002] W.T.L.R. 849.
36 *Legg v Burton* [2017] EWHC 2088 (Ch). In *Shovelar v Lane* [2012] 1 W.L.R. 637 at [48], Ward LJ admitted that that the executors "took a bad point" in raising the s.2 defence where the agreement underpinning the mutual wills concerned a bungalow.
37 See *Birch v Curtis* [2002] EWHC 1158 (Ch).
38 *Robinson v Ommanney* (1883) 23 Ch. D. 285; *Beswick v Beswick* [1968] A.C. 58.

estate. In the normal course of events, the survivor will instead change his own will as he is now released from obligations under the agreement.[39]

5-007

Thirdly, as mentioned, if the survivor revokes his will after the death of the other party, a constructive trust attaches to the property that passes to his executor (under any new will) or his administrator (if the survivor dies intestate).[40] If the agreement identifies specific property, this property can be recovered by the beneficiary from the survivor's estate. Indeed, it would seem that the beneficiary can obtain an injunction restraining any dealing with that specific property. Where, however, the specific property has been disposed of, the beneficiary's entitlement will be for its financial equivalent. If the subject matter of the trust (as is common) is identified as being the survivor's residuary estate, different considerations arise. It is, as Carnwath J acknowledged in the High Court in *Re Goodchild*, "an unusual form of trust, since it does not prevent the surviving testator using the assets during his lifetime. It is a kind of floating trust which finally attaches to such property as he leaves upon his death".[41] On a practical level, the floating trust approach entails that the value of the residuary estate to which the trust attaches can increase as well as decrease over the intervening years. A trust of such uncertain property would, in the normal course of events, be void.[42] As accepted in *Re Cleaver*,[43] it is only by the special rules of equity that such a suspended, floating obligation can crystallise into a trust on the death of the survivor.

A summary of the rules

In *Charles v Fraser*,[44] the features of mutual wills were helpfully identified by Jonathan Gaunt QC as follows:

5-008

- ■ mutual wills are wills made by two or more persons, usually in substantially the same terms and conferring reciprocal benefits, following an agreement between the parties not to revoke them without the consent of the other;

- ■ there must be what amounts to a contract between the two testators that both wills will be irrevocable and remain unaltered. A common ambition or desire is insufficient;

- ■ the mere execution of mirror wills does not imply any agreement either as to revocation or non-revocation[45];

---

39   *Re Hobley, The Times* 16 June 1997.
40   If the deceased's personal representative fails to administer the estate as required by the mutual wills, he can be replaced under s.1 of the Judicial Trustees Act 1896 (but not under s.50 of the Administration of Justice Act 1985): *Thomas & Agnes Carvel Foundation v Carvel* [2008] Ch. 395.
41   [1996] 1 W.L.R. 694 at 700.
42   *Re Jones* [1898] 1 Ch. 438.
43   [1981] 1 W.L.R. 939.
44   [2010] EWHC 2154 (Ch) at [59]; see also Y.K. Liew, "The Ambit of the Mutual Wills Doctrine" [2016] 132 L.Q.R. 664.
45   See *Marley v Rawlings* [2015] A.C. 129.

■ it is not necessary that the second testator should have obtained a personal financial benefit under the will of the first testator;

■ it is possible for there to be an agreement preventing revocability as to part of the residuary estate only, in which case the doctrine only applies to that part[46];

■ the agreement (which may be oral or in writing) might be incorporated in the will or proved by extrinsic evidence;

■ the agreement must be established on the balance of probabilities;

■ the agreement is enforced in equity by the imposition of a constructive trust on the property which is the subject matter of the agreement;

■ it is unclear whether property acquired after the death of the first testator would be the subject of the constructive trust. Mitchell, however, believes that, unless excluded in the agreement between the parties, it will cover after acquired property[47];

■ the rule relates only to the dispositive part of the will. The new will is fully effective to deal with non-dispositive matters, say as to the appointment of executors.

Secret Trusts

5-009

As shown above, testamentary dispositions (including trusts) must be executed and attested in compliance with the formalities prescribed in s.9 of the Wills Act 1837. The key features of that prescription are, it is to be recalled, writing, signature and attestation. The general rule is that any purported legacy or testamentary trust, which is not specified in a valid will is ineffective. An exception to this rule lies with so-called "secret trusts". These are testamentary trusts that usually arise in circumstances where the settlor leaves a legacy in his will on the secret understanding that the legatee (a trusted person such as a solicitor) will hold that property on trust for a third party.[48] Secret trusts can also occur when, on the strength of the recipient's under-

---

46 *Re Green* [1951] Ch. 148.

47 J.D.B. Mitchell, "Some Aspects of Mutual Wills" (1951) 14 M.L.R. 136.

48 See *Crook v Brooking* (1688) 2 Vern. 50. It is not, however, a popular form of testamentary disposition (see R. Meager, "Secret Trusts—do they have a Future?" [2003] Conv. 203).

taking, a testamentary provision is left unrevoked[49] or no will is made at all.[50] The enforcement of a secret trust appears, therefore, to be a blatant contradiction of the clear requirements of the Wills Act. Nevertheless, the secret trustee cannot deny the trust on the ground of an absence of formality. As Parker and Mellows explain:

> "It is almost inevitable that the existence of secret trusts will only be able to be proved by evidence which does not comply with these requirements; the whole object of the exercise is to exclude the identity of the beneficiary from the formally attested documents admitted to probate. Inevitably, therefore, the evidence of the communication, acceptance and terms of the secret trust in question will be either oral or contained in a document which has not been properly signed and attested. The existence of secret trusts therefore involves a departure from both the letter and the spirit of the Wills Act . . .".[51]

The purpose of a secret trust is to keep the identity of the beneficiary undisclosed (e.g. when the secret beneficiary is the testator's illegitimate child or mistress or when it is an organisation that the testator does not wish openly to be associated with). This degree of secrecy might be viewed as necessary because, once probate is granted, a will becomes a document of public record. It can be inspected by anyone who pays the appropriate fee. As Jaconelli observes, "While the publishing of wills is useful in securing certain ends, it does carry with it the risk of harming the interests of a range of persons, especially their interests in reputation and privacy".[52]

5-010

An additional reason for using a secret trust is that it caters for flexibility and allows changes and future dispositions to be made without adherence to the Wills Act 1837. In particular, the so-called "fully secret trust" (where the existence of a trust is not disclosed on the face of the will and the legacy appears to be absolute) caters well for an indecisive testator who cannot make up his mind as to what property to leave to whom. Indeed, the testator's instructions to his trustee might change many times before his death. This prompted Watkin to assert that "the courts have left the door open for the doctrine to be used, perhaps abused, by the testator who is undecided rather than secretive".[53] Hence, the testator with a fully secret trust can leave a will and thereafter communicate his intentions to his trustee as to how the property is to be held. If those instructions change, the trustee will hold under the revised directions.[54]

As will become clear, however, the same degree of flexibility does not apply to the so-called "half-secret trust" (where the existence of a trust is revealed in the will, but the benefi-

---

49   See *Tharp v Tharp* [1916] 1 Ch. 142.
50   See *Re Gardner* [1920] 2 Ch. 523, where the trustee was the deceased's intestate successor.
51   A. Oakley, *Parker & Mellows The Modern Law Of Trusts*, 9th edn (London: Sweet & Maxwell, 2008), p.123.
52   J. Jaconelli, "Wills as Public Documents—Privacy and Property Rights" (2012) 71(1) C.L.J. 147, 157.
53   T.G. Watkin, "Cloaking a Contravention" [1981] Conv. 335, 341.
54   Such was accepted by Megarry VC in *Re Snowden* [1979] 2 All E.R. 172 at 177, 178.

ciary remains undisclosed). It will be shown that, if the terms of the trust are not communicated either before or, at the latest, contemporaneously with the will, there can be no half-secret trust.[55] Watkin suggests that the same rule should be extended to fully secret trusts in order to prevent the will being used as a cloak for the shifting intentions of a testator, stating, "The reformed rule would mean that if the testator wished his plan to be backed by legal sanctions, he would have to make up his mind as to who was to benefit at the latest by the time he made his will".[56] This would ensure that "Secrecy is indulged, but not indecision".[57] Of course, this revised rule could not apply when the fully secret trust arises on intestacy (i.e. when there is no will). It would require this admittedly rare type of fully secret trust to be treated differently from others.

Origins

5-011

The equitable principles relating to secret trusts date from at least the seventeenth century and their origin is often traced back to *Crook v Brooking*.[58] There a testator bequeathed £1,500 to two brothers (Simon and Joseph) to hold on secret trust, the terms of which had been communicated only to Simon. Subsequent to the death of the testator, Simon revealed the secret trust to Joseph. The beneficiaries of the oral secret trust claimed the £1,500. It was held that, as the testator had declared the terms of the trust to Simon, a secret trust existed and was enforceable. The case demonstrated that, provided that the terms of the trust are communicated to the legatee (or here one of the legatees) during the lifetime of the testator, an equitable obligation becomes attached to the legacy. Accordingly, if an informal secret trust exists, the secret beneficiary can enforce the trust against the actual recipient of the property. Although the obligation imposed is usually to make an inter vivos transfer to the secret beneficiary, it can be to make a will in favour of the secret beneficiary.[59]

In allowing secret trusts to be binding, equity appears to disregard the statutory requirements relating to testamentary dispositions. The doctrine of secret trusts has always, therefore, been of restricted application and subject to limitations. The enforceability of these post-mortem trusts is historically thought to rest squarely on the equitable maxim that "statute cannot be used as an instrument of fraud".[60] Hence, the doctrine was originally framed to prevent provisions such as s.9 operating to cause injustice. The traditional stance is that it would be a fraud to allow the recipient to keep the property, instead of holding it on trust for the undis-

---

55   *Re Keen* [1937] Ch. 236.

56   [1981] Conv. 335, 341.

57   [1981] Conv. 335, 341.

58   (1688) 2 Vern. 50.

59   *Ottaway v Norman* [1972] Ch. 698. As Brightman J observed at 711, "The basis of the doctrine of a secret trust is the obligation imposed on the conscience of the primary donee and it does not seem to me that there is any materiality in the machinery by which the donor intends that that obligation shall be carried out".

60   See *Thynn v Thynn* (1684) 1 Vern. 296; *Devonish v Baines* (1699) Prec. Ch. 3.

closed beneficiary.[61] The court, as Lord Cairns put it in *Jones v Badley*, "engrafts the trusts on the devise by admitting evidence which the statute would in terms exclude, in order to prevent a devisee from applying property to a purpose foreign to that for which he undertook to hold it".[62] This theme was revisited by Viscount Sumner in *Blackwell v Blackwell*:

> **"For the prevention of fraud Equity fastens on the conscience of the legatee a trust, a trust, that is, which would otherwise be inoperative; in other words it makes him do what the will in itself has nothing to do with, it lets him take what the will gives him and then makes him apply it, as the Court of conscience directs, and it does so in order to give effect to the wishes of the testator, which would not otherwise be effectual".[63]**

An alternative theory of more modern vintage is that the secret trust does not run contrary to the Wills Act at all. This is because the trust operates outside the will (i.e. dehors the will) and its existence is not, therefore, dependent upon the finding of fraud or the terms of the will. This approach was advanced by Megarry VC in *Re Snowden* who admitted that, "the whole basis of secret trusts . . . is that they operate outside the will, changing nothing that is written in it, and allowing it to operate according to its tenor, but then fastening a trust on to the property in the hands of the recipient".[64] The fraud and the *dehors* theories are evaluated below (see paras **5-035, 5-036**).

Types of secret trust

There are two types of secret trust: the fully secret trust and the half-secret trust. It is crucial to any understanding of this subject area that the distinction be drawn between these two varieties of secret trust. This is because, in some situations, different rules apply to each. There is also debate as to whether each shares the same theoretic justification for its existence. As to which category of secret trust has been created, it is necessary to look at the wording of the will.

5-012

With a fully secret trust it appears from the face of the will that the legatee is entitled to take the legacy absolutely. No indication of a trust or its terms is, therefore, discernible from the will itself.[65] Take, for example, a legacy of "£500,000 for Fred".

With a half-secret trust, the existence of a trust is not secret (i.e. it is mentioned in the will), but it is the terms of the trust (particularly, the identity of the beneficiary) that will remain private and undisclosed. Take, for example, a provision that reads, "£500,000 for Fred to be

5-013

---

61   See J.G. Fleming, "Secret Trusts" [1947] Conv. 28.
62   (1868) 3 Ch. App. 362 at 364.
63   [1929] A.C. 318 at 335.
64   [1979] 2 All E.R. 172 at 177.
65   *Rawstron v Freud* [2014] EWHC 2577 (Ch); noted by M. Thomas [2014] Tr. L.I. 157.

held on trust for such purposes as I have communicated to him". The trust (but not its terms) is evident from the will itself. Jaconelli describes this as "a teasing arrangement where the existence of the trust and the property subject to it are exposed to view, but not the identity of any beneficiary".[66]

5-014

Even though the differences between the two categories of secret trust are simple to state, in practice the distinction between them is not always easy to draw. Take, for example, the provision, "£500,000 to Fred knowing that he will carry out my wishes as I have communicated to him". Is this a fully secret or a half-secret trust? As this provision employs precatory words (i.e. words of aspiration and hope, "knowing that he will") no trust obligation is imposed by the will on Fred and, therefore, this is not a half-secret trust.[67] As Brightman J admitted in *Ottaway v Norman*, "it is an essential element that the testator must intend to subject the legatee to an obligation in favour of the intended beneficiary. That will be evidenced by appropriately imperative, as distinct from precatory language".[68] If, however, the previously communicated instructions to Fred imposed a legal obligation on him, the trust will be of the fully secret variety.[69] If Fred is not subject to any fiduciary obligation whatsoever, he can keep the £500,000. In *Rawstron v Freud*,[70] the High Court made clear that a will is to be interpreted in the same manner as employed in the construction of a contract. Accordingly, the court must look at the wording used, consider the purpose of the document, appraise the facts as known to the parties when the will was drafted and utilise commonsense.

Intestacy

5-015

Although it is usual for a secret trust to be created either behind or within a will, it is possible for a fully secret trust (but not a half-secret trust) to arise when there is no will at all. In *Sellack v Harris*,[71] a father was induced by his son not to make a will. The son assured the father that he would make provision for the mother, wife and child of the intending testator. The court compelled the son to perform the secret trust. As there was no will, this was necessarily a fully secret trust.[72] A similar line of reasoning would occur when a testator is persuaded to revoke

---

66   J. Jaconelli, "Wills as Public Documents—Privacy and Property Rights" (2012) 71(1) C.L.J. 147, 163. In *Rawstron v Freud* [2014] EWHC 2577 (Ch), the secret trustees acknowledged the existence of the trust, but downright refused to disclose its terms.

67   Care should be taken with some of the older cases because, as considered in Ch.2, until the late-nineteenth century precatory words could create a trust. This is no longer the case: *Margulies v Margulies* unreported 16 March 2000 CA.

68   [1972] Ch. 698 at 711.

69   *Irvine v Sullivan* (1869) L.R. 8 Eq. 673.

70   [2014] EWHC 2577 (Ch). Evidence of the parties' subjective intentions are irrelevant unless ambiguity exists or the words used are meaningless: s.21 of the Administration of Justice Act 1982.

71   (1708) 2 Eq. Ca. Ab. 46.

72   The possibility of a secret trust arising on intestacy was accepted also by the House of Lords in *McCormick v Grogan* (1869) L.R. 4 HL 82.

a will because of the inducement by either a legatee under the replacement will or, if none, a beneficiary under the intestacy rules.

Are secret trusts express or constructive trusts?

Sheridan argues that "The secret trust which arises without mention in the will (or on intestacy) is a constructive trust, not an express trust".[73] He bases his view upon the ground that, where a person has by a representation acquired property which it would be inequitable for him to keep, a constructive trust must arise. He adds that it makes no difference whether there is a transfer by will (as with a fully secret trust) or there is an inter vivos transfer.[74] The same rule must apply in both cases. As Sheridan explains, "The fact that the transaction is a secret trust does not make it different in principle. It is but one illustration of the broad principle of constructive trusts, and should be so recognised".[75]

As regards a half-secret trust, however, Sheridan contends that this must give rise to an express trust created by the will: "That much is clear, for whatever else happens or does not happen, there is a binding trust; the contest is only as to who is the beneficiary. There is certainly no question of the legatee obtaining property which it is inequitable for him to keep".[76] He recognises a lack of clarity emerging from the decided cases as to whether the nomination of the secret beneficiary was testamentary or non-testamentary. He concludes that:

> "The decisions are the result of confusing on the one hand a specific type of constructive trust with a specific type of express trust, and on the other hand secret trusts and incorporation by reference. In consequence, a strange third institution has grown up: an express trust, partaking of some of the rules of constructive trusts and some of the rules of incorporation by reference".[77]

Sheridan's distinction between fully secret trusts and half-secret trusts is supported also by Matthews,[78] but represents unpalatable reasoning for Hodge.[79] Hodge believes that both half-secret and fully secret trusts are express trusts. This, he contends, is because in both cases the trust arises from the expressed intentions of the deceased communicated to and accepted by the trustee in the testator's lifetime. The express trust model represents the majority thinking as to the nature of secret trusts.

5-016

5-017

73   L.A. Sheridan, "English and Irish Secret Trusts" (1951) 67 L.Q.R. 314, 323.
74   See *Bannister v Bannister* [1948] 2 All E.R. 133.
75   (1951) 67 L.Q.R. 314, 324.
76   (1951) 67 L.Q.R. 314, 324.
77   (1951) 67 L.Q.R. 314, 327 (Sweet & Maxwell).
78   P. Mathews, "The True Basis of the Half-Secret Trust?" [1979] Conv. 360.
79   D. Hodge, "Secret Trusts: The Fraud Theory Revisited" [1980] Conv. 341.

The upshot of this distinction is that, if a secret trust of land is classified as an express trust, it should (as discussed in Ch.4) be evidenced in writing by virtue of s.53(1)(b) of the Law of Property Act 1925. Similarly, if it is a secret trust of a subsisting equitable interest, the disposition should be created in writing for the purposes of s.53(1)(c). This would have startling consequences in that the secrecy element would have to be sacrificed. Fortunately, the debate as to whether a secret trust is truly an express trust or a constructive trust is, for practical purposes, rendered somewhat sterile. This is because, even if the secret trust is designated as an express trust, the absence of formality would be overlooked so as to prevent fraud. A constructive trust would then emerge from the ashes of the express trust and, as implied trusts are exempt from formalities by virtue of s.53(2), this remedial trust would ensure that the secret trust is enforceable. Accordingly, the same outcome would be reached regardless of whether the secret trust itself is express or constructive.[80]

Proving a secret trust

5-018

It is usually more difficult to prove the existence of a fully secret trust in circumstances where the intended trustee falsely denies that any communication and acceptance of the trust has occurred. The scope for fraud is obviously great. The testator (and/or, where relevant, his legal adviser) should take precautionary measures such as keeping copies of letters, maintaining a private record of what was said and when and disclosing the detail of the arrangement to another confidant (e.g. the beneficiary).[81] As Brightman J put it in *Ottaway v Norman*, "If a will contains a gift which is in terms absolute, clear evidence is needed before the court will assume that the testator did not mean what he said".[82] The ordinary civil standard of proof applies (i.e. on a balance of probabilities) to show the existence of a secret trust.[83]

As regards a half-secret trust, the potential for fraud is reduced because, as the trust is evident on the face of the will, the legatee can never keep the property himself. Nevertheless, there may be future dispute as to the identity of the secret beneficiary. Again the testator should leave some private documentary record of what was agreed and disclose the terms of the trust to someone else. It is to be appreciated, moreover, that as regards half-secret trusts, evidence cannot be introduced in order to contradict the will. For example, if the will refers to the terms of the trust having been communicated to the trustee by letter, the court cannot take on board

---

80   See generally, E. Challinor, "Debunking the Myth of the Secret Trust" [2005] Conv. 492.
81   As J. Jaconelli explains in "Wills as Public Documents—Privacy and Property Rights" (2012) 71(1) C.L.J. 147, 163, "secret trusts depend for their effective functioning on one category of person—the beneficiaries—being brought into the secret. Otherwise all hinges on the integrity of the secret trustee(s) and the assurance that he or they would not be tempted to divert the trust property into their own pockets".
82   [1972] Ch. 698 at 712. As J. Jaconelli puts it, "For, if secret trusts avoid the disadvantages of will publicity, they also lack its advantages. There is no effective means whereby a person who believes that he might be the beneficiary of such a trust can ascertain the true position" ("Wills as Public Documents—Privacy and Property Rights" (2012) 71(1) C.L.J. 147, 163).
83   *Re Snowden* [1979] 2 All E.R. 172.

any oral communication that occurred.[84] In *Re Huxtable*,[85] a half-secret trust of property for unspecified charitable purposes was indicated in the will. The trustee sought to convince the court that the trust was only to survive during the trustee's lifetime and that he would be able to dispose of the property under his own will. The court would not admit evidence of this as it conflicted with the statement in the will. In *Re Keen*,[86] the testator bequeathed property on the basis that the terms would be notified to the trustees after the will. The court concluded that evidence of pre-will conversations could not be adduced as it contradicted what was said (in the future tense) in the will. Similarly, a trustee under a half-secret trust cannot take as a beneficiary.[87] Evidence can, therefore, be adduced only to complement the terms and not to conflict with those terms.[88] This, of course, does not apply to fully secret trusts.

The Creation of a Secret Trust

A leading case concerning a fully secret trust is *Ottaway v Norman*.[89] By his will, Harry Ottaway left his bungalow, half of his residuary estate and £1,500 to his housekeeper, Ms Hodges. Before his death, it was orally agreed that she, in turn, would leave by her will the bungalow (and whatever money was left) to Harry's son, William. Ms Hodges later changed her mind and left all her property by will to another. William commenced proceedings against Ms Hodges' executor (Mr Norman) for a declaration that the appropriate parts of her estate were held by him on trust for William. The fully secret trust in relation to the bungalow was upheld, but not the trust in relation to the money. The terms of the trust as regards the latter were too unclear, meaningless and unworkable. The arrangement did not require Ms Hodges to keep the Ottaway money separate and distinct from her own funds. In the words of Brightman J, "If she had the right to mingle her own money with that derived from Mr Harry Ottaway, there would be no ascertainable property on which the trust could bite at her death".[90]

5-019

In the course of his judgment, Brightman J described Ms Hodges as the "primary donee" and William as the "secondary donee".[91] He outlined the three vital ingredients of a fully secret trust:

---

84   *Johnson v Ball* (1551) 5 De. G. & Sm. 85.
85   [1902] 2 Ch. 793.
86   [1937] Ch. 236.
87   *Re Ree's WT* [1950] Ch. 204.
88   See *Blackwell v Blackwell* [1929] A.C. 318.
89   [1972] Ch. 698.
90   [1972] Ch. 698 at 714.
91   See generally D. Hayton [1972] Conv. 129.

> "The essential elements which must be proved to exist are: (i) the intention of the testator to subject the primary donee to an obligation in favour of the secondary donee; (ii) communication of that intention to the primary donee; and (iii) the acceptance of that obligation by the primary donee either expressly or by acquiescence. It is immaterial whether these elements precede or succeed the will of the donor".[92]

As regards a half-secret trust, the same ingredients must be present: intention, communication and acceptance.[93] As will become clear, however, the rules as to the timing of communication differ markedly between the two types of trust.[94]

Stage 1: intention

5-020   The Court of Appeal in *Kasperbauer v Griffith*[95] demonstrated that a secret trust (of whatever category) requires the certainty of intention that it is a trust that is to be created. There, at a family gathering, the testator declared that he was to bequeath his house and a lump sum pension benefit to his wife on the understanding that she would use the money to discharge the mortgage on the house. He explained that the house was to be sold within one year of his death and the proceeds of sale divided between his children of a former marriage. The wife remained silent throughout the meeting. The testator eventually made a will in a different form from that predicted which ensured that the wife got everything and the children received no benefit. The children alleged that a fully secret trust had been established because, at the earlier meeting, the testator had said that the wife "knew what she had to do". This argument failed as the testator's words were viewed as being equivocal and sufficient only to impose a moral (i.e. not legal) obligation on the wife. The change of emphasis within the will was deemed to be consistent with the absence of an imperative obligation.[96]

In *Re Snowden*,[97] the testatrix bequeathed her estate to her brother with the rider that "he shall know what to do". The testatrix's niece and nephew claimed the benefit of a secret trust. The High Court held that the deceased had shown the intention only to impose a moral obligation on her brother. The words used were insufficient to impose any trust obligations upon him, i.e. there was no certainty of intention to create a secret trust. Similarly, in *McCormick v*

---

92   [1972] Ch. 698 at 711.
93   *Blackwell v Blackwell* [1929] A.C. 318.
94   See generally D. Wilde, "Secret and semi-secret trusts: justifying distinctions between the two" [1995] Conv. 366.
95   [2000] W.T.L.R. 333.
96   See also *Davies v The Commissioners for Her Majesty's Revenue and Customs* [2009] UKFTT 138 (TC) where there was no evidence of a legal duty being imposed by the deceased husband on his surviving wife.
97   [1979] 2 All E.R. 172.

Grogan[98] the testator wrote a weakly worded letter which read, "I do not wish you to act strictly to the foregoing instructions, but leave it entirely to your own good judgment to do as you think I would if living, and as the parties are deserving". This again did not reveal the intention to create a secret trust and, therefore, the legatee could keep the money absolutely.[99]

Stage 2: communication

As regards both the fully secret trust and the half-secret trust, it is crucial that the obligation to hold the property on trust and the terms of the trust (including the subject matter and its beneficiaries) be communicated to the trustee. Exactly what is to be communicated will depend upon the nature of the trust obligation imposed. For example, when there is more than one beneficiary the identity of all the beneficiaries and their entitlements under the secret trust will need to be divulged to the trustee. If, as in *Ottaway v Norman*, the trustee is to be given a life interest in the property, then this must be communicated to the secret trustee.

5-021

Valid communication can be oral or take the form of, for example, a letter, fax, text message, sign language or email. Communication can also occur via the testator's agent.[100] It is possible, moreover, that communication of the terms of the trust can be constructive. The classic example is where the trustee is given a letter marked "not to be opened until after my death". Provided the letter is handed to the secret trustee in the testator's lifetime, this will amount to an effective communication of the terms of the trust. In *Re Keen*,[101] the testator made his will and this disclosed the existence of a secret trust relating to the sum of £10,000. The trustee was handed a sealed envelope that contained the name of the secret beneficiary. The letter was not to be opened until after the death of the testator. Lord Wright MR drew the parallel that "a ship which sails under sealed orders, is sailing under orders though the exact terms are not ascertained by the captain till later".[102] The trustee had the means of ascertaining the identity of the beneficiary and this amounted to a sufficient communication. This possibility was also recognised in *Re Bateman's WT*.[103]

Communication and the fully secret trust

It is as to the timing of the communication that major differences emerge between the two styles of secret trust. In relation to a fully secret trust, communication must be made during the

5-022

---

98   (1869) L.R. 4 HL 82.
99   See also *Margulies v Margulies* unreported 16 March 2000.
100 See *Moss v Cooper* (1861) 1 J. & H. 352, where one of the secret trustees (acting on behalf of the testator) communicated the trust to the other two secret trustees.
101 [1937] Ch. 236.
102 [1937] Ch. 236 at 242.
103 [1970] 1 W.L.R. 1463.

lifetime of the testator (i.e. it must be made inter vivos).[104] Communication may occur either before or after the will is drafted.[105] As Wood VC commented, "it is altogether immaterial whether the promise is made before or after the execution of the will, that being a revocable instrument".[106] The ambulatory nature of a will, therefore, entailed that pre-will communication of the trust is not essential. As without inter vivos communication there cannot be a fully secret trust,[107] it follows that, if the communication is subsequent to death (e.g. by virtue of a letter found amongst the deceased's papers), the legatee can take the property absolutely. There is nothing that affects the conscience of the legatee and equity cannot intervene.[108]

In *Wallgrave v Tebbs*,[109] the testator left £12,000 in his will jointly to Mr Tebbs and Mr Martin. After the testator's death, a draft letter was found specifying how the testator wanted them to hold the money. The court held that, because there had been no communication of this to Tebbs and Martin before the testator's death, there could be no binding trust. Tebbs and Martin could, therefore, keep the money. If, however, the trust had been communicated in the testator's lifetime the secret trust would have been effective. As Wood VC explained:

> "Here there has been no such promise or undertaking on the part of the devisees. Here the devisees knew nothing of the testator's intention until after his death . . . Upon the face of the will, the parties take indisputably for their own benefit".[110]

5-023

A less straightforward case is *Re Boyes*.[111] There the testator told the intended trustee (his solicitor) that he was going to leave him property to be applied under a secret trust. The testator said that the terms of the trust would be communicated to the trustee within the testator's lifetime. This did not, however, occur. Following the death of the testator, two documents addressed to the solicitor were discovered and these directed the solicitor to hold the property on trust for the deceased's mistress and illegitimate child. Despite the presence of these documents, the High Court held that this post-mortem communication of the terms of the trust was insufficient. The solicitor could not keep the property for himself and, instead, held it on resulting trust for the deceased's estate. The underlying rationale is that the trustee must be offered the opportunity to refuse to act as the testator would wish. If the trustee refuses, the testator can then make another will and leave the property to some other person willing to act as trustee.[112] As Kay J commented in *Re Boyes*:

---

104 *Proby v Landor* (1860) 28 Beav. 504.
105 *Rawstron v Freud* [2014] EWHC 2577 (Ch).
106 *Moss v Cooper* (1861) 1 J. & H. 352 at 367.
107 *Ottaway v Norman* [1972] Ch. 698.
108 *Re Stirling* [1954] 1 W.L.R. 763.
109 (1855) 25 L.J. Ch. 241.
110 (1855) 25 L.J. Ch. 241 at 247.
111 (1884) 26 Ch. D. 531.
112 See *Re Gardner* [1920] 2 Ch. 523.

> "I cannot help regretting that the testator's intention of bounty should fail by reason of an informality of this kind, but in my opinion it would be a serious innovation upon the law relating to testamentary instruments if this were to be established as a trust . . .".[113]

Difficulties may also arise, in relation to a fully secret trust, where the testator leaves a legacy to two or more persons jointly and does not communicate with each of them. For example, the settlor communicates with Fred, but fails to communicate with the intended co-trustee, Adrienne. The problem focuses upon whether those that were unaware of the trust will still be compelled to hold the property subject to the secret trust. The court has devised a somewhat elaborate approach to deal with this type of scenario which concentrates upon how the trustees hold the property and the timing of communication to those trustees who were aware of the trust. The mechanics of this approach were set out (albeit briefly) by Farwell J in *Re Stead*.[114] His approach unfolded as follows:

- if the property is left to the legatees as "tenants in common", so that each has a separate share (e.g. "£500,000 to Fred, Adrienne and Fiona equally"), only those with whom the testator has communicated will be bound by the trust. The others will be allowed to keep their shares because as Farwell J explained, "to hold otherwise would enable one beneficiary to deprive the rest of their benefits by setting up a secret trust".[115] In *Tee v Ferris*,[116] the legacy was to Mr Ferris and three others as tenants in common. The testator intended that they would hold the property on trust for charitable purposes. It was decided that Mr Ferris alone was bound and the others were entitled each to take a quarter share of the property. In short, an innocent tenant in common is never bound by the acceptance of another tenant in common;

- if the property is left to the legatees as "joint tenants", so that they own the property together as a single entity and have no distinct shares (e.g. "£500,000 to Fred, Adrienne and Fiona"), and the testator communicated with any of them prior to execution of the will, all three legatees are bound by the trust. This is because, as Farwell J put it in *Re Stead*, "the will is made on the faith of an antecedent promise . . . no person can claim an interest under a fraud committed by another".[117] In *Russell v Jackson*,[118] the testator communicated with some, but not all, of his intended trustees before the making of his will. The court held that the trustees were joint tenants and that all of them were bound

---

113 (1884) 26 Ch. D. 531 at 537.
114 [1900] 1 Ch. 237 at 241. B. Perrins suggests in "Can You Keep a Half Secret?" (1972) 88 L.Q.R. 225, 226 that these rules have been accepted, "generally without enthusiasm" .
115 [1900] 1 Ch. 237 at 241.
116 (1856) 2 K. & J. 357.
117 [1900] 1 Ch. 237 at 241.
118 (1852) 10 Hare 204.

by the secret trust. Accordingly, an innocent joint tenant is always bound when the trust was accepted by another joint tenant before the will was made; and

■ if the legatees are "joint tenants" and the testator's only communication with them occurred after the execution of the will, then only those who were so communicated with are bound. The others are unaffected as, "the will is left unrevoked on the faith of a subsequent promise . . . the gift is not tainted with any fraud in procuring the execution of the will".[119] For example, in *Turner v Attorney General*,[120] property was bequeathed to four persons as joint tenants. The secret trust was communicated to one of them, but after the will was executed. The living survivor of the joint tenants had known nothing of the arrangement and, hence, he was able to claim the property absolutely.[121] Accordingly, an innocent joint tenant is not bound when the only acceptance of the trust by another joint tenant occurs after the will is executed.

5-024   These complicated and admittedly arbitrary rules as to co-trustees under a fully secret trust are not, however, beyond criticism. Perrins disagrees with the approach adopted in *Re Stead*.[122] He considers the classification promoted by Farwell J to be contradictory, confusing and based upon a misunderstanding of the authorities. He suggests that the sole matter to be addressed is simply whether the legacy was procured by the co-trustee's promise. Perrins puts forward the alternative view with allusion to A and C who are the co-trustees in this example:

> **"Returning to A & C, whether they are tenants in common or joint tenants, C is not bound if his gift was not induced by the promise of A because to hold otherwise would be to enable A to deprive C of his benefit by setting up a secret trust; but C is bound if his gift was induced by the promise of A because he cannot profit by the fraud of another; and if the trust was communicated to A after the Will was made, then C takes free if this gift was not induced by the promise of A because if there is no inducement there is no fraud affecting C".[123]**

Communication and the half-secret trust

5-025   While communication must still occur before the death of the testator, as regards the half-secret trust a different dimension is added and this is that communication must occur

---

119   Per Farwell J [1900] 1 Ch. 237 at 241.
120   (1875) 10 Ir. Rep. Eq. 386.
121   See also *Moss v Cooper* (1861) 1 J. & H. 352.
122   B. Perrins, "Can You Keep Half a Secret?" (1972) 88 L.Q.R. 225, 226.
123   (1972) 88 L.Q.R. 225, 228 (Sweet & Maxwell).

either before the will or, at the very latest, when the will is created. This approach appears entrenched.[124] As indicated by Lord Wright in *Re Keen,* "The trust referred to but undefined in the will must be described in the will as established prior to or at least contemporaneously with its execution".[125] The testator, as Viscount Sumner admitted, "cannot reserve to himself a power of making future unwitnessed dispositions by merely naming a trustee and leaving the purposes of the trust to be supplied afterwards".[126] If communication takes place after the will is executed, the secret trust must fail. As the intention to create a trust is disclosed on the face of the will, the intended trustee cannot, of course, keep the property for himself. Instead, the legatee will hold the property on resulting trust for the testator's estate.[127] Hence, in *Rawstron v Freud*[128] an illegitimate son of the artist Lucian Freud argued that the creation of a half-secret trust by his father had failed because of a post-will communication of its terms to the trustees. If correct, the son would have benefited by there being an intestacy of the residue under which he would be entitled. The son's argument failed, however, as the court was able to discern the existence of a fully secret trust.

The adoption of this stricter approach was justified by Viscount Sumner in *Blackwell v Blackwell* on the basis that "To hold otherwise would indeed be to enable the testator to 'give the go-by' to the requirements of the Wills Act because he chose not to comply with them".[129] As to the need for pre-will communication and acceptance, Viscount Sumner's reasoning is unconvincing, overlooks the ability of the testator (while alive) to revoke the will and disregards the fact that the same reasoning should equally be applied to fully secret trusts (which have never been subject to the same rule). The requirement of pre-will communication and acceptance has, moreover, been rejected both in Ireland[130] and in Australia.[131]

It is thought that this requirement emerged due to an erroneous comparison drawn with a doctrine known as "incorporation by reference". This doctrine allows written memoranda, which are referred to in the will, to be allowed in as evidence as to the meaning of a testamentary disposition. The writing must, however, have been in existence before the will was made or, at the latest, the time when the will was executed.[132] While this limitation may have merit in relation to incorporation by reference, it should be distanced from the law relating to half-secret trusts. As Sheridan puts it, "no attempt has yet been made to clear up this branch of the law, which is rich in strange distinctions, and enjoys an uneasy and ill-suited association with the probate rules for incorporation by reference".[133] The communication to trustees under secret trusts, it should not be forgotten, can be oral and there may be no document whatsoever

5-026

---

124 *Rawstron v Freud* [2014] EWHC 2577 (Ch).
125 [1937] Ch. 236 at 246.
126 *Blackwell v Blackwell* [1929] A.C. 318 at 339.
127 As occurred in both *Re Keen* [1937] Ch. 236 and *Re Bateman's WT* [1970] 1 W.L.R. 1463.
128 [2014] EWHC 2577 (Ch).
129 [1929] A.C. 318 at 339.
130 *Re Browne* [1944] Ir. R. 90.
131 *Ledgerwood v Perpetual Trustee* (1997) 41 N.S.W.L.R. 532.
132 *Re Jones* [1942] Ch. 328; see further, para.**5-037**.
133 (1951) 67 L.Q.R. 314, 314.

to incorporate into the will. The two doctrines, moreover, have different backgrounds: secret trusts are based upon equitable principle whereas the doctrine of incorporation by reference is rooted in the law of probate.

In relation to the rules relating to the communication to co-trustees under a half-secret trust, the rules have been formulated somewhat haphazardly. As the trust is evident from the will itself, there is no possibility of the trustees keeping the property for themselves. Hence, if a trustee has not been communicated with, his share (co-trustees under a half-secret trust always hold as tenants in common) will either project forward for the benefit of the secret beneficiary or result back to the estate of the testator. All seems to turn upon the wording of the will.

5-027

If the will expressly allows communication to "all or any" of the trustees, the communication to one trustee (provided that such communication occurs before or at the time of the execution of the will) will bind all the co-trustees and the half-secret trust will be upheld.[134]

If the will states that the terms of the trust have been communicated to "all" the trustees and this has not occurred, the entire trust will fail because the evidence of the informed trustee will contradict the wording of the will and be inadmissible evidence. Hence, a resulting trust will exist in relation to the entire property.[135]

Stage 3: acceptance

5-028

The rules concerning the acceptance by the legatee of the obligations of trusteeship are the same whether the trust is fully secret or half-secret in nature. Acceptance is crucial because it is this that brings about the "fraud" upon which the doctrine of secret trusts is traditionally based.[136] The intended trustee is also, in this way, presented with the option of declining to act is this capacity. Acceptance can be made at any time before the testator's death. This acceptance of trusteeship can arise in one of two ways, i.e. by express agreement or by implication from silence. Assent can occur, as Lord Westbury put it in *McCormick v Grogan*, "either expressly or by any mode of action which the disponee knows must give to the testator the impression and belief that he fully assents to the request . . .".[137]

Silence, in this context, amounts to tacit acceptance.[138] Accordingly, in *Kasperbauer v Griffith* (had there been a sufficiency of intention) the silence of the wife would have signified her acceptance of the trust.[139] In *Wallgrave v Tebbs*, Wood VC made clear that the key is whether the trustee's conduct induced the testator to make the legacy and pursue the arrangement of a secret trust. This is because equity will not allow a man to profit by his fraud.

---

134 *Re Keen* [1937] Ch. 236.
135 *Re Spence* [1949] W.B.N. 237.
136 Hence, the secret trustee cannot be the sole beneficiary under the secret trust: *Re Rees* [1950] Ch. 204. As mentioned above, this case made clear also that, with a half-secret trust, such a provision would amount to a contradiction of the terms of the will itself.
137 (1869) L.R. 4 HL 82 at 97.
138 *Paine v Hall* (1812) 18 Ves. 475.
139 [2000] W.T.L.R. 333.

In *Wallgrave*, however, the legatees were able to keep the £12,000 because there had been no communication or acceptance that could act as an inducement.[140] By way of contrast, in *Strickland v Aldridge*[141] a son induced his father to leave him property on the understanding that he would pay £10,000 to his elder brother. The court compelled the younger son to hold £10,000 on trust for his elder brother.

Revoking acceptance

It is open to a person to refuse to act or to continue to act as a trustee.[142] If the disclaimer occurs after the testator's death, it is clear that, with a half-secret trust, the deceased's personal representatives will hold the property on trust for the secret beneficiary. As regards a fully secret trust, the trust should similarly be upheld. Although Cozens-Hardy LJ doubted the latter conclusion in *Re Maddock*,[143] it is an outcome that received the support of Lords Warrington and Buckmaster in *Blackwell v Blackwell*.[144] If it were otherwise, the legatee would easily be able to frustrate the entire purpose of the secret trust by renouncing the legacy.[145] As Lord Warrington recognised, "a refusal after the death of the testator to give effect to it would be a fraud on the part of the legatee".[146]

If the trustee's disclaimer occurs before the testator's death, different considerations presumably apply. In the normal course of events, the testator can invite another to act as trustee and execute a new will accordingly. The testator is admittedly inconvenienced, but is able to adapt his plans accordingly. If the testator does not do so, it is to be thought that the secret trust will fail.[147] It follows that, in relation to a fully secret trust, the former trustee should be able to keep the property for himself. In the context of a half-secret trust, the property will be held upon resulting trust for the deceased's estate. There is no fraud and nothing to attach to the conscience of the former trustee. Nevertheless, it is possible that the testator either dies before he can make a new will or is incurably insane when the disclaimer is communicated to him. The solution in this scenario is, unfortunately, far from clear. It is arguable that, unless the conscience of the former trustee is affected in some way, equity will not interfere.

To take a somewhat extreme example, say, the trustee confronted the testator and, having disclaimed the office of trusteeship, proceeded to murder him. In that scenario, and due to the rule of public policy that a wrongdoer cannot profit from her wrongdoing, the homicidal trustee

---

140 See also, *Re Falkiner* [1924] 1 Ch. 88.
141 (1804) 9 Ves. 516.
142 *Re Sharman's WT* [1942] Ch. 311.
143 [1902] 2 Ch. 220.
144 [1929] A.C. 318 at 341 and 328 respectively.
145 See generally, J. Glister, "Disclaimer and secret trusts" (2014) Conv. 11.
146 [1929] A.C. 318 at 341.
147 See *Whitton v Russell* (1739) 1 Atk. 448, where it was held that there could be no secret trust without fraud. There the testator could have changed his plans, but did not. It was held that the testator's failure to respond did not maintain any obligation on the intended trustees.

cannot benefit under the will and the legacy to her would be void. Arguably, it should follow that a fully secret trust would fail and the property would remain in the deceased's estate. As regards a half-secret trust, however, the murderous trustee would not, on the face of the will, benefit under the will. No rule of public policy would, therefore, apply. If, by her crime, the trustee stripped the half-secret trust of its validity it would be tantamount to perpetrating a fraud on the secret beneficiary. Hence, the conscience of the trustee would not be freed by having previously informed the testator that she was no longer to be bound by the trust.

Variations on a theme

5-031

For a valid secret trust to exist, therefore, it is necessary that there be sufficient intention, communication and acceptance. As regards a fully secret trust, various permutations are possible. Consider the example of "£500,000 to Fred".

- If Fred had previously agreed to the testator's request that he would hold it on trust for Adrienne, Fred will not be able to keep the money. Instead, a fully secret trust will exist and Fred will be compelled to carry out the trust.

- If Fred had assented to act as trustee, but the terms of the trust were never communicated, a resulting trust would arise in favour of the deceased's estate.

- If Fred knew nothing about the trust or had declined to act as trustee, he can keep the £500,000 for himself.

As regards a half-secret trust (e.g. "£500,000 for Fred to be held on trust for such purposes as I have communicated to him"), the following observations are to be made.

- There are no circumstances in which Fred can claim the money for himself.[148]

- If Fred had assented to be the trustee then, provided that the terms were communicated to him before or at the time the will is executed, the trust will be enforceable by the secret beneficiary.

- If Fred had assented to be trustee, but the terms were not communicated at all or were communicated after the execution of the will, the secret trust fails and the property will be held on resulting trust for the testator's estate.

- If Fred had not accepted the role of trustee, again a resulting trust of the property will arise.

---

148   *Re Rees* [1950] Ch. 204.

Predeceasing the testator

In circumstances where a fully secret trust is intended, but the sole secret trustee dies before the testator, the legacy lapses and the property will remain in the testator's estate.[149] If, however, other trustees survive the testator, the trust should remain valid in relation to the entire property. As regards half-secret trusts, however, it is thought that the death of the sole trustee will not prevent the trust from taking effect because of the rule that equity will not allow a trust to fail for want of a trustee.[150]

In the situation where the secret beneficiary predeceases the testator, the secret trust must fail. It comes into effect via the will, which in turn comes into effect on the death of the testator. If at that time, the beneficiary is no longer living, there can be no trust. The testamentary trust will, therefore, be frustrated in the same way as would occur with an inter vivos trust.[151] Hence, with a half-secret trust the property will be held on resulting trust for the testator's estate. As regards a fully secret trust, however, it should follow that the trustee can now keep the property. It is to be appreciated that, as the secret trust comes into being on the death of the settlor, it is generally revocable at any time before then and, if so, the trust will not be constituted.[152]

Changes to trust property

In circumstances where the testator wishes to add further property to the intended secret trust, these additional instructions must also be communicated to the trustee. A failure to do so will entail that, as regards the additional property, the secret trust will fail. If it is a fully secret trust, the legatee will be able to keep the excess amount.

If it is a half-secret trust, the additional property will be held on resulting trust for the deceased's estate. This was demonstrated in *Re Colin Cooper*[153] where a testator left £5,000 to trustees on terms that he had already communicated to them. Without the knowledge of the trustees, however, he increased the sum to £10,000 by codicil (i.e. a formal and attested variation of the will). It was held that the trustees held the initial £5,000 on the terms of the trust, but that the remaining £5,000 resulted back to the deceased's estate. As regards the latter sum, there had simply been no communication and acceptance of the revised terms of the trust. As Lord Greene MR explained:

---

149   See *Re Maddock* [1902] 2 Ch. 220.
150   *Re Maddock* [1902] 2 Ch. 220.
151   See *Re Corbishley's Trusts* (1880) 14 Ch. D. 846, but note the opposite conclusion drawn (it is thought incorrectly) in *Re Gardner* [1920] 2 Ch. 523. There Romer J adopted the unorthodox approach that the secret trust was created when the terms were communicated and accepted.
152   See M. Pawlowski and J. Brown, "Constituting a Secret Trust" [2004] Conv. 388. The decision in *Re Gardner (No.2)* [1923] 2 Ch. 230, however, suggests otherwise, but this is highly dubious precedent. As D. Kincaid, "The Tangled Web: The Relationship between a Secret Trust and a Will" [2000] Conv. 420, 428 noted, "it requires the death of the secret settlor to crystallise the trust and enable the transfer of the property to the trustee".
153   [1939] Ch. 811.

> "it is impossible to say that the acceptance by the trustees of the onus of trusteeship in relation to the first and earlier legacy is something which must be treated as having been repeated in reference to the second legacy or the increased legacy, whichever way one chooses to describe it . . . I cannot myself see that the arrangement between the testator and his trustees can be construed as though it had meant '£5,000 or whatever sum I may hereafter choose to bequeath'. That is not what was said and it was not with regard to any sum other than the £5,000 that the consciences of the trustees (to use a technical phrase) were burdened".[154]

Lord Greene MR went on to make two further points. First, he recognised that minor additions would be tolerated under what is known as the de minimis principle. As he put it, "It is not to be thought from what I have been saying that some trifling excess of the sum actually bequeathed over the figure mentioned in the first bequest to the trustees would necessarily not be caught".[155] Secondly, he stated that, as regards reductions, a very different approach was to be adopted. He observed:

> "Similarly it must not be thought that, if a testator, having declared to his trustees trusts in relation to a specified sum, afterwards in his will inserts a lesser sum, that lesser sum would not be caught by the trusts. In such a case the greater would I apprehend be held to include the less".[156]

The Theoretical Basis of Secret Trusts

5-034 It is apparent that, for whatever reason, secret trusts are treated differently from other forms of testamentary disposition and are properly viewed as forming an exception to the formalities imposed by the Wills Act.[157] The underlying nature of secret trusts has, not surprisingly, been the subject of both academic and judicial speculation. Nevertheless, there is an absence of unanimity as to exactly why secret trusts are treated as operating outside the realms of

---

154 [1939] Ch. 811 at 817, 818. Although *Re Colin Cooper* concerned a half-secret trust, the same general approach should also apply to a fully secret trust.
155 [1939] Ch. 811 at 818.
156 [1939] Ch. 811 at 818.
157 See E. Challinor [2005] Conv. 492.

formality. There are three schools of thought as to what comprises the underlying rationale for the law relating to secret trusts: fraud, the *dehors* theory and incorporation by reference. Unfortunately, none of these suggestions offers an entirely satisfactory explanation. Although it is certain that both fully secret and half-secret trusts will be enforced, it is unclear exactly why this should be so. In this light, the debate is predominantly designed to sate academic interest.

Fraud

As mentioned, the traditional justification for the enforcement of secret trusts is to prevent fraud.[158] This approach has fallen into some disfavour in recent times. Hodge, however, maintains that:

> "not only is the principle that equity will not permit a statute to be used as an instrument of fraud capable of being used to support the enforcement of half-secret as well as of fully secret trusts . . . it is the only principle upon which the enforcement of both kinds of secret trusts can be justified".[159]

5-035

Unfortunately, there is much divergence of opinion as to the nature of the fraud alleged and this is particularly so with trusts of the half-secret variety.[160]

As to fully secret trusts, if the legatee/trustee attempts to keep the property for himself this will be a clear fraud. In such a scenario, unless evidence is admitted contrary to the provisions of the Wills Act, the intended trustee will profit from his misconduct. As such, the justification for recognising the fully secret trust is easily made out.[161] In relation to half-secret trusts, however, this reasoning is inapplicable. If the court refused to admit evidence of the terms of the trust, the trustee could not take the property himself, but would instead hold it on resulting trust for the testator's estate. As the trustee will not profit from the failure of the trust,[162] it is thus hard to speak in terms of there being a fraud in connection with a half-secret trust. Nevertheless, it is sometimes argued that the fraud is committed on both the testator and the beneficiary if the trust is not upheld.[163] As Parker and Mellows explain:

---

158 See *McCormick v Grogan* (1869) L.R. 4 HL 82.

159 D. Hodge, "Secret Trusts: the Fraud Theory Revisited" [1980] Conv. 341, 341. P. Critchley, "Instruments of fraud, testamentary dispositions, and the doctrine of secret trusts" (1999) 115 L.Q.R. 631 is also supportive of the fraud theory.

160 See J. Andrews, "Creating Secret Trusts" [1963] Conv. 92.

161 See *McCormick v Grogan* (1869) L.R. 4 HL 82.

162 Unless, of course, he inherits the testator's residuary estate under the will. In such a case, the notion of fraud by the trustee can be readily invoked.

163 This was accepted by Lord Buckmaster in *Blackwell v Blackwell* [1929] A.C. 318 at 328, 329.

> "This view is normally expressed in this way. If evidence of the terms of the trust were not admitted contrary to the provisions of the Wills Act, the testator would be defrauded in that, on the faith of the promise made by the secret trustee, he had either made or revoked a disposition of his property. In the same sort of way, the beneficiaries of the secret trust would be defrauded in that they would be deprived of their beneficial interests".[164]

The problem with this argument is identified by Sheridan, who suggests that there is no real fraud on the beneficiary. Instead, the intended beneficiary loses out because the settlor simply did not adhere to the prescribed formalities for creating a testamentary trust.[165] This reasoning, moreover, could apply to any statute that prescribes formalities that, if not met, will frustrate the settlor's intentions and the beneficiary's expectations. As shown in Ch.4, equity is not prepared to act in this tolerant fashion in relation to a non-compliance with s.53(1)(b), (c) of the Law of Property Act 1925.

Dehors the will

5-036

In the light that the fraud theory is not an entirely satisfactory justification for the recognition of half-secret trusts, both judges and commentators have felt it necessary to look elsewhere. While both types of trust must be similarly enforceable, this has to be justified on a principled basis. Therein lies the problem. A modern view canvassed is that a secret trust (whether fully secret or half-secret) operates *dehors* (i.e. outside) the will. In other words, the trust arises not from the will, but from its lifetime communication to and acceptance by the trustee.[166] This popular approach was adopted by Viscount Sumner in *Blackwell v Blackwell*, where he admitted that "It is communication of the purpose to the legatee, coupled with acquiescence or promise on his part, that removes the matter from the provisions of the Wills Act and brings it within the law of trusts, as applied in this instance to trustees, who happen to be legatees".[167] It follows that the rules governing wills should not apply to secret trusts. Hence, in *Re Young*,[168] the testator made a bequest to his wife with a direction that on her death she should leave £2,000 for their chauffeur. Although the chauffeur had witnessed the will, he was still entitled to the money. The legacy was not void under s.15 of the Wills Act which is designed to prevent a witness to a will being a beneficiary under it. As Danckwerts J bluntly put it, "The whole theory of the formation of a secret trust is that the Wills Act 1837 has nothing to do with the matter".[169]

---

164 Oakley, *Parker & Mellows*, 9th edn (2008), p.125.
165 (1951) 67 L.Q.R. 314, 324.
166 See B. Perrins, "Secret Trusts: The Key to Dehors" [1983] Conv. 248.
167 [1929] A.C. 318 at 339, 340 see also the approach of Megarry J in *Re Snowden* [1979] 2 All E.R. 172.
168 [1951] Ch. 344.
169 [1951] Ch. 344 at 350.

The *dehors* school of thought is that secret trusts are enforceable because of the personal obligations placed on the trustee by the inter vivos declaration of trust. This trust, however, only becomes constituted on the testator's death (i.e. the property vests in the trustee by virtue of the settlor's will). The trust is not, therefore, completely independent of the will as, of course, it is the will that operates to vest title to the property in the secret trustee. Accordingly, if the will is defective (e.g. it is improperly attested or the testator does not have the legal capacity to create it), the secret trust must necessarily fail. This has prompted Penner to conclude that "The *dehors* the will theory is fundamentally unsound . . . the theory should be called the '*dehors* the Wills Act' theory to reflect what it means".[170] He argues that secret trusts are testamentary dispositions and that, simply by revoking the will or by drafting a new will, the testator can prevent the trust being constituted. The *dehors* theory is, therefore, tortuous and "just an attempt to cloak the embarrassing jam equity has got itself into with its willingness to flout the Wills Act".[171] Penner's argument enjoys some force.

Incorporation by reference

5-037

A less attractive argument is that the probate doctrine of incorporation by reference offers the true justification underlying the recognition of half-secret trusts. The doctrine permits part of a testamentary disposition to be expressed in a document which does not comply with the formal testamentary requirements, that is, secondary documents can be incorporated by reference into the will and impose legal obligations on the personal representatives.[172] This theoretical basis is put forward by Matthews.[173] This is not surprising, as there are various similarities between the two doctrines.[174] He relies on *Johnson v Ball*[175] as providing the "sheet-anchor" of his argument and providing a decision concerning "pure incorporation".[176] There the testator bequeathed the proceeds of a life assurance policy to two trustees, "to hold the same on the uses appointed by letter signed by them and myself". Although no such letter existed at the date of the will, the testator had orally communicated the terms of the trust prior to the execution of the will. The letter was written much later. Following the death of the

---

170 J.E. Penner, *The Law of Trusts* 10th edn (Oxford: Oxford University Press, 2016), para.6.62.

171 Penner, *The Law of Trusts* (2016), para.6.63; see generally P. Critchley, who concurs in "Instruments of Fraud, Testamentary Dispositions, and the Doctrine of Secret Trusts" (1999) 115 L.Q.R. 631, 641 that there must be, "a search made for a more sustainable justification for the informality of secret trusts".

172 In *Taulbut v Davey* [2018] EWHC 730 (Ch), an unattested "letter of wishes" was treated as part of the will.

173 [1979] Conv. 360.

174 As P. Critchley, "Instruments of Fraud, Testamentary Dispositions, and the Doctrine of Secret Trusts" (1999) 115 L.Q.R. 631, 642, explains, "The similarities between half secret trusts and incorporation by reference are noticeable. At the most basic level, both require there to be a validly executed will as well as the informal disposition . . . Both require the informal arrangement to be in place prior to the date of the will . . . Both require some reference in the will to the informal arrangement".

175 (1851) 5 De. G. & Sm. 85.

176 [1979] Conv. 360, 364.

testator, one of the secret beneficiaries claimed her share. The claim was dismissed because no effectual communication to the trustees had been made. Matthews explains this decision as reflecting the inability to incorporate the document by reference where it is created after the will. By a leap of logic, he concludes that it must necessarily follow that half-secret trusts are based upon the applicability of the rule of incorporation.

Matthews' reasoning is thoroughly unconvincing as it, seemingly, puts the proverbial cart before the equally proverbial horse. The *Johnson* case may well be sound authority on the central notion of incorporation that, as the will must refer to the document to be incorporated, the document must be in existence prior to the will.[177] To view it as propounding the theoretic underpinning of half-secret trusts is a very different matter. First, the *Johnson* case can be (and usually is) viewed as showing that the evidence adduced to establish a half-secret trust cannot contradict the terms of the will. Hence, if the will refers to one mode of communication, no other mode will be admissible in evidence. Secondly, the incorporation theory stands in contradiction to key authorities (whether they point in favour of the fraud or the *dehors* theories). Thirdly, it lacks force in that the communication in relation to a half-secret trust may be oral and, hence, there may be no document at all that can be incorporated into the will. Finally, the reference in the will to the communication of terms may be general (e.g. "as previously disclosed to you in writing"), whereas for the incorporation of a document into the will specificity is required to identify what document is to be read alongside the will. As Critchley concludes, any analogy between the two is strained: "It is therefore perhaps better to conclude that, whilst there may have been cross-fertilisation between incorporation by reference and half secret trusts, they are properly viewed as separate doctrines. This means that it is necessary to find some other justification for the informality permitted to half secret and fully secret trusts".[178]

Guide to Further Reading

G. Boughen, "Mutual Wills" (1951) 15 Conv. 28.

P. Critchley, "Instruments of Fraud, Testamentary Dispositions, and the Doctrine of Secret Trusts" (1999) 115 L.Q.R. 631.

D. Hodge, "Secret Trusts: The Fraud Theory Revisited" [1980] Conv. 341.

J. Glister, "Disclaimer and secret trusts" (2014) Conv. 11.

J. Jaconelli, "Wills as Public Documents—Privacy and Property Rights" (2012) 71(1) C.L.J. 147.

---

177   See also *Taulbut v Davey* [2018] EWHC 730 (Ch) where in the absence of direct evidence, it was inferred that the document pre-dated the will.

178   P. Critchley, "Instruments of fraud, testamentary dispositions, and the doctrine of secret trusts" (1999) 115 L.Q.R. 631, 645.

Y.K. Liew, "The Ambit of the Mutual Wills Doctrine" [2016] 132 L.Q.R. 664.

P. Matthews, "The True Basis of the Half-Secret Trust" [1979] Conv. 360.

P. Meager, "Secret Trusts—Do They Have a Future?" [1995] Conv. 402.

B. Perrins, "Can You Keep Half a Secret?" (1972) 88 L.Q.R. 225.

L.A. Sheridan, "English and Irish Secret Trusts" (1951) 67 L.Q.R. 314.

T.G. Watkin, "Cloaking a Contravention" [1981] Conv. 335.

6

Non-Charitable Purpose Trusts

Other chapters focus upon the enforceability of private trusts or public trusts (i.e. charitable trusts). The attention of the present chapter, however, falls upon the validity of trusts designed to further non-charitable purposes. The general rule is that non-charitable purpose trusts are void. By their very nature their object is a purpose and they lack a beneficiary to enforce the trust. Accordingly, the aim of this chapter is to consider this primary obstacle to the validity of trusts for non-charitable purposes, the "beneficiary principle". Some additional problems that arise in relation to perpetuity and uncertainty will also be considered. First, purpose trusts will be evaluated in the context of the small number of permitted historical exceptions to the general rule. Secondly, the dividing line between trusts for persons and trusts for purposes will be considered and explained. Thirdly, this chapter will focus on property-holding by unincorporated associations. Here, the difficulty posed by purpose trusts has been evaded by a movement away from equity and towards a theory based on the contractual relationship that exists between the members. Finally, this chapter will address the alternative means by which non-charitable purposes might be pursued.

The Beneficiary Principle

As indicated, the principal difficulty with private trusts for purposes lies in the absence of a beneficiary to enforce the trust. With the exception of charitable trusts, where responsibility for enforcement lies with the Attorney-General and the Charity Commission, it is a historical requirement that a trust has a beneficiary capable of enforcing it. On this basis, the courts have struck down a variety of non-charitable purpose trusts such as for "the preservation of the independence of newspapers"[1] or for "the provision of some useful monument to myself".[2] The importance of the beneficiary principle was endorsed emphatically by Lord Evershed MR who explained that "No principle perhaps has greater sanction or authority behind it than the general proposition that a trust by English law, not being a charitable trust, in order to be effective, must have ascertainable beneficiaries".[3] Similarly, in *Leahy v Attorney General of New South Wales*, Viscount Simonds explained that "A gift can be made to persons (including a corporation) but it cannot be made to a purpose or an object".[4] Put simply, the central concern behind the principle is that "there must be somebody in whose favour the court can decree performance".[5] A trustee is under no obligation unless there is a correlative right in someone else, a beneficiary, to enforce the trust.

Notwithstanding such forceful expression, the requirement of a beneficiary appears to fall short of absolute. There are two reasons underlying this observation. First, a number of anomalous case law exceptions were admitted historically as valid non-charitable trusts. Sometimes described as trusts of imperfect obligation, this group comprises cases where the court was unable to decree enforcement, but equally did not stand in the way of a person, in the shoes of trustee, prepared to carry out a testator's wishes. As regards such anomalous exceptions, the absence of a *cestui que* trust has not always proved fatal and, moreover, these decisions have never been overruled. Admittedly, however, their contemporary applicability is highly dubious. Regarded as "concessions to human weakness or sentiment",[6] or "occasions when Homer has nodded",[7] modern courts have emphasised that the scope of the cases should not be extended.

6-003

Secondly, following cases such as *Re Denley's Trust Deed*,[8] the focus of the courts in recent times has been on the practical need for someone with the capacity to enforce the trust, i.e. someone who benefits sufficiently directly. As that person need not be a beneficiary in a strict sense, *Re Denley* suggests that the court's concern lies with problems of enforcement and not with the absence of a beneficiary per se.

The need for an ascertainable beneficiary to enforce the trust is by no means the only problem associated with purpose trusts. Sometimes the courts offer alternative reasons for holding a non-charitable purpose trust void. The most frequently encountered reasons relate to perpetuity and uncertainty, but excessive delegation of testamentary power and capriciousness are viewed as further obstacles to validity. In addition, it is not uncommon for trusts to be declared invalid simply on one of these alternative grounds. The award, for example, of an annual cup for a yacht race[9] was held to be void upon the ground of perpetuity without much

---

1   *Re Astor's Settlement Trusts* [1952] Ch. 534.
2   *Re Endacott* [1960] Ch. 232.
3   *Re Endacott* [1960] Ch. 232 at 246.
4   [1959] A.C. 457 at 478.
5   Per Grant MR in *Morice v Bishop of Durham* (1804) 9 Ves. 399 at 405.
6   Per Roxburgh J in *Re Astor's Settlement Trusts* [1952] Ch. 534 at 547.
7   Per Harman LJ in *Re Endacott* [1960] Ch. 232 at 250.
8   [1969] 1 Ch. 373.
9   *Re Nottage* [1895] 2 Ch. 649.

recourse to argument based on the want of a beneficiary. It is important to recognise that, in this context, questions of uncertainty or perpetuity generally arise as a secondary concern.[10] In other words, the beneficiary principle is viewed as the primary objection to the validity of non-charitable purpose trusts. It is only when the court accepts that the lack of a beneficiary will not defeat the trust that the additional obstacles that may stand in the way of purpose trusts are usually considered. It is necessary to look at these further obstacles to validity in more detail.

Perpetuity

There are two major strands to the rule against perpetuities. The first may be described as the rule against remoteness of future vesting, which deals with the maximum length of time for which the vesting of future interests in beneficiaries can be postponed. Although the court has the ability to "wait and see" whether vesting does occur within the relevant perpetuity period,[11] if the gift does not do so then it is void. The rule against remoteness of vesting is, therefore, concerned with the commencement of interests.[12] As will become clear, there are three sets of rules that may operate (see further Ch.4):

6-004

- the common law rules, that apply to transactions created before 15 July 1964;

- the provisions of the Perpetuities and Accumulations Act 1964, which concern dealings made after 14 July 1964 and before 6 April 2010; and

- the provisions of the Perpetuities and Accumulations Act 2009 which concern transactions created after 5 April 2010.

The second strand is the so-called rule against inalienability. This rule seeks to ensure that property is not tied up in a trust for longer than an acceptable perpetuity period or, indeed, for an indefinite period. The concern, therefore, is as to duration. The Perpetuities and Accumulations Acts have no role to play here. The common law period of a specified life or lives in being plus 21 years (see below) is the yardstick to be employed. No "wait and see" rule operates in relation to the rule against inalienability. Accordingly, this second rule plays an important role in the context of the anomalous trusts for non-charitable purposes, i.e. trusts where there are no beneficiaries in whom property might vest. Where, for example, a testator seeks to cater for the maintenance of a monument or tomb (see para.**6-011**), the maximum duration of the maintenance period must be specified, as otherwise the trust might continue indefinitely.

---

10   See, e.g. *Mussett v Bingle* [1876] W.N. 170.
11   Section 3(1) of the Perpetuities and Accumulations Act 1964; s.7 of the Perpetuities and Accumulations Act 2009.
12   As Romer LJ explained in *Re Chardon* [1928] Ch. 464 at 468, the rule is "not dealing with the duration of interests but with their commencement . . . it does not matter how long that interest lasts".

It is important, therefore, that a valid perpetuity period is selected. As shown, however, the perpetuity issue arises only as an additional or peripheral obstacle to purpose trusts.[13] The purported purpose trust must first evade the invalidating reach of the beneficiary principle.

6-005

At common law, the perpetuity period is measured by a human life or lives in being plus 21 years. As Meredith J emphasised in *Re Kelly*, "there can be no doubt that 'lives' means lives of human beings, not of animals or trees in California".[14] It is possible to select a number of lives provided that they are identifiable. It used to be common to select royal lives in being because there would be no difficulty identifying the date of death of the last survivor of the group. Accordingly, a trust might continue, for example, "until the expiry of 21 years from the death of the last survivor of the descendants of Queen Elizabeth II alive at the date of my death". The effect of any uncertainty, however, is aptly illustrated in *Re Moore*, where the testator sought to create a perpetuity period of "21 years from the death of the last survivor of all persons who shall be living at my death".[15] As it is plainly impossible to ascertain when the last person within that group has died, and thus when the period of 21 years should begin, the gift was held void under the rule against perpetuities. Where no life or lives are selected, the perpetuity period is limited to 21 years from the date when the instrument creating the gift takes effect. In the case of a will, for example, a will takes effect on the date of the death of the testator.

The Perpetuities and Accumulations Act 1964 introduced a wholly new perpetuity period, that being a fixed term not exceeding 80 years.[16] Where applicable, it is open to a settlor specifically to select this statutory period, but it will not be implied. The Perpetuities and Accumulations Act 2009 adds an additional layer to the perpetuity rules, but it applies to trusts and wills created on or after 6 April 2010. Section 5 provides that the perpetuity period is 125 years. This period operates whether or not the trust instrument specifies an alternative perpetuity period and the notion of a "life in being" has no role to play. As indicated above, however, neither Act affects the rule against inalienability which applies to purpose trusts. As s.18 of the new Act expressly confirms, "This Act does not affect the rule of law which limits the duration of non-charitable purpose trusts".

Certainty

6-006

A further obstacle is uncertainty. Much litigation generated by purpose trusts occurs where there is an intention to create a charitable trust, but the attempt ends in failure. Vagueness of expression within a purported charitable trust may leave it open to the trustee to apply the gift to both charitable and non-charitable purposes. In such cases, the gift will fail because it

---

13   "The rule against inalienability is, in reality, just one of the devices that is employed to keep the development of such trusts in check" (*The Rule against Perpetuities and Excessive Accumulations* (1998) Law. Com. No.251, para.1.14).

14   [1932] I.R. 255 at 261.

15   [1901] Ch. 936.

16   Perpetuities and Accumulations Act 1964 s.1(1).

cannot be construed as exclusively charitable. Often, it is as a last resort that the court is asked to consider the alternative matter of the validity of the trust as a non-charitable purpose trust. It comes as no surprise, therefore, that outside the scope of charity, the issue of uncertainty remains a potential stumbling block for the enforcement of trusts for purposes.

Uncertainty can arise in a range of circumstances. Sometimes the purposes are not prescribed with sufficient precision or conceptual clarity.[17] Alternatively, the means by which the trustee is to achieve or to attain the specified purpose may be ill-defined or unacceptably broad.[18] In addition, the class of beneficiaries, or those people intended to benefit, must be sufficiently certain. A classic illustration is provided by *Morice v Bishop of Durham*, where a gift was upon trust "to dispose of the ultimate residue to such objects of benevolence and liberality as the Bishop of Durham in his own discretion shall most approve of . . .".[19] The especially vague description of the objects left it impossible to determine how the residue was to be applied. From a practical perspective, should the court be called upon to administer or enforce such a trust, it will be unable to do so where the purposes are not clear. Accordingly, it is said that, "a court of equity does not recognise as valid a trust which it cannot both enforce and control".[20]

Excessive delegation of testamentary power

6-007

The concern as to excessive delegation is that, where a purpose trust is created by will and there is no beneficiary to enforce the trust, it is the trustee who must determine how the trust property is to be applied. This is thought to be problematic because in such circumstances, "the testator has imperfectly exercised his testamentary power; he has delegated it, for the disposal of his property lies with them, not with him".[21] Two additional points should be noted. First, this particular objection to purpose trusts does not arise in relation to inter vivos trusts.[22] It is a rule that applies, if at all, to wills that purport to create purpose trusts. Secondly, no case law illustration can be provided of a trust that was held void for this reason. Perhaps it is because, as Hoffmann J explained, "a common law rule against testamentary delegation, in the sense of a restriction on the scope of testamentary powers, is a chimera, a shadow cast by the rule of certainty".[23] Accordingly, it is not apparent whether the commonly cited rule as to excessive delegation carries any contemporary significance.

---

17 See, e.g. *Re Endacott* [1960] Ch. 232 (for the purposes of "providing some useful monument to myself").

18 As P.A. Lovell explained of the purported trust in *Re Astor's Settlement Trust* [1952] Ch. 534, it is a case where the trust, ". . . is a sort of omnibus purpose which expresses really nothing more than an ideal" ("Non-Charitable Purpose Trusts—Further Reflections" [1970] Conv. 77, 82).

19 (1804) 9 Ves. 339.

20 Per Roxburgh J in *Re Astor's Settlement Trust* [1952] Ch. 534 at 549.

21 Per Viscount Simonds in *Leahy v Attorney General for New South Wales* [1959] A.C. 457 at 484.

22 As Goff J explained in *Re Denley's Trust Deed* [1969] 1 Ch. 373 at 387, "If this were a will, a question might arise whether this provision might be open to attack as a delegation of the testamentary power. I do not say that would be so, but in any case it cannot be said of a settlement *inter vivos*".

23 *Re Beatty's Will Trusts* [1990] 1 W.L.R. 1503 at 1509.

Capriciousness

6-008

This next obstacle to the validity of purpose trusts arises from policy considerations concerning purposes that are useless, wasteful, harmful or illegal. Capriciousness is not frequently encountered, but it does provide an additional obstacle to the acceptance of trusts for non-charitable purposes. Consider the extreme request in *Brown v Burdett*[24] that trustees block up all the rooms in a house for a period of 20 years. Needless to say, this purpose failed when Bacon VC elected to "unseal this useless, undisposed of property".[25] Similarly, in relation to gifts for the maintenance of monuments to the testator, the root of the criticism put forward by Lord Salveson appears to lie in capriciousness and offence to public policy. Memorably, he exclaimed:

> **"The prospect of Scotland being dotted with monuments to obscure persons who happened to have amassed a sufficiency of means, and cumbered with trusts for the purposes of maintaining those monuments in all time coming, appears to me to be little less than appalling".[26]**

Accordingly, it is clear that "the law will not enforce testamentary trusts for private purposes which amount to an uneconomic and extravagant deployment of resources which either manifestly impair the economic interest of beneficiaries and/or adversely impact on the community generally".[27]

Administrative workability

6-009

This is the final obstacle to the validity of a purpose trust. It will be recalled from Ch.2 that administrative workability is a necessary ingredient of any trust. The same principle applies in the pursuit of non-charitable purpose trusts. In *R. v District Auditor Ex p. West Yorkshire Metropolitan CC*,[28] a local authority in exercise of its statutory powers attempted to create a trust "for the benefit of any or all or some of the inhabitants of the County of West Yorkshire". The inhabitants, numbering some 2.5 million, comprised of a class so large that the trust was deemed to be administratively unworkable.

---

24 (1882) 21 Ch. D. 667.
25 (1882) 21 Ch. D. 667 at 673.
26 *M'Caig's Trustees v Kirk Session of United Free Church of Lismore* [1915] S.C. 426 at 434.
27 M. Pawlowski and J. Brown, "Testamentary Trusts and the Rule Against Capricious Purposes: An Underlying Rationale" (2012) Tru. L.I. 109, 111.
28 [1986] R.V.R. 24.

The Anomalous Exceptions

As referred to above, there are a number of examples of trusts for non-charitable purposes that have been regarded by the courts as valid. These include so called trusts of imperfect obligation, i.e. cases where the "trustee" is not prevented from performing the specified purposes but equally cannot be compelled by the court to do so. Although these cases are viewed in modern times as "troublesome, anomalous and aberrant",[29] they have yet to be overruled.[30] It is important to consider these exceptions to the general rule.

Monuments and graves

A notable illustration is *Mussett v Bingle*,[31] where a testator provided £300 to erect a monument in memory of the testator's wife's first husband and a further £200 to provide income for its upkeep. The former was upheld whereas the latter was held void for perpetuity. This category of case shows that the focus of the court was not on the absence of a beneficiary, but on the danger that such trusts could last for an indefinite period. Nonetheless, in applying the perpetuity rules, the courts have shown flexibility that has allowed the development of this line of authority. First, in cases where the court is concerned only with the construction of the monument (as opposed to upkeep), it has been accepted that the build will take place within the perpetuity period. Admittedly, more difficulty surrounds directions as to maintenance because to maintain a grave gives rise to concerns as to the duration of the future upkeep. A testator who provides for the upkeep of a tomb for a valid common law perpetuity period, i.e. 21 years, could create a valid gift. Where, however, no time limit is specified, the gift would fail. Secondly, somewhat arbitrary equitable intervention has operated to save a variety of gifts in circumstances where testators have stated that their wish is for the gift to last for as long as the law allows. In such circumstances, the courts have been willing to permit the purpose to be pursued for the valid common law period of 21 years.

An unusual approach can be found in *Pirbright v Salway*.[32] There a gift of income to look after a family burial enclosure "for so long as the law for the time being permitted" was deemed acceptable. Stirling J was happy to hold the gift as valid for at least a period of 21 years following the testator's death. It has been claimed that *Pirbright v Salwey* is "virtually valueless"[33] as an authority because Stirling J failed to indicate the maximum duration of the gift. Nevertheless, the case was favourably cited in *Re Hooper*[34] where a bequest to executors

---

29   *Re Endacott* [1960] Ch. 232 at 251 per Harman LJ.
30   For an argument as to the market demand for the creation of such trusts: see J. Brown, "What are we to do with Testamentary Trusts of Imperfect Obligation" [2007] Conv. 148.
31   [1876] W.N. 170.
32   [1896] W.N. 86.
33   L.A. Sheridan, "Trusts for Non-Charitable Purposes" [1953] Conv. 46, 56.
34   [1932] 1 Ch. 38.

and trustees for the upkeep of a vault, the arrangement of which was left to the discretion of the executors, was upheld for a period of 21 years from the date of the testator's death.

6-012

In *Re Endacott*,[35] the settlor left his residuary estate to North Tawton Devon Parish Council for the purpose of "providing some useful monument to myself". It was clear to the court that the words imposed a specific obligation on the trustee that the monument was to have the quality of utility and, thereby, serve a public purpose. The trust could not be deemed exclusively charitable as the use of the money was not confined to strictly charitable purposes. Accordingly, the focus of the court fell upon whether this was a trust of a public character, the type of which the courts had historically accepted as valid. Not surprisingly, the Court of Appeal held the gift to be void. Lord Evershed MR accepted the strength of case law authority, but felt that the scope of such cases "ought not to be extended".[36] Harman LJ was in full agreement, holding that "these cases stand by themselves and ought not to be increased in number, nor indeed followed, except where one is exactly like another".[37] *Re Endacott* is an excellent illustration of the contemporary judicial approach to non-charitable purpose trusts because it emphasises that the primary objection to such trusts lies in the beneficiary principle. Perhaps the Court of Appeal was particularly wary that such a large sum of money (£20,000) would be available to the trustee, without anyone to enforce the trust.[38]

6-013

Finally, it is to be appreciated that the maintenance of private graves is facilitated under s.1 of the Parish Councils and Burial Authorities (Miscellaneous Provisions) Act 1970. A burial authority or local authority may enter into a contract to maintain a monument or other memorial situated within the catchment area of the authority and in a location to which the authority has a right of access. The obligation as to maintenance runs for a period not exceeding 99 years from the date of the agreement.

Saying of masses

6-014

Trusts for the saying of masses for private individuals are treated as valid charitable trusts, provided the masses are said in public.[39] Historically, the notion of a mass for a private individual aroused suspicion of superstition and any gift on trust for such purposes was immediately void. In 1919, however, *Bourne v Keane*[40] accepted such a trust as a legitimate private purpose trust. Subsequently, the Supreme Court of the Straits Settlements has provided an addition to this category holding valid for the perpetuity period a gift for the performance of ceremonies to

35 [1960] Ch. 232.
36 [1960] Ch. 232 at 246.
37 [1960] Ch. 232 at 250.
38 As Roxburgh J explained in *Re Astor's Settlement Trusts* [1952] Ch. 534 at 542, "it is not possible to contemplate with equanimity the creation of large funds directed to non-charitable purposes which no court and no department of state can control, or in the case of maladministration reform".
39 *Re Hetherington* [1990] Ch. 1.
40 [1919] A.C. 815.

perpetuate the testator's memory.[41] The gift was not inherently charitable under the head of advancement of religion because there was no worship of a supreme being. Accordingly, the only alternative was to house it within this category of non-charitable purpose trusts.

Care of specific animals

6-015

Gifts for the care or maintenance of particular animals are not charitable. There are, however, a number of cases where gifts for the maintenance of animals have been upheld as valid purpose trusts. In *Pettingall v Pettingall*,[42] a testator provided the sum of £50 per annum for the upkeep of his favourite black mare. She was not to be ridden or put in harness and the money was intended to ensure that she was well provided for. Influenced by two separate considerations, Knight Bruce VC upheld the gift. First, there was no dispute that a bequest in favour of an animal was valid. Secondly, there were persons interested in the residue that, having regard to the decree made, would be able to have the terms of the bequest enforced. The court arrived at a workable solution because the executor under the will provided an assurance that he would use the money to look after the mare. Although he appeared from the will to be entitled to any surplus, he was obliged to provide details of the care whenever required or otherwise face an action by any party interested in the residue should the mare not be properly cared for.

6-016

This approach was followed in *Re Dean*[43] despite markedly different facts. There the testator provided for a sum of £750 per annum to be paid for a period of 50 years for the maintenance of his horses and hounds if they should live that long. It was clear from the wording that the trustee would have no entitlement to any surplus. North J upheld the direction even though he was unclear as to who might ask the court to enforce the trust. He explained:

> **"If persons beneficially interested in the estate could do so, then the present plaintiff can do so; but, if such persons could not enforce the trust, still it cannot be said that the trust must fail because there is no one who can actively enforce it".[44]**

It is clear, therefore, that North J did not regard the absence of a beneficiary or person with locus standi to enforce the trust as necessarily fatal. Nor was he concerned that a period of 50 years did not equate with an acceptable common law perpetuity period. On both points, therefore, *Re Dean* is of questionable authority.

---

41 See *Re Khoo Cheng Teow* [1932] Straits Settlements L.R. 226.
42 (1842) 11 L.J. Ch. 176.
43 (1889) 41 Ch. D. 552.
44 (1889) 41 Ch. D. 552 at 557.

Miscellaneous cases

6-017

The most frequently cited case falling into this category is *Re Thompson*.[45] The testator bequeathed a legacy of £1,000 to his friend to be applied by him in such manner as he thought fit towards the promotion and furtherance of foxhunting. His residuary estate was to go to Trinity Hall in the University of Cambridge. Interestingly, all parties concerned were happy to see the testator's wishes carried out. Even the college, as residuary legatee, described itself as "anxious" that the testator's purpose be fulfilled. It was only by virtue of its role as trustee that the college felt duty bound to challenge the validity of the bequest. The judgment of Clauson J was heavily influenced by the approach previously adopted in *Pettingall v Pettingall*. He allowed the legacy to be applied for the specified purpose subject to an undertaking from the friend that the money be used solely towards the expressed object in the testator's will. In the event that the legacy be applied in any manner other than toward the furtherance of foxhunting, the residuary legatees were at liberty to apply to the court.

The modern stance

6-018

Any tendency towards the expansion of the categories of anomalous exceptions (described above) was effectively derailed with the decision in *Re Astor's Settlement Trusts*.[46] In 1945, Viscount Astor made a life settlement of most of the shares in The Observer Ltd, the income of which was to be applied to a variety of non-charitable purposes. These included the preservation of the independence of newspapers and the maintenance of good relations between nations. Roxburgh J held that the trust was void. First and foremost, there was no beneficiary to enforce it. As he explained, "a trustee would not be expected to be subject to an equitable obligation unless there was somebody who could enforce a correlative equitable right . . .".[47] Secondly, the trust was void for conceptual uncertainty. Roxburgh J was unable to conjure certain meaning from such phrases as, "integrity of the press" or "different sections of people in any nation or community". This approach was followed by Harman J in *Re Shaw*.[48] There the court considered the will of George Bernard Shaw who wished to devote part of his residuary estate to the pursuit of a variety of purposes, such as research into the benefits of a 40-letter alphabet and an inquiry into the number of people speaking or writing English in the world at the same time. It was held that these purposes, not being charitable in nature, were invalid. In conjunction with *Re Endacott*,[49] these authorities comprise a powerful restatement of the force of the beneficial principle.

---

45 [1934] Ch. 342.
46 [1952] Ch. 534.
47 [1952] Ch. 534 at 541.
48 [1957] 1 W.L.R. 729.
49 [1960] Ch. 323.

Trusts for Persons and Trusts for Purposes

6-019

The anomalous exceptions considered above are cases involving the pursuit of abstract purposes. A possible area of confusion involves legitimate private trusts for individuals that are expressed in the form of a purpose or limited by a purpose. It is to be remembered that these trusts satisfy the beneficiary principle and adhere to the appropriate test for certainty of objects. The approach of the courts has been to determine, where possible, that the purpose is secondary to the paramount intention of the donor, which is to benefit individuals. Sometimes this has occurred where the court can construe an absolute gift to persons with the purpose merely expressing the motive for the gift (e.g. "£5,000 on trust for the planting of trees on an estate"). Alternatively, a valid fixed trust can be created where a purpose is invoked as the means by which the beneficial share is calculated. These categories of cases should be carefully distinguished from trusts for non-charitable purposes.

In *Re Sanderson's Trust*,[50] the testator's property was left upon trust "to pay or apply the whole or any part of" towards the maintenance, attendance and comfort of his brother. The question arose as to whether the funds remaining at the brother's death devolved to the brother's estate (because he was in receipt of an absolute gift) or to the residuary legatees under the testator's will (because the brother had been entitled only to the amount of income necessary for his maintenance). Wood VC decided upon the latter. The brother was a beneficiary under a fixed trust with the right to demand from trustees a distribution to meet the costs of his maintenance expenses. The purpose in this case provided the means to calculate the amount of his beneficial share.

6-020

In the course of his judgment Wood VC offered the rule of thumb that has been followed in subsequent cases where there is a trust for persons that appears to be limited by a purpose: "If a gross sum be given, or if the whole income of property be given, and a special purpose be assigned for this gift this court regards the gift as absolute and the purpose merely as the motive of the gift, and therefore holds that the gift takes effect as to the whole sum or the whole income as the case may be".[51]

In *Re Andrew's Trust*,[52] for example, a fund was set aside for the education of the children of Bishop Barclay and it was expressly made clear that the fund was "by no means intended for the exclusive use of any one of them in particular, nor for equal division among them, but deemed necessary to defray the expenses of all, and that solely in the matter of education". Kekewich J admitted that the specified object of the trust was solely the education of the children, but he was concerned to adopt a broad view, "Even if it be construed in the narrower sense it is, in Wood VC's language, merely the motive of the gift, and the intention must be taken to provide for the children in the manner (they all then being infants) most useful".[53] Accordingly, the remainder of the fund was available for distribution to the children.

---

50   (1857) 3 K. & J. 497.
51   (1857) 3 K. & J. 497 at 503.
52   [1905] 2 Ch. 48.
53   [1905] 2 Ch. 48 at 53.

6-021

In *Re Osoba*[54] a bequest to the testator's widow upon trust, "for her maintenance and for the training of my daughter Abiola up to university grade and for the maintenance of my aged mother" was held to be a trust for the specified persons absolutely. As at the date of the gift of the residue the testator's mother was deceased, there was an absolute gift to the wife and daughter in equal shares. The expression of purposes for which the gift was to be used was an indication only of the motive for the gift. As Buckley LJ maintained:

> **"The specified purpose is regarded as of less significance than the dispositive act of the testator, which sets the measure or the extent to which the testator intends to benefit the beneficiary".[55]**

Similarly, in *Re Bowes*,[56] £5,000 was left on trust to estate owners for the purpose of planting trees on the estate for shelter. The land would have benefited from £800 worth of trees, any further planting working to the disadvantage of the beneficiaries. Accordingly, it was held that the owners of the estate were absolutely entitled to the £5,000. Again, the purpose merely expressed the motive of the gift.

The Approach in *Re Denley*

6-022

The approach adopted in *Re Denley's Trust Deed*[57] appears to signal some defrosting of the beneficiary principle. The tenor of this decision is that, where a trust is expressed in the form of a purpose, it may still be deemed valid if it can be said to be for the direct or indirect benefit of one or more ascertainable individuals. In other words, the beneficiary principle should invalidate only those trusts that are for abstract non-charitable purposes.

The case concerned an inter vivos trust of land to be maintained and used for the purpose of a recreation or sports ground. It was expressed to be "primarily for the benefit of the employees of the company and secondarily for the benefit of such other person or persons (if any) as the trustees may allow to use the same". The trustees were afforded the power to raise money for improvements and to adopt such rules and regulations as appropriate to facilitate the specified user of the property. No perpetuity issue arose as the land was to be conveyed to the trustees until the expiration of 21 years from the death of the last survivor of a group of specified persons. The application of the property for the benefit of employees was, therefore, to expire at the end of a valid period of perpetuity giving effect to a gift over. Also contained in

54 [1979] 2 All E.R. 393.
55 [1979] 2 All E.R. 393 at 402.
56 [1896] 1 Ch. 507.
57 [1969] 1 Ch. 373.

the trust deed were three divesting events the occurrence of any one of which would entail that the trustees were to convey the land to the general hospital in Cheltenham.[58]

As indicated, the approach adopted by Goff J was to reassess the scope of the beneficiary principle. Importantly, he chose to fashion a distinction between trusts for purely abstract purposes and trusts that are to the benefit of identifiable individuals. He claimed:

> "in my judgment the beneficiary principle of *Re Astor* . . . is confined to purpose or object trusts which are abstract or impersonal. The objection is not that the trust is for a purpose or object per se, but that there is no beneficiary or cestui que trust . . . Where then, the trust, though expressed as a purpose, is directly for the benefit of an individual or individuals, it seems to me that it is in general outside the mischief of the beneficiary principle".[59]

The essence of the distinction drawn appears to lie in the need for someone who has sufficient capacity to seek enforcement of the trust by applying to the court. Goff J acknowledged that a line must be drawn to distinguish the *Re Denley* type enforcer:

> "I think that there may be a purpose or object trust, the carrying out of which would benefit an individual or individuals, where the benefit is so indirect or intangible or which is otherwise so framed as not to give those persons any *locus standi* to apply to the court to enforce the trust, in which case the beneficiary principle would, as it seems to me, apply to invalidate the trust, quite apart from any question of uncertainty or perpetuity . . .".[60]

In the eyes of Goff J, the beneficiary principle should not invalidate cases where persons could be found to have sufficient standing to enforce the trust. This will occur where there is a benefit to that person, provided the benefit is not too indirect or intangible. In relation to the objects of the trust before him, Goff J held that it would be possible to identify easily those employees benefiting at any given time, thus avoiding difficulty relating to certainty of objects.[61] The employees of the company comprised an ascertainable class. The reference to other persons that the trustees may seek to include did not relate to the beneficiaries under the trust but, instead, the power to permit others to use the land. As Goff J explained, "the provision as to 'other persons' is not a trust but a power operating in partial defeasance of the trust in favour

---

58 For example, where the land was no longer required for the specified purpose.
59 [1969] 1 Ch. 373 at 383.
60 [1969] 1 Ch. 373 at 382.
61 On the basis of his adoption of *IRC v Broadway Cottages Trust* [1955] Ch. 20, it appears that Goff J felt that he required a complete list of beneficiaries (see further, para.**2-038**).

of the employees which it does not therefore make uncertain".[62] The result appears to create a new qualification to the beneficiary principle, a qualification that has been the subject of judicial and academic debate.

6-024

The grounds of immediate challenge to the approach in *Re Denley* centre upon the classification of the trust as either a new type of valid purpose trust or a private trust for individuals. If viewed as a purpose trust, the primary objection remains the want of a beneficiary. As discussed above, it is a general rule that such trusts for purposes are void. By contrast, it can be argued that *Re Denley* is no more than a private trust for the benefit of individuals.[63] Viewed from this perspective, the central role afforded to the purpose in *Re Denley* may perhaps present the key obstacle on both a conceptual and a practical level. In particular, two aspects of the *Re Denley* style trust require clarification. First, if those who benefit are not beneficiaries in the true sense, what then are their entitlements in terms of enforcing the trust?[64] Secondly, of what nature and how direct must the benefit be to bring an object of the trust within the approach in *Re Denley?* As McKay argues, the right to enjoy the recreation ground "gives them a de facto interest in the carrying out of the purpose trust, but Goff J does not go on to spell out why this factual interest confers standing to enforce . . .".[65]

Re Denley interpreted: *Re Grant's WT*

6-025

The *Re Denley* type trust has been the subject of judicial comment on two principal occasions.[66] Although both purport to support the decision, each adopts a markedly different analysis. In *Re Grant's WT*,[67] Vinelott J appears to argue that *Re Denley* is akin to a discretionary trust for individuals who have sufficient standing to enforce it on their own behalf. On this view, he appears to align, on the one hand, a discretionary trust of income and, on the other, the *Re Denley* trust to facilitate the enjoyment of land for a particular purpose amongst a class of individuals. Vinelott J's reasoning unfolds as follows:

> "I can see no distinction in principle between a trust to permit a class defined by reference to employment to use and enjoy land in accordance with rules to be made at the discretion of trustees on the one hand, and, on the other hand, a trust to distribute income at the discretion of trustees among a class, defined by reference to, for example relationship to the settlor. In both cases the benefit to be

---

62 [1969] 1 Ch. 373 at 387.
63 See P.J. Millett (1985) 101 L.Q.R. 269, 282.
64 As Lawrence Collins J noted in *Re Horley Town FC* [2006] W.T.L.R. 1817 at [99], "Goff J appears to have equated the beneficiary principle with the question of enforceability and not with the issue of equitable ownership".
65 L. McKay, "Trusts for Purposes—Another View" [1973] Conv. 420 at 426.
66 *Re Grant's WT* [1980] 1 W.L.R. 360; *Re Lipinski's WT* [1976] Ch. 235. See also *Gibbons v Smith* [2020] EWHC 1727 (Ch) where the approach in *Re Denley* has been recently endorsed.
67 [1980] 1 W.L.R. 360.

> taken by any member of the class is at the discretion of the trustees, but any member of the class can apply to the court to compel the trustees to administer the trust in accordance with its terms".[68]

The approach of Vinelott J, however, is itself open to criticism. First, his approach overlooks the importance of the purpose in *Re Denley* and deflects attention from the obvious distinctions between the cases. In *Re Denley*, the heart of the direction was to achieve a specified goal (i.e. the use of the land as a sports ground). It must not be forgotten that the trustees covenanted that, should the land cease to be required or to be used by the employees as a sports ground, the land would be conveyed to the general hospital, Cheltenham. In such circumstances, the purpose is the true object of the trust and it seems unsatisfactory to hold as a matter of construction that there is a trust for individuals, and not a trust for purposes.

Secondly, the nature of the entitlement differs as between the *Re Denley* style trust and the discretionary trust.[69] The employees in *Re Denley* are not entitled to a proprietary interest of any kind. They neither have beneficial ownership of the property, nor an expectation of receiving it. They could not combine collectively to defeat the specified purpose or to enforce a distribution of the property. Their entitlement extends to the enjoyment of a sports ground, that is, an enjoyment facilitated through the pursuit of the specified purpose. Likewise, the trustees in *Re Denley* did not enjoy discretion as to the distribution of shares in the trust property. Their discretion appertained to administrative decision-making, which involved the adoption of regulations to maximise enjoyment of the land.

Thirdly, the right to benefit from the pursuit of a purpose gives rise to different questions on the issue of enforcement and different regulatory issues for the court. Questions remain unanswered regarding the rights held by the objects of the *Re Denley* type trust wherein there is a much more limited capacity to demand the performance of trustees' duties. Undeniably, it appears open to members of the specified class to restrain actions leading to the misuse of the property, for example the adoption of a regulation that operates to exclude some members, or the perpetration of fraud. It is more difficult to see how the court might positively regulate the relationship between trustees and members of the specified class. When "trustees" refuse to carry out the stated purpose, or a dispute arises as between "trustee" and "beneficiaries", there appears to be no effective means of resolution. The terms of the trust appear to dictate that the trustees be divested of the property. This is to be contrasted with the position of beneficiaries under a discretionary trust who hold prospective entitlement to rights in property on the basis that trustees may make a distribution in their favour. *Re Denley* is also very different from those valid trusts which benefit ascertainable individuals where a purpose is construed as merely the

6-026

---

68   [1980] 1 W.L.R. 360 at 370.

69   See, e.g. the arguments put forward by C.E.F. Rickett, "Unincorporated Associations and their Dissolution" (1980) 39 C.L.J. 88, 104–106. Cf. A.R. Everton, "Towards a Concept of 'Quasi-Property'?" [1995] Conv. 118, 125 who argues that they "may exhibit a common feature of a negative kind, in that it is not possible to describe as a strictly proprietary institution either a valid non-charitable non-purpose trust, or a valid discretionary trust in which it is impossible to locate the entire equitable interest".

motive for the gift.[70] The class to be benefited in *Re Denley* was a large, fluctuating group of persons, the type of beneficiaries traditionally excluded from such construction. As described above, moreover, they held inarguably more limited and non-proprietary entitlements. It is clear, therefore, that the purpose in *Re Denley* is more central than Vinelott J suggests.

6-027   Finally, Vinelott J fails to explain the distinction promoted in *Re Denley* as between abstract purpose trusts to which the beneficiary principle applies and those trusts for purposes where individuals have sufficient capacity to act as enforcers. This distinction was cited with approval by Megarry VC in *Re Northern Developments (Holdings) Ltd*[71] and by Oliver J in *Re Lipinski's WT*.[72] In addition, the distinction drawn by Goff J is at least consistent with previous case law, even though the matter had not been explicitly raised. Accordingly, in *Re Drummond*,[73] *Re Taylor*[74] and *Re Turkington*[75] the presence of ascertainable beneficiaries allowed the gift to be upheld whereas, in cases such as *Leahy v Attorney General*[76] or *Re Wood*,[77] the gift failed because there were no such beneficiaries.

▶ *Re Denley* Interpreted: *Re Lipinski's WT*

6-028   It is necessary now to consider the other instance of judicial support for the *Re Denley* principle as expounded by Oliver J in *Re Lipinski's WT*. Although *Re Lipinski's WT* too was decided in accordance with the rules governing property holding by unincorporated associations (see below), the *Re Denley* principle was viewed as an alternative justification for upholding the gift. In *Lipinski*, a testator left part of his residuary estate to an unincorporated association solely for the purpose of constructing and effecting improvements to its buildings. As this was a gift to identifiable individuals, albeit framed as a purpose, Oliver J endorsed the approach in *Re Denley* and hailed it to be "in accord with authority and common sense".[78]

Upon closer inspection, Oliver J's analysis also fails to convince. As will be shown, gifts to unincorporated associations are commonly upheld as gifts to the members of the association, subject to their contractual rights and liabilities. In *Lipinski*, therefore, it was open to the members to abandon the specified purpose because there was nothing in the terms or circumstances of the gift, or in the rules of the association, that precluded the members from dividing the subject of the gift between themselves.[79] In *Lipinski*, the superadded purpose could simply

---

70   See, e.g. *Re Bowes* [1896] 1 Ch. 507, where the specified purpose was no more than an explanation of the motive for the gift.
71   Unreported 6 October 1978.
72   [1976] Ch. 235.
73   [1914] 2 Ch. 90 (a gift to the old Bradfordians' Club).
74   [1940] Ch. 481 (a gift to the Midland Bank Staff Association).
75   [1937] 4 All E.R. 501 (a gift to the Masonic lodge to erect a suitable temple).
76   [1959] A.C. 457.
77   [1949] Ch. 498 (a gift towards "The Week's Good Cause" on the BBC).
78   [1976] Ch. 235 at 248.
79   [1976] Ch. 235 at 244.

be ignored. This approach does not sit well with *Re Denley*, where locus standi to enforce the trust can extend logically only to restraint of misapplication. It is clear, moreover, that Goff J intended the purpose to be carried out:

> **"The court can, as it seems to me, execute the trust both negatively by restraining any improper disposition or use of the land and positively by ordering the trustees to allow the employees and any such other persons (if any) as they may admit to use the land for the purpose of a recreation or sports ground".[80]**

Further confusion emerges from the claim of Oliver J that:

> **"it seems to me that whether one treats the gift as a 'purpose' trust or as an absolute gift with a superadded direction or . . . as a gift where the trustees and the beneficiaries are the same persons, all roads lead to the same conclusions".[81]**

Both absolute gifts with a superadded direction and gifts where the trustees and beneficiaries are the same persons result in absolute ownership. This is true whether the gift is to private individuals or construed under the special rules that govern property holding by unincorporated associations. More difficulty arises where one treats a gift as a purpose trust. As has been discussed, the general rule is that trusts for non-charitable purposes are void. *Re Lipinski's WT*, however, shows only that this conclusion may be avoided in the case of a gift to an unincorporated association if it is construed as a gift in favour of members even where the donor has selected a dedicated purpose for the gift. It is not clear exactly how the principle in *Re Denley* applies in this context.

Notwithstanding the conceptual and practical difficulties associated with *Re Denley*, it is now an established authority for departure from the rigours of the beneficiary principle in full, to cater for enforcement by those who benefit sufficiently directly, but fall short of being an object of the trust. It is also strongly arguable that the *Re Denley* approach might be employed to validate certain gifts upon trust to unincorporated associations (see below).

6-029

Gifts to Unincorporated Associations

6-030

Many groups and societies such as sports and social clubs are committed to the pursuit of non-charitable purposes.[82] Members adhere to the rules of their association and their funds are

---

80   [1969] 1 Ch. 373 at 388.
81   [1976] Ch. 235 at 250.
82   Note that the assets of a society may be held upon charitable trusts which are not subject to the beneficiary

devoted to the group's activities or purposes. A large number of these societies are "unincorporated associations". An unincorporated association is a body or group of individuals that has not been incorporated as a company. Unlike companies, unincorporated bodies or groups do not have legal personality and cannot hold property in their own name.[83] Property belonging to an unincorporated association must be held in the name of members on behalf of the association. Much difficulty surrounds the nature of their property holding and the construction of gifts to such societies. In the words of Lawrence Collins J, "The rule against objects trusts, combined with the rule against perpetuities, creates technical difficulty when property is given on trust to a non-charitable unincorporated association".[84] Accordingly the next part of this chapter will focus on aspects of property holding by unincorporated associations.

Definition

6-031

In *Conservative and Unionist Central Office v Burrell*,[85] Lawton LJ put forward a definition of an unincorporated association. Albeit submitted for the purpose of interpreting taxation legislation, it is a definition that is of obvious wider applicability. The definition of an unincorporated association offered was:

> **"Two or more persons bound together for one or more common purpose, not being business purposes, by mutual undertakings each having mutual duties and obligations, in an organisation which has rules which identify in whom control of it and its funds rests and on what terms and which can be joined or left at will".[86]**

Inherent difficulties

6-032

In *Leahy v Attorney General for New South Wales*,[87] the testator provided that a large sheep station known as "Elmslea" should be held upon trust "for such order of nuns as the Catholic Church or the Christian Brothers as my executors and trustees shall select". The gift could not be charitable under the head of advancement of religion because it permitted the selection of purely contemplative orders, which are not considered charitable in law.[88] Although the

---

principle or the rule against inalienability.

83   An exception relates to trade unions: Trade Union and Labour Relations (Consolidation) Act 1992 s.10.
84   *Re Horley Town FC* [2006] W.T.L.R. 1817 at [92].
85   [1982] 1 W.L.R. 522.
86   [1982] 1 W.L.R. 522 at 525.
87   [1959] A.C. 457.
88   See *Gilmour v Coats* [1949] A.C. 426.

gift was saved by virtue of a New South Wales statute which confined the power of selection to exclusively charitable objects, the Privy Council gave detailed consideration to the validity of gifts to unincorporated associations. A number of problems emerged. First, no intention to create a trust for the benefit of individuals could be discerned as the gift was of a sheep station and the members of the selected orders were so numerous and located worldwide. In addition, the property could have passed to future members of the order for an indefinite period thereby violating the rule against perpetuities. In the alternative, Viscount Simonds explored the possibility that the gift might have been construed as a valid gift to the individual members of the chosen religious orders. Unfortunately, this conclusion was deemed insupportable as the gift was expressed to be for the benefit of religious orders rather than for specified individuals.

Leahy exposed the difficulties inherent in the making of gifts for present and future members. Even in cases where a trust can be discerned, the intention to benefit future members entails that the capital must remain intact and available to future members, thereby offending the rule against remoteness of vesting.[89] If no trust could be said to exist, the only alternative was of an absolute gift to the members. In the view of the Privy Council, this was the case even where the gift purported to be for the general purposes of the society. As Viscount Simonds explained:

> **"In law, a gift to an unincorporated association *simpliciter* (i.e., where . . . neither the circumstances of the gift nor the directions given nor the object expressed impose on the donee the character of a trustee) is nothing else than a gift to its members at the date of the gift as joint tenants or tenants in common".[90]**

It was inevitable that a new theory of property holding would be developed to deliver the flexibility so patently lacking in the then extant law. In *Neville Estates v Madden*,[91] Cross J provided the foundations for what has become known as the "contract holding theory" within his outline of possible constructions of gifts to unincorporated associations. The possible constructions were threefold.

6-033

- A gift to the members of the association at the date of the gift as joint tenants so that any member can sever his share and claim it whether or not he continues to be a member.

- A gift to the members of the association at the date of the gift not as joint tenants, but "subject to their respective contractual rights and liabilities towards one another as members of the association. In such a case a member cannot sever his share. It will

---

89   Note that *Leahy* was decided prior to the enactment of the Perpetuities and Accumulations Act 1964 and thus before the wait and see rule effected a relaxation of the rules governing remoteness: see further Ch.4.
90   [1959] A.C. 457 at 477.
91   [1962] Ch. 832.

accrue to the other members on his death or resignation, even though such members include persons who become members after the gift took effect. If this is the effect of the gift, it will not be open to objection on the score of perpetuity or uncertainty unless there is something in its terms or circumstances or in the rules of the association which precludes the members at any given time from dividing the subject of the gift between them on the footing that they are solely entitled to it in equity".[92]

■ The terms or circumstances of the gift or the rules of the association show that the property in question (i.e. the subject of the gift) is not to be at the disposal of the members but is to be held on trust. In such a case, the gift will fail unless the association is a charitable body.

The contract holding theory

6-034

The second construction of there being a gift to the members subject to their contractual rights and liabilities towards one another, is the most flexible and convenient approach. The basis of their ownership is the contractual agreement between the members, which is, as Lewison J recognised in *Hanchett-Stamford v Attorney General*, "a form of beneficial ownership; that is to say that in some sense the property belongs to the members".[93] Its principal attraction lies in the ability to cater for a fluctuating membership without contravening the rules against perpetuity. As the property is held at all times by the existing members in accordance with their rules of association, members who leave or wish to join create no problems. It is not possible for an individual member to claim an individual share. His share will accrue to the remaining members on death or upon leaving the association even though the members may well include persons joining after the date on which the gift took effect. The applicability of this construction will depend upon the rules of the association and the extent to which those rules lend themselves to that construction.[94] If the rules cater for the retention of the gift within the funds of the association, the most natural construction to place upon the gift is that it is held as an accretion to the funds of the association.[95]

Adopting the contract holding theory

6-035

In *Re Recher's WT*,[96] the testatrix sought to leave part of her residuary estate to the London and Provincial Anti-Vivisection Society. It transpired that the Society had ceased to exist by the date

---

92 [1962] Ch. 832 at 849.
93 [2009] 2 W.L.R. 405 at 415. See also *Sanderson v Hi Peak Property Ltd* [2014] EWHC 4918 (Ch).
94 See generally, P. Matthews, "A Problem in the Construction of Gifts to Unincorporated Associations" [1995] Conv. 302.
95 See *Recher's WT* [1972] Ch. 526.
96 [1972] Ch. 526.

of her will, having amalgamated with the National Anti-Vivisection Society. On these facts, it was not possible to save the gift. Evidently, it could not be construed as a gift to the members of the Provincial Society subject to their contractual rights and liabilities. The Society had terminated the contract between its members and dissolved the association. There was simply no question that the gift could be construed as a gift to the members of a different association. If the Society had remained in existence, the gift would have been unproblematic. It would have been construed as a gift in favour of the members as an accretion to the funds of the society subject to their contractual rules.[97] This construction was open regardless of whether the purposes of the society were "inward looking" (to promote the common interest of the members e.g. a members' social club) or "outward looking" (to promote some outside purpose such as the abolition of vivisection).[98] Brightman J appears to have been swayed by the policy concern that, if every gift was to be construed as a purpose trust or as distributing shares to members, it would be unnecessarily hard to make a donation to such societies.

The attachment of conditions to the gift

In *Re Lipinski's WT*,[99] the testator bequeathed his residuary estate to trustees on trust "as to one half thereof for the Hull Judeans (Maccabi) Association in memory of my late wife to be used solely in the work of constructing the new buildings for the association and/or improvements to the said buildings".

6-036

As a gift to a non-charitable unincorporated association, it fell to Oliver J to consider the effect of the specification of the purpose for which the legacy was to be applied. There was no doubt that, had the gift to the unincorporated association been a gift *simpliciter*, it would have fallen squarely into the second category drawn up by Cross J in *Neville Estates v Madden*. Here, the testator had attached a seemingly specific condition to the use of the subject matter of the gift. Oliver J was, however, undaunted and held:

> "If a valid gift may be made to an unincorporated body as a simple accretion to the funds which are the subject-matter of the contract which the members have made *inter se* . . . I do not really see why such a gift, which specifies a purpose which is within the powers of the unincorporated body and of which the members of that body

---

97 As Brightman J elaborated, "In the absence of words which purport to impose a trust, the legacy is a gift to the members beneficially, not as joint tenants or as tenants in common so as to entitle each member to an immediate distributive share, but as an accretion to the funds which are the subject matter of the contract which the members have made inter se" ([1972] Ch. 526 at 539).

98 Brightman J felt it to be "undesirable and indeed impracticable that the law should depend upon an ill-defined distinction of this sort", explaining that "the most outward looking association . . . can by agreement between its members convert itself into an inward looking association and vice versa, or become a hybrid, so that the distinction is not only imprecise but not even necessarily permanent" ([1972] Ch. 526 at 542).

99 [1976] Ch. 235.

> **are the beneficiaries, should fail. Why are not the beneficiaries able to enforce the trust or, indeed, in the exercise of their contractual rights, to terminate the trust for their own benefit? Where the donee association is itself the beneficiary of the prescribed purpose, there seems to me to be the strongest argument in common sense for saying that the gift should be construed as an absolute one within the second category . . .".[100]**

Oliver J felt it to be significant that, under the constitution of the association, the members had the capacity to alter the constitution to provide for the division of the association's assets amongst the members. It was, therefore, open to the members to override the specified purpose even though it had been expressed in strong terms. Accordingly, Oliver J concluded that "the beneficiaries as members of the association for the time being, are the persons who could enforce the purpose and they must, as it seems to me, be entitled not to enforce it or, indeed to vary it".[101] From the perspective of the testator, moreover, there is merely the hope or expectation that the members will observe the spirit in which the gift was given and apply it to the furtherance of the purpose. As Vinelott J argued in *Re Grant's WT*, such gifts are made:

> **". . . in the expectation that, although the members at the date when the gift takes effect will be free, by a majority if the rules so provide or acting unanimously if they do not, to dispose of the fund in any way that they might think fit, they . . . will not in fact do so but will employ the property in the furtherance of the purpose of the association and will honour any special condition attached to the gift".[102]**

Control of the association's assets

6-037

In *Re Grant's WT*, the capacity to divide the association's assets amongst the members has been reinforced as a key requirement of the contract holding analysis. Here, the gift ("to the Labour Party property committee for the benefit . . . of the Chertsey and Walton Constituency Labour Party") did not take effect as an accretion to the funds of the Constituency Labour Party. The Chertsey and Walton CLP did not control the property sufficiently that they could dispose of it in the way they felt fit or alter the rules and direct that the property be divided amongst themselves beneficially. The rules of the constituency association were clear that its members were controlled by an outside body and did not themselves hold those powers. As Vinelott J confirmed:

---

100 [1976] Ch. 235 at 246.
101 [1976] Ch. 235 at 250.
102 [1980] 1 W.L.R. 360 at 368.

> "It must, as I see it, be a necessary characteristic . . . that the members of the association can . . . alter the rules so as to provide that the funds, or part of them, shall be applied for some new purpose, or even distributed amongst the members for their own benefit".[103]

6-038

Notwithstanding, the restrictive approach in *Re Grant's WT*, the case of *Re Horley Town FC*[104] serves to underline the judicial preference to invoke the contract holding theory. In 1948, Major Jennings settled land known as "The Defence" on trust, for the purpose of securing a permanent ground for Horley Football Club.[105] It was agreed that at the time the disposition was made, it fell into Cross J's second construction in *Madden*, that is, it was a gift to the members subject to their contractual rights and liabilities towards one another. The question was whether rule changes, which extended membership and voting rights, precluded the contract holding analysis by limiting the capacity of members to dispose of the property as they saw fit.

Lawrence Collins J held that such changes made no difference. He reached the common sense view on the facts that extensions to the membership scheme were not designed to confer the benefit of full membership on temporary or associate members. Further, the provision of voting rights to outside bodies in *Horley* could not be compared to *Re Grant*, where the level of control over the rules and destination of the association property proved too extensive. Accordingly, Lawrence Collins J concluded that the beneficial interest was held on bare trust for current full members, each entitled to a share on a per capita basis. Notably, he relied upon the views of Sir Robert Megarry VC in *Re GKN Bolts & Nuts Ltd*, as to how the court should approach its task:

> "As is common in club cases, there are many obscurities and uncertainties, and some difficulty in the law. In such cases, the court usually has to take a broad sword to the problems, and eschew an unduly meticulous examination of the rules and regulations . . . I think that the courts have to be ready to allow general concepts of reasonableness, fairness and common sense to be given more than their usual weight when confronted by claims to the contrary which appear to be based on any strict interpretation and rigid application of the letter of the rules".[106]

Dissolution

6-039

On the dissolution of an unincorporated association, the ultimate destination of any surplus property held by the association requires to be considered. Where two or more members exist

---

103 [1980] 1 W.L.R. 360 at 368.
104 [2006] W.T.L.R. 1817; see P. Luxton, "Gifts to Clubs: Contract-Holding is Trumps" [2007] Conv. 274.
105 Despite the reference to "permanent", a perpetuity period was specified with reference to royal lives.
106 [1982] 1 W.L.R. 774 at 776.

at the date of dissolution (and the contract holding theory is adopted), the distribution of property is a matter of contract. As Walton J observed in *Re Bucks Constabulary Widows' and Orphans' Fund Friendly Society (No.2)*:

> "judicial opinion has been hardening and is now firmly set upon the lines that the interests and the rights of persons who are members of any type of unincorporated association are governed exclusively by contract, that is to say the rights between themselves and their rights to any surplus assets".[107]

Walton J dealt also with the question of the proportions in which members may be entitled on dissolution. Clearly, in many cases the rules will lay down what should happen to property on the termination of a society. Where this is the case, the rules are to be regarded as decisive.[108] Where no such rules are in place, Walton J rejected any possibility of distribution amongst members according to equitable principles. Faced with the argument that the proportions may vary, he explained, "I completely deny the basic premise. The members are not entitled in equity to the fund; they are entitled at law . . . It is a matter of simple entitlement, and that entitlement must be, and can only be, in equal shares".[109]

6-040

Such cases should be distinguished from those where the society is moribund (i.e. where all or all but one of the members had died). As Walton J observed in *Re Bucks Constabulary Widows' and Orphans' Fund Friendly Society (No.2)*, "There is no association, since one can hardly associate with oneself or enjoy one's own society".[110] Walton J considered that the property must be deemed to be ownerless, such that the Crown may claim this surplus property under the doctrine of *bona vacantia*. Even in the case of a sole surviving member, he felt this was the correct destination for the surplus, as "unincorporated societies are not really tontine societies intended to provide benefits for the longest liver of the members".[111]

More recently, however, in *Hanchett-Stamford v Attorney General*,[112] Lewison J conducted a thorough review of key authorities and arrived at the contrary conclusion. He was required to determine whether a sole surviving member of an unincorporated association founded in 1914 ("The Performing and Captive Animals Defence League") could claim ownership of the outstanding association assets and transfer these to an animal charity the "Born Free Foundation".[113] The conclusion that Mrs Hanchett-Stamford, was, indeed, entitled to do so was not straightforward, but Lewison J could not accept that:

---

107 [1979] 1 W.L.R. 937 at 952.
108 Where the court is called upon to dissolve an association long inactive ("whilst it sleeps it is not dead"), the court should endeavour to reach a result "commensurate" to that which would have occurred under the rules of the association: see *Keene v Wellcom London Ltd* [2014] EWHC 134 (Ch) at [23] per Peter Smith J.
109 [1979] 1 W.L.R. 937 at 953.
110 [1979] 1 W.L.R. 936 at 943.
111 [1979] 1 W.L.R. 936 at 943.
112 [2009] 2 W.L.R 405.
113 The League could not be considered charitable as it sought a change in the law regarding the use of performing animals and, accordingly, it did not exist for exclusively charitable purposes.

> "a member who has a beneficial interest in an asset, albeit subject to contractual restrictions, can have that beneficial interest divested from him on the death of another member".[114]

This would lead, he argued, to the conclusion that:

> "if there are two members of an association which has assets of, say £2m, they can by agreement divide those assets between them and pocket £1m each, but if one of them dies before they have divided the assets, the whole pot goes to the Crown as *bona vacantia*".[115]

In the course of his judgment, Lewison J took care to construct the foundations for his conclusions via a clear analysis of the contract holding theory. He explained:

6-041

> "The thread that runs through all these cases is that the property of an unincorporated association is the property of its members, but that they are contractually precluded from severing their share except in accordance with the rules of the association; and that, on its dissolution, those who are members at the time are entitled to the assets free from any such contractual restrictions. It is true that this is not a joint tenancy according to the classical model; but since any collective ownership of property must be a species of joint tenancy or tenancy in common, this kind of collective ownership must, in my judgment, be a subspecies of joint tenancy, albeit taking effect subject to any contractual restrictions applicable as between members".[116]

On this basis, it follows that, where an unincorporated association is reduced to a single member, the last remaining member becomes solely entitled to any surplus assets by way of the principle of survivorship. As Baughan explains:

> "The property analysis now becomes the sole determinant of the destination of the unincorporated association's assets. By survivorship under the joint tenancy that subsisted prior to dissolution, the remaining member will take absolutely. The members' former contracts with one another will now have no relevance whatsoever as

---

114 [2009] 2 W.L.R. 405 at 417.
115 [2009] 2 W.L.R. 405 at 417.
116 [2009] 2 W.L.R. 405 at 420.

> these will have ceased to exist . . . on the reduction of the association to a single member".[117]

Lewison J noted that his reasoning was consistent with art.1 of the First Protocol of the European Convention on Human Rights, which guarantees the peaceful enjoyment of possessions.[118] A further consideration, perhaps underplayed in his judgment, is the lack of public interest in the state appropriation of a sole remaining member's share of an association's assets. On the facts, Mrs Hanchett-Stamford did not wish to benefit personally. As a matter of general principle, however, the effect of *Hanchett-Stamford v Attorney General* is to confer a benefit by windfall to the sole surviving member and, thereafter, on that individual's death, to their next of kin. It remains to be seen how Lewison J's approach will fare in future.

Further possible constructions

6-042 Although, the contract holding theory has developed into the preferred construction, a number of alternatives remain arguable bases for property holding by unincorporated associations. These will now be considered in turn.

Charitable purposes

6-043 Just as trusts for the furtherance of non-charitable purposes are generally void, a gift to an unincorporated association will fail if construed as creating a non-charitable purpose trust. It is possible, however, for an unincorporated association to pursue charitable objectives such as the alleviation of poverty or the advancement of education. Unincorporated charities hold their assets upon charitable trusts and do not fall subject to the rule against inalienability or the beneficiary principle.

Gifts to present individual members

6-044 It remains possible to view a gift to an unincorporated association to be for present members only. Such a gift might be an outright gift to the members,[119] or it may be held on trust for the members as joint tenants or tenants in common. Should the members hold as joint tenants, it is open to each to sever his share and become a tenant in common. On a joint tenant's death, under the right of survivorship, his share will accrue to the remaining members. Should the

---

117 S. Baughan, "Performing Animals and the Dissolution of Unincorporated Associations: The Contract-Holding Theory Vindicated" [2010] Conv. 216, 226.
118 [2009] 2 W.L.R. 405 at 420.
119 See, e.g. *Cocks v Manners* (1871) L.R. 12 Eq. 574.

members hold as tenants in common, however, each has an immediate share and is free to claim it. In contrast to the joint tenancy, on the death of a member his share will devolve by his will or the rules of intestacy. In relation to the vesting of interests in future beneficiaries, no perpetuity problem will arise under this construction. It is somewhat more difficult to avoid other inherent disadvantages. Future members will not automatically acquire any interest in property because it belongs exclusively to those members existing at the date of the gift. If the property is held on trust, the acquisition of an interest in it (being a subsisting equitable interest) appears to require of the vendor/donor a disposition in writing under s.53(1)(c) of the Law of Property Act 1925 (see para.**4-009**).

Gifts to present and future members

6-045

A gift to an unincorporated association made by way of endowment must necessarily involve a trust. In such cases, the capital sum is held separately upon trust and is used to generate an income to be applied by the members. Unless the gift is framed to be for the benefit of existing members or confined to an appropriate perpetuity period, the principal obstacle will be the rule against perpetuities.[120] The problem relates to the remoteness of future vesting. As Widdows explains:

> **"if it is interpreted as a gift to present and future members, some of the latter presumably being neither alive or ascertainable, it cannot be said by the degree of certainty required by the rule that the gift will vest completely in the period allowed".[121]**

Presumably, the court will wait and see whether, in appropriate cases, the members wind up the trust and render the capital their own within the statutory timeframe provided for by the 1964 and 2009 Acts.

It will be recalled that such problems were circumvented in *Re Denley's Deed Trust* by the limitation of duration to 21 years from the death of the last survivor of a number of specified persons. It seems, therefore, that a gift may be construed as such for present and future members who benefit sufficiently directly to have locus standi to enforce the trust under the approach in *Re Denley*. This construction will be possible where the gift is expressly confined to the perpetuity period or the rules of the unincorporated association are appropriately drafted to avoid problems of perpetuity. More difficulty surrounds the applicability of the Perpetuities and Accumulations Acts. Analysis on the basis of either Act will be dependent upon the way that the trust in *Re Denley* is classified. If perceived as a straightforward express trust for beneficiaries, it is the rule against remoteness that applies. If perceived as a valid purpose trust, however, the common law rules must apply because the applicable rule is that which strikes at inalienability.

---

120   Where an unincorporated association is at liberty to spend both capital and income a gift will not fail for perpetuity: *Re Price* [1943] Ch. 422.

121   K. Widdows, "Trusts in Favour of Associations or Societies" [1977] Conv. 179, 180.

Mandate or agency

6-046

In *Re Grant's WT*,[122] it was the inability to divide the property beneficially amongst the members that precluded the contract holding analysis. The gift failed.[123] Similarly, in *Conservative and Unionist Central Office v Burrell*,[124] the Conservative Party proved ill-suited to the definition of an unincorporated association. The Party was a historical political movement that did not display the necessary mutual rights and obligations between its members. Rules governing control, moreover, lay with the party leader.

It should be pointed out that the courts have at times strained to find the necessary elements in the structure of a given organisation. In *News Group Newspapers v SOGAT 82*,[125] for example, the local branches of a particular union were held to be unincorporated associations with sufficient capacity to take control of their assets, terminate their association and divide their property amongst the members.

6-047

In the case of political parties, however, it appears that a different theory is required to explain the structure of their property holding and the construction of gifts to their members. In *Conservative and Unionist Central Office v Burrell*,[126] Brightman LJ put forward the mandate or agency theory.[127] The theory describes the relationship between the donor and the recipient, usually the party treasurer. In essence, the donor is viewed as the principal and the party treasurer as his agent. The treasurer is required by mandate to apply the money in accordance with the donor's specifications. To the extent that he does so, the recipient discharges his mandate vis-à-vis the contributor. Money applied outside the scope of the mandate exposes the recipient to an action to restrain misapplication or the requirement to replace the money. The contributor can, furthermore, demand a return of the money not expended on the purpose. Once the money is spent the entitlement extends only to an account of expenditure. Alternatively, where the money has been mixed with other party funds, the mandate becomes irrevocable. As Brightman LJ explained, "The contributor has no legal right to have the mixed fund unscrambled for his benefit".[128] Two areas of potential difficulty arise.

- The mandate or agency theory cannot be used to classify testamentary gifts. Agency cannot be set up at the moment of death between the testator and his agent. Accordingly, there remains a problem with the construction of testamentary bequests to political parties.

---

122 [1980] 1 W.L.R. 360.
123 *Re Grant's WT* has been criticised as "a case that has shed more darkness than light, not least because it provided no explanation of how the members of the local Labour Party did in fact hold the local party's assets" (P. Luxton, "Gifts to Clubs: contract holding is trumps" [2007] Conv. 274, 280).
124 [1982] 1 W.L.R. 522.
125 [1986] I.C.R. 716.
126 [1982] 1 W.L.R. 522.
127 See further, P. Smart [1987] Conv. 415.
128 [1982] 1 W.L.R. 522 at 529.

■ More speculatively, it has been suggested that a change of the office-holder to whom the mandate is given may be detrimental to the contractual claim of any complaining contributor. As Brightman LJ conjectured, "Perhaps only the original recipient can be sued for the malpractices of his successors".[129]

Alternative Means of Pursuing Non-Charitable Purposes

Even in the context of unincorporated associations, trusts for non-charitable purposes are prima facie void under the beneficiary principle. The courts have strained to adopt a more flexible approach by developing the contract holding theory or accepting that a trust may be valid if expressed as a purpose, but construed as being directly or indirectly for the benefit of ascertainable individuals. The final matter to consider in this chapter relates to a variety of additional ways to pursue non-charitable purposes.

6-048

Using corporations

It is possible to make a gift to a corporate body to advance non-charitable ends. In *Re Chardon*,[130] a gift of income to a cemetery company for as long as it carried out a specified purpose was deemed valid and within the perpetuity period. Alternatively, incorporation of a society itself will effect a practical solution to the problem of trusts for purposes as the society becomes a legal entity.

6-049

Use of powers

The beneficiary principle applies only to trusts. Hence, it is possible to avoid the problem of trusts for purposes by drafting a power. In *Re Shaw*,[131] it was open to George Bernard Shaw to employ a power as the appropriate mechanism to pursue his non-charitable ends. However, once he manifested the intention to create a trust, it was not possible for the court to conclude that a power had been created.[132] As was emphasised in *IRC v Broadway Cottages Trust*, "a

6-050

---

129 [1982] 1 W.L.R. 522 at 530.
130 [1928] Ch. 464.
131 [1957] 1 W.L.R. 729 (see para.**7-039**).
132 Legislation would be required before trusts for non-charitable purposes could be construed as powers, which, if

valid power cannot be spelt out of an invalid trust".[133] Although the express creation of a power would have circumvented the difficulties encountered in *Re Shaw*, it is to be remembered that where a power is employed there is no obligation on the donee necessarily to pursue the purpose.

Employing conveyancing devices

6-051

In *Re Tyler*,[134] a gift was made to a charitable body (the London Missionary Society) subject to the request that they carry out the maintenance of the family tomb, but with a gift over to another charity (the Bluecoat School) if the request was not complied with. The gift was upheld. The purpose would be pursued as long as the Society felt it to be profitable and would cease when the Society declined to perform the maintenance, thereby, giving effect to the gift over. The Law Commission has acknowledged the use of this conveyancing device to evade the perpetuity rules and enforce a non-charitable purpose. It made no recommendation for change to this aspect of the law.[135] Indeed, s.2(2) of the Perpetuities and Accumulations Act 2009 confirms that the rule against perpetuities, "does not apply to an estate or interest created so as to vest in a charity on the occurrence of an event if immediately before the occurrence an estate or interest in the property concerned is vested in another charity".

Off-shore trusts

6-052

The use of off-shore trusts has become an increasingly evident means of creating trusts for non-charitable purposes. The motivation of much off-shore legislation is the facilitation of commercial transactions or off-balance sheet transactions that are made difficult in the United Kingdom.[136] In many jurisdictions, legislation has been necessary to remove the obstacles to validity that have hampered the creation of such trusts at home.[137] Accordingly, most provide for extended perpetuity periods[138] and, in some jurisdictions such as Cyprus, purpose trusts are not subject to a perpetuity period at all. In addition, legislation caters for a method of enforcement of such trusts by the use of a protector or an enforcer. The exact means of achieving

sufficiently certain, would allow trustees to elect to carry out the purposes: see, e.g. the Ontario Perpetuities Act 1966.

133 [1955] Ch. 20 at 36 per Jenkins LJ.
134 [1891] 3 Ch. 252.
135 *The Rules Against Perpetuities and Excessive Accumulations* (1998) Law Com.251, paras 7.34, 7.37.
136 The question whether a UK court would recognise and assist in the enforcement of a trust of English assets governed by an off-shore jurisdiction may, however, act to discourage the adoption of this method.
137 No such legislation appears forthcoming in the United Kingdom because, as Hayton put it, "there is a feeling that pure purpose trusts may be hijacked for shady dealings involving hiding beneficial ownership" (D. Hayton, *Modern International Developments in Trust Law* (London: Kluwer Law International, 1999), p.305).
138 See, e.g. Belize where a period of 120 years has been adopted.

this may also vary from jurisdiction to jurisdiction. Nevertheless, it has been argued that the approach in jurisdictions such as Bermuda or the Cayman Islands may serve "as appropriate role models for the introduction of new legislation in England".[139]

- In Bermuda, for example, it was not possible to create a non-charitable purpose trust until the Trusts (Special Provisions) Act 1989. This legislation required the appointment of a person to enforce the trust and provision for the appointment of a successor. Although the original Act has been amended by the Trusts (Special Provisions) Amendment Act 1998, the Supreme Court can still make an order for the enforcement of a purpose trust. This may be on the application of any person appointed by or under the trust, the settlor, a trustee or any other person whom the court considers has sufficient interest in the enforcement of the trust.[140] If the court is convinced that that there is nobody capable or willing to make an application, the Attorney-General may now himself make such an application.[141]

- In the Cayman Islands there has evolved the STAR trust,[142] which is capable of being perpetual and can only be enforced by dedicated "enforcers". Even in cases where there is a beneficiary, that beneficiary will have no right to enforce the trust as the only persons with standing are those who have been appointed as enforcers. In the case of STAR trusts the defining characteristics of the trust, such as the capacity of beneficiaries to enforce their rights against trustees, are completely missing. Hence, they provide a range of conceptual and practical problems.[143]

By appointment of an enforcer?

6-053

It has been suggested that a means of sidestepping the problem created by an absence of beneficiaries might be to permit the appointment of an enforcer of the trust.[144]

To adopt this approach would allow non-charitable purpose trusts to be valid where the settlor has appointed an enforcer provided the circumstances are such that the trust is administratively workable and restricted to a valid perpetuity period. Perhaps, unfortunately, this is the least likely alternative method of successfully pursuing non-charitable purposes. The traditional approach of the courts has been to regard the need for a beneficiary with rights enforceable against trustees as fundamental to the notion of a trust.

---

139 M. Pawlowski and J. Summers, "Private Purpose Trusts—A Reform Proposal" [2007] Conv. 440, 449.
140 Trusts (Special Provisions) Amendment Act 1998 s.12B(1).
141 For detailed analysis of the operation of offshore purpose trusts in specific jurisdictions, see P. Baxendale-Walker, *Purpose Trusts*, 2nd edn (London: Tottel, 2008).
142 Cayman Islands Special Trusts (Alternative Regime) Law 1997.
143 For a discussion of how STAR trusts might be treated by the UK courts, see A. Duckworth, "STAR Trusts" (2013) 19(2) T. & T. 215.
144 See D. Hayton, "Developing the Obligation Characteristic of the Trust" (2001) 117 L.Q.R. 96.

Guide to Further Reading

S. Baughan, "Performing Animals and the Dissolution of Unincorporated Associations: The Contract Holding Theory Vindicated" [2010] Conv. 216.

D.J. Hayton, "Developing the Obligation Characteristic of the Trust" (2001) 117 L.Q.R. 96.

P. Matthews, "A Problem in the Construction of Gifts to Unincorporated Associations" [1995] Conv. 302.

L. McKay, "Trusts for Purposes—Another View" (1973) 37 Conv. (NS) 420.

M. Pawlowski and J. Summers, "Private Purpose Trusts—A Reform Proposal" [2007] Conv. 440.

L.A. Sheridan, "Trusts for Non-charitable Purposes" (1953) 17 Conv. (NS) 46.

7

Charitable Trusts

In order to be charitable a trust must satisfy three requirements. It must be for a purpose that the law deems to be charitable; it must be for the public benefit[1] and it must be exclusively charitable in nature.[2] Until 2006, charitable trusts were required to fall within a well-established four-fold classification, that is, of trusts for the relief of poverty, advancement of education, advancement of religion or other purposes beneficial to the community.[3] As this classification was itself based on almost 300 years of case law developments,[4] the need for a modern and flexible statutory definition became essential.[5] The Charities Act 2011, which lists 13 descriptions of purposes deemed charitable at law, now provides an encompassing test of charity and more accurately reflects contemporary societal values and understandings of what charity entails.[6] In order to be charitable, therefore, a purpose is required to fall within at least one of these statutory descriptions[7] and it must be for the public benefit.[8] It is with these core characteristics of charitable trusts that this chapter is primarily concerned.

Engaging with the current law is not straightforward. Recent developments in the law of charities have been many and varied with much uncertainty as to how the law has changed and

---

1   It must be of benefit to the public at large or a sufficient section thereof: see *Verge v Somerville* [1924] A.C. 497.
2   That is, property must be capable of dedication to charitable purposes only.
3   *Commissioners for Special Purposes of Income Tax v Pemsel* [1891] A.C. 531 at 583 per Lord Macnaghten.
4   Stemming from the Preamble to the Charitable Uses Act 1601: see further para.**7-009**.
5   As stated in the Government's Strategy Unit Report, *Public Action, Private Benefit* (2002), para.4.9, "The law is confusing and unclear. The four 'heads' do not accurately represent the full range of different types of organisations with charitable status today, nor the range of organisations that should have charitable status".
6   The list of statutory descriptions was first provided by the Charities Act 2006, but the 2011 Act has consolidated in one statute much of the existing charity legislation including the Charities Act 2006, the Recreational Charities Act 1958 and the Charities Act 1993.
7   Charities Act 2011 s.3(1).
8   Charities Act 2011 s.2(1)(b).

how it might develop in the future.[9] Two reviews of the statutory reforms have been conducted. Both Lord Hodgson's statutory review of the Charities Act 2006[10] and the report of the Public Administration Select Committee (PASC)[11] contained detailed scrutiny and recommendations for change. Although the government duly responded,[12] and signalled its support for a project of charity law reforms, the suggestion that public benefit be defined by statute was not to be taken forward. Instead, the Law Commission engaged in projects focused on social investment by charities[13] and a range of technical issues in charity law.[14]

In addition, a large body of pre-existing case law continues to be relevant to the definition of charity. For this reason, a solid understanding of the general evolution of the law of charities remains challenging and essential.[15] In particular, an appreciation of historical developments explains the technical meaning ascribed to the concept of charity, to public benefit and to the approach of the courts to the key requirements of charitable trusts. Further, it elucidates the process of recognising new charitable purposes by analogy to existing charitable purposes, the essence of which has been retained within the final statutory description within the 2011 Act.[16]

7-002

This chapter aims to provide an overview of the law of charitable trusts, and includes discussion of the advantages of charitable status, the problem with political purposes, the pursuit of charity overseas and the need for exclusively charitable objects. Due regard will be had, of course, to the role of the Charity Commission in developing the law within the new statutory framework. This is because statute carves out for the Commission a prominent role in clarifying the public benefit requirement and producing guidance as to compliance for organisations seeking charitable status. It must not be forgotten nonetheless, that,

---

9 As discussed below, much of this uncertainty revolves around the public benefit requirement and the guidance and decisions of the Charity Commission.

10 Lord Hodgson, *Trusted and independent: giving charity back to charities—Review of the Charities Act 2006* (July 2012), available at: *https://www.gov.uk/government/consultations/charities-act-2006-review* (this review was a requirement of the Charities Act 2006 s.73) [Accessed 31 July 2020].

11 Public Administration Select Committee, *Third Report of 2013–14: The role of the Charity Commission and "public benefit": Post-legislative scrutiny of the Charities Act 2006* (June 2013), available at: *http://www.publications. parliament.uk/pa/cm201314/cmselect/cmpubadm/76/76.pdf* [Accessed 31 July 2020].

12 *Government Responses to 1) The Public Administration Select Committee's Third Report of 2013–14 and 2) Lord Hodgson's statutory review of the Charities Act 2006: Trusted and Independent, Giving charity back to charities* (Cm.8700, September 2013), available at: *https://www.gov.uk/government/publications/government-response-to-recommendations-on-the-legal-framework-for-charities* [Accessed 31 July 2020].

13 Its recommendations for reform were included in the Charities (Protection and Social Investment) Act 2016, which gives new powers to charities to make social investments and new powers to the Charity Commission to issue warnings and to suspend or disqualify individuals from trusteeship. See F. Quint (2017) 1 C.L. & P.R. 1.

14 Such as the application of property cy-près and certain powers of the Charity Tribunal: see Law Commission, *Technical Issues in Charity Law* (2017) Law Com. No. 375.

15 The difficulty is that, as Lord Simonds noted, "A great body of law has . . . grown up. Often it may appear illogical and even capricious. It could hardly be otherwise when its guiding principle is so vaguely stated and is liable to be differently interpreted in different ages" (*Gilmour v Coats* [1949] A.C. 426 at 443).

16 Charities Act 2011 s.3(1)(m) includes "other purposes currently recognised as charitable and any new charitable purposes which are similar to another charitable purpose".

"The Commission will be subject to the existing law of charities . . . just as it was before enactment".[17]

The Advantages of Charitable Status

7-003

Charitable trusts benefit from a range of advantages or privileges that do not attach to other trusts. Special treatment is afforded on the basis that trusts for the promotion of charitable ends are valuable in the community as providing a benefit to the public and not merely to private individuals. Much of the litigation as regards charitable trusts is spurred by the need to filter out those trusts which do not benefit a sufficient section of the community and, therefore, do not deserve the advantages bestowed on charities. These advantages range from relaxed legal rules vis-à-vis other trusts to a variety of tax exemptions that accompany charitable status. Not surprisingly, tax advantages are of particular prominence. Indeed, some have gone as far as to point to an inextricable tie between the question of whether a purpose should be deemed charitable at law and the consequent fiscal privileges which attach to charitable status.[18] Although this view is by no means universally shared,[19] it is difficult to ignore the colossal value of tax exemptions generated per annum and the motivation for manipulation of the system by individuals. As is clear from the brief categories listed below, moreover, charitable trusts benefit also from relaxed rules as to certainty and perpetuity.

Purpose trusts

7-004

As discussed in Ch.6, a trust for non-charitable purposes is prima facie void for want of a beneficiary to enforce it. This rule is redundant in the case of charitable trusts where the so-called beneficiary principle does not apply.[20] Charitable purpose trusts are, therefore, valid and responsibility for enforcement lies with the Attorney General. Hence, these trusts do not require ascertainable beneficiaries to enforce them. In addition to their wide powers of admin-

---

17   J. Hackney, "Charities and Public Benefit" (2008) 124 L.Q.R. 347 at 350.

18   As Lord Cross stated in *Dingle v Turner* [1972] A.C. 601 at 624, "In answering the question whether any given trust is a charitable trust the courts—as I see it—cannot avoid having regard to the fiscal privileges accorded to charities . . . It is of course unfortunate that the recognition of any trust as a valid charitable trust should automatically attract fiscal privileges, for the question whether a trust to further some purpose is so little likely to benefit the public that it ought to be declared invalid and the question whether it is likely to confer such benefits on the public that it should enjoy fiscal immunity are really two quite different questions".

19   See, principally, the views of Lord MacDermott in *Dingle v Turner* [1972] A.C. 601 at 614.

20   Note that charity can be carried out in a variety of legal forms which range from the charitable trust with individual or corporate trustees to unincorporated associations or registered companies.

istration, the Charity Commission can exercise powers of enforcement as are exercisable by the Attorney General.[21]

Certainty of objects

7-005

Charitable trusts differ from private trusts in that the objects of a charitable trust need not be certain. Provided the objects are wholly and exclusively charitable, the courts or the Charity Commission can remedy any vagueness by preparing a scheme for the application of funds.[22] The cy-près doctrine, which allows for the dedication of trust property to purposes as near as possible to those originally selected, is considered in Ch.8.

Perpetuity

7-006

A charity is not subject to the rule against alienability that applies to pure purpose trusts.[23] Accordingly, property can be dedicated indefinitely to charitable ends such as the relief of poverty or the advancement of religion.[24] In addition, although a gift to charity must vest within the perpetuity period, a gift over from one charity to another can occur outside the perpetuity period.[25] In this regard, the Perpetuities and Accumulations Acts 1964 and 2009 do not apply a rule against remoteness.[26] Where, however, the gift is from a non-charitable source to a charity, or from a charity to a non-charitable recipient, the rule against remoteness will apply. It was, thus, a major innovation of the 1964 Act that it became possible to wait and see whether a gift took effect within the perpetuity period. The principle of "wait and see" is retained by s.7 of the 2009 Act.

Tax advantages

7-007

Last but most certainly not least, charitable status attracts a range of significant tax advantages. These include:

- relief from income tax on investment income applicable to exclusively charitable purposes[27];

---

21   Charities Act 2011 s.114. The agreement of the Attorney General is required on each occasion.
22   Charities Act 2011 s.69.
23   See para.**6-004.**
24   Note that restrictions are imposed in relation to the accumulation of income by charity trustees under the Perpetuities and Accumulations Act 2009 s.14.
25   *Christ's Hospital v Grainger* (1849) 1 Mac. & G. 460.
26   See Ch.4 for a detailed discussion of the perpetuity rules.
27   The income must, in fact, be applied to charitable purposes: *IRC v Educational Grants Association Ltd* [1967] Ch. 993.

■ exemption from tax on trading income where either the trade is exercised in the course of carrying out a primary purpose of the charitable trust or the work in connection with the trade is mainly carried out by beneficiaries of the charitable trust[28];

■ exemptions from capital gains tax[29];

■ a claim to at least 80 per cent relief from the payment of non-domestic rates for premises wholly or mainly used for charitable purposes; and

■ exemptions from payment of stamp duty on conveyances.

It should be noted that the Finance Act 2010 introduced for tax purposes a new definition of a charity entitled to UK charity tax reliefs and exemptions.[30] In defining "charity", the Act entails that a charity must be established for charitable purposes only[31] and that it must meet new conditions relating to "jurisdiction", "registration" and "management".[32] The implication of failing to meet this new test appears to be that a charity will lose entitlement to charity tax reliefs.

The Definition of Charity

Legal meaning

The legal meaning of charity has always been somewhat elusive and stands distinct from any understanding of charity in a general or popular sense. As Lord Wright observed, the word "charitable" in its legal sense is, "a word of art, of precise and technical meaning".[33] It is curious, therefore, that prior to the enactment of the Charities Act 2006 a prominent characteristic of the development of charity was the reluctance both of the courts and of the Legislature to provide an authoritative definition.[34] Rather, in the course of past centuries, it was necessary to have regard to any prevailing or accepted understanding of charity by charting case law

7-008

---

28   Income Tax Act 2007 s.525.
29   See Taxation of Chargeable Gains Act 1992 s.256.
30   The redefinition of charity is in response to the decision of the European Court of Justice in *Persche v Finanzamt Ludenscheid* [2009] P.T.S.R. 915 that a Member State is not permitted to confine tax reliefs only to those organisations established in that Member State.
31   As defined by reference to the Charities Act 2011 s.178 (Finance Act 2010 Sch.6 para.1).
32   The management condition imposes a "fit and proper person" test (Finance Act 2010 Sch.6 para.4).
33   *National Anti-Vivisection Society v IRC* [1948] A.C. 31 at 41.
34   In *Baddeley v IRC* [1955] A.C. 572 at 583, Viscount Simonds remarked that, "while no comprehensive definition

developments in order to determine whether a trust or an institution was of an inherently charitable nature.[35] The Charities Act 2006 (now Charities Act 2011), was the first attempt to provide a modern statutory definition of charity by listing 13 descriptions of purposes deemed to be charitable at law. A charitable purpose is a purpose which falls within the list and is for the public benefit. Both the statutory descriptions and the public benefit requirement are considered in detail below, but it is first necessary to consider more closely the key developments in the evolution of the general law.

The historical development of charitable purposes

7-009

A natural starting point in tracing the development of the law is the Preamble to the Charitable Uses Act 1601.[36] The Preamble, containing a detailed list of purposes then regarded as charitable, was to assume a central role for the courts as a reference point, or catalogue of accepted instances of charity. The list was as follows:

> **"The relief of aged, impotent and poor people; the maintenance of sick and maimed soldiers and mariners, schools of learning, free schools and scholars in universities; the repair of bridges, ports, havens, causeways, churches, sea banks and highways; the education and preferment of orphans; the relief, stock or maintenance for houses of correction; the marriage of poor maids, the supportation, aid and help of young tradesmen, handicraftsmen and persons decayed; the relief or redemption of prisoners or captives; the aid or ease of any poor inhabitants concerning payment of fifteens, setting out of soldiers and other taxes."**

The Preamble became pivotal to the development of the law. As Picarda notes, "the practice of the courts was to refer to the preamble as a guide and gradually this practice became an accepted rule of law".[37] The interpretation of charitable objects, furthermore, was not confined merely to those purposes enumerated. Any purpose listed or analogous thereto was deemed to be charitable at law. As Sir William Grant spelled out in *Morice v Bishop of Durham*, "Those purposes are considered charitable, which that statute enumerates, or which by analogies are

---

of legal charity has been given either by the legislature or in judicial utterance, there is no limit to the number and diversity of the ways in which man will seek to benefit his fellow men".

35   In the view of Lord Normand in *Oppenheim v Tobacco Securities Trust Co Ltd* [1951] A.C. 297 at 309, it is this, "empirical development which has so often baffled efforts to reduce the law to systematised definitions".

36   Otherwise referred to as the Statute of Elizabeth I, the Act was repealed by the Mortmain and Charitable Uses Act 1888. Although s.13(2) of the 1888 Act expressly preserved the Preamble, both were repealed by the Charities Act 1960 s.38(4).

37   H. Picarda, *The Law and Practice Relating to Charities*, 3rd edn (London: Butterworths, 1999), p.10.

deemed within its spirit and intendment".[38] Accordingly, by reference to the Preamble and analogous purposes thereto, the categories of charitable purposes had the capacity to grow. In the equity of the statute (or its spirit and intendment), the courts found the necessary flexibility to develop the law to meet the needs of changing times. A responsive approach was necessary. In the view of Lord Greene MR:

> **"The Preamble set out what were then regarded as purposes which should be regarded as charitable in law. It is obvious that as time passed and conditions changed common opinion as to what was properly covered by the word charitable also changed".[39]**

Two hundred years were to pass before any further re-classification of charitable objects was put forward[40] and almost one hundred years more before Lord Macnaghten, in *Pemsel's Case*, famously classified charitable objects in the form to be adopted from then until the 2006 Act.[41] He claimed that charity in its legal sense comprised four principal divisions:

7-010

- trusts for the relief of poverty;

- trusts for the advancement of education;

- trusts for the advancement of religion; and

- trusts for other purposes beneficial to the community not falling under any of the preceding heads.

The alleviation of poverty and the advancement of education or religion were evidently clear in terms of the types of purposes contained therein. The fourth division or head was to prove the most cumbersome as not every purpose of possible benefit was deemed to be a purpose "beneficial to the community". Accordingly, the spirit and intendment of the Preamble continued to have a pervasive influence, in that it remained necessary to look at the Preamble and the decided cases under the Preamble to determine whether a given purpose was sufficiently analogous.[42]

In *Re Strakosch*, for example, a gift for the purpose of strengthening bonds between South

---

38 (1804) 9 Ves. 399 at 405. In order to be within the spirit and intendment of the Preamble, Lord Greene MR identified that the court, "must find something charitable in the same sense as the recited purposes are charitable" (*Re Strakosch* [1949] Ch. 529 at 537).

39 [1949] Ch. 529 at 537.

40 By Sir Samuel Romilly, in *Morice v Bishop of Durham* (1805) 10 Ves. 522.

41 *Commissioners for Special Purposes of Income Tax v Pemsel* [1891] A.C. 531 at 583.

42 A less restrictive approach to the Preamble is promoted by Russell LJ in *Incorporated Council of Law Reporting for England and Wales* [1972] 1 Ch. 73 at 88 where he argues as regards a given purpose, ". . . the proper question to ask is whether there are any grounds for holding it to be outside the equity of the Statute".

Africa and the United Kingdom was perceived by Lord Greene MR to be "undoubtedly for the benefit of the community . . . [but] not charitable in the sense in which the benefits to the community instanced in the preamble are charitable".[43] Similarly, in *Williams' Trustees v IRC*,[44] a trust to promote the interests of Welsh people living in London was of clear benefit to the public in a general sense. As the purpose could not be said to be sufficiently distinguishable from mere social or recreational purposes, however, it was not within the spirit and intendment of the Preamble. It was not beneficial in a way the law regarded as charitable.

Proceeding by analogy

7-011   A valuable illustration of the process of drawing analogies from the Preamble is to be found in *Scottish Burial Reform and Cremation Society v Glasgow City Corp*.[45] There the House of Lords was required to consider whether the provision of a crematorium was caught by the fourth head as being within the spirit and intendment of the Preamble. Lord Upjohn objected that the spirit and intendment of the Preamble had been "stretched almost to breaking point",[46] but he highlighted the series of cases that drove him to conclude that the provision of a crematorium was charitable.[47] As a starting point the Preamble makes specific reference to the repair of churches. By analogy, a trust for the repair of a parish churchyard was held charitable in *Re Vaughan*.[48] By way of analogy to *Re Vaughan*, the provision of a burial ground for members of the Society of Friends was held charitable, there being no distinction to be drawn between a gift to repair God's house and God's acre.[49] Building further, a link could be drawn to validate a public burial ground in *Re Eighmie*[50] and, accepting that, the provision of a crematorium on the instant facts.

7-012   By far the most enterprising approach is to be found in the Canadian authority of *Vancouver Regional Freenet Association v Minister of National Revenue*,[51] where the provision of internet access was held charitable by analogy to the repair of bridges or highways referred to in the Preamble. Although doubtless creative in adapting long-standing principles to meet the needs of contemporary society, it is difficult to imagine a more compelling case for statutory reform. On the evidence of such cases, the spirit and intendment of the Preamble had long ceased to function as a sensible measure of the appropriateness of adopting new charitable purposes.

43   [1949] 1 Ch. 529 at 538.
44   [1947] A.C. 447.
45   [1968] A.C. 138.
46   [1968] A.C. 138 at 153.
47   [1968] A.C. 138 at 152.
48   (1886) 33 Ch. D. 187.
49   *Re Manser* [1905] 1 Ch. 68.
50   [1935] Ch. 524.
51   (1996) 137 D.L.R. 406; see A. Iwobi, "Rolling Down the Information Highway in Search of Charitable Status" (1998) 5 Web JCLI.

The Charities Act 2011

The question of the inherent charitable nature of any given purpose or institution is no longer answered by reference to the four heads of charity as laid down in *Pemsel*. Regard must be had to the new statutory descriptions of purposes contained in paras (a)–(m) of s.3(1) of the 2011 Act. These are as follows:

(a) the prevention or relief of poverty;

(b) the advancement of education;

(c) the advancement of religion;

(d) the advancement of health or the saving of lives;

(e) the advancement of citizenship or community development;

(f) the advancement of the arts, culture, heritage or science;

(g) the advancement of amateur sport;

(h) the advancement of human rights, conflict resolution or reconciliation or the promotion of religious or racial harmony or equality and diversity;

(i) the advancement of environmental protection or improvement;

(j) the relief of those in need, by reason of youth, age, ill-health, disability, financial hardship or other disadvantage;

(k) the advancement of animal welfare;

(l) the promotion of the efficiency of the armed forces of the Crown, or of the efficiency of the police, fire and rescue services or ambulance services;

(m) other purposes currently recognised as charitable and any new charitable purposes which are similar to another charitable purpose.

The idea is that in order for a trust or institution to exist for the furtherance of charitable purposes, it must fall within at least one of the statutory purposes listed above. In addition, a charitable purpose must be for the public benefit and exclusively charitable in nature. The approach adopted in this chapter is briefly to introduce the general concepts of public benefit and exclusivity of charitable nature before examining in detail each of the statutory purposes in the Charities Act 2011. It is important throughout to have regard to the context in which the law is interpreted and applied, in particular, to the role played by the courts and the Charity Commission in assessing charitable purposes in the public benefit.

The role of the Charity Commission

7-014

The Charity Commission acts as the independent regulator of charities in England and Wales. With some 168,000 registered charities generating income of some £79 billion,[52] its regulatory role places it at the heart of day-to-day developments in the charitable sector. The objectives of the Commission are detailed in the Charities Act 2011 s.14. These are as follows:

- the public confidence objective, which is to increase public trust and confidence in charities;

- the public benefit objective, which is to promote awareness and understanding of the operation of the public benefit requirement;

- the compliance objective, which is to promote compliance by charity trustees with their legal obligations in exercising control and management of the administration of their charities;

- the charitable resources objective, which is to promote the effective use of charitable resources; and

- the accountability objective, which is to enhance the accountability of charities to donors, beneficiaries and the general public.

As an unelected regulator, the Charity Commission was not intended to act as a lawmaker. Nonetheless (and leaving aside the controversy that has surrounded its provision of public benefit guidance (para.**7-020**)), there are two important aspects to the Commission's work that have driven recent legal developments. First, the Commission has a statutory responsibility to keep and maintain a Register of Charities.[53] The advantages that flow from registration are considerable, and it is the Charity Commission that determines whether a new organisation will be registered as a charity[54] or an existing charity removed from the register.[55] In determin-

---

52 See Charity Commission, *Annual Report and Accounts 2018/19 (July 2019)*, p.12.
53 Charities Act 2011 s.29.
54 The effect of registration is that an institution is, for all purposes other than rectification of the register, "conclusively presumed to be or to have been a charity" at any time when it is or was on the register (Charities Act 2011 s.37).
55 See R. Meakin, *The Law of Charitable Status: Maintenance and Removal*, (Cambridge University Press: 2008).

ing charitable status, the Commission operates not unlike a court to interpret the law and to apply it to organisations in accordance with principles laid down in previous decisions. In this way, the Commission's decisions have become a source of precedent. Secondly, in its review of the register of charities,[56] the Commission has been instrumental in updating the law in line with changing social circumstances. This has been in evidence when the Commission has recognised new charitable purposes (through the process of drawing analogies with existing charitable purposes). It can be seen also in its identification of purposes which were once charitable that, in its view, have ceased, or should cease, to be so. One illustration is the Commission's refusal to register rifle clubs as charitable despite case law pointing to the charitable benefit of such groups.[57]

Appealing Commission decisions

7-015

Prior to the enactment of the Charities Act 2006, an appeal against a decision of the Charity Commission was required to be made to the High Court, and involved the applicant in a process which was both expensive and time-consuming. It was hoped that access to justice might be improved by the establishment of a Charity Tribunal to hear appeals against the decisions of the Commission in a timely and cost-effective manner. Following the Tribunals, Courts and Enforcement Act 2007, the Charity Tribunal was restructured. The First-Tier Tribunal (Charity) now hears increasing numbers of appeals from the legal decisions of the Charity Commission.[58] Although its decisions "turn on their own facts and have no precedent value",[59] the First-tier Tribunal offers an important avenue of redress for disgruntled applicants and an opportunity to have their case considered afresh.[60] From there, an appeal may be made to the Upper Tribunal and then to the Court of Appeal.[61] Commission decision-making is also subject to application for review.[62] In a case of procedural irregularity, for example, the Tribunal may quash a Commission decision and refer it back.

More broadly, the Charity Commission (albeit with the consent of the Attorney General)[63] may refer to the Tribunal a question that has arisen in connection with the exercise of its functions.[64]

---

56   See RR1, *The Review of the Register of Charities* (1999).

57   *Re Stephens* (1892) 8 T.L.R. 792.

58   See A. McKenna, "How Does Charity Law Develop in the Age of the Tribunal" (2018) 20 C.L. & P.R. 25.

59   See A. McKenna, "The Charity Tribunal – Where To and From" (2014) 4 PCB 213, p.214.

60   For a critique of Commission decision-making and discussion of recent FTT appeals, see L. McMurtry, "Charitable Purposes, Demonstrable Benefit and the Role of the Charity Commission: The Fourth *Pemsel* Head Recast" (2019) 70(4) N.I.L.Q. 445.

61   In a suitably important case, there is scope for the case to start in the Upper Tribunal.

62   At the request of the Attorney General or by specified persons (Charities Act 2011 s.321). General administrative complaints may be made to the Charity Commission itself and from there to the Parliamentary and Health Service Ombudsman (PHSO).

63   For a critical appraisal of the need for this consent, see M. Synge, "The Attorney General and the Charity Commission: One Rule Without Reason" [2016] P.L. 409.

64   Charities Act 2011 s.325(1)(a).

There is scope for both the Attorney General[65] and the Charity Commission[66] to refer matters to the Tribunal which relate to the operation of charity law in any respect or the application of charity law to a particular state of affairs. References differ from appeals and reviews in the sense that wider questions of charity law may be considered without the need for a specific case to have arisen. This process is important and distinctive in that it allows for clarification of the law before any decision on that aspect of law has been made. By way of illustration, the Attorney General asked the Upper Tribunal to consider whether benevolent funds and some other poverty charities satisfy the public benefit test where beneficiaries are defined by membership of a particular family or by an employment link to a particular company.[67] The Upper Tribunal confirmed that the status of these charities had been unaffected by the 2006 and 2011 Acts.[68]

Public Benefit

Statutory requirements

7-016

Section 2(1)(b) of the Charities Act 2011 makes clear that a charitable purpose is a purpose that is for the public benefit, "as that term is understood for the purposes of the law relating to England and Wales".[69] No new statutory definition of public benefit is, therefore, provided. It follows that regard must be had as to how the concept of public benefit evolved under the general law.[70] Under s.4(2), it is not to be presumed that a purpose of a particular description is for the public benefit.[71] Public benefit must be demonstrated in all cases.[72]

The approach of the courts

7-017

Traditionally, the public benefit requirement for charitable trusts could be stated succinctly, that is, the benefit must be available to the public at large, or to a sufficient section of the

---

65 Charities Act 2011 s.326(1).
66 Charities Act 2011 s.325(1)(b) (again with the consent of the Attorney General).
67 For discussion of the public benefit case law preceding the 2006 Act, see para.**7-032**.
68 *Attorney General v Charity Commission for England and Wales* [2012] UKUT 420 (TCC).
69 Charities Act 2011 s.4(3). See generally, J. Garton, *Public Benefit in Charity Law* (Oxford: Oxford University Press, 2013).
70 For a discussion of early developments, see M. Mills, "The Development of the Public Benefit Requirements for Charitable Trusts in the Nineteenth Century" (2016) 37(3) J. Leg. Hist. 269.
71 Previously (in the absence of evidence to the contrary), it was common to speak of trusts falling under the first three *Pemsel* heads as presumed to be for the public benefit.
72 See further, J. Hackney, "Charities and Public Benefit" (2008) 124 L.Q.R. 347.

community.[73] In the words of Lord Wrenbury in *Verge v Somerville*, "To ascertain whether a gift constitutes a valid charitable trust . . . a first inquiry must be whether it is public—whether it is for the benefit of the community or of an appreciably important class of the community".[74] Thus, the need for public benefit in this technical or legal sense has always been paramount. In practice, different "tests" of public benefit evolved to meet the specific concerns of the courts arising under the four *Pemsel* heads of charity. Invariably, therefore, the answer as to what amounted to a "sufficient section of the community" reflected the mix of pragmatic, economic and social concerns arising under each of these separate heads.

The personal nexus test

7-018

A prominent example of the specificity of public benefit is to be found under the advancement of education case law where the presence of a personal link (of blood or contract) between potential beneficiaries would indicate a private trust.[75] In contrast, as regards a trust for the alleviation of poverty, the cases show that no such constraints were operative. The relief of poverty was considered so altruistic that trusts under this head were exempt from the rule that there could be no personal nexus. Either public benefit to the whole community could be derived indirectly or a narrow class in this context could still be viewed as a sufficient section of the community. In a trust for the relief of poverty, therefore, it was perfectly permissible to define objects by reference to a class of poor employees or poor relatives. As will be demonstrated, however, the distinction between a trust to benefit a class of poor persons (public trust) and a trust to benefit particular poor persons (private trust) was sometimes difficult to draw. This difficulty is addressed in detail below.[76]

As regards trusts for the advancement of religion, again there was the need for a benefit to the public or a sufficient section thereof. Unlike education, a less rigorous approach applied which reflected the absence of specific concerns regarding exploitation of charitable benefits under this head. It is difficult to see what possible objection might be raised to a trust for the advancement of religion amongst one's employees, for example.

The "class within a class" test

7-019

The final *Pemsel* head contained "other purposes beneficial to the community", i.e. purposes other than those for the advancement of religion, education and for the alleviation of poverty. The development of its public benefit test was influenced by the nature of purposes collectively charitable under the fourth head. As Viscount Simonds emphasised, "It is, . . . in my opinion,

---

73 The question whether a trust is exclusively charitable may then be considered separately (para.**7-022**).
74 [1924] A.C. 497 at 499.
75 *Oppenheim v Tobacco Securities Trust Co Ltd* [1951] A.C. 297 (para.**7-047**).
76 See para.**7-034**.

particularly important . . . to keep firmly in mind the necessity of the element of general public utility and I would not relax this rule".[77] By the very nature of trusts that fell under this head, the benefits provided required to be available to the public at large.

Accordingly, the courts enforced a particular public benefit requirement, that the possible beneficiaries must not be "a class within a class". In *IRC v Baddeley*, benefits were confined to inhabitants of a particular area who were members of a particular church.[78] In effect, a class had been specified and then made subject to a further restriction, thus creating a class within a class.[79] It was necessary to distinguish between "a form of relief extended to the whole community yet, by its very nature, advantageous only to the few, and a form of relief accorded to a selected few out of a larger number equally willing and able to take advantage of it".[80] The former was charitable; the latter was not. Viscount Simonds' oft quoted illustration is that:

> **"a bridge which is available for all the public may undoubtedly be a charity and it is indifferent how many people use it. But confine its use to a selected number of persons, however numerous and important: it is then clearly not a charity. It is not of general public utility for it does not serve the public purpose which its nature qualifies it to serve".[81]**

Accordingly, it was not possible to create a trust of general public utility for those people living in London, if its benefits were confined arbitrarily to those of a particular nationality or a particular church.

Admittedly, the purposes charitable under the old fourth *Pemsel* head have now been divided up into a range of statutory descriptions, but there is nothing to suggest that the "class within a class" test will not continue to apply to future cases.

The Charity Commission guidance

7-020

The Charity Commission has a statutory obligation to consult, issue (and from time to time revise) guidance as to the operation of the public benefit requirement.[82] It is a stated statutory objective that the Commission "promote awareness and understanding" of how the requirement operates.[83] The Commission's guidance does not create a new definition of public benefit or alter the general law. Nonetheless, the Charity Commission plays a key role in assessing

---

77 *IRC v Baddeley* [1955] A.C. 572 at 591.
78 [1955] A.C. 572.
79 For a further example, see *Williams v IRC* [1947] AC 447 ("Welsh people living In London").
80 [1955] A.C. 572 at 592.
81 [1955] A.C. 572 at 592.
82 Charities Act 2011 s.17.
83 Charities Act 2011 s.14(2).

public benefit and in determining whether an organisation should acquire, or continue to hold, charitable status on this basis.[84]

In 2008, the Commission published *Charities and Public Benefit*, its general interpretative guidance on public benefit.[85] Two clear principles were promoted. The first was that there must be an identifiable benefit or benefits, thus focusing on the "benefit" element of public benefit. The second principle was designed to promote the need for benefit to the public or a sufficient section of the public, thus focusing on the "public" element to public benefit. Crucially the Commission felt that where the benefit was to a section of the public, the opportunity to benefit could not be unreasonably restricted by geographical or other restrictions or by the ability to pay any fees charged. In addition, people in poverty were not to be excluded from the opportunity to benefit and any private benefit was to be merely incidental.

In *Independent Schools Council v Charity Commission for England and Wales*,[86] however, aspects of the Commission's guidance were successfully challenged in the Upper Tribunal, forcing the Commission to rethink its approach and jettison its specific guidance on fee-charging. It has since altered its guidance which now exists in the form of three public benefit guides and a wide range of other public benefit related material.[87]

More detailed analysis of public benefit may be found within the substantive discussion of each head of charity below, but a summary of the key principles underpinning the Charity Commission's approach may be summarised as follows.[88]

7-021

- In general, for a purpose to be "for the public benefit" it must satisfy both the "benefit" and "public" aspects.[89]

- The "benefit aspect" of public benefit is about whether the purpose itself is beneficial.

- The "public aspect" of public benefit concerns who the purpose benefits.

- For a purpose to be charitable, it must be beneficial in a way that is identifiable and capable of being proved by evidence where necessary and not based on personal views.

- A purpose cannot be a charitable purpose where any detriment or harm resulting from it outweighs the benefit.

---

84 See generally, M. Synge, *The "New" Public Benefit Requirement: Making Sense of Charity Law?* (Oxford: Hart, 2015).
85 Charity Commission, *Charities and Public Benefit* (January 2008).
86 [2011] UKUT 421 (TCC).
87 See *https://www.gov.uk/government/publications/public-benefit-an-overview/public-benefit-an-overview* [Accessed 31 July 2020].
88 *https://www.gov.uk/government/publications/public-benefit-the-public-benefit-requirement-pb1/public-benefit-the-public-benefit-requirement* [Accessed 31 July 2020].
89 Different rules apply if the purpose is to relieve or prevent poverty (para.**7-036**).

■ For a purpose to be charitable it must benefit either the public in general or a sufficient section of the public.[90]

■ In general, a charity must not have a purpose which defines who can benefit by reference to their family relationship, their employment by an employer or their membership of an unincorporated association. The law allows this only where the purpose is the relief (and in some cases the prevention) of poverty.

■ A charitable purpose may only confer personal benefits if these are "incidental" to carrying out the purpose.

Exclusivity of Charitable Purpose

7-022

The final principle of a general nature is that the objects of a trust (or the purposes of a charitable institution) must be exclusively charitable. It follows that in determining the charitable nature of a trust, the courts are called upon to look closely at the terms of a trust to work out whether trust property can be dedicated to non-charitable purposes. Sometimes the distinction between cases is fine and almost imperceptible. The awkwardness in drawing firm principles derives from the sheer volume of case law decided over hundreds of years in which the courts have engaged with the subtleties of construction. Nowhere is this better illustrated than in the similarly worded provisions of *Farley v Westminster Bank*[91] and *Re Simson*.[92] In the former, a gift to a vicar "for parish work" was deemed invalid; Lord Atkin considered parish work "to be of such vague import as to go far beyond the ordinary meaning of charity".[93]

In *Re Simson*, however, a gift to a vicar "for his work in the parish" was upheld as a gift to that person limited to purposes defined by his office. Hence, there was a sufficient nexus between the vicar and his charitable work for Romer J to distinguish from previous authority. He concluded:

> **"A gift to a vicar and churchwardens 'for parish work' is a general phrase covering a multitude of activities, and, as such, was held to be too wide, but a gift to a vicar 'for his work in the parish' involves**

---

90   The guidance takes on board the Equality Act 2010, which permits charities to benefit people defined by reference to a "protected characteristic", such as age, disability, or race or nationality, provided the restriction of benefits to people having that characteristic may be justified in relation to the purpose.

91   [1939] A.C. 430.

92   [1946] Ch. 299.

93   [1939] A.C. 430 at 435.

> a totally different conception. It merely means that the gift is to be used for the purposes of such part of his work, i.e. his functions connected with the care of souls in the particular district—as lie within the particular parish. In my judgment, such work is both sufficiently definite and is charitable".[94]

Difficulties in determining the ambit of a trust extend also to cases where the precise description of objects is not stated such as in a gift on trust for "charitable purposes" or "deserving purposes". A gift on trust for "charitable purposes" is unproblematic. It may be, for example, that the trustee is given a discretion or a power to allocate property to charitable purposes of his own choosing. Whatever objects are selected, the trustee must ensure they are charitable. Where, however, a gift is on trust for "benevolent" purposes[95] or "public" purposes[96] or "deserving" purposes,[97] the gift will fail because its use is not confined to exclusively charitable purposes. Although purposes benevolent, public or deserving may incorporate much that falls within the definition of charity, there is a chance that some part of the gift may be applied outside the confines of charity and, for this reason, the gift will fail. Despite such a seemingly strict approach, there are a variety of means to construe as exclusively charitable, trusts which appear, at first glance, to provide for both charitable and non-charitable ends. It is open to the court to:

- ■ adopt a conjunctive construction;

- ■ sever charitable and non-charitable ends;

- ■ deem non-charitable ends to be merely incidental; or

- ■ apply the Charitable Trusts (Validation) Act 1954.

Each will now be considered in turn.

Conjunctive/disjunctive construction

Sometimes a charitable purpose is linked with another purpose and it is necessary to look at matters of construction to determine whether the trust property must necessarily be devoted to exclusively charitable purposes. Generally speaking, it is clear that the courts have been minded to accept that purposes linked by the word "and", such as "charitable *and* deserving"

7-023

---

94   [1946] Ch. 299 at 305.
95   See e.g. *Re Barnett* (1908) 24 T.L.R. 788 (benevolent objects or purposes of a company).
96   *Blair v Duncan* [1902] A.C. 37.
97   See *Harris v Du Pasquier* (1872) 26 L.T. 689.

or "charitable *and* educational" should be viewed conjunctively and not disjunctively. This entails that such gifts are exclusively charitable as there is no possibility that property can be applied to deserving objects or educational objects that are not also charitable. By way of illustration, in *Re Best* property was left upon trust, "for such charitable and benevolent institutions" in the city of Birmingham as the Lord Mayor should choose.[98] Farwell J had no difficulty declaring this to be a good charitable gift and claimed, "I think the testator here intended that the institution should be both charitable and benevolent; and I see no reason for reading the conjunction 'and' as 'or'".[99]

By contrast, purposes linked by the word "or" such as "charitable or deserving" should be viewed disjunctively. When construed in this way, such purposes are not exclusively charitable as they permit the dedication of property to purposes which are either charitable or non-charitable. Accordingly, in *Houston v Burns*,[100] a gift made for "public, benevolent or charitable" purposes in a Scottish parish failed because the words were wide enough to justify the trustees in disposing of the fund to benevolent or public purposes which were not charitable. Similarly, in *Attorney General v National Provincial & Union Bank of England*, a gift "for such patriotic purposes or objects and such charitable institution or institutions or charitable object or objects in the British Empire" as the trustees may select was construed disjunctively and failed.[101] There were several categories of objects, each of which could not be said to be charitable.

7-024

Although it is possible to find a large number of authorities that adhere to the general rule as to conjunctive/disjunctive construction, it is necessary to adopt a cautious approach to the case law. For example, it is not difficult to unearth authorities with markedly different standpoints. In *Attorney General Bahamas v Royal Trust Co*,[102] a gift for the "education and welfare" of young people was interpreted disjunctively on the ground that welfare could not be said to be restricted to educational welfare. Lord Oliver remarked, "it is not easy to imagine a purpose connected with the education of a child which is not also a purpose for the child's welfare. Thus if 'welfare' is to be given any separate meaning at all it must be something different from and wider than mere education, for otherwise the word becomes otiose".[103] Perhaps, therefore, this is a legitimate point of distinction from, say, the conjunctive reading of "charitable and benevolent" in *Re Best*. There, Farwell J found it easy to conceive of charitable purposes which were not also benevolent[104] and found it of no surprise that the testator should seek to ensure that the objects of the trust were both charitable and benevolent. Furthermore, as

---

98 [1904] 2 Ch. 354.

99 [1904] 2 Ch. 354 at 356. See also, *Re Sutton* (1885) 28 Ch. D. 464 at 465, where Pearson J considered that the words "charitable and deserving objects" in the will before him connoted "only one class of objects, and the word 'charitable' governs the whole sentence. It means objects which are at once charitable and deserving".

100 [1918] A.C. 337; see also *Chichester Diocesan Fund and Board of Finance v Simpson* [1944] A.C. 341, where the words "charitable or benevolent" were construed as sufficiently wide to allow property to be applied to benevolent objects which were not also charitable.

101 [1924] A.C. 262.

102 [1986] 1 W.L.R. 1001.

103 [1986] 1 W.L.R. 1001 at 1005.

104 Such as in advancing the writings of Joanna Southcote: see *Thornton v Howe* (1862) 31 Beav. 14 (see para.**7-053**).

proffered by Sargant J in *Re Eades,* "The more qualifications or characteristics enumerated, the more probable it is that there was an intention to multiply rather than restrict the scope of the disposition".[105] As to his approach to construction of the specified class of "religious, charitable and philanthropic objects", Sargant J observed that "the ordinary careful student of English language and literature would, I think, almost certainly come to the conclusion that the three epithets here are epithets creating conjunctive or cumulative classes of objects, not epithets creating conjunctive or cumulative qualifications for each object".[106] As one or more of the selected objects might be merely philanthropic and not necessarily charitable, however, the gift in favour of charity failed.

Severing charitable and non-charitable parts

A charitable trust will fail for uncertainty where the property to be applied for the charitable purpose is not stated and no guidance is provided as to how that property might be ascertained. Commonly, moreover, difficulties are created where a variety of beneficiaries are specified, but there is uncertainty as to the beneficial share. In *Salusbury v Denton*,[107] the court was able to sever purposes where it found that the trust comprised charitable and non-charitable objects. There, a testator left property by will to his widow to apply in part to the foundation of a charity school and, as to the rest, for the testator's relatives. On the facts, the courts ordered an equal division between the charitable and the non-charitable parts in line with the maxim "equity is equality". Two points require consideration. First, severance is possible only where it is not open to the trustee to apply the property solely towards the non-charitable ends. As Page-Wood VC claimed:

7-025

> "It is one thing to direct a trustee to give *a part* of a fund to one set of objects, and the *remainder* to another, and it is a distinct thing to direct him to give 'either' to one set of objects 'or' to another . . . This is a case of the former description. Here the trustee was bound to give a part to each".[108]

Secondly, equal division will be patently inappropriate in some cases. If so, the court may endeavour to calculate the percentage to be held on invalid trusts in order to hold the remaining part charitable.[109]

---

105 [1920] 2 Ch. 353 at 357.
106 [1920] 2 Ch. 353 at 357.
107 (1857) 3 K. & J. 529.
108 (1857) 3 K. & J. 529 at 539.
109 See *Re Coxen* [1948] Ch. 747 at 753 where Jenkins J admitted that, had the provisions under consideration been invalid, the court, "would find means to quantify the income applicable to the invalid trusts rather than divert from purposes admittedly charitable (say) eleven twelfths of the income of a fund because a part of such

Incidental non-charitable purposes

7-026

Provided it is truly ancillary to the achievement of the main charitable purpose, an incidental non-charitable purpose will be accommodated. In *Re Coxen*,[110] therefore, a sum of money set aside for an annual dinner for trustees did not taint the whole trust as the amount was an insignificant fraction of the total and provided for the better administration of the trust. Jenkins J considered of the testator that:

> **"his motive and object in providing for the annual dinner . . . was I think clearly to benefit the charity and not the members for the time being . . . It cannot be said that these particular modes of furthering his charitable purpose are in fact incapable of furthering it. On the contrary I think there is every reason to suppose that it will be furthered thereby".**[111]

It is important not to confuse the stated charitable purposes of a trust with the incidental consequences of carrying out those purposes. In *London Hospital Medical College v IRC*,[112] Brightman J held that a students' union would be charitable if it existed to further the educational and therefore charitable purposes of the college to which it was attached. He claimed that "If, put shortly, the union existed for the benefit of the college, it would be immaterial that the union also provided a personal benefit for the individual students who were elected members of the union and chose to make use of its facilities".[113] This is much in line with the thinking of Atkin LJ in *IRC v Yorkshire Agricultural Society* that:

> **"if the benefit given to its members is only given to them with a view of giving encouragement and carrying out the main purpose which is a charitable purpose, then I think the mere fact that the members are benefited in the course of promoting the charitable purpose would not prevent the society being established for charitable purposes only".**[114]

A problem arises where non-charitable activities are not incidental or subsidiary, but form part of the trust purposes. Clearly, the determination of whether a benefit is an incidental benefit falls to be addressed in the circumstances of the case. The more substantial the non-charitable

---

income incapable of exact quantification but incapable on any reasonable estimate of exceeding (say) one twelfth is directed to be held on invalid trusts".

110 [1948] Ch. 747 (a trust for orthopaedic hospitals).
111 [1948] Ch. 747 at 755.
112 [1976] 1 W.L.R. 613.
113 [1976] 1 W.L.R. 613 at 620.
114 [1928] 1 K.B. 611 at 631.

activity or the weaker the connection between the activity and the main charitable purpose, the greater the assumption that the activity is an object in its own right.

Charitable Trusts (Validation) Act 1954

The Charitable Trusts (Validation) Act 1954 applies to trusts taking effect before 16 December 1952. The confinement of its ambit in this manner has ensured that the Act is of increasingly less relevance with the passage of time.[115] It was enacted to render charitable the so called "imperfect trust provisions" invalid under the common law in that the property thereof could be applied either for exclusively charitable purposes or, indeed, non-charitable purposes. The effect of the Act was to allow for the terms of such trusts to be treated as though they were capable of application for charitable purposes only. By way of example, in *Chichester Diocesan Fund and Board of Finance v Simpson*, trusts for "charitable or benevolent purposes" were not deemed to be trusts for exclusively charitable purposes.[116] The Charitable Trusts (Validation) Act 1954 would have allowed this wording to permit the disposal of property towards charitable ends alone. More difficulty is involved in cases where there is no express mention of charitable purposes. Harman J preferred a restrictive view in the case of a trust for "worthy causes",[117] but in *Re Wykes*[118] the use of the phrase "welfare purposes" had a "sufficient flavour of charity"[119] that Buckley J was prepared to deem this to fall within the meaning of the Act. In essence, the court is required to make an assessment as to whether anyone would have a legitimate complaint if the whole were applied for charity. Thus in *Ulrich v Treasury Solicitor*, where Hart J was called upon to construe the vague language used by a testator, he was happy to follow *Re Wykes* and hold that the entirety of a fund was one to be devoted to the relief of poverty amongst the specified class.[120] On the facts, the class was in practice limited to those exposed to financial hardship and the size of the fund was not calculated to be of much obvious use except as a fund to be resorted to in the case of genuine hardship. Accordingly, it is now clear that the Act is not confined to cases where a specific charitable purpose has been expressed.

7-027

---

115   As Cross J professed in *Re Harpur's Will Trusts* [1961] Ch. 38 at 48, "The Act leaves the law untouched for the future but, for some reason which I do not pretend to understand, validates retrospectively a limited number of dispositions which had already failed. I do not know on what principle these particular dispositions were selected for favourable treatment and I see no reason for construing this Act liberally".
116   [1944] A.C. 341.
117   *Re Gillingham Bus Disaster Fund* [1958] Ch. 300.
118   [1961] Ch. 229.
119   To adopt the phrase used by Cross J in *Re Saxone Shoe Co Ltd's Trust Deed* [1962] 1 W.L.R. 943 at 957.
120   [2006] 1 W.L.R. 33. The approach of Hart J was endorsed by Blackburne J in *Cawdron v Merchant Taylors' School* [2010] P.T.S.R. 507 at 518, by Arnold J in *Re St Andrews (Cheam) Lawn Tennis Club* [2012] 1 W.L.R. 3487 at 3500 and by Deputy Judge Andrew Simmonds QC in *Buckley v Barlow* [2016] EWHC 3017 (Ch) at [48].

The Statutory Descriptions of Charitable Purposes

7-028 Bearing in mind that for a purpose to be charitable it must be for the public benefit and exclusively charitable in nature, it is appropriate now to consider the 13 descriptions of charity as listed in the Charities Act 2011. In order to be charitable within the law's definition, a purpose must fall within at least one of the statutory descriptions of purposes contained in s.3(1). As indicated above, the first three of Lord Macnaghten's *Pemsel* heads are ostensibly retained. Thereafter, other purposes beneficial to the community (the fourth head) are sub-divided and added to in order that the new descriptions reflect closely the contemporary understanding of the types of purposes charitable at law. Accordingly, each description will be considered in turn and any particular requirement as to public benefit will be highlighted and analysed.

(a) The Prevention or Relief of Poverty

7-029 The "prevention or relief of poverty" is the first purpose, listed in s.3(1)(a) of the 2011 Act. This description is amended from that adopted by Lord Macnaghten in *Pemsel's Case*, in that it refers both to the "prevention" and "relief" of poverty. "Prevention" and "relief" can be read disjunctively, examples of the former ranging, perhaps, from "providing debt or money management advice" to "providing emergency aid in the wake of a natural disaster to people who are at imminent risk of becoming poor because of the loss of their home, possessions, crops or business".[121] As to the latter, much can be gleaned from the case law preceding the Act as to purposes inherently charitable and the public benefit requirement.[122]

The meaning of poverty

7-030 Although relieving poverty, of course, includes helping the destitute, it is a central feature of the law that poverty, as a condition, is viewed broadly. As Eve J put it in *Re Gardom*, "there are

---

121 Uncontroversial examples cited in Annex A of the Charity Commission's supplementary public benefit guidance (December 2011), *The Prevention or Relief of Poverty for the Public Benefit*, p.20.

122 It will be recalled that the Preamble to the Charitable Uses Act 1601 listed as charitable trusts for the "relief of the aged, impotent and poor persons" (para.**7-009**). The relief of the impotent and aged now falls within s.3(1)(j), "the relief of those in need by reason of youth, age, ill-health, disability, financial hardship or other disadvantage".

degrees of poverty less acute than abject poverty or destitution, but poverty nevertheless".[123] Similarly, in *Re Coulthurst* it was held that, "Poverty does not mean destitution. It is a word of wide and somewhat indefinite import, and, perhaps, it is not unfairly paraphrased for present purposes as meaning persons who have to 'go short' in the ordinary acceptation of that term, due regard being had to their status in life and so forth".[124] Nowadays, and for some time, the Charity Commission has taken the view that anyone unable to afford things taken for granted in modern society can qualify for assistance.[125] Accordingly, in dealings with the Garfield Poverty Trust,[126] the provision of interest free loans was accepted as charitable for the relief of those unable to take out a mortgage under usual commercial terms. There are further means by which trustees of charities may relieve poverty and these include grants of money,[127] the provision of domestic items whether outright or on loan,[128] payment for services,[129] or the provision of facilities such as tools, books or vocational training. When In doubt, the Charity Commission will look for tangible benefits in order to be clear that poverty is relieved.[130]

Poverty inferred from the nature of the gift

7-031

Poverty may most clearly be inferred where a gift is on trust to an organisation or body whose aim is the relief of poverty. It may also be inferred from the nature of the gift itself. Sometimes the description of the objects of the trust is illustrative. In *Re Gosling*, the provision of a superannuation fund for, "pensioning off old worn out clerks" was held to be charitable, being implicitly for the relief of poverty.[131] Similarly, the disposition for the relief of distressed gentlefolk in *Re Young* was held charitable, as "distressed" suggested to the court an implicit poverty requirement.[132] The courts have accepted, moreover, that descriptors such as "in needy circumstances"[133] or "of limited means"[134] are apt to indicate poverty, whereas the more general label of "deserving"[135] is insufficiently referable to the poverty requirement. In other cases,

---

123 [1914] 1 Ch. 662 at 668.
124 [1951] Ch. 661 at 666 per Lord Evershed MR.
125 Charity Commission, *Commentary on the Descriptions of Charitable Purposes in the Draft Charities Bill* (August 2009), para.11.
126 (1995) 3 Decisions 7–10.
127 For example, to relieve sudden distress or to meet expenses associated with visiting people.
128 Such as furniture, fridges or even radio and television.
129 Such as child-minding or meals on wheels.
130 In *Harrogate Fairtrade Shop v Charity Commission for England and Wales* CA/2013/0009 (27 March 2014) (FTT (Charity)), for example, it was not established precisely how the sale of fair-trade goods relieved the poverty of poor producers.
131 (1900) 16 T.L.R. 152.
132 [1951] Ch. 344.
133 *Re Scarisbrick* [1951] Ch. 662.
134 *Re Gardom* [1914] 1 Ch. 662.
135 *Re Cohen* [1973] 1 W.L.R. 415.

the provision of particular services may connote poverty. In *Biscoe v Jackson*,[136] the provision of a soup kitchen in Shoreditch was implicitly for the alleviation of poverty. A less clear-cut example is provided by *Re Niyazi*.[137] There, Megarry VC upheld a trust to build a working men's hostel in Cyprus. The reference to working men in conjunction with hostel accommodation was sufficient to point to poverty although he acknowledged the case was, indeed, borderline. This decision may be usefully compared to *Re Sanders' WT* where a trust to provide dwellings for the working classes around Pembroke Dock in Wales was held not charitable.[138] It appears, therefore, that the mere limitation of the scope of a gift to the "working classes" is not, of itself, sufficient to indicate poor persons. Neither is extrinsic evidence of poverty admissible in court to indicate need. The requirement of poverty must be imposed by the terms of the trust.[139]

Such was the case in *Cawdron v Merchant Taylors' School*,[140] where Blackburne J considered the wording of the following object together with the legal meaning of poverty and concluded that a poverty requirement had been imposed:

> **"(a) The creation of a fund the income or capital of which shall be employed in (i) paying for the education at the school of any son of an Old Merchant Taylor who has fallen in the war or who has been thereby disabled, whether directly or indirectly, or in (ii) assisting any relative of such Old Merchant Taylor as may be dependent upon him; in every case the decision as to the eligibility of the candidates and the extent and method of assistance to be in the sole discretion of the committee".**

A number of points were noted as significant, including the description of the payment as "assistance", the decision-making role of the committee in determining who should benefit and the criteria for eligibility, linked as it was to dependency. As Blackburne J explained, "it is to those who would otherwise 'go short' that the assistance is to be directed . . . the provision of financial assistance to dependent relatives of the OMTs killed or disabled in the war—is charitable in nature as being for the relief of poverty".[141]

Public benefit

7-032

It will be recalled that in order to be charitable at law, a trust must be for the benefit of a sufficient section of the community. Thus, where the community to benefit is restricted to a particular class of persons the question arises as to whether a sufficient section of the community is

---

136   (1887) 35 Ch. D. 460.
137   [1978] 3 All E.R. 785.
138   [1954] Ch. 265.
139   *Re Sanders' WT* [1954] Ch. 265.
140   [2010] P.T.S.R. 507.
141   [2010] P.T.S.R. 507 at 518.

benefited. The idea was introduced that different "tests" are applicable depending on the head of charity in question. With regard to advancement of education, a gift which defines its objects by reference to a blood relationship or a contractual relationship cannot be regarded as being of public benefit, regardless of the number of people to benefit.[142] This so-called "personal nexus test" or "blood and contract rule"[143] does not apply to trusts for the relief of poverty.

A trust for a testator's poor relations has long been accepted as charitable,[144] illustrating clearly that evidence of a blood relationship between settlor and beneficiaries was no bar to public benefit. Such trusts were seemingly always deemed to be of benefit to a sufficient section of the community. It followed that no objection was raised to trusts the object of which was the relief of poverty of poor members of an association. In *Spiller v Maude*,[145] a fund for the relief of orphans of deceased members of a theatrical society to provide medical advice and annuities to members incapacitated by age, accident or infirmity was held charitable. A number of cases demonstrate, furthermore, that objects can be limited to one's poor employees. In *Re Coulthurst*,[146] for example, a gift for the benefit of widows and orphans of deceased officers and deceased ex-officers of a bank was held by the Court of Appeal to be a charitable trust for the relief of poverty.

This generous treatment of public benefit in the context of the relief of poverty has been the subject of considerable comment. In *IRC v Educational Grants Association*, Harman J objected that, not being permitted under other heads, such cases "stick out like a sore thumb".[147] Lord Evershed MR commented in *Re Scarisbrick* that, "The 'poor relations' cases may be justified on the basis that the relief of poverty is of so altruistic a character that the public element may necessarily be inferred thereby; or they may be accepted as a hallowed, if illogical, exception".[148] The matter of the appropriate public benefit test fell to be considered by the House of Lords in *Dingle v Turner*.[149] There the testator directed his trustees to invest a specified sum on trust, "to apply the income thereof in paying pensions to poor employees" of his company. Lord Cross (giving the leading speech) decided that, even though the poor relations cases were anomalous, they were too well established to overrule. He claimed that:

7-033

> "the 'poor members' and the 'poor employees' decisions were a natural development of the 'poor relations' decisions and to draw a

---

142 As Jenkins LJ emphasised in *Re Scarisbrick* [1951] Ch. 622 at 649, "An aggregate of individuals ascertained by reference to some personal tie (e.g. of blood or contract), such as the relations of a particular individual, the members of a particular family, the employees of a particular firm, the members of a particular association, does not amount to the public or a section thereof for the purposes of the general rule".

143 See para.**7-047**.

144 *Isaac v Defriez* (1754) Amb. 595 (bequest to his wife for life and after her death to his and her poorest relations).

145 (1881) 32 Ch. D. 158.

146 [1951] Ch. 661; see also, *Gibson v South American Stores (Gath & Chaves) Ltd* [1949] 2 All E.R. 985.

147 [1967] Ch. 993 at 1011.

148 [1951] Ch. 622 at 639.

149 [1972] A.C. 601. See further, T. Watkin, "Charity: The Purport of Purpose" (1978) 42 Conv. (NS) 277.

> distinction between certain sorts of poverty trusts would be quite illogical . . . and assuming, as one must, that they are properly administered . . ., to treat such trusts as charities is not open to any practical objection".[150]

Although all were in agreement with this conclusion, Lord Cross put forward his own opinion on the unsatisfactory application of the personal nexus test.[151] Regarding the determination of charitable status, he argued that "validity and fiscal immunity march hand in hand"[152] and that the cases under the head of education were "pretty obviously influenced by the consideration that if such trusts as were there in question were held valid they would enjoy an undeserved fiscal immunity".[153] He explained:

> "To establish a trust for the education of the children of employees in a company in which you are interested is no doubt a meritorious act; but however numerous the employees may be the purpose which you are seeking to achieve is not a public purpose. It is a company purpose and there is no reason why your fellow taxpayers should contribute to a scheme which by providing 'fringe benefits' for your employees will benefit the company by making their conditions of employment more attractive. The temptation to enlist the assistance of the law of charity in private endeavours of this sort is considerable . . . and the courts must do what they can to discourage such attempts".[154]

The distinction between education and poverty was, thereby, that "In the field of poverty the danger is not so great as in the field of education—for while people are keenly alive to the need to give their children a good education and to the expense of doing so, they are generally optimistic enough not to entertain serious fears of falling on evil days much before they fall on them".[155] In the view of Lord Cross, the taking on board of this fiscal advantages point adequately explained why trusts for the relief of poverty fall legitimately outside the blood and contract rule. They are simply not the trusts at which the blood and contract rule was developed to prevent. With the exception of Lord Simon, however, each other Law Lord expressly asked to be dissociated from these further remarks. Even Lord MacDermott stressed, "I would prefer not to extend my concurrence to what [Lord Cross] . . . goes on to say respecting the fiscal privileges of a legal charity. This subject may be material on the question whether what is

---

150 [1972] A.C. 601 at 623.
151 See also the views of Lord MacDermott (dissenting) in *Oppenheim v Tobacco Securities Ltd* [1951] A.C. 297.
152 [1972] A.C. 601 at 624.
153 [1972] A.C. 601 at 625.
154 [1972] A.C. 601 at 625.
155 [1972] A.C. 601 at 625.

alleged to be a charity is sufficiently altruistic in nature to qualify as such, but beyond that, and without wishing to express any final views on the matter, I doubt if these consequential privileges have much relevance to the primary question whether a given trust or purpose should be held charitable in Law".[156]

Distinguishing a class of objects

It remains necessary, nonetheless, under the head of the prevention or relief of poverty, to distinguish between trusts of a private and, therefore, non-charitable nature and those of sufficient public character to be charitable at law. It should be noted, however, that case law has focused on a sufficient section of the community for the purpose of "relieving" poverty rather than "preventing" it. As the Commission warns in its supplementary guidance, "the more restrictive beneficial class, which can be sufficient in certain circumstances for the relief of poverty, may not be sufficient for the prevention of poverty".[157]

7-034

Historically, as regards trusts for the relief of poverty, a distinction was once made between cases where the capital sum was retained, with the income applied for the benefit of the objects (deemed charitable) and those where there was an immediate distribution of capital amongst objects (private).[158] This unhelpful distinction was emphatically rejected by the Court of Appeal in *Re Scarisbrick* and latterly (unanimously) by the House of Lords in *Dingle v Turner*. The difference depends solely, as Lord Cross put it in *Dingle v Turner*, on "whether as a matter of construction the gift was for the relief of poverty amongst a particular description of poor people or was merely a gift to particular poor persons, the relief of poverty among them being the motive of the gift".[159] Only if construed as the former would the gift be upheld as charitable.

7-035

This test was met with the most liberal of interpretations in *Re Segelman*.[160] There, a testator established a trust fund for the poor and needy of six named members of the testator's family and their issue alive at the expiry of 21 years after the testator's death. At the date of the testator's death there were 26 persons in the class. Chadwick J acknowledged that the gift could not be charitable if it was in essence a gift to the individual members of the class. In his view, the gift was not of that character. The selection of named beneficiaries focused on need and not mere closeness of relationship. In addition, Chadwick J was reassured by a similarity between the instant case and *Re Scarisbrick* in that the class of those eligible to benefit was not closed upon the testator's death, but remained open for a further period of 21 years.

It has been argued, perhaps a little harshly, that the outcome of *Re Segelman* extends, in an unwarranted way, the anomaly that is presented by the charitable trust for the relief of

---

156 [1972] A.C. 601 at 614.
157 See Charity Commission, *The Prevention or Relief of Poverty for the Public Benefit* (December 2011), p.16.
158 *Attorney General v Price* (1810) 17 Ves. 371.
159 [1972] A.C. 601 at 617.
160 [1996] Ch. 171.

poor relations.[161] There is no doubt that the case is borderline.[162] The Court of Appeal in *Re Scarisbrick* made clear that a trust for the relief of poverty would not be charitable if the poor persons to benefit are either named, or comprise a narrow class of close family.[163] With that in mind, *Re Segelman* could be seen to fall just outside the narrow class of the type excluded by Jenkins LJ. Although it is perhaps problematic that the objects comprised named individuals as well as their after born issue, the members of the class in *Re Segelman* were potentially numerous, of a number unforeseen by the testator and selected originally on the basis of need. For these reasons, it is arguable that *Re Segelman* was correctly decided, albeit positioned uncomfortably close to the dividing line between the public and the private.

A continuing anomaly

7-036

It remains to consider what impact, if any, the Charities Act 2006 (now 2011) has had on public benefit in the context of relief of poverty, a matter that has not been free of debate.[164] In *Attorney General v Charity Commission for England and Wales*,[165] however, the Upper Tribunal confirmed that the law has not changed. As regards a class of potential objects defined by reference to a personal nexus such as a common relative, an employer or membership of a particular club, this will not prevent the public benefit requirement from being met. Drawing heavily from this decision, the Charity Commission's public benefit guidance now states the following:

> **"In the case of charities for the relief (and in some cases the prevention) of poverty the courts consider the public benefit requirement can be met by satisfying the 'benefit' aspect only. In these cases there is no separate consideration of the 'public' aspect. Only charities with a purpose to relieve (and in some cases to prevent) poverty can define who can benefit by reference to:**
>
> **• their family relationship (that means their descent from one individual)**

---

161 See P. Luxton, *The Law of Charities* (Oxford: Oxford University Press, 2001), p.175, "the decision in *Re Segelman* on this point . . . must be considered to have been reached *per incuriam*".

162 See Picarda, *The Law and Practice Relating to Charities*, 3rd edn (1999), p.43.

163 As Jenkins LJ argued in *Re Scarisbrick* [1951] Ch. 622 at 651, "One can conceive of a testator making a limited provision . . . for a child or children whose conduct in his view had reduced their claims on his bounty to a minimum. A disposition of that sort would obviously not be for the relief of poverty in the charitable sense. The same must be said of gifts to named persons if in needy circumstances, or to a narrow class of near relatives, as for example to such of a testator's statutory next of kin as at his death shall be in needy circumstances".

164 See, e.g. A. Rahmatian, "The Continued Relevance of the 'Poor Relations' and the 'Poor Employees' Cases under the Charities Act 2006" [2009] Conv. 12.

165 [2012] UKUT 420 (TCC).

> • their employment by an employer
> • their membership of an unincorporated association.
>
> A charity must not have a purpose which is for the benefit of named individuals, whether or not they are poor. This is so even if the motive is to relieve poverty and the named individuals happen to be poor".[166]

Exclusivity

However weak the public benefit test is in relation to trusts to relieve poverty, any such trust must aim exclusively at the relief of poverty. In *Re Gwyon*[167] a testator left his residuary estate on trust to establish a clothing foundation to provide trousers for boys in the Farnham district aged between five and 15 years old. The further conditions imposed were as follows: first, "that he shall not belong to or be supported by any charitable institution"; secondly, "that neither he nor his parents shall be in receipt of parochial relief"; thirdly, "that he shall not be black"[168]; and, finally, "that on a second or subsequent application he shall not have disposed of any garment received within the then preceding year from the Foundation and that when he comes for a new pair of knickers or trousers the legend 'Gwyon's Present' shall still be decipherable on the waist band of his old ones".

Eve J was adamant that the trust was not limited to the relief of poverty in that there were no grounds for exclusion of the well off. He claimed, "None of these conditions necessarily import poverty nor could the recipients be accurately described as a class of aged, impotent or poor persons".[169]

7-037

(b) Advancement of Education

The meaning of education

The head of advancement of education is derived from the Preamble to the Statute of Elizabeth wherein there is reference to "the maintenance of schools . . . and scholars in universities" as well as to the "education and preferment of orphans". The Charities Act 2011 retains this head

7-038

---

166   Charity Commission, *Public Benefit: The Public Benefit Requirement (PB1)* (September 2013), p.15.
167   [1930] 1 Ch. 255.
168   See generally, T. Watkin, "Discrimination and Charity" [1981] Conv. 131.
169   [1930] 1 Ch. 255 at 260.

and, consequently, much of the case law preceding the Act remains of relevance in determining what is charitable under the statutory description. In its supplementary guidance, the Charity Commission maintains that education covers both formal education, which may take place in schools and universities and other educational institutions, and less formal education which may take place in the community. This could include training, research in specific areas of study and expertise or broader education in the development of individual capabilities, competencies, skills and understanding.[170] The copious case law detailing all things inherently charitable under this head is here categorised as follows:

(i)   knowledge and research;

(ii) formal teaching and study;

(iii) public services and facilities;

(iv) art and aesthetics; and

(v)   sport and education.

(i)   Knowledge and research

7-039

The conventional understanding of the head of advancement of education is that there must be more than simply an accumulation of knowledge. Learning needs to be imparted.[171] In *Re Shaw*,[172] for example, George Bernard Shaw directed his trustees to use his residuary estate for a number of designated purposes. In particular, trustees were to make inquiries into the number of persons speaking or writing the English language by the official alphabet of 26 letters and to determine how much time could be saved by the use of an alphabet containing at least 40 letters. In addition, a phonetics expert was to be employed to transliterate his play entitled "Androcles and the Lion" into the proposed new alphabet and to advertise and publish the transliteration. Harman J perceived the object "merely to tend to the increase of public knowledge in a certain respect".[173] Unless combined with an element of teaching or education, this was not, of itself, a charitable object.

Logically, different considerations must apply to the work of academic researchers who are not engaged in the teaching process. The ambit of education in this respect was exam-

---

170   Charity Commission, *The Advancement of Education for the Public Benefit* (December 2011), p.8.
171   As Eve J recognised in *Re De Noailles* (1916) 114 L.T. 1089 at 1094, "The mere stuffing of information into a boy or girl may make them very priggish, but it does not make them of much use in life, unless they know how to apply that information for the purpose of becoming useful citizens".
172   [1957] 1 W.L.R. 729.
173   [1957] 1 W.L.R. 729 at 738.

ined in *Re Hopkin's WT*.[174] There a testatrix gave part of her residuary estate to the Francis Bacon Society to be applied towards the discovery of the Bacon-Shakespeare manuscripts. A central aim was to "encourage the general study of the evidence of Francis Bacon's authorship of plays commonly ascribed to Shakespeare". Wilberforce J was clear that a bequest for the purposes of "search, or research, for the original manuscripts of England's greatest dramatist (whoever he was)" fell well within the law's conception of a charitable purpose.[175]

As to the absence of an element of active teaching or education, Wilberforce J took a wider view than that of Harman J in *Re Shaw*. As discussed above, *Re Shaw* appears to suggest that a mere increase in knowledge could not be a charitable purpose unless combined with an element of active teaching or education. Wilberforce J felt that this could not apply to researchers engaged in work of educational value. He claimed that the words "combined with teaching or education" were "not easy to interpret in relation to other facts", and concluded that he would be "unwilling to treat them as meaning that the promotion of academic research is not a charitable purpose".[176] Accordingly, he put forward the requirements to be met before research could be regarded as charitable. The research must:

> "either be of educational value to the researcher or must be so directed as to lead to something which will pass into the store of educational material, or so as to improve the sum of communicable knowledge in an area which education may cover—education in this context extending to the formation of literary taste and appreciation".[177]

By way of a recent Illustration, in *Hipkiss v Charity Commission*,[178] the First-tier Tribunal held that speculative research into cryonics and cryopreservation carried out by the Human Organ Preservation Research Trust (HOPRT) was a useful subject of study which "comfortably passes" the test of charitable research In *Re Hopkin's WT*.[179] It is noteworthy in that the Charity Commission failed in its attempt to have HOPRT removed from the register of charities on the basis that its true purposes were not those set out in its trust deed, but the promotion and furtherance of cryopreservation.

---

174 [1965] Ch. 669; see also, *McGovern v Attorney General* [1982] Ch. 321 for discussion of research into human rights abuses.
175 [1965] Ch. 669 at 679.
176 [1965] Ch. 669 at 680.
177 [1965] Ch. 669 at 680.
178 [2018] FTT (Charity) CA/2017/0014.
179 [2018] FTT (Charity) CA/2017/0014 at [116].

(ii) Formal teaching or study

7-040

The head of advancement of education clearly embraces formal teaching including the study or promotion of individual subjects. The many illustrations are varied and uncontroversial. *Re British School of Egyptian Archaeology*,[180] for example, concerned a school whose objects were the discovery of knowledge connected with ancient Egypt, the publication of related works and the training of students in the craft or art of excavation. Harman J concluded that the School had "a direct educational purpose".[181]

Further examples include objects such as general advancement of mechanical science,[182] typing and book-keeping,[183] the study of economics[184] or the provision of postgraduate scholarships.[185]

More difficulty surrounds objects that might be considered too trivial or frivolous to fulfil a truly educational purpose. Care must be taken not to confuse the development of skill or understanding by learning, with a mere hobby or pastime to which there is an educational element. Whilst the former is charitable, the latter is not.

(iii) Public services or facilities

7-041

Advancement of education extends to the provision of educational public services and facilities such as museums,[186] botanical gardens,[187] zoos,[188] training opportunities for the unemployed[189] or public libraries.[190] Even the preparation of law reports by the Incorporated Council of Law Reporting was held by a majority in the Court of Appeal to fall under the head of advancement of education.[191] In *IRC v White*, Fox J highlighted a substantial range of activity which would foster, promote and increase the interest of the public in craftsmanship, such as the holding of public exhibitions of works of modern craftsmanship,[192] the preservation and

---

180 [1954] 1 All E.R. 887.
181 [1954] 1 All E.R. 887 at 890.
182 *Institute of Civil Engineers v IRC* [1932] 1 K.B. 149.
183 *Re Koettgen's WT* [1954] Ch. 252.
184 *Re Berridge* (1890) 63 L.T. 470.
185 *Re Gott* [1943] Ch. 193.
186 *Re Holburne* (1885) 53 L.T. 212.
187 *Townley v Bedwell* (1801) 6 Ves. 194.
188 *Re Lopes* [1931] 2 Ch. 130.
189 See further, Charity Commission RR3, *Charities for the Relief of Unemployment* (March 1999).
190 *IRC v White* (1980) 55 T.C. 651 (maintenance of a collection of books on craftsmanship).
191 *Incorporated Council of Law Reporting v Attorney General* [1972] Ch. 73 (Russell LJ dissenting). The court was unanimous in finding this purpose charitable also under the then fourth head containing other purposes beneficial to the community.
192 As Fox J illustrated in *IRC v White* (1980) 55 T.C. 651 at 655, "it seems to me that an exhibition of modern works of, say, good quality stained glass, or fine book binding or engraving, or of the silversmith's craft, would be educative of the public taste in a field in which it is to the general public benefit that such instruction should be available".

exhibition to the public of works of good craftsmanship of earlier centuries[193] and, as was directly in issue, the maintenance for the public use of a collection of books relating to craftsmanship whether old or modern. In doing so he was influenced by the approach of Farwell J in *Re Cranstoun*, who had explained why a devise of ancient cottages to the Royal Society of Arts was inherently charitable. Farwell J claimed:

> "It must be for the advantage of the whole of the people of this country that they should have an opportunity of seeing beautiful and picturesque buildings and cottages of this kind, which have in addition the historical interest which such buildings necessarily bear; and it must also be for the benefit of the community that any devices of good craftsmanship in the building of these cottages should be preserved".[194]

Such an explanation is readily illustrative of the educational value attached by the courts to the advancement of culture and heritage.

(iv) Artistic and aesthetic education

The advancement of the arts, culture, heritage and science is now recognised as a charitable purpose in its own right and it is no longer necessary to think of, say, the arts as charitable merely by advancing education. In the vast body of case law concerned with the advancement of education, however, it is clear that the promotion of artistic and aesthetic objects has been very much embraced. In *Associated Artists Ltd v Commissioners of Inland Revenue*, for example, Upjohn J claimed it to be a charitable object "to foster, promote and increase the interest of the public in the dramatic art and in the co-related arts as well by the presentation of dramatic works as by other means".[195] A further illustration is provided by *Royal Choral Society v IRC* wherein the object was the promotion, practice and performance of choral works.[196] Lord Greene MR argued strongly in favour of a broad inclusive approach on the basis that "the education of artistic taste is one of the most important things in the development of a civilised human being".[197] Further, he argued that it does not matter that the persons involved derive pleasure from the given activity, provided that it is incidental and not the primary purpose of the trust. "Curiously enough", he observed, "some people find pleasure in providing education. Still more curiously, some people find pleasure in being educated: but the element of pleasure in those processes is not the purpose of them, but what may be called a by-product which is necessarily there".[198]

7-042

---

193   As occurred in *Re Cranstoun* [1932] 1 Ch. 537.
194   [1932] 1 Ch. 537 at 545.
195   [1956] 1 W.L.R. 752 at 759.
196   [1943] 2 All E.R. 101.
197   [1943] 2 All E.R. 101 at 105.
198   [1943] 2 All E.R. 101 at 104.

In *Re Delius*,[199] the wife of the composer Delius bequeathed her residuary estate for the advancement of her late husband's work. This object was to be achieved by the production of gramophone recordings, the publication of his works and the financing of public performances. Roxburgh J perceived the purpose of the trust to be "the spreading and establishment of knowledge and appreciation of Delius' works amongst the public of the world".[200] Following *Royal Choral Society v IRC*, he was clear that a charitable trust had been created.[201]

7-043

Whereas there is little doubt surrounding the inherent educational value of advancing the works of great writers and composers such as Shakespeare or Beethoven, the same cannot be assumed of less meritorious artists or, indeed, more mundane gifts for the furtherance of appreciation of the arts. As Russell LJ observed in *Re Pinion*, "The mere fact that a person makes a gift of chattels to form a public museum cannot establish that its formation will have a tendency to advance education in aesthetic appreciation or in anything else. Inquiry must first be made . . .".[202] The danger of subjective evaluation is undeniably present where the court is called upon to adjudicate the quality of lesser-known artists' work. As will become clear, the court must draw on expert evidence in order that, in the end, it is satisfied as to the artistic merit of the object in question. Where no benefit or utility to the public can be discerned, there cannot be a sufficient educational and, thereby, charitable element.[203]

Such difficulties came to the fore in *Re Pinion*. There, an art enthusiast bequeathed his studio and its contents to trustees to enable it to be used as a museum to display his collection of works. Harman LJ pointed to "a strong body of evidence" that as a means of education the collection was "worthless".[204] The testator's own paintings (of which there were around 50), were described as being "atrociously bad".[205] The assembly was so haphazard and without purpose or style that it could not properly be called a collection. Particularly telling was the surprise expressed by one expert that "so voracious a collector should not by hazard have picked up even one meritorious object".[206] Although there were some items that were not altogether worthless, these were "stifled by a large number of absolutely worthless pictures and objects".[207] Memorably, Harman LJ concluded, "I can conceive of no useful object to be served in foisting on the public this mass of junk. It has neither public utility nor educative value".[208]

7-044

Understandably, more success was occasioned by the wife of George Bernard Shaw, who gave the residue of her estate to be held on trust for "the teaching promotion and encouragement in Ireland of self-control, elocution, oratory deportment, the arts of personal contact, of

---

199 [1957] Ch. 299.
200 [1957] Ch. 299 at 305.
201 See also *Re Shakespeare Memorial Trust* [1923] 2 Ch. 389.
202 [1965] Ch. 85 at 108.
203 See e.g. *Re Hummeltenberg* [1923] 1 Ch. 237 (a college for the training of spiritualist mediums).
204 [1965] Ch. 85 at 106.
205 [1965] Ch. 85 at 106.
206 [1965] Ch. 85 at 107.
207 [1965] Ch. 85 at 107.
208 [1965] Ch. 85 at 107.

social intercourse and the other arts of public private professional and business life".[209] Vaisey J likened this to a finishing school and was satisfied as to the inherent educational benefit in "the promotion or encouragement of those arts and graces of life which are, after all, perhaps the finest and best part of the human character".[210] A sharp contrast might be drawn between qualities deemed admirable and those less fine parts of the human character. Needless to say, as Harman LJ did in *Re Pinion*, a public library devoted entirely to works of pornography or of a corrupting nature would, by contrast, not be permitted.[211]

(v) Sports, activities and educational institutions

The promotion of amateur sport is a head of charity in its own right, but the traditional approach of the courts has been to deny that sport per se is of charitable or, indeed, educational benefit.[212] This reservation has never been pertinent where sport is ancillary to another charitable purpose, for example, the formal education of the young.[213] In *Re Mariette*, therefore, a gift for the provision of five squash courts to Aldenham school was held charitable on the ground that learning to play games at a boarding school was just as important as learning from books.[214] It is necessary, as Eve J, put it, "to provide for both mental and bodily occupation".[215]

7-045

Similarly, in *IRC v McMullen*,[216] the House of Lords upheld a trust to provide facilities in schools and universities to play football and other sports. Lord Hailsham embraced the idea that education of the young should not be limited to formal education and he painted a picture of "a balanced and systematic process of instruction, training and practice containing . . . spiritual, moral, mental and physical elements".[217] He continued:

> "I reject any idea which would cramp the education of the young within the school or university syllabus, confine it within the school or university campus, limit it to formal instruction, or render it devoid of pleasure in the exercise of skill".[218]

---

209 *Re Shaw's WT* [1952] Ch. 163.
210 [1952] Ch. 163 at 172.
211 [1965] Ch. 85 at 106.
212 As Lopes LJ affirmed in *Re Nottage* [1895] 2 Ch. 649 at 656, "I am of the opinion that a gift, the object of which is the encouragement of a mere sport or game . . . cannot upon the authorities be held to be charitable, though such sport or game is to some extent beneficial to the public" (the instant case concerned the provision of a cup to "encourage the sport of yacht racing").
213 The advancement of the physical education of young people not undergoing formal education is a recognised charitable purpose: see Charity Commission RR11: *Charitable Status and Sport* (April 2003).
214 [1915] 2 Ch. 284.
215 [1915] 2 Ch. 284 at 288.
216 [1981] A.C. 1.
217 [1981] A.C. 1 at 18.
218 [1981] A.C. 1 at 18.

Besides activities that might generally be classified as sport, the courts have considered the educational benefit of a wide range of pursuits. To adopt the approach of Lord Hailsham, it is probably the case that where an activity contains something of the process of instruction, training and practice, perhaps involving some spiritual, moral, mental and physical elements, an argument can be made as to its inherent charitable nature. Thus, in *Re Lopes*, Farwell J claimed that "A ride on an elephant may be educational. At any rate it brings the reality of the elephant and its uses to a child's mind, in lieu of leaving him to mere book learning. It widens his mind, and in that broad sense is educational".[219]

7-046

Re Dupree's Deed Trusts[220] involved a trust to promote chess playing through the organisation of an annual tournament for boys under the age of 21 in the Portsmouth area. Vaisey J made apparent his discomfort in admitting "One feels perhaps that one is on a rather slippery slope. If chess, why not draughts? If draughts, why not bezique? And so on, through to bridge, whist, and by another route stamp-collecting and the acquisition of birds' eggs".[221] Notwithstanding this practical concern, there is nothing in the remainder of his judgment to cast doubt as to his view of the educational worth in learning and playing the game. Such is evident from his admission in the opening paragraph of his judgment that:

> **"the nature of the game is such as to encourage the qualities of foresight, concentration, memory and ingenuity. Even unguided by actual evidence, I should not have been surprised if the conclusion could have been reached that the game is essentially one which does possess an educational value".[222]**

Essentially, it is possible to argue that those qualities are present in a very much wider range of activities undertaken by children. Picarda, for example, is happy to make the argument that "stamp-collecting may bring the reality of geography and history to a child's mind" or that the acquisition of birds' eggs may stimulate "his or her enthusiasm for natural history".[223] Perhaps more problematic are the activities where educational value is not so readily apparent or where chance plays a greater role, as in many card or board games.

Public benefit

7-047

It is clear that a trust is incapable of being charitable unless it is for the benefit of the public or a sufficient section of the public. Unlike trusts for the relief of poverty, a more stringent rule

---

219 [1931] 2 Ch. 130 at 136.
220 [1945] Ch. 16.
221 [1945] Ch. 16 at 20.
222 [1945] Ch. 16 at 19.
223 Picarda, *The Law and Practice Relating to Charities*, 3rd edn (1999), p.53.

applies to trusts for the advancement of education to deny the benefits of charitable status to those who seek to benefit their relatives or employees at the expense of the taxpayer. In *Re Compton*,[224] for example, a trust providing for the education of the descendants of three named persons was not a valid charitable trust because the objects were defined by reference to a personal nexus. The trust lacked a sufficiently public quality.

Guidance as to the operation of the personal nexus test was supplied by the House of Lords in *Oppenheim v Tobacco Securities Trust Co.*[225] The case concerned a settlement to provide for the education of children of employees and ex-employees of British American Tobacco or any allied company, of which there were over 110,000 potential beneficiaries. Despite the large number to benefit, the nexus between them was employment by a particular employer. Accordingly, there could not be said to be a benefit to a sufficient section of the community.[226] Lord Simonds explained:

> **"These words 'section of the community' have no special sanctity, but they conveniently indicate first, that the possible (I emphasise the word 'possible') beneficiaries must not be numerically negligible, and secondly, that the quality which distinguishes them from other members of the community, so that they form by themselves a section of it, must be a quality which does not depend on their relationship to a particular individual ... A group of persons may be numerous, but, if the nexus between them is their personal relationship to a single propositus or to several propositi, they are neither the community nor a section of the community for charitable purposes."[227]**

In essence, therefore, if beneficiaries are "numerically negligible" or ascertained by reference to some personal tie (whether of blood or contract), this cannot amount to the public or a sufficient section thereof.[228] This test has been accepted despite the legitimate criticisms of its utility voiced by Lord MacDermott in his dissenting speech. He highlighted that whilst there was no problem with a trust to advance the education of railwaymen, there could be no charitable trust for the advancement of education of the workers of a particular railway even where there would be little difference in the make-up of the group to benefit. He explained:

---

224 [1945] 1 Ch. 123.
225 [1951] A.C. 297, noted at (1951) 67 L.Q.R. 162 (A.L. Goodhart).
226 In the words of Lord Normand, "there is no public element to be found in the bare nexus of common employment" ([1951] A.C. 297 at 310).
227 [1951] A.C. 297 at 306.
228 With the exception of poverty trusts, the Charity Commission cites as a rule of general application that "where the number of people who can benefit (now and in the future) is numerically negligible", there will not be a benefit to a sufficient section of the community (*Public Benefit: The Public Benefit Requirement (PB1)* (September 2013), p.12).

> "if the bond between those employed by a particular railway is purely personal, how should the bond between those who are employed as railwaymen be so essentially different? Is a distinction to be drawn in this respect between those who are employed in a particular industry before it is nationalised and those who are employed therein after that process has been completed and one employer has taken the place of many?"[229]

The arbitrariness of the test was such that, "had the present trust been framed so as to provide for the education of the children of those engaged in the tobacco industry in a named county or town, it would have been a good charitable disposition, and that even though the class to be benefited would have been appreciably smaller and no more important than is the class here".[230] Accordingly, Lord MacDermott (alone) was of the view that public benefit should be a matter of evidence in each case without out the need to resort to a hard-and-fast rule.

A preference to a private class

7-048

It was once thought permissible to create a charitable trust for a primary class wherefrom the trustees have a power to prefer a smaller private class. Controversially, in *Re Koettgen's WT*,[231] Upjohn J held charitable a trust containing an imperative duty upon trustees to prefer, as to up to 75 per cent of the income, the employees of a selected company or any of their family members. The trust in issue was established to further the education of "persons of either sex who are British born subjects and who are desirous of educating themselves or obtaining tuition for a higher commercial career but whose means are insufficient or will not allow of their obtaining such education or tuition at their own expense". Upjohn J was influenced by the argument that it could not be certain in any future year how much (if any) of the 75 per cent would be used by the preferred class. By looking at the primary class, he was satisfied that the trust was of a sufficiently public character, and he maintained that it is "when the primary class of eligible persons is ascertained that the question of the public nature of the trust arises and falls to be decided".[232] This conclusion is essentially problematic and cannot safely be followed. Upjohn J looks to have accepted as charitable a trust whereby trustees have a discretion as to the distribution of income between charitable and non-charitable ends. It is difficult to see, therefore, how such a trust can be regarded as exclusively charitable.

A different approach prevailed in *IRC v Educational Grants Association Ltd*[233] in relation to a charitable corporation the object of which was "to advance education in such ways as shall

229 [1951] A.C. 297 at 317.
230 [1951] A.C. 297 at 318.
231 [1954] Ch. 252.
232 [1954] Ch. 252 at 258.
233 [1967] Ch. 123.

from time-to-time be thought fit and in particular by making grants to or for the benefit of and for the education of all such persons as shall be considered likely to benefit from education at a preparatory, public or other independent school, including boarding schools, and at technical colleges". The Association was supported by payments under a deed of covenant by the Metal Box Company. The question arose as to whether the payments were made for charitable purposes only, when it emerged that 80 per cent of the income of one year was paid towards the education of children connected to the company. *Re Koettgen's WT* was considered but Pennycuick J was clearly minded not to follow the thinking previously employed by Upjohn J.[234] Instead he felt compelled to follow *Oppenheim* and held that a charitable corporation was not entitled to recover income tax on income applied for the non-charitable purposes of advancing the education of a preferred group within a wider class of charitable objects. This sensible and practical approach is much to be preferred.

Independent schools and fee-charging

In *Independent Schools Council v Charity Commission for England and Wales*,[235] the Upper Tribunal addressed the question whether independent schools which charge fees are operating for the public benefit. It was clearly one of the most significant and eagerly anticipated post-2006 developments, sparking much debate as to the impact of the legislation, the operation of the public benefit requirement and the role, remit and viability of the Charity Commission in meeting its statutory objectives. It was also an inevitable development. Since the introduction of the new public benefit requirement, a high level of Charity Commission scrutiny had fallen upon educational providers which charge fees and, thereby, restrict benefit to those who can afford to pay.[236] The Charity Commission had adopted the position that, where charities charge fees, those who are unable to pay must not be entirely excluded from benefit. As the Commission explained in its initial guidance:

7-049

> **"This does not mean that charities have to offer services for free. Nor does it mean that people who are unable to pay the fees must actually benefit, in the sense that they choose to take up the benefit. They must not be excluded from the opportunity to benefit, whether or not they actually do so."[237]**

234 He cited the criticism levied at Upjohn J's judgment by Lord Radcliffe in *Caffoor v Income Tax Commissioner (Colombo)* [1961] A.C. 584 at 604, that the *Re Koettgen* decision "edges very near to being inconsistent with *Oppenheim's* case".

235 [2011] UKUT 421 (TCC).

236 As J. Jaconelli notes in "Adjudicating on Charitable Status: A Reconsideration of the Elements" [2013] Conv. 96, 98, "It is one of the peculiarities of the law that a body may qualify as charitable even though it charges a price for the services that it provides and, moreover, the price is set at such a level as to place these services beyond the reach of the great majority of individuals".

237 Charity Commission, *Charities and Public Benefit* (January 2008), p.23.

It promoted the sense that "not excluding" people from benefit required more than providing "minimal or nominal benefit".[238] The opportunity to benefit should be "genuine and meaningful".[239]

Examples of ways in which education providers might satisfy the public benefit requirement were listed, and included a demonstration of "the educational benefits to pupils in state schools arising from collaboration and partnerships between state schools and independent schools" or "the educational benefits to state school pupils who are able to attend certain lessons or other educational events at independent schools".[240] Nonetheless, in 2009 when the Charity Commission completed its public benefit assessments of fee-charging schools,[241] two schools failed by neglecting to provide a sufficient number of bursaries. Accordingly, the Independent Schools Council moved to challenge the legitimacy of the Charity Commission guidance. Its challenge was successful and the Commission has now re-drafted its public benefit guidance to take on board the ruling.

7-050

The Tribunal identified two aspects to public benefit: that the purpose itself must be beneficial and the class to benefit must be a sufficient section of the public. The ISC case was directly concerned with the latter and the issue of whether those able to pay the fees charged by schools were a sufficient section of the community.[242] The Tribunal noted that a trust whose purposes exclude the poor from benefit could not be charitable, nor could a trust where the poor were de facto excluded.[243] As to whether a school was in compliance with the public benefit requirement, fee-charging schools had to demonstrate that they were doing enough for those who could not afford the fees. In doing so, it was necessary that there be more than a mere token benefit, but once that threshold was reached, what trustees decided to do in the running of a school was a matter for them to decide. Warren J explained the correct approach:

> **"It is to look at what a trustee, acting in the interests of the community as a whole, would do in all the circumstance of the particular school under consideration and to ask what provision should be made once the threshold of benefit going beyond the de minimis or token level had been met . . . It is for the charity trustees of the school concerned to address and assess how their obligations might best be fulfilled in the context of their own particular circumstances."[244]**

---

238 Charity Commission, *Charities and Public Benefit* (January 2008), p.23.
239 Charity Commission, *Public Benefit and Fee Charging* (December 2008), p.12.
240 Charity Commission, *Charities and Public Benefit* (January 2008), p.25.
241 Charity Commission, *Emerging findings for charity trustees from the Charity Commission's public benefit assessment work: 2008–09* (July 2009).
242 The Tribunal concluded readily that the nature of the education provided was for the public benefit in the first sense.
243 [2011] UKUT 421 (TCC) at [178].
244 [2011] UKUT 421 (TCC) at [215].

The judgment of the Tribunal sent a clear message to the Commission that it was not for it (or indeed the court) to impose on trustees of a school what it thinks is reasonable. As Warren J made clear, "This is all a matter of judgment for the trustees. There will be no one right answer".[245] The amended Charity Commission approach is now to cite a range of illustrative examples of ways in which charitable educational establishments might make provision for the poor to benefit, which fits within its completely restructured guidance.[246]

Political objects

A final reference needs to be made regarding the potential for a variety of non-charitable purposes to be dressed up as educational. As the Charity Commissioners warned in their Annual Report for 1966:

7-051

> **"Ingenious draftsmen have found it possible to embrace within this word a vast variety of activities, mainly propagandist, which do not come within the meaning of the 'advancement of education' as it is used in charity law. A purpose which is not charitable cannot be made charitable merely by representing it to be a form of education".[247]**

Accordingly, a trust to educate the public that peace is best secured through pacifism and disarmament was held not charitable on the ground that the object was political albeit advanced by educational means.[248]

(c) Advancement of Religion

7-052

Section 3(1)(c) of the 2011 Act lists the "advancement of religion" as falling within the new statutory descriptions of charitable purposes. No definition of religion is provided although further clarification can be found in s.3(2)(a), which states that "religion" includes "a religion which involves belief in more than one God", and "a religion which does not involve belief in a God". The clarification was deemed necessary to take account of the growing diversity of faiths

---

245 [2011] UKUT 421 (TCC) at [220].
246 Charity Commission, *Charging for Services: Illustrative Examples of Benefits to the Poor* (September 2013).
247 At [38].
248 *Southwood v Attorney General* [2000] W.T.L.R. 1199 (see para.**7-086**).

practised in England and Wales and the consequent concern that the law should be flexible and inclusive. Accordingly, the large body of case law as to charitable trusts which advance religion will remain relevant although, in the view of the Charity Commission, the decisions as to what is charitable must now be considered "in the context of current social and economic circumstances".[249]

Meaning of religion

7-053

In approaching "advancement of religion" the courts adopted a stance of neutrality and declined to distinguish between different religions.[250] The case law is littered with examples of trusts for the advancement of religions ranging from the long-established, such as Islam or Catholicism, to the more peripheral or New Age, such as the Unification Church or small spiritualist groups.[251] Both polytheistic and monotheistic religions are embraced alike.[252] The presumption, furthermore, is that any religion is better than none.[253] Naturally, the existence of a wide variety of fringe religious groupings or sects has tested the boundaries of what is generally an inclusive approach. As Romilly MR accepted in *Thornton v Howe*, "It may be that the tenets of a particular sect inculcate doctrines adverse to the very foundations of all religion, and that they are subversive of all morality. In such a case, if it should arise, the Court will not assist the execution of the bequest, but will declare it to be void . . .".[254] This test has been adopted as the appropriate point at which the pursuit of one's "religion" ceases to be regarded as charitable. Whilst some groups readily fall to be excluded,[255] an interesting variety of trusts for the advancement of religion have been held to be charitable.

Thornton v Howe concerned the publication of the obscure works of Joanna Southcote, who alleged that she had been impregnated by the Holy Ghost and would give birth to the second Messiah. Romilly MR described her as an "ignorant woman, of an enthusiastic turn of mind, who had long wished to become an instrument in the hands of God to promote some great good on earth".[256] Although he deemed her writings to be foolish, he could find noth-

---

249 Charity Commission, *The Advancement of Religion for the Public Benefit* (December 2011), p.22.

250 As Deputy Judge Andrew Simmonds put it in *Buckley v Barlow* [2016] EWHC 3017 (Ch) at [33], "It is a fundamental principle of this branch of charity law that the courts do not take it upon themselves to pass value judgments on different religions or on different sects within religions. This, no doubt, reflects the long tradition of religious tolerance in this country which has persisted for most of the last three centuries . . .".

251 In practice, however, it has appeared more difficult for newly established religions to persuade the Charity Commission of the genuineness of belief. See, e.g. the problems encountered by the Church of Scientology discussed below (see para.**7-055**).

252 This development might be regarded as relatively recent. In *Bowman v Secular Society* [1917] A.C. 406 at 449, the House of Lords embraced the more restrictive view that "a trust for the purpose of any kind of monotheistic theism would be a good charitable trust".

253 *Gilmour v Coats* [1949] A.C. 426.

254 (1862) 31 Beav. 14 at 20.

255 For example, Satanists and devil-worshippers.

256 (1862) 31 Beav. 14 at 18.

ing that was "likely to make persons who read them immoral or irreligious".[257] Accordingly, the publication of her work was held charitable for the advancement of religion.[258] Similarly, in *Re Watson,* property was left on trust "for the continuance of the work of God as it has been maintained by Mr HG Hobbs and Myself".[259] Expert evidence showed that Mr Hobbs' numerous fundamentalist writings were of no intrinsic worth. Following *Thornton v Howe*, Plowman J acknowledged that the court did not prefer one religion over another or one sect over another. There being nothing properly subversive in the teachings, a valid charitable trust was created.

By way of a final illustration, in *Holmes v Attorney General,*[260] Walton J was called upon to determine whether the purposes of a particular trust deed were charitable, i.e. to enable a meeting-house to be built and used for the benefit of an ultra-puritan sect known as the "Exclusive Brethren" or the "Plymouth Brethren". Despite the well-documented, historical opposition of the Charity Commissioners to some of the group practices, Walton J was bound to consider the only evidence that had been put in front of him. He could find nothing in their doctrines "to which exception could properly be taken".[261] Accordingly, he declared the "Kingston Meeting Rooms Trust, Feltham", a valid charitable trust, with the reminder that "it has long been settled that the law presumes that it is better for a man to have a religion—a set of beliefs which take him outside his own petty cares and lead him to think of others—rather than to have no religion at all".[262] More recently, and with some reluctance, the Charity Commission has accepted an application for registration of the Preston Down Trust, a Plymouth Brethren Christian Church meeting hall,[263] concluding that it had a "beneficial impact through its instruction and edification of the public in a Christian way of life".[264] Nonetheless, there remains considerable uncertainty in the law as to how public benefit might be demonstrated (an earlier application by the Trust was rejected in 2012) and the extent to which pre-2006 cases, based on the so-called presumption of public benefit, might now be relied upon. Unlike poverty and education, where References have been heard by the Charity Tribunal, the Attorney General is thus far unwilling to seek clarification as to how the law has changed in the context of religion.[265]

---

257 (1862) 31 Beav. 14 at 19.
258 Echoing Romilly MR, a similar conclusion was reached by Deputy Judge Andrew Simmonds QC in *Buckley v Barlow* [2016] EWHC 3017 (Ch) at [35] that "foolish and delusional" claims did not disqualify a trust from charitable status.
259 [1973] 1 W.L.R. 1472.
260 *The Times*, 11 February 1981.
261 *The Times*, 11 February 1981.
262 *The Times*, 11 February 1981.
263 Application for Registration of the Preston Down Trust (3 January 2014). The Brethren acknowledged some of their past mistakes, amended some of their disciplinary practices and altered their trust deed.
264 At [78].
265 As Synge notes, "The lack of a Reference in the context of religion is highly unsatisfactory and the explanation for it unconvincing" ([2016] P.L. 405, 415).

Belief in a supreme being

7-054

Traditionally, a trust for the advancement of atheist or agnostic purposes could not be charitable because belief in, and worship of, a god were deemed essential features of religion.[266] Nowhere was this principle more emphatically demonstrated than in *Re South Place Ethical Society*.[267] There Dillon J observed that:

> **"It seems to me that two of the essential attributes of religion are faith and worship; faith in a god and worship of that god. This is supported by the definitions of religion given in the Oxford English Dictionary".[268]**

The society before him existed to "study and disseminate ethical principles" and to cultivate "rational religious sentiment". It was an agnostic society interested in the values of love, truth and excellence, the members of which neither believed in nor denied the existence of God. It led Dillon J to assert the logical proposition that "Religion is concerned with man's relations with God and ethics are concerned with man's relations with man".[269] As there was no belief in a Supreme Being, the society could not be a charity for the advancement of religion.

The requirement of belief in a Supreme Being posed problems even for established religions. A prominent example was that of Buddhism. In *R. v Registrar General Ex p. Segerdal*, Lord Denning MR treated it as something of an exception to the rule requiring belief in a god.[270] In *Re South Place Ethical Society*, however, Dillon J readily accepted that Buddhism was a religion but admitted to possessing insufficient knowledge to determine whether there was belief in a god.[271]

The need to address the adequacy of the accepted definition of religion in the case law led to a broad new description in the Charities Act, that specifically embraces "religion which does not involve belief in a God".[272] As made clear by the Supreme Court, "Unless there is some compelling contextual reason for holding otherwise, religion should not be confined to religions which recognise a supreme deity. First and foremost, to do so would be a form of religious discrimination unacceptable in today's society".[273] Indeed, the Charity Commission

---

266 As mentioned, the Charities Act 2011 now includes "a religion which does not involve belief in a god" (s.3(2)(a)(ii)).
267 [1980] 1 W.L.R. 1565.
268 [1980] 1 W.L.R. 1565 at 1572.
269 [1980] 1 W.L.R. 1565 at 1571.
270 [1970] 2 Q.B. 697 at 707. In the view of Lord Toulson, the meaning given to "worship" in the case was too narrow, and he clarified that, "even if it was not unduly narrow in 1970, it is unduly narrow now" (*R. (on the application of Hodkin) v Registrar General of Births, Deaths and Marriages* [2014] 2 W.L.R. 23 at 38).
271 [1980] 1 W.L.R. 1565 at 1573.
272 Section 3(2)(a)(ii).
273 *R. (on the application of Hodkin) v Registrar General of Births, Deaths and Marriages* [2014] 2 W.L.R. 23 at 36 per Lord Toulson.

response to the new statutory description has been to recognise the need for more inclusivity but also to acknowledge that in its view adherents must have:

> **"belief in a god (or gods) or goddess (or goddesses), or supreme being, or divine or transcendental being or entity or spiritual principle, which is the object or focus of the religion".[274]**

Evidence of an organised belief system certainly helped in the successful application for charitable status made by the Druid Network, a group which cited "nature" as its Supreme Being or entity.[275] By contrast, the Temple of the Jedi Order (a group advancing Jediism, a 'religion' inspired by characters in Star Wars and based on observance of the Force), lacked the "necessary spiritual or non-secular element" to fall within the new definition.[276]

The act of worship

7-055

Traditionally, there has been much judicial focus on the act of worship as a necessary facet of religious practice. This has seen the courts and the Charity Commission spell out the types of activities that constitute worship. In *R. v Registrar General Ex p. Segerdal*, Buckley LJ argued that worship must have some of the characteristics of "submission to the object worshipped, veneration of that object, praise, thanksgiving, prayer, or intercession".[277] The absence of such qualities in the practice of the Church of Scientology led directly, in that case, to the conclusion that a building used for instruction in Scientology was not a "place of meeting for religious worship" under the Places of Worship Registration Act 1855.

Similar difficulties beset the Church of Scientology in its application to the Charity Commissioners in 1999. Like the Court of Appeal, the Charity Commissioners decided that at least some elements of worship were required. The Commissioners accepted that there was a belief in a supreme being, but they could find no evidence of worship. Rather, the dominant practices were "auditing" and "training". The former, which could be described as the one to one exploration of an individual's past life, was more akin to counselling than worship. The latter was no more than intensive scripture study and, therefore, more of an educational activity than an act of worship.

In light of the 2006 Act, however, the requirement of worship is now construed liberally so as not to exclude legitimate religious groups where there is no worship of a supreme being or entity.[278] Indeed, the Supreme Court ruling to allow a woman the right to marry in

---

274 See Charity Commission, *The Advancement of Religion for the Public Benefit* (December 2011), p.8.
275 Druid Network, Charity Commission Decision (September 2010); see N. Evans and P. Luxton [2011] Conv. 144.
276 Decision of the Commission (16 December 2016).
277 [1970] 2 Q.B. 697 at 709.
278 The Commission cites the example of Jainism where adherents do not "connect" with a Supreme Being or entity, but adopt a belief system based on attainment of a state of purity or oneness after death by living

a Scientology church overrules the decision in *Ex p. Segerdal* and suggests that the Church of Scientology may now qualify for charitable status should charitable status once again be pursued.[279]

Churches and the clergy

7-056

Trusts for the repair, maintenance or enhancement of churches are charitable trusts. Accordingly, there have been valid trusts to provide for stained-glass windows in a church,[280] to maintain the church organ[281] and to assist in the training of the clergy.[282] A gift for the advancement of religion that fails to specify a particular faith to be benefited will be presumed to be for the established church.

Advancement of religion

7-057

Valid charitable trusts under this head are required positively to advance religion. In *United Grand Lodge of Ancient, Free and Accepted Masons of England v Holborn BC*, Donovan J explained that:

> **"to advance religion means to promote it, to spread the message ever wider among mankind; to take some positive steps to sustain and increase religious belief . . .".[283]**

For Lord Denning, the question of advancement inevitably brought to mind the concept of public benefit. In *National Deposit Friendly Society Trustees v Skegness UDC*, he provided the simple and effective illustration that, "When a man says his prayers in the privacy of his own bedroom, he may be truly concerned with religion but not with the advancement of religion".[284] This serves to emphasise that in a trust that purports to advance religion, there is a required 'public' element.

---

good lives: see Charity Commission, *The Advancement of Religion for the Public Benefit* (December 2011), p.23.

279 *R. (on the application of Hodkin) v Registrar General of Births, Deaths and Marriages* [2014] 2 W.L.R. 23. It would, of course, need to demonstrate its public benefit.

280 *Re King* [1923] 1 Ch. 243.

281 *Adnam v Cole* (1843) 6 Beav. 353.

282 *Re Williams* [1927] 2 Ch. 283.

283 [1957] 1 W.L.R. 1080 at 1090.

284 [1959] A.C. 293 at 322.

Public benefit

Under the head of advancement of religion, the distinction between practice in public and practice in private is uppermost. As the Charity Commission reflected in the 1999 application for registration as a charity by the Church of Scientology, "the decided cases indicated that the public or private nature of the 'religious practice' of the organisation in question was central to determining the presence or absence of public benefit".[285] As will become clear, nowhere is a public benefit more lacking than in the case of enclosed orders where religious practice is carried out in private.[286] Although the practices that occur behind closed doors are no doubt devoutly religious, they will seldom provide a tangible public benefit. There must, therefore, be a benefit beyond that experienced by adherents to the religion itself. By way of illustration, the public benefit test will be analysed by reference to the following:

- enclosed orders;

- retreat houses; and

- the saying of masses.

Enclosed orders

The line of authority as regards enclosed orders dates back to the nineteenth century. In *Cocks v Manners*,[287] Wickens VC held that a gift to the Dominican convent was not a gift on charitable trust. He reasoned that "It is said, in some of the cases, that religious purposes are charitable, but that can only be true as to religious services tending directly or indirectly towards the instruction or the edification of the public".[288] As the gift was for the purposes of an enclosed order of nuns, there was no benefit to the public, direct or otherwise. *Cocks v Manners* was cited by Lindley J in *Re White*, who argued, similarly, that "A society for the promotion of private prayer and devotion by its own members, and which has no wider scope, no public element, no purposes of general utility, would be a 'religious' society, but not a 'charitable' one".[289] More recently, the House of Lords has emphasised that no public benefit accrues from the religious activities of enclosed orders. In *Gilmour v Coats*,[290] property was left on trust for the purposes of a Carmelite convent. Although the Carmelites are a purely contemplative order that

---

285 Decisions of the Charity Commissioners (17 November 1999), p.47.

286 See Charity Commission, *Public Benefit: The Public Benefit Requirement* (PB1) (September 2013), p.12 (no public benefit where a purpose is "confined to a closed religious organisation").

287 (1871) L.R. 12 Eq. 575.

288 (1871) L.R. 12 Eq. 575 at 585.

289 [1893] 2 Ch. 41 at 51.

290 [1949] A.C. 426. See R. Meakin, *"Gilmour v Coats* Revisited: A study in the Law of Public Benefit in Charity Law Today" (2016) Law & Just. 157.

remain strictly cloistered, the Roman Catholic Church maintained that there was, nonetheless, a public benefit. First, through intercessory prayer the nuns prayed to God to help members of the public. Secondly, their cloistered lives brought spiritual edification to the community. Lord Simonds disregarded those arguments. In his view, intercessory prayer and spiritual belief were not capable of judicial proof and the benefit to the public was, therefore, intangible and vague.[291] Any benefit was felt not by the public at large or even a sufficient section of it, but by individuals within the walls of the convent.

The order of Carmelite nuns in *Gilmour v Coats* may be usefully compared with the closed community of Anglican nuns in the Society of the Precious Blood.[292] In the 1990s, the Society of the Precious Blood applied for charitable status.[293] Its constitution disclosed purposes similar to those of the Carmelite nuns in that they concerned themselves with contemplation and intercessory prayer. In distinction to *Gilmour v Coats*, however, they were not entirely cut off from the outside world. The Society had associate members who lived outside in the community. It ran a counselling and support programme that involved the community. In addition, community members, particularly school children, were permitted to visit the Abbey, to take classes on the history and archaeology of Burnham Abbey and to hear talks on religious issues. The Abbey also offered retreat facilities to needy outsiders.[294] In light of these substantially charitable activities, the Charity Commissioners felt that the constitution did not reflect the truly charitable purposes carried out by the nuns. Crucially, much of its real work was carried out in public. Accordingly, the Society was asked for amendments to be made to its constitution to reflect its inherently charitable work. The Society was duly registered as a charity.

Retreat houses

7-060

At first glance, the arguments about the absence of public benefit in relation to closed orders are also applicable to retreat houses. In *Re Warre's WT*, Harman J explained that a retreat house is "a form of religious experience well understood in the Church of England. It is a retirement from the activities of the world for a space of time for religious contemplation and the cleansing of the soul".[295] Holding that the provision of a retreat house for the Church of England was not charitable, Harman J explained, "No doubt that is a highly beneficial activity for the person who undertakes it, but it is not an activity, which for the reasons so often set out in English law is a charitable activity".[296] No public benefit attached to a trust where only the few who stayed there derived benefit. Unfortunately, this perspective ignores the indirect,

---

291 Lord Simonds regarded the benefit derived by others from the example of pious lives, as too "indirect, remote, imponderable and . . . controversial" to be admitted into the category of public benefit ([1949] A.C. 426 at 447).
292 *Society of Precious Blood* (1995) 3 Decisions 11 (an Anglican contemplative community at Burnham Abbey).
293 See also, *Caldey Abbey* [1969] Ch. Com. Rep. 9, which too provides ready comparison.
294 The provision of a retreat house has been held, of itself, to carry no public benefit: *Re Warre's WT* [1953] 1 W.L.R. 725.
295 [1953] 1 W.L.R. 725 at 728.
296 [1953] 1 W.L.R. 725 at 728.

but nonetheless discernible, benefit to the public at large when individuals return to society. As Cross J acknowledged in *Neville Estates v Madden*, "the court is entitled to assume that some benefit accrues to the public from the attendance at places of worship of persons who live in this world and mix with their fellow citizens".[297] The authority of *Re Warre's WT* is now legitimately questionable.

Retreat houses were again considered in *Re Banfield*.[298] The court was required to consider a residuary bequest in favour of "Pilsdon Community House", a religious community that received and tended to members of the public who needed help for reasons such as drug or alcohol abuse. Goff J easily distinguished the *Gilmour v Coats* line of cases as dealing with "cloistered nuns whose community was essentially introspective and existed for the purpose of sanctifying the souls of the members . . .".[299] In stark contrast, the very purpose of the Pilsdon Community House in *Re Banfield* was to do good works in the community. Goff J also faced the more formidable argument that the community house was a retreat house, which for Harman J in *Re Warre's WT* lacked the necessary element of public benefit. Of the retreat house in *Re Warre's WT*, Goff J explained that:

> **"Such a house exists for private meditation and improvement only, and is therefore lacking in the necessary public element. Pilsdon Community House is quite different, as it opens out to reach the public."[300]**

Accordingly, and for the future, it may be that such evidence of reaching out to the community will be sufficient to display the public benefit patently lacking in the cases of enclosed orders.

Religious masses

Not surprisingly, the question of public benefit arises where there is a trust for the saying of masses or the performance of religious ceremonies. The position is straightforward. Where the masses or ceremonies are held in public, the trust will be charitable. If held in private, however, no public benefit attaches. In *Re Hetherington's WT*, the testatrix made a bequest of £2,000 to the Bishop of Westminster for the saying of masses for the souls of herself, her husband, her parents and her sister.[301] The bequest was deemed charitable for the advancement of religion. Although in this case the will did not specify how the masses were to be said, Browne-Wilkinson VC placed a benign construction on the words so they were construed as capable of being carried out by charitable means only.

7-061

---

297 [1962] Ch. 832 at 853.
298 [1968] 1 W.L.R. 846.
299 [1968] 1 W.L.R. 846 at 850.
300 [1968] 1 W.L.R. 846 at 852.
301 [1990] Ch. 1.

(d) The Advancement of Health or the Saving of Lives

7-062 The advancement of health or the saving of lives is now a distinct head of charity under s.3(1)(d) of the 2011 Act. Dating back to the Statute of Elizabeth I, the promotion of health has long been accepted as a charitable purpose. The Preamble makes reference to relief of the aged or impotent and to trusts for the maintenance of sick or maimed soldiers and mariners. As will be discussed, relief of the aged will be charitable under its own separate description.[302] Trusts for the advancement of health generally will fall to be considered as a separate category.

Traditionally, the advancement of public health has been served in a variety of ways, for example, in the provision of hospitals,[303] the supply of contraceptives,[304] the provision of healthcare advice[305] or recreational activities deemed to be for the betterment of public health.[306] This new description of charity also incorporates the prevention or relief of sickness, disease or human suffering.[307] This object is promoted by the Charity Commission, for which the advancement of health includes:

> **"conventional methods as well as complementary, alternative or holistic methods which are concerned with healing mind, body and spirit in the alleviation of symptoms and the cure of illness".[308]**

7-063 As to the relief of sickness, charitable purposes extend "beyond the treatment or provision of care, such as a hospital, to the provision of items, services and facilities to ease the suffering or assist the recovery of people who are sick, convalescent, disabled or infirm or to provide comforts for patients".[309] The purpose must be exclusively charitable.[310] The "saving of lives" incorporates those bodies whose work involves the provision of rescue services such as fire brigades,[311] lifeboat associations[312] and search and rescue organisations such as

---

302 "The Relief of those in Need by Reason of Youth, Age, Ill-health, Disability, Financial Hardship, or other Disadvantage" (see para.**7-073**).

303 Note that hospitals may charge fees but cannot be charitable where the poor are excluded: see *Re Resch's Will Trust* [1969] 1 A.C. 514.

304 *Family Planning Association* [1969] Ch. Com. Rep. 11.

305 For example, the *British Pregnancy Advisory Service* [1978] Ch. Com. Rep. 26.

306 Such as the provision of an ice-rink in *Oxford Ice Skating Association* [1984] Ch. Com. Rep. 11.

307 Charities Act 2011 s.3(2)(b).

308 Charity Commission, *Charitable Purposes* (September 2013) at [6]; note that sufficient evidence of the efficacy of the method is required.

309 Charity Commission, *Charitable Purposes* (September 2013), para.26. See also Charity Commission, *Example Objects—Relief of Sickness* (May 2013).

310 In *Derby Teaching Hospital NHS Foundation Trust v Derby City Council* [2019] EWHC 3436 (Ch), the purposes of NHS Foundation Trusts were not deemed to be exclusively charitable purposes for the advancement of public health.

311 *Re Wokingham Fire Brigade Trusts* [1951] Ch. 373 (provision for a local fire brigade).

312 Such as the Royal National Lifeboat Institution.

mountain[313] or cave rescue.[314] It also includes charities that ensure the proper standards of medical practice,[315] charities set up to assist the victims of natural disasters or war[316] the provision of life-saving or self-defence classes and the provision of blood transfusion services.[317]

Public benefit

A legitimate and sometimes difficult question arises as to whether charities which charge fees (e.g. in this context private hospitals or care homes) are of benefit to a sufficient section of the community. It is acceptable that fees are charged, even if at a higher level than required for the provision of the service, as long as they are not so high as to effectively exclude the less well off.[318] Where high fees are charged, the question arises as to whether the level of fees has the effect of deterring or preventing the less well off from accessing the services. If so, there must be evidence to show that the less well off are not wholly excluded from possible benefits, whether direct or indirect. For example, the existence or otherwise of accessible medical insurance schemes may provide evidence of whether, and how, the less well off can access private hospital services.[319] Similarly, by looking at the nature and extent of the benefit provided, it might be possible to conclude that the type of service provided is one for which there is a public need and, that the service provided goes some way to meeting that need. For example, a private hospital may have, and make available, specialised equipment not available in the local NHS hospital.[320]

7-064

(e) The Advancement of Citizenship or Community Development

This purpose is found in s.3(1)(e) and includes rural or urban regeneration as well as the promotion of civic responsibility, the voluntary sector or the effectiveness or efficiency of charities.[321]

7-065

---

313 For example, Buxton Mountain Rescue Team.
314 For example, Cave Rescue Organisation.
315 Such as the General Medical Council.
316 For example, OXFAM.
317 For example, The British Blood Transfusion Society.
318 *Re Resch's WT* [1969] 1 A.C. 514.
319 This was not sufficient in the case of Odstock Private Care Ltd which was refused registration by the Charity Commission in September 2007, on the basis that those living in poverty were not able to benefit in any real sense whether directly or indirectly.
320 See Charity Commission, *Charging for Services: Illustrative Examples of Benefits to the Poor* (September 2013).
321 Charities Act 2011 s.3(2)(c).

As to urban or rural regeneration, permissible charitable purposes are required to relate to an area of social and economic deprivation. The Commission cites as key means to achieve regeneration the "maintenance or improvement of the physical, social and economic infrastructure and by assisting people who are at a disadvantage because of their social and economic circumstances".[322] An organisation might provide, therefore, public facilities, advice and assistance to businesses where it would lead to training and employment opportunities for the unemployed[323] or for the maintenance and improvement of roads and accessibility to main transport routes. It is important, however, that the benefit to the public outweighs any private benefit to individuals or companies.

As to the promotion of civic responsibility, a broad collection of associated purposes are housed here. Charities concerned with promotion of the voluntary sector are a recent and prominent example.[324] In 2011, however, the Charity Commission rejected an application from Uturn UK Ltd for registration under this description. The primary object of Uturn was to promote and set up street associations to advance citizenship and community development. More particularly, its desire was to "bring the residents of streets together in local groupings with a framework that will engender civic responsibility and volunteering". Although this purpose appeared to fall squarely within s.3(2)(c), the Commission was concerned at the lack of clarity as to how the associations might operate and that they may not be in practice confined to exclusively charitable purposes. Uturn lost its appeal to the First-tier Tribunal (Charity).[325]

(f) The Advancement of the Arts, Culture, Heritage or Science

7-066

Prior to the enactment of the Charities Act 2006, the promotion of arts, culture, heritage or science could be charitable as furthering the advancement of education. The new statutory description promotes those objects as charitable in their own right but there remains much scope for overlap. As has been discussed in the context of education, for example, the provision of a museum or an art gallery is capable of advancing education provided that the works therein are of sufficient merit. Such purposes may also be charitable under para.(f). The overlap with education is also present in relation to research carried out for the advancement of

---

322 Charity Commission RR2: *Promotion of Urban and Rural Regeneration* (March 1999), para.2.
323 See further, Charity Commission RR3: *Charities for the Relief of Unemployment* (March 1999).
324 Charity Commission RR13: *Promotion of the Voluntary Sector for the Benefit of the Public* (September 2004), Annex A, para.4; see also Charity Commission RR14: *Promoting the Efficiency and Effectiveness of Charities and the Effective Use of Charitable Resources for the Benefit of the Public* (September 2004).
325 See *Uturn UK CIC v Charity Commission for England and Wales* CA/2011/0006, 27 February 2012 (FTT (Charity)).

science and in the work of societies, such as the Royal College of Surgeons,[326] which could be considered charitable under either head. For the Charity Commission, the distinction between the descriptions seems to be important in its assessment of public benefit in that charities whose aims concern the advancement of education must show an educational benefit to the public.

More generally, there are many organisations with objects falling squarely within para. (f).[327] The purposes of the National Trust, for example, were designed to promote "the permanent preservation for the benefit of the nation of lands and tenements (including buildings) of beauty or historic interest and as regards lands for the preservation (so far as practicable) of their natural aspect features and animal and plant life".[328] Almost 20 years ago, the Charity Commission published guidance on the scope of organisations set up for the charitable purposes of preservation and or conservation.[329] Naturally, this has an impact on those bodies that seek to claim involvement in the advancement of heritage. As regards preservation, expert evidence is required that the site or building is of sufficient historical interest[330] and that there is sufficient public benefit.[331] Where a building is preserved because of its connection to a particular person, for example to commemorate a birth or death, expert evidence is required to satisfy that the person is of sufficient educational, historical or scientific interest. In addition, the building should have a real connection with the person and a significant part of the surviving fabric of the building should relate to the period during which the person occupied it. Nonetheless, considerable flexibility is maintained in that the Commission regards this as a starting point from which it is prepared to take on board other factors in assessing the merits of a particular case.[332]

Outside preservation, it remains necessary to consider whether it is charitable to erect a building or memorial for the advancement of purposes under this head. In *Re Endacott*, there was no charitable quality to the provision by a testator of "some useful monument to myself".[333] It is, perhaps, safer to suggest that some useful monument in furtherance of an accepted charitable purpose will be more readily acceptable, although there is surprisingly little authority to this effect. The provision of memorials to police officers who lost their lives in the course of their duties was deemed a charitable purpose on the ground that it promoted good citizenship and public awareness.[334] Of more long-standing authority, it was held in *Murray v Thomas* that to promote for the benefit of two villages some useful memorial prefer-

7-067

---

326 *Royal College of Surgeons of England v National Provincial Bank Ltd* [1952] A.C. 631.
327 Examples of purposes falling within this description include scientific research projects, local arts and the promotion of sculpture (Charity Commission, *Charitable Purposes* (September 2013)).
328 *Re Verrall* [1916] 1 Ch. 100 at 102.
329 Charity Commission RR9: *Preservation and Conservation* (February 2001).
330 This can be assumed in the case of a famous historic building where the existence of merit is considered obvious, or evidenced in the case of listed buildings.
331 For example, that there is sufficient public access provided.
332 Charities Commission RR9: *Preservation and Conversation* (February 2001), Annex, para.7.
333 [1960] Ch. 232.
334 *The Police Memorial Trust* [1984] Ch. Com. Rep. 10.

ably of the type of a village hall was in law a charitable purpose.[335] More broadly, where a monument is deemed a work of art, there could be little objection to its inclusion under para. (f).

(g) The Advancement of Amateur Sport

7-068

The advancement of sport per se has never been charitable.[336] If ancillary to a charitable purpose,[337] however, the promotion of sport has been held to be charitable under the applicable head. The old fourth head of "other purposes beneficial to the community" housed a number of such examples. In *Re Gray*, Romer J was happy to accept that sport in the form of shooting, fishing, cricket, football and polo would increase the efficiency of the armed forces, holding for that reason that a gift was charitable.[338] He claimed of the testator that:

> "it was his intention to benefit the officers and men of the Carabiniers by giving them an opportunity of indulging in healthy sport."[339]

In 2003, the Charity Commission recognised as charitable, first, "the promotion of community participation in healthy recreation by providing facilities for particular sports"[340] and, secondly, "the advancement of the physical education of young people not undergoing formal education".[341] Whilst the latter was merely an extension of the principles of decided cases (see para.**7-045**), the former was a new departure recognising as charitable much of the work done by many Community Amateur Sports Clubs (CASCs). It is not possible for a club with CASC status (registered with the HM Revenue & Customs (HMRC) with a separate system of tax reliefs) also to claim the advantages of charitable status. A distinction is necessary between

---

335 [1937] 4 All E.R. 545. Clauson J was persuaded that a fund collected to erect a memorial of something in the nature of a cross would also be charitable.
336 *Re Nottage* [1885] 2 Ch. 649 (yacht racing).
337 Such as the advancement of education: see *IRC v McMullen* [1981] A.C. 1 (see para.**7-045**).
338 [1925] Ch. 362.
339 [1925] Ch. 362 at 365. Similar arguments were accepted in relation to the police force in *IRC v City of Glasgow Police Athletic Association* [1953] A.C. 380, but the association was deemed to be non-charitable on the ground that the provision of recreation was a primary purpose. As Lord Normand explained at 396, "The private advantage of members is a purpose for which the association is established and it therefore cannot be said that this is an association established for a public charitable purpose only".
340 "Facilities" extends beyond the provision of lands, buildings and equipment to include the organisation of sport.
341 Charity Commission RR11: *Charitable Status and Sport* (April 2003) (currently under review).

CASCs and charities to avoid, as Nugee J put it, the "unintended and anomalous effect of enabling a CASC to benefit from the tax reliefs available to charities while at the same time not being obliged to submit to the regulatory and other requirements applicable to them".[342] It remains possible for an amateur sports club (without CASC status) to obtain charitable status where the sport in question is capable of improving health and fitness. Open membership is required, in that access to the club's facilities must be genuinely available to anyone who wishes to take advantage of them.[343] A failure to adhere to this requirement will result in private as opposed to public benefit.

The Charities Act 2011 embraces the advancement of amateur sport as a head of charity in its own right, but with the clarification that "'sport' means sport or games which promote health by involving physical or mental skill or exertion".[344] There remains some uncertainty as to how the new description will be interpreted, the type of sports or games that will qualify, and the level of mental skill or exertion necessary to promote health. Thus far, much of the focus has been on the promotion of physical health,[345] but it is clear that s.3(1)(g) is wider in scope. Accordingly, the Commission has registered the Hitchin Bridge Club, noting that, "Bridge involves logical and lateral thinking skills, planning, memory, sequencing, initiation and other higher order functions. Bridge is regarded as a game of high mental skill being one of the five component games in the World Mind Games".[346]

It remains possible, of course, that other charitable purposes may be furthered by sport. In the relief of disability, sport can be charitable where it improves the conditions of people with a mental or physical disability. The Charity Commission provides a range of examples of charities engaging in sports[347] such as bowls,[348] shooting,[349] gliding[350] and sailing.[351] In addition, physical training towards the alleviation of stiffness and immobility was cited as charitable as being for the relief of old age.[352]

7-069

---

342 *Eynsham Cricket Club v Revenue and Customs Commissioners* [2019] UKUT 286 (TCC) at [118] (eligibility of a cricket club for zero-rating for VAT).

343 A tennis and squash club with fees of £339 for adult membership did not, in the view of the Charity Commission, meet the public benefit requirement: see Charity Commission, *Public Benefit Assessments: Emerging Findings for Charity Trustees from the Charity Commission's Public Benefit Assessment Work: 2009–11* (March 2011), G4.

344 Charities Act 2011 s.3(2)(d).

345 For example, the lack of physical exertion in the sport of target shooting prevented a target shooting association from registering as a charity: see *Cambridgeshire Target Shooting Association v Charity Commission for England and Wales* CA/2015/0002, 23 November 2015 (FTT (Charity)).

346 Application for Registration of Hitchin Bridge Club (February 2011), para.17.

347 Charity Commission RR11, *Charitable Status and Sport* (April 2003), para.5.

348 British Wheelchair Bowls Association.

349 Great Britain Paraplegics Shooting Association.

350 Flyability.

351 Sailability.

352 Charity Commission RR11: *Charitable Status and Sport* (April 2003), Annex, para.8.

(h) The Advancement of Human Rights, Conflict Resolution, or Reconciliation, or the Promotion of Religious or Racial Harmony or Equality and Diversity

7-070 By analogy with existing charitable purposes,[353] it is clear that the advancement of human rights had become a recognised charitable purpose under the fourth *Pemsel* head. The Charities Act 2011 provides a statutory basis for treating the promotion of human rights as charitable. Human rights can be promoted, whether at home or abroad, in a wide variety of ways.[354] Examples range from obtaining redress for, or alleviating the need of, victims of human rights abuses, to educating the public and promoting public support for human rights.[355] In *Human Dignity Trust v Charity Commission for England v Wales*, therefore, there was nothing to prevent the registration of a company established to support individuals whose human rights had been violated by the criminalisation of consensual, homosexual conduct, by assisting in their efforts to litigate in domestic and international courts. Its purposes were the promotion and protection of human rights and the promotion of the sound administration of the law, neither of which (in the view of the First-Tier Tribunal) were deemed unclear, ambiguous or insufficiently particularised. In *HDT*, the Charity Commission had refused to register the company on the register of charities, one of its concerns being the boundary between charitable and political purposes and activities. Applying the rule that a political purpose cannot be charitable, the Charity Commission advanced the accepted wisdom that to seek to change the law whether here or abroad could not necessarily be viewed as beneficial or for the public benefit. The Tribunal held that HDT did not have a political purpose. Instead, it was "concerned with the promotion of human rights by establishing whether particular laws are valid, through a process of constitutional interpretation".[356] In other words, human rights may be promoted through litigation to interpret and enforce existing laws.

More generally, as regards public benefit, the Charity Commission holds the view that there is an obvious and clear public benefit in promoting human rights:

> **"For individuals whose human rights are thereby secured, the benefit is immediate and tangible. There is also a less tangible, but nonetheless significant, benefit to the whole community that arises**

---

353 For example, those purposes beneficial to the community by virtue of their moral or spiritual welfare and improvement: Charity Commission RR12: *The Promotion of Human Rights* (January 2005).

354 The term "human rights" should be given its "ordinary natural meaning" and is not confined to a narrow conception of human rights as consistent only with the law of England and Wales (*Human Dignity Trust v Charity Commission for England and Wales* [2015] W.T.L.R. 789 at [43].

355 See generally: RS16: *Charities Working in the Field of Human Rights* (December 2007).

356 [2015] W.T.L.R 789 at [95].

> from our perception that the fundamental rights of all members of
> the community are being protected. That provides sufficient benefit
> to the community to justify treating the promotion of human rights
> as a charitable purpose in its own right".[357]

The description of charity in s.3(1)(h) is not confined to the advancement of human rights, but extends to "conflict resolution or reconciliation". The Charity Commission has explained that the advancement of conflict resolution or reconciliation involves:

7-071

> "the resolution of international conflicts and relieving the suffering,
> poverty and distress arising through conflict on a national or inter-
> national scale by identifying the causes of the conflict and seeking to
> resolve such conflict. It includes the promotion of restorative justice
> ... It also includes purposes directed towards mediation, concilia-
> tion or reconciliation as between persons, organisations, authorities
> or groups involved or likely to become involved in dispute or inter-
> personal conflict".[358]

Accordingly, the Charity Commission has registered a wide range of organisations whose purposes are charitable in this context, such as the Restorative Justice Consortium.

The statutory description, the "promotion of religious or racial harmony or equality and diversity" will include a broad range of charitable activities such as the promotion of good race relations, the tackling of discrimination whether on the basis of age, gender or sexual orientation or the enabling of people to understand the religious beliefs of others. The Community Security Trust, for example, exists to promote good race relations between the Jewish community and other members of society, to promote the efficiency of the police within society at large, to relieve the hardship of victims of racial or religious harassment and to promote public education about racism and anti-semitism.[359]

(i) The Advancement of Environmental Protection or Improvement

The Charity Commission considers that the advancement of environmental protection and improvement, "includes preservation and conservation of the natural environment and the

7-072

---

357 Charity Commission RR12: *The Promotion of Human Rights* (January 2005), para.12.
358 Charity Commission, *Charitable Purposes* (September 2013), para.10.
359 See *Community Security Trust* (1995) 4 Ch. Com. 8 December.

promotion of sustainable development".[360] Conservation of the environment covers, "the conservation of a particular animal, bird, or other species or 'wildlife' in general; a specific plant species, habitat or area of land, including areas of natural beauty and scientific interest; flora, fauna and the environment generally".[361] Typical examples of charitable purposes falling within this description include the conservation of the environment generally, of a particular geographical area or of a particular species. In relation to the promotion of sustainable development, charitable purposes include research or practical efforts to promote biodiversity, recycling, sustainable waste management and the use of renewable energy resources. It was previously thought that no public benefit accrued from keeping the public away from the protected object or area, i.e. that public access was a key determinant of public benefit.[362] There is little evidence that such a rule will, in future, be applied rigidly. A broader view is adopted in line with developing understanding and appreciation of the need for environmental protection and improvement generally.

(j) The Relief of those in Need by Reason of Youth, Age, Ill-health, Disability, Financial Hardship, or other Disadvantage

7-073

The Preamble to the Statute of Charitable Uses 1601 contained a range of charitable purposes that now fall under this new statutory description, such as "the relief of aged, impotent and poor people". It was rapidly acknowledged that the wording thereof was to be construed disjunctively so that distinct categories evolved which concerned the relief of those in need because of age, disability and financial hardship. In *Joseph Rowntree Memorial Trust Housing Association Ltd v Attorney General*, Peter Gibson J upheld as charitable the provision of housing for the elderly without regard to any poverty requirement.[363] He claimed that the word "relief" requires that the persons in question have a need attributable to their condition as aged, impotent or poor persons which requires alleviating.[364] Accordingly, relief of the aged can be achieved in a number of ways, such as the provision of advice, medical care, rest homes or day

---

360 Charity Commission, *Charitable Purposes* (September 2013), para.11.
361 Charity Commission, *Charitable Purposes* (September 2013) at [11]. Expert evidence may be required to demonstrate the worthiness of an object for conservation: see Charity Commission RR9: *Preservation and Conservation* (February 2001).
362 See *Re Grove-Grady* [1929] 1 Ch. 557, discussed below (see para.**7-075**).
363 [1983] Ch. 159.
364 [1983] Ch. 159 at 171.

centres and is not confined to the poor and aged. Similarly, the provision of children's care homes and orphanages is charitable[365] along with the provision of apprenticeships, which are charitable in terms of the establishment in life of children or young people. Again, the development of this category of charitable purpose stems from the specific inclusion in the Preamble of "the education and preferment of orphans".

Ill health and disability can take many forms and, understandably, the relief of those who are suffering is achieved through a very wide variety of charitable purposes such as the training of guide dogs[366] and the provision of personal transportation.[367] The Charities Act 2011 s.3(2)(e) expressly includes relief given by the provision of accommodation or care to the persons outlined and in need. The reference to "other disadvantage" leaves open a variety of possibilities, such as that a trust for the relief of alcoholics or drug users may well be charitable under this head. Whilst the prevention of such social evils through the promotion of temperance will be categorised as the advancement of health, the relief of those who are suffering seems best placed under this statutory description.

As to public benefit, in *Re Duffy*[368] it was held that a legacy to help fund an old people's home for the benefit of its residents and staff was not charitable in that a home with no more than 33 residents could not be deemed to benefit a sufficient section of the community. Unfortunately, little satisfactory justification for this restrictive approach was offered, Roch J seemingly content to rely on *Oppenheim v Tobacco Securities Trust Co Ltd* (a decision on advancement of education), to deny a public benefit in this altogether different context.[369]

(k) The Advancement of Animal Welfare

7-074

The charitable nature of trusts for the protection of animals has long been accepted and its inclusion as a head in its own right has not been regarded as a significant change in the law.[370] Nonetheless, it is not entirely clear how this category developed. There is no mention of such a purpose in the Preamble and the approach of the courts has been markedly shaped by prevailing notions as to the benefit to the community of activities such as the destruction of animals, vivisection or the importance of environmental protection. Historically, charitable

365 As Lord Hailsham claimed in *D v NSPCC* [1978] A.C. 171 at 228, "the welfare of children, particularly of young children at risk of maltreatment by adults, has been, from the earliest days, a concern for the Crown, as *parens patriae*, an object of legal charities and in latter years the subject of a whole series of Acts of Parliament".
366 Guide Dogs for the Blind Association.
367 Motability.
368 [2013] EWHC 2395 (Ch).
369 See further, M. Synge, "Charitable Status: Not a Negligible Matter" [2016] L.Q.R. 305.
370 *Hanchett-Stamford v Attorney General* [2009] 2 W.L.R. 405 at 411 per Lewison J.

purposes associated with animal welfare have grown by the ready acceptance of new purposes analogous to those appearing in the decided case law. In *London University v Yarrow*, a hospital for the treatment of animals useful to mankind was held charitable.[371] This paved the way for the acceptance of, for example, the Home for Lost Dogs[372] and, further, the protection of animals.[373] Although now overruled, in *Re Foveaux*[374] Chitty J developed the category further when he declared that particular societies for the abolition of vivisection fell within the legal definition of charity.[375]

There has never been a presumption that trusts for the advancement of animal welfare are for the public benefit. The most prominent issue for the courts has been in establishing the sense in which such trusts are beneficial to the community. The pervading obstacle is that in the course of advancing welfare, a benefit must accrue to mankind. The nature of this benefit came to the fore in *Re Foveaux*, where Chitty J claimed that:

> **"Cruelty is degrading to man, and a society for the suppression of cruelty to the lower animals, whether domestic or not, has for its object, not merely the protection of the animals themselves, but the advancement of morale and education among men . . . The intention is to benefit the community".[376]**

Similarly, in *Re Wedgwood*[377] the Court of Appeal was called upon to consider the charitable nature of a trust for "the protection and benefit of animals". The trust was upheld with emphasis again placed on the benefit to humanity. As Swinfen Eady LJ commented:

> **"A gift for the benefit and protection of animals tends to promote and encourage kindness towards them, to discourage cruelty, and to ameliorate the condition of the brute creation, and thus to stimulate humane and generous sentiments in man towards the lower animals; and by these means promote feelings of humanity and morality generally, repress brutality, and thus elevate the human race. That such purposes are eminently charitable, in the accepted legal sense of that term, is amply established . . ."[378]**

---

371   (1857) 1 De F. & G. 72.
372   *Re Douglas* (1887) 35 Ch. D. 472.
373   *Armstrong v Reeves* (1890) 25 L.R. Ir. 325.
374   [1895] 2 Ch. 501.
375   *Re Foveaux* was overruled by *National Anti-Vivisection Society v IRC* [1948] A.C. 31 where it was held by the House of Lords that anti-vivisection is not a charitable purpose.
376   [1895] 2 Ch. 501 at 507.
377   [1915] 1 Ch. 113.
378   [1915] 1 Ch. 113 at 122.

7-075

Re Grove-Grady provided further elucidation.[379] There the Court of Appeal held that a sanctuary for the preservation of all animals or birds to keep them safe from molestation by man was not a charitable purpose. The court could discern no public benefit. Lord Hanworth MR identified that the sanctuary in question was not a straightforward case of a sanctuary for endangered species. He claimed that, "no such purpose is indicated—nor indeed possible".[380] Crucially, on the facts of *Grove-Grady,* the gift was neither to the advantage of the animals nor the betterment of humankind. He observed, therefore that:

> "The one characteristic of the refuge is that it is free from the molestation of man, while all the fauna within it are to be free to molest and harry each other. Such a purpose does not, in my opinion, afford any advantage to animals that are useful to mankind in particular, or any protection from cruelty to animals generally. It does not denote any elevating lesson to mankind".[381]

The advancement of animal welfare will continue to grow as a legitimate charitable purpose. As to the traditional justification for deeming it charitable, it may be that future courts adopt a lenient approach to long-standing authority.

(l) The Promotion of the Efficiency of the Armed Forces of the Crown, or of the Efficiency of the Police, Fire and Rescue Services or Ambulance Services

7-076

Trusts for national or local defence, such as those that promote the efficiency of the armed and emergency services[382] were accepted charitable purposes under the fourth *Pemsel* head. For example, a trust for training boys as officers in the Royal Navy was upheld in *Re Corbyn*.[383] Indeed, the endorsement of trusts for certain patriotic purposes had extended even to a gift to the National Revenue, as in *Nightingale v Goulbourn*, where a testator made a charitable

---

379 [1929] 1 Ch. 557.
380 [1929] 1 Ch. 557 at 573.
381 [1929] 1 Ch. 557 at 573.
382 As to the fire and rescue services, their functions are defined by the Fire and Rescue Services Act 2004 Pt 2.
383 [1941] Ch. 400.

bequest to the Chancellor of the Exchequer, "to be by him appropriated to the benefit and advantage of my beloved country Great Britain".[384]

The new statutory description specifically covers the need to ensure that the armed forces are trained and equipped in times of conflict. It extends to the provision of facilities and benefits for the armed forces. Many examples of such charitable purposes provided by the Charity Commission would be charitable under other statutory descriptions, such as increasing technical knowledge of members of the services through the provision of educational resources or maintaining a museum or other collection for the preservation of artefacts connected with a military unit.[385] Other examples of charitable purposes are more particularly relevant such as promoting and strengthening bonds between allied units or encouraging recruitment to the armed services.

(m) Any Other Purposes

7-077

Section 3(1)(m) lists as charitable any other purposes within subs.(4). These purposes are as follows.

(i) Any purposes not listed within paras (a)–(l) (above) but which are recognised as charitable purposes by virtue of s.5 (recreational or similar trusts, etc) or under the old law.

(ii) Any purposes which "may reasonably be regarded as analogous to, or within the spirit of", purposes listed in paras (a)–(l), or, indeed s.3(1)(m)(i).

(iii) Any purposes which "may reasonably be regarded as analogous to, or within the spirit of", any purposes which have been recognised under charity law as falling within s.3(1)(m)(ii).

It is important to emphasise that purposes recognised as charitable under existing law continue to be charitable purposes. The Act, furthermore, permits the inclusion of any purpose that may reasonably be regarded as analogous to, or within the spirit of the accepted charitable purposes whether new or pre-existing. The Charity Commission has identified a range of charitable purposes that will continue to be charitable, notwithstanding the absence of direct reference in the statutory descriptions of purposes discussed above. Some of the most noteworthy charitable purposes listed by the Charity Commission are as follows[386]:

---

384 (1848) 2 Ph. 594.
385 See Charity Commission, *Charitable Purposes* (September 2013), para.14.
386 Charity Commission, *Charitable Purposes* (September 2013), para.15.

- the provision of public works and services such as the repair of bridges, ports, havens, causeways and highways or the provision of water and lighting[387];

- the promotion of mental or moral improvement;

- the preservation of public order[388];

- the promotion of the sound administration and development of the law[389];

- the promotion of ethical standards of conduct and compliance with the law in the public and private sectors; and

- the rehabilitation of ex-offenders and the prevention of crime.

Public benefit

It will be recalled that charitable purposes falling within the old fourth *Pemsel* head, "other purposes beneficial to the community" developed and modernised through the process of drawing analogies with accepted charitable purposes.[390] As regards trusts classified as beneficial to the community, the courts have been vigilant to ensure a sufficient section of the community benefited, more specifically, that benefit was not restricted to a "class within a class".[391] It may be that the courts continue to adopt this test where to do so would be to draw a sensible inference from a statutory description that a purpose should benefit the public at large. There seems to be a legitimate role for the continued application of the test under para.(m), which catches purposes not expressly listed, but nevertheless charitable, or charitable by analogy thereto.

7-078

Recreational Charities

In contrast to the promotion of mere sport, a trust for the provision of public recreational facilities such as a park[392] or a recreation ground[393] is a legitimate charitable purpose.

7-079

---

387 Such purposes were contained in the Preamble and developed by analogy to include a broad range of public works and amenities (e.g. the provision of sewers, public gardens or museums).

388 See *IRC v City of Glasgow Police Athletic Association* [1953] A.C. 380.

389 *Human Dignity Trust v Charity Commission for England and Wales* [2015] W.T.L.R 789 (FTT (GRC)). Examples of charitable purposes include the provision of a court house (*Attorney General v Heelis* (1824) 2 Sim. & St. 67) and mediation services or free legal advice to those in need (such as that provided by JUSTICE to prisoners who believe they have suffered a miscarriage of justice).

390 See para.**7-011**.

391 *IRC v Baddeley* [1955] A.C. 572; see para.**7-019**.

392 *Re Hadden* [1932] 1 Ch. 133.

393 *Re Morgan* [1955] 1 W.L.R. 738.

Accordingly, a considerable number of charities have existed for many years to pursue recreational purposes.[394] The Recreational Charities Act 1958 was enacted to allay fears that many charities, such as women's institutes and miners' welfare trusts, would cease to be charitable as a result of the House of Lords' decision in *IRC v Baddeley*.[395] There, a trust to promote the moral, social and physical well-being of persons resident in West Ham and Leyton who were or were likely to become members of the Methodist Church was deemed not charitable. It was considered that the concept of well-being was too vague to be recognised as a charitable purpose under the fourth head. In addition, and most importantly, the objects were deemed to comprise a class within a class, i.e. a class restricted by reference to one criterion (e.g. geographical area) from which a further class were selected to benefit (e.g. those of a particular creed). The development of this general test of public benefit under the old fourth *Pemsel* head called into question the status of many existing charities whose beneficiaries were not only confined to a particular area, but narrowed further to a particular class within that class. The object of the 1958 Act was not to enlarge the definition of charity or to acknowledge new institutions as charitable, but to recognise by statute that the provision of recreational facilities in the interests of social welfare is a valid charitable purpose.[396] The provisions formerly contained in the Recreational Charities Act 1958 are now to be found in the Charities Act 2011.

7-080

Section 5(1) of the 2011 Act provides that "It is charitable (and is to be treated as always having been charitable) to provide, or assist in the provision of, facilities for recreation or other leisure-time occupation, if the facilities are provided in the interests of social welfare".[397] The requirement that the facilities[398] are provided in the interests of social welfare[399] is not treated as satisfied unless the facilities are provided with the object of "improving the conditions of life for the persons for whom the facilities are primarily intended".[400] In addition those persons must "have need of the facilities by reason of their youth, age, infirmity or disablement, poverty or social and economic circumstances" or "the facilities are to be available to members of the public at large or to male, or to female, members of the public at large".[401]

The intended application of s.5(1) is confirmed in s.5(4) where it is emphasised that s.5(1) applies in particular to:

---

394 For example, the Oxford Ice Skating Association.

395 [1955] A.C. 572.

396 See S. Maurice, "Recreational Charities" (1959) 23 Conv. (NS) 15.

397 The principle still applies that for a trust or institution to be charitable it must be for the public benefit.

398 Facilities provided need not be educative.

399 The "social welfare" element has been sufficient to exclude groups or societies that exist exclusively for the enjoyment of members, for example the Birchfield Harriers Athletics Club: Decisions, Vol.1 (1993), p.4.

400 No specific social disadvantage is necessary as long as facilities are provided with the object of improving the conditions of life for members of the community generally: see *Guild v IRC* [1992] 2 A.C. 310 (North Berwick Sports Centre); cf. *IRC v McMullen* [1979] 1 W.L.R. 130, where the majority of the Court of Appeal held that deprivation was necessary.

401 Charities Act 2011 s.5(3). Note the scope for overlap with the description in para.(j) "the relief of those in need by reason of youth, age, ill health, disability, financial hardship or other disadvantage".

> "the provision of facilities at village halls, community centres and women's institutes, and to the provision and maintenance of grounds and buildings to be used for purposes of recreation or leisure-time occupation, and extends to the provision of facilities for those purposes by the organising of any activity".[402]

Political Purposes

A trust for political purposes can never be a charitable trust.[403] The basis of the court's objection was explained by Lord Parker in *Bowman v Secular Society*. It is,

7-081

> "not because it is illegal, for everyone is at liberty to advocate or promote by any lawful means a change in the law, but because the court has no means of judging whether a proposed change in the law will or will not be for the public benefit".[404]

Further, as Lewison J explained in *Hanchett-Stamford v Attorney General*, "the law cannot stultify itself by holding that it is for the public benefit that the law should be changed . . . each court must decide on the principle that the law is right as it stands".[405] No charitable trust or organisation can exist, therefore, primarily to further the interests of a political party,[406] to change the law (or oppose proposed changes)[407] or to seek to influence Government to those ends, whether central or local, here or abroad.[408] It is the job of Parliament to legislate and of the courts to apply the law.

---

402 The specific provision to cater for Miners' Welfare Trusts, was repealed by the Charities Act 2006.

403 See generally, C. Forder, "Too Political to be Charitable" [1984] Conv. 263.

404 [1917] A.C. 406 at 442.

405 [2009] 2 W.L.R. 405 at 411.

406 As Finlay J held in *Bonar Law Memorial Trust v IRC* (1933) 17 T.C. 508 at 517, "it would not be right to say—that a trust for the promotion of Conservative principles, or the principles, I need hardly say, of any other political party, would be a good charitable trust".

407 *National Anti-Vivisection Society v IRC* [1948] A.C. 31.

408 See *McGovern v Attorney General* [1982] Ch. 321.

Changing the law

7-082

In *National Anti-Vivisection Society v IRC* a trust to abolish vivisection was not charitable, as it required the repeal of the Cruelty to Animals Act 1876 in order to achieve its purpose.[409] The court acknowledged the difficulties in determining whether the purpose was charitable by analogy to existing charitable purposes. Crucially, the aims could not be achieved except by the alteration of legislation. As stated above, the courts have insufficient standing to determine whether such a change is in the public benefit. If the court felt able to conclude that a change in the law was for the public benefit, this would be to confuse its role with that of the legislature.

In *McGovern v Attorney General*, Amnesty International (a non-charitable organisation) sought charitable status for the Amnesty International Trust under which charitable aspects of the organisation's work were carried into operation.[410] At this time, its objects included:

(i)   the relief of needy persons who are, were or are likely to become prisoners of conscience and their relatives;

(ii)   the attempt to secure the release of such prisoners;

(iii)   the abolition of torture or inhumane or degrading treatment or punishment; and

(iv)   the promotion and commission of human rights research and dissemination of results.

Although no objection was raised as to the part that comprised research, Slade J could not ignore the other overtly political objects. He interpreted securing the release of prisoners of conscience, for example, as involving the "direction of moral pressure or persuasion against governmental authorities".[411] Accordingly, the trust was deemed to be non-charitable on the basis that it required pressure on foreign governments to change their policies.

7-083

More recently, in *Human Dignity Trust v Charity Commission for England and Wales*,[412] the First-Tier Tribunal (Charity) was required to consider an appeal against the decision of the Charity Commission not to register as charitable the Human Dignity Trust. As an organisation for the promotion of human rights, its purposes involved supporting individuals (in litigation at home and abroad) whose rights had been violated through the criminalisation of homosexuality. Although the Charity Commission cited *McGovern*, the Tribunal did not share its view that the purposes before it could be characterised as political:

> **"We are not satisfied that the litigation supported and conducted by HDT may be described as seeking to change the law. It seems**

---

409   [1948] A.C. 31.
410   [1982] Ch. 321; see R. Nobles (1982) 45 M.L.R. 704.
411   [1982] Ch. 321 at 347.
412   [2015] W.T.L.R. 789.

> to us that the constitutional process involved in interpreting and/ or enforcing superior constitutional rights might, on one analysis, be seen as upholding the law of the state concerned rather than changing it, but it also seems to us that the paradigm of changing/ upholding the law is one more suited to an analysis of domestic provisions than it is to the arena of constitutional rights. We prefer to characterise HDT's activities as engaging in a legitimate constitutional process which occupies a different space from that occupied by the domestic law".[413]

Although a welcome development, there is no doubt that the law is now much less clear cut. Indeed, as Biehler notes, "the reality is that it will be increasingly difficult to sustain the political purposes exclusion where objects designed to advance human rights are at issue".[414]

Campaigning

7-084

Although a trust for political purposes cannot be a charitable trust, there is considerable debate as to the extent to which political and campaigning activities can (and should) be carried out by charitable bodies. In other words, the stated aims of a charitable body cannot be political, but a question arises as to what extent activities carried out in furtherance of charitable aims may, indeed, be political. Much campaigning work carried out by charities does not involve "political" campaigning, but activities such as fundraising and promoting awareness. The Government recognises the particular strengths of charities in carrying out a legitimate role in campaigning and advocacy.[415] For example, strong links between charities and local communities entail that charities are well placed to monitor, evaluate and comment upon implemented policies. Government acknowledges a benefit, moreover, from the diversity of causes represented by charities and the scope therein to give voice to a wider range of perspectives and interests than otherwise possible.

The approach of the Charity Commission has been positive in terms of emphasising the campaigning activities that are compatible with charitable purposes. Previously, it took the view that any political activity must be in furtherance of, and ancillary to, a charity's stated objects, i.e. it must serve and be subordinate to the charity's purpose.[416] Its current guidance serves to emphasise that political campaigning must not be the continuing and sole activity, but acknowledges that "a charity may choose to focus most, or all, of its resources on political

---

413 [2015] W.T.L.R. 789 at [99].
414 Biehler, "The Political Purposes Exception—Is There a Future for a Doctrine Built on Foundations of Sand?" (2015) 29 (3) Tru. L.I. 97 at 102.
415 See generally, *Private Action, Public Benefit* (September 2002).
416 See Charity Commission CC9, *Campaigning and Political Activities by Charities* (September 2004).

activity for a period".[417] The balance to be achieved by trustees is to ensure that the activity in question does not become the reason for the charity's existence.

In addition, the Electoral Commission has worked in collaboration with the Charity Commission to produce guidance for charities thinking about campaigning in the run up to a general election and who wish to understand the interaction between charity law and election law.[418] This guidance has been issued and updated following the enactment of the Transparency of Lobbying, Non-Party Campaigning and Trade Union Administration Act 2014, which introduced new rules on spending by non-party campaigners.[419]

Education and politics

7-085

Where it is clear that a trust or an organisation carries some educational benefit, it is necessary to be careful that that benefit does not mask truly political objects. In *Re Hopkinson*,[420] Vaisey J made clear that political propaganda masquerading as education is not for the public benefit. Here, a trust to educate the public in the values of a particular political party had some educational character, but it was clear that it could not be charitable. As Vaisey J claimed, "In my judgment, there can be no doubt that the testator's object was, not education in the proper sense of that word, but the furtherance of his political views and the better equipping of those who make it their business to further them".[421]

A similar conclusion befell a gift for "the advancement and propagation of the teaching of socialised medicine".[422] The testator had died in 1944. Even though the NHS was introduced after his death, at the point of his death a legislative change would have been required to bring about this purpose. There, Goulding J concluded:

> **"I am quite unable to avoid the conclusion that the main or dominant or essential object is a political one. The testator never for a moment, as I read his language, desired to educate the public so that they could choose for themselves . . .".[423]**

By way of a more recent example, in *Southwood v Attorney General* a trust for the advancement of the education of the public in the subject of militarism and disarmament was denied charitable status because the aim of the promoters was to challenge the poli-

---

417   Charity Commission CC9, *Speaking out—Guidance on Campaigning and Political Activity by Charities* (March 2008), D.8.
418   Electoral Commission, *Charities and Campaigning* (2014).
419   See *https://www.electoralcommission.org.uk/non-party-campaigners-where-start* [Accessed 31 July 2020].
420   [1949] 1 All E.R. 346.
421   [1949] 1 All E.R. 346 at 352.
422   *Re Bushnell* [1975] 1 W.L.R. 1596; noted at (1975) 38 M.L.R. 471 (R. Cotterrell).
423   [1975] 1 W.L.R. 1596 at 1605.

cies of Western governments.[424] On close examination, the object was not to educate the public in the differing means of achieving peace and avoiding war, but to educate the public to an acceptance that peace is best secured by "demilitarisation". Accordingly, Chadwick LJ concluded:

> **"The court is in no position to determine that promotion of the one view rather than the other is for the public benefit. Not only does the court have no material on which to make that choice; to attempt to do so would be to usurp the role of government."[425]**

7-086

A distinction must be drawn between political propaganda which is a political, non-charitable object and education with a political flavour. As the latter does not seek to change the law or government policy, it is capable of being charitable. *Re Koepplers' WT*, for example, concerned the purposes of the Wilton Park Project, more specifically, the provision of conferences to promote greater cooperation in Europe and the West in general, involving an exchange of views on political, economic and social questions of common interest.[426] Slade LJ identified that:

> **"(i) the conferences sought to improve the minds of the partici-pants, not necessarily by adding to their factual knowledge but by expanding their wisdom and capacity to understand;**
> **(ii) the subjects discussed at conferences were recognised aca-demic subjects in higher education;**
> **(iii) the conferences operated by a process of discussion designed to elicit an exchange of views in a manner familiar in places of higher education;**
> **(iv) the conferences were designed to capitalise on the expertise of participants who were there both to learn and to instruct".[427]**

He acknowledged, therefore, that although the topics touched on the political, the activities of Wilton Park were not of a party political nature. They were not designed to procure changes in the laws or policies of the government. As Slade LJ explained, "Even when they touch on politi-cal matters, they constitute, so far as I can see, no more than genuine attempts in an objective manner to ascertain and disseminate the truth".[428]

---

424 *The Times*, 18 July 2000.
425 *The Times*, 18 July 2000.
426 [1986] Ch. 423.
427 [1986] Ch. 423 at 436
428 [1986] Ch. 423 at 437.

Charitable Purposes Overseas

7-087

Provided a purpose or activity would be charitable in England and Wales, it is no objection that such a purpose is carried out abroad. Many well-known organisations such as OXFAM carry out valuable charitable work outside this country.[429] The principal difficulty occasioned by such trusts lies in the question as to the community to be benefited, i.e. whether the benefit must accrue to a sufficient section of the community at home or merely the community abroad.[430] Early cases appear either to ignore, or fail to recognise as important, the issue of public benefit. In *Whicker v Hulme*, for example, the House of Lords upheld a trust "for the benefit and advancement, and propagation, of education and learning in every part of the world as far as circumstances will permit".[431] Lord Evershed MR in the Court of Appeal in *Camille and Henry Dreyfus Foundation Inc v IRC*[432] adopted a more cautious approach. Recognising the existence of many charities where the benefit accrued to populations outside the United Kingdom, he claimed:

> **"It may be that, on very broad and general grounds, relief of poverty or distress in any part of the world, or the advancement of the Christian religion in any part of the world, would be regarded as being for the benefit of the community in the United Kingdom. I see formidable difficulties, however, where the objects of the trust were, say, the setting out of soldiers or the repair of bridges or causeways in a foreign country."[433]**

Accordingly, and prior to the enactment of the Charities Act 2006, it was felt that charities within the fourth head were required to be of benefit to the UK community.[434] The current approach of the courts and, indeed, the Charity Commission is more relaxed.[435] Where the purpose benefits the public, or a section of the public abroad, and that purpose would be deemed charitable if carried out at home, it will be charitable when carried out overseas provided that there is no public policy reason not to recognise it.[436] On this view, a trust to reduce the

---

429 Over 16,000 charities in England and Wales work internationally with income of some £15.95 billion: see Charity Commission, *Annual Report for 2016–17* (July 2016), p.12.

430 For example, in *Keren Kayemeth Le Jisroel Ltd v IRC* [1932] A.C. 650 (a trust for the purchase of land in Israel for the settlement of Jews) it was not possible to identify the community to be benefited, leaving open the question of whether a benefit to a sufficient section of an overseas community will suffice.

431 (1858) 7 H.L. 124.

432 [1954] Ch. 672.

433 [1954] Ch. 672 at 684.

434 As assumed in *McGovern v Attorney General* [1982] Ch. 321 at 338; see generally, H. Cohen (1983) 36 C.L.P. 241, 253–254.

435 See, e.g. the approach in *Re Carapiet's Trusts* [2002] W.T.L.R. 989.

436 *Human Dignity Trust v Charity Commission for England and Wales* [2015] W.T.L.R. 789 at [76].

national debt of a foreign state may be contrary to public policy,[437] whereas a trust to promote the protection of the environment in another nation will be accepted as charitable.

Guide to Further Reading

H. Biehler, "The Political Purposes Exception—Is There a Future For a Doctrine Built on Foundations of Sand?" (2015) 29(3) Tru. L.I. 97.

M. Chesterman, "Foundations of Charity Law in the New Welfare State" (1999) 62 M.L.R. 333.

G.H.L Fridman, "Charities and Public Benefit" (1953) 31 CBR 537.

J. Garton, "Charitable Purposes and Activities" (2014) 67(1) C.L.P. 373.

J. Hackney, "Charities and Public Benefit" (2008) 124 L.Q.R. 347.

M. Harding, "Trusts for Religious Purposes and the Question of Public Benefit" (2008) 71 M.L.R. 159.

P. Luxton, "Opening Pandora's Box: The Upper Tribunal's Decision on Public Benefit and Independent Schools" (2012/13) 15 C.L & P.R 27.

P. Luxton, "A Three-Part Invention" (2009) 11 C.L.&P.R. 19.

L. McMurtry, "Charitable Purposes, Demonstrable Benefit and the Role of the Charity Commission: The Fourth Pemsel Head Recast" (2019) 70(4) N.I.L.Q. 445

D. Morris, "The First-Tier Tribunal (Charity): Enhanced Access to Justice for Charities or a Case of David v Goliath" [2010] C.J.Q. 491.

M. Synge, "Poverty: An Essential Element in Charity After All?" [2011] C.L.J. 649.

M. Synge, "The Attorney General and the Charity Commission: One Rule Without Reason" [2016] P.L. 409.

---

437 To adopt the example provided by Jenkins LJ in *Camille and Henry Dreyfus Foundation Inc v IRC* [1954] Ch. 672 at 704.

8

Cy-près

The term cy-près loosely translated means "as near as possible". The doctrine to which it lends its name fulfils an important role in the law of charities because it determines what happens when property has been dedicated to charitable purposes, but cannot be applied in the manner intended by the donor.[1] Where cy-près is applicable, it is open to the court or the Charity Commission to draw up a scheme for the application of the property to purposes "as near as possible" to those originally selected by the donor.[2] Prior to the Charities Act 1960, cy-près was available only where it was "impossible" or "impracticable" to give effect to the donor's intentions.[3] Such would occur, for example, where the donor elected to benefit a specified institution that had ceased to exist or one which, in fact, had never existed at all. Nowadays, the circumstances in which property may be applied cy-près have been extended by statute to provide a modern, flexible framework wherein funds dedicated to charity may be utilised or channelled more effectively.[4] As will be discussed, s.62 of the Charities Act 2011 provides for cy-près in a number of situations where the original purposes of a charitable gift may now be altered, and permits consideration of both the spirit of the gift and the social and economic circumstances prevailing at the time of the proposed alteration to the original purposes.

---

1   See generally, R. Mulheron, *The Modern Cy-près Doctrine: Applications and Implications* (London: UCL Press, 2006).
2   It has never been necessary to apply the property to the very nearest possible alternative purpose: see *Attorney General v Ironmongers' Company* (1834) 2 My. & K. 576, where the redemption of Christian slaves captured by Barbary pirates was no longer capable of being carried out and the property was applied cy-près for the benefit of schools.
3   *Re Weir Hospital* [1910] 2 Ch. 124.
4   A statutory jurisdiction was first introduced by s.13(1) of the Charities Act 1960 (replaced by s.13(1) of the Charities Act 1993) and extended by the Charities Act 2006. The 2011 Act consolidates relevant provisions from the 1993 and 2006 Acts.

The Court's Inherent Jurisdiction

Impossibility and impracticability

8-002

Impossibility or impracticability may be apparent from the outset or it may become clear at some later date that the charitable purpose cannot be carried into effect. "Initial impossibility" occurs where it has never been possible for the specific charitable end to be pursued. Here, failure must occur before the date when the trust comes into existence. In the case of testamentary gifts, this initial failure covers cases where it has always been impossible for a charitable end to be achieved or where it becomes impossible at some point between the making of a will and the death of the testator.[5] Hence, initial impossibility encompasses situations such as the selection of a charity that has never existed,[6] the selection of a charity that has ceased to exist prior to the testator's death[7] or where there is an absence of certainty as to the property to be dedicated to charitable purposes.[8]

Failure or impossibility will be termed "subsequent" or "supervening" if it occurs after property has been effectively dedicated to charity (i.e. after the trust comes into effect). It is at this moment that the claims of the donor and those claiming through him are excluded permanently. In relation to cases of initial impossibility, it is necessary to infer a general or paramount charitable intention on the part of the donor before the property can be applied cy-près. In contrast, cy-près is nearly always available in instances of subsequent impossibility, regardless of the generality of charitable intention exhibited by the donor.

General charitable intention

8-003

As indicated above, the availability of cy-près to cases of initial failure will depend upon there being a general charitable intention on the part of the donor. In some cases, the generality of intention is readily apparent.[9] In many other cases, however, the discernment of this general charitable intention is by no means as straightforward.[10] The court will construe the relevant trust instrument as a whole to work out whether the primary intention was to benefit a particular object (in which case the intention is specific) or to give effect to a general mode of charity.

---

5   In *Kings v Bultitude* [2010] EWHC 1795 (Ch), a residuary gift to the "Ancient Catholic Church" failed initially as the church had ceased to exist on the date of the death of the testator.
6   *Re Harwood* [1936] Ch. 285 (gift to the "Peace Society of Belfast").
7   See, e.g. *Re Rymer* [1895] 1 Ch. 19 (St Thomas' Seminary).
8   See *Harwood v Harwood* [2005] EWHC 3019 (Ch) where a testator bequeathed the "Harwood Collection" to trustees for the purpose of establishing a museum but there was no certainty as to what comprised the collection.
9   One obvious example of general charitable intention concerns the case where a donor has expressed that the gift is to be dedicated to a charitable purpose, but has omitted to identify a mode of application, e.g. "£10,000 for the relief of poverty".
10 See generally, J. Picton [2015] Conv. 480.

Where the reference to the specific can be said to be secondary to the donor's general charitable intention, it will be possible to apply the property cy-près. As Kay J explained in *Re Taylor*:

> "If upon the whole scope and intent of the will you discover the paramount object of the testator was to benefit not a particular institution but to effect a particular form of charity . . . then, although he may have indicated the mode in which he desires that to be carried out, you are to regard the primary paramount intention chiefly, and if the particular mode for any reason fails, the court, if it sees a sufficient expression of a general charitable intention of charity, will, to use the phrase familiar to us, execute that *cy-près*, that is, carry out the general paramount intention indicated without which his intention itself cannot be effected".[11]

Where, on the other hand, the particularisation is paramount there can be no execution cy-près. As Megarry VC put it in *Re Spence*, "Where the difficulty or impossibility not only afflicts the method but also invades the concept of the alleged general charitable intention, then I think that the difficulty of establishing that the will displays any general charitable intention becomes almost insuperable".[12] Undeniably, the dividing line is difficult to draw. This has led Vinelott J to claim that to "search for such a paramount or dominant charitable purpose or intention is in many cases to follow a will-o-the-wisp".[13] The process is best illustrated through a consideration of case law examples where a general charitable intention was necessary.

Initial Failure

Although, as will become apparent, there is a marked inconsistency in approach, it is possible to categorise the cases in which the search for general charitable intention has been central.

8-004

Gifts for charitable purposes

In *Biscoe v Jackson*,[14] a testator set aside a sum of money for the provision of a soup kitchen and cottage hospital for the parish of Shoreditch. As suitable land could not be found, it was impos-

8-005

---

11   (1888) 58 L.T. 538 at 542.
12   [1979] Ch. 483 at 496.
13   *Re Woodhams* [1981] 1 W.L.R. 493 at 502.
14   (1887) 35 Ch. D. 460.

sible to carry out the testator's wishes and initially the gift failed. Despite the degree of particularity in the description of the charitable purpose, the court was able to discern a general charitable intention to benefit the sick and poor of the parish. It was simple to determine those who were intended to benefit, although a difficulty lay in the method of carrying out the testator's intention. As Lindley LJ explained, "The object here is to establish a charity for the benefit of the poor with a particular mode of doing it; and if you cannot accomplish the object in that mode, then in some other mode in which you can".[15] Accordingly, *Biscoe v Jackson* illustrates the court's readiness to execute a general charitable purpose cy-près where the impossibility extends only to the form of the gift. As explained in *Re Wilson*, "the gift is given to a particular charitable purpose, but it is possible, taking the will as a whole, to say that, notwithstanding the form of the gift, the paramount intention, according to the true construction of the will, is to give the property in the first instance for a general charitable purpose rather than a particular charitable purpose".[16]

By way of contrast, other cases suggest that the more detailed the description of the charitable purpose, the narrower the generality of charitable intention. *Re Good's WT*[17] concerned a trust to provide rest homes in Hull. The testator had drawn up extremely detailed provisions for the erection of six or more rest homes, including plans for the management and day-to-day running of the project. Insufficient funds entailed that it was impracticable to proceed with the development. Wynn-Parry J noted the specificity with which the testator's plans were developed and the technical and particular language used. He felt that both were inconsistent with the finding of a general charitable intention. The testator in *Re Good's WT* had formulated a very specific intention and, accordingly, there could be no cy-près application.

8-006

Similarly in *Re Spence*,[18] a gift to the defunct "Old Folks Home at Hillworth Lodge, Keighley" was held to be a gift for a specific charitable purpose. Megarry VC was unable to construe a general charitable intention to benefit older people in the area. The existence of the home at the time of the making of the will militated against a general intention as to charity even though that particular home had closed.

Institutions that cease to exist

8-007

As is clear from *Re Spence*, it is difficult to construe a general intention as to charity where the institution selected is specific and in existence at the time of the testator's will. *Re Rymer*,[19] for example, concerned a bequest of £5,000 "to the rector for the time being of St Thomas

---

15   (1887) 35 Ch. D. 460 at 470; see also, *Moggridge v Thackwell* (1802) 7 Ves. 36 at 69, where Lord Eldon laid down the principle that, "if a testator has manifested a general intention to give to charity, the failure of that particular mode in which the charity is to be effectuated shall not destroy the charity, the law will substitute another mode of devoting the property to charitable purposes".

16   [1913] 1 Ch. 314 at 320 per Parker J.

17   [1950] 2 All E.R. 653.

18   [1979] Ch. 483.

19   [1895] 1 Ch. 19.

Seminary for the education of priests in the diocese of Westminster for the purposes of such seminary". Before the testator's death, the seminary ceased to exist and the students moved to an alternative seminary outside Birmingham. Lindley LJ could not avoid the very specific intention evidenced in the nature of this gift. Refusing to apply it cy-près, he commented, "It is a gift of £5,000 to a particular seminary for the purposes thereof, and I do not think it is possible to get out of that".[20] His conclusion sprang from the premise that the court must "consider whether the mode of attaining the object is only machinery or whether the mode is not the substance of the gift".[21] In *Re Rymer*, impossibility afflicted both the mode and the substance of the gift.

Similarly, in *Kings v Bultitude*,[22] no general charitable intention could be discerned where the testator, Mrs Schroder, made a residuary bequest to the "Ancient Catholic Church", a church in which she had been the leading member and to which she had devoted all her time and energy. The court held that her intention was specific. Accordingly, the gift was dependent on the continued existence of the particular church. Unfortunately, it had ceased to exist on her death. As Proudman J explained:

> "there is nothing in the Will to indicate a general charitable intention which might save the gift . . . The Will contains no other charitable gift. The Church was constituted in accordance with the personal idiosyncratic beliefs of its founder, and continued by Mrs Schroder in accordance with her own particular idiosyncrasies".[23]

Accordingly, the gift failed and could not be applied cy-près.

Continuation in another form

8-008

Sometimes a testator will seek to benefit a charity that has not ceased to exist as such, but has amalgamated with other organisations and is, thereby, continued in another form. Continuation in another form can occur where the name or the objects of the charity have changed, perhaps via the making of a scheme[24] or by trustees in accordance with the trust deed.[25] It is important to distinguish those institutions that genuinely cease to exist from those that continue to exist albeit in another guise. In the latter case, there is no issue of initial failure. Where a charity has funds held on trust for its purposes, the charitable purposes will continue

20 [1895] 1 Ch. 19 at 35; see also *Re Wilson* [1913] 1 Ch. 314, where no general intention attached to the very specific provisions drawn up by the testator relating to the erection of a school and the provision of a salaried schoolmaster.
21 [1895] 1 Ch. 19 at 35.
22 [2010] EWHC 1795 (Ch); see J. Picton [2011] Conv. 69.
23 [2010] EWHC 1795 (Ch) at [53].
24 See *Re Lucas* [1948] Ch. 424.
25 See *Re Bagshaw* [1954] 1 W.L.R. 238.

despite the alteration to its constitution or its objects.[26] *Re Faraker*[27] is an oft-cited example. In 1911, a legacy was left to "Mrs Bailey's Charity, Rotherhithe". The only similar charity that had operated was Hannah Bayly's Charity founded in 1756. In 1905, it had been consolidated with 13 other charities and new trusts were declared for the benefit of the poor in Rotherhithe. It was held that the testatrix had sought to benefit Hannah Bayly's Charity. Accordingly this was not a case of initial failure. The objects of the charity had developed over the years. Rather than being destroyed by the consolidation, this charity continued in another form.[28] Accordingly, the consolidated charities were entitled to the legacy.

Gifts to incorporated and unincorporated associations

8-009

In *Re Vernon's WT*,[29] Buckley J laid down the principles governing gifts to unincorporated charities and gifts to charities with corporate status. In relation to the former he stated that:

> "Every bequest to an unincorporated charity by name without more must take effect as a gift for a charitable purpose. No individual or aggregate of individuals could claim to take such a bequest beneficially. If the gift is to be permitted to take effect at all, it must be as a bequest for a purpose, viz., that charitable purpose which the named charity exists to serve. A bequest which is in terms made for a charitable purpose will not fail for lack of a trustee but will be carried into effect . . . by means of a scheme. A bequest to a named unincorporated charity, however, may on its true interpretation show that the testator's intention to make the gift at all was dependent upon the named charitable organisation being available at the time when the gift takes effect. . . If so and the named charity ceases to exist in the lifetime of the testator, the gift fails . . .".

On this basis, a gift to an unincorporated charity will be construed as a gift for the purposes of that charity, and those purposes may continue even though the charity itself may cease to exist in the lifetime of the testator. Unless there is something to demonstrate the need for the continued existence of the donee, the gift will not fail for want of a trustee and effect will be given to it. As to the gifts to charities with corporate status, Buckley J continued:

---

26 As Kennedy LJ tentatively put it, "It seems to be the law, that an endowed charity, to whatever purpose its funds are devoted, if and so long as they are devoted to some charitable purpose under some duly authorised scheme, remains still existent so as to draw to it a sum of money given by a will for, presumably, the same purpose as the original charity" (*Re Faraker* [1912] 2 Ch. 488 at 495).

27 [1912] 2 Ch. 488.

28 As Farwell LJ concluded, "Neither the Charity Commissioners nor the Court can take an existing charity and destroy it: they are obliged to administer it" ([1912] 2 Ch. 488 at 495).

29 [1972] Ch. 300 at 303.

> "A bequest to a corporate body, on the other hand, takes effect simply as a gift to that body beneficially . . . There is no need in such a case to infer a trust for any particular purpose . . . the natural construction is that the bequest is made to the corporate body as part of its general funds, that is to say, beneficially and without the imposition of any trust. That the testator's motive in making the bequest may have undoubtedly been to assist the work of the incorporated body would be insufficient to create a trust".[30]

Accordingly, strong evidence is required to demonstrate that a corporate body is to hold property on trust for charitable purposes. In the absence of such evidence, a gift to a corporate charity will fail should the body cease to exist before the death of the testator.

Re Finger's WT[31] concerned two testamentary gifts of residue, first, to the National Radium Commission (an unincorporated charity) and, secondly, to the National Council for Maternity and Child Welfare (a corporate charity). Both had ceased to exist before the death of the testator. As to the gift to the Commission, it was interpreted as being a purpose trust that did not depend on the continued existence of the Commission. As the purposes continued, the gift would not fail for initial impossibility. By contrast, the gift to the Council was a gift to a corporate charity. As this type of gift takes effect as a gift to that body beneficially, it could not be construed as a gift on trust for its purposes. The result was a case of initial failure. Somewhat fortunately, Goff J was able to construe a general charitable intention from looking at the will as a whole and the portion of property intended for the Council was capable of application cy-près.

Although a different approach has been adopted to the construction of gifts to corporate and unincorporated charities, it is a distinction which has been criticised[32] and one capable of producing unfortunate results. In *Re Meyers*,[33] Harman J dealt with a number of legacies to both corporate and unincorporated hospitals, all of which had been taken over by the Ministry of Health under the National Health Service Act 1946. As to the legacies to unincorporated hospitals, there was no difficulty posed by the construction of those gifts as being for the purposes of the hospitals. By contrast the gifts to the corporate hospitals posed more difficulty. If viewed as gifts to those hospitals beneficially, the prima facie conclusion is that those gifts should fail. Harman J declined to accept this and held it to be "contrary to common sense"[34] not to give a like construction to each gift. He explained, "In my judgment I am doing no violence to the language that the testator has used in the context in which he has used it in saying

8-010

---

30 [1972] Ch. 300 at 303.
31 [1972] Ch. 286.
32 In *Re Roberts* [1963] 1 W.L.R. 406, for example, Wilberforce J admitted that, "The mere fact that there is a gift to an unincorporated charity does not seem to me to be enough to enable me to come to the conclusion that a gift is for charitable purposes".
33 [1951] 1 All E.R. 538.
34 [1951] 1 All E.R. 538 at 542.

that in every case when he gives money to a hospital he does not regard the fact whether it was corporate, but he gives for the purposes of the work that that hospital is carrying on".[35]

The distinction in *Re Vernon's WT* was applied in *Re ARMS (Multiple Sclerosis Research) Ltd*.[36] There (in the context of legacies made to an incorporated charity), the testator died after the charity had run into financial difficulties and a winding-up order made but before the charity had been formally dissolved. Neuberger J reasoned that if the gift is expressed to be for a company then unless there are circumstances which indicate that the recipient is to act as a trustee, the gift will take effect so long as the company is still in existence at the date of the testator's death.[37] Accordingly, the legacy took effect not as a gift on charitable trust, but as a beneficial gift to that institution such that the liquidator could claim entitlement for the benefit of the charity's creditors. In *Phillips v RSPB*,[38] moreover, a gift to the New Forest Owl Sanctuary Ltd (NFOS) failed as the company had ceased to exist following the death of the testatrix. As this was a gift to the company for its general purposes with nothing to indicate that the company should hold it on a separate trust, the funds could be applied cy-près. As Judge Cooke explained, "This case is therefore one of supervening failure . . . one where the gift was effective at the date of death to impress the funds with the charitable purpose intended to be given effect to through NFOS".[39] He concluded that, "unless the court finds that the particular method specified is the only possible way of giving effect to the donor's charitable intentions, it may direct that the funds be applied cy-près".[40]

Gifts subject to a condition

8-011   A further category of case concerns gifts that are limited by a condition. In this context, the courts have proved eager to dismiss unacceptable and specific qualifications or conditions as inessential to the testator's paramount intention.[41] For example, in *Re Lysaght*[42] there was a gift of £5,000 to the Royal College of Surgeons to create medical studentships, subject to the qualification that students must be British born and not of Jewish or Roman Catholic faith. The restriction was unacceptable to the Royal College and regarded by it as "so invidious and so alien to the spirit of the college's work as to make the gift inoperable in its present form".[43]

The gift was saved and the offensive provision deleted because the court was able to rely on the general charitable intention of the testatrix to establish the studentships. First (and somewhat questionably), it was held that the detail within the bulk of the provisions did not

---

35   [1951] 1 All E.R. 538 at 542.
36   [1997] 1 W.L.R. 877.
37   [1997] 1 W.L.R 877 at 882.
38   [2012] EWHC 618 (Ch).
39   *Phillips v RSPB* [2012] EWHC 618 (Ch) at [27].
40   *Phillips v RSPB* [2012] EWHC 618 (Ch) at [27].
41   See further paras **8-019 to 8-020**.
42   [1966] Ch. 191.
43   [1966] Ch. 191 at 200 per Buckley J.

form an essential part of her true intention. Buckley J gave an assured statement of principle when he concluded that "the fact that a testator has condescended to details cannot be conclusive that those details, or all of them, are essential parts of his true intention".[44] Less convincing, was the conclusion as a matter of construction that the details did not form part of that intention. Secondly, he determined that it did form part of her paramount intention that the College should act as trustee.[45] This enabled Buckley J to conclude that the fact that the College would not accept the gift (that is, subject to the condition) should not be allowed to deflect from her paramount intention to create the studentships. In doing so, he invoked the general principle that:

> "A general charitable intention . . . may be said to be a paramount intention on the part of the donor to effect some charitable purpose which the court can find a method of putting into operation, notwithstanding that it is impracticable to give effect to some direction by the donor which is not an essential part of his true intention—not, that is to say, of his paramount intention".[46]

A further, less troublesome, example is that of *Re Woodhams*.[47] There, a gift to the London College of Music to fund annual scholarships was expressed to be subject to the restriction that the scholarships be available only to boys coming from two specific and high-profile orphanages. Vinelott J held that the selection of orphans from those particular homes merely identified those orphans in greatest need of assistance. It was not, he claimed, "an essential part of the scheme that the scholarships be so restricted, whatever needs might present themselves in changed circumstances".[48] Accordingly, the restriction was deleted.

8-012

Non-existent institutions

8-013

In *Re Harwood*,[49] the court was called upon to consider the availability of cy-près in relation to two testamentary gifts. The first, to the "Wisbech Peace Society, Cambridge", suffered initial failure because the society had ceased to exist prior to the death of the testatrix. The second, to the "Peace Society of Belfast", had failed because there was no evidence that any such society had existed at all. As regards the first gift, Farwell J felt that the testatrix had gone out of her

---

44 [1966] Ch. 191 at 204.
45 As Buckley J explained, "It is of the essence of the trust that the trustees selected by the settlor and no one else shall act as the trustees of it and if those trustees cannot or will not undertake the office, the trust must fail" ([1966] Ch. 191 at 207).
46 [1966] Ch. 191 at 202.
47 [1981] 1 W.L.R. 493.
48 [1981] 1 W.L.R. 493 at 505.
49 [1936] Ch. 285.

way to specify that particular charity. This specific identification made it difficult to discern a general intention. As Farwell J acknowledged:

> "where the testator selects as the object of his bounty a particular charity and shows in the will itself some care to identify the particular society which he desires to benefit, the difficulty of finding any general charitable intent in such a case where the named society once existed, but ceased to exist before the death of the testator, is very great".[50]

As regards the second gift, cy-près was available. The testatrix had elected to benefit a non-existent institution and, accordingly, Farwell J readily found a general charitable intention to "benefit societies whose object was the promotion of peace".[51] Notwithstanding the doubt that such an intention was political rather than charitable, this case is an excellent illustration of the relative ease with which the court may find a general intention. The idea is that only a general charitable intention can be attributed to a donor who fails correctly to specify an existing charity. At the very least, the court, "is more ready to infer a general charitable intention than to infer the contrary".[52]

Groups of objects

8-014   In *Re Satterthwaite's WT*[53] an eccentric testatrix, who declared that she hated all human beings, left the residue of her estate to nine separate bodies concerned with the welfare of animals. There was evidence that most of the list had been compiled from the London classified telephone directory. The Court of Appeal was asked to consider whether there could be a cy-près application of the share left to the London Animal Hospital. No such charity ever existed and the share was being claimed by a vet who worked under that trade name prior to the death of the testatrix. Here, a number of factors pointed to a general charitable intention: the random selection of charities; the mode of selection (by phonebook); her public hatred of people and the nature of the charities selected, all of which were concerned with the welfare of animals.

Russell LJ was happy to construe the residuary gift as a whole. As each share was intended to go to some object connected with the care of animals, he did not question that there was a general intention to benefit that sort of charity. He explained, "Here I have no doubt from the nature of the other dispositions . . . that a general charitable intention can be discerned in favour of charity through the medium of kindness to animals".[54] Harman LJ, however,

---

50   [1936] Ch. 285 at 287.
51   [1936] Ch. 285 at 288.
52   *Re Davis* [1902] 1 Ch. 876 at 881 per Buckley J.
53   [1966] 1 W.L.R. 277.
54   [1966] 1 W.L.R. 277 at 286.

expressed "the gravest doubts" as to whether a general charitable intention had, indeed, been shown.[55] It was for another reason that he felt compelled to arrive at the same conclusion as Russell LJ, namely that the judge at first instance had discerned, in respect of a similar gift, the general charitable intention necessary to apply cy-près. As no appeal had been made as to the judge's findings in respect of that gift, Harman LJ was forced to arrive at the same conclusion as to the gift to the London Animal Hospital.[56]

8-015

Re Satterthwaite's WT suggests that a general charitable intention is easier to discern in cases where a group of objects has been selected. The approach adopted by Russell LJ appears to rely on the detection of a range of similar objects as a means of construing a general, rather than a specific, intention. It is an approach that is not without support. In *Re Knox*,[57] for example, there was a residuary gift to be apportioned in quarters to two named infirmaries, a particular nursing home and Dr Barnardo's Homes. Although the named nursing home had never existed, Luxmoore J was still able to see a general charitable intention. He explained of the name of the nursing home that "the object of each of the other charities is a kindred object to that which might be inferred from the name".[58]

In *Re Spence*,[59] however, Megarry VC was unimpressed both with the reasoning in *Re Knox* and with the argument that the principle could apply where as few as two objects had been selected. He distinguished between the case of initial failure where the object had never existed and one where the gift was to a body that had existed at the date of the will, but had ceased to exist before the death of the testator.[60] In the case of the latter, "the court is far less ready to find such an intention".[61] As Megarry VC observed, "It is difficult to envisage a testator as being suffused with a general glow of broad charity, when he is labouring and labouring successfully, to identify some particular specified institution or purpose as the object of his bounty".[62] A similar reluctance was evident in the approach of Buckley J in *Re Jenkins' WT*.[63] There, a gift to the British Union for the Abolition of Vivisection, a non-charitable association, was one non-charitable bequest amongst a group of nine gifts to charitable associations. Buckley J refused to accept that a general charitable intention motivated the gift, claiming that, "if you meet seven men with black hair and one with red hair you are not entitled to say that

---

55   [1966] 1 W.L.R. 277 at 284.
56   Diplock LJ offered no opinion, blithely stating that, "With that humility that is becoming in a common law lawyer when confronted with an arcane branch of the Chancery law, I agree with the judgments that have been delivered" ([1966] 1 W.L.R. 277 at 287).
57   [1937] Ch. 109.
58   [1937] Ch. 109 at 113. This approach was followed in *Re Hartley* unreported 15 March 1978, where a general charitable intention sufficed for a cy-près application of one part of a residuary gift in quarters to service charities where one charity no longer existed at the date of the will.
59   [1979] Ch. 483.
60   Logically, the distinction must also apply to the object that had ceased to exist before the date of the will as the intention is specific, albeit, impossible.
61   [1979] Ch. 483 at 495.
62   [1979] Ch. 483 at 493.
63   [1966] Ch. 249.

there are eight men with black hair".[64] On the basis that a non-charitable object was selected in *Re Jenkins' WT*, it appears that the case is readily distinguishable from *Re Satterthwaite's WT* where the testatrix had selected an animal hospital that had never existed.

Subsequent Failure

8-016
The application of cy-près is broader in relation to instances of subsequent or supervening failure. Unlike initial failure, no general charitable intention need be discerned on the part of the settlor. In the event that property becomes dedicated to charity, it remains dedicated to charity and it is not possible for a previous owner to assert a claim over it.[65] In the case of a will, the relevant date at which this exclusion occurs is that of the testator's death. More generally, this principle is as Jenkins LJ put it, "once the charity for which the fund was raised had been effectively brought into action the fund was to be regarded as permanently devoted to the charity to the exclusion of any resulting trust".[66]

Timing

8-017
In *Re Slevin*[67] the testator left a variety of legacies, one of which was a legacy to a Tyneside orphanage. Shortly after the testator died, but before the legacy was paid, the orphanage ceased to exist. It was held that the date of the testator's death was crucial. At that point the legacy became dedicated to charity and applicable by the Crown for charitable purposes. It did not matter that the orphanage did not obtain receipt of the legacy. As Kay LJ commented, "Obviously it can make no difference that the legatee ceased to exist immediately after the death of the testator. The same law must be applicable whether it was a day, or month, or year, or, as might well happen, 10 years after".[68] Similarly, in *Re Wright*,[69] a testatrix died in 1933 providing for the foundation, on the death of her tenant for life, of a convalescent home.

---

64 [1966] Ch. 249 at 256.
65 By way of a recent illustration, a case of supervening impossibility occurred in *Buckley v Barlow* [2016] EWHC 3017 (Ch), where it was no longer possible for funds held by trustees to be used for the purposes of a religious sect (the Agapemonites) that had ceased to function some 50 years earlier; the property was applied cy-près.
66 *Re Ulverston and District New Hospital Building Trusts* [1956] Ch. 622 at 636.
67 [1891] 2 Ch. 236.
68 [1891] 2 Ch. 236 at 241; see also, *Re Wright* [1954] Ch. 347 at 363, where Romer LJ observed that "no question of subsequent lapse, or of anything analogous to lapse, between the date of the testator's death and the time when the money actually becomes available for actual application to the testator's purpose can affect the matter so far as they are concerned".
69 [1954] Ch. 347.

Although the failure occurred during the existence of a life interest before the charity became entitled in possession to the property, it was held that the property had been dedicated to charity to the exclusion of the claims of next of kin and residuary legatees.

Surplus

A different problem was posed in *Re King*[70] wherein the question arose as to what to do with surplus remaining after the purpose had been carried out. There, a sum of money had been put aside for the setting of a stained-glass window in a parish church to the memory of the testatrix and her family. Having established that such a gift was, indeed, charitable, Romer J readily applied the surplus cy-près. As the whole fund had been dedicated to charity, the surplus was to be applied as near as possible to the original purpose and a second stained-glass window was ordered. Romer J considered this to be an application of a basic principle that, "Where a gift is made for a particular charitable purpose which is sufficiently provided for without the gift, the gift will be applied *cy-près*".[71]

8-018

Somewhat confusingly, there is authority to suggest that general charitable intention might be of some relevance in this particular context. In *Re Welsh Hospital* (*Netley*) *Fund*,[72] for example, a fund was collected for the charitable purpose of building a hospital to benefit sick and wounded soldiers. When the hospital was wound up, the question arose as to whether the surplus was available for application cy-près or whether it was, instead, to be held on resulting trust for subscribers. Unfortunately, P.O. Lawrence J sought to look for a general charitable intention as a basis for deciding upon the former, even though intention is viewed as irrelevant in cases of subsequent failure. He felt it to be clear that subscribers "did not intend that the surplus, if any, of their contributions should be returned to them".[73] Although in ordering a cy-près application the correct outcome was reached, the appropriate analysis to be employed in such cases was provided in the later case of *Re Wokingham Fire Brigade Trusts*.[74] This case concerned a voluntary fire brigade funded by donations, subscriptions and fees for attending fires. After operating a service for many years, it became no longer practicable to continue with the brigade. This was by reason of the sale of the assets to a different body charged with similar duties. Accordingly, Danckwerts J held that, "Though that purpose is no longer practicable . . . the charitable trusts do not fail. It is not necessary to consider whether there was any general charitable intention, and the trusts should be modified by means of a cy-près application".[75]

---

70   [1923] 1 Ch. 243.
71   [1923] 1 Ch. 243 at 246.
72   [1921] 1 Ch. 655; see also, *Re North Devon and West Somerset Relief Fund Trust* [1953] 1 W.L.R. 1260.
73   [1921] 1 Ch. 655 at 661.
74   [1951] Ch. 373.
75   [1951] Ch. 373 at 377.

Altering Charitable Purposes

8-019

Prior to the statutory reforms introduced by the Charities Act 1960, the court enjoyed a limited discretion to apply funds cy-près only where it was "impossible" or "impracticable" to carry out the terms of the trust. The narrow ambit of the discretion reflected the policy concern that the original wishes of the settlor should be respected. [76] In other words, the court felt constrained to give effect to the expressed wishes of the settlor and was not free to divine a more beneficial use for the property. As Kennedy LJ noted of the court's inherent jurisdiction, "neither the Court of Chancery, nor the Board of Charity Commissioners . . . is entitled to substitute a different scheme for the scheme which the donor has prescribed in the instruments which creates the charity, merely because a coldly wise intelligence, impervious to the special predilections which inspired his liberality, and untrammelled by his directions, would have dictated a different use of his money".[77]

Notwithstanding the limited application of the cy-près doctrine, it is clear that that "impossibility" had long been given a broad meaning.[78] Hence in *Re Dominion Students' Hall Trust*[79] a colour bar (i.e. a condition limiting the class of beneficiaries by reference to their colour) was removed so as to include all students of the overseas dominions of the British Empire. The rationale for so doing was that "times have changed . . . and it is said that to retain the condition, so far from furthering the charity's main object, might defeat it and would be liable to antagonise those students, both white and coloured, whose support and goodwill it is the purpose of the charity to sustain".[80]

8-020

Similarly, in looking to the question of "practicality", it was not necessary, as Evershed J points out, "to go to the length of saying that the original scheme is absolutely impracticable".[81] In *Re Robinson*,[82] for example, a condition in an endowment gift to an evangelical church requiring the preacher to wear a black gown in the pulpit was dispensed with as impracticable under the court's inherent jurisdiction. P.O. Lawrence J noted that the use of such a gown had become unusual in more modern times. In addition, he concluded that the wearing of the gown would be detrimental to the teaching and practice of evangelical doctrines and services and would, moreover, be interpreted as an act of eccentricity. He found the evidence corroborated by the fact that "no incumbent has attempted to comply with the condition during the long period which has elapsed since the fund was paid into court".[83] To negate the unwanted prac-

---

76 As Crumley and Picton explain, "The old precedents treat cy-près as a highly restrictive rule prohibiting modification of objects outside of the exceptional circumstance of the complete failure of the trust" ([2018] Conv. 262, 265).
77 *Re Weir Hospital* [1910] 2 Ch. 124 at 140.
78 See, e.g. *Re Campden Charities* (1881) 18 Ch. D. 310.
79 [1947] Ch. 183.
80 [1947] Ch. 183 at 186 per Evershed J.
81 [1947] Ch. 183 at 186.
82 [1923] 2 Ch. 332.
83 [1923] 2 Ch. 332 at 337.

tical consequence that the fund would remain in court, P.O. Lawrence J felt justified in deeming the condition to be impracticable and, hence, deleting it from the terms of the bequest.

Different considerations applied where the court was asked to make an alteration to the administration of a charity.[84] In *Re JW Laing Trust*,[85] Peter Gibson J viewed the job of the court, under its inherent jurisdiction, to consider "whether it is expedient" to regulate the administration of a charity by removing a requirement as to distribution of a capital sum. There, a trust fund worth £15,000 set up in 1922 had, by 1982, appreciated in value to an astonishing £24 million. The settlor had anticipated that trustees would distribute the fund within 10 years of his death and, in the intervening period, the income would benefit a variety of Christian evangelical causes. In recognition that the settlor had come to view the requirement as inexpedient, and that various charitable causes had come to depend on that continued support, the court approved a scheme under which the trustees were discharged from the obligation as to distribution. It is clear, therefore, that a distinction could be drawn between an alteration in the administration of a charity to cater for the continued support of selected causes, and those cases which required an alteration in the charitable purposes or objects themselves. As Peter Gibson J rationalised, "it cannot be right that any provision, even if only administrative, made applicable by a donor to his gifts should be treated as a condition and hence part of its purpose".[86]

The statutory widening of cy-près—how it happened

8-021

The cy-près doctrine now rests on a statutory footing with the relevant provisions to be found within the Charities Act 2011.[87] The modernisation of the law by statute began with the Charities Act 1960,[88] re-enacted as s.13(1) of the 1993 Act and further amended by the Charities Act 2006. The 2011 Act does not change the substantive law, but merely consolidates the existing rules within a single statutory framework. The important point to note is that cy-près is no longer confined to cases where it is "impossible" or "impracticable" to implement the terms of the trust. The statutory grounds, listed in the Charities Act 2011 s.62 (outlined below), embrace circumstances such as where the original purposes have been fulfilled as far as possible, have become harmful to the community, and where the purposes have been catered for by another means. It

---

84   The court has a well-established inherent jurisdiction as to alteration in the administration of charities: *Attorney General v Dedham School* (1857) 23 Beav. 350.

85   [1984] Ch. 143.

86   [1984] Ch. 143 at 153. See also, *Oldham BC v AG* [1993] Ch. 210, where Dillon LJ interpreted a requirement that the actual land given be used as a playing field as being administrative in nature and outside the concept of the charitable purpose.

87   Note also that the First-tier Tribunal (Charity) provides the forum to appeal Commission schemes: see B. Crumley, J. Picton, "'Still Standing': Charitable Service-users and Cy-près in the First-tier Tribunal (Charity)" [2018] Conv. 262.

88   See the recommendations of the Nathan Committee on the Law and Practice Relating to Charitable Trusts (1952) Cmd. 8710.

is, moreover, possible to invoke cy-près where the original purposes relate to an area or a class of persons that has since ceased to be suitable for the pursuit of the original charitable ends.

8-022

The effect of the Charities Act 2006 was to alter the occasions for applying property cy-près to take full account of current social and economic circumstances. Formerly, the particular focus of s.13 of the Charities Act 1993 fell upon "the spirit of the gift" or, in the words of Pennycuick VC, "the basic intention underlying the gift".[89] Indeed, the expression "spirit of the gift" appeared in four separate paragraphs within s.13(1).[90] On all but one occasion, (that is, para.(a)), s.13 was amended in 2006 to replace the words "the spirit of the gift" with a new expression, "the appropriate considerations". The expression "appropriate considerations" was defined to cover "the spirit of the gift concerned", but also "the social and economic circumstances prevailing at the time of the proposed alteration of the original purposes".[91] The effect of this change was to require the Charity Commission, when making a scheme to alter the purposes for which property is to be applied, to take into account not only the intention underlying the gift of property, but the social and economic circumstances prevailing at the time of the proposed alteration in the purpose.[92] Overall, therefore, what is now s.62 of the Charities Act 2011 expands and clarifies the jurisdiction and aims to meet the need for greater efficiency and modernisation of the cy-près doctrine.

8-023

Section 62 identifies five occasions for applying cy-près where the original purposes of a charitable gift may be altered. Each of these circumstances is considered in detail below. The power of the court or the Charity Commission to make a scheme, however, must be exercised in accordance with s.67. In the words of Briggs J, this provision "prescribes the manner by which the court decides whether, and if so how, to exercise its discretion to make, or direct the making of, a cy-près scheme for the application of charitable property".[93] There are now three matters to which the court or the Commission must have regard,[94] each of which carries equal weight. The matters are:

- "the spirit of the original gift";

- "the desirability of securing that the property is applied for charitable purposes which are close to the original purposes"; and

- "the need for the relevant charity to be able to make a significant social or economic impact".

---

89   *Re Lepton's Charity* [1972] Ch. 276 at 285.
90   Paragraphs (a), (c), (d) and (e)(iii).
91   See now s.62(2) of the 2011 Act.
92   Note that it is now the duty of trustees, where property may be applied cy-près, to take steps to have the property so applied (s.61).
93   *White v Williams* [2010] P.T.S.R. 1575 at 1579. In exercising its discretion under s.67, the Commission seeks to be "flexible and imaginative . . . balancing usefulness and practicality with respect for the existing purpose and beneficiaries" (Charity Commission, OG2: *Application of Property Cy-près* (March 2012), para.3.2).
94   Section 67(3).

Under s.67(4), the court or the Commission, when making a scheme to transfer a charity's property to another charity, can require trustees of the recipient charity to use the property for purposes as similar as practicable to the original purposes for which the property was held. The aim of the section is to cover cases where the original purposes are considered to be useful but the court or the Commission believe that the property can be more effectively used in conjunction with other property.

Paragraph (a): fulfilment or failure

Section 62(1)(a) allows for cy-près where the original purposes, in whole or in part (i) "have been as far as may be fulfilled" or (ii) "cannot be carried out or not according to the directions given and to the spirit of the gift". In interpreting para.(a), it is clear that the case law generated by the Charities Act 1960 remains of primary relevance. In *Re Lepton's Charity*,[95] a testator provided that the income from a trust would be applied in the annual payment of £3 to the minister of Pudsey with the balance being applied to poor and aged residents of Pudsey. As between the date of the testator's death in 1715 and the date at which the case was heard in 1972, the annual income had risen from £5 to almost £800. It was contended that the annual amount paid to the minister should be increased to reflect modern conditions.

8-024

Pennycuick VC was required to consider whether the expression "the original purposes" of a charitable gift in what was then s.13(1) should be construed as referring to the trusts as a whole or must be determined individually in relation to the trust for the fixed annual income and the trust for the payment of the residuary. He accepted that, "in a trust of the present character there is an obvious interrelation between the two trusts in that changes in the amount of the income and the value of the money may completely distort the relative benefits taken under the respective trusts".[96] Accordingly, Pennycuick VC concluded that the trusts comprised a single charitable gift.[97] On this basis he proceeded to hold that the original purposes could not be carried out in adherence to the spirit of the gift. Paragraphs a(ii) or e(iii)[98] provided alternative routes[99] to the same conclusion:

8-025

> "The intention underlying the gift was to divide a sum which, according to the values of 1715, was modest but not negligible, in

---

95   [1972] Ch. 276.

96   [1972] Ch. 276 at 285.

97   Note that the same conclusion would not be reached where, for example, a trust caters for the distribution of income between charities in aliquot shares, or in cases of trusts for charities in succession because "the possibility of carrying out the trusts of one share according to the spirit of the gift could hardly react upon the possibility of carrying out the trusts of the other share according to the spirit of the gift" ([1972] Ch. 276 at 285).

98   That the original purposes had "ceased in any other way to provide a suitable and effective method of using the property available by virtue of the gift, regard being had to the spirit of the gift".

99   Pennycuick VC was of the view that: "Subsection (1)(e)(iii) appears to be no more than a final writing out large of paragraph (a)(ii)" ([1972] Ch. 276 at 285).

> such a manner that the minister took what was then a clear three fifths of it. This intention is clearly defeated when in the conditions of today the minister takes a derisory £3 out of a total of £791".[100]

Thus, Pennycuick VC approved an application to increase the minister's income to £100 per annum.

Paragraph (b): A use provided for part only

8-026

Section 62(1)(b) permits cy-près where the original purposes provide a use for part only of the property available by virtue of the gift. This paragraph is straightforward in application and does not appear to alter the common law position. Hence, para.(b) will apply to facts such as those arising in *Re North Devon and West Somerset Relief Fund*.[101] There, surplus funds raised for those who suffered in the floods in 1952 were applicable cy-près. The contributors had parted with their money out and out and did not intend that the surplus, if any, would be returned to them should the immediate object of charity come to an end. In the language of para.(b), cy-près would be available because the original purposes provided a use for part only of the property.

Paragraph (c): More effective use in conjunction with other property

8-027

Section 62(1)(c) is applicable "where the property available by virtue of the gift and other property applicable for similar purposes can be more effectively used in conjunction, and to that end can suitably, regard being had to the appropriate considerations, be made applicable to common purposes".

Paragraph (c), therefore, admits schemes such as that embarked upon by the Charity Commissioners in *Re Faraker*.[102] There, it will be recalled, Hannah Bayly's Charity (established to provide for poor widows of Rotherhithe) was amalgamated with 13 other charities each of which benefited the poor. As Luxton points out, however, the Charity Commissioners acted without jurisdiction to make this alteration to the purposes of Hannah Bayly's Charity as there continued to be poor widows in Rotherhithe.[103] There is no doubt that such an alteration would now be permitted under s.62(1)(c).

---

100 [1972] Ch. 276 at 285.
101 [1953] 2 All E.R. 1032.
102 [1912] 2 Ch. 488 (para.**8-008**).
103 P. Luxton, *The Law of Charities* (Oxford: Oxford University Press, 2001), p.567.

Paragraph (d): The area or class has ceased to be suitable

Section 62(1)(d) applies where the original purposes were laid down by reference to:

8-028

> **(i)** **"an area which then was but has since ceased to be a unit for some other purpose", or**
> **(ii)** **"a class of persons or an area which has for any reason since ceased to be suitable, regard being had to the appropriate considerations, or to be practical in administering the gift".**

In *Peggs v Lamb*,[104] an application was made to the court for a cy-près scheme in relation to a longstanding trust for the benefit of the freemen of Huntingdon. The basis of the application was the decline in numbers of the particular group to be benefited. Morritt J identified the original purpose as being general in nature and for the benefit of the freemen of Huntingdon and their widows. Although hindered somewhat by the absence of a founding instrument, Morritt J divined that "the original basic intention or spirit of the gift was the benefit of the borough of Huntingdon".[105] Accordingly, he was able to apply para.(d) to hold that the original purposes had been laid down by reference to a class of persons who had since ceased to be suitable regard being had to the spirit of the gift.[106] The effect of the scheme was to enlarge the class of persons to benefit to include all of the inhabitants of Huntingdon.

Paragraph (e): Where purposes have been adequately provided for, ceased to be charitable or ceased to be suitable or effective

Section 62(1)(e) makes cy-près applicable:

8-029

> **"where the original purposes, in whole or in part, have since they were laid down:**
> **(i)** **been adequately provided for by other means; or**
> **(ii)** **ceased, as being useless or harmful to the community or for other reasons, to be in law charitable; or**
> **(iii)** **ceased in any other way to provide a suitable and effective method of using the property available by virtue of the gift, regard being had to the appropriate considerations".**

---

104 [1994] Ch. 172.
105 [1994] Ch. 172 at 197.
106 Note that s.62(2) permits consideration of the social and economic circumstances prevailing at the time of the proposed alteration in addition to the "spirit of the gift" (see para.**8-022**).

Of the occasions on which what is now s.62(1)(e) has been considered judicially, it is para.(e)(iii) that is viewed as the most encompassing.[107] Presumably, para.(e)(ii) will assume relevance only in circumstances where statute declares a purpose to be no longer charitable or legal. It has been suggested, for example, that this subsection could apply to the endowments of independent schools should charitable status be withdrawn.[108]

As indicated above in *Re Lepton's Charity*,[109] Pennycuick VC regarded para.(e)(iii) as a viable alternative to (a)(ii). On the facts before him, the original purposes could not be carried out "according to the directions given and to the spirit of the gift" (as required by para.(a)(ii)). Equally, the original purposes had "ceased to provide a suitable and effective method of using the property . . . regard being had to the spirit of the gift" (as required by para.(e)(iii)).[110] *Varsani v Jesani*[111] provides further guidance as to the breadth of para.(e)(iii). Under the court's inherent jurisdiction cy-près would not have been available on the ground that it was still possible to carry out the original purposes of the charity.[112] The case concerned a charitable trust to promote the faith of a particular Hindu sect. The sect split into rival factions following a disagreement as to the divine status of the successor to their founder, with one group refusing to continue to worship in the communal temple. Chadwick LJ was of the view that the spirit of the gift was to provide facilities for a small community of followers of a particular sect in the worship of a particular faith. The division of the community entailed that the original purposes were no longer a suitable and effective method of using the property because the fragmented community were no longer able to worship together. Regard being had to the spirit of the gift, he elected sub-para.(e)(iii) as the basis upon which a cy-près scheme could be directed, the aim being to facilitate a division of the charity property amongst the feuding groups.

8-030

The approach in *Varsani v Jesani* has been endorsed in *White v Williams*.[113] Here, the trustees of a charitable trust established by members of a congregation in Lewisham sought to have church buildings (donated for use as a place of worship) transferred to them via a cy-près scheme. The action followed on from a schism in 1997, in which the Lewisham congregation (together with two other congregations) ended their affiliation with the Bibleway Church and had since formed autonomous religious communities. The Lewisham church building had since remained in the control of the Bibleway trustees who had ceased to be part of the Lewisham congregation and had no meaningful communication with it. Accordingly, the building could not be administered in a manner consistent with the objectives of the Lewisham congrega-

---

107   Paragraph e(i) has proved useful in relation to charitable purposes which are the duty of government authorities (e.g. repair or maintenance of the roads). In such cases, the Charity Commission can use its statutory powers to apply the property cy-près towards the improvement of other local amenities.

108   See J. Jaconelli [1996] Conv. 24.

109   [1972] 1 Ch. 276.

110   Note that the expression "spirit of the gift" employed in both paragraphs before amendment in 2006 has been replaced by "the appropriate considerations" to permit consideration not only of the spirit of the gift but also the prevailing social and economic circumstances at the time of the proposed alteration: see para.**8-022**.

111   [1999] Ch. 219.

112   [1999] Ch. 219 at 237 per Chadwick LJ.

113   [2010] P.T.S.R. 1575.

tion. In addition, the trustees of the Bibleway Trust had used the Lewisham church building as security for unauthorised borrowing, a use at odds with its status as the place of worship and outside the spirit of the gift in accordance with which title was acquired. In line with para.(e)(iii) and the guidance as to the exercise of judicial discretion (located in s.67), a cy-près scheme was deemed the appropriate form of relief. As Briggs J concluded, "A scheme or schemes whereby each place of worship is transferred to separate trustees whose role is directed to the fulfilment of purposes specific to the congregation or locality associated with it seems to me to be plainly the best solution".[114]

Charities Act 2011 s.62(3)

8-031

Section 62(3) provides that s.62 "shall not affect the conditions which must be satisfied in order that property given for charitable purposes may be applied cy-près, except in so far as those conditions require a failure of the original purposes".

In *Re JW Laing Trust*, Peter Gibson J was clearly of the view that the consequence of this section would be to preserve the requirement existing prior to statutory intervention that the donor must show a general charitable intention.[115] If inclusive of cases of subsequent failure, this conclusion is open to question.[116] The majority of what are now s.62 cases concern subsequent failure where no finding of general charitable intention is, under the general law, deemed necessary.[117]

Charity Collections and Appeals

8-032

It remains to consider the statutory provisions enacted to deal with the problems of failure in the context of charity collections and public appeals.[118] Here, difficulties have arisen where charitable funds are raised by public appeal but the funds are insufficient to carry out the intended purpose (a failed appeal) or more is raised than is required (a case of surplus). Both cases raise the possibility that donations might be returned to donors but it is important to appreciate that the prospect of doing so arises in cases of initial failure alone. If the case is

---

114 [2010] P.T.S.R. 1575 at 1600.
115 [1984] Ch. 143 at 149.
116 As J. Warburton argues [1984] Conv. 319 at 320, "Peter Gibson J. has, by a back door, purported to introduce a restriction into the application of trust property cy-près which did not exist prior to 1960".
117 *Re Wright* [1954] Ch. 347.
118 The application of property cy-près, including the proceeds of fundraisers was addressed in the recent Law Commission Report, "Technical Issues in Charity Law" (Law Com No. 375, September 2017), which contains recommendations to expand and simplify the situations In which funds may be applied cy-près.

treated as one of subsequent failure, no possibility of a return of the property arises, and cy-près is available as of course.[119]

Conventionally, in the case of initial failure, a finding of general charitable intention was required before a cy-près application of property was possible. Where the intention of the donor was deemed to be specific, cy-près was not available. Instead, the courts were forced to grapple with the less attractive alternatives of a return of property to the original donors under a resulting trust or payment of the funds to the Crown as bona vacantia. Section 66 of the Charities Act provides that the purpose of an appeal fails "if any difficulty in applying property to those purposes makes that property or the part not applicable cy-près available to be returned to the donors". Sections 63 to 66 allow the Charity Commission to make cy-près schemes in a range of cases of failed appeals where contributions made by anonymous or disclaiming donors are treated as though they were made for general charitable purposes.[120]

Unknown or disclaiming donors

8-033   Section 63(1) deals with gifts by donors who are "unknown or disclaiming". Here, property given for a specific charitable purpose which fails may be applied cy-près in either of two specified cases. The first is where the donor cannot be identified or found but the prescribed advertisements and inquiries have been published and made.[121] The second covers the case of a donor who has executed a disclaimer, in the prescribed form, and who does not wish to have his property returned.[122]

There are two instances where property is conclusively presumed (without any advertisement or inquiry) to belong to donors who cannot be identified. The first covers the proceeds of cash collections made by means of collecting boxes or any "other means not adapted for distinguishing one gift from another".[123] The second covers "the proceeds of any lottery, competition, entertainment, sale or similar money-raising activity".[124] Thus, where the method of donation makes it difficult to tell one contribution from another, there is a presumption of donation to general charitable purposes. The idea is to avoid the need to impute a fictitious general charitable intention on the part of the donor, or to seek (often in vain) to return the property to the original donor.

This approach was not novel. As Wilson noted some time ago, "the general law itself would

---

119   See further, *Re Ulverston and District New Hospital Building Trusts* [1956] Ch. 622, where Jenkins LJ promotes the understanding that, where any of the property has been applied towards the charitable purpose, the failure is a subsequent failure, automatically allowing a cy-près application.

120   For details of the Charity Commission approach, see Charity Commission, OG 53 A1: *Charitable Appeals—Avoiding and Dealing with Failure* (November 2014).

121   Section 63(1)(a). This process of advertisement and inquiry has been described by the Law Commission as "cumbersome" (Law Commission (CP No.220, March 2015), para.7.31.

122   Section 63(1)(b). The procedures requiring a disclaimer or declaration have been criticised by the Law Commission as "unrealistic", and, moreover, "rarely if ever used" (Law Commission (CP No.220, March 2015), para.7.31).

123   Section 64(1)(a).

124   Section 64(1)(b).

seem to be perfectly capable of performing the task which, it appears, section 14 [now s.63 of the 2011 Act] was intended to perform".[125] In *Re West Sussex Constabulary's Fund*,[126] for example, Goff J held that those who make anonymous cash contributions to collection boxes do not intend to, and therefore do not, retain any interest in the donations. This is both sensible and correct.[127] Similarly, in relation to the proceeds from entertainment, again, this contributor retains no interest in the property. As Goff J explains, "The purchaser of a ticket may have the motive of aiding the cause or he may not. He may purchase a ticket merely because he wishes to attend the particular entertainment or to try for the prize, but whichever it be he pays his money as the price of what is offered and what he receives".[128] As such, this type of contributor attains the advantage for which he has contracted and thereby loses his entitlement to any interest in the property.

8-034

As to property not falling within the confines of s.64(1), the court or the Charity Commission[129] may direct that property be treated, without advertisement or enquiry, as belonging to donors who cannot be identified.[130] Such an order may be made if it appears that "it would be unreasonable, having regard to the amounts likely to be returned to the donors, to incur expense with a view to returning the property", or that "it would be unreasonable, having regard to the nature, circumstances and amounts of the gifts, and to the lapse of time since the gifts were made, for the donors to expect the property to be returned". Current Charity Commission guidance suggests that in cases where the total funds raised were less than £1,000 and contributed in all cases by unidentifiable donors, trustees need not seek legal authority from the Commission to apply the funds for similar purposes.[131]

Solicitations, Statements and Relevant Declarations

8-035

The Charities Act 2011 s.65 applies to property given for a specific charitable purpose in response to a solicitation or appeal. A solicitation will be within the section where it is made

---

125 D. Wilson [1983] Conv. 40 at 49.
126 [1971] Ch. 1. Although the case concerned non-charitable donations where a surplus remained after the fund was wound up, there is no distinction here to be drawn between donations for charitable and non-charitable purposes.
127 A different (and less attractive) view was taken by Harman J in *Re Gillingham Bus Disaster Fund* [1958] Ch. 300, that such donations should be held on resulting trust.
128 [1971] Ch. 1 at 11. He held, further (at 11), that in such cases "there was no direct contribution to the fund at all. It is only the profit, if any, which is ultimately received, and there may even be none".
129 Prior to the Charities Act 2006, only the court had the power to make such a direction.
130 Charities Act 2011 s.64(2).
131 Charity Commission, OG53 A1: *Charitable Appeals: Avoiding and Dealing With Failure* (November 2014), s.2.4(d).

for a specific purpose and it is accompanied by a statement to the effect that property given in response to it will, in the event of those purposes failing, be applicable cy-près as if given for charitable purposes generally. The statement will apply unless the donor makes a relevant declaration in writing at the time of making the gift that, in the event of the specific charitable purpose failing, he wishes the trustees holding the property to give him the opportunity to request the return of the property in question (or a sum equal to its value at the time of the making of the gift).[132]

Where the specific charitable purposes fail and the donor has made the relevant declaration, trustees are charged with informing the donor of the failure of the purposes, enquiring whether he wishes to request a return of the property (or a sum equal to its value), and if such a request is made within the prescribed period, to return the property (or such a sum) to him.[133] Where trustees have taken all appropriate prescribed steps but they have failed to find the donor, or the donor fails to request a return of the property (or a sum equal to its value) within the prescribed period, the property will be applied as though the donor had disclaimed any right to its return.[134] If, however, the purposes have failed and the donor has not made a relevant declaration, the property is to be applied cy-près as though the donor had disclaimed the right to have the property returned.[135]

Guide to Further Reading

B. Crumley, J. Picton, "'Still Standing': Charitable Service-users and Cy-près in the First-tier Tribunal (Charity)" [2018] Conv. 262

J. Garton, "Justifying the Cy-Près Doctrine" (2007) 21(3) Tru. L.I. 134.

P. Luxton, "In 'Pursuit of Purpose' through Section 13 of the Charities Act 1960" [1985] Conv. 313.

J. Picton, "Contradictions in the Law of Charitable Lapse" [2015] Conv. 480.

F. Quint, "Recent Developments in the Cy-Près Principle" (2009) 11(2) C.L.&P.R. 49.

J. Warburton, "*Re J. W. Laing Trust*" [1984] Conv. 319.

---

132 Section 65(3).
133 Section 65(5). "Prescribed" means prescribed by regulations made by the Commission: s.66(4).
134 Section 65(6).
135 Section 65(7).

9

Resulting Trusts

The focus of the book so far has been on express trusts wherein the settlor must comply with the three certainties[1] and adhere to requirements as to proper constitution.[2] Trusts, however, need not be express. Both the resulting trust and constructive trust are types of trust that are implied by law. Constructive trusts are considered in Ch.10. The present chapter is concerned with the resulting trust. The resulting trust is a form of implied trust in that it does not come into being by design but arises where equity stipulates that it should do so in response to particular circumstances. There are no formal requirements for its creation and it is exempt from the requirement of writing laid down in s.53(1) of the Law of Property Act 1925. Even a minor can act as a resulting trustee.[3] The term "resulting trust" is derived from the Latin *"resalire"* meaning to jump back. The essential characteristic of the resulting trust is that the settlor is also its beneficiary. Its fundamental function is to "re-direct" the beneficial ownership of trust property back to the former title owner.

9-001

The resulting trust arises in two principal contexts.[4] The first is that of apparent gifts. This includes cases where there is a voluntary transfer of property or a contribution to the purchase price of property without an express indication as to how equitable title is to be held.[5] In such cases, there is a rebuttable presumption of resulting trust. In other words, there is a presumption (capable of displacement by evidence to the contrary) that the intention of each transferor or contributor was not to make a gift, but that they should hold a proprietary right proportionate to their contribution.

The second context is that of failed trusts, where there has been an attempt to create a

---

1   *Knight v Knight* (1840) 3 Beav. 148; see Ch.2.
2   See generally, Ch.3.
3   *Re Vinogradoff* [1936] W.N. 68.
4   Per Lord Browne-Wilkinson in *Westdeutsche Landesbank v Islington LBC* [1996] A.C. 669 at 708.
5   See further, para.**9-009.**

trust and some part of the beneficial interest remains undisposed of.[6] The function of the resulting trust here is restorative. As equity is said to abhor a vacuum, someone must be entitled to that property.[7] The resulting trust is, thus, the mechanism whereby property jumps back to the settlor or it is the tool to establish that the settlor retains an equitable interest in the property.[8]

9-002

In general terms, the resulting trust might be thought of as arising in a situation where "the transferee is required by equity to hold property on trust for the transferor; or for the person who provided the purchase money for the transfer".[9] Typically broad definitions have been put forward to explain or describe a doctrine that has grown to operate in such specific, but varied circumstances. Such explanations are helpful to the extent that they point to the function of the resulting trust or to the categories in which such trusts traditionally arise. Commentators too have pondered the adaptability of the resulting trust mechanism to argue, for example, that such trusts might be imposed to reverse unjust enrichment.[10] In *Westdeutsche Landesbank v Islington LBC*,[11] however, the House of Lords rejected this liberal reasoning and effectively confined the resulting trust to its more traditional role.[12] It has also been argued that resulting trusts should play a smaller role in the modern law. Mee, for example, argues that the voluntary transfer and purchase money resulting trusts "cannot be defended in modern times and should not form part of the law".[13] He is assisted, at least in part, by recent judge-made developments that have seen the scope for resulting trusts diminish in this context where the reach of the common intention constructive trust has become more encompassing. Those developments in the law of co-ownership are discussed in Chapter 11.

9-003

The subject area of resulting trusts is notoriously difficult. Recent academic discourse has exposed its theoretical complexity and highlighted classificatory problems.[14] The principal issues of contention concern the conceptual basis of the resulting trust, the extent to which

---

6   See further, para.**9-029**.

7   As Lord Reid put it in *Vandervell v IRC* [1967] 2 A.C. 291 at 308, "the beneficial interest must belong to or be held for somebody: so if it was not to belong to the donee or to be held by him in trust for somebody it must remain with the donor".

8   As Penner notes in *The Law of Trusts*, 11th edn (Oxford: Oxford University Press, 2019), p.229, "the colourful language of 'jumping back' probably misconceives what the judges understood to be going on, but the name has stuck".

9   Hanbury and Martin, *Modern Equity*, 21st edn (London: Sweet & Maxwell, 2019), para.11-001.

10   P. Birks, "Restitution and Resulting Trusts" in S. Goldstein (ed.), *Equity: Contemporary Legal Developments* (Hebrew University of Jerusalem, 1992), p.335; R. Chambers, *Resulting Trusts* (Oxford: Clarendon Press, 1997).

11   [1996] A.C. 669.

12   As Lord Browne-Wilkinson indicated (in response to argument put forward by Birks): "As one would expect, the argument is tightly reasoned but I am not persuaded. The search for a perceived need to strengthen the remedies of a plaintiff claiming in restitution involves, to my mind, a distortion of trust principles" (*Westdeutsche Landesbank v Islington LBC* [1996] A.C. 669 at 709).

13   J. Mee, "The Past, Present, and Future of Resulting Trusts (2017) 70(1) C.L.P. 189 at 200.

14   See J. Mee "Presumed Resulting Trusts, Intention and Declaration" [2014] C.L.J. 86; W. Swadling, "Explaining Resulting Trusts" (2008) 124 L.Q.R. 72; C. Mitchell (ed.), *Constructive and Resulting Trusts* (Oxford: Hart Publishing, 2010).

such trusts give effect to the common intentions of the parties and the nature of the obligations of the resulting trustee. The primary aim of this chapter, however, is to evaluate the circumstances in which resulting trusts arise. As a corollary, the situations in which a resulting trust will be excluded are also highlighted. This chapter will draw together a range of case law illustrations to paint a comprehensive picture of the modern judicial approach to resulting trusts. In addition, the manner in which resulting trusts are classified will be evaluated and some of the principal conceptual difficulties confronted.

Classification of Resulting Trusts

9-004

As described above, the resulting trust is encountered in a variety of circumstances. In search of an analytical overview, the classification of resulting trusts has assumed a high priority for judges and commentators alike. Prior to the decision in *Westdeutsche Landesbank v Islington LBC*, the accepted categorisation of resulting trusts was that put forward by Megarry J in *Re Vandervell's Trusts (No.2)*.[15] Megarry J divided resulting trusts into two main categories: resulting trusts that arise automatically and those based on the presumed intention of the transferor of property. The former, he felt, did not depend on the intention of the parties, but arose as an automatic consequence of the transferor's failure to dispose of the entirety of the beneficial interest. For Megarry J the "automatic resulting trust" was deemed to arise:

> "where the transfer to B is made on trusts which leave some or all of the beneficial interest undisposed of. Here B automatically holds on a resulting trust for A to the extent that the beneficial interest has not been carried to him or others. The resulting trust here does not depend on any intentions or presumptions but is the automatic consequence of A's failure to dispose of what is vested in him. Since ex hypothesi the transfer is on trust, the resulting trust does not establish the trust but merely carries back to A the beneficial interest that has not been disposed of".[16]

By contrast, as regards a trust based on presumed intention:

> "the question is not one of the automatic consequences of a dispositive failure by A, but one of presumption: the property has been

15   [1974] Ch. 269.
16   [1974] Ch. 269 at 294.

> carried to B, and from the absence of consideration and any pre-
> sumption of advancement B is presumed not only to hold the entire
> interest on trust but also to hold the beneficial interest for A abso-
> lutely. The presumption thus establishes both that B is to take on
> trust and also what that trust is. Such resulting trusts may be called
> 'presumed resulting trusts'".[17]

9-005

The distinction posited by Megarry J provides a useful starting point in that he identifies two essential categories of trust that were adopted by judges in much of the case law
decided subsequently. However, the dividing line between his categories is not without difficulty. In particular, as regards the automatic resulting trust, there appears to be no focus at
all upon the intention of the parties. Megarry J sees the so-called "automatic resulting trust"
as a self-activating or mechanical response to the dispositive failure of the settlor, whereas
his "presumed intention resulting trust" arises because there is a rebuttable presumption of
trust based on inferred intention. In the latter case, the settlor makes no express indication
as to how the beneficial interest lies. Equity presumes, however, that the property belongs to
the person who advances the purchase money, that is, in the absence of evidence to rebut
the presumption. It might, nonetheless, be argued of the former that where an express trust
fails to dispose of some part of the beneficial interest, an intention can be implied on the part
of the settlor that, in so far as there is any, the unexhausted beneficial interest should revert
to him. Somewhat artificially, however, this process involves deciding what the settlor would
have intended had the thought occurred to him that some part of the beneficial interest may
remain undisposed of. It was inevitable that the distinction promoted by Megarry J would
attract further scrutiny.

In his speech in *Westdeutsche Landesbank v Islington*,[18] Lord Browne-Wilkinson clarified
the circumstances in which the resulting trust arises. First, as to category A:

> "Where A makes a voluntary transfer to B or pays (wholly or in
> part) for the purchase of property, which is vested either in B
> alone or in the joint names of A and B, there is a presumption
> that A did not intend to make a gift to B: the property is held on
> trust for A (if he is the sole provider of the money) or in the case
> of a joint purchase by A and B in shares proportionate to their
> contribution".[19]

Secondly, category B:

---

17 [1974] Ch. 269 at 294.
18 [1996] A.C. 669.
19 [1996] A.C. 669 at 708. Note that in the context of the family home, regard must be had to the approach by
the House of Lords in *Stack v Dowden* [2007] 2 A.C. 432: see Ch.11 for detailed discussion of trusts of the family
home.

> "Where A transfers property to B on express trusts, but the trusts declared do not exhaust the whole beneficial interest . . . and *Barclays Bank v Quistclose Investments Ltd . . .*".[20]

9-006

He warned, moreover, that the distinction drawn by Megarry J between the "automatic resulting trust" and the "presumed intention resulting trust" was untenable.[21] In particular, he illustrated that the so-called "automatic resulting trust" was not irrebuttable in the manner that Megarry J appeared to suggest. Lord Browne-Wilkinson argued that:

> "Megarry J . . . suggests that a resulting trust of type (B) does not depend on intention but operates automatically. I am not convinced that this is right. If the settlor has expressly, or by necessary implication, abandoned any beneficial interest in the trust property, there is in my view no resulting trust: the undisposed-of equitable interest vests in the Crown as bona vacantia".[22]

In addition, he hailed as a general feature of the resulting trust that it gives effect to the common intentions of the parties.

Despite the obvious authority underpinning Lord Browne-Wilkinson's views, his principles of resulting trusts have themselves encountered criticism. First, it is not immediately apparent that resulting trusts must give effect to the common intention of the parties. A common intention may be discerned in the case of the purchase money resulting trust where two or more people evince the intention to share the beneficial interest in property.[23] It is much less clear how, if at all, a resulting trust can give effect to common intention where it comes into being because the settlor has failed to divest himself effectively of his beneficial interest. In such cases, the only intention of relevance to the destination of the equitable interest can be that of the settlor. In addition, this explanation also fails to consider the imposition of the resulting trust where the settlor never intends that a transferee act as trustee[24] or, moreover, ever desires that the remainder of trust property result back.[25] In such cases, the imposition of a resulting trust seems antithetical to the intentions of the settlor.

Secondly, the circumstances in which one can be said to have simply abandoned property are, indeed, very rare. The courts have proved willing to uphold the resulting trust even when

9-007

---

20   [1996] A.C. 669 at 708.
21   It is to be noted that Megarry J viewed his propositions as "the broadest generalisations" which did "not purport to cover the exceptions and qualifications which doubtless exist" ([1974] Ch. 269 at 294).
22   [1996] A.C. 669 at 708.
23   The bilateral intention of the parties is, however, the distinguishing feature of the constructive trust, which arises to give effect to a bargain between the parties as to beneficial ownership.
24   In *Re Vinogradoff* [1935] W.N. 68 the transferee was a child of seven years of age.
25   In *Vandervell v IRC* [1967] 2 A.C. 291, for example, Mr Vandervell sought to dispose of his interest completely in order to avoid liability to taxation.

faced with evidence that the transferor did not intend to retain any interest. In *Air Jamaica v Charlton*,[26] for example, the Privy Council held that a resulting trust arose in favour of a company over the surplus funds of a pension trust determined to be void under the perpetuity rules. In doing so, Lord Millett overcame a formidable obstacle presented by cl.4 of the trust deed, which stated that "No moneys which any time have been contributed by the Company under the terms hereof shall in any circumstances be repayable to the Company". Nonetheless, and in elucidating further the principles of resulting trusts, he held that:

> **"Like a constructive trust, a resulting trust arises by operation of law, though unlike a constructive trust it gives effect to intention. But it arises whether or not the transferor intended to retain a beneficial interest—he almost always does not—since it responds to any absence of intention on his part to pass a beneficial interest to the recipient. It may arise even where the transferor positively wished to part with the beneficial interest, as in *Vandervell* . . . In that case the retention of a beneficial interest by the transferor destroyed the effectiveness of a tax avoidance scheme which the transferor was seeking to implement. The House of Lords affirmed the principle that a resulting trust is not defeated by evidence that the transferor intended to part with the beneficial interest if he has not in fact succeeded in doing so".[27]**

It is, therefore, a perceived limitation of both Megarry J's distinction and the views as to intention postulated by Lord Browne-Wilkinson that they fail to explain convincingly the role of intention in resulting trusts. Within his adopted category of "automatic resulting trusts", Megarry J identifies the response of equity as being detached from the question of intention altogether. For Lord Browne-Wilkinson, all resulting trusts give effect to the presumed intentions of the parties. More convincingly, both types of trust should simply be viewed as a response to the absence of intention that the recipient of property should have the benefit of it.

9-008
The remainder of this chapter is concerned to explore the operation of resulting trusts as they apply first, in the context of the voluntary transfer or the purchase in the name of another and, secondly, failed trusts. It is important to note that Lord Browne-Wilkinson positioned the *Quistclose* trust as falling within his category of trusts which fail. The *Quistclose* trust is, as Lord Millett reminds:

> **"an entirely orthodox example of the kind of default trust known as the resulting trust. The lender parts with the money to the borrower by way of loan, but he does not part with the entire beneficial inter-**

---

26 [1999] 1 W.L.R. 1399.
27 [1999] 1 W.L.R. 1399 at 1412.

> est in the money, and so far as he does not it is held on a resulting
> trust for the lender from the outset".[28]

Quistclose trusts are discussed in detail at the end of this chapter.[29] In addition to the discussion of general principles and problems of classification, the use of *Quistclose* trusts within commercial transactions is also examined.

The "Apparent Gift" Cases

The first category of case in which the resulting trust traditionally makes an appearance is that of apparent gifts. This category contains those resulting trusts that arise where there has been a contribution to the purchase price of property, but the property is held in the name of another or in joint names[30] or where a voluntary transfer of property has been made into the name of another.[31] Although both transactions have the outward appearance of a gift, equity adopts a realistic interpretation of the parties' motivations and assumes, in the absence of contrary evidence, that they intended bargains not gifts. In this manner, the imposition of the resulting trust is based on the unrebutted presumption that the transferor did not intend to benefit the transferee. In *Pettitt v Pettitt*, Lord Diplock characterised the presumption as "no more than a consensus of judicial opinion disclosed by reported cases as to the most likely inference of fact to be drawn in the absence of evidence to the contrary".[32] It is important to remember that the presumption of resulting trust may be "readily rebutted by comparatively slight evidence",[33] ousted by the more flexible constructive trust[34] or (in the context of specific relationships where a gift is deemed to have been intended), displaced by a counter-presumption of equity such as the presumption of advancement (see para.**9-015**).

9-009

---

28   *Twinsectra v Yardley* [2002] 2 All E.R. 377 at 403.
29   See para.**9-052**.
30   No presumption of resulting trust now arises in the context of the family home where legal title is held in joint names: see *Stack v Dowden* [2007] 2 A.C. 432.
31   As Bagnall J outlined in *Cowcher v Cowcher* [1972] 1 W.L.R. 425 at 431, a resulting trust arises "where a person acquires a legal estate but has not provided the consideration for its acquisition, unless a contrary intention is proved".
32   [1970] A.C. 777 at 823.
33   *Pettitt v Pettitt* [1970] A.C. 777 at 814 per Lord Upjohn.
34   Which arises to give effect to the parties' bargain as to their beneficial entitlements and prevent an unconscionable assertion of sole beneficial ownership by the holder of legal title.

Purchase in the name of another

9-010

The presumption of resulting trust is said to apply where property is purchased in the name of X, but X has provided no part of the purchase price, which in reality has been provided by Y. The resulting trust arises by operation of law in favour of Y to reflect the contribution provided by Y. Thus, if Fred was to provide the entire purchase price for property held solely by Jordan and, there is no evidence of contrary intention to fuel a constructive trust,[35] Jordan will hold legal title on resulting trust for Fred. This is because a proprietary interest, to adopt the frequently cited words of Eyre CB, "results to the man who advances the purchase money".[36] As to cases of shared legal ownership, until recently, the consistent approach of the courts has been that, "where the purchase money for property acquired by two or more persons in their joint names has been provided by those persons in unequal amounts, they will be beneficially entitled as between themselves in the proportions in which they provided the purchase money".[37] In the context of the family home, however, this approach no longer applies. Following the House of Lords' decision in *Stack v Dowden*,[38] there is a strong presumption that equity follows the law and that equitable ownership, like legal ownership, is jointly held.[39] Accordingly, as is made clear by Lord Walker and Baroness Hale, "in the case of the purchase of a house or flat in joint names for joint occupation by a married or unmarried couple, where both are responsible for any mortgage, there is no presumption of a resulting trust arising from their having contributed to the deposit (or indeed the rest of the purchase) in unequal shares. The presumption is that the parties intended a joint tenancy both in law and in equity".[40]

It was assumed that the presumption of resulting trust would continue to operate where the primary context was deemed to be commercial.[41] In *Laskar v Laskar*, for example, resulting trust principles applied where a mother and daughter had purchased a property for investment purposes.[42] In *Marr v Collie*,[43] however, the Privy Council decided that the *Stack* approach would not be confined to a purely domestic setting and might extend to commercial investments made by a couple in a close personal or emotional relationship. It remains to be seen whether such an approach proves workable and fair. Although it continues to be arguable that a role for the presumption of resulting trust remains, at least in wholly non-domestic cases, there is no question that the scope for resulting trusts has been dramatically reduced in joint names cases.

---

35 As Robert Walker J observed in *Stockholm Finance Ltd v Garden Holdings Inc* [1995] N.P.C. 162, "the equitable presumptions . . . will rarely be decisive today except where there is a complete lack of evidence as to the parties' intentions".

36 *Dyer v Dyer* (1788) 2 Cox Eq. Cas 92 at 93.

37 *Walker v Hall* [1984] F.L.R. 126 at 133 per Dillon J.

38 [2007] 2 A.C. 432.

39 As Baroness Hale explained, "cases in which the joint legal owners are to be taken to have intended that their beneficial interests should be different from their legal interests will be very unusual" ([2007] 2 A.C. 432 at 459).

40 *Jones v Kernott* [2012] 1 A.C. 776 at 786.

41 *Erlam v Rahman* [2016] EWHC 111 (Ch).

42 [2008] 1 W.L.R. 2695.

43 [2017] UKPC 17.

Voluntary conveyance or transfer

9-011

In the case of a gratuitous transfer of property into the name of the transferee or into the joint names of the transferor and transferee, it is necessary to take on board the effect of s.60(3) of the Law of Property Act 1925. As such, a distinction is drawn commonly between a voluntary transfer of land and of personalty.

Land

9-012

The subsection provides that "In a voluntary conveyance a resulting trust for the grantor shall not be implied merely by reason that the property is not expressed to be conveyed for the use or benefit of the grantee". The provision is, in essence, a word-saving mechanism to ensure that, as had been required in the past, it is no longer necessary to employ a particular formulation of words in order to render a voluntary conveyance to X effective.[44] In *Lohia v Lohia*, Judge Strauss QC was of the view that on a plain reading of the statute, s.60 abolishes the presumption of resulting trust, making it "necessary for the person seeking to establish a resulting trust to prove it".[45] Although the matter may be far from conclusively determined,[46] on this view, it is merely the presumption of resulting trust that is ousted. There is nothing to prevent a finding of resulting trust where there is other evidence to support it.[47]

In *Prest v Petrodel Resources Ltd*,[48] however, the Supreme Court proceeded on the basis that the presumption arose, but did not deem it necessary to refer at all to the effect of s.60(3). Here, in a case of a wife's claim to ancillary relief on divorce, properties vested in companies owned and controlled by her husband were held on resulting trust in what was described as "a particularly clear case of the husband using PRL [one of the companies] as a vehicle to hold legal title on trust for himself".[49] Arguably, the approach in this case was influenced by the family law context of the dispute. The effect of s.60(3) was again addressed in *National Crime Agency v Dong*,[50] a decision deemed to add to the "uncertainty on the point in question".[51]

---

44 This may have been rendered necessary after 1926 by the repeal of the Statute of Uses under which it was the practice to include the words, "unto and to the use of" where a gift was intended. For a detailed discussion of s.60(3), see J. Mee, "Resulting Trusts and Voluntary Conveyances of Land" [2012] Conv. 307.

45 [2001] W.T.L.R. 101 at 113. On the facts, the judge concluded that a gift had been intended; any presumption of resulting trust would have been rebutted.

46 On appeal, Mummery LJ was more reticent, acknowledging that on the question of whether there remained a presumption of resulting trust, it was "so inextricably bound up in centuries of English legal history that it would be bold for this court to pronounce upon it without having heard very extensive argument" (*Lohia v Lohia* [2001] EWCA Civ 1691 at [24]).

47 Morritt VC found no suggestion in *Lohia* that ousting the presumption "precludes a party to the conveyance from relying on evidence from which a resulting trust may be inferred" (*Ali v Khan* [2002] EWCA Civ 974 at [24]).

48 [2013] UKSC 34. See M. Hsiao [2017] Conv. 101.

49 [2013] UKSC 34 at [48].

50 [2017] EWHC 3116 (Ch).

51 See J. Mee, "Voluntary Conveyances of Land: The Presumption of Resulting Trust Redux" [2018] Conv. 184, 184.

The case concerned the beneficial ownership of a South London property, purchased by the defendant in 2008, renovated, and transferred three years later for no consideration into the name of a close business associate. The NCA, which sought to recover unpaid tax from the defendant, invoked the presumption of resulting trust to argue that the sole beneficial ownership had remained with the defendant.[52] In the course of his judgment, Chief Master Marsh made clear his view that the presumption of resulting trust remained in place despite the wording of s.60(3). He noted that the heading to s.60 was "unusually explicit"[53] in a part of the Act, "largely concerned with the nuts and bolts of conveying interests in land".[54] In support of his argument, he added, "if it had been the intention of the draftsman to do away with a presumption of law of long standing, it might have been expected that the Act would have said so in terms and it would be even more surprising for the presumption to have been abolished only in relation to land with a saving provision for chattels".

Personalty

9-013

It has long been established that a gratuitous transfer of personal property into the hands of a transferee gives rise to a resulting trust in the transferor's favour.[55] Some debate has centred on the question of the scope of s.60(3), in particular whether it is applicable both to real and personal property.[56] Quite legitimately, the references to "conveyance" within the section have led most commentators to the conclusion that s.60(3) operates solely in relation to transfers of land. This view is supported by the absence of decided case law on the applicability of the section to transfers of personal property. In the post-1926 case law, there is nothing to suggest that s.60(3) has altered this position. Thus, in *Re Vinogradoff*,[57] a grandmother transferred a bond into the joint names of herself and her granddaughter. Although the evidence was unclear as to her intentions, she continued to receive dividends until her death. Farwell J found that the property was held on resulting trust for the grandmother's estate. The presumption of resulting trust, arising on the voluntary transfer of personalty, was not rebutted by the evidence or displaced by the counter presumption of advancement (considered below).[58]

---

52 Although the presumption might be readily displaced by evidence to the contrary, it was clear from the evidence before the court that the defendant intended to retain the beneficial interest.

53 [2017] EWHC 3116 (Ch) at [26].

54 [2017] EWHC 3116 (Ch) at [34].

55 *Fowkes v Pascoe* (1875) 10 Ch. App. 343.

56 Section 205 of the Law of Property Act 1925 provides an inclusive definition of property that, unless the context otherwise requires, property means "any interest in real or personal property".

57 [1935] W.N. 68.

58 The grandparent was not deemed to stand in loco parentis to her grandchild. The contrary conclusion would have brought her within the category of relationships wherein the transfer would have been seen to be by way of gift "to advance" the child (see para.**9-019**).

Displacing the presumption of resulting trust

The presumption of resulting trust is occasionally displaced by evidence of intention or a counter-presumption of equity. Where there is evidence that money was provided by way of loan, for example, there can be no room for the presumption of resulting trust.[59] In *Smith v Crawshay*,[59] the presumption would not apply where the relationship between parent and adult child was a business partnership and the payments were business transactions. The debtor/creditor relationship is regulated by contract and should not entitle the lender to a beneficial interest under a resulting trust. Similarly, the presumption of a resulting trust will be displaced by evidence that the transferor or contributor intended to confer a gift. The ease with which donative intent can be assessed will obviously depend upon the strength of the evidence adduced. Not surprisingly, most of the cases arise in the context of the family. In *Walker v Walker*,[60] the public declaration by a father that he intended to give his newly wedded son the money to set up a home was sufficient to show an intention to benefit the son by way of gift. Consequently, Browne-Wilkinson LJ accepted that, "Once . . . the father had said that he was making a gift to the son, any claim based on the resulting trust must fail".

The presumption of advancement

The nineteenth-century counter-presumption of advancement arises in the context of specific relationships wherein equity recognises that there is an obligation of conscience owed by the transferor "to advance" or to support the welfare of the transferee.[61] This will occur, for example, in the case of a voluntary conveyance from the transferor to his wife, child or someone to whom he stands in loco parentis. In such narrow confines, there is no presumption of resulting trust because the transferor is presumed to transfer the property freely to the transferee on account of the relationship of obligation.[62] The transferor is deemed to intend, as Spence J explains, "to make a gift of the subject matter of the transfer to the transferee".[63] The effect of the presumption is to shift the burden of proving equitable ownership in the absence of declared intention. Hence, if Fiona transfers shares for no consideration into the name of her son, Jordan, and the presumption of advancement applies, the shares are deemed to be owned by Jordan and the onus lies with Fiona to rebut the presumption that she intended to "advance" Jordan. In *Kelly v Kelly*,[64] the claimant father brought a claim for the repayment of

---

59   [2019] EWHC 2507 (Ch).
60   Unreported 12 April 1984.
61   In *Murless v Franklin* (1818) 1 Swans 13 at 17, Lord Eldon described the duty to advance as being a "species of natural obligation to provide . . ."; see generally G. Andrews and S. Parsons, "Challenging judicial presumptions when equity is not equality" [2018] Conv. 10; G. Andrews, "The presumption of advancement: equity, equality and human rights" [2007] Conv. 340.
62   *Kelly v Kelly* unreported,12 March 2020.
63   *Goodfriend v Goodfriend* [1972] 22 D.L.R. (3rd) 699 at 703.
64   Unreported, 12 March 2020.

money allegedly loaned to his son for the purposes of buying a property. The presumption of advancement resulted in the burden of proof falling on the father to prove a loan, rather than on the son to prove a gift. The father failed on the balance of probabilities to discharge this burden. The High Court accepted that it could take into account the parties' subsequent conduct in this assessment.

The operation and rationale of the presumption of advancement has been legitimately and extensively criticised.[65] As will be clear from the discussion below, the presumption has the propensity to produce diverse outcomes and, furthermore, it reflects the prevailing moral and socio-economic values of bygone days. In the words of McHugh J, the presumption arises "where the relationship between the parties falls into a class where dependency, past, present or future, commonly exists or, at all events, commonly existed in the nineteenth century".[66] In 1970, moreover, Lord Diplock famously attacked its contemporary relevance. In *Pettitt v Pettitt*[67] he exclaimed:

> **"It would in my view, be an abuse of the legal technique for ascertaining or imputing intention to apply to transactions between the post-war generation of married couples 'presumptions' which are based upon inferences of fact which an earlier generation of judges drew as the most likely intentions of earlier generations of spouses belonging to the propertied classes of a different social era".[68]**

9-016

The operation of the presumption of advancement is considered in detail below. First, it is necessary to point out that should s.199 of the Equality Act 2010 come into force, this will lead to the prospective abolition of the presumption of advancement.[69] The desire for legislative change stems from the recognition that the presumption is outdated, weak and has much scope for unfairness. In addition, it is, as it currently operates, arguably incompatible with art.5 of the Seventh Protocol to the European Convention on Human Rights.[70] It must be emphasised, however, that s.199 is not yet in force. Unless and until the provision comes into force, modern courts will continue to grapple with parameters of advancement.[71] Such was the case

---

65 For a historical analysis, see J. Glister, "The Presumption of Advancement", in C. Mitchell (ed.), *Constructive and Resulting Trusts* (Oxford: Hart Publishing, 2010).

66 *Nelson v Nelson* (1995) 184 C.L.R. 538 at 600.

67 [1970] A.C. 777.

68 [1970] A.C. 777 at 824.

69 Except in relation to anything done (or anything done pursuant to any obligation incurred) before the commencement of the section: see Equality Act 2010 s.199(2). For criticism of the provision, see J. Glister, "Section 199 of the Equality Act 2010: How Not to Abolish the Presumption of Advancement" (2010) 73 M.L.R. 807.

70 "Spouses shall enjoy equality of rights and responsibilities of a private law character between them, and in their relations with their children, as to marriage, during marriage and in the event of its dissolution . . .". Note, for example, the views of G. Andrews, "The Presumption of Advancement: Equity, Equality and Human Rights" [2007] Conv. 340.

71 See generally, A. Blackham, "The Presumption of Advancement: A Lingering Shadow in UK Law?" (2015) 21(7) T. & T. 786.

in *Harwood v Harwood*, where Slade LJ held that the presumption of advancement "must be applied with caution in modern social conditions" but, nonetheless, he could find "nothing sufficient to displace" it on the facts of the case before him.[72] Accordingly, for the time being, it continues to be necessary to consider the relationships which give rise to the operation of this outmoded presumption.

Husband and wife

9-017

The presumption as it operates on transfers from husband to wife is long-established and historically prominent.[73] As Malins VC declared in the latter part of the nineteenth century, "The law of this court is perfectly settled that where a husband transfers money or other property into the name of his wife only, then the presumption is, that it is intended as a gift or advancement to the wife absolutely at once . . .".[74] In this context, the reach of the presumption has been somewhat limited given that it will not apply where the transfer is from wife to husband[75] as between co-habiting spouses or, furthermore, from a man to his mistress.[76]

Parent and child

9-018

The presumption of advancement is also strong where a transfer is from a parent to their child. Although the presumption applies when the child is an adult and financially independent,[77] it is less strong in such cases and more easily rebutted.[78] Historically, the presumption applied only as between father and child. As Sir George Jessel MR observed, "The father is under that obligation from the mere fact of his being the father, and therefore no evidence is necessary to shew the obligation to provide for his child. In the case of a father, you only have to prove that he is the father, and when you have done that the obligation at once arises".[79] Much less certainty surrounded the operation of the presumption in the context of other relationships. As between mother and child, for example, equity rarely construed that relationship as bestowing on the mother an obligation to advance her child either financially[80] or morally.[81] This was apparent

---

72 [1991] 2 F.L.R. 274 at 294.
73 It also operates in the case of a transfer made in contemplation of marriage: *Moate v Moate* [1948] 2 All E.R. 486.
74 *Re Eykyn's Trusts* (1877) 6 Ch. D. 115 at 118.
75 *Heseltine v Heseltine* [1971] 1 W.L.R. 342.
76 *Diwell v Farnes* [1959] 1 W.L.R. 624.
77 *Wood v Watkin* [2019] EWHC 1311 (Ch). It was emphasised that the presumption is based on parental affection as well as parental obligation.
78 *Kelly v Kelly* unreported, 12 March 2020.
79 *Bennet v Bennet* (1879) 10 Ch. D. 474 at 477.
80 See *Re De Visme* (1863) 2 De. G.J. & S 17.
81 *Bennet v Bennet* (1879) 10 Ch. D. 474.

even in cases where the father had died[82] or where the mother was the primary earner. Not surprisingly, therefore, this aspect of the operation of the presumption has been the subject of much criticism. The application of presumed advancement had, as the Grays comment,

> **"become hopelessly out of touch with the egalitarian nature of contemporary society and fails, moreover, to reflect the fact that both parents, if married to each other, are nowadays statutorily burdened with 'parental responsibility' for their minor children . . . Today it seems highly impossible that the presumption can survive, in the parental context, in its discriminatory form".[83]**

Nowadays, it is perfectly reasonable to expect the courts to adopt a more pro-active approach and eliminate indefensible gender bias. Such was the view of the High Court in Australia where in *Nelson v Nelson*[84] the presumption was deemed equally applicable to fathers and mothers.[85] This progressive approach has had the recent endorsement of Mr Simon Picken QC in *Close Invoice Finance Ltd v Abaowa*, who ventured that as between mother and daughter "It seems to me that the modern society in this country is no less egalitarian than the equivalent in Australia, and that there is no question that the presumption of advancement applies in this country in 2010 just as the High Court of Australia held it did some 15 years ago in Australia".[86] Recently, in *Farrell v Burden*[87] the High Court accepted that the presumption applied between mother and adult son. The mother failed to provide documentary evidence to the effect that the money had been provided by her to her son by way of loan and her appeal was dismissed. Accordingly, it is now readily accepted that a mother owes the same obligation to her child as does a father.

In loco parentis

9-019

Outside the relationship of parent and child, the courts will look for evidence that the donor stands in loco parentis to the transferee. This means simply that a person stands in the shoes of a parent and assumes parental obligations of support or provision.[88] Such may occur in

---

82   See, e.g. *Bennet v Bennet* (1879) 10 Ch. D. 474.
83   K. Gray and S. Gray, *Elements of Land Law*, 5th edn (Oxford: Oxford University Press, 2008), pp.856–857. Reproduced with permission of the Licensor through PLSclear.
84   (1995) 184 C.L.R. 538.
85   For a Court of Appeal of Singapore decision endorsing this approach, see *Lau Siew Kim v Terence Yeo Guan Chye* [2007] SGCA 54, noted by K. Low (2008) 124 L.Q.R. 369.
86   [2010] EWHC 1920 (QB) at [96]; see also *Musson v Bonner* [2010] W.T.L.R. 1369.
87   [2019] EWHC 3671 (QB).
88   No such obligation was assumed in *Sansom v Gardner* [2009] EWHC 3369 (QB) despite the closeness of the relationship existing between the parties.

relation to an illegitimate child,[89] or an adopted child.[90] It is also common for relatives such as uncles, aunts or grandparents to act in loco parentis where circumstances demand. In *Ebrand v Dancer*,[91] for example, a grandfather acted in loco parentis to his grandchild on the death of the child's father.

Rebutting the presumption of advancement

The effect of a presumption of equity is to shift the burden of evidential proof to the party against whom the presumption operates. Rebutting a presumption simply comes down to issues of evidence. As James LJ declared in *Fowkes v Pascoe*:

> "Where the Court of Chancery is asked, as an equitable assumption or presumption, to take away from a man that which by the common law of the land he is entitled to, he surely has a right to say: 'Listen to my story as to how I came to have it, and judge that story with reference to all the surrounding facts and circumstances'".[92]

9-020

In the context of the discredited presumption of advancement, the fiction arises in the absence of evidence as to the transferor's real intentions. Fortunately, the courts now endorse a flexible approach to the admissibility of evidence. As Lord Phillips MR explained:

> "In these cases equity searches for the subjective intention of the transferor. It seems to me that it is not satisfactory to apply rigid rules of law to the evidence that is admissible to rebut the presumption of advancement. Plainly, self-serving statements or conduct of a transferor, who may long after the transaction be regretting earlier generosity, carry little or no weight. But words or conduct more proximate to the transaction itself should be given the significance that they naturally bear as part of the overall picture. Where the transferee is an adult, the words or conduct of the transferor will carry more weight if the transferee is aware of them and makes no protest or challenge to them".[93]

Older authorities that seek to impose restrictions on the admissibility of evidence[94] must, there-

---

89 See, e.g. *Beckford v Beckford* (1774) Lofft 490.
90 *Standing v Bowring* (1886) 31 Ch. D. 282.
91 (1680) 2 Ch. Cas 26.
92 (1875) 10 Ch. App. 343 at 349.
93 *Lavelle v Lavelle* [2004] 2 F.C.R. 418 at [19].
94 See *Shephard v Cartwright* [1955] A.C. 431 at 445 per Viscount Simonds.

fore, be viewed with healthy scepticism.[95] Difficulties are, however, sometimes heightened when the transaction is designed to achieve an illegal objective and a party seeks to lead evidence of illegal behaviour in order to rebut the presumption.

Illegality

9-021

"He who comes to equity must come with clean hands" is a historic equitable principle which resonates particularly in the context of illegality and resulting trusts. It has been encountered, for example, when there was a gratuitous transfer of property from father to child as part of an illegal or fraudulent scheme. In accordance with the clean hands maxim, the presumption of advancement could not be rebutted by adducing evidence of illegality or fraudulent activity.[96] Thus, a transferor was prevented from arguing illegality to show that he intended to retain a beneficial interest in the property. For example, *Chettiar v Chettiar (No.2)*[97] concerned the evasion of regulations governing the holding of rubber plantations in Malaya. Once the father had reached the threshold of 100 acres (to hold more would subject him to further regulations), he transferred additional plantations into the name of his son. The Privy Council was unimpressed with his introduction of evidence of a fraudulent purpose to show that he did not plan to divest himself of his equitable interest in the additional plantations. Lord Denning could only conclude that the legal and equitable estate should lay where it had fallen. His clear view was that, "The father has used the transfer to achieve his deceitful end and cannot go back on it".[98] This bar gave rise to an uneasy tension in that, as the Law Commission explained in its 2010 Report, "If the courts accept the illegality defence, it often involves granting an unjustified windfall to the defendant, who may be equally implicated in the illegality. However, if the courts refuse, they may be seen to be helping a claimant who has behaved illegally".[99] This tension has recently been relieved by the decision of the Supreme Court in *Patel v Mirza*.[100]

---

95 As E. Fung argues in (2006) 122 L.Q.R. 651, 688, "The rule in *Shephard v Cartwright* is an anomalous relic of the common law from former times and should be recognised as such".

96 This rule was viewed as being a principle of policy and not a principle of justice: *Holman v Johnson* (1775) 1 Coup. 341.

97 [1962] A.C. 294.

98 [1962] A.C. 294 at 302; see also *Barrett v Barrett* [2008] 2 P. & C.R. 17 where reliance on the agreement between the parties necessitated reliance on an underlying illegal purpose.

99 Law Commission, *The Illegality Defence* (2010) Law Com. No.320, para.1.2. The Commission added (at para.1.3): "The courts have attempted to set out rules to govern this area. However, the rules are complex and confused".

100 [2016] 3 W.L.R. 399; see para.**9-025**.

Statutory Reform?

In 1999, the Law Commission published a Consultation Paper concerning the effect of illegality on contracts and trusts.[101] Following the publication of a further Consultation Paper,[102] a Final Report emerged[103] wherein the law of trusts was singled out as in need of a short, targeted Act of Parliament. The Commission felt that, since (the subsequently discredited) decision in *Tinsley v Milligan*,[104] the operation of illegality in trusts enjoyed the potential to operate arbitrarily, unfairly and without certainty and transparency.[105] As Lord Sumption explained, "denying relief not only works injustice between the parties, but in some cases actually rewards illegal conduct. The principle that the loss lies where it falls means that the past consequences of the transaction are left undisturbed".[106] The Law Commission emphasised that, "if people are to be deprived of valuable property rights, the law should be clear, proportionate, and justifiable".[107] It was particularly concerned with illegality in the context of trusts, which, it admitted, "produces complex and arbitrary results, depending on the detailed intricacies of trust law".[108] The Commission concluded that "The result depends not on the merits of the case, but on obscure legal presumptions, which are often outdated and may be discriminatory. The Commission recommended that, where a trust has been set up to conceal the beneficiary's interest in order to commit a criminal offence, legislation should provide a discretion for the court to disregard the illegality.[109] It would not matter whether the illegal purpose had been acted upon, whether it was the trustee or beneficiary who sought to conceal real ownership of the trust property or whether there were mixed motives underlying the trust.[110] The process envisaged would require the court to declare that the intended beneficiary was entitled to the equitable interest asserted.[111] Only in exceptional circumstances would illegality have an effect on this beneficial entitlement.[112]

A non-exhaustive list of factors which should influence the exercise of discretion was provided in the draft bill appended to the Report and these are:

---

101 Law Commission, *Illegal Transactions: The Effect of Illegality on Contracts and Trusts* (1999) Law Com. No.154.

102 Law Commission, *The Illegality Defence: A Consultative Report* (2009) Law Com. No.189.

103 Law Commission, *The Illegality Defence* (2010) Law Com. No.320.

104 [1994] 1 A.C. 340; see para.**9-023**.

105 As Lady Hale acknowledged in her speech entitled, "Legislation or judicial law reform: where should judges fear to tread?", Society of Legal Scholars Conference, 7 September 2016, p.8, "This was clearly an area of judge-made law where the judges had got us into a mess and Parliament was most unlikely to get us out of it", *https://www.supremecourt.uk/docs/speech-160907.pdf* [Accessed 31 July 2017].

106 "Reflexions on the Law of Illegality" Chancery Bar Association, 23 April 2012, p.4. This means that, as Lord Sumption pointed out (p.4), "the Claimant is prevented from using the court's procedures to obtain the reward of his illegal acts, but the Defendant gains a corresponding windfall from his".

107 Law Commission, *The Illegality Defence* (2010) Law Com. No.320, para.1.20.

108 Law Commission, *The Illegality Defence* (2010) Law Com. No.320, para.1.7.

109 Law Commission, *The Illegality Defence* (2010) Law Com. No.320, para.2.32.

110 Law Commission, *The Illegality Defence* (2010) Law Com. No.320, paras 2.33, 2.34.

111 Law Commission, *The Illegality Defence* (2010) Law Com. No.320, para.2.57.

112 Law Commission, *The Illegality Defence* (2010) Law Com. No.320, para.2.61.

- the conduct and intention of all the relevant parties;

- the value of the equitable interest at stake;

- the effect of allowing the claim on the criminal purpose;

- whether refusing the claim would act as a deterrent;

- the possibility that the person from whom the equitable interest was being concealed may have an interest in the value of the assets of the beneficiary.

In 2012, the government announced that it would not take forward the Commission's recommendations for statutory reform as it did not consider such reform to be a pressing priority. Nevertheless, and as will become clear, the law has been reformulated along similar lines by the Supreme Court in *Patel v Mirza*.[113]

The discredited reliance principle: *Tinsley v Milligan*

9-023

Prior to the decision of the Supreme Court in *Patel v Mirza*, the contentious reliance approach advanced by the House of Lords in *Tinsley v Milligan*[114] held sway. This entailed that where a proprietary interest can be established under a resulting or constructive trust without recourse to reliance on evidence of illegality, the "clean hands" principle had no role to play.[115] In *Tinsley*, there was the joint purchase of a home for two women as co-habiting lovers. By mutual agreement, the property was registered in Ms Tinsley's name as the sole proprietor so as to enable Ms Milligan to make false social security claims, thereby benefiting both parties. On the breakdown of their relationship, Ms Tinsley moved out and claimed possession of the house as its legal owner. Ms Milligan counterclaimed for an order for sale claiming that the house was held on trust for both of them equally. As between the ending of their relationship and Ms Tinsley's claim to possession, Ms Milligan had discontinued her fraudulent activity and had settled the matter with the relevant authorities. By a majority, the House of Lords determined that a resulting trust could be upheld where it was not necessary to rely on illegality as the basis of the claim.[116] Hence, the so-called "reliance principle" was born. The inherent problem with this approach

---

113   [2016] 3 W.L.R. 399; see G. Virgo, *"Patel v Mirza*: one step forward and two steps back" (2016) 22(10) T. & T. 1090; A. Grabiner, "Illegality and Restitution Explained by the Supreme Court" (2017) 76(1) C.L.J. 18.

114   [1994] 1 A.C. 340; see also *Gibson v Revenue & Customs Prosecution Office* [2008] EWCA Civ 645 where a drug trafficker's wife was able to assert her interest in property subject to a confiscation order.

115   See also *Slater v Simm* [2007] EWHC 951 (Ch) where lies contained in a financial statement did not prevent the assertion of a beneficial interest. Although the majority of cases concerning the reliance principle involved resulting trusts, the reliance principle was used to gauge the effect of illegality whatever type of trust was in issue: see *Collier v Collier* [2002] EWCA Civ 1095 (an express trust).

116   The decision of the House of Lords, as S. Evans, "Applying Tinsley or Snipping Tinsley?" [2008] Conv. 534 puts it, "gained textbook notoriety because of its creative side stepping of one of the maxims of equity". He added

was that, as demonstrated by the Law Commission, "The outcome of the case depended on the legal starting point or 'presumption' applied by trust law. In this case, once Ms Milligan had shown that she contributed towards the purchase price, the law 'presumed' a resulting trust".[117]

If, however, the parties had been father and daughter, the very different presumption of advancement would have operated to infer a gift to the daughter.[118] This is because, in cases where the presumption of advancement does apply, the transferor is faced with the presumption that property was transferred freely. The transferor cannot claim under a resulting trust unless and until he has rebutted that presumption of gift for those purposes. As he must rely on the underlying illegality, following *Tinsley* his claim would necessarily have failed. As Lord Browne-Wilkinson had emphasised, "A party to an illegality can recover by virtue of a legal or equitable property interest if, but only if, he can establish his title without relying on his own illegality".[119]

The reliance principle did not, however, survive for the next 21 years totally unscathed. Although expedient on the facts, *Tinsley v Milligan* showed that the outcome of future cases would pivot, often unfairly, on the nature of the relationship of the parties involved and the presumption of equity raised to cater for their inferred intentions. Understandably, therefore, *Tinsley v Milligan* was the subject of robust criticism from commentators and the Law Commission alike and ill-disguised regret in the Court of Appeal that, for at least the present time, the House of Lords authority required to be followed.[120] Stowe, for example, made the convincing argument that, "availability of relief depends entirely on a fact which is completely irrelevant from a policy perspective (viz whether there is a presumption of advancement in relation to the person to whom the property is transferred); and . . . is in no way related to the seriousness of the underlying illegality".[121]

It is noteworthy also that the High Court of Australia has long rejected the *Tinsley* approach in favour of a flexible test based on public policy considerations. Accordingly, in *Nelson v Nelson*,[122] a woman who purchased property in the name of her children in order to take advantage of particular housing subsidies was permitted to rebut the presumption of advancement by leading evidence of her illegal purpose. As a condition of equitable relief, she was obliged to repay the sums accrued improperly via the illegal scheme.[123]

---

at 538: "An earlier, more traditional holistic approach, requiring clean hands and good faith throughout had clearly been displaced".

117   Law Commission, *The Illegality Defence* (2010) Law Com. No.320, para.1.17.
118   See Lord Sumption in *Patel v Mirza* [2016] 3 W.L.R. 399 at [237].
119   [1994] 1 A.C. 340 at 375.
120   See *Silverwood v Silverwood* (1997) 74 P. & C.R. 453.
121   H. Stowe, "The 'Unruly Horse' Has Bolted" (1994) 57 M.L.R. 441, 446.
122   (1995) 132 A.L.R. 133.
123   For an overview of the Australian, Canadian and North American rejection of *Tinsley v Milligan*, see Lord Toulson in *Patel v Mirza* [2016] 3 W.L.R. 399 at [50]–[66].

The defunct withdrawal exception

9-024

A further relaxation of the "clean hands" requirement was discernible from the withdrawal exception (otherwise known as the *locus poenitentiae*) promoted by *Tribe v Tribe*.[124] There the question arose as to whether the transferor could rebut the presumption of advancement by adducing evidence of an illegal purpose that was never carried into effect.[125] The plaintiff held 459 out of 500 shares in a family company and was tenant under two leases. When a notice of dilapidations was served on him, he feared that the demands of extensive repairs would lead to losses to the family companies. In order to avoid liability by deceiving the landlord, Mr Tribe purported to sell the shares to his son for the sum of £78,000, which was never paid. It transpired that the deception was not necessary because the landlord later agreed to a surrender of one of the leases. The son, however, claimed that he was now absolutely entitled to the shares under the presumption of advancement. The Court of Appeal held that, as the father had not carried out his illegal purpose, he was able to adduce evidence of it to rebut the presumption of advancement. Hence, when the planned illegal activity is never carried out, the transferor is not precluded from relying on evidence of his proposed activities to support his claim or rebut the presumption of advancement.[126] There was, however, no need for repentance.[127] The Law Commission admitted that, "There is some uncertainty as to the exact scope of the withdrawal exception . . . It is unclear how far it is possible to go before withdrawal is no longer allowed".[128] Although in *Patel v Mirza* Lord Toulson did not examine the *locus poenitentiae* exception, the doctrine is clearly inconsistent with the new approach adopted by the Supreme Court and, hence, is no longer to be regarded as good law. Such was, moreover, the clear understanding of the Law Commission when making its recommendations.[129]

Patel v Mirza

9-025

The facts of *Patel* are straightforward. Mr Patel paid £620,000 to Mr Mirza to speculate on the price of shares in the Royal Bank of Scotland. Mr Mirza had inside information from his contacts within the Bank which would enable him to predict movements in the market price of the shares. It is to be appreciated that insider trading is a criminal offence under s.52 of the Criminal Justice Act 1993. The information was never forthcoming and the share dealing was therefore abandoned due to external circumstances rather than the action or remorse of Mr Patel. He asserted unjust enrichment based on failure of consideration, which required Mr

---

124 [1996] Ch. 107.
125 See also *Painter v Hutchison* [2007] EWHC 758 (Ch).
126 This principle was not novel: see *Symes v Hughes* (1870) L.R. 9 Eq. 475.
127 In *SMQ v RFQ* [2008] EWHC 1874 (Fam) at [125], Black J explained that "genuine repentance is not required. Justice is not a reward for merit".
128 Law Commission, *The Illegality Defence* (2010) Law Com. No.320, para.2.7.
129 Law Commission, *The Illegality Defence* (2010) Law Com. No.320, para.2.33.

Patel to establish the nature of his agreement. Mr Mirza refused to return the money, pleading illegality as a bar to its recovery. Although Mr Patel had to rely on the illegality, the Supreme Court unanimously allowed his claim. It did not serve the purpose of the legislation for Mr Mirza to retain such ill-gotten gains. This decision resulted in the abandonment of the reliance principle and the withdrawal exception.[130] Instead, the majority of the Supreme Court fashioned a new test that was intended to apply in all cases, including contract, tort, restitution and trusts.[131] The upshot, as Lord Toulson observed, is that a person, "will not *prima facie* be debarred from recovering money paid or property transferred by reason of the fact that the consideration which has failed was an unlawful consideration".[132]

The multi-factorial approach

9-026

The court was now to assess whether the public interest would be harmed by enforcement of the illegal agreement. This would not, as Lord Toulson noted, "exclude the possibility that there may be a particular reason for the court to refuse its assistance to the claimant", but as he emphasised, "such cases are likely to be rare".[133] In making this determination, the court is to consider:

- the underlying purpose of the prohibition which has been transgressed and whether that purpose will be enhanced by denial of the claim.[134] In *Stoffel & Co v Grondona*,[135] following a mortgage fraud the defence of illegality was put forward unsuccessfully by a negligent law firm. The Court of Appeal, while admitting that that dishonest mortgage applicants were a canker on society, saw no justification for allowing the negligent conveyancer to escape liability simply because unbeknownst to the firm its client has made misrepresentations to the lender[136];

- any other relevant public policy on which the denial of the claim might have an impact.

---

130   See A. Grabiner, "Illegality and Restitution Explained by the Supreme Court" (2017) 76(1) C.L.J. 18.
131   This is, perhaps, an overly ambitious goal: see N. Strauss, "Illegality decisions after Patel v Mirza" (2018) 134 L.Q.R. 538.
132   [2016] 3 W.L.R. 399 at [116].
133   [2016] 3 W.L.R. 399 at [116]. Lord Toulson (at [110]) provided the example of where to do so would be to assist the claimant in a drug trafficking operation.
134   In *Gujra v Roath* [2018] EWHC 854 (QB), the claimant who was party to a conspiracy to defraud was barred from suing his co-conspirator because to allow the action would be tantamount to implementing the conspiracy and would encourage fraudulent insurance claims.
135   [2018] EWCA 2031 (Civ).
136   In *Singularis Holdings Ltd v Daiwa Capital Markets Europe Ltd* [2018] EWCA Civ 84, the appellate court determined that to disallow a negligence claim against the bank because of the claimant's illegal act would do nothing to prevent dishonest conduct and would only undermine the duty of care imposed on the bank.

In *Stoffel & Co v Grondona*, the appellate court recognised a genuine public interest in ensuring that clients who employed solicitors were able to sue in negligence;

■ whether the denial of the claim would be a proportionate response to the illegality, considering that punishment is not a matter for the civil courts. In the *Stoffel* case, the court concluded that it would be highly disproportionate to deny the purchaser a remedy against its solicitors.[137]

9-027

The majority of the Supreme Court in *Patel v Mirza* felt that the public interest was best served by a principled and transparent assessment of those considerations, rather than by the application of any formal approach with the latter being capable of producing results that were arbitrary, unjust and disproportionate.[138] The test was to remain flexible, but relevant factors would, Lord Toulson suggested, include the seriousness of the conduct, its centrality to the transaction, whether it was intentional and whether there was a marked disparity in the parties' respective culpability.[139] In *Kliers v Schmerler*,[140] for example, the purpose of a trust of a house was to allow the legal owner to obtain mortgage funds and housing and social security benefits. He would not have been entitled to such funds if the real state of affairs had been revealed. The court raised the issue of illegality of its own motion and concluded that, following *Patel v Mirza*, the illegality should not bar the trust claim. The factors that influenced the court were that the claimant was under undue influence from family and religious leaders, the parties had not been on a level playing field when hatching and executing the plan, the claimant had jeopardised her own interests in the process and her ability to challenge the plan was limited. It would also be offensive to public policy to allow the registered proprietor to set up an illegality defence in circumstances where he was clearly aware of what was going on and had made no contributions to the purchase price. The illegal activities had to be undone.[141]

9-028

In *Patel v Mirza*, Lord Sumption (with whom Lord Clarke agreed) felt that the test as propounded by the majority was, "far too vague and potentially far too wide to serve as the basis

---

137 See also *Grove Park Properties Ltd v Royal Bank of Scotland Plc* [2018] EWHC 3521 (Comm). Cf. *Al-Dowaisan v Al-Salam* [2019] EWHC 301 (Ch) where the defendants' use of bank accounts to evade tax barred their claim to recover money paid to the claimant from those accounts.

138 J. Goudkamp, "The End of an Era? Illegality in Private Law in the Supreme Court" (2017) 133 L.Q.R. 14, 18, however, believes that, "The policy-based test is, therefore, flawed because it requires the courts to do the impossible. Requiring judges to compare the factors in play is akin to asking them whether five litres is greater than two meters".

139 [2016] 3 W.L.R. 399 at [107]. As he had earlier observed in *ParkingEye Ltd v Somerfield Stores Ltd* [2013] Q.B. 840 at [52], [53],"Rather than having over-complex rules which are indiscriminate in theory but less so in practice, it is better and more honest that the court should look openly at the underlying policy factors and reach a balanced judgment in each case for reasons articulated by it".

140 [2018] EWHC 1350 (Ch).

141 Cf. *XX v Whittington Hospital NHS Trust* [2018] EWCA Civ 2832, where a claim in negligence was allowed against the NHS Trust for causing the infertility of a patient and for costs of a commercial surrogacy arrangement in California. Although illegal in England & Wales, it was legal in the US. Accordingly, she had committed no illegal act.

on which a person may be denied his legal rights" and "leaves a great deal to a judge's visceral reaction to particular facts".[142] Lord Mance, also in the minority, felt uncomfortable with the range of factors test. As he put it, "What is apparent is that this approach, would introduce not only a new era but entirely novel dimensions into any issue of illegality".[143] Lord Mance agreed that this required the court to reach a value judgment on the basis of a varied *mélange* of ingredients and in a highly unspecific non-legal sense. Lord Sumption also disliked the notion of balancing a series of different factors and asserted that, "It would be unprincipled and uncertain, and far from confining the ambit of the illegality principle to its essential minimum, it could only broaden it beyond its proper limits. Perhaps most important of all, justice can be achieved without taking this revolutionary step".[144]

The majority view in *Patel v Mirza* marks a radical departure from the pre-existing law.[145] Although it will have initial teething problems, the range of factors approach is to be welcomed. Most certainly, it cannot be any worse that what went before.[146]

Failure of Trust Cases

9-029

The second category of case concerns failed trusts. Where an express trust fails to dispose of the entirety of the beneficial interest, the remainder is held by implication on resulting trust for the settlor. The purpose of the resulting trust in this context is to restore equitable title in property to its previous owner or to establish that that person continues to hold an equitable interest in the property. Many examples of the operation of resulting trusts feature in other parts of the book. Accordingly, some of the illustrations offered below will be familiar to the reader. Although there is no attempt to produce an exhaustive list, examples of resulting trusts will be considered under the following broad headings:

- failure to declare a trust;

- failure of a trust;

- unexhausted beneficial interests.

---

142 [2016] 3 W.L.R. 399 at [265], [263] respectively.
143 [2016] 3 W.L.R. 399 at [206]. Lord Sumption at [263] was critical of the fact that "A new body of jurisprudence would be gradually built up to identify which of a large range of factors should be regarded as relevant and what considerations should determine the weight that they should receive".
144 [2016] 3 W.L.R. 399 at [261].
145 See generally, G. Virgo, "*Patel v Mirza*: one step forward and two steps back" (2016) 22 T. & T. 1090.
146 See R.N. Nwabueze, "Illegality and trusts: trusts- creating primary transactions and unlawful ulterior purposes" [2019] Conv. 29.

Finally, *Quistclose* trusts will be analysed with a view to setting out some important general principles and problems of classification. The use of *Quistclose* trusts in commercial transactions will also be appraised.

Failure to declare a trust

9-030

Where property is conveyed to persons with the intention that they act as trustees, the failure to declare the manner in which all of the beneficial interest is to be held on trust will entail that any property unaccounted for is held on resulting trust for the grantor. The classic illustration is provided by *Vandervell v IRC*[147] (considered in detail in Ch.4). It will be recalled that in 1958 Vandervell wished to found a Chair in Pharmacology at the Royal College of Surgeons. He planned to transfer shares in Vandervell Productions Ltd to the College, in whose favour dividends on the shares would subsequently be declared. As a charity, the College enjoyed fiscal privileges, the attraction of the transaction being that the dividends (amounting to some £250,000), would not give rise to tax liability. The shares were to be transferred subject to the option to repurchase in favour of Vandervell Trustees Ltd, a company administering trusts connected to Vandervell's family and business enterprises. Once the dividends were paid, the shares could be retrieved by Vandervell Trustees Ltd. Vandervell was sure that if the option was not vested in him he could avoid any liability for tax.

Until 1961, the College was in receipt of dividend payments on the shares. The Inland Revenue sought to claim surtax on the dividends, arguing that Vandervell had failed to divest himself absolutely of the beneficial interest in the shares. The basis of this view was that, on the failure to declare a trust of the option, its benefit must be held on resulting trust for Vandervell. By a majority of three to two in the House of Lords the Inland Revenue was successful. As no trust of the option had been declared, the option was held on resulting trust. In the view of the court, retention of the option involved retention of part of the beneficial interest in the shares. As Lord Wilberforce commented, there was:

> **"no need or room to invoke a presumption. The conclusion, on the facts found, is simply that the option is vested in the trustee company as a trustee on trusts, not defined at the time, possibly to be defined later. But the equitable, or beneficial interest, cannot remain in the air: the consequence in law must be that it remains in the settlor".[148]**

9-031

In *Re Vandervell's Trusts (No.2)*,[149] the Court of Appeal concluded that the resulting trust terminated when the option was exercised. In 1961, Vandervell had sanctioned the use of money from his children's settlement to exercise the option. Legal title vested in Vandervell's

---

147 [1967] 2 A.C. 291.
148 [1967] 2 A.C. 291 at 329.
149 [1974] Ch. 269.

trust company accordingly. It was not until 1965, however, that Vandervell expressly declared that the company was to hold the shares on trust for the children's settlement. The Inland Revenue sought to argue that he had not divested himself of his equitable interest in the shares until that point and, hence, incurred liability for surtax on dividends paid during that period. At first instance, Megarry J observed that the trust company acquired the shares on trust. He held that there had been no valid declaration of trust in favour of the children's settlement. Accordingly, the shares, like the option to purchase them, were held on resulting trust for Vandervell. Ultimately successful in the Court of Appeal, Vandervell's executors fended off the Inland Revenue. The much-maligned reasoning of the decision is considered in Ch.4. Although the judgment given by Megarry J at first instance was reversed, there was nothing said in the appellate court to cast doubt on his propositions on resulting trusts. It remains a fundamental principle that, where a transfer is made on trusts which leave some or all of the beneficial interest undisposed of, the transferee holds on resulting trust for the transferor to the extent that the beneficial interest has not been carried to him or others. Here, the resulting trust functions "to fill in evidential lacunae as to the location of the beneficial interest".[150]

Failure of the trust

A trust can fail for a variety of reasons, whether it is by lapse,[151] illegality[152] or a failure to comply with the rules against perpetuity and accumulations.[153] Where such failure occurs, the resulting trust effects a transfer of property back to the settlor. It will be recalled from Ch.2 that a resulting trust can arise where a trust fails for a lack of certainty of beneficial interest or uncertain objects. Provided that a trust was intended (i.e. there is certainty of intention) there is no possibility that a trustee can take the property as an absolute gift. Thus, in *Boyce v Boyce*[154] a testator left two houses on trust to convey to Maria, "whichever house she may think proper to choose or select" and to convey the other to Charlotte. On Maria's death, it proved impossible for the court to determine which of the houses was held on trust for Charlotte. Maria had died before making her selection. Consequently, the houses were held on resulting trust for the testator's residuary estate. Similarly, in *Re Atkinson's Will Trusts*,[155] uncertainty arose in relation to a residuary gift from a testatrix to be divided between "such worthy causes as have been communicated by me to my trustees in my lifetime". This could lead only to the finding of a resulting trust when no such causes had been communicated.

Other prominent case law examples of failed trusts are consequent to the failure of a con-

9-032

---

150 C.E.F. Rickett and R. Grantham, "Resulting Trusts—The Nature of the Failing Trust Cases" (2000) 116 L.Q.R. 15, 20.
151 See, e.g. *Ackroyd v Smithson* (1780) 1 Bro. C.C. 503.
152 See paras **16-012 to 16-014.**
153 *Re Drummond's Settlement* [1986] 3 All E.R. 45.
154 (1849) 6 Sim. 476.
155 [1978] 1 All E.R. 1275.

dition precedent[156] or condition subsequent.[157] As will become clear from the following illustrations, when a transfer of property is made subject to a condition which is not achieved, the resulting trust effects a return of the property to the transferor. First, in *Essery v Cowlard*,[158] a settlement was executed in 1877 in consideration of a then intended marriage. The intended wife transferred property to trustees to be held on trust for the benefit of herself, her intended husband and any children resulting from their marriage. Although the couple cohabited and had children, no marriage took place. In 1883, an action was brought against the trustees to recover the property. Pearson J was confident that the contract to marry had been "definitely and absolutely put an end to"[159] and ordered that the property be transferred back to the woman. As the property was held on the terms of a marriage that never took place, the condition precedent had not been achieved and, accordingly, the property moved back under a resulting trust.

9-033   Failure also occurred in *Re Ames' Settlement*, which was, in the words of Vaisey J, "a simple case of money paid on a consideration which failed".[160] In a marriage settlement of 1908, the bridegroom's father covenanted to pay to trustees, within one year of the solemnisation of marriage, the sum of £10,000. This was to be held on trust, the income payable to the husband for life and after his death to the wife for life or until her remarriage, with the remainder to any issue of the intended marriage. The parties lived together until 1926 when a decree of nullity was made on the wife's petition on the grounds of non-consummation of marriage. The effect of the decree was to render the marriage void ab initio (i.e. as if it had never occurred). The husband received the income until his death some 20 years later. The question for the court was whether the capital sum was held on trust for the husband's next of kin or was, instead, payable under resulting trust to the settlor's estate. Vaisey J decided on the latter. As the money was vested on trusts which failed, the money was held on resulting trust. In *Westdeutsche Landesbank Girozentrale v Islington LBC*,[161] Lord Browne-Wilkinson described the judgment as confused and preferred the view that the ultimate trust failed because it was expressed to take effect only in the event of the failure of the issue of a non-existent marriage, which he described as an impossible condition precedent. Ultimately, as Lord Browne-Wilkinson accepted, it makes no difference because on either view the funds were vested in trusts which failed.

Finally, *Re Cochrane*[162] concerned a post-nuptial settlement into which both husband and wife brought property. In essence, the income generated was to be paid to the wife on the condition that she continued to reside with her husband. Should either die, the other would be entitled to the entirety beneficially. A problem arose when the wife left her husband and he died shortly thereafter. This was a scenario that had not been envisaged at the outset. The

---

156 For example, that X must marry, but X fails to marry.
157 For example, where the beneficiaries must remain married but they fail to do so.
158 (1884) 26 Ch. D. 191.
159 (1884) 26 Ch. D. 191 at 193.
160 [1946] 1 Ch. 217 at 223.
161 [1996] A.C. 669.
162 [1955] 1 Ch. 309.

draftsman had failed to provide for this event. Harman J felt that the gap in the trusts declared could not be filled by construction because it was difficult to see clearly what it was that would have been inserted to cover that particular eventuality. His hesitancy was evident from his reluctance to fall back on to the resulting trust in such situations. He warned, "A resulting trust is the last resort to which the law has recourse when the draftsman has made a blunder or failed to dispose of that which he has set out to dispose of".[163] Nonetheless, Harman J could arrive at no other conclusion than that there must be a resulting trust of the income of the fund in favour of the settlors in proportion to their several interests. As to the property contributed by the husband, it passed to his estate.

Excluding the resulting trust

9-034

Obviously, no resulting trust can arise where property is deemed to be the subject of an absolute gift. In *Adams and Kensington Vestry*,[164] the testator left his estate to his wife, "in full confidence that she would do what was right as to the disposal thereof between my children, either in her lifetime, or by will after her decease". No trust arose to which the widow was subject; she was entitled to retain the property as an absolute gift to herself. In other cases there is an absolute gift of property onto which failed trusts are subsequently engrafted. In such a case the rule in *Hancock v Watson*[165] might apply. As Lord Davey explained:

> **"if you find an absolute gift to a legatee in the first instance, and trusts are engrafted or imposed on that absolute interest which fail, either from lapse or invalidity or any other reason, then the absolute gift takes effect so far as the trusts have failed to the exclusion of the residuary legatee or next-of-kin as the case may be".[166]**

The court will construe the language of the instrument as a whole to determine whether there has been an initial absolute beneficial gift onto which inconsistent trusts have been engrafted. In *Palmer v Simmonds*,[167] for example, a testatrix left her estate to her husband "for his own use and benefit", subject to a trust on his death to leave "the bulk of my residuary estate" to specific named relatives. As the engrafted trust failed for a lack of certainty of subject matter, the husband took the property absolutely. This was not the case in *Boyce v Boyce*, however, where mandatory words evidenced an intention to create a trust and not to provide an absolute gift to trustees in the first instance. It is only in those cases where the rule in *Hancock v Watson* will not apply that the property will be held on resulting trust.

---

163 [1955] 1 Ch. 309 at 316.
164 (1884) 27 Ch. D. 394.
165 [1902] A.C. 14.
166 [1902] A.C. 14 at 22.
167 (1854) 2 Drew. 221.

Outside the context of private trusts, the resulting trust has also assumed a prominent role in dealing with failed charitable gifts. A purported charitable trust will fail, for example, where the purposes described are not exclusively charitable. In *Morice v Bishop of Durham*,[168] property was provided for "charitable and benevolent" purposes, but the trust failed with the consequence of a resulting trust in favour of the settlor. In this context, however, the resulting trust is by no means an automatic consequence of the failure of the trust. As discussed in Ch.8, the cy-près doctrine can, in delimited circumstances, allow the application of the trust property to purposes "as near as possible" to the original purposes specified by the settlor. In cases where failure occurs before the property has been effectively dedicated to charity, a general charitable intention is required on the part of the donor in order to exclude the resulting trust.[169]

An interesting problem arose in *Re St Andrew's (Cheam) Lawn Tennis Club Trust*.[170] Here, land was purchased by a number of contributors to be held on charitable trust for the purpose of enabling club members to play tennis. When, some 70 years later, Arnold J declared this trust to be invalid ("an attempt to achieve the legally impossible: a perpetual trust for a non-charitable purpose, namely to enable the members of the club to play tennis"),[171] it fell to the court to determine who would be beneficially entitled. Arnold J noted that the acquisition of the land had been funded in four ways. First, there was a partial gift from Mr Tweddle who accepted a much reduced price for his land. Secondly, there was a partial gift from lenders by way of waived repayments. Thirdly, there were individuals who had contributed to fund-raising activities for the purpose of acquiring the land. Finally, funding was derived from the subscriptions paid by club members. Rejecting the possibility that the gifts might be construed as gifts to the members of the club as joint tenants or, in line with the contract holding theory,[172] to the existing members subject to their respective contractual rights and liabilities towards one another, Arnold J opted for a resulting trust analysis:

> "it seems to me that the correct conclusion to be drawn is that the land is held on a resulting trust for Mr Tweddle (or now his estate). It seems clear that the land would not have been acquired by the trustees . . . if he had not made his generous offer in 1948. Furthermore, Mr Tweddle appears to have been the largest single donor, and the donations made by the smaller donors were predicated upon Mr Tweddle's donation".[173]

It was a conclusion that served to prevent the land passing to the Crown as bona vacantia.

---

168 (1805) 10 Ves. 522.
169 See para.**8-003**.
170 [2012] 1 W.L.R. 3487 per Arnold J.
171 [2012] 1 W.L.R. 3487 at 3498.
172 See para.**6-034**.
173 [2012] 1 W.L.R. 3487 at 3502.

Unexhausted beneficial interest

9-035

The next failure of trust example involves the destination of property in the event that a trust has been performed and a surplus remains. Here, the desirability of the resulting trust can depend on the context in which the trust is created. Different policy concerns arise, for example, according to whether the trust is private or charitable. In addition, different obstacles are encountered where the surplus arises from the maintenance of individuals, public appeals, the dissolution of unincorporated associations or the complex commercial arena of over-funded pension trusts. Each will be considered in turn.

(i) Maintenance cases

9-036

A resulting trust arises in respect of any surplus remaining once the purposes of the trust have been carried out. However, no resulting trust will arise where the trust instrument explicitly excludes this possibility[174] or where an inference can be drawn that some other person was intended to take the property beneficially.[175] It is merely a general principle that where money is held on trust, and the trusts declared do not exhaust the fund, the surplus will revert back to the settlor under a resulting trust. *Re Trusts of the Abbott Fund*[176] provides a classic illustration where Dr Fawcett collected a sum of money, raising subscriptions from the public, and set up a fund to be applied for the relief of two ladies who were deaf and dumb. No provision was made as to the disposal of the ultimate surplus. It was argued that the balance of the fund belonged to the survivor of the two ladies, because the subscriptions were in the form of absolute gifts and the donors could never have intended a return of any unused funds. Stirling J, in a brief judgment, could not believe that the subscriptions were "ever intended to be an absolute gift to the ladies".[177] He denied that they would have been in a position to demand a transfer of the property to themselves or that in the case of bankruptcy, for example, such sums could be claimed by their trustee in bankruptcy. Accordingly, he upheld a resulting trust of the remaining sums to the subscribers of the Abbott Fund.

A different outcome was reached, however, in *Re Andrew's Trust*[178] wherein a fund was subscribed for the education of the children of a deceased clergyman. Once the formal education of the children was complete, the court was asked to consider the destination of the surplus funds. Unlike *Re Trusts of the Abbott Fund*, where the beneficiaries had died, the children in this case were still alive. Consequently, Kekewich J would not consider the purpose exhausted merely because the children had attained ages where "education in the vulgar sense" was no

---

174 *King v Denison* (1813) 1 Ves. & B. 260.
175 *Westdeutsche Landesbank Girozentrale v Islington LBC* [1996] A.C. 669 at 708.
176 [1900] 2 Ch. 326.
177 [1900] 2 Ch. 326 at 330.
178 [1905] 2 Ch. 48.

longer necessary.[179] Instead, he ascribed the broadest possible meaning to "education" and held that the children were entitled to what remained in equal shares. Unlike *Re Trusts of the Abbott Fund*, the overriding goal of benefiting the children could still be achieved.[180]

9-037

The Court of Appeal in *Re Osoba*[181] drew a similar conclusion. This case concerned a testamentary trust for the maintenance of the testator's widow, his mother, and "for the training of my daughter Abiola up to university grade". By the time the case was heard, both the widow and mother had died. Abiola, moreover, had been fully trained up to university level. It was held that the women took the fund as joint tenants and, on the death of two of the joint tenants, the daughter would succeed to the entire fund under the principle of survivorship. Clearly anxious to avoid the contrary conclusion, Buckley LJ felt that the testator had parted beneficially with the whole fund. As the subject matter was the testator's residue, any failure of the gift would result in intestacy which was most certainly not what the testator had intended.

For Megarry VC in the High Court in *Re Osoba*,[182] the presence or absence of living beneficiaries was a key distinction to be drawn between cases. He claimed:

> **"If a trust is constituted for the assistance of certain persons by certain stated means there is a sharp distinction between cases where the beneficiaries have died and cases where they are still living . . . if the beneficiaries are still living, the major purpose of providing help and benefit for the beneficiaries can still be carried out even after the stated means have all been accomplished, and so the court will be ready to treat the standard means as being indicative and not restrictive".[183]**

9-038

Where beneficiaries are alive, it appears, therefore, that the courts are reluctant to conclude other than that the expression of a purpose is merely an indicator of motive. A similar principle is at play in the context of gifts to persons on trust for purposes,[184] where the preferred approach of the courts is to construe the gift, where possible, as an absolute gift and prevent the resulting trust. This is evident in the rule of construction laid down in *Re Sanderson's Trust* where Page Wood VC claimed, "If a gross sum be given, or if the whole income of the property be given, and a special purpose be assigned for that gift, the court always regards the gift as absolute, and the purpose merely as the motive for that gift".[185] Thus, in *Re Bowes*[186] a gift of £5,000 on trust for the purpose of planting trees on an estate was construed as an absolute

---

179 [1905] 2 Ch. 48 at 53.
180 In the alternative, he was content to construe education as being merely the motive for the gift and that the intention was to provide for the children in the manner most useful.
181 [1979] 1 W.L.R. 247.
182 [1978] 1 W.L.R. 791.
183 [1978] 1 W.L.R. 791 at 796.
184 See para.**6-019**.
185 (1857) 3 K. & J. 497 at 503.
186 [1896] 1 Ch. 507.

gift to the estate owners, the purpose being no more than an expression of motive. In all cases, it will be a matter of construction as to whether the donor parted with his property out and out. As Lord Browne-Wilkinson clarified in the *Westdeutsche* case, if the donor has expressly or by necessary implication, abandoned any beneficial interest in the trust property, there is no resulting trust and the undisposed of equitable interest vests in the Crown as bona vacantia.

(ii) Disaster appeals

In the context of public appeals for good causes, a similar approach to *Re Trusts of the Abbott Fund* was adopted in *Re Gillingham Bus Disaster Fund* where the court upheld a resulting trust.[187] There an appeal was raised in 1951 in response to a road traffic accident in which 24 Royal Marine Cadets were killed, with a number of others suffering serious injuries. Publishing the appeal in a newspaper, the mayors of the surrounding towns avowed that the memorial fund would be devoted "to defraying the funeral expenses, caring for the boys who may be disabled, and then to such worthy causes in memory of the boys who lost their lives, as the Mayors may determine". A sum of nearly £9,000 was collected via methods such as large donations from known donors, street collections, football matches and whist drives. The trustees spent £2,368 on the stated purposes and then sought guidance from the court as to how the surplus should be applied. The alternatives were as follows:

- cy-près, that is, the surplus is available to apply to a charitable purpose as near as possible to the original charitable purpose;

- resulting trust, that is, the surplus is returnable to the donors because they are deemed to hold an interest in the undisposed-of property; and

- bona vacantia, where the surplus is deemed to be genuinely ownerless and it becomes available to the Crown.

Harman J was forced to discount the possibility of cy-près. The trust fund had not been devoted to purposes deemed exclusively charitable at law and the doctrine was, thereby, unavailable to the court. Of the two remaining alternatives, he opted for the resulting trust. He applied the general principle that where money is held upon trust and the trust does not exhaust the fund it will revert to the donor under a resulting trust. He explained that the reasoning is that, "the settlor or the donor did not intend to part with his money out and out . . .",[188] but only to the extent that his wishes could be carried into effect. Harman J emphasised that the doctrine did not rest upon evidence as to the state of mind of the donor. He explained that the resulting trust arises where the expectation is for some unforeseen reason cheated of fruition, and is an

9-039

---

187 [1958] Ch. 300.
188 [1958] Ch. 300 at 310.

inference of law based on after-knowledge of the event.[189] Three aspects of Harman J's judgment are worthy of note.

9-040

First, he deemed there to be no intention on the part of donors to contribute their money out and out. This, it is submitted, has the unfortunate practical consequence that bona vacantia is excluded and that all sums from anonymous donors are paid into court awaiting unlikely claims under a resulting trust. The strong inference of his judgment is that in a case where it can be said that a donor intends to part out and out with his donation, the destination of any surplus would be as bona vacantia.

Secondly, Harman J drew no distinction between different categories of donation. He saw no difference between the person who makes a small anonymous cash donation in a collecting tin and the person who makes a large personal contribution under his own name. As Harman J concluded:

> **"I see no reason myself to suppose that the small giver who is anonymous has any wider intention than the large giver who can be named. They all give for the one object. If they can be found by inquiry the resulting trust can be executed in their favour. If they cannot, I do not see how the money could then . . . change its destination and become bona vacantia".[190]**

Despite the intuitive appeal of his argument, it was considered and rejected by Goff J in *Re West Sussex Constabulary Fund*.[191] In that case, Goff J held that people who contribute to collection boxes make their contributions out and out. This excluded the possibility of a resulting trust and entitled the Crown to the money as bona vacantia on a failure of the trusts.

Although both *Re West Sussex Constabulary Fund* and *Re Gillingham Bus Disaster Fund* are first instance decisions (and, thus, an argument can be made as to which is to be preferred in this context), Goff J did embark on a careful review of authority where he encountered strong support for his view,[192] often forcefully expressed.[193] Admittedly, it is appropriate to acknowledge the different context from which such support is derived. Goff J's supporting authorities may be distinguishable on the ground that they deal with cases of charitable funds and the question whether surplus is available cy-près. As explained above, there was no possibility that the surplus could be applied cy-près in *Re Gillingham Bus Disaster Fund* because the purposes were not exclusively charitable.

---

189 [1958] Ch. 300 at 310.

190 [1958] Ch. 300 at 314.

191 [1971] Ch. 1.

192 *Re Hillier's Trusts* [1954] 1 W.L.R. 700 at 715 per Denning LJ (approving the approach of Upjohn J at first instance); *Re Welsh Hospital (Netley) Fund* [1921] 1 Ch. 655 at 659 per P.O. Lawrence J.

193 See, e.g. the views of P.O. Lawrence J who describes it to be "inconceivable" and "absurd" that a donor to a street collection did not part with money out and out ([1921] 1 Ch. 655 at 659).

Thirdly, Harman J failed to make explicit whether there is a distinction between the proceeds of entertainment and donations by collection tin or otherwise. There is specific mention of events such as whist drives, concerts and football matches, and it is unclear whether Harman J simply lumps the proceeds from these together with other donations as forming the subject matter of a resulting trust. In any event, the view postulated by Goff J in *Re West Sussex Constabulary Fund* is, on this point, almost certainly correct. There, he claimed it to be "impossible" to apply the doctrine of resulting trust to the proceeds of entertainment and sweepstakes.[194] Goff J's reasoning unfolds on two levels. His primary objection is that the relationship is one of contract and not of trust in that "the purchaser of a ticket may have the motive of aiding the cause or he may not; he may purchase the ticket merely because he wishes to attend the particular entertainment or to try for the prize, but whichever it be, he pays his money as the price of what is offered and what he receives".[195] Quite apart from this, Goff J could see no direct contribution to the fund at all. He observed, "It is only the profit, if any, which is ultimately received and there may even be none".[196]

The facts of *Re West Sussex Constabulary Fund* raise a separate issue as to the destination of surplus funds on the winding up of an unincorporated association. Whereas *Re Gillingham Bus Disaster Fund* concerned an appeal in respect of a specific tragic event, *Re West Sussex Constabulary Fund* concerned a fund set up to benefit the widows and dependants of deceased members of the West Sussex Constabulary, an unincorporated association. Notwithstanding this very different context, Goff J's conclusions are of obvious applicability to cases such as *Re Gillingham Bus Disaster Fund*, where a surplus remains on completion of a specific appeal. Outside the cases involving unincorporated associations, therefore, the exact role of the resulting trust remains arguable. To follow *Re Gillingham Bus Disaster Fund* would see the proceeds from entertainments and the contributions from donors held on resulting trust. In the view of Goff J in *Re West Sussex Constabulary Fund*, any surplus would go to the Crown as bona vacantia.

(iii) Unincorporated associations

The construction of gifts to unincorporated associations is dealt with in detail in Ch.6 where the pursuit of non-charitable purposes is discussed. It will be recalled that, unlike companies, these associations lack legal personality and cannot hold property in their own name. Consequently, the courts have struggled with the question of how such societies hold their property and, pertinently, what happens to it on dissolution. In this context, three differing approaches have enjoyed prominence: the resulting trust, bona vacantia and distribution in accordance with the contract between members.

---

194 [1971] 1 Ch. 1 at 11.
195 [1971] 1 Ch. 1 at 11.
196 [1971] 1 Ch. 1 at 11.

(a) Resulting trust

9-044

Historically, it was thought that the destiny of property on the dissolution of an unincorporated association would be determined by the resulting trust. In *Re Printers and Transferrers Amalgamated Trades Protection Society*,[197] for example, it fell to Byrne J to decide how the unexpended funds of a society, containing the unequal contributions of two classes of member (printers and transferrers), were to be distributed. He found the correct solution to be that "there is a resulting trust in favour of those who have contributed to these funds, and I think that the proper and legitimate way of dividing, therefore, will be in accordance with the amounts contributed by the existing members at the time of the passing of the resolution".[198] This principle was followed in *Re Lead Company's Workmen's Fund Society*[199] and is also evident in *Re Hobourn Aero Components Ltd's Air Raid Disaster Fund*.[200] In the latter case, it was held that any contributor to the disaster fund was entitled to an interest in the surplus under a resulting trust in proportion to the amount contributed, but subject to any adjustment made on the basis of a benefit derived from the fund.

(b) Bona vacantia

9-045

As to the bona vacantia approach, this was approved by the Court of Appeal in *Cunnack v Edwards*[201] (and it commended itself to Goff J in *Re West Sussex Constabulary Fund*). There, a society was established in 1801 to raise a fund by the subscriptions, fines and forfeitures of its members, in order to provide annuities for the widows of its deceased members. By 1879 all the members had died. On the passing of the last widow-annuitant in 1892, there was a large surplus fund. At first instance, Chitty J followed the established approach based on the resulting trust doctrine.[202] The Court of Appeal reversed his judgment. A.L. Smith LJ contended that as each member paid money to the society, "he divested himself of all interest in this money for ever, with this one reservation, that if the member left a widow she was to be provided for during her widowhood".[203] Rigby LJ also denied that the doctrine of resulting trust could aid the personal representatives of deceased members to claim entitlement. The members, he felt, were "persons who, under contracts or quasi-contracts with the society, secured for valuable consideration certain contingent benefits for their widows which could be enforced by the

---

197 [1899] 2 Ch. 184.
198 [1899] 2 Ch. 184 at 189.
199 [1904] 2 Ch. 196.
200 [1946] Ch. 86 per Cohen J (affirmed by the Court of Appeal [1946] Ch. 194).
201 [1896] 2 Ch. 679.
202 The Society was not a charity to which the doctrine of cy-près applied. The stark choice was that the surplus was held either on resulting trust for the personal representatives or as bona vacantia for the Crown.
203 [1896] 2 Ch. 679 at 683.

widows in the manner provided".[204] Consequently, they had received everything to which they were entitled. The surplus in *Cunnack v Edwards* was, therefore, available to the Crown as bona vacantia.

Similarly, in 1968, when the West Sussex Constabulary was amalgamated with other forces, it fell to Goff J to determine how its outstanding funds were to be dealt with. Goff J identified that the fund contained four different types of contribution: the contributions of past and present members; entertainments, raffles and sweepstakes; collecting boxes and donations and legacies. In relation to the funds derived from donations and legacies, Goff J identified the resulting trust as the appropriate response in respect of the surplus. All other contributions went as bona vacantia to the Crown. The past and present members had no claim to a return of contributions under a resulting trust because as widows and dependants they had received that to which they were entitled. This entailed for Goff J that there is no question of trust. In addition, the proceeds from entertainment raised an issue of contract, this time between the seller and the buyer. An additional obstacle was evident, moreover, in the fact that the money accrued would be in the nature of profit and not a direct contribution to the fund. Finally, in relation to the proceeds of collecting boxes, this category of contributor was taken to have parted with their money out and out. This ruled out the possibility of resulting trust.

9-046

(c) Contract holding theory

As regards the approach to dissolution based on the contract between members, *Re Bucks Constabulary Fund (No.2)*[205] is the principal authority. Although based on facts markedly similar to *Re West Sussex Constabulary Fund*, Walton J arrived at a strikingly different conclusion when he held that the members were entitled to the remaining property in equal shares. Walton J criticised Goff J's approach, determining that the remaining assets on the instant facts were held "to the total exclusion of any claim on behalf of the Crown".[206] According to the developed rules regarding property holding by unincorporated associations (the contract holding theory), the distribution of property on dissolution was to be governed by the contract between the members. This is because the funds are held subject to the contractual rights and liabilities between the members in accordance with the rules of their association. Even where the rules of the association are silent as to what should happen on dissolution, Walton J saw no residuary role for the resulting trust. Instead, he deemed there to be a presumption of equal division amongst the existing members.[207]

9-047

---

204 [1896] 2 Ch. 679 at 689.
205 [1979] 1 W.L.R. 936; see para.**6-039**.
206 [1979] 1 W.L.R. 936 at 951.
207 Note that in *St Andrew's (Cheam) Lawn Tennis Club Trust* [2012] 1 W.L.R. 3487 at [63], a resulting trust analysis was invoked as the only workable solution where a gift of land on trust which failed (the property was provided for a non-charitable purpose) could not be construed as a gift to the members as joint tenants or subject to their contractual rights and obligations.

9-048

In relation to each of the types of contribution identified by Goff J in *Re West Sussex Constabulary Fund*, it is readily apparent that Walton J would have reached a contrary conclusion. Even in the case of donations and legacies, it is strongly arguable that such contributions would be held subject to the contractual rights and liabilities of the members. In *Re Recher's WT*, for example, Brightman J explicitly considered the status of a donation from an outside source and also that of a legacy:

> **"In the case of a donation which is not accompanied by any words which purport to impose a trust, it seems to me that the gift takes effect in favour of the existing members of the association as an accretion to the funds which are the subject-matter of the contract which such members have made *inter se* . . . So, in the case of a legacy. In the absence of words which purport to impose a trust, the legacy is a gift to the members beneficially".[208]**

The approach of Walton J in *Re Bucks Constabulary Fund (No.2)* is consistent with the approach adopted in the general law towards property-holding by unincorporated associations and has been followed subsequently. In *Re GKN Bolts & Nuts Ltd*, for example, Megarry VC held that proceeds from the sale of a social club should be divided equally amongst those persons who were members of the club on the date of dissolution.[209] Similarly, in *Elvidge v Coulson*, Peter Smith J hailed as a statement of the general law that:

> **"the principles of trust and resulting trust do not generally govern the principles of distribution and dissolution . . . The rules are a contract whereby persons who become members of the association are entitled to benefit and their rights and their entitlements in the funds on dissolution are governed by that contract".[210]**

Although the area has yet to be considered by the appellate courts, it is hardly contentious to argue that, as regards unincorporated associations, *Re West Sussex Constabulary Fund* follows the wrong course.

9-049

Two further points are of interest. First, outside the context of unincorporated associations, say, where a surplus remains from a specific appeal, it may be that *Re West Sussex Constabulary Fund* is correctly decided. If so, and for the reasons explored above, contributions in the form of legacies and donations from identifiable donors would be held on resulting trust, whereas those from anonymous contributors and any proceeds from entertainments would go as bona vacantia. It must not be forgotten, however, that in *Re Gillingham Bus Disaster Fund*, Harman J

---

208 [1972] Ch. 526 at 539.
209 [1982] 1 W.L.R. 774.
210 [2003] EWHC 2089 (Ch) at [7].

makes a convincing case for treating as the same the contributions from identifiable donors and those (smaller) contributions from anonymous sources. It seems right that there is no compelling reason to distinguish the two on the grounds of intention. The only difference, he argues, is the ease with which their contribution can be returned. For Harman J the principled approach is payment into court awaiting claims under a resulting trust. In practical terms, nonetheless, the resulting trust is highly problematic. Bona vacantia is much to be preferred in view of the futility of awaiting the claims of anonymous contributors for miniscule sums. In this light, a review of key case law by the appellate courts would bring a welcome clarification of the law.

Secondly, as regards the dissolution of unincorporated associations, care should be taken to distinguish cases where members are in existence at the date of dissolution from those involving moribund societies (i.e. where all or all but one of the members had died). Where a society is moribund, Goff J accepted that the property would be genuinely ownerless and, accordingly, would go bona vacantia to the Crown. In *Hanchett-Stamford v Attorney General*,[211] however, only one identifiable member remained in an association that had ceased to exist. Lewison J declined to follow Goff J's approach preferring instead the view that Mrs Hanchett-Stamford had become absolutely entitled to the association's remaining assets.[212] It is worth noting also that the court has an inherent jurisdiction to order that an unincorporated association be dissolved. In *Keene v Wellcom London Ltd*,[213] 27 years of inactivity was not of itself enough to bring about dissolution. The court exercised its jurisdiction to dissolve the association and direct that its assets be distributed to the members in existence at that date pro rata according to their contributions.

(iv) Resulting trusts and pension funds

9-050

Much has been made of dicta in the context of pension trusts where a similar problem has arisen over what to do with overfunded pensions. In *Davis v Richards and Wallington Industries Ltd*,[214] Scott J considered the winding up of a pension fund that contained contributions from three specific sources: those of employers, those of employees and money transferred from other funds. His conclusions appear to cast doubt on the approach taken by Walton J in *Re Bucks Constabulary Fund (No.2)*.[215] As regards the employers' overpayments, he observed that these would be returnable under a resulting trust. By contrast, the employees' contributions would go as bona vacantia to the Crown. Scott J acknowledged that the fact that a party had received everything he had bargained for was not necessarily a decisive argument against a resulting trust. On the facts before him, however, there could be no resulting trust in favour of the employees. First, he could see no workable scheme to apportion the surplus contribu-

---

211 [2009] 2 W.L.R. 405.
212 See para.**6-040** for detailed discussion of the reasoning in this case.
213 [2014] EWHC 134 (Ch).
214 [1990] 1 W.L.R. 1511.
215 [1979] 1 W.L.R. 936.

tions amongst different classes of employee. Scott J would not "impute to them an intention that would lead to an unworkable result".[216] Secondly, no intention could be imputed to the employees that they should receive a surplus in excess of the maximum permitted by the rules governing administration of the scheme.

In *Air Jamaica v Charlton*,[217] the Privy Council criticised the approach adopted as to imputation of intention as "erroneous". In Lord Millet's view, it was not obvious, in the case of employees promised certain benefits under a scheme to which they had contributed, that they should be regarded as having no expectation of a return of any surplus. Lord Millett pointed out that a resulting trust cannot be avoided simply because there is no intention to retain the beneficial interest:

> **"Like a constructive trust, a resulting trust arises by operation of law, though unlike a constructive trust it gives effect to intention. But it arises whether or not the transferor intended to retain a beneficial interest—he almost always does not—since it responds to the absence of any intention on his part to pass the beneficial interest to the recipient. It may even where arise the transferor positively wished to part with the beneficial interest as in *Vandervell v IRC*".[218]**

9-051

Air Jamaica v Charlton, however, concerned the failure of certain trusts of a pension scheme which were void for perpetuity. On these facts, it was impossible to say that the members had received all that they had bargained for; the surplus arose through the invalidity of the trusts. A resulting trust for employers and employees was, therefore, upheld in proportion to their respective contributions. It arose by operation of law outside the pension scheme and outside the Jamaican tax legislation. In *Davis v Richards and Wallington Industries Ltd*, Scott J could find no workable scheme to apportion the surplus funds because he had felt it necessary to value the benefits that each member had received in order to ascertain their share. In *Air Jamaica v Charlton*, it was emphasised that no such process is required. Instead there should be a pro rata division between the members and the estates of deceased members in proportion to contributions made, without regard to benefits received and irrespective of the dates on which contributions were made.

It is unlikely that this approach as to the role for the resulting trust will impact outside the limited confines of surplus pension funds. Most schemes are statutorily regulated. Some are exceedingly complex and almost all will provide expressly for what should happen in the case of any surplus. Accordingly, it is advisable to hold as distinct to its particular subject matter the judicial pronouncements as to the role of resulting trusts in this context.

---

216   [1990] 1 W.L.R. 1511 at 1544.
217   [1999] 1 W.L.R. 1399.
218   [1999] 1 W.L.R. 1399 at 1412.

The *Quistclose*-style trust

It remains to consider the Quistclose-style trust. It will be recalled that Lord Browne-Wilkinson regarded the *Quistclose* trust as falling within his category "B".[219] It is fitting, therefore, that such trusts should be discussed in detail here. In addition to general principles and problems of classification, the use of *Quistclose*-style trusts in commercial transactions is also considered.

In the commercial context, implied trusts have become increasingly prevalent and are commonly deployed as a vehicle through which assets can be protected against the insolvency of the designated holder/trustee. For example, a lender may advance money to the recipient on condition that the money is used only for a specified purpose[220] with the result that beneficial property rights in those funds do not move from the lender unless and until the money is deployed for that specified purpose.[221] The consequence of this ploy is that the obligations in respect of the funds are such that those funds are put beyond the reach of the recipient's creditors. As Deputy Judge Michael Crystal put it in *Freeman v Commissioners for Customs & Excise*, "Company liquidations create many situations where it is claimed that a company's obligations have been transformed from contract into property, or from debt to trust, so that a claimant may claim property as his own rather than it being available for distribution amongst the general body of unsecured creditors".[222] Akin to a retention of title clause,[223] the basic idea is that money advanced for a specified purpose is impressed with a trust for that purpose and does not become the recipient's property.[224] As Patten LJ explained of the trust in *Bieber v Teathers Ltd*, it "continued to subsist until the monies had been applied in accordance with the purpose for which they were lent".[225] Until that time, the transferor's beneficial interest is maintained.

While proper account needs to be taken of the structure of the arrangements and the contractual mechanisms involved, the critical focus is upon the mutual and objectively evaluated intentions of the parties. There is no need for these intentions to be set out in writing,[226] but they must be communicated.[227] The key issue is whether the money transferred was

---

219 See para.**9-005**.

220 For example, to acquire brown field sites for building purposes (*Templeton Insurance Ltd v Penningtons Solicitors* [2006] All E.R. (D) 191 (Feb)); to effect the development of a unit on an industrial estate (*Gabriel v Little* [2013] EWCA Civ 1513); or to invest in a golf course in France (*Wise v Jimenez* unreported 11 October 2013).

221 Unsurprisingly, such loan documentation tends to include an express covenant to use the loan for a stated purpose.

222 [2005] EWHC 582 (Ch) at [10].

223 See generally K.C.F. Loi, "Quistclose trusts and Romalpa clauses: substance and *nemo dat* in corporate insolvency" (2012) 128 L.Q.R. 412.

224 As Lord Millett observed in *Twinsectra v Yardley* [2002] 2 A.C. 164 at 186: "It is unconscionable for a man to obtain money on terms as to its application and then disregard the terms on which he received it . . . This is a classic situation in which a fiduciary relationship arises, and since it arises in respect of a specific fund it gives rise to a trust".

225 [2012] EWCA Civ 1466 at [13].

226 *Bellis v Challinor* [2015] EWCA Civ 59.

227 As Briggs LJ explained in *Bellis v Challinor* [2015] EWCA Civ 59 at [59], "A person creates a trust by his words or conduct, not by his innermost thoughts". There must have been a clear communication of the intention that the

intended to become the absolute property of the recipient or, instead, continued to belong beneficially to the transferor.[228] As Patten LJ acknowledged, "It is therefore necessary to be satisfied not merely that the money when paid was not at the free disposal of the payee but that, objectively examined, the contractual or other arrangements properly construed were intended to provide for the preservation of the payer's rights and the control of the use of the money through the medium of a trust".[229] Hence, the central feature is not that the recipient is bound to apply the money for a specific purpose, but that he is precluded from misapplying it.[230]

9-053

This type of trust is illustrated most famously in *Barclays Bank v Quistclose Investments Ltd*.[231] Being in serious financial difficulty, Rolls Razor Ltd borrowed £209,000 from Quistclose Investments Ltd under an arrangement whereby the loan was to be paid only for the purposes of providing a dividend for shareholders that the company had already announced. The money was deposited in a specially created bank account at Barclays Bank to whom Rolls Razor was already heavily indebted to the tune of £484,000. Before the payment of the dividend, Rolls Razor went into voluntary liquidation. Quistclose claimed the money in the special account on the ground that the parties had created a trust and that, as its purpose had failed, the funds were to result back to itself.[232] The House of Lords held that the shared, objective intentions (of the payer and the recipient) must have been that the money was to be held on trust unless it was employed for the purpose specified. If the purpose had been achieved, Quistclose would have been treated like any other unsecured creditor of the company. As the specific purpose had now failed, however, the money was to be held for the benefit of Quistclose and not Barclays Bank.[233]

9-054

In Re *Lewis' of Leicester*,[234] floor space in a department store was rented out to a number of traders. The traders agreed that their takings would be placed in a separate bank account and, pending payment over, held by the store on trust for them. The store became insolvent and the traders successfully claimed their money in priority to the store's creditors. The agreement that the money be kept separate from the store's own funds was sufficient to infer the intention to create a trust.

---

money must be returned if that purpose is not fulfilled: *Stones v Financial Conduct Authority* [2019] EWHC 3345 (Ch).

228 See *Mundy v Brown* [2011] EWHC 377 (Ch) where the recipient never acquired beneficial title to the money advanced. The money could be used only as sanctioned and the recipient had no right to use it otherwise.

229 *Bieber v Teathers Ltd* [2012] EWCA Civ 1466 at [15]. Briggs LJ added in *Bellis v Challinor* [2015] EWCA Civ 59 at [57] that, "In this respect, *Quistclose*-type trusts are no different from any other trusts. In particular they are not presumed to exist unless a contrary intention be proved, as in the case of a traditional type of resulting trust where a person makes a gratuitous transfer of property to an apparent stranger".

230 *Stones v Financial Conduct Authority* [2019] EWHC 3345 (Ch).

231 [1970] A.C. 567; see W. Goodhart and G. Jones (1980) 43 M.L.R. 489.

232 As occurred in *Toovey v Milne* (1819) 2 B. & A. 683.

233 See also *Re Nanwa Gold Mines Ltd* [1955] 3 All E.R. 219 where subscription money for shares was invited on terms that the money would be refunded if the shares were not allotted, and in the meanwhile would be kept in a separate account.

234 [1995] 1 B.C.L.C. 428.

Similarly, in *Carreras Rothmans Ltd v Freeman Mathews Treasure Ltd*[235] Carreras Rothmans employed an advertising firm, Freeman Mathews Treasure Ltd, to place advertisements in the media. The Firm incurred substantial expenses and each month invoiced Carreras Rothmans for the liabilities it had incurred on their behalf. The Firm began to experience financial difficulties and Carreras Rothmans insisted that the Firm open a special bank account into which Carreras Rothmans would make their monthly payments. The Firm agreed that the money should be used only to discharge the debts associated with Carreras Rothmans' advertisement campaign. The Firm became insolvent at a time when there was a substantial amount of money in the special bank account. Under threat that its advertisements would not otherwise run in the media, Carreras Rothmans paid some debts directly and then sought to indemnify itself from the Firm's bank account. The Firm's liquidator, however, had other ideas. The High Court found in favour of Carreras Rothmans and held that a trust arose as soon as the money was paid into the special account. As Peter Gibson J put it:

> **"Equity fastens on the conscience of the person who receives from another property transferred for a specific purpose only and not therefore for the recipient's own purposes, so that such person will not be permitted to treat the property as his own or to use it for other than the stated purpose".**[236]

The overriding factor was that Carreras Rothmans had intended that the Firm be subject to an enforceable obligation only to apply the money for the specified purpose.

Segregation

Segregation of the money received is clearly a strong evidential indicator of the objective mutual intentions of the parties. It supports heavily the argument that the transferor was intended to retain a beneficial interest in the funds and, thereby, underscores the existence of an implied trust. In *Patel v Mirza*, Deputy Judge David Donaldson QC accepted that, "it will be difficult to conclude in favour of a trust, absent exceptional circumstances, unless the parties intend that the monies shall be held separately from the agent's own monies".[237] Without segregation, he felt that the finding of a trust will require powerful evidence.

9-055

In circumstances where the funds are mingled, an inferred trust is more difficult to establish. The absence of segregation tends to weaken the inference of an intention to restrict the payee's ability to deal with the money received.[238] As Watkins LJ admitted in *Re Clowes (No.2)*,

9-056

---

235 [1985] Ch. 207.
236 [1985] Ch. 207 at 222.
237 [2013] EWHC 1892 (Ch) at [46]. As the monies were mingled the Deputy Judge concluded that there was no positive evidence of a trust.
238 *Stones v Financial Conduct Authority* [2019] EWHC 3345 (Ch).

"a requirement to keep moneys separate is normally an indicator that they are impressed with a trust, and that the absence of such a requirement, if there are no other indicators of a trust, normally negatives it. The fact that a transaction contemplates the mingling of funds is, therefore, not necessarily fatal to a trust".[239] Accordingly, when the money has been mingled with other funds, the general assumption is that the transferor has relinquished all beneficial interest in the money advanced. It is, therefore, necessary for the transferor to prove a mutual intention that the money passing between them was not to be at the free disposal of the recipient.[240] It is not enough here that the transferor has paid the money to be used in a particular way and that the recipient has agreed to this arrangement.[241] This type of arrangement may give rise to personal obligations, but is alone insufficient to create fiduciary obligations or a trust.[242] Instead, the evidence must demonstrate that the objective mutual intentions of transferor and recipient (i.e. the essence of their bargain[243]) is that the money transferred must be used wholly and exclusively in a prescribed manner.[244]

9-057

In *Twinsectra Ltd v Yardley*,[245] Twinsectra decided to make a loan of £1 million to a property developer, Mr Yardley. It was decided that the loan would be paid directly to Mr Sims (a solicitor), who was already personally indebted to Mr Yardley to the sum of £1.5 million. Twinsectra demanded that Mr Yardley's solicitor provide an undertaking (i.e. guarantee) that the money would be retained by him and used only for the purposes of purchasing property for Mr Yardley. Mr Sims furnished the clear guarantee in his official capacity.[246] After receiving the money, however, Mr Sims paid it to Mr Yardley, who in turn used it for other purposes. Twinsectra then sued both Mr Sims and Mr Yardley, arguing the money was bound by a *Quistclose* style trust.[247] Although there had been no segregation of the funds, Lord Millett held that the limitations placed upon the use of the funds advanced demonstrated the existence of a trust. Under this trust, the solicitor (Mr Sims) held the money for the benefit of Twinsectra, subject to the power of the solicitor to use it for the purposes specified. Lord Millett explained:

---

239 [1994] 2 All E.R. 316 at 325.

240 In *Bellis v Challinor* [2015] EWCA Civ 59, money was paid into a solicitor's client account in order to fund a development project which never occurred. The Court of Appeal concluded that this was an immediate loan and that no resulting trust could arise.

241 It is, therefore, woefully inadequate for the transferor merely to express a general wish that the money be utilised in a particular way: *Blackburn v HM Revenue & Customs* [2008] EWHC 266 (Ch).

242 *Twinsectra Ltd v Yardley* [2002] 2 A.C. 164.

243 A variation on this theme was considered favourably by Briggs LJ in *Bellis v Challinor* [2015] EWCA Civ 59 at [62] when he accepted that the invitation might come from a third party. The example provided was where A says to B "if you transfer money to C it will only be used for a specified purpose". A *Quistclose* trust would be created if C knew of the terms of A's invitation.

244 *Bieber v Teathers Ltd* [2012] EWCA Civ 1466. There the terms of the contracts contradicted any argument that beneficial ownership of the monies did not pass.

245 [2002] 2 A.C. 164.

246 It read: "The loan moneys will be utilised solely for the acquisition of property on behalf of our client and for no other purposes".

247 As Mr Sims was now bankrupt, it was necessary to look elsewhere for the money, hence the dishonest assistance claim made by Twinsectra against Mr Yardley.

"Money advanced by way of loan normally becomes the property of the borrower. He is free to apply the money as he chooses, and save to the extent to which he may have taken security for repayment the lender takes the risk of the borrower's insolvency. But it is well established that a loan to a borrower for a specific purpose where the borrower is not free to apply the money for any other purpose gives rise to fiduciary obligations on the part of the borrower which a court of equity will enforce. In the earlier cases the purpose was to enable the borrower to pay his creditors or some of them, but the principle is not limited to such cases".[248]

Lessons from case law

Other illustrative cases include:

9-058

- *Re EVTR*[249] in which the appellant, who had won around £250,000 on premium bonds, loaned £60,000 to his former employer. The loan was on condition that new equipment would be purchased. The company paid over the money to the supplier. Before the equipment arrived, however, the company became insolvent. The supplier then returned £48,000 to the company and the issue was whether this money was available to the company's creditors or was held on trust for the appellant. The Court of Appeal determined that a trust had been created and that, as the purpose of the loan failed, the refunded money was still subject to the trust in favour of the appellant.[250] As to the fact that the £60,000 had already been paid over to the suppliers, Dillon LJ commented, ". . . but that was only at half-time, and I do not see why the final whistle should be blown at half-time".[251] Bingham LJ agreed and spoke of giving effect to "the common fairness of the situation".[252] Nevertheless, this decision is open to the criticism that any trust should have been extinguished on the payment to the suppliers (i.e. full time had already passed). It is to be appreciated that, if the new machinery had been delivered before the insolvency, the trust would have been discharged and the company's creditors would have had priority over the appellant.

---

248 [2002] 2 A.C. 164 at 184. There must be, as Lord Mustill added in *Re Goldcorp Exchange Ltd* [1995] 1 A.C. 74 at 100, "either a mutual intention that the monies should not fall within the general fund of the company's assets but should be applied for a specified designated purpose, or that having originally been paid over without restriction the recipient has constituted himself a trustee of the money".
249 (1987) B.C.L.C. 646.
250 As Dillon LJ concluded, "a resulting trust in favour of the provider of the money arises when the money is provided for a particular purpose only, and that purpose fails" ((1987) B.C.L.C. 646 at 650).
251 (1987) B.C.L.C. 646 at 651; see also, *R. v Common Professional Examinations Board, The Times* 19 April 2000 (CA).
252 (1987) B.C.L.C. 646 at 652.

It is, however, arguable that a different outcome would arise if the goods had been delivered in a defective state and returned to the supplier before the insolvency.

■ *Neste Oy v Lloyds Bank Plc*[253] concerned a shipowner that paid money to an agent so that the agent could defray expenses incurred on its behalf. The funds were paid into the agent's general bank account. After the agent ceased trading, the shipowner made a further payment. It was held that an implied trust attached to this final payment and that, regardless of the parties' actual intentions, the beneficial interest remained with the shipowner. The reasoning was that an honest recipient of the last payment would have returned the money immediately.

■ *Cooper v PRG Powerhouse Ltd*[254] involved a director paying £34,239 to the company in order that it would discharge his debt relating to the purchase of a Mercedes car. The money was placed in the company's payroll account and a cheque was duly forwarded to the creditor. Unfortunately, the company went into liquidation before the cheque cleared. The company's general creditors claimed that the £34,239 was available for them. Mr Cooper argued that a so-called "purpose trust" had been created. Evans-Lombe J identified the key issue as being whether the money had been at the free disposal of the company. Although the funds had not been kept in a separate account, the transfer was impressed with a purpose trust. Evans-Lombe J concluded that "There was clearly to be implied into the arrangement that neither Mr Cooper nor the Company regarded the amount of the payment as part of the assets of the Company at its 'free disposal' and available, in particular, as working capital or for the payment of its creditors".[255]

■ *Dubey v HM Revenue & Customs*[256] produced a very different outcome. There the High Court rejected an implied trust in favour of the customers of the ill-fated Farepak Food & Gifts Ltd. The case dealt with the consequences for customers of Farepak following the Company's insolvency. Although the customers had made advance payments to Farepak's agents for acquiring Christmas hampers and vouchers and those specific purposes were not fulfilled by the Company, this was not a *Quistclose*-style trust.[257] Mann J based this rejection on two grounds. First, the agents were never obliged to keep the customers' money separate from other money. Secondly, there was no obligation upon Farepak to put the money on one side pending the dispatch of the customers' orders. Mann J observed that:

253 [1983] 2 Lloyds Rep. 658.
254 [2008] EWHC 498 (Ch).
255 [2000] EWHC 498 (Ch) at [24].
256 [2006] EWHC 3272 (Ch). See also *Re I* [2007] EWHC 2025 (Admin) where there was no mutual intention that the customers' money should not form part of the recipient's ordinary business cash flow.
257 The Law Commission, *"Consumer Prepayments on Retailer Insolvency"* (2016), Law Com. No.368 has made various recommendations intended to protect more effectively the purchaser in these pre-payment cases.

"If there were a *Quistclose*-style trust then that obligation would have been inherent in it, but the business model would have made no sense. It would have required Farepak to have kept all the customer moneys in a separate account from January until November, untouched until the time when the goods and vouchers were acquired and then sent out. That is completely implausible. It would turn Farepak into a very odd savings organisation. Even banks do not have to do that".[258]

The approach of Mann J appears correct. The money was part of the working capital of the company and at its free disposal. The entitlement of the disappointed customers lay in contract and not trust law.[259]

- *First City Monument Bank Plc v Zumax Nigeria Ltd*[260] where a company made various bank transfers to a Nigerian bank. The issue was whether the transfers were impressed with a *Quistclose* style trust. The Court of Appeal emphasised that a *Quistclose* trust requires more than mere payment for a specific purpose. Payments are routinely made in advance for particular goods and services, but do not constitute trust monies in the recipient's hands. Instead, the core issue is whether the parties intended the money to be at the free disposal of the recipient. The basic banker–customer relationship is one of debtor and creditor and not that of trustee and beneficiary. The present funds had not been segregated in any meaningful way and there was no intention that the particular money should not be at the free disposal of the Bank. The fact that a transfer may have been made for a particular purpose did not of itself mean that it was the subject of a trust. The Bank received the monies as the agent of its customer to whom it owed duties arising from their contractual relationship.

Understanding the *Quistclose*-style trust

Unsurprisingly, the *Quistclose* style trust can arise in many factual settings and the likelihood is that, as Parkinson points out, "the *Quistclose* trust will eventually come to be understood as an umbrella term for a variety of kinds of trust concerned with limitations of an equitable character placed on the use of money . . .".[261] The law will, therefore, develop by analogy. The legal

9-059

---

258 [2006] EWHC 3272 (Ch) at [34].
259 As Lord Millett put it in *Twinsectra v Yardley* [2002] 2 A.C. 164 at 185, "Similarly payments in advance for goods or services are paid for a particular purpose, but such payments do not ordinarily create a trust. The money is intended to be at the free disposal of the supplier and may be used as part of his cash flow. Commercial life would be impossible if this were not the case".
260 [2019] EWCA Civ 294.
261 P. Parkinson, "Reconceptualising the Express Trust" (2002) C.L.J. 657, 662, 663; see also Judge Hodge in *Gore v Mishcon De Reya* [2015] EWHC 164 (Ch) at [32].

nature of this trust has, not surprisingly, been subject to major debate both on these shores and in the Commonwealth.[262] As Briggs LJ admitted, "its jurisprudential analysis remained rather uncertain for many years".[263] In *Barclays Bank v Quistclose*, Lord Wilberforce spoke in terms of there being two trusts: a primary trust to pay the dividend (i.e. one in favour of the shareholders of Rolls Razor) and a secondary trust which would arise if the primary trust could not be carried out (i.e. one in favour of Quistclose).[264] Several difficulties, however, emerge from Lord Wilberforce's approach:

■ Lord Wilberforce did not consider whether the primary trust should properly be clas-sified as a private purpose trust and, therefore, potentially void. This has encouraged some to advance the proposition that the primary trust is a non-charitable purpose trust under which the beneficial interest is in suspense until the purpose is satisfied.[265] It is, however, best viewed as a power to apply the money for a specified purpose.[266]

■ Lord Wilberforce did not explain where the beneficial interest was to lie in the money during the period between its transfer and the failure of the primary purpose.

■ Lord Wilberforce did not make clear whether the two trusts were express trusts or implied trusts. Some have viewed them as being express trusts because of the finding of a declared intention that a trust relationship exists.[267] Others, however, have viewed them as implied trusts.[268] Additional difficulty arises as to whether these implied trusts (if they may be so properly categorised) should be classified as resulting or con-structive trusts.[269]

Much needed clarification was provided by Lord Millett in a lengthy dissenting speech in

---

262 See generally, W. Swadling (ed.), *The Quistclose Trust: Critical Essays* (Oxford: Hart Publishing, 2004); see also J.A. Glister, "The Nature of Quistclose Trusts: Classification and Reconciliation" [2004] C.L.J. 632.
263 *Bellis v Challinor* [2015] EWCA Civ 59 at [54].
264 [1970] A.C. 567 at 580; see also, the analysis of Lord Browne-Wilkinson in *Westdeutsche Landesbank Girozentrale v Islington BC* [1996] A.C. 669 at 708.
265 See Megarry VC in *Re Northern Development Holdings* unreported 6 October 1978 and Peter Gibson J in *Carreras Rothmans Ltd v Freeman Mathews Treasure Ltd* [1985] Ch. 207.
266 *Bellis v Challinor* [2015] EWCA Civ 59 at [63].
267 See, e.g. *Re Northern Development Holdings* unreported 6 October 1978, where a group of banks paid money into an account (in Northern Development's name) for the sole purpose of discharging the liability of Northern Development's subsidiary company to its general creditors. The money that was unused was held under a *Quistclose*-type trust for the benefit of the banks.
268 Although largely of academic interest, this classification does assume importance where the subject matter of the trust is land or an existing equitable interest. This is because s.53(1)(b),(c) of the Law of Property Act 1925 imposes added formalities for the enforcement and creation of such trusts if they are expressly created. By virtue of s.53(2), these formalities do not, however, apply to implied trusts.
269 For a discussion of alternative analyses, see C. Rickett, "Different Views on the Scope of the Quistclose Analysis" (1991) 107 L.Q.R. 608.

Twinsectra v Yardley, where he concluded that there was only one trust and that the lender of the money was the beneficiary under that trust.[270] Lord Millett claimed that this trust was, "an entirely orthodox example of the kind of default trust known as a resulting trust . . .".[271] His reasoning was that the recipient of the funds holds those funds on trust for the person who made the advance subject to a power to use the money only for a specified purpose.[272] It appears, therefore, that these types of trust fall properly to be regarded as a single resulting trust that comes into existence as soon as the money is paid over to the recipient.

This entails that:

9-060

■ the donor/lender does not pass over the beneficial interest in the money until the funds are applied for the purpose stipulated. It is only at that point that the trust is discharged. The claim of the transferor will from then onwards lie only in contract[273];

■ if the money is never applied for the specified purpose then, as Lord Millett explained in *Twinsectra*, "[T]he money is returnable to the lender, not under some new trust in his favour which only comes into being on the failure of the purpose, but because the resulting trust in his favour is no longer subject to any power . . . to make use of the money".[274] Accordingly, if a firm of solicitors gives an undertaking that a client's money can be used only for a specific purpose the firm cannot use any surplus for other purposes, including the payment of its own costs and expenses. [275] The money cannot be applied for unspecified purposes;

■ there is no need to analyse this style of trust as being a private purpose trust. Due to Lord Millett's view that the beneficial interest remains throughout with the lender, it does not matter whether the trust is regarded as an abstract purpose trust or a trust to benefit an ascertainable class of beneficiaries. Lord Millett's analysis explodes the myth that the beneficial interest is somehow maintained in suspense until the purpose either fails or is performed and that the lender merely retains a contractual right (enforceable by injunction) to restrain misapplication.[276]

---

270 [2002] 2 A.C. 164. Lords Hutton & Steyn agreed with this aspect of Lord Millett's reasoning. The earlier view expressed by Peter Gibson J in the *Carreras Rothmans* case to the effect that the beneficiary was the intended recipient was rejected.

271 [2002] 2 A.C. 164 at 192; see also *Blackburn v HM Revenue & Customs* [2008] EWHC 266 (Ch).

272 Writing extra-judicially, Lord Millett had previously explained ((1985) 101 L.Q.R. 269, 269) that "A loan by A to B for a specific purpose, where B is not free to apply the money for any other purpose, gives rise to a fiduciary obligation on the part of B which a court of equity will enforce".

273 As Lord Millett wrote ((1985) 101 L.Q.R. 269, 270), "This prevents B from obtaining any beneficial interest in the money, at least while the designated purpose is still capable of being carried out. When it is carried out . . . A becomes a loan creditor of B and has his normal remedy in debt".

274 [2002] 2 A.C. 164 at 192.

275 *Templeton Insurance Ltd v Penningtons Solicitors* [2006] All E.R. (D) 191 (Feb).

276 Potter LJ sponsored the latter argument at the Court of Appeal stage of the *Twinsectra* litigation ([1999] Lloyd's Rep. Bank 438 at 456).

Guide to Further Reading

J. Glister, "Section 199 of the Equality Act 2010: How Not to Abolish the Presumption of Advancement" (2010) 73 M.L.R. 807.

J. Mee, "The Past, Present and Future of Resulting Trusts" (2017) 70 C.L.P. 189.

J. Mee, "Resulting Trusts and Voluntary Conveyances of Land" [2012] Conv. 307.

P. Millett, "The *Quistclose* Trust and Who Can Enforce It" (1985) 101 L.Q.R. 269.

C.E.F. Rickett, "Different Views on the Scope of the Quistclose Analysis" (1991) 107 L.Q.R. 608.

C.E.F. Rickett and R. Grantham, "Resulting Trusts—The True Nature of the Failing Trust Cases" (2000) 116 L.Q.R. 15.

W. Swadling, "Explaining Resulting Trusts" (2008) 124 L.Q.R. 72.

G. Virgo, "*Patel v Mirza*: one step forward and two steps back" (2016) 22(10) T. & T. 1090.

T.M. Yeo, H. Tijo, "The *Quistclose* Trust" (2003) 119 L.Q.R. 8.

10

Constructive Trusts

10-001

Like the resulting trust (considered in Ch.9), the constructive trust is a form of implied trust that arises by operation of law and not by the deliberate act of the parties.[1] No formalities are required for its creation.[2] It is a trust implied in a variety of circumstances where the defendant has knowledge of some factor that affects his conscience in respect of specific property.[3] In the words of Costello J, "The principle is that where a person who holds property in circumstances which in equity and good conscience should be held or enjoyed by another he will be compelled to hold the property in trust for another".[4] The circumstances in which the constructive trust will be encountered are many and varied.[5] It follows that the constructive trust is notoriously difficult to define. As Edmund Davies LJ admitted in *Carl Zeiss Stiftung v Herbert Smith & Co*, "English law provides no clear and all-embracing definition of a constructive trust. Its boundaries have been left perhaps deliberately vague, so as not to restrict the court by technicalities in deciding what the justice of a particular case may demand".[6] It is clear, nonetheless, that the general trigger activating the constructive trust is unconscionability. Equity acts in personam to "construe" the defendant to be a trustee of property when he has knowledge of some factor that affects his conscience. Typically, equity is seen to intervene to

---

1 See Y.K. Liew, *Rationalising Constructive Trusts* (Oxford: Hart Publishing, 2017).
2 The constructive trust is exempt from the requirement of writing laid down in s.53(1) of the Law of Property Act 1925.
3 *Westdeutsche Landesbank Girozentrale v Islington LBC* [1996] A.C. 669.
4 *HKN Invest OY v Incotrade PVT Ltd* [1993] 3 I.R. 152 at 162.
5 As Lord Scott acknowledges in *Cobbe v Yeoman's Row Management Ltd* [2008] 1 W.L.R. 1752 at 1769, "It is impossible to prescribe exhaustively the circumstances sufficient to create a constructive trust but it is possible to recognise particular factual circumstances that will do so and also to recognise other factual circumstances that will not".
6 [1969] 2 Ch. 276 at 300.

remedy wrongful actions[7] or to give effect to an agreement between the parties upon which the claimant has relied.[8]

Constructive Trusts

10-002

The most notable analysis of the basis of the constructive trust is that of Lord Browne-Wilkinson in *Westdeutsche Landesbank Girozentrale v Islington LBC*.[9] The case concerned payments made under an interest rate swap agreement between a bank and a local authority.[10] The agreement entered into in 1987 was intended to run over a period of 10 years. In 1992, however, the House of Lords ruled that such agreements were ultra vires and void ab initio.[11] The Bank sought to recover the money paid to the local authority on the basis that the local authority was a constructive trustee. Lord Browne-Wilkinson held that from the point of entry into the transaction until the point at which the property ceased to be traceable, both parties believed they had entered into a valid contract. There was nothing to affect the conscience of the local authority and, accordingly, no basis upon which to impose a constructive trust. Lord Browne-Wilkinson laid down the following general principles:

> **"(i) Equity operates on the conscience of the owner of the legal interest. In the case of a trust, the conscience of the legal owner requires him to carry out the purposes for which the property was vested in him (express or implied trust) or which the law imposes on him by reason of his unconscionable conduct (constructive trust).**
>
> **(ii) Since the equitable jurisdiction to enforce trusts depends upon the conscience of the holder of the legal interest being affected, he cannot be a trustee of the property if and so long as he is ignorant of the facts alleged to affect his conscience, i.e. until he is aware that he is intended to hold the property for the benefit of others in the case of an express or implied trust, or, in the case of a constructive trust, of the factors which are alleged to affect his conscience.**

7   For example, in the case of property obtained by unlawful killing.
8   For example, the common intention constructive trust: see Ch.11.
9   [1996] A.C. 669.
10   An agreement whereby each party agrees to pay the other an amount calculated by reference to the interest that would have accrued over a given period on a notional principal sum.
11   *Hazell v Hammersmith and Fulham BC* [1992] 2 A.C. 1.

(iii) In order to establish a trust there must be identifiable trust property. The only apparent exception to this rule is a constructive trust imposed on a person who dishonestly assists in a breach of trust who may come under fiduciary duties even if he does not receive identifiable trust property.

(iv) Once a trust is established, as from the date of its establishment the beneficiary has, in equity, a proprietary interest in the trust property, which proprietary interest will be enforceable in equity against any subsequent holder of the property (whether the original property or substituted property into which it can be traced) other than a purchaser for value of the legal interest without notice".[12]

At its core, therefore, the constructive trust requires the defendant to have knowledge of factors which affect his conscience such that he is prevented from asserting his own sole beneficial entitlement to the property in question. At this level of generality, there appears much scope for the invocation of a constructive trust whether in a remedial capacity or where the justice of the case demands. Nonetheless, the English constructive trust should not be viewed as a remedial device imposed at the discretion of the court. Developed rules determine its invocation, as is evident from a close evaluation of its nature and incidents.

Institutional or remedial?

Constructive trusts may be institutional or remedial in nature (these terms are explained below).[13] Unlike other jurisdictions, however, English law recognises only the former, i.e. what is sometimes termed the "institutional constructive trust". As Lord Browne-Wilkinson further observed:

"Under an institutional constructive trust, the trust arises by operation of law as from the date of the circumstances which give rise to it: the function of the court is merely to declare that such trust has arisen in the past. The consequences that flow from such trust having arisen (including the possibly unfair consequences to third parties who in the interim have received the trust property) are also determined by rules of law, not under a discretion".[14]

---

12 *Westdeutsche Landesbank Girozentrale v Islington LBC* [1996] A.C. 669 at 705.
13 See further Y. K. Liew, "Reanalysing Institutional and Remedial Constructive Trusts" (2016) 75(3) C.L.J. 528.
14 [1996] A.C. 669 at 714.

Rather than the court imposing or creating a remedy by way of a response to the defendant's wrong, the institutional constructive trust is a substantive constructive trust where the court deems the acts of the parties already to have brought the trust into being. We will see that the obligation of trustees under express trusts is determined through the express terms of the trust instrument and also under the general law.[15] The obligations of constructive trustees will, by contrast, reflect the circumstances in which the trust has arisen.[16] Necessarily, the court is acutely aware that a constructive trustee in a pre-existing fiduciary relationship to the claimant will already have assumed onerous obligations as part of an ongoing professional relationship to the claimant. The imposition of similar levels of liability is patently unsuitable, say, where the defendant is an individual who is credited with an overpayment of the claimant's money or the payment of money by mistake. In each case, the court will determine the specific obligations of the constructive trustee when it acts to recognise the claimant's pre-existing rights.

For Lord Browne-Wilkinson in *Westdeutsche*, the distinction between institutional and remedial trusts was simple to state. Of the remedial constructive trust, he claimed, "It is a judicial remedy giving rise to an enforceable equitable obligation: the extent to which it operates retrospectively to the prejudice of third parties lies in the discretion of the court".[17] A principal practical distinction between the different forms of constructive trust lies in the date at which the claimant may assert proprietary rights. Under the institutional version, the court merely confirms the pre-existing proprietary interest in effect before the order of the court. Under the remedial constructive trust, the court creates a remedy by order of the court and exercises discretion to determine any retrospective effect. This matter of timing is of obvious relevance to third parties who acquire an interest in the property before the order of the court.

10-005

Outside England and Wales, the approach adopted in countries such as the United States is to regard the constructive trust as a remedial instrument imposed, broadly speaking, when the constructive trustee has been unjustly enriched in some way. As Cardozo J once put it, the constructive trust is thereby a "formula through which the conscience of equity finds expression".[18] It is difficult to ignore the refusal of the English courts to develop the law in line with the approach of other jurisdictions. On many occasions the remedial constructive trust has been rejected outright[19] or it has been clearly emphasised that "English law has not followed other jurisdictions where the constructive trust has become a remedy for unjust enrichment".[20] Such reluctance is, perhaps, underpinned by the fear that future equitable

---

15 See Ch.13.

16 As Millett LJ warned in *Lonrho Plc v Al-Fayed (No.2)* [1992] 1 W.L.R. 1 at 12, "it is a mistake to suppose that in every situation in which a constructive trust arises the legal owner is necessarily subject to all the fiduciary obligations and disabilities of an express trustee".

17 *Westdeutsche Landesbank Girozentrale v Islington LBC* [1996] A.C. 669 at 714.

18 *Beatty v Guggenheim Exploration Co* (1919) 225 NY 380 at 385; see also Restatement of Restitution: "Where a person holding title to property is subject to an equitable duty to convey it to another on the ground that he would be unjustly enriched if he were permitted to retain it, a constructive trust arises" (American Law Institute, 1937, para.160).

19 See, *for example, Angove's Pty Ltd v Bailey* [2016] UKSC 47.

20 *Halifax Building Society v Thomas* [1996] Ch. 217 at 229.

intervention must be principled as well as flexible. For Nourse LJ, it is simply unpalatable to grant a proprietary right by way of remedy to someone who, beforehand, had no such right. His objection is based on the established principle that property rights can be varied only by statute. As he emphasised in *Re Polly Peck International Plc (In Administration) (No.2)*, "you cannot grant a proprietary right to A who has not had it beforehand, without taking some proprietary right away from B. No English court has ever had the power to do that, except with the authority of Parliament".[21]

Notwithstanding, this consistent rejection by the courts,, Lord Browne-Wilkinson adopted a more positive stance in *Westdeutsche*, raising the possibility of future reform. He argued:

> **"Although the resulting trust is an unsuitable basis for developing proprietary restitutionary remedies, the remedial constructive trust, if introduced into English law, may provide a more satisfactory road forward. The court by way of remedy might impose a constructive trust on a defendant who knowingly retains property of which the plaintiff has been unjustly deprived. Since the remedy can be tailored to the circumstances of the particular case, innocent third parties would not be prejudiced and restitutionary defences, such as change of position, are capable of being given effect. However, whether English law should follow the United States and Canada by adopting the remedial constructive trust will have to be decided in some future case when the point is directly in issue".[22]**

Nonetheless, since the particular rejection of those ideas in the Supreme Court in *FHR European Ventures LLP v Cedar Capital Partners LLC*,[23] Lord Neuberger has since made his views abundantly clear, claiming extra-judicially,

> **"There is much to be said for the notion of a remedial constructive trust displays equity at its flexible flabby worst. I will seek to show, at least arguably, that it is unprincipled, incoherent and impractical, that it renders the law unpredictable, that it is an affront to the common law view of property rights and interests, that it involves the court usurping the role of the legislature, and, as if that were not enough, that the development of the remedial constructive trust is largely unnecessary. Apart from that, it's a pretty good concept."[24]**

---

21   [1998] 3 All E.R. 812 at 830.
22   *Westdeutsche Landesbank Girozentrale v Islington LBC* [1996] A.C. 669 at 716.
23   [2015] AC 250.
24   Lord Neuberger, "The Remedial Constructive Trust—Fact or Fiction", delivered to the Banking Services and Financial Law Association Conference, Queenstown (10 August 2014), para.6: see *https://www.supremecourt. uk/docs/speech-140810.pdf* [Accessed 31 July 2020].

10-006

It remains only to note the efforts (principally) of Lord Denning, during the 1970s to introduce a remedial constructive trust to this jurisdiction. It took the form of a constructive trust "of a new model".[25] In *Hussey v Palmer*, Lord Denning described it as a "trust imposed by law whenever justice and good conscience require it . . . It is an equitable remedy by which the court can enable an aggrieved party to obtain restitution".[26] The "new model" constructive trust failed to become established on the basis that Lord Denning's broad concepts of justice and good conscience lacked the necessary circumscription to cater for a principled and certain law. Criticism of the new model was forthcoming both here[27] and abroad.[28] As Dillon LJ memorably explained, "The court does not yet sit, as under a palm tree, to exercise a general discretion to do what the man in the street, on a general overview of the case, might regard as fair".[29]

Constructive trusts of two types

10-007

The remaining distinction of relevance to the forthcoming illustrations of constructive trusts is that put forward by Millett LJ in *Paragon Finance Plc v Thakerar & Co*.[30] There he drew a distinction between two classes of constructive trust that is, arguably, indicative of the problems of classification and definition that pervade the current law.[31]

He explained that the first type concerns cases where the defendant, although not expressly appointed as trustee, assumes the duties of a trustee by an earlier, independent lawful transaction which is not impeached by the plaintiff. As he put it:

> "the constructive trustee really is a trustee. He does not receive the trust property in his own right but by a transaction by which both parties intend to create a trust from the outset and which is not impugned by the plaintiff. His possession of the property is coloured from the first by the trust and confidence by means of which he obtained it, and his subsequent appropriation of the property to his own use is a breach of that trust. In these cases the plaintiff does not impugn the transaction by which the defendant obtained control of the property. He alleges that the circumstances in which the defend-

---

25 *Eves v Eves* [1975] 1 W.L.R. 1338.
26 [1972] 3 All E.R. 744 at 747.
27 See e.g. the approach of Fox LJ in *Ashburn Anstalt v Arnold* [1989] Ch.1.
28 See *Allen v Snyder* [1977] 2 N.S.W.L.R. 685 at 701, where it was claimed that "the legitimacy of the new model is at least suspect; at best it is a mutant from which further breeding should be discouraged".
29 *Springette v Defoe* [1992] 2 F.L.R. 388 at 393.
30 [1999] 1 All E.R. 400.
31 As Lord Sumption has noted recently in *Williams v Central Bank of Nigeria* [2014] UKSC 10 at [7], "there are few areas in which the law has been so completely obscured by confused categorisation and terminology as the law relating to constructive trustees".

10-008

> ant obtained control make it unconscionable for him thereafter to
> assert a beneficial interest in the property".[32]

The second type concerns cases where the trust obligation arises because of an unlawful transaction which is subsequently impeached by the plaintiff. It was never envisaged that the recipient would hold property as a trustee. As Millett LJ observed, "The second class of case is different. It arises when the defendant is implicated in a fraud".[33]

As to Millett LJ's adopted classification, the purpose served in distinguishing between his two types of trust lies in the application of statutory limitation periods in cases of breach of trust, where the limits to the liability of strangers to the trust has assumed relevance.[34] Detailed discussion of applicable limitation periods may be found in Ch.17.[35]

The liability of strangers to account in equity is a form of personal liability commonly described in terms of constructive trusteeship. It is encountered in two principal situations. The first is where the defendant receives property in the knowledge that receipt is pursuant to a breach of trust (knowing receipt) and, secondly, where the defendant dishonestly assists in a breach of trust (dishonest assistance). In the latter example, the language of constructive trusteeship is apt to confuse. No trust property vests in the defendant. He is merely an accessory to a trustee's breach of trust, but he is liable to account in equity as though he were a trustee.[36] As explained above, Lord Browne-Wilkinson treated, as an "apparent exception" to the rule regarding identifiable trust property, the imposition of the constructive trust on the dishonest assistant.[37] Nonetheless, the fictional nature of the constructive trust has led to convincing calls for replacement terminology. Notably, Lord Millett claimed:

> "Equity gives relief against fraud by making any person sufficiently implicated in the fraud accountable in equity. In such a case he is traditionally (and I have suggested unfortunately) described as a 'constructive trustee' and is said to be 'liable to account as a constructive trustee'. But he is not in fact a trustee at all, even though he may be liable to account as if he were. He never claims to assume the position of trustee on behalf of others, and he may be liable without ever receiving or handling the trust property . . . In this second class of case the expressions 'constructive trust' and 'constructive trustee' create a trap . . . I think that we should now discard the words

32   [1999] 1 All E.R. 400 at 408.
33   [1999] 1 All E.R. 400 at 408.
34   See, generally, *Williams v Central Bank of Nigeria* [2014] UKSC 10.
35   See para.**17-027**.
36   As Ungoed-Thomas J put it in *Selangor v Cradock (No.3)* [1968] 1 W.L.R. 1555 at 1579, the imposition of a constructive trust is "nothing more than a formula for equitable relief. The court of equity says that the defendant shall be liable in equity, as though he were a trustee"; see also, *Coulthard v Disco Mix Club Ltd* [2000] 1 W.L.R. 707 at 731.
37   *Westdeutsche Landesbank Girozentrale v Islington LBC* [1996] A.C. 669 at 705.

'accountable as constructive trustee' in this context and substitute the words 'accountable in equity'."[38]

Irrespective of the debate as to the correctness of the terminology, it remains convenient and logical to examine together third party liability in cases of dishonest assistance and knowing receipt. Detailed analysis is provided in this chapter. A broad discussion of the range of further personal and proprietary remedies for breach of trust is provided in Ch.17.

Categories of constructive trusts

10-009

It is clear that the constructive trust is imposed in a variety of circumstances and there is little agreement as to how best to categorise the many examples that are found in the case law. The approach undertaken in this chapter is to provide a selective overview of the established cases of "constructive trusts" (rightly or wrongly described), to bring into focus the more abstract discussions highlighted above. Accordingly, a variety of applications of the constructive trust will be illustrated and explained. In many cases, the illustrations will be familiar from discussions in other chapters. Where this is so, the reader will be referred to the more substantive coverage of relevant material in other chapters. The categories of cases will be considered as follows:

- unauthorised fiduciary gains;

- liability imposed on strangers to the trust who knowingly receive trust property or dishonestly assist in cases of breach of trust;

- equitable response to wrongdoing or unconscionability; and

- enforcing the agreement between the parties.

Unauthorised Fiduciary Gains

10-010

One of the clearest situations in which a constructive trust may operate is that of unauthorised fiduciary gains.[39] In essence, a fiduciary is liable to his principal in respect of unauthorised gains obtained by reason of his fiduciary office. Unauthorised gains may take a variety of forms,

---

38 *Dubai Aluminium Co v Salaam* [2002] 3 W.L.R. 1913 at 1946.
39 See generally, J. Edelman, "When do Fiduciary Duties Arise" (2010) 126 L.Q.R. 302; see Ch.13.

such as a secret profit,[40] a bribe[41] or the use of confidential information to make an unauthorised profit.[42] This principle is long-standing and well understood. As Lord Hershell observed in *Bray v Ford*, "It is an inflexible rule of the court of equity that a person in a fiduciary position, such as the plaintiff's, is not, unless otherwise expressly provided, entitled to make a profit; he is not allowed to put himself in a position where his interest and duty conflict".[43] The nature of fiduciary duty is examined in detail in Ch.13. For present purposes, it is sufficient to note that fiduciaries include not only trustees, but also others who owe similar duties of loyalty and good faith to their principal, such as solicitors and company directors, partners and agents. The imposition of a constructive trust is an important remedy to the claimant, providing him with a claim to the property in priority to general creditors. As is discussed in Ch.17, fiduciaries are under a personal obligation to account for any unauthorised gain.[44]

Supporting authority for the invocation of the constructive trust is long-standing and oft cited. In *Keech v Sandford*,[45] a landlord's trustee renewed a lease for his own purposes when it became apparent to him that the landlord was not prepared to offer a renewal to the current tenant, an infant beneficiary of the trust. Upholding the claim made on behalf of the infant beneficiary, Lord King LC explained:

> **"This may seem hard that the trustee is the only person of all mankind who might not have the lease, but it is very proper that the rule should be strictly pursued, and not in the least relaxed; for it is very obvious what would be the consequence of letting trustees have the lease on refusal to renew to *cestui que use*".[46]**

The strict application of equity's general principles has been a marked feature of more recent case law. In *Boardman v Phipps*,[47] trustees had a minor shareholding in a poorly managed company. Boardman, as solicitor to the trust, took the view that in acquiring more shares the trust could take control and, thereby, improve the fortunes of the company. As the trust was not in the financial position to purchase further shares, Boardman and a beneficiary purchased shares on their own behalf. Following the restructure of the company, both Boardman's personal investment and that of the trust increased in value. Notwithstanding that Boardman's actions were in good faith, the House of Lords held that he was a constructive trustee of the

10-011

---

40   For example, an unauthorised commission: see *Williams v Barton* [1927] 2 Ch. 9 at 11, where Russell J explained that, "A person who has the management of property as a trustee is not permitted to gain any profit by availing himself of his position, and will be a constructive trustee of any such profit for the benefit of the persons equitably entitled to the property".
41   See P. Millett, "Bribes and Secret Commissions Again" (2012) 71(3) C.L.J. 583.
42   See *Boardman v Phipps* [1967] 2 A.C. 46.
43   [1896] A.C. 44 at 51.
44   *Target Holdings v Redferns* [1996] 1 A.C. 421.
45   (1726) Sel. Cas. Ch. 61.
46   (1726) Sel. Cas. Ch. 61 at 62.
47   [1967] 2 A.C. 46. See para.**13-050**.

profit made on his personal shareholding. The opportunity to make a profit had arisen from his fiduciary office and he had used confidential information in the process.[48] Although compensation was payable to Boardman in return for the work he had completed, the fundamental principle was upheld that, unless otherwise expressly provided, a person in a fiduciary position is not entitled to make a profit because he is not allowed to put himself in a position where his interest and duty conflict.

The problem with bribes

10-012

Until the matter was finally settled by the Supreme Court in *FHR European Ventures LLP v Cedar Capital Partners LCC*,[49] there were two contrasting approaches to bribes and secret commissions. The approach which was to prevail dictates that, where a bribe is accepted by a fiduciary, a constructive trust arises which entitles the principal to make a proprietary claim against the sums received and any property acquired from those sums.[50] In the case of a depreciation of value in the property representing the bribe, the fiduciary remains liable for that difference in value. Likewise, the fiduciary cannot retain any increase in value, in line with the principle that a fiduciary must not profit from his breach. As Lord Templeman explained in *Attorney General for Hong Kong v Reid*, "the bribe and the property from time to time representing the bribe are held on a constructive trust for the person injured".[51] In *Reid*, Mr Reid, a public prosecutor in Hong Kong accepted bribes to obstruct the prosecution of criminals, the proceeds of which he invested profitably in three freehold properties in New Zealand. The Crown sought to argue his constructive trusteeship of the investments in order to assert its beneficial entitlement. Lord Templeman seemed minded to reach the politically correct outcome and did not hold back his view of the repugnant nature of the crime committed. As he put it:

> **"Bribery is an evil practice which threatens the foundations of any civilised society. In particular bribery of policemen and prosecutors brings the administration of justice into disrepute. Where bribes are accepted by a trustee, servant, agent or other fiduciary, loss and damage are caused to the beneficiaries, master or principal whose interests have been betrayed . . . In the present case the amount of harm caused to the administration of justice in Hong Kong by the first respondent in return for bribes cannot be quantified".[52]**

48 As Lord Hodson commented, [1967] 2 A.C. 46 at 106, "Mr. Boardman used the strong minority shareholding which the trustees held, that is to say eight thousand shares in the company, wielding this holding as a weapon to enable him to obtain the information of which he subsequently made use".

49 [2015] AC 250. See para.**10-015**.

50 *Attorney General for Hong Kong v Reid* [1994] 1 All E.R. 1 PC; see S. Worthington, "Fiduciary Duties and Proprietary Remedies: Addressing the Failure of Equitable Formulae" (2013) 72(3) C.L.J. 720.

51 [1994] 1 All E.R. 1 at 9.

52 [1994] 1 All E.R. 1 at 4.

The problem with the *Reid* approach is that the trust is imposed despite the absence of any pre-existing proprietary interest of the principal or any intention of the principal to obtain such an interest. On this ground alone, it has always been difficult to justify the argument that the bribe belonged to the principal from the moment the fiduciary received it.[53] As Millett LJ acknowledged in *Paragon Finance Plc v DB Thakerar & Co*:

> "He never assumes the position of a trustee, and if he receives the trust property at all it is adversely to the plaintiff by an unlawful transaction which is impugned by the plaintiff. In such a case the expressions 'constructive trust' and 'constructive trustee' are misleading, for there is no trust and usually no possibility of a proprietary remedy".[54]

In *Sinclair Investments (UK) Ltd v Versailles Trade Finance Ltd*,[55] the Court of Appeal somewhat contentiously[56] refused to follow the decision of the Privy Council in *Reid*. Lord Neuberger MR concluded that "a claimant cannot claim proprietary ownership of an asset purchased by the defaulting fiduciary with funds which, although they could not have been obtained if he had not enjoyed his fiduciary status, were not beneficially owned by the claimant or derived from opportunities beneficially owned by the claimant".[57] He identified a number of domestic authorities which supported this view and admitted, "Save where there are powerful reasons to the contrary, the Court of Appeal should follow its own previous decisions, and in this instance there are five such previous decisions. It is true that there is a powerful subsequent decision of the Privy Council which goes the other way, but that of itself is not enough to justify departing from the earlier decisions of this court".[58]

Spread over 95 years, the cases referred to all concerned whether, where an agent or employee accepts a bribe or a secret commission, his principal or employer beneficially owns the bribe. These authorities universally concluded that, although its receipt derived from a plain breach of fiduciary duty, it was not money which was part of the assets subject to his duties or derived from such assets. For example, in *Metropolitan Bank v Heiron*,[59] a bribe received by the director of a company was not to be regarded as the money of the company. In *Lister & Co v Stubbs*,[60] an employee received a bribe from one of his employer's suppliers. The Court of Appeal held that the bribe could not be considered to be the property of the employer.

---

53   See generally, A.D. Hicks, "The Remedial Principle of *Keech v Sandford* Reconsidered" (2010) 69(2) C.L.J. 287.

54   [1999] 1 All E.R. 400 at 408.

55   [2011] EWCA Civ 347. The litigation concerned profits received by a fiduciary from a fraudulent Ponzi scheme.

56   For the controversy and criticism that this decision has generated see para.**13-045**. In particular note the views of D. Hayton, "No Proprietary Liability for Bribes and other Secret Profits?" (2011) 25(1) Tru. L.I. 3 and P. Millett, "Bribes and Secret Commissions Again" (2012) 71(3) C.L.J. 583.

57   [2011] EWCA Civ 347 at [89].

58   [2011] EWCA Civ 347 at [73].

59   (1880) 5 Ex. D. 319.

60   (1890) LR 45 Ch. D. 1.

10-013

10-014

Lindley LJ explained that the relationship was one of debtor and creditor and not trustee and beneficiary[61] and that to adopt the latter categorisation would bring with it unacceptable consequences:

> "One consequence, of course, would be that, if [the employee] were to become bankrupt, this property acquired by him with the [bribe] would be withdrawn from the mass of his creditors and be handed over bodily to [the employer]. Can that be right? Another consequence would be that [the employer] could compel [the employee] to account to them, not only for the money with interest, but for all the profits which he might have made by embarking in trade with it. Can that be right? It appears to me that those consequences shew that there is some flaw in the argument".[62]

Similarly, in *Re North Australian Territory Co*,[63] a secret commission was paid to a director. Lindley LJ once more emphasised that bribes or commissions paid to a director gave rise to a debt that could be recovered by the principal from the fiduciary. It did not belong to the company in any real sense. The company had no proprietary interest in the commission or bribe received by the fiduciary. Subsequent decisions too were to follow Lord Neuberger's lead. The High Court in *Cadogan Petroleum Plc v Tolley*[64] held that, as the secret commissions generated by the fiduciary were not paid from the claimants' money, the sums paid were the defendant's property both at law and beneficially.

10-015   In *FHR European Ventures LLP v Cedar Capital Partners LLC*,[65] the Supreme Court dispelled any doubt that the approach in *Reid* was correct. Here Cedar Capital held exclusive brokerage rights in relation to the sale of a hotel. Acting as the agent of the purchaser, a price was agreed, with the agent receiving an undisclosed fee of €10 million from the seller. This was a clear breach of fiduciary duty and it fell to the court to consider the availability of a proprietary claim. At first instance, the approach in *Sinclair Investments* prevailed; this was not a case where the profit wrongly obtained could be held on a constructive trust. The principal was confined to a claim in equitable compensation. The Court of Appeal, however, arrived at a different conclusion. It saw before it a case with very different facts to those in *Sinclair Investments*. It was not a payment of money in an abstract setting. Instead, the secret commission received was an integral part of the overall arrangement surrounding the purchase of the hotel and presented an opportunity that was exploited by the fiduciary. By failing to disclose his relationship with

---

61   There is no authority which supports the notion that such a personal claim entitles the claimant to claim the value of the asset (if it is greater than the amount of the funds together with interest). Indeed, as Lord Neuberger MR pointed out in *Sinclair Investments (UK) Ltd v Versailles Trade Finance Ltd* [2011] EWCA Civ 347 at [89], "there are judicial indications which tend to militate against that notion".
62   (1890) L.R. 45 Ch. D. 1 at 15.
63   [1892] 1 Ch. 322.
64   [2011] EWHC 2286 (Ch).
65   [2015] A.C. 250. See also para.**13-046**.

the vendor, the agent denied his principal the opportunity to purchase the property at a lower price. Accordingly, it was possible to trace into the money obtained by Cedar Capital, held by it on constructive trust.

In the Supreme Court, it fell to Lord Neuberger to review and reflect upon the leading authorities on bribes and secret commissions. He considered the equitable rule that an agent who acquires a benefit in breach of fiduciary duty or in consequence of an opportunity arising from his position as fiduciary, is treated as acquiring the benefit for his principal. That rule was strictly applied, and he concluded, for reasons of principle and practicality, that it should apply also to a bribe or secret commission.[66] Wider policy concerns were also of influence, Lord Neuberger noting that "concern about bribery and corruption generally has never been greater than it is now . . . Accordingly, one would expect the law to be particularly stringent in relation to a claim against an agent who has received a bribe or secret commission".[67]

In *FHR*, the Supreme Court has now settled the issue of a principal's proprietary claim to the proceeds of his agent's bribe or secret commission. The law took a "wrong turn" in *Heiron* and *Lister* and those decisions (together with those which followed a similar line of reasoning) must now be treated as overruled.[68] Accordingly, in such cases, the principal may elect between personal and proprietary claims. The advantages of a proprietary claim are that the principal can trace the proceeds of bribes and secret commissions into other assets or into the hands of third-party recipients. In addition, in the event of an agent's insolvency, a proprietary claim will give the principal priority over the agent's unsecured creditors.

Liability Imposed on Strangers to the Trust

The second incidence of "constructive trusteeship" concerns the personal liability imposed on third parties or strangers to the trust. Speaking of the obligations of the trustee generally, Lord Selborne LC observed in *Barnes v Addy*[69] that such responsibilities "may no doubt be extended in equity to others who are not properly trustees, if they are found either making themselves trustees *de son tort*, or actually participating in any fraudulent conduct of the trustee to the injury of the *cestui que trust*".[70]

10-016

Lord Selborne LC made reference, therefore, to the constructive trust imposed on a person

---

66   As Lord Neuberger explained, "Clarity and simplicity are highly desirable qualities in the law. Subtle distinctions are sometimes inevitable, but in the present case . . . there is no plainly right answer, and, accordingly, in the absence of any good reason, it would seem right to opt for the simple answer" (at [35]).
67   [2015] A.C. 250 at [42].
68   [2015] A.C. 250 at [50].
69   (1874) 9 Ch. App. 244.
70   (1874) 9 Ch. App. 244 at 251.

who intermeddles or interferes with the trust so that he assumes the responsibilities of a trustee and faces consequent liability on that basis. He also spoke of the extension of liability to those who participate in the fraudulent conduct of the trustee. Although the courts have many times developed and reformulated the basis of liability, the personal liability of strangers to the trust now advances on two fronts. Liability will be imposed as against third parties who, first, dishonestly assist in a breach of trust or, secondly, knowingly receive trust property in breach of trust.

In the development of case law, historically, the courts have guarded against the incautious extension of these categories. As Lord Selborne LC warned:

> "strangers are not to be made constructive trustees merely because they act as the agents of trustees in transactions within their legal powers, transactions, perhaps of which a Court of Equity may disapprove, unless those agents receive and become chargeable with some part of the trust property, or unless they assist with knowledge in a dishonest and fraudulent design on the part of the trustees".[71]

This cautious approach as to the imposition of third-party liability found favour with James LJ, who added:

> "I have long thought, and more than once expressed my opinion from this seat, that this Court has in some cases gone to the very verge of justice in making good to *cestuis que trust* the consequences of the breaches of trust of their trustees at the expense of persons perfectly honest, but who have been, in some more or less degree, injudicious. I do not think it is for the good of *cestuis que trust*, or the good of the world, that those cases should be extended".[72]

Trusteeship *de son tort*

As described, where a third party intermeddles with the business or management of the trust so as to assume the responsibility for the trust or appear to act as trustee, he may be described as a trustee *de son tort* (meaning by his own wrong). As A.L. Smith LJ reflected in *Mara v Browne*:

> "Now, what constitutes a trustee *de son tort?* It appears to me if one, not being a trustee and not having authority from a trustee, takes upon himself to intermeddle with trust matters or to do acts charac-

---

71 (1874) 9 Ch. App. 244 at 251.
72 (1874) 9 Ch. App. 244 at 255.

> teristic of the office of trustee, he may thereby make himself what is called in law a trustee of his own wrong—*i.e.*, a trustee *de son tort*, or, as it is also termed, a constructive trustee".[73]

The responsibilities of the trustee *de son tort* are the same as those of the express trustee. As Viscount Cave explained in *Taylor v Davies*,[74] such persons, "though not originally trustees had taken upon themselves the custody and administration of property on behalf of others; and though sometimes referred to as constructive trustees, they were, in fact, actual trustees, though not so named".[75] More recently, in *Dubai Aluminium Co v Salaam*,[76] Lord Millett sounded his distaste for the terminology employed in the case law. He claimed:

> "we would do better today to describe such persons as de facto trustees. In their relations with the beneficiaries they are treated in every respect as if they had been duly appointed. They are true trustees and are fully subject to fiduciary obligations. Their liability is strict; it does not depend on dishonesty. Like express trustees they could not plead the Limitation Acts as a defence to a claim for breach of trust".[77]

The dishonest assistant in a breach of trust

10-018

A stranger to a trust can be liable in equity for assisting in a breach of trust, even though he has never received trust property. Where the third party assists,[78] in a dishonest manner, in the misapplication of trust property, he may be held personally liable in equity to compensate for the loss occasioned to the trust fund.[79] Originally termed liability for "knowing assistance", the elements of this personal action were laid down by Lord Selborne LC in *Barnes v Addy*.[80] There the husband of a life tenant under a trust was appointed as sole trustee. He proceeded to misappropriate trust property. The court was called upon to consider whether his solicitors, acting as trustees, were liable to make good the misappropriations. The court decided in the

---

73 [1896] 1 Ch. 199 at 209.
74 [1920] A.C. 636; see also *Williams-Ashman v Price and Williams* [1942] Ch. 219.
75 [1920] A.C. 636 at 651.
76 [2002] 3 W.L.R. 1913.
77 [2002] 3 W.L.R. 1913 at 1946. See *Williams v Central Bank of Nigeria* [2014] UKSC 10.
78 Note that the third party must assist. Mere presence does not constitute assistance: see *Brinks Ltd v Abu-Saleh (No.3)*, *The Times*, 23 October 1995, where a wife who made a number of trips to Switzerland with her husband in order to keep him company was not deemed to assist in his disposal of the proceeds of a robbery.
79 Note that an account of profits may be awarded against a dishonest assistant where a sufficiently direct causal link between the breach and the profit is established (*Novoship (UK) Ltd v Mikhaylyuk* [2015] EWCA 2 W.L.R. 526). For discussion, see W. Gummow (2015) 74(3) C.L.J. 405.
80 (1874) 9 Ch. App. 244.

negative. In the course of his speech Lord Selborne LC effectively imposed the requirement that a defendant "must assist with knowledge in a dishonest and fraudulent design on the part of the trustees".[81] This marked a shift in the development of the law as no such requirement that the breach be dishonest had hitherto been imposed.[82]

In *Royal Brunei Airlines v Tan*,[83] however, the opportunity was taken to re-evaluate the requirements for the imposition of liability on strangers to the trust.[84] Here Royal Brunei Airlines entered into an agency agreement with Borneo Leisure Travel (BLT) under which BLT was required to sell tickets for the airline and hold the money received on express trust. With the assistance of Tan, its managing director and principal shareholder, the company paid the money into its current account and, in breach of trust, used the money to cover a range of expenses incurred by BLT. The airline sought to recover the money owed. In light of BLT's insolvency, it moved against Tan on the ground of "knowing assistance" in a breach of trust. Tan was held liable for assisting in a breach of trust.

10-019

In a departure from the approach in *Barnes v Addy*, Lord Nicholls acknowledged that, in a case of an honest trustee and a dishonest third party who assists in a breach of trust, dishonesty on the part of the third party was a sufficient basis for fault-based third-party liability. There was no need for further prerequisites; his dishonesty was sufficient, "notwithstanding that the trustee, although mistaken and in breach of trust, was honest".[85] Convincingly, Lord Nicholls added, "The alternative view would mean that a dishonest third party is liable if the trustee is dishonest, but if the trustee did not act dishonestly that of itself would excuse a dishonest third party from liability. That would make no sense".[86]

In the course of his analysis, Lord Nicholls rejected outright the possibility that a third party should never be liable. He also dismissed the possibility that liability should be strict, so that a third party would be liable even if he did not know (or had no reason to suspect) that he was dealing with a trustee. In his preferred fault-based approach, Lord Nicholls hailed the criterion of dishonesty as the corner-stone of liability for the assistant in a breach of trust. Formulating what is now regarded to be the "accessory liability principle", Lord Nicholls concluded that:

> "dishonesty is a necessary ingredient of accessory liability. It is also a sufficient ingredient. A liability in equity to make good resulting loss attaches to a person who dishonestly procures or assists in a breach of trust or fiduciary obligation 'Knowingly' . . . is better avoided as a defining ingredient of the principle, and in the context of this principle the *Baden* . . . scale of knowledge is best forgotten".[87]

81 (1974) 9 Ch. App. 244 at 252.
82 See *Fyler v Fyler* (1841) 3 Beav. 550.
83 [1995] 2 A.C. 378.
84 Lord Nicholls bemoaned the tendency of judges to construe Lord Selborne's formulation, "as though it were a statute" ([1995] 2 A.C. 378 at 386).
85 [1995] 2 A.C. 378 at 384.
86 [1995] 2 A.C. 378 at 385.
87 [1995] 2 A.C. 378 at 392; see, however, *Heini v Jyske Bank (Gibraltar) Ltd* [1999] Lloyd's Rep. Bank 511, where

The test for dishonesty – conflicting authorities

Lord Nicholls also addressed the question of when a defendant will be deemed to be dishonest. He accepted that as distinct from the "objectivity of negligence", honesty has a "connotation of subjectivity",[88] in that it is "a description of a type of conduct assessed in the light of what a person actually knew at the time, as distinct from what a reasonable person would have known or appreciated".[89] Nonetheless, he was quick to dismiss a subjective test of honesty, cautioning that:

> **"these subjective characteristics of honesty do not mean that individuals are free to set their own standards of honesty in particular circumstances. The standard of what constitutes honest conduct is not subjective. Honesty is not an optional scale, with higher or lower values according to the moral standards of each individual. If a person knowingly appropriates another's property, he will not escape a finding of dishonesty simply because he sees nothing wrong in such behaviour".[90]**

This substantially objective test was reviewed in *Twinsectra Ltd v Yardley*.[91] There, the House of Lords acknowledged that the courts had frequently drawn a distinction between subjective and objective dishonesty. Lord Hutton proceeded to consider three different tests of dishonesty.[92]

- ■ A wholly subjective standard, whereby a person is deemed to be dishonest if he transgresses his own standard of honesty, even if that standard is contrary to that of the reasonable and honest person. Otherwise referred to as the "Robin Hood test", this approach has not found favour with the courts.[93]

- ■ A purely objective standard whereby a person acts dishonestly if his conduct is dishonest by the ordinary standards of the reasonable and honest person, even if he does not realise this.

....

Nourse LJ considered that the *Baden* classification, "will sometimes continue to be helpful in identifying different states of knowledge which may or may not result in a finding of dishonesty". Note that the *Baden* scale (discussed para.**10-029**) was influential in the development of the now jettisoned liability for "knowing assistance".

88   [1995] 2 A.C. 378 at 389.
89   [1995] 2 A.C. 378 at 389.
90   [1995] 2 A.C. 378 at 389.
91   [2002] 2 A.C. 164.
92   [2002] 2 A.C. 164 at 172.
93   By way of example, "A person may in some cases act dishonestly, according to the ordinary use of language, even though he genuinely believes that his action is morally justified. The penniless thief, for example, who picks the pocket of the multi-millionaire is dishonest even though he genuinely considers the theft is morally justified as a fair redistribution of wealth and that he is not therefore being dishonest" (*Walker v Stones* [2000] 4 All E.R. 412 at 444 per Sir Christopher Slade).

■ A combined test of objective and subjective elements which requires that the defendant's conduct be dishonest by the ordinary standards of the reasonable and honest person and that the defendant himself realises that by those standards his conduct is dishonest.

10-021

The majority of the House of Lords agreed that the combined test applied. To be liable as an accessory to a breach of trust, an individual must act dishonestly by the ordinary standards of reasonable and honest people and also be aware that by those standards he was acting dishonestly. This test requires knowledge by the defendant that honest people would regard his conduct as dishonest. He should not escape a finding of dishonesty if he adopts his own threshold and does not regard as dishonest that which he knows would offend the standards of honest and reasonable people. Lord Hutton identified a pragmatic consideration in support of the combined test. He claimed:

> **"A finding by a judge that a defendant has been dishonest is a grave finding, and it is particularly grave against a professional man, such as a solicitor."[94]**

10-022

Despite the logical appeal of Lord Hutton's argument, the alternative approach of Lord Millett (dissenting) was also cogently argued. Lord Millett considered that the key question was not whether Lord Nicholls used the word "dishonesty" in a subjective or objective sense in *Royal Brunei Airlines v Tan*. Instead, the issue was whether a claimant should be required to establish that an accessory to a breach of trust had a dishonest state of mind or whether it should be sufficient to establish that he acted with the requisite knowledge, i.e. so that his conduct was objectively dishonest. Although Lord Millett acknowledged that the House was free to resolve the question either way, he offered his view that "Lord Nicholls was adopting an objective standard of dishonesty by which the defendant is expected to attain the standard which would be observed by an honest person placed in similar circumstances".[95] He added, "Account must be taken of subjective considerations such as the defendant's experience and intelligence and his actual state of knowledge at the relevant time. But it is not necessary that he should actually have appreciated that he was acting dishonestly; it is sufficient that he was".[96]

Accordingly, Lord Millett discerned an essentially objective test wherein there was scope to look at very limited subjective factors. In his view, it was not necessary that the defendant realise that he acted dishonestly. The defendant did not need to know the details of the trust. It was sufficient that the defendant recognise that the money was not at the free disposal of the person to whom he lent assistance. Three reasons were put forward by Lord Millett in support of this conclusion.

10-023

First, he observed that consciousness of wrongdoing is an aspect of mens rea and, there-

---

94   [2002] 2 A.C. 164 at 174.
95   [2002] 2 A.C. 164 at 198.
96   [2002] 2 A.C. 164 at 198.

fore, an appropriate condition of criminal liability.[97] Lord Millett did not view mens rea as an appropriate condition of civil liability, which generally results from negligent or intentional conduct. He claimed, "For the purpose of civil liability, it should not be necessary that the defendant realised that his conduct was dishonest; it should be sufficient that it constituted intentional wrongdoing".[98]

Secondly, he argued that the combined test was not consistent with authority. The objective test, he claimed, was "in accordance with Lord Selborne's statement in *Barnes v Addy* . . . and traditional doctrine. This taught that a person who knowingly participates in the misdirection of money is liable to compensate the injured party. While negligence is not a sufficient condition of liability, intentional wrongdoing is. Such conduct is culpable and falls below the objective standards of honesty adopted by ordinary people".[99]

Finally, Lord Millett discussed the claim for "knowing assistance" as the equitable counterpart of the economic torts. He explained, "These are intentional torts; negligence is not sufficient and dishonesty is not necessary. Liability depends on knowledge. A requirement of subjective dishonesty introduces an unnecessary and unjustified distinction between the elements of the equitable claim and those of the tort of wrongful interference with the performance of a contract".[100]

In short, it was inevitable that the courts would revisit the appropriate test for dishonesty to be applied to dishonest assistance.

Twinsectra considered: reconciling conflicting authorities

10-024

In *Barlow Clowes International Ltd (In liquidation) v Eurotrust International Ltd*[101] the Privy Council took the opportunity to reflect on developments in *Twinsectra*, particularly as regards the approach of Lord Hutton therein to the dishonesty of the assistant. Barlow Clowes International Ltd had, in the mid-1980s, operated a fraudulent offshore investment scheme in which high returns were offered for the skilled investment of funds in UK gilt-edged securities. The scheme collapsed in 1998 and Mr Clowes was duly imprisoned. Some of the money received from investors had been diverted through offshore bank accounts held by a company providing offshore services. The principal director of the company (Eurotrust International Ltd) faced an action by Barlow Clowes (in liquidation) for dishonest assistance in the misappropriation of the investment monies.

At first instance, the defendants were found liable. The judge had proceeded on the

---

97   Under the now jettisoned Ghosh test that applied in the criminal law (*R. v Ghosh* [1982] Q.B. 1053) dishonesty required that the defendant himself must realise that what he is doing is dishonest by the ordinary standards of reasonable and honest people.
98   [2002] 2 A.C. 164 at 200.
99   [2002] 2 A.C. 164 at 200.
100 [2002] 2 A.C. 164 at 200.
101 [2006] 1 W.L.R. 1476.

basis that liability for dishonest assistance required a dishonest state of mind on the part of the assistant to a breach of trust. He found that although a dishonest state of mind was a subjective mental state, the standard by which the law assessed whether it was dishonest was objective and was to be determined by ordinary standards. In relation to one director, Mr Henwood, the judge pointed to this director's strong suspicion that the funds passing through his hands were moneys that Barlow Clowes had received from members of the public who thought that they were investing in gilt-edged securities. If those suspicions were accurate, it followed that no honest person could have assisted in the disposal of the moneys. In addition, he had consciously decided not to make inquiries so as to avoid the risk of discovering the truth of his suspicions. Accordingly, he was deemed to have had a dishonest state of mind. In the Court of Appeal, Mr Henwood succeeded on the basis that there was no evidence to show that he had acted as a dishonest assistant. Although he was deemed to be dishonest by objective standards, there was no evidence at trial as to his subjective state of mind, a seemingly clear requirement set out in *Twinsectra*.[102] Barlow Clowes appealed.

10-025

In the Privy Council, Lord Hoffmann focused on the views of Lord Hutton in *Twinsectra* upon which Mr Henwood had relied. There, Lord Hutton had spoken of the injustice in finding dishonesty where the defendant

> **"had not been aware that what he was doing would be regarded by honest men as being dishonest . . . although he should not escape a finding of dishonesty because he sets his own standards of honesty and does not regard as dishonest what he knows would offend the normally accepted standards of honest conduct".[103]**

Mr Henwood submitted that he could not be said to be consciously dishonest unless he had been aware that his actions would be dishonest by ordinary standards. The matter to be determined was, therefore, the extent to which an examination of the defendant's views about standards of honesty was required. Lord Hoffmann accepted that there was an element of ambiguity in Lord Hutton's remarks, "which may have encouraged a belief, expressed in some academic writing, that the *Twinsectra* case had departed from the law as previously understood and invited inquiry not merely into the defendant's mental state about the nature of the transaction in which he was participating but also into his views about generally acceptable standards of honesty".[104] Nonetheless, the Privy Council declined to accept that this is what Lord Hutton meant. As Lord Hoffmann explained, "the reference to 'what he knows would

---

102 The judge found that Mr Henwood may well have lived by different standards and seen nothing wrong in what he was doing, in that he had an "exaggerated notion of dutiful service to clients, which produced a warped moral approach that it was not improper to treat carrying out clients' instructions as being all important".

103 *Twinsectra Ltd v Yardley* [2002] 2 A.C. 164 at 174.

104 [2006] 1 W.L.R. 1476 at 1481.

offend normally accepted standards of honest conduct' meant only that his knowledge of the transaction had to be such as to render his participation contrary to normally acceptable standards of honest conduct. It did not require that he should have had reflections about what those normally acceptable standards were".[105]

Ruling that the judge's findings of fact should not have been set aside, Lord Hoffmann considered that the appellate court had erred in two respects. First, Mr Henwood's clear suspicions that the moneys were misappropriated in breach of trust were sufficient. It was not necessary that he conclude that the disposals were of money in breach of trust. Secondly, it was "quite unreal"[106] to suppose that Mr Henwood needed to know all the details to which the court referred before he had grounds to suspect that the moneys were misappropriated. The money "was either held on trust for the investors or else belonged to the company and was subject to fiduciary duties on the part of the directors. In either case, Mr Clowes . . . could not have been entitled to make free with it".[107]

Although it had been suggested in previous case law that a person cannot be liable for dishonest assistance in a breach of trust unless he knows of the existence of the trust or at least the facts giving rise to the trust,[108] the Privy Council did not agree. Citing *Twinsectra Ltd v Yardley*, Lord Hoffmann observed, "Someone can know, and can certainly suspect, that he is assisting in a misappropriation of money without knowing that the money is held on trust or what a trust means".[109]

This sits well with the views previously expressed by Millet J in *Agip (Africa) Ltd v Jackson*, that:

> **"it is no answer for a man charged with having knowingly assisted in a fraudulent and dishonest scheme to say that it was 'only' a breach of exchange control or 'only' a case of tax evasion. It is not necessary that he should have been aware of the precise nature of the fraud or even of the identity of its victim. A man who consciously assists others by making arrangements which he knows are calculated to conceal what is happening from a third party, takes the risk that they are part of a fraud practised on that party".[110]**

---

105 [2006] 1 W.L.R. 1476 at 1481; as T.M. Yeo argues in (2006) 122 L.Q.R. 171, 172, this clarification is unconvincing, as "It is difficult to understand the role of a combined test if the two limbs are testing for the same thing and one limb does not make sense without the other. It is also difficult to see how the question whether a person has realised that he has breached ordinary standards of honest behaviour can be answered without considering his view on what those standards are".

106 [2006] 1 W.L.R. 1476 at 1483.

107 [2006] 1 W.L.R. 1476 at 1483.

108 *Brinks Ltd v Abu-Saleh (No.3)* [1996] C.L.C. 133 at 151 per Rimer J.

109 [2006] 1 W.L.R. 1476 at 1484.

110 [1990] Ch. 265 at 295.

The essentially objective test prevails

10-026   Although *Twinsectra* clearly established an approach based on both objective and subjective tests, the *Barlow Clowes* stance is essentially objective and much more than a mere refinement of an ambiguity in the reasoning of the House of Lords. It is this approach (i.e. the objective test) that has been followed in subsequent cases, but not without the understandable need to play down the obvious differences between the House of Lords (in *Twinsectra*) and the Privy Council (in *Barlow Clowes*). Most notably, in *Abou-Rahmah v Abacha*,[111] the Court of Appeal had an early opportunity to consider this increasingly complex body of case law. There the court was required to consider an action by the claimants against a Nigerian registered bank for dishonest assistance in a fraudulent scheme.

At first instance,[112] Treacy J could find no evidence that the defendant was aware of a situation giving rise to a fiduciary duty or that any such duty had been breached. There was nothing to indicate that the funds passing through the third party's account were misappropriated funds or that they had been obtained by fraud. Accordingly, it was felt that no claim for dishonest assistance was sustainable. Treacy J appeared, nonetheless, to endorse the *Barlow Clowes* "refinement" that no subjective appreciation that conduct is dishonest by normally acceptable standards is required.

10-027   In the Court of Appeal, Arden LJ upheld the findings of the trial judge. She tackled directly the widely held view that *Twinsectra* required both an objective and subjective test of dishonesty, the application of which would entail that "the defendant would not be guilty of dishonesty unless he was conscious that the transaction fell below normally acceptable standards of conduct".[113] She was keen to promote the Privy Council approach that it is not a requirement of the standard of dishonesty that the defendant should be "conscious of his wrongdoing".[114] As to the extent that *Barlow Clowes* departs from *Twinsectra*, she cautioned that the approach in *Twinsectra* had not been jettisoned. She was very clear to emphasise that the Privy Council merely "gave guidance as to the proper interpretation to be placed on it as a matter of English law".[115]

Much more caution is evident in the approach of both Rix and Pill LJJ in the *Abou-Rahmah* decision. As to Rix LJ, his uncertainty and reticence is palpable:

> "I would merely hazard this analysis. It would seem that a claimant in this area needs to show three things: first, that a defendant has the requisite knowledge; secondly, that, given that knowledge, the defendant acts in a way which is contrary to normally acceptable standards of honest conduct (the objective test of honesty or dishonesty); and

---

111   [2007] 1 Lloyd's Rep. 115, noted D. Ryan [2007] Conv. 168.
112   [2006] 1 Lloyd's Rep. 484.
113   [2007] 1 Lloyd's Rep. 115 at [65].
114   [2007] 1 Lloyd's Rep. 115 at [65].
115   [2007] 1 Lloyd's Rep. 115 at [68].

> thirdly, possibly, that the defendant must in some sense be dishonest himself (a subjective test of dishonesty which might, on analysis, add little or nothing to knowledge of the facts which, objectively, would make his conduct dishonest)".[116]

Pill LJ, moreover, was content to "fully and respectfully acknowledge the value of *Barlow Clowes* in its explanation of *Twinsectra*", but he did not want to enter the debate.[117] In short, therefore, there is something still unsatisfactory in what Arden LJ (somewhat optimistically) described as "a consistent corpus of law"[118] which stems from *Royal Brunei* to the present day. That has not stopped the objective test from becoming entrenched.[119] In *Starglade v Nash*,[120] the Court of Appeal held that the deliberate removal (by its director) of the assets of an insolvent company for the purpose of defeating the legitimate claims of one creditor, in preference to the claims of others, was not deemed honest in accordance with honest standards of commercial behaviour. The objective standard, against which the conduct of the defendant was to be measured, was for the court to assess and then to apply. As Sir Andrew Morritt explained:

> "The relevant standard . . . is the ordinary standard of honest behaviour. Just as the subjective understanding of the person concerned as to whether his conduct is dishonest is irrelevant so also is it irrelevant that there may be a body of opinion which regards the ordinary standard of honest behaviour as being set too high. Ultimately, in civil proceedings, it is for the court to determine what that standard is and to apply it to the facts of the case".[121]

In *Ivey v Genting Casinos UK Ltd (t/a Crockford's Club)*,[122] the Supreme Court has now confirmed that an objective test should be applied in both civil and criminal cases. The

---

116 [2007] 1 Lloyd's Rep. 115 at [16].
117 "[T]he implications are in my view best considered in a case in which a real issue arises on its impact" ([2007] 1 Lloyd's Rep. 115 at [16]); see also the view of Rix LJ at [23] that he did not "need to enter into that controversy for the purposes of this appeal".
118 [2007] 1 Lloyd's Rep. 115 at [68].
119 As Newey J explained in *Al Khudairi v Abbey Bakers Ltd* [2010] EWHC 1486 (Ch) at [134], "I find Arden LJ's comments persuasive, and I shall accordingly proceed on the basis that a person can be dishonest regardless of whether he appreciates that his conduct would be considered dishonest by ordinary honest people". See also *Clydesdale Bank Plc v Workman* [2016] EWCA Civ 73, where the objective approach in *Tan* was cited by Longmore LJ without reference to *Twinsectra*.
120 [2010] EWCA Civ 1314. For a discussion of case law developments, see P. Shine, "Dishonesty in Civil Commercial Claims: A State of Mind or a Course of Conduct?" [2012] J.B.L. 29.
121 [2010] EWCA Civ 1314 at [32]. See also *Secretary of State for Justice v Topland Group Plc* [2011] EWHC 983 (QB) at 101.
122 [2017] UKSC 67 (a £7.7m win allegedly cheating at cards): see G. Virgo, "Cheating and Dishonesty (2018) 77 C.L.J. 18.

confusion in the cases (described above) was not specifically referred to but it Is clear that the approach in *Tan* prevails. Accordingly, in *Group Seven Ltd v Notable Services LLP*,[123] described by Dixon as a "a punchy Court of Appeal decision on how dishonesty is to be established",[124] Henderson LJ spelled out the position of the current law. Delivering a judgment to which each member of the Court of Appeal had contributed, he made clear,

> **"In the light of *Ivey* . . . it must in our view now be treated as settled law that the touchstone of accessory liability for breach of trust or fiduciary duty is indeed dishonesty, as Lord Nicholls so clearly explained in *Tan*, and that there is no room in the application of that test for the now discredited subjective second limb of the *Ghosh* test".[125]**

Knowing receipt of trust property

10-028

Liability to account on the basis of knowing receipt of trust property applies to strangers to the trust who receive trust property or its traceable proceeds in the knowledge that the property has been misapplied or transferred in breach of trust. It is a precondition of liability that there has been a breach of trust. Accordingly, where property is transferred to a stranger in an authorised manner or within the terms of the trust there can be no liability for knowing receipt. In addition, the success of the claim does not depend on the recipient's continued possession of the property. As Lawrence Collins J explained, "The main purpose of seeking to establish constructive trust liability on the basis of knowing receipt is when the alleged constructive trustee has disposed of the property so that a personal remedy for its value is sought against him".[126] Indeed, Sir Terence Etherton summed up the relevant principles:

> **"The claim for personal liability is for the recipient to account as a constructive trustee and will usually only be necessary where following or tracing is not possible because, for example, the property has been acquired by a bona fide purchaser for value without notice or has been dissipated and is otherwise no longer identifiable".[127]**

---

123 [2019] EWCA Civ 614.

124 M. Dixon, "Dishonest Strangers" [2019] Conv. 195, 195.

125 [2019] EWCA Civ 614 at [57], as representing the views of Peter Jackson and Asplin LJJ. See also *Re Pantiles Investments Ltd (In Liquidation)* [2019] EWHC 1298 (Ch) at [23] per ICC Judge Mullen.

126 *Re Loftus* [2005] 1 W.L.R. 1890 at 1922. For a detailed analysis of relevant case law developments, see P. Shine, "Knowledge, Notice, Bad Faith and Dishonesty; Conceptual Uncertainty in Receipt Based Claims in Equitable Fraud" (2013) 24(8) I.C.C.L.R. 293.

127 *Arthur v Attorney General of the Turks and Caicos Islands* [2012] UKPC 30 at [34].

The accepted formulation of the requirements for liability to be imposed in the context of knowing receipt are those identified by Hoffmann LJ in *El Ajou v Dollar Land Holdings*.[128] Namely, there must be:

- a disposal of assets in breach of trust or fiduciary duty;

- the receipt by the defendant of assets which are traceable as representing the assets of the claimant; and

- knowledge on the part of the defendant that the assets he received are traceable to a breach of fiduciary duty.

It is for the claimant to demonstrate, therefore, that the defendant received trust property[129] and that he knew of some breach of trust or fiduciary duty.[130] Whereas the concept of receipt is well understood, the requisite knowledge of the defendant is a markedly more complex question. Unlike liability for dishonest assistance, dishonesty is not a prerequisite. As Vinelott J emphasised in *Eagle Trust Plc v SBC Securities Ltd*, "it is not necessary, and never has been necessary, to show that the defendant was in any sense a participator in a fraud".[131]

As to what constitutes knowledge, in *Baden v Société Générale pour Favoriser le Développement du Commerce et de l'Industrie en France SA*[132] Peter Gibson J identified five categories:

(i)   actual knowledge;

(ii) wilfully shutting one's eyes to the obvious[133];

(iii) wilfully and recklessly failing to make such inquiries as an honest and reasonable man would make;

(iv) knowledge of circumstances which would indicate the facts to an honest and reasonable man; and

(v)   knowledge of circumstances which would put an honest and reasonable man on inquiry.

---

128 [1994] 2 All E.R. 685 at 700.
129 Receipt means "receipt by one person from another of assets". For example, mere entry into a binding contract cannot constitute a "receipt" of assets: see *Criterion Properties Plc v Stratford UK Properties LLC* [2004] 1 W.L.R. 1846 at 1855 per Lord Nicholls.
130 It is also a pre-requisite to a claim in knowing receipt that the disposition to the recipient is in breach of trust: *Courtwood Holdings SA v Woodley Properties Ltd* [2018] EWHC 2163 (Ch).
131 [1992] 4 All E.R. 488 at 501.
132 [1983] B.C.L.C. 325 at 407.
133 Otherwise termed "Nelsonian knowledge".

Categories (ii) and (iii) are generally considered to be types of actual knowledge or similar, where the defendant's behaviour exhibits a level of wilfulness or recklessness. Categories (iv) and (v) are not governed by similar words and appear to be aligned more clearly with mere carelessness or negligence. Unfortunately, as will become clear, there is little consensus in the case law as to the role and utility of the *Baden* categories. Indeed, the utter lack of coherence evident in much of the case law has fuelled debate as to the appropriateness of a strict liability claim to which the recipient could raise a defence of change of position.[134]

10-030

In *Re Montagu's Settlement Trusts*,[135] Megarry VC qualified the scope of the *Baden* categories of knowledge to deny a claim of knowing receipt on difficult facts. Particular chattels had been transferred to a beneficiary, the 10th Duke of Manchester, in breach of trust. During his lifetime the 10th Duke did as he pleased with the property and some of the property was disposed of. After his death, the 11th Duke argued that the trustees had been in breach of trust in failing to make an appropriate inventory of the chattels and in transferring the property to the 10th Duke. He further alleged that in taking possession of, and in dealing with the items delivered to him in the knowledge that the items were subject the trusts of the settlement, the 10th Duke held the property as a constructive trustee. Megarry VC made explicit reference to the inherent difficulties of grappling with judicial precedent. Memorably, he claimed that, "All I need do is to find a path through the wood that will suffice for the determination of the case before me, and to assist those who have to read this judgment".[136]

By way of a starting point, Megarry VC deemed the crucial question to be whether the conscience of the recipient is sufficiently affected to justify the imposition of a constructive trust. He emphasised the distinction between notice and knowledge in this context. Whereas the former is concerned with whether a person takes property subject to some equity or other property right, the latter is concerned with whether the burdens and obligations of "trusteeship" ought to be imposed. Accordingly, he concluded that,

> "The cold calculus of constructive and imputed notice does not seem to me to be an appropriate instrument for deciding whether a man's conscience is sufficiently affected for it to be right to bind him by the obligations of a constructive trustee".[137]

Cautioning against "a fertile source of confusion",[138] he suggested that the knowledge of the recipient was paramount; the word "notice" should be avoided in such cases.

10-031

Megarry VC also considered the issue of forgotten knowledge to hold that a person is not to be taken to have knowledge of a fact that he once knew but has genuinely forgotten. He claimed, "I suppose that there may be some remarkable beings for whom once known is never

---

134 See further, para.**10-033.**
135 [1987] Ch. 264.
136 [1987] Ch. 264 at 285.
137 [1987] Ch. 264 at 272.
138 [1987] Ch. 264 at 277.

forgotten; but apart from them, the generality of mankind probably forgets far more than is remembered".[139] On this basis the test to be applied is whether the knowledge continues to operate on that person's mind at the time in question. The clear implication of the decision in *Re Montagu's Settlement Trusts* is that, in order to establish liability in knowing receipt, the recipient must have actual knowledge (or its equivalent) that the assets received are traceable to a breach of trust or fiduciary duty. For these purposes actual knowledge is extended to include *Baden* types (ii) and (iii), namely, actual knowledge that would have been acquired but for shutting one's eyes to the obvious or wilfully and recklessly failing to make such enquiries as a reasonable and honest man would make. As Megarry VC admitted, "in such cases there is a want of probity which justifies imposing a constructive trust".[140] As to whether knowledge of the *Baden* types (iv) and (v) would suffice, Megarry VC felt it to be at best doubtful. In his view, he could not see that the carelessness involved would normally amount to a want of probity.

Towards a single test of knowledge?

10-032

In *Bank of Credit and Commerce International (Overseas) Ltd v Akindele*,[141] the liquidators of BCCI sued Chief Akindele, a Nigerian businessman for almost $7m he received in a divestiture payment in 1988. In 1985, Akindele had paid ICIC (a company controlled by BCCI) the sum of £10m in exchange for 250,000 shares on the basis that the company would arrange for a sale price that gave Akindele a 15% annual return on his investment. This was a fraudulent scheme designed to give a misleading impression as to the financial health of the group. The Court of Appeal held that he was not liable. It was not necessary to show that Chief Akindele had been dishonest. There was insufficient evidence to determine that he had acted unconscionably. Nourse LJ embarked on a thorough review of the relevant authorities. He noted the divergence of opinion on the degree of knowledge necessary to found recipient liability and acknowledged that, of the many authorities which suggested that mere constructive knowledge would suffice,[142] the question had not been considered in any great depth. He acknowledged the judgment of Megarry VC, as a "seminal judgment, characteristically penetrative in its treatment of authority and, in the best sense, argumentative".[143] Nevertheless, as to the *Baden* scale of knowledge, Nourse LJ concluded that there was no need for such a categorisation at all.[144] In seeking to establish a single test of knowledge, Nourse LJ claimed that all that is

---

139 [1987] Ch. 264 at 284.
140 [1987] Ch. 264 at 285.
141 [2001] Ch. 437 at 455.
142 For example, *Belmont Finance Corp v Williams Furniture Ltd (No.2)* [1980] 1 All E.R. 393; *Polly Peck International Plc v Nadir (No.2)* [1992] 4 All E.R. 769.
143 [2001] Ch. 437 at 455.
144 As Nourse LJ explained [2001] Ch. 437 at 455, "although my own view is that the categorisation is often helpful in identifying different states of knowledge which may or may not result in a finding of dishonesty for the purposes of knowing assistance, I have grave doubts about its utility in cases of knowing receipt".

necessary is the recipient's state of knowledge to be such as to make it unconscionable for him to retain the benefit of the receipt. He explained:

> "A test in that form, though it cannot, any more than any other, avoid difficulties of application, ought to avoid those of definition and allocation to which the previous categorisations have led. Moreover, it should better enable the courts to give commonsense decisions in the commercial context in which claims in knowing receipt are now frequently made".[145]

It is unfortunate that Nourse LJ did not subject his new test of unconscionability to more rigorous examination. It is not clear, for example, exactly when the recipient's knowledge will be such that he cannot in conscience retain the benefit of his receipt. Although it cannot be denied that such a test caters for maximum flexibility against diverse factual circumstances, recourse to a test of unconscionability lacks the relative certainty provided by the particular test of dishonesty now advanced in cases of dishonest assistance.[146] Although its modern-day utility is much in dispute, the *Baden* categorisation of knowledge provides, at least, a scale against which receipt can be measured and an important reference point in evaluating past cases.[147] In addition, it is as yet unclear how the relative concepts of dishonesty and unconscionability are to be distinguished in this important context. It is to be acknowledged that in *Royal Brunei*, Lord Nicholls explicitly discounted the usefulness of a test based on unconscionability. There he concluded:

> "Unconscionable is a word of immediate appeal to an equity lawyer . . . It must be recognised, however, that unconscionable is not a word in everyday use by non-lawyers. If it is to be used in this context, and if it is to be the touchstone for liability as an accessory, it is essential to be clear on what, in this context, unconscionable means. If unconscionable means no more than dishonesty, then dishonesty is the preferable label. If unconscionable means something different, it must be said that it is not clear what that something different is. Either way, therefore, the term is better avoided in this context".[148]

10-033

In his judgment, Nourse LJ engaged with the argument that, rather than impose fault-based liability, the recipient of misapplied trust property should be strictly liable to a claim in unjust

---

145 [2001] Ch. 437 at 455.
146 See para.**10-027**.
147 See, e.g. the approach of the Hong Kong Court of Final Appeal in *Thanakharn v Akai Holdings Ltd* [2010] HKEC 1692 at [136]–[137] where Lord Neuberger (delivering the leading judgment) applied *Akindele* but assessed liability by reference to the *Baden* categorisation.
148 [1995] 2 A.C. 378 at 392.

enrichment, subject to the change of position defence. He cited the view of Lord Nicholls speaking extra-judicially, [149] that "Restitutionary liability . . . would be a better-tailored response to the underlying mischief of misapplied property than personal liability which is exclusively fault-based".[150] Nourse LJ provided a committed response which doubted the wisdom and commercial workability of restitutionary liability.[151] In doing so, he accepted the lack of coherence in the law as it currently stands, but he emphasised that the law has yet to develop in the fashion outlined. He observed, "We must continue to do our best with the accepted formulation of the liability in knowing receipt, seeking to simplify and improve it where we may",[152] adding that, "if the circumstances of the receipt are such as to make it unconscionable for the recipient to retain the benefit of it, there is an obvious difficulty in saying that it is equitable for a change of position to afford him a defence".[153] In addition, it is far from clear that the approach based in unjust enrichment would bring any practical benefit or make an appreciable difference. The need to assess whether the defendant has acted in good faith such that the defence of change of position becomes available would bring the court back to an assessment of the state of mind of the recipient. As Salmons argues, "The proposition that unjust enrichment would remove the difficulties in defining the fault requirement for establishing the personal liability of third-party recipients cannot be sustained".[154]

It is clearly accepted that the approach in *Akindele* represents the current law.[155] Accordingly, "liability for 'knowing receipt' depends on the defendant having sufficient knowledge of the circumstances of the payment to make it 'unconscionable' for him to retain the benefit or pay it away for his own purposes".[156] Indeed, in *Arthur v Attorney General of the Turks and Caicos Islands*, Sir Terence Etherton states clearly that "unconscionability" is "the correct test".[157] It is a test which is extremely flexible, but it provides little clarity as to the way future cases will be decided. In *Armstrong DLW GmbH v Winnington Networks Ltd*,[158] for example, a case of a trader deemed liable in knowing receipt in the fraudulent transfer of carbon emission allowances, it proved difficult to depart from the *Baden* classification of knowledge to argue the case in any meaningful way. Deputy Judge Stephen Morris QC held that despite the approach of the court in Akindele:

10-034

149 "Knowing Receipt: The Need for a New Landmark" in Cornish, Nolan, O'Sullivan and Virgo (eds), *Restitution Past, Present and Future* (Oxford: Hart Publishing, 1998), p.238.

150 [2001] Ch. 437 at 456. See further, Lord Nicholls in *Criterion Properties Plc v Stratford UK Properties LLC Bank of Credit and Commerce International (Overseas) Ltd v Akindele* [2004] 1 W.L.R. 1846 at 1848.

151 For a rejection of the restitutionary analysis by the High Court of Australia, see *Farah Constructions Pty Ltd v Say-Dee Ltd* [2007] HCA 22.

152 *Bank of Credit and Commerce International (Overseas) Ltd v Akindele* [2001] Ch. 437 at 456.

153 *Bank of Credit and Commerce International (Overseas) Ltd v Akindele* [2001] Ch. 437 at 456.

154 D. Salmons, "Claims Against Third Party Recipients of Trust Property" (2017) 76 C.L.J. 399, 416.

155 See, e.g. *Haque v Raja* [2016] EWHC 1950 (Ch) at [46].

156 *Charter Plc v City Index Ltd* [2008] 2 W.L.R. 950 at [8] per Carnwath LJ. See also *Hollis v Rolfe* [2008] EWHC 1747 (Ch) at [172].

157 [2012] UKPC 30 at [33].

158 [2013] Ch. 156.

> "the *Baden* classification of knowledge is still useful in distinguishing different types of knowledge for the purpose of determining what kind of knowledge makes it unconscionable for the defendant to retain the trust property".[159]

He added that "other parties agreed that it was thus helpful (and indeed necessary) to consider which types of *Baden* 'knowledge' would render receipt of trust property 'unconscionable'. . .".[160] Indeed, as noted by Shine:

> "In all but the most straightforward of cases, it is inevitable that in considering questions of good faith, notice and knowledge, a court will be required to ask whether a duty to make enquiries has arisen".[161]

More generally, therefore, it is of no surprise that the courts are forced to grapple with what exactly unconscionability means in the context of the case before it. In *Uzinterimpex JSC v Standard Bank*, therefore, Moore-Bick LJ spoke of the need to show (at least) that the recipient entertained the "clear suspicion" that he was not entitled to receive the property.[162] In *Law Society for England and Wales v Habitable Concepts*,[163] where part of the proceeds of a mortgage fraud were paid away from a rogue solicitor's client account into the defendant's furniture company, the circumstances of the receipt (i.e. the absence of a commercial relationship between the parties) and a failure to enquire, pointed firmly towards liability.[164] The Hong Kong Court of Final Appeal considered, furthermore, that the recipient's "dishonest or irrational" reliance on an alleged agent's apparent authority when accepting an asset from that agent on behalf of the principal would be deemed unconscionable. Mere negligent reliance (akin to constructive knowledge) would not be.[165]

Accordingly, much seems to turn on the facts of the case before the court and it is clear that the particular mode of expression adopted by the individual judge is apt to change. Given this uncertainty, it is inevitable that the Supreme Court will at some stage review the ambit of recipient liability. Until then, as noted by Parker and Mellows, "the test is going to require virtually every claim to impose liability for knowing receipt to be litigated, something which is far from an ideal state of affairs for potential litigants".[166]

---

159 [2013] Ch. 156 at 193.
160 [2013] Ch. 156 at 193.
161 P. Shine, "Knowledge, Notice, Bad Faith and Dishonesty; Conceptual Uncertainty in Receipt Based Claims in Equitable Fraud" (2013) 24(8) I.C.C.L.R. 293, 296.
162 [2008] Bus. L.R. 1762 at 1781.
163 [2010] EWHC 1449 (Ch).
164 In the words of Norris J, "The unexplained nature of the bank credit and its sheer scale would call for enquiry to be made by anyone who wished to deal with the credit with a clear conscience" ([2010] EWHC 1449 (Ch) at [16]).
165 *Thanakharn v Akai Holdings Ltd* [2010] HKEC 1692 at [137] per Lord Neuberger.
166 A.J. Oakley (ed.), *Parker and Mellows: The Modern Law of Trusts*, 9th edn (London: Sweet & Maxwell, 2008), p.437.

Unconscionability Generally

The preceding sections have considered the constructive trust in the context of, first, unauthorised fiduciary gains and, secondly, third-party liability in cases of breach of trust. A further context in which constructive trusts arise concerns general unconscionable behaviour. This interventionist jurisdiction is one "by which a court of Equity, proceeding on the ground of fraud, converts the party who has committed it into a trustee for the party who is injured by that fraud".[167] As will be demonstrated, the courts have proved willing to apply constructive trust principles to a range of cases where the defendant acquires property belonging to another by unconscionable means. Further, the principle that a criminal should not benefit from his crime not only underpins the law as to unlawful killing (discussed below), but also as to property obtained as a result of fraud.[168]

10-035

Acquisition of property by killing

It is a statement of general principle that a person should not benefit from the commission of a criminal act.[169] A specific manifestation of this general principle is to be found in the forfeiture rule, i.e. a rule of public policy that precludes a person who has unlawfully killed another from acquiring a benefit as a consequence of the killing. As Sir Samuel Evans P stated *In the Estate of Crippen,* "It is clear that the law is, that no person can obtain, or enforce, any rights resulting to him from his own crime; neither can his representative, claiming under him, obtain or enforce any such rights. The human mind revolts at the very idea that any other doctrine could be possible in our system of jurisprudence".[170] Accordingly, when Mr Crippen murdered his wife and inherited her property, he could not leave that property by will to a legatee. As Mr Crippen was not allowed to benefit by his crime, his legatee was also unable to benefit. In the memorable words of Hamilton LJ, "A man shall not slay his benefactor and thereby take his bounty".[171]

In the cases where legal title has passed to the killer, forfeiture is enforced through the mechanism of the constructive trust. The application of the forfeiture rule may arise, for example, in the context of co-ownership. It is the essence of a joint tenancy that each co-owner individually owns nothing, but that together they are wholly entitled to the entirety of the property. The right of survivorship entails that on the death of a joint tenant the co-owned estate

10-036

---

167 *McCormick v Grogan* (1869) L.R. 4 HL 82 at 97 per Lord Westbury.
168 As Lord Browne-Wilkinson states obiter in *Westdeutsche Landesbank Girozentrale v Islington LBC* [1996] A.C. 669 at 716, "when property is obtained by fraud equity imposes a constructive trust on the recipient: the property is recoverable and traceable in equity".
169 In the words of Lord Atkin, "courts will not recognise a benefit accruing to a criminal from his crime" (*Beresford v Royal Insurance Co Ltd* [1938] A.C. 586 at 599).
170 [1911] P. 108 at 112.
171 *In the Estate of Hall* [1914] P. 1 at 7 per Hamilton LJ.

is said to "survive" to the remaining joint tenants. The last surviving joint tenant becomes the sole owner of the once co-owned property. The operation of the survivorship principle exposes the possibility that the death of a joint tenant will bestow a practical financial benefit upon the remaining co-owner(s) in whom, in consequence, entitlement to the whole of the property remains.[172] The killing of one co-owner by the other is, thus, sufficient to invite an equitable response. The prevailing understanding is that, through the imposition of a constructive trust, the killer holds legal title in the co-owned property on trust for himself and the victim's estate in equal shares.

10-037   Some limited statutory relief is provided by the Forfeiture Act 1982. The Act applies to cases of unlawful killing and permits the court to grant relief from forfeiture where the justice of the case requires.[173] As Mummery LJ explained in *Dunbar v Plant*, "The provision requires that the judge should look at the case in the round, pay regard to all the material circumstances, including the conduct of the offender and the deceased, and then ask whether 'the justice of the case requires' a modification of the effect of the forfeiture rule".[174] Accordingly, in *Dunbar v Plant*, the forfeiture rule was modified to allow the survivor of a suicide pact to claim her inheritance under the principle of survivorship.

A flurry of recent cases serve well to illustrate the modern approach of the courts. In *Macmillan Cancer Support v Hayes*,[175] where a terminally ill man unlawfully killed his wife before taking his own life (she was suffering from dementia and due to be admitted to a care home), the forfeiture rule was modified to give total relief from forfeiture. The justice of the case demanded that the court give effect to his wife's wishes that her husband inherit her property and, through the vehicle of his will, their savings would go to their chosen charities. Had the court failed to act, distant relatives stood to benefit from the property in her will to the exclusion of those chosen charities. In *Re Estate of Amos (Deceased)*,[176] the forfeiture rule was modified in the case of a 74-year-old woman who caused the death of her 81-year-old husband by careless driving, an offence to which she pleaded guilty at the first possibility. Judge Jarman QC held that It would be unjust for the forfeiture rule to apply to deny the woman her husband's share in their home or the gift in his will, claiming that the loss of either would be "significantly out of proportion to her culpability in the offence in question".[177] In *Re Ninian (Deceased)*,[178] moreover, a woman obtained relief from forfeiture following her husband's death in a Dignitas clinic in Switzerland. She had reluctantly attended and assisted him, leaving her open to prosecution for assisting suicide.[179] Chief Master Marsh acknowledged that the exercise of the court's discretion under the Forfeiture Act "is a sensitive one due to the interaction between different elements of the justice system. The court will wish to be informed about the background to the claim with

---

172   See further, T. Youdan, "Acquisition of Property by Killing" (1973) 89 L.Q.R. 235.
173   The court may grant relief in respect of all or merely part of the property: Forfeiture Act 1982 s.2.
174   [1998] Ch. 412 at 427.
175   [2017] EWHC 3110 (Ch).
176   [2020] EWHC 1063 (Ch).
177   [2020] EWHC 1063 (Ch) at [28].
178   [2019] EWHC 297 (Ch).
179   Suicide Act 1961 s.2.

complete candour".[180] He cited the decision of the Crown Prosecution Service not to prosecute in this case as a "powerful factor in favour of the grant of relief".[181] This would date back to her husband's death with the severance of their jointly owned home treated as not having taken place. As a result, the jointly owned property passed to Mrs Ninion by survivorship.

No such relief was forthcoming in *Henderson v Wilcox*,[182] however, where a son who beat his mother to death and was convicted of manslaughter and detained under the Mental Health Act 1983 "had the mental capacity to know what he was doing, understand the nature of his acts and to appreciate the difference between right and wrong".[183] The justice of the case did not warrant the provision of relief to the claimant.[184]

Absence of statutory formalities

Equity will not permit a statute to be used as an instrument of fraud.[185] *Bannister v Bannister*[186] provides a simple illustration. A widow conveyed legal title to two cottages to her brother-in-law for less than the market price. She did so on the basis of his oral promise that she could reside in one of the cottages rent free for the remainder of her life. No mention of the promise was contained in the conveyance. When the brother-in-law sought to evict the widow from the property, the Court of Appeal determined that legal title was held on constructive trust to give effect to the widow's life interest. Scott LJ identified that the constructive trust seeks to assert that the transfer of legal title to himself is absolute and unencumbered in order that he may defeat the equitable interest of another.[187] It is not open to the defendant in such cases to argue the absence of written evidence of the bargain between the parties. As Scott LJ added, "The fraud which brings the principle into play arises as soon as the absolute character of the conveyance is set up for the purpose of defeating the beneficial interest, which, according to the true bargain, was to belong to another".[188]

10-038

Property acquired expressly subject to personal rights

In delimited circumstances, and provided his conscience is affected, a constructive trust can arise to bind the purchaser of property who agrees to take subject to a pre-existing interest. In

10-039

---

180 [2019] EWHC 297 (Ch) at [54].
181 [2019] EWHC 297 (Ch) at [52].
182 [2015] EWHC 3469 (Ch).
183 [2015]EWHC 3469 (Ch) at [57] per Judge Cooke.
184 See also *Chadwick v Collinson* [2014] EWHC 3055 (Ch).
185 *Rochefoucauld v Boustead* [1897] 1 Ch. 196.
186 [1948] 2 All E.R. 133.
187 [1948] 2 All E.R. 133 at 136.
188 [1948] 2 All E.R. 133 at 136.

Binions v Evans,[189] Mr Evans was employed by Tredegar Estate and was permitted to live rent free in a cottage owned by his employer. On his death, he left a wife aged 73. Three years later the trustees of the estate entered into an agreement with Mrs Evans that she could continue to live in the cottage for the remainder of her life as a tenant at will, rent free. In return, she agreed to keep the cottage in good repair. Subsequently, the Estate sold the cottage to Mr and Mrs Binions expressly subject to the interest held by Mrs Evans. As a consequence, a reduced price was paid for the cottage. The Binions sought to evict Mrs Evans but this attempt failed. In the Court of Appeal, Lord Denning MR argued that the Binions took the property subject to a constructive trust in favour of Mrs Evans.[190] In the course of his judgment, he put forward the broad proposition that, "Whenever the owner sells the land to a purchaser, and at the same time stipulates that he shall take it 'subject to' a contractual licence, I think it plain that a court of equity will impose on the purchaser a constructive trust in favour of the beneficiary . . . It would be utterly inequitable that the purchaser should be able to turn out the beneficiary".[191]

In *Ashburn Anstalt v Arnold*,[192] Fox LJ admitted the legitimacy of this application of the doctrine of constructive trusts, but clarified the narrow principles on which it is operative. The estate had sold the cottage to the Binions expressly subject to the pre-existing agreement with Mrs Evans and for which a lower purchase price was accepted. It was, therefore, "a proper inference that on the sale to the plaintiffs, the intention of the estate and the plaintiffs was that the plaintiffs should give effect to the tenancy agreement".[193] The payment of the lower price was significant. The fact that land is expressed to be conveyed subject to a contract is not, of itself, sufficient to give rise to a constructive trust.[194] As Fox LJ emphasised, "The court will not impose a constructive trust unless it is satisfied that the conscience of the estate owner is affected".[195] In *Lloyd v Dugdale*, the crucially important question in this regard is, "whether he has taken on a new obligation, not otherwise existing, to give effect to the relevant incumbrance or prior interest".[196] If, but only if, he has done so will a constructive trust be imposed.[197] Such a "new" obligation might be demonstrated by proof that the "purchase price paid by a transferee has been reduced upon the footing that he would give effect to the relevant incumbrance or prior interest".[198]

---

189   [1972] Ch. 359.

190   Lord Denning MR sought also to argue that the contractual licence to occupy was an equitable interest in land; Megaw and Stephenson LJJ decided the case on the ground that Mrs Evans was a tenant for life under the Settled Land Act 1925.

191   [1972] Ch. 359 at 366.

192   [1989] Ch. 1.

193   [1989] Ch. 1 at 23.

194   As Fox LJ pointed out (at 26): "The words 'subject to' will, of course, impose notice. But notice is not enough to impose on somebody an obligation to give effect to a contract into which he did not enter".

195   [1989] Ch. 1 at 25.

196   [2001] EWCA Civ 1754 at [52] per Sir Christopher Slade.

197   No new obligation was evident in *Chaudhary v Yavuz* [2011] EWCA Civ 1314 in respect of a stairway that was obvious on a casual inspection of the land. A term in the contract that the purchaser take subject to rights discoverable on inspection was designed to protect the vendor from possible claims by the purchaser and not to protect the pre-existing right of a third party. See also *Graveholt Ltd v Hughes* [2013] 1 P. & C.R. 20.

198   *Lloyd v Dugdale* [2001] EWCA Civ 1754 at [52] per Sir Christopher Slade.

Property acquired by joint venture

Equity will impose a constructive trust in cases of frustrated joint venture where the so-called *"Pallant v Morgan* equity" arises.[199] In *Pallant v Morgan*, a neighbour allowed a fellow neighbour to bid for a parcel of adjoining land uncontested on the understanding that, should the land be successfully acquired, he would transfer part of that land to the neighbour. When the purchase was made and the neighbour sought to renege on the agreement, the court concluded that he had acquired the property for the benefit of both parties jointly and, hence, held it on trust on those terms. Accordingly, the *"Pallant v Morgan* equity" typically arises where property is acquired by X in furtherance of a pre-existing understanding with Y that, if Y refrains from entering the market in competition to X, Y will be granted an interest in the property.[200] It is triggered notwithstanding that their agreement falls short of creating contractual obligations that are enforceable at law. The defendant is deemed to hold property on constructive trust for the claimant.[201]

In *Banner Homes Group Plc v Luff Developments Ltd (No.1)*,[202] Luff wished to acquire a development site. It entered into negotiations with Banner to form a joint venture for the purpose of acquiring the site. The parties agreed to acquire the site through a new company owned equally between them, which would be the vehicle for the joint venture. Subsequently, Luff decided against the proposed joint venture, but omitted to inform Banner for fear that Banner would proceed itself to bid for the site. Throughout, Banner conducted itself on the basis that the joint venture was going ahead and that the parties would enter into a formal agreement reflecting their pre-agreed terms. It was not until after the site had been acquired that Luff informed Banner of its withdrawal from the proposed joint venture. Banner contended that Luff's actions gave rise to a constructive trust in its favour over half the shares in the new company.

The Court of Appeal agreed and outlined the necessary ingredients of liability. For an equity to arise, there must be a pre-acquisition understanding that the acquiring party will take steps to acquire the relevant property and that the non-acquiring party will obtain an interest in that property.[203] It is for the claimant to demonstrate the existence of this common understanding. In reliance on the understanding, the non-acquiring party should do some-

10-040

10-041

---

199 From the decision in *Pallant v Morgan* [1952] 2 All E.R. 951. As Lord Briggs notes sagely, "The reason why recourse has had to be made to a case name for this equity is, I suspect, because no-one has since been able to agree upon the principled basis for its existence, still less upon the boundaries which circumscribe its legitimate application" ("Equity in Business" (2019) 135 L.Q.R. 567, 570).

200 Where property is acquired for the joint benefit of A and B, it is not necessary that B obtain a "specific proprietorial interest (whether legal or equitable) in real property": see *Kearns Brothers Ltd v Hova Developments Ltd* [2012] EWHC 2968 (Ch) at [120].

201 See generally S. Nield, "Constructive Trusts and Estoppel" (2003) 23 L.S. 311.

202 [2000] Ch. 372; see N. Hopkins, "The *Pallant v Morgan* Equity?" [2002] Conv. 35.

203 No such understanding arose in *Button v Phelps* [2006] EWHC 53 (Ch), where the defendant had participated in rival bids (for the acquisition of bars and nightclubs) to that entered into by the claimant and defendant. This was merely "open competition" and an absence of reliance precluded the finding of a constructive trust.

thing which confers an advantage on the acquiring party or is detrimental to the non-acquiring party. In other words there must be an advantage to be gained by one party, or a detriment to the other suffered as a consequence of the understanding. It then becomes unconscionable to allow the acquiring party to retain the property for himself, in a manner inconsistent with the parties' agreement or understanding.

10-042

To that effect, it is clearly necessary that the non-acquiring party is not informed before the acquisition that the acquiring party no longer intends to honour the understanding. Equally, where negotiations are "subject to contract", it makes sense that withdrawal from such an arrangement would not involve the requisite unconscionability to give rise to a constructive trust.[204] In *London Investments Ltd v TBI Plc*, for example, Mummery LJ explained of the deal between the parties, that their "recorded intentions as to the joint venture implicitly proceeded on the basis that no concluded agreement had been reached and contemplated that such an agreement might never be reached".[205] There could be no *"Pallant v Morgan* equity". By contrast, where no such formal contract is envisaged it may be perfectly reasonable to rely on an informal agreement. This was so in *Baynes Clarke v Corless*,[206] where homeowners entered into an agreement for the acquisition of the communal parts of a housing estate. Although the informal nature of the agreement did not prevent it binding in conscience, the requisite level of reliance was not present on the facts to support the imposition of a constructive trust.

Seemingly, there is uncertainty as to whether the *"Pallant v Morgan* equity" will arise where the property is owned already by the defendant. This was a troubling aspect of the facts before Mummery LJ in *London Investments Ltd v TBI Plc*[207] and also Lord Scott in *Cobbe v Yeoman's Row Management*.[208] In the words of Lord Scott:

> **"If the property that is to be the subject of the joint venture is owned by one of the parties before the joint venture has been embarked upon (as opposed to being acquired as part of the joint venture itself), on what basis, short of a contractually complete agreement for the joint venture, can it be right to regard the owner as having subjected the property to a trust and granted a beneficial interest to the other joint venturers?"[209]**

In the case before the court, a property developer had reached an oral agreement for the purchase of land for development purposes. Although he had expended much time, money and materials and successfully received planning permission, the owner then refused to proceed

---

204 *Crossco No.4 v Jolan Ltd* [2011] EWCA Civ 1619.
205 [2002] EWCA Civ 355 at [47].
206 [2010] EWCA Civ 338.
207 [2002] EWCA Civ 355 at [48].
208 [2008] 1 W.L.R. 1752. It was not, however, an issue for Kitchin LJ in *Farrar v Miller* [2018] EWCA Civ 172, who expressed the scope of the *Pallant v Morgan* equity in very broad terms.
209 [2008] 1 W.L.R. 1752 at 1772.

on the agreed terms. At first instance, following *Banner v Luff,* the Court awarded Mr Cobbe a beneficial interest in the property. His award was upheld in the Court of Appeal. In the House of Lords, however, it was felt that no constructive trust could be imposed. The defendant had owned the property before entering into negotiations with Mr Cobbe. Further, his interest was merely speculative, in that "he never expected to acquire an interest in the property otherwise than under a legally enforceable contract".[210] This ability to walk away ruled out an estoppel-based claim. A quantum meruit payment was awarded.

In the later case of *Generator Developments Ltd v Lidl UK GmbH,*[211] where negotiations between the parties were expressly subject to contact, again no *Pallant v Morgan* equity arose. Lewison LJ offered extensive reasons for his decision, but opened with the observation that "this was a case of commercial parties, advised by lawyers, working at arm's length towards the conclusion of an agreement for a purely commercial enterprise the terms of which were never agreed".[212] He indicated clearly that the application of the principles underpinning the *Pallant v Morgan* equity, "in so far as they rest on the doctrine of common intention constructive trust", would not operate here, and that they operate "quite differently in a commercial context from the way in which they operate in a domestic context".[213] The decision in *Cobbe* had made clear that a claimant would be denied an estoppel-based claim where each party knows it is not legally bound. The same would be true of the *Pallant v Morgan* equity with the principles expounded by Chadwick in *Banner Homes*, "firmly based on the supposed congruence between the principles of proprietary estoppel and the doctrine of common intention constructive trust".[214]

The intervention of equity in this interesting context, when Invoked, is a specific illustration of the broad principle to which Millett J made reference in *Lonrho Plc v Al-Fayed (No.2).*[215] There he argued that equity will intervene by way of constructive trust, not only to compel the defendant to restore the claimant's property to him, but also "to require the defendant to disgorge property"[216] which he should have acquired for the claimant. In this latter case, the defendant's wrong arises from his subsequent failure to acknowledge the claimant's beneficial interest. Millet J concluded that "the defendant must either have acquired property which but for his wrongdoing would have belonged to the plaintiff, or he must have acquired property in circumstances in which he cannot conscientiously retain it as against the plaintiff".[217] Nonetheless, there remains much uncertainty about the scope of the *Pallant v Morgan* equity and whether it ought to be viewed as a form of common intention constructive trust or a response to the breach of fiduciary duty by the purchaser. As to the latter, support may be derived from the views of Etherton LJ in *Crossco No.4 v Jolan Ltd,*[218] where he claimed:

10-043

---

210   [2008] 1 W.L.R. 1752 at 1773.
211   [2018] EWCA Civ 396.
212   [2018] EWCA Civ 396 at [78].
213   [2018] EWCA Civ 396 at [78].
214   [2018] EWCA Civ 396 at [78].
215   [1991] 4 All E.R. 961.
216   [1991] 4 All E.R. 961 at 969.
217   [1991] 4 All E.R. 961 at 969.
218   [2011] EWCA Civ 1619 at [88].

"It is not necessary to resort to the common intention constructive trust to provide an explanation for the cases in which the *Pallant v Morgan* equity was, or is said to have been, applied. They can all be explained, and, in my judgment, ought to be explained in wholly conventional terms by the existence and breach of fiduciary duty".

Ultimately, it may be for the Supreme Court to determine at a future date its nature and precise scope for invocation.

Enforcement of Agreements

10-044   The following illustrations mark out the role of the constructive trust in preventing a defendant from unconscionably resiling from an agreement entered into with the claimant. As will be demonstrated, equity operates in diverse contexts ranging from binding contracts (such as to enforce contracts for the sale of land) to informal arrangements (such as bargains to share beneficial interests in the family home). The selection of examples considered includes specifically enforceable contracts, mutual wills and secret trusts.

Specifically enforceable contract

10-045   Under a specifically enforceable contract for sale, the vendor becomes a trustee of the property for the purchaser.[219] Equity treats as done that which ought to be done and deems the purchaser already to be the real owner of the property. In the case of a contract for the sale of land, for example, a constructive trust is imposed and the vendor of the estate is considered to assume his trusteeship from the time at which he enters into the contract. Consequently, and subject to variation by agreement, it is for the purchaser to insure against damage to the property by fire or flood in the intervening time between contract and completion.[220] If the vendor proceeds to sell to a third party, he is deemed to hold the purchase money on trust for the purchaser.[221]

Although the proposition that the vendor becomes a trustee for the purchaser dates back several centuries, the nature of that trusteeship is markedly less certain.[222] No doubt when

219 See J. Meagher, "(Re-defining) the Trust of the Specifically Enforceable Contract of Sale—the Vendor Purchaser Constructive Trust" (2018) 24(3) T. & T. 266.
220 See, however, M.P. Thompson [1984] Conv. 43.
221 *Lake v Bayliss* [1974] 2 All E.R. 1114.
222 See P. Turner (2012) 128 L.Q.R. 582.

the purchase money is paid and the purchaser has no remaining obligations to perform under the contract, the vendor is but a bare trustee who must convey legal title to the purchaser forthwith.[223] Prior to this stage, many judges point in diverse terms to a qualified trusteeship with the vendor described variously as a "constructive trustee" or a "trustee *sub modo*",[224] a "quasi-trustee",[225] or a trustee "in a modified sense".[226] It is important to recognise that the vendor-trustee occupies an unusual position. She is at liberty to safeguard her own interest in the property until conveyance. In other words, she can act in a capacity which seems at odds with the office of trustee.

In *Southern Pacific Mortgages Ltd v Scott*,[227] the Supreme Court was called upon to consider the nature of the vendor-purchaser constructive trust. Here, Mrs Scott had agreed to sell her home to a purchaser who in turn agreed to lease it back to her for the remainder of her life. In order to finance the purchase, the purchaser entered into a buy to let mortgage but did not disclose the agreement with Mrs Scott. When the purchaser defaulted on the loan and was then to disappear, the mortgagee sought to take possession of the property. Mrs Scott argued that she had an equitable interest that was binding on the bank. On exchange of contracts, she argued, the purchaser acquired an interest under a constructive trust which was itself subject to her interest arising on account of the purchaser's promise to allow her to remain in occupation of the land. The Supreme Court reached the conclusion that the rights acquired by Mrs Scott were merely personal in nature and could not bind the bank. Lord Collins accepted that a purchaser acquires rights enforceable against third parties, but it did not follow that the purchaser has "proprietary rights for all purposes".[228] Instead, he explained, "where the proprietary right is claimed to be derived from the rights of a person who does not have the legal estate, then the right needs to be 'fed' by the acquisition of the legal estate before it can be asserted otherwise than personally".[229] Mrs Scott's claim was destined to fail.

Informal trusts of the family home

As regards the informal acquisition of an interest in the family home, the so-called common intention constructive trust arises on the basis of the bargain between the parties (evidenced by their express discussions or conduct) as to their shared equitable interests.[230] A full analysis of the operation of constructive trusts in this context is provided in Ch.11.

10-046

223 *Lloyds Bank Plc v Carrick* [1996] 4 All E.R. 630.
224 Per Stamp LJ in *Berkley v Poulett* (1977) 242 E.G. 39 at 42.
225 Per Lord Greene MR in *Cumberland Consolidated Holdings Ltd v Ireland* [1946] K.B. 264 at 269.
226 Per Kekewich J in *Royal Bristol Permanent Building Society v Bomash* (1887) 35 Ch. D. 390 at 397.
227 [2015] A.C. 385.
228 [2015] A.C. 385 at [65].
229 [2015] A.C. 385 at [71].
230 *Lloyds Bank Plc v Rosset* [1991] 1 A.C. 107.

Mutual wills

10-047

It will be recalled from Ch.5 that mutual wills arise where two or more parties enter into a binding agreement that they will execute wills in a mutual form on the understanding that the wills will be irrevocable.[231] Typically, a husband and wife may enter into an agreement that each will execute a will whereby the survivor will inherit the property of the deceased spouse. On the death of the survivor, their pooled property will pass to nominated beneficiaries, usually the children of the marriage. On the date of death of the first testator, a constructive trust comes into effect[232] and it is no longer open to the surviving party to leave that property to an alternative beneficiary (e.g. to a new wife).[233] As Lord Camden explained in *Dufour v Pereira*, "It might have been revoked by both jointly . . . but I cannot be of opinion . . . that after the death of either, it could be done by the survivor by another will . . . The first that dies, carries his part of the contract into execution".[234]

Accordingly, it can be seen that a constructive trust binds the survivor and prevents disposal otherwise than under the terms of the mutual agreement. By this means, equity intervenes in order to prevent the fraud that would arise if the survivor were able to take the benefit of the agreement without performing his obligations. The imposition of a constructive trust is widely viewed as a clumsy mechanism to give effect to the parties' intentions and prevent the commission of fraud. As Mummery LJ laments, "recent cases have shown this equitable doctrine dating from the 18th century continues to be a source of contention for the families of those who have invoked it".[235] Nonetheless, the Law Commission resisted calling for its abolition in its 2017 Consultation Paper, with the rationale that the arguments in favour "can be counterbalanced by the practical consideration that, however inflexible or inconvenient, they can provide a method of protecting a person's assets. The person who makes a mutual will has some certainty as to what will happen to their assets after the death of the first person to inherit and there are situations in which that certainty is important to the testator".[236]

Secret trusts

10-048

A final illustration of the capacity of equity to enforce the agreement of the parties by means of constructive trust lies in the context of secret trusts. It will be recalled that a secret trust is a

---

231 See Y. K. Liew, "The Ambit of the Mutual Wills Doctrine" (2016) 132 L.Q.R. 677.

232 "The obligation on the surviving testator is equitable. It is in the nature of a trust of the property affected, so the constructive trust label is attached to it": *Re Walters (Deceased)* [2009] Ch. 212 at 221 per Mummery LJ.

233 As M. Pawlowski and J. Brown note, "the consequences of the constructive trust imposed upon the survivor may be particularly onerous, given that all of the survivor's property may be locked into the trust and, at the same time, he may have formed additional commitments towards new partners or children" ("Problems With Mutual Wills—A Study of Probate Practice" [2012] Conv. 467, 480).

234 (1769) Dick 419 at 420.

235 *Olins v Walters* [2009] Ch. 212 at [3].

236 Law Commission, *Making a Will* (2017) Consultation Paper No. 231, para.12.31.

trust where the testator makes a gift of property in a will to a recipient who agrees to hold that property on trust for a third party.[237] Such trusts may be fully secret (i.e. where the existence of the trust and its terms are concealed) or half secret (i.e. where only the terms are concealed). The classification of secret trusts as express or constructive remains a controversial question and one on which the commentators disagree. Hodge, for example, views both half-secret and fully secret trusts as express trusts, where the trust arises from the expressed intentions of the deceased communicated to and accepted by the trustee in the testator's lifetime.[238] Although this view appears to be widely held, not all commentators accept the express trust model. Sheridan argues that the secret trust which arises without mention in the will or on intestacy is constructive and not express.[239] He bases his view upon the ground that, where a person has by a representation acquired property which it would be inequitable for him to keep, a constructive trust must arise. He adds that it makes no difference whether there is a transfer by will (as with a fully secret trust) or there is an inter vivos transfer. The same rule must apply in both cases. As Sheridan explains, "The fact that the transaction is a secret trust does not make it different in principle. It is but one illustration of the broad principle of constructive trusts, and should be so recognised".[240] Sheridan accepts, nonetheless, that as regards a half-secret trust, this must give rise to an express trust created by the will. He holds this view on the basis that there is a binding trust with the contest concerning only the question as to the identity of the beneficiary. There is no issue of the legatee obtaining property which it is inequitable for him to keep. The relevance of the debate as to the classification of secret trusts rests in the application of formalities. If a secret trust of land is classified as an express trust, it should be evidenced in writing by virtue of s.53(1)(b) of the Law of Property Act 1925 with the attendant consequence that the desired secrecy would be lost.[241]

Guide to Further Reading

Lord Briggs, "Equity in Business" (2019) 135 L.Q.R. 567
M. Conaglen, "Proprietary Remedies for Breach of Fiduciary Duty" (2014) 73(3) C.L.J. 490.
H. Delaney and D. Ryan, "Unconscionability: A Unifying Theme in Equity" [2008] Conv. 401.

---

237 See Ch.5.
238 D. Hodge, "Secret Trusts: The Fraud Theory Revisited" [1980] Conv. 341. See also T. Cheung, "Secret Trusts and Testamentary Freedom" (2019) 25(7) T. & T. 730.
239 L.A. Sheridan, "English and Irish Secret Trusts" (1951) 67 L.Q.R. 314; see also P. Mathews, "The True Basis of the Half-Secret Trust?" [1979] Conv. 360.
240 (1951) 67 L.Q.R. 314 at 324.
241 A similar principle applies if it is a secret trust of a subsisting equitable interest, the disposition should be created in writing for the purposes of s.53(1)(c): see Ch.4.

J. Grower, "Explaining the *Pallant v Morgan* Equity'" [2016] Conv. 434.

C. Harpum, "Accessory Liability for Procuring or Assisting a Breach of Trust" (1995) 111 L.Q.R. 545.

Y. K. Liew, "The Ambit of the Mutual Wills Doctrine" (2016) 132 L.Q.R. 677.

Y. K. Liew, "Reanalysing Institutional and Remedial Constructive Trusts" (2016) 74 C.L.J. 528.

B. McFarlane, "Constructive Trusts Arising on a Receipt of Property Sub Conditione" (2004) 120 L.Q.R. 667.

P. Shine, "Dishonesty in Civil Commercial Claims: A State of Mind or a Course of Conduct?" [2012] J.B.L. 29.

P. Shine, "Knowledge, Notice, Bad Faith and Dishonesty; Conceptual Uncertainty in Receipt Based Claims in Equitable Fraud" (2013) 24(8) I.C.C.L.R. 293.

P. Turner, "Understanding the Constructive Trust Between Vendor and Purchaser" (2012) 128 L.Q.R. 582.

11

Trusts of the Family Home

11-001

This chapter is concerned with the property rights of those who jointly own a home. These persons are usually, but not necessarily, married or unmarried couples. Other persons who may share a home, of course, include friends and relatives. The Office for National Statistics revealed that, in 2019, there were 19.2 million families living in the United Kingdom. Cohabiting couple families were the fastest-growing family type with an increase of 25.8% over the decade 2008 to 2018.[1] Married or civil partner couples remain the most common family type and, in 2019, represented two-thirds of families. In 2019, there were 212,000 same-sex families, marking an increase of 40.0% since 2015.[2] The social importance of co-ownership should not, therefore, be underestimated.[3] The family home is not only the major asset that most families will possess, but also the stage upon which family life is enacted. It is, moreover, utilised as a means of raising substantial amounts of cash whether to finance lifestyle improvements or to guarantee business debts. Hence, there are a number of circumstances where it will be crucial to determine what rights, if any, each party has in the property. The issue could arise, for example:

■ on the breakdown of the relationship between the co-owners. Attention then will focus upon whether the sharers are entitled to a payment of a capital sum representing their share of the home. It is at this point that the law traditionally draws a distinction between married couples and other types of relationship. The Matrimonial Causes Act 1973 gives the court the general power to redistribute property rights on divorce.

---

1 According to the Government Actuaries Department, *Marital Status Protection for England and Wales* (2005), by 2031 one in four couples living together will be unmarried.

2 See *https://www.ons.gov.uk/peoplepopulationandcommunity/birthsdeathsandmarriages/families/bulletins/familiesandhouseholds/2019* [Accessed 31 July 2020].

3 Nor, indeed, should the financial costs to the parties: see Law Commission, *Cohabitation: The Financial Consequences of Relationship Breakdown* (2006) Law Com. No.179.

An identical stance is now adopted in relation to registered partnerships under the Civil Partnership Act 2004 (as amended the Civil Partnerships, Marriage and Deaths (Registration etc) Act 2019). As will become clear, there is (as yet) no special treatment of family assets of unmarried and non-registered partnerships;

- on the death of one of the co-owners. The issue here will concern whether the deceased had an interest in the property and, if so, what is now to happen to it;

- when the property has been purchased with the aid of a mortgage and the borrower has subsequently defaulted. The lender will seek to exercise its power of sale, obtain vacant possession and discharge the debt from the proceeds of sale. It is, therefore, imperative for the lender to ascertain whether there is anyone living in the property who can claim priority and thereby defend possession proceedings or make a superior claim against the sale proceeds;

- when a confiscation order has been made under the Proceeds of Crime Act 2002 (as amended). The issue of beneficial ownership can assume crucial importance here as the order can attach only to the property of the convicted criminal and not to, say, the beneficial interest of the offender's spouse[4];

- when an unsecured creditor seeks to sell the property so that the debt can be satisfied. The question then arises whether any co-owner can resist the creditor's claim against the home.[5] Similarly, in *Arif v Anwar* the claimant's son asserted (albeit unsuccessfully) a 50 per cent claim against the family home. The purpose was to reduce the size of the bankruptcy estate of the father[6]; and

- in relation to liability to tax or, as in *Heron v Sandwell MBC*,[7] the additional payment of owner-occupier's supplement following compulsory purchase of land.

Not surprisingly, the key purpose of this chapter is to examine when co-ownership arises and how, once it has arisen, the shares of the co-owners are quantified. Unlike with divorce or the dissolution of a registered partnership, on the breakdown of non-marital and non-registered relationships there is currently no overarching principle under which the parties' assets can be redistributed,[8] nor is there the ability for a judge always to produce a result that is fair and

---

4   See *Edwards v CPS* [2011] EWHC 1688 (Admin); *Re Ali* [2012] EWHC 2302 (Admin).

5   See *Walton v Allman* [2015] EWHC 3325 (Ch). There a charging order was made over a judgment debtor's beneficial interest in land even though that interest had yet to be quantified.

6   [2015] EWHC 124 (Fam). The son was, however, able to claim a 25% beneficial share.

7   (1980) 255 E.G. 65.

8   There is no legal concept of "a common law marriage". There have been attempts to introduce legislation in the form of the several Cohabitation Rights Bills put before Parliament since 2008. The recent Cohabitation Rights Bill 2019 has similarly failed to progress through Parliament.

reasonable in the circumstances.[9] There is no doctrine of "family assets"[10] and the entitlement of a party turns purely upon the application, as between strangers, of cold and inflexible principles of law and equity. As admitted by Waite J in *Hammond v Mitchell*:

> "Had they been married, the issue of ownership would scarcely have been relevant, because the law these days when dealing with the financial consequences of divorce, adopts a forward-looking perspective in which questions of ownership yield to the higher demands of relating the means of both to the needs of each . . . Since this couple did not marry, none of that flexibility is available to them . . . their financial rights have to be worked out according to their strict entitlements in equity, a process which is anything but forward-looking and involves, on the contrary, a painfully detailed retrospect".[11]

The concepts considered in this chapter are heavily dependent upon context (e.g. whether the property was purchased in sole or joint names and whether it is acquired for a domestic or commercial purpose) and include:

11-002

- express trusts;

- equity follows the law;

- resulting trusts;

- constructive trusts;

- estoppel.

---

9   As the Ministry of Justice admits in its *Report on the Implementation of Law Commission Proposals* (24 January 2011) HC Paper No.719, para.28, "The existing law is a patchwork of legal rules, sometimes providing cohabitants with interests in their partners' property. The law is unsatisfactory: it is complex, uncertain, and expensive to rely on. It gives rise to hardship for many cohabitants and, as a consequence, their children".

10   See *Pettitt v Pettitt* [1970] A.C. 777.

11   [1991] 1 W.L.R. 1127 at 1129.

An Express Declaration of Trust

11-003 The displacement of the working rule that legal title carries with it the equitable title will, understandably, occur when it can be shown that the legal owner holds the property subject to an express trust in favour of an ascertainable beneficiary. Retreating to basics, an express trust will arise where the legal owner expressly declares himself to be a trustee or conveys the property to a third party expressly subject to a trust. Either way, this will ensure the separation of legal and equitable title. Nominal ownership vests in the legal owner whereas true entitlement rests with the beneficiary. The terms of the express trust will usually be conclusive of the matter, even if the selection made is due to erroneous advice, but as will be shown the terms are not immutable.[12] It will, however, be recalled that express trusts of land are subject to additional formalities as prescribed in s.53(1)(b) of the Law of Property Act 1925. The statutory prescription is that, in order for an express trust of land to be enforceable, the declaration of trust must be evidenced in writing, which is signed by the settlor. As shown in Ch.4, the use of formal means of rights creation reflects the need for certainty and clarity in dealings with land.

Accordingly, if Fred is the sole legal owner of a house and seeks to declare an express trust of the land in favour of his grandson, Jordan, he is expected to comply with s.53(1)(b). Fred should, therefore, set out his intention to create a trust and its terms in writing and attach his signature to the relevant document. Only then will the express trust become enforceable by Jordan.

11-004 In *Simpson v Simpson*,[13] a daughter (Phyllis) claimed that, in 1966 when her father (James) transferred his home to a family company in return for £15,000, there was an express trust created in her favour. The property was now worth somewhere in the region of £1 million. Her difficulty was that there was no written contemporaneous evidence of what was agreed in 1966. It was clear that the ostensible sale to the Company was not the real transaction or, at least, not the whole of the transaction that took place. The father had entered the transaction in order to ensure that the family home was beyond the reach of potential creditors. There was sufficient evidence to show the intention to create an express oral trust in favour of Phyllis. In order to satisfy s.53(1)(b), the judge found documentation that prima facie qualified as evidence of the trust. In 1981, a director of the Company (Harry) had executed a statutory declaration stating that the property was held on trust for Phyllis. In 1983, Harry signed a statement that also recognised that the directors had agreed that the property was to be held on trust for Phyllis.

Harry, however, was profoundly dyslexic and the Company argued that he could not be taken to have agreed the contents of the documents. The judge was unimpressed and concluded that Harry would have had the documents explained to him at the time of his signature. Accordingly, for Harry to escape the effect of signing the documents he would have to show that they were untrue and that he was improperly persuaded to sign them. He could show neither

---

12   *Clarke v Meadus* [2010] EWHC 3117 (Ch). The stated interests can be overridden by an estoppel or a constructive trust.
13   [2005] EWHC 2098 (Ch).

of these events. Even though Harry could not read or understand the documents without assistance, they offered signed, written evidence of the oral trust in favour of Phyllis. The High Court added that, for the trust to be enforced, Phyllis would be required to pay the £15,000 or other sum due to the Company. It is to be borne in mind that, "He who seeks equity must do equity".

Of course, an implied trust might arise from the ashes of a failed express trust[14] and, indeed, it might be that any written, but unsigned, documentation will shape the terms of that implied trust.[15] It will become clear that equity attaches major significance to the underlying intent of dealings and the prevention of fraud and unconscionable conduct. Consider that Adrienne is the sole legal owner of a house in which she lives with her partner, Fred. She encourages Fred to spend money on the family home based upon the informal assurance that he will have a beneficial interest in the property. These factors should give rise to a constructive trust under which Fred will be able to claim a share even though there is no signed, written evidence in support. Such informal trusts are considered later in this chapter.

Joint names and the statutory trust

By way of a further gloss, a statutory trust of land arises automatically under s.1(2) of the Trusts of Land and Appointment of Trustees Act 1996 when two or more persons become the holders of the legal title to land. In such joint enterprises, the existence of a trust does not have to be spelled out on the face of the conveyance. The statutory trust instead arises by operation of law and, as Etherton LJ observed, "the only question is as to the size of the respective beneficial interests of the parties".[16] Understandably, the best way forward has always been to acknowledge the trust expressly and, more importantly, to specify the beneficial interests thereunder in the conveyance itself.[17] Not surprisingly, the courts have long urged conveyancers to insert an express declaration as the invariable standard practice.[18] Although a failure to do so might expose the conveyancer to an action in negligence,[19] this best practice is still not always adopted.[20] As Ward LJ lamented, "Perhaps conveyancers do not read the law reports. I will try one more time: always try to agree on and then record how the beneficial interest is to be held. It is not very difficult to do".[21]

11-005

---

14 Section 53(2) states that implied, resulting and constructive trusts are not subject to the formality of signed writing.
15 *Sleebush v Gordon* [2004] EWHC 2287 (Ch).
16 *Thompson v Hurst* [2014] 1 F.L.R. 238 at [22].
17 See C Bevan, "The search for common intention: the status of an executed, express declaration of trust post Stack and Jones" (2019) 135 L.Q.R. 660.
18 As Bagnall J in *Cowcher v Cowcher* [1972] 1 W.L.R. 425 at 442 observed, "The just resolution of future disputes would be facilitated; the additional costs would be insignificant; and I cannot think that connubial harmony would be unduly jeopardised".
19 See *Walker v Hall* [1984] 5 F.L.R. 126.
20 See *McKenzie v McKenzie* [2003] EWHC 601 (Ch).
21 *Carlton v Goodman* [2002] EWCA Civ 545 at [44].

Indeed since 1998, it has been possible (but it is not mandatory) under the Land Registration Rules that the joint registered proprietors make a declaration as to the beneficial interests under the trust of land. The Land Registry has devised a specific form for this purpose and this is known as the Land Registry Trust Information form. The transfer will, however, be valid whether or not this form is completed. As Baroness Hale pointed out in *Stack v Dowden*, "so there may still be transfers of registered land into joint names in which there is no express declaration of the beneficial interests".[22] Although this facility does not assist those involved with pre-1998 purchases, the attraction of such a compulsory declaration is that it promotes certainty and is usually determinative of whether the parties are to hold as joint tenants or as tenants in common with individual shares. The Law Commission explained that:

> **"Where two people buy a home together, there is rarely a problem. They are likely to seek legal advice. If they are married, or, although not married, are in a long-term relationship, it is very likely that they will decide to have title to the home registered in their joint names. They will also execute a declaration of trust stipulating what their respective shares in the property are to be—this will then govern the proportions into which the proceeds of sale of the house would be divided in the event of sale".[23]**

11-006   An interesting, albeit unusual, issue arose in *Sleebush v Gordon*.[24] There a declaration of a tenancy in common was duly inserted in a conveyance into the joint names of a son and his mother. Inexplicably, both had failed to sign the conveyance. Mrs Sleebush later claimed that the absence of the signatures invalidated the declaration of a tenancy in common. She asserted that, as the original purchasers had contributed to the purchase price in equal proportions, a beneficial joint tenancy should, instead, be presumed. On this understanding, and by virtue of the right of survivorship, Mrs Sleebush would become the sole legal and beneficial owner of the property. The High Court felt that the absence of the signatures did not connote a rejection of the declaration of a tenancy in common and that any presumption of a joint tenancy was effectively rebutted by the declaration in the conveyance. Accordingly, the unexecuted declaration offered conclusive proof of the parties' intentions as to beneficial ownership at the outset. Even though the declaration did not satisfy the formalities set out in s.53(1)(b), the transfer took effect according to its terms.[25] In post-Stack times (see below), this would evidence a common intention contrary to the presumption of a joint tenancy that otherwise would arise from the fact that the conveyance is taken in joint names.

The first step, therefore, is to scour the conveyance for an indication of how the parties are to hold beneficially. Absent a direct incantation, this is not always a straightforward task.

---

22   [2007] 2 A.C. 432 at 453.
23   Law Commission, *Sharing Homes: A Discussion Paper* (2002) Law Com. No.278, p.vi, para.3.
24   [2004] EWHC 2287 (Ch).
25   See also, *Roy v Roy* [1996] 1 F.L.R. 541; *Pink v Lawrence* (1978) 36 P. & C.R. 98.

In *Stack v Dowden*,[26] for example, the conveyance to the parties contained no words of trust. The parties, however, necessarily held the property on statutory trust for themselves. The issue concerned the extent of their respective beneficial interests under that trust. The conveyance contained a declaration that the survivor of them was entitled to give a valid receipt for capital money. The insertion of this type of clause is indicative of a joint tenancy as it is consistent with the right of survivorship.[27] The House of Lords considered the evidential weight (if any) to be given to the receipt clause and concluded that the mere insertion of the receipt clause did not itself amount to an express declaration of trust.[28] The House did, however, accept that, if the parties had understood the significance of the receipt clause (i.e. it was consistent only with the right of survivorship), the inference that they intended a beneficial joint tenancy could be drawn.

The involvement of conveyancers offers to the parties the ready opportunity to make an express declaration of trust. Obviously, the same opportunity is denied when the co-ownership arises after the purchase of the property. For example, where Fred buys a house in 2000 and Adrienne moves in with him in 2020 it is highly improbable that either will seek professional advice. Accordingly, as the Law Commission acknowledged:

11-007

"In this latter situation, it is relatively rare for the parties to make an express declaration of their respective beneficial entitlements. It is unusual for such persons to seek legal advice at such a time, and there is no occasion equivalent to registration of title to the property following a purchase which would afford an opportunity to advise those sharing the home of the advantages of making formal provision".[29]

Departing from the declared terms of an express trust

11-008

On the finding of an express and genuine[30] declaration of trust, only in exceptional circumstances will its terms not be definitive of the parties' true beneficial entitlement.[31] As Sir Peter Gibson put it, "Where the parties have reached a consensus on the beneficial interests in the property, the court will give effect to it, unless there is very good reason for not doing so, such

---

26   [2007] 2 A.C. 432.
27   *Re Gorman* [1990] 1 W.L.R. 616. The appropriate declaration when a tenancy in common has been created is that a valid receipt for capital monies cannot be obtained from one survivor alone.
28   See also *Huntingford v Hobbs* [1993] 1 F.L.R. 736.
29   Law Commission, *Sharing Homes: A Discussion Paper* (2002) Law Com. No.278, para.2.45.
30   A sham trust (i.e. where the parties have the common intention that the acts or documents are not to create the legal rights and obligations which they give the appearance of creating) will be ineffective: *Erlam v Rahman* [2016] EWHC 111 (Ch).
31   *Pettitt v Pettitt* [1970] A.C. 777; *Pankhania v Chandegra* [2012] EWCA Civ 1438.

as a subsequent renegotiation . . .".[32] This reluctance was further evidenced in *Goodman v Gallant*.[33] There a couple bought a house in 1978 and the conveyance defined their respective beneficial interests by stating that they held "upon trust for themselves as joint tenants". In 1983, the couple separated and Mrs Goodman served a written notice of severance on Mr Gallant. The effect of this notice was to convert the pre-existing beneficial joint tenancy into a tenancy in common. Mrs Goodman claimed that, as she had paid three-quarters of the purchase price, she was entitled to a three-quarter share of the proceeds of sale. The Court of Appeal rejected this claim on the basis that the parties could not go behind the express declaration of trust and that the declaration was conclusive.[34] On a subsequent sale, each party was thereby entitled to a half share of the proceeds. Slade LJ observed that "there is no room for the application of the doctrine of resulting implied or constructive trusts unless and until the conveyance is set aside or rectified; until that event the declaration contained in the document speaks for itself".[35] Accordingly, there is no need usually for the court to look beyond the four corners of the declaration. As the Law Commission concluded, "It is essential, in order to reward those who make proper provision, that courts continue rigorously to enforce express declarations of trust".[36]

The declaration of trust is not, however, entirely sacrosanct. It is possible that the transaction may be set aside on the basis of fraud or mistake, misrepresentation or other equitable wrongdoing (e.g. undue influence or duress).[37] This explains the (albeit unsuccessful) attempt in *Simpson v Simpson* to avoid a written declaration on the basis of severe dyslexia on the part of the signatory.[38] An express declaration of trust cannot, moreover, bind those who are not a party to the purchase. This was demonstrated in *City of London Building Society v Flegg*[39] where a house was purchased by the parties as joint tenants in law and in equity. Over half of the purchase price was provided by one party's parents and, as such, the parents were able to claim an interest in the property by virtue of a resulting trust. The arrangement between the joint tenants governed their entitlement only as regards their interests in the property, but as the parents had not executed the declaration it could not affect their entitlement.

11-009   The Privy Council was invited to look beyond the terms of a declaration of a tenancy in common in *Potter v Potter*.[40] This litigation arose out of the breakdown of the relationship between two cousins, the appellant (Mr Potter) and the respondent (Ms Potter). In 1998, they

---

32   *Crossley v Crossley* [2005] EWCA Civ 1581 at [32]; see also *Mortgage Corp v Shaire* [2001] Ch. 743.

33   [1986] Fam. 106.

34   See also *Richards v Wood* unreported 27 February 2014 CA where the contributions of the parties as recited in the declaration of trust bound the parties whether true or not.

35   [1986] Fam. 106 at 111.

36   Law Commission, *Sharing Homes: A Discussion Paper* (2002) Law Com. No. 278, para.2.52.

37   *Pink v Lawrence* (1978) 36 P. & C.R. 98. For example, in *Re Colebrook's Conveyances* [1972] 1 W.L.R. 1397 rectification was available where the parties had intended to be tenants in common, but the conveyance stated that they were joint tenants.

38   [2005] EWHC 2098 (Ch).

39   [1988] A.C. 54.

40   [2004] UKPC 41.

bought a home in New Zealand for the sum of $875,000. Before the purchase was completed, they took the precaution of sorting out the financial arrangements between them. Following the receipt of independent legal advice, the parties entered into a "Property Sharing Agreement". The agreement covered issues such as the declaration of beneficial ownership to the intention subsequently to create a formal family trust. The property was registered in their joint names. Six months after moving into the property the parties' relationship ended, but no family trust had yet been executed. Mr Potter commenced litigation, seeking an order for sale and orders that would exclude Ms Potter from any share in the proceeds. She argued that she was entitled to a share in the net proceeds of sale.

The resolution of the dispute turned upon the content and construction of the written agreement. Lord Scott read the agreement as giving the respondent a half-share. This was so even though Mr Potter had provided the purchase monies and defrayed the acquisition costs of the purchase. Mr Potter, however, attempted to vary the agreement by contending that Ms Potter's beneficial half share was impliedly subject to defeasance on the breakdown of the relationship. This argument was rejected. There was no express term to this effect and, in order for such a defeasance condition to be implied, it would be necessary to show that this was Ms Potter's intention at the time of the agreement. This was clearly not possible on the present facts. Once purchased, the property was to be held by the couple in equal shares both at law and beneficially. Although the breakdown of the relationship led to a frustration of their intentions to create a family trust, it did not justify reversing the parts of the agreement that had been implemented.

In *Wade v Grimwood*,[41] property was purchased in joint names and an ancillary trust deed was drafted. This contained a declaration that the purchasers were to hold as beneficial tenants in common and that, after all expenses and debts were discharged, the proceeds of sale were to be divided between the couple with an 80 per cent entitlement in favour of Mr Wade. Clause 4 of the trust deed stated that the parties were to bear equally the costs, expenses and outgoings payable in respect of the property. The property was sold for £510,000 and Mr Wade then commenced proceedings seeking a declaration that he was entitled to the whole of the proceeds of sale or, in the alternative, an account for the payments made solely by him of cl.4 costs. Sir Martin Nourse felt that this argument was untenable. First, cl.4 did not disturb the allocation of beneficial shares, which remained at 80 per cent in favour of Mr Wade. Secondly, the present facts gave rise to a set-off situation, with each obligation being enforceable immediately. Clause 4 imposed mutual, but independent, obligations on the parties to contribute to costs, expenses and outgoings as they became payable. Hence, if one party made an entire payment, that party acquired an immediate cause of action against the other for reimbursement. Mr Wade had, however, impliedly waived any rights to a contribution from his partner. He had led his former partner to believe that he was not going to enforce any right to reimbursement against her and she had ordered her affairs accordingly. As Sir Martin Nourse concluded, "this was not a commercial agreement between strangers . . . As between parties living happily together, that is surely enough to establish waiver.

11-010

---

41 [2004] EWCA Civ 999.

It is not appropriate to insist on the formalities of waiver in its application to an informal relationship".[42]

In *Clarke v Meadus*,[43] a property was registered in the joint names of Mrs Clarke and Mrs Meadus (her mother). An express declaration of trust was executed in 1996, under which each party was to have a beneficial half-share. Mrs Clarke subsequently claimed to be the sole beneficial owner or, in the alternative, a co-owner in such shares as the court should determine with a right for the mother to live there for life. Her claim was founded upon the assertion of a constructive trust and/or an estoppel arising from representations made by the mother. Warren J accepted that the express trust declared in 1996 could be overridden by an estoppel as a result of such subsequent promises and representations. He explained that, "It cannot, in my judgment, sensibly be argued that once beneficial interests have been declared in a formal document, those interests become immutable and incapable of being affected by a proprietary estoppel".[44] Bevan, however, sounds a more cautionary note, "To license and sanction an undoing of a written, express declaration of trust on the grounds of equitable concepts which are seemingly drawing closer to and becoming synonymous with ill-defined (if laudable) concepts of fairness and reasonableness and to permit the breakdown of the clear boundaries between formalism and equity's conscience would be to open a Pandora's box".[45]

As regards the constructive trust argument, the position was more difficult, "That claim seems to rely on a remedial constructive trust, a juridical beast which English case law has set its face against".[46] Warren J felt that the express declaration of trust did not preclude the existence in theory of a remedial constructive trust, "once Mrs Clarke has jumped the hurdle of establishing the availability of such a remedy as a matter of English law".[47] She was, of course, unable to do so. As Dixon acknowledged, "The quintessential expression of equity's conscience—the constructive trust in the family home—must yield to the formalism of the law".[48]

Significance of Legal Title

11-011 The maxim "equity follows the law" has some application here with the *prima facie* inference being that ownership of the legal estate carries with it the beneficial interest. In *Stack v*

---

42 [2004] EWCA Civ 999 at [18].

43 [2010] EWHC 3117 (Ch).

44 [2010] EWHC 3117 (Ch) at [56].

45 C. Bevan, "The search for common intention: the status of an executed, express declaration of trust post Stack and Jones" (2019) 135 L.Q.R. 660, 677.

46 [2010] EWHC 3117 (Ch) at [82].

47 [2010] EWHC 3117 (Ch) at [83].

48 M. Dixon, "To Write or Not to Write" [2013] Conv 1, 5.

Dowden,[49] the House of Lords considered the effect of a conveyance into the joint names of a cohabiting couple in circumstances when there was no explicit declaration of their respective beneficial interests.[50] Lord Hope acknowledged that the legal framework should be as simple and as accessible as possible. He explained:

> **"cohabiting couples are in a different kind of relationship. The place where they live together is their home. Living together is an exercise in give and take, mutual co-operation and compromise. Who pays for what in regard to the home has to be seen in the wider context of their overall relationship. A more practical, down-to-earth, fact-based approach is called for in their case".[51]**

Lord Hope observed that the legal title cases may be broken down into those where there is sole legal ownership and those where there is joint legal ownership.[52] Each has a different starting point. In the former, sole beneficial ownership is presumed.[53] This is so even if the parties had originally intended to purchase in joint names, but decided otherwise on the mistaken advice of a mortgage broker.[54] It follows that, as Lord Hope explained, "in a case of sole legal ownership the onus is on the party who wishes to show that he has any beneficial interest at all, and if so what that interest is".[55] This may be done only by establishing the existence of a trust (whether express, resulting[56] or constructive) or proprietary estoppel.[57] If established, the trust will establish both beneficial ownership and its extent.[58] Estoppel, as will become clear, is a less predictable vehicle. If none of these mechanisms can be successfully invoked, equitable title will be vested in the sole legal owner.[59] Such is evident from *Burns v Burns*, where

---

49   [2007] 2 A.C. 432.

50   A. Briggs, "Co-ownership and an Equitable Non Sequitur" (2012) 128 L.Q.R. 183, 183 was suitably unimpressed with this invocation of principle: "This was a textbook example of how not to resort to the maxims of equity. For on this issue the law gives no lead, and there is nothing to follow . . . It was therefore wrong for this maxim to conjure up the thought that conveyance to joint names created a joint tenancy in equity".

51   [2007] 2 A.C. 432 at 439.

52   See M. Mills, "Single name family home constructive trusts: is Lloyds Bank v Rosset still good law?" [2018] Conv. 350.

53   *Crossley v Crossley* [2005] EWCA Civ 1581; *Thompson v Hurst* [2014] 1 F.L.R. 238.

54   *Thompson v Hurst* [2014] 1 F.L.R. 238. As Etherton LJ concluded at [20], "The transfer was not in fact into the joint names of the appellant and the respondent. There is, therefore, no scope for a legal presumption that the parties intended a joint tenancy both in law and equity".

55   [2007] 2 A.C. 432 at 439; see also *Crisp v Mullings* (1976) 239 E.G. 119.

56   For example, in *R v Yuganthini Thayaparan* [2019] EWCA Crim 247, the transfer was in the sole name of the wife, but the husband was still held to be the sole beneficial owner for the purposes of a confiscation order. The purchase had been funded by his criminal activity and the wife's bank account had been operated at his behest.

57   *Gissing v Gissing* [1971] A.C. 886. The burden of proof lies with the claimant: *Rezaeipoor v Arabhalvai* [2012] EWHC 146 (Ch).

58   *Mountney v Treharne* [2003] Ch. 135.

59   As in *Hunt v Conwy CBC* [2014] 1 W.L.R. 254, where Mrs Hunt was unable to establish a beneficial interest in a seaside pier; see also *Patrick v McKinley* [2017] EWCA Civ 2068.

Ms Burns fell through the metaphorical cracks and, despite holding a family and family home together for years, was able to claim nothing.[60] More recently, in *Dobson v Griffey*[61] a co-habitant was held to have no beneficial interest in a farm which she had shared with her partner, but which he had purchased in his sole name. There was no common intention, no agreement and no detrimental reliance.

11-012

Ms Dowden and Mr Stack commenced their relationship as teenage sweethearts. In 1993, they took out a mortgage in joint names and jointly purchased a home together for £190,000. The property was registered in joint names, but the transfer did not state their beneficial interests. At this time, they had been cohabiting for 18 years and had produced four children. Nine years later, their relationship broke down. The purchase had been financed by a £129,000 payment from Ms Dowden's building society account with the outstanding sum being provided by a mortgage from Barclays Bank. Two endowment policies were taken out, one in joint names and one in Ms Dowden's sole name. Mr Stack paid the mortgage interest and the premiums on the joint policy to a total amount of approximately £34,000. Ms Dowden paid the premiums on the policy which was in her sole name. The principal of the mortgage loan was repaid by a series of lump sum payments, to which Mr Stack contributed £27,000 and Ms Dowden over £38,000. The utility bills were in Ms Dowden's name and she paid all or most of them. Accordingly, there was a substantial disparity between their respective financial contributions to the purchase of the property. The parties continued to maintain separate bank accounts and each made a number of separate investments. Mr Stack sought a declaration that the house was held upon trust by the couple as tenants in common and an order for its sale.

The case is significant because it allowed the House of Lords to establish a new working rule, designed to operate in family home, joint names cases. It adopted the form of a presumption that beneficial ownership is to be divided between the legal owners equally. As Baroness Hale put it, "It should only be expected that joint transferees would have spelt out their beneficial interests when they intended them to be different from their legal interests . . . the starting point where there is joint legal ownership is joint beneficial ownership".[62] The onus lies heavily with a party who wishes to show that the beneficial interests are otherwise divided.[63] Indeed, only in unusual circumstances will the beneficial interests be found to be different from the legal interests.[64] In *Stack v Dowden*, Baroness Hale emphasised that unequal contributions to the purchase price alone will not rebut the presumption: "It cannot be the case that all the

---

60   [1984] Ch. 317. Similarly, in *Ullah v Ullah* [2013] EWHC 2296 (Ch) the claimant unsuccessfully asserted a beneficial interest in seven properties in London. He could not establish either a common intention constructive trust or a resulting trust.

61   [2018] EWHC 1117 (Ch).

62   [2007] 2 A.C. 432 at 453.

63   See *Gibson v Revenue & Customs Prosecution Office* [2008] EWCA Civ 645 where it was a third party (HM Revenue & Customs) which attempted to challenge the presumption of equal division (there between husband and wife).

64   As Etherton LJ explained in *Thompson v Hurst* [2014] 1 F.L.R. 238 at [19], "The presumption that they intended their equitable interest to be equal could be rebutted only by evidence of their intention, actual or inferred, objectively ascertained".

hundreds of thousands, if not millions, of transfers into joint names . . . are vulnerable to challenge in the courts simply because it is likely that the owners contributed unequally to their purchase".[65] The resulting trust appears now to have no role to play in these domestic joint names cases as "It is not possible at one and the same time to have a presumption or starting point of joint beneficial interests and a presumption (let alone a rule) that the parties' beneficial interests are in proportion to their respective financial contributions".[66] It has, therefore, been argued that the rebutting party must establish some form of unjust enrichment of the other in order to shift this evidential presumption.[67] Any alteration of beneficial entitlement must, therefore, occur behind a common intention constructive trust or via an estoppel claim.

This change in the law has obvious attraction, for, as Lord Hope concluded:

> **"The advantage of this approach is that everyone will know where they stand with regard to the property when they enter into their relationship. Parties are, of course, free to enter into whatever bargain they wish and, so long as it is clearly expressed and can be proved, the court will give effect to it. But for the rest the state of the legal title will determine the right starting point. The onus is then on the party who contends that the beneficial interests are divided between them otherwise than as the title shows to demonstrate this on the facts".[68]**

This approach is not, however, without its critics.[69] Subsequently, in *Laskar v Laskar*[70] Neuberger LJ (sitting in the Court of Appeal) made clear that the joint names presumption, as advocated in *Stack v Dowden*, does not apply to commercial cases (e.g. where property is bought for development or letting).[71] In *Laskar*, the property was purchased primarily as an investment for rental income and capital appreciation. It was not purchased as a home. Hence, and even though the parties were mother and daughter, the resulting trust presumption still applied.

---

65 [2007] 2 A.C. 432 at 459. Ironically, in *Stack v Dowden* the final division of the proceeds of sale of the house was in shares roughly equating to the parties' overall financial contributions.

66 Per Lord Walker and Baroness Hale in *Jones v Kernott* [2012] 1 A.C .776 at [23]. A sentiment shared by Lord Collins at [60], "There is no presumption that the parties intended that the beneficial interest be shared in proportion to their financial contributions to the acquisition of the property".

67 See T. Etherton, "Constructive Trusts: A New Model for Equity and Unjust Enrichment" (2008) C.L.J. 265; M. Harding, "Defending Stack v Dowden" [2009] Conv. 309.

68 [2007] 2 A.C. 432 at 439. Pitchford LJ in *O'Kelly v Davies* [2014] EWCA Civ 1606 at [18] believed that the change signified "a more sympathetic approach in an evolving social environment to the assessment of beneficial property rights of cohabiting partners".

69 See W. Swadling, "The Common Intention Construction Trust in the House of Lords: An Opportunity Missed" (2007) 123 L.Q.R. 511; M. Dixon, "The Never-Ending Story—Co-Ownership After *Stack v Dowden*" [2007] Conv. 456.

70 [2008] 1 W.L.R. 2695.

71 See also *Erlam v Rahman* [2016] EWHC 111 (Ch) where domestic partners were also business partners and the property was purchased jointly as an investment for rental income and capital appreciation.

11-013

This majority view of the House, however, departs from the traditional approach[72] and was roundly rejected by Lord Neuberger. Nevertheless, as to the result, he achieved a similar outcome by employing resulting trust principles. In his dissenting speech, he accepted that equal beneficial ownership in joint names cases was a starting point, but felt that, when the parties had contributed unequally to the purchase price, it should readily be displaced by the presumption of a resulting trust.[73] Speaking extra-judicially, Lord Neuberger regarded the majority decision in *Stack* as amounting to an unjustified rewriting of the law of resulting trusts.[74] He was particularly cautious as regards changes effected by the courts and not Parliament. Accordingly, he felt that the law of resulting and constructive trusts was flexible enough to deal with these types of problems.[75]

Jones v Kernott

11-014

In *Jones v Kernott*,[76] Ms Jones and Mr Kernott bought a house in joint names in 1985. The purchase price was £30,000 and Ms Jones paid a deposit of £6,000. The balance was raised by an endowment mortgage in joint names. Mr Kernott paid £100 per week towards household expenses while they lived at the property. Ms Jones paid the mortgage and other household bills out of their joint resources. In 1986, the couple took out a loan to finance the building of an extension. The extension added around 50 per cent to the value of the property. In 1993, Mr Kernott moved out of the property. The parties had, therefore, lived together in the property for over five years, sharing household expenses. Following the separation, Ms Jones remained living in the property with the children and paid all the household expenses herself. In 1995, the couple agreed to cash in a joint life assurance policy and the proceeds were divided between them. This enabled Mr Kernott to put down a deposit on a home of his own. He was able to finance the mortgage repayments on his purchase because he was making no contributions

---

72 Which was that there was no difference between sole name cases and joint name cases and that any presumption that equity followed the law could be easily rebutted: see *McKenzie v McKenzie* [2003] EWHC 601 (Ch). A return to orthodoxy is advocated by S. Gardner and K. Davidson, "The Future of *Stack v Dowden*" (2011) 127 L.Q.R.13.

73 A glimpse behind the scenes as regards his dissenting speech was provided by Lord Neuberger in a paper entitled, "UK Supreme Court decisions on private and commercial law: The role of public policy and public interest" delivered at Centre for Commercial Law Studies Conference 2015, 4 December 2015, *https://www.supremecourt. uk/docs/speech-151204.pdf* [Accessed 31 July 2020]. He admits that it was many weeks after the hearing that he discovered that he was the sole dissenter. Until that point, he had believed that he was in the majority.

74 "Has Equity had its Day?" Hong Kong University Common Law Lecture, 12 October 2010, p.21, *http:// webarchive.nationalarchives.gov.uk/20131202164909/http://judiciary.gov.uk/media/speeches/2010/mr-speech-hong-kong-lecture-12102010* [Accessed 31 July 2020].

75 See further Lord Neuberger's Chancery Bar Association Annual Lecture, "The Conspirators, the Taxman, the Bill of Rights 1688 and a bit about the Lovers", 10 March 2008, *http://www.chba.org.uk/for-members/library/ annual-lectures/the-conspirators-the-taxman-the-bill-of-rights.pdf/view?searchterm=neuberger* [Accessed 31 July 2020].

76 [2012] 1 A.C. 776.

towards the former family home or the support of his children. This situation continued for some 14½ years until the commencement of proceedings. At the time of the hearing in 2008, the property was worth £245,000. The outstanding mortgage debt was £26,664 and the endowment policy was worth £25,209. Ms Jones commenced proceedings under s.14 of the Trusts of Land and Appointment of Trustees Act 1996, seeking a declaration of her beneficial interest.

At first instance, it was held that Ms Jones had a 90 per cent share and Mr Kernott a 10 per cent interest in the former family home.[77] The judge was able to infer from the evidence that the common intention of the parties had been to change their original beneficial entitlements. The Court of Appeal, however, concluded by a majority that the parties still owned the property in equal shares.[78] The majority felt that there was nothing to indicate that the parties had changed their intentions after the separation. The appellate court emphasised that it was improper to impute a changed intention where none was expressly uttered or inferentially formed. There was simply no evidence on which a change of intention could be based. Clearly, the Court of Appeal felt unease with this reasoning and the outcome that it produced. It granted leave to appeal and the Supreme Court duly upheld the decision at first instance (i.e. the 90/10 split).[79] Lord Walker and Baroness Hale reiterated that, in these joint names cases, the starting point is that equity follows the law and they are joint tenants in law and in equity. They added that "At its simplest the principle in *Stack v Dowden* is that a 'common intention' trust, for the cohabitants' home to belong to them jointly in equity as well as on the proprietorship register, is the default option in joint names cases. The trust can be classified as a constructive trust, but it is not at odds with the parties' legal ownership. Beneficial ownership mirrors legal ownership. What it is at odds with is the presumption of a resulting trust".[80] The Supreme Court accepted, moreover, that this common intention was not fixed in stone and might change over time. Although the "ambulatory" nature of this constructive trust had been highlighted in *Stack v Dowden*, Lord Walker and Baroness Hale now acknowledged that "It is the way in which this point was made which seems to have caused the most difficulty in the lower courts . . . It does matter that any confusion is resolved".[81] On the facts of *Jones v Kernott*, it was determined that, albeit at the outset the couple intended to provide a home for themselves and their progeny, thereafter their intentions did change significantly. Once more, the presumption of equality was rebutted.

When the Presumption of Equality does not Arise

According to Judge Poynter in *Secretary of State for Work and Pensions v London Borough Tower Hamlets*, the presumption arises only "where a couple in an intimate relationship (whether

11-015

---

77 [2010] 1 All E.R. 947.
78 [2010] 1 W.L.R. 240.
79 See generally, A. Doyle and J. Brown, "Jones v Kernott: Which Road to Rome?" (2012) 26(2) Tru. L.I. 96.
80 [2012] 1 A.C. 776 at [15].
81 [2012] 1 A.C. 776 at [13].

married or unmarried), or . . . two or more people who are friends, decide to buy a house or flat in which to live together in circumstances where the relationship is built on trust and it is unlikely that the parties intended to hold each other to a detailed financial account".[82] There it did not apply because it was a sole name, non-family home style of case and a resulting trust operated instead.[83] In *Adekunle v Ritchie*,[84] it had been argued that the *Stack* approach applied only when there was some sexual relationship between the parties. This was rejected by Judge John Behrens, but, in the context of mother and son purchasers, he accepted that "It may well be, however, that where one is not dealing with the situation of a couple living together it will be easier to find that the facts are unusual in the sense that they are not to be taken to have intended a beneficial joint tenancy".[85] The judge noted that on the facts before him the context of the acquisition of the property was very different from that of the normal cohabiting couple. This was an unusual case in that it concerned the purchase of a council house by a tenant under the right to buy scheme, with the benefit of a generous discount, in a situation where the tenant could not alone fund the mortgage. The primary purpose was to provide a home for the mother and the parties' finances were kept separate. The facts that the property was purchased in joint names, that both mother and son were jointly and severally liable under the mortgage and that her son contributed to the mortgage repayments, pointed to the conclusion that he was to have a beneficial interest in the property. Adopting a holistic approach, the judge awarded the son a one-third beneficial interest in the property.

Similarly, in *Laskar v Laskar*[86] the presumption of equality did not apply (and even if it had done would have been rebutted on the grounds that the parties' financial affairs were kept separate) because the property was not purchased as a home; there was no reason why the mother would favour this particular child over her other children; the contributions were significantly different; and the reason why the daughter became a co-owner was simply because the mother could not afford the property on her own. Again in *Edwards v CPS*,[87] the presumption of equality was rebutted by the prosecution in circumstances where the property had been purchased from the proceeds of the husband's criminal activity and was the subject of a confiscation order under the Drug Trafficking Act 1994.[88] The wife had made no contribution to the purchase of the property and Mr Edwards had paid the deposit and serviced the mortgage.

11-016 Most recently in *Marr v Collie*,[89] Mr Marr and Mr Collie were in a personal relationship with each other for 17 years. During that time, they acquired several properties in the Bahamas for investment purposes. The Privy Council had to determine the ownership of the properties fol-

---

82   [2018] UKUT 25 (AAC) at [62].
83   The default resulting trust also occurred in *Geary v Rankine* [2012] EWCA Civ 555 and *Wodzicki v Wodzicki* [2017] EWCA Civ 95. Of course, a resulting trust can be rebutted by showing a different common intention.
84   [2007] 2 P. & C.R. D20.
85   [2007] 2 P. & C.R. D20 at D21.
86   [2008] 1 W.L.R. 2695.
87   [2011] EWHC 1688 (Admin).
88   Note that this order does not in itself justify the displacement of the equality presumption: *Gibson v Revenue and Customs Prosecution Office* [2009] Q.B. 348.
89   [2017] UKPC 17.

lowing the breakdown of their relationship. Mr Marr claimed that, on a resulting trust basis, he was entitled to the full beneficial ownership of all the properties because he had made virtually all payments associated with their purchase. Mr Collie denied this claim, asserting that, as the properties were acquired in joint names, the common intention was that they were joint tenants in equity. Disappointingly, there was no decision as to outcome with the case remitted back for a determination of ownership, but several salient (albeit only persuasive) observations were made by the Privy Council[90]:

- *Laskar v Laskar* was not authority for the proposition that the principle in *Stack v Dowden* exclusively applied in "the domestic consumer context". Where a property is bought in the joint names of a cohabiting couple, even as an investment, it does not necessarily follow that the resulting trust solution must provide the answer to how its beneficial ownership is to be determined. There is no strict line of demarcation between the purchase of a family home and the acquisition of a so-called investment property. Intention is the key so, for example, it might be that partners in a relationship buy, as an investment, property which is conveyed into their joint names with the intention that the beneficial ownership should be shared equally between them. In such mixed commercial and domestic transactions, and even though they contributed in different shares to the purchase, it was felt to be illogical and wrong to impose the resulting trust solution on the subsequent distribution of the property.

- Context is also crucial and this is set either by the parties' common intention or by the lack of it. If it is the unambiguous mutual wish of the parties, contributing in unequal shares to the purchase of property, that the joint beneficial ownership should reflect their joint legal ownership, then effect is to be given to that wish. If that is not their wish (or if they have not formed any intention as to beneficial ownership), then even though the property was acquired in joint names the resulting trust solution may provide the answer. The initial intention (or lack of it) at the time of purchase may, of course, change over the years.

Rebutting the Stack presumption

11-017

Put simply, once arisen the presumption of a joint tenancy is rebuttable only if the parties had a different common intention[91] when they acquired the home or had subsequently changed their common intention.[92] The latter could occur where, for example, one party financed an exten-

---

90 See A.Y.S. Georgiou, "Marr v Collie: the ballooning of the common interest constructive trust" (2019) M.L.R. 14; J. Roche, "Returning to clarity and principle: the Privy Council on Stack v Dowden" [2017] 76(3) C.L.J. 493.

91 For example, in *Quaintance v Tandan* unreported 24 July 2012, the shared intention was that they were to be tenants in common.

92 *Fowler v Barron* [2008] 2 F.L.R. 831. Any unilateral or secret intentions do not constitute a shared intention.

sion or major construction to the property, "so that what they had now was different from what they had first acquired".[93] Cases where the parties intend that their beneficial interests should be different from their legal interests have, however, emerged as the exception rather than the norm. There is a marked reluctance of the courts to go behind the outward appearance of a joint tenancy. As Lord Walker and Baroness Hale explained in *Jones v Kernott*, "If a couple in an intimate relationship (whether married or unmarried) decide to buy a house or flat in which to live together, almost always with the help of a mortgage for which they are jointly and severally liable, that is on the face of things a strong indication of emotional and economic commitment to a joint enterprise".[94] There is also the practical problem of the parties holding each other to financial account years down the line and following, "the ups and downs of living together as an unmarried couple".[95]

The difficulty of rebutting the presumption of equality is not to be underestimated. In *Fowler v Barron*,[96] the parties had had an unmarried relationship for 23 years. The relationship began when Ms Fowler was only 17. Mr Barron was then 47 years old. In 1998, they bought a house together and they made a conscious decision to put the property into joint names, but did not take any legal advice as to the consequences of doing so. Mr Barron paid the deposit and made all the mortgage repayments. Nevertheless, Arden LJ held that the joint names presumption was not rebutted even though the claimant had made no quantifiable contributions to the purchase price or any mortgage payment. The claimant had, however, accepted joint liability under the mortgage. Arden LJ emphasised that all turns on the facts of each case. Judged objectively, the parties' intention was not that they should have unequal shares. The couple had made mutual wills, the house was their only asset of value, their resources were pooled and it was not reasonable to view the parties as intending that, if they separated, Ms Fowler would get nothing.[97] Arden LJ emphasised that equality is possible even though the parties contributed unequally to the purchase of the property.

In similar vein, in *Elithorn v Poulter*[98] Mrs Ettinger produced all of the cash for the purchase of Rose Hill. The property was transferred into the joint names of Dr Elithorn and Mrs Ettinger. Subsequently, Mrs Ettinger died and her executors claimed that the couple had intended that the size of their beneficial shares would be determined by their actual contributions to the purchase price. As Dr Elithorn had contributed nothing to the initial purchase price, it was submitted that the deceased was the sole beneficial owner. Following *Stack v Dowden*, it was held by the majority of the Court of Appeal that Dr Elithorn had throughout enjoyed a beneficial joint tenancy in Rose Hill.

11-018

In these rebuttal cases, the task of the court is to ascertain the parties' common intention in light of their whole course of conduct in relation to the property. For example, the court may

---

93 Per Lord Walker and Baroness Hale in *Jones v Kernott* [2012] 1 A.C. 776 at [14].
94 [2012] 1 A.C. 776 at [19].
95 Per Lord Walker and Baroness Hale [2012] 1 A.C .776 at [22].
96 [2008] 2 F.L.R. 831.
97 See generally, N. Piska, "Two Recent Reflections on the Resulting Trust" (2008) Conv. 441.
98 [2009] 1 P. & C.R. 19.

consider financial and indirect contributions, advice received, discussions between the parties, reasons why the property was bought in joint names, the purposes for which the home was acquired, whether it was a home for the parties' children, how the parties arranged their finances and the nature of the parties' relationship.[99] Importantly, and as demonstrated in *Jones v Kernott*, the court may also take into account how the circumstances have changed since the purchase.[100] This occurred in *Barnes v Phillips*[101] where, although the property was registered in joint names, the presumption of a beneficial joint tenancy was rebutted. The parties had separated in 2005 and the weight of the evidence supported the inference that subsequently the parties intended to alter their shares in the property. Mr Barnes had received virtually all the proceeds of a remortgage, which amounted to nearly 25 per cent of the equity in the property, just before the relationship ended. The fact that, for some six years, Mr Barnes had ceased to pay any contribution to the mortgage and paid little by way of child maintenance further supported an inference that there was a common intention to vary their interests in the property. The Court of Appeal concluded that the parties held their property interests in an 85/15 split in favour of Ms Phillips.

In *Stack v Dowden*, Ms Dowden raised a variety of factors which indicated a common intention that the beneficial interests were to be unequal and justified her successful claim to a 65 per cent share. Primarily, she had contributed far more to the acquisition of the property than Mr Stack. Similarly, she had contributed more to the repayment of the mortgage than had her partner. Although the couple had lived together for 18 years, this was not a case where the parties pooled their resources for the common good. As Baroness Hale observed, "There cannot be many unmarried couples who have lived together for as long as this, who have had four children together, and whose affairs have been kept as rigidly separate as this couple's affairs were kept. This is all strongly indicative that they did not intend their shares, even in the property which was put into both their names, to be equal . . .".[102] Both *Stack v Dowden* and *Jones v Kernott* demonstrate that rebuttal is more likely to occur where the cohabiting parties do not pool their financial resources as the unusual nature of their fiscal arrangements indicates strongly the inappropriateness of equality.

Division by inference or imputation?

Where in joint names cases a joint tenancy was not intended, or the parties had changed their original intention, the court will usually recalibrate the parties' shares with reference to

11-019

---

99   See *Adekunle v Ritchie* [2007] 2 P. & C.R. D20.
100   In *Kali & Burlay v Chawla* [2007] EWHC 2357 (Ch), the High Court felt it necessary to look at the parties' interests as at the time of their splitting up and not at the time of purchase (some 19 years earlier). It was important here that for the preceding nine years the parties had been leading separate physical and financial lives.
101   [2015] EWCA Civ 1056.
102   [2007] 2 A.C. 432 at 465.

direct evidence or by inference. As demonstrated in *Barnes v Phillips*,[103] an inferred intention is one which is objectively deduced to be the subjective actual intention of the parties, in the light of their actions and statements. Inference is, therefore, concerned with what the actual parties are taken to have intended. The majority of the Supreme Court in *Jones v Kernott* felt comfortable with inferring a change of intention on the facts. Lords Wilson and Kerr, however, felt that no such inference was possible on the evidence.[104] More recently, in *Premium Jet AG v Sutton*[105] an alternative intention was inferred from the legal co-owners' conduct. The purchase was wholly financed by the wife and, despite not having given expression to that intention, the conduct of the husband and wife gave rise to the inference that they regarded the property as being hers alone. Objectively viewed, there were clear indications that the property was to be regarded as belonging to the wife and, accordingly, it was held on constructive trust solely for her benefit.

An imputed intention, however, is one which is attributed to the parties, even though no such actual intention can be deduced from their actions and statements. Imputation requires the court "to ask what their intentions as reasonable and just people would have been if they had thought about it at the time".[106] Hence, it is concerned with issues of fairness and what the parties would have intended had they thought about the matter.[107] The Court of Appeal in *Barnes v Phillips* acknowledged that imputation is relevant only to the working out of the parties' exact entitlements under the trust. Imputation is not permissible at the stage of determining whether there exists a common intention constructive trust or there has been a common change of that intention. It is only at the stage of quantifying the share of each in circumstances where inference is not possible that imputation assumes any role. For example, if the evidence is thin or conflicting, the court is still obliged to reach a decision. The imputation of intention as to share allocation is then the only option available to the court.[108]

This type of constructive intention represents, as Lord Walker and Baroness Hale observed, "an elision between what the judge can find as a fact (usually by inference) on consideration of the admissible evidence, and what the law may supply (to fill the evidential gap) by way

---

103 [2015] EWCA Civ 1056.

104 See generally, J. Mee, "*Jones v Kernott*: Inferring and Imputing in Essex" [2012] Conv. 167.

105 [2017] EWHC 186 (QB).

106 Per Lord Walker and Baroness Hale [2012] 1 A.C. 776 at [47]. This echoes the sentiment expressed by Waite LJ in *Midland Bank v Cooke* [1995] 4 All E.R. 562 at 575 that "It would be anomalous, against that background, to create a range of home-buyers who were beyond the pale of equity's assistance in formulating a fair presumed basis for the sharing of beneficial title, simply because they had been honest enough to admit that they never gave ownership a thought or reached any agreement about it".

107 The obvious unease that imputation caused Lord Neuberger MR in *Stack v Dowden* and Rimer LJ in *Jones v Kernott* [2010] 1 W.L.R. 2401 (CA) may be an overreaction. In the Supreme Court Lord Walker and Baroness Hale [2012] 1 A.C. 776 at [34] sounded the reassuring note that, "while the conceptual difference between inferring and imputing is clear, the difference in practice may not be so great".

108 In this way, as Lord Walker and Baroness Hale acknowledged [2012] 1 A.C. 776 at [31], "the court is driven to impute an intention to the parties which they may never have had". Imputation cannot impose an outcome on the parties which is contrary to what the evidence shows that they actually intended: *Barnes v Phillips* [2015] EWCA Civ 1056.

of a presumption".[109] Lord Kerr agreed that, "As soon as it is clear that inferring an intention is not possible, the focus of the court's attention should be squarely on what is fair and . . . that is an obviously different examination than is involved in deciding what the parties actually intended".[110] As Lord Collins emphasised, "The courts are courts of law, but they are also courts of justice".[111] Imputation is, therefore, a fall-back position.

Resulting Trusts, Constructive Trusts and Estoppel

In circumstances where there is no valid express declaration of trust and the presumption in *Stack v Dowden* is not applicable (e.g. because it is a sole name case or a joint names case with a commercial dimension), the courts have devised analytical tools through which the existence of a trust may be implied and its terms divined. In such cases the solution must be found primarily in the principles of law relating to resulting and constructive trusts. It becomes necessary for the court to consider the intentions of the parties as discerned from the evidence or from presumptions to be drawn from their conduct. Unlike on divorce or the dissolution of registered partnerships, Parliament has not afforded to the court a general discretion to direct a division fair and equitable to both parties.

11-020

Unfortunately, the area of implied co-ownership is marked with some uncertainty concerning, for example, the current role of the resulting trust, the co-existence between estoppel and the constructive trust and whether the timing of intention dictates which remedial vehicle is to be adopted. The quantification of a party's beneficial share may also vary greatly according to which mechanism is employed. Be warned, however, judges and commentators alike do not always speak with one voice on such matters. As the Law Commission put it, "'Who owns what?' may be very simple to ask, but in a short time the enquirer will find themselves immersed in the off-putting, and sometimes obscure, terminology of the law of trusts and estoppel".[112]

---

109 [2012] 1 A.C. 776 at [29]. They added, at [29], that "The presumption of a resulting trust is a clear example of a rule by which the law does impute an intention, the rule being based on a very broad generalisation about human motivation".
110 [2012] 1 A.C. 776 at [75].
111 [2012] 1 A.C. 776 at [66].
112 Law Commission, *Sharing Homes: A Discussion Paper* (2002) Law Com.278, para.1.12.

The purchase money resulting trust

11-021

The purchase money resulting trust (which it is to be emphasised survives in cases where *Stack v Dowden* does not apply) arises where property is conveyed into the name of one party, but another has made a contribution to the purchase price.[113] In that scenario, it is presumed that a beneficial interest in the property passes to the contributing party.[114] As Eyre CB acknowledged over 200 years ago, "the trust of the legal estate . . . whether taken in the name of the purchasers and others jointly, or in the name of others without that of the purchaser; whether in one name or several; whether jointly or successive, results to the man who advances the purchase money".[115] This view still enjoys contemporary resonance.[116] By affording a beneficial interest to the provider of the purchase money, equity assumes bargains and not gifts. Such was demonstrated in *Karis v Lewis*,[117] where the legal title was transferred into the name of an associate, allegedly on the payment by him of £1,150,000. The issue was who really provided the purchase money. If it was the transferor himself, a resulting trust would arise in his favour. The presumption that the legal owner was also the beneficial owner was displaced by evidence which showed that the transferee could not have afforded the purchase price and that the transferor continued to treat the property as his own. The transfer was a mere cloak so that the transferor could hide real ownership of the property.

The resulting trust operates in circumstances where no common or express intention is apparent.[118] If, however, the evidence displays a common or express intention that each should have a beneficial share in the property, the case falls outside resulting trust territory.[119] As Sir Peter Gibson put it in *Crossley v Crossley*, "The presumption [of a resulting trust] yields to the intentions of the parties . . .".[120] Such facts will instead promote a claim in constructive trust or proprietary estoppel.[121] The delights of exploring these other legal concepts will be experienced later in this chapter.

11-022

Take the example where Fred and Adrienne each contribute to the purchase price, but the property is conveyed into Fred's sole name. Although Fred is the legal owner, he holds the property on trust for himself and Adrienne. Adrienne has acquired her beneficial interest by virtue of her payments to the purchase price that have triggered a resulting trust. If they each

---

113 In *Tahir v Faizi* [2019] EWHC 1627 (QB), for example, title was registered in the sole name of Mr Tahir, but was held on resulting trust for Mr Faizi who had a 100% beneficial interest.

114 Hence, if there is no financial contribution made there can be no resulting trust: *Erlam v Rahman* [2016] EWHC 111 (Ch).

115 *Dyer v Dyer* (1788) 2 Cox Eq. 92 at 93.

116 *Pettitt v Pettitt* [1970] A.C. 777.

117 [2005] EWCA Civ 1627.

118 *Themistokli v Spyrou* [2005] EWHC 1822 (Ch).

119 *Ahmad v Gould* [2005] EWCA Civ 1829.

120 [2005] EWCA Civ 1581 at [21]; see generally, M. McInnes, "Resulting Trusts, Gifts, and Unjust Enrichment in the Supreme Court of Canada" (2013) 129 L.Q.R. 473.

121 *Oxley v Hiscock* [2004] 3 W.L.R. 715.

contribute equally to the purchase price, the traditional presumption is that they have a beneficial joint tenancy. If the contributions are unequal the presumption is of a beneficial tenancy in common.[122]

Quantification

The issue of quantum is, once the facts are established, a straightforward matter. In *Arogundade v Arogundade*,[123] a flat was purchased for £207,000. The claimant contributed £62,000 to the purchase price and, by resulting trust principles, obtained a 30 per cent share in the property. Similarly, in the earlier example, the quantification of Adrienne's interest will be proportionate to her contribution to the purchase price. If she contributed 50 per cent of the purchase price, therefore, a 50 per cent share of the proceeds of any sale will result back to her. If she contributed 10 per cent, her interest will be pegged at 10 per cent.

At the outset, it is important to note that this is very unlike the assessment process under a constructive trust where the court attempts to produce an outcome that is fair and just. This divergence of treatment was made apparent in *Drake v Whipp*.[124] There the total expenditure on the purchase was £195,790 and Mrs Drake's total contribution was assessed at £38,000. Applying resulting trust principles, her entitlement would be 19.4 per cent of the current value of the property. Based upon her financial contributions, Mrs Drake's share was £43,650. The case was, however, decided on the basis that a constructive trust arose. This entitled Mrs Drake to a share now quantified at £75,000.

Rebutting the presumption

The presumption of a resulting trust may always be rebutted, in whole or in part, by contrary evidence.[125] For example, an oral or unsigned written declaration of express trust might operate to displace the presumption. Similarly, evidence of a common intention may take the bargain outside the realm of the resulting trust and into the more flexible world of the constructive trust.[126] The presumption of a resulting trust might also be defeated in circumstances where the financial contribution was by way of a loan[127] or a gift.[128]

The counter, but now anachronistic, presumption of advancement (operative, say, when a husband/father supplies the purchase money and the conveyance is taken in the wife's/

11-023

11-024

---

122 *Lake v Gibson* (1729) 1 Eq. Ca. Abr. 290.
123 [2005] EWHC 1766 (Ch).
124 [1996] 1 F.L.R. 826, noted by A. Dunn [1997] Conv. 467.
125 In *Stack v Dowden* [2007] 2 A.C. 432, the transfer of legal title into joint names rebutted the presumption of a resulting trust.
126 See *Midland Bank v Cooke* [1995] 4 All E.R. 562; *Oxley v Hiscock* [2004] 3 W.L.R. 715.
127 *Vajpeyi v Yusaf* [2003] EWHC 623 (Ch).
128 *Levin v Beatt* [2005] EWHC 828 (Ch).

child's name alone) may support the conclusion that a gift was intended.[129] Nevertheless, the presumption of advancement does not apply between cohabitants,[130] is nowadays easily dislodged[131] and, because of its gender bias, seemingly contravenes the European Convention on Human Rights.[132] In *Kyriakides v Pippas*,[133] a father purportedly made a gift of a house to his daughter upon her marriage. Although the evidence was vague and unsatisfactory, the High Court concluded that there was no intention to make an immediate gift to the daughter. The father had made statements as to the house having been a dowry merely to maintain appearances in front of fellow Greek Cypriots rather than sacrificing the interests of his wife and other children. Put simply, the donative intention was lacking and a resulting trust arose in the father's favour. As Deputy Judge Moss QC commented, "I suspect the position we have now reached is that the courts will always strive to work out the real intention of the purchaser and will only give effect to the presumptions of resulting trust and advancement where the intention cannot be fathomed and a 'long-stop' or 'default' solution is needed".[134]

11-025 Much turns, therefore, upon the strength of the presumption in favour of a resulting trust, for as Mellish LJ observed in *Fowkes v Pascoe*, "the presumption must, beyond all question, be of very different weight in different cases".[135] In some cases it will be very strong indeed, as in *Abrahams v Abrahams*[136] where a wife continued to pay her own and her estranged husband's weekly contributions to a pub lottery syndicate. It was held that the presumption of a resulting trust in her favour was not rebutted on the evidence. She was, therefore, successful in her claim to her former husband's putative share. In other cases, it will be a weak presumption and easily displaced.

In *Fowkes v Pascoe*, a woman of considerable fortune (Mrs Pascoe) purchased £250 of shares and registered them in the name of the son of her former daughter-in-law. The son lived with Mrs Pascoe and she provided for him. She also purchased a further £250 of shares in the name of her female companion. As Mellish LJ asked, "applying one's common sense to that transaction, what inference is it possible to draw, except that the purchases were intended for the purpose of gifts?"[137] The appellate court was influenced by two factors. First, that had a trust been intended there would be no reason for the two sums not to be invested in the name of a sole trustee. Secondly, Mrs Pascoe already had a large sum of stock in her own name.

---

129 *Silver v Silver* [1958] 1 W.L.R. 259. There the matrimonial home was bought in the name of the wife and was presumed to be a gift to her by the husband (see further para.**9-015**).

130 *Chapman v Jaume* [2012] 2 F.L.R. 830.

131 It is, in the words of Nourse LJ in *McGrath v Wallis* [1995] 2 F.L.R. 114 at 115, "reclassified as a judicial instrument of last resort". As Arden LJ added in *Gibson v Revenue & Customs Prosecution Office* [2009] Q.B. 348 at [26], ". . . this presumption is no longer in keeping with modern conditions or at least is much diminished, or more easily rebutted, nowadays . . .".

132 It is to be abolished when s.199 of the Equality Act 2010 comes into force.

133 [2004] EWHC 646 (Ch).

134 [2004] EWHC 646 (Ch) at [76].

135 (1875) 10 Ch. App. 343 at 352.

136 *The Times*, 26 July 1999.

137 (1875) 10 Ch. App. 343 at 353.

Mellish LJ thought that it would be absurd for a woman with so much stock to seek to invest a comparatively meagre £500 in the names of the others and yet intend for it to be held on trust for herself. As there was no plausible reason why she should transfer the shares to either the son or the companion as her nominee, the appellate court concluded from the surrounding circumstances that she intended to make a gift of the shares. This promotes a pragmatic approach that requires sensible inferences to be drawn from the available evidence.

11-026

In *Vajpeyi v Yusaf*,[138] the High Court accepted that the rebuttal of the presumption of a resulting trust might appear to be a straightforward process. Nevertheless, difficulties may arise when the transaction occurred a long time ago and the parties do not accurately remember its details or, indeed, may have died. As Deputy Judge Peter Prescott QC puzzled, "After such a lapse of time, how is the court to arrive at the truth?"[139] In the case before him, the defendant accepted that the presumption of a resulting trust arose and the onus was upon him to rebut that presumption. As to the evidence necessary to achieve this rebuttal, the Deputy Judge commented:

> "This depends on the strength of the presumption. And the strength of the presumption depends upon the facts and circumstances which give rise to it. This is because the doctrine of resulting trusts is supposed to be based on common sense. In each case the court is trying to find the answer to the question: what would the parties have intended if they had given thought to the position?"[140]

The Deputy Judge in the *Vajpeyi* case acknowledged that, depending upon the circumstances, it is possible for the presumption of a resulting trust to be rebutted by comparatively slight evidence. The evidence admissible for this purpose will focus upon the acts and declarations of the parties. He provided two examples. First, when an unmarried couple intend to live together in a property, and both contribute to the purchase price, there is a presumption that they intend to hold it in proportionate shares even though the property is conveyed into the name of one of them alone. The fact that both came up with the money calls for a common-sense explanation of which the most obvious is that they intended the property to be acquired for their joint benefit.

11-027

The second example provided concerned a young woman in her first job who raised as much as she could on mortgage to buy a flat and turned to her uncle to pay a minor part of the purchase price. The common-sense explanation in this scenario might well be that the uncle did not want an interest in the property. The Deputy Judge added, "It is more credible that it was meant to be a loan or, perhaps, a gift".[141] On a general level, this example bore some passing resemblance to the facts of *Vajpeyi* where £10,000 was advanced to the defendant (a young

---

138   [2003] EWHC 2339 (Ch).
139   [2003] EWHC 2339 (Ch) at [66].
140   [2003] EWHC 2339 (Ch) at [71].
141   [2003] EWHC 2339 (Ch) at [77].

man with limited resources) by the claimant (an older woman who was very fond of him) in order that he could purchase a house in his sole name. In concluding that the plausible explanation was that this was a loan and not an investment in the venture, the Deputy Judge added, "And we must not have our judgment clouded because of their respective sexes. Imagining they were reversed: what might we expect the position of the older and wealthier man to be?"[142]

While there is no limitation period in respect of a resulting trust, the amount of time that has elapsed before the resulting trust is asserted is also capable of helping to rebut the presumption. As the Deputy Judge in *Vajpeyi* observed, "The fact that no complaint is made for a long time calls for an explanation. If no sufficiently credible explanation is forthcoming when one might have expected this may, in my judgment, serve to rebut the presumption, or help to do so".[143] On the facts before him, the defendant was allowed to collect and keep rents from the property for nearly 21 years. This made no sense if the transaction was a shared venture. Similarly, Dr Vaipeyi's failure to seek an interest for almost 21 years told against her claim. On the facts, therefore, the presumption of a resulting trust was not a strong one and was easily rebutted by Mr Yusaf.

What payments suffice?

11-028

The presumption of a purchase money resulting trust is based upon the making of a direct contribution in money or money's worth to the purchase price.[144] The relevant principle is that the resulting trust of a property purchased arises once and for all at the date on which the property is acquired. It is at the date of purchase that the intention is presumed to exist and the entitlement under the trust fixed.[145] The working rule, therefore, is that payments made subsequent to the purchase do not generate the presumption.[146] As will become clear, such post-acquisition expenditure may well, instead, fuel a constructive trust.[147] The shift towards the latter device has diminished the currency of the resulting trust analysis and reduced it to a "judicial instrument of last resort".[148]

The clearest example of a purchase money resulting trust arises where, say, Fred purchases a house in his own name and Adrienne contributes 30 per cent of the purchase price. Adrienne will acquire her beneficial interest as a result of that contribution. Nevertheless, this is not the only type of payment that may be made and it has been left to the courts to determine which types of payment qualify and which do not.

---

142 [2003] EWHC 2339 (Ch) at [83].
143 [2003] EWHC 2339 (Ch) at [78].
144 *Solomon v McCarthy* [2020] 1 P. & C.R. DG22. There the non-legal owner was the only person who expended money on the purchase (via his right to buy discount, cash payments and the taking out of an unsecured loan). The house was held for him absolutely under a resulting trust.
145 *Pettitt v Pettitt* [1970] A.C. 777; *Gissing v Gissing* [1971] A.C. 88.
146 *Bernard v Josephs* [1982] Ch. 391.
147 *Curley v Parkes* [2004] EWCA Civ 1515.
148 Per Blackburne J in *Nightingale Mayfair Ltd v Mehta* [2000] W.T.L.R. 901.

A direct contribution to the deposit or the cash price of the property will, without more, activate the presumption of a resulting trust.[149] Nevertheless, it is not every contribution of value that will be regarded as "purchase money" for these purposes. It is useful to consider some common examples of payments that may be made and to see whether they will generate the presumption of a resulting trust.

The right to buy discount under the Housing Act 1985

11-029

In *Springette v Defoe*,[150] the sitting tenant of a local authority house was entitled to a 41 per cent discount on purchasing the property with her partner. The financial advantage achieved by her discount was regarded as her contribution to the purchase price and factored into the calculation of her equitable interest in the property. This method of contribution to the purchase price was recognised also in *McKenzie v McKenzie* where it was again held that the benefit from the discount could give rise to a resulting trust of a beneficial interest proportionate to the value of the discount in relation to the purchase price.[151] The discount obtained can be substantial. For example, in *Day v Day*[152] the discount was 60 per cent. In *Crossley v Crossley*,[153] the market value of the property was £56,500 but the price paid, reflecting a 38 per cent discount, amounted in total to £35,051.

A similar approach should be adopted in circumstances where, in the private sector, a sitting tenant and another buy the freehold reversion at a discount from the landlord.[154]

Mortgage repayments

11-030

There is no doubt that the discharge of mortgage repayments can give rise to a resulting trust, but this is not always so. The distinctions that are drawn as regards purchase by instalments reflect the difficulty of adapting the traditional resulting trust theory to such elongated transactions. In *Stack v Dowden*, Lord Neuberger acknowledged that there is no simple and clear treatment of mortgage liability and whether it can give rise to a resulting trust is questionable both in terms of principle and authority.[155] Instead, as Peter Gibson LJ acknowledged in *Curley v Parkes*, reliance is generally placed on a constructive trust where an agreement or common intention can be found or inferred from the circumstances.[156] Nevertheless, in the context of the resulting trust:

---

149 *Samad v Thompson* [2008] EWHC 2809 (Ch).
150 [1992] 2 F.L.R. 388.
151 [2003] EWHC 601 (Ch); see also, *Laskar v Laskar* [2008] 1 W.L.R. 2695.
152 [2005] EWHC 1455 (Ch).
153 [2005] EWCA Civ 1581.
154 *Carlton v Goodman* [2002] 2 F.L.R. 259.
155 [2007] 2 A.C. 432 at 471.
156 [2004] EWCA Civ 1515; see also, *Driver v Yorke* [2003] EWHC 746 (Ch).

- the assumption of legal liability under a mortgage to purchase the property will normally suffice.[157] Peter Gibson LJ explained in *Curley v Parkes* that, "Because of the liability assumed by the mortgagor in a case where monies are borrowed by the mortgagor to be used on the purchase, the mortgagor is treated as having provided the proportion of the purchase price attributable to the monies so borrowed".[158] Hence, if Fiona and Jordan buy property together with the aid of a mortgage taken out in both names, the legal liability to which each is exposed under this acquisition mortgage will usually be regarded as a contribution to the purchase price. This occurred in *Laskar v Laskar* where the parties purchased the property with the aid of a mortgage and as an investment[159];

- a mere exposure to risk because of becoming party to a mortgage will not be a qualifying condition when the evidence shows that it was not intended at the time of the initial acquisition and mortgage that the claimant should actually pay instalments.[160] This is regardless of any potential liability under the mortgage or, indeed, any payment made upon subsequent enforcement. The important factor is, instead, that it was intended that the party should be responsible for paying, and actually pay, part of the mortgage instalments;

- a voluntary and subsequent making of mortgage repayments will not be enough for resulting trust purposes.[161] As Peter Gibson LJ noted in *Curley v Parkes*, such payments "are not part of the purchase price already paid to the vendor, but are sums paid for discharging the mortgagor's obligations under the mortgage".[162] Accordingly, if Fiona is the sole borrower under the acquisition mortgage, any repayments made by Jordan will not count for resulting trust purposes. At the time the property was purchased, Jordan was under no legal compulsion to discharge the mortgage debt; and

- any payments made towards mortgage instalments on an occasional basis, or commenced some time after the original acquisition, do not enjoy, as the Deputy Judge in *McKenzie v McKenzie* put it, "the requisite direct nexus with the purchase to be treated as a contribution to the purchase price . . .".[163]

---

157 In *Samad v Thompson* [2008] EWHC 2809 (Ch), the fact that Mr Samad promised the Thompsons that he would make payments under the mortgage did not give him an interest under a resulting trust. He had no liability to the lender.

158 [2004] EWCA Civ 1515 at [14].

159 [2008] 1 W.L.R. 2695. Cf. *Close Invoice Finance v Abaowa* [2010] EWHC 1920 (QB) where there was no obligation and no payment made.

160 *McKenzie v McKenzie* [2003] EWHC 601 (Ch).

161 *Close Invoice Finance v Abaowa* [2010] EWHC 1920 (QB).

162 [2004] EWCA Civ 1515 at [14].

163 [2003] EWHC 601 (Ch) at [82].

Payment of conveyancing and other expenses

The effect of a payment of conveyancing expenses is somewhat unclear. Traditionally, such payments were thought sufficient to give rise to a resulting trust as comprising part of the composite cost of purchasing the property.[164] Nevertheless, in *Curley v Parkes* the Court of Appeal adopted the view that such expenditure is not to be regarded as a contribution to the purchase price. As Peter Gibson LJ concluded, "The payment was no part of the purchase price, though I accept that for the purposes of a constructive trust (as distinct from a resulting trust) any ancillary payment, such as the payment of expenses, may be relevant".[165] The appellate court concluded that the payment of legal fees and stamp duty could not be treated as part of the purchase cost for the purposes of a resulting trust. It also demonstrated that the payment of removal costs plainly did not form part of the purchase price and, therefore, fell to be disregarded for these purposes.[166] These payments are either non-acquisition costs or are made only after the purchase has taken place. For example, the payment of general household expenses will be insufficient.[167] Such payments are referable to the running of a home and not the acquisition of property.[168]

11-031

Domestic labour and payment of rent

Activities such as work in or on the house or child rearing do not amount to "purchase money" for the purposes of giving rise to a resulting trust.[169] Such services are geared to the running of a household rather than to the purchase of a house. As Lord Denning MR observed in relation to painting and decorating and gardening work carried out by one partner, "Those are the sorts of things that a wife does for the benefit of the family without altering the title to, or interests in, the property".[170]

11-032

The periodic payment of rent will also prove insufficient. Rent equates with a payment for the use of the property and is not to do with its purchase. As Plowman J explained in *Savage v Dunningham*, "Rent, unlike purchase-money, is not paid for the acquisition of a capital asset, but for the use of a property during the term . . . the fact that the plaintiffs and the defendant shared the rent does not establish a resulting trust in favour of the plaintiffs".[171] This, of course, stands in marked contrast to a capital contribution towards the purchase price of a lease (i.e. premium), which is clearly a contribution towards the purchase of the property.

---

164 See generally, *Davis v Vale* [1971] 1 W.L.R. 1022.
165 [2004] EWCA Civ 1515 at [21].
166 The payment of household bills also does not fuel a resulting trust: *Secretary of State for Work and Pensions v London Borough Tower Hamlets* [2018] UKUT 25 (AAC).
167 *Gross v French* (1976) 238 E.G. 39.
168 *Gissing v Gissing* [1971] A.C. 886.
169 *Burns v Burns* [1984] Ch. 317.
170 *Button v Button* [1968] 1 W.L.R. 457 at 462.
171 [1974] Ch. 181 at 185.

> ### Employer relocation packages and informal agreements

11-033

In *Curley v Parkes*, Mr Curley was asked by his employer to move to Luton and was offered a relocation package. The employer was prepared to pay removal costs, solicitor's fees and a contribution to any increased mortgage costs if the move entailed buying in a costlier housing area. Although the title to the new property and the attendant mortgage would be in the name of Ms Parkes, the employer agreed to let Mr Curley take advantage of the relocation scheme. No part of the purchase price was paid by Mr Curley. Mr Curley eventually paid the £9,213 to Ms Parkes. As it was not established that Mr Curley had incurred a liability to pay the £9,213, what arose between the parties was, as Peter Gibson LJ put it, "an agreement such as is reached between members of a family and others living together which is not intended to have legal consequences".[172] Any obligation that existed was owed by Mr Curley's employer and was owed to Mr Curley.

Doctrinal divergence

11-034

The traditional view is that the recognition and enforcement of resulting trusts ensures the realisation of the unexpressed, but imputed positive intention of the party making the financial contribution to create a trust.[173] Hence, such trusts are often referred to as "presumed intention resulting trusts". The purchase money resulting trust is one example of a presumed intention resulting trust. The other example is the gratuitous transfer resulting trust which arises when an owner of property transfers it to a third party for no consideration.

There is, however, an alternative underlying principle for the existence of resulting trusts that has assumed a popular currency. The alternative assertion is that it is the absence of any positive intention to pass by way of gift the beneficial interest to the transferee that is crucial. This absence of intention to benefit theory was, most famously, expounded by Lord Millett in *Air Jamaica Ltd v Charlton*.[174] The theory is, therefore, posited upon what the transferor did not intend as opposed to what was intended. In other words, the resulting trust is responsive to the absence of intention to pass the beneficial interest and not to the positive intention to retain it. This emphasis upon the negative entails that the resulting trust arises by operation of law and has nothing to do with any presumption as to the positive intentions of the settlor. As explained by Potter LJ at the Court of Appeal stage in *Twinsectra Ltd v Yardley*,

> "the role of intention in resulting trusts is a negative one, the essential question being whether or not the provider intended to benefit the recipient and not whether he or she intended to create a trust.

---

172 [2004] EWCA Civ 1515 at [20].

173 See the views expressed by Megarry J in *Re Vandervell's Trusts (No.2)* [1974] 2 Ch. 269.

174 [1999] 1 W.L.R. 1399 at 1412. This is, however, a decision of the Privy Council and is, thereby, only of persuasive authority.

> **The latter question is relevant to whether the provider succeeded in creating an express trust, but its relevance to the resulting trust is only as an indication of lack of intention to benefit the recipient . . .".**[175]

Although the differences between the two theories appear to carry little practical importance (i.e. in most cases both routes lead to the same destination),[176] the conundrum has stirred much intellectual argument. Rickett and Grantham[177] offer an interesting perspective that attempts to unify these seemingly opposing theories. The writers accept that all resulting trusts are a response to the presumed intention of the transferor or settlor. Nevertheless, they identify the key issue as being "whether the transfer of property to B is intended by A to be beneficial to B. It is presumed that A did not intend B to acquire a beneficial interest in the property".[178] They continue, "intention is established not by the actual evidence but by appeal to presumptions supplied by the law. Resulting trusts comprise a group of trusts that are founded upon intention, although neither express nor implied . . . All resulting trusts are more accurately termed 'presumed trusts'".[179] Hence, these commentators see the resulting trust and its associated presumptions operating as a series of default rules locating the beneficial interest in property in circumstances where there is uncertainty as to the placement of that interest.

This overarching approach has received some judicial support. In *McKenzie v McKenzie*,[180] the High Court accepted that the true doctrinal basis of a resulting trust was disputed (that is, whether it is based upon an imputed intention or, instead, the absence of intention). Nevertheless, Deputy Judge Robert Hildyard QC commented:

> **"there does seem to me to be much in the view that in the case of a resulting trust the basis for equity's intervention is not proof of a common intention; but a presumption . . . that a person is unlikely to have paid for property altruistically without some expectation of return by way of a beneficial interest in it . . . a resulting trust is equity's response to the failure of a gift or proof of lack of intention to make one. In any event, as it seems to me, conduct on the part of the contributor that it is explicable on a basis other than the expectation of return by way of beneficial interest will not suffice**

---

175 [1999] Lloyd's Rep. Bank 438 at 457. In the House of Lords [2002] 2 A.C. 164, only Lord Millett referred to this absence of intention theory. It does not, therefore, form part of the ratio of that decision.

176 This was recognised by Mummery LJ in *Carlton v Goodman* [2002] 2 F.L.R. 259 at 267.

177 C.E.F. Rickett and R. Grantham, "Resulting Trusts—The True Nature of the Failing Trust Cases" (2000) 116 L.Q.R. 15.

178 "Resulting Trusts—The True Nature of the Failing Trust Cases" (2000) 116 L.Q.R. 15, 18.

179 "Resulting Trusts—The True Nature of the Failing Trust Cases" (2000) 116 L.Q.R. 15, 19.

180 [2003] EWHC 601 (Ch).

> to give rise to the presumption that is the basis of such a resulting trust".[181]

Distinguishing a constructive trust

11-035

It is crucial that the fundamental differences between the resulting trust and the more far-reaching constructive trust are appreciated. As Lord Browne-Wilkinson writing extra-judicially observed, these types of trust "are two different animals" as to which the failure to tell them apart has led to "great confusion".[182] As shown, the resulting trust is based upon financial contributions to the purchase of land and the intention that is presumed to underlie the making of those payments. In contrast, a constructive trust is underpinned by the twin tenets of common intention and change of position. As indicated above, the reliance upon mortgage finance, and the difficulty of classifying mortgage repayments for resulting trust purposes, has reduced the importance of the resulting trust. Indeed, the Law Commission has endorsed the view that the resulting trust has become limited to those relatively rare instances where there is no evidence of the parties' actual intentions, but some contribution has been made to the purchase price.[183]

There are two distinguishing features of a constructive trust. First, it is concerned with the enforcement of the bilateral intentions of the parties arising from some antecedent arrangement, whether express or implied, relating to equitable ownership.[184] As acknowledged by Chadwick LJ in *Oxley v Hiscock*, it is the element of consensus that each should have a beneficial share which "provides the foundation for Mrs Oxley's claim in constructive trust or proprietary estoppel; and which distinguishes that claim from one founded on resulting trust alone".[185] Similarly, in *McKenzie v McKenzie* Deputy Judge Robert Hildyard QC took the view that "a constructive trust arises out of, and is equity's way of giving effect to, the common intentions of the parties. Where a common intention can be proven by reference to some express agreement or arrangement between them the technique of equity is to impose a constructive trust to fulfil it".[186] The finding of this agreement or arrangement will normally be based upon evidence of express discussions between the parties, however imprecise and imperfectly remembered. In the absence of any communicated intention, a common intention may be inferred from the conduct of the parties.

11-036

Secondly, and following *Gissing v Gissing*,[187] this common intention trust is imposed only when the claimant has acted in reliance on the bilateral intention in circumstances where it

---

181 [2003] EWHC 601 (Ch) at [76].
182 Lord Browne-Wilkinson, "Constructive Trusts and Unjust Enrichment" (1996) 10 Tru. L.I. 98, 99.
183 Law Commission, *Sharing Homes: A Discussion Paper* (2002) Law Com.278, para.2.61.
184 *Crossley v Crossley* [2005] EWCA Civ 1581.
185 [2004] 3 W.L.R. 715 at 722.
186 [2003] EWHC 601 (Ch) at [70].
187 [1971] A.C. 886.

would be inequitable to allow the other party to refuse to give it effect. As the Deputy Judge in *McKenzie v McKenzie* explained, "Consensus (whether express or inferred) will not suffice to give rise to a constructive trust without proof of detrimental reliance".[188] Conscience and the prevention of equitable fraud, therefore, underpin the constructive trust.

Under both the constructive trust and proprietary estoppel, the fundamental ingredient is that the legal owner of the property has acted unconscionably. Accordingly, in *Curran v Collins*,[189] the non-legal owner failed in her claim to a beneficial share in circumstance where she honestly, but mistakenly, reinterpreted the past. The Court of Appeal emphasised that there had to be a reasonable belief of the common intention to share. As Browne-Wilkinson LJ admitted in *Grant v Edwards*, "In both, the claimant must to the knowledge of the legal owner have acted in the belief that the claimant has or will obtain an interest in the property. In both, the claimant must have acted to his or her detriment in reliance on such belief. In both, equity acts on the conscience of the legal owner to prevent him from acting in an unconscionable manner by defeating the common intention".[190] The shared need for detrimental reliance gives rise to further difficulties in that it becomes difficult to draw a clear demarcation between the constructive trust and proprietary estoppel in this context.[191] Context is, however, paramount as demonstrated in *Burton v Liden*.[192] There the claimant paid £200 per month as a result of various representations regarding the payments being made "towards the house" and being necessary if the house was to be retained. An estoppel was upheld as the assurances concerned future ownership rather than an immediate bargain. At the time of the trial, the property was worth £435,000. On estoppel principles, the claimant was awarded a beneficial interest valued at £33,522.

As regards quantification of the beneficial interest, different rules apply according to whether the implied trust is resulting or constructive. In relation to the former, it will be remembered that the claimant should obtain a share commensurate with the value of the contribution. In the case of a constructive trust, quantification should, when possible, be according to what the parties either expressly or impliedly intended. If necessary, however, the court must resort to imputation.[193] Under a constructive trust, therefore, the court can adopt a more creative approach to the calculation of the parties' respective shares. As demonstrated in *Grant v Edwards*, this involves looking beyond direct financial contributions (which, obviously, still assume relevance) and considering the parties' entire course of conduct together.

If the intention is not expressed, the court traditionally favours a contribution-based assessment. As will become apparent, these contributions need not be to the purchase price for, as Peter

---

188 [2003] EWHC 601 (Ch) at [73]; see also *Midland Bank v Dobson* [1986] 1 F.L.R. 171.
189 [2015] EWCA Civ 404.
190 [1986] Ch. 638 at 656.
191 See *Banner Homes Ltd v Luff Developments Ltd* [2000] Ch. 372 at 397 where Chadwick LJ admitted that, "the concepts of constructive trust and proprietary estoppel have much in common in this area".
192 [2016] EWCA Civ 275; see M. Lower, "Liden v Burton: proprietary estoppel and the family home" [2018] Conv. 84.
193 *Jones v Kernott* [2012] 1 A.C. 776.

Gibson LJ put it in *Curley v Parkes*, "In a constructive trust case one looks at the entire conduct of the parties and a broader approach as to what constitutes contributions is appropriate".[194] Hence, in *Graham-York v York*[195] Ms Graham-York's share was calculated at 25 per cent, which was a fair reflection of her financial and non-financial contributions over the years.

Constructive Trusts and the Family Home

11-037
A constructive trust arises in order to prevent one party resiling from an understanding as to beneficial entitlement in circumstances where it would be unconscionable to do so.[196] This will occur primarily where the estate owner has by words or conduct induced the claimant to act to his detriment in the reasonable belief that, in so acting, he will obtain a beneficial interest in the property.[197] The concepts of bargain, change of position and conscience, therefore, lie at the heart of the constructive trust.[198] This was demonstrated by the House of Lords in *Lloyds Bank Plc v Rosset* where Lord Bridge took the opportunity to restate the law as it related to the acquisition of an interest in the family home.[199] Lord Bridge identified two rules under which a beneficial interest could arise, one following on from an express, but informal, arrangement between the parties, the other arising from their unexpressed, but inferred, common intentions.[200] It is helpful to consider these settings separately.

Rule 1: express bargain constructive trusts

11-038
The traditional context for the creation of a constructive trust is where the legal owner of land has informally agreed that another is to acquire some beneficial interest in the property.[201] As Lord Bridge explained:

---

194 [2004] EWCA Civ 1515 at [16].
195 [2015] EWCA Civ 72.
196 See *Hopton v Millar* [2010] EWHC 2232 (Ch) where there was neither a common intention nor detrimental reliance.
197 *Gissing v Gissing* [1971] A.C. 886.
198 See generally B. Sloan, "Keeping up with the Jones Case: Establishing Constructive Trusts in the 'Sole Legal Owner' Scenarios" (2015) 35 L.S. 226.
199 [1991] 1 A.C. 107.
200 See generally M. Mills, "Single name family home constructive trusts: is Lloyds Bank v Rosset still good law?" [2018] Conv. 350.
201 For example, in *Williamson v Sheikh* [2008] EWCA Civ 990 a draft declaration of trust (never executed) constituted the necessary agreement.

> "The first and fundamental question which must always be resolved is whether . . . there has at any time prior to acquisition, or exceptionally at some later date, been any agreement, arrangement of understanding reached between them that the property is to be shared beneficially. The finding of an agreement or arrangement to share in this sense can only, I think, be based on evidence of express discussions between the partners, however imperfectly remembered and however imprecise their terms may have been. Once a finding to this effect is made it will only be necessary for the partner asserting a claim to a beneficial interest against the partner entitled to the legal estate to show that he or she has acted to his or her detriment or significantly altered his or her position in reliance on the agreement in order to give rise to a constructive trust or a proprietary estoppel".[202]

Discussion and shared intention

11-039

Accordingly, there must be some discussion as to property rights between the parties and, consequently, some genuine arrangement, agreement or understanding reached between them as to ownership.[203] This discussion will usually, but need not necessarily, occur prior to the acquisition of legal title.[204] Although a constructive trust can arise years after the property has been acquired by the sole owner, "in the absence of an express post-acquisition agreement, a court will be slow to infer from conduct alone that parties intended to vary existing beneficial interests established at the time of acquisition".[205] Following *Hammond v Mitchell*,[206] and in order to avoid the case failing due to vagueness, it is necessary that the express discussions alleged should be pleaded in detail. Provided that the claimant has acted to his detriment (or significantly altered his position) in reliance upon that arrangement, either a constructive trust or a proprietary estoppel will be invoked in favour of the claimant. The trust or estoppel will be employed to give effect to the express and shared intention. This approach is well illustrated by two case law examples.

First, in *Eves v Eves*[207] Stuart told his partner, Janet, that their joint home was to be acquired in his sole name because, at the time of purchase, she was under 21 years of age. Hence, it was

---

202 *Lloyds Bank v Rosset* [1991] 1 A.C. 107 at 132; see also *Morris v Morris* [2008] EWCA Civ 257, where there was no discussion and, therefore, no "Rule 1" common intention constructive trust.

203 The agreement cannot be binding on third parties (e.g. a company controlled by one of the parties to the agreement): *Smith v Bottomley* [2013] EWCA Civ 953. There was, as Sales J explained at [60], "No equitable claim which Ms Smith had against Mr Bottomley personally carried through, or was converted into, an equitable claim against the Company, which is a distinct legal person".

204 *Clough v Killey* (1996) 72 P. & C.R. D22.

205 Per Sir John Chadwick in *James v Thomas* [2008] 1 F.L.R. 1598 at [24].

206 [1991] 1 W.L.R. 1127.

207 [1975] 1 W.L.R. 1338.

explicitly made clear that, had she been older, the property would have been transferred into joint names. The couple had already cohabited for some time and had a daughter together. Subsequently, the relationship ended and she then claimed an interest in the quasi-connubial home. Stuart ran the defence that he had used Janet's age as an excuse for not having to put the house in both names. Although it had never been Stuart's real intention that Janet should acquire any beneficial interest, his excuse was viewed as evidence of some intention to share. His positive assertion had led her to believe that she was to have an interest in the house. As Janet acted on that belief, a constructive trust was invoked under which she was entitled to a one-quarter share in the property. As Lord Denning MR explained, "he should be judged by what he told her—by what he led her to believe—and not by his own intent which he kept to himself".[208] Brightman J added that, "It seems to me that this . . . raises the clear inference that there was an understanding between them that she was intended to have some sort of proprietary inter-est in the house: otherwise no excuse would be needed".[209] This is in contrast with *Wodzicki v Wodzicki*[210] where the Court of Appeal had to consider a daughter's claim that her father had promised her that, when he had finished repaying a loan and when he thought she was "ready", he would transfer the property to her. He repaid the loan in 1996 and died some 20 years later without transferring the property to the daughter. Although the daughter claimed that, but for this promise, she would have obtained other accommodation and would not have spent money on the property, the appellate court thought that the passing of time suggested that the father had never thought that she was ready to take ownership. No common intention constructive trust was found. A further obstacle was that the property was registered in the joint names of the father and his wife. There was no evidence that he had told his wife that it was his wish or inten-tion to transfer ownership to his daughter or that his wife had agreed to that course.[211]

11-040   Secondly, in *Grant v Edwards*[212] George made a positive representation to his partner, Linda, that the only reason why the property was conveyed into his sole name was that her ongoing divorce might be prejudiced if she was to be a joint legal owner. The couple had lived together prior to the purchase and had a child together. Again, it was not the genuine desire of George that Linda become a beneficial owner. Nevertheless, by this trick she was led to believe that the property was to be theirs jointly. Hence, a constructive trust was imposed to ensure that she received the half-share in the house that George had led her to believe she would have. As Nourse LJ explained, "Just as in *Eves v Eves*, these facts appear to me to raise a clear inference that there was an understanding between plaintiff and defendant, or a common intention, that the plaintiff was to have some sort of proprietary interest in the house; other-wise no excuse for not putting her name onto the title would have been needed".[213] As Mustill

---

208 [1975] 1 W.L.R. 1338 at 1342.
209 [1975] 1 W.L.R. 1338 at 1344.
210 [2017] EWCA Civ 95.
211 David Richards LJ (at [27]) could find no support for such "a startling proposition that the beneficial interest of one joint owner of a freehold property could be terminated without his knowledge by the other joint owner".
212 [1986] Ch. 638.
213 [1986] Ch. 638 at 649.

LJ added, "Whatever the defendant's actual intention, the nature of the excuse which he gave must have led the plaintiff to believe that she would in future have her name on the title, and this in turn would justify her in concluding that she had from the outset some kind of right to the house".[214] Browne-Wilkinson VC also agreed that the representation made to Linda, albeit untrue, was clear direct evidence of a common intention that she was to have an interest in the house.[215]

The shared intention for these purposes, however, needs to be express. If no discussion occurs, as demonstrated in *Burns v Burns*,[216] there is no scope for a constructive trust under the first rule in *Rosset*.[217] The thoughts of the parties necessarily have to be communicated as, in the words of Steyn LJ, "Our trust law does not allow property rights to be affected by telepathy".[218] Nevertheless, as Arden LJ admitted in *Lightfoot v Lightfoot-Brown*, "The fact that an agreement or arrangement is reached as a result of express discussions which are imprecise in their terms does not prevent the court from finding that there was an express agreement that a party should have a beneficial interest even though he or she is not the legal owner".[219] This entails that there has to be evidence (whether direct or circumstantial) that proves the existence of a specific statement about ownership. The court will, therefore, look for some signs of a consensual understanding. This forensic exercise was described by Waite J in *Hammond v Mitchell* as involving a, "painfully detailed retrospect".[220] He added that the emphasis upon express discussions between the parties,

> **"means that the tenderest exchanges of a common law courtship may assume an unforeseen significance many years later when they are brought under equity's microscope and subjected to an analysis under which many thousands of pounds of value may be liable to turn on fine questions as to whether the relevant words were spoken in earnest or in dalliance and with or without representational intent".[221]**

In both *Eves v Eves* and *Grant v Edwards* the court could discern the necessary element of "agreement" in order to activate the constructive trust. This was despite the deceit and trickery underlying the statements made. Some commentators, however, dispute whether this finding should have been made and regard the agreement as a fiction. Clarke looks at

11-041

---

214 [1986] Ch. 638 at 653.

215 [1986] Ch. 638 at 655.

216 [1984] Ch. 317; see also *Driver v Yorke* [2003] EWHC 746 (Ch).

217 See also *Secretary of State for Work and Pensions v London Borough Tower Hamlets* [2018] UKUT 25 (AAC) where there was no consensus so no Rule 1 constructive trust.

218 *Springette v Defoe* [1992] 2 F.L.R. 388 at 394. It is also to be recalled that, where there is an intention expressed, there is no scope for a resulting trust.

219 [2005] EWCA Civ 201 at [23].

220 [1991] 1 W.L.R. 1127 at 1129.

221 [1991] 1 W.L.R. 1127 at 1139.

these excuse cases and concludes that "Surely this is not agreement: it is disagreement . . . it is surely converting the intention of one party—albeit on these facts the innocent one—into an agreement".[222] Gardner shares this incredulity and notes that, "in both, the partner had explicitly told the woman that she was not to have a share. So on the face of it, there was most decidedly no agreement that she should".[223] As he then explains, "It is hard to think that the judges concerned really believed in it. One can only conclude that they . . . were engaged in the business of inventing agreements on women's behalf . . . the judges are prepared to take an inventive approach to the facts, so as to discover a common intention when in truth none exists . . .".[224] Nevertheless, both cases survived scrutiny by the House of Lords in *Lloyds Bank v Rosset* and represent the current state of the law. Subsequently, in *Hammond v Mitchell*[225] the Court of Appeal upheld a constructive trust based upon the statement of the male partner (a second-hand car dealer) that "I'll have to put the house in my name because I have tax problems", which explained why the house was conveyed into his sole name. He added that she was not to worry as when they married (this happy event, however, never occurred) the property would be half hers. As a result, she allowed her rights in the property to be subordinated to those of a subsequent mortgagee and worked for her partner on an unpaid basis. Again, the court construed this excuse as amounting to an assurance that the house was to be shared with his partner. Such declaration of intent operated as the basis of the understanding upon which she acted to her detriment. The common intention is to be tested objectively and not subjectively.[226]

In *Oxley v Hiscock*[227] the shared intention was that the couple were to live together and to pool their financial and other resources as would a married couple. The fact that the title was registered in the sole name of Mr Hiscock was expressly stated to be to defeat any claim that Mrs Oxley's former husband may have against the property. Once more a Rule 1 constructive trust arose. By way of contrast, however, no constructive trust arose on the facts of *Curran v Collins*.[228] There the Court of Appeal took the opportunity to revisit the jurisprudence surrounding the "specious excuse" and promoted a more cautious approach. There Mr Collins purchased property in his sole name. Ms Curran had previously asked whether her name would be on the title deeds and this was emphatically answered in the negative. Mr Collins justified this response by stating that it would involve paying premiums on two life assurance policies and thus prove to be too expensive. This was viewed by the appellate court as nothing more than a statement made to avoid any embarrassment. Lewison LJ considered both *Eves v Eves* and *Grant v Edwards* and observed, "These cases are fact-sensitive and need to be carefully examined".[229] He added that:

222　P. Clarke, "The Family Home: Intention and Agreement" [1992] 22 Fam. Law 72, 74.
223　S. Gardner, "Rethinking Family Property" (1993) 109 L.Q.R. 263, 265.
224　(1993) 109 L.Q.R. 263, 265.
225　[1991] 1 W.L.R. 1127.
226　*Jones v Kernott* [2012] 1 A.C. 776.
227　[2004] 3 W.L.R. 715.
228　[2015] EWCA Civ 404.
229　[2015] EWCA Civ 404 at [66].

> "These cases do not establish the proposition that the mere giving of a 'specious excuse' necessarily or even usually leads to an inference that the person to whom the excuse is given can reasonably regard herself as having an immediate entitlement to an interest in the property in question".[230]

The court felt it significant that Mr Collins and Ms Curran had not cohabited together prior to the purchase, they had no children and the property was not intended to be a family home. There was also no positive representation that Ms Curran would otherwise be a joint owner.

Other examples of informal arrangements

The informal arrangements that might be entered between the parties are various and include the following examples:

11-042

- an agreement that Fred should retain an interest in land purchased from Fred by Jordan. In *Bannister v Bannister*,[231] a woman conveyed land at an undervalue to her brother-in-law on the oral understanding that she would be allowed to occupy rent free for the remaining years of her life. It was held that, when he tried to evict her, there was a constructive trust that enabled the enjoyment of the beneficial life interest as promised. In short, there was a bargain, detrimental reliance and equitable fraud. The attempt to defeat her equitable interest, therefore, failed;

- an agreement that Fred should retain an interest in land purchased from Adrienne by Jordan. In *Lyus v Prowsa Developments Ltd*,[232] a building plot was sold by a mortgagee to a development company subject to the subsisting rights of a named party who had paid a deposit on one of the still to be constructed houses. The contract to buy the house had not, however, been protected by an appropriate entry on the Land Register. The development company subsequently threatened not to honour its commitment. The High Court held that the development company had taken the legal title subject to a constructive trust in favour of the third party. There had been an express arrangement that formed, in part, the basis of the sale transaction which gave the house buyer new rights. For the development company to renege on that stipulation would amount to an unconscionable act;

---

230 [2015] EWCA Civ 404 at [74].
231 [1948] 2 All E.R. 133.
232 [1982] 1 W.L.R. 1044.

- an agreement that Fred should acquire an interest in land to be purchased from Adrienne by Jordan. In *Pallant v Morgan*,[233] there was a joint venture involving an antecedent and unenforceable bargain that one party could buy the land without competition from the other in return for a promise of shared rights in the land. In these circumstances, equity will not permit Jordan to acquire the property and keep it for his own benefit to the exclusion of Fred. The basis for the intervention of equity is traditionally framed around the common intention constructive trust.[234] The key ingredients of the *Pallant*-style equity are, as Sir Martin Nourse put it in *Kilcarne Holdings Ltd v Targetfollow (Birmingham) Ltd*, "first, that there be an arrangement or understanding between the parties that A will acquire the property and that if he does so B will obtain some interest in it; and secondly, that B must act in reliance on that arrangement or understanding".[235] The claim failed in the *Kilcarne Holdings* case because there was no understanding between the parties that the property should be acquired for their joint benefit or that Kilcarne would obtain some interest in it;

- an agreement that Fred should acquire an interest in land already owned by Jordan. In *Hussey v Palmer*,[236] Mrs Hussey was invited to live with her son-in-law, Mr Palmer. In return, she financed an extension to the house in which she was to be accommodated. The pair fell out and the majority of the Court of Appeal held that a constructive trust arose under which she was entitled to a share in the property because of her financial contributions. The problem with this decision is that the existence of an agreement between the parties is not readily apparent on the evidence. Indeed, in his dissenting judgment Cairns LJ felt that this was a loan and that the elderly woman was not entitled to invoke a trust; and

- an agreement that Fred should acquire a greater interest in land owned by Jordan. In *Re Densham*,[237] there was originally a purchase money resulting trust which fixed the beneficial interest of X according to the financial contributions made towards the acquisition of the property. Subsequently, it was agreed orally that X would acquire a larger share in the property. In light of X's reliance upon the agreement, a constructive trust arose to give effect to the understanding between the parties. In *Gissing v Gissing*, Lord Diplock alluded to there being "some subsequent fresh agreement, acted upon by the parties, to vary the original beneficial interests created when the . . . home was acquired".[238]

---

233 [1953] Ch. 43. See further para.**10-040**.
234 *Crossco No 4 Unlimited v Jolan Ltd* [2011] EWCA Civ 1619.
235 [2005] EWCA Civ 1355 at [21]; see also, *Banner Homes Plc v Luff Developments Ltd* [2000] Ch. 372.
236 [1972] 1 W.L.R. 1286.
237 [1975] 1 W.L.R. 1519.
238 [1971] A.C. 886 at 906.

Rule 1: change of position

Once the court has divined an express agreement, arrangement or understanding relating to the equitable ownership of the property, there must be conduct by the claimant acting upon that intention.[239] This is usually called "detrimental reliance" or "change of position". It is necessary, as Lord Diplock observed in *Gissing v Gissing*, "to show that he or she has acted to his or her detriment or significantly altered his or her position in reliance on the agreement".[240] In *Layton v Martin*, Scott J described this as some *"quid pro quo* moving from the claimant".[241] Accordingly, as in *Collins v Curran*,[242] if there is no detrimental reliance there can be no constructive trust. There has, however, to be a causal linkage between the informal understanding and the detrimental conduct. The conduct must be referable in some way to the informal arrangement reached between the parties. This required nexus was the subject of analysis, albeit somewhat divergent, by the Court of Appeal in *Grant v Edwards*.[243] There the claimant had made significant contributions to household expenses so that the other could pay the mortgage instalments.

11-043

First, Nourse LJ favoured a restrictive approach which was to consider whether the claimant would have performed the acts, but for the understanding with the defendant. He spoke in terms of "conduct on which the woman could not reasonably have been expected to embark unless she was to have an interest in the house".[244] Accordingly, no interest will accrue if the claimant would, without the understanding, have performed the acts anyway.[245] Conduct that results merely from the mutual love and affection of the parties, therefore, will not be sufficient to activate a constructive trust. Accordingly, merely moving in to live with another will not suffice.[246] In contrast, Nourse LJ felt that a woman would not be expected to wield a 14lb sledgehammer in the front garden. It remains unclear whether he would have adopted the same reasoning if it had been a male claimant who had wielded the sledgehammer.

Secondly, Mustill LJ adopted a different stance and contended that, if the bargain is express (e.g. "give up your existing Rent Act tenancy, move in with me and you will have a share in my house"), there is usually no difficulty.[247] The surrender of the tenancy and the moving in

11-044

---

239 For example, in *Culliford v Thorpe* [2018] EWHC 426 (Ch) the defendant carried out significant works of construction on the partner's property.

240 [1971] A.C. 886 at 905. The form of the reliance does not have to be specified in the agreement: *Parris v Williams* [2008] EWCA Civ 1147.

241 [1986] 2 F.L.R. 227 at 236. The court felt that she would have moved in with her partner regardless of his vague assurances as to her future financial security. Her conduct was not induced by financial considerations.

242 [2015] EWCA Civ 404.

243 [1986] Ch. 638.

244 [1986] Ch. 638 at 648.

245 *Midland Bank Plc v Dobson* [1986] 1 F.L.R. 171 (periodic decorating and household chores).

246 *Layton v Martin* [1986] 2 F.L.R. 227; see also, *Coombes v Smith* [1986] 1 W.L.R. 808 where living with her lover for 10 years and bearing him a child was an insufficient change of position for the purposes of an estoppel.

247 But see *Smith v Bottomley* [2013] EWCA Civ 953 where Ms Smith's moving out of rented accommodation was not detrimental reliance because her primary motive was that she was to be provided with rent-free

completes the bargain (it may be added without recourse to a sledge hammer) and should not now be defeated by the fact that you might have moved in with me anyway. The difficulty, of course, is when the bargain is not as clear-cut. In such a case, the court must fill in the blanks. As Mustill LJ explained, "the proprietor promises the claimant an interest in the property on the basis that the claimant will do something in return. The parties do not themselves make explicit what the claimant is to do. The court, therefore, has to complete the bargain for them by means of implication".[248] As to whether the conduct will satisfy the test, all will turn upon the nature of both the conduct and the bargain. In this default position, however, the court will again speculate as to what the claimant would have been prepared to do anyway in the absence of any informal understanding.

Thirdly, Browne-Wilkinson VC suggested what has become known as the "joint lives" approach to the linking of the intention and the acts relied upon to show detriment. Promoting a very liberal and popular approach, he explained:

> "it is impossible to say whether or not the claimant would have done the acts relied on as a detriment even if she thought she had no interest in the house. Setting up house together, having a baby, making payments to general house-keeping expenses (not strictly necessary to enable the mortgage to be repaid) may all be referable to the mutual love and affection of the parties and not specifically referable to the claimant's belief that she has an interest in the house . . . once it has been shown that there was a common intention that the claimant should have an interest in the house, any act done by her to her detriment relating to the joint lives of the parties is, in my judgment, sufficient detriment to qualify".[249]

Browne-Wilkinson VC felt that in these "joint lives" cases, the evidential inference is that the claimant acted in reliance on the understanding that a beneficial interest would be acquired and the burden lies on the legal owner to displace that inference. Of the three competing views, the approach of Browne-Wilkinson VC has much to commend it, not least because it affords flexibility and is better suited to cope with the tangled web of modern living arrangements and diverse relationships.

11-045 For the purposes of Rule 1 of *Rosset*, the conduct relied upon can adopt a variety of guises. As will become clear, this is a more liberal test than is employed in relation to Rule 2 implied bargain constructive trusts. In *Grant v Edwards*,[250] the claimant contributed to household

---

accommodation by Mr Bottomley. Sales J declined to consider the question whether a promise to marry could constitute sufficient detrimental reliance.

248 [1986] Ch. 638 at 652.
249 [1986] Ch. 638 at 657.
250 [1986] Ch. 638.

expenses so that the defendant could meet the mortgage repayments.[251] In *Eves v Eves*,[252] the claimant did not make any financial contribution, but did carry out substantial physical labour (including wielding a 14lb sledgehammer) relating to internal and external decorating, gardening and general maintenance. She also performed the role of mother and housewife. The detriment must, however, be material and not merely emotional or psychological in nature. As Lord Templeman put it, "Equity operates on conscience but is not influenced by sentimentality".[253] In *Christian v Christian*,[254] the claimant asserted as "detriment" the fact that she had to live with her partner in a house which was located near her partner's wife's property. This "social embarrassment" was not regarded as a relevant detriment and the Court of Appeal emphasised that equity was not concerned with shielding people's feelings.

The court sometimes assesses the degree of detriment by adopting a balance sheet approach. In other words, the court looks for a net disadvantage to the claimant. There must be a substantial and not trivial detriment incurred. For example, gardening work embarked upon by the claimant in his son-in-law's garden has been regarded as merely the carrying out of a hobby and, hence, it did not suffice.[255] A similar approach was adopted where housekeeping services were relied upon, but the claimant had already been compensated by the payment of a regular housekeeping allowance and free accommodation.[256]

Rule 1: quantification

11-046

If the express bargain prescribes the shares that the parties are to take, the quantification of the beneficial interest is straightforward. In *Clough v Killey*,[257] there was an express bargain that the beneficial interest be shared on a 50/50 basis. Mrs Killey argued that, under the first rule in *Rosset*, a constructive trust arose which, due to the express agreement, gave her a 50 per cent interest. After this arrangement, Mrs Killey had undeniably acted to her detriment by making the proceeds of her divorce settlement available to Mr Clough and undertaking work on the cottage. As to the extent of her share, Peter Gibson LJ admitted that "it is only common sense that where the parties form a common intention as to specific shares they are to take, those shares prima facie are the shares to which the court will give effect".[258] The correct starting point, therefore, was to take the shares as established by the parties' express common intention and to depart from this only when there was good cause. Although Peter Gibson LJ

---

251 See also *Le Foe v Le Foe* [2001] 2 F.L.R. 970.
252 [1975] 1 W.L.R. 1338.
253 *Winkworth v Edward Baron Development Co Ltd* [1986] 1 W.L.R. 1512 at 1516.
254 (1981) 131 N.L.J. 43.
255 *Hannaford v Selby* (1976) 239 E.G. 811.
256 *Layton v Martin* [1986] 2 F.L.R. 227. A similar stance is adopted in relation to satisfying an estoppel claim: see *Jennings v Rice* [2003] 1 P. & C.R. 100; *Re Knowles* [2008] UKPC 30.
257 (1996) 72 P. & C.R. D22.
258 (1996) 72 P. & C.R. D22 at D24. In *Parris v Williams* [2008] EWCA Civ 1147, the Court of Appeal emphasised that, although the contributions of the parties differ significantly, the agreement will still be enforced.

failed to indicate what would constitute such a cause, he did conclude that, on the present evidence, there was no justification for such departure: "It seems to me only just that Mr Clough should be held to, and not allowed to renege on, his promise on which Mrs Killey relied to her detriment".[259] Accordingly, *Clough v Killey* demonstrates the fundamental point that when the parties expressly agree on beneficial shares, provided there is some detrimental reliance, that understanding will almost certainly be enforced by the courts. In the absence of a further express post-acquisition agreement, therefore, the court will be slow to infer from conduct alone that the parties intended to vary their existing beneficial interests established by agreement.[260] Although the ambulatory nature of constructive trusts was accepted in principle by Baroness Hale in *Stack v Dowden*, such variations will depend on the court being able to infer an intention to alter the share in which the beneficial interest was previously held.[261] The mere fact that one party has spent time and money on improving the property will not normally be sufficient to draw such an inference.[262] Accordingly, compelling evidence will be required to infer such a change and this will usually concentrate on subsequent discussions, statements or conduct. In *Ely v Robson*,[263] Mr Ely had repeatedly assured Ms Robson that "what is mine is also yours". This would normally promote a 50/50 split of the beneficial interest. After their relationship ended, the parties met to compromise their respective property claims without their solicitors being present. This oral compromise was on terms that Mr Ely would hold the disputed property on trust for himself for life, with a remainder of 80 per cent to his heirs and assigns and 20 per cent to Ms Robson. The terms of the settlement were sufficiently clear to form the basis of a binding agreement and both had understood and intended that it should be acted upon. Accordingly, Ms Robson's interest was now limited to 20 per cent.

11-047

In *Gallarotti v Sebastianelli*[264] the parties bought a London flat together for £188,287 with the aid of a mortgage. Each of them made a cash contribution. Mr Sebastianelli contributed £86,500 while his friend paid the lesser sum of £26,896. The title to the property was registered in Mr Sebastianelli's sole name. He also took out the mortgage in his sole name and proceeded to pay the mortgage instalments. The real question, however, concerned the meaning and consequence of an express agreement between the parties, to the effect that, in return for equal beneficial shares, Mr Gallarotti would make larger payments than his friend toward the paying of the mortgage. In reality, the parties' contributions were totally asymmetric, with Mr Gallarotti making no real contribution at all. The parties could not, therefore, have intended that the agreement should operate in these circumstances. The logical result was that the understanding of an equal division was at an end.[265]

---

259 (1996) 72 P. & C.R. D22 at D24.

260 *Hopton v Miller* [2010] EWHC 2232 (Ch).

261 As, indeed, occurred in *Jones v Kernott* [2012] 1 A.C .776; see generally N. Piska, "Ambulatory Trusts and the Family Home: *Jones v Kernott*" (2010) 24(1) Tru. L.I. 87.

262 *Bernard v Josephs* [1982] 23 All E.R. 162. Cf. when s.37 of the Matrimonial Proceedings and Property Act 1970 applies (as regards married couples, engaged parties and registered partnerships).

263 [2016] EWCA Civ 774.

264 [2012] 2 F.L.R. 1231.

265 See also *Quaintance v Tandan* unreported 24 July 2012 where the common intention to share equally as tenants

Difficulties arise, however, when the express bargain is silent as to the beneficial share to be taken. The court is then forced to do its best to allocate on the basis of fairness and justice. The maxim "equity is equality" has little role to play in these circumstances.[266] As Lord Reid put it in *Gissing v Gissing*, "I think that the high-sounding brocard 'equity is equality' has been misused. There will of course be cases where a half-share is a reasonable estimation, but there will be many others where a fair estimate might be a tenth or a quarter or sometimes more than half".[267]

In *Drake v Whipp*,[268] there was an express agreement to share beneficial ownership, but the respective shares were left unstated. The issue was whether the calculation should be based upon constructive trust principles (i.e. a broad-brush approach) or resulting trust principles (i.e. an arithmetical approach). The argument promoted was that there was no scope for a constructive trust because of the lack of a common understanding or intention as to the respective shares to be taken. The Court of Appeal rejected this line of reasoning. Although it was necessary for there to be a common intention that Mrs Drake should have some beneficial interest, it was not necessary for constructive trust purposes that the exact shares be specified between them. Instead, the court could assess her share by evaluating her change of position, including direct financial contributions made, because of the informal agreement. Peter Gibson LJ acknowledged that the court would also consider:

> "the fact that Mr Whipp and Mrs Drake together purchased the property with the intention that it should be their home, that they both contributed their labour in 70 per cent/30 per cent proportions, that they had a joint bank account out of which the costs of conversion were met, but that that account was largely fed by his earnings, and that she paid for the food and some other household expenses and took care of the housekeeping for them both".[269]

Somewhat surprisingly, the same issues were once more canvassed in *Oxley v Hiscock*, where again there was an agreement to share, but in unspecified proportions.[270] The first question on appeal was whether the court was to follow the constructive trust approach or whether the shares were to be calculated simply according to the respective financial contributions to the acquisition cost. Chadwick LJ reiterated that, for the purposes of an express bargain constructive trust, the agreement need not recite the extent of the parties' beneficial interests. The primary issue was to establish an express discussion to share and, once that was demonstrated,

in common was changed by the subsequent conduct of Mr Quaintance, which amounted to the abandonment of Ms Tandan and any claim that he would have otherwise had over the property.

266 See Waite J in *Hammond v Mitchell* [1991] 1 W.L.R. 1127 at 1137.
267 [1971] A.C. 886 at 897.
268 [1996] 1 F.L.R. 826.
269 [1996] 1 F.L.R. 826 at 831.
270 [2004] 3 W.L.R. 715.

there was no practicable alternative to the determination of a fair share. Accordingly, he claimed that "It must now be accepted that . . . the answer is that each is entitled to that share which the court considers fair having regard to the whole course of dealing between them in relation to the property".[271] This includes arrangements which they make from time to time to meet the outgoings (e.g. housekeeping, mortgage contributions, council tax and utilities) which have to be met if they are to occupy the property as a home. Accordingly, the court is simply inferring a common intention as to the parties' respective shares based on that which, in the light of all the material circumstances (including the acts and conduct of the parties after the acquisition) is shown to be fair and reasonable. Chadwick LJ acknowledged that "the courts have not found it easy to reconcile that final step with a traditional, property-based approach".[272]

11-049

Chadwick LJ noted that this "fair share" approach had been criticised by Dillon LJ in *Springette v Defoe*[273] as offering palm tree justice, but he felt that the court must make such an order as the circumstances require to give effect to the beneficial interest of the one party, "the existence of which the other party (having the legal title) is estopped from denying".[274] Chadwick LJ preferred his reasoning to that adopted in *Midland Bank v Cooke*,[275] which attributed to the parties a fictitious common intention that their respective beneficial interests should be fixed as from the time of the acquisition when, in reality, they had given no thought to the matter. Chadwick LJ also believed his approach to be better than that promoted by Lord Diplock in *Gissing v Gissing*[276] which was that, at the time of acquisition, the common intention was that their respective shares should be left for later determination.

The "fair share" approach is based upon three strands of reasoning:

- the court must operate on the basis that the parties have agreed that their shares are to be determined in such a way at the end of their relationship or upon sale;

- following a review of the whole of the parties' course of dealing, the court must assume that this was the parties' assumed common intention at the time of purchase; and

- the fairness approach must operate because it invokes principles that are almost indistinguishable from those applied under the doctrine of proprietary estoppel.

---

271 [2004] 3 W.L.R. 715 at 750. This approach was approved by Baroness Hale in *Stack v Dowden* [2007] 2 A.C. 432 (cf. Lord Neuberger's view at 476).

272 [2004] 3 W.L.R. 715 at 750.

273 [1992] 2 F.L.R. 388.

274 [2004] 3 W.L.R. 715 at 750. Chadwick LJ expressed the view that the *Springette* case did not accurately reflect the state of the law even when it was decided. The primary issue was to establish an express discussion to share and, once you get to that stage, there is no practicable alternative to the determination of a fair share.

275 [1995] 4 All E.R. 562.

276 [1971] A.C. 886.

In the Court of Appeal in *Stack v Dowden*,[277] Chadwick LJ was offered the opportunity to revisit his earlier decision in *Oxley v Hiscock*. Following the decision of the House of Lords in *Stack*, his views are now relevant primarily to sole name cases. He took the opportunity to consider the relevance of financial contributions. He again rejected the proposition that, absent agreement as to shares, the property is necessarily to be held in beneficial shares proportionate to their respective contributions to the purchase price. He admitted, however, that quantification might reflect the parties' contributions when it was fair and just that this should follow. This may be, for example, where most of the purchase price has been provided by one party and the other has made a comparatively slight financial input. Although the parties may have agreed that each should have an undefined beneficial interest, it would not be fair, having regard to the whole course of dealing between the parties in relation to the property, to treat their beneficial shares as equal. An alternative conclusion would, of course, fail to give proper weight to the financial contributions made to the acquisition of the property.

11-050

Rule 1 and the role for proprietary estoppel?

Lord Bridge in *Lloyds Bank Plc v Rosset* envisaged that a beneficial interest could be acquired by proprietary estoppel as well as by constructive trust.[278] The traditional distinction between a constructive trust and an estoppel lies in the emphasis of the former upon "bargains" and the emphasis of the latter upon "representations".[279] Estoppel is an equitable jurisdiction by which a court may interfere in cases where the assertion of a strict legal right would be unconscionable.[280] There are three characteristics of proprietary estoppel: there must be an unconditional[281] representation or assurance[282]; there must be reliance or change of position[283]; and there must be substantial detriment and unconscionable disadvantage.[284] Hence, under the first rule in *Rosset*, a constructive trust and a "common expectation" proprietary estoppel can arise on the same facts. They both share common characteristics in that there is the need for

11-051

---

277   [2006] 1 F.L.R. 254; affirmed at [2007] 2 A.C. 432.

278   [1991] 1 A.C. 107 at 132.

279   *Southwell v Blackburn* [2014] EWCA Civ 1347; see generally, P. Ferguson, "Constructive Trusts—A Note of Caution" [1993] 109 L.Q.R. 114.

280   *Ely v Robson* [2016] EWCA Civ 774. This was an unusual case in that Mr Ely (unsuccessfully) pleaded estoppel in circumstances where he was already the sole legal owner of the property.

281   There must be more than a mere indication of intention: *Cooke v Thomas* [2010] EWCA Civ 227.

282   In *Morris v Morris* [2008] EWCA Civ 257, Sir Peter Gibson noted that the representation or assurance "must be specific, such as would entitle the person to whom it is made reasonably to rely on it or change his or her position" (at [28]). For example, in *Burton v Liden* [2016] EWCA Civ 275 an assurance concerned with payments 'towards the house' was sufficiently clear to mean payments "towards the ownership of the house".

283   This need not be financial detriment and, as in *Southwell v Blackburn* [2014] EWCA Civ 1347, can include the giving up of a secure rented accommodation. In *Suggitt v Suggitt* [2012] EWCA Civ 1140, the claimant devoted his entire working life to the farm and the business on the strength of the representation.

284   The detriment must be assessed and evaluated over the course of the relationship: *Southwell v Blackburn* [2014] EWCA Civ 1347.

some form of shared understanding as to ownership, detrimental reliance and equitable fraud. The conventional response is that both are "concerned with equity's intervention to provide relief against unconscionable conduct".[285] As Browne-Wilkinson VC put it in *Grant v Edwards*, "The two principles have been developed separately without cross-fertilisation between them, but they rest on the same foundation . . .".[286] It is, therefore, common for alternative arguments based upon the constructive trust and estoppel to be pleaded.[287] Nevertheless, the scope for semantic and conceptual confusion is clear from *Simpson v Simpson*, where the High Court unhelpfully spoke in terms of a constructive trust based on equitable estoppel.[288]

The role for estoppel in the co-ownership arena appears primarily to concentrate on Rule 1 cases where there has been an informal agreement as to ownership and even then only when the informal agreement is inconclusive as to the parties' beneficial shares. This is a sensible restriction as the usual outcome will be that under Rule 1 a complete informal agreement will be enforced as it stands. This is regardless of the degree of the change of position undertaken by the claimant. Under an estoppel, however, what is represented (i.e. the expectation generated) is far from determinative of the outcome of the case.[289] Such was demonstrated in *Jennings v Rice*,[290] where the Court of Appeal admitted that the court had to look at matters in the round and have regard to the nature and quality of the representation and the expectation engendered, the detriment incurred and the proportionality of any award having regard to the detriment. If the claimant's expectations are uncertain, extravagant or out of proportion to the detriment suffered, the court should recognise that the claimant's equity should be satisfied in another and generally more limited way than that which was expected.[291] To honour the representations in the *Jennings* case (i.e. to award the claimant a house worth £435,000) would have been entirely disproportionate to satisfy the equity.[292] Instead, the claimant was awarded a sum of £200,000. The touchstone of unconscionability, therefore, comes into play when satisfying the equity.[293] A disproportionate remedy is not the correct way of doing what is right to avoid an unconscionable result.[294] As in *Southwell v*

---

285 Per Robert Walker LJ in *Yaxley v Gotts* [2000] Ch. 162 at 176. Note, however, his later reluctance to accept that the two concepts can be assimilated: *Stack v Dowden* [2007] 2 A.C. 432 at 448; *Cobbe v Yeoman's Row Management Ltd* [2008] 1 W.L.R. 1752 at 1776.

286 [1986] Ch. 638 at 656.

287 See *Pinfield v Eagles* [2005] EWHC 477 (Ch). In *Wodzicki v Wodzicki* [2017] EWCA Civ 95, the daughter ran the estoppel argument to assert that she was entitled to sole beneficial ownership. This failed because it could not be shown that any promise made by her father was made with the knowledge of the co-owning wife.

288 [2005] EWHC 2098 (Ch).

289 If justified, however, they can coincide: *SMQ v RFQ* [2006] EWHC 1874 (Fam); see further, B. McFarlane and P. Sales, "Promises, detriment, and liability: lessons from proprietary estoppel" (2015) L.Q.R. 610.

290 (2003) 1 P. & C.R. 100.

291 *Powell v Benney* [2007] EWCA Civ 1283.

292 See also, *Murphy v Burrows* [2004] EWHC 1900 (Ch). In *Davies v Davies* [2016] EWCA Civ 463, for example, the lower court satisfied the estoppel by making an award of £1.3 million. This was reduced by the Court of Appeal to the sum of £500,000.

293 *Culliford v Thorpe* [2018] EWHC 426 (Ch).

294 *Moore v Moore* [2016] EWHC 2202 (Ch). There Deputy Judge Monty explained (at [174]) that, "Proportionality

Blackburn,[295] any benefits that accrued to the claimant during the relationship must also be thrown into the mix. Relevant factors there included having had rent-free accommodation for herself and for her two daughters and the financial assistance she had received enabling her successfully to complete an undergraduate degree course, which enhanced her earning ability. It is also an adage of estoppel that the court will confer only the minimum equity to do justice on the facts of each case. Such concerns do not bother the court when there is an express bargain to share in specified proportions.

Estoppel may assume particular relevance in the scenario where there has been an express agreement as to sharing, but the agreement is totally silent as to the parties' shares. It was in this context that Chadwick LJ in *Oxley v Hiscock* surveyed the relationship between the two legal concepts and concluded that "the time has come to accept that there is no difference in outcome . . . whether the true analysis lies in constructive trust or in proprietary estoppel".[296] This assimilation was, however, doubted by Lord Walker in *Stack v Dowden* as "proprietary estoppel typically consists of asserting an equitable claim against the conscience of the 'true' owner. The claim is to a 'mere equity'. It is to be satisfied by the minimum award necessary to do justice . . . which may sometimes lead to no more than a monetary award. A 'common intention' constructive trust, by contrast, is identifying the true beneficial owner or owners, and the size of their beneficial interests".[297] As Lord Collins emphasised in *Scott v Southern Pacific Mortgages Ltd*, "the difference would only be crucial in terms of remedies".[298] This, however, is not always so.[299]

As shown, in cases where there is an agreement to share and the agreement expressly allocates the parties' respective interests, a constructive trust analysis will prevail. Accordingly, where the parties have informally agreed that each is to have an equal share this will usually be definitive. It is, however, possible that, subsequent to an agreement between Fred and Jordan, Fred acts further to his detriment without there being a positive representation made by Jordan. If Jordan stands back and allows Fred to change his position in the mistaken belief that he (Fred) has rights, although there is no bargain between them, Fred's additional detriment could be recognised by an added value estoppel interest built upon the finding of a constructive trust.[300] This theme was pursued in *Sleebush v Gordon*[301] where the High Court

11-052

---

lies at the heart of the doctrine of promissory estoppel; the court must take into account whether in all the circumstances the promise and the benefit is proportionate to the detriment and the remedy must also be proportionate".

295 [2014] EWCA Civ 1347.

296 [2004] 3 W.L.R. 715 at 751.

297 [2007] 2 A.C. 432 at 448; see also Black J in *SMQ v RFQ* [2008] EWHC 1874 (Fam) who acknowledged that a claimant may well do better under a constructive trust than by relying on an estoppel.

298 [2015] A.C. 385 at [28].

299 In *Culliford v Thorpe* [2018] EWHC 426 (Ch), there was an Informal agreement to share beneficial ownership equally. Judge Paul Matthews determined, however, that whichever route was adopted (Rule 1 or estoppel) the outcome would on the facts before him be the same. The detriment far outweighed the value of the assurance.

300 *Preston & Henderson v St Helens MBC* (1989) 58 P. & C.R. 500. This case concerned who was entitled to the owner occupier's supplement on compulsory purchase of an unfit dwelling house.

301 [2004] EWHC 2287 (Ch).

felt that an express declaration of trust contained in the conveyance could be departed from by the invocation of proprietary estoppel. There the co-owner made clear and unequivocal representations and, as a result, the claimant took over total financial responsibility for the property over many years. This reliance warranted an increased entitlement to the property which was awarded on an estoppel basis. Similarly, a variation by estoppel can exceptionally arise in relation to an express declaration of trust. In *Clarke v Meadus*,[302] there was an express declaration under which each party (mother and daughter) was to have a beneficial half-share. Ms Clarke (the daughter) claimed to have a greater share due to estoppel and the detriment incurred as result of her mother's representations. Warren J accepted that the express trust could be overridden by an estoppel because of subsequent promises and representations.

Rule 2: the implied bargain constructive trust

11-053

The second rule in *Rosset* applies where there is no evidence of an express discussion having occurred between the parties. In this situation, the court looks in detail at the conduct of the parties with the prospect of presuming a common intention to share beneficial ownership.[303] There are two key ingredients. First, the claimant must convince the court that there was a common intention to share the property beneficially. As Arden LJ emphasised in *Lightfoot v Lightfoot-Brown*, "In the absence of a common intention, no common intention constructive trust will arise".[304] Secondly, the claimant must demonstrate that he changed his position because of the unexpressed common intention. The court may look at conduct both prior and subsequent to the acquisition of the property.

It will quickly become clear that, under this second rule, the role of direct financial contributions made by a non-owner is multifaceted. This was discussed by Arden LJ in *Lightfoot v Lightfoot-Brown* where she concluded that such contributions serve:

- as evidence from which a common intention can be inferred;

- as corroboration of direct evidence of intention;

- as evidence that the claimant has acted in reliance on the intention; and

- as an aid to the quantification of the size of the beneficial interest.[305]

---

302 [2010] EWHC 3117 (Ch).
303 The court must necessarily be wary of self-serving evidence of subjective intention introduced without corroborative evidence: *Thandi v Sands* [2014] EWHC 2378 (Ch).
304 [2005] EWCA Civ 201 at [24].
305 [2005] EWCA Civ 201 at [24].

Rule 2: common intention

The process of finding a common intention has been eased somewhat by the stance of the Court of Appeal in *Oxley v Hiscock*.[306] This appeal concerned a female claimant who had made a 20 per cent contribution towards the purchase of the family home. Under constructive trust principles, however, she was awarded a 40 per cent share. As regards the threshold issue relating to the intention to share beneficially, Chadwick LJ emphasised that "direct contributions to the purchase price will be conduct from which such common intention can readily be inferred".[307] The appellate court, therefore, acknowledged that proof of the common intention will normally take the form of financial contributions made by the claimant to the acquisition cost of the property. This was an approach shared also by the High Court in *McKenzie v McKenzie* where it was admitted that "the Court is unlikely to consider the inference justified unless there is proof that the claimant made direct contributions to the purchase price which are not explicable except on the basis that the parties must have intended that the property would be beneficially shared . . .".[308]

It follows that even a small contribution can afford evidence of the common intention and, as it is an inference drawn by the court from conduct, the fact that the parties never gave any thought to the matter is irrelevant.[309] The common intention is not, therefore, undermined by the lack of any consensus as to beneficial shares and is not usually difficult to establish.[310]

11-054

Rule 2: change of position

In contrast to the first rule in *Rosset*, there is a more demanding test employed here about what amounts to a change of position. It is not enough for the purposes of Rule 2 that the claimant's conduct is merely attributable to the inferred agreement between the parties. It should not be overlooked that, as Lord Bridge observed, the claimant is relying upon his own conduct, "both as the basis from which to infer a common intention to share the property beneficially and as the conduct relied on to give rise to a constructive trust".[311] Consequently, the change of position is localised only to direct financial contributions made to the initial and/or ongoing purchase of the property.[312] As Arden LJ explained in *Lightfoot v Lightfoot-Brown*, "In this respect

11-055

---

306 [2004] 3 W.L.R. 715.
307 [2004] 3 W.L.R. 715 at 734.
308 [2003] EWHC 601 (Ch) at [72].
309 *Midland Bank v Cooke* [1995] 4 All E.R. 562.
310 In *Capehorn v Harris* [2015] EWCA Civ 995, however, Mr Harris was unable to show either an express agreement (so Rule 1 could not apply) or any implied common intention (so Rule 2 could not apply). The payment by Mr Harris of £750 per week to Mrs Capehorn concerned the purchase of her frozen food business and did not give him a beneficial interest in the property registered in her sole name.
311 *Lloyds Bank Plc v Rosset* [1991] 1 A.C. 107 at 133.
312 *Gissing v Gissing* [1971] A.C. 886. Hence, it would cover mortgage repayments: *Webster v Webster* [2009] 1 F.L.R. 1240.

the expenditure has to be referable to the acquisition of the house".[313] Indeed, as Lord Bridge acknowledged, "it is at least extremely doubtful whether anything else will do".[314] Accordingly, if direct contributions are found the courts will readily imply a constructive trust,[315] whereas, if no such contributions are made then co-ownership under the second rule simply does not arise.

The insistence upon there being monetary contribution to the purchase of the property ignores other valuable contributions that a claimant may have made. This was patently demonstrated in *Burns v Burns*[316] where years of domestic labour and child rearing were disregarded. There had been no express agreement (so Rule 1 could not apply) and no direct financial contribution whatsoever (so she could not invoke a Rule 2 constructive trust or, indeed, a purchase money resulting trust). Hence, Ms Burns acquired no interest at all in the family home.[317] As Fox LJ put it, "the mere fact that the parties live together and do the ordinary domestic tasks is . . . no indication at all that they thereby intended to alter the existing property rights of either of them".[318] In a similar vein, a daughter's unpaid work managing a public house did not trigger a constructive trust in relation to the family home that was purchased out of the profits of the pub business.[319] The contribution was indirect and showed no intention that she was to acquire an interest in the house.[320] In *James v Thomas*, Sir John Chadwick said of a cohabitant's unsuccessful claims to a beneficial interest, "The true position, as it seems to me, is that she worked in the business, and contributed her labour to the improvements to the property, because she and Mr Thomas were making their life together as man and wife. The Cottage was their home: the business was their livelihood. It is a mistake to think that the motives which lead parties in such a relationship to act as they do are necessarily attributable to pecuniary self-interest".[321]

This view of the law was regarded as outmoded and too narrowly stated by the majority of the House of Lords in *Stack v Dowden*.[322] The insistence upon a direct financial contribution was criticised as being too restrictive, arbitrary and a source of injustice. Lord Walker commented that "Whether or not Lord Bridge's observation was justified in 1990, in my opinion the law has moved on, and your Lordships should move it a little more in the same direction . . .".[323] Baroness Hale believed that the court should ascertain the parties' shared

---

313 [2005] EWCA Civ 201 at [24].

314 *Lloyds Bank Plc v Rosset* [1991] 1 A.C. 107 at 133.

315 See *Pinfield v Eagles* [2005] EWHC 477 (Ch).

316 [1984] Ch. 317; see also, *Button v Button* [1968] 1 W.L.R. 457.

317 See S. Gardner, "Problems in Family Property" (2013) 72(2) C.L.J. 301.

318 *Burns v Burns* (1984) Ch. 317 at 331; see also *James v Thomas* [2008] 1 F.L.R. 1598.

319 *Ivin v Blake* (1994) 67 P. & C.R. 263.

320 See also *Morris v Morris* [2008] EWCA Civ 257.

321 [2008] 1 F.L.R. 1598 at [36]. Ms James had performed work of a heavy nature, for example, she drove a tipper, dug trenches, picked up materials, laid concrete, tarmac and gravel and generally undertook manual work associated with the business of Mr Thomas with whom she was cohabiting.

322 [2007] 2 A.C. 432.

323 [2007] 2 A.C. 432 at 445.

intentions, actual or inferred, with respect to the property in the light of their whole course of conduct in relation to it. She felt that many more factors than financial contributions might be relevant to divining the parties' true intentions. Lord Walker agreed that, "the court should in my opinion take a broad view of what contributions are to be taken into account"[324] and should proceed:

> **"by taking a wide view of what is capable of counting as a contribution towards the acquisition of a residence, while remaining sceptical of the value of alleged improvements that are really insignificant, or elaborate arguments (suggestive of creative accounting) as to how the family finances were arranged".**[325]

It remains to be seen what will unfold in the aftermath of this criticism of the contributions traditionally required under Rule 2. Some defrosting is welcome, but it is a controversial extension that comes at the expense of certainty, established authority and conventional wisdom.

A special provision

11-056

Section 37 of the Matrimonial Proceedings and Property Act 1970 deals with spousal contributions in money or money's worth to the improvement of property in which either or both parties to the marriage have a beneficial interest.[326] Provided the contribution is substantial, and in the absence of express or implied agreement to the contrary, this provision gives rise to the presumption that the contribution will operate either to acquire a beneficial share or to enlarge one that already exists.[327] In *Re Nicholson*,[328] for example, one party paid for a new central heating system and this increased that party's beneficial share in the family home. Similarly, in *Hallman v Harkins*[329] the contribution was provided by taking out a joint loan which had been used for home improvements. By way of contrast, in *Bindra v Chopra*[330] the contribution of some £2,600 towards improvements over a nine-year period of occupation, and at a time when the value of the property ranged between £231,000 and more than £400,000, was not of a sufficiently substantial nature. Unless the share is agreed, the court is given the discretion

---

324 [2007] 2 A.C. 432 at 447.
325 [2007] 2 A.C. 432 at 448. In *Fowler v Barron* [2008] 2 F.L.R. 831, Arden LJ emphasised that a holistic approach now had to be taken towards divining the intentions of the parties. She felt that post-*Stack* the contributions are no longer limited to financial contributions.
326 Section 2 of the Law Reform (Miscellaneous Provisions) Act 1970 extends this provision to the property of formally engaged couples and the Civil Partnership Act 2004 extends it to registered partnerships.
327 If there is no evidence of any significant work having been done to the property by the spouse then s.37 does not operate: *AI v MKI* unreported 10 November 2015.
328 [1974] 1 W.L.R. 476.
329 [2019] UKUT 245 (LC).
330 [2008] EWHC 1715 (Ch).

to do what is just in all the circumstances.[331] This facilitating provision does not, however, mean that the paying for improvements outside these prescribed relationships or descriptions (i.e. insubstantial improvements)[332] can never amount to a direct contribution to the purchase price for the purposes of a Rule 2 constructive trust[333] or a detriment for the purposes of proprietary estoppel.[334] It is a facilitating provision that overcomes potential obstacles concerning the need to prove common intention and appropriate reliance.

Rule 2: quantification

11-057

Although the making of direct financial contributions remains necessary to buy entry into the co-ownership arena, it is important to appreciate that, once the constructive trust is invoked, the court can look beyond the direct contributions.[335] In doing so it is able to divine a beneficial share which, on the facts of each case, accords with justice and good conscience.[336] As Chadwick LJ pointed out in *Oxley v Hiscock*, "the relevant common intention is that each party should have some beneficial interest. Direct contributions to the purchase price may lead to an inference that each party should have some beneficial interest without necessarily leading to the further inference that their respective shares should be proportionate to the amount of the direct contributions".[337] This is apparent also from *Midland Bank Plc v Cooke* where Waite LJ refused to accept that the shares were to be fixed solely by reference to the wife's direct contributions which, in turn, would make all other conduct irrelevant.[338] Instead, he believed that the court was to undertake a survey of the whole course of dealing between the parties relevant to their ownership and occupation of the property and their sharing of its burdens and advantages.[339] The contemporary tendency is, therefore, for the court to adopt a broad-brush approach to the calculation of shares under the implied bargain. Without the sanction of Parliament, and although vehemently denied by the judiciary,[340] the courts have in the post-*Rosset* world seemingly employed the flexibility of an implied bargain constructive trust to

---

331 See *Dibble v Pfluger* [2010] EWCA Civ 1005. The wife was afforded a third by way of a beneficial interest in *Cann v Ayres* (1976) 7 Fam. Law 47.

332 As in *Hameed v Qayyum* [2009] EWCA Civ 352.

333 See *Hussey v Palmer* [1972] 1 W.L.R. 1286.

334 *Morris v Morris* [2008] EWCA Civ 297. There the estoppel claim failed because there was no representation made and no unconscionability present on the facts.

335 See the Privy Council decision in *Abbott v Abbott* [2007] UKPC 53. As Baroness Hale observed at [19], "The parties' whole course of conduct in relation to the property must be taken into account in determining their shared intentions as to its ownership".

336 *Drake v Whipp* [1996] 1 F.L.R. 826.

337 [2004] 3 W.L.R. 715 at 734.

338 [1995] 4 All E.R. 562.

339 The court cannot, however, consider the abusive nature of a relationship or other factors that do not have anything to do with the property: *Graham-York v York* [2015] EWCA Civ 72.

340 As Tomlinson LJ emphasised in *Graham-York v York* [2015] EWCA Civ 72 at [22], "The court is not concerned with some form of redistributive justice"; see also Lady Hale, "Legislation or judicial law reform: where

effect some back-door redistribution of family assets according to perceptions of what is a fair and justifiable outcome.[341]

A fair share, however, does not necessarily equate with an equal share in the property.[342] This is a further area which is usually unsuited to an application of the equitable maxim, "equity is equality".[343] This maxim will only be invoked as a measure of last resort.[344] Accordingly, it is common for the determination to be of unequal shares.

11-058

The financial contributions made by the claimant may be a persuasive, but not necessarily decisive, factor in the calculation of beneficial interests. As demonstrated in *Midland Bank Plc v Cooke*, the court must look at the entire course of dealings between the parties. This flexible approach entails that factors which are totally irrelevant in discerning the existence of co-ownership can assume major relevance when calculating the parties' shares once co-ownership has been established. Accordingly, and as the Court of Appeal in the *Cooke* case made clear, when deciding the issue of quantum the court can survey the parties' shared endeavours, past family life, pooling of resources and mutual commitment.

Non-financial and indirect financial contributions assume much relevance in the evaluation process. The court can have regard to payments towards the financing of substantial improvements to the property[345] and to the discharge of utilities such as council tax, electricity and household insurance.[346] Account may be taken of indirect assistance such as the payment of other household expenses, contributions by way of labour and other unquantifiable actions of the claimant.

Rule 2 and the scope for proprietary estoppel?

11-059

In contrast with Rule 1 (see para.**11-051**), estoppel has a more limited role to play when a Rule 2 constructive trust is divined from the common intention of the parties. The latter operates in the absence of any express discussion or assurance, whereas estoppel usually requires some form of encouragement or assurance. Often, therefore, they exist in mutually exclusive spheres. When the common intention to share is inferred, and the claimant has made a direct contribution to the purchase of the property, this is constructive trust territory and the rights of the parties will be determined according to the implied bargain reached between them. If, however, no direct contributions are made by the claimant, the Rule 2 constructive trust is unavailable. In those circumstances, and because detrimental reliance for estoppel purposes

---

should judges fear to tread?", Society of Legal Scholars Conference 2016, 7 September 2016, *https://www.supremecourt.uk/docs/speech-160907.pdf* [Accessed 31 July 2020], pp.1, 2.
341 See *Hapeshi v Allnatt* [2010] EWHC 392 (Ch).
342 *Oxley v Hiscock* [2004] 3 W.L.R. 715.
343 *Hammond v Mitchell* [1991] 1 W.L.R. 1127.
344 See Neuberger J in *Mortgage Corp v Shaire* [2001] Ch. 743 at 750.
345 *Passee v Passee* [1988] 1 F.L.R. 263 where money was spent by one co-owner on re-roofing, central heating, double glazing and re-wiring.
346 *Oxley v Hiscock* [2004] 3 W.L.R. 715.

is not limited solely to financial contributions,[347] an estoppel might arise to prevent the other party from unconscionably denying a representation or encouragement.[348] These are sometimes referred to as "unilateral mistake" cases.[349] This was considered by the Privy Council in *Re Knowles*,[350] where the claimants (the brother and sister-in-law of the owner) moved into a two-bedroomed house as licensees and, over the subsequent 20 years, had it extensively renovated. An estoppel case was advanced as it was alleged that the improvements were carried out with the alleged tacit encouragement and acquiescence of the owner, George.[351] The Privy Council could find no such tacit encouragement and rejected the claimants' argument. Sir Henry Brooke concluded that:

> **"it would be unconscionable in this case to deprive George of his property when he had done nothing at all to encourage any belief that his brother and sister-in-law could treat the property as belonging to them. While recourse to the doctrine of estoppel provides a welcome means of effecting justice when the facts demand it, it is equally important that the courts do not penalise those who through acts of kindness simply allow other members of their family to inhabit their property rent free".[352]**

The Cohabitation Rights Bill 2019: A failed attempt at reform

11-060

Following reviews by the Law Commission in 2002,[353] 2006[354] and 2007,[355] a new scheme has been proposed each year since 2013 (by way of a private member's bill) based upon the 2006 and 2007 deliberations of the Commission and focused upon the relationship between the parties. As will become clear, this was designed to apply specifically to certain types of cohabiting couple (or former cohabitants) who separate. The Family Court would then have a wide range of financial settlement orders that it could make. Without doubt, a new bill will be introduced in future parliamentary sessions, but legislative reform does at present seem an unlikely prospect.

---

347 See *Jennings v Rice* (2003) 1 P. & C.R. 100 where the detriment was unpaid labour and caring duties.

348 See *Henry v Henry* [2010] UKPC 3; *Southwell v Blackburn* [2014] EWCA Civ 1347.

349 See Lord Walker in *Cobbe v Yeoman's Row Management Ltd* [2008] 1 W.L.R. 1752 at 1777.

350 [2008] UKPC 30.

351 See generally I. Samet, "Proprietary Estoppel and Responsibility for Omissions" (2015) 78 M.L.R. 85.

352 [2008] UKPC 30 at [27].

353 Law Commission, *Sharing Homes: A Discussion Paper* (2002) Law Com. No. 278, which promoted the ill thought out "property law scheme".

354 Law Commission, *Cohabitation: The Financial Consequences of Relationship Breakdown* (2006) Law Com. Consultation Paper No. 179.

355 Law Commission, *Cohabitation: The Financial Consequences of Relationship Breakdown* (2007) Law Com. No. 307

In outline, eligibility under the 2019 scheme was as follows:

- the parties must have lived as a couple in a joint household;

- they must not be married or in a civil partnership or in a 'prohibited' relationship (e.g. with a parent, grandparent, sister, brother, aunt or uncle);

- they must either have children in their family or (if none) have lived together for a continuous period of three years before their separation. For these purposes, one or more periods (not exceeding six months in all) during which the parties ceased living together as a couple is to be totally disregarded;

- the parties must not have contracted out of the scheme in signed writing and after receiving independent and separate legal advice. If they have, their entitlements will be governed by the old law;

- the claim must be brought within two years of the parties' separation. The court will have the power to extend this period only in exceptional circumstances;

- once the claimant has satisfied the qualifying conditions, the relief to be granted is at the court's discretion. The court will exercise its discretion with regard to listed criteria, including the welfare of any children, the needs and obligations of the parties and the conduct of the parties; and

- the court will have a wide range of orders that it can make (not including periodic maintenance payments) and the order will be based upon the economic impact of cohabitation and qualifying contributions made by the parties. The latter are not limited to financial contributions.

Guide to Further Reading

C. Bevan, "The search for common intention: the status of an executed, express declaration of trust post Stack and Jones" (2019) 135 L.Q.R. 660.

S. Bridge, "The Property Rights of Cohabitants—Where Do We Go From Here?" [2002] Fam. Law 743.

A. Briggs, "Co-ownership and an Equitable Non Sequitur" (2012) 128 L.Q.R. 183.

P. Clarke, "The Family Home: Intention and Agreement" [1992] 22 Fam. Law 72.

T. Etherton, "Constructive Trusts: A New Model for Equity and Unjust Enrichment" (2008) C.L.J. 265.

P. Ferguson, "Constructive Trusts—A Note of Caution" [1993] 109 L.Q.R. 114.

S. Gardner, "Rethinking Family Property" (1993) 109 L.Q.R. 263.

A.Y.S. Georgiou, "Marr v Collie: the ballooning of the common interest constructive trust" (2019) M.L.R. 14.

M. Harding, "Defending Stack v Dowden" [2009] Conv. 309.

A. Lawson, "The Things we do for Love: Detrimental Reliance and the Family Home" (1996) *Legal Studies* 218.

J. Mee, "Jones v Kernott: Inferring and Imputing in Essex" [2012] Conv. 167.

12

The Appointment, Retirement and Removal of Trustees

The trustee is the pivotal character in the trust relationship. Although it is possible to have a trust without there being a settlor (as with implied trusts) or a beneficiary (as with the small number of legitimate purpose trusts), there can be no trust without the presence of a trustee. At the heart of a trust is the vesting of legal title to the trust property in the trustee. Hence, the trustee acquires all the rights and powers relating to that property, subject to his labouring under an obligation to use the property in a prescribed manner. The trustee is the representative of the trust. It is the trustee who has the power to deal with trust property and to make investments. It is the trustee who is responsible to carry out the terms of the trust and to exercise any discretion and powers that have been given to him. The operation of the trust, the achievement of the settlor's intentions and the promotion of beneficiary's interests, therefore, rest heavily upon the shoulders of the trustee. The obligations are onerous and the consequences for breach of trust are severe.[1] Not everyone is equipped or willing to act to act as a trustee.[2] The characteristics of a trustee are, as Pettit puts it, "integrity, a willingness to spend time and trouble on trust affairs, the ability to get on with co-trustees and beneficiaries; knowledge of financial matters, business acumen, and common sense . . .".[3]

This chapter introduces the reader to the types of trustee that may exist and considers how trustees are appointed, both initially and by way of replacement. It will also examine the

---

1 As F.H. Maugham, "Excusable Breaches of Trust" (1898) 14 L.Q.R. 159, 161 put it, "no position known to the law is treated so unkindly as that of a trustee".

2 Hence, the rule is that no-one can be compelled to undertake a trust: *Robinson v Pett* (1734) 3 P. Wms. 249 at 251. It is, of course, possible that an individual could be saddled unwillingly with the role under a constructive or resulting trust.

3 P.H. Pettit, *Equity and the Law of Trusts*, 12th edn (Oxford: Oxford University Press, 2012), p.373. The reality is that, as Megarry VC observed in *Cowan v Scargill* [1985] Ch. 270 at 293, "there are some who are temperamentally unsuited to being trustees . . .".

ability of a trustee, who no longer wishes to continue to act in that capacity, to retire voluntarily from his office and explain how a trustee can be compulsorily removed from office. The focus, however, is upon the general law with the special rules governing charities and pension trusts falling outside the scope of this book. Finally, this chapter will consider the ability of a trustee to delegate his powers and discretions without ceasing to hold the office of trustee.

Types of Trustee

Ordinary trustees

12-002

The general rule is that any individual, limited company or corporation may act as a trustee. An individual can act as a co-trustee with a corporation, and a corporate trustee can act as co-trustee with another corporate body. Put simply, if you can hold property, you can be a trustee. For example, the Crown can in principle be a trustee,[4] as can a local authority.[5] There is, moreover, no problem with a foreign national holding as trustee (unless the trust property is a ship).[6] In contrast, an unincorporated association or a society cannot assume the office of trustee because such an entity does not have the legal personality to hold property. Instead, it is the members as individuals who have legal recognition, the property of the association held in accordance with the contract between them. Those with an unspent conviction for crimes of dishonesty, undischarged bankrupts, anyone who has been removed from trusteeship of a charity for misconduct or mismanagement and anyone under a disqualification order under the Company Directors Disqualification Act 1986 cannot usually be the trustee of a charity.[7] A minor cannot, moreover, be expressly appointed as a trustee and any attempt to do so will be void.[8] Nevertheless, a minor can become a trustee under a trust of personalty arising by implication or by operation of law. This was demonstrated in *Re Vinogradoff*,[9] where a grandmother transferred £800 of War Loan Stock into the names of herself and her granddaughter. At the time, the granddaughter was only four years old. It was held that the child became a trustee

---

4   See *Civilian War Claimants Association Ltd v R* [1932] A.C. 14.
5   Indeed, many local authorities hold assets subject to charitable trusts.
6   Aliens have a limited ability to own British Flag vessels: see s.17 of the Status of Aliens Act 1914 (as amended).
7   Sections 178–180 of the Charities Act 2011. Charitable trustees are, therefore, vetted before being appointed and a search should be made of the Register of Removed Trustees before any new appointment occurs. If the charity works with children or vulnerable adults, the trustees must make appropriate checks with the government's Disclosure and Barring Service. The latter body has replaced the Criminal Records Bureau and Independent Safeguarding Authority.
8   Section 20 of the Law of Property Act 1925.
9   [1935] W.N. 68.

holding the property on a resulting trust for the grandmother.[10] Although a child cannot hold a legal estate in land,[11] the same principle applies with implied trusts of land.

An ordinary trustee will not usually be able to claim remuneration for the performance of his functions.[12] This rule gives way when payment is authorised by the trust instrument or the trustee is either a trust corporation or is in the business of trust management and administration. In practice, a professional trustee (e.g. a solicitor or accountant) will undertake the task only when express provision is made for remuneration.

The number of trustees that can be appointed is, with one exception, unlimited. While there must be at least one trustee, there is no cap placed upon the maximum number permissible. The exception referred to concerns trusts of land, where a maximum of four trustees only are allowed to hold legal title.[13] If more than four are named, the first four named who are willing and able to act will be the trustees. Obviously, it is inconvenient to have too many trustees and uncommon to have in excess of four. The potential downside of having a sole trustee is that the opportunities for fraud and maladministration are increased. For some purposes, moreover, a two-trustee rule operates. These include capital money arising from land which must be paid to (or at the direction of) at least two trustees,[14] a valid receipt for capital money must be given by at least two trustees[15] and the process through which trust interests in land are overreached by a purchaser requires the involvement of at least two trustees.[16]

12-003

Trust corporations

Trust corporations play a major role in the administration of trusts. They can act jointly with ordinary trustees or, as is more usual, they can act as sole trustee. Their size, longevity, financial stability and expertise place them in an advantageous position when compared with an ordinary trustee. The most recognisable trust corporations are large banks and insurance companies that have trust departments. A law firm may also own a trust corporation. Such corporations are, moreover, usually well equipped economically to make good any breach of trust. It is crucial to appreciate that a trust corporation is a very different creature from a mere corporate trustee. A trust corporation enjoys a special status and has powers and rights that

12-004

---

10   The presumption of advancement (i.e. gift) did not apply here because it was not a parent/child situation and the grandmother did not stand in loco parentis to the girl.
11   Section 1(6) of the Law of Property Act 1925; see *Newham LBC v Ria* [2004] EWCA Civ 41.
12   For example, the great majority of charity trustees receive no payment for their work, see *https://www.gov.uk/ guidance/payments-to-charity-trustees-what-the-rules-are* [Accessed 20 April 2020]. It is possible for charity trustees to be paid either with the permission of the Charity Commission or if the charity's governing documents authorise such payment.
13   Section 34(2) of the Trustee Act 1925. By way of an exception to this limitation s.34(3) permits a greater number of trustees "in the case of land vested in trustees for charitable, ecclesiastical, or public purposes".
14   Section 27(2) of the Law of Property Act 1925.
15   Section 14(2) of the Trustee Act 1925.
16   Section 2(1) of the Law of Property Act 1925.

an ordinary company trustee does not have. For example, a trust corporation may itself give a good receipt for capital money under a trust of land. As shown, the involvement of two trustees is normally required for an effective receipt for capital money to be given to a purchaser. Traditionally, a trust corporation was in the same position as an ordinary trustee and, thereby, only able to levy a charge if there were (as is usual) express arrangements made to do so. Since s.29(1) of the Trustee Act 2000, however, a trust corporation can charge a "reasonable remuneration" for its services and this does not require the consent of the other trustees. The downside is that the involvement of a trust corporation will not come cheaply.

The status of a trust corporation is reserved for a body corporate that carries out the business of acting as a trustee and, moreover, satisfies certain conditions. These conditions[17] are that the company must:

- be expressly authorised by its constitution to carry out the business of acting as a trustee;

- have an issued share capital of not less than £250,000 (or its foreign equivalent) of which at least £100,000 (or its foreign equivalent) must be paid up in cash;

- have been incorporated in a European Union country; and

- operate from a place of business located within the United Kingdom.

12-005

In addition to these commercial trust corporations, a number of other bodies are afforded the status of a trust corporation by primary and secondary legislation. The meaning has been extended to include the Public Trustee or a corporation either appointed by the court to be a trustee or entitled under the Public Trustee Act 1906 to act as a custodian trustee.[18] The definition also includes the Treasury Solicitor, the Official Solicitor and other bodies as prescribed by the Lord Chancellor. These entities are, thereby, given the various privileges that extend to trust corporations.

Judicial trustees

12-006

A judicial trustee is a person or corporation appointed as trustee by the High Court under s.1(1) of the Judicial Trustees Act 1896[19] and in circumstances where the supervision of the court is required.[20] This appointment is at the discretion of the court[21] and is not to be confused with

---

17   See rule 30 of the Public Trustee Rules 1912 (as amended).
18   Section 68(18) of the Trustee Act 1925.
19   This is supplemented by the Judicial Trustee Rules 1983 (SI 1983/370).
20   *Re Ridsdel* [1947] Ch. 597.
21   Section 1(1) of the 1896 Act. Hence, an application can be refused: see *Re Chisolm* (1898) 43 S.J. 43.

the appointment by the court of an ordinary trustee under s.41 of the Trustee Act 1925 (see para.**12-022**). Although the appointment of a judicial trustee is usually made following the application by an existing trustee or a beneficiary, it can be made at the behest of the settlor when creating a trust. The court can appoint any fit and proper person (e.g. a solicitor or accountant) and, in the absence of a nomination or a suitable candidate, may appoint a court official so to act.[22] The appointment of a judicial trustee is usually made in circumstances where the administration of the trust by ordinary trustees is deficient in some way.[23] This could occur where, for example, there has been major mismanagement[24] or misconduct,[25] the administration of the trust has become extraordinarily problematic or the trust is facing complex litigation.[26] The court will usually not appoint a judicial trustee when the person having a power to appoint trustees has nominated trustees willing to act.[27] Not surprisingly, the procedure is invoked infrequently. Instead, the tendency is to appoint a professional, corporate trustee to sort matters out.

Once appointed, the judicial trustee will work closely with, and under the supervision of, the court.[28] The judicial trustee will usually be appointed as the sole trustee, but might act jointly with a private trustee.[29] Although the judicial trustee is essentially in the same position as any other trustee, he is throughout an officer of the court. This entails that he can obtain directions informally from the court (i.e. without making a formal application) when necessary. Unless it is a court official that is appointed, the judicial trustee will provide the court with a financial guarantee to protect the beneficiaries from loss arising from the performance of his duties. The judicial trustee is, however, allowed to charge for his services and the court will determine the amount of remuneration, which is paid from the coffers of the trust fund.

The Public Trustee

The Public Trustee is an office established by the Public Trustee Act 1906 (the 1906 Act). It is styled as a "corporation sole" (i.e. it is a trust corporation with perpetual succession that may sue or be sued like any other corporation).[30] The Public Trustee can be appointed by the court to be a new or additional trustee. He can, therefore, act either alone or in conjunction with other

12-007

---

22 Section 1(3) of the 1896 Act.
23 The Judicial Trustee is, as Jenkins J observed in *Re Ridsel* [1947] Ch. 597 at 605, "to provide a middle course in cases where the administration of the estate by the ordinary trustees has broken down".
24 *McDonald v Horne, The Times,* 12 October 1993.
25 *Re Ratcliff* [1898] 2 Ch. 352. There the court declined to appoint because there was no misconduct on the part of the existing trustee.
26 *Re Diplock* [1948] Ch. 465.
27 *Re Chisolm* (1898) 43 S.J. 43.
28 See *Re Ridsel* [1947] Ch. 597.
29 *Re Martin* [1900] W.N. 129.
30 Section 1(2) of the 1906 Act.

trustees.[31] The Public Trustee may be appointed as an ordinary trustee, a custodian trustee or as a judicial trustee.[32] If the Public Trustee is to act as an ordinary trustee, the appointment can be made expressly by a settlor/testator when the trust is created.[33] As to the subsequent appointment of a Public Trustee, this cannot be excluded by the trust instrument[34] and can be made on the application of the settlor, a trustee, a beneficiary or the person nominated expressly by the trust instrument to appoint trustees. In default, the court can of its own volition appoint the Public Trustee. An attraction of using the Public Trustee is that the Lord Chancellor will compensate individuals in respect of liability for breach of trust. The Public Trustee may charge fees on a scale set by the Lord Chancellor.[35]

The office of Public Trustee was created to administer small estates and to help people who might otherwise have difficulty finding someone prepared to act as a trustee (e.g. until the Public Trustee and Administration of Funds Act 1986 the Public Trustee enjoyed a role in the management of a psychiatric patient's estate). A further role relates to the holding of the property of a person who has died without a will (i.e. intestate), pending the appointment of an administrator of the deceased's estate by the court.[36] Although the Public Trustee may refuse to act, such refusal cannot be based solely upon the ground of the small value of the trust property.[37] In addition the Public Trustee cannot, as a general rule, accept any trust that involves the carrying on of any business or when the estate is insolvent and can never administer charitable trusts.[38] The main role of this public sector service is, therefore, to provide a trustee of last resort for small private trusts.[39]

Custodian trustees

12-008

The Public Trustee, the Official Custodian for Charities and trust corporations[40] are authorised to act as custodian trustees. An individual cannot act in this capacity, as it is a role limited to authorised corporate entities. The appointment of a custodian trustee is made by the court, the

31 Section 2(2) of the 1906 Act.
32 Section 2(1) of the 1906 Act.
33 As in *Public Trustee v Sidey* unreported 16 April 1980, where the public trustee was appointed executor under the deceased's will.
34 Similarly, a provision which prohibits the exercise of discretion by fewer than two trustees will be overridden when the public trustee becomes the sole trustee: *Re Duxbury's ST* (1995) 1 W.L.R. 425.
35 Section 2(1)(a) of the Public Trustee (Liability and Fees) Act 2002; see the Public Trustee (Fees) Order 2008.
36 Section 14 of the Law of Property (Miscellaneous Provisions) Act 1994. This occurred in *Barkatali v Davies* [2020] EWHC 753 (Ch) where the surviving relative had not applied for letters of administration.
37 Section 2(3) of the 1906 Act.
38 Section 2(4) and (5) of the 1906 Act.
39 See generally, P. Polden, "The Public Trustee—England 1906–1986: The Failure of an Experiment" (1989) 10 J.L.H. 228.
40 Accordingly, in *Re Brooke Bond & Co Ltd* [1963] Ch. 357, an insurance company was appointed the custodian trustee.

creator of the trust or the person having power to appoint a new trustee.[41] This type of trustee is different from the usual managing trustees. The custodian trustee takes custody of the trust property and documents of title (without having the management of the trust property) while the managing trustees, who have free access to the property and documents, take care of the day-to-day running of the trust.[42] For example, where a pension trust is invested in shares the legal title to those shares will be held by a custodian and then, as the Law Commission explains, "The job of a custodian is simple: to hold the asset safely and to account for its ownership correctly".[43] The custodian trustee must comply with the directions of the management trustees. Accordingly, it takes instructions from the managing trustees and not the beneficiaries. Nevertheless, as with any trustee, the custodian trustee owes a fiduciary duty to the beneficiaries.[44] A custodian trustee cannot at the same time be a managing trustee.[45] Hence, if the sole managing trustee dies, the custodian trustee cannot take his place without first giving up the role of custodian trustee.[46] In addition, in determining the number of trustees for the purposes of the Trustee Act 1925, the custodian trustee is discounted from the calculation. The custodian trustee is not, however, a bare trustee and has duties to perform relating, for example, to the receipt and paying out of income and capital of the trust.[47] The advantage of appointing the comparatively passive custodian trustee is that, with large trusts, there can be changes made to the identity of the managing trustees without the need to vest the trust property in them.[48] This may involve considerable savings in expense, time and effort.

Not surprisingly, the custodian trustee can charge fees.[49] The appointment may be terminated by the court on the application of either the custodian trustee himself, a managing trustee or a beneficiary. Such removal will occur when the court is satisfied that it is the general desire of the beneficiaries or it is otherwise expedient to do so.[50]

Appointment of Trustees

12-009

Trustees may be appointed both on the creation of a trust and during its continuance, whether as a replacement for an existing trustee or in addition to the existing trustees. The appointment

---

41 Section 4(1) of the 1906 Act.
42 Section 4(2)(a)–(c) of the 1906 Act.
43 Law Commission, *Fiduciary Duties of Investment Intermediaries* (2013) Consultation Paper No.215, para.59.
44 *Re Brooke Bond & Co Ltd* [1963] Ch. 357.
45 *Arning v James* [1936] Ch. 58.
46 *Re Squire's Settlement* (1946) 115 L.J. Ch. 90.
47 The duties, rights and liabilities of a custodian trustee are set out in s.4(2) of the 1906 Act.
48 See *Bankes v Salisbury Diocesan Council of Education* [1960] Ch. 631.
49 Section 4(3) of the 1906 Act.
50 Section 4(2) of the 1906 Act.

is usually made by deed without the involvement of the court. Indeed, it is only in exceptional circumstances that the court will appoint a trustee.

The original trustees

12-010

The settlor or the testator usually appoints the original trustees at the time the trust is set up. If it is an inter vivos (i.e. a lifetime) trust, it is common for the trustees to be parties to the trust deed and for this instrument to transfer the trust property to them. With a lifetime trust, it is possible that the settlor might appoint himself as a trustee. In the case of a testamentary trust, understandably, that is not possible. In such circumstances, the executors of the deceased's will might be the same individuals who are nominated to act as trustees. If not, the executors will hold the property on trust for the named trustees until the deceased's estate is wound up. The personal representative will then assent that the nominated trustees hold the property on trust.

If there is appointed more than one trustee, the trustees hold the trust property as joint tenants. As it is the legal estate that the trustees hold, there can be no severance of this joint tenancy into a tenancy in common. This entails that, if one of their brethren dies, the survivors retain the same duties and powers as before.[51] The trust property accrues by virtue of the right of survivorship to the living trustees.[52] The process will continue until there is only one trustee remaining. On the death of the last surviving or sole trustee, the personal representatives of that trustee (or, if he dies intestate, the Public Trustee) will hold the property on trust until replacement trustees are appointed.[53] On appointment of a new trustee(s), a personal representative automatically ceases to have the capacity to continue to act as trustee.[54]

12-011

As regards an inter vivos trust, there can be no valid trust if the trust is not completely constituted. Accordingly, if there are no original trustees named or they are dead by the time the trust is to take effect, the trust must necessarily fail. Simply put, there is no one in whom the legal title to the trust property can vest. With a testamentary trust the problem is less acute as the personal representatives of the deceased will always hold as trustees until replacement trustees are appointed.[55]

It is a very different situation that arises once the trust has been perfectly constituted. The trust will not subsequently be allowed to fail.[56] Hence, the death of an existing sole trustee will not prevent the continuation of the trust.[57] This accords with the general equitable principle that the court will not allow a trust to fail for want of a trustee.[58]

---

51 Section 18(1) of the Trustee Act 1925.
52 *Warburton v Sandys* (1845) 14 Sim. 622.
53 Section 18(2) of the Trustee Act 1925; ss.1 and 3 of the Administration of Estates Act 1925.
54 *Re Routledge's Trust* [1909] 1 Ch. 280.
55 See *Re Smirthwaite's Trusts* (1870–1871) L.R. 11 Eq. 251.
56 *Jones v Jones* (1874) 31 L.T. 535.
57 Section 18(2) of the Trustee Act 1925: see *Rafferty v Philip* [2011] EWHC 709 (Ch).
58 See, e.g. *Sonley v Clock Makers Co* (1780) 1 Bro. C.C. 81.

Disclaimer

As indicated, an individual who has been appointed as trustee and has not yet accepted the role may disclaim the responsibility. Disclaimer by the intended trustee must, therefore, occur before he does any act indicating his acceptance, such as bringing legal action in the name of the trust[59] or giving directions as to the sale of trust property.[60] Accordingly, the trustee should disclaim as soon as is possible and before acting in relation to the trust property. For example, in *James v Frearson*[61] a person was named in a will as an executor and trustee. He was present when the property was sold at the behest of the other trustees and requested information concerning the deceased's financial accounts. These acts were held to constitute acceptance of trusteeship. A similar approach was adopted in *Conyngham v Conyngham*[62] where the nominated trustee received rents from the occupier of the trust property and was therefrom unable to renounce the office of trusteeship.

When disclaiming a trust, it is advisable, albeit not essential, to do so expressly by deed.[63] The presence of a deed will offer clear and certain evidence of the disclaimer. Disclaimer can also occur by implication from conduct (e.g. by apathy and inaction).[64] It is, however, impermissible to disclaim only part of the trust.[65] Once the role has been disclaimed, the individual cannot subsequently have a change of heart. Once an individual accepts the role, however, there can no longer be a disclaimer.[66] The trustee must then elect to retire which, as will become clear, is a very different matter. If the trustee disclaiming is the intended sole trustee, the trust property will result back to the settlor or his personal representatives.[67] If there are other intended trustees, the property will remain vested in them and no resulting trust will arise.

As mentioned, the general rule is that a trust (once constituted) will not fail for want of a trustee.[68] If an existing trustee later refuses to act, then the trust continues[69] and new trustees will be appointed.

12-012

12-013

---

59 *Montford v Cadogan* (1810) 17 Ves. J.R. 485.
60 *James v Frearson* (1842) 1 Y. & C. Ch. Cas. 370.
61 (1842) 1 Y. & C. Ch. Cas. 370.
62 (1750) 1 Ves. Sen. 522.
63 *Re Schar* [1951] Ch. 280.
64 See *Re Clout & Frewer's Contract* [1924] 2 Ch. 230.
65 *Re Lord and Fullerton's Contract* [1896] 1 Ch. 228.
66 *Re Sharman's WT* [1942] Ch. 311.
67 *Stacey v Elph* (1833) 1 My. & K. 195.
68 *Re Lysaght* [1966] Ch. 191. Where the trustee subsequently declined to act as a matter of conscience he was to, as Buckley J put it at 207, "make way for a trustee who can and will do so".
69 An exception to this rule arises when the trust is made conditional upon certain people acting as trustees: *Re Lysaght* [1966] Ch. 191.

New trustees

12-014

As soon as the trust is created, the settlor has no automatic right to appoint future trustees. The authority to appoint replacement trustees can arise either from an express power, a statutory power or on the order of the court.

As to express powers, the trust instrument may reserve for the settlor or some other person the power to appoint new trustees. This is a common practice in both private and charitable trusts and will dictate the terms and mode of the appointment. As demonstrated in *Re Higginbottom*,[70] this is the primary right to make an appointment. There the existing trustee had the power to appoint new trustees and this right took priority over the wishes of many of the beneficiaries. Nevertheless, the appointor should communicate with the beneficiaries and take on board their views even though there is no obligation to act on them.[71] The court will not usually interfere with the appointment process.[72] There are, however, potential pitfalls associated with such express powers. If two or more persons are given the power to exercise it jointly, following the death of one of them the power will not be exercisable by the survivor.[73] Similarly, where two or more persons have the power, but cannot agree as to who should be appointed, the power is likely to be frustrated.[74] The ability to exercise the express power may, moreover, be curtailed by the attachment of conditions. For example, in *Re Wheeler*[75] the power was given to named donees to appoint a replacement trustee if one of the existing trustees became "incapable". One trustee became bankrupt and disappeared. The question was whether a new trustee could be appointed by the named donees. As bankruptcy did not make the trustee "incapable" (it merely made him "unfit"), the donees did not have the power to replace him. Similarly, if the power is to be exercised by deed, it cannot be exercised by a will. Furthermore, it is arguable that the donee of the power to appoint cannot nominate himself as the new trustee as this would be an improper exercise of a fiduciary power of selection.[76]

12-015

If the trust instrument does not cater for the appointment of new trustees, there are, as indicated, further ways in which replacements may be appointed:

- under the statutory power afforded by s.36(1) of the Trustee Act 1925 (as amended) to appoint replacement and/or additional trustees;

- by the more limited statutory power of beneficiaries to appoint under ss.19 and 20 of the Trusts of Land and Appointment of Trustees Act 1996 (as amended); and

---

70 (1892) 3 Ch. 132.
71 *O'Reilly v Alderson* (1849) 8 Hare 10.
72 *Re Hodson's Settlement* (1851) 9 Hare 118.
73 *Re Harding* [1923] 1 Ch. 182.
74 *Re Sheppard's ST* [1888] W.N. 234.
75 [1896] 1 Ch. 315.
76 *Re Skeat's ST* (1889) L.R. 42 Ch. D. 522; cf. *Re Sampson* [1906] 1 Ch. 435.

- as a last resort, the court can appoint new trustees under s.41 of the Trustee Act 1925 or, even less usually, under its inherent jurisdiction.

Method 1: s.36(1) of the Trustee Act 1925

12-016

Subject to its exclusion in the trust instrument,[77] s.36(1) applies generally to all trusts and allows for new, replacement trustees to be appointed in writing[78] (but not by will).[79] The appointor may appoint himself under this provision. It is permissible to appoint overseas trustees.[80] As the appointment must be "in place of" a retiring trustee, the appointment of one new trustee will never be sufficient to discharge two retiring trustees.[81] The other trustee must, accordingly, retire under the machinery provided for by s.39 (see para.**12-028**). One trustee can, therefore, only replace another trustee. The power is, however, exercisable only on the occurrence of one or more of seven eventualities.[82] These eventualities are set out in s.36 and are where a trustee (whether an original trustee or not):

- has died and this includes where a trustee was nominated in a will, but has predeceased the testator: s.36(8);

- has, for whatever reason, remained outside the United Kingdom for a continuous period of more than 12 months.[83] Where the trust is designed to operate abroad, the trust instrument should exclude the operation of this aspect of s.36(1);

- has expressed the wish to be discharged from the trust or part of the trust;

- has refused (this includes a disclaimer),[84] has become unfit to act as trustee (e.g. due to dishonesty[85] or bankruptcy)[86] or has become incapable of acting as trustee (e.g. through illness, old age or mental disorder[87]);

---

77 Contracting out is catered for by s.69(2) of the Trustee Act 1925.
78 Normally a deed is executed to obtain the benefit of the vesting provisions set out in s.40 of the Trustee Act 1925 (see below). Cf. retirements under s.39 of the Trustee Act 1925 which are required to be by deed.
79 *Re Parker's Trusts* [1894] 1 Ch. 707.
80 *Richards v Hon A.B. Mckay* [2008] W.T.L.R. 1667.
81 *Adam & Co International Trustees Ltd v Theodore Goddard* (2000) W.T.L.R. 349. F. Barlow [2003] Conv. 15, however, criticises this limitation as unsound and unjustifiable.
82 The court will interfere only if the appointment is viewed as being so inappropriate that it would not have been countenanced by a reasonable trustee: *Richards v Mackay* [1990] 1 O.T.P.R. 1.
83 If the trustee returns to the United Kingdom for a period (however short) within the 12-month time frame, s.36 does not apply: *Re Walker* [1901] 1 Ch. 259 (one week's return).
84 *Noble v Meymott* (1851) 14 Beav. 19.
85 *Turner v Maule* (1850) 15 Jur. 761.
86 See *Re Barker's Trust* (1875) 1 Ch. D. 43.
87 See *Re Watt's Settlement* (1872) L.R. 7 (Ch).

- is an infant. As a minor cannot be an express trustee, this applies only when the minor is a trustee under a resulting or constructive trust;

- has been removed under a power contained in the trust instrument (s.36(2) of the Trustee Act 1925)[88]; and/or

- is a corporation that has been dissolved (s.36(3)).

12-017

The aim of s.36 is not only to enable the appointment of a new trustee without a court order, but also to ensure that there will be someone who has the ability to exercise the power if necessary. It sets out in s.36(1)(a)–(b) a hierarchy of persons who may exercise the power to appoint. If there is no one able and willing to exercise the power in the first category, the power devolves to those in the second category and so on. If there is no person able and willing to act, the s.36 power necessarily becomes redundant.

The following characters in the following pecking order can engage s.36. The first is any person having an express power to appoint new trustees given by the trust deed. There is no need for the power to refer to the statutory scheme. If this express right to appoint is limited to some only of the eventualities listed above (see para.**12-016**), the donee of that power is not to be treated as the nominated person as far as the other non-specified eventualities contemplated by s.36 are concerned.[89]

12-018

Second in line are the "surviving or continuing" trustees (i.e. the existing trustees).[90] Some gloss is applied to the meaning of "continuing trustees" by s.36(8) and this provides that the term includes a refusing or retiring trustee (but not a trustee removed against his will[91]) who is willing to act for these purposes. This caters for a retiring trustee to nominate his successor. Indeed, it is standard practice for refusing and retiring trustees to become involved in the appointment of replacement trustees. Although the concurrence of the refusing or retiring trustee is usually necessary for a valid appointment, this rule gives way when he is unwilling to nominate. In the latter scenario, the trustee's participation is not essential.[92]

The third group are the personal representatives of the last surviving trustee. These include those who have proved the will of the dead trustee and those who have become the administrators of a trustee dying intestate (s.36(4)).[93]

---

88 It is important to appreciate that s.36 of the Trustee Act 1925 does not give the court the power to remove a trustee.

89 *Cecil v Langdon* (1885) 28 Ch. D. 1.

90 The personal representatives of the settlor can be trustees for these purposes: *Re Cockburn's WT* [1957] Ch. 438. It is to be appreciated that the beneficiaries cannot claim for themselves or otherwise control the exercise of this power: *Re Brockbank* [1948] Ch. 206.

91 *Re Stoneham's ST* [1953] Ch. 59 where a trustee was removed because he had been outside the United Kingdom for more than 12 months.

92 *Re Coates to Parsons* (1886) 34 Ch. D. 370.

93 Section 36(5) of the Trustee Act 1925 provides that a sole executor intending to renounce probate (i.e. to wish to

Appointment of additional trustees

Traditionally, and unless the trust instrument provided to the contrary, a new trustee could only be appointed when there was a vacancy. Section 36(6) of the Trustee Act 1925, however, caters generally for the appointment in writing of additional trustees (i.e. without any replacement). The appointment may be made by the person nominated by the trust instrument to appoint new trustees or, if there is no such person able and willing to act, the trustee(s) for the time being. An additional trustee can be appointed even when the existing trustee is a trust corporation. Unlike under s.36(1), it is thought that the appointor cannot appoint himself as an additional trustee.[94] Section 36(6), however, only permits an additional appointment when there are no more than three existing trustees (i.e. the general rule is that the number of trustees cannot be increased beyond four).[95] While as regards trusts of personalty the trust instrument may increase the number, the maximum ceiling for trusts of land must always remain at four trustees.[96]

12-019

Method 2: The Trusts of Land and Appointment of Trustees Act 1996

Where all the beneficiaries are sui juris (i.e. of full age and capacity) they may act in unison and direct the current trustees to appoint in writing any person(s) of the beneficiaries' collective choosing as trustee(s). The appointment is, thereby, effected by the existing trustees. This power is afforded to the beneficiaries by s.19(1) of the 1996 Act and applies retrospectively to trusts of all types of property.[97] This was not a power previously available to the beneficiaries.[98] The written direction must be given to the existing trustees or, if there are none remaining, the direction must be given to the personal representative of the last surviving trustee. The power can be excluded in the trust instrument, for example when a power to appoint trustees is vested in someone nominated for the purpose in the trust instrument. Hence, it is designed to apply only when the trust instrument makes no provision for the appointment of new trustees.

The direction can be made in tandem with a direction to some or all the trustees to retire (s.19(2)). Unlike the power granted under s.36(1) of the Trustee Act 1925, the appointment of new trustees under s.19 of the 1996 Act is not tied to such occurrences as death, unfitness, incapacity and the like. The power can, moreover, be exercised as often as the beneficiaries may

12-020

---

cease to act as a personal representative) shall have the power to appoint trustees until the time that probate is renounced.

94 *Re Power's ST* [1951] Ch. 1074.
95 This rule does not apply to charitable trusts.
96 Section 34(2) of the Trustee Act 1925.
97 It is uncertain, however, whether s.19 applies to beneficiaries under a discretionary trust.
98 *Re Brockbank* [1948] Ch. 206 (it was then necessary for the beneficiaries to terminate the trust and create a new one appointing the chosen trustees themselves).

deem appropriate. The beneficiaries may give joint or separate directions, but must nominate the same individual(s) for appointment or retirement.[99]

12-021

Section 20 of the 1996 Act deals with the situation where a trustee is rendered incapable of carrying out his office by reason of a mental disorder and there is no person willing or able to appoint a replacement under an express power of appointment or under s.36. In this situation, s.20 enables the beneficiaries of full age and capacity in unison to direct the appointment of a replacement trustee. Section 20(2) requires that the direction be given to a representative of the incapacitated trustee (i.e. a receiver, an attorney or a person authorised for the purpose under the Mental Capacity Act 2005). Again, this provision can be excluded in the trust instrument.

Method 3: appointment by the court

12-022

The court has both an inherent and a statutory jurisdiction[100] to appoint replacement or additional trustees. The inherent jurisdiction is keyed into the general role of the court to supervise trusts and trustees.[101] Although this jurisdiction remains intact,[102] in the light of statutory developments its exercise will be uncommon.[103] It is, therefore, exceptional in that it is not a jurisdiction that is usually exercised.[104] The additional jurisdiction given by s.41 of the Trustee Act 1925 appears sufficiently wide to cater for most (albeit not all) eventualities.[105]

Under s.41 of the Trustee Act 1925, the court has a broad, discretionary power to appoint new trustees in circumstances where it is "inexpedient, difficult or impracticable so to do without the assistance of the court".[106] It does not have to be "necessary" for the court to act. As mentioned, the appointment might be of an additional trustee or a replacement trustee.[107] An order can be made on the application of either a trustee or beneficiary, but no one else.[108] The

---

99   Section 21(1),(2) of the 1996 Act.

100 First afforded by the Trustee Act 1850.

101 *Buchanan v Hamilton* (1801) 5 Ves. J.R. 722.

102 *Barclay v Smith* [2016] EWHC 210 (Ch). Under this inherent jurisdiction, there is no restriction imposed regarding its being "inexpedient difficult or impracticable".

103 It might, for example, be employed to remove a trustee against his will or to remove a donee of a fiduciary power: *Bridge Trustees Ltd v Noel Penny Turbines Ltd* [2008] EWHC 2054 (Ch).

104 *London Capital and Finance Plc (in Administration) v Global Security Trustees Ltd* [2019] EWHC 3339 (Ch). There is not, however, a threshold test of exceptionality or, indeed, the need for a strong case to be made out for an application to be made under the inherent jurisdiction.

105 In *Bridge Trustees Ltd v Noel Penny Turbines Ltd* [2008] EWHC 2054 (Ch) the person to be replaced was not a trustee proper because the trust property was not vested in him. Accordingly, s.41 did not apply to this appointment.

106 In *Polly Peck International Plc v Henry* (1999) 1 B.C.L.C. 407, it was held that it could not be expedient to appoint a trustee if it was also not expedient to pay that trustee. The trust instrument provided that the trustees were not to receive remuneration or to claim for expenses.

107 The consent of the trustee who is to be replaced is, understandably, not necessary: *Re Henderson* [1940] Ch. 764.

108 Section 58 of the Trustee Act 1925; see *Davidson v Seelig* [2016] EWHC 549 (Ch).

court will not usually make an appointment when there is an express power in the trust instrument or where one of the other statutory powers can be employed.[109] If it does act, the court will not appoint someone against the wishes of the person who has a power to appoint.[110] The s.41 power becomes exercisable in situations where there is doubt as to whether a trustee is somehow unfit or "lacks capacity to exercise" the functions of trustee.[111] In *Panton v Brophy*,[112] the lack of capacity focused upon the inability of an unincorporated association to hold legal title. It could only be held by its members. It has, moreover, been employed in circumstances where the trustee has emigrated,[113] when there is no one who has the power to make an appointment or where the intention is to increase the number of trustees beyond four.[114] Section 41 bites also when the trustee becomes bankrupt or is a company that has gone into liquidation.[115]

In *Mohammed v Khan*,[116] Mr Khan sought the replacement of two management trustees of a mosque. He had founded the mosque as a private trust in 1984, but a power struggle between him and the defendants arose as to its control. A court order had previously imposed an interim remedy that a trusteeship board be appointed. Unfortunately, the interim trustees refused to work together. The court had no hesitation in appointing new management trustees under s.41 as it had become inexpedient, difficult or impracticable to appoint new trustees without the court's assistance. In *London Capital and Finance Plc (in Administration) v Global Security Trustees Ltd*[117] it was emphasised that the court would never remove a trustee lightly and would always consider the application in light of all the circumstances, with the welfare of the beneficiaries firmly in mind. If there had been misconduct by the trustees, it was likely that removal would occur, but the mere fact that the beneficiaries had argued with the trustees was likely to be insufficient.

The court enjoys the discretion as to whom to appoint as trustee. The court has, however, deemed certain types of person to be unsuitable for appointment. For example, a beneficiary will not normally be appointed,[118] nor will some person resident outside the jurisdiction.[119] A close relative of one of the parties interested in the trust will, moreover, usually make an unsatisfactory appointment.[120] This caution seemingly extends also to a solicitor acting for the

12-023

---

109 *Re Gibbon's Trust* (1882) 45 L.T. 756.
110 *Re Brockbank* [1948] Ch. 206.
111 In *Re Phelp's ST* (1886) 31 Ch. D. 351, for example, the trustee was aged, deaf and careering towards senility; see also, *Re Lemann's Trusts* (1883) L.R. 22 Ch. D. 633 where the trustee was aged and incapable.
112 [2019] EWHC 1534 (Ch).
113 *Re Bignold's ST* (1871–1872) L.R. 7 Ch. App. 223.
114 It is to be recalled that s.36(6) of the Trustee Act 1925 does not allow an additional trustee when the appointment would increase the number beyond four trustees.
115 See *Panton v Brophy* [2019] EWHC 1534 (Ch) where the former trustee company was dissolved.
116 [2005] EWHC 599 (Ch).
117 [2019] EWHC 3339 (Ch).
118 *Forster v Abraham* (1873–1874) L.R. 17 Eq. 351.
119 *Re Weston's Settlements* [1969] 1 Ch. 223.
120 *Wilding v Bolder* (1855) 21 Beav. 222.

beneficiary or the trustee.[121] In addition, the court will try to ensure that there is appointed more than a sole trustee.[122]

As regards suitable candidates, the court will exercise its discretion according to well-established principles.[123]

- It will have regard to the settlor's wishes (e.g. the settlor may have stated whom he does not want to be a trustee).

- It will not appoint a trustee against the wishes and interests of some of the beneficiaries.[124]

- It will not appoint a person excluded from being a trustee under s.36(1) of the Trustee Act 1925 (e.g. a person under a mental disability or permanently living abroad).[125]

- It will be reluctant to appoint a beneficiary as trustee if it perceives a possible conflict of interest.[126]

- It will have regard to whether the proposed appointment will promote or, instead, impede the carrying out of the trust.[127] For example, if the existing trustees refuse to work with the person who the court intends to appoint, this conflict would potentially jeopardise the effective running of the trust.[128] In *Mohammed v Khan*,[129] the court would not allow any of the parties to be appointed to the board of trustees due to their mutual animosity.

- It will not, unless there has been incompetence or malpractice, appoint a new trustee if this would inflict financial loss on the existing trustee.[130]

- It will not exercise its discretion simply to engineer the avoidance of tax (e.g. to appoint

---

121 *Re Norris* (1884) L.R. 27 Ch. D. 333.
122 *Viscountess D'Adhemar v Bertrand* (1865) 35 Beav. 19.
123 See *Re Tempest* (1865–1866) L.R. 1 Ch. App. 485.
124 *Re Parson's* [1940] Ch. 973.
125 *Re Windeatt's WT* [1969] 1 W.L.R. 692.
126 *Re Knowle's Settled Estates* (1884) L.R. 27 Ch. D. 707.
127 For example, charitable trustees should have a strong personal commitment to the aims and objectives of that charity and demonstrate the skills, knowledge and experience required for the post, see *http://www. charitycommission.gov.uk/publications/cc30.aspx* [Accessed 31 July 2020].
128 See *Re Badger* [1915] W.N. 166 where an appointment of an additional trustee was declined because it conflicted with the wishes of a sole trustee.
129 [2005] EWHC 599 (Ch).
130 See *Re Pauling's Settlement (No.2)* [1963] Ch. 576 where the removal of the trustees would have deprived them of security for the costs that might be payable to them if litigation with the beneficiaries was successful.

overseas trustees who are not liable to UK tax).[131] An attempt to do so failed in *Re Weston's ST*, where Lord Denning MR described the application as, "a cheap exercise in tax avoidance which I ought not to sanction . . .".[132]

Vesting of trust property

On the appointment of a new trustee under s.36 or s.41 of the Trustee Act 1925, or by direction of the beneficiaries under the Trusts of Land and Appointment of Trustees Act 1996, the new trustee has the same powers, authorities and discretions as the original trustee.[133] Accordingly, he may in all respects act as if he had been originally appointed under the trust instrument. It is, however, vital that the trust property becomes vested in the new trustee and this is so whether he is a sole trustee or is acting jointly with other continuing trustees.

12-024

Vesting can occur by means of the former or continuing trustees transferring title to the trust property to the new trustee.[134] The appropriate method of achieving this depends upon the nature of the trust property. For example, legal title to land requires a deed of conveyance; shares require a completed transfer form and registration of the transaction; and chattels require physical delivery with intention to transfer.[135] This type of formal transfer is not, however, always necessary as automatic vesting in relation to existing trusts is facilitated by s.40 of the Trustee Act 1925.

Section 40(1) offers a short cut and provides that automatic vesting can occur when the new trustees are appointed by deed (which explains why this is the usual practice).[136] If the deed contains a declaration that the property shall vest in the new trustees (i.e. a "vesting declaration"), vesting of title will occur without any conveyance or other transfer. In such cases, the deed of appointment will itself operate to vest the property in the new trustees. If the deed does not contain an express vesting declaration, the declaration may be implied, subject to any provision in the deed of appointment to the contrary.[137]

12-025

There are, however, important exceptions to the operation of s.40 and in such circumstances title to the property must be transferred by the usual method appropriate to that property. These exceptions concern the following types of property:

---

131 *Re Whitehead's WT* [1971] 1 W.L.R. 833 (doubted in *Richard v Mackay* [2008] W.T.L.R. 1667).
132 [1969] 1 Ch.223 at 234.
133 Sections 36(7) and 43 of the Trustee Act 1925.
134 If necessary, the existing trustees are required to join in the transfer of legal title: s.37(1)(d) of the Trustee Act 1925.
135 See para.**3-004**.
136 It does not apply where the property is held by personal representatives: *Re Cockburn's WT* [1957] 3 W.L.R. 212. Hence s.40 applies only to estates and interests which form part of the existing trust property: *Re King's ST* [1964] Ch 542.
137 Similar provisions are to be found in s.40(2) of the Trustee Act 1925 and these operate to vest trust property in the continuing trustees on the discharge of a trustee.

- land conveyed by way of mortgage as security for a loan of trust money. This means that, where trust money is invested in the mortgage of land, on the appointment of new trustees automatic vesting does not occur. Instead, there must be a separate, formal transfer of the mortgage term to the new trustee[138];

- land held under a lease or sub-lease that contains a covenant against assignment without consent, unless the consent has been obtained before the execution of the deed. This exemption prevents the appointment of a trustee causing an inadvertent breach of covenant against assignment and giving rise to a forfeiture of the lease;

- stocks and shares. This exception recognises that the legal title to shares can only be effected by registration with the relevant company[139]; and

- registered land. Section 27 of the Land Registration Act 2002 requires that the deed of appointment/retirement must be registered so that the change of registered proprietor can be duly recorded.

12-026

The court has a wide jurisdiction to make vesting orders by virtue of ss.44–56 of the Trustee Act 1925. These overlap with s.40 in that vesting orders can be made either when the appointment is made under a statutory or express power or when made by the court. Nevertheless, the court's powers become relevant where the appointment is not made by deed or one of the exceptions to s.40 applies. Similarly, a vesting order would be appropriate when it has proved difficult or impossible to obtain an express formal transfer of the legal title from the former trustees or, as regards the assignment of leases, the consent of the landlord.

Retirement and Removal of Trustees

12-027

Once the office of trusteeship is accepted, the understanding is that it is a lifelong appointment. This can cause difficulties when, say, the trustee and the beneficiaries are engaged in disagreement. Understandably, there exist ways in which a trustee can be compelled to retire or may of his own volition retire from the office. It is, however, to be appreciated that retirement does not guarantee freedom from liability. Not surprisingly, trustees will remain liable for breaches of trust that occurred during their trusteeship.[140] As to future breaches, the retiring

---

138 *London & County Bank v Goddard* [1897] 1 Ch. 642.
139 Note that s.40 cannot apply to so called "bearer" securities. Section 18 of the Trustee Act 2000, however, requires the trustees to appoint a custodian of bearer securities.
140 As the liability of trustees is both joint and several, a departing trustee will usually seek an indemnity assurance

trustee is less vulnerable. The general rule is that retirement brings with it a discharge from further responsibility and liability under the trust. Nevertheless, trustees who retire knowing that this will facilitate a breach by their successors or the continuing trustees will be jointly liable for future associated loss.[141]

The prospect of continuing liability explains why, on retirement, the trustee may seek a formal release by the beneficiaries of his liability in relation to the trust. On retiring in favour of new trustees, such a release is not available unless expressly permitted in the trust instrument. In contrast, if the trust is being wound up, the trustee can insist upon a release.[142] If a release is granted, it is effective only in so far as the beneficiaries are aware of the material facts. By way of contrast, if the retiring trustee is owed money by the trust, then the trustee is entitled to retain assets until any liabilities properly incurred by the trustee have been paid. The trustee has an equitable lien over the property and, if appropriate, the court can order sale of trust assets to discharge that debt.

Voluntary retirement

A trustee may retire in one of five ways only. Outside these five methods, a purported voluntary retirement is void and the trustee will continue to hold office.[143] Retirement may arise in the following ways:

12-028

- by a special power in the trust instrument. If express provision is made for retirement, the trustee can, of course, exercise that power. Although once customary, nowadays such a facility is rare and, since the Trustee Act 1925, unnecessary;

- under s.36(1) of the Trustee Act 1925. As discussed above, retirement under s.36 can occur only when a replacement trustee is being appointed and this retirement may relate to either the whole of the trust or merely part of the trust;

- under s.39(1) of the Trustee Act 1925.[144] This statutory escape is not, however, dependent upon the appointment of a replacement trustee.[145] Section 39(1) allows a trustee to retire from the whole of the trust (and not merely part) if there will remain at least two other trustees or a trust corporation in office. It is also necessary that the remaining trustees consent to the retirement and that the consent of any person who has an

from the continuing or new trustees. This then gives rise to a charge that assumes priority over the equitable interests of the beneficiaries.

141 *Head v Gould* [1898] 2 Ch. 250.
142 *Tiger v Barclays Bank* [1952] 1 All E.R. 85.
143 *Mettoy Pension Trustees v Evans* [1990] 1 W.L.R. 1587.
144 Previously, this was possible under the auspices of the Conveyancing Act 1881.
145 *Adam & Co International Trustees Ltd v Theodore Goddard* [2000] W.T.L.R. 349.

express power to appoint trustees has been obtained.[146] Section 39 requires that the retirement be made in deed form[147];

- with the consent of all the beneficiaries who must be of full age and capacity.[148] If this occurs, the trustee will not be liable for anything that happens in post-retirement times. If there is an infant beneficiary, therefore, no effective discharge can arise in this way; and

- by an order of the court. The court has a statutory jurisdiction under s.41 of the Trustee Act 1925 to discharge a trustee when it replaces him with a new appointment (see para.**12-022**). The court also enjoys an inherent jurisdiction to discharge a trustee without nominating any replacement.[149] This is useful when the consent of the other trustees cannot be obtained for the purposes of s.39. Provided that there will be remaining at least one continuing trustee or a suitable replacement has been found, the court will usually accede to the trustee's wish to retire.[150] Costs of the procedure will normally be borne by the retiring trustee. If there is no continuing trustee, the court will postpone the discharge but, although the trustee will remain in office, he will be effectively relieved of responsibility.[151]

Compulsory removal

12-029

As a measure of last resort, a trustee may be removed against his wishes if there is the power to do so contained in the trust instrument itself. This would be a fiduciary power to remove and would, therefore, have to be exercised to promote the interests of the beneficiaries. In such instances, the terms of any such power must be strictly complied with.[152] As shown, removal may also occur under s.36 of the Trustee Act 1925 on the appointment of a replacement trustee[153] or following an order of the court issued under the statutory jurisdiction afforded by s.41 of the same Act. Removal against the trustee's wishes can, however, arise in two further ways.

---

146 These conditions do not apply when one of the remaining trustees is the Public Trustee: s.6 of the Public Trustee Act 1906.
147 See *Re Epona Trustees Ltd's Representation* [2009] W.T.L.R. 87 (a decision of the Royal Court of Jersey). The retirement may be set aside if it was induced by the undue influence of, say, a continuing trustee: *Daniel v Drew* [2005] EWCA Civ 507. There an aged and vulnerable aunt successfully argued that her nephew had procured her resignation from the family trust by undue influence.
148 *Re Brockbank* [1948] Ch 206.
149 *Courtenay v Courtenay* (1846) 3 Jo. & Lat. 533.
150 *Re Chetwynd's Settlement* [1902] 1 Ch. 692.
151 *Courtenay v Courtenay* (1846) 3 Jo. & Lat. 533.
152 See *Von Knieriem v Bermuda Trust Co* (1994) 1 BOCM 116 (a decision of the Bermuda Supreme Court).
153 Removal being justified because the trustee has been outside the United Kingdom for a continuous period of 12 months or that the trustee refuses or is unfit to act or is incapable of acting.

The first method of removal, which operates without the need to appoint a replacement, is by ss.19–21 of the Trusts of Land and Appointment of Trustees Act 1996. The second means is via the court's inherent jurisdiction to remove a trustee compulsorily.[154]

Removal under the 1996 Act

12-030

A trustee must retire from his office if directed to do so in writing (there need not be a deed) by all the beneficiaries under s.19 of the Trusts of Land and Appointment of Trustees Act 1996.[155] The direction may be made by the beneficiaries jointly or be given by each of them. The retirement must itself be made by deed. The retiring trustee and the continuing trustees must then do whatever is necessary to vest the trust property in any new trustee. If the trustee refuses to execute a deed of retirement, the court can order the execution of the deed on the trustee's behalf.[156]

Any beneficiary may withdraw the direction in writing once given, and, as s.19 requires unanimity, the process will thus fail.[157] The direction may, either instead or in addition, require the retiring trustee to appoint a successor. If it is purely a retirement direction, it must be served on the retiring trustee(s). If it includes a direction to appoint, the direction must be served on each of the current trustees.[158]

12-031

Section 19 operates only in specified circumstances. First, there must be no person nominated by the trust instrument who has the power to appoint new trustees. The statutory provision is not activated even though the donee of any such power is unwilling to make the appointment or is incapable of exercising the power. If the donee is deceased, however, the precondition is satisfied because there is no longer a nominated person in existence.

Secondly, all the beneficiaries must be of full age (18 years old and above) and full capacity and they must act in unison (s.19(1)(a)–(b)). Albeit uncertain, this should be taken to include beneficiaries under a discretionary trust. This interpretation would rest easily with the collective ability of the beneficiaries of a discretionary trust, under the rule in *Saunders v Vautier*,[159] to terminate the trust. Section 19 should enable such beneficiaries to appoint and/or retire trustees without the need to wind up the trust. This is not a tactic available at common law or under s.36(1) of the Trustee Act 1925.[160]

Thirdly, the trustee in receipt of such a direction must retire in circumstances where there

---

154 Executors of a will can be removed by court order under s.50 of the Administration of Justice Act 1985: see *Goodman v Goodman* [2013] 3 W.L.R. 1551 where, in replacing family executors with an independent professional executor, the High Court emphasised that s.50 applied whether or not probate had been granted.

155 The operation of s.19 may, however, be excluded in the trust instrument.

156 Section 39 of the Senior Courts Act 1981.

157 Section 21(1).

158 Section 19(2)(b).

159 (1841) 4 Beav. 115.

160 *Re Brockbank* [1948] Ch. 206.

will be at least two other trustees or a trust corporation remaining and either a replacement is to be appointed or the continuing trustees consent.

Fourthly, it is also necessary that reasonable arrangements be made for the protection of the retiring trustee's rights in connection with the trust. A trustee may have rights of reimbursement or indemnity for expenses incurred in relation to the trust and may need to take action to ensure that he can enforce those rights. He may also need to guard himself against taxation liabilities for which he could be held responsible after his retirement. In a similar vein, he may have incurred contractual liabilities to third parties in dealing with the trust property. Such possibilities explain why s.19(3) provides that the trustee shall be under an obligation to execute a deed of retirement only after reasonable arrangements have been made for the protection of his interests.

Removal under the court's inherent jurisdiction

12-032

The High Court enjoys an inherent jurisdiction to control the administration of a trust and the actions of the trustee. The overarching duty is to see that trusts are properly executed and this is not excluded by reason that there is also a statutory means of removal available.[161] To this end, the court may remove a trustee on the application of any beneficiary. Indeed, it can remove a trustee of its own volition during proceedings.[162] This is, however, an exceptional jurisdiction and is exercised sparingly.[163] Most decisions are, moreover, made in Chambers and are never reported. The overriding considerations are the preservation of trust property and the promotion of the interests of the beneficiaries.[164] The inherent jurisdiction is particularly useful when there is a dispute as to the facts and/or no replacement is to be made.[165] For example, in *Letterstedt v Broers*[166] a beneficiary made several allegations of misconduct against the trustees and asked for their removal. Although the allegations were unfounded, he succeeded in his application. It was held that the duty of the court was to ensure the proper execution of the trust.[167] Accordingly, in *Agnes Carvel Foundation v Carvel*[168] the trustee was removed in circumstances that indicated dishonesty, a conflict of interest and

161 *The Pensions Regulator v Dalriada Trustees* [2013] EWHC 4346 (Ch). As Nugee J acknowledged at [36], "it can hardly be supposed that the policy of Parliament was to restrict the ability of the Court to supervise and if necessary intervene in the administration of trusts for the protection of the beneficiaries".
162 *Re Wrightson* [1908] 1 Ch. 789.
163 *London Capital and Finance Plc (in Administration) v Global Security Trustees Ltd* [2019] EWHC 3339 (Ch). The power under s.41 of the Trustee Act 1925 usually suffices.
164 *Caldicott v Richards* [2020] EWHC 767 (Ch).
165 If no such dispute exists and a replacement trustee is to be appointed, the court will tend to exercise its statutory power under s.41 of the Trustee Act 1925.
166 (1883–1884) 9 L.R. App. Cas. 371.
167 In *Jones v Firkin-Flood* [2008] EWHC 2417 (Ch), four trustees were removed because of their collective unfitness to be trustees.
168 [2008] Ch. 359.

a lack of understanding. Even if the facts are disputed, or the trustees can disprove the allegations, they may still be removed if there is disharmony as to the way the trust is to be administered.[169]

The welfare and best interests of the beneficiary are the paramount concerns[170] and the court must, therefore, evaluate whether the trustee's continuance in office would be prejudicial to the interests of the beneficiaries.[171] Accordingly, the court can consider the expense to the trust of a change of trustees and, even where there has been a minor breach of trust, decide against removal.[172] Such occurred in *Re Wrightson*[173] where the test advocated was whether the trust property could safely be left in the control of the trustees. This demonstrates that not every error on the part of the trustee will be viewed as a ground for removal. It also emphasises that a trustee cannot be removed merely at the whim of a beneficiary.[174] Reasonable cause must be established to justify the removal.[175] For example, a case for removal was made out in *Cowan v Scargill*[176] in circumstances where the trustees persisted with an investment policy that was not in the best interests of the beneficiaries. The court felt that the trustees were endangering trust funds. Similarly, a trustee who sets up a rival business to the trust might not be in breach of trust and yet the conflict of interest could be a ground for his removal.[177] Other more mundane examples include where the trustee refuses to act,[178] has mismanaged the trust,[179] allowed a property to fall into disrepair, neglected to re-let that property and failed to obtain possession of another property,[180] committed a criminal offence[181] or has been adjudged bankrupt.[182]

12-033

---

169 See *Re Consiglio Trusts* [1973] 3 O.R. 326, where all the trustees were removed and replaced by a trust corporation. In *Kershaw v Micklethwaite* [2010] EWHC 506 (Ch), however, the court emphasised that friction and hostility were not in themselves reasons for removing a trustee. Such matters were merely factors to be taken on board.

170 *London Capital and Finance Plc (in Administration) v Global Security Trustees Ltd* [2019] EWHC 3339 (Ch).

171 *E v E* [1990] 2 F.L.R. 233; *Walker v Walker* unreported 30 January 2007.

172 In *Caldicott v Richards* [2020] EWHC 767 (Ch), there was a breach of the self-dealing rule, but the trustees were not removed.

173 [1908] 1 Ch. 789. There the trustees made unauthorised investments and were in breach of trust.

174 See *Lee v Young* (1843) 2 Y. & C.C.H. 532.

175 The judge, however, need not give reasons for making an order: *Re Edwards' WT* [1981] 2 All E.R. 941.

176 [1985] Ch. 270.

177 *Moore v M'Glynn* [1894] 1 Ir. R. 74.

178 *Palairet v Carew* (1863) 32 Beav. 564.

179 *Ex parte Phelps* (1742) 9 Mod. Rep. 357. In *Walker v Walker* unreported 30 January 2007, the trustee favoured his own interests over those of the beneficiaries and maintained suspect accounts. He was removed from office by the court.

180 *Brudenell-Bruce v Moore* [2014] EWHC 3679 (Ch).

181 *Re Danson* [1895] W.N. 102.

182 *Re Barker's Trusts* (1875) 1 Ch. D. 43.

Delegation of Trusteeship

12-034

The general rule is that, while a trustee can delegate ministerial and administrative functions,[183] he cannot delegate his powers and discretions to a third party or, indeed, another trustee.[184] This principle is known as *delegatus non potest delegare*. As the role of trustee involves a high degree of personal trust, confidence and judgment, the settlor may have selected the trustee because of his personal characteristics and beliefs. In the absence of an express power given in the trust instrument, a trustee cannot, therefore, delegate his discretion to select who gets what under the auspices of a discretionary trust or as to how the trust fund is to be invested. At common law, any attempt to do so will be ineffective.[185] It was viewed as amounting to "a betrayal of the settlor's wishes . . .".[186]

Exceptions to the rule against delegation do exist and are to be found in s.25 of the Trustee Act 1925 (as amended) and s.1 of the Trustee Delegation Act 1999. These provisions deal with delegation by individual trustees. A further statutory incursion allows collective delegation by the trustees of land to a beneficiary and is to be found in s.9 of the Trusts of Land and Appointment of Trustees Act 1996. If the trustee delegates outside the parameters of an express power or a statutory provision, he will be liable as if he had acted personally.[187]

Section 25 of the Trustee Act 1925

12-035

Under s.25(1),[188] a trustee can delegate, by power of attorney, any or all his duties, powers and discretions vested in him as trustee. This applies whether the trustee is a sole trustee or one of a number of joint trustees. The delegation cannot exceed a period of 12 months from the commencement date of the power.[189] This provision was designed to cater for the situation where, say, a trustee emigrates abroad or the trust property is situated on foreign shores. There are no restrictions upon the number of delegations that can occur and, since the Trustee Delegation Act 1999, delegation can be made in favour of anyone, including an existing trustee and a trust corporation.[190] The delegating trustee must, at the latest within seven days of the granting of the power of attorney, provide the other trustees and anyone else who has an express power to appoint new trustees with notice in writing.[191] The notice must state the terms

---

183 Section 11 of the Trustee Act 2000. This is, however, no new thing: see *Attorney General v Scott* (1750) 1 Ves. Sen. 413.
184 *Re May* [1926] 1 Ch. 136.
185 *Fry v Tapson* (1884) 28 Ch. D. 268.
186 The Law Commission, *The Law of Trusts: Delegation by Individual Trustees* (1994) Law Com. 220, para.2.1.
187 *Turner v Corney* (1841) 5 Beav. 517.
188 As amended by the Trustee Delegation Act 1999.
189 Trustee Act 1925 s.25(2).
190 Trustee Act 1925 s.25(3).
191 Trustee Act 1925 s.25(4).

of the power of attorney, its commencement date and duration, the identity of the donee, the reason for the delegation and the powers and discretions that are delegated. Once delegation has occurred, the donee is in the same position as the delegating trustee, except that the donee has no power to delegate. The delegating trustee is liable for the acts of the donee as if they were his own.[192]

Section 25 is seldom invoked and is used only when delegation is essential. This is largely to do with the continuing liability of the delegating trustee. Instead, trustees prefer collectively to appoint agents to undertake their functions. The trustees are liable for an agent's actions only if the trustees have themselves failed in their duty of care.[193] Accordingly, there is a markedly reduced threat of liability for the acts of an agent than is the case with an attorney. As Parker and Mellows comment, "Section 25 of the Trustee Act 1925 could therefore work in a completely unjust way, particularly since the donor is likely to have no more control over the donee than he would over an agent".[194]

Section 1 of the Trustee Delegation Act 1999

12-036

A further power of delegation arises under s.1 of the Trustee Delegation Act 1999. The power operates only where the delegating trustee has a beneficial interest in land held by the trust and when the provision is not excluded in the trust instrument. Put simply, it was designed to cater for an express trust of land where the trustees are also the beneficiaries. For example, a father, mother and son buy a house together. The title is conveyed into their joint names so that they hold the land on trust for themselves (whether as joint tenants or tenants in common). It might be that the parents are aged and unwell and wish to delegate their trust powers to their son. The advantages of s.1 are, first, that it enables the parents to delegate without having to jump through the hoops set by the Trustee Act 1925. Secondly, it enables the parents to make effective provision for the disposal of the land where they fear the onslaught of senility or other mental incapacity. To this end, a lasting power of attorney in favour of their son is an option available to the parents. The son as donee of the power is, thereby, delegated to act on behalf of his parents.

Section 1 allows such a trustee to delegate indefinitely all trustee functions, relating to the land and income and proceeds of sale from land, by power of attorney. The delegating trustee remains liable for the actions of the donee, but the s.1 facility is not limited to a 12-month period. Trustees who are not also beneficiaries cannot take advantage of this facility and must delegate under the more restricted s.25 of the Trustee Act 1925 procedure. A trustee who has granted an existing power of attorney under that procedure cannot also take advantage of s.1 of the 1999 Act.[195]

---

192 Trustee Act 1925 s.25(7).
193 Section 1 of the Trustee Act 2000.
194 A. Oakley, *Parker & Mellows: The Modern Law Of Trusts*, 9th edn (London: Sweet & Maxwell, 2008), p.636.
195 Trustee Delegation Act 1999 s.1(8).

12-037   Under both the s.25 and s.1 procedures, one trustee can delegate to another trustee by a power of attorney. Two trustees, moreover, can delegate to the same donee. This creates a potential problem with trust interests in land, which can be overreached only on the payment of the purchase money to two trustees or a trust corporation. Section 7 of the 1999 Act makes it plain that this requirement is not satisfied when the payment is made to an attorney who is acting in the dual capacity of a trustee and donee or as a donee representing two or more trustees. A further trustee would have to be appointed in such circumstances.

Section 9 of the Trusts of Land and Appointment of Trustees Act 1996

12-038   Section 9(1) expressly enables trustees of a trust of land collectively to delegate their powers, including the power of sale, to any beneficiary or beneficiaries of full age entitled with an interest in possession to the trust land. Delegation can only be of powers relating to land and no other trust property. The delegation must be by power of attorney given by all the trustees and may be revoked subsequently by any one of them. It ceases also on the appointment of a new trustee.[196] The delegation may be made for any period of time or indefinitely.[197] Beneficiaries, to whom the powers have been delegated, have the same duties and liabilities as the trustees, but are not regarded as trustees for any other purpose.[198] They cannot sub-delegate their functions nor can they receive capital monies to overreach the equitable interest of any beneficiary. If the donee subsequently ceases to be a person beneficially interested in the land (e.g. his interest is bought out), his ability to exercise powers under the delegation also ceases.[199]

Delegation to agents under the Trustee Act 2000

12-039   Section 11 of the 2000 Act introduced a new regime under which, as considered further in Ch.14 in the context of investment, trustees are permitted collectively to delegate tasks to agents. Importantly, by s.11(2) this does not extend to distributive duties and discretions or the ability to appoint trustees or nominees and custodians. Although the trustees may appoint one of their brethren to act as agent (s.12(1)), they cannot instruct a beneficiary to act in this capacity (s.12(3)). This power can be restricted or excluded by the trust deed (s.26) and the terms of the appointment are as the trustees shall determine (s.14(1)), subject to certain limitations set out in s.14(3). The remuneration (s.14(1)) and expenses (s.31(2)) of the agent will be reimbursed by the Trust. There is no vicarious liability for the acts or omissions of the agent.

---

196 Trusts of Land and Appointment of Trustees Act 1996 s.9(3).
197 Trusts of Land and Appointment of Trustees Act 1996 s.9(5).
198 Trusts of Land and Appointment of Trustees Act 1996 s.9(7).
199 Trusts of Land and Appointment of Trustees Act 1996 s.9(4).

Guide to Further Reading

F. Barlow, "The Appointment of Trustees: A Disappointing Decision" [2003] Conv. 15.

C. Bell, "Some Reflections on Choosing Trustees" (1988) 2(3) T. L. & P. 86.

M. Clements, "The Changing Face of Trusts: The Trusts of Land and Appointment of Trustees Act 1996" [1998] M.L.R. 56.

N. Hopkins, "The Trusts of Land and Appointment of Trustees Act 1996" [1996] Conv. 411.

M. Jacobs, "Trustees—Obtaining an Effective Discharge on Retirement" (1986) 1(1) T. L. & P. 16.

M. Jacobs, "To be or not to be . . . Trustee Act 1925, s.37(1)(c) Revisited Again" (1993) 7(3) Tru. L.I. 73.

G.H. Jones, "Delegation by Trustees: A Reappraisal" [1959] M.L.R. 381.

13

The Duties of a Trustee

13-001

At the heart of a trust lies the fact that, while the trustee may have legal title to the trust property, real entitlement rests with the beneficiaries. A trustee has no personal stake in the trust property, unless of course that trustee is also a beneficiary. Despite outward appearances, the trustee simply cannot deal with the property as if it were his own.[1] Instead, he labours under a variety of duties and obligations. Understandably, the trustee's actions are, therefore, policed and controlled and the parameters of the trustee's duties and powers closely regulated. As Sir James Bacon VC put it in *Payne v Evens*:

> **"No doubt the court acts with strictness and rigour against trustees because it requires for the public interest that the duties assumed by trustees should be discharged with the utmost punctuality and regularity. When trustees have failed in these duties and wrong has been done in consequence of that failure the court is in the habit of visiting the trustees with severity . . .".[2]**

The rights and responsibilities of the trustee are as prescribed by the trust instrument, imposed by equity and set out in statutory form. The extent of a trustee's duties also varies according to the nature of the trust, e.g. whether it is a constructive trust, a bare trust, a charitable trust or a pension trust. There is, as Lord Browne-Wilkinson pointed out, "a mistaken assumption that all fiduciaries owe the same duties in all circumstances. That is not the case".[3] Not surprisingly, the more onerous duties fall upon the trustee of an express trust, particularly so with pension trusts. The failure to discharge the duties

---

1   *Frith v Cartland* (1865) 2 Hem. & M. 417.
2   (1874) LR 18 Eq. 356 at 361, 362.
3   *Henderson v Merrett Syndicates Ltd* [1995] 2 A.C. 145 at 206.

of trusteeship may, of course, mean that the trustee will incur personal liability to the beneficiaries.[4]

The duties that may rest upon the shoulders of a trustee are onerous and diverse. As Millett LJ stated in *Armitage v Nurse*, "there is an irreducible core of obligations owed by the trustees to the beneficiaries and enforceable by them which is fundamental to the concept of a trust. If the beneficiaries have no rights enforceable against the trustees there are no trusts".[5] He continued, "The duty of the trustees to perform the trusts honestly and in good faith for the benefit of the beneficiaries is the minimum necessary to give substance to the trusts".[6] By way of an overview, the trustee's duties may be divided into three categories:

- the general duties owed by a trustee in relation to the running of the trust (i.e. the administrative and managerial obligations). The trustee must both hold and deal with the property in a fashion that furthers and protects the interests of the present and future beneficiaries. The overarching duty is, therefore, to administer the trust for the benefit of all the beneficiaries. In doing so, the trustee must act impartially and in the best interests of all the beneficiaries.[7] This requires that the trustee manage the trust in a way that safeguards the capital value of the property and generates an income for the beneficiaries.[8] Of course, the trustee is able to employ agents (e.g. an accountant or a solicitor) to carry out key administrative tasks[9];

- the fiduciary duties that automatically arise from the relationship of trustee and beneficiary (see paras **13-022 to 13-052**). As all trustees stand in a fiduciary relationship with the beneficiaries (which entails that the trustee must always act in utmost good faith), an obligation of loyalty, prudence and faithfulness is expected of a trustee.[10] It is to be appreciated, however, that negligence and breach of fiduciary duty are different creatures and that it is possible to be in breach of fiduciary duty and yet to have acted honestly and reasonably.[11] The trustee is not permitted to advance the interests of one beneficiary at the expense of another. Similarly, a trustee is not entitled to profit from

---

4   As regards charitable trusts, s.115(5) of the Charities Act 2011 allows a "person interested" in the charity to issue proceedings and then only with the consent of the Charity Commission or permission of the High Court: see *Rosenzweig v NMC Recordings Ltd* [2013] EWHC 3792 (Ch).

5   [1998] Ch. 241 at 253.

6   [1998] Ch. 241 at 253, 254.

7   *Lloyds Bank v Duker* [1987] 3 All E.R. 193.

8   In *Walker v Walker* [2007] All E.R. (D) 418, the trustee failed to take reasonable steps to ensure that the trust income was optimised for the benefit of the beneficiaries.

9   Section 11 of the Trustee Act 2000; cf. the more limited ability to delegate the role of trustee to a third party: see para.**12-034**.

10   *Bray v Ford* [1896] A.C. 44. Hence, in *Roberts v Frohlich* [2011] EWHC 257 (Ch), the directors of a company continued with a development project which was against the interests of the company. As they did so deliberately and knowingly, they were in breach of their fiduciary duty.

11   *Forstater v Python (Monty) Pictures Ltd* [2013] EWHC 1873 (Ch).

his position or to place himself in a position where his interests conflict with those of the trust; and

- the duties that concern the distribution of capital and income in favour of the beneficiaries (i.e. the distributive or dispositive obligations of the trustee). The trustee will have to dispose of the trust property according to the directions of the settlor and must not distribute trust money to someone who is not entitled.[12] In cases of a distribution under a discretionary trust or the exercise of a dispositive power such as the power of advancement, the trustee must exercise his discretion sensibly and responsibly while taking on board relevant matters and disregarding irrelevant concerns. As Sir Richard Scott put it in *Edge v Pensions Ombudsman*:

> **"The trustees are entitled to be partial. They are entitled to exclude some beneficiaries from particular benefits and to prefer others. If what is meant by 'undue partiality' is that the trustees have taken into account irrelevant or improper or irrational factors, their exercise of discretion may well be flawed. But it is not flawed simply because someone else, whether or not a judge, regards their partiality as 'undue'. It is the trustees' discretion that is to be exercised".[13]**

The Trustee's Duty of Care

13-002

Before considering the categories of duty owed by trustees, it is perhaps useful to depict the standards against which a trustee's actions are to be measured. This is known as the trustee's "duty of care". Each trustee owes a duty to take care (i.e. to avoid loss and injury arising from their conduct in relation to the trust).[14] At common law, unpaid (i.e. amateur) trustees were required to utilise such due diligence and care as would be expected of an ordinary prudent

---

12   The trustee must not to deviate from the trust: *Re Hulkes* (1886) 33 Ch. D. 552.

13   [1998] Ch. 512 at 534. In *JSC Mezhdunarodniy Promyshlenniy Bank v Pugachev* [2016] 1 W.L.R. 160, Lewison LJ added (at [13]) that "A beneficiary under a discretionary trust has a right to be considered as a potential recipient of benefit by the trustees. That is an interest which equity will protect. The trustees must apply some objective criterion in deciding whether or not to exercise their discretion in favour of a particular beneficiary; so that each beneficiary has more than a mere hope. But that right is not a proprietary interest in the assets held by the trustees . . .".

14   In *Buttle v Saunders* [1950] 2 All E.R. 193, the trustees had entered into a "gentleman's agreement" to sell a house. Before contracts were exchanged, a higher offer was made by another. The trustees were obliged to obtain the best price.

man of business managing his own affairs.[15] A higher expectation, however, operated in relation to the duty to invest. As Lindley LJ explained, "The duty of a trustee is not to take such care only as a prudent man would take if he had only himself to consider; the duty rather is to take such care as an ordinary prudent man would take if he were minded to make an investment for the benefit of other people for whom he felt morally bound to provide".[16] This approach prevented the trustee from engaging in a speculative investment.

With the emergence of paid (i.e. professional) trustees and corporate trustees, an additional and higher standard of care was devised. These mercenary trustees fell to be judged by the standards they professed and which had led to their employment as trustees. As Brightman J put it, "a professional corporate trustee is liable for breach of trust if loss is caused to the trust fund because it neglects to exercise the special skill and care that it professes to have".[17] The objective standard applicable at common law, therefore, depended upon the presence of payment, the nature of the trustee and the special skills that he claimed.[18] As such, it was not the most straightforward test to employ and took no account of the subjective standard that the trustee would actually have adopted in relation to his own affairs.[19]

13-003

The common law duty of care has now been subsumed, albeit strictly speaking not entirely, by s.1 of the Trustee Act 2000, which imposes a statutory duty of care on trustees.[20] This new duty applies to the activities carried out by trustees as listed in Sch.1 to the Act. The ambition was to produce a uniform duty that would apply across the spectrum of trustees' duties and thereby instil more certainty and consistency into the regulation of the trustee's behaviour.[21] These listed activities include, for example, the making of investments,[22] the acquisition of land, the employment of agents, the taking out of insurance, the carrying out of valuations of the trust property and beneficial interests and the auditing of trust accounts. This prescription, therefore, encompasses all of the trustee's key functions. The list is not, however, exhaustive and omits reference to a trustee's functions concerning the custody and management of trust property other than land and the commencement and defence of legal proceedings by or against the trust. As regards the few activities that are not so listed, it is an inescapable conclusion that the common law yardstick will still operate. The statutory duty can be excluded[23] and this suggests that, in such cases, the common law duty might be reactivated.

Subject to exclusion by the trust instrument, s.1(1) blends the objective with the subjective. It requires a trustee to "exercise such care and skill as is reasonable in the circumstances". In determining what is reasonable, particular regard is to be had to:

---

15   *Speight v Gaunt* (1883) 9 App. Cas. 1.
16   *Learoyd v Whiteley* (1886) 33 Ch. D. 347 CA at 355.
17   *Bartlett v Barclays Bank Trust Co* [1980] Ch. 515 at 534.
18   *Bray v Ford* [1896] A.C. 44.
19   *Re Lord de Clifford's Estate* [1900] 2 Ch. 707.
20   The Law Commission, "Trustees' Powers and Duties" (1999) Law Com. No.260, para.2.35 admitted that the statutory duty, "was no more than a codification of the existing common law duty".
21   For a background to this reform, see S. Panesar, "The Trustee Act 2000" (2001) I.C.C.L.R. 151.
22   The power to invest is considered in Ch.14.
23   Trustee Act 2000 Sch.1, para.7. Professional trustees will often exclude or modify the statutory duty.

■ any special knowledge or experience that he has or holds himself out as having.[24] This necessitates that, unlike at common law, the personal characteristics of a trustee can assume relevance. Although the general intention was that the statutory standard would be higher than that set by the common law, this may not always be the case. As Parker and Mellows speculate, "So it may be that a trustee who is unintelligent or unworldly owes a lower statutory duty of care, not just than that of a trustee who is neither but also than that of the prudent man of business under the pre-existing law".[25] It is to be emphasised that the standard is geared not only to the expertise that the trustee actually has, but as at common law it also reflects the expertise that the trustee claims to have. The claim must somehow have been communicated to the settlor, an appointing trustee or the beneficiaries. The claim could emerge from conversations, publicity material, advertisements and the like; and

■ whether the trustee acts in the course of a business or profession and, if so, any special knowledge or experience reasonably expected of such a person in the same business or profession.[26] This must entail that a higher standard of care is expected from a paid trustee who specialises in trust work than from, say, an accountant or a solicitor who acts as a trustee as part of his general practice.[27]

As to the trustee's duty when investing, the Trustee Act 2000 is modelled upon the common law test. The requirement is that the trustee must behave like a prudent person acting for others when making investments, reviewing investments and obtaining investment advice.[28] This can, however, be excluded or modified in the trust instrument.[29] The contemporary approach is as advocated by Hoffmann J in the High Court in *Nestle v National Westminster Bank*[30] that modern trustees are entitled to be judged by the standards of the "portfolio theory". The burden was on the claimant to prove that she would have been better off if the investments had been properly diversified. She could not do this and her claim, therefore, failed. This issue is revisited in Ch.14.

Provided that the trustee crosses the minimum threshold applicable, he will not be liable for subsequent loss that occurs. The trustee is able to apply to the High Court for directions prior to the taking of any action that might compromise his position as trustee. If the trustee

13-004

---

24 Trustee Act 2000 s.1(1)(a).
25 A.J. Oakley, ed., *Parker and Mellows: The Modern Law of Trusts* 9th edn (London: Sweet & Maxwell, 2008), p.640.
26 Trustee Act 2000 s.1(1)(b). As regards pension trustees, this duty is extended by a duty to take all reasonable steps to meet the requirements of ss.35–36 of the Pensions Act 1995 and associated Investment Regulations (see *Independent Trustee Service Ltd v GP Noble Trustees Ltd* [2010] EWHC 1653 (Ch)).
27 See *Forstater v Python (Monty) Pictures Ltd* [2013] EWHC 1873 (Ch).
28 Trustee Act 2000 Sch.1, paras 1, 2; see *Jeffrey v Gretton* [2011] W.T.L.R. 809, where the trustees were held to be in breach of their obligations to regularly review the trust portfolio and to take professional advice.
29 Trustee Act 2000 Sch.1, para.7.
30 Unreported 29 June 1988.

does not take such pre-emptive action, it is still possible to apply to the court for relief under s.61 of the Trustee Act 1925 (see para.**13-054**). This enables the court to exonerate (in whole or in part) a trustee who has acted honestly and reasonably and who ought fairly to be excused for the breach and the failure to obtain the directions of the court. Case law demonstrates that an unpaid trustee is more likely to be released from liability than his professional counterpart.[31]

Exoneration clauses

13-005

It is common practice for an exemption clause to be present in the trust instrument that will operate to restrict the potential liability of a trustee for breach of trust. There are, moreover, no statutory provisions which regulate the reasonableness of trustee exemption clauses. As the Law Commission pointed out in its Consultation Paper, "As the powers of trustees have increased . . . so has the breadth of trustee exemption clauses. When coupled with the less restrictive approach recently adopted by the courts to the construction of exemption clauses, it can be strongly argued that the protection offered to beneficiaries, one of the prime concerns of trust law, is weaker than in the past".[32] It is to be appreciated, however, that there can be no exclusion of liability arising from fraud or intentional wrongdoing.[33] Otherwise blanket protection may be afforded to shield a trustee from his extreme, but honest, folly,[34] to excuse a breach of fiduciary duty[35] and to exonerate even a professional trustee from mishandling trust affairs.[36] In each case, the wording of the clause must be construed in order to determine whether liability for the conduct complained of was excluded. Such a clause might be drafted as follows: "No Trustee shall be liable for any loss or damage which may happen to the Trust Fund at any time or from any cause whatsoever unless such loss or damage shall be caused by his own actual fraud". If there is dispute concerning the wording of such clauses, the interpretation to be given is one that does not favour the trustee.[37] An illustration as to the effects

---

31 *Re Pauling's ST* [1964] Ch. 303; *Re Rosenthal* [1972] 1 W.L.R. 1273.

32 Law Commission, *Trustee Exemption Clauses* (2003) Consultation Paper No.171, p.vi. In *Bonham v Fishwick* [2008] EWCA Civ 373, for example, the clause exempted the trustees from all liability except in the case of "wilful and individual fraud or wrongdoing".

33 See *Baker v JE Clark & Co (Transport) Ltd* [2006] EWCA Civ 464.

34 *Barraclough v Mell* [2005] EWHC 3387 (Ch).

35 *Barnsley v Noble* [2016] [2016] EWCA Civ 799 (breach of self-dealing rule). It was, however, recommended in the "Final Report on UK Equity Markets and Long Term Decision Making" (BIS/12/917, 12 July 2012) that there should be no contracting out whatsoever of fiduciary duties. This recommendation did receive governmental support ("Government Response to the Kay Review" BIS/12/1188, 22 November 2012), but no change has occurred.

36 "[A]n absolute owner of property can settle his affairs . . . on such terms as would relieve his trustees from the responsibility to exercise the degrees of care and prudence which would otherwise be inferred" (per Murphy J in *Stacey v Branch* [1995] 2 I.L.R.M. 136 at 143).

37 *Wight v Olswang (No.1) The Times*, 18 May 1999. As Kitchen J pointed out at first instance in *Bonham v Blake Lapthorn Linell* [2006] EWHC 2513 (Ch) at [177], "A liability can be excluded only by clear and unambiguous words. Nevertheless, trustees accept office on the terms of a document for which they are not responsible, and they are entitled to have the document fairly construed according to the natural meaning of the words used".

of an exclusion clause is to be found in *Barraclough v Mell*.[38] In that case, there was a trustee exemption clause which, in effect, made the trustee liable for breach of duty for her own personal acts when she knew that the relevant acts were wrongful or when she had no belief that the act was right and did not care if it was wrong.[39] The trustee misapplied trust money by paying £64,000 to the wrong beneficiaries. Although the trustee admitted negligence, she still sought to avoid liability under the exemption clause. The High Court concluded that, as she had genuinely thought that she was acting within the terms of the trust, she was protected by the exemption clause.

In *Armitage v Nurse*,[40] a clause that purported to exempt trustees from any liability to the trust unless it was caused by their own "actual fraud" was upheld.[41] The Court of Appeal interpreted "fraud" as meaning "dishonesty" and requiring, at the least, an intention to pursue a course of action either knowing that it ran contrary to the interests of the beneficiaries or being recklessly indifferent as to its impact on them.[42] Exploitation of position alone is, therefore, not enough to fall beyond the reach of exclusion.[43] Hence, there has to be some wilful misconduct to deprive the trustee of the protection otherwise afforded.[44] This approach is interesting in that it allows a clause to exempt a trustee not only for ordinary negligence,[45] but also for gross negligence.[46] It also gives rise to the possibility that a trustee who knowingly acts outside his powers, but does so in the belief that this will promote the best interests of the beneficiaries, would be shielded from liability.[47] All seems to turn upon how "fraud/dishonesty" is defined.[48] In *Nurse*, Millett LJ viewed the latter type of conduct as falling beyond the scope of the fraud

---

38   [2005] EWHC 3387 (Ch).

39   In *Bonham v Fishwick* [2008] EWCA Civ 373, Mummery LJ expressed the view that a trustee who acted upon legal advice could not be accused of wilful wrongdoing.

40   [1998] Ch. 241.

41   A trust deed which allowed the trustee to act fraudulently without giving the beneficiaries any recourse would seemingly fail as a trust: see *Baskerville v Thurgood* (1992) 100 Sask L.R. 214.

42   This was a theme echoed by Sir Christopher Slade in *Walker v Stones* [2001] 1 Q.B. 902. As he explained at 939: "A person may in some cases act dishonestly, according to the ordinary use of language, even though he genuinely believes that his action is morally justified. The penniless thief, for example, who picks the pocket of the multi-millionaire is dishonest even though he genuinely considers the theft is morally justified as a fair redistribution of wealth and that he is not therefore being dishonest".

43   Only if it is designed to release the trustees from the core obligations of honesty and good faith will it fail as a valid clause: *Halliwells LLP v Austin* [2012] EWHC 1194 (Ch).

44   *Spread Trustee Co Ltd v Hutcheson* [2012] 2 A.C. 194 PC.

45   Nothing contentious there: see *Bogg v Raper, The Times*, 22 April 1998.

46   Cf. the position in Scotland where there can be no exclusion of liability for gross negligence: *Lutea Trustees Ltd v Orbis Trustees* [1998] S.L.T. 471.

47   *Sofer v Swiss Independent Trustees* [2019] EWHC 2071 (Ch).

48   The difference between fraudulent breaches of trust and other types of breach is reflected also in the limitation period in which action must be commenced. Section 21 of the Limitation Act 1980 provides that there is no limitation period applicable to fraudulent breaches of trust when the action is brought against the trustee. If the action is, instead, brought against a dishonest assistant to a breach of trust, then the limitation period of six years applies in the normal fashion: *Williams v Central Bank of Nigeria* [2014] UKSC 10.

carve-out. By way of stark contrast, in *Royal Brunei Airlines v Tan*[49] Lord Nicholls believed that such conduct would indeed be fraudulent because the trustees were taking a risk that they knew they had no right to take. It is suggested that the latter stance is likely to prevail and, therefore, trustees would be most unwise deliberately to take unauthorised action in the hope that they are protected by an exemption clause.[50] Akin to the criminal test of dishonesty, recent authorities have supported the notion that the trustee will not be acting dishonestly unless he does something that ordinary people would regard as dishonest and he knew that ordinary people would so regard it.[51] In *Ivey v Genting Casinos UK Ltd*,[52] the Supreme Court emphasised that the court must ascertain the actual state of the individual's knowledge or belief as to the facts. As to whether the conduct was honest or not, this was then to be determined by applying the objective standards of ordinary decent people. There is no requirement in the definition of dishonesty that the defendant should appreciate that what they were doing was dishonest by the standards of ordinary honest folk.[53]

13-006   In the Trust Law Committee Consultation Paper entitled *Trustee Exemption Clauses* (published in June 1999) it was proposed that a distinction should be drawn between lay trustees and professional trustees. While the existing law would essentially be preserved as regards the former, professional trustees would no longer be able to claim protection against negligence. The attitude is that professional trustees should always be expected to act with reasonable care and, in any event, are likely to be covered by liability insurance. As the Committee explained, "There is much to be said for trust corporations and professional individuals paid for their services as trustees (like solicitors, barristers and accountants) to accept the price of liability for negligence in acting as a paid trustee and to insure against such risk, with the premiums being reflected in the fees for the services provided".[54] Four years later, the Law Commission echoed this sentiment and agreed that, while exclusion clauses should not be abolished, there should be further regulation. It believed that the present law was too deferential to professional trustees. The Commission provisionally concluded that professional trustees (i.e. trust corporations and any other trustees acting in a professional capacity) should not be allowed to rely on exclusion clauses as regards negligent breaches of trust or to claim indemnity from the trust fund.[55] These proposals were, however, rejected in the Law Commission's subsequent report.[56] The Report warned of "dangers in taking an oversimplified view of the role of trustee

---

49   [1995] 2 A.C. 378 at 390.

50   *Barnsley v Noble* [2016] EWCA Civ 799.

51   *Fattal v Walbrook Trustees (Jersey) Ltd* (2010) EWHC 2767 (Ch). In *Cavell USA Ltd v Seaton Insurance Co* [2009] EWCA Civ 1363, Longmore LJ warned that there remains "scope for considerable debate about what constitutes 'fraud' as a matter of English law" (at [11]) and acknowledged that "the concept of fraud is notoriously difficult to define" (at [15]).

52   [2018] A.C. 391. This concerned a £7.7 million win at a casino allegedly by cheating at cards.

53   Accordingly, the test previously propounded in *R. v Ghosh* (1982) Q.B. 1053 was rejected.

54   *Trust Law Committee Consultation Paper* (1999), para.7.8.

55   Law Commission, *Trustee Exemption Clauses* (2003) Consultation Paper No.171, p.viii.

56   Law Commission, *Trustee Exemption Clauses* (2006) Law Com. No.301, Cm.6874.

exemption clauses"[57] and proposed a scheme of regulation ("a rule of practice") to be enforced by the relevant professional bodies. The cynic might conclude that the decision not to regulate was taken primarily to ensure that professional trustees did not relocate to jurisdictions which have less restrictive controls and to keep trust funds in England and Wales. This proposed rule of practice would apply only to paid trustees and would operate when the trustee caused a settlor to include an exemption clause. In such cases, the trustee is expected to take "such steps as are reasonable to ensure that the settlor is aware of the meaning and effect of that clause".[58] This promotion of settlor awareness is designed to respect settlor autonomy and to prevent a deleterious impact on both trustees and beneficiaries. The Society of Trust and Estate Practitioners, for example, has acted to protect both the public and trustees by ensuring the disclosure of clauses in trusts or wills exempting trustees or executors from liability. The Society, which has a history of involvement with the reform agencies as to the possible regulation of exclusion clauses, hopes that other professional bodies will follow suit to ensure that such rules of practice become the standard in the private client industry. It still remains to be seen what, if any, benefits this code of practice will bring.

Administrative Duties

The trustee is subject to a range of duties that arise on appointment and continue for the duration of the trust. As will become clear, these duties relate to the preservation of and dealings with trust property, the managerial actions taken by trustees and the information to be given to beneficiaries. These include various types of obligation.

13-007

Duties on appointment

Upon accepting the office, the trustee is expected to ascertain the terms of the trust and to confirm that he has been validly appointed and that the trust property has been vested in him.[59] As Kekewich J put it, "I think that when persons are asked to become new trustees, they are bound to inquire of what the property consists that is proposed to be handed over to them, and what are the trusts. They ought also to look into the trust documents and papers to ascertain what notices appear among them of incumbrances and other matters affecting the

13-008

---

57   Law Commission, *Trustee Exemption Clauses* (2006) Law Com. No.301, Cm.6874, para.3.41.
58   Law Commission, *Trustee Exemption Clauses* (2006) Law Com. No.301, Cm.6874, para.6.65. This is, however, little more than an affirmation of what has always been expected of the draftsman of a trust.
59   *Harvey v Oliver* [1887] 57 L.T. 239.

trust".[60] The trustee will, therefore, be expected to study the contents of the trust instrument and the trust accounts and to identify any co-trustees, the beneficiaries, the nature of the trust and the trust assets.

To enable a new trustee to obtain basic information, an existing or retiring trustee can be required to produce any documents maintained which relate to the management of the trust. As Jenkins LJ explained, "If . . . [an] executor or trustee does, in fact, reduce his deliberations to writing, as, for instance, by recording them in a diary relating to the administration of the estate or trust, we see no reason in principle why he should not be required to produce it to his successor in office".[61] This entails that, if previously there had been meetings held between trustees, the new trustee will be entitled to see the recorded minutes of those encounters. Similarly, the new trustee will wish to read all correspondence and other documents related to the trust. In addition, a new trustee is advised to question an existing or retiring trustee and elicit information via that means. If the existing or retiring trustee is a corporation, the new trustee should also call for the internal memoranda of that company.

13-009

A new trustee is entitled to operate on the basis that an existing or retiring trustee has carried out his functions properly[62] and need not conduct a detailed examination of past conduct.[63] In *Hallows v Lloyd*,[64] the trustees could not discover the existence of a marriage settlement from the trust documentation and, therefore, were not in breach of duty. They did not have derivative notice from the retiring trustee who knew of the settlement. Nevertheless, any suspicions that the trustee may have as to the prior administration of the trust should be investigated and, if necessary, appropriate steps taken against the party responsible (i.e. a former or current trustee).[65] These preliminary steps are necessary to shield the new trustee from liability.

Safeguarding trust property

13-010

If the trust was in existence before his appointment, a new trustee must ensure that he understands the provisions of the trust and that the trust property has been properly invested.[66] Hence, if a trust investment has fallen in value and threatens to jeopardise the trust fund, the trustee should consider whether to reinvest elsewhere. Otherwise, he will be liable for the failure to review. In *Re Medland*,[67] for example, trust money was lent on mortgage, but the security for the loan had depreciated in value and now risked the interests of the trust. North J held that the trustee should have deliberated whether or not to call in the mortgage.

Except where expressly allowed in the trust instrument, the trustee should never lend trust

---

60   *Hallows v Lloyd* (1889) 39 Ch. D. 686 at 691.
61   *Tiger v Barclays Bank* [1952] 1 All E.R. 85 at 87.
62   *Re Miller* [1978] L.S. Gaz. R. 454.
63   *Harvey v Oliver* [1887] 57 L.T. 239.
64   (1889) 39 Ch. D. 686.
65   *Re Strahan* (1856) 8 De GM. & G. 291.
66   *Nestle v National Westminster Bank* [1993] 1 W.L.R. 1260 CA.
67   (1889) 41 Ch. D. 476.

money or allow it to remain outstanding on an unsecured basis.[68] In *Bhullar v Bhullar*, for example, a director was in breach of fiduciary duty in making substantial loans without express provision for repayment or for the payment of interest.[69] If the trust property includes chattels, the trustee should also obtain an accurate inventory.[70] The trustee is expected to ensure that all securities and chattels are in safe custody.[71] As regards land, the trustee should ensure that it is secure and free from the adverse claims of a trespasser. Perhaps surprisingly, there appears to be no duty to insure the trust property.[72]

Calling in loans

The trustee should, moreover, ensure that, where part of the trust property is a loan due for repayment, this loan should be called in.[73] This action is required because of the general notion that the trustee must take all reasonable steps to safeguard trust assets. This is subject to the trustee's overarching obligation to act in the interests of all the beneficiaries.[74] The danger for the trustee is that, if he allows the debt to become statute-barred under the Limitation Act 1980, he will assume personal liability for the ensuing loss to the trust. If necessary, therefore, the trustee must institute legal action to enforce repayment.[75]

13-011

The trustee who decides not to bring an enforcement action should ask the court for directions under s.57 of the Trustee Act 1925 that support the intended inaction.[76] If not, the trustee might show, by way of a defence, that he held a well-founded belief that any enforcement action would be pointless.[77] It is, however, no defence for the trustee to argue that he thought it somehow indelicate or inappropriate to ask for the loan to be repaid and to initiate recovery proceedings. This was demonstrated in *Re Brogden*[78] where the trustees decided not to sue on a £10,000 debt owed to the trust because they feared a crisis in the family of the beneficiary would ensue. This excuse was held to be an inadequate justification for the trustees' failure to enforce the debt and liability followed accordingly for breach of duty. As Fry LJ put it:

---

68 *Pickard v Anderson* (1872) L.R. 13 Eq. 608.
69 [2017] EWHC 407 (Ch).
70 In *Ali v Taj* [2020] EWHC 213 (Fam), the trustees were ordered to provide an inventory and to account properly to the beneficiaries. They had been without a proper understanding of the administration of their inheritance for over a decade and it was unconscionable to allow the situation to continue.
71 *Re Miller's Deed Trusts* [1978] L.S. Gaz. 454.
72 *Bailey v Gould* (1840) 4 Y. & C. Ex. 221; *Revenue & Customs Commissioners v The Peter Clay Discretionary Trust* [2008] 2 W.L.R. 1052.
73 *M'Gachen v Dew* (1851) 15 Beav. 84.
74 See *Madison Pacific Trust Ltd v Shakoor Capital Ltd* [2020] EWHC 610 (Ch).
75 *Buxton v Buxton* (1835) 1 My. & Cr. 80.
76 *Public Trustee v Cooper* [2001] W.T.L.R. 901; see also *Angus v Emmott* [2010] EWHC 154 (Ch). Section 57 allows the court to authorise an action concerning the management or administration of trust property according to a notion of expediency.
77 *Re Brogden* (1888) 38 Ch. D. 546.
78 (1888) 38 Ch. D. 546.

> "A trustee undoubtedly has a discretion as to the mode and manner, and very often as to the time in which and at which he shall carry his duty into effect. But his discretion is never an absolute one; it is always limited by the duty—the dominant duty, the guiding duty—of recovering, securing, and duly applying the trust fund. And no trustee can claim any right of discretion which does not agree with that paramount obligation".[79]

In contrast, in *Ward v Ward* the court decided that the trustee acted reasonably in failing to sue a debtor, who was also a beneficiary, in circumstances where to bring an action would have financially ruined the debtor and impacted deleteriously upon other beneficiaries (his children).[80]

Joint control

13-012

The trust property ought to be placed in the joint control of all the trustees. It must be kept distinct from the trustee's personal property or the property of any other trust. Accordingly, a new trustee should ensure that investments are in the names of all the trustees. If not, and where trust property is misapplied by a trustee, the co-trustees are potentially liable for any loss that arises.[81] For example, in *Lewis v Nobbs*,[82] the trust property included bearer bonds which were in the sole control of one trustee. When this trustee went off with the bonds in his custody, the other trustee was held liable because by his negligence he had facilitated the misappropriation. As Hall VC pointed out, "care should have been taken that there could not be any improper disposition . . . he is liable for the illegal dealing with the moiety of the bonds of his co-trustee".[83] In order to protect themselves, trustees are now given the right by the Trustee Act 2000 to appoint custodians of trust property and documents. Indeed, in relation to so-called "bearer securities" (i.e. securities which are not registered in the name of anyone), the trustees must appoint a custodian unless exempted by the trust instrument or by statutory provision. By their very nature, these securities cannot be placed in the names and joint control of the trustees.

---

79 (1888) 38 Ch. D. 546 at 571. Lopes LJ added that, "No consideration of delicacy, and no regard for the feelings of relatives or friends, will exonerate him . . ." (at 574).
80 (1843) 2 H.L. Cas. 777.
81 *Rodbard v Cooke* (1877) 36 L.T. 504.
82 (1878) 8 Ch. D. 591.
83 (1878) 8 Ch. D. 591 at 595.

The duty to account

The obligation to provide financial accounts is central to the relationship of trustee and beneficiary.[84] It is the first duty of the trustee, as Plumer MR noted in *Pearse v Green*, "to be constantly ready with his accounts".[85] This is not generally a reference to annual financial statements, but is, instead, referring to the very notion of accounting itself.[86] Trustees must be ready to account to the beneficiaries for what they have done with the trust assets. The right is an aspect of the court's inherent jurisdiction to supervise and, if appropriate, to intervene in the administration of a trust. Although the court enjoys the discretion as to whether to make such an order, and the form it will adopt, it will ordinarily exercise its discretion in favour of a beneficiary.[87] As Master Matthews noted, "This may be done with formal financial statements, or with less formal documents, or indeed none at all. It is no answer for trustees to say that formal financial statements have not yet been produced by the trustees' accountants".[88]

The motivation underlying this duty to account is that all beneficiaries have the opportunity to discover whether a breach of trust has occurred. There is, however, no set rule as to what kind of accounting, and in relation to what, different classes of beneficiary are entitled. As Master Matthews explained:

> **"I do not think that it necessarily follows that all such documents must be disclosed to all beneficiaries. It must depend on what is needed in the circumstances for the beneficiaries to appreciate, verify and if need be vindicate their own rights against the trustees in respect of the administration of the trust. That will vary according to the facts of the case".[89]**

As regards remuneration claimed by the trustee, for example, each item must be noted and presumptions may be made against the trustee if he has not kept proper records.[90] Understandably, the trustee will appoint an agent (i.e. a qualified accountant) to prepare and maintain the trust accounts. Trustees who do not maintain proper accounts can be directed to do so by the court and may face liability for costs in those and future proceedings.[91] As

---

84 See *Tiger v Barclays Bank* [1952] 1 All E.R. 85. As Deputy Judge Roger Kaye QC put it in *Walker v Walker* [2007] All E.R. (D) 418, "A trustee must keep accounts, provide them when required and provide to the beneficiaries all reasonable information as to the manner in which the trust estate has been dealt with" (at [249]).

85 (1819) 1 Jac. & W. 135 at 140.

86 *The Royal National Lifeboat Institution v Headley* [2016] EWHC 1948 (Ch).

87 *Henchley v Thompson* [2017] EWHC 225 (Ch).

88 *The Royal National Lifeboat Institution v Headley* [2016] EWHC 1948 (Ch) at [11].

89 *The Royal National Lifeboat Institution v Headley* [2016] EWHC 1948 (Ch) at [14].

90 *Pullan v Wilson* [2014] EWHC 126 (Ch).

91 *Re Skinner* [1904] 1 Ch. 289. This is so where there is either gross negligence or where the refusal to provide accounts is wholly indefensible.

Farwell J observed in *Re Skinner*, "beneficiaries have a right to expect the performance of their duty by executors, and not the less when one of them has power to make professional charges".[92]

Every beneficiary is entitled physically to inspect the trust's financial accounts[93] and this rule applies equally to fixed and discretionary trusts[94] and whether or not the beneficiary's interest is in possession.[95] It appears that, if the beneficiary wants a copy of the accounts, it is to be paid for out of the pocket of that beneficiary.[96] The beneficiary may challenge the accounts and this is traditionally known as "falsifying" and "surcharging" accounts. "Falsifying" refers to the ability of the beneficiary to show that an entry in the accounts was erroneous and should be rectified (i.e. the falsification of accounts). In *Bonham v Blake Lapthorn Linell*, Kitchen J explained that falsification is "the means by which that loss is made good. The trust is restored by disallowing the payment away of the funds in issue".[97] "Surcharging" concerns a credit entry which was omitted entirely and which should be included in the accounts. The trustee is under a duty to correct any errors detected in the accounts.

13-014

The trustee has the power to have the accounts audited by an independent accountant. There is, however, no duty upon a trustee of a private trust to take such action.[98] Section 22(4) of the Trustee Act 1925 imposes limitations upon the ability of the trustee to have the accounts audited at his own behest. It provides that, as a general rule, an audit cannot occur more than once every three years. The idea is that the expense to the trust fund should be minimised. The three-year rule gives way, however, when the nature of the trust or special dealings with trust property make it desirable to have more frequent audits.

Any beneficiary or trustee can, however, apply to the Public Trustee for an audit to be carried out under s.13 of the Public Trustee Act 1906. In *Re Oddy*, Parker J noted the potential breadth of this provision:

> **"Section 13, when carefully examined appears to be an exceedingly drastic enactment. It enables any trustee or beneficiary to apply for an audit of the whole accounts of a trust at any time whatever . . . There is no limit backwards beyond which the audit is not to be extended, and, therefore, in a trust which has lasted 30 or 40 years**

92 [1904] 1 Ch. 289 at 292. This is not an unlimited right. In *The Royal National Lifeboat Institution v Headley* [2016] EWHC 1948 (Ch), for example, the disclosure sought by a capital beneficiary did not entitle him to accounts as regards fees and expenditure that concerned only the income beneficiary.

93 *Kemp v Burn* (1863) 4 Giff. 348.

94 *Murphy v Murphy* [1999] 1 W.L.R. 282.

95 *Armitage v Nurse* [1998] Ch. 241. This duty is placed upon Charity Trustees by the Charities Act 2011.

96 *Ottley v Gilbey* (1845) 8 Beav. 602.

97 [2006] EWHC 2513 (Ch) at [180].

98 Cf. the trustee of a charitable trust who, subject to certain conditions, is under an obligation to audit imposed by the Charities Act 2011. Similarly, under the Judicial Trustee Rules there is provision for an annual audit following the appointment of a judicial trustee.

> it is open to a *cestui que trust* to go back to the very beginning, unless of course, the court otherwise orders . . .".[99]

There are, however, two limitations on this statutory right to an audit. First, an audit cannot occur within one year of a prior audit. Secondly, an applicant runs the risk of having to pay the costs of the process himself. As Parker J demonstrated, "The only penalty for insisting improperly for an investigation of the trust accounts is . . . to order the applicant to pay the costs of the audit".[100] Due to this fear of costs, the s.13 route is rarely followed.

The duty to provide information

Apart from the keeping of accounts, the trustees must be prepared to provide information and documents to the beneficiaries as to the current state of the trust property and any dealings that have occurred in relation to it. The beneficiary is entitled to receive explanations as to what the trustees have been doing with the trust property (e.g. concerning income, investments and distributions). In particular, the trustees must be able to give full and accurate information as to the value of the trust fund.[101] There is, moreover, a positive duty to inform a beneficiary of full age and capacity of his entitlement under a fixed trust.[102] It is thought that the trustees are also under a duty to reveal their names and addresses to the beneficiaries.[103] The trustees need not, however, provide reasons for their decision whether or not to exercise their discretion in a particular way. Hence, in *Re Beloved Wilkes' Charity* when the trustees selected a boy to be educated at Oxford University, they were entitled not to disclose the reasons underlying their selection.[104]

It is the duty of the trustees to produce trust documents (including, as shown, accounts) at the request of a beneficiary whether under a discretionary trust or a fixed trust.[105] The problem, of course, concentrates upon what is properly to be classed as a "trust document" in a particular case. In *Re Londonderry's Settlement*, Salmon LJ admitted that "The category of trust document has never been defined. Nor could it be—certainly not comprehensively by me".[106] He managed, however, to identify certain characteristics of a trust document and these were, first, that the document is to be in the possession of the trustees as trustees. Secondly,

13-015

---

99   [1911] 1 Ch. 532 at 537.
100 [1911] 1 Ch. 532 at 538.
101 *Re Tillott* [1892] 1 Ch. 86. There it was made clear by Chitty J (at 89) that a trustee is not bound to give a beneficiary information about a share in which he has no interest.
102 *Hawkesley v May* [1956] 1 Q.B. 304. As regards a discretionary trust, the trustees should, if practical, make the beneficiaries aware of their ability to make a possible claim.
103 *Murphy v Murphy* [1999] 1 W.L.R. 282.
104 (1851) 3 Mac. & G. 440.
105 See *Schmidt v Rosewood Trust Ltd* [2003] 3 All E.R. 76 where Lord Walker accepted that "The right to seek the court's intervention does not depend on entitlement to a fixed and transmissible beneficial interest" (at 91).
106 [1965] Ch. 918 at 938.

the document is to contain information about the trust which the beneficiaries are entitled to know. Thirdly, the beneficiaries are entitled to see such documents. It can, therefore, be said that a trust document is, essentially, one that is in the possession of the trustee in his capacity as trustee and which contains information about the trust. Accordingly, in *Blades v Isaac*[107] the trustees obtained the opinion of specialist counsel and were obliged to disclose this documentation to the beneficiary. The opinion had been obtained by the trustees for the benefit of the trust and it was, therefore, properly classified as a trust document. Master Matthews emphasised that, as the object of a discretionary trust had the standing to complain of a breach of trust by the trustees, the beneficiary also had the standing to require relevant information about the management of the trust.

13-016   The ability of the court to order such production emerges from its general supervisory role. As Lord Walker put it in the Privy Council decision in *Schmidt v Rosewood Trust Ltd*, "the more principled and correct approach is to regard the right to seek disclosure of trust documents as one aspect of the court's inherent jurisdiction to supervise, and if necessary to intervene in, the administration of trusts".[108] Lord Walker rejected the view that a beneficiary has any proprietary right to see all trust documents. He felt that the court had to engage in a balancing exercise, "Especially when there are issues as to personal or commercial confidentiality, the court may have to balance the competing interests of different beneficiaries, the trustees themselves and third parties. Disclosure may have to be limited and safeguards may have to be put in place".[109] For example, the court might order disclosure of only certain types of document, either completely or in a redacted form, and might limit the use which may be made of the documents disclosed whether by undertakings to the court or by arrangements for professional inspection. Although in principle an order can be made at the behest of a beneficiary under a discretionary trust, Lord Walker accepted the uncertain nature of this type of beneficial interest. He observed that "In many cases the court may have no difficulty in concluding that an applicant with no more than a theoretical possibility of benefit ought not to be granted any relief".[110]

The documents that a beneficiary may call for would include, for example, trust deeds, documents relating to the settlement of assets, documentation relating to any change of the trustees or any amendment to the terms of the trusts, any trust diary maintained by the trustees which records their decisions, any other *aide-memoire* such as the minutes of meetings between the trustees and correspondence or written advice from an agent of the trustee.[111] In *Re Cowin*, North J admitted that this is not an absolute rule: "I do not say that he is entitled as of right, but only that he is entitled under the circumstances, because there might be a state of circumstances under which the right to production would not exist".[112]

---

107 [2016] EWHC 601 (Ch).
108 [2003] 3 All E.R. 76 at 91.
109 [2003] 3 All E.R. 76 at 97.
110 [2003] 3 All E.R. 76 at 97.
111 See *North Shore Ventures v Anstead Holdings Inc* [2012] EWCA Civ 11.
112 (1886) 33 Ch. D. 179 at 187. There the beneficiary sought title deeds and other documents.

The right to information is, therefore, subject to limitations. First, there is no right to see documents that are not classified as trust documents. As indicated, not all documents held by trustees are "trust documents". For example, as Harman LJ observed in *Re Londonderry's Settlement*, "I cannot think that communications between individual trustees and appointors are documents in which beneficiaries have a . . . right . . . I do not think that letters to or from an individual beneficiary ought to be open to inspection by another beneficiary".[113] This limitation arises because the beneficiary's entitlement to "trust documents" is traditionally thought to be justified only on the ground that, as Lord Wrenbury explained, "They are in a sense his own".[114] Hence, there is no right to see advice provided by the trustee's solicitor which was paid for out of his own pocket and relates to proceedings waged against the trustee personally.[115] As mentioned, the beneficiary will be able to see documents such as the trust instrument,[116] all instruments concerning a change in trustee, all receipts for payments made by or on behalf of the trustees[117] and written legal advice as to the administration of the trust.[118]

Secondly, the right to see trust documentation does not extend to those documents that state the reasons why the trustees made particular decisions when exercising their discretionary powers. In *Schmidt v Rosewood Trust Ltd*, Lord Walker described this as "the need to protect confidentiality in communications between trustees as to the exercise of their dispositive discretions, and in communications made to the trustees by other beneficiaries".[119] The classic demonstration of this was by the Court of Appeal in *Re Londonderry's Settlement*.[120] There the beneficiary was refused access to documentation that would show why the trustees chose to distribute the fund in the way that they did. The trustees determined that it would not be in the interests of family harmony to disclose documents which included minutes and agendas of trust meetings and correspondence between the trustees and their agents and other beneficiaries. If they were compelled to do so, the rule that trustees do not need to disclose their reasons would be defeated and the trustees felt that they would be unable to do their job effectively. As Harman LJ acknowledged, "they are protected for the special reason which protects the trustees' deliberations on a discretionary matter from disclosure. If necessary, I hold that this principle overrides the ordinary rule".[121] The upshot of this decision is, therefore, that in trust law the right to inspect documents does not extend to documents that the trustees desire to be private and which contain the reasons for their decisions.[122]

---

113 [1965] Ch. 918 at 934.
114 *O'Rourke v Darbishire* (1920) A.C. 581 at 626.
115 *Talbot v Marshfield* (1865) 2 Dr. & Sm. 549.
116 *Ex p. Holdsworth* (1838) 4 Bing. N.C. 386.
117 *Re Ellis* [1908] W.N. 215.
118 *Devaynes v Robinson* (1855) 20 Beav. 42.
119 [2003] 3 All E.R. 76 at 91.
120 [1965] Ch. 918.
121 [1965] Ch. 918 at 938.
122 *See Wilson v Law Debenture Trust Corp* [1995] 2 All E.R. 337. There Rattee J held that the rule applied equally to a pension trust (where the beneficiaries purchase their interests) as to any other type of trust (where the beneficiaries are volunteers).

13-018

The *Londonderry* case, however, does nothing to prevent a trustee being ordered to disclose such documents in the course of civil proceedings that allege that the trustees have exercised their discretion in some improper fashion. Indeed, discovery of such documents was ordered in *Talbot v Marshfield*.[123] Writing extra-judicially, Megarry questioned whether the courts will "permit the bonds of secrecy to be invaded by the simple process of commencing hostile litigation against the trustees? It is not easy to see how the courts can prevent this".[124] It is, however, apparent that the court will not order disclosure as part of a "fishing expedition" by the claimant, seeking to establish a case. The claimant must at least be able to demonstrate a prima facie case before disclosure of documents is ordered.

Thirdly, the right gives way in exceptional circumstances where the trustees decide that, in providing the requested information to a particular beneficiary, the interests of the beneficiaries as a whole will be compromised[125] and the administration of the trust prejudiced.[126] This is likely to arise when the trust concerns the running of a business and the beneficiary seeks commercially sensitive information. A disgruntled beneficiary can test the correctness of the trustee's refusal to disclose by seeking directions of the court.

13-019

Finally, as regards so-called "letters of wishes", further restrictions may apply. These "letters of wishes" are no more than guidance provided by a settlor to his trustees as to how they should exercise their powers and discretions. This guidance is important in that it must be considered when a trustee exercises his discretion and must be passed on to new trustees. In *Breakspear v Ackland*,[127] Briggs J noted that the large increase in the use of wish letters went hand in hand with the increased popularity of discretionary trusts and that they were useful in terms of both flexibility for trustees and privacy for the settlor. He accepted also that there is an inevitable tension between the advantages of confidentiality and the advantages of disclosure. As to whether the beneficiaries enjoy a right to inspect a letter of wishes, however, the answer appears to be in the negative. They seem to fall within the *Londonderry* range of documents that enjoy immunity as they intimate the reasons underlying the exercise of discretion by the trustees.[128] Letters of wishes are, therefore, confidential between the settlor and trustee and will as a general rule remain private.

The duty to act jointly

13-020

The general rule is that, where there are two or more trustees, they must act unanimously in that decisions have to be made jointly by all the trustees.[129] This is sometimes referred to as

---

123 (1865) 2 Drew. & Sm. 549. Disclosure is now governed by Pt 31 of the Civil Procedure Rules.
124 R.E. Megarry (1965) 81 L.Q.R. 192, 196.
125 *Rouse v 100F Australia Trustees Ltd* [2000] W.T.L.R. 111.
126 *Re Rabaiotti's 1989 Settlement* [2000] W.T.L.R. 953 (a Channel Islands case).
127 [2008] 3 W.L.R. 698.
128 *Breakspear v Ackland* [2008] 3 W.L.R. 698.
129 See J. Jaconelli, "Decision-taking by Private and Charitable Trustees" [1991] Conv. 30.

the "unanimity principle".[130] The actions of a majority cannot bind the trust estate.[131] This rule flows from the fact that the settlor has given all the trustees the collective and generally non-delegable duty to act in furtherance of the trust. Hence, no cognisance is usually taken of a majority decision and the acts of some trustees cannot bind others.[132] The notion underlying the requirement of unanimity is that it puts in place a safeguard for beneficiaries and militates against incautious action by the trustees.[133] In *Fielding v Christie-Miller*, for example, it was unsuccessfully alleged that representations made by one trustee to a beneficiary gave rise to an estoppel that would bind the other trustees and beneficiaries.[134] Sir William Blackburne concluded that "Elementary fairness requires that before a person can be bound by the acts of another purporting to act on his behalf, that other must have his authority to bind him in the matter".[135] As with any general rule, however, there exist limited exceptions:

- the trust instrument may expressly cater for majority or unilateral decision making[136] or such action might be authorised by all the beneficiaries provided that they are of full age and capacity[137];

- under the normal rules of agency, one trustee can bind another if that trustee has actual or apparent authority so to act[138];

- the court may order that a majority decision be implemented[139];

- the trustees may authorise one trustee to receive income when it is in the interests of convenience[140]; and

- majority action is permissible in relation to charitable trusts[141] and pension trusts.[142]

The law does not differentiate between an "active" and a "passive" (or "sleeping") trustee. Each is liable by virtue of the mere assumption of the office of trustee. Hence, a trustee will maintain liability even though the management of the trust has been left to a co-trustee.

---

130 *Preedy v Dunne* [2015] EWHC 2713.
131 *Luke v South Kensington Hotel Co* (1879) 11 Ch. D. 121.
132 *Boardman v Phipps* [1967] 2 A.C. 46.
133 *Naylor v Goodhall* (1877) 47 L.J. Ch. 53.
134 [2015] EWHC 752 (Ch).
135 [2015] EWHC 752 (Ch) at [26].
136 *Re Butlin's ST* [1976] Ch. 251 (e.g. to cater for the illness or infirmity of a trustee).
137 A possibility acknowledged in *Preedy v Dunne* [2015] EWHC 2713.
138 *Fielden v Christie-Miller* [2015] EWHC 87 (Ch).
139 See *Cowan v Scargill* [1984] 2 All E.R. 750 where Megarry VC accepted that the particular inclinations of the majority could, in exceptional circumstances, be decisive as to investment policy.
140 *Townley v Sherbourne* (1634) J. Bridg. 35.
141 *Wilkinson v Malin* (1832) Cr. & J. 636.
142 Section 32 of the Pensions Act 1995.

This also entails that a trustee who disagrees with the majority decision of his brethren might be well advised to stand firm and not bow to the predominant wish. In *Bahin v Hughes*,[143] for example, three trustees held property on trust for Mrs Bahin for life with remainder to her children. One trustee made unauthorised investments and a loss arose. Mrs Bahin sued the three trustees and the "passive" trustees were held to be as liable as the "active" trustee. As Fry LJ noted, "I can see no principle in law for such a distinction".[144] As the investing trustee had acted honestly (albeit improperly), the other trustees were not even entitled to an indemnity from the "active" trustee. Fry LJ explained that if it were otherwise, "each trustee will be looking to the other or others for a right of indemnity and so neglect the performance of his duties. Such a doctrine would be against the policy of the court in relation to trusts".[145] The "passive" trustees had neglected their duty by doing nothing and could not be in a better position than an active trustee striving to fulfil his duty. Cotton LJ concluded that "All the trustees were in the wrong, and everyone is equally liable to indemnify the beneficiaries".[146] The trustees were, therefore, jointly and severally liable to Mrs Bahin.[147]

The duty to consult

13-021

Subject to modification in the trust instrument, s.11 of the Trusts of Land and Appointment of Trustees Act 1996 relates to trusts of land and requires that the trustees should, as far as is practicable, consult the beneficiaries of full age when exercising their functions.[148] In addition, and so far as is consistent with the general interest of the trust, trustees should give effect to the expressed wishes of the beneficiaries. If there is a divergence of opinion, the wishes of the majority should be followed or, if not, the approval of the court sought.[149] This duty can be excluded.

---

143 (1886) 31 Ch. D. 390.

144 (1886) 31 Ch. D. 390 at 397, 398.

145 (1886) 31 Ch. D. 390 at 398.

146 (1886) 31 Ch. D. 390 at 396.

147 In a suitable case, the Civil Liability (Contribution) Act 1978 allows one trustee who has been held liable for a breach of trust to claim a contribution from the other trustees. This is at the discretion of the court and available only when it is "just and equitable" to make such an order.

148 As it must relate to the exercise of a function of the trustee, the unilateral giving of a notice to quit by one joint tenant without consulting the other is not caught by this provision: *Notting Hill Housing Trust v Brackley* [2002] H.L.R. 10.

149 In *Cotton v Earl of Cardigan* [2014] EWCA Civ 1312, the beneficiaries unsuccessfully attempted to stop the sale of the family estate by the trustees at a certain price. The trustees bypassed these objections by obtaining the approval of the court to the sale.

The General Fiduciary Duty

What is a fiduciary?

The trustee is not the only type of fiduciary. The classic examples of a status-based fiduciary relationship are as between principal and agent, director and company,[150] partner and co-partner, solicitor and client, mortgagee and mortgagor[151] and, of obvious importance for present purposes, trustee and beneficiary.[152] The categories of fiduciary are not, however, closed and the mantle can be adopted expressly or impliedly by agreement. Such ad hoc fiduciary relationships are common, and fiduciary duties may be owed provided the circumstances justify the imposition of such duties. A fiduciary duty typically arises where one person is entrusted with authority to manage the property or affairs of another who is reliant or dependent on such exercise of powers.[153] Arden LJ considered these fact-based relationships in *Sinclair Investment Holdings SA v Versailles Trade Finance Ltd* and explained that, "in my judgment if it is alleged that a person who does not fall within the usual categories of a fiduciary relationship, such as trustee and director, made manifest his intention to enter into a fiduciary relationship—that is, to undertake to the other a duty of loyalty—there would be sufficient pleading of fiduciary relationship".[154] She emphasised that an obligation of loyalty lies at the heart of the fiduciary relationship and this entails that the fiduciary will relegate his interests and act solely in the interests of his principal.[155] Nevertheless, she noted that there was a need for the relationship to relate to an item of property. This requirement explains why a fiduciary relationship might be specific and concern only an aspect of a party's relationship with another.[156]

13-022

---

150 The fiduciary duties of company directors are set out in ss.170–180 of the Companies Act 2006. These statutory duties are, however, modelled upon the equitable duties. For example, the no profit and the no conflict rules are expressly included In the 2006 Act.

151 In *O'Kane v Rooney* [2013] N.I.Q.B. 114, the Irish court held that a receiver was effectively in the same position as a mortgagee. Consequently, a receiver had to be under a duty to act in good faith and honestly, as well as to obtain the true market value of the property.

152 Although all trustees are fiduciaries, it is thought that only express trustees owe fiduciary duties. Accordingly, constructive trustees and, possibly, resulting trustees owe no fiduciary obligations: see P. Millett, "Restitution and Constructive Trusts" (1998) 114 L.Q.R. 399.

153 *Courtwood Holdings SA v Woodley Properties Ltd* [2018] EWHC 2163 (Ch). There a company which had contracted to provide advice regarding land acquisition and planning matters owed a fiduciary duty because the other party was entirely dependent on the advice for its day-to-day decision-making.

154 [2005] EWCA Civ 722 at [20]; see *Hageman v Holmes* [2009] EWHC 50 (Ch). This may take the form of what is termed "a best efforts clause".

155 In *Al-Dowaisan v Al-Salam* [2019] EWHC 301 (Ch), however, there was no fiduciary relationship between the parties as theirs was purely a business relationship with no trust and confidence reposed in the defendants by the claimants.

156 In *John v James* [1991] F.S.R. 397, the claimant (Elton John) asserted fiduciary duties against his manager, publisher and associated companies under agreements for the exploitation of compositions, accompanied by the assignment of the copyright in the compositions. Nicholls J held that fiduciary duties did exist, even though the copyrights were assigned outright to the defendant.

Outside the established status-based categories of fiduciary relationship, therefore, the decision as to whether a fiduciary tie exists is a fact sensitive and somewhat unpredictable exercise.[157] It must be shown that one party undertook to act in relation to the property or affairs of another in circumstances that give rise to a relationship of trust and confidence.[158] In *Ross River Ltd v Waveley Commercial Ltd*,[159] a development project concerning land was categorised as a joint venture between the parties and, in these special circumstances, the duties owed were held not merely to be contractual in nature, but amounted to fiduciary obligations. Similarly, in *Vivendi SA v Richard*s Newey J concluded that so-called "shadow directors" (i.e. "persons in accordance with whose directions or instructions the directors of the company are accustomed to act") owe fiduciary duties.[160] In the employment context, "the courts typically look to the employee's contractual obligations and the circumstances of his employment, for example seniority, managerial responsibility, decision-making autonomy, independence and the vulnerability of the employer".[161]

In *Bristol & West Building Society v Mothew*, Millett LJ highlighted the defining characteristics of a personal fiduciary relationship: "The core liability has several facets. A fiduciary must act in good faith; he must not make a profit out of his trust; he must not place himself in a position where his duty and his interest may conflict; he may not act for his own benefit or the benefit of a third party without the informed consent of his principal".[162] Millett LJ did not intend this to be an exhaustive list, but felt that it offered a useful indication of the nature of fiduciary obligations. He also made the point that, as regards a fiduciary who acts for two principals with potentially conflicting interests, a breach of fiduciary duty will arise unless he is authorised to do so by the contracts under which he is employed.[163] If so authorised, the normal fiduciary duties are modified and the fiduciary must serve each as faithfully and loyally as the other. Accordingly, as Eder J acknowledged, "where an individual is employed by and owes fiduciary duties to one company in a group, he may also be held to owe duties to other companies in the same group".[164]

---

157   See *Courtwood Holdings SA v Woodley Properties* Ltd [2018] EWHC 2163 (Ch); see further J. Edelman, "When do Fiduciary Duties arise?" (2010) 126 L.Q.R. 302.

158   In its Consultation Paper entitled *Fiduciary Duties and Regulatory Rules* (1992) Law Com. No.124, para.2.4.6, the Commission stated that the test is based on, "discretion, power to act and vulnerability".

159   [2013] EWCA Civ 910; see also *R v R* [2013] EWHC 4244 (Fam) where the court restrained a husband from acting in commercial competition with the family company. As a shadow director of the company, he owed fiduciary duties, one of which was a duty to act in the interests of the company and not to act in his own separate interests.

160   [2013] EWHC 3006 (Ch) at [124].

161   Per Eder J in *Otkritie International Investment Management Ltd v Urumov* [2014] EWHC 191 (Comm) at [72].

162   [1998] Ch. 1 at 18. Accordingly, employing trust money for unauthorised purposes is a breach of fiduciary duty: *Abraaj Investment Management Ltd v Bregawn Jersey Ltd* [2010] EWHC 630 (Comm).

163   *Moody v Cox* [1971] 2 Ch. 71.

164   *Otkritie International Investment Management Ltd v Urumov* [2014] EWHC 191 (Comm) at [73].

What is a fiduciary duty and how is it breached?

In *Bristol & West Building Society v Mothew*, Millett LJ considered what was meant by the concept of a "fiduciary duty" and warned that "this branch of the law has been bedevilled by unthinking resort to verbal formulae . . . The expression 'fiduciary duty' is properly confined to those duties which are peculiar to fiduciaries and the breach of which attracts legal consequences differing from those consequences upon the breach of other duties . . . It is obvious that not every breach of duty by a fiduciary is a breach of fiduciary duty".[165] While acknowledging that there is no need for dishonesty on the part of a fiduciary, Millett LJ explained, "The various obligations of a fiduciary merely reflect different aspects of his core duties of loyalty and fidelity. Breach of fiduciary duty, therefore, connotes disloyalty and infidelity. Mere incompetence is not enough".[166] The duty to act bona fide in the interests of the trust is a subjective one. As Jonathan Parker J observed in *Regentcrest Plc v Cohen*, "The question is not whether, viewed objectively by the court, the particular act or omission which is challenged was in fact in the interests of the company; still less is the question whether the court, had it been in the position of the director at the relevant time, might have acted differently. Rather, the question is whether the director honestly believed that his act or omission was in the interests of the company. The issue is as to the director's state of mind".[167] In addition, and as Lord Browne-Wilkinson warned in *Henderson v Merrett Syndicates Ltd*:

> **"The phrase 'fiduciary duties' is a dangerous one, giving rise to a mistaken assumption that all fiduciaries owe the same duties in all circumstances. That is not the case . . . the fiduciary duties owed, for example, by an express trustee are not the same as those owed by an agent . . . in the case of an agent employed under a contract, the scope of his fiduciary duties is determined by the terms of the underlying contract".[168]**

The core proposition that emerges is that a trustee owes undivided loyalty to the beneficiary, labours under a duty of confidentiality, may not profit from the office of trusteeship and must not allow self-interest to conflict with his duty to the trust.[169] As Lord Herschell explained in

---

165 [1998] Ch.1 at 16. There a solicitor acted for both the borrower and the lender in a mortgage transaction. The solicitor was held not to be in breach of a fiduciary duty to the lender because of an inadvertent and non-conscious failure to act with care.

166 [1998] Ch.1 at 18. M. Conaglen, "The extent of fiduciary accounting and the importance of authorisation mechanisms" (2011) 70 C.L.J. 548, 556 acknowledges that "Fiduciary doctrine is based on a fundamentally cynical view of human nature".

167 [2001] 2 B.C.L.C. 80 at [120].

168 [1995] 2 A.C. 145 at 206. As Lewison J pointed out in *Fattal v Walbrook Trustees (Jersey) Ltd* [2010] EWHC 2767 (Ch) at [113], "it is the wrong approach to label someone a fiduciary and then reach for a 'one size fits all' package of supposed fiduciary duties. The contract is the starting point".

169 *Boardman v Phipps* [1967] 2 A.C. 46. As W. Bishop and D. Prentice observe, "The rules have been designed to

Bray v Ford, where a solicitor-trustee unsuccessfully claimed for costs from the trust fund in bringing a libel action for defamatory comments made against himself in his capacity as trustee of a college:

> **"It is an inflexible rule of a Court of Equity that a person in a fiduciary position . . . is not, unless otherwise expressly provided, entitled to make a profit; he is not allowed to put himself in a position where his interest and duty conflict . . . human nature being what it is, there is a danger, in such circumstances, of the person holding a fiduciary position being swayed by interest rather than by duty, and thus prejudicing those whom he was bound to protect. It has, therefore, been deemed expedient to lay down this positive rule".[170]**

The no profit and the no conflict rules are best viewed as imposing mainly distinct, but sometimes overlapping, standards that tend to be strictly applied by the courts. The decided cases have focused primarily upon instances where the trustee obtains an unauthorised remuneration,[171] acts in such a way as to benefit both himself and the trust or acts solely for his own profit.[172] Writing extra-judicially, Millett offered the following insight: "The no conflict and no profit rules are policy driven. They have nothing to do with compensating the principal for loss or with restoring to him property which belonged to him or ought to have been obtained for him . . . They are based on a pessimistic but realistic appraisal of human nature, and are directed to the avoidance of temptation".[173]

Trustees' remuneration

13-024

Until the Trustee Act 2000, the general rule (being based upon the no conflict of interest and duty principle) was that the role of trustee had to be performed without remuneration or profit.[174] The underlying notion was that a trustee might undertake unnecessary work in order to receive payment and, hence, provide a potential conflict between interest and duty. As Chitty J commented in *Re Barber*, "The difficulty would be in saying in each particular case that the

---

operate prophylactically and place the maximum deterrent on a fiduciary benefiting from his position" ("Some Legal and Economic Aspects of Fiduciary Remuneration" [1983] M.L.R. 289, 309).

170 [1896] A.C. 44 at 51, 52.

171 As in *Psycare Ltd v Mundy* unreported 11 December 2013, where a company director unlawfully misappropriated over £600,000 of company funds pursuant to a fictitious charging clause.

172 See *Ultraframe (UK) Ltd v Fielding* [2006] F.S.R. 17.

173 P. Millett, "Bribes and Secret Commissions Again" (2012) 71(3) C.L.J. 583, 590. As M. Conaglen, "The Extent of Fiduciary Accounting and the Importance of Authorisation Mechanisms" (2011) 70 C.L.J. 548, 560 puts it, "It is that risk that is the target at which fiduciary doctrine is aimed—not the idea that there is always harm where there is a conflict between duty and interest".

174 *Robinson v Pett* (1734) 3 P. Wms. 249.

business was not required to be done".[175] It is also thought that the professional services of an individual trustee are difficult to value and that, in any event, a person can always decline to accept the role of trustee. The argument runs that, if the trustee voluntarily accepts the office, then he cannot complain if he is not paid for his services.[176] Traditionally, the onus was upon the trustee to show that there was an express charging clause[177] or some other legal validation for remuneration.[178] Prior to the 2000 Act, justification might come from a variety of sources.

By virtue of contract

13-025

This would operate when the trustee has entered into a contract allowing payment directly with all the beneficiaries when all are of full age and capacity.[179] This need for unanimity reduces the potential for exploitation and unfairness. The consideration for this contract can be the performance by the trustee of existing or future services (but not past services).[180] Of course, the contract can be set aside if it is induced either by undue influence, misrepresentation or duress.[181] Indeed, this occurred in *O'Sullivan v Management Agency & Music Ltd*[182] where a contract between a singer (the once famous Gilbert O'Sullivan) and his agent was avoided on the ground of undue influence.

By order of the court

13-026

Under the inherent jurisdiction to ensure the adequate administration of the trust, the court might award payment to a trustee. This will occur only when the services of the trustee are regarded as being of exceptional benefit to the trust.[183] As Fox LJ acknowledged in *Re Duke of Norfolk's Settlement Trusts*:

> **"In exercising that jurisdiction the court has to balance two influences which are to some extent in conflict. The first is that the office**

---

175 (1887) 34 Ch. D. 77 at 81. This case concerned the profit costs of a solicitor-trustee.
176 In *Interactive Technology Corp Ltd v Ferster* [2018] EWCA Civ 1594, a former director was in breach of his fiduciary duty by causing the company to pay him substantial, unauthorised remuneration.
177 For example, in *Robinson v Pett* (1734) 3 P. Wms. 249 the executors were allowed to charge £100 for their services; see also, *Ellison v Airey* (1748) 1 Ves. Sen. 111.
178 *Gavriel v Davis* [2019] EWHC 2446 (Ch) makes clear that, subject to exceptions, in the absence of a charging clause a trustee is not entitled to be remunerated other than to be reimbursed out of pocket expenses.
179 *Ayliffe v Murray* (1740) 2 Atk. 58.
180 *Williams v Roffey Brothers & Nicholls (Contractors) Ltd* [1990] 1 All E.R. 512.
181 *Stilk v Myrick* (1809) 2 Camp. 317.
182 [1985] 3 All E.R. 351.
183 *Re Barbour's Settlement* [1974] 1 All E.R. 1188, where a bank's claim for an allowance failed as there was no benefit to the beneficiaries upon which it could be justified.

> of trustee is, as such, gratuitous; the court will accordingly be careful to protect the interests of the beneficiaries against claims by the trustees. The second is that it is of great importance to the beneficiaries that the trust should be well administered".[184]

In *Foster v Spencer*,[185] for example, two trustees sought remuneration for past and future services designed to enhance greatly the development value of the trust property (a cricket ground). Paul Baker QC sitting in the High Court allowed payment for the past services (but not the proposed future services because they did not call for any specific expertise). Payments for past services were justified on the basis that otherwise the beneficiaries would be unjustly enriched. Similarly, in *Perotti v Watson* a solicitor undertook the administration of an estate that in time became unexpectedly complex.[186] Although the services provided were not always of a high standard, the Court of Appeal allowed the solicitor to claim fees, albeit scaled down to 75 per cent to reflect the varying quality of those services. In *Gavriel v Davis*, however, the lay trustee unsuccessfully sought to charge £27,300 for services provided.[187] The court emphasised that its power was only to be exercised having regard to all aspects of the case including a trustee's honesty and the nature of the evidence adduced.

13-027

Even when a charging clause has been inserted into the trust instrument, the court can employ its inherent powers to vary or increase the amount that can be charged. For example, in *Re Duke of Norfolk's Settlement Trusts*,[188] a trust corporation accepted the administration of the trust for a low annual fee. As trustee, it subsequently became involved in an extensive redevelopment project and was allowed an increase in remuneration because the duties became unexpectedly onerous. As Fox LJ reasoned, "if the court has jurisdiction . . . upon the application of a trustee to authorise remuneration though no such power exists in the trust instrument, there is no reason why the court should not have the power to increase the remuneration given by the instrument".[189] In the *O'Sullivan* case, and even though the contract was set aside, the court allowed the agent to recover some payment in acknowledgement of his role in advancing his client's career.[190] An application for approval of remuneration was, however, rejected in *Guinness Plc v Saunders*.[191] The House of Lords emphasised that payment will not be permitted in circumstances where there is a possible conflict between personal interest and fiduciary duty. There a

---

184 [1982] Ch. 61 at 79; see also *Brudenell-Bruce v Moore* [2014] EWHC 3679 (Ch) where the High Court emphasised that this jurisdiction be exercised sparingly and only in exceptional circumstances.

185 [1996] 2 All E.R. 672.

186 [2001] EWCA Civ 116.

187 [2019] EWHC 2446 (Ch).

188 [1982] Ch. 61.

189 [1982] Ch. 61 at 78. In *Re Portman Estate* [2015] EWHC 536 (Ch), the payment provision in the trust deed was varied to ensure that each trustee was paid the same for the same work. The efficient administration of the trust was the overriding principle for altering the trustee remuneration clause.

190 It appears that the court's jurisdiction is employed more readily when it is a variation style case as opposed to when there is no provision whatsoever for payment: *Re Portman Estate* [2016] EWHC 536 (Ch).

191 [1990] 1 All E.R. 652.

director of one company unsuccessfully claimed £5.2 million for advice and services provided in facilitating the takeover of another company. His personal interests were in stark conflict with his fiduciary duty as a director. Lord Goff spoke of limiting the jurisdiction to cases, "where it cannot have the effect of encouraging trustees in any way to put themselves in a position where their interests conflict with their duties as trustees".[192] He declined, however, to comment upon whether a director could claim an equitable allowance if the director was not also a trustee.

Special treatment of solicitors' profit costs in litigation work

13-028

Although a fiduciary relationship would prevent a solicitor-trustee from getting ordinary profit costs of non-litigious legal business done by him as solicitor,[193] a solicitor-trustee's costs of litigation are the subject of special treatment. According to the oft-criticised and curious rule in *Cradock v Piper*,[194] a solicitor-trustee is entitled to profit costs (i.e. solicitors' charges that involve a profit element) in litigation where he acts as solicitor on behalf of himself and a co-trustee or beneficiary in relation to trust affairs.[195] This is provided that the costs are no more than they would have been had he acted for the co-trustee alone (i.e. no additional expense has been incurred by his acting for himself).[196] Stebbings explains that, "the two characters of trustee and solicitor would remain distinct, and there could be no conflict between duty and interest. If no conflict existed, there would be no reason for prohibiting remuneration for professional work done".[197] Although the reasoning underlying this distinction is somewhat unclear, the rule does not apply when a solicitor-trustee employs his firm to do non-litigious work.[198] It is thought that this distinction is to do with the difficulties of costing work that is not subject to judicial scrutiny.[199] Upjohn J later described the *Cradock* rule as "exceptional and anomalous and not to be extended . . .".[200]

Overseas property

13-029

If the trust property is located abroad, and the law of the country where it is situated permits the remuneration of trustees, it appears that the trustees are entitled to keep any payments

---

192 [1990] 1 All E.R. 652 at 667.
193 *Re R Gertzenstein Ltd* [1937] Ch 115.
194 (1850) 1 Mac. & G. 664. This overruled the contrary authority of *Bainbrigge v Blair* (1845) 8 Beav. 588.
195 The rule was reaffirmed in *Broughton v Broughton* (1854) 5 De G.M. & G. 160; see generally, C. Stebbings, "The Rule in *Cradock v Piper* (1850): Exception or Principle?" (1998) 19(3) J. Leg. Hist. 189.
196 *Re Worthington* [1954] 1 All E.R. 677.
197 C. Stebbings, "The Rule in *Cradock v Piper*" (1998) 19(3) J. Leg. Hist. 189, 195.
198 See *Re Corsellis* (1887) 34 Ch. D. 675 where the solicitor's firm was unable to recover costs for work done in passing receivers' accounts and granting leases. It is apparently irrelevant as to whether any profits made by the firm are actually going into the pocket of the trustee: *Re Hill* [1934] Ch. 623.
199 See *Broughton v Broughton* (1854) 5 De G.M. & G. 160.
200 *Re Worthington* [1954] 1 All E.R. 677 at 679.

made. In *Re Northcote's WT*,[201] a testator left property both in England and the United States. The executor was obliged to obtain probate in the United States relating to the assets located there. Harman J held that the executor could charge for those costs because there was no conflict of interest and duty.

Statutory authority

13-030
Remuneration is payable in those circumstances where Parliament has authorised its payment, for example, on the appointment by the court of a trust corporation (under s.42 of the Trustee Act 1925), on the appointment of a judicial trustee (under s.1(5) of the Judicial Trustees Act 1896) and on the appointment of the public trustee (under s.9 of the Public Trustee Act 1906).

With the emergence of professional trustees (such as banks, solicitors and accountants), the need for payment became more pronounced and the existing provisions were revealed as woefully inadequate. The Law Reform Committee in its 1982 Report concerning trustees' powers and duties highlighted such defects.[202] As Parry commented in 1984, "It is time to recognise that the changed social and economic circumstances in which trusts today operate call for increasing professionalism on the part of trustees. If a professional is appointed to undertake this function . . . he should be entitled to reasonable remuneration for his services".[203] Of course, if the appointment of a professional trustee was anticipated by the settlor, a well-drafted charging clause could easily be included in the trust instrument. Nevertheless, in cases of uncertainty or ambiguity, the courts construe such clauses strictly. In *Re Chalinder & Herington*,[204] a clause which allowed the solicitor-trustee to claim for "all professional and other charges for his time and trouble" was held not to cover costs incurred in non-professional work.

13-031
Not surprisingly, difficulties arise when no express facility is reserved. This omission would effectively prevent a professional trustee from acting as an original or a replacement trustee. The reason is that when a trustee receives unauthorised remuneration, he is liable to account to the trust and the money will be held by him on constructive trust. This was the problem that Pt V of the Trustee Act 2000 sought to address.[205] Remuneration is specifically catered for in ss.28–29 of the 2000 Act and these provisions operate in two situations.

■ Section 28 operates when there is an express charging clause in the trust deed. As regards trust corporations or trustees acting in "a professional capacity",[206] s.28 ena-

---

201 [1949] 1 All E.R. 442.
202 Law Reform Committee 23rd Report, *The Powers and Duties of Trustees* (1982) Cmnd.8733.
203 N.B.M. Parry, "Remuneration of Trustees" [1984] Conv. 275, 285.
204 [1907] 1 Ch. 58.
205 This does not apply fully to charitable trusts. The appropriate Secretary of State has the power to issue regulations for the provision of remuneration to such trustees: s.30.
206 For these purposes, this requires the trustee to act in the course of a profession or a business that is connected with the management or administration of trusts: s.28(5).

bles these trustees to claim remuneration under such a clause. This rule relaxes the strict construction previously given to charging clauses and applies even if a lay trustee could have effectively provided those services.[207] The trustee will, however, be liable to account for any charges made that are unreasonable or excessive.[208] Although s.28 applies to trusts whenever created, it only covers services provided after the commencement date of the 2000 Act (1 February 2000). Section 28 can be excluded in the trust instrument.[209]

■ Section 29 only operates in relation to certain trustees and only when there is no express provision made for remuneration.[210] Subsections (1)–(2) provide that a trust corporation and trustees (other than sole trustees) who act in a professional capacity for a private trust are entitled to receive "reasonable remuneration". A "reasonable remuneration" means such sums as are reasonable in the circumstances for the provision of those services by the trustees to or on behalf of the trust.[211] Whereas a trust corporation is automatically entitled to such remuneration, other trustees who act in a professional capacity are entitled to receive reasonable remuneration only with the written agreement of all other trustees. It is implicit, moreover, that the trustee's firm is entitled to receive reasonable remuneration for services provided by the firm if the other trustees agree in writing that the trustee may be remunerated.[212] A professional trustee is not necessarily entitled to charge by reference to his normal or standard charging rates.[213] Instead, the court must have regard to the nature and the value of the services performed and to the propriety, reasonableness and proportionality of using the services of the level of fee earner who is providing them. This is because, "To hold otherwise would be inconsistent with the trustee's duty to avoid any conflict between his duties to the trust and his personal interests".[214] The charges are clearly open to challenge by the trust for as Deputy Judge Hodge QC explained *Pullan v Wilson*, "a beneficiary is entitled to have the charges made by a professional trustee investigated, and the trustee will be liable to account for any charges made insofar as they are unreasonable or excessive. This is in accordance with the principle in equity

---

207 Section 28(2); cf. the former rule in *Re Chapple* (1884) 27 Ch. D. 584 where a solicitor-trustee was not allowed to claim for services of a non-professional character.

208 In *Pullan v Wilson* [2014] EWHC 126 (Ch), for example, the court applied a 7.5 per cent discount for excess administration and other non-productive time.

209 Section 28(1).

210 Section 29(5); see *Pullan v Wilson* [2014] EWHC 126 (Ch).

211 Section 29(3). In *Pullan v Wilson* [2014] EWHC 126 (Ch), Deputy Judge Hodge QC emphasised that the trustee must be prepared to document each item of charges and expenditure and presumptions may be made against him if he has not kept proper records.

212 *Pullan v Wilson* [2014] EWHC 126 (Ch).

213 As Deputy Judge Hodge QC acknowledged in *Pullan v Wilson* [2014] EWHC 126 (Ch) at [55], "To hold otherwise would be to deprive a court of equity of any effective control over a trustee's remuneration".

214 Per Deputy Judge Hodge QC in *Pullan v Wilson* [2014] EWHC 126 (Ch) at [56].

for the taking into account against a fiduciary to ensure the due administration of a fund which he holds".[215]

As with s.28, this provision applies to trusts whenever created[216] and to services that could otherwise have been provided by a lay trustee.[217] Despite the improvements offered by s.29, it remains best practice for the settlor to insert a comprehensive charging clause in the trust deed or to specify clearly what the trustee may charge in the letter of engagement. This should, at the least, deter disputes as to what amounts to a fair and reasonable hourly rate.

Director's fees

13-032

Often a trustee will obtain remuneration as a director of a company connected with the trust. As shown in *Re Macadam*,[218] when the directorship was acquired because of his position as a trustee, the trustee is accountable to the trust for fees received. This rule does not apply, however, when the directorship was obtained independently of the trust. In *Re Gee*,[219] for example, the trustee became a director without any reliance upon trust votes and was able to retain the remuneration received. Similarly, as in *Re Dover Coalfield Extension Ltd*,[220] payments may be kept when the directorship was obtained before assuming the office of trustee. The rule, therefore, focuses upon preventing a serving trustee becoming a director and claiming a profit from acting as such. In that scenario, the possibility of self-advancement at the expense of the better interests of the trust is evident. The will or settlement may, however, authorise the trustee to keep any remuneration obtained from a directorship whenever obtained.[221] As Jenkins LJ admitted in *Re Llewellin's Will Trusts*, "there is no rule of equity which says that a testator, if so minded, may not provide that the trustees can hold salaried offices in companies which the testator's estate controls and receive the emoluments attached to those offices without liability to account . . . indeed as a matter of business it is often a very sensible provision to make".[222] Such was illustrated in *Deir v Al Athel*[223] where a director acted on the strength of an oral contract with the settlor and was able to claim and retain director's fees under the terms of that agreement.

---

215 [2014] EWHC 126 (Ch) at [26].
216 Trustee Act 2000 s.33(1).
217 Trustee Act 2000 s.29(4).
218 [1946] Ch. 73.
219 [1948] Ch. 284.
220 [1908] 1 Ch. 65.
221 *Pullan v Wilson* [2014] EWHC 126 (Ch).
222 [1949] Ch. 225 at 227.
223 [2011] EWHC 354 (QB).

Out-of-pocket expenses

13-033

Not surprisingly, a trustee is entitled to be reimbursed for out-of-pocket expenses properly incurred while acting for the trust.[224] The design is to ensure that trustees are not out of pocket when acting on behalf of the trust and that the trust is efficiently and properly administered. Conversely, no indemnity claim can be made for expenses that are unreasonably and improperly incurred or when the trustee is clearly acting on her own behalf and not that of the trust.[225] Misconduct might deprive a trustee of an indemnity[226] and this might also occur when a trustee is removed on grounds of conflict of interest.[227] Accordingly, in *Wood v Gorbunova*[228] Morgan J disallowed 15 per cent of the costs claimed by court-appointed receivers because they had acted unwisely in applying without notice for the delivery-up of documents from the deceased's former solicitors. The trustee is not, moreover, able to claim interest in respect of any outlay.[229] Reimbursement extends both to money spent and liabilities to pay that may arise. Any expenses claimed, however, must be reasonable and appropriate in the circumstances.[230] Hence, in *Malcom v O'Callaghan*[231] the trustee's claim for expenses for frequent trips to Paris on trust business was disallowed because his presence there was not necessary. Mundane examples of recoverable expenditure include the payment of insurance premiums, fees paid to agents and money spent on repairs to trust property. A less obvious scenario arose in *Benett v Wyndham*[232] where a trustee employed woodcutters to topple some trees on the trust land. Due to their negligence, a branch fell on a passing stranger causing injury. The trustee, as legal owner of the land, was successfully sued and had to compensate the victim. The trustee was able to claim the cost of the damages paid from the trust fund.

A trustee will be allowed his litigation costs if all the beneficiaries approve the action or the High Court grants leave to sue or to defend.[233] The latter is known as a "*Beddoe* Order" and derives its name from the decision of the Court of Appeal in *Re Beddoe*.[234] An application

---

224 Section 31(1) of the Trustee Act 2000. For example, this would include legal costs incurred by a trustee acting on behalf of the trust: *Close Trustees (Switzerland) SA v Vildosola* [2008] EWHC 1267 (Ch).

225 *London Capital & Finance Plc (in Administration) v Global Security Trustees Ltd* [2020] EWHC 597 (Ch)

226 *Price v Saundry* [2019] EWCA Civ 2261. This concerned costs incurred by the trustee and awarded against her in litigation. There was misconduct and breaches of trust of a nature that warranted the removal of the trustee's indemnity.

227 *London Capital & Finance Plc (in Administration) v Global Security Trustees Ltd* [2020] EWHC 597 (Ch).

228 [2013] EWHC 1935 (Ch).

229 *Foster v Spencer* [1996] 2 All E.R. 672. There the trustees were allowed to recover for business class flights to Malaysia as a reasonable expense.

230 In *Re Chapman* (1895) 72 L.T. 66, the trustee incurred unnecessary expenditure in establishing whether or not a life tenant was dead or alive. As he saw risk when none existed and had acted unreasonably, the trustee was unable to claim back the expenses incurred.

231 (1835) 3 Myl. & Cr. 52.

232 (1862) 4 De G.F. & J. 259.

233 See CPR r.46.3 . The trustee has an equitable lien (or right of retention) over trust assets as a means of discharging these potential liabilities: *Jennings v Mather* [1905] 1 K.B. 108.

234 [1893] 1 Ch. 547.

for a *Beddoe* Order should be made in separate preliminary proceedings.[235] Trustees making a *Beddoe* application are essentially asking the court to adjudge that their participation in the litigation is neither unreasonable nor for the benefit of anyone other than the fund.[236] For example, directions are particularly appropriate when the defendant to possible proceedings is a beneficiary and other beneficiaries have a different interest in their outcome[237] or where the trustees seek to appeal to the Supreme Court and wish to recover the costs of doing so.[238]

Where a *Beddoe* Order is not sought, the trustee will obtain costs only if the action was properly brought or defended for the benefit of the trust estate.[239] In other words, the trustee will be shielded where a *Beddoe* Order would have been made had the trustee applied for it.[240] As in *Beddoe*, trustees who act without the approval of the beneficiaries or the court run the risk that they may have to pay their own (and possibly also the other party's) costs themselves.[241] In contemporary conditions it is no longer possible for trustees to obtain guidance from the court inexpensively. Hence, the normal rule is that, absent improper conduct,[242] the costs of the trustee will be indemnified from trust funds.[243] The failure to apply for a *Beddoe* Order does not amount to a breach of trust.[244]

Matters are more complex when, as in *Blades v Isaac*,[245] it is a beneficiary who is bringing an action against the trustees. The beneficiary succeeded in her claim against the defendants as to disclosure of information and it would normally follow that the trustees, as the unsuccessful parties, would be ordered to pay the claimant's costs. The issue then became whether the trustees would be entitled to an indemnity from the trust fund for those costs properly incurred.[246] It was determined that, absent misconduct, a trustee who is accused of breach of duty not causing loss to the trust fund was prima facie entitled to the indemnity, whether he

---

235 *Alsop v Neary* [1995] 1 All E.R. 431.
236 *Pettigrew v Edwards* [2017] EWHC 8 (Ch). There the court said that the application was unlikely to serve any useful purpose in claims brought against the trustees for breach of trust because the court was unlikely to be able to judge the strength of the trustees' defence at such an early stage.
237 *Davies v Watkins* [2012] EWCA Civ 1570; *Abdulla v Abdulla* [2013] EWHC 4281 (Ch).
238 *Airways Pension Scheme Trustee Ltd v Fielder* [2019] EWHC 29 (Ch)
239 *Holding & Management Ltd v Property Holding & Investment Trusts Plc* [1990] 1 All E.R. 938.
240 *McDonald v Horn* [1994] P.L.R. 33. The burden lies on the trustee to show that the costs were properly incurred.
241 See *Singh v Bhasin, The Times*, 21 August 1998, where the trustee acted unreasonably in defending an action and could not, therefore, claim the costs of that litigation from the trust.
242 For example, in *Three Professional Trustees v Infant Prospective Beneficiary* [2007] EWHC 1922 (Ch) it was acknowledged that the protection afforded by a *Beddoe* order could be weakened or undone if full disclosure of all relevant matters was not made by the applicant trustee.
243 *Davies v Watkins* [2012] EWCA Civ 1570. This is a particular example of the general proposition as to indemnity as set out in s.31(1) of the Trustee Act 2000. *Beddoe* orders and indeed indemnity clauses, however, are only worth having as long as the person or the fund providing the indemnity can afford to pay. In *Davies*, the protection afforded was illusory.
244 *Bonham v Blake Lapthorn Linnel* [2006] EWHC 2513 (Ch). The order is designed merely to protect the trustee.
245 [2016] EWHC 601 (Ch).
246 As Master Matthews observed at [72], "If so, then the Claimant would effectively be obtaining her costs out of the trust fund. Thus, since she or her family are the main beneficiaries of the trust, she would be in substance paying for the litigation which she won".

is found to be in breach of duty or not. The trustees had not acted unreasonably in defending or conducting the proceedings. In these circumstances, it would be unfair to deprive them of their indemnity.

Purchase of trust property

Traditionally, the prevention of a trustee from purchasing trust property was classified as merely one aspect of the trustee's duty not to profit from his position. The modern approach, however, is to view this type of purchase as being the subject of two distinct rules, namely, the "self-dealing" rule and the "insider dealing" rule (sometimes known also as the "fair dealing" rule).[247] As Megarry J explained, "there are two rules: the consequences are different, and the property and the transactions which invoke the rules are different. I see no merit in attempting a forced union which has to be expressed in terms of disunity".[248] The former rule caters for purchases by a trustee of property that is legally owned by the trustees as a body.[249] The latter rule deals with the situation where a trustee buys out a beneficiary's equitable interest under the trust. It is necessary to look at these rules in some detail.

13-034

The self-dealing rule

Where a trustee purchases trust property, for example he buys the freehold or takes a lease of trust land,[250] the beneficiaries can subsequently set the transaction aside (i.e. it is voidable at the behest of the beneficiaries).[251] The notion is that the trustee should not profit from his office and it reflects the possibility that the trustee might not give the best price obtainable.[252] This self-dealing rule applies to all types of property and the transaction can be set aside as against the trustee as well as against any purchaser from the trustee who has notice of the breach of trust.[253] The rule will be invoked when, for example, a co-trustee buys trust property from himself and the other trustees.[254] Accordingly, in *Caldicott v Richards*[255] a sale of shares

13-035

247 See *Tito v Waddell (No.2)* [1977] Ch. 106 at 240, 247–249; see further, M. Conaglen, "A Re-Appraisal of the Fiduciary Self-Dealing and Fair-Dealing Rules" (2006) 64 C.L.J. 366.
248 [1977] Ch. 106 at 240.
249 The rule applies also to dispositive powers which the trustees, therefore, cannot exercise in their own favour: *Rafferty v Philp* [2011] EWHC 709 (Ch).
250 *Attorney General v Earl of Clarendon* (1810) 17 Ves. 491.
251 *Campbell v Walker* (1800) 5 Ves. 678.
252 The self-dealing rule cannot apply when there is no trust relationship with the property: *Hollis v Rolfe* [2008] EWHC 1747 (Ch).
253 *Aberdeen Town Council v Aberdeen University* (1877) 2 App. Cas. 544.
254 In *Brudenell-Bruce v Moore* [2012] EWHC 1024 (Ch), for example, Newey J set aside the purchase by a trustee of a lease from the trust.
255 [2020] EWHC 767 (Ch).

in a family company held under a discretionary trust to one of the trustees (who was also a beneficiary) was rescinded. The trustees had not provided a full and frank disclosure and, hence, the beneficiaries had not given their fully informed consent to the transaction. Matters are, understandably, different when it is a sole trustee who purports to sell. In this instance, the transaction is necessarily void ab initio.[256] The trustee cannot intelligibly be said to buy property from himself.[257]

The self-dealing rule gives way when the purchase is authorised by Parliament,[258] the trust instrument or all the beneficiaries. In *Sargeant v National Westminster Bank Plc*, the sale of certain farms to the trustees was expressly permitted by the settlor and the transactions were upheld.[259] As Nourse LJ admitted, "the rule is expressed by saying that a trustee must not put himself in a position where his interest and duty conflict. But to express it that way is to acknowledge that if he is put there, not by himself, but by the testator or settlor under whose dispositions his trust arises, the rule does not apply".[260]

13-036

A transaction is tainted by the self-dealing rule even in the absence of unfairness or sharp practice[261] and regardless of whether or not the trustee makes a profit.[262] The rule applies even if the trustee bought the property at public auction.[263] The operation of the rule is well illustrated in *Wright v Morgan*[264] where the trustee took an assignment of an option to purchase trust property (land and the stock thereon) at a valuation to be provided by another trustee. The Privy Council held that, despite the air of an independent valuation, there was still a conflict of interest and duty.

As the underlying ethos is that the trustee's interests must not collide with his fiduciary duty, the rule has no application if the contract to sell or the sale itself occurred before assuming the role of trustee.[265] Similarly, a person who at the outset disclaims the role of trustee may make an effective purchase[266] and it appears that a bare trustee with no active duties to carry out also falls outside the scope of the rule.[267] In *Holder v Holder*,[268] a son was appointed

---

256 *Franks v Bollans* (1868) 3 Ch. App. 717.
257 See *Rye v Rye* [1962] A.C. 496.
258 For example, s.68 of the Settled Land Act 1925 enables the tenant for life to purchase trust property.
259 (1990) 61 P. & C.R. 518.
260 (1990) 61 P. & C.R. 518 at 519.
261 *Dyson v Lum* (1866) 14 L.T. 588; see also *Breitenfeld UK Ltd v Harrison* [2015] EWHC 399 (Ch) at [70] where Norris J admitted that "The honesty of the fiduciary is irrelevant to the question whether a breach of this fiduciary duty has occurred, so that a breach may be attended by perfect 'good faith' on the part of the fiduciary . . .".
262 *Ex p. Lacey* (1802) 6 Ves. Jr. 62.
263 *Lister v Lister* (1802) 6 Ves. 631.
264 [1926] A.C. 788.
265 *Vyse v Foster* (1874) L.R. 7 H.L. 318. In *Re Mulholland's Will Trusts* [1949] 1 All E.R. 460, an option to purchase land was granted to a bank before it assumed the role of trustee. The bank was still entitled to exercise the option.
266 *Stacey v Elph* (1833) 1 My. & K. 195.
267 *Parkes v White* (1805) 11 Ves. Jr. 209.
268 [1968] 1 All E.R. 665.

as one of the executors under his father's will. He attempted to renounce his executorship and announced his intention to buy part of the estate (a farm) at public auction. Although he acquired the farm at a fair price, a beneficiary under the will sought to have the sale set aside. The Court of Appeal could see no sufficient conflict of interest and duty to activate the rule against self-dealing and upheld the transaction. It was important that the son had never become actively involved in the administration of his father's estate, had not acquired any special knowledge in his capacity as executor and had exerted no pressure on the other executors as to the sale or the timing of sale.[269]

13-037

Not surprisingly, the self-dealing rule cannot be sidestepped simply by the trustee retiring in order to purchase trust property.[270] The rule will cease to apply, however, after a long period of retirement.[271] The rule cannot be circumvented by the trustee employing a nominee company to act on his behalf,[272] selling to his children,[273] selling to his wife,[274] transferring the property into the name of a partnership between the trustee and others[275] or acting as the agent for a third party.[276] In *Campbell v Walker*,[277] an apparent conflict emerged when the trustee attempted to sell to a party who was, in reality, a trustee for the selling trustee. The rule bites also when the trustee sells to a business partner, but only when there is some benefit (direct or indirect) for the trustee.[278] In contrast, where the trust property is sold bona fide to a third party, there is nothing to prevent a trustee from subsequently purchasing the property from the new owner.[279]

The advisable course for a trustee who seeks to purchase trust property from his co-trustees is to apply to court for approval of the sale. Such leave will be given when the transaction is to the manifest advantage of the beneficiaries[280] and usually only with the consent of the beneficiaries.[281] It is, therefore, recommended that, in all cases, the purchasing trustee should obtain the beneficiaries' informed consent to the proposed transaction.[282] It is also important to note the affect that an exclusion clause may have on the personal liability of a self-dealing trustee. In *Caldicott v Richards*, the exclusion clause did not prevent the transaction from being

---

269 This was, as Harman LJ concluded at 392, "a case where the reasons behind the rule do not exist . . .".
270 *Holder v Holder* [1968] 1 All E.R. 665.
271 In *Re Boles & British Land Co's Contract* [1902] 1 Ch. 244, Buckley J held that a trustee who had retired 12 years before the purchase was able to buy trust property as there was no evidence that there was any longer a potential conflict of interest and duty.
272 *Silkstone & Haigh Moore Coal Co v Edey* [1900] 1 Ch. 167.
273 *Gregory v Gregory* (1815) G. Coop. 201.
274 *Ferraby v Hobson* (1847) 2 Ph. 255.
275 *Re Thompson's Settlement* [1986] Ch. 99. There the trustees granted a lease to a company and partnership of which the trustees were directors and partners. This was a clear breach of the self-dealing rule.
276 *Ex p. Bennett* (1805) 10 Ves. Jr. 381.
277 (1800) 5 Ves. Jr. 678.
278 *Ex p. Moore* (1881) 45 L.T. 558.
279 See *Whitcomb v Minchin* (1820) 5 Madd. 91.
280 *Farmer v Dean* (1863) 32 Beav. 327.
281 *Tennant v Trenchard* (1869) 4 Ch. App. 537.
282 *Randall v Errington* (1805) 10 Ves. 423.

set aside, but it did prevent a claim for equitable compensation, the repayment of dividends received and an account for profits.[283]

The insider dealing (fair dealing) rule

13-038

A different approach is adopted when the trustee or other fiduciary intends to purchase the equitable interest of a beneficiary, for example when the trustee wishes to buy out the beneficiary's interest in land. Whereas the self-dealing rule is based upon the relationship between the parties, the fiduciary rule against insider dealing is framed around the conduct of the trustee. In order for the sale to be effective, the transaction must be fair and honest.[284] This means that the consideration provided must be adequate,[285] there must be no undue influence exerted by the trustee and the beneficiary must be given full and accurate information about the extent of the beneficial interest to be bought.[286] As Megarry J observed in *Tito v Waddell (No.2)*, "the fair dealing rule is essentially a rule of equity that certain persons (including trustees) are subject to certain consequences if they carry through certain transactions without, where appropriate, complying with certain requirements".[287]

The purchase of a minor's interest will, for obvious reasons, usually fall foul of the fair dealing rule.[288] It is also a relevant factor if it is the beneficiary who initiates the sale. In *Coles v Trecothick*,[289] for example, the sale was upheld in circumstances where the beneficiary took control of the sale by auction. The beneficiary had chosen both the venue and the auctioneer and, moreover, was content with the price obtained on the sale. As Lord Eldon explained, a trustee may buy from a beneficiary provided that, "there is a distinct and clear contract, ascertained to be such after a jealous and scrupulous examination of all the circumstances, proving that the *cestui que trust* [the beneficiary] intended the trustee should buy; and there is no fraud, no concealment, no advantage taken, by the trustee of information acquired by him in the character of trustee".[290] In *Morse v Royal*,[291] an ex-army officer sold his interest to the trustee. There was no concealment or deceit by the trustee. When the property went up in price, the beneficiary, who had pressed the trustee to buy the property, regretted the sale and sought to have it set aside. The beneficiary was unsuccessful in his action.

---

283 [2020] EWHC 767 (Ch).

284 The onus of proof is upon the trustee: *Sharma v Farlam Ltd* [2009] EWHC 1622 (Ch).

285 *Dougan v MacPherson* [1902] A.C. 197.

286 *Randall v Etherington* (1805) 10 Ves. 427; see further M. Conaglen, "A Re-appraisal of the Fiduciary Self-dealing and Fair-dealing Rules" (2006) 64 C.L.J. 366.

287 [1977] Ch. 106. For example, the rule does not apply when the sale is by an independent person acting in pursuance to a court order: *Bank of Scotland v Neath Port Talbot County BC* [2008] B.C.C. 376.

288 See *Sanderson v Walker* (1807) 13 Ves. 601.

289 (1804) 9 Ves. 234.

290 (1804) 9 Ves. 234 at 247.

291 (1806) 12 Ves. 355.

In contrast, in *Dougan v Macpherson*[292] two brothers were beneficiaries under a trust. One brother was also a trustee. The trustee purchased his brother's beneficial interest without disclosing to him a valuation report of the trust estate. The beneficial share was worth much more than the trustee paid for it. The transaction here was set aside. As the Earl of Halsbury LC concluded, "it is to my mind an absolute novelty to hear it gravely argued that such a transaction as that can stand".[293] Lord Ashbourne observed, "It was the absolute and obvious duty of the defender in this case, if he thought he could maintain the transaction upon which he had entered, to have present in his mind the distinct duty which he owed to his brother".[294]

Incidental profit

In light of the rule that a trustee may not put himself in a position where his interest and duty conflict, the derivation of a direct profit by a trustee clearly contravenes the fiduciary relationship existing with the beneficiaries. Unless authorised by the trust instrument, the beneficiaries, the court or Parliament, a trustee is under a strict duty to account for any profits made by exploiting trust property or the office of trustee. For example, in *Williams v Barton*[295] the trustee worked as a clerk to a stockbroker. His salary was partly commission based. He instructed the stockbroker to act on behalf of the trust and was then liable to account for the commission he earned in respect of that business. As Russell J acknowledged, "the case falls within the mischief which is sought to be prevented . . . The case is clearly one where his duty as trustee and his interest in an increased remuneration are in direct conflict".[296] The profit arose out of and by reason of his trusteeship. More recently, in *Burns v The Financial Conduct Authority*[297] the fiduciary had misused her position as a non-executive director to seek to advance her own commercial interests by entering a commission arrangement and had failed to disclose conflicts of interest.

In modern times, the means by which a trustee can make a direct profit from his position are various. It is, therefore, convenient to categorise the common scenarios within which a conflict of interest and duty may potentially arise.

Sale of property to the trust

A sale by the trustee of property to the trust is apt to be set aside by the beneficiaries in circumstances where the trustee does not fully disclose the nature of his interest in the property sold.

---

292 [1902] A.C. 197.
293 [1902] A.C. 197 at 202.
294 [1902] A.C. 197 at 203, 204.
295 [1927] 2 Ch. 9.
296 [1927] 2 Ch. 9 at 12.
297 [2017] EWCA Civ 2140.

The honesty of the trustee and the fairness of the consideration paid are irrelevant factors.[298] Indeed, a sale may be set aside even if it was negotiated prior to the vendor assuming the role of trustee. The same principle operates where the trustee runs a business that trades with a business carried out by the trust.

Competing with the trust

13-042

The general rule is that a trustee or other fiduciary may not enter into business competition with the trust.[299] This rule gives way if the business is authorised by the trust, the beneficiaries or the shareholders as appropriate.[300] The basic premise is that the duty cannot impose an unreasonable restraint on the ability of an ex-fiduciary to earn a living.[301] In *Re Thomson*,[302] the trustee claimed the right to carry on a yacht broker's business in the same town as a similar business operated by the trust. The trustee's commercial activities were reined in by Clauson J on the basis that business competition within the same locality was unavoidable. He explained:

> **"The rule of universal application is that an executor and trustee having duties to discharge of a fiduciary nature towards the beneficiaries under the will—in this particular case the duty of a fiduciary nature was to carry on the business of the testator to the best advantage of the beneficiaries—he shall not be allowed to enter into any engagement in which he has or can have a personal interest conflicting, or which may possibly conflict, with the interests of those whom he is bound to protect".[303]**

Several observations may be made about this rule. First, the specialist nature of the businesses in *Thomson* may exert some significance in that it highlights the inevitability of conflict. Clauson J placed great emphasis upon the nature of a yacht agent's business and limited his decision to the business operated on the facts before him.[304] It is unclear whether the same rule would apply to a general business carried out by the trustee. For example, it is doubtful whether the court would prevent the trustee opening up a rival greengrocer's shop in the same

---

298 *Gillett v Peppercone* (1840) 3 Beav. 78.
299 *Balston Ltd v Headline Filters Ltd* [1990] F.S.R. 385 (competitive tendering for the business of a client of the company of which he had been a director and poaching a former employee of that company).
300 In *Sharma v Sharma* [2013] EWCA Civ 1287, for example, the sole director of a family company was allowed to acquire some dental practices for her own benefit by the shareholders. This was not a breach of fiduciary duty.
301 *A.G. v Blake* [2001] 1 A.C. 268. There a retired intelligence officer published a memoir and the Crown sought £90,000 (author's royalties) from the publisher. It was concluded that the author no longer owed a fiduciary duty to the Crown.
302 [1930] 1 Ch. 203.
303 [1930] 1 Ch. 203 at 215.
304 [1930] 1 Ch. 203 at 213, 216.

town. Unless the shops are in close proximity, there appears to be no meaningful conflict of interest and duty that could justify such drastic action.[305] Obviously, in modern times and with the growth of online trading, physical proximity might not be as an important Indicator of conflict.

Secondly, the trustee in the *Thomson* case commenced his rival business after accepting the office of trustee. If the conflicting business of the trustee was in existence prior to his appointment, the outcome would depend upon whether the settlor knew of the trustee's business. Presumably, if the settlor does possess such knowledge then the trustee will be allowed to continue with his commercial activity until a real and meaningful conflict of interest and duty emerges.

Thirdly, the rule appears to apply more strictly to trustees than other types of fiduciary (e.g. company directors).[306] In *Island Export Finance Ltd v Umunna*,[307] it was held by the High Court that, although his fiduciary duties did not automatically end upon his resignation, a former director could enter a competing business provided that he did not exploit a maturing business opportunity of his former company.[308] The company was not actively seeking such contracts when he resigned or, indeed, when he later obtained the contracts for himself. There was, moreover, no improper use by him of confidential information acquired while he was a director. The judicial attitude is that directors "acquire a general fund of knowledge and expertise in the course of their work and it is plainly in the public interest that they should be free to exploit it in a new position".[309] Similarly, in *Foster Bryant Surveying Ltd v Bryant*[310] a director was forced out of his company and later set up another company. The new company was engaged by one of his former company's clients and the former company sought an account of profits for breach of fiduciary duty. This was not a case, therefore, where Mr Bryant resigned in order to attempt to take work or clients from the company. The re-engagement of Mr Bryant's services was, moreover, at the customer's insistence. As Rix LJ put it, "This is not a case where a director has used corporate property. It is not a case where a director has resigned in order to make use of a corporate opportunity. It is not a case where a director has solicited corporate business in competition with his company. It is not a case where a director has acted in bad faith, deceitfully or clandestinely".[311] The most that could, therefore, be argued was that Mr Bryant was still

---

305 See *Moore v M'Glynn* [1894] 1 Ir. R. 74. If the trustee is allowed to continue his business, however, he may be required to resign or be removed from office.
306 This is because s.175 of the Companies Act 2006 does not impose the same strict standard as imposed by equity. Also at common law there is no rigid rule that a director could not be involved in a competing business: *London and Mashonaland Exploration Co Ltd v New Mashonaland Exploration Co Ltd* [1891] W.N. 165.
307 [1986] B.C.L.C. 460.
308 See also *Framlington Group Plc v Anderson* [1995] 1 B.C.L.C. 475; *Foster Bryant Surveying Ltd v Bryant* [2007] EWCA Civ 200.
309 Per Hutchinson J in *Island Export Finance Ltd v Umunna* [1986] B.C.L.C. 460 at 482. Cf. *British Midland Tool Ltd v Midland International Tooling Ltd* [2003] 2 B.C.L.C. 523 where the directors failure to prevent a former director poaching the company's employees put them in breach of their duties.
310 [2007] EWCA Civ 200.
311 [2007] EWCA Civ 200 at [48].

obtaining for himself a business opportunity or putting himself in a position of conflict with the company, Here, however, there was no breach of fiduciary duty as Mr Bryant had not diverted any business opportunity to himself, but instead merely acquiesced in the client's solution to the problem caused to its business by his departure. By way of contrast, in *Breitenfeld UK Ltd v Harrison*[312] a managing director, who caused his company to enter into contracts and to undertake dealings with a newly founded company owned by his son and his daughter-in-law, was clearly in breach of his fiduciary duty. He was ordered to pay £90,500 by way of equitable compensation. His son and daughter-in-law had to pay the same sum for their dishonest assistance in that breach of fiduciary duty.

All, therefore, turns upon the facts of a particular case for as Etherton J explained in *Shepherds Investments Ltd v Walters*:

> **"It is obvious, for example, that merely making a decision to set up competing business at some point in the future and discussing such an idea with friends and family would not of themselves be in conflict with the best interests of the company and the employer. The consulting of lawyers and other professionals may, depending on the circumstances, equally be consistent with a director's fiduciary duties and the employee's obligation of loyalty. At the other end of the spectrum, it is plain that soliciting customers of the company and the employer or the actual carrying on of a trade by a competing business would be in breach of the duties of a director and the obligations of an employee. It is the wide range of activity and decision making between the two ends of the spectrum which will be fact sensitive in every case".[313]**

Renewal of trust lease

13-044 This aspect of the non-profit rule is illustrated by *Keech v Sandford*[314] where a trustee of a lease of Romford Market applied for its renewal for the benefit of an infant beneficiary. The landlord refused to renew the lease in favour of the beneficiary, but agreed to renew the lease in the trustee's own favour. In the genuine knowledge that a lease renewal would not be granted to the beneficiary, the trustee went ahead and took the grant. The infant then sought to have the lease assigned to him. Although there was no question of fraud, Lord King LC concluded that the trustee held the lease on constructive trust for the infant and that he had to account for profits received. The underlying reason was that there would be less incentive on the trustee

---

312 [2015] EWHC 399 (Ch).
313 [2006] EWHC 836 (Ch) at [108].
314 (1726) Sel. Cas. Ch. 61; see further A.D. Hicks, "The Remedial Principle in *Keech v Sandford* Revisited" (2010) 69 C.L.J. 285.

to press for a renewal for the trust if he knew that he would benefit by a refusal. As Lord King LC put it:

> "I very well see, if a trustee, on the refusal to renew, might have a lease for himself, few trust estates would be renewed to *cestui que use*; though I do not say there is a fraud in this case, yet he should have rather let it run out, than to have had the lease to himself . . . for it is very obvious what would be the consequences of letting trustees have the lease, on refusal to renew to *cestui que use*".[315]

The rule in *Keech v Sandford*, however, applies only when it is the trustee (or some other fiduciary) who obtains the benefit.[316] As Lord King LC acknowledged, "the trustee is the only person of all mankind who might not have the lease".[317] In *Re Biss*,[318] for example, a yearly tenant of a shop died intestate and a renewal was refused to his widow. Although one of their children subsequently obtained a renewal, he was entitled to keep the lease for himself. No fiduciary duty was owed to the estate.[319]

Abuse of position: bad faith

13-045

Understandably, where the trustee or other fiduciary has acted in bad faith, and by doing so made a profit or unlawfully paid monies away,[320] he will have to account for those sums.[321] This was illustrated in *Aerostar Maintenance International Ltd v Wilson*.[322] There a company director, who was also an employee of the company, acted in breach of fiduciary duty by setting up his own company and entering into a contract that he had originally been negotiating on behalf of his employer. He had not acted in good faith and, by using information he had acquired as an employee for his own purposes, had placed himself in a position where his

---

315 (1726) Sel. Cas. Ch. 61 at 62.
316 In *Foreman v King* [2008] EWHC 592 (Ch), a business partner purchased the freehold of the premises from which the partnership operated. Following the dissolution of the partnership, it was determined that he held the freehold on consultative trust.
317 (1726) Sel. Cas. Ch. 61 at 62.
318 [1903] 2 Ch. 40.
319 S. Cretney, "The Rationale of *Keech v Sandford*" [1969] Conv. 161, 176 disputes the validity of this distinction, arguing that trustees should also be able to rebut a presumption of wrongdoing.
320 For example, in *Northampton BC v Cardoza* [2019] EWHC 26 (Ch) the managing director of a football club took out a loan for the benefit of the club, but used the money for the benefit of himself and another director.
321 See *Gresport Finance Ltd v Battaglia* [2016] EWHC 964 (Ch). In *Parr v Keystone Healthcare Ltd* [2019] 4 W.L.R. 99, a director was in breach of fiduciary duty by failing to report his own wrongdoing. As a result, the other directors entered into a share dealing with the wrongdoer that they otherwise would not have entertained.
322 [2010] EWHC 2032 (Ch); see also *FHR European Ventures LLP v Cedar Capital Ventures LLC* [2015] A.C. 250 where an agent, who received a secret commission from the seller of a Monte Carlo hotel, held that money on constructive trust for its principal.

duty to his employer and his own interest conflicted. In *Reading v Attorney General*,[323] an army sergeant earned £19,000 by transporting smuggled goods in an army vehicle and while in army uniform. The profit was confiscated and, on his release from prison, he took action for its return. His action failed because he was a fiduciary and was liable to account for the profits to the Crown. As Lord Normand commented, "he owes to the Crown a duty as fully fiduciary as the duty of a servant to his master or of an agent to his principal, and in consequence that all profits and advantages gained by the use or abuse of his military status are to be for the benefit of the Crown".[324] In *Islamic Republic of Iran Shipping Lines v Denby*,[325] a solicitor accepted a cash inducement from the opposing side to settle a case initiated by his client. It was held that the solicitor was liable to pay the money received to his client. Similarly, in *English v Dedham Vale Properties*,[326] agents were held liable to account for profits when they allowed Ms English to sell her property to them for £7,750 without her knowing that the agents had previously applied for planning permission. The agents were fiduciaries and, as such, should have disclosed the application before the contract was entered.[327]

The Privy Council in *Attorney General for Hong Kong v Reid*[328] adopted a similar approach in circumstances where a fiduciary (the Acting Director of Public Prosecution for Hong Kong) accepted bribes (for discontinuing certain criminal proceedings) during the course of his employment by the Crown. It was held by the Privy Council, albeit somewhat contentiously, that the Crown was able to recover the property acquired by the proceeds of the bribes (three houses in New Zealand) even though the houses were of a higher value than the bribes received.[329] Accordingly, this was a proprietary claim against the bribes received. A different approach was, however, signalled (albeit fleetingly) in *Sinclair Investments (UK) Ltd v Versailles Trade Finance Ltd*.[330] There Lord Neuberger MR concluded that the *Reid* case was unsound.[331] He determined instead that the claimant could not assert a proprietary interest in a shareholding purchased by a defaulting fiduciary with funds that were not beneficially owned by the claimant or deriving from opportunities beneficially owned by the claimant.[332] Although the claimant enjoys a personal remedy in equity to repayment of the funds, Lord Neuberger MR

---

323 [1951] A.C. 507.

324 [1951] A.C. 507 at 517. See also, *Dyson Technology Ltd v Curtis* [2010] EWHC 3289 (Ch), where an employee of Dyson was in breach of fiduciary duty in receiving bribes from other manufacturers.

325 [1987] 1 Lloyd's Rep. 367.

326 [1978] 1 All E.R. 382.

327 See also *Page v Hewetts Solicitors* unreported 8 February 2011, where a legal executive made a secret profit in the form of unauthorised commission on the sale of a client's property.

328 [1994] 1 A.C. 324.

329 G. Virgo, "Profits Obtained in Breach of Fiduciary Duty: Personal or Proprietary Claim?" (2011) 70 C.L.J. 502, 503 dismissed this decision as "inconsistent with authority, principle and policy".

330 [2011] EWCA Civ 347. The *Sinclair* denial of a proprietary claim is no longer good law as the decision was overruled by the Supreme Court in *FHR European Ventures LLP v Cedar Capital Ventures LLC* [2015] A.C. 250.

331 See generally, R. Goode, "Proprietary Liability for Secret Profit—a Reply" (2011) 127 L.Q.R. 493.

332 It was mistakenly predicted by G. Virgo, "Profits Obtained in Breach of Fiduciary Duty: Personal or Proprietary Claim?" (2011) 70 C.L.J. 502, 503 that Lord Neuberger's judgement would become "a classic of equitable jurisprudence".

felt that this should be limited to the amount of the funds, together with interest. The rules of equitable compensation may then be used to ensure that the fiduciary does not profit from his breach of duty. Lord Neuberger's reasoning was structured around the much earlier decision of the Court of Appeal in *Lister v Stubbs*.[333] There Mr Stubbs was the foreman of a textile mill and employed by Lister. He was tasked to buy dyestuffs at market value for his employer and received secret commissions from the supplier. He invested these ill-gotten gains profitably in shares and land in York. It was held that, although there was a debt due in consequence of the corrupt bargain, the money was not the plaintiffs' and was not held on trust for them. The plaintiffs were unable to go against the shares or the land.

The *Sinclair* case proved to be highly controversial and, for the period that it enjoyed some validity, "divided legal scholars and the common law world".[334] Clearly in a state of high dudgeon, Millett voiced his concerns:

> **"*Lister v Stubbs* and *Sinclair v Versailles* are contrary to principle and authority, fail to give effect to the policy of the law, reduce English law to a state of incoherence, and leave this country in the uncomfortable position of being the only common law jurisdiction where a dishonest fiduciary is allowed to retain a profit he has made by profitably investing a bribe or otherwise exploiting the fiduciary relationship for his own benefit without the fully informed consent of his principal".**[335]

A return to orthodoxy came with the Supreme Court decision in *FHR European Ventures LLP v Cedar Capital Partners LCC*.[336] There Cedar Capital (a company established by Mr Mankarious) had the exclusive brokerage rights in relation to the sale of a hotel. The Company acted as the agent of the purchaser and negotiated the price of the deal (€211.5 million). The agent received an undisclosed fee of €10 million from the seller. This clearly amounted to a breach of fiduciary duty by the agent, but the key issue was whether the purchaser's remedy against Cedar Capital was a personal remedy or a proprietary one. It is to be appreciated that the advantages

13-046

---

333 (1890) 45 Ch. D 1. As P. Millett, "Bribes and Secret Commissions Again" (2012) 71(3) C.L.J. 583, 583 comments of this reinvigoration of *Lister v Stubbs*, "Like old soldiers some old cases, wrongly decided, never die; unfortunately they do not simply fade away either. As with Humpty Dumpty after his great fall, someone will always be found to try to put the pieces back together again".

334 Per Sir Terence Etherton, *FHR European Ventures LLP v Mankarious* [2013] 3 W.L.R. 466 at [70]. Pill LJ agreed at [61] that, "Consideration of the views of commentators and practitioners generally on the subject of constructive trusts in the law of England and Wales reveals passions of a force uncommon in the legal world".

335 P. Millett, "Bribes and Secret Commissions Again" (2012) 71(3) C.L.J. 583, 614. This sentiment is shared by others, for example R. Hedlund, "Secret Commissions and Constructive Trusts: Yet Again!" (2013) J.B.L 747, denounced the judgment as being "erroneous in law, principle and policy" and D. Hayton, "No Proprietary Liability for Bribes and other Secret Profits?" (2011) 25 Tru. L.I. 3, 5 offered the warning that *Sinclair Investments* could "undermine the integrity of the trust concept".

336 [2015] A.C. 250.

of having a proprietary remedy arise where a fiduciary becomes insolvent and the dispute concerns priorities; where money has been invested profitably in an asset that has increased in value; or, as here, where the defaulting fiduciary no longer has the profit and the principal seeks to recover it from a third party. Accordingly, the argument in FHR focused upon the availability of following and tracing.

In the Supreme Court, the President, Lord Neuberger, revisited the equitable rule that an agent may acquire a benefit in breach of fiduciary duty or in consequence of an opportunity which arose from his fiduciary position and be treated as having acquired the benefit for his principal. In such instances, the benefit is owned by the principal and the equitable rule is that the latter enjoys a proprietary claim in addition to his personal remedy and, therefore, can elect between the two remedies. Cedar Capital, however, contended that the equitable rule did not apply because the money received was not a benefit which could properly be said to be the property of the principal. FHR argued that in any case where an agent receives a benefit, which results from a breach of fiduciary duty, the agent holds the benefit on trust for the principal. It was held that the argument of FHR prevailed. Any notion that the rule should not apply to a bribe or secret commission received by an agent, because it could not have been received by or on behalf of the principal, was viewed as unattractive and inconsistent with the longstanding authorities such as *Keech v Sandford*.[337] As Lord Neuberger commented, "The whole reason that the agent should not have accepted the bribe or commission is that it puts him in conflict with his duty to his principal".[338] Elementary economics indicated a strong possibility that the bribe had disadvantaged the principal. On the present facts, if the vendor was prepared to pay a secret commission of €10 million then it would be quite likely that it would have sold the share capital for €10 million less.

Lord Neuberger felt that wider policy issues also supported the case that bribes and secret commissions received should be treated as the property of the principal. Bribery is an evil practice and secret commissions are objectionable in that they tend to undermine faith in the commercial world. As Lord Neuberger observed, "Accordingly, one would expect the law to be particularly stringent in relation to a claim against an agent who has received a bribe or secret commission".[339] Policy, practicality and principle justified the conclusion that a bribe or secret commission accepted by an agent is held on trust for his principal.[340]

13-047

Hence, the law had taken a wrong turn in cases such as *Lister v Stubbs* and any subsequent cases which followed that route (including *Sinclair Investments*) were to be treated as overruled.[341] Speaking extra-judicially, Lord Neuberger appreciated the irony of overruling, while in the Supreme Court, his own earlier decision in the Court of Appeal.[342] Somewhat

---

337 (1726) Sel. Cas. Ch. 61.
338 [2015] A.C. 250 at [37].
339 [2015] A.C. 250 at [42].
340 See also *Parr v Keystone Healthcare Ltd* [2019] 4 W.L.R. 99.
341 See further, M. Conaglen, "Proprietary Remedies for Breach of Fiduciary Duty" (2014) 73(3) C.L.J. 490.
342 Lord Neuberger, "Twenty Years a Judge: Reflections and Refractions", Neill Lecture 2017, Oxford Law Faculty, 10 February 2017, *https://www.supremecourt.uk/docs/speech-170210.pdf* [Accessed 31 July 2020].

tongue in cheek, he commented: "But Lord Neuberger is not on his own when it comes to judicial tergiversations on the issue of a principal's proprietary interests in his agent's bribe. His volte-face is by no means an exception in what is seen by some as the placid waters of equity".[343]

Abuse of position: good faith

13-048

In the above cases there was clearly bad faith shown by the fiduciary, but this is not a necessary requirement before a fiduciary is compelled to account for abuse or exploitation of position.[344] For example, in *Industrial Development Consultants Ltd v Cooley*[345] a managing director of a company had been negotiating a contract with the Eastern Gas Board. The Gas Board did not wish to enter into any dealings with the company, but it was prepared to enter a contract with the managing director privately. Consequently, he terminated his association with the company on the false basis of illness and signed the contract with the Gas Board. The first issue was whether he was a fiduciary and Roskill J answered this in the affirmative: "The defendant had one capacity and one capacity only in which he was carrying on business at the time. That capacity was as managing director of the plaintiffs".[346] The second issue concerned whether he was in breach of fiduciary duty. Although a contract between the company and the Gas Board would never have come to fruition, its former managing director had to account to the company for the benefit of the contract he had personally entered. As Roskill J observed, "he was guilty of putting himself into the position in which his duty to his employers . . . and his own private interests conflicted and conflicted grievously".[347] The conflict was that he had negotiated the contract in the company's time and had a platform for negotiation with the Gas Board because of his association with the company. As Roskill J explained, "Information which came to him while he was managing director and which was of concern to the plaintiffs and relevant for the plaintiffs to know was information which it was his duty to pass on to the plaintiffs".[348] Instead, he guarded the information for his own personal profit. As Roskill J continued, "if the defendant is not required to account he will have made a large profit as a result of having deliberately put himself into a position in which his duty to the plaintiffs who were employing

343 Lord Neuberger, "Equity—The soul and spirit of all law or a roguish thing?", Lehane Lecture 2014, Supreme Court of New South Wales, Sydney, 4 August 2014 at [10], *https://www.supremecourt.uk/docs/speech-140804.pdf* [Accessed 31 July 2020].
344 *Parr v Keystone Healthcare Ltd* [2019] 4 W.L.R. 99. There Lewison LJ accepted that a breach of fiduciary duty did not require fraud or an absence of bona fides. The liability arose from the mere fact of a profit having been made. The purpose was to take from the fiduciary the unauthorised profits made whilst in a position of conflict of duty.
345 [1972] 1 W.L.R. 443.
346 [1972] 1 W.L.R. 443 at 451.
347 [1972] 1 W.L.R. 443 at 453.
348 [1972] 1 W.L.R. 443 at 451. Cf. acquisition by directors of a general fund of knowledge which can be exploited subsequently in a new position: *CMS Dolphin Ltd v Simonet* [2001] 2 B.C.L.C. 704.

him and his personal interests conflicted".[349] More recently, in *Sharma v Sharma* a company director was in breach of his fiduciary duty to avoid a conflict of interest when, for his personal gain, he exploited opportunities which came to his attention through his role as director which he could and should exploit for the company's benefit.[350] In a like vein, in *Davies v Ford* directors of a recycling company breached their fiduciary duties by diverting its business to their own company.[351] It did not matter that the recycling company had been close to insolvency and had been unable to take up the business opportunities itself.

Two of the most illustrative cases concerning the abuse of position by a fiduciary are *Regal (Hastings) Ltd v Gulliver*[352] and *Boardman v Phipps*.[353] In *Regal (Hastings) Ltd v Gulliver*, Regal operated a cinema and wished to buy two further motion picture theatres in the vicinity. The directors determined to set up a subsidiary company which would acquire the leases to the other cinemas. The idea was that Regal would then sell its interest in all three venues as a going concern. Unless the subsidiary company had a paid-up capital of at least £5,000, the landlord of the two cinemas demanded a financial guarantee from the directors. The directors were reluctant to offer a personal guarantee and elected for the alternative course. As Regal could fund only £2,000 of the required £5,000, the directors decided to club together and to raise the shortfall themselves in return for a share issue. The leases were duly acquired, but Regal did not sell its business interest. Instead, the directors sold their shares in both Regal and the subsidiary company and made a substantial profit. A new board of directors was appointed and the board sought an account of the profits personally made from the sale of the shares in the subsidiary company. The directors argued that they had acted in good faith and had secured a benefit for Regal in the process. Reversing the decision of the Court of Appeal, the House of Lords held that the directors were liable to account for the profits made. Lord Russell explained:

> **"The rule of equity which insists on those, who by use of a fiduciary position make a profit, being liable to account for that profit, in no way depends on fraud, or absence of *bona fides*; or upon such questions or considerations as whether the profit would or should otherwise have gone to the plaintiff, or whether the profiteer was under a duty to obtain the source of the profit for the plaintiff, or whether he took a risk or acted as he did for the benefit of the plaintiff, or whether the plaintiff has in fact been damaged or benefited by his action. The liability arises from the mere fact of a profit having, in the stated circumstances, been made. The profiteer, however honest or well intentioned, cannot escape the risk of being called to account."[354]**

---

349 [1972] 1 W.L.R. 443 at 453.
350 [2013] EWCA Civ 1287.
351 [2020] EWHC 686 (Ch).
352 [1942] 1 All E.R. 378.
353 [1967] 2 A.C. 46.
354 [1942] 1 All E.R. 378 at 386. This strict approach has, however, been rejected by both the Supreme Court

The outcome of this decision was to provide the new purchasers of Regal and its subsidiary with a windfall bonus because they were able to recoup some of the money that had been spent on acquiring the businesses. Nevertheless, as Lord Porter acknowledged, "the principle that a person occupying a fiduciary relationship shall not make a profit by reason thereof is of such vital importance that the possible consequence in the present case is in fact as it is in law an immaterial consideration".[355] Lord Wright stated that the directors should have "let the opportunity pass".[356] Viscount Sankey reiterated the traditional line, "no-one who has duties of a fiduciary nature to perform is allowed to enter into engagements in which he has or can have a personal interest conflicting with the interests of those whom he is bound to protect. If he holds any property so acquired as trustee, he is bound to account for it . . .".[357]

13-049

By way of an aside, Lord Russell believed that this liability to account could have been sidestepped had the trustees obtained the prior approval of Regal's shareholders to the purchase of the shares in the subsidiary company. In *Sharma v Sharma*,[358] Jackson LJ accepted that, if the shareholders with full knowledge of the relevant facts consented to the director exploiting those opportunities for his own personal gain, then that conduct was not a breach of fiduciary or statutory duty. The acquiescence by the shareholders in the director's proposed conduct might constitute consent. It matters not that the shareholders did not appreciate that the proposed action could be characterised as a breach of duty. Following *Queensland Mines v Hudson*, ratification might be an effective shield even when coming from the board of directors provided that the fiduciary is not a controlling shareholder of the company.[359] Indeed, s.175 of the Companies Act 2006 deals with the situation where there is a conflict of interest between a director and the company and allows the board of directors, if authorised by the company's constitution, to permit what would otherwise be a breach of duty.

In *Boardman v Phipps*, a testator set up a trust for the benefit of his widow and children. The trust solicitor was Mr Boardman. In time, Mr Boardman became concerned about a trust investment in an ailing private company. He concluded that the only way to protect the trust investment was for the trust to obtain a majority shareholding in the company and to appoint a new management team. Two of the three trustees were willing to do this, but the third trustee was an old woman who was in poor health and she was not consulted. Wrongly believing that they had the support of the beneficiaries, Mr Boardman and one of the beneficiaries (Tom Phipps) went ahead and bought the outstanding shares themselves. During the phase leading

13-050

---

of Canada (*Peso Silver Mines v Cropper* (1966) 58 D.L.R. (2d) 1) and the High Court of Australia (*Consul Development v DPC Estates* (1975) 132 C.L.R. 373). Both jurisdictions favour a more flexible approach in keeping with modern times.

355 [1942] 1 All E.R. 378 at 394. See also, *Apcoa Parking UK Ltd v Perera* unreported 14 October 2010 (Ch), where the employee of a car park set up his own company to make a profit by subletting parking spaces to his employer's customers. The employee intended that the employer would benefit as well from increased trade.

356 [1942] 1 All E.R. 378 at 394.

357 [1942] 1 All E.R. 378 at 381.

358 [2013] EWCA Civ 1287.

359 (1977) 18 A.L.R. 1 (PC). There the Board of Directors waived a fellow director's breach of duty in exploiting a business opportunity for personal gain; cf. *Cook v Deeks* [1916] 1 A.C. 554.

up to the takeover Mr Boardman had claimed to represent the trust and had obtained information that was not available to the public at large. With the support of two of the three trustees, the pair took control of the company. As a consequence, the trust benefited by £47,000. Mr Boardman and the beneficiary made a profit in the region of £75,000. One of the other beneficiaries (John Phipps) claimed that the profit had been made by the use of information that had been acquired by the pair while acting on behalf of the trust and in a fiduciary capacity. The claim, which was based on the principle enunciated in the *Regal (Hastings)* case, succeeded before the House of Lords by virtue of a 3:2 majority decision.[360] As Millett points out, however, "In view of the diversity of opinions expressed by the members of the Appellate Committee, it is not easy to extract the *ratio*".[361]

It was concluded by Lords Guest, Cohen and Hodson that the rule in *Keech v Sandford* (see para.**13-044**) operated in the present case. They classed both Mr Boardman and the beneficiary as fiduciaries and, as they had made a profit from speculating with trust property (i.e. trust information and contacts), they were liable to account to the trust for the profit made. It was immaterial that the pair had acted honestly in a fashion that was of great benefit to the trust. Lord Cohen felt that Mr Boardman would have been incapable of giving independent advice to the trust if it had been sought as he was himself negotiating privately for the purchase of shares.[362] Put shortly, there was a conflict between his interest and his duty. While the reasoning of the majority is convincing as regards Mr Boardman, it does not sit as comfortably with the position of Tom Phipps. It could be argued that, as the latter acquired the information in his capacity as beneficiary, he was not a fiduciary and, hence, there was no conflict of interest and duty. It appears that his refusal to be severed from Boardman during the litigation, and his admission that he owed fiduciary duties presumably as an agent of the trust, sealed his fate.

13-051   Viscount Dilhorne and Lord Upjohn were the dissenting voices in *Boardman v Phipps*. Lord Upjohn concluded that the "no conflict" rule should not be applied strictly and automatically and that it should be tempered by the concept of reasonableness, "In my view it means that the reasonable man looking at the relevant facts and circumstances of the particular case would think that there was a real sensible possibility of conflict; not that you could imagine some situation arising which might, in some conceivable possibility in events not contemplated as real sensible possibilities by any reasonable person, result in a conflict . . .".[363] Viscount Dilhorne advocated an alternative test to be applied when considering the liability of a fiduciary to account for a profit. In his eyes, it should be shown that the fiduciary made a profit within the scope and ambit of his duty and in circumstances where there was a real and sensible possibility of conflict between interest and duty. He commented that "On the facts of this case there

---

360 Mr Boardman was, however, allowed an equitable allowance for his valuable services. In *Gavriel v Davis* [2019] EWHC 2446 (Ch), the court admitted that it can have regard to the services provided and the possible unjustness of the defendant having undertaken work for which the claimants take the benefit, but emphasised that to award the trustee payment is both discretionary and exceptional.

361 P. Millett, "Bribes and Secret Commissions Again" (2012) 71(3) C.L.J. 583, 610.

362 [1967] 2 A.C. 46 at 103, 104.

363 [1967] 1 A.C. 46 at 124.

was not, in my opinion, any conflict or possibility of a conflict between the personal interests of the appellants and those of the trust".[364] Although Viscount Dilhorne's test does not represent the present state of the law, it is attractive in that it would instil flexibility and alleviate the harshness of outcome as occurred in *Boardman v Phipps*.

Despite the conclusion of Lords Guest and Lord Hodson that information could properly be categorised as trust property, Lord Cohen concluded that it could never be so classified. Lord Upjohn took the view that, although "knowledge" was not property in the strict sense, it should be regarded as such only when it is confidential information and its use would amount to a breach of confidence and put him in a place where his duty and personal interest might conflict.[365] On the facts, he concluded that it was not injurious to the trust and felt that the majority decision of the House was unreasonable and inequitable.[366] Viscount Dilhorne agreed and admitted that the information gathered here was of no value to the trust.[367] Of this diversity of opinion, it is thought that Lord Upjohn's take on information as property represents the modern view.

13-052

Dispositive Duties

13-053

After the payment of all debts of the trust, the basic duty of the trustee in relation to the distribution of remaining trust property (i.e. income and capital) is to hand over the property to the proper persons in accordance with the directions contained in the trust instrument. Once this is done, and following the timely presentation of final accounts[368] and the disclosure of any breaches of trust,[369] the trustee will seek a formal discharge by the beneficiaries.[370] The release is usually by deed and paid for out of the trust fund.

The trustees must take this distributive responsibility seriously as, if there is an unauthorised allocation, it will amount to a breach of trust and the trustee will not be automatically relieved of liability even if he acted following legal advice. It is for the aggrieved beneficiary to decide whether to sue the trustee or, instead, to follow the money into the hands of the wrongful recipient. For example, in *Eaves v Hickson*[371] the trustees wrongly paid money to beneficiaries on the strength of a forged marriage certificate, which led the trustees to believe falsely

---

364 [1967] 2 A.C. 46 at 88.
365 [1967] 2 A.C. 46 at 128. As P. Millett observed in "Bribes and Secret Commissions Again" (2012) 71(3) C.L.J. 583 (fn.89), "If information is property it is of a very unusual kind, since it can at one and the same time be disposed of and yet retained".
366 [1967] 2 A.C. 46 at 133, 134.
367 [1967] 2 A.C. 46 at 91.
368 *Wedderburn v Wedderburn* (1838) 4 My. & Cr. 50.
369 *Cole v Gibson* (1750) 1 Ves. Sen. 507.
370 *King v Mullins* (1852) 1 Drew. 311.
371 (1861) 30 Beav. 136.

that the recipients were legitimate children and entitled under the trust. The trustees were required to account to the rightful beneficiary for such payments. Similarly, in *Re Hulkes*[372] the trustees adopted an honest, but mistaken, meaning of the trust instrument and, as a result, paid sums to the wrong beneficiaries. The trustees were again held to be liable.

And s.61 of the Trustee Act 1925?

13-054

It is to be appreciated that since s.3(1) of the Judicial Trustees Act 1896 the court enjoys the discretion to relieve a trustee (but no other fiduciary) of personal liability (e.g. for an irregular distribution).[373] This is now afforded by s.61 of the Trustee Act 1925 (see further para.**17-025**). It is a pioneering jurisdiction that focuses upon the ethically sensitive issue of when it is reasonable to break the law.[374] It was enacted at a time when the use of professional trustees was frowned upon and when it was apparent that lay trustees were often ill-equipped and untutored to deal with novel and increasingly sophisticated responsibilities. Against a backcloth of high standards, unrealistic expectations and no-fault liability, there emerged a serious trustee recruitment problem. It was never envisaged that the jurisdiction would shield professional trustees and, indeed, the reform was designed to slow the march to professionalism by making lay trusteeship more appealing. Nevertheless, as will become clear, professional trustees are nowadays protected by s.61.

Relief applies to all breaches of duty by a trustee, including a breach of fiduciary duty and negligence. Many of the cases in which relief was originally sought, concerned the making of unauthorised investments or authorised investments imprudently made.[375] Its modern manifestation, however, focuses on solicitors being unwittingly embroiled in conveyancing fraud and unlawfully paying away the mortgage monies to a fraudster.[376]

The discretion will, however, be exercised only in circumstances where it appears to the court that the trustee has acted honestly[377] and reasonably[378] and, moreover, ought fairly to

---

372 (1886) 33 Ch. D. 552.

373 Equivalent provisions include s.191(1) of the Charities Act 2011 (which affords the Charity Commission a discretion to grant relief to trustees and others) and s.1157 of the Companies Act 2006 (which offers the court the ability to grant relief to officers of a company).

374 See M. Haley, "Section 61 of the Trustee Act 1925: A Judicious Breach of Trust?" (2017) 76 C.L.J. 537.

375 As, for example, in *Daniel v Tee* [2016] 4 W.L.R. 115 where the trustees had acted to the best of their abilities and invested in reliance on what they reasonably believed to be competent professional advice.

376 A bare trust is imposed on the conveyancer in receipt of mortgage monies and persists until the completion of the transaction: *DB UK Bank Ltd v Edmunds & Co* [2014] P.N.L.R. 12. No exclusion clause is permitted within that retainer.

377 There has never been a universally accepted definition of "honesty" for these purposes. It gives rise to questions that are "impossible to answer fully" (F.H. Maugham, "Excusable Breaches of Trust" (1898) 14 L.Q.R. 159 at 163). Honesty, as L.A. Sheridan, "Excusable Breaches of Trust" [1953] 19 Conv. 420, 423 rightly points out, "seems to denote being motivated by the interests of the trust".

378 The trustee must act "with exemplary professional care and efficiency . . ." and be "careful, conscientious and thorough . . ." (per Rimer LJ in *Lloyds TSB Bank Plc v Markandan & Uddin* [2012] 2 All E.R. 884 at [60], [61]).

be exonerated (in whole or in part) for the consequences of the breach of trust or the failure to obtain directions.[379] The onus rests with the trustee to convince the court to grant relief, hence the obvious advantage of having an exclusion clause included in the trust deed. The court must, therefore, investigate whether the trustee should be relieved from personal liability and this will involve consideration of all the relevant factors.[380] Although in *Barraclough v Mell* the trustee was shielded behind the very wide terms of an exclusion clause, Deputy Judge John Behrens added that he would have refused relief to the trustee under s.61. He explained that, "Her conduct was in my view grossly negligent. Whilst I think she has acted honestly I do not think that she has acted reasonably. Nor do I think she ought fairly to be excused for the breach of trust".[381] In *Re Evans*,[382] a daughter distributed her father's estate on the basis that her brother was dead. He reappeared four years later and claimed that his sister (as trustee) was in breach of trust. The court granted the trustee partial relief against her brother's claims. Although each case will turn upon its own facts, the primary focus will be upon whether the trustee acted reasonably or not.[383] On the facts of *Evans*, the trustee had acted honestly and reasonably. Similarly, in *Perrins v Bellamy*[384] the trustees mistakenly believed that they had a power to sell some leasehold property. As a result there was a major drop in trust income. The trustees were in breach of trust and responsible, but as they had acted honestly and reasonably they were excused.[385]

Mortgage fraud is an endemic problem within contemporary society and has given rise to an increased use of the s.61 jurisdiction by conveyancing solicitors.[386] In *Lloyds TSB Bank Plc v Markandan & Uddin*,[387] the fraudster was an imposter who pretended to be operating a branch office of a well-known firm of solicitors. The purchaser's solicitors failed to check whether that branch office existed. Rimer LJ accepted that "The careful, conscientious and thorough solicitor, who conducts the transaction by the book and acts honestly and reasonably in relation to it in all respects but still does not discover the fraud is, however, likely to be treated mercifully by the court on his s.61 application".[388] The Court of Appeal, however, refused to grant this solicitors' firm relief when, as part of a scam conveyancing transaction, it innocently paid over

379 This requires the court to make an ethical judgment as to whether the demands of justice require the trustee to be relieved and, if so, to what extent: see Farwell J in *Lord De Clifford's Estate* [1900] 2 Ch. 707 at 713.
380 *Davis v Hutchings* [1907] 1 Ch. 356.
381 [2005] EWHC 3387 (Ch) at [98]. See also *Martin v Triggs Turner Bartons* [2009] EWHC 1920 (Ch).
382 [1999] 2 All E.R. 777.
383 *Chapman v Browne* [1902] 1 Ch. 785. In *Kemp v Sims* [2008] EWHC 2579 (Ch), a trustee was denied relief under s.61 because he was a qualified lawyer and had not acted reasonably in that capacity.
384 [1899] 1 Ch. 797.
385 In *Bairstow v Queens Moat Houses Plc* [2000] B.C.C. 1025, the directors of QMH unlawfully paid dividends to shareholders. The High Court held that relief was unavailable as the directors could not establish honesty and had not acted reasonably. In *Sheffield v Sheffield* [2013] EWHC 3927 (Ch), the trustee was granted relief against a claim that trust property had been sold at an undervalue because he acted as a prudent man of business and followed the advice of a professional valuer.
386 See P. Davies, "Section 61 of the Trustee Act 1925: Deus Ex Machina?" [2015] Conv. 379.
387 [2012] 2 All E.R. 884.
388 [2012] 2 All E.R. 884 at [61].

£742,500 of the Bank's money without obtaining the proper documentation and authorisation and without checking the identity of the recipient. There was also a failure by the trustee solicitor to have regard to an earlier breach of undertaking by the fraudster. These failings clearly increased the risk that the fraudster would succeed in his plan.[389] By way of contrast, in *Nationwide Building Society v Davisons Solicitors*[390] the fraudster used the name of a genuine solicitor, but offered a fictitious business address. The scam was so designed that, when the firm checked the address (as it did), it would appear as a genuine place of business. The Court of Appeal concluded that the duped firm had acted reasonably in accepting the apparently genuine replies to its requisitions and taking an appropriate undertaking from the person it reasonably believed to be the seller's solicitor to redeem a prior mortgage.

13-055   The issue of mortgage fraud and s.61 was also before the Court of Appeal in *Santander UK Plc v R.A. Legal Solicitors*.[391] Briggs LJ set the scene, "Section 61 of the Trustee Act has become the principal mechanism by which the law tempers the rigour of a trustee's otherwise strict (i.e. not fault based) liability where a fraudulent intervention in a conveyancing transaction of which the purchaser's solicitor is entirely unaware causes an unauthorised disposal of the lender's advance in breach of trust".[392] The solicitors acting for Santander released £200,000 to what it thought was the vendor's solicitors. The money simply disappeared from the recipient's client account and became untraceable. Unusually on the present facts the fraud was perpetrated by a solicitor. Since the funds were released without completion ever taking place, R.A. Legal was sued for breach of trust. The firm, however, sought to be exonerated from liability under s.61. There was no suggestion that R.A. Legal had not acted honestly, but there were doubts raised as to the reasonableness of the firm's actions. As mentioned, the burden is on the solicitors to show that s.61 applied and that it should be operated in its favour. Consequently, as Briggs LJ pointed out, "the solicitor will need to be able to provide a paper-trail demonstrating that the whole of his or his firm's conduct sufficiently connected with the loss satisfied the reasonableness test".[393] Looking at matters in the round, he explained, "The question is whether the trustee's relevant conduct was reasonable, taken as a whole".[394] He took a dim view of R.A. Legal's numerous departures from best practice and concluded that, in the light of these serious and consequential breaches, it would not be fair to excuse the firm from liability in whole or in part.

Conveyancing fraud also featured in *Purrunsing v A'Court & Co*[395] and *P&P Property Limited v Owen White & Catlin LLP*.[396] In both cases, the solicitors were not allowed to shield themselves behind s.61 as they had not acted as reasonable solicitors during the conveyancing process. The growing number of mortgage fraud authorities mark a departure from the tradi-

389 See also *Ikbal v Sterling Law* [2013] EWHC 3291 (Ch).
390 [2012] EWCA Civ 1626.
391 [2014] EWCA Civ 183.
392 [2014] EWCA Civ 183 at [19].
393 [2014] EWCA Civ 183 at [56].
394 [2014] EWCA Civ 183 at [97].
395 [2016] 4 W.L.R. 81.
396 [2018] EWCA Civ 1082.

tional application of s.61. Unlike with conventional trusts and trustee malfeasance, the courts are weighed down by a painstaking analysis of the lender-solicitor retainer, which in inevitably arcane form dictates whether a trust is in existence and, if so, whether there has been a breach of that trust. It can be argued that the current application of the s.61 in such instances is overly technical, seemingly without any element of fairness or merit and fraught with difficulty.

Further protection for trustees

There exist several further ways in which a trustee can shield himself from the perils of adverse claims. First, if the trustee makes an overpayment to a beneficiary, he may recoup the over-payments by deducting the amount from any future payments made to that beneficiary. This occurred in *Re Ainsworth* when the executors wrongly paid legacy duty out of capital and not from income.[397] Secondly, there are opportunities to involve the court in the distribution process.

13-056

- If it is unclear whether someone is entitled or not, the safest course is for the trustee to apply to the court for directions.[398] Provided those directions are adhered to, the trustee will be protected from ensuing liability. As Megarry put it, "It is well settled that trustees confronted by a particular problem may surrender their discretion to the court, and so be relieved of the agony of decision and the responsibility for the result".[399] The Law Reform Committee, however, recognised that the costs of going to court for directions are sometimes out of all proportion to the amount of money at stake.[400] In such circumstances, the Committee recommended that trustees should be allowed to take the advice of counsel and to distribute on the basis of that advice if proceedings are not commenced by a beneficiary within three months of receiving a copy of counsel's opinion. This is in part now enshrined in s.48 of the Administration of Justice Act 1985, which allows the High Court to authorise action to be taken in reliance on senior counsel's opinion as regards a will or a trust.

- Under s.63 of the Trustee Act 1925, a trustee who is in doubt as to who is entitled is permitted to pay the trust fund into court and, on the issue of a receipt by the court, is then discharged from liability for future breaches.[401] For example, in *Boyle v Collins*[402] an unincorporated association was dissolved and its land sold. The addresses of

---

397 [1915] 2 Ch. 96.
398 See *Re Allen-Meyrick's WT* [1966] 1 W.L.R. 499 where the trustees did not agree as to the application of trust income.
399 R.E. Megarry (1966) 82 L.Q.R. 306, 307.
400 Law Reform Committee 23rd Report, *The Powers and Duties of Trustees* (1982) Cmnd.8733.
401 They do, however, remain responsible for previous breaches: *Barker v Peile* (1865) 2 Drew & Sm. 340.
402 [2004] EWHC 271 (Ch).

certain members could not be discovered, despite three advertisements in the local paper. The trustees paid money into court such part of the fund as represented the entitlement of those untraceable members. Although the payment into court will mark the retirement of the trustee,[403] he will remain liable for past breaches of trust and be responsible for any trust money that comes to him in future. A new trustee can then be appointed by the court or the person nominated as appointor by the trust instrument. The disadvantage attached to this process is that, unless the trustee has reasonable cause for the payment into court, he is likely to be made liable for costs.[404] The trustee's doubts have to be bona fide and be such that they would concern legal counsel.[405] Although the general rule is that, where there is more than one trustee, they must act jointly (see para.**13-020**), by way of an exception s.63 allows a majority decision to pay money into court.

■ If there is the real possibility of an undiscovered beneficiary, the trustee can apply for a "Benjamin order", which takes its name from *Re Benjamin*,[406] that authorises the distribution of trust property. As David Richards J explained in *Re Global UK Ltd (in special administration) (No.3)*, "In those cases where the trustees are faced with a practical difficulty in establishing the existence of possible beneficiaries or other claimants, the court will give a direction to the trustees enabling them to distribute the trust property on an assumption of fact that there is no such beneficiary or claimant".[407] The order does not vary or destroy beneficial interests, but merely enables trust property to be distributed according to the practical probabilities. The onus then shifts from the trustee to those beneficiaries who receive a distribution, and it is they who usually will be required to provide some security so that any later discovered claimant will not be deprived of his entitlement. In *Re Green's WT*,[408] the testatrix's son had gone missing during a war-time bombing raid and had subsequently been certified as presumed dead. Nourse LJ identified the issue as being "whether in all the circumstances the trustees ought to be allowed to distribute and the beneficiaries to enjoy their apparent interests now rather than later".[409] As Luxton points out, however, this "disturbing" decision to distribute was against the settlor's expressed wishes and her enduring belief that her son was alive.[410]

---

403 *Re Williams' Settlement* (1858) 4 K. & J. 87.
404 *Re Giles* (1886) 34 W.R. 712; see A.J. Hawkins, "The Release of Powers" (1968) 84 L.Q.R. 65.
405 *Re Knight's Trusts* (1859) 27 Beav. 45.
406 [1902] 1 Ch. 723. There the beneficiary was presumed to be dead, but not declared to be dead. In *Re Gess* [1942] Ch 37, a similar order was made as regards any creditors of the deceased in war-time Poland.
407 [2013] 1 W.L.R. 3874 at 3881. He added at 3882, "Those cases permit the trustee to act on a presumed fact in circumstances where it is impossible or impracticable to establish the fact one way or the other".
408 [1985] 3 All E.R. 455.
409 [1985] 3 All E.R. 455 at 462.
410 P. Luxton, "Eluding the Dead Hand: A Live Issue?" [1986] Conv. 138.

By way of an alternative, it is possible to take out missing beneficiary insurance, which will provide the funds to meet any future claim by a missing beneficiary. Although at a cost, but much less than applying for a *Benjamin* order, this will prevent the trustee being exposed to liability to meet any such prospective claims and will also shield the known beneficiaries from being liable to account. Insurance coverage will, therefore, offer "a practical answer to such problems . . . to the advantage of all . . .".[411]

13-057

Thirdly, the trustee may take advantage of s.27 of the Trustee Act 1925 (as amended), which offers protection by advertisement. This allows a trustee to advertise publicly in order to discover the existence of potential claims under the trust, whether it is fixed or discretionary.[412] Under s.27, the trustee must advertise in the *London Gazette*, in a local newspaper and anywhere else as directed by the court. Those advertisements must invite interested parties to forward to the trustees their personal details within a stated time limit. The time limit for claims must allow at least two months from the publication of the last advertisement within which a response is to be given. On the lapse of the stated time limit, the trustee can distribute the property to the beneficiaries of whom he is aware whether as a result of the advertisements or otherwise.[413] Provided that the conditions of s.27 are satisfied, the trustee will not be liable for breach of trust to any beneficiary of whom he has no notice (e.g. the assignee of a beneficial interest who has not notified the trustee of the transaction).[414] The concept of notice is, therefore, pivotal to the operation of s.27. If the statutory prescription is followed and there is an absence of notice (whether in actual, constructive or imputed form), the trustee will be in the same position as if he had administered the estate under the directions of the court. Of course, s.27 cannot protect trustees in respect of claims by persons entitled, even where those persons had not responded to an advertisement placed by the trustees, if the trustees had notice of the claims at the time of distribution.[415] This ability cannot be modified or excluded in the trust instrument.[416] Section 27(2)(a) expressly preserves the right of an aggrieved beneficiary to trace the property into the hands of a person who has received it.

---

411   Per Judge Richard McCombe QC in *Re Evans* [1999] 2 All E.R. 777 at 785.
412   In *MCP Pension Trustees Ltd v AON Pension Trustees Ltd* [2011] 3 W.L.R. 455, a pension fund was being wound up and the trustees employed s.27. The court emphasised that the trustees are protected only against claims of which they had no notice when distribution occurs and accepted that s.27 applies to pension trusts as well as other trusts.
413   Section 28 of the Trustee Act 1925 provides that notice acquired in the capacity as trustee of another trust does not, absent the trustee's fraud, count for these purposes.
414   As required by s.137 of the Law of Property Act 1925.
415   *Re Land Credit Company of Ireland* (1872) 21 W.R. 135.
416   Section 27(3).

Guide to Further Reading

W. Bishop and D. Prentice, "Some Legal and Economic Aspects of Fiduciary Remuneration" [1983] M.L.R. 289.

M. Haley, "Section 61 of the Trustee Act 1925: A Judicious Breach of Trust?" (2017) 76 C.L.J. 537.

J. Lowry, "Directorial Self-Dealing: Constructing a Regime of Accountability" (1997) 48 N.I.L.Q. 211.

J. Lowry, "*Regal (Hastings)* Fifty Years On: Breaking the Bonds of the *Ancien Regime?*" (1994) 45 N.I.L.Q. 1.

P. Matthews, "The Efficacy of Trustee Exemption Clauses in English Law" [1989] Conv. 42.

P. Millett, "Bribes and Secret Commissions Again" (2012) 71(3) C.L.J. 583.

N.D.M. Parry, "Remuneration of Trustees" [1984] Conv. 275.

C. Stebbings, "The Rule in *Cradock v Piper* (1850): Exception or Principle?" (1998) 19(3) J. Leg. Hist. 189.

G. Virgo, "Profits Obtained in Breach of Fiduciary Duty: Personal or Proprietary Claim?" (2011) 70 C.L.J. 502.

14

Trustees' Powers: Investment, Maintenance and Advancement

As demonstrated in the previous chapter the trustee labours under a variety of duties as imposed by the trust instrument, equity and statute. By way of a correlative, the trustee is afforded a wide range of administrative powers. Some of these powers concern how the trustees may deal with the trust property, while others may focus upon how the trustees deal with the beneficiaries. The starting point is that trustees have all the powers of a legal owner of the property and that such powers can be exercised only by the trustee and not by an equitable owner.[1]

Although for the purposes of this chapter the key powers of investment, maintenance and advancement will be considered in more detail, it is to be appreciated that there is a variety of other powers that may be exercised by a trustee. At the outset, it is useful to provide illustrations of such powers. This may be done by a cursory examination of Pt II of the Trustee Act 1925 (as amended) as this offers a short catalogue of powers. Subject to exclusion or modification in the trust instrument,[2] these powers include:

- the s.12 power to sell the whole or a part of the property at public auction or by private treaty;

- the s.14 power to give a purchaser a good receipt for money paid (except when the property is land in which case the receipt must be by at least two trustees or a trust corporation);

---

1   *Schalit v Joseph Nadler Ltd* [1933] 2 K.B. 79 (the beneficiary unsuccessfully sought to exercise the remedy of distress instead of the trustee landlord).
2   Trustee Act 1925 s.69(2).

■ the s.15 power to compound liabilities by, for example, the payment of debts, accepting security for debts, allowing time for payment of debts and compromising or settling any debt;

■ the s.16 power to raise money by the sale or mortgage of trust property. This operates when the trustee is authorised to pay or apply capital money for any purpose or in any manner. This power has been limited to those cases where the money is required either to preserve assets or to advance capital[3]; and

■ the s.19 power to insure trust property. This enables a trustee to insure fully the trust property against risk of loss and damage. The insurance premiums can be met from the trust fund. It is to be appreciated that there is no power to take out life assurance and, thereby, protect against the ravages of inheritance tax on the death of a beneficiary.

The Power to Invest

14-002

The investment of trust funds is a major aspect of the administration of trusts and will be a feature of all but the most primitive of trusts. The power to invest is, therefore, administrative rather than dispositive in nature. In particular, if the subject matter of the trust is money (as opposed to, say, a house) the trustee will be under a duty to invest the trust fund to the advantage of the beneficiaries. Modest-sized trusts might only make simple investments, such as depositing the money in a bank or building society account. Nevertheless, such trustees should ensure the best interest return available in the circumstances. The trustees in *Abdulla v Abdulla*,[4] for example, agreed to reimburse the trust for additional interest (totalling £18,000) which the beneficiary claimed should have been accrued by investment of the trust assets. The claim was that the trustees could and should have obtained some 5 per cent by way of interest when they had in fact received only some 3 per cent. By way of contrast, larger trusts will employ discretionary trust managers and invest heavily on the stock market. This is facilitated by the wider powers of delegation offered in the Trustee Act 2000 (see para.**14-010**).

Investment is an attractive option as it should shield the trust fund from the depreciating effects of inflation (which is especially desirable where the trust is designed to run for a number of years). Investment of capital should also ensure that there is an income stream from which interim payments can be made to the beneficiaries (which is especially pertinent where there is a beneficiary who enjoys merely a life interest). Although there is usually a duty to invest, the

---

3 *Re Suenson-Taylor's Settlement* [1974] 3 All E.R. 397.

4 [2013] EWHC 4281 (Ch).

trustee is not given an unbridled ability to invest as he wishes. This power is subject to regulation by Parliament, the courts and the trust instrument. Unfortunately, the area of investment
is complex and not without difficulty. As the Law Commission pointed out in its short paper,
"In some areas there may be a difference between what the law actually is and how some may
perceive it. In others the law is uncertain. There may also be limited areas in which the law is
problematic".[5]

The first port of call is to examine the trust instrument. Not surprisingly, in many contemporary trusts there will be found an express investment clause. This will reflect the vision of the
settlor as to how trust property is to be invested for the better advantage of the beneficiaries.
If no express power of investment is contained in the trust instrument, the trustee is given a
statutory power to invest which is now to be found in the Trustee Act 2000.[6]

Express powers

As mentioned, common practice is to insert an express investment clause into the trust instrument. Although such a clause may operate to narrow the field of investments open to a trustee,[7]
it is usual for it to broaden the choice beyond that which is permissible under statute.[8] By way of
a simple example, such a clause might allow the trustees "to invest in or upon such investments
as to them may seem fit and as if they were the absolute owners of the fund". Accordingly, in
Khoo Tek Keong v Ch'ng Joo Tuan Neoh the extraordinarily wide scope of the investment clause
entailed that it was not a breach of duty for the trustee to make interest-bearing loans on the
security of jewellery.[9] The Privy Council did, however, conclude that the provision of unsecured
loans could not be deemed "investments" and constituted a breach of trust. This type of wide
power is intended to offer the trustees the utmost flexibility as to how and where they may
invest trust money. As will become clear, this does not give a trustee *carte blanche* to do exactly
what he wishes. The trustee throughout remains subject to the general duty to take care and
the other duties now imposed by the Trustee Act 2000. Although the trustee's statutory power
to invest has been greatly extended by the 2000 Act, it is still possible for an express power to
confer more freedom of choice and action than its statutory counterpart.

An express power must be carefully drafted so as to be clear, understandable and
capable of enforcement.[10] Traditionally, the clause is to be construed strictly with the onus
upon the trustee to establish that the investment is within its scope.[11] Hence, in *Bethell v*

14-003

---

5   Law Commission, *Fiduciary Duties of Investment Intermediaries: Initial Questions* (May 2013), para.1.7.
6   This replaces the more limited power previously contained in the Trustee Investments Act 1961.
7   See *Re Hill* [1914] W.N. 132, where a power was given to invest in specified investments only and no others.
8   See the aptly named *Re Power* [1947] Ch. 572, where the clause allowed the trustee to invest in land.
9   [1934] A.C. 529. It could, of course, be a breach of duty if, at the time of the loan, the security offered is
    insufficient.
10 See *Re Kolb's WT* [1962] Ch. 531, where a provision allowing investment in "blue chips" was void for uncertainty.
11 As will be discussed in Ch.15, the trustees may apply under the Variation of Trusts Act 1958 for the investment
    clause to be widened: *Trustees of the British Museum v Attorney General* [1984] 1 W.L.R. 418.

Abraham[12] the clause offered the trustees a wide discretion to change investments "from time to time". Sir George Jessel MR held that this did not enable the trustees to make certain speculative and substantive investments of a type substantially different from the investments chosen by the settlor before his death. Nevertheless, and as demonstrated in *Re Harari's ST*,[13] the court will strive to give an investment clause a plain and ordinary meaning. In that case, the settlor gave his trustees the power to invest trust money "in or upon such investments as to them may seem fit". Existing investments included certain Egyptian bonds and securities which, at the time, were not authorised investments. The court had to determine whether the express power was to be limited to the statutorily permitted range of investments or whether the trustees could lawfully invest outside that limited range. Jenkins J could see no justification for reading into the clause such a restriction and added, "I think the trustees have power, under the plain meaning of those words, to invest in any investments which . . . they 'honestly think' are desirable investments . . .".[14]

Statutory regulation

14-004

Until the eighteenth century, there had been little fetter placed upon the ability of a trustee to invest trust money. There was no statutory regulation and no effective guidance from the courts. Trustees were allowed to invest in any manner that was deemed appropriate. This *laissez faire* approach, however, came to an abrupt end with the misguided speculation of trustees in the South Sea Company and other high-risk ventures. As Lord Neuberger speaking extra-judicially put it, "In the heady days of the South Sea Bubble in 1720, many highly dubious company prospectuses were being hawked around the City of London to induce foolish folk to part with their money. They included a prospectus for a company which proposed to reclaim sunshine from vegetables, one for a company which allegedly intended to build mansions floating in the sea, and another for a company which allegedly was aimed at constructing a wheel for perpetual motion".[15] The so-called "bursting of the South Sea bubble", as well as the financially draining Napoleonic wars, promoted a response from the Court of Chancery. While the Court of Chancery restricted the types of investment that the trustee could select without express authorisation in the trust instrument (i.e. it frowned upon commercial speculation), it encouraged investment in government stock by offering trustees immunity from ensuing liability for breach of trust.[16] Prior to the modern Trustee Acts, the trustee's power to invest outside the terms of an express power remained limited. The emphasis was then upon the preservation

---

12 [1873] L.R. 17 Eq. 24.
13 [1949] 1 All E.R. 430.
14 [1949] 1 All E.R. 430 at 434.
15 The Blackstone Lecture, "Tweaking the Curial Veil", Pembroke College Oxford, 15 November 2014 at [1], *https://www.supremecourt.uk/docs/speech-141115.pdf* [Accessed 31 July 2020]. Lord Neuberger also alluded to a prospectus which sought subscriptions for "an undertaking of great advantage, but nobody to know what it is".
16 *Pocock v Reddington* (1801) 5 Ves. Jr. 794.

of the trust fund rather than the maximisation of benefit for the beneficiaries. Indeed, trustees could not invest in stock of a private company or Bank of England stock, lend money on security or invest in mortgages.

The nineteenth century and the advent of industrialism brought a need for a broader view of trustee investment. This was satisfied to a small extent by the now largely repealed Law of Property Amendment Act 1859 which allowed investment in stocks of the Bank of England, the Bank of Ireland and the legendary East India Co. These powers were extended piecemeal by further legislation. The range of authorised investment, however, still excluded major classes of stock and focused largely upon safe, fixed-rate investments. The next significant developments were the Trustee Investment Act 1889 and Trustee Act 1893 which brought with them a greater freedom to invest in railway stock, local authority stock and public utility stock. In 1925, the government considered whether to widen the range of trustee investment, but concluded that the cautious approach remained the best way forward. A gradual defrosting process was to continue, with further stocks added incrementally to (and, indeed, sometimes removed from) the list of permissible investments until the Trustee Investments Act 1961.

Following World War II, the nature of the trust changed dramatically. Moving away from strict settlements under which there were successive interests (i.e. tenant for life and remainderman), trusts became employed to redistribute family property in a tax-efficient manner. In addition, the vehicle of the trust was hijacked to facilitate investment in unit trusts and to provide pension trusts for employees. The ambitions of the trustee necessarily shifted in the wake of these changes. In short, the emphasis was soon to be placed upon generating the best financial returns for beneficiaries. With the emergence of inflation, coupled with the realisation that government stock was declining in value at a time when the shares of large industrial companies were increasing in worth, the clamour for greater investment powers intensified. The Trustee Investments Act 1961 was designed to cater for these modern developments.

14-005

The 1961 Act introduced a new scheme of trustee investment. The ambition was to provide a compromise between the competing objectives of safety and flexibility. The Act prescribed three classes of authorised investment which were to govern the trustee's power. The first category was styled as "narrower range investments not requiring advice". This comprised a limited band of investment that the trustee could make at any time and without consultation. It included such cautious investments as National Savings Certificates, Post Office savings accounts, bank deposits and defence bonds. The second category was described as "narrower range investments that required advice". It included government stock and the stock of nationalised industries. The third category was termed as "wider range investments requiring advice" and these concerned securities and shares of UK companies and UK unit trusts. There was no power to invest in land.

14-006

The 1961 Act also introduced changes to procedure. Although a trustee could invest exclusively in narrow range investments, when making wider-range investments the trustee was originally required to divide the trust fund into two equal parts. One part only could then be invested in the wider range, with the other part remaining in narrower range investments.[17] In

---

17   This was later modified to allow a trustee to invest as little as 25 per cent in the narrow range with potentially

the making of (and changing of) wider range investments, moreover, the trustee was required to obtain proper written advice from a qualified person as to the wisdom of the proposed dealings. The trustee also was to have regard to the need to diversify the investments and to evaluate their suitability for the trust. In 1982, the Law Reform Committee described the 1961 Act as "tiresome, cumbrous and expensive in operation with the result that its provisions are now seen to be inadequate".[18] The Committee appreciated that, in a large number of instances, the 1961 Act was modified or excluded in the trust instrument. Not surprisingly, the Committee recommended that the 1961 Act should be repealed and replaced by a new statutory code. It rejected the suggestion that trustees should enjoy a general freedom to invest, subject only to the requirement of sound prudent management. Instead, it favoured a formal scheme that categorised investments into those that could be made without advice and those which could be made only subsequent to advice being taken. The Committee did not see the justification of retaining restrictions upon the proportions of the trust fund that might be invested in either of these categories.

This theme was developed further by the Law Commission in its 1999 Report entitled "Trustees' Powers and Duties",[19] which claimed that the Trustee Act 1961 was out of date, needlessly restrictive and usually operated to the detriment of the trust. The Commission also lamented that the law as it was then did not offer adequate statutory powers to enable trustees to appoint custodians and nominees in connection with a range of modern investment services. The Commission took the opportunity to put forward a number of wide-ranging reforms that formed the basis of the Trustee Act 2000.

The Trustee Act 2000

14-007 Unless the trust instrument contains an express investment clause, which is unlikely in the case of homemade trusts, the power to invest is now widened and regulated by Pt II of the Trustee Act 2000.[20] This regulation is retrospective in application.[21] The so-called "general power of investment" is set out in s.3(1) which authorises the trustee to make "any kind of investment that he could make if he were absolutely entitled to the assets of the trust". The statutory power can, however, be modified or excluded by the trust instrument.[22] An investment for these purposes requires an anticipation of profit or income (e.g. granting a mortgage on terms that it will be repaid with interest) and "investments of the trust" refers to "the assets of the

75 per cent of the trust fund being invested in the wider range.

18   Law Reform Committee, *The Powers and Duties of Trustees* (1982) Cmnd.8733, para.3.17.
19   Law Commission, *Trustees' Powers and Duties* (1999) Law Com. No.260.
20   It does, not, however extend to pension trusts, unit trusts or charitable trusts (ss.36–38). These are regulated by different and specific legislative codes.
21   Section 7(1) of the Trustee Act 2000.
22   Section 6(1) of the 2000 Act. It cannot be limited or excluded in a trust instrument created before 3 August 1961 (i.e. the coming into force of the Trustee Investments Act 1961).

trust" or "the trust fund".[23] This power does not extend to investments in land (except loaning money by way of mortgage) as the power to invest in land is specifically governed by s.8. Unlike its predecessor, the new Act does not restrict the trustees to listed investments. Instead, the power is broadened to facilitate any investment. As will be discussed in para.**14-014**, the trustee labours under the duty of care prescribed in s.1 of the 2000 Act.[24]

Standard investment criteria and reviews

Trustees when exercising the statutory power of investment are required to have regard to what are styled as "standard investment criteria".[25] Section 4(3)(a) requires the trustees, when making any investment or reviewing existing investments, to have regard to the suitability of particular investments. This will involve consideration of the extent to which the investments are appropriate in light of the nature of the trust and the needs of the beneficiaries.[26] In *Re Buckley*,[27] for example, an aged woman executed a lasting power of attorney in favour of her niece. Following advice by the business owner, the niece used some £88,000 of her aunt's money to invest in a reptile breeding business. The power of attorney was revoked on the basis that the niece had acted in a way that was not in the aunt's best interests, taking into account the age and life expectancy of the aunt. As Senior Judge Lush observed, "The investment was very high risk. When investing funds on behalf of older people, the perceived wisdom is that the investments should be safe and that very little risk is acceptable as can be seen from the short-term investment tables . . . Even when investing funds long-term on behalf of a younger person, a hazardous and speculative investment of this kind would have been inappropriate for anyone in a fiduciary position to make".[28] Section 4(3)(b) also emphasises the need for diversification and this is designed to ensure that there will be a range of investments and a minimisation of investment risk.

The trustees are obliged by virtue of s.4(2) to carry out periodic reviews of the investment portfolio and, if necessary, to vary the investments. The duty to review applies equally to an investment which is settled on a trustee and one which is purchased by a trustee in the exercise

---

23 See *Gregson v HAE Trustees Ltd* [2008] EWHC 1006 (Ch).
24 For an overview of the scope of the Act, see S. Panesar, "The Trustee Act 2000" (2001) I.C.C.L.R. 151. He concludes (at 157) that "The provisions of the Trustee Act 2000 are a reflection of the fact that the trust is now operating in conditions far different from those that existed at the beginning of the twentieth century".
25 Section 4(1) of the 2000 Act. Similar provisions were previously to be found in s.6(1) of the Trustee Investment Act 1961.
26 *Gregson v HAE Trustees Ltd* [2008] EWHC 1006 (Ch). There Ms Gregson, the beneficiary, alleged that the trustee company, HAE Trustees, was in breach of duty in failing to review the need to diversify investments. The Company had no assets so the beneficiary sued the directors directly (this is sometimes called a "dog leg" claim). This was, however, unsuccessful as the directors owe a duty to the Company and not the beneficiaries (s.174 of the Companies Act 2006).
27 [2013] EWHC 2965 (COP).
28 [2013] EWHC 2965 (COP) at [51].

of his powers.[29] This requirement was imposed at common law by virtue of cases such as *Bartlett v Barclays Bank Trust Co Ltd*.[30] A trustee who fails to carry out periodic reviews will be in breach of trust. For most purposes, an annual review carried out at the end of each tax year will be appropriate.

Taking advice

14-009

Section 5 of the 2000 Act requires the trustees to obtain and consider proper investment advice from a suitable source before exercising any power of investment or before reviewing the existing investments of the trust. There is no requirement that the advice be given in writing. The need to take advice is not limited to investment under the statutory power, but applies also to any investment under an express power. The rule requiring advice only gives way when it would be reasonable to proceed without such advice (e.g. if the investment is small or the investments proposed are low risk).[31]

Section 5(4) states that the advice must come from "a person who is reasonably believed by the trustee to be qualified to give it by his ability in and practical experience of financial and other matters relating to the proposed investment". The adviser must be licensed under the Financial Services and Markets Act 2000. Hence, the source could be an expert trustee or an outside adviser. As to the niece's unwise investment in *Re Buckley*, Senior Judge Lush lamented, "She did not obtain and consider proper advice from someone who is qualified to give investment advice. One can hardly describe a man who runs a reptile breeding business as someone who is qualified to give investment advice by his ability in and practical experience of financial and other matters relating to investment".[32] Although trustees are not obliged to follow the advice received, if they decline to do so they run the risk of personal liability for any resultant loss.[33] In principle, moreover, it is possible that a trustee who relies on erroneous advice of a professional adviser could still be personally liable for breach of trust. The trustee must not follow such advice blindly, but must exercise his own independent judgment and, if he feels that the advice is obviously or glaringly wrong, it should not be followed.[34] Understandably, the more specialist the nature of the advice, the more reasonable is it likely to be for a trustee to act on it.[35]

---

29 *Gregson v HAE Trustees Ltd* [2008] EWHC 1006 (Ch).
30 [1980] 1 All E.R. 139.
31 Section 5(3) of the 2000 Act.
32 [2013] EWHC 2965 (COP) at [50].
33 See *Adams v Bridge* [2009] Pens. L.R. 153. It is, therefore, wise for trustees to document in writing why they have not followed Investment advice. In *Daniel v Tee* [2016] 4 W.L.R. 115, for example, aspects of advice were ignored to minimise risk to the trust.
34 *Locke v Camberwell HA* [1991] 2 Med. L.R. 249. The honest and reasonable trustee might, however, be relieved of liability under s.61 of the Trustee Act 1925 (see para.**13-054**).
35 See *Daniel v Tee* [2016] 4 W.L.R. 115.

Delegation, nominees and custodians

As the investment of trust funds is a complex and potentially risky venture, it is a desirable practice that the task as regards substantial trusts should be delegated to someone with the necessary skills and expertise (e.g. an asset manager). Until the enactment of the Trustee Act 2000, the rule was that the trustee could delegate only administrative functions. This entailed that the trustee could not delegate discretions relating to which investments should be made and when those investments should be changed.[36] This unsatisfactory state of affairs has been remedied in Pt IV of the Trustee Act 2000. Section 11 allows the trustees collectively to delegate to an agent discretion relating to asset management.[37] Absent such a power, the trustees would be required to give instructions to a broker on each sale or purchase of an investment. The agent is bound by any restrictions imposed on the trustee by the trust deed and must operate subject to the standard investment criteria (s.13(1)). If the agent is a qualified financial adviser, there is no requirement that the agent seek professional advice (s.13(2)). Legal title to the investments throughout remains with the trustees. Section 15, however, imposes some special restrictions on this power to delegate and, if they are not complied with, there can be no lawful delegation.[38] It provides that the employment of the investment manager be in writing or, at the least, evidenced in writing. Section 15 also requires the trustee to draft a policy document which details how the asset manager is to go about his business. This policy statement will provide a set of trust objectives that the agent must follow. When appropriate, the statement can be revised by the trustee at a later date.

Subject to modification by the trust instrument, the 2000 Act contains other powers so as to facilitate a more effective trust administration and these include the appointment of custodians (s.16) and nominees (s.17). These characters are not trustees, but are controlled by the trustees. Such appointments, therefore, do not undermine the fiduciary relationship between trustee and beneficiary. The Act restricts those who can be appointed as a custodian or nominee to professionals or a company controlled by the trustees (s.19(2)) and describes their terms of appointment (s.20). Appointments of both must be in writing or, at least, evidenced in writing (ss.16(2),17(3)). Custodians and nominees can recover expenses and receive reasonable remuneration for their services (s.32)). The trustees are obliged to keep the arrangement under review (s.22).

A custodian is a necessary appointment when the trustees retain or invest in bearer securities (s.18). Whereas the function of a custodian is to manage (i.e. to take care of trust documents and other indicia of title), a nominee will be vested with legal title to trust assets, such as shares. The employment of a nominee might be designed so as:

■ to offer an administrative service in relation to investments;

---

36   An exception to this rule, however, applied in relation to pension trusts under the Pensions Act 1995.
37   Section 12 states who may act as an agent and this includes an existing trustee, but not a beneficiary.
38   *Daniel v Tee* [2016] 4 W.L.R. 115.

- to facilitate dealings by a discretionary fund manager;

- to enable the use of CREST (i.e. the United Kingdom's electronic registration and settlement system for equity share trading) which allows shares to be held in electronic form rather than in physical form; and

- if registered land is held in trust, to avoid the need for repeated changes to the identity of the registered proprietors as and when trustees change.

A trustee is not vicariously liable for any act or default of the agent, nominee or custodian unless the trustee has failed to comply with the duty of care applicable to him regarding the appointment and review of the arrangements (s.23(1)).

Investment in land

14-011

As mentioned, traditionally the trustee could not purchase land as an investment. This rule gave way in the face of express authority in the trust instrument or when such investment is permitted by s.6 of the Trusts of Land and Appointment of Trustees Act 1996 (the 1996 Act). As to express authority, land could be acquired only for the purposes of generating an income for the trust[39] and not, say, to provide rent-free accommodation for a beneficiary.[40] The 1996 Act, however, operates with a different ethos. This allows trustees of land (not personalty) to purchase land for occupation by a beneficiary or for any other purpose. Accordingly, a house might have been acquired initially for resale at a profit, but subsequently the trustee may decide instead to allow the beneficiary to take up residence.

Section 8 of the Trustee Act 2000 is modelled upon the 1996 Act provision and allows the trustee of personalty to purchase freehold or leasehold land in the United Kingdom as an investment, for occupation by a beneficiary or for any other reason. It does not have to be intended to generate a rental income. It might, therefore, be purchased simply to provide a home for a beneficiary. On acquiring land, the trustee under both statutory schemes has the same powers as would an absolute owner and this allows the trustee to sell, mortgage, lease or otherwise deal with the land. The trustee, of course, remains subject to the duty of care set out in s.1 of the Trustee Act 2000. The application of s.8 can be excluded or modified[41] in the trust instrument and, if not so excluded, operates regardless of when the trust was created.

---

39 *Re Wragg* [1919] 2 Ch. 58.
40 *Re Power* [1947] Ch. 572. As there was no income stream from the property, it could not be said to be an investment.
41 In *Alexander v Alexander* [2011] EWHC 2721 (Ch), for example, the trustees were denied the power to purchase leasehold land with an unexpired term of less than 60 years.

Investing in mortgages of land

Section 3 of the 2000 Act permits the trustee to invest in land by means of providing a loan secured on the land (i.e. the granting of a mortgage). The mortgage may be legal or equitable. Understandably, private mortgages are now uncommon. Mortgage funds are in modern times provided by banks, building societies and other lending institutions. For the trustee, the grant of a mortgage is not an attractive form of investment. Instead, investment in stocks and shares is the preferred option. Some guidance to the trustee who wishes to grant a mortgage is to be found in s.8 of the Trustee Act 1925. This sets standards which the trustee should (but is not obliged to) follow. Section 8 deals with issues of value and is not concerned with whether the investment by way of mortgage is prudent. It states that:

- the trustee should not lend a sum greater than two-thirds of the value of the property;

- the trustee should obtain a valuation report from a surveyor or valuer; and

- the trustee should grant the mortgage on the advice of the surveyor or valuer.

In circumstances where a trustee complies with the statutory guidance, he will be protected as regards any loss that arises from an incorrect valuation of the mortgaged property. If he does not follow such steps, however, the trustee will be liable for loss which is suffered by the trust estate by reason of his failure to do so.[42] Accordingly, if the trustee lends more than two-thirds of the value of the security, the trustee's liability will (if the mortgage is otherwise a proper investment) be scaled down to the excess sum with interest. In *Shaw v Cates*,[43] the maximum advance authorised was £3,400, but the trustee advanced £4,400. The trustee's liability was capped at making good the £1,000 excess with interest.

The trustee's duty of care

At common law, the duty of care placed upon a trustee when investing trust funds was higher than that imposed on him when carrying out his other administrative functions. The general yardstick was that the trustee must invest the trust property wisely acting as an ordinary prudent man making investments.[44] At the Court of Appeal stage in *Learoyd v Whiteley*, Lindley LJ explained that, "The duty of a trustee is not to take such care only as a prudent man would take if he had only himself to consider; the duty rather is to take such care as an ordinary prudent man would take if he were minded to make an investment for the benefit of other

---

42 See *Re Solomon* [1912] 1 Ch. 261, where Warrington J surveyed the relationship between the valuer and the trustee.
43 [1909] 1 Ch. 389.
44 See generally *Daniel v Tee* [2016] 4 W.L.R. 115.

people for whom he felt morally bound to provide".[45] The distinction is framed around the acceptance that a prudent man of business might still invest in risky ventures. As Lord Watson commented in the House of Lords in *Learoyd v Whiteley*, "businessmen of ordinary prudence may, and frequently do, select investments which are more or less of a speculative character; but it is the duty of trustees to confine themselves to the class of investments which are permitted by the trust, and likewise to avoid all investments of that class which are attended with hazard".[46] This test was, however, to prove ill-suited to developing investment practices. The objective standard of a prudent businessman became relatively meaningless in a complex commercial environment where businessmen display varying degrees of skill and aspire to different objectives. A further gloss was added by Hoffmann J at first instance in *Nestle v National Westminster Bank Plc*.[47] He advocated what is known as the "portfolio theory", which entails that, as trustees will often introduce an element of diversity to their investment portfolio, they are to be judged on their overall performance and not on the failure or success of a particular investment. As Hoffmann J observed, "modern trustees acting within their investment powers are entitled to be judged by the standards of the current portfolio theory, which emphasises the risk level of the entire portfolio rather than the risk attaching to each investment taken in isolation".[48] Hence, it is possible for a trustee to engage in a high risk venture which would alone be a breach of trust and yet falls not to be classified as such due to the profitability of other investments. Unsurprisingly, Thornton takes the stance that the portfolio theory offers trustees de facto immunity and adds that, "due to the risk and uncertainty inherent in the making of investment choices, it will be very difficult in practice for aggrieved beneficiaries to prove loss arising from breach of their trustees' duties in this respect".[49]

As discussed in Ch.13, the standard of care expected of a trustee has been redefined in s.1 of the Trustee Act 2000. This overhauled duty is not limited merely to investment and extends widely to such diverse functions as, for example, the acquisition of land, the entering into arrangements to appoint agents and nominees, the exercise of powers of compromise and insurance and the valuation of trust property.

14-014

Subject to exclusion in the trust instrument, s.1 of the 2000 Act provides that the trustee must exercise such care and skill as is reasonable in the circumstances having regard, first, to any special knowledge or experience that he has or holds himself out as having. This instils a subjective element into the test. Secondly, and if he acts as trustee in the course of a business or profession, regard must be had to any special knowledge or experience that it is reasonable to expect of a person acting in the course of that business or profession. This instils an objective element into the test. The standard of care prescribed in the 2000 Act confirms

---

45 (1886) L.R. 33 Ch. D. 347 at 355.
46 (1897) L.R. 12 A.C. 727 at 733.
47 Unreported 29 June 1988.
48 Unreported 29 June 1988.
49 R. Thornton, "Ethical Investments: A Case of Disjointed Thinking" [2008] C.L.J. 396, 415. Indeed, such was demonstrated in *Daniel v Tee* [2016] 4 W.L.R. 115, where it was emphasised that, no matter how imprudent the trustee had acted, liability would arise only if loss to the trust could be established.

that a professional trustee is expected to show a higher degree of care than a lay trustee.[50] A lay trustee who makes investments will, therefore, be judged against a different standard of reasonableness than his professional counterpart. Hence, as is evident from *Bartlett v Barclays Bank Trust Co Ltd*, a trust company with specialist staff will be judged on a different level to an unpaid, family trustee.[51] This case was in its time described by Schindler as marking "a radical departure from the single standard of competence expected from trustees".[52]

In the *Bartlett* case, the trustee Bank allowed a management company to invest trust money in two ambitious development projects which were described by Brightman J as "a gamble and not, on the evidence I have heard, a very good gamble".[53] The Bank did not ask for or receive much information about the transactions. Subsequently, the beneficiaries sued the Bank as trustee for breach of trust for the substantial losses that were incurred by the failure of the two projects. The Bank attempted to shield itself behind the management company, claiming that it should be entitled to rely on the expertise and skills of the company's experienced board of directors. Brightman J accepted that there is an element of risk inherent in any investment, but noted that "The distinction is between a prudent degree of risk on the one hand, and hazard on the other".[54] This was such a hazardous investment that it should not have been made without express authorisation in the trust instrument. The judge considered the Bank's position as if, first, it had been an ordinary trustee and, secondly, as a specialist trustee. The Bank had failed in its duty whether it was judged by the standard of the prudent businessman or the skills of a trust corporation. In relation to the former, Brightman J determined that such a trustee, as a prudent man of business, would have been more proactive and sought out more information about the activities of the management company. The Bank should have overseen the company's use of the trust money. The judge, however, concluded that the Bank was an expert trustee and, therefore, plainly owed a higher level of care. Brightman J explained:

> "A trust corporation holds itself out in its advertising literature as being above ordinary mortals. With a specialist staff of trained trust officers and managers with ready access to financial information and professional advice, dealing with and solving trust problems day after day, the trust corporation holds itself out, and rightly, as capable of providing an expertise which it would be unrealistic to expect and unjust to demand from the ordinary prudent man or woman who accepts, probably unpaid and sometimes reluctantly from a sense of family duty, the burdens of trusteeship . . . a profes-

---

50   See generally, Law Commission, *Fiduciary Duties of Investment Intermediaries* (2013) Consultation Paper No.215.
51   [1980] 1 All E.R. 139.
52   G.A. Schindler [1980] 44 Conv. 155, 158; see also, P. Pearce and A. Samuels, "Negligent Investment by Trustees" [1983] Conv. 127.
53   [1980] 1 All E.R. 139 at 147.
54   [1980] 1 All E.R. 139 at 150.

sional corporate trustee is liable for breach of trust if loss is caused to the trust fund because it neglects to exercise the special care and skill which it professes to have".[55]

Consecutive interests

14-015

As regards trusts with consecutive interests (i.e. where there is a tenant for life and a remainderman), the trustees are under a duty to treat income and capital beneficiaries in an impartial manner.[56] This might be described as a duty to act fairly between all types of beneficiary. The trustee must, therefore, ensure that a fair balance is drawn between high income and high-risk investments and those safer and less lucrative investments that will preserve the capital. As Hoffmann J put it at first instance in *Nestle v National Westminster Bank Plc*, "The trustees must act fairly in making investment decisions which may have different consequences for different classes of beneficiaries".[57] The general duty was to require certain returns and outgoings of a trust to be shared in a particular way between capital and income. In some cases, this imposed a duty to sell certain investments. These became known as rules of apportionment. It had long been clear, however, that the apportionment rules were either excluded in the trust instrument or plainly ignored. The problem was that the rules generated considerable inconvenience by requiring complex calculations often in relation to small sums of money. Parliament has now intervened in the form of the Trusts (Capital and Income) Act 2013.[58] The Act abolishes the rules for trusts coming into existence after 1 October 2013. Settlors who wish the rules to apply can, however, make express provision to that effect in the trust instrument.

In the *Nestle* case, the settlor left £54,000 in shares on trust for his widow for life and thereafter for his children and grandchildren. Eventually, his granddaughter (as remainderman) became entitled to the trust fund (then worth £269,000). The investment portfolio had throughout been managed by the Bank as trustee. The granddaughter claimed that the Bank was in breach of trust because it had mismanaged the trust investments by failing to diversify and to review the portfolio. She argued that, had the Bank not acted in an overly cautious manner, the fund should have been worth more than £1 million. In the Court of Appeal,[59] it was determined that the Bank was not in breach of trust. This was so even though it had misunder-

---

55 [1980] 1 All E.R. 139 at 152.
56 See *Close Trustees (Switzerland) SA v Vildosola* [2008] EWHC 1267 (Ch) where the trustees sought to make a one-third retention of future income of a life tenant in order to secure their anticipated legal costs. In rejecting the trustees' claim, Deputy Judge Mark Herbert observed, "the trustees and the court should not favour one party against the other . . ." (at [29]).
57 Unreported 29 June 1988.
58 This gave effect to the recommendations contained in the Law Commission's Report, *Capital and Income in Trusts: Classification and Apportionment* (2009) Law Com No.315.
59 [1994] 1 All E.R. 118; noted at [1993] Conv. 63 (A. Kenny).

stood the scope of its investment powers, failed to conduct periodic reviews, did not diversify effectively and in the past had shown symptoms of what Staughton LJ described as "incompetence or idleness".[60] The trustee had nevertheless satisfied the required standard of care. By the undemanding standard of prudence, the Bank was not shown to have been in breach of its duty. Leggatt LJ explained that the Bank's, "engagement was as a trustee, and, as such, it is to be judged not so much by success as by absence of proven default".[61] Staughton LJ added that Ms Nestle failed because she was unable to show that "the trustees made decisions which they should not have made or failed to make decisions which they should have made".[62]

As to consecutive interests, in the *Nestle* case the trustee had attempted to balance the income needs of the tenant for life with the longer-term capital interests of the granddaughter. It is for the trustee to reconcile this conflict of interest. As Staughton LJ accepted, "At times it will not be easy to decide what is an equitable balance. A life tenant may be anxious to receive the highest possible income, whilst the remainderman will wish the real value of the trust fund to be preserved. If the life tenant is living in penury and the remainderman already has ample wealth, common sense suggests that a trustee should be able to take that into account, not necessarily be seeking the highest possible income at the expense of capital but by inclining in that direction".[63] The trustee has merely to maintain a fair, impartial and equitable balance between the two camps. Although this does not require the interests to be evenly balanced, the appellate court accepted that, where there are successive interests under a trust, at least 50 per cent of the investments should lie in ordinary shares issued by companies. The reasoning is that such investments tend to keep pace with inflation. It will suffice if, as in *Nestle*, those investments are in the "safest" (but often financially less rewarding) shares such as in banks and insurance companies.

14-016

Non-financial considerations

The duty of a trustee is to act in the best financial interests of the beneficiaries both present and future, which is part of the general obligation to promote the purpose for which the trust was created and not for any extraneous purpose.[64] This entails that the trustee must obtain the best rate of return available coupled with diversification of risks.[65] This is so even

14-017

---

60   [1994] 1 All E.R. 118 at 133.
61   [1994] 1 All E.R. 118 at 142.
62   [1994] 1 All E.R. 118 at 133, 134.
63   [1994] 1 All E.R. 118 at 137.
64   *Re Merchant Navy Ratings Pension Fund* [2015] EWHC 448 (Ch). As Asplin J explained (at [228]), "It is necessary first to decide what is the purpose of the trust and what benefits were intended to be received by the beneficiaries before being in a position to decide whether a proposed course is for the benefit of the beneficiaries or in their best interests".
65   In *Buttle v Saunders* [1950] 2 All E.R. 193, the trustees sought to sell trust land to Mrs Saunders at lower price than another offer that had been made. The trustees had an overriding duty to obtain the best price which they could obtain. Although there might be cases where trustees could properly refuse a higher offer, each case must depend on its own facts. Here the trustees should at least have tested the strength of the later offer.

where it is against the political, social or moral views of some of the beneficiaries.[66] In *Cowan v Scargill*,[67] the investment policy of the mineworkers' pension fund was challenged by five union-appointed trustees. The fund was managed by 10 trustees, half of whom were appointed by the National Union of Mineworkers and the rest appointed by the Coal Board. The dispute concerned investments in foreign energy companies. The trustees appointed by the Trade Union objected to the investments on the ground that these companies were in direct competition with the domestic coal mining industry. The five trustees were motivated by their personal views and the wish to promote union policy. The other trustees countered that many of the beneficiaries (e.g. widows) would not directly be affected by the success or otherwise of the mining industry and that any claimed social benefits were too speculative and remote. The High Court held that the trustees had to act in the best financial interests of the beneficiaries and, hence, that they would be in breach of duty if they failed to invest in the overseas energy companies. The trustees, therefore, had to put aside their personal interest and views. Megarry VC considered the relevance of non-financial concerns:

> "Trustees may have strongly held social or political views. They may be firmly opposed to investment in South Africa or other countries, or they may object to any form of investment in companies concerned with alcohol, tobacco, armaments or many other things. In the conduct of their own affairs, of course, they are free to abstain from making any such investments. Yet under a trust, if investments of this type would be more beneficial to the beneficiaries than other investments, the trustees must not refrain from making the investments by reason of the views that they hold".[68]

It has been argued by Farrar and Maxton that the stance adopted by Megarry VC is too rigid, in that "The pension scheme in question was not an ordinary private trust. It was an extraordinary trust with certain public characteristics set up under a scheme for nationalization. The object of the nationalization was to develop the industry in the national interest and safeguard the welfare of employees".[69] Perhaps this overstates the nature of the trust and overlooks the fact that the primary aim was to benefit individuals. Some have interpreted *Cowan* as imposing on a trustee an absolute duty to invest funds in the most profitable investments available.[70] It is, however, important to appreciate that ethical investment is not prohibited by the decision in *Cowan*. Even Megarry VC admitted, "I am not asserting that the benefit of the beneficiaries which a trustee must make his paramount concern inevitably and solely means their financial

---

66   See R. Thornton, "Ethical Investments: a Case of Disjointed Thinking" [2008] C.L.J. 396.
67   [1985] Ch. 270.
68   [1985] Ch. 270 at 287, 288. He added at 288, "trustees may even have to act dishonourably (though not illegally) if the interests of their beneficiaries require it".
69   J.H. Farrar and J.K. Maxton, "Social Investment and Pension Scheme Trusts" (1986) 102 L.Q.R. 32, 33.
70   Fair Pensions, "Protecting Our Best Interests: Rediscovering Fiduciary Obligation" (March 2011), p.20.

benefit . . .".[71] It is still possible for the trust instrument to sanction ethical investment or to prohibit investment in certain companies.[72] The beneficiaries, moreover, may collectively sanction such an investment policy and the trustees always retain the ability to choose ethical investing when the financial returns will be equivalent to an alternative, "non-ethical" portfolio.[73]

As regards charitable trusts, however, a modified approach is adopted.[74] The trustees are entitled to decline investments that run contrary to the objectives of that trust (e.g. investing in armament companies). As Nicholls VC put it in *Harries v Church Commissioners for England*:

> **"There will be some cases, I suspect comparatively rare, when the objects of the charity are such that investments of a particular type would conflict with the aims of the charity. Much cited examples are those of cancer research companies and tobacco shares, trustees of temperance societies and brewery and distillery shares, and trustees of charities of the Society of Friends and shares in companies engaged in production of armaments".[75]**

Although logically the trustees could take this course even if it was to the financial detriment of the charity, this is unlikely to arise in practice. As Nicholls VC observed, "It is not easy to think of an instance where in practice the exclusion for this reason of one or more companies or sectors from the whole range of investments open to trustees would be likely to leave them without an adequately wide range of investments from which to choose a properly diversified portfolio".[76] The trustees cannot, therefore, totally disregard the financial implications of their restrictive decision making. As demonstrated in the *Harries* case, charitable trustees are not allowed to pursue a blanket policy of ethical investment if this would be detrimental to the value of the trust fund. In *Martin v Edinburgh DC*,[77] the trustees, as a protest against apartheid in South Africa, decided to withdraw their trustee investments in that country. The court restrained this action because the trustees had not considered whether it was in the best interest of the beneficiaries to do so and had not obtained professional advice as to whether what was proposed was in the best interest of the beneficiaries.

---

71 [1985] Ch. 270 at 288.

72 *Harries v Church Commissioners for England* [1992] 1 W.L.R. 1241. There the trustees wanted to invest with the object of promoting the Christian faith.

73 See *Martin v City of Edinburgh DC* [1989] Pens. L.R. 9. Thornton regards this exception as being "based in unreality" and believes that "the occurrence of such a choice is a practical impossibility" ([2008] C.L.J. 396, 405). It has been argued that statutory clarification is needed so as to liberate trustees from any perceived restrictions upon their ability to invest as they see fit: Fair Pensions, *Protecting Our Best Interests: Rediscovering Fiduciary Obligation* (March 2011), p.78.

74 See R. Nobles, "Charities and Ethical Investment" [1992] Conv. 115, 116, who makes the astute point that, "if they can be trusted to make these judgments when giving away the charity's property, they can be trusted to make its investments on the same basis".

75 [1992] 1 W.L.R. 1241 at 1246.

76 [1992] 1 W.L.R. 1241 at 1246.

77 [1989] Pens. L.R. 9.

Investment and charitable trusts

14-018

The powers and duties of charitable trustees as regards investment are broadly similar to those of private trustees.[78] Such powers will be prescribed either expressly in the trust instrument or by legislation. Accordingly, charitable trustees have the general power of investment conferred by s.3 of the Trustee Act 2000 and this allows them to invest as if they were absolutely entitled to the fund, subject to the standard investment criteria and the taking of expert advice. These provisions only assume relevance where the trust fund is so substantial that diversification of investments and the associated professional costs can be absorbed. Many charities, however, have such small trust funds that the prescription of the Trustee Act 2000 is unsuitable and inappropriate. To cater for such small funds, s.96 of the Charities Act 2011 permits the court and the Charity Commission to devise schemes ("common investment schemes") which allow participating charities to have their investments pooled under the control of management trustees appointed by the court.[79] The aim is to allow separate charitable trusts to be combined into one scheme. Section 96 provides that such a scheme can be devised on the request of two or more charities and this remains so even if the trustees are the same persons. As Wilberforce J acknowledged in *Re University of London Charitable Trusts*, "The result of that would be that the university has power to consolidate any other charitable trusts of which the university might become trustee so as to be part of the combined pool without coming back to court . . .".[80] By way of an alternative strategy, charitable trustees can apply for the authorisation of a "common deposit fund" which allows the funds to be pooled and placed in an interest-bearing account.[81]

Maintenance of Minor Beneficiaries from Income

14-019

Absent an express provision in the trust instrument or statute, trustees are not authorised to pay trust income or capital to a minor. The basic idea is that a person under the age of 18 years (unless married)[82] is legally incapable of giving a valid receipt for such payments. Similarly,

---

78 Since 1 January 2014, the Trusts (Capital and Income) Act 2013 allows the trustees of charities with a permanent endowment (normally grant-giving foundations that have been left endowments) to adopt a "total return" approach to investment. This allows charities to make a wider range of investments and to put money into assets that have good growth prospects, but pay little income.

79 The rules regulating common investment schemes are governed by ss.96–99 of the Charities Act 2011.

80 [1964] Ch. 282 at 285.

81 These funds are governed by ss.100–103 of the Charities Act 2011.

82 The capacity for a married minor to give a good receipt is afforded by s.21 of the Law of Property Act 1925.

a minor's parents or guardian cannot give a receipt on the infant's behalf.[83] As to payments made from trust income for the maintenance and education of a minor beneficiary, however, a paternalistic approach has long been adopted. This is of obvious merit in the situation, say, where Fred leaves shares by will to his grandson, Jordan, conditional upon Jordan reaching 18 years of age. At Fred's death, Jordan is 14 years old. The trustees will retain the legal title to the shares until the contingency is met (i.e. Jordan reaches majority age). In the intervening period, those shares will attract dividend payments (i.e. they will generate income for the trust). As (and only because) Jordan is beneficially entitled to that intermediate income, the income can be employed (either at the discretion of the trustees or pursuant to a court order) to promote his welfare. The power to make such maintenance payments is claimed by the court under an inherent jurisdiction and is afforded to trustees either expressly in the trust instrument or by virtue of s.31(1) of the Trustee Act 1925.[84]

The court's inherent jurisdiction

14-020

The court claims an inherent jurisdiction to authorise payments from income to maintain or educate an infant beneficiary.[85] The inherent jurisdiction to apply trust income for the benefit of a minor beneficiary exists even where the minor's interest is contingent (e.g. conditional upon attaining 18 years of age) or is otherwise defeasible (e.g. by the exercise by the trustees of a power of appointment). As Pearson J pointed out *Re Collins*, the underlying notion is that a testator who has put property on trust for children could not intend, "that these children should be left unprovided for or in a state of such moderate means that they should not be educated properly for the position and fortune which he designs them to have . . .".[86] He continued that "to deprive the children for 21 years of all the income would be to make the property, when it comes to them, an injury rather than a benefit".[87] This inherent jurisdiction is remarkable as it permits the court to disregard the clearest wording of a testator's will in order to promote an outcome that, it is assumed, the testator would have wished for had he given any thought to the matter.[88] It is not, however, to be used to deflect the living parents' responsibility to look after their own children. Accordingly, and even if there is a substantial trust fund, the parent must shoulder the burden of maintaining the child and cannot shift that

---

83 *Harvell v Foster* [1954] 2 All E.R. 736.

84 Sections 31 and 32 (the advancement provision) are amended by the Inheritance and Trustees' Powers Act 2014, which gives effect to the recommendations of the Law Commission, *Intestacy and Family Provision Claims on Death* (2011) Law Com. No.331.

85 In rare circumstances, moreover, the jurisdiction has been employed to maintain an adult beneficiary: *Revel v Watkinson* (1748) 1 Ves. Sen. 93.

86 (1886) L.R. 32 Ch. D. 229 at 232. The court authorised £2,000 a year in total for the maintenance and education of three minor beneficiaries.

87 (1886) L.R. 32 Ch. D. 229 at 233.

88 See the speech of Lord Morton in *Chapman v Chapman* [1954] A.C. 429 at 456, where he acknowledged that this was an exception to the general rule that the court cannot alter a man's will because it thinks it beneficial.

responsibility on to the child.[89] In the light of the emergence of express and statutory powers, this jurisdiction is now seldom exercised.

Express powers

14-021

Despite the existence of the inherent jurisdiction of the court to provide for minors, it became common for express provision to be made in professionally drafted trust instruments enabling trustees to use trust income for maintenance purposes. Tax considerations (particularly as regards inheritance tax) traditionally shape when and in what form an express power will appear. Understandably, the precise effect of an express clause turns upon the construction given to the words employed by the settlor. In *Re Peel*,[90] for example, the express provision was couched in such imperative language that the court concluded it to be a trust and not a power at all. Hence, the income had to be used for the maintenance of the minor beneficiaries and could not be accumulated. In *Re Borwick's Settlement*,[91] there was an express power, but it was drafted to exclude maintenance while the minor was in the custody and control of his father or while his father "had anything to do with the education or bringing up" of the minor. This restriction was effective to narrow the scope of the trustee's power which could not be exercised unless the father abandoned all parental control over the infant.

If the court discerns the existence of a power to maintain then the trustees enjoy the discretion to make payments. There is no obligation to make an award. The trustees must, therefore, honestly decide whether or not to exercise the power and make the payment to the parent or guardian of the minor.

14-022

In reaching their decision, the trustees must have regard to the interests of the minor and not take on board the interests of the settlor or anyone else (e.g. the infant's parents). Although the exercise of the power (say, to pay for school or medical fees) may in its wake be of incidental benefit to a parent, this does not prevent the trustees exercising their power. As Lightman J commented in *Fuller v Evans*, "I find it very difficult to read the settlement as paralysing the trustees in this situation, barring them from exercising the powers conferred on them merely because a by-product of their exercise is an advantage to the settlor".[92] He concluded that, "If the trustees reach the conclusion that it is in the best interests of the beneficiaries to make such provision out of trust funds, they are free to do so".[93]

In addition, and as demonstrated in *Wilson v Turner*,[94] the trustees have to make a separate decision each time that payment is claimed or made. There the trustees handed over the

---

89 *Douglas v Andrews* (1849) 12 Beav. 310.
90 [1936] Ch. 161. The clause read, "upon trust to pay or apply the same in manner thereinafter provided to or for the benefit of the children".
91 [1916] 2 Ch. 304.
92 [2000] 1 All E.R. 636 at 638.
93 [2000] 1 All E.R. 636 at 639.
94 (1883) 22 Ch. D. 521.

entire income of the trust fund to the father during the infancy of the minor beneficiary without periodically considering the continuing merits of the minor's claim and, thereby, without exercising their discretion.[95] The money was recoverable from the father's estate. Similarly, the trustees cannot decide upon a blanket refusal ever to make a maintenance payment. If they do so, the beneficiary can apply to court for an appropriate order.[96] In the light of the statutory power to maintain (considered immediately below), an express power is no longer a necessary feature of the trust instrument.[97] Those that remain, however, are usually modelled upon the statutory power with customised features as are desired by the settlor.

The statutory power

Parliament has, since Lord Cranworth's Act 1860, demonstrated a concern for infants and allowed trustees to make payments for the "maintenance or education" of minors. There has never been a statutory power to maintain adult beneficiaries. The current and wider statutory power is to be found in s.31 of the Trustee Act 1925 (as amended) and, subject to exclusion or modification in the trust instrument,[98] this automatically applies to all trusts coming into operation after 1925.[99] The statutory power applies whether the trust is established by will or is an inter vivos (i.e. a lifetime) trust and operates regardless of the nature of the property.[100] Its purpose is "to simplify the task of the draftsman of a trust instrument and to fill gaps which he might unwittingly leave in the disposal of trust income".[101] Unfortunately, s.31 is difficult to navigate and, as Lord Evershed MR admitted in *Re Vestey's Settlement*, "The language . . . I confess, is by no means easy to follow, nor does it seem to me that the section has been put together in a way which makes the task of apprehending its effect as easy as might be".[102]

As originally drafted, s.31(1) of the Trustee Act 1925 provided that "trustees may, at their sole discretion, pay to his parent or guardian, if any, or otherwise apply for or towards his maintenance, education or benefit, the whole or such part of the income of that property as may, in all the circumstances, be reasonable . . .".[103] Hence, the trustees could pay, say, fees directly to a school. The Law Commission recommended that the words "as may, in all the circumstances,

---

95 See also, *Re Greenwood* (1911) 105 L.T. 509.
96 *Stopford v Lord Canterbury* (1840) 11 Sim. 82.
97 See *Fine v Fine* [2012] EWHC 1811 (Ch) where the trust deed expressly incorporated the terms of s.31.
98 *Re Turner's WT* [1937] Ch. 15. There the Court of Appeal emphasised that s.31 of the Trustee Act 1925 bestowed a power and did not impose a duty.
99 Trustee Act 1925 s.31(5). Earlier trusts are governed by the partially repealed Conveyancing Act 1881.
100 *Stanley v IRC* [1944] K.B. 255.
101 *Re Delamere's ST* [1984] 1 All E.R. 584 at 592 per Walker LJ.
102 [1950] 2 All E.R. 891 at 897. The amendments to be introduced in the Inheritance and Trustees' Powers Act 2014, have had an improving effect.
103 This can be problematic when the trustee is also the father of the beneficiary. In *Walker v Walker* [2010] W.T.L.R. 1617, for example, the parent/trustee consistently preferred his own interests over his daughter's interest and, in breach of trust, did not pay income due to her under s.31.

be reasonable" be replaced with "as the trustees think fit".[104] The Commission concluded that the existing wording "is perceived as imposing an additional requirement that the exercise of the trustees' discretion must be objectively reasonable . . .".[105] This reform has now been implemented by s.8(a) of the Inheritance and Trustees' Powers Act 2014 which applies only to a trust created or arising (or an interest under a trust which arises as a result of the exercise of any power arising) after 1 October 2014. Section 8 of the 2014 Act is not, therefore, retrospective in effect. The change also brings s.31 into line with both s.32 (see para.**14-032**) and routine professional practice in the drafting of wills and trust documents.

Section 31(1) adds that the discretion is unaffected by there being another fund applicable for the maintenance of the minor or the existence of someone bound at law to provide for the minor's maintenance and education. The rider originally attached by s.31(1)(ii) was that, if the trustees are aware of another trust fund available for the maintenance of the minor, a principle of proportionality applies. This entailed that, as far as is practicable and unless the court directs otherwise, a proportionate part of each fund should be used for maintenance purposes. The trustees of the respective funds were, if possible, to reach agreement concerning the proportion to be paid from each fund. This proviso attracted the attention of the Law Commission who felt that "this requirement is too rigid, and an impractical and potentially costly administrative burden which is out of step with modern practices and requirements".[106] The recommendation was to delete this rider to s.31(1) (ii) and this has now been achieved by s.8(b) of the Inheritance and Trustees' Powers Act 2014. As with s.8(a), this reform is not retrospective in effect.

A contrary intention?

14-024

As indicated, the statutory power can be modified or even dispensed with entirely, whether expressly or by implication.[107] An example of such modification would be when the trustees are expressly given an absolute discretion, as opposed to the statutory temperance afforded by the concept of "reasonableness". In *Re Delamere's ST*,[108] for example, the trust instrument provided that the income of the trust was to be held for the settlor's grandchildren in "equal shares absolutely". While they were minors, the sum of £120,000 had been accumulated in income. Even though the settlor probably had no notion of the existence of s.31, the use of the word "absolutely" displaced its operation because it made clear that the children's interests were indefeasible.[109] In order to avoid this potential trap, Slade LJ proffered some advice for those drafting settlements: "In many cases the draftsman may well be advised out of caution

---

104 Law Commission, *Intestacy and Family Provision Claims on Death* (2011) Law Com. No.331, para.4.95.
105 Law Commission, *Intestacy and Family Provision Claims on Death* (2011) Law Com. No.331, para.4.80.
106 Law Commission, *Intestacy and Family Provision Claims on Death* (2011) Law Com. No.331, para.4.89.
107 This is permitted by s.69(2) of the Trustee Act 1925. In *Price v William-Wynn* [2006] EWHC 788 (Ch), the mistaken omission to exclude the operation of s.31 was rectified by the court; see also *Bullard v Bullard* [2017] EWHC 3 (Ch).
108 [1984] 1 All E.R. 584.
109 For a criticism of this decision see R. Griffith [1985] Conv. 153.

either expressly to provide that the section is to apply with or without stated modifications or expressly to exclude its application altogether".[110]

A further example of how the statutory power may be excluded is to be found in *Re Erskine's ST* where the settlor made provision for the income to be accumulated.[111] Although the direction was void for offending the perpetuity rules (see **Ch.4**), this otherwise ineffective provision demonstrated an intention to exclude the s.31 power to maintain. Stamp J explained that "Income cannot at one and the same time be both accumulated in accordance with a direction . . . and dealt with under s.31".[112] In short, as Lord Evershed MR put it, "it suffices to make the statutory power . . . inapplicable if, on a fair reading of the instrument in question, one can say that such application would be inconsistent with the purport of the instrument".[113] The overriding rule is that the settlor's expressed intentions are paramount.

Entitlement to income

14-025

Section 31 offers the trustees a broad, discretionary power to apply trust income for the benefit of a minor (but not an adult) beneficiary. This power may be exercised as regards any trust interest whether or not it has vested or remains contingent.[114] All that is required by virtue of s.31(3) is that the trust interest carry the entitlement to intermediate income (i.e. income generated between the date that the gift is made and the date that it vests in the beneficiary). Not all gifts, however, carry this entitlement to income.[115] Nevertheless, this is a necessary requirement in the light that statutory maintenance is payable only from income. For example, a trust of shares for Jordan if he reaches the age of 18 will vest only when Jordan reaches majority age. In the intervening period, he has what is described as a "contingent" interest. Whether the trust was created inter vivos or by will, Jordan will be entitled to any intermediate income (i.e. the dividends) and can, therefore, benefit from the statutory power to maintain.

As discussed below, the general rule remains that, subject to a contrary intention, vested gifts or inter vivos and testamentary contingent gifts will carry the intermediate income. A contrary intention might arise where, for example, there is a settlement that gives an adult a life interest and leaves the minor as the remainderman. The statutory power cannot then arise. The life tenant is entitled to income and there is nothing from which the infant remainderman can be maintained. Similarly, and as demonstrated in *Re Vestey's Settlement*,[116] if the minor is a beneficiary under a discretionary trust there is no entitlement to income sufficient to activate

---

110 [1984] 1 All E.R. 584 at 592.
111 [1971] 1 All E.R. 572.
112 [1971] 1 All E.R. 572 at 574.
113 *IRC v Bernstein* [1961] Ch. 399 at 413. There a trust for accumulation of income showed a conflicting intention to exclude the closely allied provision relating to advancement contained in s.32 of the Trustee Act 1925.
114 See generally, A.M. Prichard, "Acceleration and Contingent Remainders" [1973] C.L.J. 246.
115 See generally, B.S. Ker, "Trustees' Power of Maintenance" (1953) 17 Conv. 273.
116 [1950] 2 All E.R. 891.

s.31. It also remains open for the settlor to direct that a party other than the minor is entitled to the income and, thereby, disarm s.31.

14-026 A vested interest will, subject to a contrary intention, carry the right to income.[117] Consider the example of a legacy of £100,000 to Jordan who is 14 years of age when the testator dies. Although the trustees will hold legal title to the capital sum until Jordan can give a valid receipt for it (on his reaching majority or entering into an earlier marriage), his interest has vested and he is entitled to the income.

As regards contingent interests, however, the rules are more complicated. Three key propositions emerge. First, an inter vivos contingent gift will carry the right to income. A lifetime trust of shares for Jordan when he becomes 18 years old, for example, does not vest until that time is reached and, in the interim, remains a contingent interest. Secondly, s.175(1) of the Law of Property Act 1925 provides that a contingent testamentary disposition of real or personal property will usually carry the intermediate income. Accordingly, a legacy of land to benefit Jordan when he marries will bring with it the entitlement to income. Finally, and subject to delimited exceptions, a contingent pecuniary testamentary disposition will not usually carry the right to income. The gift is in suspense.[118] Take, for example, a legacy of £100,000 to Jordan when he reaches 18. If the general rule is followed, and as this is a pecuniary legacy (i.e. purely monetary), it does not fall within s.175(1) and attracts income only when it becomes payable and not during the intervening period.[119]

14-027 To complicate matters further, there are several exceptions to the general restriction concerning pecuniary legacies. Such a contingent legacy will carry the income when:

- the legacy was given to a minor by his father (but not his mother[120]) or some person standing in loco parentis.[121] As Ker points out, "The idea is simple; a father is under an obligation to maintain his child and is therefore presumed to intend the income of the gift to be paid for his child's maintenance until the contingency happens".[122] The contingency, however, has to be of the minor reaching 18 years (not, say 30 years)[123] or making an earlier marriage.[124] In addition, there must be no other fund available for the infant's maintenance. In *Re West*,[125] an aunt made two distinct provisions for her niece's welfare. First, a contingent pecuniary legacy of £900 and, secondly, a separate provision for maintenance. It was held that the availability of this other source prevented the niece being entitled to income from the £900 legacy;

---

117 *Berry v Geen* [1938] A.C. 575.
118 *Re George* (1877) L.R. 5 Ch. D. 837.
119 *Re Raine* [1929] 1 Ch. 716.
120 *Re Eyre* [1917] 1 Ch. 351.
121 This would include a mother: *Re Eyre* [1917] 1 Ch. 351.
122 B.S. Ker, "Trustees' Power of Maintenance" (1953) 17 Conv. 273, 277.
123 *Re Abrahams* [1911] 1 Ch. 108.
124 See Farwell J in *Re Jones* [1932] 1 Ch. 642 at 649, 651.
125 [1913] 2 Ch. 345.

- the will demonstrates an intention (whether expressly or by implication) that the beneficiary should be maintained out of the testator's bounty. There is no need for any special relationship here nor does the legacy have to be contingent upon attaining majority or earlier marriage. In *Re Churchill*,[126] for example, the testatrix gave a pecuniary legacy to her grandnephew. She directed her trustees to pay money "towards the advancement in life or otherwise for the benefit" of the legatee. The court determined that this demonstrated a sufficient intention for the s.31 power to maintain to operate[127]; and

- the testator has directed (whether expressly or by implication) that the pecuniary legacy be put aside to be available to the infant legatee as soon as the contingency occurs. For example, a gift of £100,000 to Jordan on reaching 18 years of age. This ring-fencing of the £100,000 shows the intention for Jordan to have the accretions earned meanwhile.[128]

Maintenance, education or benefit

14-028

This statutory expression alludes to recurring expenditure and is of wide ambit. In addition to any run-of-the-mill living expenses, it may embrace the purchase of a house in which the minor beneficiary can live or a share in a business partnership for the minor.[129] It can also include the payment of the beneficiary's debts.[130] Income may be employed to pay past maintenance expenses and, albeit exceptionally, it might be used to make donations to charity.[131] The money can be employed for school fees and medical expenses and might properly be used to provide a holiday for the minor.

Decision making

14-029

Unless the minor is married, the payments may be made to the parent or guardian of the minor. The payments made may exhaust the entire trust income and (unlike with the inherent jurisdiction) are not affected by the legal liability of a parent to maintain the minor beneficiary. As discussed above, the trustees are directed by the rider to s.31(1) to, "have regard to the age

---

126 [1909] 2 Ch. 431.
127 See also, *Re Selby-Walker* [1949] 2 All E.R. 178, where the trustees had the power to apply the legacy so as to promote the education of the legatee.
128 In *Re Medlock* (1886) 55 L.J. Ch. 738, the testator segregated a sum of £750 to be divided between three people on their attaining 21 years. This was a definite fund that was divorced from the remainder of the estate.
129 *Re Heyworth's Contingent Reversionary Interest* [1956] Ch. 364.
130 A possibility recognised in *Re Spencer* [1935] Ch. 533.
131 *Re Walker* [1901] 1 Ch. 879. This was, as Farwell J noted at 887, "keeping up the reputation of the family and estate . . .".

of the infant and his requirements and generally to the circumstances of the case, and in particular to what other income, if any, is applicable for the same purposes". The Law Commission recommended the abolition of the allusion to "other income", asserting that it, "serves no substantive purpose; it duplicates the existing law and is unlikely in practical terms to assist trustees in their decision-making".[132] This became law (but of prospective effect only) by virtue of s.8 of the Inheritance and Trustees' Powers Act 2014. The trustees must focus upon the best interests of the minor beneficiary and these will vary according to the age of the minor and his family circumstances. The trustees should, as Cotton LJ explained in *Re Lofthouse*:

> "take into account that the father is not of sufficient ability properly to maintain his child, and that it is for her benefit not merely to allow him enough to pay her actual expenses, but to enable him to give her a better education and a better home. They must not be deterred from doing what is for her benefit because it is also to the father, though, on the other hand, they must not act with a view to his benefit apart from hers".[133]

Provided that the trustees act in a bona fide and prudent manner and periodically direct their minds to whether or not the power should be exercised, the court will not interfere.[134] As discussed above (see para.**14-022**), the trustees, however, cannot make a blanket decision never to pay maintenance or pay over the entire trust fund to the beneficiary's parents for them to decide how best to use the money. As it is a power, the trustees cannot be compelled to pay maintenance. Short of making a payment under its inherent jurisdiction, all the court can do is direct a trustee to consider whether or not to make a payment.

Ceasing to be a minor

14-030

The power to maintain ceases when the beneficiary attains the age of majority. The primary issue then concerns what is to happen to the surplus income. The now adult beneficiary will be entitled either to all the income or none of it. Section 31(1) deals with the scenario where the beneficiary attains 18 years of age.

First, if in accordance with the terms of the trust, the beneficiary acquires a vested interest (in income or capital) on attaining majority[135] there is little problem. Understandably, the beneficiary becomes entitled to the unused income.

Secondly, where the beneficiary attains the age of majority, but still has merely a contingent interest in the trust property, s.31(1)(ii) obliges the trustees to pay the income to the

---

132 Law Commission, *Intestacy and Family Provision Claims on Death* (2011) Law Com. No.331, para.4.95.
133 (1885) 29 Ch. D. 921 at 932.
134 *Re Bryant* [1894] 1 Ch. 324.
135 Or by previous marriage if that is the prescribed contingency.

beneficiary until his interest either vests or fails. This provision accelerates the beneficiary's interest, as, in its absence, he would not be entitled to the income until the contingency was satisfied.[136] Any maintenance paid is not recoverable from the beneficiary (or his estate) if the contingency is not met. Take, for example, a trust of shares for the benefit of Jordan when he reaches the age of 21 years. Although now 18 years old, Jordan's interest remains contingent until he achieves the greater age of 21 years. His interest will vest if and when he becomes 21 years old. The gift, of course, fails if the contingency is not satisfied. Nevertheless, Jordan will be entitled to the intermediate income.

This facilitating rule, however, gives way in the face of a contrary direction in the trust instrument. In *Re McGeorge*,[137] the testator bequeathed land to his daughter. The bequest was not to take effect until after his wife's death. The 21-year-old daughter claimed the income. Cross J held that she was not entitled to maintenance from the income because the gift was deferred (i.e. it was limited to take effect only on a future specified event). This deferral indicated a contrary intention and she was not entitled to the interim income. Similarly, if the settlor has directed that the surplus income is to be accumulated, the beneficiary has no entitlement to the income produced until the interest vests. In *Re Turner's WT*,[138] the interest was contingent upon the beneficiaries attaining 28 years of age. The settlor had directed the trustees to accumulate surplus income. The beneficiaries that reached majority age were not entitled to claim the income generated prior to their becoming 28 years old. The direction, thereby, excluded the statutory power of maintenance.

Entitlement to accumulated income

14-031

Subject to a contrary intention in the trust instrument, and until the beneficiary reaches majority age, s.31(2) of the Trustee Act 1925 provides that the trustees must accumulate and invest the income that has not been applied for the maintenance of the beneficiary. This has the effect of, as Lord Greene MR observed in *Stanley v IRC*, "engrafting upon the vested interest originally conferred on the infant by the settlement or other disposition a qualifying trust of a special nature which confers on the infant a title to accumulations if, and only if, he attains [the age of majority] or marries".[139] During the infancy of the beneficiary, however, the accumulated income may also be used for maintenance purposes.[140] A thorny and technical issue concerns the entitlement to any surplus accumulated income once the beneficiary achieves the age of 18 years or marries under that age.

First, s.31(2)(i)(a) provides that, if the interest vests upon majority or previous marriage (as appropriate), the beneficiary is entitled to the accumulated income.

---

136 See *Swales v Inland Revenue* [1984] 3 All E.R. 16.
137 [1963] 1 All E.R. 519.
138 [1936] 2 All E.R. 1435.
139 [1944] K.B. 255 at 261.
140 Section 31(2)(ii) of the Trustee Act 1925.

Secondly, s.31(2)(i)(b) provides that the right to accumulated income also arises where, on attaining the age of 18 years or earlier marriage, the beneficiary has become entitled to the trust property (i.e. the capital), "in fee simple, absolute or determinable, or absolutely, or for an entailed interest". The reference to "fee simple" exclusively applies to trusts of land whereas the allusion to "absolutely" concerns trusts of personalty. The words "for an entailed interest" extend to both realty and personalty. In *Re Sharp's ST*,[141] the High Court held that, when the beneficiaries were entitled to capital (personalty) on attaining majority age, they were not entitled to accumulated income as they were not "absolutely" entitled. This was because the settlor had given the trustees an overriding power of appointment and this prevented the beneficiaries from having complete beneficial ownership of the property. Their interest could be defeated if the power was exercised. Pennycuick VC identified the anomaly that a beneficiary with a determinable interest in realty will qualify for accumulated income under s.31(2)(i)(b) whereas a beneficiary having a similar interest in personalty will not.[142] Although he criticised the distinction "as little short of disgraceful to our jurisprudence",[143] it was too well established to be disturbed.

Thirdly, in any other case s.31(2)(ii) requires that the accumulated income be added to the capital of the property from which it was derived. Hence, if an interest in the capital devolves to Jordan on reaching 21 years, he will not be able to claim the accumulated income when he reaches 18 years of age. It will instead be an accretion to the capital to which he will become entitled in three years' time. In a like vein, if Jordan was given merely a life interest then any surplus accumulated income (in the guise of capital) must belong to the remainderman.

Advancement from Capital

14-032

As shown, maintenance concerns the trustee's ability to use trust income to promote the welfare of a minor beneficiary by defraying recurrent expenditure. The power of advancement, however, caters for the deployment of part of the trust capital to benefit permanently a minor or adult beneficiary before her entitlement under the trust has vested. To put it simply, it is designed to set a beneficiary up in life. The key distinction between the two powers, therefore, lies with the source of the funds given to the beneficiary. Other differences are that advancement is not geared to the age of the intended recipient[144] and is designed primarily to make particular, permanent and substantial long-term provision for a beneficiary rather than to meet the payment of day-to-day expenses.

---

141   [1973] Ch. 331 at 340.
142   [1973] Ch. 331 at 340.
143   [1973] Ch. 331 at 340.
144   For example, in *Hardy v Shaw* [1975] 2 All E.R. 1052, advancement was made to a middle-aged beneficiary.

The trustee's ability to make advance payments from capital will arise either from an express power in the trust instrument or under s.32 of the Trustee Act 1925 (as amended). These sources will, in due course, be considered in turn. At the outset, however, it is perhaps useful to consider the circumstances in which the power of advancement has been utilised. These are as follows:

- to buy premises for a beneficiary to set up business as a doctor.[145] In *Re Kershaw's Trusts*,[146] the trustees were able to advance £5,000 to set the husband of the beneficiary up in business in England because it was in the interests of the beneficiary wife that he remain in this country and not set up business abroad. As Malins VC observed, "in such a case what is for the benefit of the husband is for the benefit of the wife"[147];

- to provide a dowry on the marriage of a woman[148];

- to purchase a commission in the armed forces[149];

- to pay the beneficiary's emigration costs[150];

- to discharge the beneficiary's debts[151] and this is so even if it is without the consent of the beneficiary[152];

- to finance improvements to land[153];

- to minimise the beneficiary's tax liability to death duty and surtax[154];

- to promote a legal career at the Bar[155]; and

- to allow the beneficiary to fund a sub-trust/new settlement in favour of, say, his wife

---

145 *Re William's WT* [1953] Ch. 138. Danckwerts J would have upheld the advance even if it had been to provide a home without a surgery for the doctor/beneficiary.

146 (1868) L.R. 6 Eq. 322.

147 (1868) L.R. 6 Eq. 322 at 323.

148 *Lloyd v Cocker* (1860) 27 Beav. 645.

149 *Lawrie v Bankes* (1858) 4 K. & J. 142.

150 *Re Long's ST* (1868) 38 L.J. Ch. 125.

151 *Marshall v Crowther* (1874) 2 Ch. D. 199.

152 See *Pilkington v IRC* [1962] 3 All E.R. 622; but note the view of Pennycuick J in *Re Clore's ST* [1966] 2 All E.R. 272 at 275 that, in relation to a charitable donation, "It is not open to trustees to pay away the beneficiary's prospective capital over his head or against his will in discharge of what they consider to be his moral obligation".

153 *Re Walker's Settled Estate* [1894] 1 Ch. 189 (the rebuilding of an old mansion house).

154 *Pilkington v IRC* [1962] 3 All E.R. 622.

155 *Roper-Curzon v Roper-Curzon* (1871) L.R. 11 Eq. 452.

and children.[156] As Farwell J commented, "To some extent it would be to benefit objects other than the objects of the power, because the wife and children might be the persons to benefit. But I cannot doubt that it would be for the plaintiff's benefit that some provision should be made for them".[157]

14-033

For example, Fiona is the beneficiary under a trust of £100,000, which is contingent upon her becoming 35 years of age. Now, at the age of 30 years, Fiona wishes to open a hairdressing salon, but has insufficient funds to buy the necessary premises and equipment. Maintenance from income is unavailable as she is an adult and, in any event, it is unlikely that sufficient income will be generated to finance such a project. Hence, an advance payment from capital before she reaches the magic age of 35 years is the option that Fiona might pursue.

Benefit?

14-034

Although in the above example the "needy" beneficiary (Fiona) might be directly helped out by an advance from capital, it would be naïve to think that this is the only purpose underlying the exercise of the power of advancement. As with maintenance, it is often used as a tax-saving device and the premature movement of capital might be employed to reduce the beneficiary's prospective liability to such duties.[158] A good illustration of this is where capital is advanced to the remainderman in order to reduce the tax liability arising on the death of the tenant for life.[159]

The concept of "benefit" will embrace any use of the money which improves the material situation of the beneficiary. In *Re Clore's ST*[160] the trustees, as part of a tax-saving scheme, used one-seventh of the trust capital to make large donations to a family charitable foundation. Pennycuick J, however, accepted that the improvement of the material situation of the beneficiary was not confined to his direct financial situation, but could include the discharge of certain moral or social obligations, particularly providing for family and dependants. He noted also that the court has long recognised that a wealthy person is under a moral obligation to make donations to charity. Pennycuick J reasoned, moreover, that it is to the donor's material advantage that the moral obligation be discharged out of the trust capital rather than from his own pocket. Nevertheless, he pointed out that the nature and amount of those donations must depend upon the circumstances, including the position in life of the intended donor, the amount of the trust fund and the amount of the donor's other resources. Quantum of the donation is a necessary ingredient in the proper exercise of the power to advance capital.

---

156 *Re Halsted's WT* [1937] 2 All E.R. 570; see generally D.W.M. Waters, "The Creation of Sub-Trusts under a Power of Advancement" [1959] 23 Conv. 27.
157 [1937] 2 All E.R. 570 at 571.
158 *Pilkington v IRC* [1962] 3 All E.R. 622.
159 *Re Ropner's ST* [1956] 1 W.L.R. 902.
160 [1966] 2 All E.R. 272.

In these circumstances, therefore, a benefit can be discerned even when the advance proposed will operate to deprive the beneficiary of a material benefit currently available. In *Re CL*,[161] the transaction approved the extinction of the beneficiary's interest in favour of her adopted children and a consequential saving on estate duty. In *Re Hampden's ST*,[162] an advance in favour of the beneficiary's children was of benefit as it relieved the beneficiary of the considerable obligation of making further provision for their future. There the approach adopted was that the capital must be dealt with in a way which, when viewed objectively, can fairly be said to be for the benefit of the donor and the donor subjectively believes it to be so. The proposed advance may be generous, but cannot be excessive. Accordingly, it cannot objectively be regarded as being to the benefit of a beneficiary with no resources to make an advance from capital of £500,000 in order to provide for his children.

The issues of quantum and reasonableness were returned to in *X v A* where Hart J emphasised that there has to be the objective existence of a moral obligation.[163] It was not enough that the beneficiary wife subjectively believed it to be her moral obligation to give away to charity a substantial part of the capital (around £2.5 million). Hart J accepted that, in distinguishing between the objective existence of a moral obligation on one hand and the beneficiary's own recognition of it on the other, "there is a danger of the court being cast adrift in an open sea".[164] Nevertheless, the answer had to be found in concrete examples provided by the decided cases and generally accepted norms applicable in the context of dealings with settled wealth. Hart J concluded that, "No such case goes anywhere near recognising the existence of a moral obligation of the extent in question here". Accordingly, he could not see how this transaction could be said to benefit the wife:

> "It cannot be said that the proposed advance is relieving the wife of an obligation she would otherwise have to discharge out of her own resources if only because the amount proposed exceeds the amount of her own free resources. In any event the court has no reason to suppose that, in relation to her free assets, she will regard the advance as having discharged her moral obligation. The moral imperative informing her request to the trustees might logically be thought to apply to her own assets regardless of whether or not an advance is made out of the trust fund".[165]

---

161   [1969] 1 Ch. 587.
162   [1977] T.R. 177.
163   [2005] EWHC 2706 (Ch).
164   [2005] EWHC 2706 (Ch) at [43].
165   [2005] EWHC 2706 (Ch) at [42].

Express powers

14-036
As indicated, a power to apply capital for the advancement or benefit of a minor or contingent beneficiary may be afforded expressly by the trust instrument. The precise extent of such a power will turn upon the skills of the draftsman and the construction given by the court to the exact words employed.[166] An express power might be employed where the settlor regards the statutory power of advancement (see below) to be too limited. For example, until recently the statutory power limited the proportion of the trust capital that can be advanced to a beneficiary. Although this limitation is prospectively abolished by the Inheritance and Powers of Trustees Act 2014, traditionally an express power might have been desirable in order to allow a greater proportion to be advanced to the beneficiary. It might also give a tenant for life a right to capital without the consent of the remainderman.[167] An express power might also overcome problems of classifying what expenditure should properly come from income and what should come from capital. Take, for example, routine repairs carried out to the beneficiary's house. The cost of such repairs should be defrayed from income (i.e. via the power of maintenance). Nevertheless, it is open to the settlor to provide expressly that this expenditure be made from capital. Similarly, as will become clear, the statutory power does not apply to settled land. Hence, an express power of advancement would be appropriate as regards such settlements.

The statutory power

14-037
Prior to 1926, it was usual for there to be an express power of advancement inserted into the trust instrument. The statutory power of advancement is now to be found in s.32 of the Trustee Act 1925. This provides that, absent the finding of a contrary intention, every trust created after 1925[168] offers the trustees an absolute discretion to apply capital money and, under s.9(2)(a) of the Inheritance and Trustees' Powers Act 2014, "any other property forming part of the capital of the trust", for "the advancement or benefit" of a beneficiary. It does not matter whether the trust is inter vivos or testamentary in nature. The use of the word "benefit", therefore, widens the scope of the power to make payments.[169] In *Pilkington v IRC*, Viscount Radcliffe accepted that the term should be given a wide construction.[170] He commented that "I have not been able to find in the words of s.32 . . . anything which in terms or by implication restricts the width of the manner or purpose of advancement".[171] He was of the opinion that s.32 offered the trustees the discretion to employ capital in any way that would improve the lot of a beneficiary.

---

166 See generally, D.W.M. Waters [1958] 22 Conv. 413, 417–428. In *Martin v Triggs Turner Bartons* [2009] EWHC 1920 (Ch), the settlor's solicitors negligently drafted an express power of advancement and were held liable to the settlor's widow who suffered loss as a result.
167 *Re Marquess of Abergavenny's Estate Act Trusts* [1981] 1 W.L.R. 843.
168 Section 32(3).
169 See generally, D.W.M. Waters [1958] 22 Conv. 413.
170 [1962] 3 All E.R. 622; noted at [1963] 27 Conv. 65 (F.R. Crane).
171 [1962] 3 All E.R. 622 at 627, 628.

Section 32 of the Trustee Act 1925 makes clear that this power applies where there is a minor beneficiary with a vested interest as well as where there is a beneficiary with a contingent interest (e.g. £100,000 to Fiona when she reaches 35 years of age). Hence, even though the contingency may never be satisfied (by Fiona failing to attain 35 years), the statutory power to advance capital to Fiona remains available during the interim period. Section 32 goes on to state that the power is exercisable even though the interest of the beneficiary is liable to be defeated by the exercise of a power of appointment or revocation or to be diminished by an increase in the class of beneficiary. An example of the latter would be where Fred leaves £100,000 on trust for any of his children who reach 35 years of age. Although when the trust is created Fred might have two children, it is possible that there might be future offspring who will live to the age of 35 years and satisfy the specified contingency. The existing children's interests are, therefore, capable of being diminished. Nevertheless, this does not affect the availability of the power of advancement.

Limitations to s.32 of the Trustee Act 1925

There were traditionally five limitations to the operation of s.32. First, as regards trusts created or established before 1 October 2014, s.32(1)(a) imposes what is known as the half-share rule. This entails that the money advanced cannot exceed "altogether in amount one-half of the presumptive or vested share or interest of that person in the trust property". In the example where Fiona is entitled to the £100,000 on reaching 35 years of age, the maximum amount in total that could be advanced under s.32 is capped at £50,000. If the trust had been of £100,000 for the benefit of Fiona and Jordan upon attaining 35 years of age, however, Fiona's entitlement to an advance payment would have a ceiling of £25,000, that is, one-half of her presumptive share. The half-share rule has proved contentious with the Law Commission concluding that s.32 was in much need of an update. The Commission sensibly recommended that the power should be extended to the whole, rather than one-half, of the beneficiary's share in the trust fund.[172] This reform is achieved by s.9(3)(b) of the Inheritance and Trustees' Powers Act 2014, but does not have retrospective effect.

A novel gloss on s.32 arose from the decision in *Re Marquess of Abergavenny's Estate Act Trusts*.[173] There the beneficiary was advanced the then maximum one-half share of his trust interest. Subsequently, the capital value of the trust (mainly land) appreciated considerably and the beneficiary asked for a further advance. The trustees were willing to do this, but as a precaution sought directions from the High Court. Goulding J felt that the answer was plain and held that there could be no further exercise of the statutory power because the one-half share had been exhausted at the time of the original advance. He concluded:

14-038

---

172 Law Commission, *Intestacy and Family Provision Claims on Death* (2011) Law Com. No.331, para.72.
173 [1981] 1 W.L.R. 843; noted at [1982] 46 Conv. 158 (J.W. Price).

> "All that the settlor authorised has been done. It would to my mind be strange and unexpected if the object of the power as such retained an interest or possibility of interest in the fund still in settlement, so that he could require accounts from the trustees and demand reconsideration of his position whenever there should be an appreciation of assets . . . There is no reason that I can see why such . . . exposure to fortune, should be continued to the possible disadvantage of other beneficiaries after the limit has been reached".[174]

Albeit a little unconvincingly, Price defends this decision, arguing that, "It would surely be undesirable to allow a beneficiary to obtain his or her full share at a given date and then to return and 'milk' the trust fund of further sums as inflation or wise investment caused increases in the value of the fund. There could never effectively be an end to the exercise of such a power".[175] As Price adds, "Trustees need to know easily when a power is exhausted".[176] The irony is that had the beneficiary initially obtained an advance of less than his half-share, he could subsequently have taken advantage of the increased value and received a greater advance overall. In order to retain flexibility, therefore, the beneficiary should never be paid his full share. Such problems no longer exist as regards post-1 October 2014 trusts.

The one-half share rule has never been immutable in its operation. In *CD (a minor) v O*,[177] for example, Lloyd J held that the one-half share rule could be varied by the court under the jurisdiction afforded by s.1 of the Variation of Trusts Act 1958.[178] This case concerned the proceeds of two life assurance policies that were held on trust for three minors in equal shares. The claimant's school fees had originally been paid from trust income (i.e. under the power of maintenance), but the income became exhausted with fees remaining to be paid. The trustees then resorted to making an advance payment from capital under s.32. The claimant wanted her entire share in the capital to be available for these purposes and sought to sidestep the one half-share rule. Lloyd J approved the requested extension of the statutory power of advancement. He was influenced by the fact that the trust instrument made no provision for the use of capital and income and that the claimant would, had it not been for her age, be entitled absolutely to her share. He noted also that the rule is commonly relaxed in modern trust instruments. Lloyd J was satisfied that it would be for C's benefit for the limit imposed by s.32 of the 1925 Act on the application of the capital of the fund for her education to be lifted. The key question was whether, and on what basis, the court has power to achieve this result. He considered the source of this jurisdiction. Although in exceptional circumstances the variation could be justified under the court's inherent jurisdiction to provide for a minor,[179] Lloyd

---

174 [1981] 2 All E.R. 643 at 646.
175 [1982] 46 Conv. 158.
176 [1982] 46 Conv. 158, 159.
177 [2004] 3 All E.R. 780.
178 See Ch.15.
179 See *Chapman v Chapman* [1954] 1 All E.R. 798.

J preferred to frame his decision around the Variation of Trusts Act 1958. Alluding to s.1 of that Act, he concluded that the whole fund, as well as C's fund separately was, "property . . . held on trusts arising . . . under any will, settlement or other disposition". The court allowed the entire capital fund to be used for advancement purposes under the 1958 Act because it was satisfied that the proposed variation of the trusts was for the benefit of the relevant beneficiary.

The second limitation was that s.32, in its original form, allowed the trustees to make payments only out of "any capital money". "Capital" for these purposes comprises personalty (e.g. money and securities) and realty that is subject to a trust of land under the Trusts of Land and Appointment of Trustees Act 1996. Its meaning does not extend to settled land or the proceeds of sale of settled land.[180] Advancement, moreover, is concerned with trust property itself and not an interest in the trust property.[181] It was noted by the Law Commission that the trust fund might be made up of a range of other assets and that the trustees might seek to transfer assets (other than cash) for the benefit of the beneficiary. As it would be nonsensical to require the trustees to advance cash purely to enable the beneficiary to buy the trust asset,[182] the Commission recommended that s.32 be amended to make it clear that such a transfer can be made straightforwardly. The reform will ensure "that the trustees have power to transfer or apply other property subject to the trust on the same basis as the power to pay or apply capital money to or for the advancement or benefit of a beneficiary".[183] This recommendation has found its way into s.9(6) of the Inheritance and Trustees' Powers Act 2014, which states that the trustees "may pay, transfer or apply money or other property on the basis (express or implied) that it shall be treated as a proportionate part of the capital . . .". This provision is of full retrospective effect.

14-039

The third limitation is that s.32(1)(b) imposes an obligation on the beneficiary to account for money advanced or property transferred when he "becomes absolutely and indefeasibly entitled to a share in the trust property". Hence, the money is to be deducted from the beneficiary's eventual share under the trust. This is sometimes known as "hotchpot" and, being designed to ensure equality of distribution between the beneficiaries, operates to give effect to the settlor's presumed intentions. For example, where Fiona is advanced £25,000 under a settlement of £100,000 for herself and Jordan, she must deduct that payment from her eventual entitlement under the trust. Hence, Fiona will subsequently receive a further £25,000 and Jordan will receive £50,000. This rule makes no allowance for inflationary tendencies, as the property is valued as at the time the advance was made. The Law Reform Committee recommended that the calculation should be based upon fractional distributions of entitlement and not geared to the cash sums advanced.[184] Unfairness might otherwise

---

180   Section 32(2) (as amended).
181   *Southgate v Sutton* [2011] EWCA Civ 637, where an attempt was made to advance a contingent interest under the trust rather than to advance property subject to the trust.
182   *Re Collard's WT* [1961] Ch. 293.
183   Law Commission, *Intestacy and Family Provision Claims on Death* (2011) Law Com. No.331, para.4.76.
184   Law Reform Committee, *The Powers and Duties of Trustees* (1982) Cmnd.8733, paras 4.43–4.47.

arise because, as the Committee explained, "The result might well be that the beneficiary who has received part of his share by way of advancement will, in fact, in the long run, receive a larger portion of the whole fund than would be expected given the value of his initial, undivided, share".[185]

14-040

The fourth exception is that s.32(1)(c) provides that no payment or asset transfer shall be made to prejudice any interest prior to that of the beneficiary's interest. For example, take the situation were property is held on trust for Noel for life with remainder to Fiona. If sums from capital were advanced to Fiona while Noel was still with us, it would reduce the fund from which Noel's income was to be derived. It would, thereby, prejudice her prior interest. Not surprisingly, the Act only allows such advances when Noel is of full age and gives written consent to the payment. The court will be slow to infer any contrary intention on the part of the settlor. In *Henly v Wardell*,[186] a trust was established under which the testator gave his widow a life interest with remainder to his two sons. The trust instrument gave the trustees an "absolute and uncontrolled" discretion to advance capital to the benefit of the testator's children. The court had to consider whether the latter provision was sufficient to override the need for the life tenant's written consent to an advance from capital. On a proper construction of the instrument, it was held that the word "uncontrolled" was not strong enough to disarm s.32(1)(c). The modification instead was merely to enlarge the provision so that the whole of a beneficiary's share could be advanced if the trustees thought fit. It did not do away with the need for the consent of the life tenant. Indeed, it was unlikely that the testator would have wished for his sons to have the capital at his widow's expense.

Finally, the section gives way in the face of a contrary intention.[187] This means that the power can be excluded either expressly by an appropriate declaration in the trust instrument or by implication. As regards the latter option, this occurred in *Re Evans' Settlement* where the trust instrument stated that the trustees were to have a power to advance capital up to a specified amount.[188] As this contradicted the traditional statutory half-share rule, the intention was that s.32 was not to apply. Obviously, if s.9(3)(b) of the Inheritance and Trustees' Powers Act 2014 applies (and the half-share rule is inapplicable), *Re Evans* will cease to have such relevancy. In *Re Craven*,[189] the express power was limited by a clause that permitted advancement only for specified purposes. The limitation imposed was sufficient to prevent the application of the wider statutory power. Similarly, the Court of Appeal in *IRC v Bernstein*[190] concluded that a trust, under which income was to be accumulated during the settlor's lifetime, demonstrated the intention to exclude s.32.

---

185 Law Reform Committee, *The Powers and Duties of Trustees* (1982) Cmnd.8733, para.4.43.
186 *The Times*, 29 January 1988.
187 Section 69(2) of the Trustee Act 1925.
188 [1967] 3 All E.R. 343.
189 [1937] Ch. 431.
190 [1961] Ch. 399.

Discretion

As the notion of "benefit" is now divorced from the concept of "need", the trustees have to take special care to ensure that their discretion is exercised properly. Trustees, of course, have always been liable for negligently making an advance. In *Simpson v Brown*,[191] on coming of age a beneficiary successfully recovered from his trustee money that had been advanced to provide the beneficiary with an apprenticeship with a chemist. The problem was that the chemist was unqualified and, therefore, unable to provide the beneficiary with the appropriate training. Beyond this, however, a trustee who could show that the advancement was to alleviate a "need" of the beneficiary will generally be shielded.[192] Different considerations necessarily apply when the advancement is instead to confer a benefit. More is expected from a trustee when making an advance to benefit the beneficiary rather than to assuage his need.[193] The trustees are expected to take on board all relevant considerations and determine that it is a proper case for advancement. The court can, therefore, prevent trustees from an exercise of discretion that is wrong or unreasonable. As Lindley LJ pointed out in *Hampden v Earl of Buckinghamshire*, "A honest trustee may fail to see that he is acting unjustly towards those whose interests he is bound to consider and to protect; and, if he is so acting, and the Court can see it although he cannot, it is in my opinion the duty of the Court to interfere".[194] If, however, there is no injustice, the court will not readily interfere. This was demonstrated in *Re Charteris* where there was an allegation that trustees unreasonably exercised a discretion to postpone the payment of a legacy.[195] Swinfen-Eady LJ concluded that this was a proper exercise of discretion as the trustees had acted fairly and properly in the general interest of the estate, and in the interests of all the beneficiaries.

Continuing supervision

Regardless of the terms of the power of advancement, on exercising the discretion the trustees must ensure that the funds advanced are actually used for the purposes stated by the beneficiary. This continuing responsibility was highlighted in *Re Pauling's ST*[196] where the trustees (Coutts & Co) advanced numerous capital sums to beneficiaries from their presumptive share. Although nominally for the benefit of their children, the capital was really used to finance the luxurious lifestyle of their parents. The children were of full age and did not complain about the manner in which the money was used. It was presumed, however, that they were under the undue influence of their parents. The belief of the trustees was that they had acted law-

---

191   (1864) 11 L.T. 593.
192   See *Re Brittlebank* (1881) 30 W.R. 99.
193   See D.W.M. Waters [1958] 22 Conv. 413, 431–434.
194   [1893] 2 Ch. 531 at 544.
195   [1917] 2 Ch. 379.
196   [1963] 3 All E.R. 1.

fully in making the advances to the children and what the children did with the money was not their concern. Subsequently the children succeeded in suing the trustees for breach of trust in making improper advances. The Court of Appeal concluded that the power had been improperly exercised and that, as the payments had been made for a particular purpose, the trustees had an obligation to inquire as to the actual use of the money. Willmer LJ reading the majority judgment made clear that what the trustees cannot do "is to prescribe a particular purpose, and then raise and pay the money over to the advancee leaving him or her entirely free, legally and morally, to apply it for that purpose or to spend it in any way he or she chooses, without any responsibility upon the trustees even to inquire as to its application".[197] The trustees had to pay the money back into the trust fund. The moral is that a trustee must not abandon the beneficiary to her own folly.

If, as opposed to a direct payment, the money is to be paid to an agent of the beneficiary, the trustee must ensure that the agent is authorised. On payment to an unauthorised agent (e.g. one with a forged power of attorney), the general rule is that (barring ratification, estoppel or contributory negligence) the trustee will remain liable to the beneficiary.[198]

Setting Aside the Exercise of a Dispositive Discretion

14-043

Past cases provide scant guidance as to what matters (beyond the expressed wishes of the settlor and the needs of the beneficiaries) the trustees ought to take into account when making distributive or dispositive decisions.[199] The issue took centre stage in the conjoined appeals of *Pitt v Holt; Futter v Futter*.[200] Both appeals concerned the exercise of a discretionary power and the subsequent realisation that the effect of what the trustee did was fiscally different from that intended. Hence, both cases were motivated by the emergence of unintended tax consequences of the trustees' actions.[201] Understandably, HM Revenue & Customs resisted the applications. In *Futter* the trustees were given incorrect legal advice from a reputable source as to the charging of capital gains tax in respect of gains realised by non-resident trustees. In consequence, and within their powers, the trustees distributed capital to Mr Futter and advanced

---

197 [1963] 3 All E.R. 1 at 8.
198 *Welch v Bank of England* [1955] 1 Ch. 508.
199 See generally, R.C. Nolan, "Controlling Fiduciary Power" [2009] C.L.J. 293.
200 [2013] 2 A.C. 108.
201 The mistaken attempt to minimise tax liability dominates modern case law: see, for example, *Payne v Tyler* [2019] EWHC 2347 (Ch); *Hartogs v Rothschild Trust (Schweiz) AG* [2019] EWHC 1915 (Ch) and *Smith v Stanley* [2019] EWHC 2168 (Ch).

money to Mr Futter's three children. In *Pitt* the claim was made by the personal representatives who received inaccurate financial advice as to the liability to inheritance tax. Consequently, a trust was established that failed to minimise such liability. Two issues arose on these conjoined appeals.

First, when trustees exercise a discretionary power intending to change the beneficial ownership of trust property, but the effect of what they do turns out to be different from that which they intended, there was the question whether the court can set their act aside. If so, the court had to consider what was the correct legal test to determine in what circumstances and on what basis the court could intervene. Focus fell upon the so-called rule in *Re Hastings Bass*,[202] which was traditionally (mis)employed as authority for the principle that the exercise of a discretionary power by a trustee might be declared void and set aside on the basis that the trustees failed to take into account relevant matters when exercising the power.[203] While accepting that "The true ratio of the decision has been much debated, both in forensic argument and by legal scholars",[204] Lord Walker felt that a justifiable criticism of the *Hastings Bass* rule was that it was too general in making reference to unintended consequences. It unlocked a door that was pushed wide open in later cases and thereby engendered a culture whereby trustees asserted and relied on their own or their adviser's failings in seeking the assistance of the court.[205] He acknowledged that the *Hastings-Bass* rule was not about mistake nor did it turn on an inquiry as to what was actually in the minds of the trustees in exercising their power of advancement. Lord Walker emphasised, moreover, that the operation of the rule was to make the trustees' disposition voidable at the discretion of the court. It was not void ab initio. This had previously been an issue of some uncertainty.

In order to limit the scope of the *Hastings-Bass* rule, the Supreme Court determined that a breach of fiduciary duty[206] was an essential prerequisite for a successful claim to be made.[207] As Lord Walker demonstrated, "It is not enough to show that the trustees' deliberations have fallen short of the highest possible standards, or that the court would, on a surrender of discretion by the trustees, have acted in a different way. Apart from exceptional circumstances (such as an impasse reached by honest and reasonable trustees) only breach of fiduciary duty

---

202 [1975] Ch. 25. This much criticised rule, as illustrated in *Mettoy Pension Trustees Ltd v Evans* [1990] 1 W.L.R. 1587, was concerned with trustees who make decisions without having given proper consideration to matters that they ought to have taken into account. It was readily invoked in cases where tax-planning arrangements involving trusts went wrong.

203 The decision in *Re Hastings Bass* [1975] Ch. 25 concerned the scope of a fiduciary power rather than with the decision-making process which led to its being exercised in a particular way; see generally, S. Evans, "It's 'clean hands' again: the dirtiness of not paying tax considered in the Supreme Court" (2015) Conv. 61.

204 [2013] 2 A.C. 108 at [22].

205 As C. Mitchell, "Reining in the Rule in re Hastings-Bass" (2006) 122 L.Q.R. 35, 41, 42 questioned, "Why should a beneficiary be placed in a stronger position than the outright legal owner of property if he wishes to unwind a transaction to which he has given his consent, but which turns out to have unforeseen tax disadvantages?"

206 Here the concept of fiduciary duty is necessarily wider than the no-conflict rule: see R. Nolan, "Fiduciaries and their flawed decisions" (2013) 129 L.Q.R. 469.

207 As previously held to be so in *Abacus Trust Co (Isle of Man) v Barr* [2003] Ch. 409.

justifies judicial intervention".[208] The trustees' duty does not extend to being right on every occasion. As in neither appeal were the trustees personally in breach of fiduciary duty, the rule could not unravel the actions of the trustees. In short, there must be a serious breach before the courts can intervene.

Of course, if the trustees act *ultra vires* (i.e. outside their powers), that exercise of a power will always be void. For example, in *Roadchef (Employee Benefits Trustees) Ltd v Hill*[209] a power to transfer shares from an employee benefit trust to another trust arose only when the transfer would benefit the beneficiaries. A transfer that benefited the trustee personally and not the beneficiaries was fatally flawed.

14-044

Secondly, the issue was raised as to whether the trustees' gratuitous actions in *Pitt* could be rescinded on the ground of mistake.[210] It is to be appreciated that, for present purposes, the focus is upon the rescission of voluntary settlements and not commercial bargains.[211] The presence or absence of consideration, therefore, is the critical distinction. Although the fact that the mistake is a mistake about tax is irrelevant,[212] the court will not exercise its discretion to grant relief merely to unravel an artificial tax avoidance measure that has gone wrong. This refusal to intervene is because the claimant has acted on expert advice,[213] must be taken to have accepted the risk or to grant relief would otherwise offend public policy.[214]

Following a survey of the authorities, Lord Walker identified the three-stage test for setting aside a voluntary disposition on the ground of mistake. These impose strict limits on the circumstances in which a voluntary disposition may be set aside on the ground of mistake and, as Judge Hodge QC emphasised, "should not be viewed as an available 'get-out-of-jail-free' card, which may be invoked wherever a taxpayer finds himself facing a charge to tax which has not been anticipated".[215] Lord Walker's test requires that the donor must have made a mistake, the mistake must be of a relevant type (i.e. as to the effect of the transaction, key facts or relevant law) and it must be of such a serious nature as to make it unconscionable for it not to be corrected.[216] He concluded that the gravity of the mistake must be

---

208 [2013] 2 A.C. 108 at [73]. See *Brewer v Iqbal* [2019] EWHC 182 (Ch)
209 [2014] EWHC 109 (Ch).
210 A mistake must be distinguished from mere ignorance, inadvertence or misprediction as to future events: *Payne v Tyler* [2019] EWHC 2347 (Ch). The distinction is not always clear-cut for, as Lord Walker put it [2013] 2 A.C. 108 at [105], "Forgetfulness, inadvertence or ignorance is not, as such, a mistake, but it can lead to a false belief or assumption which the law will recognise as a mistake".
211 Different rules apply according to whether it is a contractual transaction under which the other party has given consideration or is, instead, a voluntary settlement (whether or not created by deed): see *Van der Merwe v Goldman* [2016] 4 W.L.R. 71.
212 *Van der Merwe v Goldman* [2016] 4 W.L.R. 71.
213 Even if no advice is sought, the court can still refuse to set aside the transaction: *Estera Trust (Jersey) Ltd v Singh* [2019] EWHC 2039 (Ch).
214 See *Kennedy v Kennedy* [2014] EWHC 4129. This anti-tax avoidance sentiment was echoed also in *Freedman v Freedman* [2015] EWHC 1457 (Ch).
215 *Hartogs v Rothschild Trust (Schweiz) AG* [2019] EWHC 1915 (Ch) at [37].
216 R. Lee, "Correcting mistakes in trust planning: a comparative post-Pitt analysis" (2018) Conv. 45, 46 feels that this restatement "has been unhelpful in practice, particularly because the courts have generously interpreted

assessed on a close examination of the facts, including the circumstances of the mistake and its consequences. The injustice of leaving a mistaken disposition uncorrected had to be evaluated objectively, but with an intense focus upon the facts of the particular case.[217] Lord Walker concluded:

> **"The court cannot decide the issue of what is unconscionable by an elaborate set of rules. It must consider in the round the existence of a distinct mistake (as compared with total ignorance or disappointed expectations), its degree of centrality to the transaction in question and the seriousness of its consequences, and make an evaluative judgment whether it would be unconscionable, or unjust, to leave the mistake uncorrected. The court may and must form a judgment about the justice of the case".[218]**

This test was satisfied on the facts of *Pitt* and the trust was set aside on the ground of mistake.[219] Similarly, in *Bainbridge v Bainbridge*[220] transfers of the partnership land to the trustees took place and unexpectedly incurred a liability of more than £200,000 by way of capital gains tax. Master Matthews reiterated that, for the transactions to be rescinded on the ground of mistake, there had to be a distinct mistake as distinct from mere ignorance or inadvertence. Even if causative, mere ignorance was insufficient to found the cause of action. The Master noted, however, that forgetfulness, inadvertence or ignorance can lead to a false belief or assumption, which might be recognised as a legally relevant mistake. He explained further that a mistake may still be a relevant even if it was due to carelessness, unless the circumstances show that the claimant deliberately ran the risk. It was again emphasised that the causative mistake must be sufficiently grave as to make it unconscionable on the part of the donee to retain the property. In a like vein, in *Smith v Stanley* the court set aside a deed of appointment executed by trustees on the basis of erroneous advice that it would be a potentially exempt transfer for the purposes of inheritance tax.[221] The mistake here as to tax law was of so serious a character as to render it manifestly unjust not to set aside the disposition. This was not a case where there

---

mistakes based on mere ignorance, bringing about the unintended effect of liberalising the doctrine of equitable mistake".

217 In *Wright v National Westminster Bank Plc* [2014] EWHC 3158 (Ch), a husband created a discretionary trust of which the bank was the trustee. The settlor had wrongly believed that the income of the settlement could be applied for his wife's benefit during his lifetime. It was just and appropriate to rescind the disposition due to this grave mistake.

218 [2013] 2 A.C. 108 at [128]. See generally R. Lee, "Correcting mistakes in trust planning: a comparative post-*Pitt* analysis" (2018) Conv. 45.

219 See further, T. Etherton, "The Role of Equity in Mistaken Transactions" (2013) 27(4) Tru L.I. 159; S. Watterson, "Reversing Mistaken Voluntary Dispositions" (2013) 72(3) C.L.J. 501.

220 [2016] EWHC 898 (Ch). This case demonstrates also that the right to rescind is an equity which attaches to the property in whosoever's hands it may be, unless and until it comes to the hands of a good faith purchaser for value without notice.

221 [2019] EWHC 2168 (Ch). There an ignorance of tax consequences was regarded as a relevant mistake.

has been an element of artificial tax avoidance so as to require the court to withhold relief on the grounds of public policy. The trustees had simply followed expert advice.

Guide to Further Reading

T. Etherton, "The Role of Equity in Mistaken Transactions" (2013) 27(4) Tru. L.I. 159.

B.S. Ker, "Trustees' Powers of Maintenance" [1953] 17 Conv. 273.

R. Lee "Correcting mistakes in trust planning: a comparative post-Pitt analysis" (2018) Conv. 45.

A.M. Prichard, "Acceleration and Contingent Remainders" [1973] C.L.J. 246.

R. Thornton, "Ethical Investments: A Case of Disjointed Thinking" [2008] C.L.J. 396.

D.W.M. Waters, "The 'New' Power of Advancement" [1958] Conv. 413.

15

Variation of Trusts

The working rule is that the terms of a properly constituted trust are to be followed strictly. The trustees are obliged to apply the property in accordance with the terms of the trust and, if they do not do so, are potentially liable for breach of trust. As Romer LJ put it, "As a rule, the court has no jurisdiction to give, and will not give, its sanction to the performance by the trustees of acts with reference to the trust estate which are not, on the face of the instrument creating the trust, authorised by its terms".[1] This rule of strict fidelity is, however, subject to exceptions and these recognise that, as a trust may last for many years, it is likely that, in time, the original terms might become tired, unreasonable and undesirable. This might occur in relation to the original management and administrative provisions of the trust or, indeed, might focus upon the beneficial interests as originally allocated by the settlor.

A variation of the trust terms might be catered for by the settlor giving to the trustees an express power to amend a trust. This is a common feature of modern pension trusts. It might be described as a power to amend or might adopt the form of a power to add to, vary, modify or alter the terms of the trust. If such ability is given by the trust instrument, the court will be vigilant to ensure that it is properly exercised for the purpose for which it was granted and as intended by the settlor.[2] As Lord Steyn commented in *Society of Lloyds v Robinson*, "This principle is closely linked with the general proposition that the power must not be exercised beyond the reasonable contemplation of the parties . . .".[3] Accordingly, any restrictions on the power of amendment must be complied with. For example, if the power is expressed to allow only administrative or managerial changes, it cannot be employed to vary the beneficial interests under the trust.

Beyond the presence of an express power, only in limited circumstances will the law allow the terms of a trust to be varied. First, it is possible that the beneficiaries might collectively

---

1   *Re New* [1901] 2 Ch. 534 at 544.
2   *Hole v Garnsey* [1930] A.C. 472.
3   [1999] 1 W.L.R. 756 at 766.

authorise a variation. Secondly, and where the beneficiaries are not sui juris or unanimous, an application for variation can be made to the court. The application will usually be made in open court, but in exceptional circumstances might be held in private.[4] The variation might be ordered under the court's inherent jurisdiction or its statutory jurisdiction. The primary example of Parliamentary intervention in this area takes the form of the Variation of Trusts Act 1958. Such inroads upon the sanctity of the trust instrument illustrate that the clearest expressed intentions of a settlor are most certainly not sacrosanct.[5]

Consensual Variation

15-003

The general ability of beneficiaries to redraft the trust emerges from the consent principle embodied in the rule in *Saunders v Vautier*,[6] which was concerned with the premature termination of the trust by the beneficiaries. Once it was accepted that the beneficiaries could end a trust, it followed naturally that the rule in *Saunders v Vautier* could instead be employed to vary the terms of an existing trust.[7] The greater thereby subsuming the lesser.[8] Hence, it offers a prime example of when the current interests of the beneficiaries take priority over the original prescription of the settlor.[9] The validity of the rule has, however, been challenged on the basis that it defeats the settlor's purpose without any off-setting gain and, by ignoring the fiduciary duties of the trustees, is mistaken conceptually.[10] The trustees are, however, protected as the beneficiaries have authorised the deviation and are, thereby, unable to pursue successfully an action for breach of trust.[11] No court approval or other involvement is necessary. As the Law Reform Commission of Saskatchewan explained, "The rule in *Saunders v Vautier* provides what amounts to a self-help remedy . . . No application to court is necessary

---

4   In *V v T&A* [2014] EWHC 3432 (Ch), a public hearing occurred, but reporting restrictions were imposed to protect the child beneficiaries. An anonymity order, moreover, should only be made when there is clear, cogent evidence that a derogation from the principle of open justice is required: *MN v OP* [2019] EWCA Civ 679.

5   This is evident also in the context of charitable trusts with the scope for variation afforded by the cy-près doctrine: see Ch.8.

6   (1841) 4 Beav. 115.

7   *Re Holt's Settlement* [1969] 1 Ch. 100; Re *Holmden's ST* [1968] A.C. 685 at 713; *Berry v Geen* [1938] A.C. 575.

8   See P. Luxton, "Variation of Trusts: Settlors' Intention and the Consent Principle in *Saunders v Vautier*" (1997) 60 M.L.R. 719; J. Nitikman, "Variation under the Rule in *Saunders v Vautier*: yes or no?" (2015) 21(8) T. & T. 923.

9   See generally, P. Mathews, "The Comparative Importance of the Rule in *Saunders v Vautier*" (2006) 122 L.Q.R. 266.

10 See J.H. Langbein, "Why the Rule In *Saunders v Vautier* Is Wrong" in P.G. Turner (ed.), *Equity and Administration* (CUP, 2016), Ch.10.

11 *Re Pauling's ST* [1963] 3 All E.R. 1.

unless the trustee improperly refuses to distribute the trust property or disagrees that the rule is applicable".[12]

The modification contemplated here will usually involve a recasting of the beneficial interests and be motivated by tax considerations, especially the fear of inheritance tax. It is also thought that a variation of an existing trust is not a disposition for the purposes of Capital Gains Tax, whereas the revocation of the existing settlement and the creation of a new one is most definitely a taxable disposal.[13] The overriding goal is, therefore, usually to minimise potential fiscal liabilities. As Lord Denning MR acknowledged in *Re Weston's Settlements*, "Nearly every variation that has come before the court has tax avoidance for its principal object: and no one has ever suggested that this is undesirable or contrary to public policy".[14]

Under the rule in *Saunders v Vautier* a beneficiary who is of full age (i.e. 18 years and above), of sound mind and entitled to the entire equitable interest can at any time direct the trustees to transfer the trust property (or part of it[15]) to him and, thereby, put a premature end to the trust.[16] The rule will also allow two or more beneficiaries who are absolutely entitled to the trust assets to require an outright transfer of their shares.[17] Indeed, Walton J considered it to be "trite law that persons who between them hold the entirety of the beneficial interests in any particular trust fund are as a body entitled to direct the trustees how that fund is to be dealt with. . .".[18]

The facts of *Saunders v Vautier* concerned a testator who bequeathed £2,000 of East India stock upon a fixed trust for Daniel Vautier, with a direction that the dividends were to be accumulated until Mr Vautier achieved 25 years of age. On reaching 21 years, however, Mr Vautier claimed to be entitled to the entire trust fund. The trustee opposed his claim. It was held that, although it was the settlor's intention that enjoyment be postponed until Mr Vautier reached 25 years, the interest vested on his reaching majority (then 21 years). He was entitled to have the property transferred to him. As Lord Langdale MR explained, "where a legacy is directed to accumulate for a certain period, or where the payment is postponed, the legatee, if he has an absolute indefeasible interest in the legacy, is not bound to wait until the expiration of that period, but may require payment the moment he is competent to give a valid discharge".[19] Accordingly, as Swinfen Eady MR put it in *Re Nelson*, "where there is what amounts to an absolute gift, that absolute gift cannot be fettered by prescribing a mode of enjoyment".[20]

Subsequently, the rule was extended so that it could be applied collectively. If there is

15-004

15-005

---

12   The Law Reform Commission of Saskatchewan, *The Rule in Saunders v Vautier and the Variation of Trusts*, Consultation Paper (1994) No.1, p.15.
13   *Wyndham v Egremont* [2009] EWHC 2076 (Ch).
14   [1969] 1 Ch. 234 at 245.
15   *Hughes v Bourne* [2012] EWHC 2232 (Ch).
16   See *Tod v Barton* [2002] 4 I.T.E.L.R. 715, where the two beneficiaries (a charity and the testator's son) agreed to end the trust prematurely.
17   *Berry v Green* [1938] A.C. 575.
18   *Stephenson v Barclays Bank* [1975] 1 All E.R. 625 at 637.
19   (1841) 4 Beav. 115 at 116.
20   [1928] Ch. 920 at 921.

more than one beneficiary, the conditions as to age and mental capacity must be satisfied by each, they must act unanimously, and together they must be entitled to the entire beneficial interest.[21] The rule in *Saunders v Vautier* has no application, therefore, when one beneficiary refuses to join in, is underage or is mentally unequipped to make his own decisions.

The rule in *Saunders v Vautier* applies equally to discretionary trusts.[22] The operation of the rule in this sphere was demonstrated in *Re Smith*.[23] There the Public Trustee held a fund on a discretionary trust to pay any part of the income or capital for the benefit of Mrs Aspinall. Any surplus income was to be accumulated and the fund remaining at Mrs Aspinall's death was to pass to her children in equal shares. Mrs Aspinall was alive when all her children reached majority age. Subsequently, Mrs Aspinall and her children mortgaged their trust interests to the Legal and General Assurance Co. The mortgagee sought payment of the whole income by the trustees until the mortgage was paid off. Romer J held that the Public Trustee was obliged to utilise the income in this way. The key factor was that Mrs Aspinall and her children were together entitled to the whole fund. It did not matter that the Public Trustee enjoyed a discretion vested in it as to what sums Mrs Aspinall would receive and whether this would be funded from capital as well as from income. The beneficiaries were collectively entitled to require the trustee to hand over the fund to them.

15-006

The following propositions can be distilled from *Re Smith* and all turn upon the nature of the beneficiary's equitable ownership of the trust property.

First, if the trustees have the discretion to apply the whole or part of a fund to or for the benefit of a particular person, that person cannot come to the trustees and demand the fund. This is because the whole fund has not been dedicated to that person and her entitlement is only to so much as the trustees think fit to afford to her.

Secondly, where the entire fund is available to be applied for the benefit of a particular person there is nothing to prevent that person claiming the whole trust fund. The fact that the trustees enjoy the discretion as to the method in which the whole fund is to be applied for the benefit of that person makes no difference.

15-007

Thirdly, where the trustees have the discretion whether to apply the whole or part of the fund for the benefit of one person, but are obliged to apply the rest of the fund for the benefit of a second named person, collectively the beneficiaries can claim the fund. They are together the sole objects of a discretionary trust and between them are entitled to the entire fund. As Romer J commented, "in such a case as that you treat all the people put together just as though they formed one person, for whose benefit the trustees were directed to apply the whole of a particular fund".[24]

The situations in which a consensual rearrangement of beneficial interests might be sought traditionally arose around consecutive trust interests. The classic example is that of a

---

21 Once consent is given, it may be that it cannot be revoked: see *Re IMK Family Trust* [2009] 1 F.L.R. 664 (a Channel Islands case).
22 This includes pension trusts: *Thorpe v Revenue & Customs Commissioner* [2010] EWCA Civ 339.
23 [1928] Ch. 915.
24 [1928] Ch. 915 at 919.

life tenant and a remainderman. Although there are various permutations possible, the following illustrate methods through which beneficial interests can be varied by agreement:

- the surrender by a life tenant of his interest to the remainderman (i.e. the person entitled to the property on the death of the life tenant). For example, Adrienne sets up a trust in shares which gives Fiona a life interest with remainder to Jordan. If Fiona decides to sell her life interest to Jordan, she will be surrendering her interest up to Jordan;

- the surrender by the remainderman of his interest to the life tenant. This would occur when it is Jordan who disposes of his remainder interest to Fiona;

- the disclaimer of a life interest created by will;

- the release of an annuity created by will; and

- the division of the trust fund between the life tenant and the remainderman. This would arise where Fiona and Jordan agree to allocate the shares between them and put an end to the trust.

The Court's Inherent Jurisdiction

As made clear, consensual variation cannot occur if unanimity is absent or the beneficiaries are not all adults and of sound mind. If, for example, the trust is designed to benefit children or, as yet, unborn beneficiaries the rule in *Saunders v Vautier* is rendered inoperative. In such circumstances, therefore, variation can occur only following the authorisation of the court. A variation can be justified under the, admittedly limited, inherent jurisdiction of the court. The parameters of this jurisdiction remain as charted by the House of Lords in *Chapman v Chapman*.[25] There it was made clear that apart from compromise (see para.**15-011**) and maintenance (see para.**15-013**), the court's inherent powers of variation extend only to management and administrative matters. As Marshall explains, "This decision makes it clear that the court does not possess plenary powers to alter a trust because alteration is thought to be advantageous to beneficiaries who are infants or not yet born, even though paradoxically, such beneficiaries could of their own volition and without the assistance of the court have made the desired alteration, had they been *in esse* and *sui juris*".[26]

15-008

---

25   [1954] A.C. 429; noted by J.D.B. Mitchell [1954] 17 M.L.R. 473.
26   O.R. Marshall, "Deviations from the Terms of a Trust" [1954] M.L.R. 420, 420.

In the *Chapman* case, the House was, simply put, invited to rewrite the trust interests to avoid death duties. The House concluded that it had no power to vary the trust in the circumstances before it. Indeed, this restrictive stance provided the momentum behind greater statutory intervention, namely the Variation of Trusts Act 1958. Lord Morton justified his decision by invoking a policy argument:

> "if the Court had power to approve, and did approve, schemes such as the present scheme, the way would be open for a most undignified game of chess between the Chancery Division and the legislature. The alteration of one settlement for the purposes of avoiding taxation already imposed might well be followed by scores of successful applications for a similar purpose by beneficiaries under other settlements. The legislature might then counter this move by imposing fresh taxation upon the trusts as thus altered. The beneficiaries would then troop back to the Chancery Division . . . So the game might go on, if the judges of the Chancery Division had the power which the appellants claim for them, and if they thought it right to make the first move".[27]

The upshot of this approach was that the courts had to pay more respect to the expressed intention of the settlor and that the possibilities of varying trusts for tax-saving purposes were greatly diminished. Lord Morton did, however, identify the limited circumstances in which the court can invoke its inherent jurisdiction to vary the terms of a trust.[28] These are:

- salvage and emergency;

- compromise; and

- maintenance.

Salvage and emergency

15-009   The first occasion on which the inherent jurisdiction emerges is when the court sanctions some special managerial act in accordance with the so-called "salvage principles". The traditional notion is that, in an emergency, the court can sanction a transaction (e.g. the sale or mortgage of part of an infant's trust interest) in order that the trustees can raise money to carry out necessary repairs to land. The idea is that the beneficiary's inheritance can thus be

---

27   [1954] A.C. 429 at 468.
28   [1954] A.C. 429 at 451. As will become clear, further statutory exceptions emerged (e.g. s.57(1) of the Trustee Act 1925).

preserved. This is, however, a limited jurisdiction. In *Re De Teissier's Settled Estates*,[29] Chitty J refused to allow the money to be used to rebuild, repair and improve a mansion house because there were two life interests preceding that of the infant beneficiary. There was no suggestion that the life tenant in possession could not afford the works and it was clear that, if the works were carried out, it would be chiefly for the benefit of the current tenant in possession. Chitty J concluded that, "unless the Court is firm in a matter such as this the Court will be flooded with similar applications".[30] This reticence is evident also in *Re Jackson*[31] where Kay J felt it necessary to conduct a limited inquiry as to what repairs were absolutely necessary. There an infant was entitled to real estate in possession, but the property was in a very dilapidated condition. While expressing the view that the jurisdiction should be jealously exercised, he felt that it was in the infant's interests that the absolutely essential works be authorised. Hence, it is not sufficient that the repairs are merely desirable or beneficial.[32] Accordingly, in *Re Montagu*[33] the Court of Appeal declined to sanction a scheme to demolish and rebuild certain houses even though it was clearly in the interests of the tenant for life and his children (who enjoyed an interest in remainder) that it do so. As Lopes LJ admitted, "That is not enough. If the buildings were falling down it would be a case of actual salvage and would stand differently".[34]

In *Re New*,[35] however, the salvage rules were extended into less conventional territory. There the trustees held legal title to shares in a particular company and, as an emergency matter, sought to become involved in the capital reconstruction of that company. As a result, the existing shares would be exchanged for new shares in the reconstructed company. This fell outside the trustees' powers of investment as set out in the trust instrument. The court sanctioned the transaction on the basis that it was analogous to the salvage cases. Romer LJ explained:

> **"In a case of this kind, which may reasonably be supposed to be one not foreseen or anticipated by the author of the trust, where the trustees are embarrassed by the emergency that has arisen and the duty cast upon them to do what is best for the estate, and the consent of all the beneficiaries cannot be obtained by reason of some of them not being *sui juris* or in existence, then it may be right for the Court, and the Court would in a proper case have jurisdiction, to sanction on behalf of all concerned such acts on behalf of the trustees . . .".[36]**

---

29   [1893] 1 Ch. 153.
30   [1893] 1 Ch. 153 at 165.
31   (1882) 21 Ch. D. 786.
32   See *Conway v Fenton* (1888) 40 Ch. D. 512.
33   [1897] 2 Ch. 8.
34   [1897] 2 Ch. 8 at 11.
35   [1901] 2 Ch. 534.
36   [1901] 2 Ch. 534 at 545.

Romer LJ provided the further example of a testator who declared that land is to be sold by a stipulated date. If, due to an unforeseen change of circumstances sale by the prescribed time would prove ruinous to the estate, he felt that the court would authorise the trustees to postpone sale in order to effect a proper sale at a later time.[37]

15-010

Re New was later described by Cozens-Hardy LJ in *Re Tollemache* as representing "the high-water mark of the exercise by the court of its extraordinary jurisdiction in relation to trusts".[38] In *Re Tollemache*, the trustees sought permission to invest in a mortgage using trust money. They argued that it would benefit the life tenant by generating an increased income and would not prejudice the position of the remainderman. The court, however, refused to approve this unauthorised use of trust funds as it could not be said to be an emergency transaction. The clear inference to be drawn from *Re Tollemache* is that the salvage and emergency rule does not cater for a scheme designed directly to vary existing beneficial entitlements under the trust. Such variation may be a consequence, but it is not a justification.

Compromise

15-011

The second inroad is, as Lord Morton confirmed in the *Chapman* case, that the court enjoys an inherent jurisdiction to approve compromises reached on behalf of an infant beneficiary. In this context, it is important to note that the infant does not enjoy the legal capacity to enter the compromise of its own volition. This aspect of the court's inherent jurisdiction is, however, dependent upon there being a real dispute concerning the infant's interest under the trust and a real compromise of that dispute that is proposed.[39] The dispute might concern the powers of the trustees or the beneficial interests created under the trust. Hence, the court's approval may engineer a variation of beneficial entitlement. As Lord Cohen put it in *Chapman v Chapman*, "The very essence of a compromise is that it may give each party something other than that which the will or settlement would, on its true construction, confer on them".[40]

The *Chapman* case emphasised that a proposed exchange or bargain is not a compromise. A fictitious or manufactured dispute will not, moreover, operate to engage the jurisdiction. In *Re Powell-Cotton's Resettlement*,[41] there was an investment clause of uncertain meaning and a proposed new investment clause was approved by the adult and infant beneficiaries. As there was not really any dispute, the court was invited to accede to a compromise so as to resolve a doubt or difficulty. This it refused to do. Although Lord Evershed MR sought, "to avoid laying down any hard and fast rule",[42] he concluded that, "it seems to me very doubtful, to say the least, whether it could be said that as between the beneficiaries in this case there

---

37   [1901] 2 Ch. 534 at 545.
38   [1903] 1 Ch. 955 at 956.
39   See *Re Lord Hylton's Settlement* [1954] 1 W.L.R. 1055.
40   [1954] A.C. 429 at 472.
41   [1956] 1 W.L.R. 23.
42   [1956] 1 W.L.R. 23 at 27.

is any dispute as to their rights".[43] Put simply, there was nothing to compromise. In *Mason v Farbrother*,[44] ambiguity again descended upon the extent of the trustees' power to invest as given by the trust instrument. In this case, however, the High Court held that a genuine difference of potential meaning allowed it to exercise its inherent jurisdiction at the behest of the trustees. This was so even though there was no contested dispute involving third parties. As Judge Blackett explained, "I do not think there need be open warfare before the court may approve a compromise, provided that there are genuine points of difference requiring determination or settlement".[45] In theory, the jurisdiction to vary exists even if the compromise will have the effect of reducing a beneficiary's eventual entitlement.

In the *Chapman* case, there was no such dispute and no suggestion of a compromise. All that was sought there was a simple rearrangement of existing and undisputed interests. As Lord Simonds noted, "It is the function of the court to execute a trust, to see that the trustees do their duty and to protect them if they do it, to direct them if they are in doubt and, if they do wrong, to penalise them. It is not the function of the court to alter a trust because alteration is thought to be advantageous to an infant beneficiary".[46]

15-012

Maintenance

15-013

The third example of where the inherent jurisdiction of the court arises is when the court awards maintenance from income that the testator has directed should be accumulated. The testator may make provision for his family, but might seek to postpone the enjoyment of the gift while the estate is increasing in value. As examined in Ch.14, the court will assume that the testator did not intend for his family to go short in the interim period and can override his express directions by ordering the payment of maintenance.[47] The court will, therefore, interfere with the accumulation. Any such order will necessarily result in a variation of the beneficial interests. The jurisdiction is not limited to urgent cases[48] and maintenance is not limited to minor beneficiaries.[49] In *Revel v Watkinson*, the Lord Chancellor expressed the view that "she stands entirely in the light of a child unprovided for during that time, and at the mother's pleasure, and the court will not, in favour of a remainder man . . . leave a daughter and heir at law to starve".[50]

---

43   [1956] 1 W.L.R. 23 at 28.

44   [1983] 2 All E.R. 1078.

45   [1983] 2 All E.R. 1078 at 1085. Nevertheless, the court preferred to utilise its jurisdiction under s.57 of the Trustee Act 1925 to insert a new investment clause.

46   [1954] A.C. 429 at 446.

47   *Re Collins* (1886) 32 Ch. D. 229; *Havelock v Havelock* (1881) 17 Ch. D. 807.

48   *Haley v Bannister* (1820) 4 Madd. 275.

49   *Revel v Watkinson* (1748) 1 Ves. Sen. 93. There an adult daughter was entitled to maintenance during her mother's lifetime.

50   (1748) 1 Ves. Sen. 93 at 95.

Statutory Jurisdiction: Miscellaneous Provisions

15-014

Prior to the Variation of Trusts Act 1958, the statutory exceptions to the duty of the trustee not to depart from the terms of the trust were piecemeal and scattered across a number of Acts of Parliament. As these provisions (albeit in amended form) still retain validity in the post-1958 Act era, it is convenient to consider them at the outset in isolation from the Variation of Trusts Act. The provisions to be considered in turn are:

- s.53 of the Trustee Act 1925;

- s.57(1) of the Trustee Act 1925;

- s.64 of the Settled Land Act 1925;

- s.24 of the Matrimonial Causes Act 1973; and

- s.16 of the Mental Capacity Act 2005.

Section 53 of the Trustee Act 1925

15-015

Section 53 of the Trustee Act 1925 provides that, when an infant is beneficially entitled to any property, the court may order certain dealings with the property with a view to the application of capital or income for the maintenance, education or benefit of that infant.[51] For example, the court may order that the property be conveyed for the infant's advantage or vest in any person the right to receive income or dividends from the property to further the interests of the infant. In *Re Lansdowne's WT*,[52] the barring of an estate in tail to minimise the liability for estate duty was categorised as an application for the benefit of the infant. The disentailing deed was a necessary and integral part of the scheme for carrying the arrangement into effect. The statutory provision is wider than the inherent jurisdiction to maintain in that it allows for capital to be employed for these purposes and alludes to "benefit" and not merely to "maintenance". As Upjohn J noted in *Re Heyworth*, "It covers not merely expenditure but capital investment such as the purchase of a house to live in or a share in a partnership, or even in some cases placing of money on deposit for an infant".[53] Accordingly, in *Re Meux's WT*[54] the court authorised deal-

---

51 See O.R. Marshall, "The Scope of Section 53 of the Trustee Act 1925" [1957] 21 Conv. 448.
52 [1967] Ch. 603.
53 [1956] 2 W.L.R. 1044 at 1048, 1049.
54 [1958] Ch. 154.

ings under which an infant's reversionary interest was sold to the tenant for life with the ambition of reducing estate duty and thereby advancing the interests of the infant beneficiary. The proposed conveyance of the reversionary interest was with a view to an application for the benefit of the infant reversioner within s.53. It was central to the decision that the proceeds of sale were to be held on new trusts for the infant. This was viewed as a single transaction which was overwhelmingly to the benefit of the infant. In *Re Gower's Settlement*,[55] the court was invited to sanction the raising of money by a mortgage of the interest of an infant beneficiary under a settlement. The infant was a tenant in tail subject to a preceding life interest and the mortgage was to benefit the infant. The court authorised the dealing under s.53 even though the mortgage would take priority over the potential claims of remote beneficiaries. In *Re Bristol's Settled Estates*,[56] a transaction was authorised by Buckley J to bar an entail and thus pave the way for an infant's subsequent application under the Variation of Trusts Act 1958. This was for the benefit of the beneficiary and amounted to an application of capital or income.

Section 53 does not, however, allow the court to vary the infant's actual beneficial interest under the trust. This was demonstrated in *Re Heyworth* where Upjohn J refused to countenance a dealing under which the proceeds of sale of an infant's reversionary interest were to be given to the infant absolutely.[57] Although the bargain was undoubtedly beneficial to the infant, there was no present need of the cash for the infant. Upjohn J explained:

> **"The deed is not in the least degree entered into with a view to the application of, or for the purpose of applying, any capital or income of the infant for her benefit . . . If I sanctioned this scheme on behalf of the infant I should be reading the section as though it empowered the court to convey the property of an infant whenever it was for her benefit. Unfortunately, the section only confers a more limited jurisdiction".[58]**

Section 57(1) of the Trustee Act 1925

It is not uncommon for trustees to experience difficulties in the management or administration of trust property and to discover that they do not have the necessary legal powers to effect a transaction that is considered to be in the best interests of the beneficiaries.[59] For example, in *Re Portman Estate* the trustees sought the insertion of a power to trade so that the trust could

15-016

---

55   [1934] Ch. 365.
56   [1964] 3 All E.R. 939.
57   [1956] 2 W.L.R. 1044.
58   [1956] 2 W.L.R. 1044 at 1049.
59   In *Gelber v Sunderland Foundation* [2018] EWHC 2344 (Ch), the trustees successfully sought new powers to authorise them to enter into a deed of covenant and pay part of the proceeds of sale of land to a charitable company, whose primary objective was restoring and preserving Blenheim Palace.

open a hotel and run a farm business[60] and, in *South Downs Trustees Ltd v GH,* a trustee wished to sell the trust's entire shareholding in a company, even though the trust deed expressly restricted the power to sell where it would lead to a loss of control over the company.[61] Section 57(1) caters for this difficulty and provides a cost-effective and convenient means through which trustees (other than trustees under the Settled Land Act 1925)[62] can be authorised to do any act relating to the management or administration of trust property, which the court deems to be expedient.[63] Accordingly, as demonstrated in *Alexander v Alexander,*[64] there are several matters that the court must consider as to whether a variation is appropriate under s.57(1). It must determine whether it has jurisdiction to act under s.57, decide whether it is expedient to confer the power that is sought and decide whether it should exercise its discretion to confer that power.[65] The court must consider the interests of the beneficiaries collectively and hold the scales fairly between the various interests. The court should also take on board the interests of the settlor.[66]

For example, in *Southgate v Sutton*[67] the trustees sought powers of appropriation and partition as regards the trust property vested in them. As they had no existing powers to do so, the trustees successfully applied to court under s.57(1) of the Trustee Act 1925. Similarly, in *Re English & American Insurance Co Ltd*[68] the claim concerned trust arrangements that were established to deal with certain protected liabilities of the now defunct company. The application was made because of the existence of a small subset of 19 beneficiaries, who potentially had rights to benefit from the trust fund, which prevented the trustees from distributing the fund to the clear majority of beneficiaries whose claims would soon be ascertained. The trust deed contained no power of amendment or resettlement and this stalemate was likely to last for years to come. The High Court decided to apportion the fund under s.57(1) to create a principal sub-trust for the majority of the beneficiaries and a residual sub-trust for the other 19 beneficiaries.

As demonstrated in *Re Salting,*[69] the statutory authorisation operates as if it was an overriding power inserted into the trust instrument. Nevertheless, Eve J could not accept that the revised terms were to be treated as if they were originally in the trust instrument.[70] The

---

60   [2015] EWHC 536 (Ch).
61   [2018] EWHC 1064 (Ch).
62   Section 57(4). Such trustees are offered an alternative and wider route under s.64 of the Settled Land Act 1925 (see para.**15-018**).
63   Note that trustees do not usually initiate the more expensive proceedings under the Variation of Trusts Act 1958: see *Re Druce's ST* [1962] 1 W.L.R. 363. Unlike under the 1958 Act, there Is no need for the beneficiaries to be joined to the proceedings: *Re Portman Estate* [2015] EWHC 536 (Ch).
64   [2011] EWHC 2721 (Ch).
65   There the court was satisfied that it was expedient to sell a cottage, but acknowledged that it was still in its discretion as to whether the order sought would be made.
66   *Alexander v Alexander* [2011] EWHC 2721 (Ch).
67   [2011] EWCA Civ 637.
68   [2013] EWHC 3360 (Ch).
69   [1932] 2 Ch. 57.
70   [1932] 2 Ch. 57 at 64.

underlying ethos is that trust property should be managed as effectively as possible in the best interests of the beneficiaries. The court will be invited to sanction specific dealings with the property that would otherwise be unauthorised and yet are to the overall advantage of the beneficiaries.[71] In *Re Mair*,[72] a scheme was approved under which the life interest given to two women was to be sold, primarily to enable one of them to pay her debts. The scheme involved the payment out of capital of a considerable sum to the two women.[73] In *Re English & American Insurance Co Ltd*,[74] the proposed variation was viewed as being commercially rational as well as the most cost-effective and administratively efficient means of proceeding. If the court did not intervene, real and material prejudice would be inflicted upon the majority of the beneficiaries. It was emphasised by the High Court that expediency did not require it to be satisfied that the change was advantageous to the interests of each and every beneficiary separately. It is also to be appreciated that the power of the court is not limited to a one-off transaction and that additional and more general administrative powers could be authorised. Accordingly, in *Re Portman Estate* it was accepted that a general power to trade could be authorised to avoid repeated applications and to cater for changing circumstances.[75]

Section 57(1) clearly overlaps with the narrower "salvage" jurisdiction (see para.**15-009**). Two major differences, however, emerge. First, the inherent jurisdiction is framed around the existence of an "emergency", whereas, s.57(1) is based upon the more generous concept of "expediency". Secondly, as regards the statutory jurisdiction there is no requirement that the reason for intervention be one that the settlor could not reasonably have foreseen.[76] Accordingly, s.57(1) offers greater scope than the salvage principles and has, for most practical purposes, subsumed the traditional jurisdiction.

15-017

Section 57(1) cannot, however, be operated merely to promote the position of one beneficiary at the expense of others.[77] In *Re Craven's Estate (No.2)*,[78] the testatrix left her residuary estate on trust for several beneficiaries, including her son. The trustees were given an express power of advancement for the limited purpose of buying a business. The son sought to become a member of Lloyds, which required the payment of a deposit, and asked the court to vary the terms of the advancement provision under its s.57 jurisdiction. It was clear that the use of the money did not amount to the purchase of a business. Although it would clearly benefit the son, Farwell J concluded that it would not be expedient to the other beneficiaries to allow part of the

---

71   See Lord Evershed MR in *Re Downshire's Settled Estates* [1953] Ch. 218 at 248.
72   [1935] Ch. 562.
73   In *Trustees of the British Museum v Attorney General* [1984] 1 All E.R. 337, s.57 was employed to widen the trustees' existing powers of investment.
74   [2013] EWHC 3360 (Ch).
75   [2015] EWHC 536 (Ch).
76   *Re Downshire's Settled Estates* [1953] Ch. 218.
77   Such a jurisdiction is instead offered by the Variation of Trusts Act 1958 (see para.**15-022**). If the sole purpose of the application is to alter the trustees' powers, with no variation of the beneficial interests, s.57 offers the most effective route as there is no need to obtain the court's approval on behalf of minor or unborn beneficiaries: *Edward v Fitzgerald* [2019] EWHC 726 (Ch).
78   [1937] Ch. 431.

trust fund to be used in this unauthorised fashion. The court refused to sanction the variation. Farwell J explained:

> "The word 'expedient' there quite clearly must mean, expedient for the trust as a whole. It cannot mean that however expedient it may be for one beneficiary if it is inexpedient from the point of view of the other beneficiaries concerned the Court ought to sanction the transaction. In order that the matter may be one which is in the opinion of the Court expedient, it must be expedient for the trust as a whole".[79]

The provision is designed to promote the "management" and "administration" of property vested in the trustees. These terms, however, remain undefined in the Act and, although most proceedings occur in private and the decisions are unreported, it has been left for the courts to ascribe some meaning to these words. Section 57(1) has been utilised to authorise, for example, a modernisation of the trustees' investment powers,[80] the sale of settled chattels,[81] the sale of land where the necessary consents could not be obtained,[82] the sale of a cottage and the purchase of an alternative residential property,[83] distributions in the form of taxable payments,[84] the widening of the investment powers of a charitable corporation,[85] the sale of a reversionary interest,[86] and the expedient partition of property.[87] By way of further examples, in *Re Portman Estate*[88] the variations afforded the trustees powers to trade, to provide guarantees for beneficiaries, to accept good receipts for the payment of income to beneficiaries under 18 years, to hold trust property via nominees and to appoint a manager of trust property. Accordingly, s.57 is focused upon the supervision and control of trust property. It has nothing directly to do with the variation of beneficial interests (these are not vested in the trustees) or stimulating tax advantages. As Marshall concludes, "The object of the section is to enable the court to authorise specific dealings with the trust property which it might not have been able to do on the basis of salvage or emergency, but it was no part of the legislative aim to disturb the rule that the court will not rewrite a trust".[89]

Nevertheless, this does not mean that the proposed variation cannot have some impact

---

79 [1937] Ch. 431 at 436.
80 *Mason v Farbrother* [1983] 2 All E.R. 1078.
81 *Re Hope's WT* [1929] 2 Ch. 136. Three valuable family portraits were amongst the chattels concerned. Eve J described the sale as "beneficial to all parties interested, and indeed is almost unavoidable" (at 140).
82 *Re Beale's ST* [1932] 2 Ch. 15. There the trustee in bankruptcy wished to sell, but the bankrupt refused his consent.
83 *Alexander v Alexander* [2011] EWHC 2721 (Ch).
84 *NBPF Pension Trustees Ltd v Warnock-Smith* [2008] 2 All E.R. (Comm) 740.
85 *Re Shipwrecked Fishermen & Mariners' Benevolent Fund* [1959] Ch. 220.
86 *Re Cockerell's ST* [1956] Ch. 372. The benefit sought here was the avoidance of death duties.
87 *Re Thomas* [1930] 1 Ch. 194. This concerned the allocation (partition) of real and personal property held on trust amongst the beneficiaries.
88 [2015] EWHC 536 (Ch).
89 O.R. Marshall [1954] 17 M.L.R. 420, 425; see *Re Downshire's Settled Estate* [1953] Ch. 218.

on the existing beneficial interests. As demonstrated in *Southgate v Sutton*, it is permissible for the proposal to have an incidental effect upon the interests of the beneficiaries, but it cannot amount to creating a different set of beneficial interests.[90] As Mummery LJ cautioned, "The court must decide, on the particular facts of each case, on which side of the line the application falls. That may be difficult, especially when, as is the case here, the application is not opposed. The court is nervous about the fundamental matter of jurisdiction if it is asked to act without the benefit of adversarial argument that normally disciplines its decision-making processes".[91] In *Re English & American Insurance Co Ltd*[92] the court exercised its s.57 jurisdiction to grant the trustees the power to partition the trust fund. Deputy Judge Clive Freedman QC explained that "I find that whilst the effect of the foregoing would be to affect the beneficial interests in the trust, it does so only incidentally".[93] Although there was no guarantee that the overlapping beneficiaries would receive exactly what they would have received if the fund had remained undivided, it was very likely that any variation would be minuscule. The reserve fund should be sufficient to cover the entire claim of the minority beneficiaries, and any risk otherwise was negligible.

Section 64 of the Settled Land Act 1925

15-018

Section 64 of the Settled Land Act 1925 affords the court a generous jurisdiction to authorise the tenant for life of settled land to carry out a wide variety of transactions as if he were the absolute owner. The transactions include "any sale, extinguishment of manorial incidents, exchange, assurance, grant, lease, surrender, reconveyance, release, reservation or other disposition, any purchase or other acquisition, any covenant, contract, or option and any application of capital money . . . and any compromise or other dealing or arrangement . . .".[94]

With the rider that the provision operates only when the trust is of settled land,[95] this is a more flexible and much wider power than that offered under s.57(1) of the Trustee Act 1925. First, there is no requirement that the authorisation may only be of management and administrative actions. This was demonstrated in *Hambro v Duke of Marlborough*, where variation of the beneficial interest of an adult beneficiary was proposed.[96] Section 64 merely requires that the transaction be for the benefit of either the settled land or the persons interested under the

---

90   [2011] EWCA Civ 637. Similarly, in *Re Portman Estate* [2015] EWHC 536 (Ch) the authorised changes were to have only minimal impact on beneficial interests.
91   [2011] EWCA Civ 637 at [8].
92   [2013] EWHC 3360 (Ch).
93   [2013] EWHC 3360 (Ch) at [44].
94   Section 64(2).
95   Accordingly, it has no application to a settlement of personalty or to trusts of land governed by the Trusts of Land and Appointment of Trustees Act 1996. Section 64 is, therefore, of diminishing importance as new settlements created after the 1996 Act will not be subject to the Settled Land Act.
96   [1994] Ch. 158.

settlement.[97] Secondly, under s.64 the court can vary beneficial interests in order to generate tax savings. In *Raikes v Lygon*,[98] Peter Gibson J upheld the transfer of capital assets from one settlement to another to ensure the maintenance of a mansion house and its grounds. The key motivation behind the proposal was to mitigate foreseeable inheritance tax consequences. Nevertheless, this was a transaction within s.64 as the property consisted of the settled land and those interested under the settlement were to be benefited. It was, moreover, a transaction that could have been effected by an absolute owner.

15-019

The types of transaction that are subject to s.64 are widely defined.[99] The section covers a conveyance by the tenant for life to trustees of a new settlement. This was demonstrated in *Hambro v Duke of Marlborough*,[100] where the Duke (as tenant for life) and the trustees concluded that the Marquess of Blandford (the tenant in tail in remainder) was ill-suited to managing the Blenheim Estates on the death of the Duke. This heir apparent displayed unbusinesslike habits and lack of responsibility. Against the wishes of the Marquess, they floated a scheme under which the estate would be transferred to trustees of a new trust. This redesigned trust would provide the Duke with the income for his life and, following his death, the estate would be held on protective trusts for the Marquess for life. Following the death of the Marquess, the estate was to be held on the trusts of the original settlement. Morritt J held that this was a transaction within s.64 and this was so despite the opposition of the adult beneficiary. As Cooke comments, "The amusing point is that the 1925 legislation, which aimed to make land freely alienable, will be the means of keeping this estate intact for future generations".[101]

By way of a further example, in *Re Scarisbrick Resettlement Estates*[102] the sale of investments to raise £10,000 to facilitate the continued occupation of the tenant for life in a stately home (Scarisbrick Hall) and, thereby, assuring the preservation of the property was held to be a transaction for these purposes. As indicated, s.64 might also be employed to adjust existing beneficial interests to avoid tax liabilities, particularly those relating to inheritance tax.[103]

Section 24 of the Matrimonial Causes Act 1973

15-020

Section 24 of the Matrimonial Causes Act 1973 allows the court, when making an order for divorce or annulment of marriage, to make a property adjustment order.[104] It is to be appreci-

---

97   If the land has been sold, s.64 has no application: see *Re Simmons* [1956] Ch. 125.
98   [1988] 1 W.L.R. 281.
99   See *Re Downshire's Settled Estates* [1953] Ch. 218.
100   [1994] Ch. 158; noted at [1994] Conv. 492 (E. Cooke).
101   [1994] Conv. 492, 495.
102   [1944] Ch. 229.
103   See *Raikes v Lygon* [1988] 1 W.L.R. 281.
104   This applies also to registered partnerships under the Civil Partnership Act 2004. Section 23A allows such an order to be made pre-decree and on the separation of the parties.

ated that the s.24 jurisdiction is unfettered and, in theory, unlimited.[105] As Black LJ explained, "The breadth of the discretion to vary a nuptial settlement is considerable, including the power to exclude a beneficiary entirely from the settlement and to transfer an asset to a non-beneficiary free from all trusts".[106] The court must, however, have regard to all the circumstances of the case and to the specific matters listed in s.25(2)(a)–(h). The overall ambition is to achieve a fair result for both sides and the court should not do any more than is necessary to achieve justice. [107]

Section 24 can operate to vary the trusts contained in any nuptial settlement that was made in contemplation of marriage or post marriage for the benefit of the parties to the marriage or the children of that marriage. The court can then make the order directly against the trust and the trustees. If the trust is not nuptial in nature, s.24(1)(c) does not apply. As Mostyn J pointed out, "Trusts have always aroused controversy in this exercise. This is because assets held in trust are not legally owned by either party. They are owned by third parties—the trustees".[108] The court, moreover, should be slow to deprive innocent third parties (e.g. children of the marriage) of rights under a settlement.[109] This jurisdiction caters for the remoulding of beneficial interests.[110] In *Brooks v Brooks*,[111] a company pension scheme of which the husband was the sole member was varied under s.24. Under the scheme, the husband had the power to surrender part of his pension to provide his wife with a deferred pension for life. On the company ceasing to trade, the pension fund was valued at £440,000. When looked at in the round, the House of Lords considered this to be a post-nuptial settlement that fell squarely within the statutory jurisdiction. The settlement was made after the marriage and contained the nuptial element of providing for the wife in her capacity as wife.[112] Lord Nicholls explained that, "The section gives the court power to vary a settlement. Inherent in this provision is the notion that the court's jurisdiction extends to all property comprised in the settlement. This includes any interest the settlor himself thenceforth may have in the settled property by virtue of his own settlement".[113] As Lord Nicholls further observed, "it is also implicit in the section that the court's power does not extend to property which is not part of the settled property".[114] This case, therefore, turned upon the fact that there was an express ability for the wife to benefit

---

105 *Ben Hashem v Al Shayif* [2008] EWHC 2380 (Fam).
106 *AB v CB* [2015] EWCA Civ 447 at [45].
107 In *HRH Luxembourg v HRH Luxembourg* [2018] EWFC 77, however, the court could not make a property adjustment order in favour of a wife in circumstances where the husband did not enjoy any beneficial interest in the matrimonial home.
108 *BJ v MJ* [2011] EWHC 2708 (Fam) at [1].
109 In *Ben Hashem v Al Shayif* [2008] EWHC 2380 (Fam) at [290], Munby J admitted that an impact on third party rights "should be permitted only if, after taking into account all the terms of the intended order, all monetary considerations and any other relevant factors, however intangible, it can be said, on the whole, to be for their benefit or, at least, not to their disadvantage".
110 *Thomson v Thomson* [1956] P. 384.
111 [1996] 1 A.C. 375; noted at [1997] Conv. 52 (M. Thomas).
112 See also *AB v CB* [2015] EWCA Civ 447.
113 [1996] 1 A.C. 375 at 392.
114 [1996] 1 A.C. 375 at 392, 393.

under the scheme and that there was only one member of that scheme. He cautioned that "Not every pension scheme constitutes a marriage settlement".[115]

The decision does not concern entitlement under the usual style of multi-member pension scheme. As regards this common type of pension scheme, so-called "pension-sharing" or "pension splitting" on the breakdown of a marriage or registered partnership is now catered for by Pts III and IV of the Welfare Reform and Pensions Act 1999. For divorce proceedings begun after 1 December 2000, this enactment gives the court new discretionary powers to deal with pensions in matrimonial proceedings.[116] Pension offsetting is the simplest form of dealing with pensions. The total value of pension funds is offset against other assets. Pension sharing is where the court calculates a percentage share of the ex-partner's pension and that share is then allocated to the other.[117] A pension attachment order ("ear marking") provides an agreed amount of the other's net pension income or lump sum, or both, when it starts being paid to them. This entails that no pension is payable until the ex-partner has begun taking his or her pension, which could be problematic if the ex-partner is much younger or retires later than the other.

Section 16 of the Mental Capacity Act 2005

15-021

Section 16(1)(b) of the Mental Capacity Act 2005 gives the Court of Protection the power to make a settlement of an incapacitated patient's property, whether for the benefit of the patient[118] or the benefit of others (s.18(1)(h)).[119] Section 16(7) allows the court to vary that settlement in such manner as it thinks fit in the best interests of the person (as defined in s.4) and with regard to the statutory principles listed in s.1. There is no hierarchy as between the factors which must to be borne in mind and the determinative issue is the judicial evaluation of what is in the individual's best interests.[120] In *Re CWHT*,[121] the Court of Protection ordered that certain property of a patient be settled on trust. This gave the patient's sister a life interest with remainder for the patient's children and remoter issue. No power of revocation was reserved. Subsequently, the trust was varied during the lifetime of the patient so that the property was to be divided (i.e. a partition was effected) between tenant for life and the remaindermen.

---

115   [1996] 1 A.C. 375 at 396.

116   This introduced new provisions into the 1973 Act (i.e. ss.24B–24G) which deal specifically with pensions.

117   See *Martin-Dye v Martin-Dye* [2006] 1 W.L.R. 3448 where a 57:43 ratio was employed for the purpose of determining the pension sharing order. The idea is that the share awarded (i.e. a pension credit) will set up the spouse/registered partner with a pension of his/her own. Pension sharing does not apply to the State Pension.

118   See *Re PV* [2015] EWCOP 22.

119   In *Re Jones* [2014] EWCOP 59, for example, the Court of Protection ordered that a statutory will be drafted on behalf of an 81-year-old intestate man who suffered from dementia and lacked testamentary capacity. It was in his best interests to be remembered with affection by his family as having done the right thing by his will.

120   *Re M* [2011] 1 W.L.R. 344.

121   [1978] Ch. 67. This concerned the equivalent provisions then contained in the Mental Health Act 1959.

The Variation of Trusts Act 1958

15-022

As shown, the decision of the House of Lords in *Chapman v Chapman*[122] had the effect of narrowing the scope for the variation of trusts for the purposes of tax planning. It also left the law in an uncertain and unpalatable state. Indeed, Lord Simonds acknowledged that the way the law had developed might not be logical, but was not prepared to claim for the court "a certain jurisdiction, merely because we think it ought to have it".[123] He continued that, "It is for the legislature, which does not rest under that disability, to determine whether there should be a change in the law and what that change should be".[124] In response, during 1957 the Law Reform Committee was invited to consider whether the powers of the court to sanction variations of trusts should be widened. The Committee reported later in the year and unanimously recommended that the court should be given an extensive jurisdiction to authorise variations.[125] The Committee said of the *Chapman* decision that "it has created distinctions between cases in which the trusts can be varied and cases in which they cannot be varied which have nothing to do with the merits of the proposed variations".[126] The recommendations of the Committee shortly afterwards became embodied in the Variation of Trusts Act 1958. The central ambition of the Committee was to restore the jurisdiction of the court to its pre-*Chapman* days. As it admitted, "In our view the only satisfactory solution of the problem is to give the Court the unlimited jurisdiction to sanction such changes which it in fact exercised in the years immediately preceding the decision in *Chapman v Chapman* . . . Logically, there is no satisfactory stopping place short of an unlimited jurisdiction".[127]

The Committee rejected the view of Lord Morton that variation for tax purposes was analogous to an undignified game of chess between the court and the legislature. The Committee concluded that lawful tax avoidance was a legitimate strategy goal for the court to condone. Indeed, most applications under the 1958 Act are framed to avoid tax that would arise if the existing provisions remained unaltered.[128] As Evans puts it, "This financial incentive is the main inducement to incur the expense of an application".[129]

---

122 [1954] A.C. 429.
123 [1954] A.C. 429 at 444.
124 [1954] A.C. 429 at 444.
125 Law Reform Committee, *The Court's Power to Sanction Variation of Trusts* (1957) Cmnd.310.
126 Law Reform Committee, *The Court's Power to Sanction Variation of Trusts* (1957) Cmnd.310, para.9.
127 Law Reform Committee, *The Court's Power to Sanction Variation of Trusts* (1957) Cmnd.310, para.13.
128 See, e.g. *Re Clitheroe's ST* [1959] 3 All E.R. 789. In *Re Weston's Settlement* [1969] 1 Ch. 223 Stamp LJ explained that the court "is not the watchdog of the Commissioners of Inland Revenue" (at 232).
129 S. Evans, "Variation Clarification" [2011] Conv. 151, 152.

The discretionary power

15-023

Section 1 of the Variation of Trusts Act 1958 confers on the court what Lord Evershed MR in *Re Steed's WT* described as a "very wide and, indeed, revolutionary discretion".[130] This, by virtue of s.1(1), extends to trusts arising "under any will, settlement or other disposition". In such circumstances, the court is afforded the discretionary power to approve "any arrangement (by whomsoever proposed, and whether or not there is any other person beneficially interested who is capable of assenting thereto) varying or revoking all or any of the trusts, or enlarging the powers of the trustees of managing or administering any of the property subject to the trusts".[131] Section 1 makes clear that the discretion applies to trusts whether created by will or inter vivos and regardless of whether the subject matter is real or personal property. It is retrospective in effect and, therefore, operates in relation to trusts whenever established.[132] It has also been accepted that the 1958 Act extends to property held on a bare trust, at least for a minor.[133] The key consideration is whether, in the context of the arrangement as a whole, the proposed variation is for the benefit of each beneficiary or group on whose behalf approval is sought.[134]

Some uncertainty, however, has concerned whether the 1958 Act applies to the statutory trusts which arise on intestacy by virtue of ss.46, 47 of the Administration of Estates Act 1925. In *S v T*,[135] all turned upon what was meant by "disposition" and whether the fact the trusts were statutory in origin meant that they were excluded from variation under the Act by s.1(5).[136] Etherton J concluded that s.1(5) had no application and that the statutory trusts arose under a disposition effected by the death of the deceased and not solely because of the statutory provisions. He could see no policy reason to justify an alternative conclusion. In *Re Bernstein*,[137] Blackburne J had to determine whether the term "trusts" as employed in s.1(1) included the duties incident to the office of personal representative or was, instead, confined to the duties of

---

130 [1960] Ch. 407 at 420, 421. It is, therefore, surprising that, as Mummery LJ pointed out in *Goulding v James* [1997] 2 All E.R. 239 at 246, "For a jurisdiction invoked thousands of times over almost forty years there are remarkably few reported cases on its construction".

131 In *A v B* [2016] EWHC 340 (Ch), there were, in addition to the parties, many potential beneficiaries. The court determined that it was neither sensible nor appropriate to join this wider class as parties to the proceedings and for them to make representations.

132 In *Re Seale's Marriage Settlement* [1961] 3 W.L.R. 262, the trust was created in 1931 and varied under the Act in 1961.

133 *CD (A Minor) v O* [2004] EWHC (Ch) 1036.

134 *Edward v Fitzgerald* [2019] EWHC 726 (Ch). There the settlor and adult beneficiaries supported the proposed variation (including an extension of the perpetuity period) and the court was satisfied that it was for the benefit of the unborn and unascertained beneficiaries on whose behalf the application was made.

135 [2006] W.T.L.R. 1461.

136 This provides that "Nothing in the foregoing provisions of this section shall apply to trusts affecting property settled by Act of Parliament".

137 [2008] EWHC 3454 (Ch); noted by S. Evans, "Variation Clarification" [2011] Conv. 151 who claims (p.151), "Like rural buses, reported cases concerning applications to the court under the Variation of Trusts Act 1958 . . . seem to come along rather infrequently".

a trustee holding identified property for an identified beneficiary. He concluded that the wording of s.1(1) was well capable of extending to property held by personal representative on trusts, whether express or implied and added:

> "the fact that during the period of administration of an estate the beneficiaries, whether legatees or otherwise, have no legal or equitable interest in the assets comprised in the estate, but have no more than a right to require the deceased's estate to be duly administered, does not mean that even if it can be said that the property comprised in the estate is held on trusts arising under a will, settlement or other disposition, the legatees cannot establish an interest under those trusts so as to come within section 1(1)(a). It is clear that the reference to 'interest' in that paragraph is not so confined".[138]

The 1958 Act does not affect the powers, already discussed, which the court already enjoyed under either its inherent jurisdiction or its pre-1958 statutory jurisdiction. As Mowbray puts it, "The jurisdiction given by the new Act takes its place among other powers of the court to vary trusts. It differs from most of the other powers, however, in that it is a mere power to assent and (with few exceptions) no order made under the new Act can override the wishes of any beneficiary ascertained and capable of making up his own mind on the proposed variation".[139] In *CD (A Minor) v O*,[140] it was emphasised that it is more appropriate that the court proceed under the 1958 Act if that is possible.[141]

Any person interested can make an application, for example a beneficiary, trustee[142] or settlor.[143] Nevertheless, the court can only approve an arrangement entered on behalf of the limited classes of beneficiary listed in s.1(1) (see para.**15-029**). Even then, with the exception of a discretionary beneficiary under a protective trust (i.e. a trust under which the beneficial interest is liable to be forfeited on the occurrence of some event), the court can only sanction the arrangement if it will work to the benefit of the person on whose behalf the application is made. Again apart from discretionary beneficiaries under a protective trust, the rule is that the court cannot agree on the behalf of ascertained beneficiaries who are sui juris. Hence, the court is unable to override any objection or the need for consent of such a beneficiary. The underlying design of s.1 is, therefore, to allow the court to approve arrangements on behalf of beneficiaries who cannot give consent themselves. Mummery LJ considered that, "In relation to the mem-

15-024

---

138 [2008] EWHC 3454 (Ch) at [29].
139 W.J. Mowbray, "Varying Trusts" [1958] 22 Conv. 373, 375.
140 [2004] EWHC (Ch) 1036.
141 There are, however, drawbacks as the process is costly and cumbersome. All adults with a beneficial interest must be joined to the proceedings, which usually occur in the High Court, and each might be separately represented: see S. Evans, "Variation Clarification" [2011] Conv. 151, 152.
142 Although it is unusual for a trustee to make an application under the 1958 Act, in all cases the trustees must at least be joined to the proceedings: *TM v AH* [2016] EWHC 572 (Fam).
143 In *Re Clitheroe* [1959] 1 W.L.R. 1159, unusually it was the settlor who made the application.

bers of the specified class who cannot act for themselves, the court is almost in the position of a 'statutory attorney' . . .".[144] He appraised the 1958 Act as being "a statutory expansion of the consent principle embodied in the rule in *Saunders v Vautier*".[145] Lord Reid explained in *Re Holmden's ST*:

> "The beneficiaries are not bound by variations because the court has made the variation. Each beneficiary is bound because he has consented to the variation. If he was not of full age when the arrangement was made he is bound because the court was authorised by the Act to approve of it on his behalf and did so by making an order. If he was of full age and did not in fact consent he is not affected by the order of the court and he is not bound. So the arrangement must be regarded as an arrangement made by the beneficiaries themselves. The court merely acted on behalf of or as representing those beneficiaries who were not in a position to give their own consent and approval".[146]

Types of variation

15-025

The 1958 Act allows for administrative variations as well as variations affecting beneficial interests. Although usually employed to enlarge a trustee's powers, the court has the jurisdiction to approve a variation removing or restricting such powers as part of a wider variation of the trust.[147] It has been employed to authorise a wide range of changes. These include:

- the insertion of a power of advancement[148] and the modification of such a power[149];

- the insertion of an accumulation period for income[150] and the termination of a trust for accumulation[151];

- the inclusion of a new perpetuity period[152];

---

144 *Goulding v James* [1997] 2 All E.R. 239 at 249.
145 [1997] 2 All E.R. 239 at 247.
146 [1968] A.C. 685 at 701. Lord Guest added (at 711) that "The court thus supplied the capacity which the incapax lacked".
147 *Edward v Fitzgerald* [2019] EWHC 726 (Ch).
148 *Re Lister's WT* [1962] 1 W.L.R. 1441.
149 See *CD (A Minor) v O* [2004] EWHC (Ch) 1036 where the application was intended to secure that, if necessary, the whole capital could be applied for advancement purposes.
150 *Re Holt's Settlement* [1969] 1 Ch. 100.
151 *Re Tinker's Settlement* [1960] 1 W.L.R. 1011.
152 *Wyndham v Egremont* [2009] EWHC 2076 (Ch); see also *A v B* [2016] EWHC 340 (Ch).

- the widening of the investment powers of the trustees[153] and the substitution of one investment clause by another[154];

- the addition of a clause which prevented the settlor or his wife from taking any benefit under a charitable trust and sidestepped the potential tax liability of the settlor[155];

- the variation of a settlement in which the applicant held a life interest[156] and the variation of a testamentary trust so as not to disadvantage the next generation of beneficiary[157];

- the variation of a trust in order to defer vesting of capital[158];

- a variation of the original settlement, which placed a sum of money in trust for the purpose of purchasing a property for an ex-wife, by means of a partition of the fund partly in her favour and partly in favour of the children and their subsequent issue yet to be born or ascertained[159];

- to extend the trust period[160] and to widen the class of beneficiaries to include civil partners and those in same-sex marriages[161];

- a variation to allow the accumulation of income to meet future periodic inheritance tax charges[162];

- a change to the provision for the appointment of new trustees[163];

- the appointment of a Canadian Trust Corporation in place of the existing English trustees following the emigration of the beneficiaries under a marriage settlement[164]; and

---

153 *Re Coates' Trusts* [1959] 1 W.L.R. 375.
154 *Re Byng's WT* [1959] 1 W.L.R. 379. These investment cases will now usually be dealt with under the Trustee Act 2000.
155 *Re Roberts' ST, The Times*, 27 February 1959.
156 *Re Oake's Settlement* [1959] 1 W.L.R. 502; *Ridgwell v Ridgwell* [2007] EWHC 2666 (Ch).
157 *Re Cohen's WT* [1959] 1 W.L.R. 865.
158 *Wright v Gater* [2012] 1 W.L.R. 802; *Bailey v Bailey* unreported 12 November 2004 (Ch). In the latter case, there were in addition variation orders relating to the extension of administrative powers and the ability to accumulate income.
159 *Re King* [2010] EWHC 3939 (Ch).
160 *DC v AC* [2016] EWHC 477 (Ch).
161 *Pemberton v Pemberton* [2016] EWHC 2345 (Ch).
162 *Allfrey v Allfrey* [2015] EWHC 1717 (Ch).
163 *Bathurst v Bathurst* [2016] EWHC 3033 (Ch).
164 *Re Seale's Marriage Settlement* [1961] 3 W.L.R. 262.

■ the enlargement of a protective life interest into a life interest free of the protective trusts.[165]

An arrangement?

15-026

The term "arrangement" was regarded by Lord Evershed MR in *Re Steed's WT* as "deliberately used in the widest possible sense so as to cover any proposal which any person may put forward for varying or revoking the trusts".[166] Accordingly, Lord Evershed MR makes clear that the term is not limited to a scheme that is inter partes and worked out between two or more persons. Evans defines an "arrangement" as "any dealing with the trust property, or any disposition of the beneficial interests therein which are not sanctioned by nor contemplated in the trust instrument creating the trust".[167]

A major limitation has, however, emerged from the decision of Wilberforce J in *Re Towler's ST*.[168] In this case, the arrangement emerged because of concerns by a mother over the financial recklessness and immaturity of her daughter, a minor beneficiary. It was argued that the possession of a large sum of free capital would expose the daughter and her fortune to considerable hazards. The proposal was to transfer the child's share of settled funds to trustees to hold on protective trusts for the child's lifetime with remainders over. The minor would otherwise have become absolutely entitled on reaching 21 years of age. The court refused to approve the arrangement as it would be tantamount to creating an entirely new trust and could not be viewed as a variation. As Wilberforce J explained, "the proposal goes much too far, because it is not confined to dealing in a beneficial way with the special requirements of this infant but seeks authorisation for a complete resettlement".[169] This was a sentiment later echoed by Megarry J in *Re Ball's Settlement*:

"If an arrangement changes the whole substratum of the trust, then it may well be that it cannot be regarded as merely varying that trust. But if an arrangement, while leaving the substratum, effectuates the purpose of the original trust by other means, it may still be possible to regard that arrangement as merely varying the original trusts, even though the means employed are wholly different and even though the form is completely changed".[170]

---

165 *Re Burney's ST* [1961] 1 W.L.R. 545.
166 [1963] 3 All E.R. 759 at 762.
167 D.M.E. Evans, "The Variation of Trusts Act in Practice" [1963] 27 Conv. 6, 10.
168 [1964] Ch. 158.
169 [1964] Ch. 158 at 162. Instead, Wilberforce J deferred vesting and imposed protective trusts in the intervening period.
170 [1968] 2 All E.R. 438 at 442.

In the *Ball* case, Megarry J felt able to approve an arrangement that preserved the general tenor of the existing trust even though the old trusts were remoulded by the disappearance of a life interest and the defining of the interests of the other beneficiaries. He added that "the differences between the old provisions and the new may, I think, fairly be said to lie in detail rather than in substance".[171] In *Re Towler's ST*, the court approved a revised arrangement under which the minor's right to capital should be deferred for a period, leaving her entitled to a life interest during the period of deferral. It was a different and palatable way of achieving a broadly similar result.[172]

The distinction between a variation and a resettlement came to the fore again in *Allfrey v Allfrey*.[173] There Deputy Judge Jeremy Cousins QC explained that there was no single litmus test for deciding the question and that the issue was one of construction of the settlement in the light of the surrounding circumstances.[174] The matter must be determined according to the view that would be taken of the transaction by a person with knowledge of trusts who uses language in a practical and common sense manner. The Deputy Judge determined that the proposal before the court was a mere variation. The terms of the settlement were to remain in force, save that the trust period was extended. The purpose of the arrangement was to further the interests of the settlement by protecting it from the need to realise assets to meet the periodic charge to Inheritance Tax. The beneficial interests were not exhausted, the administrative powers originally established were to remain and the same trustees continued in office. As the Deputy Judge explained, "The intention was to supplement the provisions of the existing Settlement, thereby enhancing its operation. In my judgment, the arrangement quite clearly is to be described as a variation rather than a resettlement".[175] More recently, in *Edward v Fitzgerald* an application to convert an existing Settled Land Act trust into a trust of land was not a resettlement.[176]

On whose behalf?

It will be recalled that the 1958 Act empowers the court to approve arrangements on behalf of those beneficiaries who cannot give consent themselves.[177] It does not operate as regards a beneficiary who is sui juris. It follows that, before an application is lodged, the consent of all adult and able beneficiaries should be obtained. Take, for example, a scenario where property

---

171   [1968] 2 All E.R. 438 at 443.
172   [1964] Ch. 158; see also *Ridgwell v Ridgwell* [2007] EWHC 2666 (Ch) where the addition of a life interest in this case did not fundamentally alter the entire basis of the original trusts.
173   [2015] EWHC 1717 (Ch).
174   Blackburne J acknowledged in *Wyndham v Egremont* [2009] EWHC 2076 (Ch) at [22] that there is no "bright-line test".
175   [2015] EWHC 1717 (Ch) at [22].
176   [2019] EWHC 726 (Ch).
177   The instruction of separate counsel for the infant or incapacitated party is a fundamental requirement: *Wright v Gater* [2012] 1 W.L.R. 802.

is held on trust for Fiona and Jordan for life with remainder to Adrienne. Jordan is an infant. The trustees seek to divide the trust property so as to afford Adrienne a half share absolutely. The court can only approve the arrangement on behalf of Jordan.[178] The others (i.e. Fiona and Adrienne) will have to consent expressly to the remodelling of the beneficial interests. If either of the adult beneficiaries declines to consent, the general rule is that the arrangement will not be sanctioned or effective.[179] As Mowbray points out, "In this it differs from the court's other statutory powers, which are powers, if necessary, to override the wishes of some of the beneficiaries".[180] The fact that the arrangement if approved would override the wishes of the settlor is a consideration to be taken on board,[181] but it is merely one factor that can exert influence on the exercise of judicial discretion. Approving a variation that would defeat the testator's intentions, Pennycuick J said in *Re Remnant's ST* that such intentions are "a serious but by no means a conclusive consideration".[182]

In *Goulding v James*,[183] the testatrix, Mrs Froud, left her residuary estate on trust for her daughter, June, for life, remainder to June's son, Marcus, provided that he attained the age of 40 years. If Marcus predeceased June (whether or not he reached 40 years of age) or died before reaching the stipulated age, Marcus' children living at his death would take the capital absolutely. The testatrix died in 1994, leaving an estate valued at £1.14 million. June and Marcus (who was still childless) applied to the court for the approval of an arrangement which would recast the beneficial interests. The proposal was that June would have a 45 per cent interest, Marcus would have a 45 per cent interest and Marcus' as yet unborn children would have the remaining 10 per cent. This was demonstrated to be an improvement on the estimated value of the unborn children's contingent interests under the existing trust. The evidence also showed that the testatrix had never wanted June to get her hands on the capital. Nevertheless, the Court of Appeal approved the arrangement. Mummery LJ recognised that the court must take care not to allow "extrinsic evidence of the subjective wishes of Mrs Froud . . . to outweigh considerations of objective and substantial benefit to the class on whose behalf the court is empowered to act".[184]

The four classes

15-029

There are four specified classes of beneficiary or potential beneficiary on whose behalf the arrangement may be made for the purposes of s.1. The first category includes any person having, directly or indirectly, a vested or contingent interest who by reason of infancy or other

---

178 See *Collins v Collins* [2016] EWHC 1423 (Ch) where the proposed arrangement was financially more beneficial to the youngest child.
179 See the views of Buckley J in *Re Suffert's Settlement* [1960] 3 All E.R. 561 at 563.
180 W.J. Mowbray [1958] 22 Conv. 373, 375.
181 *Re Steed's WT* [1960] Ch. 407.
182 [1970] Ch. 560 at 567.
183 [1997] 2 All E.R. 239; noted at [1997] 60 M.L.R. 719 (P. Luxton).
184 [1997] 2 All E.R. 239 at 251.

incapacity is incapable of assenting (s.1(1)(a)). This is a straightforward classification that embraces those too young to consent[185] and those of unsound mind who cannot consent.[186] Hence, a settlement made in favour of a beneficiary who becomes mentally incapacitated can be varied under this paragraph as long as it is for his benefit.[187] By way of illustration, take the situation where property is held on trust for Adrienne for life with remainder to Fiona. If either (or both) are infants or insane, para.(a) will then become engaged. In *ET v JP*,[188] an application was made on behalf of a severely autistic, child beneficiary. The issue which arose was whether the benefit of the variation fell to be determined by the Court of Protection or by the Chancery Court. The High Court concluded that he lacked capacity because he was a minor and not solely because he was unable to make a decision due to an impairment or disturbance of the mind or brain. In the case of a beneficiary who was under 18, the question of benefit was always a matter for the High Court.

The second type of beneficiary is "any person unborn" (s.1(1)(c)). Such beneficiaries obviously cannot consent to a variation and the trustees should act as "the watchdog" for the unborn beneficiary.[189] A practical limitation was, however, imposed in *Re Pettifor's WT*[190] where it was held that it was unnecessary to seek approval on behalf of the unborn children of a 78-year-old woman. Pennycuick J concluded that, "It does not seem to me that protection against this impossible contingency is a matter which can properly be dealt with by way of variation of existing trusts".[191] He commented that, "In the case of a woman in her seventies, not only would trustees be authorised to distribute a fund on that footing without any doubt or question, but the court would, I think, normally consider it an unnecessary waste of money to come to court and ask for leave so to distribute. Trustees can with complete safety and propriety deal with their funds on the basis that a woman of 70 will not have a further child".[192]

The third category includes any person[193] who has a discretionary interest under a protective trust[194] provided that the interest of the principal beneficiary (e.g. a life tenant) has not failed or determined (s.1(1)(d)). Put more simply, this caters for the variation of protective trusts. A protective trust is employed when the settlor wishes to protect property against an improvident beneficiary and/or the claims of his creditors. Traditionally, the settlor will give the beneficiary what is known as a "determinable life interest", which upon forfeiture is succeeded by a discretionary trust for a class of beneficiaries. Take, for example, a trust for "Fiona for life

---

185 In *CD (A Minor) v O* [2004] EWHC (Ch) 1036, the application was made on behalf of a 12-year-old girl.

186 Section 1(6) states that this provision does not limit the powers of the Court of Protection.

187 *Re CL* [1969] 1 Ch. 587.

188 [2018] Ch. 565.

189 *Re Druce's ST* [1962] 1 W.L.R. 363.

190 [1966] Ch. 257.

191 [1966] Ch. 257 at 260.

192 [1966] Ch. 257 at 260.

193 This includes unascertained or unborn persons: *Re Turner's WT* [1960] Ch. 122. Danckwerts J admitted that the words "any person" are "perfectly general" and embrace "any person who might take under the provisions of a discretionary trust" (at 127).

194 Defined by reference to s.33 of the Trustee Act 1925; see *Re Wallace's Settlements* [1968] 2 All E.R. 209.

until she becomes bankrupt with remainder to be held on discretionary trust for Jordan". Fiona has a determinable life interest, which will be forfeited on her becoming a bankrupt. Until that time, Jordan has a discretionary interest under a protective trust for the purposes of para.(d). The court may, for example, approve an arrangement on Jordan's behalf under which Fiona's protected life interest is enlarged to become an absolute life interest.[195] Alternatively, it might sanction an arrangement under which Fiona releases her life interest in favour of Jordan. It is irrelevant whether Jordan is an adult and, under para.(d), it does not matter that the arrangement might be to Jordan's disadvantage. As Danckwerts J observed in *Re Turner's WT*, "the court may, if it likes, disregard the question whether any benefit is provided or not".[196]

15-030
Although there is no need to show benefit for the purposes of para.(d), it should not be overlooked that the court's power is discretionary and the presence or absence of benefit may still play an important role. As Wilberforce J commented in *Re Burney's ST*, "a specific and substantial benefit . . . makes the arrangement as a whole appreciably more attractive of the court's discretionary approval".[197] The court must still consider the evidence and will require the applicant to make out a case to justify the variation of a protective trust. In *Re Baker's ST*, Ungoed-Thomas J adjourned an application to convert a protected life interest into an absolute interest in both capital and income, stating, "evidence, including evidence of the financial position of the applicant and her husband, must be laid before the court to show to what extent the protective trusts continued to serve any useful purpose".[198]

The fourth and final categorisation is by far the most problematic. It is defined in s.1(1)(b) so as to include "any person (whether ascertained or not) who may become entitled, directly or indirectly, to an interest under the trusts as being at a future date or on the happening of a future event a person of any specified description or a member of any specified class of persons . . .". By way of a proviso, it goes on to exclude "any person who would be of that description, or a member of that class, as the case may be, if the said date had fallen or the said event had happened at the date of the application to the court". This opaque provision does not lend itself well to ready interpretation and demands more detailed attention.

Deconstructing para.(b)

15-031
The allusion in s.1(1)(b) to the future ("who may become entitled") entails that those who already have an interest, whether vested or contingent, are outside its scope. This was demonstrated in *Knocker v Youle*[199] where property was held on trust for the settlor's wife for life, with remainder to appointees under her will. In default of any such appointment, there was a gift over in favour of the settlor's son or, if the son was dead, to the settlor's four sisters living at the

---

195 *Re Burney's ST* [1961] 1 W.L.R. 545.
196 [1960] Ch. 122 at 127.
197 [1961] 1 W.L.R. 545 at 550, 551.
198 [1964] 1 W.L.R. 336 at 337.
199 [1986] 2 All E.R. 914; noted at [1987] Conv. 144 (J.G. Riddall).

son's death or, if they were dead, their issue who should reach 21 years of age. The settlor's wife and four sisters died prior to the application. Approval of an arrangement was sought by the settlor's son and daughter on behalf of numerous individuals who were the issue of the four sisters. As some lived in Australia, it was thought to be impracticable to obtain each individual's consent. Warner J was unable to sanction the arrangement because they already held contingent beneficial interests. The wording of para.(b) prevented the court giving its approval and the cousins' consent to the variation was necessary. As Warner J concluded regretfully, "people in the position of cousins in this case have an interest that is extremely remote. None the less, it is an interest, and the distinction between an expectation and an interest is one which I do not think that I am entitled to blur".[200]

Among the classes that can fall within para.(b) are the prospective next of kin of a living person.[201] These persons do not enjoy even a contingent interest and, instead, have a mere hope of succeeding. As Buckley J recognised in *Re Moncrieff's ST*,[202] such persons might become interested in the settlor's estate at a future date. This type of interest is sometimes referred to as a *spes successionis*. Similarly, the future spouse of an unmarried beneficiary may fall within para.(b).[203] Take, for example, where property is settled on Jordan for life with remainder to Jordan's wife, with remainders over. At a time when Jordan is an adult, but is unmarried, the court can approve an arrangement on behalf of his future unascertainable spouse. If it were otherwise no variation in that situation would be possible because the consent of an unknown future spouse is obviously impossible to obtain.

Matters are further complicated by the express and speculative exclusion in s.1(1)(b) of any person who would be of that description or a member of the class if the future date/event had already occurred at the date of the application to the court. In *Re Suffert's Settlement*,[204] a 61-year-old spinster was entitled to the income under a protective trust. After her death, the property was destined to go to her statutory next of kin (three cousins). She sought a variation under which a fund of £500 would be held on trust for her cousins with the remainder of the fund (some £8,300) to be held on trust for herself absolutely. One cousin consented to the application, but the others did not. She invited the court to approve the arrangement on behalf of the other two cousins as well as any unborn or unascertained persons who might become entitled. Buckley J held that, while he could approve the variation on behalf of the unborn and the unascertainable, the court could not approve the arrangement on behalf of the two cousins. The cousins would have been entitled as next of kin had the tenant for life been dead at the date of the court application. The cousins had themselves to decide whether or not to consent.

In *Re Moncrieff's ST*,[205] property was assigned by the settlor, Mrs Parkin, to trustees to be held on trust for herself for life with remainder to such of her children as by deed or by

15-032

---

200 [1986] 2 All E.R. 914 at 918.
201 See *Re Suffert's Settlement* [1960] 3 All E.R. 561.
202 *Re Moncrieff's ST* [1962] 1 W.L.R. 1344.
203 *Re Clitheroe's ST* [1959] 3 All E.R. 789.
204 [1960] 3 All E.R. 561
205 [1962] 1 W.L.R. 1344.

will she should appoint. In default of appointment, the property was to be held on trust for her next of kin as if she died a widow and intestate. An application to court for approval of an arrangement was made by Mrs Parkin. At the date of the application, her next of kin was her adopted adult son, Alan. If he predeceased her, however, the next of kin would be her four infant cousins. The approval was sought on behalf of Alan and the cousins as persons who might "become entitled . . . on the happening of a future event". On this occasion, Buckley J approved the arrangement on behalf of the cousins. Alan, however, fell outside para.(b) because of the proviso. He was the next of kin if at the date of the application Mrs Parkin was deceased. As to the cousins, "none of them would be within the class of next of kin if she died today".[206] Their interest depended not only upon the death of Mrs Parkin, but also on the demise of Alan. The arrangement could, therefore, become effective only with the consent of Alan.

Benefit

15-033

As mentioned earlier, except for "discretionary beneficiaries" under protective trusts, the arrangement must be for the benefit of the persons on whose behalf approval is sought. Although the 1958 Act is silent on the matter, the court has adopted a broad view of what constitutes "benefit" for these purposes. Although most cases concern a financial (particularly tax) advantage,[207] this is not the only factor that the courts will consider. As Megarry J admitted in *Re Holt's Settlement*, "The word benefit . . . is . . . plainly not confined to financial benefit, but may extend to moral or social benefit".[208] This theme was pursued also by Ungoed-Thomas J in *Re Van Gruisen's WT*:

> **"The court is not merely concerned with this actuarial calculation . . . The court is also concerned whether the arrangement as a whole, in all the circumstances, is such that it is proper to approve it. The court's concern involves, *inter alia*, a practical and business like consideration of the arrangement, including the total amounts of the advantages which the various parties obtain, and their bargaining strength".[209]**

The court must, therefore, look at matters in the round and not focus unduly upon a balance sheet approach.[210] The prospect of financial gain is not always decisive nor, indeed, is

---

206 [1962] 1 W.L.R. 1344 at 1346.
207 *Re Drew's Settlement* [1966] 1 W.L.R. 1518.
208 [1968] 1 All E.R. 470 at 479.
209 [1964] 1 All E.R. 843 at 844.
210 See *Ridgwell v Ridgwell* [2007] EWHC 2666 (Ch) where the theoretical postponement of the children's interests was outweighed by the practical advantages associated with the tax savings to be made.

it always necessary. Accordingly, the court will not sanction an arrangement, even though it might promise monetary savings, if it is not for the overall benefit of those on whose behalf the application is made. Financial advantage and benefit will, however, usually go hand in hand. As Lord Reid put it in *Re Holmden's ST*, "an arrangement which would avoid large payments of estate duty could hardly fail to be for the benefit of such an infant and potential beneficiaries".[211] Nevertheless, in *Re Weston's Settlements*,[212] the settlor sought approval of an arrangement under which property settled on his sons would be transferred from the existing English settlements to settlements based in the Channel Isles. The purpose was to avoid capital gains tax in the region of £163,000. Harman LJ described the proposal as "an essay in tax avoidance naked and unashamed".[213] The drawback was that the settlor's sons would have to take up residence in the Channel Isles. Even though they had already moved to Jersey some months earlier, the Court of Appeal held that the arrangement was not for the overall benefit of the children. As Lord Denning MR admitted, "There are many things in life more worthwhile than money. One of these things is to be brought up in this our England, which is still 'the envy of less happier lands'. I do not believe it is for the benefit of children to be uprooted from England and transported to another country simply to avoid tax . . . Children are like trees: they grow stronger with firm roots".[214] Harman LJ also voiced his concerns: "It seems to me most unlikely that two wealthy young men of this sort will be content at the threshold of their lives to settle down in the island . . .".[215] Accordingly, it was the judicially perceived welfare of the beneficiaries that was the important consideration. The decision of the Court of Appeal, as Harris observes, "is overtly based upon a rather surprising balancing of cash gains against non-cash losses".[216] In a more cynical vein, Baker ponders, "How is the court to know whether a person who has professed to go away for good has in reality only gone for a holiday at the expense of the Revenue?"[217]

In *Re Seale's Marriage Settlement*,[218] however, the court felt able to approve the exportation of an English trust to Quebec. Although this was to achieve tax advantages and involved child beneficiaries living in Canada, the court concluded that it was for their benefit. It avoided many administrative difficulties and financial disadvantages. The key influences were that the children already lived in Canada and had been brought up there by their parents.[219] It was a case of genuine and long-standing emigration. As Lord Denning MR later commented in *Re Weston's Settlement*, "The family has emigrated to Canada many years before, with no thought

15-034

---

211 [1968] A.C. 685 at 699.
212 [1969] 1 Ch. 223; noted at [1969] 85 L.Q.R. 15 (P.V. Baker).
213 [1969] 1 Ch. 223 at 246.
214 [1969] 1 Ch. 223 at 245, 246. He commented further "I cannot help wondering how long these young people will stay in Jersey" (at 245).
215 [1969] 1 Ch. 223 at 248.
216 J.W. Harris [1969] 32 M.L.R. 320, 322.
217 P.V. Baker [1969] 85 L.Q.R. 15, 16.
218 [1961] 3 All E.R. 136.
219 A similar approach was adopted in *Re Windeatt's WT* [1969] 2 All E.R. 324 as regards the exportation of a trust to Jersey where the beneficiaries had lived for 19 years.

of tax avoidance, and had brought up the children there as Canadians. It was very proper that the trust should be transferred to Canada".[220]

In *Re CL*,[221] the Court of Protection approved an arrangement on behalf of a 78-year-old widow who was a Mental Health Act patient under the now repealed Pt VIII of the Mental Health Act 1959. Under the arrangement, the widow sacrificed her life interest, for no consideration, for the benefit of her daughters. The purpose was to reduce her estate's liability to tax, but there was no financial advantage to her personally. The benefit was a moral one. It appears that Cross J was influenced by the fact that her income greatly exceeded her outgoings, that she was unlikely ever to be discharged from care and that this is what she would have wished for had she been of full mind.[222]

15-035

Albeit rare, it is also possible that the court might approve an arrangement that operates to the financial disadvantage of the persons on behalf of whom it was sanctioned. Such was demonstrated in *Re Towler's ST*[223] where an application to postpone the vesting of a capital fund in a beneficiary was successful on the basis that the fund would otherwise be dealt with in a reckless fashion. It did not matter that the beneficiary would claim to be disadvantaged by the arrangement. In a like vein, in *Re Remnant's ST*[224] the High Court allowed the deletion of a forfeiture clause that was to operate on any of the beneficiaries becoming or marrying a Roman Catholic. Taking a broad view, Pennycuick J acknowledged that this variation potentially worked to the financial disadvantage of the beneficiaries, but it was for their general benefit. He explained, "There are the non-financial considerations which seem to me to loom large in this matter" and added, "Obviously, a forfeiture provision of this kind might well cause very serious dissension between the families . . .".[225] The usual rule of thumb, however, is that the court will not leave the beneficiary materially out of pocket as a result of the arrangement.[226]

In *Wright v Gater*,[227] the court's approval on behalf of a child (Rory) was sought by the child's mother and uncle. They sought the postponement of vesting beyond majority and until the child reached 30 years of age. They contended that it would not be beneficial for Rory to be in absolute control of substantial sums of money before reaching that greater age. Norris J acknowledged that the postponement of vesting beyond the age of majority was not beneficial in principle and he would have to be persuaded that a variation incorporating such a feature

---

220 [1969] 1 Ch. 234 at 245.

221 [1969] 1 Ch. 587.

222 [1969] 1 Ch. 587 at 593.

223 [1963] 3 All E.R. 759.

224 [1970] Ch. 560; noted at [1971] 34 M.L.R. 96 (R.B.M. Cotterrell).

225 [1970] Ch. 560 at 566. Pennycuick J cautioned at 567 that, "The effect of any particular forfeiture provision must depend on the nature of the provision itself and upon the circumstances in which it is likely to operate. A forfeiture provision is by no means always intrinsically undesirable".

226 See *Ridgwell v Ridgwell* [2007] EWHC 2666 (Ch) where the variation was to ensure that, on the death of the settlor, the settlor's spouse was to have a life interest under the settlement. The beneficial impact of the change as felt by children and the unborn outweighed any detriment incurred by deferring their interests.

227 [2012] 1 W.L.R. 802.

was justified on the facts. As he put it, "in assessing whether a proposed variation conferred a non-financial benefit, the court should consider whether a prudent adult, motivated by intelligent self-interest and after sustained consideration of the proposed trusts and powers and the circumstances in which they might fall to be implemented, would be likely to accept the proposal?"[228] The proposal, which went close to being a resettlement rather than a variation, would not be approved as there was nothing in the character of the child to demonstrate a real risk that he would be incapable of dealing with any income or capital inherited without supervision before he attained the age of 30. Norris J considered it wrong to approve "the establishment of a long-term trust where close family members controlled the purse strings because the child was entitled to have his future independence and autonomy as a young adult respected".[229] Instead, taking an overview, the court approved a revised variation that "provided proportionate measures to address those risks but went no further than was necessary to do so".[230] Following what he described as "A degree of mental contortion",[231] Norris J felt able to identify a benefit for the infant. The revised arrangement would serve to introduce Rory gradually to control of his wealth and deter him from going off the rails.

No benefit?

15-036

The general requirement that there must be a benefit has caused few applications to be unsuccessful. Even where there is the chance of disadvantage arising from foreseeable circumstances, the court will still be prepared to take the risk. In *CD (A Minor) v O*,[232] for example, the court authorised the use of the whole trust fund for the purposes of advancement of a minor even though this might operate to accelerate her benefit and entail that the trust property never becomes vested in her. As Megarry J explained in *Re Holt's Settlement*, "the court should be prepared to take a risk if the arrangement appears on the whole to be for their benefit".[233] This was, however, no new observation as it had previously been made in *Re Cohen's WT*. In that case, Danckwerts J admitted, "if it is a risk that an adult would be prepared to take, the court is prepared to take it on behalf of an infant".[234] The risk under the proposed arrangement there was that infants and unborn persons would benefit except in the unlikely scenario of one of the testator's three children predeceasing the testator's widow, who was aged 80 years. Indeed, writing extra-judicially, Megarry translated this as meaning that the arrangement must

228 [2012] 1 W.L.R. 802 at [11].
229 [2012] 1 W.L.R. 802 at [16].
230 [2012] 1 W.L.R. 802 at [21]. He was to be entitled to income on reaching 18 with 10% of the capital fund vesting on his attaining the age of 21 and the balance of the fund vesting on attaining the age of 25.
231 [2012] 1 W.L.R. 802 at [21].
232 [2004] EWHC 1036 (Ch).
233 [1968] 1 All E.R. 470 at 480, where the arrangement was approved even though it might conceivably operate to the detriment of as yet unborn children.
234 [1959] 1 W.L.R. 865 at 868; noted at [1960] 76 L.Q.R. 22 (R.E. Megarry).

be shown, on a balance of probabilities, to be for the benefit of the person on whose behalf approval is requested.[235]

The risk should, it is to be emphasised, be one that a prudent and well-advised adult would be prepared to take.[236] The exercise undertaken by the court is to weigh the benefits of the arrangement against the magnitude of the risk and the degree of potential loss. It might be that the arrangement will contain a provision requiring insurance against the unlikely prospect of loss arising.[237] On this point, Megarry commented:

> **"Only if the credit balance on such a reckoning is sufficiently great ought insurance to be dispensed with. Even so, it is suggested that the principle of insurance ought to be the rule rather than the exception. Certainly it seems improbable that the legislature envisaged the court as performing the function of a superior form of gambling expert, with the duty of certifying whether the odds are sufficiently good for infants and the unborn".[238]**

15-037

It is, however, useful to consider a brace of cases in which the court felt that there was no benefit. In *Re Tinker's Settlement*,[239] the settlor gave property on trust for his son and daughter. If the son died before reaching 30 years of age, his share was to pass to the daughter for life with remainder to her children. The settlor applied to court to vary the trust so that, if the son died before reaching 30 years, his share would pass to the son's issue. The application was made on behalf of the unborn children of the daughter, but as the variation was entirely without benefit for those unborn it was destined to fail. As Russell J observed, "I cannot think that I would be benefiting the daughter's children if I gave away half of that which they would come into if the son dies under 30".[240]

Similarly, in *Re Cohen's ST*[241] property was to be held on trust until the settlor's last surviving son died. At that point, the property was to be divided between the settlor's grandchildren and surviving issue of any deceased grandchild. By 1965, only one son survived. The son applied for the approval of a tax advantageous arrangement on behalf of unborn beneficiaries that would allow the trust fund to be distributed in June 1973. The application was rejected because it would operate to debar any issue of a grandchild born between June 1973 and the son's eventual death. The proposal, as Stamp J acknowledged, "deprives him of any chance of taking . . .".[242]

---

235 [1960] 76 L.Q.R. 22; or at the least the beneficiary should not be worse off than under the original settlement: *Re King* unreported 15 December 2010.
236 *Bailey v Bailey* unreported 12 November 2014 (Ch).
237 *Re Robinson's ST* [1976] 1 W.L.R. 806.
238 [1960] 76 L.Q.R. 22 at 23 (Sweet & Maxwell).
239 [1960] 1 W.L.R. 1011.
240 [1960] 1 W.L.R. 1011 at 1013.
241 [1965] 3 All E.R. 139. This is a different case and Cohen family from that previously considered.
242 [1965] 3 All E.R. 139 at 141.

Guide to Further Reading

S. Evans, "Variation Clarification" [2011] Conv. 151.

P. Luxton, "Variation of Trusts: Settlors' Intentions and the Consent Principle in *Saunders v Vautier*" [1997] 60 M.L.R. 719.

O.R. Marshall, "Deviations from the Terms of a Trust" [1954] 17 M.L.R. 420.

O.R. Marshall, "The Scope of Section 53 of the Trustee Act 1925" [1957] 21 Conv. 448.

M. Mowbray, "Varying Trusts" [1958] 22 Conv. 373.

16

Setting Trusts Aside

Unless there is a power of revocation in the trust instrument, the general rule is that, once a trust has been completely constituted, it cannot be revoked by the settlor or, indeed, by anyone else.[1] Unless the settlor is also a trustee, the trust property moves outside his legal control. It is never to be forgotten that, in the eyes of equity, the true owners of the trust property are the beneficiaries. All general rules, however, must have their exceptions and so it is here. No trust that contravenes the law or undermines the principles of public policy will be upheld. In addition, so-called "sham trusts" and "illusory trusts" can be revoked. Similarly, a settlement may be set aside when such avoidance is catered for by statute. Parliamentary concern has focused upon trusts designed to put property unfairly beyond the reach of creditors, spouses and other members of the family. It is these three types of invalidating factor that will be examined in this chapter.

Although outside the scope of the present chapter, it is to be appreciated that there exist other means by which a trust may be rendered void. These include, first, where the trust offends the rules against perpetuity and inalienability. These rules are considered in detail within Ch.4. Secondly, the settlor may be induced to make the settlement for one of the following reasons.

■ Duress—duress comprises any threat (usually physical or economic) that brings about a coercion of the will sufficient to vitiate consent. For example, in *Ayliffe v Murray*[2] a beneficiary executed a deed under duress. The deed was set aside because of the excessive pressure exerted on the beneficiary by his trustees.

16-001

---

1   This is subject to the rule in *Saunders v Vautier* (1841) 4 Beav. 115, which allows all the beneficiaries of full age and capacity consensually to terminate the trust; see generally, P. Matthews, "The Comparative Importance of the Rule in *Saunders v Vautier*" (2006) 122 L.Q.R. 266.

2   (1740) 2 Atk. 58.

■ Mistake—in *Forshaw v Welsby*,[3] the settlor, during a period of illness, executed a deed of settlement that was not read to him and knowing nothing of its contents. The court revoked the settlement on his recovery from illness. The mistake had tainted the legitimacy of the settlement.[4] A mistake recently came to the fore in the decision of the Supreme Court in *Pitt v Holt; Futter v Futter*.[5] Mrs Pitt established a trust that failed to achieve the tax advantages as had been expected and advised. The mistake was sufficiently serious to warrant the setting aside of the trust. As unconscionability is the cornerstone of this interventionist jurisdiction,[6] there must be something more than mere ignorance, inadvertence or misprediction.[7]

■ Misrepresentation—an illustration of this arises from *Re Glubb*.[8] There a charity innocently misrepresented to subscribers that it would be entitled to a substantial legacy if additional funds were donated to it. Unfortunately, the opportunity to obtain the legacy had passed and the court ordered that the charity return the sums obtained by its misrepresentation. In *Bom v Bok*,[9] a declaration of trust signed by a husband whereby he settled all his assets on trust for their son was set aside for misrepresentation. He had been wrongly told by his wife that the trust would take effect only on his death.

■ Fraud—a settlement induced by the fraud of the beneficiary can be revoked by the settlor. Although fraud has proved elusive to exact definition, an example of where it operated to unravel a transaction is *Baker v Monk*.[10] There an infirm and illiterate woman executed a deed without understanding its nature. As she had been the victim of a fraud, the deed was set aside.

■ Undue influence—this is to do with the application of improper pressure on an individual and is, therefore, wider than the concept of duress. The traditional approach is that a settlement of an improvident nature, which is entered into without independent legal advice and without a fully informed and free will, is liable to be avoided on the basis of undue influence.[11] The wife in *Bom v Bok*[12] had exerted actual undue influence

---

3   (1860) 30 Beav. 243.

4   In *Wilson v Wilson* [1969] 1 W.L.R. 1470, a declaration of trust under which two brothers declared that they were joint tenants of the property in equity was rectified for mistake. They had clearly intended that one brother should be the sole beneficial owner.

5   [2013] 2 A.C. 108.

6   *Rogge v Rogge* [2019] EWHC 1949 (Ch).

7   *Ogilvie v Littleboy* [1897] 13 T.L.R. 399

8   [1900] 1 Ch. 355.

9   [2018] SGA 83 (Court of Appeal (Singapore)); see also *Walker v Walker* [2010] W.T.L.R. 1617 where a father/trustee unduly influenced his daughter/beneficiary.

10   (1864) 33 Beav. 419.

11   See *Allcard v Skinner* (1887) 36 Ch. D. 145; *Singh v Singh* [2014] WHC 2762.

12   [2018] SGA 83.

over her husband while he was grieving over his mother's death. She had taken advantage of him by pressuring him to sign the trust declaration. The law relating to undue influence, and how it is to be proved, was the subject of major overhaul by the House of Lords in *Royal Bank of Scotland Plc v Etridge (No.2)*.[13]

■ Illegality—the general rule is that the court will not come to assist anyone who seeks to enforce a trust set up for an illegal purpose (*ex turpi causa non oritur actio*). The primary example of an illegal purpose trust is to be derived from *Re Great Berlin Steamboat Co*.[14] In this case, an individual paid £1,000 into the company's bank account. The aim was to mislead others as to the credit worthiness of the company. In short, it was for a fraudulent purpose. Although it was agreed that the money was to be held on trust, the company spent some of it without the individual's consent. The company was later wound up and the individual sought to recover the remaining balance of some £99. The Court of Appeal declined to offer any assistance. Cotton LJ reasoned that "He left the money at the bank as long as the possibility of carrying out the illegal purpose continued, and it is now too late for him to reclaim it".[15] In light of the traditional stance that private purpose trusts are void,[16] there are few examples of express trusts avoided on this basis. Nevertheless, as Harman LJ noted in *Re Pinion*, a trust to set up a school for prostitutes and pickpockets would necessarily be void.[17] Similarly, a trust to evade (as opposed to avoid) tax will be invalid.[18] The traditional response is that, as regards illegal purpose trusts, the court will not aid the beneficiary or assist a settlor that seeks to recover the property in issue. As Truro LC commented, "Those who violate the law must not apply to the law for protection".[19] Illegality, however, has generated much difficulty in the context of implied resulting trusts. Speaking in an extra-curial capacity, Lord Sumption highlighted the problem:

> "An illegal transaction will not be enforced, but where does that leave the parties? Broadly speaking, two approaches are possible. The law may set about reversing the consequences, financial or proprietary, of the transaction so far as the parties have given effect to them. Or it may simply decline to have anything to do with it. The first approach seeks to regulate the consequences of the illegal transaction, so as to put the parties so far as possible in the position they

---

13   [2002] 2 A.C. 773; see M. Haley, "The O'Brien Defence Refined: Legal Rights, Equitable Wrongs and Commercial Responsibilities" (2010) 61(2) N.I.L.Q. 141.
14   (1884) 26 Ch. D. 616.
15   (1884) 26 Ch. D. 616 at 620.
16   See Ch.6.
17   [1965] Ch. 85 at 105.
18   See *Sekhon v Alissa* [1989] 2 F.L.R. 94.
19   *Benyon v Nettlefold* (1850) 3 Mac. & G. 94 at 102.

would have been in had the transaction not occurred. The second simply withholds legal remedies, and generally leaves the loss to lie where it falls".[20]

This aspect of Illegality Is considered in detail in Ch.9.

Public Policy and Illegality

16-002 As previously indicated, a trust or gift that is regarded as being offensive to public policy or is otherwise unlawful will not be enforced.[21] Although it is beyond the scope of this book to provide a comprehensive list of such events, it is possible to illustrate the role of public policy and illegality by considering the major examples of where trusts have failed or conditions struck out on this basis. The attachment of conditions is generally designed to control and manipulate the future conduct of the beneficiaries.[22] As will become clear, in some cases the gift will be absolute and free from the condition while in others both the condition and the gift will be void. The outcome depends primarily upon whether the condition is a condition precedent or is a condition subsequent.[23] The former relates to a gift that is not to take effect until the condition occurs (e.g. a gift to Fiona if she marries). The latter concerns a gift that vests at once, but is to be forfeited on the occurrence of some event (e.g. a gift to Fiona on condition that she does not marry). A condition precedent that is illegal or against public policy will render the entire gift void. If it is a condition subsequent that is void, the gift will be valid and freed from the condition attached.

Trusts for illegitimate children

16-003 The traditional stance was that a trust to benefit a future illegitimate child is void.[24] The underlying notion is that such a trust is designed to encourage immorality. As regards a trust to ben-

---

20 "Reflexions on the Law of Illegality", Chancery Bar Association, 23 April 2012, p.3 *https://www.supremecourt.uk/docs/speech_120423.pdf* [Accessed 31 July 2020].
21 Perhaps surprisingly, the provisions contained in the Race Relations Act 1976 and the Sex Discrimination Act 1975 do not taint a discriminatory trust.
22 For example, a testator leaving his estate to his teetotal ex-wife on the condition that she drinks a bottle of wine per day for the rest of her life or a provision for a daughter on condition that she does not enlist in the armed forces.
23 See J.H.C. Morris (1947) 11 Conv. 218.
24 *Medworth v Pope* (1859) 27 Beav. 71. This still applies to trusts made before 1 January 1970.

efit an embryonic or otherwise existing illegitimate child, the law has always taken a different approach and concluded that, as the immorality had already occurred, the trust was good.[25] In *Occleston v Fullalove*,[26] the testator left property for the benefit of his three illegitimate children. Two had been born at the date of the will and the other was *en ventre sa mere* (i.e. in an embryonic state). By a majority, the Court of Appeal upheld the trust as valid in relation to all three of the testator's offspring. There was no promotion of future immorality. The rule, therefore, applies to both inter vivos and testamentary trusts. Mellish LJ explained:

> **"If a man, at the commencement of an illicit intercourse with a particular woman could make a valid settlement on his expected illegitimate children, this would I think, manifestly encourage the immoral connection and discourage marriage, which the law favours . . . Now if a will was so worded as to give a bequest to illegitimate children to be begotten after the death of the testator, I think it would be subject to the same objection as a settlement by deed".[27]**

As regards settlements created after 1969, these are now governed by the Family Law Reform Act 1987. This legislative intervention is based on the acceptance that, as Maugham J put it, "no useful purpose is served by penalising illegitimate children, and that the true interests of public policy do not require innocent persons to be punished in that manner".[28] The Act, therefore, abolishes the iniquitous rule that a settlement benefiting an illegitimate child not in being is void. This about turn demonstrates that public policy is not set in stone and, as Danckwerts LJ acknowledged in *Nagle v Feilden*, "the law relating to public policy cannot remain immutable. It must change with the passage of time. The wind of change blows on it".[29] The same anti-inequality stance was demonstrated more recently as regards illegitimate children in *Holden-Hindley v Holden Hindley*[30] and *PQ v RS*.[31]

Trusts in restraint of marriage

Trusts, conditions or gifts over that impose a general restraint of marriage[32] are wholly void and this is so even when the total restraint is merely the *probable* outcome of the trusts or

16-004

---

25   *Ebbern v Fowler* [1909] 1 Ch. 578; see also *PQ v RS* [2019] EWHC 1643 (Ch).
26   (1874) 9 Ch. App. 147.
27   (1874) 9 Ch. App. 147 at 171.
28   *Re Hyde* [1932] 1 Ch. 95 at 98. His comment concerned the Legitimacy Act 1926.
29   [1966] 1 All E.R. 689 at 696. The Court of Appeal was concerned with whether it was against public policy for a woman to hold a licence to train horses.
30   [2013] EWHC 3053 (Ch).
31   [2019] EWHC 1643 (Ch).
32   Since the Marriage (Same Sex Couples) Act 2013 and the Civil Partnerships, Marriages and Deaths (Registration Etc.) Act 2019 this would include a restraint on entering civil partnerships.

condition.[33] A trust to promote celibacy in an individual, therefore, will be void. This prohibition does not, however, apply to total restraints on second or subsequent marriages. In *Allen v Jackson*,[34] a condition in restraint of the second marriage of the deceased's husband was held to be valid. James LJ noted that this had long been the case with a provision that was designed to prevent a widow from remarrying and explained that this exception came about because her husband, "if she were a widow with children . . . might think that his children would not be so well cared for and protected if his widow formed a second alliance and became the mother of a second family".[35] Nevertheless, he concluded that there was no justification for treating the second marriage of a man in a different manner as "The case before us seems to me to shew what immense mischief one would be doing if one were to introduce a different rule of law in the case of a widower to that in the case of a widow".[36]

A partial restraint of marriage does not, however, contravene notions of public policy. For example, a trust that prohibits the marriage to a particular person or class of person is not deemed to offend public policy.[37] In *Hodgson v Halford*,[38] a restriction as to religious faith (i.e. the interest would be forfeited if the children married a person not of the Jewish denomination) was upheld. A son who married a Christian thereby lost his share of the trust fund. Similarly, in *Jenner v Turner*[39] a disposition of land by a testatrix that was to be forfeited on her brother marrying anyone that was or had been a domestic servant was upheld. The brother married a former domestic servant and thereby sacrificed his interest in the property. As Bacon VC explained, "The condition is not in restraint of marriage generally, for it was open . . . to choose a wife from the whole female world, except only that portion of it which comprises domestic servants".[40]

16-005   A trust or gift with a condition that requires a named party's consent to the marriage is also acceptable. In *Re Whiting's Settlement*,[41] a mother made it a condition subsequent of a trust that her daughter's interest was to be forfeited if she married without the mother's consent. On this event, the property was to go to the Police Relief Fund. The Court of Appeal regarded the clause as valid and this was so even though the refusal of consent would prohibit marriage as effectively as the imposition of any general restraint. As Vaughan Williams LJ acknowledged, "This branch of the law is one with which it is not very satisfactory to deal, and I cannot say that I think the mode in which it has been dealt with is very easy to weld into one consistent whole".[42]

---

33   *Lloyd v Lloyd* (1852) 2 Sim. (NS) 255; see generally O. Browder, "Conditions and Limitations in Restraint of Marriage" (1941) 39 Michigan Law Review 1288 who states at p.1288 that, "Just what social evil may be expected to result from these provisions has never been agreed upon".

34   (1875) 1 Ch. D. 399.

35   (1875) 1 Ch. D. 399 at 403.

36   (1875) 1 Ch. D. 399 at 403.

37   For example, not to marry an Irish woman. Cf. a proviso not to marry someone of the same sex.

38   (1879) 11 Ch. D. 959.

39   (1880) 16 Ch. D. 188.

40   (1880) 16 Ch. D. 188 at 197.

41   [1905] 1 Ch. 96.

42   [1905] 1 Ch. 96 at 115. O. Browder, "Conditions and Limitations in Restraint of Marriage" (1941) 39 *Michigan Law*

It is also to be appreciated that a provision that the trust or gift is to exist only until marriage is perfectly valid. In *Re Lovell*,[43] a testator was living with his mistress who had been deserted by her husband. The testator bequeathed to her an annuity of £750 provided that she did not return to her husband, did not remarry and lived "a clean moral and respectable life". The bequest did not offend public policy because it was neither an inducement to maintain the separation from her husband nor operated to deter remarriage. It was designed instead to provide for her until such an eventuality occurred. Although at first sight curious, the long-standing logic is that such a provision creates merely a determinable interest (i.e. a limitation) and is not construed as a bequest upon a condition that operates as a penalty on the event of marriage. Whereas the latter will be void, the former interest determines according to its terms and is unaffected by notions of unlawfulness. In other words, it is not against public policy to provide for someone prior to that person's marriage.

Conditions violating marital harmony

The approach of the court to the sanctity of marriage is encapsulated in the judgment of Turner LJ in *Hope v Hope* where he said:

16-006

> "There is nothing which the courts of this country have watched with more anxious jealousy, and I will venture to say, with more reasonable jealousy, than contracts which have for their object the disturbance of marital relations. The peace of families—the welfare of children, depends to an extent almost immeasurable, upon the undisturbed continuance of those relations. . .".[44]

In the scenario where a husband and wife have elected to separate and, subsequent to that decision, enter into a deed of separation the terms of that agreement will, however, remain valid.[45] The key factor is that the trust contained in the separation agreement does not encourage the separation, but instead is a consequence of the breakdown of the relationship. The separation has already been decided upon and is, thereby, viewed as inevitable. If the parties do not then separate, the trusts will be void as the condition underpinning them has failed.[46] This is to be distinguished from a trust that is established by a husband and wife, while living together, in contemplation of their future separation. As such a trust might generate a separa-

---

Review 1288, 1289 agrees that the rules "have been devised haphazardly . . . and produced a confusion possibly without parallel in the law".

43   [1920] 1 Ch. 122.
44   (1857) 8 D.M. & G. 731 at 744.
45   *Wilson v Wilson* (1848) 1 H.L. Cas. 538.
46   *Bindley v Mulloney* (1869) L.R. 7 Eq. 343.

tion that would not otherwise occur, the trust will be void. In *Re Moore*,[47] for example, a provision for weekly maintenance made by a testator for his sister, "during such time as she may live apart from her husband" was entirely void. As Bowen LJ concluded, "There can be no question that the object of this gift was to promote separation, an object which is against the policy of the law . . .".[48] This was not an absolute gift subject to a void condition. Although she later separated from her husband, the funds were unavailable to her. As Bowen LJ lamented, "One regrets taking away a dead man's bounty from the object of it under the very circumstances in which he intended her to have it, but we must not depart from the law".[49]

This rule does not apply to ante-nuptial settlements that deal with the aftermath of divorce. As Denning LJ observed in *Egerton v Egerton*, "A settlement which contains provisions for what should happen in the event of divorce is not contrary to public policy".[50]

16-007

The effect of the provision has to be evaluated in each case. At one extreme, a condition attached to a legacy to a married woman that she should separate from her husband must necessarily be invalid.[51] In *Re Caborne*,[52] a testatrix left her residuary estate to her son subject to a proviso that reduced the gift so long as he remained married to his wife. The gift was to become absolute if the wife should predecease him or the marriage otherwise be ended. The condition was struck out as being against public policy. As Simonds J admitted, "I re-assert the sanctity of the marriage bond and with it the importance of maintaining the integrity of family life, and, therefore, denounce and declare void a provision which is designed or tends to encourage an invasion of that sanctity".[53] Similarly, in *Re Johnson's WT*[54] the residue of the testator's estate (some £11,000) was left to his daughter for life. The problem was that the legacy was subject to a proviso that reduced her entitlement to a comparatively meagre £50 p.a. so long as she was married and living with her husband. She was to be entitled to the entire income on the termination of the marriage or on separation. The proviso was void and disregarded because it encouraged the breakdown of marriage. It was irrelevant that the testator had been concerned to protect his daughter against her untrustworthy and disliked husband. The proviso was, as Buckley J concluded, "an incentive to the break-up of a marriage that the court will not assist in any way".[55] She was entitled to the gift without the strings that her father sought to attach.

By way of contrast, a trust to benefit a deserted wife so long as she remained abandoned by her husband was upheld in *Re Charleton*.[56] This did not encourage marital breakdown,

---

47   (1888) 39 Ch. D. 116.
48   (1888) 39 Ch. D. 116 at 131.
49   (1888) 39 Ch. D. 116 at 132, 133.
50   [1949] L.J.R. 1683 at 1684; for a discussion of this aspect of the law and possible reform see the Law Commission Report, *Matrimonial Property, Needs and Agreements* (2014) Law Com. No.343.
51   *Wren v Bradley* (1848) 2 De. G. & Sm. 49.
52   [1943] Ch. 224.
53   [1943] Ch. 224 at 228.
54   [1967] Ch. 387.
55   [1967] Ch. 387 at 396.
56   [1911] W.N. 54.

but was instead designed to provide for the welfare of the wife because her husband had left. As shown, in *Re Lovell*[57] the object was not to induce the woman to maintain the separation from her husband, but to care for her until he returned or she remarried. In a like vein, in *Re Hope Johnstone*[58] a trust set up by a husband in favour of a wife for as long as she lived with him, with a gift over to the husband if she ceased to live with him, was held valid. Of this provision, Kekewich J observed, "That seems to be a provision rather in favour of morality than against it, rather to secure the continuance of cohabitation than to encourage a severance".[59] It was a limitation and not a gift defeasible by the performance or non-performance of a void condition. Hence, the wife, who was no longer cohabiting with her husband, was not entitled under the trust he had previously declared.

The key factor is whether the purpose of the gift is construed as encouraging divorce or separation. If the court discerns a different motive then the gift will be upheld. In *Re Thompson*,[60] the testator provided that his daughter would receive an annuity of £300 while she remained married to her present husband. The testator intensely disliked his son-in-law. If she became a widow, divorced or remarried, however, she would be entitled to the entire income of the estate. It was held that the provision was not contrary to public policy. The object was merely to prevent the money falling into the hands of the spendthrift husband. It was not to induce a separation.

16-008

Conditions undermining parental duties

If a trust contains a condition that is framed to separate a parent from a child, the condition will be void as it offends public policy.[61] As demonstrated in *Re Piper*,[62] this is regardless of whether the parents are still married. There a condition precedent was attached to a legacy that prevented children from living with their father. This non-residence condition was invalidated even though, at the time of the will, the parents had divorced. The gift, therefore, took effect without the offending provision. A further illustration of this invalidating tendency emerges from *Re Sandbrook*[63] where the testatrix left her estate on trust for her two grandchildren. It was a condition that, if one or both lived with their father, was in his custody, control or guardianship or under his direct influence, the interest should be forfeited. The condition was struck out on the basis of both uncertainty and public policy and the remainder of the gift upheld as valid. The condition, as Parker J acknowledged:

16-009

---

57   [1920] 1 Ch. 122.
58   [1904] 1 Ch. 470.
59   [1904] 1 Ch. 470 at 478.
60   [1939] 1 All E.R. 681.
61   *Re Sandbrook* [1912] 2 Ch. 471.
62   [1946] 2 All E.R. 503.
63   [1912] 2 Ch. 471.

> "is inserted in the will with the direct object of deterring the father of these two children from performing his parental duties with regard to them, because it makes their worldly welfare dependent upon his abstaining from doing what it is certainly his duty to do, namely, to bring his influence to bear and not give up his right to custody, the control and education of his children".[64]

Other cases decided upon this basis include *Re Morgan* where the bequest was to grand-children on condition of them living with their mother if the parents separated.[65] The condition was dispensed with on the ground of public policy. A more indirect condition that was designed to prohibit an infant's residence abroad was invalidated in *Re Boulter* because, as the father was seeking employment overseas and the mother was a German national, it catered for the possible separation of child and parent.[66] Sargant J explained that, "It seems to me that the whole tendency of this provision is one which in many sets of circumstances . . . might have a very prejudicial effect indeed on the position of the infants and upon the judgment that has to be exercised by their parents for their benefit".[67]

16-010   A more contentious gloss was applied in *Re Borwick* where a condition subsequent was imposed to the effect that a child beneficiary would forfeit his interest if he "be or become a Roman Catholic or not be openly and avowedly Protestant".[68] It was held that this condition was void as it restrained and hampered their parents in the performance of their parental duties.[69] Bennett J observed that "The parents' duty is to be discharged solely with a view to the moral and spiritual welfare of their children, and ought not to be influenced by mercenary considerations affecting the infant's worldly welfare".[70] This strict approach has, however, been diluted by the House of Lords in *Blathwayt v Baron Cawley*.[71] There the House upheld a forfeiture clause which was to operate on a male descendant becoming a Roman Catholic. Lord Wilberforce emphasised that not every condition, which might affect or influence the child-rearing process, will be void. He concluded that "I do not find myself able to discern a rule of public policy sufficiently clear and definite for total invalidation of conditions of the kind now in question. To say that any condition which in any way might affect or influence the way in which a child is brought up, or in which parental duties are exercised seems to me to state far too wide a rule".[72] The House signalled that a condition as to religious persuasion is

---

64   [1912] 2 Ch. 471 at 476.
65   (1910) 26 T.L.R. 398.
66   [1922] 1 Ch. 75.
67   [1922] 1 Ch. 75 at 84.
68   [1933] Ch. 657.
69   See also, *Re Tegg* [1936] 2 All E.R. 878 where a condition that a child was not to be sent to any Roman Catholic school for education was void because it fettered the parents' judgment as to what was in the best interests of the child.
70   [1933] Ch. 657 at 666.
71   [1975] 3 All E.R. 625.
72   [1975] 3 All E.R. 625 at 637.

not void simply because it makes parents choose between the path of money or spirituality for their child. As Lord Wilberforce added, "After all, a choice between considerations of material prosperity and spiritual welfare has to be made by many parents for their children—and, one may add, by judges in infants' interests—and it would be cynical to assume that these cannot be conscientiously and rightly made".[73] Lord Fraser made the distinction that, "deterring a father from performing his parental duty and from exercising any control at all over his children seems to me quite different from influencing him to exercise his authority in a particular way, as the will in the present case might tend to do".[74]

Accordingly, the current state of the law appears to be that, while a condition that prevents a parent from carrying out his parental duty is void, a condition which merely influences the way in which that duty is performed remains valid.

Name and Arms Clauses

16-011

Although a quaint and old-fashioned notion,[75] and based on the concept of lineage, it is possible that a name and arms clause may be inserted into a trust.[76] A modern demonstration of this is *Howard v Howard-Lawson,* which concerned the construction and effect of such a clause.[77] There the testator had sought to ensure the continuance of the association of his family name and arms with his landed estates. A names and arms clause declared that the heir under a will had to use the Howard name and bear the Howard coat of arms within one year of becoming entitled. The will contained a forfeiture provision under which the heir was required, within the year, to "apply for and endeavour to obtain the Royal Licence or take such other steps as might be requisite to authorise the user and bearing of the said surname and arms". The heir would be disentailed if he should refuse or neglect to do so.[78] The appellant was the embittered son of the heir and he claimed that his father had been disentailed by his failure to comply with the names and arms clause, which had been hidden from him for the last 50 years. Accordingly, the father had forfeited his interest and the son now claimed to be entitled to the estate absolutely. The Court of Appeal dismissed the son's argument, confirming that

---

73 [1975] 3 All E.R. 625 at 637.

74 [1975] 3 All E.R. 625 at 649, 650.

75 See generally B. Wells-Furby, "The Origin of the 'Name and Arms' Clause and the Development of the Lineage Culture in Fourteenth-Century England" (2015) *Nottingham Medieval Studies* 77. She traces it back to the 14th century and, as she puts it (at 104), "the first burgeoning of the lineage culture among landowners . . .".

76 Such a clause, however, cannot bind an infant tenant for life: *Re Edwards* [1910] 1 Ch. 541.

77 [2012] 3 All E.R. 60.

78 The expression "refuse or neglect" is not equivalent to "fail" or "omit" as it implies a conscious act of volition: *Re Quintin Dick (No 1)* [1926] Ch. 992.

the father had applied for a Royal Licence within the year and that it had not been necessary to obtain it or, indeed, use the name and arms within that time frame.

The names and arms clause traditionally might require a bride on marriage to "take, use and bear on all occasions" her maiden name and her family coat of arms. The courts have had to consider on a number of occasions whether such a clause is void as running contrary to public policy. No objection to such clauses emerged until post-World War II when, as Wilberforce J observed, "From 1945 onwards a wind of change of increasing force developed against them".[79] Indeed, such a clause was in *Re Fry* held to be void on the grounds of public policy.[80] Vaisey J was of the opinion that "the use of different surnames by a man and his wife cannot fail to be productive of many embarrassments and inconveniences, not only to themselves, their children and relatives, but to their friends and acquaintances, and indeed to society generally".[81] A different judicial approach was, however, adopted in *Re Howard's WT*.[82] There Wilberforce J saw no policy justification for invalidating a name and arms clause which applied to men. In the light of previous authority, however, he did feel that a clause that was applicable to a married woman would still be against public policy.[83] This has subsequently been held to be an untenable distinction by the Court of Appeal in *Re Neeld (No 1)* where a clause was held to apply equally to spinsters and married women.[84] Hence, the name and arms clause seemingly no longer offends public policy.[85]

Sham and Illusory Trusts

16-012

A trust that at face value appears perfectly valid may be set aside if it is a sham trust or an illusory trust. The presumption is, however, that a trust remains valid until a court of competent jurisdiction determines otherwise.[86] As Norris J put it in *Swift Advances Plc v Ahmed,* "The phenomenon of the 'deed in the drawer' is one that is now frequently encountered. X appears to be the owner of a property, and people lend to him or otherwise deal with him on the footing that he owns it. But if X becomes bankrupt or the subject of enforcement proceedings a

79 *Re Howard's WT* [1961] Ch. 507 at 516. In *Re Neeld* [1962] Ch.643, Upjohn LJ observed that, "this wind was but a light, fickle and variable breeze" (at 680).
80 [1945] Ch. 348; see also, *Re Kersey* [1952] W.N. 541.
81 [1945] Ch. 348 at 354.
82 [1961] Ch. 507.
83 [1961] Ch. 507 at 523, 524.
84 [1962] Ch. 643.
85 See also *Blathwayt v Baron Cawley* [1975] 3 All E.R. 625.
86 See the Royal Court of Jersey case *Heinrichs v Pantrust International SA* [2018] 21 I.T.E.L.R. 955. There it was emphasised that a valid trust does not become a sham simply because the trustee subsequently departed from its terms and administered it in a particular way.

deed is produced which shows that in truth he holds the property upon trust for somebody else".[87] The court must look at the reality and substance of the purported transaction and determine whether the settlor has given the false impression that a trust has been created.[88] The court is not, however, restricted to examining the four corners of the document and may take on board external evidence, such as evidence of the subsequent conduct of the parties.[89] Understandably, the burden of proof rests with whoever asserts that the trust should not take effect according to its outward appearance.[90] It can be proved by inference[91] and can arise from reckless indifference.[92] As Mowbray observes, "In practice, it is bound to be difficult to prove this in a case where the trust is declared in a trust deed to which the trustees are parties without also proving that they shared the intent, or at least went along with the settlor without either knowing or caring what they were signing".[93]

The term "sham" connotes, as Diplock LJ explained in *Snook v London and West Riding Investments Ltd*, "acts done or documents executed by the parties to the 'sham' which are intended by them to give to third parties or to the court the appearance of creating between the parties legal rights and obligations different from the actual rights and obligations (if any) which the parties intend to create".[94] Accordingly, if the settlor retained the full beneficial interest and did not pass any interest in the property to the proclaimed beneficiaries, the "trust" is a mere fiction, i.e. sham.[95] It will give rise to no legal obligations or rights.[96] It is necessary, therefore, that all the parties thereto must have a common intention that the acts or documents are not to create the legal rights and obligations which they give the appearance of creating. The test of intention is, moreover, subjective. The parties must have intended to create different rights and obligations from those appearing from the document and to give a false impression of those rights and obligations to third parties.[97] The mere fact that the

---

87 [2015] EWHC 3265 (Ch) at [1].

88 *Abdel Rahman v Chase Bank (CI) Trust Co* [1991] J.L.R. 103 (a Channel Islands case). There the settlor retained such dominion and control over the property throughout his life that the trust was categorised as a sham by the Royal Court of Jersey, "in the sense that it was made to appear to be what it was not" (at 168).

89 *Erlam v Rahman* [2016] EWHC 111 (Ch). As Patten LJ acknowledged in *Pankhania v Chandegra* [2013] 1 P. & C.R. 16 at [20], "The question of what constitutes a sham trust has been the subject of considerable discussion in recent years, particularly in the context of attempts to shield assets from the claims of divorced spouses or creditors".

90 For example, in *ND v SD* [2017] EWHC 1507 (Fam) a wife failed prove that an offshore trust set up by the husband, which benefited the parties' two children and into which family assets were placed, was a sham.

91 *Ali v Bashir* [2014] EWHC 3853 (Ch). All that matters is that the primary facts support that inference.

92 *A v A* [2007] EWHC 99 (Fam).

93 J. Mowbray, "Shams, Pretences, Blackmail and Illusion: Part 1" (2000) P.C.B. 28, 30.

94 [1967] 1 All E.R. 518 at 528. Of course, there has to be demonstrated some proper basis for overturning the transaction. As Munby J put it in *A v A* [2007] EWHC 99 (Fam) at [17], "the court cannot grant relief merely because the . . . arrangements appear to be artificial or even 'dodgy'".

95 In *Pankhania v Chandegra* [2013] 1 P. & C.R. 16, there was no attempt as Patten LJ acknowledged at [22], "to mask the true nature of their agreement from other parties". The parties were, therefore, bound by the legal consequences of what they had signed.

96 *Kali v Chawla* [2007] EWHC 2357 (Ch).

97 *Erlam v Rahman* [2016] EWHC 111 (Ch).

document is unfavourable or artificial does necessarily entail that it is a sham, provided that the parties intend the agreement to take effect according to its terms.[98] If the parties subsequently depart from the agreement, this does not necessarily mean that they never intended that agreement to be effective and binding.

In *Midland Bank Plc v Wyatt*,[99] for example, following legal advice a settlor underwent the pretence of declaring a trust in favour of his wife and two daughters. This was a ploy to put the property beyond the reach of the Bank, who he never informed of the arrangement. Deputy Judge Young was unimpressed with Mr Wyatt's behaviour and noted, "It follows that even if the Deed was entered into without any dishonest or fraudulent motive but was entered into on the basis of mistaken advice, in my judgment such a transaction will still be void and therefore an unenforceable transaction if it was not intended to be acted upon but was entered into for some different or ulterior motive".[100] A similar approach was adopted by Munby J in *Re W*, "the court will not allow itself to be bamboozled by husbands who put their property in the names of close relations in circumstances where, taking a realistic and fair view, it is apparent that the recipient is a bare trustee and where the answer to the real question—whose property is it?—is that it remains the husband's property".[101] It was held that the trust was a sham and that the Bank could lay claim to the property. In both cases, the courts considered the settlor's conduct after the disputed declaration of trust. As Conaglen puts it, "in conceptual terms, the relevance of the sham doctrine is that it justifies the court in stepping outside of the normal construction process in order to ascertain 'the truth of the matter' by reference to material which would normally be excluded as irrelevant to that process".[102]

More recently, in *JSC Mezhdunarodniy Promyshlenniy Bank v Pugachev*[103] five discretionary trust deeds in which the settlor, Mr Pugachev, was named as a beneficiary together with members of his family, were held to be shams. Under the trust deeds, the settlor was appointed as a "protector" with extensive powers (including the power to remove trustees "with or without cause") and the companies that were the trustees were controlled by his lawyer. Mr Pugachev had intended to mislead other people by creating the false appearance that the assets did not belong to him.

Illusory trusts

16-013

A further exception to the rule that a constituted trust cannot be revoked takes the form of so-called "illusory trusts".[104] Although properly to be viewed as a particular type of "sham

---

98   *National Westminster Bank Plc v Jones* [2001] 1 B.C.L.C. 98.
99   [1995] 1 F.L.R. 697.
100 [1995] 1 F.L.R. 697 at 707.
101 [2000] 2 F.L.R. 927 at 938.
102 M. Conaglen, "Sham Trusts" (2008) 67(1) C.L.J. 176, 182.
103 [2017] EWHC 2426 (Ch).
104 In *Clayton v Clayton* [2016] NZSC 29, the Supreme Court of New Zealand felt that the expression "illusory trust"

trust",[105] the illusory trust concerns the transfer of property to trustees merely as a convenient mode of paying the settlor's debts.[106] As Sheridan puts it, "The peculiar feature of this type of assignment is that, in general, the debtor is accorded a power of revocation although nothing is said about revocability in the trust instrument".[107] These assignments are also known as "deeds of arrangement". The transaction does not give rise to a real trust in that it passes no beneficial interest in the property to the creditors.[108] The settlor, as Pepys MR admitted in *Bill v Cureton*, "proposes only a benefit to himself by the payment of his debts—his object is not to benefit his creditors".[109] Hence, the creditors have no right to complain as they are not injured by the revocation, have waived no right of action and are not executing parties to the deed of arrangement.

This is, however, to be contrasted with an arrangement that is, instead, designed to benefit the creditors. In this latter scenario, an irrevocable trust can be created if that accords with the settlor's intentions.[110] The difficulty for the court is to determine which side of the divide a transaction falls. The forensic approach adopted by the court is as described by Turner VC in *Smith v Hurst*:

> "the motive of the party executing the deed may have been either to benefit his creditors or to promote his own convenience; and the Court there has to examine into the circumstances for the purpose of ascertaining what was the true purpose of the deed; and this examination does not stop with the deed itself, but must be carried on to what has subsequently occurred, because the party who created the trust may, by his own conduct, or by the obligations which he has permitted his trustee to contract, have created an equity against himself".[111]

In relation to an illusory trust, as no beneficial interest passes the trustees hold the property on resulting trust for the settlor.[112] They are the settlor's agents and they are to apply the property according to his directions and for his benefit. The creditors, as Shadwell VC observed in *Garrard*

16-014

---

added nothing. It held that, when a sham is not detected, the only question is whether there is, or is not, a valid trust. See further G. Young, "Sham and illusory trusts—lessons from *Clayton v Clayton*" (2018) 24(2) T. & T. 194.

105 As J. Mowbray, explains in "Shams, Pretences, Blackmail and Illusion: Part 2" (2000) P.C.B. 105, 108, "They are indeed not intended to operate quite as their wording would at first indicate, and they are ineffective to a large extent. But the reasoning behind the way that the courts have treated them is different from the reasoning about sham trusts that we have seen so far".

106 *Garrard v Lord Lauderdale* (1830) 3 Sim. 1.

107 L.A. Sheridan, "Trusts for Paying Debts" [1957] Conv. 280.

108 See J. Mowbray, "Shams, Pretences, Blackmail and Illusion: Part 2" (2000) P.C.B. 105.

109 (1835) 2 My. & K. 503 at 511.

110 *Mackinnon v Stewart* (1850) 1 Sim. 76.

111 (1852) 10 Hare 30 at 47.

112 *Smith v Hurst* (1852) 10 Hare 30.

v Lord Lauderdale, "are merely persons named there for the purpose of showing how the trust property under the voluntary deed shall be applied for the benefit of the volunteers".[113] The settlor, therefore, retains control and power and the creditors have no say in what happens to the property set aside.[114]

An example of where an illusory trust might be employed is to be found in *Cornthwaite v Frith*.[115] There the debtor was to spend some time abroad and found it convenient to set up an arrangement by which he would transfer property to his agents on the understanding that they would sell the property and discharge his debts from the proceeds of sale. Knight Bruce VC held that the creditors could make no direct claim against the property. The arrangement did not create a deed of trust in favour of the creditors. Instead, it created a general agency whereby his agent could discharge his debts. This entailed that the settlor was free to revoke or vary the agent's mandate and, indeed, could at any time call for the property to be transferred back to him.

16-015

A noteworthy feature is that an arrangement that starts out in the guise of a revocable, illusory trust might metamorphose into an irrevocable and enforceable trust in favour of the creditors.[116] This has occurred in the following examples. First, where the settlor provides that the arrangement is to take effect following his death.[117] The logic here is that, as it was only the settlor that could countermand the trustee's instructions, the arrangement by that stage becomes irrevocable. Accordingly, the deceased's next of kin cannot lay claim to this property. If the arrangement is, instead, to pay debts both during the lifetime and after the death of the settlor, it would appear that it becomes irrevocable only following the death of the debtor.[118]

A second illustration is where the creditor is a party to the deed of arrangement and executes the deed, the deed is irrevocable as against him. The creditor becomes a beneficiary and can call upon the trustee to account. As Lord Cranworth VC explained, "A valid trust is created in his favour; and the relation between the debtor and trustee is no longer that of mere principal and agent".[119]

16-016

Thirdly, where the deed is communicated to any of the creditors,[120] and they assent and act to their detriment in reliance upon the arrangement, the deed cannot be revoked as against those creditors. For example, in *Harland v Binks*[121] it was demonstrated that, if a creditor assented to a trust for the payment of a debt and indicated that he would rely on the trust and

---

113 (1830) 3 Sim. 1 at 12.
114 *Ellis & Co v Cross* [1915] 2 K.B. 654.
115 (1851) 4 De. G. & Sm. 552.
116 Note, however, the additional restrictions imposed by the Deeds of Arrangement Act 1914 appertaining to the need to register most deeds of arrangement and to obtain the written consent of the majority of creditors in some circumstances.
117 *Re Fitzgerald's ST* (1888) 37 Ch. D. 18.
118 *Montefiore v Browne* (1858) 7 H.L. Cas. 241.
119 *Mackinnon v Stewart* (1850) 1 Sim. 75 at 89, 90.
120 The creditor need not see the deed and it suffices that its existence is made known to the creditor (e.g. in correspondence with the trustees): *Re Baber's Trusts* (1870) L.R. 10 Eq. 554.
121 (1850) 15 Q.B. 713.

not the debt, the trust becomes irrevocable. The election is the requisite detrimental act. The assent may be expressed or be discerned from some act that amounts to acquiescence.[122] It is not necessary that the debtor knows of the creditor's assent or acquiescence.[123]

Fourthly, the conduct or language of the settlor may demonstrate the intention to create an enforceable trust. In *New Prance and Garrard's Trustee v Hunting*,[124] a deed was executed two days before the bankruptcy of the transferor. The purpose was that the property could be used to raise money so as to remedy several breaches of trust committed by the transferor. The intention was to create a valid trust in favour of those from whom he had previously misappropriated money. It was to shield himself against criminal action as regards his breaches of trust. Put simply, there was nothing illusory about this trust.

Trusts to Defeat Creditors

16-017

Since the innovation of the trust, settlors have attempted to employ the concept as a means of putting property beyond the grasp of potential creditors. The transfer of property to trustees on trust for named family members generally has the effect of negating the settlor's interest in those assets. Consequently, those assets will be shielded from the claims of the settlor's creditors. When the beneficiary is a close family member (e.g. a husband or wife), it is the settlor who will usually retain the physical enjoyment of the property. The self-serving attitude that pervades such transactions is evident. It is, as Sir George Jessel MR summed up, "If I succeed in business, I make a fortune for myself. If I fail, I leave my creditors unpaid. They will bear the loss".[125] Not surprisingly, Parliament has taken steps to protect creditors from the consequences of this type of debt evasion. It has long done so by imposing restrictions upon the use of trusts for these purposes.[126] Outside such legislative restrictions, however, a trust can be employed effectively to sidestep a creditor's claims. Indeed, the use of offshore trusts (often situated in the Channel Isles) is usually to achieve the protection of assets against adverse claims, whether by a private creditor or HM Revenue & Customs.

The present law is to be found within the Insolvency Act 1986, which is not limited merely to transactions which take place in England and Wales.[127] This chapter will now examine the jurisdiction of the court to set aside transactions that are at an undervalue and operate unfairly

---

122 *Field v Lord Donoughmore* (1841) 1 Dr. & War. 227.
123 *Siggers v Evans* (1855) 5 El. & Bl. 367.
124 [1897] 2 Q.B. 19.
125 *Re Butterworth* (1882) 19 Ch. D. 588 at 598.
126 The initial regulation was contained in the Statute of Elizabeth 1571.
127 For this extra-territorial effect and the need for a sufficient connection with England and Wales, see *Concept Oil Services v En-Gin Group LLP* [2013] EWHC 1897 (Comm); *Fortress Value Recovery Fund 1 LLC v Blue Skye Special Opportunities Fund LP* [2013] EWHC 14 (Comm).

to disadvantage creditors. Albeit governed by different statutory provisions and different rules, the court has a jurisdiction to do so where the transferor remains solvent or when he is subsequently adjudged bankrupt. These possibilities will be considered in turn.

Transactions defrauding creditors

16-018   Other than on the bankruptcy of the debtor, a transaction at an undervalue may only be set aside under the auspices of ss.423–425 of the 1986 Act. These are, as Lady Arden explained, "provisions designed to bring assets back into the pot for the settlor's creditors . . ."[128] Under these provisions there is no need that the transferor be insolvent.[129] Although the provisions can be invoked by a trustee in bankruptcy or liquidator, the overwhelming majority of applications are made by individual creditors. There are three conditions underlying the s.423 jurisdiction:

- the transaction, which by virtue of s.436 includes a "gift, agreement or arrangement", must be otherwise effective[130] and must involve a significant undervalue[131];

- the purpose of the transaction must be either to place assets beyond the reach of a person who is making, or may in future make, a claim against the transferor[132] or to prejudice in some other way the interests of such a person in relation to any present or future claim made against the transferor.[133] The evidential burden lies, of course, with the applicant and, despite the recommendation of the Cork Committee,[134] there is no evidential presumption available to assist the applicant. If there is no intention to place assets out of the reach of potential claimants, the s.423 jurisdiction does not arise.[135]

---

128   "Family Trusts Today" speech delivered at the Trusts and Wealth Management Conference, Singapore Asian Wealth and the Global Context, 1 August 2019 at [30]. This is available at *https://www.supremecourt.uk/docs/speech-190801.pdf* [Accessed 31 July 2020].

129   If the transferor is adjudged bankrupt before the s.423 application is made, leave of the court is required: see *Godfrey v Torpy* [2007] EWHC 919 (Ch).

130   *Re Farrell (A Bankrupt)* [2019] EWHC 119 (Ch).

131   "Transaction" is to be given a wide meaning, "entirely consistent with the statutory objective of remedying the avoidance of debts . . ". (per Jonathan Parker LJ in *Feakins v DEFRA* [2005] EWCA Civ 1513 at [76]). In *Payroller Ltd (In Liquidation) v Little Panda Consultants Ltd* [2018] EWHC 3161 (QB), the High Court felt it to be arguable that money paid by the sole director to discharge the bona fide obligations of innocent third parties was a "transaction" for these purposes.

132   It is not necessary to show that the intention was to put assets beyond the reach of the particular s.423 applicant: *Jyske Bank (Gibraltar) Ltd v Spjeldnaes (No.2)* [1999] 2 B.C.L.C. 101.

133   See *Midland Bank Plc v Wyatt* [1995] 1 F.L.R. 697 where the transfer was attempted so as to prevent the bank making future claims against the matrimonial home.

134   Insolvency Law Review Committee, *Insolvency Law and Practice* (1982) Cmnd.8558, para.1215.

135   *Wood v Watkin* [2019] EWHC 1311 (Ch). For example, it was accepted in *Premium Jet AG v Sutton* [2017] EWHC 186 (QB) that, if the declaration of trust was merely the formal expression of a pre-existing state of affairs, it would not be caught by s.423. Cf. if the transaction created new proprietary rights.

Accordingly, in *Re Farrell (A Bankrupt)*[136] a man who had made gifts before being made bankrupt had done so pursuant to tax-planning advice and for tax-planning purposes. The gifts were not, as his trustees in bankruptcy had alleged, transactions defrauding creditors. Nevertheless, as admitted in *Midland Bank Plc v Wyatt* by Deputy Judge Young, "the more hazardous the business being contemplated is, the more readily the court will be satisfied of the intention of the settlor or the transferor"[137]; and

■ the claimant must demonstrate that he is a victim of the transaction and this is adjudged as at the time of the application and not the transfer.[138] The victim will usually be a creditor of the transferor, but could, instead, be a non-creditor who is in litigation with the transferor[139] or who has a cause of action against the transferor.[140] The inbuilt elasticity of s.423 is evident for, as Arden LJ explained in *Hill v Spread Trustee Ltd*, "all that has to be shown is that the person is making or may at some time make a claim".[141] Indeed, a person can be a victim even though he was not in the transferor's mind when the transaction was entered[142] or not even a creditor at the date of the transaction.[143] As Sales J commented, "It is enough that the transferor acted with the purpose of defrauding any person who had made or might make a claim against him".[144]

As mentioned, there is no requirement that a debt exists at the time of the transaction. For example, a wealthy individual might make a settlement in favour of his wife prior to embarking upon a high-risk venture with a view to putting the property beyond the claims of future creditors.[145] The transaction is clearly vulnerable to being set aside. There is, moreover, no special time limit beyond which the transaction is immune for these purposes.[146] The attraction of the s.423 route is outlined by Keay:

"It is a trite point that creditors often do not fare well when distributions are made by bankruptcy trustees or liquidators out of

---

136 [2019] EWHC 119 (Ch).

137 [1995] 1 F.L.R. 697 at 709. By way of contrast, in *Wood v Watkin* [2019] EWHC 1311 (Ch) the court refused to infer an intention where the individual commanded an annual income of £1.6million and the transactions concerned no more than a small fraction of that income.

138 *Clydesdale Financial Services Ltd v Smailes* [2009] EWHC 3190 (Ch).

139 *Pinewood Joinery v Starelm Properties Ltd* [1994] 2 B.C.L.C. 412.

140 *Moon v Franklin* [1996] B.P.I.R. 196 Ch D.

141 [2007] 1 W.L.R. 2404 at [136].

142 *Sands v Clitheroe* [2006] B.P.I.R. 1000.

143 *Random House UK Ltd v Allason* [2008] EWHC 2854 (Ch).

144 [2009] EWHC 2633 (Ch) at [22].

145 See *Re Butterworth* (1882) 19 Ch. D. 588, where a successful baker went into business as a grocer which, it turned out, was ill-suited to his abilities.

146 The Limitation Act 1980 does, however, apply to s.423 actions: *Hill v Spread Trustee Co Ltd* [2007] 1 W.L.R. 2402; *Giles v Rhind* [2008] EWCA Civ 118.

the estates of insolvents. So any action, other than the initiation of formal insolvency proceedings, will usually be worth considering. One possible option that creditors might consider, if they are aware that a debtor . . . has disposed of any assets improperly at an under-value, is to seek relief under s.423 of the Insolvency Act 1986".[147]

What can the court do?

16-019 Once satisfied that the transaction meets the above-stated requirements, the court may make an order as it thinks fit from the range of options set out in ss.423(2) and 425 of the 1986 Act. Section 423 is not, however, to be regarded as a form of punishment of wrongdoers and, moreover, the recipient of a transfer which is ultimately set aside might be entirely innocent.[148] The court, however, does not enjoy an unlimited jurisdiction to grant relief.[149] The court will do its best to restore the status quo ante[150] and to protect the interests of those who were prejudiced or are potentially prejudiced by the transaction.[151] These orders include, but are not limited to:

- setting the transaction aside either in whole or in part;

- requiring any property transferred to be vested in any person, either absolutely or for the benefit of all the victims of the transaction;

- damages where the assets acquired by the transaction have been put beyond the claimant's reach[152];

- requiring any property representing the proceeds of sale of the property to be so vested; and

- requiring any person who has received benefits from the transferor to pay to any other person such sums as the court may direct. In *4 Eng Ltd v Harper*, a husband transferred property to his wife to prevent it being claimed in litigation and the court ordered that

---

147 A. Keay, "Transactions Defrauding Creditors: The Problem of Purpose under s.423 of the Insolvency Act" [2003] Conv. 272, 272.
148 *Deansgate 123 LLP v Workman* [2019] EWHC 2 (Ch).
149 *Johnson v Arden* [2018] EWHC 1624 (Ch).
150 As Nourse LJ put it in *Chohan v Sagger* [1994] B.C.C. 134 at 141C, "the judge must ask himself is what assets have been lost to the debtor. His order should, so far as practicable, restore that loss".
151 Account should be taken of matters such as the mental state of the transferee and the degree of involvement in the fraudulent scheme of the transferor/debtor: *4 Eng Ltd v Harper* [2009] EWHC 2633 (Ch).
152 *New Media Distribution Co SEZC Ltd v Kagalovsky* [2018] EWHC 2876 (Ch).

she repay money and restore property to her husband in order that it could be used to fund damages awarded against him.[153]

And third parties?

16-020

To be effective, it is necessary that the powers of the court can be exercised against third parties. This is explicitly recognised in s.425(2), which states that an order made may affect the property of, or impose an obligation on, a third party whether or not that person was a party to the impugned transaction.[154] Obviously, the immediate transferee is most at risk from the transaction being unravelled. As regards subsequent transferees, however, they are protected provided that the transaction was entered in good faith, for value and without notice of the circumstances which made s.423 applicable in the first place.[155] The same change of position defence is available to a person who has acquired a benefit under the impugned transaction.[156]

Purpose and motive

16-021

There is no requirement that the transferor must act dishonestly[157] and a transaction can be impugned even if the transferor was following legal advice.[158] It is the purpose of entry into the transaction[159] and not the agreement itself that is the central issue.[160] It is not even necessary that a s.423 purpose be the predominant motive underlying the transaction.[161] As Evans-Lombe QC noted, the provision would be frustrated, "if it were possible successfully to contend that if the owner was able to point to another purpose, such as the benefit of his family, friends or the advantage of his business associates, the section could not be applied".[162] Accordingly,

---

153 [2009] EWHC 2633 (Ch). In *Dornoch Ltd v Westminster International BV* [2009] EWHC 1782 (Admlty), the court made an order requiring a ship to be transferred to the claimant's nominee with a view to its sale.

154 *Johnson v Arden* [2018] EWHC 1624 (Ch). There it was held that the jurisdiction did not extend to directors whose only role had been to direct the company to enter into the transaction or give the preference, and who had received no benefit.

155 *Claridge v Claridge* [2011] EWHC 2047 (Ch).

156 *4 Eng Ltd v Harper* [2009] EWHC 2633 (Ch). For example, if a gift is received in good faith and the money is spent on a world cruise it might be regarded as unfair to require the innocent donee to repay the money.

157 *Midland Bank v Wyatt* [1995] 1 F.L.R. 696.

158 See *Arbuthnot Leasing International Ltd v Havelet Leasing Ltd (No.2)* [1990] B.C.C. 636.

159 *Re Farrell (A Bankrupt)* [2019] EWHC 119 (Ch) where gifts made before bankruptcy were pursuant to tax-planning advice and for tax-planning purposes and not within s.423.

160 As was made clear in *Hill v Spread Trustee Co Ltd* [2007] 1 W.L.R. 2402, s.423 requires the person entering the transaction to have a particular purpose. It is not sufficient to show that the transaction has a particular result.

161 It is not, however, enough that the prejudicing of the interests of the potential claimant is simply a by-product or consequence of the transaction: *Swift Advances Plc v Ahmed* [2015] EWHC 3265 (Ch).

162 *Chohan v Saggar* [1992] B.C.C. 306 at 321; see also *Fox v Mohammed* [2019] EWHC 3409 (Ch).

the fact that it was also his intention to benefit a third party does not prevent the operation of s.423.[163] Arden LJ developed this theme further in *IRC v Hashmi*:

> **"it will often be the case that the motive to defeat creditors and the motive to secure family protection will co-exist in such a way that even the transferor himself may be unable to say what was uppermost in his mind . . . for something to be a purpose it must be a real substantial purpose; it is not sufficient to quote something which is a by-product of the transaction under consideration, or to show it was that it was simply a result of it . . . or an element which made no contribution of importance to the debtor's purpose of carrying out the transaction . . . trivial purposes must be excluded".[164]**

Hence, it is sufficient if the ambition of the transferor is to deprive creditors of speedy access to property that would otherwise be applicable for their benefit.[165] In certain circumstances, the intention to put assets beyond the creditors' reach will readily be inferred by the court. As Schiemann LJ put it in *Barclays Bank Plc v Eustice*, "when action by the creditor was clearly anticipated by the debtor and that these transfers were at an undervalue and that what remains in the hands of the debtor barely if at all covers the debt, there is in my judgment a strong prima facie case that the purpose of the transactions was to prejudice the interests of the creditor".[166] The court must make its determination, as Deputy Judge Evans-Lombe QC observed in *Chohan v Saggar*, "bearing in mind the mischief against which the section . . . is aimed".[167] In *Papanicola v Fagan*,[168] the transfer was designed to avoid divorce proceedings and, amounting to valuable consideration, fell outside the mischief of s.423.[169]

What is an undervalue?

16-022

It is to be appreciated that a transaction entered for adequate consideration is not a transaction at an undervalue and thereby falls outside the statutory machinery.[170] In that scenario,

---

163   *Curtis v Pulbrook* [2011] EWHC 167 (Ch).
164   [2002] W.T.L.R. 1027 at 1035. It is, therefore, a substantial purpose test that is to be applied rather than the stricter dominant purpose test that courted favour in earlier times (see *Lloyds Bank Ltd v Marcan* [1973] 1 W.L.R. 1387).
165   *Northampton BC v Cardoza* [2019] EWHC 26 (Ch). There, in relation to the transfer of the matrimonial home at an undervalue, Judge Simon Barker QC emphasised (at [228]) that "the applicability of s.423 is fact sensitive".
166   [1995] 1 W.L.R. 1238 at 1248.
167   [1992] B.C.C. 306 at 321.
168   [2008] EWHC 3348 (Ch).
169   See also *Burnden Holdings (UK) Ltd (In Liquidation) v Fielding* [2019] EWHC 1566 (Ch), where the defendants' real substantial purpose in making a share distribution was not to put the shares beyond the reach of creditors. The purpose instead was principally to benefit the business.
170   Cf. *Harvey v Nuruz-Zaman* [2018] EWHC 1742 (Ch) where £60,000 had been given for the transfer of the property into the wife's sole name, but the property was worth £170,000.

it matters not that the transaction was designed to defeat creditors. In *Delaney v Chen*,[171] for example, the sale and leaseback of a property at a price substantially lower than the unencumbered freehold value did not amount to a sale at an undervalue as the premium value of the tenancy made up the shortfall in the purchase price. It did not matter that the evidence showed that the purpose of the transaction was to harm the interest of creditors generally.

A transaction at an undervalue is defined in s.423(1) as being either a gift, a transaction in consideration of marriage or formation of a civil partnership[172] or a transaction for consideration which, in terms of money or money's worth, is "significantly less than" the equivalent value of the property transferred.[173] In some cases, the task is straightforward. Obviously, this is particularly so with the gift and the marriage transactions. In *Moon v Franklin*,[174] for example, a husband, facing legal proceedings, made a substantial gift to his wife. The purpose was to prevent the property being affected by the outcome of the case. The court rejected an argument that the gift was an expression of gratitude for the services rendered by the wife and set aside the gift under s.423. The most difficulty lies with those cases when consideration is given and the court must compare in monetary terms the value of the consideration provided by both parties.[175] All will turn upon the court's view of the expert valuation evidence introduced by the parties.[176]

In *Re Kumar*[177] the wife agreed to take sole responsibility for the mortgage in return for acquiring her husband's share in the matrimonial home. Although she gave consideration for the transaction, Ferris J calculated that the obligations undertaken were worth much less than the value of the husband's share. As the consideration she gave was significantly less than that given by her husband, the transaction was at an undervalue and set aside in favour of his creditors. This shows that, in assessing whether a transaction is at an undervalue, the court must view the transaction in its entirety.

A similar approach was adopted in *Agricultural Mortgage Corp Plc v Woodward*.[178] There a farmer, whose farm was subject to a £700,000 mortgage, granted a tenancy to his wife at the full rental value (£37,250) in order to ensure that the mortgagee would be unable to take possession when he defaulted on the mortgage. The tenancy was set aside on the basis that the wife would obtain benefits under the transaction beyond those that she had paid for. Those benefits were that she would be able to retain her home, allowed to operate the family business free from the claims of the husband's creditors and effectively hold the mortgagee to ransom. The latter arose because the tenancy reduced the value of the mortgagee's security by more

16-023

---

171 [2010] EWHC 6 (Ch).
172 Obviously, this has no application to transactions by a body corporate.
173 The payment of a dividend by a company is capable of constituting a transaction at an undervalue, which is designed to put funds beyond the reach of creditors: *BTI 2014 LLC v Sequana SA* [2019] EWCA Civ 112.
174 [1996] B.P.I.R. 196.
175 See *Williams v White* unreported 27 July 2007 where Judge Behrens said by way of obiter that a shortfall of 4.09% would not be significant.
176 *Pagemanor Ltd v Ryan (No.2)* [2002] B.P.I.R. 593.
177 [1993] 1 W.L.R. 224.
178 (1995) 70 P. & C.R. 53.

than 50 per cent and offered her a high surrender value (or ransom value) if the mortgagee was to buy her out. As she had paid nothing for such additional benefits, the transaction was at an undervalue and the tenancy set aside.[179] As Sir Christopher Slade concluded, "when the transactions are viewed as a whole, the benefits which the first defendant thereby conferred on her were significantly greater in value, far greater in value, in money or money's worth than the value of the consideration provided by her. To hold otherwise would seem to me to fly in the face of reality and common sense".[180]

Who may apply?

16-024

Section 424 lists the persons who may apply to court for an order under s.423. The rider is attached by s.424(2) that, regardless of which party makes the application, it is treated as being made on behalf of every victim of the transaction (i.e. it is a class action under which the actual applicant obtains no priority).[181] The persons who can make an application are:

- where the debtor has been adjudged bankrupt or it is a company that is being wound up or is in administration: the official receiver, the trustee of the bankrupt's estate, the liquidator, the administrator (including a foreign administrator)[182] or, with leave of the court, a victim of the transaction;

- where there exists a voluntary settlement (i.e. compromise) made between the debtor and his creditors: the supervisor of the voluntary agreement or any person who is a victim of the transaction; or

- in any other case: a victim of the transaction, as defined in s.423(5) as being someone "who is, or is capable of being, prejudiced by it". As David Richards J noted, "In choosing the term 'victim' and this definition, it is I think clear that it was intended to be a wider category than simply creditors. The words used are ordinary English words with no technical meaning and the correct approach in any given case is to ask whether, on the facts of the case, the claimant is a person who is, or is capable of being, prejudiced by the transaction".[183]

---

179 In *Barclays Bank v Eustice* [1995] 1 W.L.R. 1238 the "ransom point" was decisive in showing that the transferee obtained more than was paid for when he took the tenancy of a farm.

180 (1995) 70 P. & C.R. 53 at 64; see also *Feakins v DEFRA* [2005] EWCA Civ 1513 where the debtor persuaded the bank to sell the farm to his girlfriend at a price which took account of the subsisting agricultural tenancy. The tenancy was then quickly terminated. It was held that the tenancy was merely a device to depress the value of the farm and induce the bank to sell it to his girlfriend at an undervalue.

181 *Dora v Simper* [2000] 2 B.C.L.C. 561.

182 *Schmitt v Deichmann* [2013] Ch. 61.

183 *Clydesdale Financial Services Ltd v Smailes* [2009] EWHC 3190 (Ch) at [73]. A party who was not itself a creditor,

Additional provisions on bankruptcy

The Insolvency Act 1986 contains a number of further provisions that operate on the bankruptcy of a debtor and which enable the court to set aside transactions made at an undervalue (s.339)[184] or by way of preference (s.340).[185] The basic aim is to facilitate the trustee in bankruptcy in recovering the bankrupt's property for the benefit of creditors.[186] These provisions co-exist with those dealing with undervalue transactions independently of bankruptcy.[187] As will become clear, the two sets of provisions are similar, but are not identical. The trustee in bankruptcy will, however, usually prefer this route rather than instituting proceedings under s.423 because there is no need to show intention to defeat a creditor by an undervalue transaction.[188] As Miller comments of these provisions:

> **"They are an integral part of the insolvency code which is directed at securing *pari passu* distribution amongst the insolvent's creditors. They apply only to transactions within a limited period before insolvency and the intention of the insolvent is irrelevant. The rationale of s.423 . . . is quite different being directed at improper, if not dishonest, conduct by a debtor vis-a-vis a creditor or creditors".[189]**

The orders that can be made resemble those available under ss.423, 425 (see para.**16-019**) and the overarching goal is the same, that is, to restore the position to what it would have been had the transaction not taken place.[190] The treatment of third parties is similar, that is, no order can be made against a bona fide purchaser for value without notice.[191] There are, however, some differences between s.423 and the bankruptcy provisions. First, these provisions operate subsequent to the bankruptcy of the transferor. Secondly, they only allow an application to court by the trustee of the bankrupt's estate. Thirdly, they may only invalidate transactions that were entered into within specified periods prior to bankruptcy (this is known as the "relevant time"). Fourthly, and as mentioned above, in relation to an undervalue transaction there is no reference to any intention to be held by the transferor. Finally, whereas s.423(2) allows the

---

but could be subrogated to the creditor's claims against the transferor, might be regarded as a victim for these purposes.

184 See *Durkan v Patel* [2018] EWHC 3231 (Ch). In *Thomas v Rathore* [2018] B.P.I.R. 501, two transfers of shares from husband to wife were caught by s.339.

185 See *Abdulali v Finnegan* [2018] EWHC 1806 (Ch). There the repayment of a loan by a man who later became bankrupt was not a voidable preference because the requisite desire to prefer the lender was not present.

186 The trustee has 12 years within which to initiate a claim (s.8 of the Limitation Act 1980). It is thought that the period of 12 years runs not from the bankruptcy order, but from the later date when a trustee in bankruptcy is first appointed: *Stonham v Ramrattan* [2011] 1 W.L.R. 1617.

187 *Wood v Watkin* [2019] EWHC 1311 (Ch).

188 *Kavuma v Hunt* [2017] EWHC 3888 (Ch).

189 G. Miller, "Transactions Prejudicing Creditors" [1998] Conv. 362, 363, 364.

190 Insolvency Act 1986 s.342.

191 Insolvency Act 1986 s.342(2).

court to protect the interests of persons who are victims of the transaction, there is no equivalent provision in s.339.

Undervalue and creditor's preference

16-026   The meaning of "undervalue" is as considered above. This entails, for example, that a trustee in bankruptcy of the husband may claim the wife's share in the matrimonial home to the extent that she did not contribute towards its purchase.[192] The 1986 Act also caters for a property adjustment order made in divorce proceedings to be overturned by one party's trustee in bankruptcy.[193] This interaction between the matrimonial and insolvency courts was analysed in *Hill v Haines*,[194] where the divorce court ordered the husband to transfer his beneficial interest in the former matrimonial home to the wife. A bankruptcy order was subsequently made against the husband and the trustee sought to set aside the transaction as being at an undervalue. The Court of Appeal held that the now ex-wife had given consideration (i.e. her right to ancillary relief) and that it was to be assumed, in the absence of evidence as to collusion, that the award "is, prima facie, the measure of the value of the right".[195] The trustee was, therefore, unsuccessful. In *Re MC Bacon Ltd*,[196] the company granted a debenture in favour of its bank to secure an overdraft facility. Millett J refused to classify this as an undervalue transaction because the granting of the debenture was not a gift and, in any event, did not involve the company suffering any loss or parting with something of value.[197] As he noted, "That gives the game away. The applicant's real complaint is not that the company entered into the transaction at an undervalue but that it entered into it at all".[198]

A "preference" arises where the debtor places one of his creditors or a guarantor in a more favourable position, should the debtor's bankruptcy ensue, than would otherwise have been the case. Accordingly, it strikes at a transaction that improves the position of one creditor above those of others.[199] Section 340 allows the court to make any order as it thinks fit for restoring the position to what it was prior to the preference. For example, if the preference involves the transfer of money, the starting proposition is that the money should be returned by the recipient creditor.[200] It is a precondition that the debtor was influenced in deciding

---

192   *Re Densham* [1975] 1 W.L.R. 1519; *Stonham v Ramrattan* [2011] 1 W.L.R. 1617.

193   Insolvency Act 1986 Sch.14; see *Re Flint* [1993] Ch. 319. Such is, moreover, recognised in s.39 of the Matrimonial Causes Act 1973.

194   [2008] Ch. 412.

195   Sir Andrew Morritt [2008] Ch. 412 at [29].

196   [1990] B.C.L.C. 324.

197   See also *Doyle v Saville* [2002] B.P.I.R. 947.

198   [1990] B.C.L.C. 324 at 340.

199   An argument that a spouse under a property adjustment order should be classified as a creditor was rejected in *Re Jones* [2008] 2 F.L.R. 1969. The agreement reached between divorcing spouses was unenforceable without an order of the court and did not give rise to a liability.

200   *Re Oxford Pharmaceuticals Ltd* [2009] EWHC 1753 (Ch).

to give the preference by a desire to better the creditor's position in the event of the debtor's bankruptcy. It has been decided that, if the preferential transaction is entered into because of economic necessity, it is not to be regarded as being influenced by a desire to give the creditor a preference.[201] The requisite influence will, however, be presumed, unless the contrary is shown, where the preference is given to an "associate". For these purposes an "associate" includes family members, partners, employers, employees and related companies.[202]

Timing of the transaction: undervalue cases

16-027

As regards a transaction (including a preference) made at an undervalue, s.341 prescribes a two-tier time limit. First, it provides that the standard period is two years, which put simply means that, if a bankruptcy petition is presented within two years of an undervalue transaction, an order can be made in respect of it.

Secondly, an increased period of five years applies where the debtor was insolvent at the time of the transaction. For these purposes, "insolvency" is defined in s.341 as meaning either that the debtor is unable to pay his debts as they fall due or that the value of his assets is less than the amount of his existing liabilities. In *Tanner v Miller*, Sales J concluded that "the bankrupt did not have sufficient assets of his own to meet his liability to pay damages. He was therefore insolvent".[203] As regards the latter calculation, therefore, regard must be had to the debtor's possible and prospective liabilities. In relation to an undervalue transaction with an associate (see above), it is a rebuttable presumption that the debtor was insolvent at the time of the transaction (s.341(2)).

Timing of the transaction: giving a preference

16-028

In relation to a preference, different time limits apply.[204] The standard period afforded by s.341 is six months. Accordingly, the general rule is that the court can make an order concerning a preference (which is not also at an undervalue) given within the six months preceding the bankruptcy petition.

If the preference is given to an associate, the court can make an order relating to a preference given in the two years preceding the bankruptcy petition unless the individual was (discounting the property included in the preference) solvent at the time.

---

201 *Re MC Bacon Ltd* [1990] B.C.L.C. 324.
202 Insolvency Act 1986 s.435.
203 [2013] EWHC 750 (Ch) at [15]. He added at [15] that, "The fact that he had a generous friend . . . on hand who might have been prepared to help him (but had no legal obligation to do so) does not meet the point . . ".
204 For s.340 to apply, the preference must always be granted before the presentation of the bankruptcy petition: *Official Receiver v Bathurst* [2008] EWHC 2572 (Ch).

> ## Transactions by companies

16-029 The above provisions, which operate on bankruptcy, extend only to transactions by individuals. Similar provisions that apply to transactions by bodies corporate are to be found in ss.238 and 239 of the Insolvency Act 1986. There are, however, differences between the two sets of rules and these will now be considered.

As to undervalue transactions, s.238 limits the ability of the court to make an order. It states that no order will be made when the court is satisfied that the company entered into the transaction in good faith for the purpose of carrying out its business and, at the time, there were reasonable grounds for believing that the company would be benefited by the transaction.[205] The burden of proving that a transaction was entered into at an undervalue lies upon the applicant.[206] The consideration for the transaction is, moreover, valued as at the date of the transaction[207] and assuming the existence of a market for the asset.[208] The applicant does not, however, have to establish any intention to sell at an undervalue or other subjective element.[209]

In addition, a transaction may be set aside only if the company was unable to discharge its debts at the time of the transaction or became unable to do so as a consequence of the transaction. The time requirement here is that the transaction must have been entered within a period of two years prior to the insolvency of the company.

16-030 In relation to transactions by way of preference, under s.239 the general rule is that the preference must have been given within six months prior to the insolvency, but this period is enlarged to two years if the preference was given to a party connected with the company. As with transactions at an undervalue, the transaction will be unravelled only if the company was unable to pay its debts at the time it was entered or ceased to be able to do so because of the transaction.

Family Claims

16-031 In the same way as a debtor might seek to transfer property in order to put it beyond the reach of creditors, it is possible that a transaction is designed to place property outside the grasp of a spouse or other dependant. Statutory restrictions have, not surprisingly, been imposed on the ability of a transferor to avoid maintenance and to sterilise her estate against claims for financial provision. Two incursions upon the freedom of a property owner to deal with property are

---

205 See *Clements v Henry Hadaway Organisation Ltd* [2007] EWHC 2953 (Ch).
206 *Stone & Rolls Ltd v Micro Communications Inc* [2005] EWHC 1052 (Ch).
207 *Phillips v Brewin Dolphin* [2001] W.L.R. 143.
208 *Ailyan and Fry (Trustees in Bankruptcy of Kevin Foster) v Smith* [2010] B.P.I.R. 289.
209 *Stanley v TMK Finance Ltd* [2010] EWHC 3349 (Ch).

to be found in the Matrimonial Causes Act 1973 and the Inheritance (Provision for Family and Dependants) Act 1975. The former, as the name suggests, applies to claims made in the course of matrimonial proceedings. The latter concerns the rights of dependants upon the death of the person who provided for them.

Section 37 of the Matrimonial Causes Act 1973

Section 37 protects one spouse (including a former spouse) against dealings by the other that may deplete the assets available for the funding of financial relief under the 1973 Act.[210] It was designed as a divorce centred, statutory alternative to the equitable right to seek rescission procured by misrepresentation. As Purchas LJ acknowledged in *Kemmis v Kemmis*, "The clear purpose of s.37 is to give a power to the court to prevent a party acting to diminish the assets of the family which would otherwise be available for consideration by the court when making orders for financial relief".[211] If the transaction has not yet been made, the court can prevent it taking place (i.e. by making a freezing order).[212] This is so even if the property is situated abroad. In *Hamlin v Hamlin*, for example, the property was a villa in Spain.[213] If the transaction has occurred, the transaction is classified as a "reviewable disposition" and may be set aside by the court.[214] If there is no disposition, the jurisdiction is not, of course, engaged.[215]

As considered by Mostyn J in *AC v DC*,[216] there are several qualifications to the operation of s.37. First, an application under s.37 can be made only after proceedings for financial relief have been commenced. The s.37 jurisdiction ceases to be available if, say, the other spouse dies before an order for financial relief has been made.[217] Nevertheless, it can catch transactions that were made at an earlier date.

Secondly, the court may intervene when one spouse is to make or has made a transfer or other disposition of property[218] (e.g. a declaration of a trust)[219] with the subjective intention of

16-032

16-033

---

210 This also applies to registered partnerships under the Civil Partnership Act 2004.
211 [1988] 1 W.L.R. 1307 at 1315. There the issue was whether the husband had procured a mortgage over the matrimonial home with the intention of defeating the wife's claim for financial relief.
212 See *Chaudhri v Shafi* [2019] EWHC 1272 (Fam).
213 [1985] 2 All E.R. 1037.
214 As in *Everclear Ltd v Agrest* [2011] EWCA Civ 232, where a $5 million transaction entered into by the husband in favour of a former business associate and designed to leave the ex-wife destitute was set aside under the similar provisions (dealing with foreign divorces) contained in s.23 of the Matrimonial and Family Proceedings Act 1984.
215 *Read v Panzone* [2019] EWCA Civ 1662.
216 [2012] EWHC 2032 (Fam).
217 *Cadogan v Cadogan* [1977] 1 W.L.R. 1041. The surviving spouse would be able to pursue a claim under s.10 of the Inheritance (Provision for Family and Dependants) Act 1975.
218 This would not include where one joint tenant has served a notice to quit on the landlord to terminate the joint tenancy: *Newlon Housing Trust v Alsulaimen* [1999] 1 A.C. 313. This expired notice was not a disposition of property.
219 Matrimonial Causes Act 1973 s.37(6).

reducing the capital source from which financial relief can be awarded (s.37(1)).[220] The requisite intention will be presumed when the transaction occurs within three years preceding the application for financial relief (s.37(5)). It is then up to the transferor to rebut this evidential presumption.[221] Outside the three-year period, however, the applicant must prove affirmatively that this was the other spouse's subjective intention. This motive does not, however, have to be the dominant motive in the transaction and will suffice even if it was a subsidiary (but material) motive.[222] In *Kemmis v Kemmis*, Purchas LJ observed that, although there is no limit as to the retrospective effect of s.37, the task of showing the necessary intention "will become increasingly difficult with the passage of time".[223]

Thirdly, the execution of the charge had the consequence of defeating, frustrating or impeding the claim to relief in whole or in part (s.37(1)) and the court feels it appropriate to exercise its discretion to set aside the charge (s.37(2)). In *AC v DC*, for example, the court set aside the transaction because it was fair and just to do so and as, if it had not done so, "the very vice that s.37 is directed towards would be given full rein".[224] Mostyn J explained that "'Avoidance' is the language of nullity not of repayment or revesting. Etymologically it refers to the concept of 'voidity'".[225]

Fourthly, and by way of an exception to the general rule that all dispositions are liable to be set aside, s.37(4) offers a defence to a third party caught in the cross-fire between husband and wife.[226] In this way a s.37 order "can co-exist with the preservation of subsequently completed transactions entered into in good faith".[227] This provides that a transaction cannot be set aside when made for valuable consideration (other than marriage) to a bona fide purchaser without notice of any intention to defeat the matrimonial claim.[228] For these purposes the concept of "notice" embraces the actual, constructive and imputed varieties.[229] The onus of proof lies on the third party to demonstrate that the ingredients of this defence are satisfied.[230] In *Green v Green*[231] the husband and wife sold part of the grounds of their matrimonial home to a company which, in turn, charged the land to a bank as security for certain advances. She received no part of the proceeds of sale. The marriage broke down and the wife sought financial relief. She applied to have the transfer to the company set aside

---

220 In *Akhmedova v Akhmedov* [2018] EWFC 23 (Fam), the court set aside transactions designed by a husband to conceal assets in off-shore companies to evade enforcement of ancillary financial relief orders.

221 See *Shipman v Shipman* [1991] 1 F.L.R. 250.

222 *Lazard Brothers and Co (Jersey) Ltd v Norah Holdings Ltd* [1988] 1 W.L.R. 1307.

223 [1988] 1 W.L.R. 1307 at 1315.

224 [2012] EWHC 2032 (Fam) at [12].

225 [2012] EWHC 2032 (Fam) at [18]. Mostyn J stated at [13] that the s.37 order had the legal effect of nulling the transaction *ab initio*, "so that for all legal (including fiscal purposes) they are treated as never having happened . . .".

226 See J. Fortin, "Can She Avoid His Diverting Ploys" [1989] Conv. 204.

227 *AC v DC* [2012] EWHC 2032 (Fam) at [23].

228 *Ansari v Ansari* [2010] Fam. 1.

229 *Kemmis v Kemmis* [1998] 1 W.L.R. 1307.

230 *AC v DC* [2012] EWHC 2032 (Fam).

231 [1981] 1 All E.R. 97.

under s.37. As the bank had no notice of the husband's intention, the court refused to set aside the transaction and to deprive the bank of its statutory defence.[232] By way of contrast, in *Sherry v Sherry*[233] a friend of the husband bought several properties at an undervalue. The purchaser knew that the couple were experiencing marital difficulties and that the husband feared that the wife would lay claim to his property. The purchaser was held to have constructive notice of the husband's intention and could not, therefore, rely upon the s.37(4) defence.[234] The moral of this case is that a third party who is aware of the matrimonial difficulties between husband and wife should make full enquiries of the other spouse before dealing with the selling spouse. Similarly, in *Everclear Ltd v Agrest*, the purchaser knew of the matrimonial order before completing the purchase and this prompted Sir Nicholas Wall to conclude that "the edifice of the *bona fide* purchaser evaporates, and it was open for the judge to set the purchase aside".[235]

The Inheritance (Provision for Family and Dependants) Act 1975

16-034

In order to ensure that a surviving spouse or registered partner and/or surviving dependants are provided for, the 1975 Act gives the court a broad, discretionary jurisdiction to make an award to an applicant.[236] Section 2 empowers the court to allocate part of the deceased's estate to make reasonable financial provision[237] for a surviving spouse or registered partner, former spouse or registered partner who has not remarried or entered into a new registered partnership,[238] cohabitant,[239] child (which under the Inheritance and Trustees' Powers Act 2014 includes anyone treated by the deceased as a child of his or her family outside the context of a marriage or civil partnership) and any other person who was, at the time of the death,

232 In *Ansari v Ansari* [2010] Fam. 1, the third-party bank was not part of any conspiracy and did not even know of the husband's intention to defeat the wife's claims.
233 (1991) 1 F.L.R. 307.
234 See J. Fortin, "The Diversions of a Fugitive Husband" [1991] Conv. 370.
235 [2011] EWCA Civ 232 at [11]. As Sedley LJ added in the course of argument, "he bought a pig in a poke, the English law as I read it, does not entitle him on the facts of this case to retain it" (at [28]).
236 See generally, C. Sachs [1985] Conv. 258; C. Sachs [1990] Conv. 45. Section 4 imposes a time limit of 6 months from the date that personal representatives are appointed, but this is readily extended by the courts: see *Cowan v Foreman* [2020] 2 W.L.R. 61. In *Re Bhustate* [2019] EWHC 470 (Ch), for example, the claim was nearly 26 years out of time, but the application was still allowed.
237 Reasonableness is adjudged by reference to the needs of the applicant for maintenance and by reference to the standard appropriate to the circumstances: *Barkatali v Davies* [2020] EWHC 753 (Ch).
238 This is qualified by s.15 (as amended) which allows the court to order in "clean break" matrimonial proceedings that a spouse shall not make a claim on the death of the other spouse. This also applies to registered partnerships.
239 Provided that they have lived in the same household for the two years preceding death. In *Barkatali v Davies* [2020] EWHC 753 (Ch), no provision for maintenance was deemed necessary as the claimant had an income entirely satisfactory to meet his needs.

maintained wholly or partly by the deceased.[240] The court is directed by s.3 to a number of factors which it must take into account. These include: the present and future financial resources and needs of the applicant; any obligations and responsibilities which the deceased owed to the applicant; the size and nature of the estate; the conduct of the parties and any physical and mental disability of the applicant. Baroness Hale in *Ilott v The Blue Cross* added that, "One factor which is not in the list, but which does feature elsewhere in family law, is the public interest in family members discharging their responsibilities towards one another so that these do not fall upon the state".[241] The order will override the provisions of the will or the operation of the intestacy rules. In *Re Ubbi*,[242] for example, a lump sum of £386,290 was ordered to be paid to two young children by way of reasonable financial provision from the estate of their late father, who had made a will before they were born which made no provision for them. In *Thompson v Raggett*[243] a couple had cohabited for 42 years and the claimant (who was 79 years old, in ill-health and with very modest savings) had been financially and physically dependent on her deceased partner. The deceased's estate was valued at £1.5 million and she was awarded the outright transfer of a cottage (worth £225,000), plus a monetary award (£160,000) to cover outgoings, maintenance and renovations.

Oliver J described the approach that the court should adopt and stated that "these matters have to be considered at two stages—first in determining the reasonableness of such provision (if any) as has been made by the deceased for the applicant's maintenance and, secondly, in determining the extent to which the court should exercise its powers under the Act if, but only if, it is satisfied that reasonable provision for the applicant's maintenance has not been made".[244] As Lord Hughes emphasised in *Ilott v The Blue Cross*, "The test of reasonable financial provision is objective; it is not simply whether the deceased behaved reasonably or otherwise in leaving the will he did, or in choosing to leave none. Although the reasonableness of his decisions may figure in the exercise, that is not the crucial test".[245] In *Cattle v Evans*,[246] for example, Ms Cattle sought reasonable provision from the estate of her late partner Mr Evans, who died intestate. The couple had enjoyed a long-standing relationship and had planned their future together. No provision whatsoever had been made for Ms Cattle who was now 60 years of age, unemployed and in receipt only of a small income. In contrast, the deceased's children were self-supporting adults without any particular financial needs. The judge concluded that she reasonably required a property in which to live and ordered the estate to purchase a new property to the value of £110,000. The property purchased was to be

---

240 See S. Bridge, "Money for Nothing? Family Provision in Dire Straits" (1991) C.L.J. 42. The claim does not, however, survive the death of a potential applicant: *Roberts v Fresco* [2017] Ch. 433.

241 [2017] UKSC 17 at [63]. This case concerned a deceased mother making no testamentary provision for her long estranged, adult daughter (who was in straitened financial circumstances and on benefits) and leaving the majority of her estate to various animal welfare charities.

242 [2018] EWHC 1396 (Ch).

243 [2018] EWHC 688 (Ch).

244 *Re Coventry* [1980] 1 Ch. 461 at 469; affirmed on appeal [1980] 1 Ch. 478.

245 [2017] UKSC 17 at [2].

246 [2011] EWHC 945 (Ch).

held on trust for the deceased's children, subject to a life interest in favour of Ms Cattle. In other instances, a transfer of land or the payment of an appropriate sum from the estate may be the solution promoted by the court.[247] As Lord Hughes pointed out in *Ilott v The Blue Cross*, "It will very often be more appropriate, as well as cheaper and more convenient for other beneficiaries and for executors, if income is provided by way of a lump sum from which both income and capital can be drawn over the years".[248]

Sections 10 and 11 of the 1975 Act cater for the possibility that the deceased may have given away property prior to death with the intention of not providing for his spouse (or registered partner) and dependants. The Act puts in place anti-avoidance machinery by giving the court the power to require the donee to make available a sum of money up to, but not in excess of, the value of the gift received.[249] Except as to cash, the valuation is at the date of the death of the donor. This power, however, arises only when the gift was made within six years before the donor's death and was made with the intention of defeating an application for financial provision under the 1975 Act.[250] This intention, which need not be the donor's sole or dominant motive, must be demonstrated before the statutory machinery can be employed.[251] In *Re Dawkins*,[252] a husband left his entire estate to his daughter. Indeed, he had transferred the matrimonial home to her for £100 during his lifetime. His widow made a successful claim under the 1975 Act. As Bush J concluded, when the deceased transferred to house to his daughter, "he did so with the intention, though not necessarily the sole intention, of preventing an order for financial provision being made under the Act, or reducing the amount of the provision which might otherwise have been granted . . .".[253]

Guide to Further Reading

J. Fortin, "Can She Avoid His Diverting Ploys" [1989] Conv. 204.

J. Fortin, "The Diversions of a Fugitive Husband" [1991] Conv. 370.

J. Goudkamp, "The End of an Era? Illegality in Private Law in the Supreme Court" (2017) 133 L.Q.R. 14.

---

247 *Williams v Seals* [2014] EWHC 3708 (Ch).
248 [2017] UKSC 17 at [15].
249 This is a different ethos to that considered above in the context of s.37 of the Matrimonial Causes Act 1973. As Mostyn J noted in *AC v DC* [2012] EWHC 2032 (Fam) at [18], "the draftsman of s.10 of the 1975 Act expressly did not want a reversing transaction to operate as an avoidance *ab initio* . . ".
250 Inheritance (Provision for Family and Dependants) Act 1975 s.10(2).
251 Inheritance (Provision for Family and Dependants) Act 1975 s.12.
252 [1986] 2 F.L.R. 360.
253 [1986] 2 F.L.R. 360 at 366.

A. Grabiner, "Illegality and Restitution Explained by the Supreme Court" (2017) 76(1) C.L.J. 18.

A. Keay, "Transactions Defrauding Creditors: The Problem of Purpose under s.423 of the Insolvency Act" [2003] Conv. 272.

G. Miller, "Transactions Prejudicing Creditors" [1998] Conv. 362.

L.A. Sheridan, "Trusts for Paying Debts" (1957) 21 Conv. 280.

G. Virgo, "*Patel v Mirza*: one step forward and two steps back" (2016) 22(10) T. & T. 1090.

17

Breach of Trust and Associated Remedies

Breach of Trust

As considered in Ch.13, a trustee assumes a range of duties and responsibilities, breach of which exposes her to liability in an action by the beneficiary. This chapter focuses on possible breaches of duty and the range of remedies that a beneficiary may pursue of both a personal and proprietary nature. Analysis of the case law on breach of trust will produce many examples of breach in a variety of different circumstances. It is difficult, therefore, to lay down any exhaustive list of possible breaches that will give rise to trustee liability. Confronted with this difficulty in *Armitage v Nurse*, Millett LJ explained:

> "Breaches of trust are of many different kinds. A breach of trust may be deliberate or inadvertent; it may consist of an actual misappropriation or misapplication of the trust property or merely of an investment or other dealing which is outside the trustees' powers; it may consist of a failure to carry out a positive obligation of the trustees or merely of a want of skill and care on their part in the management of the trust property; it may be injurious to the interests of the beneficiaries or be actually to their benefit".[1]

It is important to distinguish between different types of breach of trust because the nature of the breach will determine the available claims or responses that are open to the beneficiary.

---

1   [1997] 3 W.L.R. 1046 at 1053.

There are three principal types.[2] The first involves some misapplication of trust money or property, such as an unauthorised investment, misappropriation or mistaken payment away. Here the trustee is simply not permitted to deal with the property in that way and it causes a loss to the trust. The second involves the breach of a duty of loyalty where the trustee makes a profit at the expense of the trust. The third concerns a failure to do something or do something properly; it involves a negligent or careless course of action. Concerned about the stewardship of the trust, the beneficiary may call for an account to be taken. Where a breach of trust can be established, the beneficiary will look to the trustee to account for profits or compensate for loss. As Chief Master Marsh explained in *Henchley v Thompson*, "It is *possible* that claims for breach of trust might follow from the provision of an account but, in the first instance, the beneficiaries will be better off than they were before by having obtained information about the trust assets which they did not previously possess".[3]

Taking an account

17-002

The starting point in understanding a trustee's liability lies in the trustee's obligation to account for her stewardship of the trust.[4] As Lindley LJ commented in *Low v Bouverie*, "The duty of the trustee is properly to preserve the trust fund, . . . and to give all his *cestuis que trust* on demand information with respect to the mode in which the trust fund has been dealt with and where it is".[5] A beneficiary's challenge to the account is known as "falsifying" or "surcharging" the account. To falsify is to show that an entry is erroneous and to disallow the payment away.[6] Surcharging is concerned with the omission of an entry which should be included. The trustee is under a duty to correct such errors. As Millett explained (in an extrajudicial capacity):

> "If the beneficiary is dissatisfied with the way in which the trustee has carried out his trust—if, for example, he considers that the trustee has negligently failed to obtain all that he should have done for the benefit of the trust estate, then he may surcharge the account. He does this by requiring that the account be taken on the footing of wilful default . . . The trustee is made to account, not only for what he has in fact received, but also for what he might with due diligence have received . . .".[7]

---

2   See *Auden McKenzie (Pharma Division) Ltd v Patel* [2019] EWCA Civ 2021 at [31] per David Richards LJ.
3   [2017] EWHC 225 (Ch) at [35].
4   "The taking of an account is the means by which a beneficiary requires the trustee to justify his stewardship of trust property" (*Ultraframe (UK) Ltd v Fielding* [2005] EWHC 1638 (Ch) at [1513] per Lewison J).
5   [1891] 3 Ch. 82 at 99. In *Walker v Walker* [2007] All E.R. 418, Deputy Judge Roger Kaye QC explained that the trustee must "keep accounts, provide them when required and provide to the beneficiaries all reasonable information as to the manner in which the trust estate has been dealt with".
6   See *Bonham v Blake Lapthorn Linell* [2006] EWHC 2513 (Ch) at [180].
7   P. Millett, "Equity's Place in the Law of Commerce" (1998) 114 L.Q.R. 214, 224 (Sweet & Maxwell).

In cases of misapplication, however,

> "he falsifies the account, that is to say, he asks for the disbursement to be disallowed. If, for example, the trustee lays out trust money on an unauthorised investment which falls in value, the beneficiary will falsify the account by asking the court to disallow both the disbursement and the corresponding asset on the other side of the account. The unauthorised investment will then be treated as having been bought with the trustee's own money and on his own behalf. He will be required to account to the trust estate for the full amount of the disbursement—*not* for the amount of the loss. That is what is meant by saying that the trustee is liable to restore the trust property . . .".[8]

Whether the account is falsified (and the trustee must restore the value of the misapplied assets) or surcharged (made liable for what the trust might have received had the trustee acted diligently[9]), the trustee must restore the trust estate or compensate the trust for any losses incurred. Not every breach, however, will result in a financial loss to the beneficiary. Consider, for example, a trustee who misapplies trust property in a lucrative investment. In such a case, the beneficiary may well be content with it. Again, as Millet explained:

> "[The beneficiary] is not obliged to falsify the account which the trustee renders; he can always accept it. (It goes without saying that the trustee cannot simply 'borrow' the trust money to make a profitable investment for his own account and then rely on the fact that the investment was unauthorised to avoid bringing the transaction into the account. He must account for what he has done with the trust money, not merely for what he has properly done with it). Where the beneficiary accepts the unauthorised investment, he is often said to affirm or adopt the transaction. That is not wholly accurate. The beneficiary has a right to elect, but it is really a right to decide whether to complain or not".[10]

17-003

It is conceivable, moreover, that a claimant may have two potential avenues of redress, from which one remedy must be elected. In *Tang Man Sit (Personal Representatives) v Capacious Investments Ltd*,[11] for example, it was open to the claimant to seek an account of profits from rents paid for the occupation of 16 properties or, alternatively, equitable compensation for the

---

8   P. Millett, "Equity's Place in the Law of Commerce" (1998) 114 L.Q.R. 214, 224.
9   Described by Deputy Judge Jules Sher QC in *Coulthard v Disco Mix Ltd* [2000] 1 W.L.R. 707 at 734 as "a roving inquiry as to what, but for his negligence or fraud, the defendant should have received".
10   P. Millett, "Equity's Place in the Law of Commerce" (1998) 114 L.Q.R. 214, 226.
11   [1996] 1 All E.R. 193.

simultaneous loss sustained as a result of the deterioration and use of those properties and the claimant being deprived of it. As Lord Nicholls explained,

> "Faced with alternative and inconsistent remedies a plaintiff must choose, or elect, between them. He cannot have both ... He is required to choose when, but not before, judgment is given in his favour and the judge is asked to make orders against the defendant ... the court should not make orders which would afford a plaintiff both of two alternative remedies".[12]

17-004

It is clear that the personal liability of the trustee is an important and immediate avenue for redress for a beneficiary; it may prove the only available source of redress in the circumstances. It may also prove to be one of a variety of claims that may be pursued on the facts of a particular case. Alternative options must be considered, say, where the trustee is insolvent as, here, a personal claim against the trustee will be fruitless.[13] As will be discussed in this chapter, many of the cases involve the misappropriation of trust property and the beneficiary may prefer to pursue a proprietary claim to recover the assets or their traceable proceeds. The significance of the choice between personal and proprietary remedies came to the fore in *FHR European Ventures LLP v Cedar Capital Partners LLC*.[14] This case concerned a secret commission obtained by an agent while brokering the sale of a Monte Carlo hotel. This was, of course, a breach of fiduciary duty wherein the agent became liable to account to its principal. It fell to the court to determine, however, whether the claimant was confined to its personal remedy (equitable compensation to a sum equivalent to the commission) or may be permitted, instead, a proprietary claim to the property (and any proceeds) in the hands of a third party. Lord Neuberger considered the divergent approaches in the case law but decided in the end that bribes and secret commissions accepted by an agent must be held on trust for his principal. A proprietary claim was open to the claimant.

Equitable Compensation

17-005

Having considered the traditional means by which the beneficiary obtains a remedy, it is necessary to look more closely at the modern approach to explaining and calculating equitable

---

12   [1996] 1 All E.R. 193 at 197.
13   As has been discussed in Ch.10, a personal action may be available against third parties who are liable in equity when they knowingly receive trust property or dishonestly assist in a breach of trust.
14   [2015] A.C. 250.

compensation.[15] Again, it is essential to pay attention to the type of breach committed. The label "equitable compensation" is "used to encompass remedies of distinctly different types"[16] and is, for that reason, apt to confuse.[17]

Where trust property is paid away or invested without authority and a loss occurs (the "misapplication" type of breach), the immediate duty of the trustee is to restore the trust property (i.e. make specific restitution). Where this is not possible, the trustee must pay a money sum equivalent to the value of the property misapplied, or, as Millett puts it, "account to the trust estate for the full amount of the disbursement".[18] This is not compensation for loss, as such, but an award which "compels performance in money of the trustee's primary obligation to maintain the trust fund and disburse it in an authorised manner".[19] Edelman and Elliott prefer the term "substitutive compensation" for this type of claim. The amount claimed is the "objective value of the property which the trustees should be able to produce".[20]

By contrast, in cases where the trustee has failed to safeguard the value of the trust (through negligence or some omission), the trustee is made liable to compensate for losses. This compensation is calculated by reference to what the trustee might with due diligence have obtained for the benefit of the trust. The remedy, as Edelman and Elliott explain, is not offered by way of, "substitutively enforcing the performance of the trustee's primary duties. Rather, compensatory damages require the trustee to make good losses occasioned by his breach of trust. The compensation is reparative rather than substitutive in nature".[21]

It makes sense that compensation for losses caused by a failure to exercise care and skill might be comparable to damages at common law. As Millett LJ argued in *Bristol & West Building Society v Motthew,*

> **"Equitable compensation for breach of the duty of skill and care resembles common law damages in that it is awarded by way of compensation to the plaintiff for his loss. There is no reason in principle why the common law rules of causation, remoteness of damage and measure of damages should not be applied by analogy in such a case".[22]**

---

15 In *Creggy v Barnett* [2016] EWCA Civ 1004 at [22] Patten LJ referred to the modern tendency to seek equitable compensation for breach, "without going through the cumbersome and often extremely lengthy process of taking an account".

16 S. Elliott, J. Edelman, "Money Remedies Against Trustees" (2004) 18 Tru. L. I. 116, 116.

17 As David Richards L.J. noted in *Interactive Technology Corp Ltd v Ferster* [2018] EWCA Civ 1594, "Equitable compensation is apt to include a payment made to restore to a claimant the value of assets or funds removed without authority by a trustee or other fiduciary, such as a director. It may also include reparation for losses".

18 P. Millett, "Equity's Place in the Law of Commerce" (1998) 114 L.Q.R. 214, 224.

19 S. Elliott, J. Edelman, "Money Remedies Against Trustees" (2004) 18 Tru. L. I. 116, 118.

20 D. Hayton, P. Matthews & C. Mitchell (eds), *Underhill and Hayton: Law Relating to Trusts and Trustees*, 19th edn (London: LexisNexis Butterworths, 2016), para.87.11.

21 S. Elliott, J. Edelman, "Money Remedies Against Trustees" (2004) 18 Tru. L. I. 116, 119.

22 [1998] Ch. 1 at 17.

Millett LJ was also keen to warn that equitable compensation in this regard was not to be confused with equitable compensation for breach of fiduciary duty. As he made clear, "The expression 'fiduciary duty' is properly confined to those duties which are peculiar to fiduciaries and the breach of which attracts legal consequences differing from those consequent upon the breach of other duties".[23] Accordingly, "not every breach of duty by a fiduciary is a breach of fiduciary duty".[24]

Traditional principles and the modern context

17-006
In *Target Holdings Ltd v Redferns*,[25] Lord Browne-Wilkinson was required to consider the basis and measure of equitable compensation arising from a commercial conveyancing transaction in which the defendant solicitors had misapplied trust property. He took the opportunity to forge a distinction between the application of rules to traditional trusts where an account may be falsified (and the trust "restored"), and the response required to a breach of trust that arises in the course of a fleeting, modern commercial transaction. He did so by introducing the element of causation to limit compensation to losses caused by the breach. In this context, he claimed, "Equitable compensation for breach of trust is designed to achieve exactly what the word compensation suggests: to make good a loss in fact suffered by the beneficiaries and which, using hindsight and common sense, can be seen to have been caused by the breach".[26] His speech has been regarded as the "highest authority for the proposition that, in order to recover equitable compensation, the trustee must show actual loss caused by the breach".[27]

It is instructive to consider the facts to which the Court of Appeal and the House of Lords responded with divergent approaches. Target Holdings (a mortgage lender) sought to provide a loan of around £1.7 million to Crowngate secured against a property it believed to be valued at £2 million. Target Holdings paid loan moneys to Redferns solicitors on trust to facilitate the acquisition. In breach of trust, Redferns paid away the sums received contrary to the instructions from its lender client. The money was not paid to Crowngate, but to an intermediary company. In due course, however, the transaction was completed as intended and Target Holdings received a charge over the property as security for the loan. Unfortunately, however, the value of the property had been artificially inflated by the series of sales between the connected companies. Crowngate became insolvent and, on enforcing its security, Target Holdings discovered that the property was worth only a fraction of the original loan. Instead of the expected value of £2 million, sale achieved only £500,000. Target Holdings brought proceedings against Redferns claiming their net loss of £1.2 million.

17-007
The Court of Appeal identified a breach of trust occurring when Redferns made an improper

---

23 [1998] Ch. 1 at 16.
24 [1998] Ch. 1 at 16.
25 [1996] 1 A.C. 421.
26 [1996] 1 A.C. 421 at 439.
27 *Re Ahmed (A Debtor)* [2018] EWCA Civ 519 at [35] per Gloster LJ.

and unauthorised payment of trust moneys to the intermediary company (i.e. a stranger to the trust). As a result, the trust estate suffered an immediate loss. Subsequent events, which reduced the loss suffered, were irrelevant save for imposing on the claimant an obligation to discount any benefit it subsequently received. The Court of Appeal drew a distinction between a case of administrative failure (where it is necessary to wait to establish what loss, if any, is occasioned by the breach)[28] and the case of a wrongful payment of trust moneys to a third party. As regards the latter, the appellate court held that "there is an immediate loss, placing the trustee under an immediate duty to restore the moneys to the trust fund".[29] Accordingly, the Court of Appeal held that no inquiry was necessary to establish whether the loss would have resulted notwithstanding the breach of trust.

The House of Lords reversed the Court of Appeal decision on the basis that the defendant was liable to pay equitable compensation for the losses caused by his breach measured at the date of judgment and with the benefit of hindsight. As the lender had got precisely what it would have received had there been no breach of trust, it was not entitled to compensation because it had suffered, "no compensatable loss" flowing from the breach.[30] It was clear that the transaction would have gone ahead even if there had been no breach of trust. Accordingly, there was no causal link between the breach and the loss occasioned. It was not possible, as the Court of Appeal had held, to "stop the clock" at the date the moneys were paid away and ignore events that occurred between the date of breach and the date of trial.

As regards the approach adopted in *Target Holdings*, it is worthy of comment that Lord Browne-Wilkinson endeavoured to forge a distinction between principles of trust law (developed in the context of traditional trusts) and those principles that might be employed in relation to bare trusts in the commercial context. He emphasised that, in *Target Holdings*, the solicitors held money on bare trust for their client as part of a conveyancing transaction. This had the consequence that following the breach there was no sense in restoring the trust estate. Rather, the appropriate remedy was the payment of compensation to the beneficiary. He warned that it is "wrong to lift wholesale the detailed rules developed in the context of traditional trusts and then seek to apply them to trusts of quite a different kind".[31] Emphasising that the trust has become an important device in commercial and financial dealings, he claimed, "it is important, if the trust is not to be rendered commercially useless, to distinguish between the basic principles of trust law and those specialist rules developed in relation to traditional trusts which are applicable only to such trusts and the rationale of which has no application to trusts of quite a different kind".[32]

The apparent scope of the *Target Holdings* causation principles excited some debate. Nolan, for example, argued that the case had "not done a great deal to clarify the rules of causation employed in equity".[33] A similar confusion was expressed by Sir Peter Millett, when

17-008

---

28   The assessment of compensation takes place at the date of trial.
29   [1994] 1 W.L.R. 1089 at 1103, per Peter Gibson LJ.
30   Per Lord Browne-Wilkinson [1996] 1 A.C. 421 at 440.
31   [1996] 1 A.C. 421 at 435.
32   [1996] 1 A.C. 421 at 435.
33   R. Nolan, "A Targeted Degree of Liability" [1996] L.M.C.L.Q. 161, 164.

he objected that, "It is difficult to know what to make of this . . . Is it seriously to be supposed that the result in *Target Holdings Ltd v Redferns* would be different if the trust in question had been a traditional trust?"[34] Indeed, Millett puts forward the proposition that the *Target Holdings* case might have been decided on the basis of the trustee's liability to account, that is, the unauthorised use of the trust money entitled the claimant to falsify the account.[35] In any event, the defendant solicitors were to comply, eventually, with their instructions and obtain the authorised security. If Millett's approach had been applied, the outcome would have been the same as that reached by Lord Browne-Wilkinson albeit via a different, more palatable route. As Millett explained:

> "The plaintiff could not object to the acquisition of the mortgage or the disbursement by which it was obtained; it was an author-ised application of what must be treated as trust money notionally restored to the trust estate on the taking of the account. To put the point another way; the trustee's obligation to restore the trust property is not an obligation to restore it in the very form in which he disbursed it, but an obligation to restore it in any form authorised by the trust".[36]

17-009

The Supreme Court looked again at the application of the *Target* principles in *AIB Group (UK) Plc v Redler & Co Solicitors*.[37] This case concerned Mr and Mrs Sondhi whose home was valued at £4.5m. It was subject to an existing mortgage (in favour of Barclays Bank) and their out-standing indebtedness was £1.5m. The couple sought to remortgage and approached AIB for a loan of some £3.3m. AIB agreed, provided that the pre-existing mortgage was redeemed and that AIB obtain a first charge executed in their favour. Redler and Co Solicitors acted for both the borrower and the lender. They contacted Barclays to obtain an exact redemption figure, but were negligent in noting a lesser sum as representing the total required to discharge the debt to Barclays. In due course, the solicitors paid that sum to Barclays and, minus expenses and costs, the remainder to the borrowers. The borrowers executed what was meant to be a first legal charge in favour of AIB but, eventually, AIB had no option but to recognise Barclays' prior charge and to seek registration as a second mortgagee. When the borrowers defaulted, Barclay's exercised its power of sale. The property sold for only £1.2m. AIB received only £868,000.

Both parties purported to follow *Target*. The solicitors argued that the loss should be cal-culated by reference to the position the Bank would have been in had the solicitors not been in breach. The actual loss caused by their negligence was confined to £275,000, that is, the sum

---

34   P. Millett (1998) 114 L.Q.R. 214, 224 (Sweet & Maxwell).
35   No argument to this effect was considered (proceedings were, in fact, brought for professional negligence as the claimant only later became aware of the breach of trust).
36   (1998) 114 L.Q.R. 214 at 217.
37   [2014] UKSC 58.

it failed to set aside to fully discharge Barclay's prior charge. AIB, however, argued that it was entitled to recover some £2.5m, the full amount of its loan minus what it received on sale. It argued on the basis that the primary entitlement of the claimant was to the reconstitution of the trust in full, an entitlement which must endure until the transaction was completed. The transaction, it felt, was never completed.

The Supreme Court dismissed the Bank's appeal. Although equitable compensation is designed to restore to the claimant what has been lost as a result of the breach, the idea is to restore the trust fund to the position it would have been in had the trustee performed its obligations.[38] With the benefit of hindsight, only part of the £3.3m had been misapplied. The solicitors could not be deemed responsible for the depreciation in market value of the property as in all common sense this loss could not have been seen to be caused by the breach.

Albeit glossing over the clear distinction between the circumstances in *Target* and those before the court,[39] the Supreme Court endorsed the approach in *Target*, that equitable compensation involves making good only that loss which, using hindsight and common sense, can be seen to be caused by the breach. The principles in *Target* and *Redler* have been much criticised,[40] but the language of causation and equitable compensation is now entrenched.

- In *Main v Giambrone & Law*,[41] the claimants were investors in a development to build luxury homes in Italy, which failed. The case concerned a claim against a firm of solicitors (Giambrone) for equitable compensation for loss arising from its wrongful payment away of the claimants' deposit monies, without the appropriate guarantees in place. The investors argued that they were entitled to compensation to the value of their lost deposits. Giambrone argued that the breach did not cause the loss as the collapse of the scheme did not trigger a pay-out under the terms of the guarantees. Its argument entailed that, had the guarantees been obtained, the claimant would still have lost their deposits. The Court of Appeal found for the investors, a result recognised by one commentator to be "more generous to the claimants than that reached in *Target* and *AIB*".[42] Focusing on the content of the firm's obligations, Jackson LJ drew a distinction between a duty to take positive steps (in Target, to secure a charge over the property; in AIB, to remove prior charges before releasing the money) with the duty of Giambrone which was one of custodianship, to do nothing until guarantees were

---

38 "[T]he amount of the award is measured by the objective value of the property lost determined at the date when the account is taken and with the benefit of hindsight", per Lord Millett NPJ in *Libertarian Investments Ltd v Hall* [2014] 1 HKC 368 at [168].

39 As Man Yip notes, "The precise effect of *AIB* is difficult to articulate. This is because notwithstanding the obvious differences between the reasoning in *Target Holdings* and *AIB*, the latter had unreservedly affirmed the former ("The Commercial Context in Trusts Law" [2016] Conv. 347, 362).

40 See for example, Lord Millett, who argues in "AIB v Redler" (2018) 32(1) Tru. L. I. 44, 44 that the Supreme Court "granted the wrong remedy and did not take the opportunity to revisit the unfortunate reasoning of the House of Lords in *Target Holdings v Redferns*".

41 [2017] EWCA Civ 1193.

42 P. Davies, "Equitable Compensation and the SAAMCO Principle" (2018) 134 L.Q.R. 165, 165.

produced. As Jackson LJ explained, "I would characterise the solicitors' obligation as an obligation to act as custodians of the deposit monies indefinitely. Compliant guarantees never appeared. Therefore Giambrone should have remained as custodians of the deposit monies until the preliminary contracts were rescinded, and then paid those monies back to their clients. In *Target* the plaintiff's claim failed on the "but for" test. In the present case the claimants' claim passes the "but for" test.[43]

- In *Auden McKenzie (Pharma Division) v Patel*,[44] the Court of Appeal considered whether in a claim for equitable compensation arising from a director's misappropriation of company funds, it was open to the director to argue that, had the misappropriation not taken place, those funds would have transferred lawfully to the same persons (himself and his sister) in the form of dividends. He sought to argue that the company had suffered no loss flowing from the breach. Richards LJ accepted that *Target* and *AIB* "are of great importance because of the qualification that they introduced to the previously strict application of the obligation of a trustee to restore to the trust fund the value of any assets transferred".[45] Nonetheless, in ascertaining the loss suffered he could not take into consideration the effect that "hypothetical intervening events might have had on the claimant's "loss".[46] The hypothetical dividends had not been paid; neither were directors obliged to pay them.

A selection of further illustrations

17-010

Having considered the modern approach of the courts to the calculation of equitable compensation, it is finally necessary to consider a range of specific situations and subsidiary rules as may be gleaned from the case law. These include:

(i) making unauthorised investments;

(ii) improper retention of trust property;

(iii) failure to invest;

(iv) interest; and

(v) set-off of profit against loss.

----

43   [2017] EWCA Civ 1193 at [62].
44   [2019] EWCA Civ 2291.
45   [2019] EWCA Civ 2291 at [38].
46   [2019] EWCA Civ 2291 at [51].

(i)   making unauthorised investments

Trustees involved in the purchase of unauthorised investments are exposed to liability to replenish the trust for the loss that has occurred together with any adjustment necessary to replace the unauthorised investment with authorised investments.[47] In *Knott v Cottee*,[48] a trustee made an unauthorised investment in Exchequer bills. In 1846, the bills were sold at a loss by order of the court. In 1848, when sale would have produced a profit, the court declared that the investment was improper. Holding the trustee liable for the difference between the two prices, Romilly MR commented that, "The case must either be treated as if these investments had not been made, or had been made for his own benefit out of his own monies, and that he had at the same time retained monies of the testator in his hands".[49] In *Re Massingberd's Settlement*,[50] trustees procured a sale of authorised investments and re-invested the proceeds in unauthorised mortgages. Although all of the money was recovered, the authorised investments had risen in value. Accordingly, the trustees were liable to replace the sold investments or replenish the trust estate to the equivalent value.

(ii)   improper retention of trust property

In *Fry v Fry*,[51] trustees were instructed to sell the testator's house as soon as convenient following the death of the testator. Although an initial offer for the property was made and rejected, no sale of the property was achieved in the lifetime of the trustees. The trustees' estates were held to be liable for the difference in price between the current value of the property and the price that would have been achieved had the property been sold at the appropriate time. In *Re Ahmed (A Debtor)*,[52] moreover, the recipients of shares transferred away in breach of trust (who had returned the shares before trial) were treated as trustees of the shares and made liable for the diminution in value.

(iii) failure to invest

The failure to invest within a reasonable period of time will constitute a breach of the trustee's statutory duty of care. Where the failure to invest is as regards one specified investment, the trustee will be liable to provide the amount of the specified investment as would have been obtained with trust funds at the time at which the investment ought to have been

---

47   It is, of course, open to beneficiaries of full capacity to adopt the unauthorised investment.
48   (1852) 16 Beav. 77.
49   (1852) 16 Beav. 77 at 79.
50   (1890) 63 L.T. 296.
51   (1859) 28 L.J. Ch. 591.
52   [2018] EWCA Civ 519.

made.[53] More frequently, however, trustees have a discretion to choose from a range of investments. In this case and, where no investment is made at all or, regard has not been had to the true scope of investment powers, liability should be assessed by reference to the value which a prudent trustee might have achieved.[54]

(iv) interest

17-014

A trustee who misapplies trust funds in breach of trust will be liable not only to replenish the trust fund, but to do so with interest from the date of the misapplication.[55] As Buckley LJ explained in *Wallersteiner v Moir (No.2)*, "This is on the notional ground that the money so applied was in fact the trustee's own money and that he has retained the misapplied trust money in his own hands and used it for his own purposes".[56] It is a discretionary matter for the court to determine the rate of interest applied. In *Attorney General v Alford*,[57] for example, Lord Cranworth LC indicated the discretionary nature of the exercise when he suggested that "What the Court ought to do, I think, is to charge him only with the interest which he has received, or which it is justly entitled to say he ought to have received, or which it is so fairly to be presumed that he did receive that he is estopped from saying that he did not receive it".[58] The usual practice is to charge the trustee with simple interest only. If trust funds have been ploughed into the trustee's trade or business, however, he will be held to account for profits or, if preferable to the beneficiary, the sums involved plus compound interest. The justification for charging compound interest "normally lies in the fact that profits earned in trade would be likely to be used as working capital for earning further profits".[59]

More broadly, in *Westdeutsche Landesbank Girozentrale v Islington Borough Council*,[60] Lord Browne-Wilkinson conducted a review of the case law and concluded that compound interest is awarded not to compensate for loss of profit but to ensure that the defendant does not retain a profit for which he must account. He explained, "in the absence of fraud, equity only awards compound (as opposed to simple) interest against a defendant who is a trustee or otherwise in a fiduciary position, by way of recouping from such a defendant an improper profit made by him".[61] As no fiduciary duties were owed by the local authority to the bank in respect of the payments made, compound interest could not be awarded in the case before him.

---

53 *Byrchall v Bradford* (1822) 6 Madd. 235.
54 *Nestlé v National Westminster Bank Plc* [1993] 1 W.L.R. 1260.
55 Historically interest was awarded at a rate of 4%: see e.g. *Hall v Hallet* (1784) 1 Cox Eq. Cas. 134.
56 [1975] Q.B. 373 at 397.
57 (1855) 4 De. G. M. & G. 843.
58 (1855) 4 De. G. M. & G. 843 at 851.
59 Per Buckley LJ in *Wallersteiner v Moir (No.2)* [1975] Q.B. 373 at 397.
60 [1996] A.C. 669.
61 [1996] A.C. 669 at 702.

In *Watson v Kea Investments Ltd*,[62] the Court of Appeal recently reviewed the basis upon which interest is awarded in equitable compensation cases. McCombe LJ acknowledged that the courts have "consistently tried to make awards that were suited to investment of trust funds and the economic realities of the times".[63] He explained that, "In the 19th century the task was relatively simple; trust investments could be expected to yield 4%; trustees who mixed trust assets with their own for the purposes of commerce could safely be presumed to have earned at least 5% which they should restore to the trust".[64] In the different economic climate of the late twentieth century, however, traditional rates were not high enough to deprive the wrongdoer of his profit, and accordingly, a convenient borrowing rate was applied.[65] In the case before him (a long-running saga of litigation between former business partners), McCombe LJ, rejected a borrowing rate as "not the realistic proxy"[66] where it was unrealistic to assume that the deprived fund would have borrowed to invest. He felt it appropriate instead to determine the rate of interest by reference to the available evidence of how the trustee might have invested the funds throughout the period including any element of capital return. As Hamblen LJ added, "If, as the case law shows, interest is meant to reflect the return that should have been obtained on the trust funds then, in the modern world of trustee investment, there is no reason why in an appropriate case it should not reflect total return".[67] Compound interest of 6.5% was awarded.

(v)   set-off of profit against loss

As a general rule, where a trustee is liable in respect of distinct breaches of trust, one of which has resulted in a loss and the other in a profit, the trustee is not entitled to set off the profit against the loss.[68] In *Bartlett v Barclays Bank Trust Co Ltd*,[69] however, there appears to have been a softening of this general approach. There, the Bank had neglected its duty as trustee to ensure that it received sufficient information as regards the investment activities of a board of company directors. Two property development projects were highlighted: the "Guildford" project (which was successful), and the "Old Bailey" project (which was unsuccessful and described by Brightman J as "imprudent and hazardous and wholly unsuitable for a trust").[70] Brightman J reflected on the development of authority and decided that the cases were not easy to reconcile. Nonetheless, he permitted the profit to be set off against a loss because both the profit and the loss arose out of the same course of speculative investment. He claimed:

17-015

---

62   [2019] EWCA Civ 1759. See T. Graham, T. McPhail, "How Equity Should Assess a Rate of Interest Against a Defaulting Trustee" (2020) 26(3) T. & T. 227.
63   [2019] EWCA Civ 1759 at [71].
64   [2019] EWCA Civ 1759 at [71].
65   *Wallersteiner v Moir (No.2)* [1975] Q.B. 373.
66   [2019] EWCA Civ 1759 at [73].
67   [2019] EWCA Civ 1759 at [79].
68   *Dimes v Scott* (1828) 4 Russ. 195.
69   [1980] Ch. 515.
70   [1980] Ch. 515 at 534.

> "The relevant cases are, however, not altogether easy to reconcile. All are centenarians and none is quite like the present. The Guildford development stemmed from exactly the same policy and (to a lesser degree because it proceeded less far) exemplified the same folly as the Old Bailey project. Part of the profit was in fact used to finance the Old Bailey disaster. By sheer luck the gamble paid off handsomely, on capital account. I think it would be unjust to deprive the bank of this element of salvage in the course of assessing the cost of the shipwreck. My order will therefore reflect the bank's right to an appropriate set-off".[71]

Liability of Trustees Inter Se

17-016   Co-trustees who have acted in breach of trust are jointly and severally liable to beneficiaries.[72] Accordingly, a beneficiary may seek to recover a loss in its entirety from any one or more individual trustees or all of the trustees jointly. As between trustees, where any one trustee is compelled to pay more of his share of the liability for a breach of trust, he is entitled in equity to enforce an equal contribution from his complicit co-trustees.[73] As A.L. Smith LJ put it in *Chillingworth v Chambers*, "As between two trustees who are in *pari delicto*, the one who has made good a loss occasioned by a breach of trust for which the two are jointly and severally liable may obtain contribution to that loss from the other".[74] Historically, the rules of equity ensured that a passive trustee could not, through inactivity, evade the liability incurred by an active trustee who acted honestly but fell into error. This principle was aptly prescribed by Cotton LJ in *Bahin v Hughes*, where he claimed that it "would be laying down a wrong rule to hold that where one trustee acts honestly, though erroneously, the other trustee is to be held entitled to indemnity who by doing nothing neglects his duty more than the acting trustee".[75]

The capacity to recover contribution from co-trustees now rests on a statutory basis. The Civil Liability (Contribution) Act 1978 confers on the court discretion as to the amount that can be recovered by one trustee from another. Section 2(1) highlights that the sums recoverable must be "such as may be found by the court to be just and equitable having regard to the

---

71   [1980] Ch. 515 at 538.
72   See further, para.**13-020.**
73   *Fletcher v Green* (1864) 33 Beav. 426.
74   [1896] 1 Ch. 685 at 707.
75   (1886) 31 Ch. D. 390 at 396. As Fry LJ perceived it, "the loss which has happened is the result of the combination of the action of Miss Hughes with the inaction of Mr Edwards" (at 398).

extent of that person's responsibility for the damage in question".[76] It is open to the court, therefore, to depart from the equitable presumption of equal responsibility where the facts of the case demand. The Act does not, however, cover cases where a trustee is not liable to contribute but, instead, is entitled to an indemnity against his own liability from his co-trustees. Instances of indemnity might usefully be confined to three key categories:

17-017

- where one trustee alone is solely liable for a breach. Thus, in *Re Smith*, where in the course of a joint investment one trustee had acted dishonestly, Kekewich J concluded, "The fact that he took a bribe is conclusive against him. Honesty seems to be out of the question after that; and I must hold that he is liable to make good the loss occasioned by the investment. I do not think that it is a case of joint and several liability".[77] This category, therefore, catches a variety of cases where one trustee alone has acted in a dishonest manner;

- where a trustee is a solicitor on whose advice co-trustees have relied. Here, the court is cautious to ascertain the extent of the solicitor's control. As Kekewich J warned in *Head v Gould*, a solicitor trustee is not bound to indemnify his co-trustee against loss, "merely because he was a solicitor, when that co-trustee was an active participator in the breach of trust complained of, and is not proved to have participated merely in consequence of the advice and control of the solicitor"[78]; and

- where one of the trustees in breach of trust is also a beneficiary who obtains, as between himself and his co-trustee, an exclusive benefit from the breach. The trustee beneficiary must, in this case, indemnify his co-trustee to the extent of his interest in the trust estate.[79]

Criminal Liability

17-018

The criminal liability of trustees who act in breach of trust is secured under the Theft Act 1968.[80] Hence, the dishonest appropriation of property (including land or anything forming

---

76 In *Dawson v Bell* [2016] EWCA Civ 96 (a case of misapplied company funds), it was not deemed just and equitable under s.2(1) for one director to contribute to another's share of what was owed to the company, despite her knowledge of the misappropriation. Equitable principles did not require her to contribute for money received solely for the claimant's benefit and put to uses that included (as was highlighted by Tomlinson LJ at [52]), the services of a prostitute in the Czech Republic.

77 [1896] 1 Ch. 71 at 77.

78 [1898] 2 Ch. 250 at 265.

79 *Chillingworth v Chambers* [1896] 1 Ch. 685.

80 Historically, the trustee was considered to be the owner of the trust property with the consequence that a breach of trust did not infringe the criminal law.

part of it)[81] with the intention of permanent deprivation exposes a trustee to criminal sanction. Trust property, for the purposes of the Act belongs to "any person having a right to enforce the trust".[82] This appears to include potential beneficiaries under a discretionary trust. In addition, the Fraud Act 2006 s.4 makes fraud by abuse of position a criminal offence for a trustee acting dishonestly for his own gain.[83]

Protection of Trustees

17-019

A trustee may take advantage of a wide range of defences to an action for breach of trust. It might be argued, for example, that another trustee committed the breach[84] or that a particular course of conduct was reasonable and that no breach has, therefore, been committed.[85] In addition, the principal defences relied upon by trustees to escape liability are as follows:

- the trustee exemption clause;

- the principle of consent;

- breach at the instigation of a beneficiary;

- statutory relief under s.61; and

- limitation of actions.

Exemption clauses

17-020

The protection afforded to a trustee by virtue of an exemption or exclusion clause has been considered in depth in Ch.13.[86] It will be recalled, therefore, that a trustee may, by virtue of a pro-

---

81　Under the Theft Act 1968 s.4(2)(a), a trustee may be deemed to steal land if "he appropriates the land or anything forming part of it by dealing with it in breach of the confidence reposed in him".
82　Theft Act 1968 s.5(2).
83　See J. Collins, "Fraud by Abuse of Position: Theorising Section 4 of the Fraud Act 2006" (2011) 7 Crim. L.R. 513.
84　On the ground that a trustee is not always liable for the acts or omissions of another trustee: *Townley v Sherborne* (1633) Bridg. 35.
85　*Nestlé v National Westminster Bank Plc (No.2)* [1993] 1 W.L.R. 1260.
86　See para.**13-005**.

vision in the trust instrument, claim relief from liability.[87] In *Armitage v Nurse*,[88] consideration was given to the scope of the so-called "exemption clause" and its capacity to exclude liability for a trustee's negligence in the course of his duties. The exemption clause in *Armitage* read, "No trustee shall be liable for any loss or damage which may happen . . . at any time or from any cause whatsoever unless such loss or damage shall be caused by his own actual fraud . . .". Millett LJ considered it, "apt to exclude liability for breach of trust in the absence of a dishonest intention on the part of the trustee whose conduct is impugned".[89] As long as he had not acted dishonestly, the trustee was free from liability for loss or damage to the trust property, "no matter how indolent, imprudent, lacking in diligence, negligent or wilful he may have been".[90]

The law on trustee exemption clauses is frequently criticised.[91] In 2003, the Law Commission published a consultation paper which highlighted the inadequacy of the current position whereby a professional trustee can escape liability for breach of trust occasioned by his negligence and proposed that professional trustees should no longer be allowed to exclude this liability.[92] Millett LJ himself conceded that "it must be acknowledged that the view is widely held that these clauses have gone too far, and that trustees who charge for their services and who, as professional men, would not dream of excluding liability for ordinary professional negligence should not be able to rely on a trustee exemption clause excluding liability for gross negligence".[93] Nonetheless, the Law Commission has since changed its view. Instead, it proposes a rule of practice, that where a paid trustee causes a settlor to include a clause limiting liability, trustees must take such steps "as are reasonable to ensure that the settlor is aware of the meaning and effect of the clause".[94] This radical shift of position has, understandably, left many disappointed. [95]

17-021

Consent to a course of dealing

17-022

A trustee might seek to escape the prospect of liability for breach of trust by arguing that the beneficiary consented to, or acquiesced in, a given course of conduct. The classic statement of the principle of consent is that of Lord Eldon LC in *Walker v Symonds*:

> "if the *cestui que trust* joins with the trustees in that which is a breach of trust, knowing the circumstances, such a *cestui que trust* can never complain of such a breach of trust. I go further, and agree that either

---

87   See generally, P. Matthews, "The Efficacy of Trustee Exemption Clauses in English Law" [1989] Conv. 42.
88   [1997] 2 All E.R. 705.
89   [1997] 2 All E.R. 705 at 710.
90   [1997] 2 All E.R. 705 at 711.
91   In *Barraclough v Mell* [2005] EWHC 3387 at [89], Behrens J pointed to "an area of law ripe for reform".
92   Trustee Exemption Clauses (2003) Law Com. Consultation Paper No. 171.
93   *Armitage v Nurse* [1997] 2 All E.R. 705 at 715.
94   Law Commission, *Trustee Exemption Clauses* (2006) Law Com. 301, para.6.65.
95   See, for example, A. Kenny, "The Good, The Bad and the Law Commission [2007] Conv. 103.

> concurrence in the act, or acquiescence without original concurrence, will release the trustees: but that is only a general rule, and the court must inquire into the circumstances which induced concurrence or acquiescence".[96]

The court must be convinced that it is fair and equitable to deny a beneficiary a claim against the trustee. Matters must be looked at in the round. It must be shown that there was an exercise of independent judgment by a beneficiary in full knowledge of the facts. A beneficiary cannot be deemed to consent or acquiesce in conduct of which he has no knowledge or understanding.[97] In *Re Pauling's ST*, Lord Wilberforce considered the requirements for consent. He explained, "it is not necessary that [the beneficiary] should know that what he is concurring in is a breach of trust, provided that he fully understands what he is concurring in".[98] Neither Is It necessary to show that the beneficiary benefited directly from the breach of trust. In addition, it is clear that consent must be freely obtained[99] and it cannot be obtained from a minor.[100]

17-023

Closely related to the defence of consent, a trustee may argue that conduct or words after the breach should release a trustee from liability. Although delay in bringing a claim may, legitimately, point to the beneficiary's acquiescence or release post-breach, it is not, of itself, an sufficient ground to protect the trustee from liability. Comparatively less additional evidence is required to demonstrate acquiescence than release. In all cases, the court is guided by the same broad concepts of equity and justice on the facts of the case.

Breach at the beneficiary's instigation

17-024

Where a beneficiary instigates or requests a trustee to commit a breach of trust the court enjoys a jurisdiction in equity to impound the beneficiary's interest, i.e. apply it as far as possible towards the provision of an indemnity for the trustee. Where a breach of trust is instigated or requested it is not necessary to show that the beneficiary was in receipt of a benefit.[101] The underlying motive of personal benefit is sufficient. This principle does not apply, however, where a beneficiary merely consents to or concurs in a breach of trust. Here a benefit derived by

96 (1818) 3 Swan. 1 at 64; see generally, J. Payne, "Consent" in P. Birks and A. Pretto (eds), *Breach of Trust* (Oxford: Hart Publishing, 2002), pp.297–318.
97 *Re Somerset* [1894] 1 Ch. 231.
98 [1962] 1 W.L.R. 86 at 108.
99 As the Court of Appeal emphasised in *Re Pauling's ST* [1964] Ch. 303 at 338, "a trustee carrying out a transaction in breach of trust may be liable if he knew, or ought to have known, that the beneficiary was acting under the undue influence of another, or may be presumed to have done so, but will not be liable if it cannot be established that he so knew, or ought to have known".
100 *Lord Montford v Lord Cadogan* (1816) 19 Ves. Jr. 635. Note that a minor who misrepresents his age will not be permitted to deny the effectiveness of his consent.
101 *Trafford v Boehm* [1746] 3 Atk. 440.

the beneficiary must be demonstrated.[102] As Romer LJ identified in *Fletcher v Collis*, "If a beneficiary claiming under a trust does not instigate or request a breach of trust, is not the active moving party towards it, but merely consents to it, and he obtains no personal benefit from it, then his interest in the trust estate would not be impoundable in order to indemnify the trustee liable to make good loss occasioned by the breach".[103]

The statutory jurisdiction of the court to impound the beneficiary's interest is broader, at least to the extent that the receipt of a personal benefit is not an explicit consideration in the exercise of discretion. It is clear, nonetheless, that the statutory jurisdiction to impound in the case of consent will only apply where consent was secured in writing.[104] Section 62(1) of the Trustee Act 1925[105] provides:

> "Where a trustee commits a breach of trust at the instigation or request or with the consent in writing of a beneficiary, the court may, if it thinks fit, . . . make such order as to the court seems just, for impounding all or any part of the interest of the beneficiary in the trust estate by way of indemnity to the trustee or persons claiming through him".

Two short points require attention. First, old cases remain a guide to the application of the statute. Accordingly, the court will refuse to impound a beneficiary's interest unless it can be shown that the beneficiary, whether by instigation or in concurrence, was aware that the proposed course of action would result in breach of trust. Secondly, the power to impound remains notwithstanding the appointment of a new trustee. As Wilberforce J exclaimed in *Re Pauling's Settlement (No.2)*, "It seems to me to be an absurdity to suppose that there is a requirement, as a condition of exercising the right to obtain an impounding order, that the trustee, who *ex hypothesi* is in breach of trust, must remain a trustee in order to acquire a right of indemnity".[106]

Statutory relief under s.61

Section 61 of the Trustee Act 1925 is considered in detail in Ch.13.[107] It confers on the court the power to relieve a trustee from personal liability.[108] It reads:

17-025

> "If it appears to the court that a trustee . . . is or may be personally

---

102 *Lord Montford v Lord Cadogan* (1816) 19 Ves. Jr. 635.
103 [1905] 2 Ch. 24 at 32.
104 The requirement of writing relates only to consent: *Re Somerset* [1894] 1 Ch. 231.
105 Replacing the Trustee Act 1893 s.45.
106 [1963] Ch. 576 at 584.
107 See para.**13-054**.
108 See M. Haley, "Section 61 of the Trustee Act 1925: A Judicious Breach of Trust?" (2017) 76 C.L.J. 537.

liable for any breach of trust . . . but has acted honestly and reasonably, and ought fairly to be excused for the breach of trust and for omitting to obtain the directions of the court in the matter in which he committed such breach, then the court may relieve him either wholly or partly from personal liability for the same".[109]

Applications for relief typically involve the trustee's payment of funds to an incorrect beneficiary or the entry into an unauthorised investment.[110] In all cases, the court is called upon to exercise its discretion judiciously. In *Marsden v Regan*, Evershed MR drew attention to "the threefold obligation" on a trustee seeking relief, namely, "that he must show that he himself acted honestly and reasonably, and he must further satisfy the court that he ought 'fairly' to be excused".[111] The burden of establishing honesty and reasonableness lies with the trustee.[112] The court then enjoys a wide discretion to consider the facts of the case before it and whether the trustee ought fairly to be excused from liability. *Santander UK Plc v R.A. Solicitors*[113] is one of a growing number of cases dealing with the availability of s.61 where a solicitor has been drawn into a mortgage or conveyancing fraud.[114] Here, a firm of solicitors failed to persuade the court that it had acted reasonably, in all aspects connected with a loss, where money transferred to it by Santander was released in breach of trust to a fraudulent solicitor.[115] Briggs LJ identified particular failures on the part of R.A. Legal as "departures from a sophisticated regime, worked out over many years, whereby risks of loss to lenders and lay clients are minimised".[116] He explained, "Where solicitors fail, in serious respects, to play their part in that structure, and at the same time are swindled into transferring and then releasing trust money to a fraudster without authority, they cannot expect to persuade the court that it is fair to excuse them from liability, upon the basis that they have demonstrated that they have in all respects connected with that loss, acted reasonably".[117] In *Purrunsing v A'Court & Co (a Firm)*,[118] the claimant sued both the vendor's solicitors and the conveyancing firm he had himself instructed for parting with the purchase money in breach of trust. The purported sale was a fraud and completion never took place. The defendants admitted liability but were unsuccessful in their attempt to claim relief under s.61. Although each played different roles in relation to the transaction,

---

109 Potential liability must relate to a past incident and not a future anticipated breach: *Re Rosenthal* [1972] 1 W.L.R. 1273.

110 See *Perrins v Bellamy* [1898] 2 Ch. 521 (Judicial Trustees Act 1896 s.3).

111 [1954] 1 W.L.R. 423 at 435.

112 *Re Stuart* [1897] 2 Ch. 583.

113 [2014] EWCA Civ 183.

114 See P. Davies, "Section 61 of the Trustee Act 1925: Deus Ex Machina?" [2015] Conv. 379.

115 The trustee is required to show that he acted reasonably only as regards those aspects of his conduct which are connected to the beneficiary's loss: see *Nationwide Building Society v Davisons Solicitors* [2013] 1 E.G.L.R. 73.

116 [2014] EWCA Civ 183 at [100].

117 [2014] EWCA Civ 183 at [100].

118 [2016] EWHC 789 (Ch).

neither had acted to the required standard of reasonableness. Each was to bear equal liability for the loss.

In a completely different context, *Re Evans*[119] concerned an administratrix who took out insurance to cover the share of a missing beneficiary (her brother) before effecting a distribution of her father's estate. She acted reasonably in taking legal advice and honestly in the belief that her brother was dead. Somewhat unexpectedly, her brother returned to claim his share. It transpired that the insurance covered only the capital sum to which the beneficiary was entitled. When he claimed for interest, the administratrix sought to employ s.61 as a defence to his action. Judge Richard McCombe QC was influenced by the judgment of Evershed MR in *Marsden v Regan*. He claimed that that authority "clearly shows that to act on legal advice is not a 'passport to relief' under s.61, but that it is important to have regard to the nature of the estate, the circumstances of the defaulting representative and his or her actions in the light of the advice received".[120] On the instant facts, the judge identified a relatively small estate and that the administratrix was a lay person unaccustomed to problems of this nature. She had, at all times, been willing to abide by the advice of solicitors. Accordingly, her liability was excused to the extent that the claim could not be satisfied by assets she retained from the estate. As a matter of general principle, Judge Richard McCombe QC was no doubt influenced by the policy-driven need to avoid discouraging personal representatives, particularly of small estates, from tackling difficult administration problems and without the expense of resort to the court. Not surprisingly, there is markedly less sympathy for professional trustees who receive payment for services.[121]

Limitation

In cases of breach of trust it is important that the beneficiary comply with the rules as to limitation of actions. Put simply, the beneficiary must sue within the permitted timeframe. The equitable nature of a claim for breach of trust exposes the claimant to a minefield of limitation rules, in essence, an unpalatable mix of historical doctrine and complex statutory intervention. More particularly, in determining the permitted time limit, regard must be had both to the applicable provisions of the Limitation Act 1980[122] and the equitable doctrine of *laches*.[123]

---

119 [1999] 2 All E.R. 777, noted by P. Kenny [1999] Conv. 375, 376 as a "sad little case tried over five days in the Chancery Division".

120 [1999] 2 All E.R. 777 at 789.

121 See, e.g. *Re Rosenthal* [1972] 1 W.L.R. 1273.

122 The limitation rules are viewed by the Law Commission, *Limitation of Actions* (2001) Law Com. No.270, para.1.5 as "unfair, complex, uncertain and outdated"; see also W. Swadling, "Limitation" in P. Birks and A. Pretto (eds), *Breach of Trust* (Oxford: Hart Publishing, 2002), where it is claimed at p.344 that "The current limitation regime for breach of trust is a mess".

123 See para.**17-032**. Under the Limitation Act 1980 s.36, "nothing in the Act shall affect any equitable jurisdiction to refuse relief on the ground of acquiescence or otherwise".

The Limitation Act 1980

17-028

Section 21(3) establishes the general rule that an action to recover trust property must be brought within a period of six years from the date of the breach:

> **"An action by a beneficiary to recover trust property or in respect of any breach of trust, not being an action for which a period of limitation is prescribed by any other provision of this Act, shall not be brought after the expiration of six years from the date on which the right of action accrued".**

Nonetheless, s.21(1) outlines the exceptional circumstances in which a trustee will be unable to seek protection from the Act:

> **"No period of limitation prescribed by this Act shall apply to an action by a beneficiary under a trust, being an action—**
> **(a) in respect of any fraud or fraudulent breach of trust to which the trustee was a party or privy; or**
> **(b) to recover from the trustee trust property or the proceeds of trust property in the possession of the trustee, or previously received by the trustee and converted to his use".**

Paragraph (a) appears to be limited by the concept of dishonesty. In *Armitage v Nurse*, Millett LJ confined its scope to "cases of fraud or fraudulent breaches of trust properly so called, that is to say cases involving dishonesty".[124] By contrast, dishonesty is not a relevant factor for the purposes of para.(b) where trust property or its proceeds are in the hands of the trustee. In *Re Howlett*,[125] therefore, the trustee was considered to have retained possession of the trust property and the application of the usual period of limitation was thereby excluded.

In general terms, the appropriate limitation period for a breach of fiduciary duty has proved problematic for the courts and will depend upon the nature of the claim. It should be made clear that a breach of non-fiduciary duty by a fiduciary (that may lead to an action in contract or tort) will mean the imposition of the usual six-year limitation period. In *Coulthard v Disco Mix Club Ltd*,[126] however, a six-year limitation period was imposed in a case of an alleged breach of fiduciary duty stemming from the liability to account. Here, no statutory period of limitation applied, but it was appropriate to apply the common law limitation period by analogy. As Deputy Judge Jules Sher QC made clear, the alleged dishonest breaches were no more than the equitable counterparts of the claims at common law, such that "one could scarcely imag-

---

124 [1997] 2 All E.R. 705 at 719. See also *First Subsea v Balltec* [2018] Ch. 25 at [64] (Patten LJ).
125 [1949] Ch. 767 (occupation rent obtainable in respect of the trustee's continued possession of a wharf until his death).
126 [2000] 1 W.L.R. 707.

ine a more correspondent set of remedies as damages for fraudulent breach of contract and equitable compensation for breach of fiduciary duty in relation to the same factual situation, namely, the deliberate withholding of money due by a manager to his artist".[127] It would, he said, "have been a blot on our jurisprudence if those self-same facts gave rise to a time bar in the common law courts but none in a court of equity". It follows, however, that where the breach of fiduciary duty complained of pertains to the obligation of loyalty, say, where the no profit rule or no conflict rule is contravened, there is no analogous claim at common law and no statutory period of limitation applies.[128]

It is important to note that s.21(1) requires a relationship of trustee and beneficiary to exist between the parties and that under s.38(1),[129] the word "trust" extends to include "implied and constructive trusts". In *Paragon Finance Plc v Thakerar*,[130] Millett LJ supported a two-fold classification of constructive trusts.[131] The first class is where constructive trusteeship arises because the constructive trustee has assumed fiduciary duties prior to the wrongful conduct complained of by the claimant. The second is where a constructive trust is imposed on the defendant as a direct result of his wrongful conduct rendering him personally liable to account. As regards the 1980 Act, this distinction is directly in point. Millett LJ explained:

17-029

> **"The importance of the distinction between the two categories of constructive trust lies in the application of the statutes of limitation. Before 1980 constructive trusts of the first kind were treated in the same way as express trusts and were often confusingly described as such; claims against the trustee were not barred by the passage of time. Constructive trusts of the second kind however were treated differently. They were not in reality trusts at all, but merely a remedial mechanism by which equity gave relief for fraud".[132]**

In *JJ Harrison (Properties) Ltd v Harrison*,[133] Chadwick LJ held that a company director who obtained the company's property for himself by the misuse of the powers entrusted to him in his capacity as director was a constructive trustee within Millett LJ's first class of constructive trust. He argued that the director was vested with powers and duties to deal with the company property in the interests of the company. In that sense, he owed a fiduciary duty to the company in respect of those powers, the breach of which would be treated as a breach of trust. Chadwick LJ held, therefore, that Mr Harrison was prevented by s.21(1)(b) of the 1980 Act from raising the

---

127   [2000] 1 W.L.R. 707 at 730.
128   As Millett LJ explained in *Bristol and West Building Society v Mothew* [1998] Ch. 1 at 18, such duties are "those duties which are special to fiduciaries and which attract those remedies which are peculiar to the equitable jurisdiction and are primarily restitutionary or restorative rather than compensatory".
129   Applying the Trustee Act 1925 s.68.
130   [1999] 1 All E.R. 400 (see paras **10-007 to 10-008**).
131   See Ch.10.
132   [1999] 1 All E.R. 400 at 409.
133   [2002] 1 B.C.L.C. 162; see also *Bank of Credit and Commerce International (SA) v Saadi* [2005] EWHC 2256 (QB).

defence of limitation. The appropriate remedy (in the light that the property had been sold) was an account of the value of the property and attendant profits.

In *Burnden Holdings (UK) Ltd v Fielding*,[134] Lord Briggs clarified the scope of s.2(1)(b). He affirmed the orthodox position that directors of English companies are to be regarded as trustees for all purposes connected with s.21.[135] This is because company directors are entrusted with the stewardship of company property and owe fiduciary duties in respect of it. On the assumed facts of *Burnden Holdings*, directors of a company had improperly diverted its shareholding to another company in which they were the majority shareholders and directors. They argued that as they had not personally received the diverted shareholding and converted it to their use, s.21(1)(b) could have no application. This argument was rejected by the Supreme Court. As Lord Briggs made clear, "It was a conversion of the shareholding to their own use because of the economic benefit which they stood to derive from being the majority shareholders in the company to which the distribution was made. By the time of that conversion the defendants had previously received the property because, as directors of the claimant company, they had been its fiduciary stewards from the outset".[136] Accordingly, s.2(1)(b) was engaged. In cases where s.2(1)(b) is not engaged, i.e. other breaches of fiduciary duty by company directors, absent fraud, those claims will be subject to the usual limitation period.[137]

17-030
It is also now clear that a personal action against a third part accessory to a breach of trust must be brought with the conventional six-year limitation period because, although the label of constructive trustee is attached to the third party, he is not a constructive trustee within Millett LJ's first class.[138] The Supreme Court confirmed this in *Williams v Central Bank of Nigeria*.[139] Here, Dr Williams alleged that he had entrusted a UK-based solicitor with some $6.5 million and that, in the course of a fraud in which the Bank was involved, the money had been paid into an account in that Bank. Unfortunately, some 28 years had elapsed and the question for the Supreme Court was whether his claim (if proven) would be statute barred. By a majority of 3:2, it held that a stranger to the trust liable in dishonest assistance or knowing receipt was not a true trustee for the purposes of s.21(1)(a). Nor did the words "any action in respect of any fraud or fraudulent breach of trust to which the trustee was party or privy" in s.21(1)(a) make possible an action against a party who was not a true trustee. Accordingly, the Bank would be under a merely ancillary form of liability in equity and the six-year period of limitation would apply. It was admitted by Lord Neuberger that dishonest assistants and knowing recipients would be placed in a better position than defaulting trustees, but he felt this was "plainly justifiable, as defaulting trustees have pre-existing fiduciary duties to claimants which dishonest assisters and knowing recipients do not".[140]

---

134 [2018] UKSC 14.
135 See *Davies v Ford* [2020] EWHC 686 (Ch) at [310] per Deputy Judge Johnson.
136 [2018] UKSC 14 at [22] per Lord Briggs.
137 *Gwembe Valley Development Co v Koshy* [2004] 1 B.C.L.C. 131; *First Subsea v Balltec* [2018] Ch 25.
138 See *Cattley v Pollard* [2007] Ch. 353 (endorsed by Lord Hoffman in the Hong Kong Court of Final Appeal in *Peconic Industrial Development Ltd v Lau Kwok Fai* [2009] HKFCA 16); the alternative view of Evans-Lombe J in *Statek Corp v Alford* [2008] EWHC 92 (Ch) at [125] has now been discredited.
139 [2014] UKSC 10.
140 [2014] UKSC 10 at [118].

More generally, the following considerations are relevant in applying the Limitation Act 1980:

■ in the case of a beneficiary with a future interest, a right of action is not deemed to have accrued until the interest has fallen into possession;

■ under s.28, the limitation period is capable of extension where the person to whom the action accrues is under a disability.[141] In such cases, time will only begin to run when that disability ends;

■ s.32 caters for an extension or exclusion of ordinary time limits in cases of fraud, concealment or mistake. Hence, s.32 applies to any action (for which a period of limitation is prescribed) based upon the fraud of the trustee, the trustee's deliberate concealment of a right of action or to cases where the action is for relief from the consequences of a mistake. In these delimited circumstances the period of limitation will not begin to run until the fraud, concealment or mistake has been discovered or could, with reasonable diligence, have been discovered; and

■ s.22 provides an alternative time limit for actions in respect of claims to the personal estate of a deceased person. Here, subject to the s.21 exceptions, a limit of 12 years is provided.

Laches

The doctrine of *laches* may be raised as a defence where it can be established that an acquiescent beneficiary knew of the existence of a breach of trust and delayed unacceptably in bringing his claim. A strong case for denying a remedy might arise in a commercial context where the claimant had "cynically waited to see whether there was value in pursuing his claim".[142] Generally, as Lord Selbourne LC explained in *Lindsay Petroleum Co v Hurd*,

"the doctrine of *laches* in Courts of Equity is not an arbitrary or a technical doctrine. Where it would be practically unjust to give a remedy, either because the party has, by his conduct, done that which might fairly be regarded as equivalent to a waiver of it, or where by his conduct and neglect he has, though perhaps not waiving that remedy, yet put the other party in a situation in which it would not be reasonable to place him if the remedy were afterwards

---

141 Typically mental incapacity or infancy.

142 *Davies v Ford* [2020] EWHC 686 (Ch) at [360]. See, for example, *Excalibur Ventures LLC v Texas Keystone Inc* [2013] EWHC 2767 (Comm).

> to be asserted, in either of these cases, lapse of time and delay are most material".[143]

Indeed, the modern approach to the defence was detailed in *Frawley v Neill*[144] and endorsed by the Court of Appeal in *Green v Gaul*.[145] In *Frawley v Neill*, Aldous LJ confirmed that:

> "I my view the more modern approach should not require an enquiry as to whether the circumstances can be fitted within the confines of a preconceived formula derived from earlier cases. The inquiry should require a broad approach, directed to ascertaining whether it would in all the circumstances be unconscionable for a party to be permitted to assert his beneficial right."[146]

Of course, where an action falls within s.21(1) (discussed above), no statutory period of limitation applies. The current view (although not uncontested)[147] is that this does not prevent the trustee raising the defence of *laches*.[148]

Associated Remedies

17-033

Having considered the personal liability of trustees in cases of breach of trust, it is now necessary to examine the availability of remedies to the claimant beneficiary. The primary focus of the remainder of the chapter is on the availability of proprietary claims. Where property is misappropriated in breach of trust the beneficiary may track its movement in order to recover the specific property or its traceable proceeds. The problem lies in ascertaining exactly what has happened to the property. Misappropriated property may remain in the hands of a wrongdoing trustee or it may pass into the hands of a third party, whether it be a bona fide purchaser, an innocent volunteer or a knowing recipient. Trust property may be exchanged for different property, it may become inextricably mixed with other property, such as in a bank account, or

---

143 (1874) L.R. 5 P.C. 221 at 239.
144 *The Times*, 5 April 1999.
145 [2007] 1 W.L.R. 591 (also known as *Re Loftus (Deceased)*.
146 *The Times*, 5 April 1999; see also *Patel v Shah* [2005] W.T.L.R. 359.
147 See *Gwembe Valley Development Co v Koshy* [2004] W.T.L.R. 97 at [140], where Mummery LJ claimed, "The defence of *laches* is not available. As already explained no period of limitation is specified by the 1980 Act in respect of the cause of action for dishonest breach of fiduciary duty. The effect of s.21(1)(a) is that either as a result of direct application, or of analogy, there is no period of limitation applicable to that cause of action".
148 *Green v Gaul* [2007] 1 W.L.R. 591.

it may be dissipated altogether. Notwithstanding obvious evidential difficulties, if beneficiaries can identify the trust property or its substitute or the value of that property in a mixture of trust property and other property, the beneficiary can seek to make a proprietary claim.[149]

The advantages of a proprietary claim

Consider the case of a trustee who wrongfully misappropriates trust property and uses it solely for the acquisition of a different asset for his own benefit. Here the beneficiary can establish either his beneficial ownership of the proceeds (i.e. the new asset) or bring a personal claim against the trustee for breach of trust secured by an equitable lien (a charge on the proceeds to secure restoration of the trust fund). Understandably, the beneficiary will choose the course of action most beneficial to him. As Keene LJ explained in *Serious Fraud Office v Lexi Holdings Plc (In Administration)*:

17-034

> **"These are true alternatives. In the first kind of claim, the beneficiary is in effect saying: 'Those proceeds (or part of them) belong to me.' In the second, alternative, kind of claim the beneficiary is in effect saying 'The trustee is obliged to account personally to me for his misappropriation and those proceeds stand charged as security for his personal obligation to me'."[150]**

The advantages of a proprietary claim lie on two fronts. First, a proprietary claim affords priority to the claimant in the event of the defendant's insolvency. Thus, whether the beneficiary asserts a claim to ownership of the asset itself or an equitable proprietary interest in its traceable proceeds, the trustee cannot claim that the asset forms part of his estate. The proprietary claim of a beneficiary to trust property or its traceable proceeds can be maintained against the wrongdoer and anyone who derives title from him save for a bona fide purchaser for value without notice of the breach of trust.[151] As such, it is not relevant to the beneficiary that the trustee is insolvent. If, however, the beneficiary is unable to trace the trust property into its proceeds, he will opt to pursue a personal claim against the trustee, although this claim will be unsecured.

Secondly, a proprietary claim (but not a personal claim) will entitle the beneficiary to any appreciation in value generated from the appropriation of his asset.[152] It would be improper to allow the trustee to benefit from the fruits of his misappropriation and illogical that anyone deriving title from him could assert a better title. Where there has been depreciation in the value of an asset, the claimant may choose, in addition, to embark on a personal action in order

---

149   See, generally, L. Smith, *The Law of Tracing* (Oxford: Clarendon Press, 1997).
150   [2009] Q.B. 376 at 389.
151   See *Sinclair Investments (UK) Ltd v Versailles Trade Finance Ltd (In Administration)* [2011] EWCA Civ 347.
152   *FHR European Ventures LLP v Cedar Capital Partners LLC* [2015] A.C. 250.

to recover the difference in value to the trust. In the alternative, he will opt for a personal claim from the outset.

Following or tracing?

17-035

Logically, there are two stages to the process of obtaining a remedy. The first is the identification of the trust property. This may be achieved by the process of "following" or "tracing". Lord Millett has recognised that following and tracing "are both exercises in locating assets which are or may be taken to represent an asset belonging to the [beneficiaries] and to which they assert ownership".[153] He explains further that "the processes of following and tracing are, however, distinct. Following is the process of following the same asset as it moves from hand to hand. Tracing is the process of identifying a new asset as a substitute for the old".[154]

The second step is the selection of an appropriate remedy to bring in respect of that property. Whether identification is achieved by the process of following or tracing, neither provides, by itself, a remedy.[155] At all times, the choice of remedies available to the claimant will depend on the circumstances of the case. For example, a constructive trust might be imposed, say, where property has been identified in the hands of the defendant, who has acted unconscionably.[156] An equitable charge or lien might be appropriate where trust money is used to provide part of the cost of acquiring an asset that has depreciated in value. Here the claimant will be entitled to enforce a charge to secure his personal claim for the amount of the misapplied money. Further, where the claimant's money has been used to discharge a mortgage on the defendant's land, the court may treat the land as subject to a charge by way of subrogation in favour of the claimant.[157]

Streamlining the process of tracing

17-036

Historically, different rules have applied to tracing at common law and in equity. The common law rules are characterised by a restrictive approach. Here, once trust property has become mixed with other property (e.g. in the bank account of the trustee or a third party), the claimant is no longer permitted to trace. As misappropriated property is frequently mixed in this way, the utility of common law tracing is evident in only delimited circumstances. It is, however, possible

---

153 *Foskett v McKeown* [2001] 1 A.C. 102 at 127.
154 [2001] 1 A.C. 102 at 127.
155 As Lewison J noted in *Ultraframe v Fielding* [2005] EWHC 1638 (Ch) at [1464], "the tracing exercise must be carried out first. Only then can the court consider what rights (if any) the claimant has in the assets that have been identified as being trust property or their identifiable substitutes".
156 *Westdeutsche Landesbank v Islington* [1996] A.C. 669.
157 See *Boscawen v Bajwa* [1996] 1 W.L.R. 328.

to "follow" an asset into the hands of a third party in order to recover the specific item or its "clean" substitute.[158]

In contrast, tracing in equity will assist a claimant beneficiary in establishing a proprietary claim over property that has been mixed.[159] Equity will allow the claimant to trace into a mixed fund and charge the fund. It is a pre-requisite to equitable tracing, however, that the claimant has some equitable, proprietary interest in the property and that as between the wrongdoer and claimant, there is a fiduciary relationship.[160] Although perfectly understandable from a historical perspective, the insistence on preconditions is viewed by some as inconvenient, hampering the logical development of the law towards a unitary process for all claimants.

In past decades, judges and commentators alike have voiced regret that the law had failed to develop a single system of rules to determine the availability of proprietary claims. In particular, the lack of a unitary process was a frequent topic for critical comment in the 1990s. As Millett LJ observed in *Jones (FC) & Sons v Jones*, "There is no merit in having distinct and differing tracing rules at law and in equity, given that tracing is neither a right nor a remedy but merely the process by which the plaintiff establishes what has happened to his property and makes good his claim that the assets which he claims can properly be regarded as representing his property".[161] More recently, however, in *Foskett v McKeown* both Lord Millett and Lord Steyn spoke of a single set of tracing rules applicable to claimants in equity or the common law.[162] Birks too has been a key proponent of the view that there is a unified regime for tracing which "allows tracing to be cleanly separated from the business of asserting rights in or in relation to assets successfully traced".[163] He explained:

> "the modern law is equipped with various means of coping with the evidential difficulties which a tracing exercise is bound to encounter. The process of identification thus ceases to be either legal or equitable and becomes, as is fitting, genuinely neutral as to the rights exigible in respect of the assets into which the value in question is traced. The tracing exercise once successfully completed, it can then be asked what rights, if any, the plaintiff can, on his particular facts, assert. It is at that point that it becomes relevant to recall that on

17-037

---

158 Whereas mixed substitutions occur where a new asset is acquired using a mixture of trust property and the defendant's assets, clean substitutions occur where the new asset is acquired solely with trust property: *Foskett v McKeown* [2001] 1 A.C. 102 at 130.

159 Note that tracing may occur in the context of other fiduciary relationships and is not strictly confined to claims between trustee and beneficiary: see *Re Hallett* (1880) 13 Ch. D. 696 at 709.

160 As Fox LJ claimed in *Agip (Africa) Ltd v Jackson* [1991] Ch. 547 at 566, "there must be a fiduciary relationship which calls the equitable jurisdiction into being".

161 [1996] 3 W.L.R. 703 at 712.

162 [2001] 1 A.C. 102 at 128 and 113, respectively.

163 Ross Cranston, "The Necessity of a Unitary Law of Tracing" in *Making Commercial Law, Essays in Honour of Roy Goode* (Oxford: Clarendon Press, 1997), p.257.

> some facts those rights will be personal, on others proprietary, on some legal, and on others equitable".[164]

In *Foskett v McKeown*, Lord Steyn described this as a "crystalline analysis", stating "I regard this explanation as correct. It is consistent with orthodox principle. It clarifies the correct approach to so-called tracing claims. It explains what tracing is about without providing answers to controversies about legal or equitable rights to assets so traced".[165] Similarly, Lord Millett was persuaded that, "Given its nature, there is nothing inherently legal or equitable about the tracing exercise. There is thus no sense in maintaining different rules for tracing at law and in equity. One set of tracing rules is enough".[166]

On the basis of *Foskett v McKeown*, there appears to be authoritative support for future courts to depart fully from the historical approach which was in favour of a robust application of different legal and equitable rules. In this light, it is surprising that in *Shalson v Russo*,[167] Rimer J was not persuaded that he should regard *Foskett* as having decided that there is no longer any difference between the common law and equitable rules. He claimed, "I do not regard *Foskett* as having decided that".[168] Admittedly, Lord Millett's remarks in *Foskett* are obiter. Having put forward his view, Lord Millett tellingly remarked that this was not the occasion to explore these matters further.[169]

17-038

In *Shalson v Russo*, Rimer J found that support for his view was strengthened having considered the other speeches of the House in *Foskett*. Lord Hoffmann, for example, agreed with Lord Millett's speech, and he could not be deemed thereby to have decided any more on the point than Lord Millett. Similarly, Lord Browne-Wilkinson agreed with Lord Millett's speech, but he expressly made clear that he did "not want to enter into the dispute whether the legal and equitable rules of tracing are the same or differ".[170] Lord Hope did not deal at all with the point. Although Rimer J accepted that Lord Steyn might be regarded as having adopted a more positive stance, the overall conclusion was clear that "it cannot be said that *Foskett* has swept away the long recognised difference between common law and equitable tracing".[171] Accordingly, the distinction between the legal and equitable rules must, at least for the present time, be maintained.[172]

---

164 *Making Commercial Law* (1997), p.258. Reproduced with permission of the Licensor through PLSclear.
165 [2001] 1 A.C. 102 at 113.
166 [2001] 1 A.C. 102 at 129.
167 [2005] 2 W.L.R. 1213.
168 [2005] 2 W.L.R. 1213 at 1246.
169 [2001] 1 A.C. 102 at 129.
170 [2001] 1 A.C. 102 at 109.
171 [2005] 2 W.L.R. 1213 at 1247.
172 See *FHR European Ventures LLP v Cedar Capital Partners LLC* [2015] A.C. 250 at [44] where Lord Neuberger accepted that, "at least as the law is currently understood", there are differences in the operation of legal and equitable rules.

Tracing at Common Law

As indicated above, the process of tracing at common law establishes that the claimant's misappropriated property has passed into the hands of the recipient. The claimant is, thereby, positioned to pursue a remedy that recognises his ownership of that property at common law. This may take the form of an action against the recipient for money had and received (misappropriated money) or for conversion (chattels). At its most simple, the claimant may be able to follow the specific property into the hands of the recipient, in which case he will seek a return of that specific property. In the alternative, a clean substitution of the original trust property may be traced. The claimant will trace his property into its product "to assert his title to the product in place of his original property".[173] For example, if misappropriated money is used to pay the total purchase price of a number of shares, there has been a "clean" substitution of the money for the shares. Accordingly, the substitute property can be the subject matter of a common law claim. In *Lipkin Gorman v Karpnale Ltd*,[174] therefore, a firm of solicitors was able to trace money misappropriated from the firm's client account (and gambled by a partner of the firm at the Playboy Club) into the hands of the defendant recipient club owner. Although the solicitors had no proprietary interest in the money in their client account, at common law they were owners of the chose in action which arose through the indebtedness of the Bank to them. They were thereby able to trace their property into its direct product (the money drawn from the account) and follow It into the hands of the club owner. The rationale was, as Lord Templeman explained, "The club received stolen money by way of gift from the thief; the club, being a volunteer, has been unjustly enriched at the expense of the solicitors from whom the money had been stolen and the club must reimburse the solicitors".[175]

It is clear from this formulation of words that the House of Lords viewed the personal action for money had and received as achieving a form of restitution, i.e. a means of reversing the unjust enrichment of the recipient. To this, the Playboy Club had a defence that their payment of winnings in good faith constituted a "change of position" as a consequence of which the solicitors' firm should not be able to claim the entire shortfall.

Accordingly, the solicitors' firm was entitled to claim only the net profit of the Playboy Club and not the total value of the misappropriated funds.

The principle that the common law rules allow tracing into substitute assets has been said to derive from *Taylor v Plumer*.[176] There Sir Thomas Plumer gave money to a stockbroker for the purpose of buying exchequer bills. Contrary to instruction, the stockbroker instead used the money to buy American securities for his own purposes. Sir Thomas was able to trace his property into the securities held by the stockbroker so to defeat a claim made to them by the stockbroker's assignees in bankruptcy. As Lord Ellenborough CJ explained:

17-039

17-040

---

173   *Lipkin Gorman v Karpnale Ltd* [1991] 2 A.C. 548 at 573 per Lord Goff.
174   [1991] 2 A.C. 548; noted at [1992] Conv. 124 (M. Halliwell).
175   [1991] 2 A.C. 548 at 565.
176   (1815) 3 M. & S. 562; see, e.g. *Agip (Africa) Ltd v Jackson* [1990] Ch. 265 at 285 per Millett LJ.

> **"It makes no difference in reason or law into what other form, different from the original, the change may have been made . . . for the product of or substitute for the original thing still follows the nature of the thing itself . . .".[177]**

Although it has been shown that *Taylor v Plumer* was in fact decided on the rules of equity,[178] both *Lipkin Gorman v Karpnale Ltd*[179] and *Banque Belge pour L'Etranger v Hambrouck*[180] cite this case as authority for the proposition that tracing into exchanged assets was permissible at common law. In *Jones (FC) & Sons v Jones*,[181] Millett LJ underlined the jurisdiction of the common law maintaining that Lord Ellenborough CJ in *Taylor v Plumer* "gave no indication that, in following assets into their exchange products, equity had adopted a rule which was peculiar to itself or which went further than the common law".[182] The principle, therefore, may be simply stated. Provided the trust property or its clean substitute is segregated and identifiable, i.e. it has not been mixed with other property, tracing at common law remains possible.

Common law tracing seemingly extends also to cases where the original property has been substituted and it is from the use of the new property that some profit is derived. The leading authority is that of *Jones (FC) & Sons v Jones*.[183] There the sum of £11,700 was loaned, lawfully, from the partnership account of a firm to Mrs Jones, the wife of one of the partners, who made a successful investment in potato futures. She returned a very healthy profit and proceeded to place the sum of almost £50,000 (comprising both capital and profit) in a bank account separate from all her other assets. It emerged that under the Bankruptcy Act 1914 the partnership was deemed to have been bankrupt before the payment to Mrs Jones. Accordingly, the partnership assets were to pass to the Official Receiver retrospectively. The Official Receiver and not Mrs Jones was, thereby, entitled to the original £11,700 at the point at which the loan was made. Although there was no question that the Official Receiver was entitled to recover the original amount, more difficulty surrounded the profits. Importantly, the rules of equitable tracing could not be employed to facilitate a claim in the light that no fiduciary relationship existed between the Official Receiver and Mrs Jones.[184] The court was left to decide the case solely on the basis of the common law rules.

17-041

At common law, the appropriate remedy in such cases is an action for money had and received. Unfortunately, however, this would enable a claim for the original amount but not as to any profit.[185] Although at first glance, a claim to the original amount could be of little help

---

177   (1815) 3 M. & S. 562 at 575.
178   L. Smith, "Tracing in *Taylor v Plumer*: Equity in the Court of King's Bench" [1995] L.M.C.L.Q. 240.
179   [1991] 2 A.C. 548.
180   [1921] 1 K.B. 321.
181   [1996] 3 W.L.R. 703.
182   [1996] 3 W.L.R. 703 at 712.
183   [1996] 3 W.L.R. 703.
184   The pre-requisites of equitable tracing are discussed below (see para.**17-043**).
185   As Fox LJ explained in *Agip (Africa) Ltd v Jackson* [1991] Ch. 547 at 563, "Liability depends upon receipt by the defendant of the plaintiff's money and the extent of the liability depends on the amount received".

to the Official Receiver's case, both Millett and Nourse LJJ swayed in its favour, albeit by different reasoning.[186] Millett LJ countenanced a proprietary claim to the entire sum on the basis that the property in issue had been retained in a separate bank account. He derived support from *Banque Belge pour L'Etranger v Hambrouck*[187] and the House of Lords in *Lipkin Gorman v Karpnale Ltd*,[188] and saw "no reason for concluding that the common law does not recognise claims to substitute assets or their products".[189] He held the claimant entitled to the contents of the account stating that "the fact that it included profits made by the use of that money is immaterial".[190] Undeniably, his approach marks an extension to the traditional understanding of the ambit of the common law rules.[191]

Nourse LJ immediately acknowledged that they had gone further than the House of Lords in *Lipkin Gorman v Karpnale Ltd* to accept the proposition that "the action for money had and received entitles the legal owner to trace his property into its product, not only in the sense of property for which it is exchanged, but also in the sense of property representing the original and the profit made by the defendant's use of it".[192] Interestingly, he agreed with the result, but by means of a broader justification. Focusing upon the personal action for money had and received, Nourse LJ endorsed the view that the action "is a liberal action in the nature of a bill in equity".[193] Accordingly, he embraced an argument of conscience to deny Mrs Jones. For Nourse LJ, the defendant could not "in conscience retain the profit any more than the original £11,700. She had no title to the original. She could not have made the profit without her use of it. She cannot, by making a profit through the use of money to which she had no title, acquire some better title to the profit".[194]

Loss of the right to trace at common law

17-042

Most cases of misappropriated property require a claimant to trace into a mixed bank account, typically, where the defendant has mixed those monies with other funds and insufficient funds remain to satisfy all claims. In such cases there is no scope for tracing at common

---

186 For a discussion of their respective approaches, see *Armstrong DLW GmbH v Winnington Networks Ltd* [2012] EWHC 10 (Ch) at [77].

187 [1921] 1 K.B. 321.

188 [1991] 2 A.C. 548.

189 [1996] 3 W.L.R. 703 at 711.

190 [1996] 3 W.L.R. 703 at 712.

191 It is noteworthy that Millett LJ had previously argued extra-judicially that curtailment of the common law rules was appropriate, stating that "A unified and comprehensive restitutionary remedy should be developed based on equitable principles, and attempts to rationalise and develop the common law action for money had and received should be abandoned" (P. Millett, "Tracing the Proceeds of Fraud" (1991) 107 L.Q.R. 71, 85).

192 [1996] 3 W.L.R. 703 at 714.

193 [1996] 3 W.L.R. 703 at 714, citing the words of Lord Mansfield CJ in *Clarke v Shee and Johnson* (1774) 1 Cowp. 197 at 199.

194 [1996] 3 W.L.R. 703 at 714.

law.[195] In the words of Lord Goff, "at common law, property in money, like other fungibles is lost as such when it is mixed with other money".[196] By way of example, in *Agip (Africa) Ltd v Jackson*,[197] the defendant accountants laundered the claimant's money through the bank accounts of a number of shell companies which were subsequently liquidated. The claimant's funds were transferred telegraphically from its bank in Tunis through the New York clearing system into accounts in London controlled by the defendants. In the course of the complex transactions, therefore, the trust money was combined with other monies and changed into different currencies. As a partial remedy, the claimant sought to trace into the defendant's accounts. In the Court of Appeal, Fox LJ held that, on the basis that mixing of the funds had occurred in the New York clearing system, common law tracing was unavailable. The rationale, highlighted by Millett J in the High Court, was that "Nothing passed between Tunisia and London but a stream of electrons".[198]

The limitations of common law tracing are patently displayed in the case law. Although it is clearly possible in straightforward circumstances to trace cheques paid into bank accounts, the presence of telegraphic transfer, telexed instructions or the engagement of inter-bank clearing systems have operated to obscure the identity of the original property with the consequence that tracing at common law has failed. As will be demonstrated, such mixing is no barrier to tracing in equity. As in most cases mixing will have occurred, the common law rules maintain only a limited practical value.

Tracing in Equity

The requirement of fiduciary relationship

17-043

The requirement of a fiduciary relationship or equitable proprietary interest in the property is frequently cited as a prerequisite to tracing in equity. In *Box v Barclays Bank*, for example, Ferris J stated this requirement in strict terms. He claimed, "Equitable tracing is only available where there is an equity to trace, which requires that there must be an initial fiduciary relationship between the person claiming to trace and the party who is said to have misapplied that person's money".[199] In *Re Diplock's Estate*, Lord Greene noted that:

---

195 It appears that tracing into a substantially unmixed account is permissible: see *Banque Belge pour L'Etranger v Hambrouck* [1921] 1 K.B. 321.
196 *Lipkin Gorman v Karpnale Ltd* [1991] 2 A.C. 548 at 572.
197 [1991] Ch. 547.
198 [1990] Ch. 265 at 286.
199 *The Times*, 30 April 1998.

> "Lord Parker and Lord Haldane both predicate the existence of a right of property recognized by equity which depends upon there having existed at some stage a fiduciary relationship of some kind (though not necessarily a positive duty of trusteeship) sufficient to give rise to the equitable right of property. Exactly what relationships are sufficient to bring such an equitable right into existence for the purposes of the rule which we are considering is a matter which has not been precisely laid down. Certain relationships are clearly included, e.g., trustee (actual or constructive) and cestui que trust; and "fiduciary" relationships such as that of principal and agent".[200]

Indeed, *Re* Diplock Is a frequently cited case on establishing an equity to trace, Caleb Diplock, who died in 1936, directed the executors under his will to apply his residuary estate, "for such charitable institution or institutions or other charitable or benevolent object or objects in England" as his executors should in their discretion select. His executors distributed £203,000 amongst 139 charitable institutions, but the gift was subsequently declared invalid on the basis that it was not exclusively charitable. In addition to an action against the executors for misappropriation of the residuary estate, the next of kin sought to trace (and recover) the property in the hands of the recipient charities. In the Court of Appeal it was held that "equity may operate on the conscience not merely of those who acquire a legal title in breach of some trust, express or constructive, or of some other fiduciary obligation, but of volunteers provided that as a result of what has gone before some equitable proprietary interest has been created and attaches to the property in the hands of the volunteer".[201]

This seeming precondition of a fiduciary relationship has been the subject of criticism and confusion. In *Agip (Africa) v Jackson*, Millett J accepted that the restriction on the ability of equity to follow assets in that there must be some fiduciary relationship which permits the assistance of equity to be invoked. but he viewed the requirement as resting on authority rather than principle. He was prepared to push further, taking the view that "it is not necessary that the fund to be traced should have been the subject of fiduciary obligations before it got into the wrong hands".[202] In his view, it would be sufficient that the payment to the defendant could itself give rise to a fiduciary relationship.

As a consequence of the need to establish a fiduciary relationship as a precondition to tracing in equity, the courts have strained to accept that fiduciary relationships can exist in circumstances where fiduciary duties would not usually arise. This enthusiasm to discern a fiduciary relationship has, of course, been motivated purely by the practical need to permit a claimant's use of the equitable tracing rules. The classic illustration is the thief who may be deemed to owe a fiduciary duty to his victim such that the victim can trace his property through

17-044

---

200 [1948] Ch 465 at 540.
201 *Re Diplock's Estate* [1948] Ch. 465 at 530. As will be discussed, they successfully brought a personal action to recover money from the charities: see [1951] A.C. 251 (considered by the House of Lords).
202 [1990] Ch. 265 at 290.

a subsequent sale from which the proceeds have become mixed in a bank account.[203] Any development of the law in this manner is patently unsatisfactory, although the continuing need to establish a fiduciary relationship as a prerequisite to tracing is offset somewhat by the ease with which one may be established.

Equitable tracing rules in operation

17-045

The operation of the equitable tracing rules and consequent claims is best explained by a series of illustrations drawing on the typical contexts in which the rules will be invoked. The trust property (or its substitute) may remain intact in the hands of a third party or it may have been mixed with other property, in a physical mixture, e.g. oil or grain. Trust funds may be mixed with the funds of the wrongdoer, or with the funds of other contributors, most commonly in a bank account. Logically, different rules will operate to determine what may be traced and claimed. The detailed workings of these rules will now be considered.

Physical mixtures

17-046

Where trust property such as grain or oil is physically mixed with other property, it remains possible to divide the mixture into identical parts. Although it ceases to be clear exactly which part of the commingled mass belongs to each contributor, it is clear that the contribution of each contributor lies somewhere in the mixture. If some part of the mixture is consumed or dissipated, insufficient property remains to satisfy the claims of all contributors. In the case of wrongdoing, for example, where a trustee mixes trust property with his own property, the rules will operate in favour of the beneficiary as the innocent contributor.[204] Accordingly, the trustee will be deemed to use his own property first. Only when the beneficiary's claim is satisfied will the trustee be permitted to trace his own contribution to the mixture. By contrast, in the absence of wrongdoing, contributors share rateably, i.e. in proportion to their contributions.

Pro rata division is appropriate in the case of mixtures of fungibles such as grain or oil. More problematic is the case where mixing of assets creates an entirely new product. Under the doctrine of specification, the prima facie conclusion must be that the original asset has been destroyed and the ability to follow that asset is lost. This principle appears to give way where the mixing is carried out by a wrongdoer. In the Canadian case of *Jones v De Marchant*,[205] a husband used 18 beaver skins belonging to his wife together with four skins of his own and made a fur coat as a present for his mistress. Although the mistress was an innocent volunteer who had no knowledge of the ownership of the skins, the wife was deemed entitled to recover the coat. It was clear that the mistress, as an innocent volunteer in receipt of misappropriated property, could

203 See, e.g. the view of Lord Templeman in *Lipkin Gorman v Karpnale Ltd* [1991] 2 A.C. 548 at 565.
204 See *Indian Oil Corp Ltd v Greenstone Shipping SA (Panama)* [1987] 2 Lloyd's Rep. 286.
205 (1916) 28 D.L.R. 561.

stand in no better a position than the donor. The coat was a new asset created from the comingled skins of the claimant wife and her wrongdoing husband. Division of the coat into shares in proportion to their respective contributions was patently inappropriate. Accordingly, the facts gave rise to an "all or nothing case" in which the coat should be assigned to one or other of the parties. As the wrongdoer carried out the mixing and it was by virtue of this mixing that the mistress acquired the asset, the maximum that the wrongdoer and his donee can ask for is pro rata division. With this possibility excluded, the wrongdoer and his donee were entitled to nothing.

Trustee's own money mixed with misappropriated trust money

Where there is competition as between a wrongdoing trustee and a beneficiary seeking to trace into the funds in a mixed bank account, there follows a "cherry picking" exercise[206] in which equity permits the beneficiary to elect the more beneficial of two rules that might be invoked. Take, for example, a trustee, Fred, who mixes £5,000 of his own money with £5,000 of trust money. Were he to proceed to squander £3,000 and then to invest a further £6,000 profitably, only £1,000 would remain in the account. Between the parties, the question arises as to the proportion of money dissipated, the proportion profitably invested and the proportion untouched in the account. Under the rule in *Re Hallett's Estate*,[207] it is presumed that if a trustee uses money from a fund in which he has mixed his own money with trust money, he uses his own money first. The principle is that which Jessel MR famously declared: "Wherever it can be done rightfully, he is not allowed to say, against the person entitled to the property or the right, that he has done it wrongfully".[208] Accordingly, as the trustee has acted wrongfully, it is not open to him to assert that he lost anything other than his own money first.

In *Re Oatway*,[209] however, the trustee solicitor used funds from a bank account containing a mixture of his own and his clients' money to make a profitable investment in shares before proceeding to waste the rest of the funds. Joyce J made clear that in these circumstances the trustee could not be deemed to spend his own money first. The claim of the beneficiary stood first in priority. As Joyce J spelt out, "when any of the money drawn out has been invested, and the investment remains in the name or under the control of the trustee, the rest of the balance having been afterwards dissipated by him, he cannot maintain that the investment which remains represents his own money alone, and that what has been spent and can no longer be traced and recovered was the money belonging to the trust".[210]

Looking again at the example above, Fred has wasted £3,000 and invested £6,000 at a profit. £1,000 remains in the account. Under the rule in *Re Hallett*, he would be deemed to

17-047

17-048

206 Per Rimer J in *Shalson v Russo* [2005] 2 W.L.R. 1213 at 1261.
207 (1880) 13 Ch. D. 696.
208 (1880) 13 Ch. D. 696 at 727.
209 [1903] 2 Ch. 356.
210 [1903] 2 Ch. 356 at 360.

spend his own money first. As to the beneficiary, it is logical that he may wish to trace into the property purchased from the mixed fund (and, thereby, the profit) before any claim to the sum that remains in the account. In *Re Tilley's WT*, Ungoed-Thomas J expressed the view "that if, having regard to all the circumstances of the case objectively considered, it appears that the trustee has in fact, whatever his intention, laid out trust moneys in or towards a purchase, then the beneficiaries are entitled to the property purchased and any profits it produces to the extent to which it has been paid for out of trust money".[211]

Further clarification can be gleaned from *Foskett v McKeown*.[212] Here, Lord Millett described as a basic rule that where a trustee wrongfully uses trust money to provide part of the cost of acquiring an asset, the beneficiary is entitled at his option either to claim a proportionate share of the asset or to enforce a lien upon it to secure his personal claim against the trustee for the amount of the misapplied money. In *Foskett v McKeown*, Timothy Murphy took out a life assurance policy of £1 million and proceeded to pay the first two annual premiums out of his own funds. The next two premiums (from five in total) were paid from money held by Murphy as an express trustee for a group of purchasers who had paid substantial sums to Murphy pending the transfer to them of building land in the Algarve. Before his suicide in 1991, Murphy settled the life assurance policy on trust for his mother and his children. On his death, the sum assured was paid to the trustees of the policy. The purchasers claimed that they were entitled to recover 40 per cent of the policy proceeds (i.e. some £400,000), a sum in proportion to the premiums paid. The beneficiaries argued that if the purchasers were entitled at all, it was to the amount of their premiums (£20,000) and not to a pro rata share in the policy proceeds. By a majority, the House of Lords upheld the purchasers' claim to a pro-rata share on the basis that they could assert an equitable proprietary interest in the mixed fund.

17-049
It seems both sensible and just that, as between the beneficiary and the wrongdoing trustee, the operation of the rules should overtly favour the beneficiary. In the case of the profitable investment, therefore, the beneficiary is entitled to claim a proportionate share in the asset. As Rimer J explained in *Shalson v Russo*, "The justice of this is that, if the beneficiary is not entitled to do this, the wrongdoing trustee may be left with all the cherries and the victim with nothing".[213] In the example provided, the beneficiary can enforce a proprietary claim to a proportionate share of Fred's profitable investment, i.e. £5,000 plus profits.

Lowest intermediate balance

17-050
It should be noted that beneficiaries are confined to tracing into what has been referred to as the lowest intermediate balance of the account. Consider where a trustee, Fred mixes £5,000 of his own money with £5,000 of trust money and proceeds to waste £7,000 of the entire fund.

---

211 [1967] Ch. 1179 at 1193. On the facts, nonetheless, the trustee was deemed to have used her overdraft facility and not trust moneys towards the purchase of properties.
212 [2001] 1 A.C. 102.
213 [2005] 2 W.L.R. 1213 at 1261.

Even if, at some future date, Fred replenishes the fund, only £3,000 of the trust money can be traced. In the absence of evidence that Fred intended to replace the claimant's funds, tracing can take effect only in relation to the lowest balance in the intervening period.[214] Speaking of the defendant in *Roscoe v Winder*, Sargant J emphasised:

> **"I think it is impossible to attribute to him that by the mere payment into the account of further moneys which to a large extent he subsequently used for purposes of his own he intended to clothe those moneys with a trust in favour of the plaintiffs".[215]**

This principle has been upheld in respect of the wrongful diversion of oil stocks in *Glencore International AG v Alpina Insurance Co Ltd*.[216] There Moore-Bick J applied *Roscoe v Winder* claiming that "an intention to transfer title cannot be inferred simply from the fact that a wrongdoer has added to a commingled bulk a quantity of his own goods . . . sufficient to reverse the effect of previous wrongful withdrawals".[217]

Overdrawn bank accounts

The right to trace in equity is lost when trust funds pass into an overdrawn account.[218] As Rimer J explained in *Shalson v Russo*,[219] this is simply because an overdrawn account is not an asset, but a liability. In such a case, "the claimant cannot show that his money has become represented by an asset into which it is possible to trace: all his money has done is to reduce a liability, and so has ceased to exist".[220] In *Bishopsgate Investment Management Ltd v Homan*,[221] therefore, no equitable tracing was available in respect of the improper payment of pension funds into an overdrawn account.

17-051

Backwards tracing

The question arises as to whether beneficiaries might be permitted to trace backwards through the payment of a debt using trust money, into an asset purchased with the borrowed funds.[222]

17-052

---

214 See, e.g. *Campden Hill Ltd v Chakrani* [2005] EWHC 911 (Ch) at [79].
215 [1915] 1 Ch. 62 at 69; see also *Re BA Peters Plc* [2008] EWHC 2205 (Ch).
216 [2004] EWHC 66 (Comm).
217 [2004] EWHC 66 (Comm) at [18].
218 *Re Goldcorp Exchange Ltd* [1995] 1 A.C. 74 at 104–105; *Serious Fraud Office v Lexi Holdings Plc* [2009] Q.B. 376 at 393.
219 [2005] 2 W.L.R. 1213.
220 [2005] 2 W.L.R. 1213 at 1260.
221 [1995] Ch. 211.
222 See generally, M. Conaglen, "Difficulties with Backwards Tracing" (2011) 127 L.Q.R. 432.

A simple example is of the trustee, Fred who uses £3,300 of his overdraft to buy a car and one day later pays the same sum into his account using misappropriated trust funds. The issue of whether a claimant to the misappropriated funds can (or should be entitled to) trace through the repayment into the asset has excited much debate. In *Foskett v McKeown*,[223] the matter was considered in the Court of Appeal where, Scott VC openly regarded it to be undecided. He claimed:

> "I do not regard the fact that an asset is paid for out of borrowed money with the borrowing subsequently repaid out of trust money as being necessarily fatal to an equitable tracing claim by the trust beneficiaries. If, in such a case, it can be shown that it was always the intention to use the trust money to acquire the asset, I do not see why the order in which the events happen should be regarded as critical to the claim".[224]

At first instance in *Bishopsgate Investment Management Ltd v Homan*, moreover, Vinelott J would not rule out the possible invocation of so-called backwards tracing, arguing that proof that trust moneys were paid into an overdrawn account of the defaulting trustee might not always be sufficient to bar a claim to an equitable charge. In the Court of Appeal,[225] however, Leggatt LJ was markedly less enthusiastic. Effectively ruling out such an application of the rules, he explained:

> "there can be no equitable remedy against an asset acquired before misappropriation of money takes place, since ex hypothesi it cannot be followed into something which existed and so had been acquired before the money was received and therefore without its aid. The concept of a 'composite transaction' is in my judgment fallacious. What is envisaged is (a) the purchase of an asset by means of an overdraft, that is, a loan from a bank, and (b) the discharge of the loan by means of misappropriated trust money. The judge thought that the money could be regarded as having been used to acquire the asset . . . [but] there can ordinarily be no tracing into an asset which is already in the hands of the defaulting trustee when the misappropriation occurs".[226]

In line with this conventional understanding of tracing as a process which allows a claimant to trace the value of specific assets through real-time substitutions into specific, identifiable property, there is no room for backwards tracing.[227]

223 [1998] Ch. 265.
224 [1998] Ch. 265 at 283.
225 [1995] Ch. 211.
226 [1995] Ch. 211.
227 As Buckley LJ identified in *Borden (UK) Ltd v Scottish Timber Products Ltd* [1981] Ch. 25 at 46, "it is a

The latest case law development occurred in *Brazil v Durant International Corp.*[228] Here, the Privy Council upheld the decision of the Court of Appeal in Jersey and allowed a claim supported by backwards tracing. The claimant was the municipality of Sao Paulo[229] and its claim concerned companies under the control of the former mayor of the municipality and his son. The claimant sought to trace the proceeds of bribes (some US$10.5 million) paid to the former mayor and laundered through mixed accounts, one of which was the Deutsche Bank in Jersey. The account from which they sought to claim was Account "K". Through 13 separate payments, the bribe proceeds had been paid initially into Account "C" between January and February 1998. Six payments were made from Account "C" into Account "D", also in January of that year. Moneys then moved from Account "D" to Account "K". In all, some US$13.5 million was transferred to Account "K" In four payments. The obstacle facing the claimant was that some of the payments into Account "C" arrived there only after the final transfer of money away from that account, destined for Account "K". Using conventional tracing rules, only US$7.7 million could be traced because the outstanding moneys in Account "K" were paid in before the deposit of the bribe proceeds. Nonetheless, the Privy Council permitted recovery of the full amount. The idea that there could never be backwards tracing or that it would never be possible to trace into an overdrawn account was rejected. To permit recovery, however, there was a need for a close transactional link between the depletion of the trust and the acquisition, such that the court could attribute the value of what has been acquired with that of the misused funds. As Lord Toulson explained:

> **"The development of increasingly sophisticated and elaborate methods of money laundering, often involving a web of credits and debits between intermediaries, makes it particularly important that a court should not allow a camouflage of interconnected transactions to obscure its vision of their true overall purpose and effect. If the court is satisfied that the various steps are part of a co-ordinated scheme, it should not matter that, either as a deliberate part of the choreography or possibly because of the incidents of the banking system, a debit appears in the bank account of an intermediary before a reciprocal credit entry".[230]**

The outcome in *Brazil v Durant International Corporation* (that backwards tracing be permitted) reflects the maxim that Equity regards substance over form, but only in the case of a clearly coordinated scheme designed purposefully to defraud. Although a decision of the Privy

---

fundamental feature of the doctrine of tracing that the property to be traced can be identified at every stage of its journey through life".

228 [2016] A.C. 297. See P. Turner, "Tracing To and Fro" (2016) 75(3) C.L.J 462.

229 The Republic of Brazil was required by its constitution to be listed as the nominal claimant in legal proceedings brought outside Brazil.

230 [2016] A.C. 297 at [38].

Council, it is an interesting development in the law of tracing that may, perhaps, signal the future direction of English courts where circumstances demand.[231]

Swollen assets theory

17-053

A related (and unsuccessful) attempt to relax the rules of tracing can be found in the much discredited swollen assets theory as derived from *Space Investments Ltd v Canadian Imperial Bank of Commerce Co (Bahamas) Ltd*.[232] There, Lord Templeman suggested obiter that beneficiaries could trace misappropriated trust money into all the assets of a bank without the need to point to the specific assets into which the value could be traced. The justification for this flexible approach was said to be that the trust money swelled the total assets held by the bank and that a claimant needed merely to show that its value had gone into the bank's general assets. As Lord Templeman explained, "equity allows the beneficiaries . . . to trace the trust money to all the assets of the bank and to recover the trust money by the exercise of an equitable charge over all the assets of the bank . . . that equitable charge secures for the beneficiaries and the trust priority over the claims of the customers . . . and . . . all other unsecured creditors".[233] Rejected in *Re Goldcorp Exchange Ltd*[234] and also by the Court of Appeal in *Bishopsgate Investment Management Ltd v Homan*,[235] it is clear that the tracing rules do not permit the claimant to move beyond specific identifiable property (into which the value of its assets have passed) and to treat all of the defendant's assets as a large single fund in which trust assets have been mixed.

Addressing specifically Lord Templeman's dictum in *Space Investments*, in *Serious Fraud Office v Lexi Holdings Plc (In Administration)*, Keene LJ claimed that:

> "This cannot be right, in our view. For the equitable charge to attach it must attach to assets in existence which derive from the misappropriated trust funds. There must be a nexus. Were it otherwise the principles of following and tracing could become otiose. On the contrary, tracing in this area is a vital process: just because it is by that process that the necessary nexus is established and the proprietary remedy, be it by way of constructive trust or equitable charge, made effectual. It is for that reason that if all the misappropriated trust funds in any given case are paid into an account which was and remains overdrawn then the proprietary remedy is lost: for there

---

231 For a discussion of the developing case law in New Zealand, see A. Butler, N Walker, "New Zealand Developments in Equitable Tracing and Subrogation: Overuse and Underuse" (2018) 24(9) T. & T. 879.
232 [1986] 1 W.L.R. 1072.
233 [1986] 1 W.L.R. 1072 at 1074.
234 [1995] 1 A.C. 74.
235 [1995] Ch. 211.

> are no identifiable assets left in existence deriving from the misap-
> propriated trust funds, to which a constructive trust or an equitable
> charge could attach . . .".[236]

Mixed funds consisting of two trust funds or trust moneys with moneys of an innocent volunteer

The cases and illustrations above apply where there has been a mixture of trust money with the trustee's own money (i.e. claimant and wrongdoer). Frequently, however, it is necessary to consider the position where a mixed fund contains property from two or more trust funds or where trust property has become mixed with the property of an innocent volunteer. In such cases, different rules apply to tracing claims.

17-054

Innocent volunteers and other claimants

As regards the mixing of trust property with that of an innocent volunteer, the matter was duly considered in *Re Diplock's Estate*.[237] It will be recalled that the litigation concerned the distribution by executors of the testator's residuary estate to around 139 charities under a bequest later held by the House of Lords to be invalid. Accordingly, the question arose as to how to balance the competing equitable claims of the beneficiary and the innocent volunteer. The answer provided by Lord Greene MR was that:

17-055

> **"Where an innocent volunteer (as distinct from a purchaser for value
> without notice) mixes 'money' of his own with 'money' which in equity
> belongs to another person, or is found in possession of such a mix-
> ture, although that other person may not claim a charge on the mass
> superior to the claim of the volunteer, he is entitled, nevertheless, to
> a charge ranking *pari passu* with the claim of the volunteer".[238]**

This principle is open to the criticism that it is unduly favourable to the innocent volunteer. Consider, for example, an innocent volunteer who purchases investments in part with trust money and in part with his own funds. He takes the proceeds of the investments and dissipates a large sum of money. As the proceeds are derived in part from trust money and in part from his own resources, he is deemed to have dissipated money rateably from the trust fund and his own funds. He is not presumed to spend his own money first.

---

236 [2009] Q.B. 376 at 393.
237 [1948] Ch. 465.
238 [1948] Ch. 465 at 524.

The potential for unfairness is even more pronounced where the mixing occurs in a current bank account. Where an account contains misappropriated funds from two or more trusts or there is a mixture of trust moneys and the money of an innocent volunteer, the court can elect to apply one of three different approaches.[239] These are as follows:

- the "first in, first out" approach;

- proportionate shares; or

- the North American rolling charge.

First in, first out

17-056
The "first in, first out" rule established by *Clayton's case*[240] is the rule adopted traditionally where the property of different trusts has been mixed in a current or running bank account. The essence of the approach in *Clayton's case* is that when sums become mixed in a bank account, the withdrawals from that account are deemed to occur in the same order as the money was deposited. Historically, the rule achieved the most efficient means of balancing the respective interests of a banker and his customer in a bank account. What was an effective tool of accounting, however, quickly became regarded as the primary means to determine the distribution of property from a fund containing mixed trust funds from two or more trusts or a mixture of trust funds with funds belonging to an innocent volunteer.[241] This is particularly important where there is insufficient money to meet the respective claims.

Even at first glance, it is clear that any rigid application of this rule is apt to produce arbitrary and unacceptable results. Consider a bank account into which £1,000 from Trust X is deposited, followed by £1,000 from Trust Y, followed by £1,000 from Trust Z. Imagine that £1,500 is withdrawn and invested profitably, whereas the remaining £1,500 in the account is dissipated. Under the rule in *Clayton's case*, Trust X would be entitled to trace the first £1,000 into the profitable investment. This opens the way to a full recovery of the value of the misappropriated funds and a claim to a proportionate share of the profit. Trust Y, by contrast, will recover only £500 and the proportion of the profit thereby generated. Purely on the basis of the timing of the deposit of moneys in the account, the rule in *Clayton's case* reduces the claim of Trust Y to half of the value it added to the account. Trust Z can recover nothing.

17-057
It should come as little surprise that the first in, first out rule has attracted criticism. As Judge Learned Hand said in *Re Walter J Schmidt & Co Ex p. Feuerbach*:

---

239 See *Charity Commission for England & Wales v Framjee* [2015] 1 W.L.R. 16 at [48].
240 (1816) 1 Mer. 529.
241 In *Barlow Clowes International v Vaughan* [1992] 4 All E.R. 22 at 33, Dillon LJ recognised, a "long-established general practice" of the courts in applying *Clayton's Case* in such circumstances.

> "The rule in *Clayton's case* is to allocate the payments upon an account. Some rule had to be adopted, and though any presumption of intent was a fiction, priority in time was the most natural basis of allocation. It has no relevancy whatever to a case like this. Here two people are jointly interested in a fund held for them by a common trustee. There is no reason in law or justice why his depredations upon the fund should not be borne equally between them. To throw all the loss upon one, through the mere chance of his being earlier in time, is irrational and arbitrary, and is equally a fiction as the rule in *Clayton's case*. When the law adopts a fiction, it is, or at least it should be, for some purpose of justice. To adopt it here is to apportion a common misfortune through a test which has no relation whatever to the justice of the case".[242]

Notwithstanding, its frequent invocation, the rule in *Clayton's case* is merely a rule of convenience based on a presumption as to intentions.[243] In the words of Leggatt LJ in *Barlow Clowes International v Vaughan*, "neither its acclaim nor its application has been universal".[244] Accordingly, as Woolf LJ made clear, the modern approach is to apply the rule when it is convenient to do so and when its application can be seen to do broad justice having regard to the nature of the competing claims.[245]

Proportionality

As indicated above, the approach based on proportionality would entail that the available assets and moneys would be distributed rateably in proportion to the amounts contributed to the fund. This solution disregards the date at which investments were made. Instead, it is necessary to share the remaining assets on a proportionate basis among all contributors. The clear advantage of this approach lies in the capacity to minimise the potential for injustice where *Clayton's case* is applied. This principle of proportionate shares was adopted in the House of Lords in *Foskett v McKeown* where Lord Millett held that, "Where a beneficiary's claim is in competition with the claims of other innocent contributors, there is no basis upon which any of the claims can be subordinated to any of the others. Where the fund is deficient, the beneficiary is not entitled to enforce a lien for his contributions; all must share rateably in the fund. The primary rule in regard to a mixed fund is that gains and losses are borne by the contributors rateably".[246]

17-058

---

242 (1923) 298 F. 314 at 316. Reproduced with permission.
243 See Lord Greene MR in *Re Diplock's Estate* [1948] Ch. 465 at 553.
244 [1992] 4 All E.R. 22 at 43.
245 See generally, M. Pawlowski, "The Demise of the Rule in Clayton's Case" [2003] Conv. 339.
246 [2001] 1 A.C. 102 at 132.

Accordingly, in the example cited above, Trusts X, Y and Z would claim equally between them. Their contributions to the fund were exactly the same.

Rolling charge

17-059

The North American solution is termed "the rolling charge". In the United States and Canada it has been adopted (where appropriate) in preference to the rule in *Clayton's case* as establishing a fairer and more equitable result.[247] As Woolf LJ explained in *Barlow Clowes*, "This solution involves treating credits to a bank account made at different times and from different sources as a blend or cocktail with the result that when a withdrawal is made from the account it is treated as a withdrawal in the same proportions as the different interests in the account . . . bear to each other at the moment before the withdrawal is made".[248] It has the advantage that "each debit to the account, unless unequivocally attributable to the moneys of one depositor or source (e.g. as if an investment was purchased for one), should be attributed to all the depositors so as to reduce all their deposits pro rata".[249]

Consider, for example, a trustee who mixes £1,000 from Trust A with £1,000 from Trust B. He then gambles away £800. One day later, he adds £2,000 from Trust C. The balance of the account now stands at £3,200. If the "first in, first out" rule fell to be applied, Trust A would be disadvantaged (only £200 could be claimed by A), but both B and C could recover fully. Applying the rolling charge, however, the timing of deposits and withdrawals is factored in. In the example provided, C's money was not added until after the defendant loses £800. Under the rolling charge approach, only A and B should shoulder this loss in proportion to their respective contributions to the fund prior to the defendant's wasteful act. Accordingly, prior to the payment of £2,000 from Trust C into the account, the balance stands at £1,200. This is a balance to which A and B are entitled rateably (i.e. 1:1 ratio). Once Trust C's money is added to the account, a subsequent loss or gain will be shared in the same proportion as their interests bear to each other at the point at which the loss or gain was made (i.e. a 3:3:10 ratio).

17-060

Admittedly, on complex facts, the rolling charge will be difficult and expensive to apply.[250] In *Barlow Clowes*, for example, thousands of investors had contributed money to BCI. When the company went into liquidation, the question arose as to who was entitled to the remaining assets. Although the rolling charge was deemed to be fairest in the sense that claimants would share losses in proportion to their interest in the fund prior to each withdrawal, the method

---

247 See, e.g. the decision of the Ontario Court of Appeal in *Re Ontario Securities Commission and Greymac Credit Corp* (1986) 55 O.R. (2d) 673.
248 [1992] 4 All E.R. 22 at 35.
249 [1992] 4 All E.R. 22 at 27. As Henderson J put it in *Charity Commission for England and Wales v Framjee* [2015] 1 W.L.R. 16 at [48], it is a "methodology, which combines the pari passu approach with the lowest intermediate balance principle. Its effect is that the position has to be analysed whenever a payment is made out of the fund, and no contributor can be paid more than his rateable share of the lowest intermediate balance while his money remained in the fund".
250 See *Russell-Cooke Trust Co v Prentis* [2003] 2 All E.R. 478.

was deemed to be inapplicable. For example, Woolf LJ noted that, "it might just be possible to perform the exercise", but he felt that "the costs involved would be out of all proportion even to the sizeable sums which are here involved".[251] Accordingly, the rule in *Clayton's case* was reaffirmed as the rule of convenience in such cases. On the facts of *Barlow Clowes*, however, the rule in *Clayton's case* was not applied. The available assets were ordered to be distributed rateably to investors in proportion to their contributions to the fund.[252] A similar outcome was reached in *Commerzbank Aktiengesellschaft v IMB Morgan Plc*, where the rule in *Clayton's case* was deemed to be impracticable and unjust.[253] Albeit attractive in theory, the rolling charge is yet to displace the more traditional rules of equitable tracing in this context.[254]

The limits to tracing and equitable proprietary claims

Notwithstanding the operation of the rules of tracing, there are various situations in which the capacity to trace is lost or it is clear that the claimant will be unsuccessful with any resulting claim. Key considerations are as follows.

17-061

(i) The bona fide purchaser

Where misappropriated trust property falls into the hands of a bona fide purchaser for value without notice it ceases to be possible for a beneficiary to pursue a proprietary claim. Although, technically, it is possible to trace property into the recipient's hands, bona fide purchasers take free from the claims of beneficiaries. In *Sinclair Investments (UK) Ltd v Versailles Trade Finance Ltd (In Administration)*,[255] therefore, the defendant banks were partially entitled to rely on the bona fide purchaser defence in that they had no notice of the claimant's proprietary interest until July 2001. The right to trace was lost in respect of payments to the banks before that point. In addition, in *Independent Trustee Services Ltd v GP Noble Trustees Ltd*,[256] the Court of Appeal addressed a novel question regarding the availability of the defence when faced with a transaction, relied upon by the recipient of property to show that she was a bona fide purchaser, which had been set aside. Mrs Morris, wife of Mr Morris, had been paid some £1.5 million by him by way of a divorce settlement, endorsed by judicial consent order under the Matrimonial Causes Act 1973. Faced with growing evidence of her husband's lavish lifestyle, Mrs Morris successfully applied to have the order set aside in the expectation that she could claim for more

---

251 [1992] 4 All E.R. 22 at 35.
252 For Woolf LJ this outcome had "the virtue of relative simplicity and therefore relative economy and also the virtue of being in this case more just than the first solution [*Clayton's case*]. It would have the effect of sharing the pool of assets available proportionately among the thousands of investors in a way which reflected the fact that they were all the victims of a 'common misfortune'" ([1992] 4 All E.R. 22 at 35).
253 [2005] 1 Lloyd's Rep. 298 at 306.
254 See, however, *Shalson v Russo* [2005] 2 W.L.R. 1213 where Rimer J clearly preferred the rolling charge solution.
255 [2011] EWCA Civ 347.
256 [2012] 3 W.L.R. 597. See B. Häcker, "The Effect of Rescission on Bona Fide Purchase" (2012) 128 L.Q.R. 493.

by way of settlement. She had no idea that the funds paid to her had been misappropriated from a pension trust. In the meantime and pending the new hearing, Mrs Morris was permitted to retain the money already paid out to her. Before the hearing could take place, however, Mrs Morris became aware of the fraudulent activities of her husband and of the action against her by ITS, the pension scheme trustees, to recover its misapplied funds. The question for the Court was whether these sums were recoverable. The Court of Appeal acknowledged that there was a point in time when Mrs Morris was able to assert the bona fide purchaser defence. This was when she had no knowledge of events and, by virtue of the consent order, she was deemed to have given value or consideration. This did not, however, render her immune to subsequent events. On the setting aside of the order, and regardless of lack of knowledge on her part, she could no longer claim to be a "purchaser" and had instead become a volunteer. As discussed above, the bona fide purchaser defence is not available to the volunteer who acts in good faith or otherwise.[257] Accordingly, the claimants could recover any property (or traceable proceeds) still in her hands. Any property that had been dissipated by her or now in the hands of a third party bona fide purchaser had ceased to be recoverable.

(ii) Destruction or Dissipation

Where trust property or its traceable value is consumed, dissipated or destroyed, the beneficiary will not succeed in making a proprietary claim. Typically, for example, a trustee or third party might dissipate funds by going on a holiday or discharging a personal debt. In such circumstances, a proprietary claim is destined to fail. It is important to remember that in complex commercial cases it can be difficult to determine exactly where the value of misappropriated funds now lies. In other words monies can become so inextricably mixed that it seems impossible to disentangle the relevant financial transactions in order to trace successfully. In *Sinclair Investments (UK) Ltd v Versailles Trade Finance Ltd (In Administration)*,[258] the Court of Appeal dealt with exactly this contention that, in such circumstances, tracing must fail. Lord Neuberger MR rejected this argument outright and explained:

> **"I do not see why this should mean that a proprietary claim is lost simply because the defaulting fiduciary, while still holding much of the money, has acted particularly dishonestly or cunningly by creating a maelstrom. Where he has mixed the funds held on trust with his own funds, the onus should be on the fiduciary to establish that part, and what part, of the mixed fund is his property".[259]**

This rule will work in favour of the claimant and against the wrongdoing recipient. Note, however, that no tracing claim will be permitted where it is shown to be more probable than not that the claimant's property (or its identifiable substitute) does not lie in the wrongdoer's mixed

---

257 See para.**17-055**.
258 [2011] EWCA Civ 347.
259 [2011] EWCA Civ 347 at [138].

fund. In terms of legitimate examples of consumption, dissipation or destruction, money paid into an overdrawn bank account ceases to be identifiable[260] and it is not currently open to the beneficiary to trace backwards[261] or to argue that the assets of the bank have swollen and that trust funds must be located within the general assets of the bank.[262] Different considerations apply where a trustee uses trust money to effect improvements to land or to pay off a secured debt such as a mortgage. In the case of the former, the land will be charged with the payment to the claimant of a sum reflecting the extent to which the recipient's land has been improved by use of the misappropriated money. As to the latter, the court may treat the land as subject to a charge by way of subrogation in favour of the claimant.[263] The claimant's position is said to be subrogated (i.e. substituted) to that of the original mortgagee.

(iii) Change of Position Defence

The claim of a beneficiary may possibly be met by the defence of change of position, i.e. that it is inequitable for a beneficiary to pursue a proprietary claim on the basis that a bona fide recipient's position has changed. Although this defence applies to a claim of unjust enrichment, consider the recipient charities in *Re Diplock's Estate*.[264] Where the charities, as innocent donees, had spent the claimant's money on improvements to their property, the Court of Appeal deemed it inequitable to permit the claimant to pursue a proprietary action. The charge, enforceable by sale, would have required the charities to sell their own property to meet the claims of the next of kin. It is, as yet, unclear how the restitutionary defence of change of position will mesh with the rules governing equitable proprietary claims. It is to be remembered that in *Foskett v McKeown*[265] Lord Millett kept separate the defences available in each context. He observed, "a claim in unjust enrichment is subject to a change of position defence, which usually operates by reducing or extinguishing the element of enrichment. An action like the present is subject to the bona fide purchaser for value defence, which operates to clear the defendant's title".[266]

---

260 *Shalson v Russo* [2005] 2 W.L.R. 1213.
261 *Bishopsgate Investment Management Ltd v Homan* [1995] Ch. 211; see **17-052**.
262 As argued by Lord Templeman in *Space Investments Ltd v Canadian Imperial Bank of Commerce Co (Bahamas) Ltd* [1986] 1 W.L.R. 1072; see para.**17-053**.
263 *Boscawen v Bajwa* [1995] 4 All E.R. 769.
264 [1948] Ch. 465.
265 [2001] 1 A.C. 102.
266 [2001] 1 A.C. 102 at 129.

In Personam Claims

17-062

It remains to examine the alternative claim made by the next of kin in *Re Diplock's Estate*.[267] It will be recalled that the personal representatives of the testator (whose residuary disposition was invalid) distributed his residuary estate to charities upon the footing that the disposition was, indeed, valid. In the Court of Appeal, it was held that the next of kin could recover by means of a personal action in equity. In the light that the original wrong payment was due to the mistake of the personal representatives, however, the beneficiary's primary claim was against the personal representatives. Any in personam claim against those wrongly paid must be limited to the amount not recoverable from the party responsible. Accordingly, it was held that any amount recovered from the executors must be apportioned among the charities in proportion to the grants they had received, so that the maximum recoverable from any individual charity by the next-of-kin would be rateably reduced.

It fell to the House of Lords to consider the question of a direct claim in equity against the charities.[268] The House of Lords endorsed the approach of the Court of Appeal upholding the right of an unpaid legatee to bring a personal action in equity against the persons to whom the estate had been wrongfully distributed. It is to be noted, nonetheless, that this principle may not extend to otherwise analogous cases in the context of execution of trusts. Indeed, Lord Simonds appears to indicate that the approach extends only to cases dealing with the administration of the deceased's estate. He claimed:

> **"I think that it is important in the discussion of this question to remember that the particular branch of the jurisdiction of the Court of Chancery with which we are concerned relates to the administration of assets of a deceased person. While in the development of this jurisdiction certain principles were established which were common to it and to the comparable jurisdiction in the execution of trusts, I do not find in history or in logic any justification for an argument which denies the possibility of an equitable right in the administration of assets because, as it is alleged, no comparable right existed in the execution of trusts".[269]**

---

267 [1948] Ch. 465.
268 [1951] A.C. 251.
269 [1951] A.C. 251 at 265.

Guide to Further Reading

M. Conaglen, "Difficulties with Backwards Tracing" (2011) 127 L.Q.R. 432.

T. Cutts, "Tracing Value and Transactions" (2016) 79 M.L.R. 381.

P. Davies, "Section 61 of the Trustee Act 1925: Deus Ex Machina?" [2015] Conv. 379

S.B. Elliott and J. Edelman, "Money Remedies Against Trustees" (2004) 18 Tru. L.I. 116.

P. Millett, "Equity's Place in the Law of Commerce" (1998) 114 L.Q.R. 214.

P. Millett, "Tracing and the Proceeds of Fraud" (1991) 107 L.Q.R. 71.

M. Pawlowski, "The Demise of the Rule in Clayton's Case" [2003] Conv. 339.

L. Smith, "Tracing into the Payment of a Debt" [1995] C.L.J. 290.

Man Yip, "The Commercial Context in Trust Law" [2016] Conv. 347.

18

Injunctions

The remaining chapters are dedicated to an analysis of two principal equitable remedies: the injunction and the order for specific performance. The focus of this chapter falls upon injunctions. An injunction is issued to direct a person to commit or to refrain from committing a specified act. Like the order for specific performance, the injunction is an equitable and, therefore, discretionary remedy, developed largely in accordance with settled principles.[1] This chapter will evaluate the general jurisdiction of the court to grant an injunction, the nature of the remedy, the different types of injunction obtainable and the principles upon which judicial discretion is exercised. Due consideration will be given to the capacity of the court to award damages in lieu of, or in addition to, the award of injunctive relief or specific performance. As regards either remedy, moreover, the failure to comply with an order of the court is a contempt of court, ultimately punishable by imprisonment. Accordingly, the means of enforcement at the disposal of the court also fall to be detailed in this chapter.

---

1   Note that the power to grant an injunction may also be conferred upon the court by statute such as in the protection of copyright and patents: see, e.g. Copyright, Designs and Patents Act 1988. By way of a recent illustration, this Act was utilised to require ISPs to block web customer access to streaming that infringed copyright during the Premier League broadcast of live football matches (*Football Association Premier League Ltd v British Telecommunications Ltd Plc* [2017] EWHC 480 (Ch)).

General Issues

Jurisdiction

18-002

The High Court jurisdiction to grant injunctions is contained in s.37(1) of the Senior Courts Act 1981.[2] It provides: "The High Court may by order (whether interlocutory or final) grant an injunction . . . in all cases in which it appears to the court to be just and convenient to do so". As with the remedy of specific performance, this discretion is exercised "not by the caprice of the Judge, but according to sufficient legal reasons or on settled principles".[3] Being an equitable remedy, an injunction was originally obtainable only from the Court of Chancery. Subsequent statutory developments[4] saw a limited power to grant injunctions extend to the common law courts.[5] Thereafter, the effect of the Judicature Acts 1873 and 1875 was to vest in the High Court, the jurisdiction of the Chancery and the common law courts to grant injunctions.

There has been considerable and detailed discussion of the impact of these statutory developments, for example whether s.25(8) of the Judicature Act 1873 enlarged the court's jurisdiction to embrace cases where no injunction would previously have been granted[6] and likewise whether the 1981 Act enlarged the pre-existing jurisdiction.[7] A much-promoted view is that, "if no court had the power of issuing an injunction before the Judicature Act, no part of the High Court has power to issue such an injunction".[8] This restrictive approach has House of Lords' approval in *Gouriet v Union of Post Office Workers* where it was claimed that such provisions "dealt only with procedure and had nothing to do with jurisdiction".[9]

Notwithstanding such clear statements of principle, there is also a discernible reluctance to accept that the statutory jurisdiction under s.37 is fettered by the pattern of historical intervention or that the power of the court should be limited to "exclusive categories".[10] As Lord Nicholls recognised in *Mercedes Benz AG v Leiduck*, "As circumstances in the world change, so must the situations in which the courts may properly exercise their jurisdiction to grant injunctions".[11] By way of an illustration, in *Cartier International AG v British Sky Broadcasting*

---

2   The jurisdiction of the county court is governed by s.38 of the County Courts Act 1984 (as amended).

3   *Beddow v Beddow* (1878) 9 Ch. D. 89 at 93 per Jessel MR.

4   See Ch.1.

5   See, e.g. the Common Law Procedure Act 1854 s.79.

6   As argued by Lindley and Chitty LJJ in *Cummins v Perkins* [1899] 1 Ch. 16.

7   In *Chief Constable of Kent v V* [1983] Q.B. 34 at 42, Lord Denning MR argued that "The section as it now stands plainly confers a new and extensive jurisdiction . . . It is far wider than anything that had been known in our courts before".

8   *North London Rly Co v Great Northern Rly Co* (1883) 11 Q.B.D. 30 at 36 per Brett LJ.

9   [1978] A.C. 435 at 516.

10   See generally, Lord Goff in *South Carolina Insurance Co v Assurantie Maatschappij de Zeven Provincien NV* [1987] A.C. 24.

11   [1996] A.C. 284 at 308. As Lord Nicholls added, "The exercise of the jurisdiction must be principled, but the criterion is injustice. Injustice is to be viewed and decided in the light of today's conditions and standards, not those of yester-year" (at 308).

Ltd,[12] the Court of Appeal confirmed the jurisdiction of the court to grant injunctions which required ISPs (intermediaries themselves not guilty of any wrongdoing, but whose services were used to infringe trademarks) to block access to particular websites selling counterfeit goods.[13] Rejecting a restrictive reading of s.37(1) (that the circumstances in which an injunction might be granted were limited), Kitchin LJ acknowledged that, "pursuant to general equitable principles injunctions may issue in new categories when the course appears appropriate".[14] To hold otherwise, he felt, "would impose a straightjacket on the court and its ability to exercise its equitable powers which is not warranted by principle".[15]

The protection of rights

In the enforcement of a claimant's private rights, it is a general requirement that a claimant show some legal or equitable cause of action. Equity will not intervene merely on the ground that there has been some perceived injustice to the claimant. As Lindley LJ claimed in *Holmes v Millage*, "It is an old mistake to suppose that, because there is no effectual remedy at law, there must be one in equity".[16] In *Day v Brownrigg*,[17] for example, the claimants alleged that their house had been called "Ashford Lodge" for a period of 60 years and that the adjoining house belonging to the defendants had been called "Ashford Villa" for a period of 40 years. When the defendants altered the name of their house to the same name as the claimant's house, the claimants sought an injunction to restrain the inconvenience, annoyance and depreciation in value of their property. The Court of Appeal refused injunctive relief. James LJ explained that, "This Court can only interfere where there is an invasion of a legal or equitable right. No such legal or equitable right exists . . .".[18] In *Paton v Trustees of British Pregnancy Advisory Service*, moreover, it was held that a husband seeking to prevent his wife from aborting their child had "no legal right enforceable in law or in equity to stop his wife having this abortion or to stop the doctors from carrying out the abortion".[19]

A wide range of rights might be protected, nonetheless, and, as indicated above, the approach of modern courts is flexible and responsive to changing times. Such was the sentiment of Fox LJ in *Bayer AG v Winter* when he observed, "Bearing in mind we are exercising a jurisdiction which is statutory and which is expressed in terms of considerable width, it seems to me that the court should not shrink, if it is of opinion that an injunction is necessary for the

18-003

---

12 [2016] EWCA Civ 658.
13 In an appeal concerned with costs, the Supreme Court has since held that ISPs should not bear the Implementation costs of those orders. The availability of blocking orders for brand owners was nonetheless confirmed: see *Cartier International AG v British Telecommunications Plc* [2018] UKSC 28.
14 [2016] EWCA Civ 658 at [54].
15 [2016] EWCA Civ 658 at [54].
16 [1893] 1 Q.B. 551 at 555.
17 (1878) 10 Ch. D. 294.
18 (1878) 10 Ch. D. 294 at 305.
19 [1979] Q.B. 276 at 281 per Sir George Baker P.

proper protection of a party to the action, from granting relief, notwithstanding it may, in its terms, be of a novel character".[20] In *Re Oriental Credit Ltd*,[21] therefore, Harman J granted an injunction ancillary to an order under s.561 of the Companies Act 1985 to prevent the director of a company from leaving the jurisdiction prior to examination under the order. He claimed, "I had the power to make my order although it is not an order made in aid of a legal right or in protection of an equitable interest".[22] The grant of the injunction was deemed necessary to ensure that the order under s.561 was obeyed.

18-004

As to the enforcement of a claimant's public rights, the leading authority remains the House of Lords decision in *Gouriet v Union of Post Office Workers*.[23] There, a member of the public had sought an injunction to restrain a threatened disruption to postal communications between South Africa and England and Wales. This presented a difficulty for the claimant in that it is the Attorney General who protects public rights either by an act on his own initiative or on behalf of a member of the public. In *Gouriet*, the Attorney General refused to consent to a relator action and provided no justification for his refusal.

The House of Lords denied that the court had the jurisdiction to grant the injunction or that it had the power to review the exercise of the Attorney General's discretion in any way. It reinforced the fundamental principle of English law that public rights can only be enforced in a civil action by the Attorney General, as an officer of the Crown, representing the public. Save where statute provides otherwise, a private individual can only bring an action to restrain a threatened breach of the law where the threatened breach would infringe his private rights or inflict special damage upon him. Lord Wilberforce was adamant:

> **"The distinction between public rights which the Attorney-General can, and the individual (absent special interest) cannot seek to enforce, and private rights is fundamental to our law. To break it, as counsel for Mr Gouriet frankly invited us to do, is not a development in the law, but a destruction of one of its pillars".[24]**

18-005

Further concerns were voiced in the House as to the use of the civil courts as a means of criminal law enforcement. It was accepted that instances of applications by Attorneys General to the civil courts for aid in enforcing the criminal law are "few in number and exceptional in character".[25] In the view of Viscount Dilhorne, it is appropriate that the criminal law is enforced in the criminal courts by the process of conviction and punishment of offenders and not in the civil courts. He accepted, however, that there may be circumstances where it is appropriate for an Attorney General to seek an injunction to restrain the commission of a criminal act, not

---

20   [1986] 1 W.L.R. 497 at 502.
21   [1988] 1 All E.R 892.
22   [1988] 1 All E.R. 892 at 895.
23   [1978] A.C. 435.
24   [1978] A.C. 435 at 482.
25   [1978] A.C. 435 at 489 per Viscount Dilhorne.

least where the penalties imposed for the offence are inadequate to deter its commission.[26] It is inevitable that such occasions will be rare. As Viscount Dilhorne put it, "It has been and in my opinion should continue to be exceptional for the aid of the civil courts to be invoked in support of the criminal law, and no wise Attorney General will make such an application or agree to one being made in his name unless it appears to him that the case is exceptional".[27]

The scope of an injunction

In granting an injunction, the court acts in personam. Equity fastens on the conscience of the defendant, "compelling the wrongdoing litigant himself to comply with the rule prescribed by equity".[28] The fact that a person is resident abroad, i.e. outside the jurisdiction of the court, will not necessarily place him outside the reach of the court if service out of the jurisdiction can be achieved under the Civil Procedure Rules.[29] It is also of note that the injunction can be framed in surprisingly wide terms. It used to be said that "you cannot have an injunction except against a party to the suit".[30] The modern day approach of the courts is significantly changed and there is a growing array of examples of injunctions granted against unnamed defendants,[31] or even *contra mundum* (as against the world).[32] It is important to note that injunctions are effective not only against persons to whom the order is directed, but also third parties who knowingly act in breach of the injunction resulting in impedance to, or interference with, the administration of justice.[33] Two particular developments have helped to shape the contemporary approach of the courts. First, the Civil Procedure Rules provide the court with a procedural code, the overriding objective of which is to deal with cases justly.[34] Secondly, following the coming into force of the Human Rights Act 1998, the influence of European jurisprudence is increasingly manifest.[35]

18-006

---

26 See, e.g. *Attorney General v Sharp* [1931] 1 Ch. 121 (unlicensed carriage plying for hire in circumstances where the defendant intended to pursue his illegal activities).

27 [1978] A.C. 435 at 491.

28 *R Griggs Group Ltd v Evans* [2005] Ch. 153 at 164 per Peter Prescott QC.

29 CPR Pt 6. In *Sweden v Serwin* [2020] EWHC 1251 (Comm), for example, a worldwide freezing order was enforced in the UK against Swedish assets of individuals who were the subject of fraud proceedings in Sweden.

30 Per Lord Eldon in *Iveson v Harris* (1802) 7 Ves. Jr. 251 at 257.

31 See, e.g. *Bloomsbury Publishing Group Plc v News Group Newspapers Ltd* [2003] 1 W.L.R. 1633 where an injunction was issued against "the person or persons who have offered the publishers of The Sun, The Daily Mail and the Daily Mirror newspapers a copy of the book Harry Potter and the Order of the Phoenix by JK Rowling . . .".

32 For example, to protect the confidentiality of information regarding the killers of Jamie Bulger: *Venables v News Group Newspapers Ltd* [2001] 1 All E.R. 198.

33 See *Attorney General v Times Newspapers* [1992] 1 A.C. 191 at 206.

34 For example, there is no requirement that a defendant must now be named: see *Bloomsbury Publishing Group Plc v News Group Newspapers Ltd* [2003] 1 W.L.R. 1633.

35 As Dame Elizabeth Butler-Sloss noted almost 20 years ago in *Venables v News Group Newspapers Ltd* [2001] 1 All E.R. 908 at 939, "in light of the implementation of the 1998 Act, we are entering a new era, and a

18-007

Particular attention in recent times has been focused upon the use of the so-called "super-injunction", where the very existence of the injunction, and thereby any details relating to it, may not be reported.[36] In 2009, solicitors Carter Ruck obtained an injunction on behalf of the oil trader Trafigura preventing disclosure of its internal report on the dumping of toxic waste in the Ivory Coast.[37] It was only when reference to this issue was made in a Parliamentary question[38] (the fact of which it appeared could not be reported by the press) that the information came into the public domain by way of its wide circulation on the internet. There was no option for Carter Ruck but to drop its objection to the media reporting of the question. The use of these super-injunctions is extremely controversial as it involves a lack of transparency and derogates from the principles of open justice. It was, at the time, far from clear how often and for what purpose the courts had resort to such measures. Although there may be a legitimate need for a high level of caution and anonymity where lives are at risk, it had seemingly become commonplace for celebrities to seek[39] (and to obtain)[40] injunctions to prevent the reporting of sexual scandals in their private lives.[41] Some of these have been "super-injunctions", but the majority are anonymity orders, where the fact of the proceedings is in the public domain, but not the identity of the applicant or the parties.[42] Public concern led directly to the formation of Lord Neuberger's Committee on Super-Injunctions in April 2010, tasked to examine the use of super-injunctions and the increasing frequency of anonymised reporting. Its report, *Super-Injunctions, Anonymised Injunctions and Open Justice* made a series of recommendations to ensure that:

> **"exceptions to the principle of open justice will only be allowed when they are strictly necessary in the interests of justice, and that when allowed they will go no further than is strictly necessary. This should mean that super-injunctions will only be granted in very limited circumstances and, at least normally, for very short periods of time".[43]**

requirement that the courts act in a way which is compatible with the convention, and have regard to European jurisprudence, adds a new dimension to those principles".

36   As David Eady explained in "Injunctions and the Protection of Privacy" (2010) 29 C.J.Q. 411, ". . . although the usage of the term is by no means consistent, what is generally referred to is an injunction which includes within it an express prohibition upon those to be served with it against revealing even the fact that the injunction has been granted".

37   *RJW & SJW v Guardian Newspaper & Person or Persons Unknown* [2009] EWHC 2540 (QB).

38   Note that the rules on Parliamentary privilege apply.

39   *Terry v Persons Unknown* [2010] 1 F.C.R. 659 (application on behalf of footballer John Terry).

40   See, e.g. *Ntuli v Donald* [2010] EWCA Civ 1276 (granted to a well-known member of the band Take That and then set aside on appeal).

41   Actions for breach of confidence and misuse of private information are considered in detail at para.**18-051**.

42   Where the names of the parties to the action are referred to by unrelated, random letters, e.g. *CTB v News Group Newspapers* [2011] EWHC 1232 (QB) (famous Premiership footballer who obtained an interim injunction to prevent the publication of details of an affair).

43   See *https://www.judiciary.uk/wp-content/uploads/JCO/Documents/Reports/super-injunction-report-20052011. pdf* [Accessed 31 July 2020].

The Report appears to have had the desired effect with low numbers of privacy injunctions granted in recent years. The latest statistics from the Ministry of Justice (issued quarterly) show something of a resurgence, however, with 10 new privacy injunctions granted in 2019, six of which were issued between July and December of that year.[44]

Failure to comply with an injunction

The next matter to consider is the enforcement of injunctions. Where a person breaches intentionally the terms of an injunction (or indeed an order for specific performance), he is liable for contempt of court.[45] Nonetheless, non-compliance can take a variety of forms and the court will weigh up a variety of considerations such as the conduct of the defendant and the history of the case before it decides on an appropriate course of enforcement. The range of penalties at the disposal of the court includes imprisonment, a writ of sequestration of property,[46] the provision of a fine or simply an order to pay costs.[47] The ultimate sanction against the individual is, of course, committal to prison.[48] The justification for imprisonment is evident on two levels.[49] First, there is a punitive element based on the need to punish the defendant for his continuing disregard of the court.[50] Secondly, there is a coercive element, whereby the court aims to force compliance with its order.[51] Accordingly, where continuing imprisonment is deemed to have no further coercive effect, the court can cut short the term of imprisonment imposed on the contemnor.[52] The power to order release should be exercised sparingly because the value of the coercive element of a prison sentence is in jeopardy if it is clear to a contemnor that the court will order release if he is simply to state his intention not to comply. As Neuberger J admitted in *Shalson v Russo*, "if it became known that the court would let a contemnor out of prison early whenever he made it clear that there was no pos-

18-008

---

44 Ministry of Justice, *Civil Justice Statistics Quarterly* (5 March 2020), available at: *https://assets.publishing.service. gov.uk/government/uploads/system/uploads/attachment_data/file/870184/civil-justice-statistics-quarterly-Oct- Dec.pdf* [Accessed 31 July 2020].

45 Contempt of Court Act 1981. See *Absolute Living Developments Ltd v DS7 Ltd* [2018] EWHC 1717 (Ch) for a discussion of relevant principles.

46 Usually in the case of corporations.

47 As Underhill LJ recognised In *Cuadrilla Bowland Ltd v Persons Unknown* [2020] EWCA Civ 9 at [112], it is "important for the rule of law that deliberate breaches of court orders attract a real penalty".

48 *JSC BTA Bank v Solodchenko* [2010] EWHC 2404 (Comm). For principles applicable to sentencing see *Crystal Mews Ltd v Metterick* [2006] EWHC 3087 (Ch).

49 See *Asia Islamic Trade Finance Fund Ltd v Drum Risk Management Ltd* [2015] EWHC 3748 (Comm).

50 For example, in *Re King Thompson* [2019] EWHC 2962 (QB) at [38], Murray J considered the breach of an injunction by a young urban explorer determined to climb the exterior of The Shard as "deliberate, knowing and contumacious"; he was sentenced to 24 weeks' detention in a Young Offenders' Institution.

51 See *Re Barrell Enterprises Ltd* [1972] 3 All E.R. 631.

52 See generally, *Enfield LBC v Mahoney* [1983] 2 All E.R. 901, where a landowner refused to hand over a Saxon artefact to the local borough council.

sibility of his complying, then much of the value of the coercive element of a prison sentence would be at risk".[53]

Generally, committal to prison will be avoided in circumstances where the court has a viable alternative,[54] but it may be especially appropriate where an order of the court is met with unwavering defiance. Thus, in *Burton v Winters*[55] a sentence of two years' imprisonment (the maximum term permitted by s.14(1) of the Contempt of Court Act 1981) was held to be justified because the claimant, in proceedings in trespass and nuisance against the defendants, persisted in attempts to build a wall on the defendant's land, ignoring the terms of an injunction against her.

In addition, a third party who aids and abets the breach of an injunction becomes an accessory and liable for contempt.[56] The problems are somewhat different with regard to strangers. In the light that they are neither accessories to the breach nor party to the order, such third parties cannot be said to be in breach of an order of the court. As regards interim proceedings, however, an exception has evolved to the effect that third parties are in criminal contempt of court if they wilfully interfere with the administration of justice in the proceedings in which the order was made, notwithstanding that their actions were wholly independent of the defendant.[57] Intentional interference with the manner in which a judge is conducting a trial is a basis of criminal rather than civil contempt.[58] When a claimant brings an action to preserve an alleged right of confidentiality, for example, a third party who, with knowledge of the order, publishes the information and thereby destroys its confidentiality, will be in contempt of court.[59] This reasoning will apply in the case of an interim but not a final injunction.[60] As Lord Phillips MR acknowledged in *Attorney General v Punch*, "the offence lies not simply in the commission of the act prohibited by the order, but in the effect that the act has of interfering in the conduct of the trial".[61]

---

53 [2002] EWHC 399 (Ch) at [20].
54 *Danchevsky v Danchevsky* [1974] 3 All E.R. 934; see also, *Larkman v Lindsell, The Times*, 30 November 1985, where a property owner could have sought to enforce an order to vacate property by committal proceedings, but the grant of a possession order was a reasonable alternative to secure compliance.
55 [1993] 3 All E.R. 847.
56 *Acrow (Automation) Ltd v Rex Chainbelt Inc* [1971] 3 All E.R. 1175. Of course, the defendant is always potentially liable for the actions of his agent.
57 *Attorney General v Punch* [2003] 1 All E.R. 289.
58 *Attorney General v Times Newspapers Ltd* [1991] 1 A.C. 191.
59 *Attorney General v Times Newspapers Ltd* [1991] 1 A.C. 191.
60 See *Jockey Club v Buffham* [2003] Q.B. 462.
61 [2001] Q.B. 1028 at 1055.

The Award of Damages in Equity

Section 50 of the Senior Courts Act 1981 provides that, "Where the Court of Appeal or the High Court has jurisdiction to entertain an application for an injunction or specific performance, it may award damages in addition to, or in substitution for, an injunction or specific performance". This provision is a substantial re-enactment of powers conferred on the court by Lord Cairns' Act[62] (hence the tendency to continue to refer to it as such) to award damages in addition to or in substitution for an injunction, "in all cases in which the Court of Chancery has jurisdiction to entertain an application for an injunction".[63] The mischief at which this Act was addressed was, as noted by Turner LJ, that "great complaints were constantly made by the public, that when plaintiffs came into a court of equity for specific performance the court of equity sent them to a court of law in order to recover damages so that parties were bandied about, as it was said from one court to another".[64]

    The Act, therefore, enabled the court of equity to award damages in cases where a court of law had done so previously as well as to award an injunction to prevent the continuance or repetition of the prohibited activity. Lord Cairns' Act is also the basis of the court's jurisdiction in cases where there is no right to damages at law, for example where the breach in question is a breach of an equitable rather than a legal right[65] or where an injury is threatened and has not yet occurred. Where injury was merely threatened or apprehended, no damages could be recovered at law because "such damages were given only in respect of a cause of action which had accrued at the date of the commencement of the action".[66] Nonetheless, equity can restrain a threatened breach with the issue of a quia timet injunction[67] and, accordingly, it lies open to the court to award damages in lieu of (or in addition to) the grant of an injunction or an order for specific performance.

    It should be remembered that the award of damages is dependent on the court's jurisdiction to grant an injunction (or to order specific performance) and this is so even if the court is likely to refuse relief. The claimant must show that he has a prima facie case for equitable relief. Where the claimant is unable to do so, there can be no award of damages under Lord Cairns' Act.

18-010

Damages in lieu of injunction

The reluctance of the court to award damages instead of an injunction is premised upon the view that to do so would allow the defendant to purchase the right to persist in committing a

18-011

---

62 Chancery Amendment Act 1858.
63 Chancery Amendment Act 1858 s.2.
64 *Ferguson v Wilson* (1866) 2 Ch. App. 77 at 88.
65 See *Baxter v Four Oaks Properties Ltd* [1965] Ch. 816 (restrictive covenant).
66 *Leeds Industrial Co-Operative Society Ltd v Slack* [1924] A.C. 851 at 856 per Viscount Finlay.
67 See para.**18-025.**

wrongful act. In *Shelfer v City of London Electric Lighting Co*, Lindley LJ commented that, "ever since Lord Cairns' Act was passed the Court of Chancery has repudiated the notion that the legislature intended to turn that court into a tribunal for legalizing wrongful acts".[68] Similarly, as Buckley J emphasised in *Cowper v Laidler*, "The court has affirmed over and over again that the jurisdiction to give damages where it exists is not so to be used as in fact to enable the defendant to purchase from the plaintiff against his will his legal right . . .".[69] Accordingly, the courts developed the practice of refusing to award damages in substitution for an injunction save for exceptional circumstances. Of the many attempts to draw guidelines as to when damages in lieu are appropriate, the most cited is that made in *Shelfer v City of London Electric Lighting Co*.[70] Here, A.L. Smith LJ laid down what he described as "a good working rule"[71] that damages may be given in substitution for an injunction where:

(i)   the injury to the claimant is small;

(ii) the injury is one which is capable of being estimated in money;

(iii) the injury is one which can be adequately compensated by a small money payment; and

(iv) the case is one in which it would be oppressive to the defendant to grant an injunction.

There is no shortage of critical discussion in the case law as to how the working rule in *Shelfer* ought to be applied. In *Fishenden v Higgs and Hill Ltd*, for example, Lord Hanworth MR doubted the wisdom in formulating specific rules. He described the prescription as the "high-water mark of what might be called definite rules".[72] Romer LJ, moreover, was without any doubt that the discretion of the court could not be fettered. He emphasised that, "Where the four conditions . . . are fulfilled, I do not doubt that a court will grant damages in lieu of an injunction, but it by no means follows that A. L. Smith LJ intended to say or did say or in fact could say that in all cases in which those four conditions do not prevail, the injunction must be granted; he could not have intended to fetter the discretion imposed upon the court by Lord Cairns' Act".[73] Maugham LJ, too, questioned the scope of the rule, arguing that it was "not a universal or even sound rule in all cases of injury to light".[74] On the facts of *Fishenden*, substantial

---

68   [1895] 1 Ch. 287 at 315. Here, the Court of Appeal awarded injunctive relief where the defendant electricity company had caused structural damage to the claimant's property and nuisance to the claimant.
69   [1903] 2 Ch. 337 at 341. As Lord Sumption noted in *Coventry (t/a RDC Promotions) v Lawrence* [2014] UKSC 13 at [160], however, to adopt such a view "seems an unduly moralistic approach to disputes, and if taken at face value would justify the grant of an injunction in all cases, which is plainly not the law".
70   [1895] 1 Ch. 287.
71   [1895] 1 Ch. 287 at 322.
72   (1935) 153 L.T. 128 at 138.
73   (1935) 153 L.T. 128 at 141.
74   (1935) 153 L.T. 128 at 144.

damages were awarded to a claimant whose right to light was obstructed by the defendant's construction of a new building. Here, in particular, the conduct of the claimant militated against the provision of injunctive relief.

If many older authorities are overtly critical, modern courts have appeared generally ready to accept the longstanding influence of *Shelfer*. In *Jaggard v Sawyer*,[75] Millett LJ accepted the legitimacy of the *Shelfer* guidelines, commenting that, "Laid down just 100 years ago, A.L. Smith LJ's test has stood the test of time".[76] He proceeded to single out the fourth limb of A.L. Smith LJ's rule as being of particular importance, stating that, "The outcome of any particular case usually turns on the question: would it in all circumstances be oppressive to the defendant to grant the injunction to which the plaintiff is prima facie entitled?"[77] Here, the defendant built a house in a cul-de-sac in breach of covenant. When the claimant sought to restrain the defendant's continuing trespass and breach of restrictive covenant, injunctive relief was deemed oppressive. It was clear to Sir Thomas Bingham that the visual amenity of the claimant's house had not been impaired, nor had its value been affected.[78] Accordingly, the Court of Appeal held damages to be the appropriate remedy. In *Kennaway v Thompson*, moreover, the Court of Appeal acknowledged that "The principles enunciated in *Shelfer's* case, which is binding on us, have been applied time and time again over the past 85 years".[79] On the facts, however, the first three limbs of A.L. Smith LJ's rule had not been met. Although damages were awarded at first instance, the Court of Appeal granted an injunction to restrict the noise generated by motorboat racing, which constituted nuisance to the claimant.

18-012

Two more recent Court of Appeal decisions appeared to provide clarification as to the appropriate approach of the court to awarding damages in lieu of injunction. In *Regan v Paul Properties*,[80] the claimant, Mr Regan, alleged that the defendant property developers had infringed his right to light when they erected, directly opposite to his property, a 16-unit development complete with penthouse. When Regan complained about the loss of light caused by the penthouse, the defendants relied on misleading legal advice (that there was no actionable injury) and continued with the development, undeterred. At first instance, it was accepted that nuisance was committed, but that the appropriate remedy was an award of damages in lieu of injunction. Somewhat surprisingly, the Court of Appeal found in Regan's favour. In doing so, the opportunity was taken to affirm some basic principles and to warn developers in future cases that an award of damages is by no means certain. Mummery LJ noted that the claimant was prima facie entitled to an injunction because of the nuisance caused by the defendants. He emphasised, moreover, that damages in lieu of injunction was appropriate for exceptional cases only, i.e. the burden of proof did not lie with the claimant to convince the court not to

18-013

---

75 [1995] 1 W.L.R. 269.
76 [1995] 1 W.L.R. 269 at 287.
77 [1995] 1 W.L.R. 269 at 288.
78 [1995] 1 W.L.R. 269 at 282.
79 [1981] Q.B. 88 at 93.
80 [2006] 3 W.L.R. 1131. See P. Chynoweth, "Rights to Light: Radical Consequences of an Orthodox Decision" [2007] Conv. 175.

award damages as the trial judge had directed. On the facts, the injury to light was not small. It could be estimated in money terms, but it could not be compensated by the payment of a small money sum. Further, as regards the oppression caused to the defendant should part of the building works be required to be dismantled, Mummery LJ found that this was not, of itself, decisive. It was, he claimed, "necessary to consider all the surrounding circumstances of the dispute and the conduct of the parties".[81] In contrast to Mr Regan, whose conduct could not be criticised and who acted on advice which was correct, the defendants had taken a calculated risk to adhere to advice which turned out to be wrong. Accordingly, as Mummery LJ explained, the court could not be justified in "denying [Regan] an injunction and effectively forcing him to accept compensation from the defendants for losing the light in respect of his home".[82]

18-014

Renewed enthusiasm for the grant of injunctive relief was also reflected in *HKRUK II (CHC) v Heaney*,[83] where the addition of two floors to an office block in Leeds city centre caused an actionable interference with Heaney's right to light. Despite a "catalogue of reasons" put forward by the developer to show that oppression would result from the grant of an injunction,[84] Judge Langan QC was unimpressed.[85] Highlighting that all four *Shelfer* requirements had not been met, he drew the following conclusions in the case before him:

> **"(1) The infringement was not a trivial one. (2) The infringement was not inadvertent. It was, rather, committed in the knowledge that what was being done was actionable. (3) The infringement was committed with a view to profit. (4) The claimant was not driven by necessity, but could have very easily, if somewhat less profitably, built sixth and seventh floors of reduced dimensions. In my judgment, it would be wholly wrong for the court effectively to sanction what has been done by compelling the defendant to take monetary compensation which he does not want".[86]**

18-015

On the basis of the cases above, it appeared no longer safe for defendants to rely on the oppression that would result from the grant of an injunction, particularly where their conduct showed insufficient regard for the risk of infringement to the claimant's rights.[87] Nonetheless,

---

81   [2006] 3 W.L.R. 1131 at 1144.
82   [2006] 3 W.L.R. 1131 at 1144.
83   [2010] EWHC 2245 (Ch). See also *Jacklin v Chief Constable of West Yorkshire* [2007] EWCA Civ 181.
84   Not least the cost of between £1 million and £2 million to remove the offending part of the completed works.
85   Note that M. Dixon, "Shining a Light on Easements" [2013] Conv. 85, 86, viewed this as "a fully reasoned judgment, which does not appear to stray from existing principles".
86   [2010] EWHC 2245 (Ch) at [80].
87   As Richard Arnold QC acknowledged, however, in *Site Developments (Ferndown) Ltd v Barratt Homes Ltd* [2007] EWHC 415 (Ch) at [64], "whether it would be oppressive depends on all the relevant circumstances existing as at the date the court is asked to grant an injunction . . . [including] the conduct of the parties and the reality on the ground at the time that the question falls to be decided".

the notion that all four elements in *Shelfer* must be satisfied before the court will award damages seemed legitimately open to question. In *Coventry (t/a RDC Promotions) v Lawrence*,[88] the *Shelfer* principles were to come under renewed scrutiny as the Supreme Court had its say on the applicable principles by which the court may award damages in lieu of injunction. In the words of Dixon, "Such anguish as may have been caused by *Heaney* was, no doubt, soothed by the Supreme Court's decision.[89] Lord Sumption, for example, regarded *Shelfer* as "out of date" commentating that:

> "it is unfortunate that it has been followed so recently and so slavishly. It was devised for a time in which England was much less crowded, when comparatively few people owned property, when conservation was only beginning to be a public issue, and when there was no general system of statutory development control. The whole jurisprudence in this area will need one day to be reviewed in this court. There is much to be said for the view that damages are ordinarily an adequate remedy for nuisance . . .".[90]

Lord Neuberger, too, was concerned to stress the court's discretionary powers which he felt should not, "as a matter of principle, be fettered, particularly in the very constrained way in which the Court of Appeal has suggested in Regan . . .".[91] Rejecting the need for *Shelfer*-style guidelines, he felt that each case was "likely to be so fact-sensitive that any firm guidance is likely to do more harm than good".[92] Accordingly, Lord Neuberger preferred "a modified version" of the view expressed by Romer LJ in *Fishenden*,[93] that "it would, in the absence of additional relevant circumstances pointing the other way, normally be right to refuse an injunction if those four tests were satisfied".[94] The fact that the tests were not all satisfied would not mean necessarily that an injunction should be granted.

Although the Supreme Court has opened the way for the award of damages largely free from the constraints of *Shelfer*,[95] the principles may continue to prove a useful starting point for the court. Such was the case in *Rogers v Humphrey*,[96] where the claimant obtained an injunction to enforce a restrictive covenant entered into by his neighbour not to build without permission. The judge used *Shelfer* as a starting point but also factored in a range of relevant considerations such as the priorities of the claimant who had, in this case, chosen a

---

88 [2014] UKSC 13 (noise from a speedway track alleged to constitute nuisance).
89 "Green Light for Development" [2015] Conv. 1, 2.
90 [2014] UKSC 13 at [161].
91 [2014] UKSC 13 at [120].
92 [2014] UKSC 13 at [120].
93 (1935) 153 L.T. 128 at 141 (see para.**18-011**).
94 [2014] UKSC 13 at [123].
95 As Deputy Judge N. Strauss QC declared confidently in *Charlie Properties Ltd v Risetall Ltd* [2014] EWHC 4057 (Ch) at [8], "the court now has an unfettered discretion to award damages in lieu of injunction".
96 [2017] EWHC 3681 (QB).

rural area to live in, without many neighbours nearby. Slade J ruled that the judge had exercised his discretion appropriately, noting that "a court does not err by considering the *Shelfer* tests, as long as it does not apply them mechanically and also takes into account all relevant circumstances".[97]

More broadly, there is no doubt that the conduct of the defendant will continue to exert influence, for example where behaviour is high-handed or where a breach is flagrant and deliberate.[98] In such cases, an injunction may be necessary to do justice to the claimant and serve as a warning to others. It was on this basis that in *Ottercroft Ltd v Scandia Care Ltd* an order to compel the removal of an external staircase which had caused only a minor infringement of a neighbour's right to light was upheld by the Court of Appeal.[99] In *Charlie Properties Ltd v Risetall Ltd*,[100] moreover, the defendants had deliberately trespassed on land with a view to appropriating it for construction and, unsurprisingly, failed in their efforts to resist the injunction.

Measure of damages in lieu

18-016

Where damages are awarded in lieu of an injunction, they are a "monetary substitute for an injunction"[101] and as Lord Sumner recognised in *Leeds Industrial Co-Operative Society v Slack*, "No money awarded in substitution can be justly awarded, unless it is at any rate designed to be a preferable equivalent to an injunction and therefore an adequate substitution for it".[102] Accordingly, in *Wroth v Tyler*[103] (a case where specific performance was refused), Megarry J embraced that sentiment and awarded damages for loss of bargain calculated not as at the date of breach, but at the date of the judgment of the court.[104] He did so on the basis that the case was one within Lord Cairns' Act 1858. His decision was taken to suggest that a higher sum in damages may be awarded under the Act than is available at common law. In *Johnson v Agnew*,[105] however, Lord Wilberforce emphasised that "equity follows the law" and that there should be no difference between the measure of damages obtainable under Lord Cairns' Act

---

97   [2017] EWHC 2681 (QB) at [61].

98   Note that in *Coventry v Lawrence* at [121], Lord Neuberger cautiously approved the statement made by Lord MacNaghten in *Home and Colonial Stores Ltd* [1904] A.C. 179 at 193 that, "In some cases, of course, an injunction is necessary—if, for instance the injury cannot fairly be compensated by money—if the defendant has acted in a high-handed manner—if he has endeavoured to steal a march upon the plaintiff or to evade the jurisdiction of the Court".

99   [2016] EWCA Civ 867.

100 [2014] EWHC 4057.

101 *Morris-Garner v One Step (Support) Ltd* [2018] UKSC 20 at [44] per Lord Reed.

102 [1924] A.C. 851 at 870.

103 [1974] Ch. 30.

104 As Megarry J put it, "the damages that may be awarded are not limited to the £1,500 that is appropriate to the date of the breach, but extend to the £5,500 that is appropriate at the present day, when they are being awarded in substitution for specific performance" ([1974] Ch. 30 at 60).

105 [1980] A.C. 367 (again a claim for specific performance).

and at common law. His comments make sense when it is appreciated that both cases involved the court in assessing damages "for loss occasioned by a single, once and for all, past breach of contract on the part of the defendant".[106] As Millett LJ explained, "It cannot sensibly have any application where the claim at common law is in respect of a past trespass or breach of covenant and that under the Act is in respect of future trespasses or continuing breaches of covenant".[107] It follows that damages under the Act will not necessarily be measured in the same way as damages recoverable at law. As Lord Reed observed in *Morris Garner v One Step (Support) Ltd*, "That is hardly to be expected, given that the damages are available on a different basis, in different circumstances, and in respect of different types of wrong (past, on the one hand, and future or continuing, on the other)".[108]

A distinctive approach developed under Lord Cairns' Act where damages are awarded in lieu of an injunction to restrain breaches of restrictive covenant or interferences with property rights. In *Wrotham Park Estate Co v Parkside Homes Ltd*,[109] the claimant could not demonstrate financial loss flowing from a breach of covenant. The court awarded damages on what became known as the *"Wrotham Park"* basis, by reference to the value of the use wrongfully made of the property.

Wrotham Park damages

18-017

Wrotham Park[110] involved a developer who built houses in breach of a covenant only to build in accordance with the claimant's plans. The claimant sought an injunction, but omitted to seek interim relief with the consequence that the houses were complete when the issue was tried. The claimant sought a mandatory order requiring the houses to be pulled down. Brightman J recounted the social and economic reasons that were to inform his decision, noting specifically the "unpardonable waste of much needed houses",[111] were he to direct that they now be pulled down. He was in no doubt that the order should be refused.

In assessing damages in lieu, it was clear that the claimant had suffered no financial damage as a result of the breach of the layout stipulation. The claimant's use of the estate was, moreover, in no way impeded. To adopt that measure would result (at most) in purely nominal damages. Nominal damages were not, however, awarded. By way of a just substitute for an injunction, Brightman J held that the claimants would be entitled to such a sum as they might reasonably have demanded in return for the relaxation in the covenant (i.e. 5 per cent of the developer's anticipated profit).

---

106 *Jaggard v Sawyer* [1995] 1 W.L.R. 269 at 291, per Millet LJ.
107 [1995] 1 W.L.R. 269 at 291.
108 [2018] UKSC 20 at [47]
109 [1974] 2 All E.R. 321.
110 [1974] 2 All E.R. 321.
111 [1974] 2 All E.R. 321 at 337.

The opportunity to review *Wrotham Park* arose in *Jaggard v Sawyer*.[112] Here, the defendant erected a house in breach of covenant to which his only means of access was by way of trespass over a private road. The claimant sought an injunction. The Court of Appeal openly followed the *Wrotham Park* case. To avoid the undesirable consequence of an injunction, i.e. that the defendant's property would be landlocked, the claimant was awarded a sum that reflected what the defendant ought to have paid for the right of way and for release of the restrictive covenant. Accordingly, these cases demonstrate the jurisdiction of the court to compensate a claimant without the need to establish loss, posited on the need to avoid injustice.

18-018

In *Morris-Garner v One Step (Support) Ltd*,[113] Lord Reed jettisoned the term "Wrotham Park damages" in favour of "negotiating damages", a term employed by Neuberger LJ in *Lunn Poly Ltd v Liverpool & Lancashire Properties Ltd*.[114] With no further need to refer to the *Wrotham Park* decision (described by Lord Reed as "a source of potential confusion"[115]), the term "negotiating damages" should now be used to represent the sum of money that might reasonably be demanded by the claimant from the defendant as a quid pro quo for permitting the continuation of a breach of covenant or other invasion of rights. In *One Step*, Lord Reed emphasised that measuring loss by reference to the economic value of that permission was "one possible method of quantifying damages", but that it was not the only approach to assessing damages under Lord Cairns' Act. He proceeded to make clear that "It is for the court to judge what method of quantification, in the circumstances of the case before it, will give a fair equivalent for what is lost by the refusal of the injunction".[116]

By way of illustration, in the earlier case of *Tamares (Vincent Sq) Ltd v Fairpoint Properties (Vincent Sq) Ltd*, Deputy Judge Gabriel Moss QC deduced the principles to be applied in the assessment of *Wrotham Park* damages in the context of a right to light. Clearly tailored to this particular type of claim, these were as follows:

> **"(1) The overall principle is that the court must attempt to find what would be a 'fair' result of a hypothetical negotiation between the parties.**
> **(2) The context, including the nature and seriousness of the breach, must be kept in mind.**
> **(3) The right to prevent a development (or part) gives the owner of the right a significant bargaining position.**
> **(4) The owner of the right with such a bargaining position will normally be expected to receive some part of the likely profit from the development (or relevant part).**
> **(5) If there is no evidence of the likely size of the profit, the court**

---

112   [1995] 1 W.L.R. 269.
113   [2018] UKSC 20 at [3].
114   [2006] EWCA Civ 430 at [22].
115   [2018] UKSC 20 at [3].
116   [2018] UKSC 20 at [95].

can do its best by awarding a suitable multiple of the damages for loss of amenity.

(6) If there is evidence of the likely size of the profit, the court should normally award a sum which takes into account a fair percentage of the profit.

(7) The size of the award should not in any event be so large that the development (or relevant part) would not have taken place had such a sum been payable.

(8) After arriving at a figure which takes into consideration all the above and any other relevant factors, the court needs to consider whether the 'deal feels right'."[117]

Accordingly, in *Tamares (Vincent Sq) Ltd v Fairpoint Properties (Vincent Sq) Ltd*, the sum of £50,000 was deemed a fair result for an infringement to the claimant's right to light.

Types of Injunction

Having considered by way of introduction some important general matters regarding injunctions, it is now necessary to address the variety of injunctions that are issued by the court and the differences between them. The following categories are considered:

18-019

- prohibitory and mandatory injunctions;

- perpetual and interim injunctions;

- mandatory injunctions and orders for specific performance;

- without notice injunctions; and

- quia timet injunctions.

---

117   [2007] 1 W.L.R. 2167 at 2171. These principles were endorsed in *HKRUK II (CHC) v Heaney* [2010] EWHC 2245 (Ch) at [82].

Prohibitory or mandatory?

18-020

A prohibitory injunction is restrictive in nature and requires the defendant to refrain from initiating or committing the prohibited act. For example, an injunction ordered to prevent the defendant from building an extension to his property will be prohibitory in nature.

A mandatory injunction, however, is positive in the sense that it requires the defendant to act. Such an injunction will be necessary where the prohibited act has been committed and an order restraining the defendant would be pointless. For example, where the defendant has begun to build his extension, an order restraining him from doing so will not be an effective remedy. A mandatory injunction will, however, require positive steps to ensure that the act be undone[118] and, for this reason, "it is not the practice of the court to grant mandatory injunctions as readily as prohibitory injunctions".[119] It is irrelevant, moreover, that a mandatory order is couched in negative terms,[120] for example that the defendant "refrains from permitting the extension to remain". The action required is that he takes the positive steps necessary to demolish it.

Perpetual or interim?

18-021

A perpetual injunction simply means an injunction that (the court having heard the arguments put forward in full by both sides) finally settles or resolves the dispute between the parties.[121] Such injunctions are also referred to as "final" or "permanent". Interim injunctions (formally termed interlocutory injunctions) are granted pending the full hearing of the case and in circumstances where the claimant requires (until the case is heard in full) the immediate restraint of the defendant's proposed course of action. The object of an interim injunction is as Lord Wilberforce put it, "to prevent a litigant, who must necessarily suffer the law's delay, from losing by that delay the fruit of his litigation".[122] As will be discussed, the principles upon which an interim injunction is granted are specific to the role of that particular injunction and are not tied to the general equitable considerations which underpin the grant and refusal of perpetual injunctions or, indeed, specific performance.

---

118 Usually evidenced by the need for expenditure on the part of the defendant.
119 *Shillings International LLP v Scott* [2018] EWHC 1210 (Ch) at [44] per Norris J.
120 An injunction that is in substance mandatory should now be worded in positive terms: *Jackson v Normanby Brick Co* [1899] 1 Ch. 438.
121 It is not perpetual in the sense that it endures indefinitely.
122 *Hoffman-La Roche & Co v Secretary of State for Trade and Industry* [1975] A.C. 295 at 355.

Mandatory injunctions and specific performance

Both the mandatory injunction and the order for specific performance[123] compel the defendant positively to act in order that positive obligations will be enforced. Being part of the armoury of equitable remedies, both bring with them the same sanctions should the defendant fail to perform the stipulated positive act.[124] It is perhaps possible to distinguish between them on two fronts. First, the grounds upon which specific performance will be refused are more numerous and far-reaching. As will be discussed, the court must test the justice and wisdom of compelling an unwilling defendant to perform his positive contractual obligations. In contrast, the grant of an injunction requires no positive act unless, of course, the defendant has by his own wrongdoing initiated a course of action that requires a mandatory order to effect a return to the status quo.

Secondly, it has been emphasised by Lord Hoffmann that an order for specific performance is a final order, i.e. it is not available on an interim basis.[125] Clearly, this represents a restriction to the claimant where interlocutory relief is sought. In *Sky Petroleum Ltd v VIP Petroleum Ltd*,[126] however, the judgment of Goulding J suggests that the matter is not so straightforward. There, the claimant applied for an interim injunction restraining the defendant company from failing to supply it with petrol. Goulding J acknowledged that, if he granted the injunction, he would be specifically enforcing the contract until the date of the hearing. Nonetheless, he treated it as a claim for specific performance and issued the injunction. On the basis that the contract with the defendant appeared to be the sole means by which the plaintiff could keep his business, damages did not offer a sufficient remedy.

Without notice injunctions

Where the interim relief sought is particularly urgent in nature (i.e. where irreparable damage or prejudice would be caused by following the usual procedure), an injunction may be applied for without notice. Such injunctions were previously referred to as ex parte, meaning in the absence of the party against whom the injunction is sought. The availability of injunctive relief in such circumstances is given sparingly and only where necessary[127] on the basis that "no order should be made to the prejudice of a party unless he has the opportunity of being heard in defence".[128] On occasion, however, the balance of justice will militate against the defendant where the need for immediate intervention outweighs his interest in being heard. In the context of family

18-022

18-023

---

123 See Ch.19.
124 For example imprisonment, a fine or sequestration of assets (see para.**18-008**).
125 *Co-operative Insurance Society Ltd v Argyll Stores (Holdings) Ltd* [1998] A.C. 1 at 18.
126 [1974] 1 W.L.R. 576.
127 As Ormrod LJ explained in *Ansah v Ansah* [1977] 2 All E.R. 638 at 642, "Orders made *ex parte* are anomalies in our system of justice which generally demands service or notice of the proposed proceedings on the opposite party".
128 *Thomas A. Edison Ltd v Bullock* (1912) 15 C.L.R. 679 at 681.

disputes, for example, a claimant will succeed only where there is a real immediate danger of serious injury or irreparable damage. Indeed, the more intrusive the order, the more the court will require by way of proof that the order is necessary and that it should be made in the form sought. For example, in *Harris v Moat Housing Group South Ltd*, Brooke LJ emphasised, "It is one thing to restrain a defendant from what would in any event be anti-social behaviour for a short time until a hearing can be arranged at which both sides can be heard. It is quite another to make a 'without notice' order directing the defendant to leave their home immediately and banning them from re-entering a large part of the area where they live".[129] There, the Court of Appeal held that an antisocial behaviour injunction under the Housing Act 1996, excluding the appellant and her children from their home, should not have been made on a without notice application. By way of a further example, in the context of patent infringement no without notice injunction will be granted unless there is real urgency. As between the without notice application and the subsequent hearing of the effective application, there must be an "element of threatened damage that requires the immediate intervention of the court".[130] This requirement is more difficult to meet where an early effective hearing date is available.

Injunctions without notice are also available where service on the defendant cannot readily or easily be achieved and there is an immediate need to prevent a threatened act. In *Bloomsbury Publishing Ltd v Newsgroup Newspapers*,[131] injunctive relief was granted without notice against an unnamed individual to restrain the unauthorised publication of the fifth book in the *Harry Potter* series. The claimant had an arguable case that loss would be substantial (i.e. measurable in millions of pounds) and inflicted in a very short time. The recipient (who had tried to sell the book to three national newspapers) would be in no doubt that the injunction was directed at him. The order was effective also against all those who, knowing of the order, assisted in attempts to sell the book.

18-024

When granted, the injunction without notice is effective for only a limited period and subject to review on the defendant's application.[132] Particularly stringent rules apply to the claimant seeking an injunction without notice. A claimant is required to disclose all facts relevant to the exercise of judicial discretion and this extends to revealing any defences that might have been employed by the defendant if present. Should the claimant be in breach of duty to do so, the court will discharge the injunction and leave the claimant to apply again.

Quia timet injunctions

18-025

A quia timet injunction is issued to prevent an infringement of the claimant's rights where the infringement is threatened but has not yet occurred. It requires both a strong probability

---

129 [2006] Q.B. 606 at 625.
130 *Mayne Pharma (USA) Inc v Teva UK Ltd* [2004] EWHC (Ch) 3248 at [14] per Pumfrey J.
131 [2003] 1 W.L.R. 1633.
132 It is open to the defendant to request a hearing at any time before the end of the period in order to have the injunction discharged or varied.

that, unless restrained, the defendant will act in breach of the claimant's rights and, were the defendant to breach the claimant's rights, grave and irreparable harm.[133] In the words of Lord Buckmaster, "a mere vague apprehension is not sufficient to support an action for a *quia timet* injunction".[134] In *Drury v Secretary of State for the Environment, Food and Rural Affairs*,[135] where a possession order was sought against trespassers, the claimant failed to show "convincing evidence of real danger of actual violation".[136] As Wilson J explained, this danger might have been demonstrated by evidence of "an expression of intention to decamp to the other area . . . a history of movement between the two areas from which a danger of repetition can be inferred . . ." or evidence of "such propinquity and similarity between the two areas as to command the inference of a real danger of decampment of one to the other".[137] In *British Telecommunications Ltd v One in a Million Ltd*,[138] furthermore, the registration of Internet domain names comprising the name or trademark of well-known companies was a threatened "passing off" and trademark infringement. The registration was patently calculated to infringe the plaintiffs' rights in future. Aldous LJ drew attention to the general rule that a quia timet injunction will be issued in these circumstances only where the defendant has equipped himself with or intends to equip another with an instrument of fraud.

Principles Governing the Grant of Final Injunctions

Unlike the principles governing the grant of interim relief, the jurisdiction of the court as to the grant of final injunctions is based on settled equitable principles. As will be clear from Ch.19, similar principles guide the court in determining whether to order specific performance.

18-026

Adequacy of damages and other legal remedies

It was once declared by Lindley LJ that "the very first principle of injunction law is that prima facie you do not obtain injunctions to restrain actionable wrongs, for which dam-

18-027

---

133 *Vastint Leeds BV v Persons Unknown* [2019] 4 W.L.R. 2 (quia timet order restraining entry onto an industrial site without the company's consent).
134 *Graigola Merthyr C Ltd v Swansea Corp* [1929] A.C. 344 at 353.
135 [2004] 1 W.L.R. 1906.
136 [2004] 1 W.L.R. 1906 at 1912 per Wilson J. See also, *Ministry of Agriculture Fisheries and Food v Heyman* (1989) 59 P. & C.R. 48 per Saville J.
137 [2004] 1 W.L.R. 1906 at 1913.
138 [1999] 1 W.L.R. 903.

ages are the proper remedy".[139] The test as to appropriateness of damages was hailed by Turner LJ to be "whether this is a case in which the remedy at law is so inadequate that the court ought to interfere, having regard to the legal remedy, the rights and interests of the parties, and the consequence of the court's interference".[140] Accordingly, the court considers factors such as the danger of repetition (i.e. the need to relieve the applicant of the necessity of bringing a series of actions) or the damage done to the applicant and whether this was assessable in monetary terms. Nowadays, the central question appears to be when taking on board a fuller range of considerations whether it is more just to grant an injunction than to award damages.[141] Principally, the court may consider the following matters:

- the conduct of the claimant;

- equity will not act in vain;

- delay and acquiescence;

- hardship; and

- public interest.

Conduct of the claimant

18-028

Such maxims of equity as "he who comes to equity must come with clean hands" and "he who comes to equity must do equity" are prominent illustrations of equity's regard for proper conduct.[142] Naturally, therefore, the gaze of equity falls on the conduct of the claimant. As an application of the clean hands principle, a claimant who has behaved unconscionably or improperly may be denied equitable intervention. Mere "general depravity" will not suffice.[143] The court will exercise its discretion only where there is a strong link between the poor conduct of the claimant and the relief sought, such that one has "an immediate and necessary relation" to the other.[144] In *Littlewood v Caldwell*,[145] therefore, the wrongful removal of partnership books by the claimant led to the refusal of an injunction for the claimant in the midst of proceedings to dissolve the partnership.

---

139 *London and Blackwell Rly Co v Cross* (1886) 31 Ch. D. 354 at 369.
140 *AG v Sheffield Gas Consumers Co* (1853) 3 De G. M. & G. 304 at 321.
141 *Beswick v Beswick* [1968] A.C. 58 at 102; see further, para.**19-012.**
142 Also explored in the context of specific performance: see para.**19-025.**
143 Per Eyre CB in *Dering v Earl of Winchelsea* (1787) 1 Cox 318 at 319.
144 (1787) 1 Cox 318 at 319; see also *Moody v Cox* [1917] 2 Ch. 71 at 87.
145 (1822) 11 Price 97.

By contrast, the maxim "he who comes to equity must do equity" focuses on the claimant's future conduct. Accordingly, no injunction will be granted to a claimant unless he is ready, willing and able to carry out any contractual obligations owed to the defendant. Thus, in an action to restrain breach of covenant, Cozens-Hardy MR explained that "the plaintiffs who are seeking equitable relief by way of injunction, cannot obtain such relief unless they . . . are ready and able also to perform their part in future".[146]

Equity will not act in vain

18-029

This further equitable maxim can be employed to justify the refusal of the court to issue an injunction on the grounds of impossibility or futility of performance. In *Evans v Manchester, Sheffield and Lincolnshire Rly Co*,[147] it was impossible for the defendant to comply with the terms of an injunction to prevent further subsidence of the foundations of a canal and its banks because the extent of any further subsidence could not be foreseen. As Kekewich J explained, "I think it would be wrong to enjoin a company or an individual from permitting that to be done which is really beyond his control . . . in the sense that he cannot by any precaution or by any works with reasonable certainty prevent [further subsidence]".[148] More recently, in *Attorney General v Observer Ltd*,[149] the futility of continuing with existing injunctions led directly to the discharge of orders against national newspapers prohibiting the publication of confidential information. The worldwide publication of *Spycatcher* (Peter Wright's memoirs) had destroyed any secrecy as to its contents. As copies were readily available to any individual who wished obtain them, the injunction had ceased to serve any legitimate or useful purpose.

Delay and acquiescence

18-030

The related matters of delay and acquiescence have the capacity to influence any exercise of discretion by the courts. The former demands of a claimant that equitable relief is sought without unreasonable delay. The latter entails that the knowing failure to object to wrongdoing may prevent the claimant from seeking to object to it at some future juncture. Unfortunately, many of the authorities on the defence of delay are contradictory and inconsistent, some questioning whether at all delay can act as a bar to relief. Recent authorities appear to stress that an "inordinate" delay would be required to prevent the grant of an injunction.[150]

A shorter period is sufficient to bar enforcement of rights in the case of acquiescence.[151]

---

146 *Measures Bros Ltd v Measures* [1910] 2 Ch. 248 at 254.
147 (1887) 36 Ch. D. 626.
148 (1887) 36 Ch. D. 626 at 639.
149 [1990] 1 A.C. 109.
150 *H.P. Bulmer Ltd & Showerings Ltd v Bolinger SA (No.3)* [1977] 2 C.M.L.R. 625.
151 *Sayers v Collyer* (1884) 28 Ch. D. 103 per Baggallay LJ.

The defence of acquiescence arises where the claimant has assented to the acts of the defendant or has been passively inactive in a case where the defendant changes his position and violates the claimant's rights. In consequence, it may be unjust to grant relief. A classic statement of principle was provided by Lord Wensleydale, that "If a party, who could object, lies by and knowingly permits another to incur an expense in doing an act under the belief that it would not be objected to, and so a kind of permission may be said to be given to another to alter his condition, he may be said to acquiesce".[152] Thus, in *Sayers v Collyer*[153] a house was used for the sale of beer in clear breach of covenant. The claimant was denied an injunction on the grounds that he had knowledge of the breach for a period of three years and that he, himself, had purchased beer there. This was held to be a sufficient bar to any remedy.

18-031

Acquiescence may be an entire bar to all relief[154] or it may be a ground for inducing the court to give damages in lieu of injunction. In the words of Fry LJ, "an amount of acquiescence less than what would be a bar to all remedy, may operate on the discretion of the Court and induce it to give damages instead of an injunction".[155] In *Shaw v Applegate*,[156] the claimant sought to enforce a covenant prohibiting the use of land as an amusement arcade. The claimant had been unsure as to whether the actions of the defendant were in breach of covenant. Although he began proceedings after a delay and failed to seek interlocutory relief, it was not "unconscionable or dishonest" for him to seek to enforce his rights. There was sufficient acquiescence to rule out the availability of an injunction in that the defendant had been lulled into a false sense of security by the claimant's delay and failure to apply for interlocutory relief when the action was commenced. The defendant had, furthermore, continued to build up his business. The proper course was, therefore, to award damages in lieu of an injunction.

No such acquiescence was evident in *Mortimer v Bailey*, where a mandatory injunction to pull down the defendant's extension was granted notwithstanding the claimant's failure to commence proceedings in a timely manner.[157] Peter Gibson LJ accepted that delay was a relevant consideration, but took the view that,

> **"the defendants had been warned by the claimants that if the construction continued proceedings would be brought against them . . . They chose to rely on the advice of their legal advisers and to proceed with the construction. In so doing they took a gamble that it was unreasonable for the claimants to have refused consent. They lost that gamble".[158]**

---

152 *Archbold v Scully* (1861) 9 H.L.C. 360 at 383.
153 (1884) 28 Ch. D. 103.
154 See *Gafford v Graham* (1999) 3 E.G.L.R. 75, where knowledge of a breach of a restrictive covenant coupled with a failure to complain for three years was a bar to all relief by virtue of acquiescence.
155 *Sayers v Collyer* (1884) 28 Ch. D. 103 at 110.
156 [1977] 1 W.L.R. 970.
157 [2005] P. & C.R. 9; see G. Watt [2005] Conv. 14.
158 [2005] P. & C.R. 9 at [35].

Hardship

18-032

Any element of hardship is a key consideration for the court where the injunction sought is interim or mandatory in nature. In the case of an interim injunction, the rights of the parties have not yet been determined and it is appropriate that the court safeguard the defendant from potential hardship as he has not yet been found to be in breach of the claimant's rights. In the case of the mandatory injunction, the court inevitably guards against the hardship that may result from compelling the defendant positively to act (usually by expenditure). Here, there is an obvious risk that hardship to the defendant can outweigh the benefit to the claimant.[159]

Albeit less weighty, hardship remains a consideration where a final order is sought. Where disproportionate hardship will be caused to the defendant by the grant of an injunction than to the claimant in being confined to a remedy of damages, the court can, in its discretion, refuse to grant an injunction.[160] Generally, this discretion will be exercised only in exceptional circumstances. The defendant's position must, of course, be weakened in cases where he knew he was acting in breach of the claimant's rights.[161]

Public interest

18-033

As will be discussed with regard to specific performance, considerations of public policy impact upon the availability of equitable relief. Thus, with a breach of contract the courts are loath to enforce private rights that conflict with public policy. A different emphasis appears to prevail where an injunction is sought to restrain commission of a tort. Indeed, the difficulties inherent in the exercise of judicial discretion came markedly to the fore in *Miller v Jackson*.[162] There, an established cricket ground was alleged to cause a nuisance due to the frequency that cricket balls landed in the garden of a newly erected, nearby house. Both Geoffrey Lane and Cumming-Bruce LJJ accepted that the activity constituted nuisance, but they disagreed as to whether an injunction ought to be granted (the former in favour; the latter against). Lord Denning MR denied the presence of nuisance on the facts and agreed with Geoffrey Lane LJ (but for different reasons) that the injunction should be refused. He argued that, even if the tort of nuisance had been committed, an injunction should be refused on the basis of the greater public interest in "protecting the environment by preserving our playing fields in the face of mounting development, and by enabling our youth to enjoy all the benefits of outdoor games".[163] As a statement of principle, he declared obiter that "I am of the opinion that the public interest should prevail over the private interest".[164]

---

159 See para.**18-046** for a discussion of hardship in the context of interim mandatory orders.
160 *Wood v Sutcliffe* (1851) 61 E.R. 303 at 305.
161 *Smith v Smith* (1875) L.R. 20 Eq. 500 at 505.
162 [1977] Q.B. 966.
163 [1977] Q.B. 966 at 981.
164 [1977] Q.B. 966 at 982.

In light of the divergence of opinion, it is unsurprising that more recent courts have not felt bound by *Miller v Jackson*. Nor is it surprising that the views of Lord Denning MR have been singled out for attack. In *Kennaway v Thompson*, Lawton LJ criticised his conclusion holding that, "The statement of Lord Denning MR that the public interest should prevail over the private interest runs counter to the principles enunciated in *Shelfer's* case[165] and does not accord with the reasoning of Cumming-Bruce LJ for refusing an injunction".[166] Accordingly, the Court of Appeal denied that the public interest in motor-boat racing could prevail over a claimant's right to quiet enjoyment of her property. The claimant in that case had sought an injunction to restrain the defendants from creating excessive noise in the pursuit of their chosen sport. Lawton LJ highlighted the considerable public interest in the club and the fact that the public attended in large numbers. On the basis of this public interest, the claimant was denied an injunction restraining all of the club's activities. Instead, the court decided on a form of order that made restrictions in the number and type of event, to the number of permitted racers and users and as to acceptable levels of noise. The effect was to protect the claimant from intolerable noise while at the same time allowing the club to organise activities about which the claimant could not legitimately complain.[167] The Court of Appeal accepted that a balance must be achieved and that the question of public interest was one matter to be taken into account in performing that balancing function.

More recently, the Supreme Court has emphasised that, where it arises, public interest will almost always be a relevant consideration. As Lord Neuberger made clear in *Coventry (t/a RDC Promotions) v Lawrence*, "I find it hard to see how there could be any circumstances in which it arose and could not, as a matter of law, be a relevant factor".[168] Here, in a case of noise nuisance alleged to occur from the use of land as a speedway track, the court considered the relevance of public interest to the grant of planning permission. In the words of Lord Neuberger:

> "the existence of a planning permission which expressly or inherently authorises carrying on an activity in such a way as to cause a nuisance by noise or the like, can be a factor in favour of refusing an injunction and compensating the claimant in damages. This factor would have real force in cases where it was clear that the planning authority had been reasonably and fairly influenced by the public benefit of the activity, and where the activity cannot be carried out without causing the nuisance complained of. However, even in such cases, the court would have to weigh up all the competing factors".[169]

---

165   *Shelfer v City of London Electric Lighting Co* [1895] 1 Ch. 287 (see para.**18-011**).
166   [1981] Q.B. 88 at 93.
167   See also *Watson v Croft Promo-Sport Ltd* [2009] 2 All E.R. 249, where an injunction was granted restricting the use of the defendant's land as a motor racing circuit.
168   [2014] UKSC 13 at [124].
169   [2014] UKSC 13 at [125].

Dennis v Ministry of Defence emphasises that the effect of public interest will "depend on the circumstances, not least the strength of the public interest in question".[170] Here, the claimants brought an action for a declaration[171] and damages in relation to nuisance and/or interference with human rights, constituted by noise emanating from a nearby air force base. It was accepted that there was a strong and legitimate public interest served in the continuation of the training of RAF pilots. The court concluded, however, that the claimants should not bear the cost of the public benefit. Accordingly, although the declaration was refused on the ground of public interest, damages of £950,000 were awarded for loss of capital value together with past and future loss of use and amenity. In short, these cases serve to illustrate that the interest of the public and third parties generally can impact upon the remedy adopted, i.e. there are cases where it is not in the public interest to grant an injunction and damages are instead awarded.

18-034

Principles Governing the Grant of Interim Injunctions

It will be recalled that the principles upon which the court will issue an interim injunction differ in their particularity and their origin from those that apply at the trial. At the interim stage, the court is not in a position to decide the case or to resolve uncertainty. Its role is to minimise the risk of injustice to the parties in circumstances where it is unclear that the claimant will succeed.[172] As Lord Diplock put it, "It was to mitigate the risk of injustice to the plaintiff during the period before that uncertainty could be resolved that the practice arose of granting him relief by way of interlocutory injunction".[173]

18-035

An undertaking in damages

The grant of an interim injunction requires (unless the court orders otherwise) that the claimant enter into the "usual undertaking" that he will abide by any order as to damages which the court may make if it transpires that the claimant was not entitled to the interim injunction

18-036

---

170 [2003] 2 E.G.L.R. 121 at 126 per Buckley J.
171 As required where an injunction is sought against the Crown.
172 As Judge Keyser QC put it in *Happy Camper Productions Ltd v BBC* [2019] EWHC 558 (Ch) at [17], "the purpose of the exercise, without adjudicating on the case, is to seek to ensure that if one makes a mistake it is the least bad mistake one can make".
173 *American Cyanamid Co v Ethicon Ltd* [1975] A.C. 396 at 406.

and the defendant has suffered damage thereby.[174] Its function is to aid the court "in doing that which was its great object, viz abstaining from expressing any opinion upon the merits of the case until the hearing".[175] The court, however, has no power to compel a claimant to enter into an undertaking, but the claimant will be aware that the court will be reluctant to grant the injunction unless the undertaking is given. In *Bunn v BBC*,[176] for example, relief was sought to protect the confidentiality of a statement made to the police. Lightman J admitted that an applicant's lack of means would not "be a sufficient ground in itself to prevent him obtaining relief".[177] Conveniently, however, he was not required to test this on the facts. The applicant was barred by delay and the injunction would have been in vain as the statement was already in the public domain.

Although the undertaking is for the benefit of the defendant, the undertaking is made to the court. Accordingly, a failure to perform is a contempt of court and not a breach of contract. The court then enjoys the discretion as to whether to enforce the undertaking.[178] If it does so, the measure of damages is calculated as though the claimant had breached a contract with the defendant.[179] If there is doubt as to the capacity of the claimant to pay any damages, the court can require the claimant to deposit sums with solicitors or to give security to the court. No undertaking is required from the Crown when it is seeking to enforce the law by means of a law enforcement action.[180] An undertaking will be extracted in cases where the Crown seeks to enforce its own proprietary or contractual rights.[181] In this respect, the Crown is placed in the same position as an individual as regards the usual undertaking in damages.

18-037   Until the decision in *American Cyanamid Co v Ethicon Ltd*,[182] it was understood that a claimant was required to show a strong prima facie case that he would succeed at trial and that damages would be an inadequate remedy.[183] In *American Cyanamid*, however, Lord Diplock

---

174 As Lewison LJ put it in *JSC Mezhdunarodniy Promyshlenniy Bank v Pugachev* [2015] EWCA Civ 139 at [68], "The default position is that an applicant for an interim injunction is required to give an unlimited cross-undertaking in damages. That is regarded as the price for interfering with the defendant's freedom before he has been found liable for anything". Note that as a condition of refusing to grant the injunction, the court can require the defendant to make an undertaking that, should the claimant succeed at trial, he will compensate the claimant for damage suffered.

175 *Wakefield v Duke of Buccleugh* (1865) 12 L.T. 628 at 629 as cited by Lord Diplock in *American Cyanamid Co v Ethicon Ltd* [1975] A.C. 396 at 408.

176 [1998] 3 All E.R. 552.

177 [1998] 3 All E.R. 552 at 558.

178 *Cheltenham & Gloucester v Ricketts* [1993] 1 All E.R. 1545.

179 See the views of Lord Diplock in *Hoffmann La-Roche (F) & Co v Secretary of State for Trade and Industry* [1975] A.C. 295 at 361.

180 This involves proceedings brought by the Crown to prevent a subject from breaking the law and causing harm to the general public.

181 *Hoffmann La-Roche (F) & Co v Secretary of State for Trade and Industry* [1975] A.C. 295.

182 Which concerned a quia timet interlocutory injunction to restrain infringement of a patent; see P. Prescott (1975) 91 L.Q.R. 168.

183 In *Stratford & Sons Ltd v Lindley* [1965] A.C. 269 at 323, for example, Lord Reid made reference to "a sufficient prima facie case".

criticised as unnecessary this seemingly accepted requirement. He was of the view that the "use of such expressions as, 'a probability', 'a prima facie case', or 'a strong prima facie case' in the context of the exercise of a discretionary power to grant an interlocutory injunction leads to confusion as to the object sought to be achieved by this form of temporary relief".[184] His speech has been taken to lay down firm guidelines as to the balancing function of the court in such cases. It is the "balance of convenience" that lies at the heart of the *Cyanamid* approach. The *Cyanamid* principles are discussed in detail below. It is important to note that the court will address key issues as it applies the *Cyanamid* principles, namely:

■ whether there is a serious issue to be tried;

■ the adequacy of damages to the parties; and

■ where the balance of convenience lies.

The *American Cyanamid* principles

The court must be satisfied that the claim is not frivolous or vexatious.[185] In other words, there must be a serious issue to be tried.[186] Thereafter, the balance of convenience must be considered. The balance of convenience is not by any means a new consideration, but it is a most important element in the *Cyanamid* guidelines. The balance of convenience or "balance of justice"[187] is the result of weighing up respective risks that injustice may result from deciding the case in one way rather than the other in the face of incomplete evidence. In other words, it is a balancing exercise whereby the court determines how best it can minimise the risk of injustice to the parties. The court takes "whichever course appears to carry the lower risk of injustice if it should turn out to be wrong".[188]

18-038

The inadequacy of damages to each party is the primary focus. Accordingly, in *ESL Fuels Ltd v Fletcher*,[189] an order preventing the defendants from selling a product allegedly manufactured in breach of confidence and exploiting a trade secret was refused by the court. The balance favoured the defendants in that their fledgling company might well be "strangled

---

184   [1975] A.C. 396 at 407.
185   That is, that the claimant's case is not, for example, futile or misconceived.
186   There was no "seriously arguable case" in *Seele Middle East FZE v Raiffeisenlandesbank Oberösterreich Aktiengesellschaft Bank* [2014] EWHC 343 (TCC), for example, where the claimant failed to convince the court that a demand made for payment under a performance guarantee may have been invalid (at [23] per Akenhear J).
187   See *Attorney General v Barker* [1990] 3 All E.R. 257 per Lord Donaldson MR.
188   *Films Rover International Ltd v Cannon Films Sales Ltd* [1987] 1 W.L.R. 670 at 680 per Lord Hoffmann. As Jacob LJ notes in *SmithKline Beecham Plc v Apotex Europe Ltd* [2007] Ch. 71 at 83, "the expression 'wrongful injunction' is used, but in truth there is nothing wrongful about it. The decision whether or not to grant it is made on the basis of a necessarily incomplete picture".
189   [2013] EWHC 3726 (Ch).

near birth"[190] if an interim order was to prevent the development of business and the meeting of start-up costs. The claimant, by contrast, had a well-established business.[191] The effect of the interim order was to preserve the confidentiality of the alleged trade secret but to allow the defendants to continue to sell their product subject to the preservation of net profits to compensate the claimant should he succeed at trial.[192]

In general terms, the balancing process is as follows. If an injunction is refused, the court will consider whether damages will be an inadequate remedy to compensate the claimant were he to succeed at trial and suffer losses in the intervening period. If damages can compensate, and the defendant is able to pay, the court will lean towards refusal of interim relief. If the loss to the claimant is not remediable,[193] the court will consider the possibility of granting the injunction. If an injunction is granted, the court must question whether the claimant would be in a position to compensate the defendant for any loss suffered by him pending trial, if at trial the defendant were to succeed. Where damages will *not* compensate the claimant in circumstances where an interim injunction is wrongly refused, but *will* compensate the defendant if an interim injunction is wrongly granted, the court will favour the grant of an injunction, provided the claimant can make an undertaking in damages.

18-039

Frequently, however, damages are inadequate for both parties or there is doubt as to the adequacy of the respective remedies in damages.[194] In such cases, other aspects of the balance of convenience come into play. Although Lord Diplock considered it "unwise" to attempt to list the various matters to be taken into consideration in determining where the balance lies,[195] the court will address matters such as public interest[196] or the particular circumstances of the case.[197] Where these factors appear to be evenly balanced, Lord Diplock

---

190   [2013] EWHC 3726 (Ch) at [54] (a phrase borrowed from Laddie J in *Series 5 Software Ltd v Clarke* [1996] 1 All E.R. 853 at 868).

191   As Judge Hodge QC noted, "ESL can be adequately compensated in damages for any pecuniary loss it may suffer if interim injunctive relief is withheld but ESL succeeds at trial. As for any damage to ESL's commercial reputation and standing, in my judgment this will be adequately redressed if ESL is vindicated by victory over the defendants at trial" ([2013] EWHC 3726 (Ch) at [53]).

192   See also *Roper Insurance Services Ltd v Wood* unreported 6 December 2016, where an interim injunction (to enforce non-compete and confidentiality clauses) was granted against the former employee of an insurance broker on the basis that the balance of justice favoured the claimant who would suffer more respective hardship in the marketplace.

193   For example, loss of trade caused by picketing the claimant's business: see *Hubbard v Pitt* [1976] Q.B. 142.

194   Most cases will not be resolved at this stage because as Laddie J explained in *Series 5 Software v Clarke* [1996] 1 All E.R. 853 at 863, "evidence relating to the adequacy of damages normally will be contradictory and there will be no possibility of resolving the differences by cross-examination"; cf. *Factortame Ltd v Secretary of State for Transport (No.2)* [1991] 1 All E.R. 70 at 118, where Lord Goff argued that, "At this stage . . . many applications for interim injunctions can well be decided".

195   [1975] A.C. 396 at 408.

196   Where the defendant is a public body, allegedly in breach of its statutory duty, the court will weigh up the interests of the general public in determining the balance of convenience: see *Smith v Inner London Education Authority* [1978] 1 All E.R. 411.

197   For example, the courts are reluctant to grant an interim injunction in cases of industrial disputes or political decisions.

emphasised that it is "a counsel of prudence to take such measures as are calculated to pre-serve the status quo".[198]

Finally, Lord Diplock addressed the circumstances in which it may be appropriate to evalu-ate prospects of success. It will be recalled that, prior to *Cyanamid*, the assessment of the strength of each party's case was the most significant matter. The court was, understandably, reluctant to subject a claimant to the risk of irrecoverable loss by refusing injunctive relief in a case where it was felt that the claimant was likely to succeed at trial. Post-*Cyanamid*, it appears that the court should refrain from immediate recourse to this test. As is clear from the caution with which Lord Diplock discussed the issue, the court should assess the strength of their cases as a last resort and only where the strength of one party's case is evidently disproportionate to that of the other party. As Lord Diplock put it:

> **"If the extent of the uncompensatable disadvantage to each party would not differ widely, it may not be improper to take into account in tipping the balance the relative strength of each party's case as revealed by the affidavit evidence adduced on the hearing of the application. This, however, should be done only where it is apparent upon the facts disclosed by evidence as to which there is no credit-able dispute that the strength of one party's case is disproportionate to that of the other party. The court is not justified in embarking upon anything resembling a trial of the action upon conflicting affidavits in order to evaluate the strength of either party's case".[199]**

Finally, and without elaboration, Lord Diplock accepted that special factors arising in the par-ticular case can be considered.

The *American Cyanamid* approach considered

The *American Cyanamid* principles appear, at first glance, emphatic and constraining. In the face of such firm House of Lords' guidance, there seems little doubt as to the appropriate framework to be adopted in interim proceedings. It looks impossible to reconcile these princi-ples with the previous practice of requiring the claimant to make a strong prima facie case. In short, *Cyanamid* relegates any assessment of the relative strength of each party's case as far as possible behind the need to assess the balance of convenience. Not surprisingly, it is a decision that has been met with criticism and consternation and to which there is a growing body of

18-040

---

198 [1975] A.C. 396 at 408. In *ESL Fuels Ltd v Fletcher* [2013] EWHC 3726 (Ch) at [19], the status quo was deemed to be the state of affairs before the most significant recent change affecting the parties, although generally, as Zuckerman notes, "the status quo is not as simple a concept . . . What the plaintiff may consider to be staying put the defendant may see as a fundamental change" ((1991) 107 L.Q.R. 196, 200).

199 [1975] A.C. 396 at 409.

exceptions. Much judicial focus has fallen on the extent to which the court is bound to follow *Cyanamid*. In addition, the role of special factors has been a concern, particularly whether the presence of such factors enables the court to move outside the balance of convenience to assess prospects of success or, alternatively, that they merely form part of the balance of convenience.[200]

In *Fellowes & Son v Fisher*,[201] the claimant firm of solicitors sought to restrain a breach of restrictive covenant in the contract of a former employee. The employee contended that the covenant was invalid. No interlocutory relief was granted. Browne LJ accepted that the court was "bound to follow and apply" the decision in *American Cyanamid*.[202] In the absence of evidence as to the adequacy of damages to either party, the balance of convenience favoured refusal of the interlocutory injunction. Sir John Pennycuick agreed, but regarded it as "the most serious difficulty" that the prospects of success have been disregarded, "except as a last resort when the balance of convenience is otherwise even".[203] He pointed out that there are many classes of case "where the prospect of success is within the competence of the judge hearing the interlocutory application and represents a factor which can hardly be disregarded in determining whether or not is just to give interlocutory relief".[204] Accordingly, he confessed to difficulty in arriving at a just conclusion without considering the prospects of success at trial. Both he and Browne LJ felt unduly constrained to apply *American Cyanamid*. On the other hand, Lord Denning MR found it impossible to reconcile the statements made by Lord Diplock in *American Cyanamid* with those in *JT Stratford & Son v Lindley*.[205] The latter was a House of Lords' decision (not considered by Lord Diplock) where all members of the House of Lords agreed that a claimant must establish a strong prima facie case. Lord Denning MR viewed the instant case as one of many individual cases that allowed the court to depart from *American Cyanamid* and to look to whether a strong prima facie case was established. Alternatively, he considered the case to be one of "uncompensatable disadvantages" (where damages on either side would not be an adequate remedy), thus permitting consideration of the prospects of success.

18-041

In *Hubbard v Pitt*,[206] Lord Denning MR again took the opportunity to argue that special factors were not merely an aspect of the balance of convenience, but permitted the court to move outside *Cyanamid* altogether. The case concerned a campaign against an estate agency in Islington that involved demonstrating and leafleting outside the claimant's office. At first instance, an injunction was granted restraining the picketing of the premises. This was upheld by a majority of the Court of Appeal. Stamp LJ explicitly raised Lord Denning's interpretation of the role of "special factors" and admitted nonetheless that "it appears to me clear beyond

---

200 For a discussion of post-*Cyanamid* developments in the case law, see A. Keay, "Whither American Cyanamid?: Interim Injunctions in the 21st century" (2004) 23 C.L.Q. 132.
201 [1976] Q.B. 122.
202 [1976] Q.B. 122 at 138.
203 [1976] Q.B. 122 at 141.
204 [1976] Q.B. 142 at 185.
205 [1965] A.C. 269.
206 [1976] Q.B. 142.

peradventure that Lord Diplock was . . . referring to special factors affecting the balance of convenience and not to special factors enabling the court to ignore the general principles there laid down".[207]

Both *Fellowes & Son v Fisher* and *Hubbard v Pitt* provide examples of cases where the Court of Appeal has felt constrained to follow (or in the case of Lord Denning to reinterpret) the House of Lords' guidelines. Other cases reveal markedly less concern that the discretion of the court has been so patently restricted. As Kerr LJ declared in *Cambridge Nutrition Ltd v BBC*, for example, "The *American Cyanamid* case contains no principle of universal application. The only such principle is the statutory power of the court to grant injunctions when it is just and convenient to do so. The *American Cyanamid* case is no more than a set of useful guidelines which apply in many cases. It must never be used as a rule of thumb, let alone a strait-jacket".[208] Similarly, Lord Goff has emphasised that the court should not feel shackled by *Cyanamid*. In *R. v Secretary of State for Transport Ex p. Factortame Ltd (No.2)* he claimed:

> "I do not read Lord Diplock's speech as intended to fetter the broad discretion conferred on the courts by s.37 of the Supreme Court Act 1981; on the contrary a prime purpose of the guidelines established . . . was to remove a fetter . . . that a party seeking an interlocutory injunction had to establish a *prima facie* case . . . It is now clear that it is enough if he can show that there is a serious question to be tried. If he can establish that, then he has, so to speak, crossed the threshold; and the court can then address itself to the question whether it is just or convenient to grant an injunction".[209]

18-042

Perhaps the most interesting attempt to re-evaluate Lord Diplock's *Cyanamid* guidelines was provided by Laddie J in *Series 5 Software v Clarke*.[210] This is another case where the perceived inconsistency between past practice and the *Cyanamid* guidelines came to the fore. Laddie J was acutely aware that, as recently as four months before *Cyanamid* was decided, Lord Diplock himself had cited with approval the traditional need for the claimant to show a strong prima facie case.[211] He could not accept that Lord Diplock had radically changed his view in such a short space of time. Laddie J was of the opinion, therefore, that there was "no significant inconsistency" between *Cyanamid* and *La Roche* and that the prospects of success remained an important factor. He argued that there was nothing in what Lord Diplock said to suggest that it is not legitimate to look at the relative strength of the parties' cases. Although Lord Diplock appears to suggest that the court cannot take this step where there is a dispute on the evidence, Laddie J was unperturbed. He emphasised that relief must be flexible, and

---

207 [1976] Q.B. 142 at 185.
208 [1990] 3 All E.R. 523 at 534.
209 [1991] 1 All E.R. 70 at 118.
210 [1996] 1 All E.R. 853.
211 *Hoffmann La-Roche v Secretary of State for Trade and Industry* [1975] A.C. 295 at 360.

calculated that Lord Diplock did not intend to prevent consideration of likelihood of success. Accordingly, he argued that where "the court is able to come to a view as to the strength of each party's case on credible evidence then it can do so".[212]

Although the interpretation offered by Laddie J has received judicial support[213] and, as illustrated above, the *Cyanamid* guidelines have been convincingly criticised, it is clear that a more literal reading of *Cyanamid* may yet at times prevail.[214] By way of illustration, in *Epoch Co Ltd v Character Options Ltd*,[215] Hacon J took the view that he "must apply *American Cyanamid* according to the traditional, as opposed to a more radical reading . . . Lord Diplock's ruling should be interpreted in line with the many cases other than *Series 5* in which it has been applied since 1975". Not least, the approach in *Series 5* seems to ignore the clear requirement that the court concern itself with the balance of convenience and not the parties' prospects of success. As Lord Diplock made clear in *NWL Ltd v Woods*, the *Cyanamid* approach "enjoins the judge on an application for an interim injunction to direct his attention to the balance of convenience as soon as he has satisfied himself that there is a serious issue to be tried".[216]

Qualifications to *Cyanamid*

18-043

As has been discussed, the *American Cyanamid* guidelines are those generally applicable to the grant of an interim injunction. The guidelines are subject to important judge-made qualifications and refinement, in the following cases:

- where there is no arguable defence;

- where the grant or refusal of relief will put on end to the action or finally resolve the case;

- where an interim mandatory injunction is sought.

---

212 [1996] 1 All E.R. 853 at 865. See also *ESL Fuels v Fletcher* [2013] EWHC 3726 at [27], where Judge Hodge QC remarked that "the American Cyanamid principles have a degree of flexibility, and do not prevent the court from giving proper weight to any clear—and I stress the word clear—view which the court can form at the time of the application for interim relief (and without the need for a mini-trial on copious written evidence) as to the likely outcome at trial".

213 For example, see Robert Walker LJ in *Barnsley Brewery Co Ltd v RBNB* [1997] F.S.R. 462. Note that with the introduction of the Civil Procedure Rules and the emergence of a new approach to case management, the more flexible approach in *Series 5* is, perhaps, to be preferred.

214 The decision in *Talaris (Sweden) AB v Network Controls International Ltd* [2008] EWHC 2930 (TCC) (breach of exclusive distribution agreement), for example, has been described as a "methodical application of the *American Cyanamid* principles" (B. Roy (2009) 15 C.T.L.R. 86, 87).

215 [2015] EWHC 3436 (IPEC) at [6] (interim injunction refused in a patent infringement case concerning the marketing and sale of beaded toy products).

216 [1979] 1 W.L.R. 1294 at 1306.

No arguable defence

18-044

Where a defendant has no arguable defence, there is no basis upon which to consider the *American Cyanamid* guidelines.[217] The reason is logical, because as James LJ explained, "Balance of convenience has nothing to do with a case of this kind; it can only be considered where there is some question that must be decided at the hearing".[218] This point was expanded upon recently in *Royal Bank of Scotland Plc v Hicks*, where Floyd J offered the following explanation:

> **"The court is not concerned in such a case about whether its decision to grant or refuse an injunction might turn out later to be wrong. In that context, there is no need for the balancing exercise which is otherwise necessary to determine which course carries the least risk of injustice. In such a case there should not, therefore, be a two stage approach withholding relief from a party until a second hearing at which there is no prospect of a different result being achieved".[219]**

Accordingly, in cases where the defendant has no arguable defence, the appropriate course is to grant the injunction until trial. In *Amazon UK Service Ltd v Tejan-Kella*,[220] for example, a former employee put forward no defence to the claim that he was acting in breach of contract regarding his use of confidential information. The injunction applied for was granted as sought.

Final resolution of case

18-045

In *NWL Ltd v Woods*,[221] the House of Lords acknowledged that where the grant or refusal of an interim injunction will have the practical effect of putting an end to the action, such that the parties would not proceed to trial, the *Cyanamid* guidelines would require modification.[222] In such cases, it is necessary to attach greater significance to the relative strength of the parties' claims. In the words of Lord Diplock, the claimant's likelihood of success becomes,

---

217 See *Official Custodian for Charities v MacKey* [1985] Ch. 168; *Quick Draw LLP v Global Live Events LLP* [2012] EWHC 233 (Ch).
218 *Stocker v Planet Building Society* (1879) 27 W.R. 877 at 878.
219 [2010] EWHC 2568 (Ch) at [26].
220 [2020] EWHC 84 (QB).
221 [1979] 1 W.L.R. 1294.
222 In *Global Gaming Ventures (Group) Ltd v Global Gaming Ventures (Holdings) Ltd* [2018] EWCA Civ 68 at [43], Patten LJ described this as the type of case where, "if an injunction was to be granted at all it had, so to speak, to be now or never".

> "a factor to be brought into the balance by the judge in weighing the risks that injustice may result from his deciding the application one way rather than the other".[223]

In *Cayne v Global Natural Resources Plc*,[224] it was clear that there would be no trial of the action if the claimant obtained an injunction. Here, the applicant sought to restrain a share issue, the effect of which would be to determine the constitution of a board of directors of a company. If the applicants were to succeed, they were likely to take control of the company. The court acknowledged that it would then be inconceivable that they would continue with the present proceedings. For Kerr LJ, therefore, the overriding concern was that, "if an injunction is granted, the effective contest between the parties is likely to have been finally decided summarily in favour of the plaintiffs".[225] Similarly, In *Global Gaming Ventures (Group) Ltd v Global Gaming Ventures (Holdings) Ltd*[226] the appellants sought an order for disclosure and inspection of financial documentation in order that they could monitor and protect their rights as shareholders and, if necessary, challenge the action of receivers conducting a share sale. Disclosure needed to be immediate as there would be no further opportunity to make any challenge before the completion of the sale. In the circumstances it was appropriate that Cyanamid was modified to reflect the reality that the interim hearing was decisive of the contest between the parties.

Under markedly different circumstances, the Court of Appeal in *Cambridge Nutrition Ltd v BBC*[227] also viewed the *Cyanamid* guidelines as pertaining to situations where the substantial issues between the parties required to be resolved at trial. The appellate court found that a different set of considerations must be relevant where the crucial issues did not depend on trial, but on the grant of interim relief. The claimants sought an injunction to restrain the BBC from broadcasting a programme until after the publication of a government report on the same issue. If successful, the trial of the action would be unlikely. The claimants would have secured their goal with the grant of interlocutory relief in that the crucial consideration was the postponement of the broadcast. Kerr LJ expressed himself narrowly in holding that the *Cyanamid* guidelines could not extend to "cases in which the subject matter concerns the right to publish an article, or to transmit a broadcast whose importance may be transitory but whose impact depends on timing, news value and topicality".[228] Such cases do not lend themselves easily to the application of the *Cyanamid* guidelines in that the availability of interim relief will be decisive of the case and make trial of the action unlikely indeed. Instead, the court will assess the merits of the case. On the facts, the existence of a contract was doubtful and could not support the grant of an injunction which would prevent the broadcast by the BBC of a programme on a matter of public interest. No injunction was issued.

---

223 *NWL Ltd v Woods* [1979] 1 W.L.R. 1294 at 1307.
224 [1984] 1 All E.R. 225.
225 [1984] 1 All E.R. 225 at 236.
226 [2018] EWCA Civ 68.
227 [1990] 3 All E.R. 523. See A. Zuckerman (1991) 1107 L.Q.R. 196.
228 [1990] 3 All E.R. 523 at 535.

> ### Interim mandatory injunctions

Where an interim mandatory order is sought, the court has jurisdiction to grant it, but will very rarely do so, "for the Court would not compel a man to do so serious a thing as to undo what he had done except at a hearing".[229] Sensibly, therefore, a high degree of assurance is required that at trial it will appear that the injunction was rightly granted. In *De Falco v Crawley BC*, Bridge LJ emphasised that the guidelines laid down by Lord Diplock in *Cyanamid* had "no relevance"[230] to the issue of whether a local authority could be ordered to provide accommodation for the homeless claimant.[231] The higher standard required of the applicant was that he show "a strong prima facie case".[232] Similarly, in *Leisure Data v Bell*[233] the Court of Appeal was of the view that the *Cyanamid* guidelines were not applicable to the issue of interim mandatory orders. In *National Commercial Bank Jamaica Ltd v Olint Corp Ltd (Practice Note)*,[234] however, the Privy Council preferred a different starting point for the court, rejecting a "box-ticking approach" where the nature of the injunction is assessed and a lower or higher threshold test applied depending on the prohibitory or mandatory nature of the order applied for.[235] This, Lord Hoffmann thought, did not do justice to the complexity of the decision before the court. Indeed, Lord Hoffmann went as far as to state of the *Cyanamid* principles, "There is . . . no reason to suppose that . . . Lord Diplock was intending to confine them to injunctions which could be described as prohibitory rather than mandatory. In both cases, the underlying principle is the same, namely, that the court should take whichever course seems likely to cause the least irremediable prejudice to one party or the other".[236] Nonetheless, it is abundantly clear that, in the case of mandatory orders, the possibility of irremediable hardship to the defendant is greater than when a prohibitory order is sought.[237] The *Cyanamid* principles require amendment in light of the greater risk of injustice should the claimant fail to succeed at trial.[238]

Where a mandatory order is sought, the particular concerns affecting the court at an interim stage have been outlined by Megarry J in *Shepherd Homes v Sandham*.[239] First, a mandatory order is larger in scope. The prohibitory injunction focuses on restraining continuance of the act or conduct in the period between the issue of the interim order and the date of the effec-

---

229 *Gale v Abbot* (1862) 10 W.R. 748 at 750 per Kindersley VC. See also *Edwin Shirley Productions Ltd v Workspace Management Ltd* [2001] 23 E.G. 158.
230 [1980] 1 All E.R. 913 at 924.
231 Under the Housing (Homeless Persons) Act 1977, now repealed.
232 [1980] 1 All E.R. 913 at 922 per Lord Denning MR.
233 [1988] F.S.R. 367 at 371 per Dillon LJ.
234 [2009] 1 W.L.R. 1405.
235 [2009] 1 W.L.R. 1405 at 1410. Lord Hoffmann took the view that "arguments over whether the injunction should be classified as prohibitive or mandatory are barren".
236 [2009] 1 W.L.R. 1405 at 1410.
237 From the perspective of the court, such orders may also present the problem of constant supervision: see *Shillings International LLP v Scott* [2018] EWHC 1210 (Ch).
238 *Warm Zones CIC v Thorley* unreported 2 February 2014.
239 [1971] Ch. 340.

tive hearing. In the words of Megarry J, "it does not attempt to deal with what has happened in the past".[240] By contrast, the mandatory injunction looks at least in part to what has happened in the past because it will require the taking of positive steps to dismantle or undo something already done. Secondly, the danger at an interim stage of requiring the defendant to take positive steps is pronounced. Megarry J drew attention to the "consequent waste of time, money and materials" if it later transpires that the defendant had been wrongly mandated.[241] Thirdly, Megarry J described the interim mandatory injunction as a "once and for all"[242] order in that, once granted, the claimant will receive all that is required. In the destruction of a building, for example, there is no need for the continuance of a mandatory order. Once demolished, the claimant has achieved all that was sought by the action. Accordingly, Megarry J felt that a case must be "unusually strong and clear" before the court could exercise its discretion.[243]

Exceptions to *Cyanamid*

18-047
In addition to the general qualifications outlined above, there are a variety of specific contexts in which it is inappropriate to import the *Cyanamid* guidelines. A selection of examples will now be considered and explained. These include:

- trade disputes;

- restraining the presentation of a winding-up petition;

- Human Rights Act 1998 s.12(3).

Trade disputes

18-048
Section 221(2) of the Trade Union and Labour Relations (Consolidation) Act 1992 provides an exception in the context of an application for an interim injunction where the defendant claims that he acted in contemplation or furtherance of a trade dispute. Here the court can exercise its discretion and have regard to that party's likelihood of succeeding at trial in establishing

---

240 [1971] Ch. 340 at 348.
241 [1971] Ch. 340 at 348.
242 [1971] Ch. 340 at 348.
243 [1971] Ch. 340 at 349. For discussion of those exceptional cases where the court might intervene, even though it does not feel a "high degree of assurance" about the applicant's prospects of establishing his rights, see Hoffmann J in *Film Rover International Ltd v Cannon Film Sales Ltd* [1987] 1 W.L.R. 670 at 680.

a defence under the Act conferring immunity from liability in tort. Accordingly, the *Cyanamid* guidelines have been modified in this particular context.

Restraining the presentation of a winding-up petition

Where a company seeks to restrain a creditor from presenting a winding-up petition, the company must show a prima facie case that the petition will fail and be an abuse of process of the court. As Buckley LJ noted in *Bryanston Finance Ltd v de Vries (No.2)*, the fact that the action is "an action designed to prevent the commencement of proceedings *in limine* is a special factor. In such a case the court shall not, in my judgment, interfere with what would otherwise be a legitimate approach to the seat of justice unless the evidence is sufficient to establish prima facie that the plaintiffs will succeed in establishing that the proceedings sought to be restrained would be an abuse of process".[244] Although Buckley LJ purported to follow *American Cyanamid* in treating the case as one involving "special factors", both Stephenson LJ and Sir John Pennycuick regarded the facts as properly outside *Cyanamid's* reach. All three, nonetheless, were minded to refuse the injunction. This exception to *Cyanamid* was endorsed in *Southern Cross Group Plc v Deka Immobilien Investment GmbH*.[245] There, the applicant sought an injunction restraining the respondent from presenting a winding-up petition. There was no dispute as to the debts owed by the claimant in the form of unpaid rent and service charges. The applicant, however, alleged substantial cross-claims on the basis that the respondent had unreasonably refused its consent to the assignment of the lease. Nicholas Warren QC held that, on the basis of insufficient evidence to support the claim of alleged losses, the court was unable to restrain the respondent. The applicant had failed to present a genuine and serious case to establish a counter-claim greater than the debt on which the statutory demands underlying the petition were based.

18-049

The Human Rights Act 1998

The application for interim injunctions also requires to be considered in the context of art.8 (right to respect for private and family life) and art.10 (right to freedom of expression) of the European Convention. More particularly, s.12 of the Human Rights Act 1998 provides a specific test that must be employed by the courts before relief is granted which might affect the exercise of the Convention right to freedom of expression. Under s.12(3), "No relief is to be granted so as to restrain publication before trial unless the court is satisfied that the applicant is likely to be able to establish that publication should not be allowed".[246] Lord Phillips has acknowl-

18-050

---

244 [1976] Ch. 63 at 78.
245 [2005] B.P.I.R. 1010.
246 Section 12(4) emphasises that "The court must have particular regard to the importance of the Convention right of freedom of expression and, where the proceedings relate to material which the respondent claims, or which

edged that this is "a particularly high threshold test"[247] where an applicant seeks interim relief in an action against the media. The *American Cyanamid* threshold of "a serious question to be tried" is, clearly, a more readily surmountable obstacle than the higher test imposed in this context.

The protection of privacy

18-051

Since the enactment of the Human Rights Act 1998, the use of injunctions in the protection of privacy has grown at an astonishing rate.[248] Most of the early case law developments were framed as breaches of confidence, although, as was recognised in *A v B Plc*, the adoption of the values that arts 8 and 10 protect was providing a "new strength and breadth" to this cause of action.[249] Accordingly, a duty came to be imposed, "whenever a person receives information he knows or ought to know is fairly and reasonably to be regarded as confidential".[250] It is important to note that these circumstances were strikingly different from those that traditionally gave rise to a duty of confidence.[251] In the absence of a pre-existing relationship between the parties (where an action for breach of confidence is apposite), an applicant was able to proceed on the basis that there had been a "misuse of private information".[252] Testing the capacity of the courts to protect privacy both within pre-existing relationships[253] and in cases where no such relationship exists,[254] a host of celebrities and high-profile figures have sought to restrain publication of articles and photographs pertaining to weddings,[255] photographs posted on

---

appears to the court to be journalistic, literary or artistic material (or to conduct related to such material), to (a) the extent to which—(i) the material has, or is about to, become available to the public; or (ii) it is, or would be, in the public interest to be published; (b) any relevant privacy code".

247 *Douglas v Hello!* [2005] 3 W.L.R. 881 at [258].

248 As Lord Nicholls recognised in *Campbell v MGN Ltd* [2004] 2 A.C. 457 at 464, "In this country, unlike the United States of America, there is no over-arching, all-embracing, cause of action for 'invasion of privacy' . . . But protection of various aspects of privacy is a fast developing area of the law, here and in other jurisdictions".

249 [2002] 2 All E.R. 545 at 549 per Lord Woolf CJ. As Buxton LJ acknowledged in *McKennitt v Ash* [2008] Q.B. 73 at [11], "in order to find the rules of the English law of breach of confidence we now have to look in the jurisprudence of Articles 8 and 10".

250 *Campbell v MGN Ltd* [2004] A.C. 457 at 465 per Lord Nicholls.

251 See *Coco v AN Clark (Engineers) Ltd* [1969] R.P.C. 41 at 47 per Megarry J. An overview of developments in the law of confidence is provided by Lord Phillips in *Douglas v Hello!* [2005] 3 W.L.R. 881.

252 To adopt the phrasing of Lord Nicholls in *Campbell v MGN Ltd* [2004] A.C. 457. As Nicol J notes, "Although this tort had its origin in remedies for breach of confidence it has outgrown those confines under the influence of Article 8 of the ECHR" (*ERY v Associated Newspapers* [2016] EWHC 2760 (QB) at [44]).

253 See *McKennitt v Ash* [2008] Q.B. 73 (publication of a book by a former friend of a Canadian folk artist revealing personal details about the artist's private life). As Eady J acknowledged at first instance, "it seems to have been accepted . . . that she protected her reputation and her privacy 'with the iron safeguard of a chastity belt'"([2005] EWHC 3003 (QB) at [6]).

254 For example, where "private" information as to medical health, finances or personal or sexual relationships has been purloined for misuse.

255 *Douglas v Hello!* [2001] Q.B. 967.

Facebook,[256] their extramarital affairs,[257] details of drug use,[258] visits to brothels[259] or being the subject of a criminal investigation.[260]

In *Peck v United Kingdom*, Mr Peck attempted suicide in a public location such that any passer-by may have witnessed it. Nonetheless, the court held he had a reasonable expectation of privacy, as the broadcast of CCTV images in which Peck's identity was barely shielded "far exceeded any exposure to a passer-by or to security observation".[261] Similarly, in *Murray v Express Newspapers Plc*, the Court of Appeal held that the infant son of J.K. Rowling arguably had a reasonable expectation of privacy in relation to the publication of a photograph of him in his buggy with his parents in a public street.[262] Admittedly, there had to be a cut-off point in that "a point *may* be reached where the information sought to be restricted, by an order of the Court, is so widely and generally accessible 'in the public domain' that such an injunction would make no practical difference".[263] Such was the case in *Mosley v News Group Newspapers*,[264] where an application to restrain the defendant from making available on its website video footage of Mosley (president of the FIA) engaged in sexual activities with five prostitutes was refused. There was nothing left that the law could protect.

Where the applicant's art.8 rights are engaged, the court must consider whether there is a justification for disclosure. In other words the courts must balance the defendant's rights under art.10 with the applicant's rights under art.8. Neither article takes precedence.[265] In a contest between values, the court must apply an intense focus to the specific facts and the rights being claimed.[266] As to whether there is a compelling public interest in disclosure (such that greater weight should be attached to freedom of expression), the courts now construe public interest as an increasingly narrow concept. It is no longer sufficient to satisfy the public interest test merely on the basis that public figures must expect higher levels of media intrusion or that such figures are viewed as role models,[267] although such arguments may or may not be relevant on the facts.[268] Disclosure will be justified, however, to expose crime or wrongdoing,

---

256 *Rocknroll v News Group Newspapers Ltd* [2013] EWHC 24 (Ch).

257 See, e.g. *ETK v News Group Newspapers* [2011] EWCA Civ 439.

258 *Campbell v MGN Ltd* [2004] 4 A.C. 457.

259 *Theakston v MGN Ltd* [2002] E.M.L.R. 22.

260 *ZXC Bloomberg LP* [2019] EWHC 970 (QB). See also *Richard v BBC* [2019] Ch 169.

261 (2003) 36 E.H.R.R. 41 at [62].

262 [2008] E.M.L.R. 12; see also *Weller v Associated Newspapers Ltd* [2014] EWHC 1163 (QB).

263 *Mosley v News Group Newspapers* [2008] EWHC 687 (QB) at [33].

264 [2008] EWHC 687 (QB).

265 *PJS v News Group Newspapers* [2016] 2 W.L.R. 1253.

266 *Re S (A Child)* [2005] 1 A.C. 593.

267 As occurred in *Theakston v MGN Ltd* [2002] E.M.L.R. 22 where a report (but not photographs) of a well-known TV presenter's visit to a brothel was justified on the basis that he was a role model to young people. See, however, *McClaren v News Group Newspapers Ltd* [2012] EWHC 2466 (QB) at [34], where Lindblom J accepted that a former manager of the England football team was "a prominent public figure who has held positions of responsibility in the national game" and in a "category of those from whom the public could reasonably expect a higher standard of conduct".

268 See *Mosley v News Group Newspapers* [2008] EWHC 1777 (QB) at [12].

to protect the health and safety of the public or to set the record straight where the public has been misled.[269] As Simon LJ put it in *ZXC v Bloomberg* LP, "The Court must not allow itself to be drawn into confining the important rights of the press under article 10 , so that it ceases to be the public watchdog of freedoms in a democratic society and becomes the muzzled lapdog of private interests".[270]

18-054

The tendency of the courts in recent times has been to favour the right to respect for private and family life. In *K v News Group Newspapers*,[271] the Court of Appeal held that a judge had been wrong to refuse to grant an interim injunction preventing a newspaper from publishing details of an affair between the applicant (a leading figure in the entertainment industry) and his work colleague, and the subsequent termination of that colleague's employment contract. The arguments in favour of free speech were substantially outweighed by the harm done by the contravention of art.8.[272] The decision is noteworthy due to the emphasis placed upon protecting the rights of children.[273] As Ward LJ explained, "The purpose of the injunction is both to preserve the stability of the family while the appellant and his wife pursue a reconciliation and to save the children the ordeal of playground ridicule when that would inevitably follow publicity".[274] In *CTB v News Group Newspapers*,[275] moreover, an anonymity order restricting the press from naming a footballer involved in an alleged adulterous affair was continued despite his identity having been revealed in Parliament and globally on Twitter. Tugendhat J did so with the following justification:

> "It is obvious that if the purpose of this injunction were to preserve a secret, it would have failed in its purpose. But in so far as its purpose is to prevent intrusion or harassment, it has not failed. The fact that tens of thousands of people have named the claimant on the internet confirms that the claimant and his family need protection from intrusion . . . The order has not protected the claimant and his family from taunting on the internet. It is still effective to protect them from taunting and other intrusion and harassment in the print media".[276]

---

269 See *Campbell v MGN Ltd* [2004] 2 A.C. 457, where the publication of the fact that Naomi Campbell had taken drugs and was receiving treatment for addiction was necessary to set the record straight given her previous statements to the press. Further information (including photographs) was deemed to be intrusive and should not have been disclosed.

270 [2020] EWCA Civ 611 at [108]. See also *Rocknroll v News Group Newspapers Ltd* [2013] EWHC 24 (Ch) at [30] per Briggs J.

271 [2011] EWCA Civ 439.

272 Ward LJ warned, nonetheless, that "This restriction can only be justified if it is proportionate and is no more than is necessary . . . To restrict publication simply to save the blushes of the famous . . . could have the wholly undesirable chilling effect on the necessary ability of publishers to sell their newspapers" (at [13]).

273 See T. Bennett, "The Relevance and Importance of Third Party Interests in Privacy Cases" (2011) 127 L.Q.R. 531.

274 [2011] EWCA Civ 439 at [17].

275 [2011] EWHC 1334 (QB).

276 [2011] EWHC 1334 (QB) at [3].

This approach was endorsed by the majority of the Supreme Court in *PJS v News Group Newspapers Ltd*.[277] There an injunction was held in place to restrain publication of the details of PJS's extramarital sexual encounters, despite arguments that knowledge of the story had become so widespread that the injunction had ceased to be effective. Notwithstanding the significant coverage of the story online and more limited disclosure in print publication overseas, the majority held that an injunction continued to serve a useful protective purpose. To permit publication in mass circulation print media would be to allow for that information "to be recorded in eye catching headlines and sensational terms" in national newspapers which would only serve to magnify the intrusion and distress to PJS and his family.[278]

It appears, therefore, that at the risk of seeming to act in vain[279] (and, for some, exposing the law to ridicule),[280] the courts are prepared to fetter the freedom of the press to uphold an individual's art.8 rights to prevent further or magnified distress and intrusion, notwithstanding that the information is in the public domain. This use of injunctions to prevent continuing harassment is in line with European case law,[281] but the approach in *PJS* does provide a very clear sense of how far the law has moved towards the protection of privacy.[282] As Eady J was anxious to explain in *CTB v News Group Newspapers Ltd*, "It is important always to remember that the modern law of privacy is not concerned solely with secrets: it is also concerned importantly with intrusion".[283]

18-055

Applying s.12(3)

At an interim stage of proceedings, it is the s.12(3) test that is of primary importance. Not surprisingly, the meaning of "likelihood" in s.12(3) has been extensively litigated. In *Cream Holdings v Banerjee*,[284] Ms Banerjee had been an employee of the Cream group of companies. Cream began a successful nightclub in Liverpool and diversified into areas such as the organisation of music festivals and merchandising. When Banerjee's contract of employment was terminated, she copied company files and made these available to two principal Merseyside newspapers. Her story was one of considerable public interest and suggested that Cream had

18-056

---

277 [2016] UKSC 26. See J. Rowbottom (2017) 133 L.Q.R. 177; C. Rae (2016) 35(4) C.J.Q. 26.
278 [2016] UKSC 26 at [68] per Lord Neuberger.
279 As Jackson LJ argued in the Court of Appeal, it is inappropriate for the court to seek "to ban people from saying that which is common knowledge" (*PJS v News Group Newspapers* [2016] EWCA Civ 393 at [47]).
280 The concern of Lord Toulson (the sole dissenting voice in the Supreme Court) was that the court may lose "public respect for the law by giving the appearance of being out of touch with reality" ([2016] UKSC 26 at [88]).
281 See, e.g. *Von Hannover v Germany* (2005) 40 E.H.R.R. 1.
282 See, however, E. Reid, "Rebalancing Privacy and Freedom of Expression" (2012) 16(2) Edin. L.R. 253, who highlights the "rebalancing exercise in Strasbourg" in light of *Axel Springer AG v Germany* (2012) 55 E.H.R.R. 6 and *Von Hannover v Germany (No.2)* (2012) 55 E.H.R.R 15 and notes at p.258, "a discernible degree of realignment towards freedom of expression at the expense of respect for private life".
283 [2011] EWHC 1326 (QB) at [23].
284 [2004] 4 All E.R. 617. See P. Devonshire (2005) 24 C.L.Q. 194.

been involved in serious instances of illegal and improper conduct. On this ground, the House of Lords concluded that the applicants had failed to show that they were more likely than not to succeed at trial in preventing the publication of information. The opportunity was taken explicitly to address the higher threshold that the court must impose in the context of breach of confidence cases.

Lord Nicholls indicated that s.12(3) makes the likelihood of success at trial an "essential element" in the court's assessment of whether to make an interim order.[285] As to the degree of likelihood that might make a claimant's prospects of success sufficiently favourable, he took the view that the court must be "exceedingly slow to make interim restraint orders where the applicant has not satisfied the court that he will probably ('more likely than not') succeed at trial".[286] Noting that there can be "no single, rigid standard governing all applications for interim restraint orders", he also warned of difficult cases where this higher standard should not be imposed, such as where the "potential adverse consequences of disclosure are particularly grave, or where a short-lived injunction is needed to enable the court to hear and give proper consideration to an application for interim relief pending the trial or any relevant appeal".[287]

Lord Nicholls, therefore, clarified that the word "likely" in s.12(3) cannot have been intended to mean "more likely than not" in all situations; as a test of universal application, this would be a degree of likelihood too high. He deemed the intention of Parliament to set a threshold which was higher than the commonplace *American Cyanamid* standard but which "permits the court to dispense with this higher standard where particular circumstances make this necessary".[288]

Principles Governing the Grant of Injunctions in Specific Situations

18-057   Finally, it remains to discuss two specialist injunctions and the principles governing their award, namely the search order (issued to prevent the removal or destruction of evidence) and the freezing injunction (issued to prevent the removal of assets). The search order and the freezing injunction are two particular types of interim injunction, operative in their own

---

285 [2004] 4 All E.R. 617 at 625. As Sir David Eady warned in *AXB v BXA* [2018] EWHC 588 (QB) at 55, however, "that can be a difficult question to answer at the early stages of litigation simply because of the lack of evidence. One can easily be wrong . . ."

286 [2002] 4 All E.R. 617 at 625.

287 [2004] 4 All E.R. 617 at 625.

288 [2004] 4 All E.R. 617 at 624.

special circumstances[289] and governed by a distinct body of case law. Described as the law's "nuclear weapons",[290] detailed guidelines have been developed to circumscribe their use and safeguard the defendant from the obvious risk of oppression.

The search order

The search order (formerly known as an *Anton Piller order*)[291] is mandatory in nature and requires the defendant to permit the claimant to enter the defendant's premises for specified purposes, usually to inspect and copy documents, including information stored on digital devices.[292] Technically, a search order is not a search warrant because it does not empower the holder to enter or search premises. Instead, it requires the defendant to allow the holder access to the premises. The order does, however, have much in common with a search warrant. The first reported use of such an order was in 1974,[293] causing Lord Wilberforce to cite the development of this modern day jurisdiction as "an illustration of the adaptability of equity to new situations".[294] The utility of the order is most evident in cases of breach of copyright, passing off or infringements of patents,[295] where there is a risk that vital documents or files may be destroyed and it is crucial that the claimant be allowed to inspect them.[296] If the claimant goes beyond what the court empowers, i.e. by seizing non-specified materials, the court will require the claimant to hand over materials unlawfully taken and provide an account of what use was made of those materials.[297]

In *Anton Piller KG v Manufacturing Processes Ltd*,[298] for example, the claimant believed that the defendant was selling confidential information to its competitors. In order to prove this, it required access to documents filed in the defendant's premises. The Court of Appeal made an order requiring the defendant to permit the claimant to enter the premises and inspect the relevant documentation. The order in *Anton Piller* was made ex parte, i.e. without notice to the defendant. This is to ensure that the defendant is not warned in advance for, as

18-058

---

289 Although frequently issued in conjunction.

290 *Bank Mellat v Nikpour* [1985] F.S.R. 87 at 91 per Lord Donaldson MR.

291 Taking its name from *Anton Piller KG v Manufacturing Processes Ltd* [1976] Ch. 55.

292 See *A v B* [2019] EWHC 2089 (Ch).

293 See *EMI Ltd v Pandit* [1975] 1 All E.R. 418.

294 *Rank Film Distributors Ltd v Video Information Centre* [1982] A.C. 380 at 439. Lord Neuberger MR in his Hong Kong University Common Law Lecture 2010 entitled, "Has Equity had its Day?" traced its origins back to a nineteenth-century remedial equitable measure and commented, "And so the search order was born, by refinement and the extension of principle by precedent, of a 174-year-old equitable power" (at p.5).

295 Hence, its description by Hoffmann J in *Lock International Plc v Beswick* [1989] 1 W.L.R. 1268 at 1279 as the "ultimate weapon against fraudulent copyright pirates". These orders are frequently sought in actions against former employees who have joined competitors or started competing businesses of their own.

296 For example, in *Indicci Salus Ltd v Chandrasekaran* [2007] EWHC 406 (Ch), a search order was issued to prevent software and other confidential material owned by a company from being used by former business associates.

297 *TBD (Owen Holland) Ltd v Simons* [2020] EWHC 30 (Ch).

298 [1976] Ch. 55.

Templeman LJ put it in *Rank Film Distributors Ltd v Video Information Centre*, "If the stable door cannot be bolted, the horse must be secured . . . If the horse is liable to be spirited away, notice of an intention to secure the horse will defeat the intention".[299]

As demonstrated in *Alfa Laval Tumba AB v Separator Spares International Ltd*, obstructing the execution of a search order is a contempt of court.[300] There the defendant was in possession of thousands of the applicant's technical drawings, copies of which he had hidden on a website accessible only by a link on his computer system. Following the making of the search order he had deleted all evidence of that link.[301] Similarly, in *Microsoft Corp v Mbaezue*, the defendant was committed to prison for contempt for continuous and serious breaches of freezing and search orders where he had deliberately attempted to prevent or delay the discovery of assets and information and had failed to comply with the orders.[302] The burden of proving the contempt rests with the claimant and the standard of proof is that of the criminal law (i.e. beyond a reasonable doubt). As May J observed in *Hewlett Packard Enterprise Company v Sage*, "The judgmental exercise involves a holistic consideration of all the available documentary evidence, the oral evidence the court has received, and the inferences which the court is driven to draw from that evidence".[303]

18-059

The power to make a search order is now placed on a statutory footing.[304] Section 7(1) of the Civil Procedure Act 1997 provides the High Court[305] with a power to issue a search order for the purpose of securing, in the case of any proposed or existing proceedings in court, the preservation of evidence which is or may be relevant or the preservation of property which is or may be the subject matter of the proceedings or as to which any question arises or may arise in the proceedings.[306] The order may direct any person to permit any person described in the order (or secure that any person so described is permitted) to enter premises in England and

---

299 [1982] A.C. 380 at 418.

300 [2010] EWHC 674 (Ch). The court's powers are wide and range from fines and sequestration, to suspended and final orders of committal to prison. As May J acknowledged in *Hewlett Packard Enterprise Co v Sage* [2017] EWHC 66 (QB) at [80], "The sanction of committal to prison is reserved for cases of serious, contumacious flouting of orders of the court . . .". Mr Sage was committed to prison for a period of 18 months.

301 See also *Aspect Capital Ltd v Christensen* [2010] EWHC 744 (Ch) where the defendant had deliberately attempted to interfere with the contents of his computer and to put it beyond reach by triggering an encryption program.

302 [2009] EWHC 51 (Ch). His catalogue of sins included failing to deliver up his passport, failing to disclose his email address and password, deleting emails and dissipating relevant assets. In *Northamber Plc v Genee World Ltd* [2020] EWHC 31 (Ch), the penalty imposed was a fine of £25,000 for failing to provide data and not providing audited accounts.

303 [2017] EWHC 66 (QB) at [15].

304 It is to be appreciated that the court also has a general power to order disclosure of documents or inspection of equipment or other property under the Civil Procedure (Modification of Enactments) Order 1998.

305 In appropriate circumstances the application can also be made before a judge of the Patents County Court: *Suh v Ryu* [2012] EWPCC 20. In addition, a High Court judge sitting in the county court can make a search order or freezing order: see the County Court Remedies Regulations 2014.

306 Different search and seizure orders can be issued under other legislative provisions, for example, s.365 of the Insolvency Act 1986 and s.47G(2) of the Proceeds of Crime Act 2002.

Wales,[307] and while on the premises to take in accordance with the terms of the order any of the steps specified in the Act. Those steps are to carry out a search for, or inspection and removal of, anything described in the order and to make or obtain a copy, photograph, sample or other record of anything so described. The order may also direct the person subject to the order to provide any information[308] or article described in the order and to retain for safe keeping anything described in the order. The search order can also be directed at a non-party to the proceedings, which was a development promoted in the recent decision in *Abela v Baadarani*.[309] There the claimants obtained a judgment debt against the defendant (Mr Baadarani) for $20 million. They subsequently sought a search order against Mr Baadarani's bank for documents relating to his assets. The search order was granted as it related to ongoing "proceedings" to enforce the judgment even though the bank was a third party.

Use and abuse

18-060

By the 1980s there was considerable concern that the grant of search orders had become commonplace. This is particularly problematic because as Mann J observed, "one will not normally know until one gets to a trial whether the search and seizure order really was justified".[310] The ex parte use of search orders clearly gives rise to the potential for hardship and oppression. As Scott J recognised in *Columbia Picture Industries Inc v Robinson*, "the practice of the court has allowed the balance to swing much too far in favour of the plaintiffs and that *Anton Piller* orders have been too readily granted and with insufficient safeguards for respondents".[311] Such was illustrated in *Lock International v Beswick*[312] where the claimant's solicitors were permitted to search the premises and the homes of three individual defendants. In addition to documents that belonged to the claimant (documents containing specified confidential information), virtually all the defendants' drawings, documents, records and prototypes were removed. In total, 12 boxes of drawings, five filing cabinet drawers and five prototypes were taken. Hoffmann J accepted that the order should never have been granted and, with particular regret as to the searches of individuals' private homes, confessed that he could "only sympathise with the sense of outrage that they must have felt".[313]

Such concerns are, however, no new thing. In *Anton Piller KG v Manufacturing Processes Ltd*, Lord Denning MR felt that it was important that the inspection did no real harm to the defendant or his case. In addition, various judges have highlighted that a balancing exercise is required to measure, on the one hand, the applicant's right to his property and to ensure the preservation of

---

307 Premises includes any vehicle: s.7(8).
308 For example, PINs, user names, combinations, passwords, codes and any other information which may be necessary to give access to such computers, other electronic storage devices, email accounts and websites.
309 [2017] EWHC 269 (Ch).
310 *Hewlett Packard Enterprise Co v Manchester Technologies Data (Holdings) Ltd* [2019] EWHC 2301 (Ch) at [1].
311 [1987] Ch. 38 at 76.
312 [1989] 1 W.L.R. 1268.
313 [1989] 1 W.L.R. 1268 at 1283.

evidence as against, on the other, the invasion of privacy of a defendant where he has no opportunity to put his case.[314] As Scott J pointed out in *Columbia Picture Industries Inc v Robinson*, search orders potentially involve serious inroads on civil rights such as the presumption of innocence, the right not to be condemned unheard, protection against arbitrary searches and seizures and the sanctity of the home.[315] By way of illustration, the court will not grant a search order against a person of good standing who is deemed likely to respond to an order of the court to deliver up. In the words of Hoffmann J, "Not everyone who is misusing confidential information will destroy documents in the face of a court order requiring him to preserve them".[316]

Pre-conditions

18-061

Underpinned by the Civil Procedure Rules,[317] more recent practice is to exercise considerable caution in the grant of search orders.[318] As Judge Jones rightly pointed out, the court should be concerned with the rights infringed by the order, "the right to privacy in one's own home; the right to be fully protected against unjustified and arbitrary searches and seizures; the right to be heard in defence of a claim before an order is made".[319] Before a search order can be granted certain basic requirements need to be satisfied[320]:

- the facts and circumstances surrounding the case must be appropriate to justify this type of order;

- given that the application is made without notice, and may in an extreme emergency be made over the telephone, it is crucial that the applicant make a full and fair disclosure of all material facts[321];

- as the defendant may be entitled to damages for any loss sustained if the order is wrongly granted, the applicant must give an undertaking in damages,[322] which

---

314 For example, in *Lock International v Beswick* [1989] 1 W.L.R. 1268, Hoffmann J acknowledged that "The making of an intrusive order ex parte even against a guilty defendant is contrary to normal principles of justice and can only be done when there is a paramount need to prevent a denial of justice to the plaintiff. The absolute extremity of the court's powers is to permit a search of a defendant's dwelling house, with the humiliation and family distress which that frequently involves" (at 1281).

315 [1987] Ch. 38.

316 [1989] 1 W.L.R. 1268 at 1281. See also Tugendhat J in *CBS Butler Ltd v Brown* [2013] EWHC 3944 (QB) at [38].

317 See CPR Pt25, PD 25A, para.7.

318 See further, the comments of Sir Donald Nicholls VC in *Universal Thermosensors Ltd v Hibben* [1992] 1 W.L.R. 840.

319 *Lasytsya v Koumettou* [2020] EWHC 660 (Ch) at [24].

320 See Warren J in *Indicci Salus Ltd v Chandrasekaran* [2007] EWHC 406 (Ch) at [10]; affirmed on appeal at [2008] EWCA Civ 67.

321 *Brink's MAT Ltd v Elcombe* [1988] 3 All E.R. 188 CA.

322 For example, in *Al-Rawas v Pegasus Energy Ltd* [2008] EWHC 617 (QB), the court had to assess damages,

(depending on the financial status of the claimant[323]) may be required to be supported by some form of security.[324] If the applicant gets it wrong, therefore, the financial consequences could be serious;

- there must be an extremely strong prima facie case which shows that the damage, whether potential or actual, must be very serious for the applicant[325];

- there must be clear evidence that the defendant has in his possession incriminating documents or things and that there is a real possibility that the defendant may destroy such material before a without notice application is made (see below); and

- the harm likely to be caused by the execution of the search order on the defendant and his business affairs must not be out of proportion to the legitimate object of the order.[326] In *Coca-Cola v Gilbey*, however, the risk of violence to the defendant which would follow from the disclosure of the information was a factor to be considered, but did not prevent the issue of a search order.[327]

Evidencing a real possibility

18-062

In *Indicii Salus Ltd v Chandrasekaran*, Warren J accepted that search orders had traditionally been granted too readily by the courts and that "Judges became concerned that it had become all too easy to obtain this sort of relief which could often have serious and permanent adverse consequences for a defendant".[328] In particular, the courts now place emphasis upon the requirement that there should be a "real possibility" that the defendants may destroy evidence.[329] As Dillon LJ explained in *Booker McConnell Plc v Plascow*:

---

payable under the applicant's undertaking, for the serious disruption to the defendant's business while the search process had been undertaken.

323 See, e.g. *Re DPR Futures Ltd* [1989] I W.L.R. 778 where a company in receivership gave an undertaking limited to the amount of the assets it held.

324 If there is a change to the applicant's financial position affecting his ability to honour the undertaking in damages, he is under a duty to disclose it to the respondent: *Staines v Walsh* [2003] EWHC 1486.

325 In *Lock International v Beswick* [1989] 1 W.L.R. 1268, for example, the evidence was insufficiently strong and the High Court set aside the search order.

326 As Hoffmann J explained in *Lock International v Beswick* [1989] 1 W.L.R. 1268 at 1281, "the court must employ a graduated response . . . there must be proportionality between the perceived threat to the plaintiff's rights and the remedy granted".

327 [1995] 4 All E.R. 711. Police protection was an option for the defendant.

328 [2007] EWHC 406 (Ch) at [12].

329 In principle, the same applies to hiding as well as destruction: *Indicci Salus Ltd v Chandrasekaran* [2007] EWHC 406 (Ch).

> "The phrase 'a real possibility' is to be contrasted with the extravagant fears which seem to afflict all plaintiffs who have complaints of breach of confidence, breach of copyright or passing off. Where the production and delivery up of documents is in question, the courts have always proceeded, justifiably, on the basis that the overwhelming majority of people in this country will comply with the court's order, and that defendants will therefore comply with orders to, for example, produce and deliver up documents without it being necessary to empower the plaintiffs' solicitors to search the defendant's premises".[330]

Nevertheless, it is unusual for the court to obtain cogent or actual evidence of a threat to destroy material or documents.[331] Hence, it is necessary to draw inferences from the evidence with the inevitable outcome that the probability of disappearance or destruction is readily inferred when the evidence shows that "the defendant is engaged in a nefarious activity which renders it likely that he is an untrustworthy person".[332] An issue that the court should address is whether a lesser order would be complied with for, as Warren J explained, "If there is no reason to think that a defendant would disobey an order, for instance for delivery up of a claimant's property, then it would not be appropriate to seek to obtain a search order".[333]

18-063
As indicated above, the applicant must make full and fair disclosure of all material facts. For these purposes, materiality is to be decided by the court and not by the applicant. This entails that the applicant must make proper inquiries before making the application and the duty is not limited to facts actually known to the applicant, but extends also to facts which would have been discovered on the making of such enquiries.[334] A failure to disclose may result in any order granted being discharged.[335] The outcome, of course, depends upon the discretion of the court and the importance of the undisclosed fact to the initial making of the order.[336] The court will, therefore, take on board the gravity of the breach,

---

330 [1985] R.P.C. 425 at 441.
331 As Warren J put it in *Indicci Salus Ltd v Chandrasekaran* [2007] EWHC 406 (Ch), "the Court does not have to be satisfied before making a search order that the defendant actually would destroy evidence" (at [14]).
332 Per Oliver LJ in *Dunlop Holdings Ltd v Staravia Ltd* [1982] Comm. L.R. 3 at [3].
333 *Indicci Salus Ltd v Chandrasekaran* [2007] EWHC 406 (Ch) at [15]. There the defendants were willing to deliver up certain computers, but the real risk was that they would remove sensitive material from them before doing so. A search order was, therefore, appropriate.
334 *Brink's MAT Ltd v Elcombe* [1988] 3 All E.R. 188 CA.
335 For example, in *Irish Response Ltd v Direct Beauty Products* [2011] EWHC 37 (QB), the claimant had acted in breach of the duty of fair presentation by failing to disclose certain correspondence and the order was discharged.
336 *Behbehani v Salem* [1989] 1 W.L.R. 723.

the explanation offered and the severity and duration of the prejudice occasioned to the defendant.[337]

Executing the order

There are additional regulations set out in Practice Direction 25A which govern the way that the search order is performed. These are designed, of course, to protect the defendant's interests. These require that the order should be carried out in the presence of a court-approved supervising solicitor (ideally with experience and not a member of the firm of solicitors acting for the claimant). If the material sought is contained on a computer (e.g. an email account or file system), it is advisable also to take along a forensic computer expert (named in the order) so as to avoid damage to the system or data. The order should normally be executed during office hours, i.e. between 9.30 and 17.30, Monday to Friday. If the search is to be of a private dwelling, and the supervising solicitor is a man and the respondent is female, the solicitor serving the order should be accompanied by a woman. The supervising solicitor is obliged to explain the process to the respondent. Unless it is impracticable, a list of items to be removed should be prepared at the premises and the defendant afforded an opportunity to check this list. Understandably, no items should be taken from the defendant's premises unless covered by the terms of the order. The supervising solicitor is to compile a written report on the execution of the order and a copy should be delivered immediately to the defendant's solicitors. The court will consider this report and set down a further hearing if the respondent wishes to apply to set aside the order. If the claimant or his solicitor has acted improperly, the order can be discharged and exemplary (i.e. punitive) damages may be awarded to the defendant.

18-064

The privilege against self-incrimination

In *Rank Film Distributors Ltd v Video Information Centre*,[338] the House of Lords held, reluctantly, that the defendant could invoke the privilege against self-incrimination where to comply with the search order (by answering questions or disclosing documents) would give rise to a real and appreciable risk of criminal proceedings being brought against him for conspiracy to defraud. As Lord Wilberforce emphasised, no civil court "has any power to decide in a manner which would bind a criminal court that evidence of any kind is admissible or inadmissible in that court".[339] In other words, the court could not compel disclosure at the same time as safeguarding the defendant from the consequences of self-incrimination. This development threatened

18-065

---

337 *Memory Corp Plc v Sidhu* [2000] F.S.R. 921.
338 [1982] A.C. 380.
339 [1982] A.C. 380 at 442.

to make it increasingly difficult to obtain disclosure of information from defendants. There are, however, two relevant qualifications to this rule.

First, it does not apply to material which is independent of the search order. Such is demonstrated in *OTL v P*,[340] where the High Court confirmed that the application of the privilege against self-incrimination did not apply to material that was free-standing evidence. The public interest required that the offending material should be passed to the police. This theme was revisited in *C Plc v P*,[341] where again highly indecent images of children were recovered from a computer following the execution of a search order made in intellectual property proceedings. The appellant argued that the privilege against self-incrimination entailed that these images should not be disclosed to the police. The Court of Appeal held that the privilege against self-incrimination was not an absolute privilege available regardless of the circumstances. Even before the enactment of the Human Rights Act 1998, the privilege against self-incrimination could not be invoked in respect of evidence which existed independently of any compulsory questioning of the defendant or any application of the court's compulsory discovery process. There was no privilege in the offending material as it was material that existed independently of the court order.

Secondly, s.72 of the Senior Courts Act 1981 assumes relevance in proceedings for infringement of intellectual property rights or passing off. It provides that a person shall not be excused from answering questions or from complying with any order made simply because to do so would expose that person (or spouse) to proceedings for a related offence. In *Cobra Golf Ltd v Rata*,[342] a search order was granted to enable the applicants to recover and preserve evidence in their passing off action against the defendants. The applicants sought to use information obtained in subsequent committal proceedings against the defendants for contempt of court. The defendants pleaded the privilege against self-incrimination, but the High Court accepted that the general protection was abrogated by the statutory exception. In *Phillips v Mulcaire*,[343] the Supreme Court was called upon to consider whether the voicemail messages of an employee of the celebrity publicist, Max Clifford, fell within the scope of "intellectual property" as defined by s.72(5).[344] Adopting an expansive interpretation that went beyond the understanding of intellectual property in any traditional sense, the court held that commercially confidential information fell within the s.72 definition and that this was consistent with the intention of Parliament. Accordingly, the private investigator Glen Mulcaire could not rely on the privilege against self-incrimination to avoid complying with an order that he disclose the details of his instructions to intercept messages in the *News of the World* phone-hacking scandal.

---

340 [2006] EWHC 1226 (Ch). Illegal images of children were found on a computer subject to the search order.
341 [2007] EWCA Civ 493.
342 [1998] Ch. 109.
343 [2013] 1 A.C. 1.
344 Defined by s.72(5) as "any patent, trademark, copyright, design right, registered design, technical or commercial information or other intellectual property".

The freezing order

Formerly known as the *Mareva* injunction,[345] the freezing injunction (as with the search order) is comparatively recent in origin.[346] It has, however, acquired contemporary popularity and relevance.[347] As Longmore LJ put it:

18-066

> **"Freezing injunctions are now an accepted part of our legal land-scape. They can only be granted when the claimant has a good arguable case and there are reasonable grounds to suppose that a defendant may dissipate his assets before judgment is pronounced. The purpose of the injunction is to preserve a defendant's assets, subject to dealings in the ordinary course of business so that, if and when a judgment is pronounced, the defendant still has assets to meet that judgment".[348]**

The freezing injunction is, therefore, an order of the court to restrain the defendant from hiding, disposing of or removing assets from the jurisdiction where there is a risk that any judgment will go unsatisfied by reason of that concealment, disposal or removal.[349] A straightforward example arises from *Vause v* Bray,[350] where a freezing injunction was obtained in circumstances when the plaintiff claimed that he had bought a defective car from the defendant and, facing legal action, the latter threatened to put his assets beyond the reach of the plaintiff. As in *Vause*, the order is normally issued on an interim basis pending trial, but it may also be issued post-trial where the claimant can show the risk that the defendant will dispose of his assets to avoid execution of the judgment.[351] The order will usually be limited to assets not exceeding the value of the claim.[352] Often ancillary to the freezing order, the court will also

---

345 Taking its name from *Mareva Compania Naviera SA v International Bulkcarriers SA* [1975] 2 Lloyd's Rep. 509.

346 Its first reported use was in *Nippon Yusen Kaisha v Karageorgis* [1975] 1 W.L.R. 1093. As Lord Neuberger MR speaking extrajudicially observed, "And so one of the oldest equitable remedies was extended—or refined—to give birth to a new form, but one born of a long-established jurisdiction" ("Has equity had its day?" Hong Kong University Common Law Lecture, 2010, p.5).

347 For example, under the Proceeds of Crime Act 2002, the National Crime Agency utilises interim freezing orders in unexplained wealth cases: see *National Crime Agency v Hussain* [2020] EWHC 432 (Admin). Similarly, a freezing order may be made under s.37 of the Matrimonial Causes Act 1973: see *YM v NM* [2020] EWFC 13.

348 *JSC BTA Bank v Kythreotis* [2010] EWCA Civ 1436 at [52]. For a statement of the elementary principles and safeguards relating to freezing injunctions see *UL v BK* [2013] EWHC 1735 (Fam).

349 This is sometimes known as the "enforcement principle": see *JSC Mezhdunarodniy Promyshlenniy Bank v Pugachev* [2015] EWCA Civ 139.

350 [1987] 3 WLUK 289.

351 See, e.g. *Babanaft International Co SA v Bassatne* [1990] Ch. 13; *Nomihold Securities Inc v Mobile Telesytems France SA* [2011] EWHC 337 (Comm).

352 If the claim fails in whole or in part, the claimant will be potentially liable in damages for loss caused to the defendant because of the improperly obtained order: see *Fiona Trust & Holding Corp v Privalov* [2016] EWHC 2163 (Comm).

order that the defendant remain in the United Kingdom pending full disclosure of his assets and that he deliver up his passport. It might also be appropriate to seek a search order to search the defendant's premises and seize evidence.

The jurisdiction of the court is now on a statutory basis and s.37(3) of the Senior Courts Act 1981 provides that the power to grant a freezing injunction "shall be exercisable in cases where that party is, as well as in cases where he is not, domiciled, resident or present within that jurisdiction".[353] As is evident from s.37(1) of the Act, the High Court enjoys the jurisdiction to grant an injunction when it is "just and convenient" to do so. The Civil Procedure Rules emphasise that a party may be restrained from removing or dealing with assets wherever situated.[354]

18-067

Prior to 1982, the court was unable to grant interlocutory injunctive relief where the substantive proceedings were taking place abroad.[355] This had the effect that a claimant in a foreign court seeking control of a defendant's assets in England was unable to do so. The English courts did not have jurisdiction over the provision of substantive relief.[356] Following s.25 of the Civil Jurisdiction and Judgments Act 1982,[357] as extended by Civil Jurisdiction and Judgments Act 1982 (Interim Relief) Order 1997,[358] the High Court can now grant interim relief in aid of substantive proceedings anywhere else, "of whatever kind and wherever taking place".[359] The claim must be such, however, that an English court could identify the relief as interim relief in relation to the final order sought abroad.[360]

General guidelines

18-068

Despite the seemingly broad discretion bestowed by s.37, which is sometimes called the "flexibility principle", guidelines applicable for obtaining a freezing injunction were laid down by Lord Denning MR in *Third Chandris Shipping Corp v Unimarine SA*.[361] Ultimately, of course, the court must ensure that its remedy is not used oppressively against the defendant and the ultimate question is whether it is convenient, just and reasonable in the circumstances of the

---

353 Originally, the freezing injunction was a remedy against a defendant located outside the jurisdiction with assets inside the jurisdiction.

354 CPR r.25.1(1)(f). For worldwide freezing orders: see para.**18-072**. In *Sinclair Investment Holdings Ltd v Cushnie* [2004] EWHC 218 (Ch), the order related to Mr Cushnie's house in France.

355 See *The Siskina* [1977] 3 All E.R. 803.

356 *Mercedes-Benz AG v Leiduck* [1995] 3 All E.R. 929.

357 This gave power to the High Court to grant interim relief where substantive proceedings were pending in a Brussels or Lugano Convention state and the subject matter of the proceedings was within the scope of the Brussels or Lugano Conventions.

358 SI 1997/302; the order extends the effect of s.25 to non-Convention countries and to proceedings outside the scope of the Conventions.

359 *Crédit Suisse Fides SA v Cuoghi* [1998] Q.B. 818 at 825 per Millett LJ. In *JSC Mezhdunarodniy Promyshlenniy Bank v Pugachev* [2015] EWCA Civ 139, for example, the proceedings were commenced in Russia.

360 *Fourie v Le Roux* [2005] EWCA Civ 204; see also *Sweden v Serwin* [2020] EWHC 1251 (Comm).

361 [1979] 2 All E.R. 972; see also *Lord Chancellor v Blavo* [2016] EWHC 126 (QB).

case to grant the relief sought.[362] For example, in *Charles Russell LLP v Rehman*[363] the mere possibility that a client might recover costs from the other side was no substitute for a freezing order sought by the solicitor against his client. There was no guarantee that such further money would be forthcoming or that, if it was paid, that it would ever be paid over to the solicitor. A freezing order, moreover, must do no more than is necessary to protect the applicant's claim and is not to be employed as a weapon of oppression. This entails that the terms of a freezing injunction may subsequently be varied so as to cater, say, for additional living or legal expenses of the defendant,[364] to allow the defendants to raise money for a defence[365] or to permit the registered owners to grant tenancies of the properties pending the determination of the beneficial ownership of the properties.[366] It is, however, necessary for the applicant to demonstrate a change of circumstances such that a different decision would have been made at the earlier hearing.[367] The order must, therefore, be clear and unequivocal and falls to be narrowly construed[368] and this is sometimes called the "strict interpretation principle". In *Haederle v Thomas*,[369] the order was unclear because after each of four "£" signs in the order, which were to indicate the minimum assets to be maintained in the jurisdiction (i.e. £560,000), no figure was actually inserted.

Lord Denning's guidelines are as follows. First, the claimant must make a full and frank disclosure of all matters in his knowledge which are material for the judge to know.[370] If the applicant fails to disclose information that is of a significant nature,[371] the court might be persuaded to refuse, discharge[372] or modify the order[373] and make an order of costs against

18-069

---

362 See *Lord Chancellor v Blavo* [2016] EWHC 126 (QB), where the High Court continued a freezing injunction against a solicitor who (it was alleged) had been engaged in large-scale, legal aid fraud. There was an arguable case and, in light of the alleged dishonesty, the defendant's financial difficulties and his lack of full disclosure, it was clearly just and convenient to do so.

363 [2010] EWHC 202 (Ch).

364 *Willetts v Alvey*, [2010] EWHC 155 (Ch).

365 *Stewart v Franey* unreported 16 June 2016.

366 *Kazakhstan Kagazy Plc v Zhunus* [2019] EWHC 97 (Comm).

367 *Kea Investments Ltd v Watson* [2020] EWHC 472 (Ch). There, the court was satisfied that it would have made no difference. The claimant was simply trying to unpick the consequences of the injunction.

368 See *JSC BTA Bank v Ablyazov* [2015] UKSC 64.

369 [2016] EWHC 1866 (Ch).

370 This involves the applicant in the making of proper inquiries prior to his application: see *Brink's Mat Ltd v Elcombe* [1998] 3 All E.R. 188.

371 It must be an omission that is more than of peripheral relevance: *VTB Commodities Trading DAC v JSC Antipinsky Refinery* [2020] EWHC 72 (Comm).

372 As occurred in *DBI Innovations (UK) Ltd v May Fair Avenue General Trading LLC* [2019] EWHC 2235 (QB) where, at the original *ex parte* hearing, the claimant had made a material non-disclosure and showed a lack of candour. Similarly, in *Fimbank Plc v Discover Investment Corp* [2020] EWHC 254 (Comm) a freezing order was discharged because the claimant had failed to provide full and frank disclosure of the pre-existing arrangements between it and the defendant.

373 *Charles Russell LLP v Rehman* [2010] EWHC 202 (Ch). But this is not necessarily the case, as in *Guerrero v Monterrico Metals Plc* [2009] EWHC 2475 (QB) where the order was continued even though the judge had not been presented with a full picture of the evidence at the hearing of the without notice application.

the claimant.[374] If the claimant has complied with the disclosure and demonstration of risk of dissipation requirements, however, it is unlikely that the court will vary or discharge the original order.[375] The duty of full and frank disclosure might even require a "without prejudice" document or meeting to be disclosed, if it would otherwise mislead the court.[376] It is for the court to determine whether any fact that was undisclosed is material and, if so, what the consequence of that non-disclosure should be.[377]

Secondly, the claimant should give the particulars of his claim against the defendant, stating the ground of his claim[378] and the amount thereof,[379] and fairly anticipating the points that might be advanced in response if the defendant knew of the application. As regards the latter, in *Complete Retreats Liquidating Trust v Logue* the order was discharged because the applicant made no attempt to inform the court of the likely defences that the defendant might seek to put forward.[380] This omission was designed to paint a highly prejudicial picture of the defendant without any attempt to put before the court any material that might show otherwise. Put generally, the applicant must demonstrate a good arguable case[381] and this is particularly so as most applications are made "without notice".[382] In *Polly Peck International v Nadir (No.2)*,[383] Scott LJ refused an application for a freezing injunction against a bank on the ground that the claimant had no arguable case for liability.[384] Unlike *Cyanamid*, therefore, the court necessarily engages with the question of the strength of the claimant's case.[385]

Thirdly, the claimant must give some grounds for believing that the defendant has assets

---

374   As, indeed, happened in *Rugby B.C. v Tayton* [2020] EWHC 898 (QB).
375   *Abdullah v Siddiqi* [2020] 2 WLUK 395.
376   *Linsen International Ltd v Humpus Sea Transport PTE Ltd* [2010] EWHC 303 (Comm).
377   *BCS Corporate Acceptances Ltd v Terry* [2016] EWHC 533 (QB). For example, it would be material if the applicant was being investigated by the police for dishonesty at the time of the ex parte hearing.
378   Hence, if no breach of duty is specified (*Yossifoff v Donnerstein* [2015] EWHC 3357 (Ch)), or no identification of any judgment to be enforced is made (*Lemos v Lemos* [2016] EWCA Civ 1181), there can be no freezing order granted.
379   The freezing injunction will usually specify the monetary value of assets to be preserved to reflect this sum and potential costs. Any assets in excess of that amount can be freely dealt with by the defendant.
380   [2010] EWHC 1864 (Ch).
381   For the difficulties in the face of conflicting evidence, see *Antonio Gramsci Shipping Corp v Lembergs* [2012] I.L.Pr. 36, summarised on appeal at [2013] I.L.Pr. 36 at [15].
382   As Lord Scott observed in *Fourie v Le Roux* [2007] 1 W.L.R. 320 at 334, "I find it very difficult to visualise a case where the grant of a freezing order, made without notice, could be said to be properly made in the absence of any formulation of the case for substantive relief that the applicant for the order intended to institute".
383   [1992] 4 All E.R. 769.
384   In *Alliance Bank JSC v Zhunus* unreported 30 January 2015 (Comm), a freezing order was discharged by Leggatt J in circumstances where the claimant failed to state what the provisions of foreign law were alleged to have been breached.
385   Three unexplained interim, wealth freezing orders were set aside in *National Crime Agency v Baker* [2020] EWHC 822 (Admin) because they had been based upon unreliable assumptions reached by the NCA and the fact that its case was, as Lang J put it at [217], "flawed by inadequate investigation into some obvious lines of enquiry . . .".

in the United Kingdom.[386] It is accepted that the claimant will rarely have precise information, but he is required to furnish some evidential indication. For example, the existence of a bank account in England will suffice, regardless of whether it is in overdraft or not.[387]

Fourthly, the claimant should give some grounds for believing that there is a real risk (judged objectively)[388] of the assets being removed before the judgment or award is satisfied.[389] The court must, however, be cautious and particularly so in ex parte proceedings.[390] In *Montechi v Shimco*, Lord Bridge spoke of the need for a "real reason to apprehend" that the claimant would be denied a remedy.[391] In *ABC v P*,[392] the defendant was convicted of two offences of voyeurism and of making an indecent image of his step-daughter and was sentenced to imprisonment. She commenced proceedings for damages and sought a freezing order. The court declined her application because, although the step-father's actions involved deceit and a betrayal of trust, this was inadequate to prove that he would deliberately dissipate assets from the court's jurisdiction. The court will consider the nature of the assets and the ease with which they can be dissipated, the nature and financial standing of the defendant's business, the length of time the defendant has been in business, any statement of intent made by the defendant in respect of dissipating assets, whether the substantive claim relates to dishonesty and the defendant's previous compliance history with court orders.[393] In *BCS Corporate Acceptances Ltd v Terry*,[394] Mr Terry was resident out of the jurisdiction in Geneva; he was plainly experienced in international finance; he had in the past given a false address; the judgment against him reflected his fraudulent activity; he had made transfers of valuable assets to his wife following his unsuccessful appeals against judgment; he had failed to make any reference to a large, residential property which he jointly owned and had misled the court as to his employer. In these circumstances, May J concluded unsurprisingly that there was a risk of dissipation.

---

386 The term "assets" is widely defined to include movable and immovable property, e.g. land, bank accounts, cars, ships, aircraft, antiques, jewellery, shares, securities, trade goods, office equipment, choses in action and money.

387 *Third Chandris Shipping Corp v Unimarine SA* [1979] 2 All E.R. 972 at 985 per Lord Denning MR.

388 As Gloster LJ admitted in *Candy v Holyoake* [2017] EWCA Civ 92 at [34], "Solid evidence will be required to support a conclusion that relief is justified, although precisely what this entails in any given case will necessarily vary according to the individual circumstances . . .".

389 There must be a real risk that, unless restrained by injunction, the defendant will dissipate or dispose of his assets other than in the ordinary course of business and that assets are likely to be dealt with in such a way as to make enforcement of any award or judgment more difficult: *Congentra AG v Sixteen Thirteen Marine SA* [2008] EWHC 1615.

390 *Thane Investments Ltd v Tomlinson* [2003] EWCA Civ 1272. As Peter Gibson LJ noted (at [27]), "The requirements are imposed on applicants for a freezing order in order to protect persons who are not in a position to protect themselves".

391 [1979] 1 W.L.R. 1180 at 1183.

392 Unreported 4 May 2011.

393 *Shepherd Construction Ltd v Berners (BVI) Ltd* [2010] EWHC 763 (TCC).

394 [2016] EWHC 533 (QB).

Fifthly, the claimant must give a cross-undertaking in damages.[395] As has been discussed in relation to interim injunctions more generally, the undertaking is required because liability has yet to be determined. It is, however, fairness rather than the likelihood of loss that justifies the taking of a cross-undertaking. Accordingly, in *Guerrero v Monterrico Metals Plc*,[396] the applicants had to give a cross-undertaking in damages so that the defendant was not deprived of a right of recourse against them if it was later found that the defendant had suffered damage because of the injunction. If no set sum is ordered, the default position is that the cross-undertaking will be unlimited in amount. It can also be "fortified", which usually means that the court will require money to be paid into an English bank account under the control of the court.[397] However, this is relevant only when the claimant has no assets in England and Wales and the defendant is at risk of loss.[398]

Third parties

18-070

A third party who has notice of a freezing injunction against a defendant will be in contempt of court if he knowingly assists in the removal or disposal of assets.[399] Equally, of course, any other asset held by any other person and covered by the terms of the freezing order is subject to the same principle. A third party must not allow the defendant to have access to the asset so as to enable him to dispose of it. Such would be in contempt of court. Unsurprisingly, many of the case law illustrations involve banks and bank accounts. It is to be appreciated that banks do not owe a duty of care towards a claimant to ensure that funds falling within the scope of a freezing order are not dissipated.[400] The expectation of banks is that, as Lord Denning MR described in *Z Ltd v A-Z*:

> **"As soon as the bank is given notice of the freezing injunction, it must freeze the defendant's bank account . . . It must not allow any drawings to be made on it, neither by cheques drawn before the injunction nor by those drawn after it. The reason is because, if it allowed any such drawings, it would be obstructing the course of**

---

395 Unless there are special circumstances. this does not apply to public bodies such as HMRC: *Revenue and Customs Commissioners v Rhino Television and Media Ltd* [2020] EWHC 364 (Ch).

396 [2009] EWHC 2475 (QB).

397 In *Candy v Holyoake* [2017] EWCA Civ 92, Gloster LJ did not rule out the possibility of an insurance policy being adequate fortification, even in a case where allegations of fraud were being made.

398 *JSC Mezhdunarodniy Promyshlenniy Bank v Pugachev* [2015] EWCA Civ 139.

399 See *Trafigura PTE Ltd v Emirates General Petroleum Corp* [2010] EWHC 3007 (Comm) where committal to prison for 12 months for contempt was deemed to be both just and necessary.

400 See *Customs and Excise Commissioners v Barclays Bank Plc* [2007] 1 A.C. 181, where (at 196) Lord Bingham claimed that it would be "unjust and unreasonable that the bank should, on being notified of an order which it had no opportunity to resist, become exposed to a liability which was in this case for a few million pounds only, but might in another case be for very much more".

> justice, as prescribed by the court which granted the injunction, and would be guilty of a contempt of court".[401]

In light of the obvious scope for inconvenience to third parties, the claimant is under an obligation to indemnify a third party for any expenses and liabilities incurred because of the issue of the injunction. Where a bank is asked to undertake a search to identify the defendant's assets, for example, the claimant must undertake to cover the costs. It is vital that assets subject to the order are clearly identified and that third parties are provided with a detailed explanation of what they are permitted to do and restrained from doing. In addition, the court is mindful of the inconvenience caused to third parties by the issue of a freezing injunction. Accordingly, in *Galaxia Maritime SA v Mineralimportexport*,[402] the third-party owner of a ship containing the defendant's assets was permitted to sail outside the jurisdiction of the court, his rights ranking in preference to the desire of the claimant to maintain control of those assets.

Trust assets

18-071

In *JSC BTA Bank v Kythreotis*,[403] the bank claimed that it could freeze the assets of Mr Kythreotis which he claimed he held in the capacity of trustee or nominee. The Court of Appeal had to consider whether trust assets could be the subject of a freezing order. It was accepted that, following amendments made in 2009 to the standard form of freezing injunction, the order could now embrace assets, "whether the Respondent was interested in them legally, beneficially or otherwise".[404] This amendment was sufficiently radical to include trust assets within the definition of "Respondent's assets". The bank was, thereby, given the opportunity of investigating the truth of the claim that the assets were held on trust. Longmore LJ acknowledged that international fraud is of increasing concern and that the court must take drastic action to deal with shadowy offshore trusts and companies formed in countries were secrecy is prized and regulation low. In *JSC Mezhdunarodniy Promyshlenniy Bank v Pugachev*,[405] there existed various discretionary trusts, each of which was subject to New Zealand law, under which Mr Pugachev and his family were the beneficiaries. There were layers of corporate holdings in various offshore places. Mr Pugachev dismissed the old trustees and appointed replacements. It was strongly arguable that the trust assets were, in reality the assets of, or under the control of, Mr Pugachev and that the new trustees would do his bidding. At his behest, they had already paid $800,000 out of trust funds in breach of the freezing order. The freezing order was maintained.

---

401 [1982] Q.B. 558 at 574. Obligations to third parties must be honoured and, accordingly, payments under letters of credit or under bank guarantee are not prevented: see *Intraco Ltd v Notis Shipping Corp* [1981] 2 Lloyd's Rep. 256. The bank must also honour all credit cards issued to the defendant.
402 [1982] 1 All E.R. 796.
403 [2010] EWCA Civ 1436 at [52].
404 See Practice Direction 25A.
405 [2016] EWHC 248 (Ch).

> ### Worldwide freezing orders

18-072

A remaining issue concerns the extent of the freezing order and whether it should be confined to the United Kingdom or made to operate worldwide. It is because the court acts in personam that the injunction may be granted in relation to assets, "whether located within the jurisdiction or not".[406] Nevertheless, and as illustrated in *Barwa Real Estate Co v Rees*,[407] the court making the order must be in a position to enforce it. There the court declined to continue an order freezing the worldwide assets of a defendant because, although the claimant had a good arguable case and there was a risk of the dissipation of assets, the defendant had since left the United Kingdom. The court admitted that, if the order was continued, it would have grave difficulty in enforcing it and, hence, the order was no longer expedient.

The worldwide injunction is justified only in exceptional circumstances where it can be made effectively, without oppression and where no conflict exists with the ordinary principles of international law.[408] The claimant is not allowed to "forum shop" so as to provide jurisdiction against a foreign domiciled defendant.[409]

Worldwide freezing orders usually assume relevance when the defendant has perpetrated a fraud on a large scale,[410] has the facility internationally to transfer large sums of money and/or can secrete assets away behind companies or in countries which have lax financial regulation.[411] For example, in *BCCI SA (No.9)*,[412] following a major international fraud bringing about the collapse of BCCI, a worldwide freezing order was granted against the defendant employees of the bank. More recently, in *Gerald Metals SA v Timis*, a worldwide freezing order sought over Senegal oil assets was refused because it could not be shown that Mr Timis had effective control of those assets.[413]

18-073

Where a worldwide freezing order is deemed appropriate, the court will insist upon an undertaking by the claimant that the claimant will seek permission of the English court before attempting to enforce the order in a foreign jurisdiction. The need for such an undertaking is clearly to protect the defendant from the risk of oppression where the claimant is able to bring proceedings in different jurisdictions. As to the circumstances in which permission should be granted, the Court of Appeal laid down non-exhaustive guidelines for the exercise of judicial

---

406 CPR r.25.1(1)(f); see also *Babanaft International Co SA v Bassatne* [1990] Ch. 13, where it was accepted by the Court of Appeal that there is no geographical limitation to the jurisdiction of the court to issue such an injunction. For a recent illustration, see *Credit Suisse Trust Ltd v Intesa Sanpaolo Spa* unreported 10 March 2014 (steps to enforce a worldwide freezing order including property and assets in Italy).
407 [2009] EWHC 2134 (Comm).
408 See *Derby & Co Ltd v Weldon* [1990] Ch. 48.
409 *PJSC Commercial Bank Privatbank v Kolomoisky* [2019] 1 All E.R. (Comm) 971.
410 See *Paylor v Bowers* [2018] EWHC 2244 (Ch), which involved an international "Ponzi" scheme to defraud investors.
411 As in *JSC Mezhdunarodniy Promyshlenniy Bank v Pugachev* [2016] EWHC 248 (Ch).
412 [1994] 3 All E.R. 764.
413 [2016] EWHC 2327 (Ch).

discretion in *Dadourian Group International Inc v Simms*.[414] In particular, the guidelines state that:

- the grant of permission should be "just and convenient" and "not oppressive to the parties". Accordingly, in *Arcelormittal USA LLC v Ruia* the serious impact that a freezing injunction would have on the defendants' business entailed that it was not just and convenient to make the order[415];

- all the relevant circumstances and options need to be considered and the interests of the applicant should be balanced against the interests of the other parties to the proceedings. A cross-undertaking in damages will usually be required and, if the undertaking is insufficient, this is the factor that will militate against the making of the order[416];

- permission should not normally be given in terms that would enable the applicant to obtain relief in the foreign proceedings which is superior to that offered by the worldwide freezing order;

- the evidence in support of the application for permission should contain all the information necessary to enable the judge to reach an informed decision. In particular, the court will expect the highest standards of disclosure from those who seek relief without notice. The evidence should cover the applicable law and practice in the foreign court, the nature of the proposed proceedings to be commenced, the assets believed to be located in the jurisdiction of the foreign court and the names of the parties who are holding such assets.[417] If there is non-disclosure by the applicant, the order may subsequently be discharged, but this is not an automatic outcome[418];

- the applicant must show that there is a real prospect that assets are located within the jurisdiction of the foreign court in question;

- there must be "solid evidence" of a risk of dissipation of the assets in question.[419] If not

---

414 [2006] 1 W.L.R. 2499 at 2502 at 2503.
415 [2020] EWHC 740 (Comm).
416 *Delagio v Maxwell* [2009] EWHC 2888 (Ch).
417 Of course, it can also order the defendant to disclose relevant information. In *Allergy Therapeutics (UK) Ltd v Inflamax Research Inc* [2019] EWHC 2526 (Comm), for example, the court ordered disclosure as to whether the assets of a defendant had been transferred to a trust and whether the defendant was the effective controller of the trust assets.
418 In *Alphasteel Ltd v Shirkhani* [2009] EWHC 2153 (Ch), there were a number of admitted non-disclosures, but the order was allowed to continue as the without notice injunction would have been granted in any event. The court did, however, narrow its operation to the defendant's property situated in the United Kingdom.
419 *Ninemia Maritime Corp v Trave Schiffahrtsgesellschaft mbH* [1983] 2 Lloyd's Rep. 600. In *Shepherd Construction*

the order will be refused or, if already granted, discharged. In *Cherney v Neuman*,[420] for example, the claimant delayed making an application for a worldwide freezing injunction for eight months after the commencement of proceedings. As the defendant would by the commencement of the proceedings know of the claim against him, the delay indicated that there was no real risk that the assets would be dissipated. Similarly, in *Delagio v Maxwell* there was no basis for the continuation of a worldwide freezing order against a property agent when there was insufficient evidence of dishonest conduct on his part or of any likelihood that he would attempt to avoid a judgment against him[421]; and

■ in cases of urgency, and where it is just to do so, the permission may be given without notice to the party against whom relief will be sought in the foreign proceedings. The party should then have the earliest practicable opportunity of having the matter reconsidered by the court at a hearing of which he is given notice.

Guide to Further Reading

M. Dockray and H. Laddie, "*Piller* Problems" (1990) 106 L.Q.R. 601.
D. Eady, "Injunctions and the Protection of Privacy" (2010) 29(4) C.J.Q. 411.
S. Gee, "The Undertaking in Damages" [2006] L.M.C.L.Q. 181.
A. Keay, "Whither American Cyanamid: Interim Injunctions in the 21st Century" (2004) 23 C.J.Q. 133.
A. McColgan, "Privacy, Freedom of Expression and the Grant of Interim Injunctions" (2008) 27(1) C.L.J. 23.
P. McGrath, "The Freezing Order: A Constantly Evolving Jurisdiction" (2012) 31(1) C.J.Q. 12.
G. Phillipson, "Transforming Breach of Confidence? Towards a Common Law Right of Privacy under the Human Rights Act" (2003) 66 M.L.R. 726.
A. Zuckerman, "Interlocutory Injunctions on the Merits" (1991) 107 L.Q.R. 196.

Ltd v Berners (BVI) Ltd [2010] EWHC 763 (TCC) the evidence took the form of broken promises, the defendant's history of non-payment, non-compliance with previous judgments and a pattern of giving dishonoured cheques.
420 [2009] EWHC 1743 (Ch).
421 [2009] EWHC 2888 (Ch). In *National Bank Trust v Yurov* [2020] EWHC 757 (Comm), an admittedly narrow, worldwide freezing order was lifted in relation to one defendant who gave an undertaking to the court not to deal with her house.

19

Specific Performance

An order for specific performance is an order of the court directing a party to a contract positively to perform his obligations according to the terms of the order. The remedy operates in personam, i.e. it imposes a personal obligation on the defendant to fulfil his promise. Specific performance developed as part of the jurisdiction of equity to do justice where the common law was inadequate. Traditionally regarded as an "exceptional remedy",[1] it is available only where damages will not adequately compensate the claimant for a breach of contract.

Being equitable in origin, the award of specific performance is a discretionary remedy. Accordingly, a variety of factors can influence the exercise of discretion, such as the conduct of the claimant,[2] any delay in seeking equitable assistance[3] or hardship resulting from the compelled performance of contractual obligations.[4] Nonetheless, as will become evident, the principles upon which specific performance is awarded are established equitable principles.[5] Hence, it has long been possible to say with some certainty that specific performance will be awarded in respect of some types of contract,[6] but not in the case of others.[7] The law is not, however, static, for as Millett LJ observed, "The court is entitled and bound to re-examine its practice to see whether it accords with modern requirements".[8] Notwithstanding the foundation of settled principle, the general trend appears to be to expand the scope of the remedy to

---

1   *Co-operative Insurance Society Ltd v Argyll Stores (Holdings) Ltd* [1998] A.C. 1 at 11 per Lord Hoffmann.
2   In accordance with the equitable maxim, "he who comes to equity must come with clean hands".
3   Under the doctrine of laches.
4   *Tamplin v James* (1880) L.R. 15 Ch. D. 215.
5   As Lord Chelmsford put it in *Lamare v Dixon* (1873) L.R. 6 H.L. 414, the discretion in the court is "not an arbitrary or capricious discretion, but one to be governed as far as possible by fixed rules and principles".
6   For example, contracts relating to the sale of land.
7   For example, contracts for personal services.
8   *Co-operative Insurance Society Ltd v Argyll Stores (Holdings) Ltd* [1996] Ch. 286 at 306.

order specific performance where it is just and practicable to do so.[9] As will be demonstrated, recent decisions have brought important incremental developments[10] and modern courts have, on occasion, moulded longstanding principles to meet the needs of contemporary society.[11] The aim of this chapter is to provide a helpful analytical introduction to the key features of the remedy, the principles upon which it is nowadays awarded and the main grounds for its refusal.

Preconditions

19-002

An important precondition is that there can be no specific performance of an agreement unless it is in the form of a legal and binding contract. As equity will not assist a volunteer, it is required that the contracting parties provide consideration.[12] The provision of money or money's worth is, seemingly, adequate consideration,[13] but past consideration will not suffice.[14]

The award of specific performance is not necessarily dependent on a pre-existing breach of contract and can be made in circumstances where there can be no recovery of damages at common law.[15] In *Marks v Lilley*,[16] the claimant commenced an action for specific performance of a contract for the sale of land after the date fixed for completion, but without serving a notice making time of the essence of the contract. Vaisey J acknowledged that in a strict sense there had been no default and that, subject to the clearing away of the difficulties that were besetting the defendant, the contract would be completed in a reasonable time. Nevertheless, the defendant was under an equitable obligation to make good his promise and the claimant was, therefore, in a position to enforce his rights. Specific performance was awarded.

In *Airport Industrial GP Ltd v Heathrow Airport Ltd*,[17] moreover, specific performance of a covenant to build a 280-space car park on a site at Heathrow Airport was ordered before the contractual date specified for completion of the works.[18] Although the defendant would not

---

9   See *Beswick v Beswick* [1968] A.C. 58 at 102 per Lord Upjohn, "Equity will grant specific performance when damages are inadequate to meet the justice of the case".

10 For example, in the context of enforcement of leasehold repairing covenants.

11 See, e.g. the development of the case law on the doctrine of mutuality (para.**19-026**).

12 "The court will never lend its assistance to enforce the specific execution of contracts which are voluntary, or where no consideration emanates from the party seeking performance, even though they may have the legal consideration of a seal": Fry, *A Treatise on the Specific Performance of Contracts*, 6th edn (India: Universal Law Publishing Co, 2002), p.53.

13 *Mountford v Scott* [1975] Ch. 258.

14 *Robertson v St John* (1786) 2 Bro. C.C. 140 (agreement to renew a lease in consideration of previous expenditure).

15 Conversely, of course, damages may be available where specific performance is refused.

16 [1959] 1 W.L.R. 749.

17 [2015] EWHC 3753 (Ch).

18 Morgan J cited *Marks v Lilley* as well as the Privy Council decision in *Hasham v Zenab* [1960] A.C. 316, but

have breached its obligations before October of the following year, the order of the court was designed to facilitate compliance with its obligations.

The effect of an order

Where an order for specific performance is made the contract remains in existence and is not merged in the judgment of the court.[19] Hence, in the event that the defendant fails, or is unable, to comply with the order, the claimant can seek to dissolve the order and obtain common law damages. In claiming specific performance, however, the claimant essentially surrenders to the court control of how the contract is carried out.[20] As such it is necessary that the claimant return to court either to enforce the order or to terminate the contract.[21] The principles governing the entitlements of the parties are authoritatively laid down in *Johnson v Agnew*.[22] Here, the claimant sought specific performance of a contract to sell mortgaged properties to the defendant. The defendant purchaser delayed and the claimant's mortgagee duly sought to enforce its security and sell the properties. As performance of the contract was no longer possible, the claimant was entitled to ask for the order for specific performance to be discharged, for the contract to be terminated and for an award in damages as an alternative remedy.

It is noteworthy also that an order for specific performance is a final order.[23] Unlike the injunction, it is an equitable remedy that is seemingly not available on an interim basis.[24]

19-003

Enforcement

Enforcement can take a variety of forms. Section 39 of the Senior Courts Act 1981, for example, allows the court to appoint a nominated person other than the defendant to execute a contract or conveyance which the defendant has neglected or refused to execute. Ultimately, however, failure to comply with an order may see the defendant committed to prison for contempt of court. Other options include sequestration of assets pending compliance and the imposition of fines.

19-004

---

decided (at [111]) that with no authority directly in point, he would "go beyond what has been expressly held . . ." and require the taking of action before the date for completion.

19   Per Greene MR in *Austins of East Ham Ltd v Macey* [1941] Ch. 338 at 341.
20   As Megarry VC clarified in *Singh v Nazeer* [1978] 3 All E.R. 817 at 822, "it is the provisions of the order and not the contract which regulate how the contract is to be carried out".
21   *GKN Distributions Ltd v Tyne Tees Fabrication Ltd* [1985] 2 E.G.L.R. 181.
22   [1980] A.C. 367.
23   *Co-operative Insurance Society Ltd v Argyll Stores (Holdings) Ltd* [1998] A.C. 1 at 18 per Lord Hoffmann.
24   See, however, *Sky Petroleum Ltd v VIP Petroleum Ltd* [1974] 1 W.L.R. 576 where an interim injunction restraining the defendant company from failing to supply the claimant with petrol was tantamount to specific enforcement of the claimant's contract until the date of the full hearing.

Damages in addition to or in substitution for specific performance

Principles governing the award of damages have been considered in Ch.18 in the context of injunctions. The same principles operate in the context of specific performance. Damages may be awarded in addition to or in lieu of specific performance,[25] but also in conjunction with other equitable remedies. In *Seven Seas Properties Ltd v Al-Essa (No.1)*, therefore, an order for specific performance was combined with a *Mareva* injunction restraining the vendor from dealing with the purchase money from a sale.[26] Hoffmann J regarded it as "excessively formalistic" to require the result to be achieved by two orders rather than one and he was happy that the court had jurisdiction to create a combined order.[27]

Inadequacy of Common Law Damages

The following section considers a key principle governing the award of specific performance, that is, no decree of specific performance will be awarded where the plaintiff can obtain an adequate remedy at law.[28] The laudable aim of the court is to interfere "only when it can by that means do more perfect and complete justice".[29] Damages will be inadequate where the obligation is such that successive breaches would necessitate successive actions for damages,[30] where damages are insufficient to meet the justice of the case[31] or where loss is impossible to quantify.[32] Specific performance will not be awarded where, on the true construction of the contract, the parties have agreed to the payment of a sum of money as an alternative to the performance of an obligation.[33] This is because the court will construe a "formal recognition" by the parties that the award of damages is an adequate remedy for the particular breach.[34]

---

25 See para.**18-010**.
26 [1989] 1 All E.R. 164.
27 [1989] 1 All E.R. 164 at 166.
28 As Lord Neuberger and Lord Sumption put it in *Makdessi v Cavendish Square Holdings BV* [2015] UKSC 67 at [30], "the minimum condition for an order of specific performance is that the innocent party should have a legitimate interest extending beyond pecuniary compensation for the breach".
29 *Wilson v Northampton and Banbury Junction Railway Co* (1874) 9 Ch. App. 279 at 284 per Lord Selbourne.
30 *Beswick v Beswick* [1968] A.C. 58 (payment of an annuity).
31 For example, where only nominal damages were recoverable by an action at law: *Beswick v Beswick* [1968] A.C. 58.
32 *Hart v Herwig* (1873) 8 Ch. App. 860; see, however, *Zinc Cobham 1 Ltd (in administration) v Adda Hotels* [2018] EWHC 1025 (Ch).
33 *Legh v Lillie* (1860) 6 H. & N. 165.
34 See *Warner Bros v Nelson* [1937] 1 K.B. 209 at 220 per Branson J.

Ultimately, however, the court's discretion to award or to refuse specific performance cannot be fettered by agreement between the parties.[35] The court cannot be bound by the terms of the contract because otherwise, as Stocker LJ noted, "the function of the court would be reduced to that of a rubber stamp".[36]

The following illustrations provide evidence of the approach of the courts to the issue of adequacy of damages. As is clear, the principle operates in the context of many different types of contract. The types of contract considered here are as follows:

- contracts for the sale or other disposition of interests in land;

- contracts for the sale of personalty;

- contracts for transient interests; and

- contracts to pay money.

Contracts for the sale or other disposition of interests in land

19-007

The remedy of specific performance is almost always granted to compel performance of land contracts. As Sir William Grant said of the Court of Equity, it is "as much a course in this court to decree specific performance, as it is to give damages at law".[37] Land is deemed to be unique and, hence, damages are considered an inadequate remedy to compensate for the failure of a vendor to complete a contract for its sale.[38] In respect of contracts entered into on or after 27 September 1989, however, the Law of Property (Miscellaneous Provisions) Act 1989 requires that a contract for the sale or disposition of any interest in land must be made in writing[39] and signed by or on behalf of each party.[40] The contract must incorporate all express terms in one document, or, where contracts are exchanged, in each. Failure to comply with the formalities

---

35 Although it remains common practice for the parties to contract that breach of a particular term shall "sound only in damages".

36 *Quadrant Visual Communications Ltd v Hutchinson Telephone (UK) Ltd* [1993] B.C.L.C. 442 at 451.

37 *Hall v Warren* (1804) 9 Ves. Jr. 605 at 608.

38 As Sir John Leach VC explained in *Adderley v Dixon* (1824) 1 Sim. & S.T. 607 at 610, "a Court of Equity decrees performance of a contract for land, not because of the real nature of the land, but because damages at law, which must be calculated upon the general money value of land, may not be a complete remedy to the purchaser, to whom the land may have a peculiar and special value".

39 Previously a contract was required only to be evidenced in writing and could be enforced under the doctrine of part performance: Law of Property Act 1925 s.40.

40 The Law of Property (Miscellaneous Provisions) Act 1989 s.2(5) exempts from the requirement of signed writing a contract to grant a short lease taking effect in possession for a term not exceeding three years, a contract made in the course of a public auction and a contract regulated under the Financial Services and Markets Act 2000 other than a regulated mortgage contract.

renders the contract void. As a precondition to the award of specific performance of land contracts, therefore, the 1989 Act imports the requirement of a written and signed contract.

Contracts for the sale of personalty

19-008 Most items of personal property cannot be said to be unique or of such rarity that a claimant will not be compensated adequately by damages. Traditionally, therefore, specific performance has not been granted to enforce contracts for the sale of most goods and personal property. Such was the case in *Cohen v Roche*[41] where the subject matter of the contract was a set of eight Hepplewhite chairs. McCardie J declared that the discretion was not to be exercised where the property concerned was no more than an "ordinary article of commerce and of no special value or interest".[42] Accordingly, he declined to order specific performance and instead awarded damages. The contrasting approach towards contracts for the sale of land was addressed in *Adderley v Dixon* by Sir John Leach VC, who explained that "Courts of Equity decree the specific performance of contracts not upon any distinction between realty and personalty, but because damages at law may not in the particular case, afford a complete remedy".[43] Accordingly, it is not the personal nature of goods that serves to explain the approach of the courts, but simply that, in the case of most items of personalty, damages is as satisfactory a remedy as the delivery of the items themselves.

19-009 By contrast, where a chattel can be shown to have special value or interest, damages may not be deemed to be an adequate remedy. Hence, in *Behnke v Bede Shipping Co*,[44] specific performance was awarded to compel the sale of a steamship. Wright J noted that the ship was of "peculiar and particularly unique value" to the claimant and that it was required for immediate use.[45] He accepted the evidence of an experienced ship valuer, who knew of only one other comparable ship, which by then might have been sold. Specific performance was granted, he claimed, "in order that justice may be done".[46] Similarly, in *Falcke v Gray*, two china jars were considered to be articles of unusual beauty, rarity and distinction such that damages could not adequately compensate for their loss.[47] In addition, it has been accepted that heirlooms or articles of particular personal value to the claimant can fall into this category.[48]

Where there is no readily available market (e.g. in the case of particular stocks and shares), damages may not be an adequate remedy.[49] Damages will be adequate, however, where the

---

41 [1927] 1 K.B. 169.
42 [1927] 1 K.B. 169 at 181.
43 (1824) 1 Sim. & S.T. 607 at 610.
44 [1927] 1 K.B. 649.
45 [1927] 1 K.B. 649 at 661.
46 [1927] 1 K.B. 649 at 661.
47 (1859) 4 Drew. 651.
48 *Thorn v Commissioners of Public Works* (1863) 32 Beav. 490 (stones from the old Westminster Bridge).
49 *Duncuft v Albrecht* (1841) 12 Sim. 189.

shares are such that "anyone can go out and buy them".[50] Shares in private limited companies are subject to limitations on transfer and availability to the public. As such, a legitimate claim for specific performance might be made in respect of a contract for the sale of such shares. In *Sky Petroleum Ltd v VIP Petroleum Ltd*,[51] specific performance of a contract for the sale of fuel was ordered on the ground that the contract with the defendant's company was the sole means of keeping the claimant's business afloat. Goulding J acknowledged the "well established and salutary rule" that there was no specific performance of contracts for the sale of non-specific chattels.[52] Nonetheless, due to the unusual state of the petroleum market at that time, the award of damages was not an adequate remedy.

Notably, a statutory jurisdiction is provided by the Sale of Goods Act 1979. Section 52 enables the court to decree specific performance of contracts for the sale of "specific or ascertained goods", i.e. goods identified and agreed by the parties when the contract is entered into. In respect of contracts for the supply of goods, services and digital content, the rights and remedies of consumers have been strengthened by the Consumer Rights Act 2015.[53] It is clear that the statutory remedies available to consumers under this new Act do not prevent the consumer from seeking other remedies, including specific performance.

19-010

Contracts for transient interests

Historically, a court of equity would not protect so called "transient interests". The recent trend in judicial thinking, however, is to disregard the reasoning in earlier authorities and exercise discretion according to the justice of the case.[54] Accordingly, the contemporary approach is encapsulated by Roskill LJ who pitched the duty of the court to be "to protect, where it is appropriate to do so, any interest, whether it be an estate in land or a licence, by injunction or specific performance as the case may be".[55] As will be shown, adequacy of damages has emerged as the prevailing consideration in the enforcement of such contracts.

The most prominent illustration of equitable intervention is that of *Verrall v Great Yarmouth BC*.[56] Here, the Court of Appeal awarded specific performance of a contractual licence to use a public hall for the purposes of the two-day party conference of the National Front. Specific performance had not hitherto been available because, in the words of Lord Greene MR, "If a

19-011

---

50   *Re Schwabacher* (1907) 98 L.T. 127 at 128 per Parker J.
51   [1974] 1 W.L.R. 576.
52   [1974] 1 W.L.R. 576 at 578.
53   The Act came into force on 1 October 2015 and repeals Pt 5 of the Sale of Goods Act 1979 (the relatively recent amendments to the 1979 Act providing the courts with powers, for example, to enforce a seller's obligation to repair or replace defective goods).
54   See, e.g. *Mexfield Housing Co-operative Ltd v Berrisford* [2012] 1 A.C. 955 at 973 where Lord Neuberger doubted why a contract for the occupation of land for an uncertain term "should not be capable of taking effect as a contract, enforceable as between the parties personally".
55   *Verrall v Great Yarmouth BC* [1981] Q.B. 202 at 220.
56   [1981] Q.B. 202.

licence is revoked in breach of contract, the remedy is damages and nothing else, the reason being that the licensee has no estate in the land at all".[57] In *Verrall*, a newly constituted council had tried to force a cancellation of the event at the last minute. The National Front claimed that it was unable, at such short notice, to locate a suitable alternative venue. The award of damages was not an adequate remedy because even with damages in hand, the claimant was unable to reorganise the planned event. Only performance of the contract would enable the conference to take place.

Contracts to pay money

19-012
The adequacy of common law damages also precludes the award of specific performance in relation to contracts to pay money.[58] For example, of a contract to make a loan, Lord Herschell stated unequivocally, "I do not think that it is open to any doubt that a person with whom a contract to lend money has been entered into cannot obtain specific performance of that contract".[59] Perhaps, surprisingly, an agreement to grant an annuity is specifically enforceable.[60] The remedy of specific performance is deemed to be the preferred alternative to a "series of actions at law to enforce the performance of a continuing obligation".[61] Its availability, moreover, is frequently justified on the basis that it is difficult to assess damages with accuracy and, thereby, unjust to leave a claimant to his common law remedy.[62] It is certainly questionable whether this reasoning carries force in modern times. For example, such calculations have become commonplace with the growth of life assurance and the ease with which annuities can be bought and sold. This clearly points to damages as the appropriate remedy for the breach of such contracts.

In *Beswick v Beswick*,[63] however, specific performance was awarded in respect of a contract to pay money and in circumstances where, for the House of Lords, justice, seemingly, outweighed settled principles. Peter Beswick entered into an agreement with his nephew that he would transfer his business to him in consideration of his nephew employing him (Peter) as a consultant for the remainder of his life and, thereafter, the payment to Peter's widow of an annuity at the rate of £5 per week for life. Subsequent to Peter Beswick's death, the nephew made only a single payment to the widow. Personally, and in her capacity as administratrix of Beswick's estate, she sued for specific performance.

19-013
Arguments for the claimant looked insurmountable. Although the widow had suffered loss

---

57 *Booker v Palmer* [1942] 2 All E.R. 647 at 677.
58 A statutory exception can be found in the Companies Act 2006 s.740, where a contract with a company to take up and pay for debentures can be enforced by an order for specific performance.
59 *South African Territories Ltd v Wallington* [1898] A.C. 309 at 315.
60 *Keenen v Handley* (1864) 2 De. G. J. & Sim. 283.
61 *Beswick v Beswick* [1968] A.C. 58 at 78 per Lord Hodson.
62 See the approach of Leach VC in *Adderley v Dixon* (1842) 1 Sim. & St. 607 at 611 who emphasised the principle that "Damages might be no complete remedy, being to be calculated merely by conjecture".
63 [1968] A.C. 58.

personally, she was not a party to the contract and, accordingly, she had no right of action.[64] In her capacity as administratrix, moreover, only nominal damages appeared to be recoverable. The estate had suffered no loss. In the circumstances, it seemed difficult to maintain that nominal damages would be inadequate. Lord Upjohn, however, seized on the injustice of the claimant's predicament to hold that, "the court ought to grant a specific performance order all the more because damages are nominal".[65] It was felt to be "wholly repugnant to justice and commonsense" that the defendant had received the whole benefit of his bargain, failed to perform his obligations and that the breach would attract only nominal damages.[66] Justice demanded an equitable remedy.

Grounds for Refusal

19-014

Whereas the inadequacy of common law damages is the central principle motivating the award of specific performance, there are a number of grounds upon which the remedy may be refused. In some cases the court enjoys a flexible discretion as to whether on the facts of a given case specific performance is the appropriate remedy. In others, the jurisdiction of the court is more tightly constrained. Accordingly, the refusal to award specific performance might be justified on the following bases:

- the need for constant supervision;

- the contract is for personal services;

- the conduct of the claimant;

- want of mutuality;

- impossibility and futility;

- part of a contract;

- illegality and public policy;

---

64 This case pre-dates the Contracts (Rights of Third Parties) Act 1999 under which it is possible for a third party to enforce the contract and obtain substantial damages. It remains unlikely that specific performance will be awarded as equity will not assist a volunteer.

65 [1968] A.C. 58 at 102.

66 [1968] A.C. 58 at 89 per Lord Pearce.

- hardship and prejudice to third parties;

- *laches* or delay; and

- mistake, misdescription and misrepresentation.

Constant supervision of the court

19-015

Specific performance has historically been refused where enforcement would require the constant supervision of the court. In the nineteenth-century case of *Ryan v Mutual Tontine Westminster Chambers Association*,[67] for example, the Court of Appeal was asked to construe a term in a lease which required the constant attendance of a resident porter or, in the event of some temporary absence, a trustworthy assistant. Lord Esher MR appeared concerned at the period of time over which the court would be required to compel performance. Declining on the ground of constant superintendence, he explained, "The contract is that those services shall be performed during the whole term of the tenancy; it is therefore a long continuing contract, to be performed from day to day, and under which the circumstances of non-performance might vary from day to day".[68]

More recently, and on very similar facts, the rationale underpinning *Ryan* has been called into question. *Posner v Scott-Lewis*[69] also concerned the enforcement of a landlord's covenant to employ a resident porter, facts that Mervyn Davies J was prompted to admit were "difficult to distinguish" from the *Ryan* case.[70] Here, however, specific performance was granted. Mervyn Davies J felt that *Ryan* had to be viewed in the context of its re-evaluation by many later authorities.[71] The modern approach of the court is to focus on the practicality of enforcing the individual contract before it. In *Tito v Waddell (No.2)*, therefore, Megarry VC emphasised that "The real question is whether there is sufficient definition of what has to be done in order to comply with the order of the court. That definition may be provided by the contract itself, or it may be supplied by the terms of the order, in which case there is the further question whether the court considers that the terms of the contract sufficiently support by implication or otherwise the terms of the proposed order".[72] Accordingly, in *Posner v Scott-Lewis*, Mervyn Davies J embraced a refinement of general principle. He considered the pertinent questions to be as follows:

67 [1893] 1 Ch. 116.
68 [1893] 1 Ch. 116 at 123.
69 [1987] Ch. 25.
70 [1987] Ch. 25 at 34.
71 Principally, *Giles & Co Ltd v Morris* [1972] 1 W.L.R. 307 per Megarry J; *Shiloh Spinners v Harding* [1973] A.C. 691 at 724 per Lord Wilberforce; *Tito v Waddell (No.2)* [1977] Ch. 106 at 321 per Megarry VC.
72 [1977] Ch. 106 at 321.

> "(a) Is there a sufficient definition of what has to be done in order to comply with the order? (b) Will enforcing compliance involve super-intendence by the court to an unacceptable degree? (c) What are the respective prejudices and hardships that will be suffered by the parties if the order is made or not made".[73]

On the facts, the work was sufficiently defined and there was no unacceptable level of super-intendence.[74] In addition, the award of damages was not an adequate remedy. Although the landlord had arranged for the functions to be carried out by a non-resident, damages could not adequately compensate for the loss of the feeling of security and opportunities to ask for help that arose from the porter's presence.[75]

Running a business

19-016

The constant supervision principle fell to be reviewed by the House of Lords in *Co-operative Insurance Society Ltd v Argyll Stores (Holdings) Ltd*.[76] The facts are straightforward. The defend-ants were granted the lease of the largest unit in a shopping centre. It was envisaged that the unit would be an anchor unit, attracting trade to the smaller businesses in the shopping centre. As any closure of the anchor unit would have a disastrous effect on the other tenants, the defendants were required to covenant to keep their premises open for retail trade during the usual hours of business in the locality. Subsequently, however, the defendants experienced financial loss and sought, in breach of contract, to close down the supermarket. The claimant sought damages and an order for specific performance of the keep-open covenant.

At first instance, the court endorsed the settled approach to award damages. It was a showing of what Leggatt LJ later described as "unwarrantable reluctance" to award the remedy of specific performance.[77] In the appellate court, he called for the court to intervene and exercise its discretion "afresh unfettered by shibboleths which will otherwise continue to be unthinkingly applied".[78] Leggatt LJ was patently struck by the "gross commercial cyni-cism" of Argyll.[79] Roch LJ too reluctantly faced what he described as the "unedifying specta-cle of a large commercial company seeking to rely on its own wanton and quite unreasonable

---

73 [1987] Ch. 25 at 36.
74 The porter was to carry out specific domestic functions pertaining to the cleaning of common parts, maintenance of heating services and refuse disposal. Compare *Ryan v Mutual Tontine Westminster Chambers Association* [1893] 1 Ch. 116, where the porter was subject to such ill-defined obligations as "to be and act as the servant of the tenants".
75 As Mervyn Davies J explained, "There is to my mind a world of difference between living in a block with a porter in residence and living in a block where there is no porter in residence" ([1987] Ch. 25 at 33).
76 [1998] A.C. 1.
77 [1996] Ch. 286 at 294.
78 [1996] Ch. 286 at 294.
79 [1996] Ch. 286 at 294.

conduct".[80] Forming a majority view in the Court of Appeal,[81] specific performance was awarded on the grounds that damages would be inadequate and that the tenant's obligations were defined with sufficient precision. The defendants appealed.

19-017

In the House of Lords, Lord Hoffmann was focused and categorical in denying the availability of the remedy. He drew attention, first, to the long settled practice of the court that orders requiring the defendant to run a business would not be made. The practice was not only premised on the adequacy of damages, but also that the order would require the constant supervision of the court (i.e. that it would draw the court into the undesirable position of having to give an indefinite series of rulings to ensure compliance with the order).[82] Secondly, he highlighted deficiencies in the means of forcing compliance. The prospect of imprisonment for contempt of court was a heavy-handed enforcement mechanism wholly ill-suited to the adjudication of disputes in the running of a business. In Lord Hoffmann's view, it would force the defendant "to make decisions under a sword of Damocles which may descend if the way the business is run does not conform to the terms of the order".[83] Thirdly, Lord Hoffmann was persuaded that an order for specific performance would allow the claimant to enrich himself at the defendant's expense. The damage suffered by the defendant in running a business at a loss for an indefinite period would be greater than that suffered by the claimant through breach of contract. Accordingly, the landlord would be in a position to extract a high price from the defendant in order to release it from its obligations.[84] Finally, he felt that it was perfectly satisfactory that the defendant rely on legal advice as to the settled practice of the court.[85] In other words the parties entered into the transaction with the knowledge that specific performance was not awarded to enforce performance of such contracts. The obligation was not, therefore, one which the House of Lords was prepared to specifically enforce.

As to the principle of constant supervision generally, Lord Hoffmann emphasised a distinction between orders requiring the defendant to carry out an activity over a more or less extended period of time and orders requiring the defendant to achieve a result. In the former case there was a danger of repeated actions for rulings on compliance with the order, whereas in the latter case that risk was less apparent. In addition to the risk of wasteful litigation, a further objection to an order to carry out an ongoing activity was the inevitable imprecision in the

---

80 [1996] Ch. 286 at 296.

81 Millett LJ gave a dissenting judgment.

82 See also *Zinc Cobham Ltd (in administration) v Adda Hotels* [2018] EWHC 1025 (Ch) where similar obstacles to the availability of specific performance were apparent.

83 [1998] A.C. 1 at 13. It was not, furthermore, in the interest of public policy to award a remedy which "yokes the parties together in a continuing hostile relationship" (per Lord Hoffmann at 16).

84 This finding can be criticised on the basis that the lease could be assigned with the landlord's consent and that the cost to the defendant would be no more than that required to find a new assignee. In any event, as Tettenborn argues in [1998] Conv. 23, 36, "it is hard to see any injustice in this when the defendant can avoid having to pay up by the simple expedient of providing what the plaintiff was justifiably entitled to in the first place".

85 This was despite the view of Leggatt LJ in the Court of Appeal that there was no evidence of the parties receipt of advice to the effect that the promise could be disregarded upon payment of damages ([1996] Ch. 286 at 294).

terms of the order. Lord Hoffmann foresaw a risk of oppression in such cases, noting, "The less precise the order, the fewer signposts to the forensic minefield which he has to traverse".[86]

Whatever the merits of this practical assessment, two final observations can be made. First, it is not clear that, even by Lord Hoffmann's own test, the defendant's obligations were not sufficiently precise and geared to achieve a particular result. Arguably, this was a straight-forward case where all concerned knew exactly what would be required of the defendant. Secondly, the decision of the House of Lords is a noteworthy failure to respond to the justice of the case before it. Tettenborn describes it as an "unfortunate failure to liberalise the rules of specific performance and grant an effective remedy to a plaintiff who is clearly deserving and who is liable to be severely short-changed by a mere award of damages".[87] Perhaps, on this basis, the approach of the Court of Appeal is to be preferred.

It remains to discuss two further contexts in which the courts have grappled with the principle of constant supervision, namely, building contracts and the enforcement of leasehold repairing covenants. Notwithstanding the somewhat intransigent stance of the House of Lords in *Argyll*, the courts have been generally favourable to expanding the scope of the remedy.

19-018

Building contracts

Building agreements appear to fall readily into the class of contract for which, on the ground of constant supervision, the court might decline to award specific performance. As Kay LJ explained in *Ryan v Mutual Tontine Westminster Chambers Association*, "Ordinarily the court will not enforce specific performance of works, such as building works, the prosecution of which the court cannot superintend; not only on the ground that damages are generally in such cases an adequate remedy, but also on the ground of the inability of the court to see that the work is carried out".[88] This category has, nonetheless, been the subject of notable exceptions. Of particular historical prominence, a number of cases involved railway companies that had acquired land on condition that they carry out specified works on the land. When such companies acquired the land and then sought to evade their contractual obligations, specific performance was required to compel performance. In general, these were cases where the award of damages was not an adequate remedy, the works required were sufficiently definite and the companies in question had taken possession of the lands.[89] In addition, judges also appear to have been motivated by the need to respond to the justice of the case. In *Wilson v Furness Railway Company*, for example, Sir W.M. James VC commented of the company's refusal to build a road, "It would be monstrous if the company, having got the whole benefit of the agreement,

19-019

---

86   [1998] A.C. 1 at 14.
87   [1998] Conv. 23, 38.
88   [1893] 1 Ch. 116 at 128.
89   See, e.g. *Storer v Great Western Railway* (1842) 2 Y. & C. Ch. Cas. 48 at 54, where the defendant was required to construct and maintain "one neat archway sufficient to permit a loaded carriage of hay to pass under the railway".

could turn round and say, 'This is the sort of a thing that the court finds a difficulty in doing, and will not do'. Rather than allow such a gross piece of dishonesty, the court would struggle with any amount of difficulties in order to perform the agreement".[90]

19-020

As regards building contracts more generally, it is nowadays established that specific performance will be available where the conditions listed by Romer LJ in *Wolverhampton Corp v Emmons*[91] are satisfied. *Emmons* involved the sale of a plot of land by the urban sanitary authority in Wolverhampton, part consideration for the sale being the purchaser's covenant to erect a number of houses in line with the Corporation's scheme of improvement for the area. The parties entered into a further written agreement containing the detailed plans for the building scheme.[92] Upon the builder's breach, the Corporation commenced an action for specific performance. Although all three judges admitted to confusion as to the principles upon which courts of equity had acted previously, the Court of Appeal was unanimous in its support for the plaintiff. It fell to Romer LJ to reiterate the criteria that had, for many years past, allowed a plaintiff to bring himself within the exception generated for building contracts.

19-021

First, the building work must be defined by the contract, to the extent that "the court can sufficiently see what is the exact nature of the work of which it is asked to order the performance".[93] Hence, in any future proceedings between the parties, it can be determined accurately what the defendant is required to do.

Secondly, the plaintiff must have "a substantial interest in having the contract performed".[94] This element serves simply to emphasise that there can be no equitable remedy where damages are adequate. Here, it was of great importance to the sanitary authority that the land, situated in the middle of the town, would not be left vacant and that the houses built upon it would contribute to the rates.

Thirdly, it is a requirement that the defendant has obtained possession of the land on which the work is contracted to be done.[95] The crucial consideration here is that it is the defendant alone who can carry out the works. In such circumstances specific performance will be available to the plaintiff and completion of the works compelled by order of the court.

---

90 (1869) Law Rep. 9 Eq. 28 at 33.
91 [1901] 1 K.B. 515.
92 Smith LJ felt that it would have been "hopeless" to seek specific performance of the covenant contained in the conveyance, but endorsed the view of the lower court that the subsequent agreement was sufficiently specific to justify an order for its specific performance.
93 [1901] 1 K.B. 515 at 525.
94 [1901] 1 K.B. 515 at 525.
95 Romer LJ appears to require the defendant's possession to be obtained by contract. Cf. *Carpenter's Estates Ltd v Davies* [1940] Ch. 160 at 165 where Farwell J did not consider it a "complete bar" to the granting of specific performance that the defendant "had not obtained by the contract" possession of the land on which the work is to be done.

Specific performance of a landlord's covenant

In *Jeune v Queens Cross Properties Ltd*,[96] Sir John Pennycuick VC successfully crafted an analogy with building agreements to allow the court to specifically enforce a lessor's repairing covenant. The tenants of Westbourne Terrace, London had sought specific performance of a covenant requiring the landlord to restore a collapsed balcony to the standard in which it existed before its disrepair. Pennycuick VC considered that the work to be completed was sufficiently defined by the contract, that damages would not be adequate and that the defendant's entitlement to possession of the balcony ensured that the plaintiff could not have the work carried out without committing a trespass. Although the *Wolverhampton Corp v Emmons* conditions were satisfied, a potential obstacle remained in the lack of mutuality in the availability of the remedy to the parties. Indeed, Pennycuick VC referred to the decision of Lord Eldon LC in *Hill v Barclay* that a landlord cannot obtain against his tenant an order for specific performance of a covenant to repair.[97] Nonetheless, he could see no reason in principle why an order should not be made against a landlord to carry out the specific work, although he admitted that "obviously, it is a jurisdiction which should be carefully exercised".[98]

In the case of dwellings, the jurisdiction to award specific performance of a landlord's repairing covenant has now been placed on a broad statutory footing. Section 17 of the Landlord and Tenant Act 1985[99] provides:

> **"In proceedings in which a tenant of a dwelling alleges a breach on the part of a landlord of a repairing covenant relating to any part of the premises in which the dwelling is comprised, the court may order specific performance of the covenant, whether or not the breach relates to a part of the premises let to the tenant and notwithstanding any equitable rule restricting the scope of the remedy, whether on the basis of a lack of mutuality or otherwise".**

The approach of Pennycuick VC in *Jeune v Queens Cross Properties Ltd* has, in any event, been endorsed by subsequent case law[100] and fits with the generally progressive approach of the courts as to the exercise of discretion in this context.[101]

---

96   [1974] Ch. 97.
97   (1810) 16 Ves. Jr. 402 (see para.**19-027**).
98   [1974] Ch. 97 at 101.
99   Replacing the Housing Act 1974 s.125.
100 See, e.g. *Gordon v Selico Ltd* (1986) 18 H.L.R. 219 where specific performance was awarded to compel a landlord to remove dry rot.
101 By way of a recent illustration, in *Blue Manchester Ltd v North West Ground Rents Ltd* [2019] EWHC 142 (TCC), an order for specific performance compelled the defendant to restore the glass panelling of the Beetham Tower in Manchester (home to the Hilton Hotel) to create "substantially the same external appearance as was present at the date of the lease" (at [108]).

> ## Specific performance of a tenant's covenant

19-023

Where a tenant is in breach of a negative leasehold covenant, it has always been possible for a landlord to seek injunctive relief to restrain the breach. As is evident from the discussion above, the same flexibility has been traditionally lacking where the landlord wishes to compel performance of a tenant's positive covenant to repair.[102] Despite admissions that, in light of *Jeune v Queens Cross Properties Ltd*, the strength of older authority "may logically be much weakened",[103] it took almost 25 years before doubt was dispelled as to the applicability of specific performance to a tenant's repairing covenant. The decision in *Rainbow Estates Ltd v Tokenhold Ltd*[104] signalled a change in judicial tack that would see specific performance available against a tenant in cases where damages are inadequate, but subject to the "overriding need to avoid injustice and oppression".[105]

The appropriateness of specific performance was plainly evident on the facts. First, the landlord had no adequate alternative remedy. The lease contained no forfeiture clause or proviso for re-entry. Thus, even a breach of repairing covenant did not entitle the landlord to forfeit the lease. Neither did the lease contain a term permitting the landlord to enter for the purpose of carrying out the necessary works and later recovering the costs.[106] Secondly, the property was in a state of serious disrepair and deterioration. Thirdly, the schedule of works was sufficiently certain that the court could see with precision exactly what was required to be done. Quite uncommonly, there was an absence of any dispute regarding the repairs to be carried out. Finally, Epping Forest District Council had served notices pursuant to the Housing Act 1985 and the Environmental Protection Act 1990, non-compliance with which allowed the Council to step in, carry out the repairs and recover its costs. Accordingly, in the view of the court, there was no clearer a case to demonstrate how "a modern law of remedies requires specific performance of a tenant's repairing covenant to be available in appropriate circumstances".[107]

Contracts for personal services

19-024

It is an established equitable rule that equity will not intervene to compel the performance of personal services or the maintenance of a personal relationship between the parties. As Jessel

---

102 *Hill v Barclay* (1810) 16 Ves. Jr. 402.
103 Per Oliver J in *Regional Properties Ltd v City of London Real Property Co Ltd* [1981] 1 E.G.L.R. 33 at 34.
104 [1999] Ch. 64.
105 The court must be astute to ensure that the landlord is not "seeking the decree simply in order to harass the tenant", the mischief at which the Leasehold Property (Repairs) Act 1938 was enacted to prevent ([1999] Ch. 64 at 73 per Lawrence Collins QC).
106 As M Pawlowski argues, "The presence of these alternative remedies would, in my view, militate strongly against any successful claim for the grant of specific performance" ((2016) 20(6) L. & T. Review 236, 238).
107 [1999] Ch. 64 at 72.

MR declared in 1878, the courts "have never dreamt of enforcing agreements strictly personal in nature whether they are agreements of hiring or service, being the common relation of master and servant, or whether they are agreements for the purpose of pleasure, or for the purpose of scientific pursuits or for the purpose of charity and philanthropy".[108] Accordingly, on this ground, specific performance has been refused to compel performance of contracts of employment,[109] apprenticeship[110] and, more recently, as between school and parent.[111] Indeed, s.236 of the Trade Union and Labour Relations (Consolidation) Act 1992 provides that no court can decree specific performance so as to compel an employee to work.[112] A significant underlying motivation in the rule against specific performance is one of public policy. In the memorable language of Fry LJ, "the courts are bound to be jealous lest they should turn contracts of service into contracts of slavery".[113]

It is also true that the enforcement of contracts for personal services has been rejected as necessitating continuous supervision. In *Giles & Co Ltd v Morris*,[114] however, Megarry J insisted that the reason was more the futility of equitable intervention:

> "The reasons why the court is reluctant to decree specific performance of a contract for personal services (and I would regard it as a strong reluctance rather than a rule) are, I think, more complex and more firmly bottomed on human nature. If a singer contracts to sing, there could no doubt be proceedings for committal if, ordered to sing, the singer remains obstinately dumb. But if instead the singer sang flat, or sharp, or too fast, or too slowly, or too loudly or too quietly, or resorted to a dozen of the manifestations of temperament traditionally associated with some singers, the threat of committal would reveal itself as a most unsatisfactory weapon: for who could say whether the imperfections of performance were natural or self-induced? To make an order with such possibilities of evasion would be vain".[115]

As is apparent, moreover, Megarry J did not feel that the rule against specific performance in the case of such contracts is an unbending one. In support of his contention, there is authority that in cases where a high degree of confidence exists between the parties the court may be jus-

---

108 *Rigby v Connol* (1878) 14 Ch. D. 482 at 487.

109 As Geoffrey Lane LJ commented in *Chappell v Times Newspapers* [1975] 1 W.L.R. 482 at 506, "The reason is obvious: if one party has no faith in the honesty, integrity or the loyalty of the other, to force him to serve or to employ that other is a plain recipe for disaster".

110 *Webb v England* (1860) 29 Beav. 54.

111 *R. v Incorporated Froebel Institute Ex p. L* [1999] E.L.R. 488.

112 Nor can the same result be achieved by use of the injunction.

113 *Francesco v Barnum* (1890) 45 Ch. D. 430 at 438.

114 [1972] 1 W.L.R. 307.

115 [1972] 1 W.L.R. 307 at 318.

tified in departing from the general rule. Such was the case in *Hill v CA Parsons & Co Ltd* where an employer was restrained from terminating by invalid notice the contract of an employee, Mr Hill.[116] The decision to terminate his contract had been taken a mere two years before his planned retirement and solely on the basis of his refusal to join a particular trade union. Denning LJ noted that Mr Hill's employers had acted "under pressure from a powerful trade union", and that they had attempted to terminate Mr Hill's employment by a notice "which is too short by far".[117] The majority decision of the Court of Appeal was to award injunctive relief which amounted to an order for specific performance of a contract for services. Admittedly, the circumstances were exceptional and a remedy in damages (as would be usual in this context) was not deemed adequate. First, Mr Hill's pension entitlement under the company pension scheme would be affected by early retirement. Secondly, moreover, should the employers have sought at a future date to serve the valid notice required lawfully to terminate his contract, this would have been sufficient to bring him under the protection of the newly enacted Industrial Relations Act 1971. This Act had yet to come into force but it was soon to confer rights on workers in respect of trade union membership. The effect of judicial intervention was, therefore, to safeguard Mr Hill's job in the intervening period.

More broadly, any order for specific performance must be workable.[118] As Stamp LJ argued in his dissenting judgment in *Hill v CA Parsons & Co Ltd*, the court "will not exercise its discretion where the order will be nugatory, uncertain or as a practical matter impossible to enforce".[119] In the vast majority of cases, it is manifestly doubtful that a court can compel the re-establishment of a relationship of trust and confidence between the parties that would render the order workable. Such was the case in *Ashworth v Royal National Theatre*,[120] where the court refused an application made by professional musicians to require the National Theatre to continue to engage their services in the critically acclaimed West End production of *War Horse*. Cranston J acknowledged that "the production of a play necessarily involves close cooperation between all those involved",[121] that there was an "absence of personal confidence" on the part of the National Theatre and that "the claimants themselves would be affected by knowing that the National Theatre does not want them and believes that the play is better without them".[122] This was, he claimed, "a standard case where on a traditional analysis loss of confidence is the primary block" to compelling performance.[123]

---

116 [1972] Ch. 305.
117 [1972] Ch. 305 at 316.
118 *Robb v Hammersmith and Fulham LBC* [1991] I.C.R. 514.
119 [1972] Ch. 305 at 323.
120 [2014] EWHC 1176 (QB).
121 [2014] EWHC 1176 (QB) at [23].
122 [2014] EWHC 1176 (QB) at [25].
123 [2014] EWHC 1176 (QB) at [23].

The conduct of the claimant

The court's concern as to the conduct of the claimant is summed up by two equitable maxims: "he who seeks equity must do equity", and "he who comes to equity must come with clean hands". In relation to the former, any claimant who wishes to enlist the help of equity must do equity, i.e. fulfil his own obligations of conscience arising out of the disputed agreement. Accordingly, a claimant must show that he has performed his own contractual obligations,[124] or has tendered performance and is willing to perform his future obligations[125] before specific performance will be awarded to him. As to the latter, unconscionable conduct in relation to the contract will also disbar a claimant from the equitable remedy. If the conduct of the plaintiff is "tricky or unfair", the court may refuse the remedy, for "he who comes to equity must come with clean hands".[126]

Want of mutuality

The doctrine of mutuality has had a prominent influence on equitable intervention. Indeed, want of mutuality has been viewed as a traditional barrier to the award of specific performance. The principle upon which discretion is exercised is clearly explained in *Price v Strange*.[127] The court "will not compel a defendant to perform his obligations specifically if it cannot at the same time ensure that any unperformed obligations of the plaintiff will be specifically performed, unless, perhaps, damages would be an adequate remedy to the defendant for any default on the plaintiff's part".[128] The classic illustration of a lack of mutuality appears in *Flight v Bolland*.[129] Here, it was held that a minor is unable to obtain specific performance for the reason that specific performance cannot be decreed against him. Leach MR was confident that "No case of a bill filed by an infant for the specific performance of a contract made by him has been found in the books"[130] and he did not dispute the general principle of equity to interpose "only where the remedy is mutual".[131] Similarly, it is often said that a person whose contractual obligation amounts to the performance of personal services cannot obtain specific performance for the reason that the remedy cannot be obtained against him.[132]

---

124 This requirement does not extend to "non-essential or trivial breaches": see *Dyster v Randall* [1926] Ch. 932 at 942 per Lawrence J (failure to submit "unexceptionable" plans for the approval of the defendant's architect).

125 As Lord Radcliffe explained in *Australian Hardwoods Pty Ltd v Railways Commissioner* [1961] 1 W.L.R. 425 at 435, "he must fail unless he can show that he is ready and willing on his part to carry out those obligations, which are in fact part of the consideration for the undertaking of the defendant that the plaintiff seeks to enforce".

126 *Quadrant Visual Communications Ltd v Hutchinson Telephone (UK) Ltd* [1993] B.C.L.C. 442; see C. Harpum [1992] C.L.J. 263.

127 [1978] 1 Ch. 337.

128 [1978] 1 Ch. 337 at 368 per Buckley LJ.

129 (1828) 4 Russ. 298.

130 (1828) 4 Russ. 298 at 301.

131 (1828) 4 Russ. 298 at 301.

132 See, e.g. *Ogden v Fossick* (1862) 4 De. G.F. & J. 426. Note, however, that "some small element of personal service . . . does not destroy the quality of mutuality (otherwise plainly present) want of which may in general

Historically, much debate has focused upon the time at which the requirement of mutuality must be satisfied, i.e. whether there was a requirement of mutuality at the time at which the contract was entered into,[133] or at all material times later.[134] The issue has now been resolved by the Court of Appeal in *Price v Strange*,[135] wherein a liberal approach was adopted and any need for mutuality at the time of entering into the contract firmly rejected. As Goff LJ made clear, "want of mutuality raises a question of the court's discretion to be exercised according to everything that has happened up to the decree".[136] *Price v Strange* concerned the enforcement of an oral agreement to grant a new underlease of a flat to the plaintiff in return for the performance of repair works on the property. When the works were only partially completed by the plaintiff, the defendant landlord sought to repudiate the agreement. The plaintiff in turn sought specific performance. At the date of the agreement, there was an absence of mutuality. By the date of the hearing the repair works had been performed. Although it was the defendant landlord who had performed some of the plaintiff's obligations, specific performance was awarded on terms that the plaintiff pay to the defendant appropriate compensation for the actual cost of the works carried out. In any event, as Goff LJ noted, the defendant had waived any potential defence based on want of mutuality by allowing the plaintiff to start the prescribed works and in accepting the increased rent payments under the terms of the new agreement.

19-027

Nowadays, want of mutuality is emphasised as a discretionary matter for the court. As Lawrence Collins QC put it in *Rainbow Estates v Tokenhold Ltd*, "it does not follow from the fact that specific performance is not available to one party that it is not available to the other: want of mutuality is a discretionary, and not an absolute, bar to specific performance".[137] The absence of mutuality, after all, does nothing to oust the jurisdiction of the court to award damages in lieu of specific performance. Accordingly, modern courts will award the remedy if it can be done without injustice or unfairness to the defendant.[138] It is, in addition, possible for a claimant to counter the absence of mutuality by agreeing to perform an obligation that cannot be specifically enforced against him[139] or by waiving the benefit of a term in the contract.[140]

The comment of Lawrence Collins QC was made in the context of repairing covenants in leases. It will be recalled that the classic explanation for the failure of the courts to award specific performance of a landlord's repairing covenant was want of mutuality, that is, that

---

terms properly be a ground for refusing a decree of specific performance" (*Beswick v Beswick* [1968] A.C. 58 at 97 per Lord Upjohn).

133 As famously promoted by Fry, *A Treatise on the Specific Performance of Contracts* (2002), p.219.

134 See, e.g. Spry, *Equitable Remedies: Injunctions, Specific Performance and Equitable Remedies*, 3rd edn (London: Sweet & Maxwell, 1984), p.91.

135 [1978] 1 Ch. 337.

136 [1978] 1 Ch. 337 at 354.

137 [1999] Ch. 64 at 69.

138 *Price v Strange* [1978] Ch. 337 at 357 per Goff LJ.

139 See *Scott v Bradley* [1971] Ch. 850, where a purchaser consented to be bound by an omitted term that he pay half of the defendant's legal costs incurred on sale.

140 *Heron Garage Properties v Moss* [1974] 1 W.L.R. 148.

tenant's covenants could not be specifically enforced.[141] As Lord Eldon LC claimed in *Hill v Barclay*, "The difficulty upon this doctrine of a court of equity is, that there is no mutuality in it. The tenant cannot be compelled to repair".[142] The enforcement of leasehold covenants provides a telling illustration of the movement away from the slavish adherence to older authority. It will also be recalled that following *Jeune v Queens Cross Properties*, s.17 of the Landlord and Tenant Act 1985 provided a statutory incursion into the principle of mutuality. The section allows the court to order specific performance of a landlord's covenant and despite the existence of equitable rules "based on mutuality or otherwise". Accordingly, the section appears to carve an important exception to the general principle of mutuality.

In 1999, however, the decision in *Rainbow Estates v Tokenhold Ltd*, (which allowed for the specific performance of a tenant's repairing covenant) had the effect of restoring a semblance of parity to the availability of the remedy to landlords and tenants. It is interesting that the court downplayed the significance of the principle of mutuality in modern judicial thinking, yet emphasised that mutuality is clearly to be preferred. As Lawrence Collins QC admitted, "even if want of mutuality were any longer a decisive factor (which it is not) the availability of the remedy against a tenant would restore mutuality as against the landlord".[143] In view of these more recent case law developments, it seems difficult to argue, as Megarry did in 1951, that "the doctrine of mutuality still broods heavy over specific performance".[144]

19-028

Impossibility and futility

19-029

Equity does not act in vain. Where performance is impossible, equity will not seek to enforce what cannot be done. In *Ferguson v Wilson*, therefore, there could be no specific performance of a contract to allot shares as the shares had been validly allotted to other shareholders before equitable relief was sought.[145] The defence of impossibility can be raised whatever the manner in which the impossibility arises. Simply put, the remedy will be awarded only where the defendant is able to perform his obligations. In *Jones v Lipman*,[146] the defendant had transferred his property to a company and the concern was that sale to the purchaser would not now be possible. It was held that the company was controlled by the defendant and that the transfer had been made with the sole object of defeating the claimant's unprotected contractual interest. Russell J recognised that the defendant's company was no more than a "creature" of the defendant, "a device and a sham, a mask which he holds before his face in an attempt to avoid recognition by the eye of equity".[147] Specific performance was ordered. By his ownership

141 Other justifications for a refusal included inadequate definition of the works to be carried out and that an award of specific performance would require the constant supervision of the court.
142 (1810) 16 Ves. Jr. 402 at 405.
143 [1999] Ch. 64 at 73.
144 R.E. Megarry (1951) 67 L.Q.R. 300.
145 (1866) L.R. 2 Ch. 77.
146 [1962] 1 W.L.R. 832.
147 [1962] 1 W.L.R. 832 at 836.

and control of the company in which the property was vested, the defendant was, indeed, in a position to complete the contract, i.e. performance was possible.

Similarly, where performance is not technically impossible an order for specific performance may be denied on the ground that intervention would be futile. Again, this defence is rooted in the argument that to act would be to act in vain. Accordingly, specific performance has been refused in respect of leases for terms that had already expired[148] and for an agreement to execute a deed constituting a partnership determinable at will.[149]

Part of a contract

19-030

The court will decline to award specific performance of a part of a contract if it is not in a position to order performance of the whole. In *Ogden v Fossick*[150] there was an agreement between the parties that the claimant would be granted a lease of a coal wharf and that the defendant would be appointed manager of the wharf. An action for specific performance of the agreement to grant the lease failed because the court could not enforce the employment aspect to the contract, i.e. it could not enforce the whole of the contract. Where, however, an agreement can be construed as a series of separate and distinct contracts, enforcement of one part will cease to depend on whether the court is able to enforce performance of the others.[151]

Illegality and public policy

19-031

Not surprisingly, there can be no specific performance of an illegal contract. As such contracts are void, there is no valid agreement capable of enforcement. Equally, an agreement the enforcement of which would be contrary to public policy may not be enforced specifically. An illustration is provided by *Wroth v Tyler*.[152] The defendant Edmund Tyler entered into a contract to sell his bungalow with vacant possession. On the following day, his wife entered a notice in the charges register at the Land Registry, which, under the Matrimonial Homes Act 1967,[153] secured her personal right to occupy the property. When the existence of the charge came to light and the wife refused to vacate it, the husband was unable to deliver the property with vacant possession. The vendor sought specific performance of the contract.

Two public policy reasons were put forward by Megarry J to justify the refusal to award specific performance. First, Mr Tyler could only carry out his contractual obligation by embarking

---

148 In *Mundy v Joliffe* (1839) 9 L.J. Ch. 95, the object of the action was to enable a further action to be brought on the covenants contained in the lease.
149 *Hercy v Birch* (1804) 9 Ves. Jr. 357, on the basis that the defendant could simply dissolve the partnership.
150 (1862) 4 De. G.F. & J. 426.
151 See *Wilkinson v Clements* (1872) L.R. 8 Ch. App. 96.
152 [1974] Ch. 30.
153 Now Family Law Act 1996.

on litigation to terminate his wife's right of occupation. Megarry J warned that the court should be "reluctant to make an order which requires a husband to take legal proceedings against his wife, especially when they are still living together".[154] Secondly, as a consequence of awarding specific performance, the purchaser would take the property subject to the wife's right of occupation. As both the husband and children would be subject to eviction, the inevitable splitting up of the family was against public policy. Accordingly, Megarry J felt disobliged to award specific performance and he opted for damages as the only feasible alternative. Somewhat unfortunately, however, the award of damages resulted in the husband's bankruptcy and entailed that the property was sold by his trustee in bankruptcy with vacant possession and free from the wife's right of occupation.

Hardship and prejudice to third parties

19-032

It is at the discretion of the court to refuse to award specific performance where unnecessary hardship would result for either of the parties to the contract or, indeed, a third party. In *Warmington v Miller*, for example, the court refused to order specific performance of an agreement to grant an underlease of a ground floor workshop, where to do so would leave the defendant landlord in breach of a covenant contained in his head lease.[155] As Stamp LJ acknowledged, "To order him specifically to perform the contract . . . so allowing the tenants to retain possession would be to . . . expose him to a forfeiture".[156] Accordingly, the tenants were left to their remedy in damages.

Ordinarily, it is to be expected that the parties to a contract for the sale of land might envisage that some hardship may result from some future change in circumstances. For this reason, the defence of hardship has traditionally been confined to hardship existing at the date of the contract or hardship arising from the conduct of the plaintiff.[157] In *Patel v Ali*,[158] however, the court resisted performance of a land contract where the hardship was supervening and in no way attributable to the plaintiff.[159] The defendant co-owners entered into a contract for the sale of their house, but the husband's bankruptcy precipitated a long delay for which neither the plaintiffs nor the defendants sought to blame each other. Completion was further hampered by a disastrous change in personal circumstances that befell the defendant. Shortly after the making of the contract, she was diagnosed with bone cancer and, whilst in an advanced state of pregnancy, underwent an operation to amputate her right leg. Thereafter, she came to

---

154 [1974] Ch. 30 at 51.
155 [1973] Q.B. 877.
156 [1973] Q.B. 877 at 886.
157 Fry, *A Treatise on the Specific Performance of Contracts* (2002), p.199.
158 [1984] Ch. 283.
159 As Stephen Davies J recognised in *Matila Ltd v Lisheen Properties Ltd* [2010] EWHC 1832 (Ch) at [245], "the court's discretion is wide enough, in a proper case, to refuse specific performance on the ground of hardship subsequent to the contract and not caused by the claimant, and that it does not have to be hardship related to the subject matter of the contract as opposed to personal hardship of the defendant".

rely heavily on the support provided by friends and relatives in the neighbourhood. Her reliance became acute in the months that followed as her husband was imprisoned and she continued to speak virtually no English. At the time of the hearing, the defendants had three children and argued that their enforced removal would be unjust.

19-033

Goulding J accepted that to award specific performance would "inflict upon her a 'hard-ship amounting to injustice'".[160] Of particular significance was the four-year delay, within which the defendant's circumstances had altered in an unforeseeable way, and after which she was being asked to do what had not been contemplated, i.e. complete a sale at that much later time. Accordingly, he felt the proper course was to leave the plaintiffs to their remedy in damages.[161] Although *Patel v Ali* serves to emphasise the width of judicial discretion, it is important to note that future cases will continue to turn on their own facts.[162] Goulding J felt that it took such "extraordinary and persuasive circumstances" to supply an excuse for resisting performance of a contract for the sale of immovable property.[163] Perhaps rarely, therefore, will such compelling evidence be presented to the court.

Laches and delay

19-034

The general equitable rule is that time is not the essence of a contract[164] and, accordingly, a claimant may obtain specific performance in circumstances where he has failed to carry out his contractual obligations by the time specified.[165] Nonetheless, a claimant who brings an action after an unreasonable delay may well be unsuccessful. Although there is no statutory period of limitation on the time at which a claim for specific performance may be brought, it is a statement of general principle that, in the absence of special circumstances rendering the position unjust, "relevant equitable rules should accord with comparable legal rules".[166]

Unfortunately, there is no easily applicable definition of an unreasonable delay and little can be gleaned from the copious case law on the doctrine of *laches* to be dug up from previous centuries.[167] As Aldous LJ put it in *Frawley v Neill*, "the more modern approach should

---

160 [1984] Ch. 283 at 288 adopting the phrase employed by James LJ in *Tamplin v James* [1880] 15 Ch. D. 215 at 221.

161 There was evidence that sympathetic members of the Muslim community were willing to put up the money to meet the costs of the damages.

162 As Master Bowles noted in *Shah v Greening* [2016] EWHC 548 (Ch) at [83], "The court is exercising an equitable discretion and must do so on a case by case basis".

163 [1984] Ch. 283 at 288.

164 Where the parties agree that time is of the essence of a contract, or the circumstances indicate that completion is of the essence, specific performance will not be awarded if the time limit has not been respected: see *Steedman v Drinkle* [1916] 1 A.C. 275.

165 The delaying party may, however, be liable to damages for breach of contract: see *Raineri v Miles* [1981] A.C. 1050.

166 I.C.F. Spry, *Equitable Remedies: Injunctions and Specific Performance*, 5th edn (London: Sweet & Maxwell, 1997), p.419; see further, *P & O Nedlloyd BV v Arab Metals Co* [2007] 1 W.L.R. 2288.

167 As Laddie J indicated in *Nelson v Rye* [1996] 1 W.L.R. 1378 at 1396, "some of the factors which must be

not require an inquiry as to whether the circumstances can be fitted within the confines of a preconceived formula derived from earlier cases".[168] The award of specific performance in *Lazard Bros & Co Ltd v Fairfield Property Co (Mayfair) Ltd*[169] is illustrative of the modern judicial approach. Megarry VC argued that, if specific performance was to be regarded as a prize to be awarded by equity to the zealous and denied to the indolent, then the claimants in the case before him should fail. His view was that whatever the position over a century ago that was the wrong approach today. If it was just that the claimant should obtain his remedy, the court ought not to withhold it merely because he was guilty of delay. This is a long way from the nineteenth-century view of Lord Alvanley that "a party cannot call upon a Court of Equity for a specific performance unless he has shewn himself ready, desirous, prompt and eager".[170] The essence of the contemporary approach, therefore, is to question whether the claimant's actions render it unconscionable for him to assert his rights.[171]

Delay will not be a bar to specific performance where the claimant has taken possession under the contract and, as equitable owner, seeks to have the legal estate vested in him. In *Williams v Greatrex*,[172] a delay of 10 years was no bar by *laches* because the purchaser had equitable title to the property by virtue of the contract and he had entered into possession of it.[173] Different considerations apply where it is the transaction creating the proprietary interest that is in dispute.[174] Here the doctrine of *laches* unquestionably applies. It is clear also that the subject matter of the contract is a relevant consideration in determining unreasonableness. Where the subject matter has a "speculative and fluctuating value", for example, delay on the part of the claimant will be prominent in the exercise of judicial discretion.[175]

Further consideration is required of a claimant who commences a timely action for specific performance, but delays in bringing the matter to trial. Generally, delay will not in itself be sufficient to defeat the claim. Neither will detriment to the defendant of itself be sufficient as a ground for the court's refusal of leave to enforce an order. Such was the case in *Easton v Brown*[176] where the plaintiff property developers delayed by eight years an action to enforce an order for specific performance of a contract for the sale of property with vacant possession. Although the defendant argued that such late enforcement was to his detriment, the plaintiffs had acted reasonably throughout and had provided a legitimate explanation for the delay. The delay had been caused by the defendant's former wife and their nine children who remained in

19-035

---

taken into consideration in deciding whether the defence runs . . . include the period of the delay, the extent to which the defendant's position has been prejudiced by the delay and the extent to which that prejudice was caused by the actions of the plaintiff".

168 [2000] C.P. Rep. 20.
169 (1977) 121 S.J. 793.
170 *Milward v Earl of Thanet* (1801) 5 Ves. Jr. 720.
171 *Frawley v Neill* [2000] C.P. Rep. 20.
172 [1956] 3 All E.R. 705.
173 The possession claimed must be possession under the contract: *Mills v Haywood* (2000) 6 Ch. D. 196.
174 *Joyce v Joyce* [1979] 1 W.L.R. 1170.
175 *Mills v Haywood* (1877) 6 Ch. D. 196 at 202 per Cotton LJ.
176 [1981] 3 All E.R. 278.

occupation of the property. Legal advice suggested litigation to remove them would be unsuccessful. Accordingly, it was not until agreement was reached between the parties that the plaintiffs pressed ahead to enforce their rights. It seems, therefore, that the court will require both an insufficient explanation of the delay by the claimant and a detriment to the defendant before it is unjust to enforce the order.

Mistake, misdescription and misrepresentation

19-036

Where a contract cannot be avoided in equity by reason of a mistake or misrepresentation, both can be grounds to defend an action for specific performance.[177] In other words, X may not succeed in his efforts to rescind a contract, but equity will not provide to Y the remedy to compel performance of it. To succeed with the defence of mistake, a defendant is usually required to show "hardship amounting to injustice".[178] Ignorance as to the legal implications of an agreement[179] or evidence of some fault or mistake solely on the part of the defendant will generally not suffice. In *Tamplin v James*,[180] for example, the defendant purchaser made a unilateral mistake as to the extent of the property being sold; the vendor had accurately described the property by reference to plans. The purchaser, who had first-hand knowledge of the property, failed to consult the plans and mistakenly assumed he was buying a portion of land that did not, in fact, belong to the vendor. Specific performance was awarded against the defendant on the basis that his mistake was solely attributable to his own negligence. There was nothing misleading in the particulars. In the words of James LJ, "If a man will not take reasonable care to ascertain what he is buying, he must take the consequences. The defence on the ground of mistake cannot be sustained. It is not enough for a purchaser to swear, 'I thought the farm contained 12 fields which I knew, and I find it does not contain them all' or 'I thought it contained 100 acres and it only contains 80'. It would open the door to fraud if such a defence was to be allowed".[181]

A markedly less rigorous (and frequently criticised) approach[182] was adopted in *Malins v Freeman* where the defendant at auction was mistaken as to the lot put up for sale.[183] Despite the defendant's failure to draw attention to the mistake immediately and that the mistake itself was solely attributable to the defendant, specific performance was refused.[184]

19-037

Where the claimant has contributed to, or somehow induced the defendant's mistake,

---

177   As Lindley LJ put it in *Re Terry and White's Contract* (1886) 32 Ch. D. 14 at 29, "it is well known that a less serious misleading is sufficient to enable a purchaser to resist specific performance than is required to enable him to rescind the contract".
178   *Tamplin v James* (1880) 15 Ch. D. 215 at 221 per James LJ.
179   *Powell v Smith* (1872) L.R. 14 Eq. 85.
180   (1880) 15 Ch. D. 215.
181   (1880) 15 Ch. D. 215 at 221.
182   See, e.g. the discussion of Kekewich J in *Van Praagh v Everidge* [1902] 2 Ch. 266.
183   (1837) 2 Keen 25.
184   Lord Langdale admitted that the defendant was "hurried and inconsiderate" and that when the mistake

the court is legitimately less likely to award specific performance on the ground that it is inequitable to do so. In *Denny v Hancock*,[185] the purchaser's mistake as to the accuracy of the boundary of a property arose due to the misleading layout of the vendor's plans. Mellish LJ questioned whether the plan and particulars were "naturally calculated to deceive" and concluded, "I cannot but think that they were".[186] Even on a more generous interpretation of the vendor's intentions (i.e. that the inducement was unintentional) the defendant's mistake was at least attributable to the negligence of the vendor's agents in the production of the plans. The more complicit the claimant in the defendant's mistake, therefore, the less likely the court is to award specific performance. In *Webster v Cecil*,[187] the defendant's error was unilateral, but the purchaser, who must have known of the error, sought to take full advantage. Negotiations as to the sale price of property had been conducted by letter. The vendor mistakenly offered to sell at £1,250. His intention had been to write down a figure of £2,250. The purchaser readily accepted. Immediately, upon realising his mistake, the vendor gave notice of his error. Nonetheless, the purchaser sought to compel the vendor to sell at £1,250. As he had a previous offer of £2,200 rejected by the vendor, the purchaser must have realised the mistake. No specific performance was awarded.

In the case of a misdescription of subject matter the approach of the courts will depend on the justice of the case. It may be that specific performance will be ordered with an appropriate abatement in the purchase price. In the case of a serious misdescription, the court will refuse to compel performance and, indeed, allow rescission of the contract.

Guide to Further Reading

P.S. Davies, "Being Specific about Specific Performance" [2018] Conv. 324.
A. Dowling, "Vendors' Application for Specific Performance" [2011] Conv. 208.
A. Tettenborn, "Absolving the Undeserving: Shopping Centres, Specific Performance and the Law of Contract" [1998] Conv. 23.

---

was made known to him, he was "not so prompt as he ought to have been in declaring it" ((1837) 2 Keen 25 at 35).
185 (1870) 6 Ch. App. 1.
186 (1870) 6 Ch. App. 1 at 14
187 (1861) 30 Beav. 62.

Index

LEGAL TAXONOMY
FROM SWEET & MAXWELL

This index has been prepared using Sweet and Maxwell's Legal Taxonomy. Main index entries conform to keywords provided by the Legal Taxonomy except where references to specific documents or non-standard terms (denoted by quotation marks) have been included. These keywords provide a means of identifying similar concepts in other Sweet & Maxwell publications and online services to which keywords from the Legal Taxonomy have been applied. Readers may find some minor differences between terms used in the text and those which appear in the index.

Suggestions to *sweetandmaxwell.taxonomy@tr.com*.

(All references are to paragraph number)